*Photograph: Courtesy Yardena Youner*

# ESSAYS ON
# INTERNATIONAL LAW
# AND ORGANIZATION

## VOLUME I

BY

LEO GROSS

Springer-Science+Business Media, B.V.

**Library of Congress Cataloging in Publication Data**

Gross, Leo, 1903–
Essays on international law and organization.

Includes index.
1. United Nations. 2. International law. 3. International agencies. I. Title.
JX1977.G759 1983 341 83-9136

**ISBN 978-0-941320-15-3 978-94-017-7048-4 (eBook)**
**DOI 10.1007/978-94-017-7048-4**



Originally published by Transnational Publishers, Inc. in 1984.
Softcover reprint of the hardcover 1st edition 1984

# SUMMARY OF CONTENTS

## VOLUME 1



## VOLUME 2

# CONTENTS

## VOLUME I



### I. Development of International Law



### II. Development of International Law by the United Nations

## III. International Law and Individual Responsibility



## IV. Problems of Interpretation



## V. Problems of Voting

## VI. Some Problems of Organization in the United Nations



# VOLUME II



## VII. Settlement of Disputes by the International Court of Justice

## VIII. Settlement of Disputes by the Political Organs of the United Nations: Some Aspects of the Arab-Israel Dispute

## IX. Domestic Jurisdiction and Peace-Keeping Operations

# Preface

Professor Leo Gross turned eighty years of age in 1983 and happily, for the cause of international law and organization, the causes of candor and common sense in international relations, and for his own good sake, he continues to turn out some of the finest expositions of our era in the field of international law. It is altogether fitting and felicitous that, in his eightieth year, a selection of his papers should be published in these two volumes.

These papers are but a partial reflection of a life of distinguished scholarship. Leo Gross's books are of course not included, nor are his extensive articles written in German. His contributions as an editor of books—notably, *International Law in the Twentieth Century* and *The Future of the International Court of Justice*—are not included. His work as an editor of scholarly journals, particularly as an editor, and as the book review editor for some 25 years, of the *American Journal of International Law,* are not reflected. And his distinguished teaching of more than forty years at the Fletcher School of Law and Diplomacy and elsewhere is still another aspect of his life as a leading international lawyer which these two volumes cannot represent.

Nevertheless, if these papers do not reflect the whole Leo Gross, they capture his essence as an exceptional international lawyer and exceptionally acute observer of international affairs. They reflect his singular combination of idealism and realism, his taste for a more effective international law heavily salted with a sense of the limitations imposed by the hard facts of international life. Leo Gross has never pretended that we have the sort of international law we need simply because we need it. He has preferred to promote a more effective international law within more realistic bounds. If some have found his approach positivistic, his analyses rigorous, his concern for legal integrity unyielding, Leo Gross pleads guilty on all counts. He could also plead in his defense the facts of international affairs, and particularly of international organization, as they have developed the last twenty-five years. The looser that standards at the United Nations have become, the more appealing are the strictures which Leo Gross has laid down, not to suit this or that trend and turn of United Nations majorities, but steadily and impartially from the outset of the life of the Organization. As these papers repeatedly show, Leo Gross has manifested an abiding concern for the proper application of the principles, rules and procedures of international organizations in a lawyer-like appreciation of the importance which procedure has for the fair achievement of substance. He has appreciated no less that precedent may be a two-edged sword, which can be applied to its makers in the fullness of time.

Leo Gross is at once master of the theory and of the practice of international law. His hold on the historical antecedents of modern international law is reflected in the first paper republished, on "The Peace of Westphalia, 1648–1948," a classic article which perhaps more than any other has given currency to the term, "Westphalian State System". His subtle analysis of the theory of international law is illustrated in his essay on "States as Organs of International Law and the Problem of Autointerpretation," which is notable for its sympathetic but not uncritical appreciation of the jurisprudence of Hans Kelsen. And his incisive critiques of the conduct and misconduct of States and of international organs are found in a multiplicity of the papers that follow. Leo Gross is not sparing in his criticism—as his most recent essay, his editorial comment "On the Degradation of the Constitutional Environment of the United Nations" illustrates. Why should he be, when there is too much in this world to criticize, and too few who are prepared to withstand the winds of the fashionable to say what needs saying?

Yet Leo Gross is a constructive critic. His concern for and contribution to the development of more effective international institutions is particularly reflected in his preoccupation with invigorating the processes of international adjudication. There are few scholars who have contributed more, particularly in the last twenty years, to the literature of the International Court of Justice than has Leo Gross—as the dozen articles on the Court in these volumes demonstrate. He has played an especially notable role as analyst of the causes—or the paucity of the case load which the Court has suffered during those years. He has come forth with valuable proposals for expanding the role of the Court (see, in particular, his article on "The International Court of Justice: Consideration of Requirements for Enhancing Its Role in the International Legal Order"), and has been a leading figure in stimulating others to consider what can and should be done to nurture the processes of international adjudication.

While Leo Gross thinks for himself, he thinks not of or only by himself; he has, on the contrary, manifested a facility not only for educating his students but for working with his colleagues in common endeavours of importance. Two of those exercises have concentrated on invigorating the role of the Court, and, insofar as the world of scholarship and the collective concern of the community of international lawyers can contribute to achieving that goal, they have done so in significant measure. One wonders whether the American Bar Association and the Congress of the United States would have moved as far as they have in supporting wider jurisdiction for the Court, had it not been for the ideas of Leo Gross and his colleagues, particularly those of the American Society of International Law.

Leo Gross has done all this and more in style; that is to say, he is a pleasure to read. His prose is as lucid, direct, straightforward and at times as astringent as the man himself. Long may he continue to grace the world of international legal scholarship.

Stephen M. Schwebel
The Hague
June, 1983

# ACKNOWLEDGMENTS

"The Peace of Westphalia, 1648–1948." Reprinted by permission of the American Society of International Law from THE AMERICAN JOURNAL OF INTERNATIONAL LAW, Vol. 42, No. 1, pp. 20–41, (January, 1948).

"Ways and Means of Making the Evidence of Customary International Law More Readily Available: Preparatory Work Within the Purview of Article 24 of the Statute of the International Law Commission." Reprinted by permission of the Secretariat of the United Nations from United Nations Publication, Sales No. 1949, Vol. 6, pp. 1–100, (March 7, 1949).

*Note:* The publication of this study in its original form was authorized by and prepared for the Secretariat of the United Nations, and was subsequently converted into an official document of the International Law Commission (A/CN.4/6 of 7 March 1949).

"International Law and Peace." Reprinted by permission of the International Law Association of Japan from THE JAPANESE ANNUAL OF INTERNATIONAL LAW, NO. 11, pp. 1–14, (1967).

"Sources of Universal International Law." Reprinted by permission of Vikas Publishing House Pvt Ltd from ASIAN STATES AND THE DEVELOPMENT OF UNIVERSAL INTERNATIONAL LAW, R.P. Anand, Ed. (Pp. 189–212), (1972).

"The United Nations and the Role of Law." Reprinted by permission of the Massachusetts Institute of Technology (MIT) Press from the journal INTERNATIONAL ORGANIZATION, Vol. XIX, No. 3, pp. 537–561, (1965).

"The Development of International Law Through the United Nations." Reprinted by permission of the publisher from THE UNITED NATIONS: PAST, PRESENT, AND FUTURE, James Barros, Ed. Copyright © 1972 by The Free Press, a Division of Macmillan Publishing Company (pp. 171–217).

"Family Planning as a Human Right: Some Jurisprudential Reflections on Natural Rights and Positive Law." Reprinted by permission of the Indian Law Institute from LAW QUARTERLY: JOURNAL OF THE INDIAN LAW INSTITUTE, Vol. 2, No. 2, pp. 85–96, (June, 1974).

"Some International Law Aspects of the Freedom of Information and the Right to Communicate." Reprinted by permission of the Ablex Publishing Corp. from NATIONAL SOVEREIGNTY AND INTERNATIONAL COMMUNICATION, Kaarle Nordenstreng and Herbert I. Schiller, Eds. (Pp. 195–216), (1979).

"The Right of Self-Determination in International Law." Reprinted by permission of the publishers from NEW STATES IN THE MODERN WORLD, Martin Kilson, Ed. Cambridge,

Ma: Harvard University Press, (pp. 136–157). Copyright © 1975 by the President and Fellows of Harvard College.

"Immunities and Privileges of Delegations to the United Nations." Reprinted by permission of the MIT Press from INTERNATIONAL ORGANIZATION, Vol. XVI, No. 3, pp. 483–520, (Summer Issue, 1962).

"The Criminality of Aggressive War." Reprinted by permission of the American Political Science Association from THE AMERICAN POLITICAL SCIENCE REVIEW, Vol. XLI, No. 2, pp. 205–225, (April, 1947).

"The Punishment of War Criminals: The Nuremberg Trial." Reprinted by permission of Martinus Nijhoff Publishers B.V. and T.M.C. Asser Instituut from NETHERLANDS INTERNATIONAL LAW REVIEW, Issue 4, pp. 1–34, (1955).

"International Terrorism and International Criminal Jurisdiction." Reprinted by permission of the American Society of International Law from THE AMERICAN JOURNAL OF INTERNATIONAL LAW, Vol. 67, No. 3, pp. 508–511, (July, 1973).

"States as Organs of International Law and the Problem of Autointerpretation." Reprinted by permission of the University of California Press from LAW AND POLITICS IN THE WORLD COMMUNITY: ESSAYS ON HANS KELSEN'S PURE THEORY AND RELATED PROBLEMS IN INTERNATIONAL LAW, George A. Lipsky, Comp. and Ed. (Pp. 1–32), (1953).

"Problems of International Adjudication and Compliance with International Law: Some Simple Solutions." Reprinted by permission of the American Society of International Law from THE AMERICAN JOURNAL OF INTERNATIONAL LAW, Vol. 59, No. 1, pp. 48–59, (January, 1965).

"Treaty Interpretation: The Proper Role of an International Tribunal." Reprinted by permission of the American Society of International Law from PROCEEDINGS OF THE AMERICAN SOCIETY OF INTERNATIONAL LAW, pp. 108–122, (1969).

"Voting in the Security Council: Abstention from Voting and Absence from Meetings." Reprinted by permission of the Yale Law Journal Company and Fred B. Rothman & Company from THE YALE LAW JOURNAL, Vol. 60, pp. 209–257, (February, 1961).

"The Double Veto and the Four-Power Statement on Voting in the Security Council." Reprinted by permission of the Harvard Law Review Association from the HARVARD LAW REVIEW, Vol. 67, No. 2, pp. 251–280, (December, 1953). Copyright © 1953 by the Harvard Law Review Association.

"The Question of Laos and the Double Veto in the Security Council." Reprinted by permission of the American Society of International Law from THE AMERICAN JOURNAL OF INTERNATIONAL LAW, Vol. 53, No. 1, pp. 118–131, (January, 1960).

"Voting in the Security Council: Abstention in the Post-1965 Amendment Phase and Its Impact on Article 25 of the Charter." Reprinted by permission of the American Society of International Law from THE AMERICAN JOURNAL OF INTERNATIONAL LAW, Vol. 62, No. 2, pp. 315–334, (April, 1968).

"Voting in the Security Council and the PLO." Reprinted by permission of the American Society of International Law from THE AMERICAN JOURNAL OF INTERNATIONAL LAW, Vol. 70, No. 3, pp. 470–491, (July, 1976).

"Was the Soviet Union Expelled from the League of Nations?" Reprinted by permission of the American Society of International Law from THE AMERICAN JOURNAL OF INTERNATIONAL LAW, Vol. 39, No. 1, pp. 35–44, (January, 1945).

"The Charter of the United Nations and the Lodge Reservations." Reprinted by permission of the American Society of International Law from THE AMERICAN JOURNAL OF INTERNATIONAL LAW, Vol. 41, No. 3, pp. 531–554, (July, 1947).

"Election of States to United Nations Membership." Reprinted by permission of the American Society of International Law from PROCEEDINGS OF THE AMERICAN SOCIETY OF INTERNATIONAL LAW, pp. 37–59, (1954).

"Progress Towards Universality of Membership in the United Nations." Reprinted by permission of the American Society of International Law from THE AMERICAN JOURNAL OF INTERNATIONAL LAW, Vol. 50, No. 4, pp. 791–827, (October, 1956).

"The United Nations and the United States." Reprinted by permission of the publisher, Duncker & Humblot, from VÖLKERRECHT UND RECHTSPHILOSOPHIE, pp. 403–424, (1980).

"On the Degradation of the Constitutional Environment of the United Nations." Reprinted by permission of the American Society of International Law from THE AMERICAN JOURNAL OF INTERNATIONAL LAW, Vol. 77, No. 3, pp. 569–584, (July, 1983).

"Some Observations on the International Court of Justice." Reprinted by permission of the American Society of International Law from THE AMERICAN JOURNAL OF INTERNATIONAL LAW, Vol. 56, No. 1, pp. 33–62, (January, 1962).

"Participation of Individuals in Advisory Proceedings Before the International Court of Justice: Question of Equality Between the Parties." Reprinted by permission of the American Society of International Law from THE AMERICAN JOURNAL OF INTERNATIONAL LAW, Vol. 52, No. 1, pp. 16–40, (January, 1958).

"Bulgaria Invokes the Connally Amendment." Reprinted by permission of the American Society of International Law from THE AMERICAN JOURNAL OF INTERNATIONAL LAW, Vol. 56, No. 2, pp. 357–382, (April, 1962).

"Expenses of the United Nations for Peace-Keeping Questions: The Advisory Opinion of the International Court of Justice." Reprinted by permission of the MIT Press from INTERNATIONAL ORGANIZATION, Vol. XVII, No. 1, pp. 1–35, (1963).

"The Jurisprudence of the World Court: Thirty-Eighth Year (1959)." Reprinted by permission of the American Society of International Law from THE AMERICAN JOURNAL OF INTERNATIONAL LAW, Vol. 57, No. 4, pp. 751–780, (October, 1963).

"Limitations Upon the Judicial Function." Reprinted by permission of the American Society of International Law from THE AMERICAN JOURNAL OF INTERNATIONAL LAW, Vol. 58, No. 2, pp. 415–431, (April, 1964).

"The Time Element in the Contentious Proceedings in the International Court of Justice." Reprinted by permission of the American Society of International Law from THE AMERICAN JOURNAL OF INTERNATIONAL LAW, Vol. 63, No. 1, pp. 74–85, (January, 1969).

"The International Court of Justice and the United Nations." Reprinted by permission of Martinus Nijhoff Publishers B.V. from the RECUEIL DES COURS, Vol. II, 117 pp., (1967).

"The International Court of Justice: Consideration of Requirements for Enhancing Its Rôle in the International Legal Order." Reprinted by permission of the American Society of International Law from THE AMERICAN JOURNAL OF INTERNATIONAL LAW, Vol. 65, No. 2, pp. 253–326, (April, 1971).

"What Future for the International Court of Justice? A Comment." Reprinted by permission of the American Society of International Law from PROCEEDINGS OF THE AMERICAN SOCIETY OF INTERNATIONAL LAW, pp. 278–280, (April, 1971).

"Review of the Rôle of the International Court of Justice." Reprinted by permission of the American Society of International Law from THE AMERICAN JOURNAL OF INTERNATIONAL LAW, Vol. 66, No. 3, pp. 479–490, (July, 1972).

"The Dispute Between Greece and Turkey Concerning the Continental Shelf in the Aegean." Reprinted by permission of the American Society of International Law from THE AMERICAN JOURNAL OF INTERNATIONAL LAW, Vol. 71, No. 1, pp. 31–59, (January, 1977).

"On the Justiciability of International Disputes." Reprinted by permission of the publisher, The New Republic Book Company, Inc., from A TRIBUTE TO HANS MORGENTHAU, Kenneth Thompson and Robert J. Myers, Eds. (Pp. 203–219), (1977).

"The Case Concerning United States Diplomatic and Consular Staff in Tehran: Phase of Provisional Measures." Reprinted by permission of the American Society of International Law from THE AMERICAN JOURNAL OF INTERNATIONAL LAW, Vol. 74, No. 2, pp. 1143–1158, (April, 1980).

"Passage Through the Suez Canal of Israel-Bound Cargo and Israel Ships." Reprinted by permission of the American Society of International Law from THE AMERICAN JOURNAL OF INTERNATIONAL LAW, Vol. 51, No. 3, pp. 530–568, (July, 1957).

"The Geneva Conference on the Law of the Sea and the Right of Innocent Passage Through the Gulf of Aqaba." Reprinted by permission of the American Society of International Law from THE AMERICAN JOURNAL OF INTERNATIONAL LAW, Vol. 53, No. 3, pp. 564–594, (July, 1959).

"Passage Through The Strait of Tiran and in the Gulf of Aqaba," (From the Symposium on the Middle East Crisis: Test of International Law. Reprinted by permission of Duke University Press from LAW AND CONTEMPORARY PROBLEMS, pp. 125–146, (Winter Issue, 1968). Copyright © 1968 by the Duke University School of Law.

"Domestic Jurisdiction, Enforcement Measures and the Congo." Reprinted by permission of the Australian National University from the AUSTRALIAN YEAR BOOK OF INTERNATIONAL LAW, J. G. Starke, Q.C., Ed. (Pp. 137–158), (1965).

# I

# DEVELOPMENT OF INTERNATIONAL LAW

# THE PEACE OF WESTPHALIA, 1648–1948

The acceptance of the United Nations Charter by the overwhelming majority of the members of the family of nations brings to mind the first great European or world charter, the Peace of Westphalia. To it is traditionally attributed the importance and dignity of being the first of several attempts to establish something resembling world unity on the basis of states exercising untrammeled sovereignty over certain territories and subordinated to no earthly authority.

The next attempt, the settlement of Vienna of 1815 and the Congress of Aix-la Chapelle of 1818, which in a sense completed the former, gave birth to that loose system of consultation between the Great Powers known as the Concert of Europe. Born of the cataclysm of the Napoleonic Wars and anchored in the Protocol of the Aix-la Chapelle of November 15, 1818, the Concert provided some sort of a self-appointed directing body for the maintenance and manipulation of that balance of power on which the European peace precariously reposed for about a hundred years. Uncertain in its foundations, devoid of much organization or continuity, it was characterized as much by the devotion of the Great Powers which composed it to the policy of a free hand as it was, in consequence, by the absence of definite commitments. Consultation and conference on problems of mutual interest was a frequent practice but no obligation of the Great Powers. It was precisely this flexibility, frequently regarded and praised as the chief virtue of the concert system, which ultimately brought about its ruin at a moment when it was most desperately needed. The policy of free hands reaped a large harvest in World War I.

Faced with the devastating results of World War I and the bankruptcy of the Concert, the Paris Settlement of 1919, without essentially departing from the Peace of Westphalia, attempted a novel solution, drawing for its inspiration on the Concert, the Hague Peace Conferences, the experience of the nineteenth and twentieth centuries in non-political international collaboration, and the wartime collaboration between the Allied and Associated Powers. It produced the League of Nations, in which the member states assumed certain commitments to coöperate in various fields and, above all, without abolishing the right of war, *jus ad bellum,* to establish "the undertakings of international law as the actual rule of conduct among governments." It is a moot question whether the failure of the League should be attributed to a defective legal technique in organizing international security or to a kind of fatal and gradual relapse of the Great Powers into the traditional methods of consultation untrammeled by and frequently in open disregard of their obligations under the Covenant. The climax in this process of degeneration was reached in 1939 when alliances were hurriedly tossed around and when Poland, though attacked by Germany on September 1, 1939, found it convenient to manifest its contempt of the League of Nations by not even appealing to it under Article 10 of the Covenant, and when Great Britain and France went to the assistance of Poland not because they were legally bound to do so by the Covenant but because they felt in honor bound to fulfill their obligations as allies in Poland. Thus World War II started in the customary way, even as if the League were non-existent; as a consequence the League was doomed.

Critics of the United Nations Charter point out that it includes some of the elements of the League organization and that it relies even more heavily than did the League on the notion of consultation, on limited obligations in the political, and the method of voluntary coöperation in the non-political, field. The Charter proclaims that the organization is based on the sovereign equality of all the members only in order the firmer to establish the hegemony of a group of Great Powers. On the other hand, in Articles 24 and 25, the principal framers of the Charter almost obtained what the Concert never succeeded in obtaining, namely, the recognition by the lesser nations of the preëminent position of the Great Powers as the guardians of international peace and security. In spite of this and other important indications of a new approach to the problem of international security and relations, the Charter at first glance would seem to have left essentially unchanged the framework of the state system and of international law resulting from the Peace of Westphalia.

Thus the Peace of Westphalia may be said to continue its sway over political man's mind as the *ratio scripta* that it was held to be of yore. What is the explanation of this curious phenomenon? In view of this continued influence of the Peace of Westphalia, it may not be amiss to discuss briefly its character, background and implications.

It should be clear from the outset that the actual provisions of the Treaties of Osnabrück between the Empire and Sweden, and of Münster between the Empire and France and their respective confederates and allies, have undergone more than one substantial change in the course of time. The political map of Europe as outlined in these Treaties is no longer. It should be noted, however, that the chief political idea underlying the Franco-German settlement of 1648 has undergone relatively little change. Then the axiom of French politics was, as it appears to be today, that the best guarantee of French security lies in a divided and impotent Germany, and that this division and impotence must be secured by appropriate provisions such as those which gave France a right to intervene when necessary in order to vindicate the principle of the sanctity of treaties.

The Thirty Years' War had its origin, at any rate partially, in a religious conflict or, as one might say, in religious intolerance. The Peace of Westphalia consecrated the principle of toleration by establishing the equality between Protestant and Catholic states and by providing some safeguards for religious minorities. To be sure, the principle of liberty of conscience was applied only incompletely and without reciprocity.[1] The religious Peace of Augsburg of 1555 and the rule *cujus regio ejus religio* were confirmed. With a view to alleviating the lot of religious minorities, however, the Treaty of Osnabrück provided that[2]

> subjects who in 1627 had been debarred from the free exercise of their religion, other than that of their ruler, were by the Peace granted the right of conducting private worship, and of educating their children, at home or abroad, in conformity with their own faith; they were not to suffer in any civil capacity nor to be denied religious burial, but were to be at liberty to emigrate, selling their estates or leaving them to be managed by others.

Moreover, in an effort to assure equality between Catholic and Protestant members of the German Diet, the Treaty of Osnabrück laid down the important rule that in matters pertaining to religion[3]

> a majority of votes should no longer be held decisive at the Diet; but that such questions should be settled by an amicable 'composition' between its two parts or *corpora*. . . . In the same spirit of parity it was agreed that when possible there should be equality of consulting and voting power between the two religions on all commissions of the Diet, including those *Deputationstage* which had come to exercise an authority nearly equalling that of the Diets themselves.

The principle of religious equality was placed as part of the peace under an international guarantee.[4] The Peace of Westphalia thereby established a precedent of far-reaching importance. One or two illustrations may be in order. The Constitution of the Germanic Confederation of June 8, 1815, which forms part of the Final Act of the Congress of Vienna of June 9, 1815, stipulates in Article XVI that the difference between the Christian religions should cause no difference in the enjoyment by their adherents of civil and political rights, and, furthermore, that the German Diet should consider the grant of civil

[1] Sir A. W. Ward, *The Peace of Westphalia*, The Cambridge Modern History, Vol. IV, 1934, p. 416: ". . . the provision made for individual freedom in the exercise of any of the recognized religions was insufficient; and from the dominions of the House of Austria as a whole, Protestant worship was deliberately excluded." But see Yves de la Brière, *La Société des Nations?*, 1918, p. 57.

[2] Ward, work cited, p. 412. See also Andrea Rapisardi Mirabelli, "Le Congrés de Westphalie," 8 *Bibliotheca Visseriana* (1929), p. 75.

[3] Ward, work cited, p. 414; Mirabelli, work cited, pp. 13, 76.

[4] Mirabelli, work cited, p. 13: *Mais une circonstance ultérieure—importante au point du vue international—c'était que le principe de l'égalité des confessions (basé jusqu'alors sur la tolérance des Princes ou sur des lois révocables) prenait alors la forme d'engagement international, fixé conventionnellement par les traités et pour cela assuré par leur force et leur durée.*

rights to Jews on condition that they assume all civic duties incumbent on other citizens.[5] By the time the Congress of Berlin convened the principle of religious tolerance had become so firmly established that the delegate of France, M. Waddington, could make the following statement:[6]

> Mr. Waddington believes that it is important to take advantage of this solemn opportunity to cause the principles of religious liberty to be affirmed by the representatives of Europe. His Excellency adds that Serbia, who claims to enter the European family on the same basis as other states, must previously recognize the principles which are the basis of social organization in all states of Europe and accept them as a necessary condition of the favor which she asks for.

The representatives of Great Britain, Germany, Italy, Austria-Hungary, and of the Ottoman Empire concurred in the view propounded by M. Waddington and the Congress acted accordingly in the case of Serbia, Montenegro, and Rumania.

This precedent was relied upon by the Principal Allied and Associated Powers in submitting to Poland the Treaty of June 28, 1919, concerning the protection of minorities. In his covering letter to M. Paderewski, the President of the Paris Peace Conference stated that "This treaty does not constitute any fresh departure," and continued as follows:[7]

> It has for long been the established procedure of the public law of Europe that when a state is created, or even when large accessions of territory are made to an established state, the joint and formal recognition by the Great Powers should be accompanied by the requirement that such State should, in the form of a binding international convention, undertake to comply with certain principles of government.

The latest step in this long line of evolution is represented by the United Nations Charter, the Preamble of which declares that the peoples of the United Nations are determined "to reaffirm faith in fundamental human rights, in the dignity and worth of the human person, in the equal rights of men and women, and of nations, large and small," and, "to practice tolerance and live together in peace with one another as good neighbors." It is one of the basic purposes of the United Nations to achieve international coöperation "in promoting and encouraging respect for human rights and for fundamental freedoms for all without distinction as to race, sex, language, or religion." If the efforts of the United

[5] 2 *British and Foreign State Papers*, 1814–1815, p. 132. The Final Act of Vienna and its Annexes include several interesting provisions designed to ensure freedom of religion. A particularly illuminating example is to be found in Article II of the Annex to the Treaty between the King of the Netherlands and Austria of May 31, 1815, which reads: *Il ne sera rien innové aux Articles de cette Constitution qui assurent à tous les Cultes une protection et une faveur égales, et garantissent l'admission de tous les Citoyens, quelle que soit leur croyance religieuse, aux emplois et offices publics.* Work cited, p. 141.

[6] Protocol of June 28, 1878. 69 *British and Foreign State Papers*, 1877–1878, p. 960; English translation from the "Letter addressed to M. Paderewski by the President of the Conference (M. Clemenceau) transmitting to him the Treaty to be signed by Poland under Article 93 of the Treaty of Peace with Germany" of June 24, 1919. 112 *British and Foreign State Papers*, 1919, p. 226. See also George A. Finch, "The International Rights of Man," in this JOURNAL, Vol. 35 (1941), p. 662.

[7] See letter quoted in the preceding note.

Nations are crowned with success by the adoption of an international bill of the fundamental rights of man, they will have accomplished the task which originated in the religious schism of Europe and which had found its first, albeit an inadequate, solution on an international basis in the Peace of Westphalia.

Another aspect of the Peace of Westphalia which exercised considerable influence on future developments relates to the guarantee of the peace itself. Both treaties declare that the peace concluded shall remain in force and that all parties to it "shall be obliged to defend and protect all and every article of this peace against anyone, without distinction of religion."[8] This was by no means a new departure. As Van Vollenhoven pointed out, the promise of guarantee in the treaties of 1648 merely followed earlier precedents.[9] Nevertheless this guarantee of the observance and the execution of an agreed international transaction, including as it did clauses of a constitutional character, as far as the Empire was concerned, came to assume in the following decades an overriding significance. It was pointed out that "no guarantee was more important or has been more often referred to than that included in the treaties of Westphalia."[10]

> These treaties contain clauses by which Sweden and France not only make peace with the Emperor on certain terms, but pledge themselves to their allies, the subordinate German Princes, that they will ensure that the privileges and immunities conferred on the Princes and free cities of Germany in the treaty shall be upheld and maintained. This is constantly referred to in later treaties as the guarantee for the execution of the terms of the treaty and, as Sir Ernest Satow has pointed out, it continued to be regarded as valid almost down to the outbreak of the French Revolution. Here, again, the fact of the guarantee was of the highest importance in ensuring that the treaties should be observed and that they should continue to hold their place as part of the general European System.

For the first time Europe thus received "what may fairly be described as an international constitution, which gave to all its adherents the right of intervention to enforce its engagements."[11] That this attempt to guarantee effectively a peace so laboriously achieved was not wholly successful needs hardly to be emphasized.[12] In this respect the Settlement of Westphalia is in good company with many other international instruments of historical importance.

In addition to the guarantee, the Settlement of Westphalia formulated certain extremely interesting rules for the peaceful settlement of disputes and collective sanctions against aggressors. Thus the Treaty of Münster, in Articles CXIII and CXXIV stipulates that[13]

[8] Text from Article CXXIII of the Treaty of Münster, in *A General Collection of Treatys,* Vol. I, 1710, p. 36.

[9] See C. Van Vollenhoven, *The Law of Peace,* 1936, p. 85.

[10] Sir James Headlam-Morely, *Studies in Diplomatic History,* 1930, p. 108. The statement quoted in the text continues, as follows:

[11] David Jayne Hill, *A History of Diplomacy in the International Development of Europe,* Vol. II, 1925, p. 602; but see La Brière, work cited, p. 67.

[12] Christian L. Lange, *Histoire de l'Internationalisme,* Vol. 1, 1919, p. 498.

[13] From Articles CXXIII and CXXIV of the Treaty of Münster, in work cited. C. Van Vollenhoven, "Grotius and Geneva," 6 *Bibliotheca Visseriana,* p. 72.

> if it happens that any point should be violated, the Offended shall before all things exhort the Offender not to come to any Hostility, submitting the Cause to a friendly Composition, or the ordinary Proceedings of Justice. Nevertheless, if for the space of three years the Difference cannot be terminated, by any of those means, all and every one of those concern'd in this Transaction shall be oblig'd to join the injur'd Party, and assist him with Counsel and Force to repel the Injury, being first advertis'd by the Injur'd that gentle Means and Justice prevail'd nothing; but without prejudice, nevertheless, to every one's Jurisdiction, and the Administration of Justice conformable to the Laws of each Prince and State; and it shall not be permitted to any State of the Empire to pursue his Right by Force and Arms; but if any difference has happen'd or happens for the future (between the states of the Empire), every one shall try the means of ordinary Justice, and the Contravener shall be regarded as an Infringer of the Peace. That which has been determin'd (between the States of the Empire) by Sentence of the Judge, shall be put in execution, without distinction of Condition, as the Laws of the Empire enjoin touching the Execution of arrests and Sentences.

This was a "novel feature"[14] in international treaty and peacemaking. The provisions for a moratorium of war, the settlement of disputes by peaceful means, and for individual and collective sanctions against the aggressor, after a delay of three years, although proclaimed primarily for the Empire, the members of which had been given their sovereign rights to conclude treaties of alliance, have nevertheless served as a model for numerous subsequent treaties.[15] They constitute, in a sense, an early precedent for Articles 10, 12, and 16, of the Covenant of the League of Nations. Writers on the subject, of course, have not failed to point out the shortcomings of the above-quoted provisions which admittedly were serious.[16]

The grave dislocations in the social and economic life of Europe caused by the long war prompted the delegates to the Congress of Westphalia to discuss means designed to facilitate reconstruction. For this purpose two clauses were inserted in the Treaties of Münster and Osnabrück. One aimed at restoring freedom of commerce by abolishing barriers to trade which had developed in the course of the war, and the other intended to provide a measure of free navigation on the Rhine.[17] In this respect, as in many others, there is apparent the particular character of the Westphalian peace which distinguishes it sharply from routine peace treaties and which points out its kinship with the great peace settlements of 1815 and 1919.

As the above rapid survey of some of the salient features of the Peace Settlement of 1648 discloses, the actual terms of the settlement, interesting and novel as they may be, would hardly suffice to account for the outstanding place attributed to it in the evolution of international relations. In order to find a more adequate explanation it would seem appropriate to search not so much in the text of the treaties themselves as in their implications, in the broad conceptions on which they rest and the developments to which they provided impetus.

[14] Van Vollenhoven, *The Law of Peace,* p. 86; see also p. 88.

[15] Van Vollenhoven, *The Law of Peace,* p. 86.

[16] Lange, work cited, p. 498. More definite provisions for arbitration were included in the Treaty between Spain and the United Provinces signed at Münster on January 30, 1648. See Van Vollenhoven, work cited, p. 88.

[17] Mirabelli, work cited, p. 84.

In this order of ideas it has been affirmed that the Peace of Westphalia was the starting point for the development of modern international law.[18] It has also been contended that it constituted "the first faint beginning of an international constitutional law" and the first instance "of deliberate enactment of common regulations by concerted action."[19] In this connection the special merits of the work of Grotius have been stressed. On the one hand it has been argued that "Grotius adapted the (old) Law of Nature to fill the vacuum created by the extinction of the supreme authority of Emperor and Pope."[20] On the other hand it has been affirmed that Grotius developed a system of international law which would equally appeal to, and be approved by, the believers and the atheists, and which would apply to all states irrespective of the character and dignity of their rulers.[21] It can hardly be denied that the Peace of Westphalia marked an epoch in the evolution of international law. It undoubtedly promoted the laicization of international law by divorcing it from any particular religious background, and the extension of its scope so as to include, on a footing of equality, republican and monarchical states. Indeed these two by-products of the Peace of 1648 would seem significant enough for students of international law and relations to regard it as an event of outstanding and lasting value. It would seem hazardous, however, to regard the Settlement of Westphalia and the work of Grotius as more than stages in the gradual, though by no means uniform, process which antedates and continues beyond the year 1648.[22] As to the contention that Grotius filled the vacuum created by the deposition of Pope and Emperor, more will be said about this in a different context.

Closely related with the stimulus to international law is the impetus said to have been given by the Peace of Westphalia to the theory and practice of the balance of power. Indeed, the existence of a political equilibrium has frequently been regarded as a necessary condition for the existence of the Law of Nations.[23] It has also become virtually axiomatic that the maintenance of the state system depends upon the preservation of a balance of power between its component and independent parts.[24] There is substantial evidence for the fact that while the principle of the balance of power had been evolved prior to 1648,[25] the Peace of Westphalia first illustrates its application on a grand scale.

[18] Paul Fauchille, *Traité de Droit International Public,* Vol. I, Pt. I, p. 75; see also P. H. Winfield, *The Foundations and the Future of International Law,* 1941, p. 18.

[19] F. S. Dunn, "International Legislation," 42 *Political Science Quarterly* (1927), p. 577.

[20] Winfield, work cited, p. 20.

[21] W. Van der Vlugt, "L'Oeuvre de Grotius et son Influence sur le Développement du Droit International," 7 *Recueil des Cours* (1925), p. 448; Mirabelli, work cited, pp. 54, 92. But see John N. Figgis, *From Gerson Grotius, 1414–1625,* 1916, p. 284, n. 13. This merit is now claimed for Gentili: A. P. Sereni, *The Italian Conception of International Law,* 1943, p. 114, "His first merit lies in having cleared the field of international law from the dogmas of a particular religion and of having distinguished the juridical from the ethical and political aspects of the problems debated."

[22] Van Vollenhoven, *The Law of Peace,* p. 1; Mirabelli, work cited, p. 7; Sereni, work cited, p. 124.

[23] Oppenheim, *International Law,* 4th ed., edited by Arnold McNair, Vol. I, 1928, p. 99; but see La Brière, work cited, pp. 62, 68.

[24] Van Vollenhoven, work cited, p. 91.

[25] Mirabelli, work cited, p. 10. See E. Kaeber, *Die Idee des europäischen Gleichgewichts in der publizistischen Literatur vom 16. bis zur Mitte des 18. Jahrhunderts,* 1907, pp. 8, 20.

The operation of the maxim *partager pour équilibrer*[26] can be traced in the territorial clauses of the Treaties of Münster and Osnabrück. This is notably the case in those referring to the aggrandizement of France and Sweden, to the independence of the United Provinces, of the Swiss Confederation, and to the consolidation of about nine hundred units of the Empire into about three hundred. Henceforth, in the organization of Europe resulting from the Peace, *tout repose sur la convenance de balancer les forces et de garantir les situations acquises par l'éstablissement de contrepoids.*[27] It is interesting to note that the advocacy of a political equilibrium in the literature of the Renaissance has been interpreted as having the character of a protest against the rival principle of a universal monarchy.[28] It was argued, in effect, that the freedom of all states would be brought about as a result of the establishment of a political equilibrium.[29] In this sense the balance of power doctrine forms an important part of that body of political thought which came to fruition in the Peace of Westphalia. It assumed, thereby, increased significance and prestige.

Of even greater importance than any of these particular aspects of developments of the Treaties of Osnabrück and Münster were the general political ideas, the triumph of which they apparently consecrated in the mind of man. The Peace of Westphalia, for better or worse, marks the end of an epoch and the opening of another. It represents the majestic portal which leads from the old into the new world.[30] The old world, we are told, lived in the idea of a Christian commonwealth, of a world harmoniously ordered and governed in the spiritual and temporal realms by the Pope and Emperor.[31] This medieval world was characterized by a hierarchical conception of the relationship between the existing political entities on the one hand, and the Emperor on the other.[32] For a long time preceding the Peace of 1648, however, powerful intellectual, political, and social forces were at work which opposed and, by opposing them, undermined, both the aspirations and the remaining realities of the unified control of Pope and Emperor. In particular the Reformation and the Renaissance, and, expressive of the rising urge of individualism in politics, nationalism, each in its own field, attacked the supreme authority claimed by the Pope and the Emperor. The combined impact of these centrifugal forces could not, in the long run, be resisted solely by the writings of the defenders of their authority. To maintain the claims it would have been necessary to display a real overpowering authority. Neither the Pope nor the Emperor, however, was at that time in the position to re-

[26] Charles Dupuis, *Le Principe d'Equilibre et le Concert Européen,* 1909, p. 23.

[27] Dupuis, p. 22; see also pp. 12, 20, and 21; La Brière, work cited, p. 60, 62.

[28] Lange, work cited, p. 133: *Au fond le principe d'équilibre implique une protestation contre le principe de l'Empire universel.* A publication in the year 1632 espoused the notion of the *système des contrepoids* and argued that the King of France *tiendra la balance du monde en ses mains, qu'il a apporté du Ciel.* Kaeber, work cited, p. 32.

[29] Kaeber, work cited, p. 41; G. L. Comte de Garden, *Histoire Générale des Traités de Paix,* Vol. I, 1848, pp. 246, 250.

[30] Robert Redslob, *Histoire des Grands Principes du Droit des Gens,* 1923, p. 223.

[31] Dupuis, work cited, p. 9: *Le moyen âge avait revé d'organiser l'Europe sur la double base de l'unité de la chétienté et de la hiérarchie des pouvoirs. Le pape et l'empereur, placés au sommet de la société internationale devaient, en théorie, maintenir l'unité, en se partageant la domination dans l'ordre spirituel et dans l'ordre temporel; ils devaient, en même temps, sauvegarder les droits de tous, en offrant un recours suprême contre les abus auxquels se pouvaient livrer les mille détenteurs de la souveraineté morcelée par régime féodal.* See also Julius Goebel, *The Equality of States,* 1923, p. 22.

[32] Van de Vlugt, work cited, p. 448.

strain effectively the centrifugal tendencies. The latter was ultimately forced to abandon all pretenses on the field of battle and the former's protest against the Peace of Westphalia, the Bull *Zel Domus* of November 26, 1648,[33] failed to restrain the course of history. In the spiritual field the Treaty of Westphalia was said to be "a public act of disregard of the international authority of the Papacy."[34] In the political field it marked man's abandonment of the idea of a hierarchical structure of society and his option for a new system characterized by the coexistence of a multiplicity of states, each sovereign within its territory, equal to one another, and free from any external earthly authority.[35] The idea of an authority or organization above the sovereign states is no longer. What takes its place is the notion that all states form a world-wide political system or that, at any rate, the states of Western Europe form a single political system.[36] This new system rests on international law and the balance of power, a law operating between rather than above states and a power operating between rather than above states.

It is true that the powers assembled at the Congress of Westphalia paid homage to the old conception of world unity by proclaiming in the preamble of the Treaty of Münster that it was made *ad Christianae Reipublicae salutem* and in that of the Treaty of Osnabrück *au salut de la Republique Chrestienne.*[37] Nevertheless, there is a notable lack of consensus in the appreciation of the major implications of the Peace of Westphalia according to one view the old system was simply superseded by a modern, the present political, state system, a world-wide system.[38] On the other hand the view is also held that the Peace of Westphalia marks a decisive date in the history of the disorganization of the public law of Europe.[39] In this order of ideas it was argued that the system inaugurated by the Peace, while it may be new, was "as utterly remote as possible from a juridical order founded on a common respect for law";[40] and that in spite of all the appearances of the

[33] J. Du Mont, *Corps Universel Diplomatique du Droit des Gens,* Vol. VI, Part I, 1708, p. 463.

[34] John Eppstein, *The Catholic Tradition of the Law of Nations,* 1935, p. 192; see also p. 325.

[35] Sir Paul Vinogradoff, "Historical Types of International Law," 1 *Bibliotheca Visseriana* (1923), p. 45.

[36] Van Vollenhoven, *The Law of Peace,* p. 81.

[37] Du Mont, work cited, p. 450, 469.

[38] Van Vollenhoven, work cited, p. 81; G. F. de Martens, *Traité de Droit International,* Vol. I, 1883, p. 117; similarly Paul Fauchille, work cited, p. 75. Fauchille underscores *la reconnaissance par les Etats européens de la solidarité de leurs intérêts politiques, . . . dans l'application de l'idée qu'un certain équilibre politique était l'un des facteurs* de la paix; Oppenheim, work cited, p. 69; H. Treitschke, *Politics* (English translation), Vol. II, 1916, p. 569; Montagu Bernard, *Four Lectures on Subjects Connected with Diplomacy,* 1868, p. 6; T. J. Lawrence, "The Work of Grotius as a Reformer of International Law, "*Essays on Some Disputed Questions of International Law,* 1885, p. 189; Edwin L. Borchard, "International Law," 8 *Encyclopaedia of the Social Sciences,* 1935, p. 169; James Bryce, *The Holy Roman Empire,* 1866 (revised edition), p. 372; see also Mirabelli, work cited, p. 8; Jacob ter Meulen, *Der Gedanke der Internationalen Organisation in seiner Entwicklung, 1300–1800,* 1917, p. 24; Hill, work cited, Vol. III, p. vii; same, Vol. II, 1906, p. 599, 604; Wolfgang Windelband, *Die auswärtige Politik der Grossmächte in der Neuzeit. Von 1494 bis zur Gegenwart,* 4th ed. (1936), p. 126 f.; see also Singer, "Völkerrechtsgeschichte," *Wörterbuch des Völkerrechts,* edited by Strupp, Vol. III, 1929, p. 193; Dupuis, work cited, pp. 13, 21; T. A. Walker, *A History of the Law of Nations,* 1899, Vol. I, pp. 147 and ff.; The Collected Papers of John Westlake on Public International Law, ed., by L. Oppenheim, 1914, pp. 55 ff.; E. H. Carr, *Nationalism and After,* 1945, p. 1.

[39] de la Brière, work cited, p. 58.

[40] Same, p. 53. The passage quoted with approval in Van Vollenhoven, at p. 83, appeared in the following context: *Dans leur modalités politiques et diplomatiques, en effet, les tractations de Westphalie portent le caractère d'un empirisme tellement brutal, tellement immoral, tellement incohérent, qu'on est en droit de les proposer aux négociateurs futurs de la paix du XXe siècle comme un parfait exemple des erreurs et des fautes dont il faudra désormais nous préserver à tout prix. Bien plus, dans son principe même (et c'est là surtout que nous voulons en venir), le règlement européen adopté à Münster et à Osnabrück constituera la première application général et solonnelle de la politique d'équilibre, système diplomatique aussi radicalement éloigné que possible de l'ordre juridique, fondé sur le respect du droit des tous, qui est aujourd'hui le très noble objectif des promoteurs de la 'Société des Nations.'*

birth of a new international society of nations "even the germ of such a society was likely to be absent under a system in direct opposition to any impingement upon the sovereign independence of each individual state."[41] Which of these conflicting views is accurate? The answer is difficult in the extreme for the materials regarding the basic problems of the origin of our state system lack coördination and clarity[42] and all the necessary sources are not readily available. For these reasons the following remarks are necessarily tentative and intended to indicate rather than to solve the problems connected with the rise of the modern state system and the particular role of the Peace of Westphalia in this vital process.

The imperial authority, the gradual weakening of which is sometimes said to have set in as early as the Treaty of Verdun of 843, probably received a serious blow in the course and as a result of the Great Interregnum (1254–73) on the one hand, and the rise of independent or quasi-independent communities in Italy and of national states in England,[43] Spain, and France, on the other. The discovery of the New World and the extension of intercourse between the Western Christian and Eastern non-Christian world provided those opposing the claim of the Emperor to universal dominion with arguments of considerable persuasiveness. The Great Schism in the Church (1378–1417) and the rise of sects and eventually of the Reformation weakened correspondingly the authority of the Pope. These developments in the secular and spiritual fields which finally culminated in the Thirty Years' War and the Peace of Westphalia, were reflected in and stimulated by contemporaneous political thought.

One of the early opponents of the Emperor was Bartolus of Sassoferrato, who drew a fine distinction between the *de jure* overlordship of the Emperor and the *de facto* existence of *civitates superiorem non recognoscentes.*[44] The formula, said to be of French origin, was later cast by Baldus in a sharper form: *Rex in regno suo est Imperator regni sui.*[45] In that sentence, observed Professor Barker, "we may hear the cracking of the Middle Ages."[46] Bartolus, however, in spite of his insistence on the *de facto* independence of Italian city states, still recognized the Empire and the Emperor as the Lord of the world albeit on an idealistic or spiritualistic plane.[47] In France a similar movement against the universalistic

[41] Van Vollenhoven, *The Law of Peace,* p. 93.

[42] Professor Sereni's book referred to above constitutes a recent and useful contribution.

[43] Sir Henry Maine, *Ancient Law,* 1930, p. 129, Pollock's Notes, to the effect that the Kings of England never owed or rendered any temporal allegiance to the Empire. Figgis, work cited, p. 213 suggests that "the dream of a universal state had disappeared with the failure of Charles V to secure the Empire for his son."

[44] Sereni, work cited, p. 59.

[45] Same, note 11.

[46] Ernest Barker, *Church, State, and Study,* 1930, p. 65.

[47] Sereni, p. 60: "All the cities, however, all the states, are in Bartolus' mind coordinated within the empire. The emperor is the Lord of the world: to deny it would be heresy. . . . Thus the superiority of the empire over the cities is admitted on a purely ideal plane. Bartolus' elevation of the empire to the function of a spiritual institution amounts to a complete denial of its political authority, in accordance with the reality of the age. The empire is envisaged by Bartolus as the necessary universal society, in which all the powers of Christendom must co-operate. In Italy, Dante, Marsilio of Padua, Cino da Pistoia, and many other political thinkers, jurisconsults, and poets had invoked the authority of the empire on the same ideal plane. The empire was to have been the unifying force of the Christian world, to have appeased all discords, suppressed wars and reprisals, affirmed the reign of peace and justice on the earth. For Bartolus as well as for these other Italians the empire was then but a messianic dream, an ideal aspiration." Cf. also Sir Paul Vinogradoff, work cited, p. 43.

claims of both Emperor and Pope was on foot. The development of the theory of sovereignty by Bodin may be regarded as marking the end, on the doctrinal level, of the efforts to throw off the overlordship of the Emperor and vindicate the independence of states.[48] This movement was not unopposed. Imperialist writers continued to defend and support the claims of the Emperor. Their argument was, broadly, that being of divine origin, the rights of the Emperor existed irrespective of their actual exercise. No voluntary abandonment, not even an express grant, was susceptible of impairing them. As late as the seventeenth century, imperialist lawyers repeated the claim that the King of France, like other princes, was of right, and must forever remain, subject to the Roman Emperor.[49]

While some of the jurists of the sixteenth century questioned with increasing boldness the claim of any single potentate to be *totius orbis dominus*[50] others combined their opposition with the exposition of a new positive doctrine, that of an international community of states. This doctrine is admittedly of ancient origin. The conception of the entire human race forming a single society goes back to the Stoa and the teachings of the early church fathers.[51] It experienced a revival in the works of some of the early writers of international law, notably those of Victoria, Suarez, and Gentili. They denied, on the one hand, the claim of the Emperor to exercise temporal jurisdiction over princes,[52] and affirmed, on the other, the existence of an international community governed by international law.

Victoria, in a famous passage arguing the binding force of laws made by a king upon the king himself, irrespective of his will, and of pacts entered into by the free will of the contracting parties upon them, declares:[53]

> From all that has been said, a corollary may be inferred, namely: that international law has not only the force of a pact and agreement among men, but also the force of a law; for the world as a whole, being in a way one single State, has the power to create laws that are just and fitting for all persons, as are the rules of international law. Consequently, it is clear that they who violate these international rules, whether in peace or in war, commit a mortal sin; moreover, in the gravest matters, such as the inviolability of ambassadors, it is not permissible for one country to refuse to be bound by international law, the latter having been established by the authority of the whole world.

Gentili referred with approval to the teachings of the Stoics that[54]

[48] Maine, work cited, p. 129: "Modern National sovereignty may be regarded, in a general way, as a reaction against both the feudal and the imperial conceptions. Rulers of the Middle Ages, as and when they felt strong enough, expressly or tacitly renounced both homage to any overlord and submission to the Emperor."

[49] Bryce, work cited, p. 243. Sereni, work cited, p. 65, n. 33. "As late as the end of the sixteenth century there were still Italian jurisconsults who endeavored to maintain the supremacy and universality of the authority of the pope and the emperor."

[50] Walker, work cited, p. 149.

[51] Barker, work cited, p. 62; James Brown Scott, *The Law, the State, and the International Community*, Vol. II, 1939, p. 255.

[52] Walker, work cited, p. 149; Sereni, work cited, pp. 64, 115.

[53] Relectio of the Reverend Father, Brother Franciscus de Victoria Concerning Civil Power, a translation by Gwladys L. Williams. In James Brown Scott, *The Spanish Origin of International Law*, 1934. Appendix C, p. xc.

[54] Alberico Gentili, *De Iure Belli Libri Tres*, translation of the edition of 1612 by John C. Rolfe, *The Classics of International Law*, by James Brown Scott, 1933, p. 67. See also Sereni, work cited, p. 64.

> the whole world formed one state, and that all men were fellow citizens and fellow townsmen, like a single herd feeding in a common pasture. All this universe which you see, in which things divine and human are included, is one, and we are members of a great body. And, in truth, the world is one body.

And again, he declared:[55]

> Now what Plato and those expounders of the law say of private citizens we feel justified in applying to sovereigns and nations, since the rule which governs a private citizen in his own state ought to govern a public citizen, that is to say a sovereign or a sovereign people, in this public and universal state formed by the world. As a private citizen conducts himself with reference to another private citizen, so ought it to be between one sovereign and another, says Baldus.

Suarez' conception of the international society is expounded in the following "perhaps the most memorable passage of the 'Law of Nations.' "[56]

> The rational basis . . . of this phase of law consists in the fact that the human race howsoever many the various peoples and kingdoms into which it may be divided, always preserves a certain unity . . . enjoined the natural precept of mutual love and mercy; a precept which applies to all, even to strangers of every nation.
>
> Therefore, although a given sovereign state, commonwealth, or kingdom, may constitute a perfect community in itself, consisting of its own members, nevertheless, each one of these states is also, in a certain sense, and viewed in relation to the human race, a member of that universal society; for these states when standing alone are never so self-sufficient that they do not require some mutual assistance, association, and intercourse, at times for their own greater welfare and advantage, but at other times because also of some moral necessity or need. This fact is made manifest by actual usage.
>
> Consequently, such communities have need of some system of law whereby they may be directed and properly ordered with regard to this kind of intercourse and association; and although that guidance is in large measure provided by natural reason, it is not provided in sufficient measure and in a direct manner with respect to all matters; therefore, it was possible for certain special rules of law to be introduced through the practice of these same nations. For just as in one state or province law is introduced by custom, so among the human race as a whole it was possible for laws to be introduced by the habitual conduct of nations. This was the more feasible because the matters comprised within the law in question are few, very closely related to natural law and most easily deduced therefrom in a manner so advantageous and so in harmony with nature itself that, while this derivation (of the law of nations from the natural law) may not be self-evident—that is, not essentially and absolutely required for moral rectitude—it is nevertheless quite in accord with nature, and universally acceptable for its own sake.

[55] Gentili, work cited, p. 68. Affirming that it is right to make war upon pirates, Gentili says: "And if a war against pirates justly calls all men to arms because of love for our neighbor and the desire to live in peace, so also do the general violation of the common law of humanity and the wrong done to mankind. Piracy is contrary to the law of nations and the league of human society": p. 124.

[56] James Brown Scott, *The Spanish Conception of International Law and of Sanctions*, 1934, p. 90. The English translation of the above quotation from Suarez, *De Legibus*, Book II, Ch. XIX, paragraph 9, is taken from Scott, *The Law, the State, and the International Community*, Vol. II, p. 257.

It is this conception of an international society embracing, on a footing of equality, the entire human race irrespective of religion and form of government which is usually said to have triumphed in the seventeenth century over the medieval conception of a more restricted Christian society organized hierarchically, that is, on the basis of inequality. As the dominating political position of the Roman Emperor had gradually but decidedly declined in the centuries and decades preceding the Peace of Westphalia, it is probably correct to say that the Peace merely finally sealed an existing state of affairs. Lord Bryce said that the Peace of Westphalia "did no more than legalize a condition of things already in existence, but which, by being legalized, acquired new importance."[57] It is probably also true, in a broad sense, that with the Congress of Westphalia the various states entered into the legal concept of a *societas gentium* which had long before been established by the science of natural law.[58] It is equally correct that the so-called Grotian Law of Nature school continued to expound the concept of a society of states. Christian Wolff's idea of a *civitas gentium maxima* is a noteworthy and well-known example. A sideline of this type of thinking and writing is represented by the writers who in one form or another, on a restricted or universal basis, advocate the establishment of a more definite society of states than in their view appeared to be actually in existence. One might mention as representatives of this school of thought Dante, Pierre Dubois, George of Podebrad, Erasmus, Emeric Crucé, Sully, William Penn, the Abbé de Saint-Pierre, Rousseau, Jeremy Bentham, Immanual Kant, William Ladd, William Jay, Elihu Burritt, Saint-Simon, Jean de Bloch, A. H. Fried, J. Novicov, and others. To some extent their writings should have served as evidence that the *pluriversum* which emerged in the sixteenth and seventeenth centuries was not quite an international community and that the states did not always behave as members of one body politic.

Be that as it may, it would seem not altogether unjustified to observe that the development of international law, a determining factor of any conception of an international community, did not come to a standstill with the Peace of Westphalia. It would seem possible to distinguish at least three trends of thought on the subject of the binding force of international law prior to 1648. In Victoria one might discern the attempt to base international law on an objective foundation irrespective of the will of the states and to conceive international law as a law above states. In Suarez the objective foundation is at least overshadowed if not replaced by a subjective foundation in the will of the states. Suarez presented the *jus gentium* as a law between states.[59] In Gentili, of whom it has been said that he had taken the first step towards making international law what it is,[60] namely, almost exclusively positive, international law still appears to be based on natural reason and derived from a law of nature superior to the nations.[61] Gentili's doctrine "marked

[57] Bryce, work cited, p. 372; Mirabelli, work cited, p. 15 ff.
[58] Ter Meulen, work cited, p. 34.
[59] Walker, work cited, p. 155; Introduction by Coleman Phillipson to Gentili in the above-quoted edition, p. 23a, n. 4.
[60] T. E. Holland, *Studies in International Law,* 1898, p. 23.
[61] Sereni, p. 107: "With Gentili there thus begins the naturalistic conception of international law, later accepted by Grotius."

progress because it affirmed the existence of an autonomous system of rules of law distinct from the precepts of religion and ethics and directed at regulating international relations according to abstract principles of justice."[62] But what, precisely, we may ask, was the nature of that autonomy? An indication of its meaning may perhaps be gleaned from Gentili's doctrine of the just war. One of the essential conditions of a just war is that it must be waged for a just cause. Gentili affirms that war may be waged with justice on both sides.[63] He is said to come close to Machiavelli's opinion that all necessary wars are justified.[64] But who decides whether there is a just cause, whether the necessity is of such a nature as to justify war? The answer to this question must obviously be of decisive importance for the understanding not only of Gentili's doctrine of just war but equally for his conception of international law. Now it is extremely interesting to note that the decision "concerning the lawfulness of war is on the whole left to each belligerent."[64] If this is an accurate interpretation of Gentili's doctrine, then the autonomy of international law would seem to assume a deeper meaning. It would indicate not merely the independence of international law from precepts of civil law, religion, and ethics. It would also seem to indicate that the contents of international law as well as the existence or non-existence of international law depends upon the insight of the states concerned, or, to use a modern phrase, upon the will of the states.[65]

Grotius and several subsequent writers still maintain natural or divine law alongside of customary law as a source of international law. It would seem, however, that with Grotius the accent begins to be transferred from the Law of Nature or divine law to that branch of human law which "has received its obligatory force from the will of nations, or of many nations."[66] Zouche, the "second founder of the Law of Nations," rather than Grotius, is called the father of positivism for the emphasis given by him to customary international law.[67] Without any attempt to trace the development of the doctrine of the will of states as the basis of international law, it may be useful to conclude this brief survey with a few remarks about Vattel. Vattel, regarded as a Grotian, still maintains the distinction between different types of branches of the Law of Nations. Within the positive law of nations, based on the agreement of nations, he differentiates three divisions:

[62] Sereni, p. 107.

[63] Gentili, Book I, Ch. VI, p. 31.

[64] Sereni, p. 109.

[65] Gentili, while affirming that "some law of nature exists," stressed the difficulty involved in discovering "what that law is and how we shall prove that it is this or that": Book I, Ch. I, p. 5. His reasoning on this subject, particularly at p. 7, is illustrative of the difficulty inherent in any law of nature doctrine. Gentili seems to accept the agreement of states, not necessarily of all states, and usage, as a test of the existence of rules of international law: p. 8. See Phillipson's *Introduction*, p. 22a. It is also interesting to note that in discussing arbitration of dispute between sovereigns Gentili starts from the proposition that "the sovereign has no earthly judge." Book I, Ch. III, p. 15. Having referred to a number of arbitrations, he says: "But why do I multiply examples, as if any one could not call to mind a great number of such occurrences in every age? Why, to be sure, in order that those who avoid this kind of contest by arbitration and resort at once to the other, that is, to force, may understand that they are setting their faces against justice, humanity, and good precedent, and that they are rushing to arms of their own free will, because they are unwilling to submit to any one's verdict": p. 16.

[66] Grotius, *De Jure Belli Ac Pacis*, Translated by Francis W. Kelsey, *The Classics of International Law*, Edited by James Brown Scott, Vol. II, 1925, Book I, Ch. I, paragraph 14. Phillipson's *Introduction*, p. 22a.

[67] L. Oppenheim, International Law, 5th ed., edited by H. Lauterpacht, 1937, Vol. I, p. 87.

the voluntary, the conventional, and the customary law. The voluntary law proceeds from their presumed consent, the conventional law from their express consent, and the customary law from their tacit consent. Positive international law is distinguished from the natural or necessary law of nations which Vattel undertakes to treat separately. In order to understand the respective functions of natural and positive international law Vattel draws the following distinction:

> But after having established on each point what the necessary law prescribes, we shall then explain how and why these precepts must be modified by the voluntary law; or, to put it in another way, we shall show how, by reason of the liberty of nations and the rules of their natural society, the external law which they must observe towards one another differs on certain points from the principles of the internal law, which, however, are always binding upon the conscience.

With these nice distinctions in mind one may ask legitimately what precisely is the role of these branches of the law of nations with respect to the conduct of states in relation to one another. Vattel leaves no doubt about it, for he declares that while the necessary law is at all times obligatory upon the conscience, and that a nation must never lose sight of it when deliberating on the course it must pursue in order to fulfill its duty, it must consult the voluntary law "when there is question of what it can demand from other states."[68] It may not be unreasonable to conclude that according to Vattel only those rules of the law of nations which proceed from and are based on the consent of states are enforceable in international relations. This rather significant feature of Vattel's doctrine, it is believed, may not have entirely escaped the attention of diplomats to whom it was addressed, and it may, therefore, account at least partially for his immense popularity. But Vattel's international law is no longer above but beside the diplomat.[69]

Although he does not rank as a strict positivist, Vattel prepared the ground for the era of uninhibited positivism. He helped to establish, precisely because of his popularity, perhaps more than any of his predecessors or successors, the consensual character of international law and to reduce natural law from the function of supplying an objective basis for the validity, the binding force, of the law of nations to the function of supplying rules for filling gaps in positive international law. This distinction between the dual function of natural law in relation to the law of nations is not always observed and yet it would seem to deserve close attention.

The development of international law along the lines indicated above, was bound to influence the concept of an international society of states. In the course of time it became purely formal. *Ubi ius, ibi societas.* Those who argued the existence of a law of nations accepted the use, though rarely more, of the phrase, "Family of Nations." In the period

[68] E. Vattel, *The Law of Nations,* translated by Charles G. Fenwick, *The Classics of International Law,* Edited by James Brown Scott, Vol. III, 1916, p. 9.

[69] Albert de Lapradelle's introduction to the above edition of Vattel, Vol. III, p. liv: "Writing for courts and for the leaders of nations, he could only place law beside diplomacy as wise counsel; he could not set it above diplomacy as a strict rule."

following the Peace of Westphalia the development of international relations would seem to have followed decidedly not the conception of an objectively founded international law and community of Victoria but that indicated in the teachings of Suarez, if indeed it be accurate to assume an essential difference between their doctrines.[70] From the 18th century and, in particular, from Vattel onward, however, there can be no doubt as to the trend of the development. It was predominately positivist and consensual. The will of states seems to explain both the contents and the binding force of international law. The concept of the Family of Nations recedes in the background.[71] To have paved the way for this development by liquidating, with a degree of apparent finality, the idea of the Middle Ages of an objective order of things personified by the Emperor in the secular realm, would seem to be one of the more vital aspects of the consequences of the Peace of Westphalia and of its place in the evolution of international relations. Viewed in this light the answer to the question formulated above cannot be doubtful. Instead of heralding the era of a genuine international community of nations subordinated to the rule of the law of nations, it led to the era of absolutist states, jealous of their territorial sovereignty to a point where the idea of an international community became an almost empty phrase and where international law came to depend upon the will of states more concerned with the preservation and expansion of their power than with the establishment of a rule of law. In the period immediately following the Peace, of the objective validity of international law there may be some doubt. Of the subjective character of much of modern international law there can hardly be any doubt.[72]

It may be said, by way of summary, that on the threshold of the modern era of international relations there were two doctrines with respect to the binding force of international law and the existence of an international community of states. The doctrine of

[70] Scott, *The Spanish Conception of International Law and of Sanctions*, 1934, p. 91: "If the two passages (quoted above in the text), however, be compared from the standpoint of international law, the statement of Suárez seemed to lack that sense of ultimate completeness which always seems to have been in the mind of Victoria; his is not merely an international community with law, but it is an international community with a power to create law and to punish the violations of that law. It may well be that the presence of law in Suárez' community implies both the right consciously to create and the power to preserve that law inviolate; but neither the right nor the power are express, as in the case of Francis of Victoria's international community. For does not Victoria say expressly that the *jus gentium* has 'the force of a pact and agreement among men'? Whereas Suárez implies in the succeeding chapter of this very book that the law of nations may have been introduced simply through 'usage and tradition,. . . and without any special and simultaneous compact or agreement on the part of all peoples.' This conception of Suárez looks to an inorganic association; Victoria's conception looks to an organized society, with a law of nations having the force of a pact, the obligations of which are enforceable, not merely under the law of nations but under the natural law."

[71] Lapradelle, as cited, p. liv: "It would be vain to look in his work for a reflection of the fine passage of Suárez on the solidarity of nations; but, on the other hand, it would be too much to require in a diplomat of the end of the eighteenth century, even though he were permeated with the spirit of the Encyclopaedia, the same freedom of speech as in a monk of the sixteenth. Vattel, who does not develop to any great extent the idea of arbitration, would probably have no place as an organizer of the society of the future."

[72] Emphasizing the destructive character of Vattel's elegant doctrine of the law of nations, Van Vollenhoven concludes: "Henceforth, there will be not merely no positive law, even on a limited scale, there will be not merely the claims of the governments to a limitless sovereignty; from that time onward there will be a nominal law of peace, exacting in character, elaborated in detail, full of celestial principles and unctuous rhetoric, but one that is rendered utterly futile by the reservation, ceaselessly reiterated, that it is for the sovereign states to judge the extent to which those principles and that rhetoric shall bind them in the sphere of reality." *The Law of Peace*, p. 107 f. See also J. L. Brierly, The Law of Nations, 1936 (2d ed.). p. 32.

Victoria is characterized by an objective approach to the problem of the binding force of international law and by an organic conception of the international community of states. The other doctrine, characterized by the voluntaristic conception of the binding force of international law, is adumbrated in the work of Suarez.[72a] It is developed in the writings of Gentili, Grotius and Zouche, and it breaks to the fore in the work of Vattel who, emphasizing the independence rather than the interdependence of states, wrote the international law of political liberty.[72b] The growth of the voluntaristic conception of international law is accompanied by a weakening of the notion that all states form and are part of an international community. It is still very strong in the writings of Suarez and Gentili, although it seems to have assumed a character different from that attributed to it by Victoria. The test of the strength of the community doctrine may be said to have come in the seventeenth century. The liquidation of the universalistic claims of the Empire and the recognition of a multiplicity of states wielding the same powers as those hitherto reserved for the Emperor should have created a political and juridical condition favorable for the establishment of a genuine society of states. The opportunity which may have existed at the end of the Thirty Years' War for substituting a new order based on the impersonal supremacy of international law for the old order based on the personal supremacy of the Empire, was not, however, utilized. Instead of creating a society of states, the Peace of Westphalia, while paying lip service to the idea of a Christian commonwealth, merely ushers in the era of sovereign absolutist states which recognized no superior authority. In this era the liberty of states becomes increasingly incompatible with the concept of the international community, governed by international law independent of the will of states. On the contrary this era may be said to be characterized by the reign of positivism in international law. This positivism could not admit the existence of a society of states for the simple reason that it was unable to find a treaty or custom, proceeding from the will of states, which could be interpreted as the legal foundation of a community of states. In the nineteenth century, after the Napoleonic wars, there may be discerned in the Congress and Concert system the beginning of a conscious effort to establish a community of states based on the will of all states or at least on the will of the Great Powers. The Hague Peace Conferences, the League of Nations and, we may confidently assert, the United Nations are further stages in this development cognizable by positive international law.

This reaction against the unrestrained liberty of states, recognized as self-destructive in its ultimate implications was accentuated by a reaction against the prevailing voluntaristic conception of international law. The attempts to provide international law with an

[72a] Joseph Delos. *La Société Internationale et les Principes du Droit* Public, 1929, p. 229 f: *Considérable dés son vivant, traditionnelle aujourd'hui encore, l'oeuvre de Suarez a dépassé de beaucoup le cercle des théologiens. Suarez est, lui aussi, l'un des Fondateurs du Droit International, le plus connu peut-être, et l'un de ceux qui ont le plus influé sur les destinées de la doctrine. Son rôle dans de conflit du Droit à fondement objectif et du Droit subjectif, nous semble avoir été décisif à plus d'un égard. Son oeuvre offre de plus le cas topique que nous cherchions: elle permet de saisir, à un moment donné, et particulièrement important, puisqu'il se place aux origines mêmes du monde moderne, la cause du mal dont souffre la science politique internationale: la substitution du point de vue volontariste au point de vue du Droit à fondement objectif.*

[72b] Lapradelle, as cited, pp. liv, lv.

objective foundation, without, however, abandoning altogether the will of states doctrine, are illustrated by Bergbohm's and Triepel's theory of the *Vereinbarung*. A radical departure from the consensual view of international law is characteristic of Kelsen's theory of the initial hypothesis, and of the recent revival of natural law thinking in the field of international law. Other writers follow this trend away from the purely consensual nature of international law by emphasizing the role of *pacta sunt servanda* as the fundamental norm in international law. Others still suggested that international law is based on the maxim *voluntas civitatis maximae est servanda.*[73] The sociological interpretations of the binding force of international law should not be forgotten in this connection. It is common to all these schools of thought that they strive to vindicate for international law a binding force, independent of the will of the states and to substitute for the doctrine that international law is a law of coordination, the old-new doctrine, that international law is, and, if it is to be law, must be, a law of subordination, that is, a law above states.

An international law thus conceived could be interpreted as a law of an international community constituting a legal order for the existing states. It would seem doubtful, however, whether this result can be achieved without the creation of some new institutions or the strengthening of existing institutions. It was pointed out that the efforts to establish the binding force of international law independent of the will of states are bound to cause international lawyers to advocate the creation of an international legislature or, as a very minimum, of an international tribunal endowed with compulsory jurisdiction over disputes between states. While the creation of an international legislature would be concomitant with the formation of a super-state "the objective ascertainment of rights by courts is one (manifestation of the legal nature of international law) which could be effected within the frame of the existing practice and doctrine of international law."[74] The absence of an international court of justice with compulsory jurisdiction over disputes between states does not merely strain the legal character of international law to the breaking point.[74] In truth, it would seem to jeopardize altogether the conception of international law as a body of rules governing the conduct of states.

The history of the past three hundred years tends to show that international law, increasingly separated from its roots in right reason and natural law and deprived of its sources of objective and heteronomous validity, could but inadequately perform the task which devolved upon it following the disappearance of the secular rule of the Empire and its aspiration to be the Universal Monarchy envisioned by Dante. Such an international law, rugged individualism of territorial and heterogeneous states, balance of power, equality of states, and toleration,—these are among the legacies of the Settlement of Westphalia. That rugged individualism of states ill accommodates itself to an international rule of law reënforced by necessary institutions. It would seem that the national will to self-control which after a prolonged struggle first threw off the eternal shackles of

[73] H. Lauterpacht, *The Function of Law in the International Community*, 1933, p. 421. A brief survey of recent doctrines on international law will be found on p. 415.
[74] Lauterpacht, p. 426.

Pope and Emperor is the same which *mutatis mutandis* persists today in declining any far-reaching subordination to external international controls. It was one of the essential characteristics of the League of Nations and it is one of the chief weaknesses of the United Nations.

The approaching tercentenary of the Peace of Westphalia would seem to invite a thorough reëxamination of the foundations of international law and organization,[75] and of the political, economic, ideological and other factors which have determined their development. It may not be unreasonable to believe that such a broad inquiry, along with important insights into the forces which have shaped in the past and which shape at present the course of international law and organization, might also yield some precise data regarding the ways and means of harmonizing the will of major states to self-control with the exigencies of an international society which by and large yearns for order under law.

[75] Such a revision has been proposed by Dr. Lauterpacht in a different context: p. 437.

# WAYS AND MEANS OF MAKING THE EVIDENCE OF CUSTOMARY INTERNATIONAL LAW MORE READILY AVAILABLE

Preparatory work within the purview of
article 24 of the Statute of the
International Law Commission

# PART ONE

## The problem of making the evidence of customary international law more readily available

# THE PROBLEM OF MAKING THE EVIDENCE OF CUSTOMARY INTERNATIONAL LAW MORE READILY AVAILABLE

The memorandum on "Methods for Encouraging the Progressive Development of International Law and its Eventual Codification",[1] submitted by the Secretariat to the Committee on the Progressive Development of International Law and its Codification, which met at Lake Success from 12 May to 17 June 1947, suggested that the General Assembly might recommend to Governments the preparation of digests of materials illustrating their point of view in questions of international law. The memorandum stated:

"Such a recommendation might be implemented through the creation of a small committee which would consult with the Governments concerned on the manner in which the preparation of the digests could most effectively be undertaken. This body, with the consent of the respective Governments, might, for instance, nominate in each country a certain number of experts who would undertake the preliminary work of research with regard to the practice of [any] State."[2]

The same memorandum further suggested:

"That the collection and publication of decisions of national courts dealing with international law problems, possibly in connexion with the preparation of digests of State practice . . . will provide a useful indication of the *opinio juris* of States. . . . As far as collections of international law cases are concerned, a useful method would be to encour-

[1] A/AC.10/7,6 May 1947.

[2] *Ibid.*, p. 6.

Note: Part I was added by the U.N. Secretariat, and it is included here as an introduction. Professor Gross' article begins on page 33.

age the continuation of the collection of cases undertaken in the *Annual Digest and Reports of Public International Law Cases, 1919–1942,* as well as the continuation, in respect to the International Court of Justice, of the publications of the Permanent Court of International Justice.''[3]

The matters dealt with in the memorandum referred to were discussed at various meetings of the Committee. Thus at the second meeting, held on 13 May 1947, the United States delegate advocated the stimulation by the United Nations of the publication by Governments and private initiative ''of digests or other compilations revealing . . . the customary practice of States'', the continuation by the International Court of Justice of the model system of documenting cases developed by the Permanent Court of International Justice, and the making more accessible of the decisions of other tribunals.[4] And, at a subsequent meeting, the Yugoslav delegate spoke of the need for an international collection comprising not merely treaties, as is envisaged in the United Nations Treaty Series, but also ''municipal instruments connected with international law''.[5]

Following the discussion in the Committee, the Rapporteur, Professor J. L. Brierly, submitted a report on item 3 *(a)* of the agenda (Study of the methods by which the General Assembly shall encourage the progressive development of international law and its eventual codification), paragraph 18 of which reads:

''In connexion with the development of customary international law, as well as with the development of the law through the judicial process, the Committee desired to recommend that the International Law Commission consider ways and means for making the evidences of customary international law more readily available by the compilation of digests of State practice, and by the collection and publication of the decisions of national or international courts of[6] international law questions.''[7]

This paragraph, which was stated by the Chairman not to mean

''that there were no other sources of international law, but only that the evidence of customary international law was not easily available in contradistinction to evidence of scientific international law which was always laid down in books.'',[8] was incorporated in the report of the Committee presented to the General Assembly. The paragraph in question was amended slightly with a view to greater clarity in Sub-Committee 2 of the Sixth Committee, to which the report was ultimately referred, and became without further change article 24 of the statute of the International Law Commission. The English and French texts of that article are as follows:[9]

[3] *Ibid.*, pp. 6–7.
[4] A/AC.10/11, 13 May 1947, pp. 4, 7–8.
[5] A/AC.10/SR.8, 27 May 1947, p. 2.
[6] ''of'' became ''on'' in the draft adopted by the Committee.
[7] A/AC.10/40, 5 June 1947.
[8] A/AC.10/SR.27, 20 June 1947, p. 11.
[9] Resolution 174 (III), A/519, 8 January 1948, p. 109.

"The Commission shall consider ways and means for making the evidence of customary international law more readily available, such as the collection and publication of documents concerning State practice and of the decisions of national and international courts on questions of international law, and shall make a report to the General Assembly on this matter."

*"La Commission examine les moyens susceptibles de rendre plus accessible la documentation relative au droit international coutumier, par exemple la compilation et la publication de documents établissant la pratique des Etats et des décisions de juridiction nationales et internationales sur des questions de droit international, et elle fait rapport à l'Assemblée générale sur ce sujet."*

It is clear from the text of article 24 and from the preparatory work that the function assigned to the International Law Commission under that article is distinct from the other functions of the Commission, namely, the progressive development and the codification of international law. As part of the process of codification the Commission is indeed, through the Secretary-General, to "address to Governments a detailed request to furnish the texts of laws, decrees, judicial decisions, treaties, diplomatic correspondence, and other documents relevant to the topic being studied and which the Commission deems necessary" (article 19 (2) of the statute). But its task under article 24 is on the one hand much broader, and, on the other, more restricted. It relates exclusively to evidence of customary international law, yet it is concerned not merely with any particular topic but with the whole range of customary international law. The task, specifically stated, is to explore ways and means of remedying the present unsatisfactory state of documentation. This is made clearer by the French text, which speaks of "documentation", than by the English text, which employs the word "evidence". The French text, again, makes it clearer than does the English that the collection and publication of documents concerning the practice of States, and of decisions of national and international courts[10] in questions of international law are not necessarily the only methods for the discharge of the task which may be examined. Any other category of material relating to customary international law and any other method of making it more readily available may therefore be considered by the Commission. In singling out for mention two sources of customary international law article 24 merely gives prominence to those which during the past two decades have perhaps received more attention than others.

[10] The use in the French text of the more general term "jurisdiction", in contradistinction to the word "courts" in the English text, is also to be noted.

# PART TWO

## The existing state of the evidence of customary international law and suggestions hitherto made for its improvement

# I. GENERAL SURVEY OF COMPILATIONS AND DIGESTS OF EVIDENCE OF CUSTOMARY INTERNATIONAL LAW

Numerous collections of evidence to the practice of States already exist; of earlier works, it is sufficient to mention Leibnitz' *Codex Juris Gentium Diplomaticus* (1693), Dumont's *Corps Universel Diplomatique du Droit des Gens* (eight volumes covering the period from 800 to 1718, published 1726–1731), and G. F. von Martens' *Erzählungen merkwürdiger Rechtsfälle des neueren europäischen Völkerrechts* (1800–1802), Ch. de Martens' *Causes célèbres de droit des nations* (two volumes, 1827) and his *Nouvelles causes célèbres* (two volumes, 1843) were sufficiently successful to warrant a second edition in 1858–1861. G. F. von Martens began in 1791 the *Recueil des Traités,* which has continued to appear ever since. All these works, it will be noted, were the result of individual initiative. Governments began to contribute to digests only in more recent times, although some of them already published material of international legal import. Thus the British practice of issuing Blue Books began in the eighteenth century, though it assumed first importance only in the century following, when it was imitated by other States. The first official digest of State practice, however, was compiled and published by the United States Department of State in 1877, incidentally, primarily for the Department's own convenience.

This part of this paper is designed to offer a brief summary of the principal collections and digests, of use to the international lawyer, which are now in existence.

## A. COLLECTIONS OF DOCUMENTS RELATING TO THE STATE PRACTICE OF PARTICULAR COUNTRIES

At the present time a large number of Governments publishes, either in series or less regularly, State papers containing material of interest to the student and practitioner of international law. This brief survey is arranged by countries as follows: (1) Latin America; (2) United States; (3) United Kingdom; (4) France; (5) Russia and the Union of Soviet Socialist Republics; (6) Germany; (7) other countries.

### 1. Latin-American countries

#### *Official publications*

Nearly all the Latin-American Republics have, almost from the time of their establishment, published through their Ministries of Foreign Affairs annual reports or other compilations containing diplomatic correspondence and other materials on international law. These countries for the most part also publish so-called Colour Books as occasion warrants. There can be no doubt but that this mass of material, of which a by no means exhaustive list is given here, is very rich. It has unfortunately been little used hitherto, perhaps because it is not always easy to come by, and because it is largely unindexed.

ARGENTINA. There are several serial publications of the *Ministerio de Relaciones Exteriores y Culto;* the most important is the *Memoria,* which has appeared fairly regularly (though with some intervals, e.g., between 1905 and 1910), and which contains the texts of treaties and diplomatic correspondence.[11] The Ministry also issues collections of documents from time to time in a special *Libro Azúl.*

BOLIVIA. The Ministry of Foreign Affairs publishes, in addition to the *Memoria,* which has appeared fairly regularly since 1825, a treaty series, reports of national delegates to conferences, and since 1920 has published several volumes of diplomatic documents on special topics, e.g., the Chaco and the Tacna-Arica disputes.[12]

BRAZIL. The *Ministerio das Relações Exteriores* has published regularly since 1922 the *Archivo Diplomatico da Independencia,* in addition to various bulletins and to the *Relatorio,* publication of which seems to have started in the first half of the nineteenth century.

CHILE. The *Memoria,* published since 1829 and appearing annually since 1927, contains documents on the foreign relations of Chile, international conferences and negotiations, and also presidential messages, laws, decrees, and regulations of international import. The Ministry of Foreign Affairs also publishes from time to time special volumes of diplomatic documents on particular problems.[13]

COLOMBIA. Reports on foreign relations presented to the Congress have been published under various titles since 1823. The present title is *Memoria de Relaciones Exteriores Presentada al Congreso.* The Ministry of Foreign Affairs also publishes from time to time volumes of documents supplementary to the *Memoria,* and a bulletin entitled *Revista Colombiana de Derecho Internacional.* The *Anales Diplomaticos y Consulares Colombia* edited by Antonio José Uribe (six volumes, 1900 to 1920) are also of interest.[14]

[11] *A Guide to the Official Publications of the Other American Republics, Argentina;* General editor, James B. Childs, Library of Congress, Washington, 1945, pp. 109–110.
[12] *Ibid., II, Bolivia,* pp. 48–50.
[13] *Ibid., IV, Chile,* pp. 36–38.
[14] *Ibid., V, Columbia,* pp. 69–71.

COSTA RICA. The *Secretaria de Relaciones Exteriores, Justicia, Gracia y Culto,* has published a large number of volumes on boundary questions and other international legal problems, and since 1844 (apparently with some gaps) a series of *Memorias.*[15]

CUBA. Since 1904 the *Ministerio de Estado* has published an official bulletin of information on international affairs and on particular questions has issued Grey Books. The Ministry does not publish regular reports but its work is reviewed in presidential messages to the Congress.[16]

DOMINICAN REPUBLIC. The Ministry of Foreign Affairs has published *Memorias* irregularly since 1877, and also an official bulletin, besides several volumes on special questions.[17]

ECUADOR. The *Memorias* cover, with some gaps, the period from 1837 to the present day. There are other official publications, devoted to arbitration, disputes, etc.[18]

EL SALVADOR. *Memorias* have appeared since 1827, regularly since 1849. Some are published separately and some in the *Diario Oficial* as part of the annual presidential message to the Congress. The Ministry of Foreign Affairs has also published the texts of some laws, e.g., on claims of foreigners, and some volumes of diplomatic documents on special questions.[19]

GUATEMALA. *Memorias* have appeared since 1849, regularly since 1879. Some volumes contain documents on boundary disputes and arbitrations. The Ministry of Foreign Affairs issued a White Book on the Belize question in 1938 and an Addendum thereto in 1940.[20]

HAITI. The Ministry of Foreign Affairs has published various volumes of diplomatic documents.[21] The report of the Ministry is generally contained in the President's annual message to the National Assembly.[22]

HONDURAS. Documents relating to State practice have been published in the *Memoria* since 1897, and in several volumes separately published by the Ministry of Foreign Affairs.[23]

MEXICO. The *Memoria* has appeared since 1821 under slightly differing titles, though with important gaps. The Ministry of External Relations has issued thirty-odd volumes of the *Archivo Historico Diplomatico Mexicano* since 1923, as well as six volumes of diplomatic correspondence relating to the years 1878 to 1892, and three volumes covering the years 1910 to 1913.

NICARAGUA. The *Memoria* has appeared since 1869–1870. The volume for 1885, en-

[15] *A Guide to the Official Publications of the Other American Republics, VI, Costa Rica,* pp. 25–28; cf. also Childs, *The Memorias of the Republics of Central America and of the Anthilles,* 1932, pp. 24 ff.
[16] *Ibid., VII, Cuba,* pp. 21–22; cf. also Childs, *op. cit.,* p. 67.
[17] *Ibid., VIII, Dominican Republic,* Childs, *op. cit.,* p. 67.
[18] *Ibid., IX, Ecuador,* pp. 34–37.
[19] *Ibid., X, El Salvador,* pp. 55–58; *op. cit.,* p. 166.
[20] *Ibid., XI, Guatemala,* pp. 75–81.
[21] *Ibid., XII, Haiti,* pp. 17–18.
[22] Childs, *op. cit.,* pp. 47 ff.
[23] *A Guide to the Official Publications of the Other American Republics, XII, Honduras,* pp. 22–25; Childs, *op. cit.,* pp. 124 ff.

titled *Derecho de Gentes Positivo de la Republica de Nicaragua,* is principally a collection of treaties.[24]

PANAMA. The *Memoria* has appeared biannually since 1904–1906.[25]

PARAGUAY. The *Memoria* is available for the period since 1877, with some gaps. There have been published several volumes of documents on special questions, including the White Books of 1928 and 1933–1934.[26]

PERU. The *Memorias* seem to have begun in 1832. A series entitled *Archivo Diplomatico Peruviano* began in 1930 with a volume on the Panama Congress of 1826.

URUGUAY. *Memorias* are currently published.

VENEZUELA. Under such titles as *Memoria, Informe, Exposicion and El Libro Amarillo* (apparently the current title), official papers have been published since 1835.

### *Unofficial publications*

A wealth of relevant materials has been published in the numerous learned journals.[27] Amongst the latter may be mentioned the *Revista de Derecho Internacional (Organo del Instituto Americano de Derecho Internacional)* edited by Antonio S. de Bustamante (vol. I, 1922, *et seq.*); the *Revista Peruvuana de Derecho Internacional (Organo de la Sociedad Peruana de Derecho Internacional,* vol. I, 1941 *et seq.*); the *Anuario de la Sociedad Panamena de Derecho Internacional* (vol. I, 1934–37, vol. II, 1944–46); the *Boletin da Sociedade Brasileira di Direito Internacional* (vol. I, 1945, *et seq.*); and the *Revista Argentina de Derecho Internacional* (vol. I, 1930, *et seq.*).

## 2. United States

### *Official publications*

A substantially complete record of the foreign relations of the United States since 1861 has been published by the Department of State under the title, *Papers Relating to the Foreign Relations of the United States.* The latest volume (for the year 1932) appeared in 1948 as *Foreign Relations of the United States—Diplomatic Documents.* The Department has published several volumes on the War of 1914–1918, two volumes on relations with Japan from 1931–1941, two volumes entitled *The Lansing Papers, 1914-1920,* and thirteen volumes of the Paris Peace Conference, etc., as supplements to the *Foreign Relations.* The procedure for the compilation of the *Foreign Relations* is dictated by the Secretary of State. The Departmental Order of Secretary of State Frank B. Kellogg, dated 26 March 1925, recommended that the Chief of the Division of Publications should, with the aid of the Solicitor, "give special attention to the publication of all important decisions made by the

[24] *A Guide to the Official Publications of the Other American Republics, XIV, Nicaragua,* pp. 24–26; Childs, *op. cit.,* pp. 142 ff.

[25] *Ibid., XV, Panama,* pp. 19–21; Childs, *op. cit.,* p. 151.

[26] *Ibid., XVI, Paraguay,* pp. 50–52.

[27] For a list of periodicals published in Latin-American countries see H. C. Gutteridge, *Comparative Law* (1946), pp. 202 f.

Department relating to international law, with a view to making available for general study and use the annual contributions of the Department to this important branch of jurisprudence''.[28] The same directive suggested that a record of treaty negotiations be included in the series.[29] The *Foreign Relations* consists simply in State papers, without editorial comment or official interpretation. The volumes are, however, elaborately indexed. They appear about fifteen years after the events with which they deal. This gap arose by accident, the War of 1914–1918 having delayed the publication programme, and the Department hopes ultimately to diminish it. But to close the gap altogether is less easy. The series prints no paper originating with a foreign Government without its consent. Some Governments being reluctant to allow recent papers to be published, it has proved impossible to make the series more topical without sacrificing its claim to completeness. But under a Departmental Order of 27 October 1947,[30] it is provided that Governments are to be asked for their permission to include documents it is desired to print, so that some further progress in closing the gap is to be hoped for.

Since 1929 the Department has, in order to make available material on current diplomatic affairs, published *Press Releases* and a *Treaty Information Bulletin.* These were combined, as from 1 July 1939, into the *Department of State Bulletin,* which appears weekly and is indexed semi-annually. In April 1948, the Department began to publish a new series, entitled *Documents and State Papers,* which constitutes a monthly complement to the Bulletin. Other important publications of the Department of State are the *International Organization and Conference Series,* which began on 1 January 1948, and which absorbed the *Conference Series,* the *United States and United Nations Report Series* and the *United States and United Nations Information Series;* the *European,* the *Near Eastern,* and the *Commercial Policy Series* (all begun 1 October 1929); the *Economic Cooperation,* the *General Foreign Policy,* and the *International Information and Cultural Series* (begun 1 January 1948). It is also necessary to note that the series *Treaties and other International Acts of the United States of America* (ed. Hunter Miller, 1931–1938), of which eight volumes, covering the period 1776 to 1863, have so far appeared, contains numerous notes illustrating the practice of the United States and other States.[31]

### *Unofficial publications*

Unofficial compilations on United States diplomatic practice are numerous. Worthy of special mention, if only because they fill a gap in the official documentation, are the *Diplomatic Correspondence of the United States Concerning the Independence of the Latin-American Nations, 1810–1830* (three vols., 1925) and the *Diplomatic Correspondence of the United*

[28] Cf. *Papers Relating to the Foreign Relations of the United States 1914 Supplement. The World War* (1928), p. iii.

[29] *Ibid.*

[30] Department of State Regulation, 297.1 of 27 October 1947; *Foreign Relations of the United States—Diplomatic Papers, 1932,* vol. I (1948), pp. iii to iv.

[31] Cf. Report of the Committee on Publications of the Department of State submitted to the 29th Annual Meeting of the American Society of International Law, *Proceedings* (1935), pp. 206–207.

*States: Inter-American Affairs, 1831–1860* (twelve vols., 1932–1939), both edited by Professor W. R. Manning, which contains some 7,000 documents not published elsewhere. Professor Manning has also selected and arranged four volumes of *Diplomatic Correspondence of the United States—Canadian Relations, 1784–1860* (1940–1945).

The following review of the first three volumes of the Canadian series is of interest:

"These three volumes show, perhaps even more clearly than the other volumes of the *Diplomatic Correspondence of the United States,* the full significance and usefulness of Dr. Manning's monumental undertaking. Most of the documents reproduced in these volumes are printed for the first time. Together with those previously available, they throw new light on many a question. This applies in particular to the Caroline incident (in volume III) and to the interesting story of the rejection of the award of the King of the Netherlands in the matter of the northeastern boundary. There is also in these volumes a wealth of material on the subjects of discovery and occupation of territory and river navigation.

"The various volumes of the entire series edited by Dr. Manning cover most subjects of international law. It is not certain that under the present arrangement of the index they are as useful to the student as their contents warrant. At present the indices contain references mainly to names. They are not analytical guides to subjects from the point of view of their legal interest to the international lawyer. It is only by way of exception that the index, as at present arranged, contains references of this nature as is the case, for instance, with regard to 'piracy' in volume III. In connexion with the Nyon Agreements of 1937 for the suppression of attacks, there described as piratical, by submarines of unknown nationality, the question was discussed whether that designation can properly be applied to acts other than that of piracy committed *animo furandi.* In connexion with the Caroline incident the British Government spoke repeatedly of 'British Rebels and American Pirates' and insisted repeatedly that the use of the latter expression was proper in the circumstances. But the index contains only one reference to the matter, and even this is exceptional. It may perhaps be a subject for consideration whether the time has not come for a cumulative and analytical index of the volumes published so far under the scholarly and painstaking editorship of Dr. Manning."[32]

Another important, but very different, unofficial collection, is the series *Documents on American Foreign Relations,* issued under the auspices of the World Peace Foundation, of which eight volumes, covering the years 1938 to 1946, appeared between 1939 and 1948. The purpose of this series is to present in a convenient form selected material, primarily on the contemporary foreign policy of the United States.

[32] H. L. in *British Yearbook of International Law,* vol. 21 (1944), pp. 254–256.

## 3. United Kingdom
### *Official publications*

The practice of the British Government to make diplomatic documents available to the public is probably older and more sustained than that of any other Government. The well known series, *British and Foreign State Papers,* comprising 139 volumes covering the period from 1812 to 1936, began to appear in 1852. The first volume published, volume 16 of the series, covering the years 1828 to 1829, contained an "advertisement" which is still of interest:

"This Publication is intended to comprise the principal documents which have been made public, relating to the Political and Commercial Affairs of Nations, and to their Relations with each other from the termination of war in 1814 to the latest Period. The Work has hitherto been printed exclusively for the use of the Government and of its Diplomatic Agents abroad. But the general interest attached to these Collections has led to its Publication."

The Series has always been compiled in the Foreign Office. Hertslets' *Commercial Series* was incorporated with it in 1925, with the issue of volume 116 (for 1922). The scope of the series is very wide. It prints the texts of treaties, both bi-partite and multipartite, the proceedings of international conferences, diplomatic correspondence with various Governments, official pronouncements on foreign affairs, emanating from different capitals, and the constitutions and important laws of many countries. Whilst in general the material included is selected from papers already published, from time to time other documents have been printed. In contrast to the United States *Foreign Relations,* which usually lags fifteen years behind, the British State Papers Series has on the whole been kept fairly up to date. But the two series are not, of course, comparable. The British State Papers are not intended to be a complete record of British diplomacy, nor a record of British State practice exclusively. However, the importance of the contribution the series makes to knowledge of the practice of many States in matters of foreign policy and international law cannot be over-estimated.

British State practice itself is perhaps reflected more fully and with greater accuracy in the *Parliamentary Papers,* one of the most important collections of State papers in the world, though not comprising a complete record of the correspondence of the Foreign Office. Many guides to the papers issued since 1800 exist.[33] The *Foreign Office List and Diplomatic Consular Yearbook,* published annually since 1859, gives each year a list of "Papers Relating to Foreign Affairs Laid before Parliament." Such papers have also been recently listed in an invaluable publication entitled *"A Century of Diplomatic Blue Books, 1814–1914",* by H. W. V. Temperly and L. M. Penson.

In addition to the documents periodically published as White Papers or Blue Books the British Government has issued an important collection entitled *British Documents on the Origin of the War, 1898–1914* (Ed. G. P. Gooch and H. W. V. Temperly, 10 vols.,

[33] Cf. S. F. Bemis and G. G. Griffin, *Guide to the Diplomatic History of the United States,* 1775–1921 (1935), p. 838.

1926–1933) and has recently undertaken a new series, *Documents on British Foreign Policy, 1919–1939,* of which five volumes have so far appeared, under the editorship of E. L. Woodward and R. Butler.

### *Unofficial publications*

Amongst the most important unofficial collections devoted to the practice of the United Kingdom is the series of *Documents on International Affairs* published under the auspices of the Royal Institute of International Affairs. Volumes covering the years from 1928 to 1938 have so far appeared, and also a special volume entitled *Norway and the War, September 1939 to December 1940.* The series is not designed especially for international lawyers, but it is of assistance to, and has come to be widely used by, them.

## 4. France

### *Official publications*

The earlier period of French State practice is portrayed and documented in the important series: *Recueil des Instructions Données aux Ambassadeurs et Ministres de France depuis les Traités de Westphalie jusqu'à la révolution française,* published under the auspices of the *Commission des Archives Diplomatiques* at the Ministry of Foreign Affairs. Between 1884 and 1929 there appeared in this series twenty-five volumes covering the relations of France with most European countries. The French Government has frequently published more recent documents in so-called Colour Books. Several lists of the Colour Books issued since 1861 exist,[34] but there is no digest of the international legal material contained in them. The collection *Documents Diplomatiques Français* published by the *Commission de Publication des Documents relatifs aux Origines de la Guerre de 1914–1918,* is divided into three series, 1871 to 1901, 1901 to 1911, and 1914. Although thirty-one volumes in all have been published only series three is complete as yet. The French Government has also published an official edition of the Proceedings of the Paris Peace Conference of 1919. This, however, is confidential, and has been made available only to the participating Governments.

### *Unofficial publications*

One of the prime sources of State practice of the period is the *Archives Diplomatiques, Recueil de Diplomatie, d'Histoire et de Droit International,* of which 193 volumes were issued between 1861 and 1914. There is no index, analytical or otherwise, to this collection.

[34] Cf. D. P. Myers, *Manual of Collections of Treaties and Collections Relating to Treaties* (1922), pp. 156–159; and R. Doré, *Bibliographie des "Livres Jaunes" à Date du 1er Janvier 1922* (1922), completed to 1929 and reprinted in *Official Publications of European Governments,* Part I, compiled by Jose Mayer (1929), pp. 211–249.

## 5. Russia and the Union of Soviet Socialist Republics

Printed documents on Russian diplomatic relations are very numerous. The Imperial Government published, in Russian and French, an *Annuaire diplomatique de l'Empire de Russie (Ezhegodnik)* from 1861 to 1917. A two-volume history of Russian relations with the Western Powers from 1814–1822 *(Dokumenty dlia istorii diplomaticheskikh snoshenii Rossii s zapadnymi derzhavami evropeiskimi ot zakliucheniia vseobschago mira v 1814, do Kongressa v Verona v 1822 g.)* was published, as were also the well-known *Orange Books* (1914) of documents respecting negotiations preceding the War of 1914–1918; and the *Material pertaining to the History of French-Russian Relations during 1910–1914 (Materialy po istorii franko-russkikh otnoshenii za 1910–1914 gg. Sbornik sekretnykh diplomaticheskikh dokumentov byvsh. Imperatorskogo Rossiiskogo Ministerstva inostrannykh diel).* Special volumes were issued on events in Armenia 1912–1914 *(Sbornik diplomaticheskikh dokumentov. Reformy v Armenii.);* Persia 1911–1913 *(Sbornik diplomaticheskikh dokumentov kasaiushchikhsia sobytii v Persii).* Furthermore, the *Recueil des traités et documents diplomatiques concernant l'Extrême Orient* (1895–1905) *(Sbornik dogovorov i diplomaticheskikh dokumentov po dielam Dal'niego Vostoka);* and a collection of consular reports for the period 1898 to 1910 *(Sbornik konsulskikh donesenii)* also appeared. A list of State papers and treaties kept in the State Board of Foreign Affairs covering the period 1265–1696 *(Sobranie gosudarstvennykh gramot i dogovorov khraniaschikhsia v Gosudarstvennoi kollegii inostrannykh diel)* was completed in five volumes in 1895.

The Soviet Government was the first to publish diplomatic documents on the origins of the War of 1914–1918, the celebrated *Collection of Secret Documents from the Archives of the Former Ministry of Foreign Affairs (Sbornik sekretnykh dokumentov iz Arkhiva byvshago Ministerstva inostrannykh diel)* appearing in 1917 and 1918. This collection was supplemented by special collections relating to Greece *(Evropeiskie derzhavy i Gretsiia v epokhu mirovoi voiny),* Turkey *(Evropeiskie derzhavy i Turtsiia vo vremia mirovoi voiny),* and Constantinople and the Straits *(Konstantinopol' i prolivy po sekretnym dokumentaum b. Ministerstva inostrannykh diel).* An official record of the peace negotiations at Brest-Litovsk *(Mirnye peregovory v Brest-Litovske s 22/9 dekabria 1917 g. po 3 marta (18 fevralia) 1918 g.)* was also printed. And the Soviet Government has published a collection entitled *Modern International Policy Presented in Treaties, Notes and Declarations (Mezhdunarodnaia politika noveishego vremeni v dogovorakh, notakh i deklaratsiiakh)* covering the period from the French Revolution to the tenth anniversary of the October Revolution. The publication *International Relations during the Epoch of Imperialism (Mezhdunarodnye otnosheniia v epokhu imperializma. Dokumenty iz arkhivov tsarskogo i vremennogo pravitel'stv)* is in three series covering the period 1878 to 1917; five volumes, relating to the year 1914 up to the outbreak of war, have so far appeared. The more recent period is covered by a *Yearbook Series,* begun in 1917, the successive reports of the Peoples' Commissariat for Foreign Affairs *(Mezhdunarodnaia politika za . . . god)* and the series *International Life (Mezhdunarodnaia zhizn')*. There is also the useful *Ten Years of Soviet Diplomacy (Desiat' let sovetskoi diplomatii)*.

The Royal Institute of International Affairs, London, issued in 1948 a compilation entitled *A Calendar of Soviet Documents on Foreign Policy* (prepared by J. Degras).

## 6. Germany

### *Official publications*

The German Government never published any systematic series of diplomatic documents comparable to the United States *Foreign Relations* or the *British and Foreign State Papers*, although from time to time it issued White Books, to which there are some guides.[35] But among collections dealing with specific phases of German foreign policy may be mentioned *Die Diplomatischen Akten des Auswärtigen Amtes zu Bismarcks Nordschleswigpolitik 1864–1879* (1925), issued on behalf of the German Foreign Office. There are several collections of German documents on the origins of the War of 1914–1918, the official series, entitled *Die Grosse Politik der Europäischen Kabinette 1871–1914* (1922–1927), comprising forty volumes. An official account of the negotiation of the Armistice, entitled *Amtliche Urkunden zur Vorgeschichte des Waffenstillstandes, 1918* (1924), was also published by the German Foreign Office.

It appears that the foreign departments of France, the United Kingdom, and the United States are contemplating the publication of a series of volumes dealing with the origins of the War of 1939–1945 on the basis of the large numbers of documents from the German official archives which fell into Allied hands.[36]

### *Unofficial publications*

The best known German serial publication is the semi-official *Das Staatsarchiv, Sammlung der Offiziellen Aktenstücke zur Geschichte der Gegenwart,* of which eighty-six volumes, covering the period from 1861 to 1919, were published. This series attempted a comprehensive survey of contemporary State practice. Some phases of diplomatic negotiations were made the subject of special supplementary volumes. The series contains several index volumes. There appears to be no complete index. An attempt to revive the *Staatsarchiv* failed after the publication of one further volume in 1928.

## 7. Other countries

Collections of diplomatic documents published by the Governments of other countries are too numerous to be mentioned here. Those issued by the Governments of Aus-

[35] Cf. J. Sass, *Die deutschen Weissbücher zur auswärtigen Politik, 1879–1914* (1928).
[36] Cf. *Department of State Bulletin,* vol. 18 (1948), p. 180.

tria, Belgium, Bulgaria, Czechoslovakia, Denmark and Finland are conveniently listed in Part I of Meyer's *Official Publications of European Governments.*[37]

In addition to published documents, there is, of course, an immense mass of manuscript material in the archives of different Governments. No attempt has been made to indicate here the quantity of this material, its availability, or its bearing upon questions of international law. Much useful information concerning it is to be found in the *Guide International des Archives—Europe* published in 1934 by the Institute of Intellectual Co-operation, and in other well-known books of reference.

## B. DIGESTS OF STATE PRACTICE WITH REFERENCE TO PARTICULAR COUNTRIES

### 1. United States

The term digest, properly used in this connexion, should probably be confined to publications of the United States Department of State, under the auspices of which no less than four such compilations relating to American State practice have appeared. The first in time, entitled *A Digest of the Published Opinions of the Attorneys General and of the Leading Decisions of the Federal Court with Reference to International Law, Treaties and Kindred Subjects,* was prepared by John L. Cadwalader, Assistant Secretary of State, and published in 1877. The purpose of this work was to supply the staff of the Department with a means of ready reference to precedents in matters of international legal concern.[38] It was followed, and replaced, in 1886 by Francis Wharton's *Digest of the International Law of the United States,* published under an Act of Congress and arranged systematically instead of alphabetically, as was its forerunner. One noteworthy omission from the scheme of Wharton's work was the topic of international tribunals and commissions, this being explained by the circumstance that John Bassett Moore was simultaneously preparing a digest on this topic to be published "in a separate volume".

The "separate volume" proved, on publication in 1898, to be Moore's six-volume *History and Digest of International Arbitrations to which the United States was a Party.*[39] And this work was itself followed in 1908 by Moore's *Digest of International Law as embodied . . . especially in documents . . . of the United States.* This eight-volume work completely superseded Wharton's *Digest* and set a standard in compilations of its kind which has yet to be surpassed. Moore drew upon a greater number of papers than did his predecessors and abandoned the practice of printing mere extracts from documents and decisions, aiming instead to give the complete history of any question considered and the fullest account of the opinion prevailing in relation to it. Further, again in contrast to his predecessors,

[37] See also *Papers and Documents relating to the Foreign Relations of Hungary,* vol. I, 1919–1920. Collected and edited by Francis Deak and Dezso Ujvary. 1939.

[38] Cf. Preface.

[39] See pp. 40–41.

Moore endeavoured in connexion with manuscript material "to avoid giving brief glosses which convey no intimation of the question under consideration but to follow and, whenever practicable, quote the text, and to give, besides, enough of the facts to render the application apparent" this being "of the essence of a digest".[40]

A reviewer of Moore's work observed that the writer took care:

*"de donner à ses citations diplomatiques, non plus le caractère d'une règle que celui d'une espèce, d'où l'on peut tirer un précédent, et, puisque le droit des gens est universel, de rapprocher les opinions des auteurs, même européens, de celles des diplomates ou des juges américains. Par là son œuvre prend un caractère scientifique plus large".*[41]

The work achieved a striking success and was much used at the Second Hague Peace Conference, as the records of the conference show. Even thirty years later it could be stated that Moore's *Digest* was "one of the most frequently quoted works in the field and has found its way into practically all the Foreign Offices of the world, leaving a permanent impress upon the development of international law".[42]

Moore's *Digest* was not replaced, but rather brought up to date, by that published in eight volumes between 1940 and 1944 by Judge Green C. Hackworth. Hackworth's *Digest* is arranged in substantially the same fashion as Moore's in order to facilitate their consultation together. Neither work is concerned with any real or supposed "international law of the United States"—as the titles of the earlier digests might misleadingly suggest these to be—but is intended rather to outline the position taken in legal questions by the Government of the United States in so far as it is to be ascertained from the records of the Department of State and, in a lesser degree, from the decisions of the federal courts, the opinions of the Attorneys General and other similar sources. There are perhaps fewer references to the literature of international law in Hackworth's *Digest* than in Moore's. And extracts from easily accessible documents, e.g., those published in the *Foreign Relations of the United States,* have been curtailed. On the other hand, there are many expositions of particular questions by the editor himself. The eighth volume contains an extensive index and list of cases.

The diplomatic archives of virtually every State are now so extensive that their examination and digesting is beyond the capacity of any one individual. Thus, whilst Moore was solely responsible for the work which bears his name and took nine years over its compilation, Judge Hackworth, who was at the time legal adviser to the Department of State, was aided in the preparation of his digest by a team of assistants. This circumstance is of considerable importance in so far as it shows that an eminently satisfactory work of this character can be prepared, as it inevitably must be, in collaboration under Governmental sponsorship.

[40] Page iv.

[41] A. P. in *Revue Générale de Droit International Public,* vol. 14 (1907), pp. 785–787.

[42] Report of the Committee on the Publications of the Department of State, 23 April, 1938. *Proceedings* of the American Society of International Law, 1938, p. 236.

## 2. United Kingdom

There is no official United Kingdom digest of international law comparable to the work of either Moore or Hackworth, though undoubtedly there exist materials from which it might be compiled, richer even than those which have been drawn upon in the United States, and including in particular some 200 manuscript volumes of Opinions of the Law Officers in international legal questions.[43]

Whilst no such official digest exists, the materials extant have been used in several individual works, inspired by American models. Amongst these may be mentioned Dr. H. A. Smith's *Great Britain and the Law of Nations* (vol. I, 1932, vol. II, 1935), a work similar in its general purpose to Moore's *Digest* in that it aims at explaining the official attitude of the United Kingdom towards contemporary problems of international law by reference to official documents.[44] But the work is unofficial and makes no claims to completeness. It omits judicial decisions and, in the first volume at least, gives virtually as much prominence to the editorial commentary as to the documents which illustrate this.[45] The second volume, however, sets out documents more fully and contains less by way of comment, but presents only selected documents on disputed points. Both volumes contain historical materials in addition to purely legal opinions. But no more than two volumes have appeared, confined to the topics of the nature, sources and scope of international law, the dependence, independence, recognition and territory of States, the high seas, and territorial waters. The work, though remarkable and undoubtedly valuable because of the vivid picture of a Foreign Department "in action" which it gives, thus serves mainly to show what a wealth of material concerning the State practice of the United Kingdom exists to be drawn upon.

The subjects dealt with in volume I are: nature, sources and scope of international law; dependence and independence of States; and recognition. The second volume contains documents on title to territory, high seas and territorial waters. In the second volume documents occupy nearly four-fifths of the space and nearly all of them were previously unpublished.

Neither volume I nor volume II is equipped with an index. Some writers, commenting upon the first volume of this work, felt that being "neither digest nor treatise, the volume's usefulness is limited," and that "the documents included are insufficient to provide a textual exposition of British views on international law".[46]

Others, while appreciating that this series would endeavour to some extent to do for Great Britain what Moore did for the United States, observed that "the book is as much, if not more, a contribution to diplomatic history as to the history of international law, though, as is almost invariably the case, diplomacy and law are closely related. It

[43] Cf. H. A. Smith, *Great Britain and the Law of Nations*, vol. I (1932), p. iii.
[44] Preface to vol. I, p. viii.
[45] *Ibid.*, p. ix.
[46] E. D. Dickinson in *American Journal of International Law*, vol. 27 (1933), p. 203.

may possibly be objected that the extracts are not sufficiently long to give the whole story, but it appears that Professor Smith has made a judicious selection and his own contributions by way of exposition are well done''.[47]

After the appearance of the second volume it was stated by one writer that ''so valuable is it for a study of international law that most readers . . . will have been eagerly awaiting its appearance, as they are no doubt looking forward to its successor''.[48]

A more specialized work which has been compiled from unpublished sources is Judge Sir Arnold McNair's *Law of Treaties, British Practice and Opinions.* This book, which was published in 1938 under the auspices of the Columbia University Research in International Law, is designed to state the practice of the United Kingdom in relation to treaties and is intended ''to reproduce or reflect views which have been expressed or would be likely to be expressed in British official quarters'' and ''is not a treatise, but a collection of opinions and practice''.[49] It is compiled principally from the opinions of the Law Officers of the Crown and from decisions of British Courts. Whilst reference is occasionally made to international arbitrations and awards to which the United Kingdom has been a party, diplomatic correspondence is not drawn upon, and the part of the author is confined to introductory comments and remarks connecting the various documents printed.

Other recent specialized works which are based to a greater or less extent on the practice of the United Kingdom but which do not, however, purport to be collections of legal opinions or judicial decisions include: J. Mervyn Jones, *British Nationality, Law and Practice* (1947), and H. Lauterpacht, *Recognition in International Law* (1947).

### 3. Other countries

There appear to be no digests, official or unofficial, in any way comparable to the works of Moore or Hackworth, or of Smith, in countries other than the United States or the United Kingdom. To some extent, however, State practice is reported or digested in legal periodicals and in general international legal literature. Thus there are several international legal journals published in France, but these are more concerned to report judicial decisions than to publish diplomatic correspondence. And though some journals, such as the *Revue Générale de droit international public* (France) and the *Zeitschrift für ausländisches öffentliches Recht und Völkerrecht* (Germany) from time to time published, or have published, such correspondence, they do not in any sense take the place of digests properly so called.

In Switzerland there has appeared since 1944 the *Annuaire* of the *Société suisse de droit international,* the second part of which contains documents illustrating the contemporary State practice of Switzerland, including opinions of the Federal Department of Justice and Police on questions of international law, extracts from reports and decisions of the Federal

[47] A. P. H. in *British Year Book of International Law,* vol. 14 (1933), pp. 218–219.
[48] E. in *British Year Book of International Law,* vol. 17 (1936), p. 230.
[49] Preface, pp. vii–viii.

Council, judicial decisions and the like. In the Netherlands the latest (1948) issue of the *Grotius Annuaire International,* which publication has appeared since 1914, contains documents on Netherlands State practice during the years 1940 to 1946. There are also documentary sections in the *Revue Egyptienne de droit international* (founded 1945), and in the *Annuaire* of the Yugoslav Association for International Law (1931–1937). But, useful as these publications are, they are not digests of international law in any proper sense of the term.

## C. DIGESTS OF STATE PRACTICE IN GENERAL

The nearest approach to a digest of the practice of States in general is the *Digest of the Diplomatic Correspondence of the European States* in the *Fontes Juris Gentium* series,[50] edited by Viktor Bruns (two volumes, covering the period 1856–1878).

This *Digest,* of which only two volumes were published, covers the period from 1856–1871 and 1871–1878 respectively. It is limited as the title indicates to European States and provides a systematic treatment of official papers which have already been published. The official papers from which extracts were taken are, first, diplomatic notes exchanged between Governments and, secondly, instructions to diplomatic representatives and the reports of diplomatic representatives to their Governments.

The *Digest* offers extracts of varying lengths. The extent to which a passage is quoted is governed by the desire of the editor "to convey to the reader an approximate general impression of the meaning of the passage reproduced and of the manner and context in which the statement was made, in order that he may be spared superfluous research of all appropriate records". The editor is at pains to point out, however, that the *Digest* "does not render it superfluous for a conscientious scientific worker to read and investigate the whole of the original text" for, in his view, "the meaning and scope of a sentence or paragraph can only be ascertained in connexion with the whole". This is rendered all the more necessary for two reasons. First, the *Digest* does not distinguish between legal and political statements, and therefore it is necessary, by examining the original document in its entirety, to ascertain whether "the statements made in individual cases are of a legal nature or embody a political claim". The second reason is that the *Digest* does not purport to present passages "which in the opinion of the editors convey a rule or principle of active international law".[51]

More specifically the material on which the *Digest* is based includes: (1) notes submitted by diplomatic representatives to the Government to which they are accredited; (2) Foreign Office instructions to diplomatic representatives; (3) reports of diplomatic representatives to their Foreign Offices; (4) letters written by one Sovereign to another; (5) minutes of international congresses and conferences; and (6) documents attached as annexes to the notes proper.

[50] Series B. *sectio* I, *tomi* I and II (1932–1938).

[51] This and other quotations are from the preface to tomus I of series B, sectio I.

The material covered concerns only European States, but notes dispatched from American Ministries to their representatives in Europe and *vice versa* are included.

The *Digest* starts with the Peace of Paris, signed 30 March 1856. The chief reason for choosing 1856 as the initial date was that it "is only since the middle of the nineteenth century that [published] material is available which shows the diplomatic practice of a number of States". While the British practice of presenting Blue Books to Parliament goes back to the beginning of the eighteenth century, corresponding practice "does not, on the European continent, reach further back than the sixties of the nineteenth century".[52] The same is true of unofficial collections such as the *Archives Diplomatiques* and the *Staatsarchiv* which were inaugurated in the sixties of the last century.

The published source material was used in the following order: (1) "Colour Books"; (2) official publications of diplomatic documents other than "Colour Books" such as *Les origines diplomatiques de la guerre 1870–1871;* (3) private collections such as the *Archives Diplomatiques,* the *Staatsarchiv,* collections of important statesmen and, finally, (4) collections on particular questions.[53]

Regarding languages the editor states that the extracts were always reproduced in the original language. Where the original text was in German, French or English no translation was provided. On the other hand, "the original texts in other languages are provided in the footnotes with translation into one of the three languages just mentioned, in so far as such translations were to be found in the source collections utilized".[54]

Each abstract is preceded by annotations containing the names of the sender and recipient, etc. However, no detailed editorial or explanatory notes are attached to the extracts "because this work is not intended to replace the original texts of diplomatic correspondence, but only to serve as a signpost to these texts".[55]

A remarkable tribute was paid to the series *Fontes Juris Gentium,* at that time comprising several volumes, by the Fifth Conference of Teachers of International Law and Related Subjects, which after a thorough discussion went "on record as expressing its appreciation of the preparation of the volumes . . . which have already appeared, and its earnest hope that this very valuable and important work will be continued with all practicable speed".[56]

[52] Preface, *loc. cit.,* p. xxxiv.

[53] *Op. cit.,* p. xxxiv.

[54] *Op. cit.,* p. xxxv.

[55] *Ibid.*

[56] *Proceedings of the Fifth Conference of Teachers of International Law and Related Subjects,* held at Washington, D.C., 26–27 April 1933, p. 174.

## D. GENERAL COLLECTIONS OR REPORTS OF DECISIONS OF INTERNATIONAL TRIBUNALS

### *Official publications*

The series entitled the *United Nations Reports of International Arbitration Awards* is prepared by the Registry of the International Court of Justice. Its preparation was undertaken in connexion with the function of progressive development of international law conferred on the General Assembly by Article 13 of the Charter of the United Nations. The series is to be confined strictly to awards between States and will not include either the judgments and advisory opinions of the Permanent Court of International Justice or the decisions of the Mixed Arbitral Tribunals, which are published elsewhere. The starting-point of the series is, however, the end of the war of 1914–1918 and the first volume, which has already been published, contains thirteen decisions, arranged in chronological order, dating from the years 1920–1925. Certain awards falling within this period and listed in A. M. Stuyt, *Survey of International Arbitrations, 1794–1938,*[57] do not appear in this volume.

The *Reports* generally supply the following information and in this order: title or name of case; parties; date of *compromis* or agreement to arbitrate; the arbitrator or arbitrators; the date of the decision; summary of the case; text of *compromis* or relevant treaty provisions; text of decision. There are generally no indications concerning the source or sources from which the texts of the decisions were taken. However, for bibliography, index and tables the reader is referred to volume III.

### *Unofficial publications*

Moore's *International Adjudications, Ancient and Modern*[58] is the most recent and most comprehensive collection in its intended scope.[59] It has for its object "to furnish an intelligible and fully documented report of all judicial decisions of international questions not recorded in the ordinary law reports" and thus "to bring together all discoverable records of international judicial action, ancient and modern, into one comprehensive publication, in which there shall be given, in appropriate historical setting, the full text of every

[57] See pp. 37–38.

[58] Full title: *International Adjudications. Ancient and Modern.* History and Documents Together with Mediatorial Reports, Advisory Opinions, and the Decisions of Domestic Commissions on International Claims. Ed. by John Bassett Moore. The *Modern Series* comprises six volumes, covering the following cases: vols. I and II (1929), Saint Croix River Arbitration; vol. III (1931), Arbitration of Claims for Compensation for Losses and Damages Resulting from Lawful Impediments to the Recovery of Pre-war Debts; vol. IV (1931), Compensation for Losses and Damages Caused by the Violation of Neutral Rights, and by the Failure to Perform Neutral Duties; vol. V (1933), I—Spanish Spoliation, 1795, II—French Indemnity, 1803, III—French Indemnity, 1831; vol. VI (1933), Arbitration of the Title to Islands in Passamaquoddy Bay and the Bay of Fundy. The *Ancient Series* comprises only one volume numbered vol. II, entitled: Emil Usteri, *Bienne-Beppet Arbitration.* Relating to disputes between the town of Bienne (Biel) and the town clerk, John Serriant, and Benedict Beppet. 1491-1504. (1936).

[59] Charles Rousseau, *Principes Généraux du Droit International,* vol. I (1944). p. 113.

international judicial decision, or opinion, and in addition certain affinitive matter lying, as the case might be, within the sphere or border of judicial action''.[60]

The reason for including in the series mediatorial reports or recommendations on questions of international law, as stated by Moore was ''not because they are supposed to result from the exercise of judicial power, or to have the binding force of judicial decisions, but by reason of their tenor and the character and learning of the persons by whom they were made, they have brought an end to controversy, or contributed to its eventual solution, on legal grounds''. A further reason may be sought in that Moore was ''less concerned with nice classifications and exclusive categories'' than ''with adding as much as possible to the materials with which the international structure may, especially on its legal side, be enlarged and strengthened and made more convenient and useful''.[61]

A further factor in determining the choice of materials for inclusion in the *International Adjudications* was Moore's conviction that ''judicial judgments, in order to be intelligible and of constructive value, must be read in the light of the circumstances which gave rise to them''. Judgments frequently give only a meagre indication of the origins of the dispute and of the reasons underlying the judgment. ''In such cases'', affirmed Dr. Moore, ''the meaning of the document, if only the text were read, might be practically lost, while, in reality, the decision may have been the culmination of a transaction of the first order. It is only in their historical and circumstantial setting that the individual significance and relative importance of judicial judgments can be correctly estimated''.[62]

For the sake of convenience Moore divided *International Adjudications* into an ancient and modern series. The latter begins with the three cases decided by the mixed commissions set up by Great Britain and the United States under the so-called Jay Treaty of 19 November 1794 which ''marks the revival in modern times of the practice of international arbitration''. The ancient series was intended to begin with a volume on arbitration among the Greeks.

The material in *Modern Series,* in which six volumes were published, is organized according to a pattern which consists of: the agreement to arbitrate; the nature of the dispute; the organization of the mixed commission and the claims of the parties; the evidence; the arguments on behalf of the parties; and, finally, bibliographical notes. One of the distinctive features of this series is that the arguments of the agents are printed in full with the exception of the Arbitration of the Title to Islands in Passamaquoddy Bay where the arguments are summarized.[63]

This series, as indicated above, was planned on a broad basis so as to include not merely arbitrations properly so-called but also ''to embrace various processes or forms of

[60] Preface to *Modern Series,* vol. I, p. vii f.
[61] *Modern Series,* vol. I, p. vii.
[62] *Ibid.*
[63] See *Modern Series,* vol. VI, p. x.

process, all judicial in their nature, some of which do not strictly fall within the scope of the word 'arbitration' ".[64]

The appearance of the first volumes of *International Adjudications,* which constituted the achievement of a design conceived by Dr. Moore some forty years ago, was deemed to mark a date in the literature of international law. Thus one international lawyer expressed himself as follows:[65]

*"Les premiers volumes de cette collection viennent de paraître et ils méritent de figurer dans ces livres d'or que sont, pour les internationalistes, les grands recueils de textes conventionnels ou de sentences arbitrales. La nouvelle collection entreprise par le professeur Moore se situe d'emblée au premier rang des ouvrages fondamentaux du droit des gens . . .*

*"La haute portée scientifique de cette publication n'a pas à être soulignée. Par la richesse de la documentation et la rigueur de la méthode, elle forme à coup sûr une des plus belles collections de jurisprudence internationale dont puisse s'enorgueillir la littérature juridique contemporaine."*

The distinctive feature of *International Adjudications* was not only that it "set a standard of meticulous scholarship which has probably never been excelled" but that it aimed at completeness, something that, it is probably safe to say, has never been attempted by any collection of international decisions either before or after the appearance of the *Modern Series,* the publications of the Permanent Court of International Justice apart. The volumes of the *Modern Series* were regarded as definitive works; there was no need to go beyond the material presented in the text and footnotes.[66]

The degree of completeness achieved in the *Modern Series* will appear from one or two comparisons with the *History and Digest of International Arbitrations* published by Moore in 1898. The Saint Croix River Arbitration occupied 43 pages in the *History and Digest,* in the *Modern Series* it occupies two volumes. The Arbitration of Claims for Compensation for Losses and Damages resulting from Lawful Impediments to the Recovery of Pre-war Debts, which occupies the entire third volume in the *Modern Series* comprising 564 pages, was presented on 27 pages in the *History and Digest.*[67] The Compensation Claims which cover all of the fourth volume in the *Modern Series,* covered only 50 pages in the *History and Digest.*[68] The various cases dealt with in volume V of the *Modern Series* are based largely on newly discovered material.[69] Finally, the Passamaquoddy Bay Arbitration in volume VI of the *Modern Series* covered only 20 pages in the *History and Digest.*[70]

It was reported when the first volumes of *International Adjudications* appeared, that there was enough edited material in a forward state of preparation to comprise from

[64] See *Modern Series,* vol. I, p. xii. The considerations which led Dr. Moore to determine the scope and title of his work are set forth in "Notes on the Historical and Legal Phases of the Adjudication of International Disputes", *Modern Series,* vol. I, pp. xv–xcvi.

[65] Charles Rousseau, *Revue Générale de Droit International Public,* vol. 40 (1933), pp. 90–91.

[66] Philip C. Jessup in *Political Science Quarterly,* vol. 47 (1932), pp. 118, 120.

[67] Jessup, *Ibid.*

[68] Kuhn in *American Journal of International Law,* vol. 26 (1932), p. 443.

[69] Kuhn in *American Journal of International Law,* vol. 27 (1933), p. 802.

[70] Kuhn in *American Journal of International Law,* vol. 28 (1934), p. 198.

30–40 volumes.[71] However, as noted before only six volumes of the *Modern Series* and only one volume of the *Ancient Series,* which will be discussed presently, were published.

The Carnegie Endowment for International Peace under whose auspices this series was inaugurated and published decided several years ago to discontinue this project and, therefore, no further volumes will be published. The historical papers and materials collected by Judge Moore in connexion with the project were turned over by him to the Library of Columbia University.[72]

The *Ancient Series* was intended to begin with "the earliest known arbitrations, and it is expected that the first volume will be devoted to the arbitrations among the Greeks".[73] This volume, however, having been unavoidably delayed, the first and only volume published in this series is devoted to a medieval arbitration, the Bienne-Beppet Arbitration 1491–1504,[74] which "furnished ample material for a close study of the medieval Swiss methods of dealing with controversies which were submitted to an arbitral tribunal for settlement".[75]

As pointed out by Dr. Moore, in this case "the use of the procedures employed for the purpose of avoiding a decision on strictly legal grounds is happily exemplified. . . . In the proceedings before the Council of Fribourg the arbitrators at first tried to effect a direct settlement by means of good offices, and, this effort having failed, they succeeded in persuading the parties to consent to a decision *ex aequo et bono*".[76]

While ordinarily all documents were to be given in the original text, together with an English translation, in this case they were reproduced in the original only as an English translation proved impracticable. However, the essence of the proceedings is included in a Commentary by Dr. Emil Usteri which precedes the documentary part. The latter comprises numerous hitherto unpublished documents.[77]

The Bienne-Beppet Arbitration was not one between two States. One party was an individual and the other a semi-independent community under the sovereignty of the prince-bishop of Basle. Nevertheless, it was included in the *Ancient Series* as it was deemed "much more interesting and more significant than many a conflict between the most powerful city-states or rural cantons of the Swiss Confederation".

The next work which must be mentioned is the de La Pradelle and Politis Collection of International Arbitrations.[78]

The objective of this collection was essentially to present the documentation relative

[71] Kuhn in *American Journal of International Law,* vol. 25 (1931), p. 603.
[72] From a communication from the Carnegie Endowment for International Peace.
[73] Cf. Dr. Moore's Preface, *Modern Series,* vol. I, p. x.
[74] For full title see p. 49, footnote 58.
[75] Cf. Dr. Moore's Foreword, *Ancient Series,* vol. I, p. ix.
[76] *Ibid,* p. x.
[77] Dr. Usteri's Preface, *ibid.,* p. xiii.
[78] Full title: A. de La Pradelle and N. Politis, *Recueil des Arbitrages Internationaux.* vol. I, 1798–1855 (1905), vol. II, 1856–1872 (1923). A second edition was published in two volumes in 1932.

to "all instances of international arbitration since the end of the eighteenth century which it is possible to trace and to analyse".[79]

The collection was to serve as source for a new *droit des gens judiciaire,* and, therefore, the editors decided to concentrate on cases of arbitration properly so-called. Arbitration was taken to mean the procedure to solve international disputes by the application of the rule of law *(la régle du droit).*

The editors excluded cases of mediation, diplomatic mixed commissions and also the work of domestic claims commissions. On the other hand they decided to include in the collection some cases of diplomatic commissions which preceded or followed an arbitration proceeding.

The collection, however, is not strictly limited to arbitrations between States as the editors included some affairs concerning individuals, or States and individuals, which involve points of international law and are outside any national jurisdiction.

Although the editors excluded cases where the *compromis* was not followed by arbitration, they included cases where there has been a beginning of arbitral procedure.

The editors encountered considerable difficulties in assembling official documentation on the known cases of arbitration. They were led to limit their collection to those arbitral proceedings with reference to which it was possible *"de reconstituer les dossiers d'une manière suffisamment complète".*[80]

The total number of cases reported in volume I is 22 and in volume II it is 30. Six instances of arbitration during the period covered by the first volume and 12 instances during the period covered by the second volume were not included in the collection for one of the following reasons: (1) *compromis* not followed up; (2) lack of documentation; and (3) final settlement occurred at a later time.

The cases are presented in the chronological order of their final settlement and not, as in La Fontaine's *Pasicrisie Internationale* in the chronological order of the *compromis.*

Great emphasis is placed upon maintaining the unity of the case without separating the awards from the arguments of the parties or the special agreements from the facts which had led to their conclusion. Emphasis is also placed upon uniformity of presentation and all the material is given in French. In reconstructing a case the editors have drawn upon published and unpublished documentation which they have endeavoured to make more accessible by means of résumés, analyses, and extracts.

Accordingly each case is presented as follows: (1) statement of fact; (2) text of special agreement and procedure along with an analysis of the claims and counterclaims *(mémoires);* (3) the award and its execution, which in case of a mixed commission is given separately for each of the several claims under this head; (4) in case of the more important affairs a critical evaluation after the manner of the great collections of internal jurisprudence. These commentaries, written in some cases by the editors and in others by well-

[79] *Ibid.,* vol. I, p. xix.
[80] *Ibid.,* p. xxiii.

known international lawyers in the different countries, form one of the distinctive features of the de La Pradelle and Politis collection.

While it was perhaps intended to bring this collection up to date and publish international arbitral awards currently, there is no information available with regard to the possible continuation of this collection which does not even cover the last and probably most important third of the nineteenth century.

The qualities of the collection which ranks as an *ouvrage fondamental*[81] were recognized immediately. Renault, in his Preface to the *Recueil,* declared that de La Pradelle and Politis *"ont rendu un service éminent à la pratique et à la science du droit international".*[82] This collection, he said[83]

*"donne ce qui manquait pour les grands procès entre les Etats qui attirent de plus en plus l'attention publique. Il permettra à ceux qu'intéresse le droit international de compléter les exposés dogmatiques par la jurisprudence des tribunaux d'arbitrage présentée avec tous les éclaircissements désirables. Les diplomates et les praticiens aux prises avec une difficulté verront s'il y a un précédent. Des tables détaillées, faites avec grand soin, permettront de trouver facilement la renseignement dont on a besoin".*

An American authority on the subject of international arbitrations, agreeing with Renault's judgment, declared that this publication was "one of the most valuable yet issued covering questions of international law as administered upon reference either to mixed commissions, or to special persons". Comparing the de La Pradelle and Politis *Recueil* with Moore's earlier *History and Digest of International Arbitrations,* the same authority found that[84]

"the plan of the *Recueil* differs markedly from that adopted by Professor Moore in that . . . all questions arising under a given commission are grouped together, falling as well under the common head. It also differs in the greater fullness naturally given to the arbitrations of Continental Europe and in that the doctrinal and footnotes bring the general subject up to a later date, many of the doctrinal notes being so extensive as almost to constitute treatises upon the matters to which they relate".

In spite of these differences in method or scope, or perhaps because of them, these two collections are really complementary.

La Fontaine's *Pasicrisie Internationale,*[85] which appeared four years after Moore's *History and Digest of International Arbitrations* was intended as *"le premier et modeste recueil d'une jurisprudence internationale sans cesse grandissante et pacificatrice".*[86] Its objective[87]

*"a été mettre à la disposition des Etats et de leurs représentants officiels, ainsi que des juristes et des arbitres éventuels, des renseignements absolument précis et indiscutables, à la réunion desquels*

[81] Charles Rousseau, *Principes Généraux de Droit International,* vol. I, p. 112.
[82] *Recueil,* vol. I, p. xi.
[83] *Ibid.,* p. xiii.
[84] Jackson H. Ralston, *American Journal of International Law,* vol. I (1907), pp. 252–254.
[85] Full title: H. La Fontaine, *Pasicrisie Internationale, Histoire Documentaire des Arbitrages Internationaux, 1794–1900.* (1902).
[86] *Op. cit.,* p. xvi.
[87] *Op. cit.,* p. vii.

*ils auraient à consacrer un temps considérable. Il est évident, en effet, que les décisions arbitrales, intervenues dans les conflits du passé, constituent une jurisprudence précieuse au point de vue du droit public international, au même titre que les arrêts et les jugements des cours et des tribunaux dans les procès civils entre des personnes privées".*

A total of 369 documents were collected by the author. With reference to each arbitration the author endeavoured to reproduce the text of the *compromis,* of the award and, in some cases, of the rules of procedure.

The documents are mostly printed in the original language, but some are printed in a translation if the original text was not available. The author endeavoured to follow a chronological order. The difficulties encountered in assembling the necessary data were such, however, that the project had to be abandoned. Therefore the order adopted was that of the date of the *compromis.*

Altogether during the period from 1794 to 1900 the author was able to trace 177 *instances arbitrales.*[88]

The *Pasicrisie* was considered as useful but suffering from certain defects. Thus it was pointed out that the *Pasicrisie* which[89]

*"s'attache à l'ordre des traités d'arbitrage, tient beaucoup plus compte des compromis que des jugements; toute procédure en est absente; par d'exposé de faits; pas d'analyse de mémoires; pas de renseignements sur les suites de la sentence".*

Similarly it was noted that it *"n'est pas seulement limitée dans le temps, elle est défectueuse également à divers points de vue".*[90]

The absence of translations and commentaries was also considered as detracting from the value of the compilation.[91]

In spite of imperfections it is probably correct to say that quite apart from its historical importance the *Pasicrisie* continues to render service.

*The Annual Digest* and *Reports of Public International Law Cases* was originally conceived as a Digest, and only with the volume for 1933–1934 (1940) were full reports of cases included. For this reason and also because this series is equally devoted to decisions of national courts on questions of international law, it has been thought better to discuss it in its entirety in connexion with digests of municipal courts.

Moore's *History and Digest of International Arbitrations to Which the United States has been Party,* the first and one of the principal standard works on international jurisprudence, will be discussed in connexion with collections and digests of arbitrations with reference to specific countries, as its principal concern, indicated in the title, was with the arbitrations "to which the United States has been a party". It merits reference in this context because, as indicated in its sub-title, it contains "Historical and Legal Notes on Arbitrations Ancient and Modern".

[88] *Op. cit.,* p. viii.
[89] De La Pradelle et Politis, *Recueil des Arbitrages Internationaux,* vol. I, p. xix.
[90] Rosseau, *Principes Généraux de Droit International,* vol. I, p. 112.
[91] D. Anzilotti, *Cours de Droit International,* vol. I (1929), p. 77.

De La Pradelle's *Recueil Général Périodique et Critique des Décisions, Conventions et Lois Relatives au Droit International Public et Privé,* founded by Albert de La Pradelle and edited with the collaboration of French and foreign jurists, was published during the years 1934 to 1938 and comprises altogether five volumes. It reported current decisions of the Permanent Court of Arbitration, of the Permanent Court of International Justice, of individual tribunals, of mixed commissions, and of the Mixed Arbitral Tribunals established after World War I. The reports include head-notes summarizing briefly the main points of the decision. There is also in some cases a commentary on the decision. Dissenting or separate opinions are sometimes reported in full but in some cases only extracts are given. All the texts are in French or in French translations.

This *Recueil* was said to "respond to a real need, but perhaps it is too ambitious, it is difficult to obtain, and one wonders whether it presents a secure prospect for permanence".[92] The outbreak of World War II has interrupted the publication of the *Recueil* and no information is available as to whether it will be resumed.

The Descamps and Renault *Recueil International des Traités du XIXe Siècle*[93] was intended to supplement the *Recueil International des Traités du XXe Siècle* edited by the same authors. The purpose of this collection was to furnish a complete and systematic presentation of conventional international law and of international jurisprudence in its entirety.

With reference to arbitral decisions Descamps and Renault declared that *"elles predront place à côté des traités et seront reproduites* in extenso, *de manière à offrir le tableau intégral de la jurisprudence arbitrale internationale pendant le siècle qui vient de s'écouler".*[94]

However, only one volume appears to have been published in this series. The material is arranged in chronological order and includes some *compromis* and some arbitral decisions. There is no table of contents and no analytical index, these being intended to be included in the final volume.

The Descamps and Renault *Recueil International des Traités du XXe Siècle*[95] was inaugurated by Descamps and Renault in order to provide, in addition to national collections, *"un Recueil de haute et incontestable utilité internationale".*[95] It was intended that each volume would contain the treaties concluded in that year. Arbitral awards would also be included in chronological order *"comme faisant suite aux Conventions qui organisent les juridictions d'arbitres".* The *Recueil* would thus embrace *"non seulement le développement d'ensemble du droit conventionnel entre les Etats, mais encore la marche de la jurisprudence internationale et, en première ligne, les décisions de la Cour permanente d'arbitrage de La Haye".*[96]

[92] Manley O. Hudson, "Twelve Casebooks on International Law", *American Journal of International Law,* vol. 32 (1938), p. 455.

[93] Full title: *Recueil International des Traités du XIXe Siècle Contenant l'Ensemble du Droit Conventionnel entre les Etats et les Sentences Arbitrales (Textes Originaux et Traduction Française). Publié par le baron Descamps et Louis Renault.* Vol. I, 1801–1825 (1914).

[94] *Ibid.,* p. vi.

[95] Full title: *Recueil International des Traités du XXe Siècle Contenant l'Ensemble du Droit Conventionnel entre les Etats et les Sentences Arbitrales (Textes Originaux avec Traduction Française). Publié par le baron Descamps et Louis Renault. Année* 1901 (1910)—1907.

[96] *Ibid.,* p. vii.

Each volume contains a chronological table, an alphabetical table of States and an analytical table. There is no separate list of arbitral decisions.

## E. GENERAL REGISTERS OF DECISIONS OF INTERNATIONAL TRIBUNALS

As appears from the foregoing there is no complete collection of arbitral decisions neither in the broad sense employed by Moore in his *International Adjudications* or in his *History and Digest* nor in the narrower sense adopted by de La Pradelle and Politis in their *Recueil.* However, the *Survey of International Arbitrations 1791-1938* published in 1939 by A. M. Stuyt endeavours to provide in a simplified form an index or register of international jurisprudence more complete and more up-to-date than any compiled so far.

The *Survey* comprises 408 arbitrations; twenty-four international postal arbitrations based on the Conventions of the Universal Postal Union since 1874;[97] four cases of international commissions of inquiry; one case before the Central American Court of Justice 1907–1918, and briefer references to nine other cases before that Court; one report of the Committee of Jurists appointed by the Council of the League of Nations on 12 July 1920 to report on some legal aspects of the dispute between Finland and Sweden regarding the Aaland Islands; and, finally, six cases of international conciliation commissions.

Dr. Stuyt did not include in his *Survey* decisions and advisory opinions of the Permanent Court of International Justice, decisions of Prize Courts or of the Mixed Arbitral Tribunals as all these had been published and are easily accessible.

As far as the material included in the *Survey* is concerned no claim to completeness is made, as during the period from 1794 to 1938 there may have been international arbitrations which have not been published.

As a criterion for determining what constitutes international arbitration, Dr. Stuyt adopted the definition given in article 27 of the Hague Convention for the Pacific Settlement of International Disputes. It may be noted, however, that among the 408 cases of arbitration Mr. Stuyt included some (18) cases in which one of the parties was not a State. He also included several cases where it may be doubtful whether one or both parties were States within the meaning of international law, such as disputes between Swiss cantons and between German states, etc.

The analysis of the cases follows a standard pattern which provides information on the following points: (1) parties; (2) dispute; (3) arbitrator or arbitral tribunal; (4)arbitral treaty or special agreement: *(a)* date, *(b)* law to be applied, *(c)* text (e.g. source of treaty or special agreement); (5) award or other disposition of the case; *(a)* date, *(b)* in favour of, *(c)* execution, *(d)* text (source of award), *(e)* bibliography.

As regards point (2) the author supplies the information that "the matter of difference is described in the terms set down in the treaty or special agreement" in the original language and without translation.

[97] These were said to have been published for the first time. See Denys P. Myers, in *American Journal of International Law,* vol. 24 (1940), p. 554.

This *Survey* which has been found "entirely accurate" though it may not be a definitive list of arbitrations[98] may well be found to furnish a satisfactory basis for a comprehensive collection of arbitral decisions. As a guide to international jurisprudence it has great usefulness.

The well-known collection, Darby's *International Tribunals,*[99] developed out of a resolution of the International Law Association adopted at Brussels on 1 October 1895 to study the question of an international court of arbitration. Its broad purpose was to present materials on "the literary, political, and diplomatic work done in connexion with international arbitration during the past 300 years".[100] In this context the list of "Instances of International Settlements involving the Application of the Principle of International Arbitration" is of special interest. The arbitrations, in this list, are divided into three groups: the eighteenth, the nineteenth and twentieth century arbitrations. Beginning with the Jay Treaty of 1794, six arbitration cases are listed for the eighteenth century. The list of nineteenth century arbitrations contains 471 cases which are classified as follows: (1) formal arbitrations: 222 cases; (2) arbitral boards and commissions: 97 cases; (3) delimitation commissions: 119 cases; (4) national commissions: 33 cases. The group of twentieth century arbitrations consists of 63 cases of which 21 cases are classified as formal arbitrations, 19 cases of arbitral boards and commissions, 20 cases of boundary commissions, and 3 cases of national arbitrations and commissions.

The author gives in a few lines a survey of each case, followed by bibliographical references. It may be noted, however, that among the "instances of international arbitrations" there are included not merely awards of international tribunals but also agreements to arbitrate without regard to subsequent developments. It is thus not clear from this list whether such agreements have actually led to an international arbitration.

## F. REPORTS AND DIGESTS OF DECISIONS OF INTERNATIONAL TRIBUNALS WITH REFERENCE TO SPECIFIC COUNTRIES

### 1. United States

#### *Official publications*

The Department of State of the United States of America undertook in 1929 the publication of the *Arbitration Series.* This series comprises international arbitrations to which the United States was a party and contains the following cases:

[98] Myers, *loc. cit.*, p. 554.
[99] Full title: *International Arbitration. International Tribunals, A Collection of the Various Schemes which have been Propounded; and of Instances in the 19th Century.* By W. Evans Darby, 4th edition (1904). The first edition was presumably published in 1897.
[100] *Ibid.*, p. vii.

(1) Arbitration of the claims of Charles J. Harrah. 1929.

(2) "I'm Alone" case. 1931–1935. 7v.

(3) Shufeldt Claim. 1932.

(4) Salem Claim. 1932–1935. 7v.

(5) Arbitration between the United States and Sweden under Special Agreement of 17 December 1930. 1932–1934.

(6) American and Panamanian General Claims Arbitration. 1934.

(7) Special Mexican Claims Commission. Report to the Secretary of State. 1940.

(8) Trail Smelter Arbitral Tribunal. Trail Smelter Arbitration between the United States and Canada under Convention of 15 April 1935. 1941.

(9) American Mexican Claims Commission. Report to the Secretary of State. 1948.

It appears that the material included in this series is not of uniform completeness in all cases. Thus the Harrah Case comprises only the Memorial of the United States before the Tribunal selected under the Protocol of 1 October 1929 between the United States of America and Cuba. The relevant documentation in the "I'm Alone" Case, the Shufeldt Claim, the Salem Claim and in the Arbitration between the United States and Sweden runs to several volumes, while the Report to the Secretary of State relating to the American Mexican Claims Commission consists of decisions showing the reasons for the allowance or disallowance of claims.

It may be of interest to refer here to a suggestion of the Fifth Conference of Teachers of International Law and Related Subjects to the effect that the *Arbitration Series* "be continued to include the awards in all arbitrations in which the United States participates, in a separate indexed series, and the supplementary documentation, including *compromis,* diplomatic correspondence, cases, counter-cases, and oral arguments, in another series adequately indexed".[101]

The *Arbitration Series* has so far, however, published, as in the Salem Case or in the Arbitration between the United States and Sweden, the award along with cases, counter-cases, replies and oral arguments in one series, though spread over a number of volumes.

[101] Proceedings of the Fifth Conference of Teachers of International Law and Related Subjects. 26–27 April 1933, p. 197.

*Unofficial publications*

Moore's *History and Digest of the International Arbitrations to which the United States has been a Party*[102] began to take shape at the time when Moore was engaged in assisting in the compilation of Wharton's *Digest of the International Law of the United States.*[103] It was planned as a one-volume supplement to the *Digest* containing opinions of international commissions between the United States and other Governments, but it grew to six volumes as Dr. Moore discovered the vast body of materials accumulated in the Department of State of the United States.

The first two volumes cover arbitrations from the St. Croix River Commission under article V of the Jay Treaty to the Behring Sea Damage Commission in 1897; volumes III and IV contain material illustrating various special problems such as procedure, intervention, nationality, domicile, denial of justice, etc.; volume V has three appendices as follows: appendix I, Domestic Commissions for the Adjustment of International Claims; appendix II, Treaties Relating to Arbitrations to which the United States has been a Party; appendix III, Historical Note including Notes on Arbitrations in the nineteenth century between various Powers. There is also a detailed index in volume V, while volume VI is made up of maps.

The method adopted by Moore in presenting the arbitrations is somewhat difficult to summarize. Broadly speaking the general course followed comprised a brief history of the dispute, the steps leading to an agreement to arbitrate or to refer the dispute to commissioners, the agreement itself, the constitution of the tribunal or commission, the summaries of the arguments presented by both sides, the decision, and, finally, the execution of the decision and incidental information.

There was some criticism of the method and of the scope of Moore's *History and Digest.* The form of a digest, in the view of one writer, was responsible for the fact that *"l'unité de la procédure, quand elle renferme plusieurs affaires, l'unité d'une même affaire, quand elle offre plusieurs aspects, se trouvent profondément rompues".*[104]

## 2. The Netherlands

*Unofficial publications*

E. O. van Boetzelaar's *Les arbitrages néerlandais de 1581 à 1794* (1930), is a survey of international arbitrations, including some instances of mediation and conciliation, only in the sense that it lists arbitration and conciliation agreements. The author does not often indicate whether such agreements were implemented and, in fact, gives only seven in-

[102] Full title: *History and Digest of the International Arbitrations to which the United States has been a Party,* together with Appendices containing the Treaties relating to such Arbitrations, and Historical and Legal Notes on Other Arbitrations Ancient and Modern, and on the Domestic Commissions of the United States for the Adjustment of International Claims. By John Bassett Moore. 6 vols. (1898).

[103] See p. 43 *supra.*

[104] De La Pradelle and Politis, *loc cit.,* p. xix.

stances of actual arbitrations culminating in an award. But the work is complemented by G. A. van Hamel's *Les arbitrages internationaux néerlandais de 1813 à nos jours* (1939), which contains analyses in the Dutch language of some ten arbitrations to which the Netherlands has been a party. Decisions of tribunals of the Permanent Court of Arbitration are not included. The work is based partly on unpublished archives of the Dutch Government.

## G. REPORTS OR COLLECTIONS OF DECISIONS OF SPECIFIC INTERNATIONAL COURTS OR TRIBUNALS

### 1. The International Court of Justice

The official publications of the Court consist at present of:

(1) Reports of Judgments, Advisory Opinions and Orders, 1947.

(2) Reports of Judgments, Advisory Opinions and Orders, 1948.

(3) Series D—Acts and Documents concerning the Organization of the Court No. 1 (first edition 1946, second edition 1947): Charter of the United Nations, Statute and Rules of Court, and other Constitutional Documents.

(4) Yearbook 1946–1947 (no publication date).
Yearbook 1947–1948.

For a complete list of the publications which the Court intends to issue, see *Yearbook*, 1947–1948, pp. 69–70.

It is doubtful, however, if the *Yearbook* should be regarded as a publication of the Court in view of the statement in the Preface by the Registrar of the Court: "It is to be understood that the Yearbook of the International Court of Justice is prepared and published by the Registrar and in no way involves the responsibility of the Court."

The *Reports* 1947 and 1948 are paginated consecutively and include, in addition to several Orders of the Court, the Corfu Channel Case, Judgment on Preliminary Objection, Judgment of 25 March 1948 and the Advisory Opinion of 28 May 1948 relating to the Conditions of Admission of a State to Membership in the United Nations (Article 4 of the Charter).

### 2. The Permanent Court of International Justice

#### *Official publications*

The work of the Permanent Court of International Justice was officially reported in several serial publications in French and English issued by the Registry.

*Series A:* comprising in nos. 1 to 24 the judgments of the Court and some of its orders, was issued from 1922–1930;

*Series B;* comprising in nos. 1–18 (1922–1930) the advisory opinions;

*Series A/B:* since 1931 the former A and B Series were combined into this new Series which comprises in nos. 40 to 80 (1931–1940) the judgments of the Court, its advisory opinions and such orders as were directed by the Court to be printed in it;

*Series C;* contains in nos. 1 to 19 (1922–1930) and nos. 52 to 88 (1931–1942) acts and documents relating to the judgments and advisory opinions given by the Court;

*Series D:* contains the acts and documents concerning the organization of the Court in nos. 1 to 6 (1926–1932);

*Series E:* is a series of annual reports on the activities of the Court and comprises nos. 1–16 (1925–1945).

*Series F:* this series, nos. 1 to 4 (1927–1937) contains general indexes to the publications of the Court and no. 4 is an index to the Statutes and Rules of the Court.

It is important to note that Series C includes, among the acts and documents relating to the judgments and advisory opinions of the Court, the written proceedings, orders not published in Series A/B, texts of diplomatic correspondence relating to the cases, and of relevant treaties, and also the records of oral proceedings. Thus there exists a virtually complete and official record of each case before the Court.

Indeed, the Court's publication programme was considered so satisfactory that it has been said "that no public institution in the world is better documented; certainly it is doubtful whether any other judicial institution publishes such a complete record of its activities".[105]

### *Unofficial publications*

(1) *In German.* "With the authorization of the Registrar of the Court and subject to his supervision" the *Institut für Internationales Recht* at Kiel, published the series *Entscheidungen des Ständigen Internationalen Gerichtshofs.*[106] This series reached 12 volumes, published between 1929–30 and 1937, and covered the Court's judgments, advisory opinions and orders rendered between 1922 and 1935.

(2) *In Spanish.* The *Instituto Ibero-Americano de Derecho Comparado,* at Madrid, published the *Colección de decisiones del Tribunal Permanente de Justicia Internacional.* However, only two volumes, covering the period from 1922 to 1926 were issued (in 1924 and 1927).

(3) *In English. The World Court Reports* edited by Manley O. Hudson and published by the Carnegie Endowment for International Peace cover the activities of the Court during the twenty-year period from 1922 to 1942.[107] This series contains judgments, advis-

[105] Manley O. Hudson, *The Permanent Court of International Justice, 1920–1942* (1943), p. 308.

[106] See Series E, no. 4, p. 325.

[107] Hudson's *World Court Reports* consist of four volumes as follows: vol. I (1922–26), vol. II (1927–1932), vol. III (1932–1935), vol. IV (1936–42), 1934–43.

ory opinions and orders of the Court. Information and instruments relative to the Court, such as its Statute, etc. are also included. All material is reproduced from official publications. The judgments and orders do not always follow the chronological order. Where there are several judgments or orders relating to the same case, e.g. the Mavrommatis Palestine Concessions Case, they are printed as a group.

Each entry begins with an editor's note which summarizes the history of the case "before, during, and after action by the Court, where information is available".[108] Then follows a bibliography of official publications and unofficial legal analyses in comments relating to the case. Next are reproduced from Series C of the Court's publications, the instruments relating to the submission of the dispute. Then follows the text of the decisions or advisory opinions including dissenting or separate opinions.

Numerous tables, lists and indices add to the usefulness of these *Reports.*

### 3. The Permanent Court of Arbitration

#### *Official publications*

The International Bureau of the Permanent Court of Arbitration published:

(1) The *Recueils* comprising the *compromis,* the protocols of the sittings and the decisions of the Court in the following cases: I. The Pious Fund Case, 1902; II. The Venezuelan Preferential Claims Case, 1904; III. The Japanese House Tax Case, 1905; IV. The Mascat Dhows Case, 1905; VII. The North Atlantic Coast Fisheries Case, 1910; VIII. The Orinoco Steamship Company Case, 1910; IX. The Savarkar Case, 1911; X. The Canevaro Case, 1912; XVI. The Expropriated Religious Properties in Portugal Case, 1920; XVII. The French Claims against Peru, 1921; XVIII. The Norwegian Claims Case, 1922; and;

(2) The *Awards* in the following cases: V. The Casablanca Case, 1909; VI. The Grisbadarna Case, 1909; XI. The Russian Indemnity Case, 1912; XII. The Manouba Case, 1913; XIII. The Carthage Case, 1913; XV. The Island of Timor Case, 1914; XIX. The Island of Palmas Case, 1928; XX. The Chevreau Case, 1931.

In the Tavignano, Camouna and Gaulois Cases (case No. XIV) no decision was rendered by the Tribunal, the matter being settled out of court by Agreement of 2 May 1904 between France and Italy.[109]

The Bureau of the Court was not authorized to compile *Recueils* relating to Cases V, VI, XI–XIII and XX mentioned above. No *Recueil* was published concerning cases XV and XX mentioned above as the proceedings in these two cases were exclusively in writing.[110]

[108] *World Court Reports,* vol. I, 1922–1926 (1934), p. x.

[109] *Bureau International de la Cour Permanente d'Arbitrage, Analyses des Sentences rendues par les Tribunaux d'Arbitrage, constitués conformément aux stipulations des Conventions de La Haye de 1899 et 1907 pour le règlement pacifique des conflits internationaux, ainsi que par les juridictions spéciales d'arbitrage qui ont fonctionné en application de l'article 47 de la Convention de 1907, 1899–1934* (1934), p. 65.

[110] *Analyses des Sentences, op. cit.,* p. 111, note 2.

No information is available concerning the official publication by the International Bureau of *Recueils* or *Awards* in the Nordsjernan Case, 1932, the China v. Radio Corporation of America Case, 1935, and the Radio Orient Case, 1940, listed in the *Affaires d'arbitrages jugées à la Cour permanente d'arbitrage ou avec la coopération de son Bureau International.*[111]

The Bureau had become increasingly aware that there was a need for a *"vue d'ensemble des sentences de la Cour ainsi que des matières de droit qui y sont traitées"*. With a view to satisfying this demand the Bureau decided to publish *"un recueil contenant des analyses de toutes les sentences rendues depuis la création de la Cour, par les tribunaux d'arbitrage constitués conformément aux stipulations des Conventions de La Haye de 1899 et 1907 pour le règlement pacifique des conflits internationaux, ainsi que par les juridictions spéciales d'arbitrage qui ont fonctionné, sous son égide, en application de l'article 47, alinéa 1, de la Convention de 1907"*.[112]

This volume, the *Analyses des Sentences, 1899–1934,* comprises the analysis of twenty awards. For each case the following information is supplied: parties to the dispute; date of the *compromis;* the name or names of the arbitrator or of members of the tribunal; date of the award. Then follows: a brief history of the dispute and the points of law involved; a statement of the facts; the questions submitted for arbitration by the *compromis;* a summary of the award. The legal grounds on which the awards are based are indicated in italics. An analytical index and a bibliography are included.

### *Unofficial publications*

Scott's *Hague Court Reports*[113] is a collection of awards made during the period from 1902 to 1928. The award in the Chevreau Case of 9 June 1931 is not included, nor any award rendered after that date. The texts of the awards, of the *compromis* and of other essential documents "have been obtained in translated form from the most reliable sources available. . . . Where translations have been obtained from official sources, they have been reproduced in their official forms." In some instances unofficial translations were used. However, the original official texts of all translated documents are printed in an appendix.

The presentation of each case includes: a short title of the dispute; the parties; date of the award; a syllabus giving a brief history of the dispute; the composition of the tribunal and the material part of the award; the text of the award; the text of the *compromis;* and in some cases certain additional documents deemed useful for the understanding of the dispute and of its settlement.

[111] Cf. *Rapport du Conseil Administratif de la Cour Permanente d'Arbitrage. Quarante-septième année 1947* (1948).

[112] *Op. cit.,* Preface.

[113] Full title: *The Hague Court Reports,* comprising the awards, accompanied by syllabi, the agreements for arbitration, and other documents in each case submitted to the Permanent Court of Arbitration and to Commissions of Inquiry under the provisions of the Conventions of 1899 and 1907 for the Pacific Settlement of International Disputes. Edited with an introduction by James Brown Scott. (1916). A second series was published in 1932.

As Wilson's *Hague Arbitration Cases,*[114] the first collection to be made, covers less ground than Scott's *Hague Court Reports* and has been substantially superseded by it, there is no need for further discussion of its scope and method.

## 4. The International Military Tribunal, Nürnberg

### *Official publications*

In accordance with the direction of the International Military Tribunal, a series of volumes covering the judgments and proceedings of this Tribunal is in process of publication by the secretariat of the Tribunal, under the jurisdiction of the Allied Control Authority for Germany.

As is stated in the preface to volume I:

"Recognizing the importance of establishing for history an authentic text of the trial of major German war criminals, the International Military Tribunal directed the publication of the record of the trial. The proceedings are published in English, French, Russian and German, the four languages used throughout the hearings. The documents admitted in evidence are printed only in their original language.

"The first volume contains basic, official, pre-trial documents together with the Tribunal's judgment and sentence of the defendants. In subsequent volumes the trial proceedings are published in full from the preliminary session of 14 November 1945 to the closing session of 1 October 1946. They are followed by an index volume. Documents admitted in evidence conclude the publication."[115]

The complete record is to be 37 volumes, consisting of one volume of pre-trial documents as indicated above, 22 volumes of testimony, 12 volumes of exhibits and 2 volumes of index. Approximately one half of the whole has appeared so far.

In the United Kingdom there is in process of publication under the authority of H.M. Attorney-General, by H.M. Stationery Office, a series entitled *The Trial of German Major War Criminals, Proceedings of the International Military Tribunal Sitting at Nürnberg, Germany.*

A brief description is given in the foreward to part I as follows:

"This is the first of a series of publications which will, in due course, cover the whole trial of major war criminals now in progress at Nürnberg. The publication will be issued in fortnightly parts.

"A copy of the official text of the transcript has been made available to the Attorney-General for this purpose by the International Military Tribunal, who, however, accept no responsibility for this publication."

[114] Full title: George Grafton Wilson, *The Hague Arbitration Cases. Compromis* and awards with maps in cases decided under the provisions of the Hague Conventions of 1899 and 1907 for the Pacific Settlement of International Disputes and texts of the Conventions. 1915.

[115] *Trial of the Major War Criminals Before the International Military Tribunal, Nürnberg, 14 November 1945—1 October 1946.* Published at Nürnberg, Germany. Vol. I (1947). Official text in the English language. p. vii.

Part I of this series was issued in London in 1946. So far 17 parts have been published.

In the same manner but not as part of the series, one volume was published in 1946 containing the speeches of the Chief Prosecutors for the United States of America, the French Republic, the United Kingdom and the USSR, at the close of the case against individual defendants.

5. The Central American Court of Justice

The decisions of this Court "were not published in any uniform style".[116] During the initial period of the Court's functioning its decisions or resolutions were printed individually at San José. Thus the decision in the case of Honduras *v.* Guatemala and El Salvador rendered in 1908, and the resolution in Diaz *v.* Guatemala of 6 March 1909 were published at San José in 1908[117] and 1909 respectively.[118] Subsequent decisions and resolutions, beginning with the resolution of 14 October 1911, Cerdá *v.* Costa Rica, were published in the seven volumes of the *Anales de la Corte de Justicia Centro Americana,* of which the Secretary of the Court was the director. The *Anales* were published from 1911 to 1917. They were, however, not confined to reporting exclusively the resolutions and decisions of the Court but contained also other matters. Certain documents pertaining to the organization of the Court were printed in the *Anales* as were, in some cases, documents relating to matters of which the Court was seized.

6. The Mixed Arbitral Tribunals

The decisions of these Tribunals, created in 1919 and 1920, were published in an unofficial collection entitled *Recueil des Décisions des Tribunaux Arbitraux Mixtes institués par les Traités de Paix, publié sous les auspices de l'Office Français des Biens et Intérêts Privés.* The series comprises ten volumes issued between 1922 and 1930.

The Director of the series declared in the preface to volume I that *"le Recueil des Décisions de T.A.M. nous paraît répondre à un véritable besoin, non seulement en raison de l'intérêt qu'il présentera pour les juristes curieux des manifestations du Droit International, mais aussi pour les plaideurs qui trouveront dans cette publication les éléments de jurisprudence dans cette matière absolument nouvelle".* He also believed that *"à juste titre, la jurisprudence de la haute juridiction formera un monument important de Droit International nouveau, qui, créé à la suite d'une conflagration sans précédent dans l'histoire, ne sera pas sans avoir des répercussions sur l'état de paix qui va suivre".*

The *Recueil* makes no claim to completeness and gives no clue as to how the cases were selected.

[116] Manley O. Hudson, "The Central American Court of Justice." *American Journal of International Law,* vol. 26 (1932), p. 767.

[117] *Corte de Justicia Centroamericana. Cartago, Costa Rica. Sentencia En El Judicio Promovido Por La República de Honduras Contra Las Repúblicas de El Salvador y Guatemala. Impenta de Avelino Alsina.* San José. Costa Rica.

[118] Hudson, *op. cit.,* pp. 769 f.

The report of a case generally indicates the title of the tribunal, the name of the president, the title of the claim and its number. The headnotes are in English, French, Italian or German depending upon the language of the tribunal. Catchwords are in these four languages. In some cases there is a brief summary of the facts and of the decision. The text of the decision is in the official language of the tribunal concerned.

The *Recueil* contains also the rules of procedure of the different tribunals, national legislation on the questions involved, as well as pertinent decisions of domestic courts, bibliographical notes and tables.

## 7. The Arbitral Tribunal for Upper Silesia

This tribunal was established pursuant to the Geneva Convention of 15 May 1922 between Poland and Germany to decide all conflicts concerning the interpretation or application of the provisions of that Convention.[119] Article 592, paragraph 1 provided for the official publication of its decisions, *"lorsqu'elles sont d'un réel intérêt jurisprudentiel"*.

The Tribunal between 1922 and 1937 decided 3,726 cases[120] of which 127 leading cases were published in Polish and German. The official collection in German and Polish comprises seven volumes published from 1929 to 1937.[121]

## 8. Claims Commissions and *ad hoc* Arbitral Tribunals

Decisions of claims commissions instituted by agreement between two or more States to dispose of a more or less substantial number of accumulated claims have frequently been published officially and unofficially, as were the awards of arbitral tribunals created for the settlement of a particular dispute. It is probably safe to say that all of the decisions and awards have not been made available in print. And one of the characteristics of the present situation with regard to this material is that there is no serial publication in existence which would provide a complete collection of such awards and decisions.

There are several volumes of decisions rendered by particular claims commissions, and many of the decisions were also published by periodicals in the field of private and public international law. As mentioned above, one or two projects were started, but not consummated, to provide a complete collection not merely of the awards or decisions ever rendered, but also of other pertinent documentation such as *compromis,* cases and counter-cases, oral proceedings, etc.

The situation for the past twenty or thirty years is somewhat less unsatisfactory than for the preceding period, partly because the Governments themselves have published more material, and partly because of the existence of the *Annual Digest and Reports of Public International Law Cases.* The greater attention and space devoted to international case

[119] *League of Nations Treaty Series,* vol. 9.

[120] Georges Kaeckenbeeck, *The International Experiment of Upper Silesia* (1942), p. 857.

[121] The official collection is entitled: *Amtliche Sammlung von Entscheidungen des Schiedsgerichts für Oberschlesien—Zbior Urzedowy Orzeczen Trybunalu Rozjemczego dla Górnego Slaska.*

materials in leading journals must not be overlooked as an important factor in the picture. In spite of all these improvements, certain recent awards are extremely hard to find.[122]

The compilation of a complete list of available published reports containing the texts of awards and decisions handed down by mixed commissions and *ad hoc* arbitral tribunals cannot be attempted here. There are, however, numerous references in Stuyt's *Survey of International Arbitrations,*[123] in Sandifer's *Evidence before International Tribunals* (1939) and of course in Ralston's *The Law and Procedure of International Tribunals.*[124]

## H. DIGESTS OF DECISIONS OF INTERNATIONAL TRIBUNALS

### 1. General Digests

The only general digest of decisions of international tribunals which appears to exist is *The Annual Digest and Reports of Public International Law Cases, 1919–1942.*[125] The title of this publication was originally *The Annual Digest of Public International Law Cases* but was changed in 1940 in conformity with the change in editorial policy which has resulted in a partial transformation of the series into law reports proper. The work was originally undertaken by Sir Arnold McNair and Professor Lauterpacht with the assistance of an advisory committee and some twenty-five contributors from different countries. Since 1935 Professor Lauterpacht has been the sole editor.

The ten volumes of the series which have so far appeared contain reports or digests of nearly 3,000 decisions of the years 1914–1942, including not only decisions of international tribunals, but also those of national tribunals upon points of international law. The original method by which the work was compiled was this: the contributors collected the decisions of the tribunals or countries for which they were individually responsible and these were then, when necessary, translated into English; the editors then selected the cases to be published and cast them into a common form consisting of a heading, a statement of facts and a condensed and paraphrased "Held" which gave the substance of the decision. Where a decision dealt with more than one point of law, it was dissected and printed in different entries. With the volume for 1929–1930 the dissection of decisions was, however, abandoned in order to give a trial to the policy, recommended by readers, of reporting each case as a whole and inserting cross references indicating the various

[122] Cf. Briggs, "Finding International Law", *American Journal of International Law,* vol. 42 (1948), p. 103.

[123] See pp. 55–56 *supra.*

[124] See also Ralston, *Supplement* to 1926 revised edition of *The Law and Procedure of International Tribunals.*

[125] *Digest of Public International Law Cases.* Being a selection from the decisions of international and national courts and tribunals given during the years 1925 and 1926. Editors: Arnold D. McNair and H. Lauterpacht (1929); volume II, years 1927 and 1928. Edited by McNair and Lauterpacht (1931); volume III, years 1919 and 1922 (1932) and volume VI, 1923 and 1924 (1933), edited by Sir John Fischer Williams and H. Lauterpacht; volume V, 1929 and 1930 (1935) edited by H. Lauterpacht as were the following volumes: volume VI, 1931 and 1932 (1938), volume VII, 1933 and 1934 (1940), volume VIII, 1935 and 1937 (1941), volume IX, 1938–1940 (1942), volume X, 1941 and 1942 (1945), volume XI, 1919–1942 (supplementary volume, 1947). Beginning with volume VII the work appeared under the title *Annual Digest and Reports of Public International Law Cases.*

points of law covered by it. And with the volume for 1931–1932 a further change of method was introduced, decisions being printed partly or wholly verbatim instead of being merely summarized. The original method of providing digests was thereafter retained only with respect to unimportant decisions and to certain bulky and easily accessible decisions such as those of the Permanent Court of International Justice and "the verbatim, although often abridged, report [ultimately became] the rule"[126] rather than the exception. Thus in the preface to the ninth volume the editor could say that "little remains to be done" to transform the *Digest* into international law reports proper"[127] and the tenth volume is "predominantly—though not exclusively—a volume of, in most cases, complete law reports reproduced verbatim (in the case of reports in the English language) or in a translation".[128] Another important change in editorial policy at present in process of being achieved is the transformation of the series into one appearing at annual intervals and providing an almost contemporaneous report of decisions of international legal interest.

Two other features of the *Annual Digest and Reports* are noteworthy. The first is that the series contains a profusion of notes by either editor or contributors, appended to individual cases reported or digested. The second is that with the volume for the years 1933–1934 there was begun the practice of reporting cases previously omitted because of oversight, inaccessibility or other similar reason, but subsequently considered of sufficient importance, to warrant inclusion. The culmination of this practice was the publication in 1947 of a supplementary volume covering the entire period of the *Digest* and containing, in addition to numerous cases not previously published, comprehensive tables of all cases reported or cited and a consolidated index to the first ten volumes of the series.

The arrangement of the *Annual Digest and Reports* is systematic. Cases are arranged under numerous sub-headings falling under the following main headings: I. International law in general; II. States as international persons; III. State territory; IV. Jurisdiction; V. State responsibility; VI. The individual and international law; VII. Diplomatic and consular intercourse and privileges; VIII. Treaties; IX. International organization; X. Disputes; XI. War and neutrality. The decisions included thus cover the whole field of international law. One exception, however, may be noted: the original editorial policy was not, as a rule, to print decisions of prize courts arising out of the war of 1914–1918; but some important decisions of prize courts during the war of 1939–1945 appear in the volume for the years 1941–1942.

The value of the *Annual Digest and Reports* is very generally acknowledged. It has, of course, been criticized, but successive changes in editorial policy have very largely met criticisms. Thus, the point that the work endeavoured to do two things, to be an index of decisions on the one hand and to be a primary source on the other, and that it really did neither, has ceased to have validity since the virtually complete transformation of the

[126] *Annual Digest 1935–1937*, p. ix.
[127] *Annual Digest 1938–1940*, p. ix.
[128] *Annual Digest 1941–1942*, p. ix.

series from a digest into reports. The view has also been expressed that "bulk is no substitute for new principles" and that it is "merely a waste of the reader's time to report cases which do not appear to embody any new principle or even a modification of an established principle".[129] This raises the fundamental question whether the selection of cases according to their weight and novelty should be done by the editor, or by readers. Clearly any system whatsoever of editorial selection is open to criticism. The policy of Professor Lauterpacht and his collaborators has been to include "even cases of minor importance in a note or footnote", on the ground "that even a seemingly insignificant or purely domestic decision may on occasion become of importance to the specialist and that, unless the case is recorded in the *Digest* in some form, it may easily become lost for the purposes of international law".[130] The reputation and utility of the work, in any event, are now beyond question. But it is to be noted that unsold stocks of the earlier volumes were unfortunately destroyed in the bombing of London and are now virtually unobtainable; and further, that the editor depends for the expenses of publication upon grants from various sources. In this connexion, it may be remarked that it has been suggested that official support might be given to the undertaking through the United Nations, with a view to its development "into a genuine international law reporter".[131]

## 2. Digests of Decisions of Specific International Tribunals

### (i) The International Court of Justice

With the second issue of the Yearbook of the International Court of Justice there was inaugurated a digest of the decisions and advisory opinions of the Court upon the same lines as the digest which appeared in the annual reports of the Permanent Court of International Justice.[132]

### (ii) The Permanent Court of International Justice

#### *Official publications*

In conformity with the request of the Council of the League of Nations, dated 23 December 1924, the Registry of the Permanent Court of International Justice began to publish, as Series E of the publications of the Court, annual reports in which were included summaries of judgments and advisory opinions. The section of the report devoted to decisions was transformed into a digest with its third issue and this feature was retained so long as the Court continued to exist.

It was pointed out by the Registrar, that "this summary of judgments and advisory

[129] G. Schwarzenberger, "The Inductive Approach to International Law," *Harvard Law Review*, vol. 60 (1947), p. 565.
[130] *Annual Digest 1933–1934*, p. x.
[131] Herbert W. Briggs, "Finding International Law," *American Journal of International Law*, vol. 42 (1948) p. 102.
[132] See *infra*.

opinions, the object of which is to present a general view of the Court's work, may not be cited in argument against the actual text of the judgments and opinions and does not constitute an interpretation of them''.[133]

The method of a digest was adopted because it was thought that it would ''afford a firm foundation for the codification of the Court's decisions—both past and future—and . . . lend itself more readily to consultation: under each article of the Statute are grouped the provisions for the Rules connected therewith and the practice adopted by the Court in the application of the terms of its Statute and Rules''.[134] The chapter containing the digest was originally followed by an analytical index. Subsequently the number of indexes was increased.[135] The sixteenth annual report for the period from 15 June 1939 to 31 December 1945, embodies in chapter VI all the decisions taken by the Court during the years from 15 June 1933 to 31 December 1945. The Digest of Decisions ''is followed by three indexes: (1) an analytical index; (2) an index of articles of the Statute; (3) an index of the Rules to which the decisions relate. The three indices cover all decisions since 1922''.[136]

*Unofficial publications*

The decisions and advisory opinions of the Permanent Court of International Justice during the period 1922–1934 are digested in *Fontes Juris Gentium: Digest of the Decisions of the Permanent Court of International Justice,* 1922–1930 and 1931–1934.[137] Decisions and Opinions of the Court issued in the Series A/B Nos. 63–80 have not been digested in this series.

This *Digest* of decisions, advisory opinions and separate and dissenting opinions, is divided into two parts. The first part deals with substantive international law and the second with adjective international law, more specifically with questions of the jurisdiction and procedure of the Court. Within each part the material is arranged in accordance with a simple classification. All extracts are printed in French and English. The classification is printed in French, English and German. All tables and indexes are also in these three languages.

In these two volumes ''the basic principles and special rules on which the Court has relied in the arguments underlying its decisions and opinions have been collected and systematically classified''. In the opinion of the editor of this series, ''even a cursory survey

[133] Series E, No. 1, p. 162.
[134] Series E, No. 3, p. 173.
[135] Series E, No. 12, p. 186.
[136] Series E, No. 16, p. 159. Chapter VI of the Tenth Annual Report, Series E, No. 10, contains at p. 151 the following note: ''It should be noted that, since the publication of the ninth annual report, a work entitled *Statut et Règlement de la Cour permanente de Justice internationale (éléments d'interprétation)* has been published by the *Institute für Ausländisches öffentliches Recht und Völkerrecht of Berlin.* This work includes, *inter alia,* a digest of decisions taken by the Court in application of the Statute and Rules up to and including those recorded in the ninth addendum (Series E, No. 9). Accordingly, for those who are able to consult the work above mentioned, the present chapter may be regarded as the first addendum thereto.''
[137] *Fontes Juris Gentium,* Series A, sectio I, *tomus* I and *tomus* 3 published in 1931 and 1935 respectively.

of these extracts shows a small system of international law complete in itself, a system of rules which are in great part neither treaty rules nor rules of customary law''.[138]

The broad objective of the editors of the *Digest* was to furnish a source book and for this reason they have endeavoured to select statements ''of more general import'' and they have not attempted to formulate themselves ''a single rule of law corresponding to a legal conception of the Court derived from the combination of several passages''.[139] To enable the user of the *Digest* to assess properly the import of certain passages, the context in which it appears has frequently been reproduced. However, the editors insist that ''the study of the decisions themselves remains indispensable for all more profound research''.[140]

It is characteristic for the methodological conception underlying the *Digest* that the decisions ''of international tribunals have not been included . . . as decisions of individual cases, but simply and solely as material, in so far as they contain the legal views of international decisional bodies. For this reason no distinction could be drawn in these volumes between the *rationes decidendi* and *obiter dicta.* In the opinion of the editor it is inadmissible to apply to the field of international law the distinction between different kinds of reasons for a decision which is shown by the Anglo-American jurisprudence, as the condition on which such a distinction is made, viz. the general binding force of the decision, is not found in the same way in international law. A collection of material must be made with the greatest possible impartiality''.[141]

It naturally follows from this conception that any attempt to distinguish between different parts of the decision would have introduced individual or even subjective judgments which the *Fontes Juris Gentium* series was at pains to avoid. It also follows that ''the selection was not restricted to those utterances which served to direct the decision of the questions before the Court, but included also such passages which possess no decisive significance for the case at bar, but which are nevertheless characteristic of the legal viewpoint of the Court''.[142]

The publication of this *Digest* was on the whole well received by international lawyers. The view of one writer was that: *"Il y a là un effort scientifique de la plus haute importance et dont l'utilité juridique est inappréciable"*[143] and that *"la valeur scientifique de l'œuvre est au-dessus de tout éloge".*[144] Another writer recognized that the Digest was ''the first product of a monumental undertaking which should be greeted with gratitude and approval by the legal profession throughout the world'', but cautioned that ''while such a work must be used with the reservation that a paragraph in a judgment or opinion is al-

[138] *Fontes Juris Gentium,* Series A, sectio I, tomus I, p. xxv.
[139] *Ibid.,* p. xxxiii.
[140] *Ibid.*
[141] *Fontes Juris Gentium,* Series B, sectio I, *tomus* I, p. xx.
[142] *Fontes Juris Gentium,* Series A, sectio I, *tomus* 1, p. xxxiv.
[143] Charles Rousseau in *Revue Générale de Droit International Public,* vol. 38 (1931), p. 785.
[144] Charles Rosseau in *Revue Générale de Droit International Public,* vol. 42 (1935), p. 706.

ways qualified by its setting, it should prove to be of inestimable value and convenience to students of current international law. The amount of the Court's output has grown very large, and such a digest fills a real need. The execution of the plan is admirable down to the last detail. The reproduction of the several languages ensures the wide use of the digest''.[145]

Another writer, appreciating the objective of the *Digest* ''to facilitate a greater measure of objectivity in practice and in research'' raised the question: ''May it not be that something rather less than the editors have provided, something more in the nature of a full and reasoned index to the decisions, might have been equally useful? At present there may be a danger that the considerable length of many of the citations, divorced though they are from the full context in which they occur, may encourage the habit of relying on the authority of the digest alone''.[146]

Several critical voices were raised at the Fifth Conference of Teachers of International Law and Related Subjects. It was reported that, according to one view, the extracts ''may be a legal conclusion, a parenthetical observation, a mere *obiter;* it is served up either as law, or having the appearance of law—one cannot know which''.[147] One of the editors of the *Digest* made this statement, however: ''Ever since the *Digest of the Decisions of the Permanent Court of International Justice* was issued, practically every member of the Permanent Court has been urging us continually to get out a supplement. I might add that those volumes which are in the possession of the members of the Permanent Court have been practically destroyed through constant use''.[148]

It may be noted as indicative of the recognition with which the *Digest* was received, that half of the first edition was sold in the course of the first year after publication.[149]

### (iii) The Permanent Court of Arbitration

The decisions of tribunals of this Court are digested in *Fontes Juris Gentium: Digest of the Decisions of the Permanent Court of Arbitration, 1902–1928.*[150]

This *Digest* was prepared in the conviction that the decisions of the tribunals of the Permanent Court of Arbitration ''are of lasting value for the study of international law'' and ''of great importance as sources of legal rules''.[151] The method applied was, as far as possible, the same as that employed in the *Digest of the Decisions of the Permanent Court of International Justice.* The editors found it necessary to stress again that ''the catchwords placed above the passages reproduced are not intended as systematic subdivisions of the chapter headings, but as aids to the reader'' and that the *Digest* ''is intended merely as a

145 Manley O. Hudson in *American Journal of International Law,* vol. 25 (1931), p. 795–796.
146 J. L. B. in *British Year Book of International Law,* vol. 13 (1932), p. 200.
147 *Proceedings,* 1933, p. 168.
148 *Ibid.,* p. 174.
149 *Fontes Juris Gentium,* Series B, sectio I, *tomus* 1, p. xxi.
150 *Fontes Juris Gentium,* Series A, sectio I, *tomus* 2 (1931).
151 *Ibid.,* p. xi.

guide and that the study of the decisions themselves remains indispensable for all more profounded research".[152]

Altogether 19 decisions are digested. The texts of the *compromis* relating to these arbitrations are reproduced *in extenso* in an annex. The abstracts are classified under 16 main headings and a larger number of sub-headings or "catchwords".

The extracts reproduced in the *Digest* are taken from the official publications of the International Bureau of the Permanent Court of Arbitration and are marked as such. However, all extracts are given in French, English and German, the necessary translations being made by the editors.

The abstracts themselves are reproduced without reference to the decision from which they were taken. In order to facilitate their identification there are printed on the margin numbers referring to the Index of passages reproduced from the decisions which concludes the volume.

## I. REPORTS OR COLLECTIONS OF DECISIONS OF MUNICIPAL COURTS ON QUESTIONS OF INTERNATIONAL LAW

### 1. General Collections

No attempt has yet been made to prepare a systematic and comprehensive collection of decisions on questions of international law rendered by the courts in the different countries over a period of time. It is possible, however, to point to the *Annual Digest and Reports of Public International Law Cases*[153] which since 1940 began to report cases *in extenso*, and which "has served to reveal the wealth of material which may lie buried". The number of countries, however, whose decisions are reported in this work, although substantial, is limited and therefore, as has been pointed out, "a general global collection of cases on international law" would be still more valuable.[154]

In addition to the *Annual Digest*, several legal periodicals in different countries published regularly a selection of decisions of municipal courts, in their own country and abroad, on questions of international law. A fairly representative cross-section of such decisions was offered in the *Bulletin* of the *Institut Intermédiaire International* at The Hague 1919–1940.[155] Some of the decisions are reported *in extenso* and others in the form of a

[152] *Ibid.*, pp. xi and xii.

[153] See pp. 68–70.

[154] Manley O. Hudson, "Twelve Casebooks on International Law", *American Journal of International Law*, vol. 32 (1938), p. 455.

[155] The Institute was established at The Hague on 18 January 1918 as *un office de virements documentaires, un 'clearinghouse' pour renseignements internationaux*. Its name was subsequently changed to *Institut Juridique International*. In addition to publishing treaties, decisions of prize courts, and various diplomatic documents, it was the purpose of the Institute to prepare *un aperçu de décisions judiciares présentant un caractère international, soit que ces décisions soient rendues par des juges internationaux, soit qu'elles émanent de juges nationaux, pour autant que ces dernières touchent à des questions d'un caractère international. Bulletin*, vol. I (1919), pp. 20–22. The *Bulletin* comprises 42 volumes, the forty-second appeared in January 1940.

very brief digest or extract. More complete summaries or the full text could be obtained on request from the Institute. The Institute, however, informed the reader that the decisions printed in the *Bulletin* under the heading. *Jurisprudence en Matière de Droit International* represented only a fraction of the jurisprudence which it had collected and which was available in its archives. Also of interest is the collection *Comparative Judicial Decisions on Commercial or Maritime Law, the Law of the Air, International Law and the Law of Copyright,* the first volume of which was issued by the *Istituto di Studi Legislativi* at Rome in 1938.

2. Collections with Reference to Particular Countries

There is likewise a scarcity of comprehensive collections of decisions upon points of international law of the courts of particular countries. Official or unofficial reports exist, of course, in most countries, but very rarely are such decisions as are of interest to international lawyers extracted from the mass and published separately. There are, however, several such collections, some of which may be briefly mentioned here:

(i) Germany

There was issued in the *Fontes Juris Gentium* collection a series consisting of the decisions of the German Supreme Court in questions of international law, covering the period from 1879 to 1929.[156] As, however, this series partakes more of the nature of a digest than of a law report, it is more appropriate to list it elsewhere in this survey.[157] Parallel collections of the decisions of the highest courts of other countries were planned by the editors of this series, but they failed to materialize.

(ii) United States

Decisions of the Supreme Court and of other courts in the United States have been reproduced in the *American Journal of International Law* and other periodicals. The important cases are also conveniently represented in the different casebooks of international law. The first casebook was Freeman Snow's *Cases and Opinions,* published in 1893, upon which was based Scott's *Cases on International Law* (1902). Stowe and Munroe's casebook followed in 1916, that of Evans in 1917, those of Dickinson and Hudson in 1929, that of Fenwick in 1935, and that of Briggs in 1938. Though primarily intended for students, these publications have been of much assistance to practitioners as well. The method of presentation employed in them varies somewhat. Thus some approximate to digests, whilst others resemble law reports proper. The majority of them include not only American cases but decisions of international tribunals and of the courts of the United Kingdom and other countries.

[156] Series A, sectio II, *tomus* 1 (1931).
[157] See pp. 80–82.

### (iii) United Kingdom

Decisions of the courts of the United Kingdom on questions of international law are reproduced in the legal journals and notably in the *British Yearbook of International Law*. Pitt Cobbett's *Leading Cases and Opinions on International Law* (1885), the first casebook on international law to be published anywhere, now in its sixth edition, contains a selection of decisions. But this work is less of a law report than a collection of paraphrased decisions. American casebooks, as has been already noted, also contain decisions of the courts of the United Kingdom.

### (iv) France

There is no general collection of French case law of international legal import nor yet any French casebook on French international law. But the numerous French decisions are extensively reported in legal journals, in particular in the *Revue de droit international* (1927–1940, edited by de La Pradelle), the *Journal de droit international* (founded by Clunet in 1874) and the *Revue générale de droit international public*. The different *Recueils Dalloz* and the *Répertoires Dalloz* also contain international law cases. There exists, with respect to French cases, the important *Recueil général périodique et critique des décisions, conventions et lois relatives au droit international public et privé,* founded by Albert de La Pradelle in 1934, but unfortunately discontinued in 1938, part III of which is devoted to *Jurisprudence interne française et étrangère*. Finally there must be mentioned Darras' *Répertoire de droit international* (edited by de La Pradelle and Niboyet, 1929-1931), which is further discussed in this survey in connexion with digests of municipal decisions on questions of international law.[158]

### (v) Canada

A collection of Canadian cases[159] on international law was published by Mackenzie and Laing in 1938.

### (vi) Other Countries

Decisions of the courts of other countries on questions of international law are reported in the periodical literature of many such countries. Thus, Egyptian decisions are to be found in the *Revue égyptienne de droit international* and Yugoslav cases in the *Annuaire* of the Yugoslav Association for International Law.

[158] See p. 80.
[159] *Canada and the Law of Nations.*

## 3. Collections of Municipal Decisions on Special Topics

Several collections of the decisions of municipal courts on particular questions of international law exist. The following would appear to be the most important categories of these:

### (i) Prize Cases

The decisions of prize courts of different countries have at various times been collected. Thus, there exist the three volumes of the *Prize Cases in the United States Supreme Court, 1789–1918,* published under the auspices of the Carnegie Endowment for International Peace in 1923, and Roscoe's *English Prize Cases* (two volumes, 1905, covering the years 1745 to 1859). Reports of the principal Russian and Japanese Prize Cases decided in 1904–1905 were published by Judge Sir Cecil Hurst and F. E. Bray in 1912 and 1913. Further, various collections of prize cases decided during the war of 1914–1918 were published, of which it is sufficient to mention Lloyd's *Reports of* [British] *Prize Cases* (ten volumes, 1915–1924, new series, one volume, 1940–1947); *British and Colonial Prize Cases* (three volumes), 1916–1922); Fauchille and Basdevant's *La guerre de 1914, Jurisprudence Britannique en Matière de Prises Maritimes* (two volumes, 1922 and 1927; *Décisions du Conseil des Prises et Décrets Rendus en Conseil d'Etat en Matière de Prises Maritimes* (two volumes, 1916, 1932; Fauchille, *La Guerre de 1914, Jurisprudence Française en Matière de Prises Maritimes* (two volumes; 1916, 1919); *Sentenze della Commissione delle Prede, Guerra Europea, 1915–1918* (1927); Fauchille and Basdevant's *La Guerre de 1915, Jurisprudence Italienne en Matière de Prises Maritimes* (1921); *Entscheidungen des Oberprisengerichts in Berlin* (two volumes, 1918, 1921); Fauchille and Visscher's *La Guerre de 1914, Jurisprudence Allemande en Matière de Prises Maritimes* (two volumes, 1922,1924); J. H. W. Verzyl, *Le Droit des Prises de la Grande Guerre, Jurisprudence de 1914 et des années suivantes en matière de prises maritimes;* published under the auspices of the *Institut Intermédiaire International* (Leyden 1924).

### (ii) Labour Cases

The International Labour Office published an *International Survey on Legal Disputes on Labour Laws* covering the years 1925 to 1938 which, though only partially concerned with international law, possesses certain features of interest in connexion with the general problem of collecting and publishing municipal decisons. The *Survey* was at first confined to the four most important European legal systems and, although United States decisions were added to it in 1927, Italian decisions had to be omitted in later years. Decisions were grouped by countries and then subdivided in accordance with an elaborate system. A standard method of presentation of cases was adopted, but the actual selection of cases was in the hands of individual experts from the countries concerned. In respect of each country there was printed a note on jurisdiction to enable the reader to assess the importance of decisions of courts with which he might not be familiar. This information is normally lacking in casebooks and digests on international law but would be very valuable.

### (iii) Civil Aviation

The secretary of the Legal Committee of the International Civil Aviation Organization reported at its second session that the secretariat had collected certain judicial, administrative and arbitral decisions on questions affecting civil aviation and the Legal Committee recommended to the council of the Organization the publication of this material.[160]

### (iv) War Crimes

The United Kingdom Stationery Office is in process of publishing 20 volumes comprising a total of 122 cases of war crimes tried by municipal tribunals, military and civil, on behalf of the United Nations War Crimes Commission. Eight volumes have so far appeared, entitled *Law Reports of Trials of War Criminals Selected and Prepared by the United Nations War Crimes Commission.*

## J. DIGESTS OF DECISIONS OF MUNICIPAL COURTS ON QUESTIONS OF INTERNATIONAL LAW

### 1. General Digests

It is believed that the *Annual Digest and Reports of Public International Law Cases* is the only work which systematically reports and digests decisions of courts of a plurality of countries on questions of international law. As has been already seen, this work incorporates also decisions of international tribunals. Its general characteristics have been discussed, therefore, under the heading of Digests of Decisions of International Tribunals.[161] To the observations already made concerning it, however, it may be added that the number of countries covered by the *Annual Digest* varies somewhat from volume to volume, relevant materials for all countries not being always discoverable or accessible. The volume for 1919–1922 contained a varying number of digests for the following countries: Argentina, Austria, Belgium, Bolivia, Brazil, Canada, Chile, Costa Rica, Cuba, Czechoslovakia, Egypt, England, France, Germany, Greece, Holland, Hungary, Italy, Japan, Latvia, Mexico, Nicaragua, Norway, Panama, Peru, Poland, Scotland, Union of South Africa, Sweden, Switzerland, the USSR, and Venezuela. The last pre-war volume (for the years 1935–1937) contained digests for the following countries: Argentina, Australia, Austria, Belgium, Brazil, British Empire, Canada, Danzig, Egypt, England,

[160] *International Civil Aviation Organization, Legal Committee, Second Session* (1948). Doc. 6014, L.C./III, 16/8/48, p. 100.

[161] See p. 68 f.

Estonia, France, Guatemala, Germany, Greece, Holland, Hungary, Italy, Luxembourg, Mexico, Norway, Palestine, Panama, Poland, South Africa, Sweden, Switzerland, and the United States. There may also be noted a criticism of the work for its lack of background material on the ground that "decisions of national courts cannot—any more than diplomatic material—be properly understood in isolation. They have to be analysed against the background of the legal systems to which they belong and seen in their place in the hierarchy of courts".[162]

Though the *Annual Digest* is thus the only general digest of decisions of municipal courts, various periodicals publish such decisions, notably the *Bulletin* of the *Institut Intermédiaire International*, the *Revue générale de droit international public*, and the *Journal de droit international*. The *American Journal of International Law* and the American casebooks also contain such decisions.

## 2. Digests of Decisions of Courts of Specific Countries

### (i) United States

Summaries of decisions of American courts on questions of international law are contained in Moore's Digest, in Hackworth's Digest,[164] in some of the casebooks, and in legal periodicals. In connexion with the last-mentioned source, the recent decision of the board of editors of the *American Journal of International Law* to extend greatly the reporting of decisions in that *Journal* is to be noted. This decision was prompted by the fact that "the digest system, used by American lawyers as a guide through the multitude of American cases in the court reports, does not furnish a very satisfactory means for finding even the decisions in this country on international law points".[163] Thus, it was reported, "the *General Digest* for the years 1941-1942, listed only 42 decisions under the section 'International Law'. By making his own index and by diligent effort, the writer was able to discover a total of 124 cases decided by United States courts during that period in which the decision turned upon some questions of international law".[164] Similarly, the *General Index* for 1943–1944 lists only 40 cases, but further research yielded 74 cases.[164a]

As a further aid to finding American cases on international law questions perhaps the *Annual Survey of American Law*, published since 1942 by the New York University School of Law should be mentioned. This *Annual Survey* contains regularly a chapter on international law in which current American cases on international law are discussed and American legislation on questions of international law and organization reviewed.

[162] G. Schwarzenberger, "The Inductive Approach to International Law," *Harvard Law Review*, vol. 60 (1947), p. 565.
[164] Herbert W. Briggs, "Finding International Law", *American Journal of International Law*, vol. 42 (1948), p. 101.
[163] William W. Bishop, Jr., "Recent American Judicial Decisions involving international law", *American Journal of International Law*, vol. 42 (1948), p. 194.
[164] Herbert W. Briggs, "Finding International Law", *American Journal of International Law*, vol. 42 (1948), p. 101.
[164a] *Ibidem*.

## (ii) United Kingdom

Legal journals, notably the *British Yearbook of International Law,* periodically report decisions upon questions of international law. The *English and Empire Digest* comprises decisions of English, Scottish, Irish, Canadian, Indian, Australian, Newfoundland, and South African Courts, but contains no general heading International Law, so that relevant cases must be sought under such headings as Aliens, the Crown in Foreign Relations, etc. Also of assistance in tracing relevant British decisions is the *Annual Survey of English Law,* published since 1928 by the London School of Economics and Political Science, and containing chapters on international law and relations. British decisions are further to be found in Pitt Cobbett's *Cases and Opinions on International Law,*[165] in Moore's and Hackworth's *Digests,* in the American casebooks and in some French journals.

## (iii) France

Perhaps the most valuable guide to French decisions on international legal questions is, apart from periodicals, de La Pradelle and Niboyet's *Répertoire de droit international,* consisting of ten volumes and one supplement (1929–1934). This work, which is systematically arranged, is not confined exclusively to French cases; thus the title on Nationality therein refers to the legislation and decisions of sixty-three different countries.

## (iv) Germany

The decisions of the German Supreme Court relating to international law, from 1879 to 1929, are published in the *Fontes Juris Gentium* series[166] both as a collection of decisions and also in the form of a systematic digest. Decisions of lower courts were omitted on the ground that although this omission would result in the exclusion of some cases of interest from the viewpoint of international law, these decisions were not of equal authority with those of the Supreme Court.

The digest is based on 412 decisions of which 76 had not been previously published. The majority of the decisions were taken from official reports, but some were taken from legal periodicals.

Not all of the 412 decisions deal with questions of international law. The editors also took into consideration "such cases as show the effect of international legal relationships on domestic affairs and others which pronounce on facts, domestic in themselves, but which are capable of being considered from the point of view of international law. It was indeed inevitable that material of this kind—extradition, for example—should occupy a comparatively large space in this collection. In accordance with the purpose of the

[165] See p. 76 *supra.*
[166] Series A, *sectio* 2, *tomus* 1 (1931).

work, the relevant utterances have been classified under the appropriate headings of international law''.[167]

As indicated above, this volume consists of two parts. The first part ''contains, in the form of a systematic digest, the most important rules taken from the decisions, either literally reproduced, or else closely moulded on the actual words of the report''. This digest is divided into a general and special part. ''The special part deals with particular questions with which the *Reichsgericht* had to deal after the war in consequence of Germany's position under the Versailles Treaty. Cross-references preserve the connexion between the general and the special part''.[168]

The material in the general part is classified as follows: I. General principles; II. International law and municipal law; III. Subjects of international law; IV. Nationality; V. Territory of States; VI. Jurisdiction of States; VII. Legal position of aliens; VIII. Extradition; IX. Succession of States; X. Organs of international intercourse; XI. Consular jurisdiction; XII. Treaties; XIII. International offences; XIV. International organs and commissions; XV. War.

The special part consists of the following main headings: Armistice Agreement; Treaties of Peace; Occupation of the Rhineland; Saar Basin; Upper Silesia; Occupation of the Ruhr.

All extracts in the first part are reproduced in the German language, followed by translations into the French and English languages.

The second part contains the text of the 412 decisions on which the digest is based, ''showing the rules in their proper content''. In general, ''only the facts of the case and the passages relevant from the point of view of international law are printed. Part two is thus a necessary supplement, furnishing the reader of part one with the possibility of immediate control without the inconvenience of searching for the individual decisions in the various collections''.[169]

The decisions are printed in chronological order and each decision is numbered consecutively. The numbers are repeated above each of the rules printed in part one, so as to facilitate as far as possible the finding of any particular decision. Reference to the source from which the text of the decision is taken is also provided. All decisions are reproduced exclusively in German.

This volume of the *Fontes Juris Gentium* was favourably received. As one international lawyer observed: *"Le droit interne, en effet, est des plus importants à connaître de nos jours et entre pour une part non négligeable dans l'élaboration des grandes règles internationales. Le droit allemand est donc assuré de gagner, par le canal de ces publications, une notoriété qui facilitera au juge international certaines interprétations ou applications".*[170] In the opinion of another, the editor of the series ''pointed the way toward a new equipment for the legal profession to

[167] *Ibid.*, p. xi.
[168] *Ibid.*, p. xii.
[169] *Ibid.*, p. xiii.
[170] R. G. in *Revue Générale de Droit International Public*, vol. 39 (1932), p. 225.

deal with problems of international law. Similar digests are needed on the decisions of the highest courts in other countries, and it is to be hoped that the *Institut*[171] will be able to publish a digest of the decisions of the Supreme Court of the United States''.[172]

## K. NATIONAL LEGISLATION RELATING TO INTERNATIONAL LAW

The great scarcity of publications setting out national legislation dealing with or affecting questions of international law makes it perhaps useful to mention in this survey such works of this type as do exist.

### 1. General Publications

There is no comprehensive publication on national legislation relating to international law. The international lawyer is forced to look for information to a variety of legal periodicals of different countries, and notably to the *Annuaire de Législation Etrangère,* published since 1872 by the *Société de législation comparée.* There exists also the *Recueil Universel de Lois et Décrets* (four volumes, 1938) published by the International Legislative Information Center; the *Legislazione Internazionale* and the *Repertorio della Legislazione Internazionale,* both published by the *Istituto di Studi Legislativi* from 1932 onwards. De La Pradelle's *Recueil Général Périodique et Critique des Décisions, Conventions et Lois relatives au Droit International Public et Privé* represented an ambitious attempt to provide legislative texts periodically. Altogether five volumes appeared between 1934 and 1938, part VI in each volume being devoted to *Lois et Règlements internes d'ordre international.*

### 2. Publications on Specific Topics

*Official publications*

(i) League of Nations

The Library of the League of Nations published annually from 1930 to 1939 a *Chronology of International Treaties and Legislative Measures* derived from treaty and legislative texts printed in the *Official Gazettes* of nearly all countries and having reference to matters within the sphere of activity of the League. The material so published is classified under the following headings: I. Foreign affairs and public administration; II. Military questions; III. Educational, social and health questions; IV. Economics and finance; V. Finance; VI. Communications and transit; and VII. Commerce and clearing.

[171] Reference is made to the *Institut für ausländisches öffentliches Recht und Völkerrecht* which was responsible for the compilation of the *Fontes Juris Gentium.*
[172] Manley O. Hudson, in *American Journal of International Law,* vol. 26 (1932), p. 428.

## (ii) Labour Law

The *Legislative Series,* published since 1920 by the International Labour Office, contains reprints or translations of the texts of the most important laws and regulations affecting labour adopted in the different countries, issued in leaflet form and distributed every two months. The series has so far appeared in French and English, but a Spanish edition is contemplated.

The International Labour Office also published in 1944 a volume entitled *Constitutional Provisions Concerning Social and Economic Policy.* This work is not confined to labour matters but includes, for instance, constitutional provisions whereby international law is declared to be part of internal law on the ground that, with the growth of the customary law of nations and the increase of its social and economic content, such provisions may have significance in relation to social and economic policy.

## (iii) Human Rights

At its second session the United Nations Economic and Social Council, on the recommendation of the Nuclear Commission on Human Rights, adopted on 21 June 1946, a resolution requesting the Secretary-General to make arrangements for:

*(a)* The compilation and publication of a year book on law and usage relating to human rights, the first edition of which should include all declarations and bills on human rights now in force in the various countries;

*(b)* The collection and publication of information on the activities concerning human rights of all organs of the United Nations;

*(c)* The collection and publication of information concerning human rights arising from trials of war criminals, quislings, and traitors, and in particular from the Nürnberg and Tokio trials;

*(d)* The preparation and publication of a survey of the development of human rights; and

*(e)* The collection and publication of plans and declarations on human rights by specialized agencies and non-governmental national and international organizations.

*The Yearbook on Human Rights,* was prepared pursuant to that resolution and contains constitutional and some legislative provisions, in force on 31 December 1946. All countries were considered and "all constitutional provisions relating to human rights have been included".[173]

The reason for including legislative enactments was stated to be: "Even where the constitution contains specific provisions relating to human rights and fundamental freedoms it is sometimes useful to supplement the study of these provisions by examination of the machinery established for their application and enforcement (ordinary laws, some-

[173] *Yearbook on Human Rights for 1946* (1948), p. ix.

times supplemented by decrees, by-laws, edicts, etc.). Thus the exercise of freedom of the Press or freedom of association is often governed by elaborate rules. The decisions of courts also contribute to the development of the law.

"The laws and regulations relating to human rights were found to be so numerous that only a selection could be included in the *Yearbook*. Since each issue relates to a single year, only those laws and regulations which came into force in 1946 would normally appear in this volume. However, some ordinary legislation adopted before 1946 has been added in the case of countries liberated in 1944 and 1945 in order to give a clear picture of the recent development of human rights in those countries".[174]

In addition to constitutional and legislative texts the *Yearbook* "contains statements and studies describing and commenting on the law relating to human rights in 16 countries, and indicating any recent changes in the law. The statements are in lieu of written constitutional texts where none exist or where the constitution does not mention human rights. The studies, on the other hand, deal with certain countries where there are constitutional provisions relating to human rights. In addition to five statements, there are eight studies which deal with the principles of human rights in general, and five studies which deal with specific questions in this field or describe the recent evolution of the law governing human rights".[175]

The five statements referred to above relate to Great Britain, Australia, Canada, New Zealand, and China. Studies relate to the following countries: Czechoslovakia, Poland, Sweden, USSR, Belgium, Cuba, France, Italy, Lebanon, Mexico and Australia. There are two studies concerning human rights in the United States of America.

Concerning the authorship of these statements and studies, the *Yearbook* says: "The statements or studies relating to Australia, China, Czechoslovakia, New Zealand, Poland, Sweden, Union of Soviet Socialist Republics and United Kingdom were written by experts designated by these Governments, or by delegates or officials of the Government concerned. Those concerning Belgium, Canada, Cuba, France, Italy, Lebanon, Mexico, and the United States of America were prepared by experts selected by the Secretariat. These statements and studies, however, are to be considered as representing the personal views of their authors".[176] Moreover, a large number of persons assisted in the preparation of the *Yearbook* by supplying information and suggestions.

### (iv) International Civil Aviation

At the eleventh meeting of the second session of the Legal Committee of ICAO, the Secretary recalled "that at its first session the Legal Committee had charged the Secretariat first of all with a permanent task, that was to keep up-to-date and as complete as possible the documentation on all questions referred to the Committee". The Secretariat had

[174] *Ibid.*, p. x.
[175] *Ibid.*
[176] *Ibid.*

accordingly "compiled a list of all the national laws and regulations on civil aviation. That covered about 1,500 documents which could be published and used by national Governments and air lines. The Secretariat was prepared to publish all these documents if the Committee considered it as useful and if the Council decided to give the appropriate funds for that purpose".[177]

It may be of interest to quote here the following observations on the "Collection of National Aviation Laws and Regulations" from the "Report submitted by the Secretariat on questions referred to it by the Legal Committee":[178]

"To date, twenty-six Contracting States[179] have responded to the request made in November 1945 that they forward to the Organization copies of their national aviation laws and regulations. Some have provided very complete sets of their national laws and regulations as well as additional documents such as executive decisions concerning permits to airlines, approval of tariffs, etc., and some have also supplied texts relating to their colonies, protectorates and mandated territories. Extensive research by the Secretariat in official publications and aviation periodicals issued by the States which have not replied has resulted in the collection of a large number of references which have enabled requests to be addressed to them for specific texts. With a view to keeping in touch with the latest developments and trends in aviation laws and regulations, the Secretariat has also procured, whenever possible, the texts of draft laws or codes, among them the draft Air Code of Chile received during the past year.

"During the year 1947 the number of national laws and regulations in the files of the Organization has increased by nearly 500. Among these are laws concerning the ratification of the Chicago Convention, the ratification of the Warsaw Convention and the establishment of national air authorities, and regulations relating to air navigation, air insurance, quarantine, customs, accident investigations, etc.

"The list of national laws and regulations issued during the First Assembly is being reviewed for the purpose of eliminating references to laws which are no longer in force or which have been amended. A revised list will be ready for distribution in the near future".

The Legal Committee, acting upon the report submitted by the Secretariat, adopted on 18 June 1948 the following resolution:[180]

"The Legal Committee, considering the importance of the legal documentation collected by the Secretariat, both for the Committee and for Governments, decrees that this documentation be published as soon as possible: instructs the Secretariat to prepare, in particular, a plan for the publication of national laws, and requests the Council that in the budget for publications, appropriation be made for the aforesaid publications."

[177] ICAO Legal Committee. 2. Second session, 28 May—18 June 1948. Minutes and documents. Document 60N. LC/111, 16/8/48, p. 100.

[178] *Ibid.*, pp. 155-156.

[179] Argentina, Australia, Belgium, Bolivia, Brazil, Canada, Chile, China, Colombia, Czechoslovakia, Denmark, Egypt, Greece, India, Ireland, Mexico, New Zealand, Nicaragua, Peru, the Philippines, Portugal, Sweden, Switzerland, Union of South Africa, United Kingdom and its colonies, protectorates, etc., Venezuela.

[180] *Ibid.*, p. 101.

### *Unofficial publications*

### (i) Nationality

*A Collection of Nationality Laws of Various Countries*[181] was prepared in connexion with the Research in International Law under the auspices of Harvard Law School and its work on a draft convention on nationality intended to assist the First Conference for the Codification of International Law.

Part I of the volume contains nationality legislation of some 87 States, dominions, colonies, and mandates. Part II contains 12 multipartite and 54 bipartite conventions and agreements on nationality.

The material for the *Collection* was largely obtained from official sources and where necessary, translated into English. Regulations and instructions were included. As the editors point out "it might have been a more desirable course that the laws of the various countries should have been collected and published by an international authority, in the original language as well as translation", but this proved not practicable.

Under each political division there is provided a brief editorial summary of the history of the legislation in the country concerned. Bibliographies under each heading with comments from technical journals and an exhaustive analytical index are valuable features of this *Collection.*

In the judgment of an international lawyer, "the International Law Division of the Carnegie Endowment for International Law have made all international lawyers their debtors by this publication, and the editors will receive from them a unanimous vote of thanks for their arduous labours".[182]

It was also pointed out that "this collection will be of indispensable value to jurists, legislators and administrative officers of the Governments throughout the world, and to practitioners in this field. It should also be of great service to future international conferences which may be called for the purpose of eliminating the inconveniences resulting from nationality conflicts".[183] Another collection giving the texts of laws, decrees, etc., in force at the time of publication is that of E. Bourbousson, *Traité général de la nationalité dans les cinq parties du monde. Du statut de la femme mariée, de la naturalisation, de la perte de la nationalité* (Paris 1931), with Supplement A (1938).

Lastly should be mentioned the volume which has appeared in the series of Leske-Loewenfeld, *Die Rechtsverfolgung im internationalen Verkehr,* vol. VII, *Das Recht der Staatsangehörigkeit der europäischen und aussereuropäischen Staaten, 1. Teil, Die europäischen Staaten* (Berlin 1934–1940).

[181] Full title: *A Collection of Nationality Laws of Various Countries: As contained in Constitutions, Statutes and Treaties.* Ed. by Richard W. Flournoy, Jr., and Manley O. Hudson (1929), Carnegie Endowment for International Peace.

[182] A. P. H., in *British Year Book of International Law,* vol. 12 (1931), p. 216.

[183] Henry B. Hazard, in *American Journal of International Law,* vol. 25 (1931), p. 177.

## (ii) Diplomatic and Consular Laws

*A Collection of the Diplomatic and Consular Laws and Regulations of Various Countries* edited by A. H. Feller and M. O. Hudson, was published by the Carnegie Endowment for International Peace in 1933 in 2 volumes. No collection of such laws and regulations had ever been published before and this was made available "in the hope that an up-to-date collection might fill a need not only in connexion with any attempted codification, but also in connexion with the current activities of the diplomats and consuls and in connexion with the work of jurists and publicists". The collection was undertaken to facilitate "the preparation of draft conventions with a view to the codification of the law as to Diplomatic Privileges and Immunities and the Legal Status and Functions of Consuls" by the Research in International Law.[184]

This *Collection* includes selected material of varying degrees of completeness for over 70 countries, dominions, colonies, protectorates and territories under mandate, etc. As the editors point out "two general divisions have been made with respect to each State: (1) the organization of its own diplomatic and consular services, (2) the laws relating to diplomats and consuls sent by other States. Under (1), an attempt has been made to set forth the outlines of the organization of the services, particularly as regards recruitment and classification; details in regard to salaries, leaves of absence, consular fees, office management, and similar matters have been reduced to a minimum; provisions in regard to functions, on the other hand, have generally been given *in extenso*. Under (2), provisions relating to the status of foreign diplomatic officers and consuls have been reproduced in full, except for the omission of some details of ceremonial. In some cases, official memoranda which contain résumés of administration and application of the laws have been included".[185]

The Department of State of the United States "co-operated with the editors very generously" in procuring the necessary texts. The Department of State also permitted the compilers "to reproduce portions of the Instructions to Diplomatic Officers which have not heretofore been published".[186]

The *Collection* contains, besides a detailed analytical index and bibliographical notes, a "List of Treaties dealing with Consuls", running to over 50 pages.

As one international lawyer pointed out, *"les deux volumes . . . rendront les plus appréciables services aux juristes et aux praticiens du droit international . . . L'utilité d'un pareil recueil est certaine: si l'on excepte le livre déjà ancien du baron de Cussy (1851), cette œuvre n'avait guère tenté les juristes. Le soin ave lequel a été menée une entreprise aussi délicate, l'ampleur et la rigueur de la documentation, la clarté de la présentation font de ces deux volumes un précieux instrument de travail"*.[187]

[184] *A Collection of the Diplomatic and Consular Laws and Regulations of Various Countries*. Ed. by A. H. Feller and Manley O. Hudson. Vol. I (1933), p. vii.

[185] *Ibid.*

[186] *Ibid.*, p. viii.

[187] Charles Rousseau, in *Revue Générale de Droit International Public*, vol. 41 (1934), p. 343.

In the opinion of another "obviously this collection is of the greatest possible utility as a work of reference, and international lawyers of all countries may be grateful to the publishers for placing it at their disposal. . . . The completeness of the collection in regard to individual countries depends upon a factor which is beyond the editor's control, namely, the extent to which, in the case of each country, the matter is dealt with by special laws and regulations, as opposed to being dealt with either as part of the general law (as, for instance in the United Kingdom where diplomatic privilege is largely a matter of common law) or by merely executive action in the form of consular instructions".[188]

### (iii) Neutrality

The materials for the *Collection of Neutrality Laws*[189] were assembled in connexion with the preparation of a draft Convention on Rights and Duties of Neutral States in Naval and Aerial War for the Research in International Law under the auspices of the Faculty of the Harvard Law School, and published in the hope that they might also prove "of general value to Government officials and to students of the subject of neutrality".

The *Collection* comprises the laws, regulations and treaties of every State whose laws were accessible—altogether over seventy countries, dominions, protectorates, territories, colonies, etc.—for the period from 1800 to 1 October 1938. However, "believing that the United States has, more than any other nation, furnished the pattern for the development of some aspects of the international law of neutrality, the editors felt justified in departing from the temporal limitation in this case by including laws, regulations and treaties of the United States in the last two decades of the eighteenth century".[190] As the object of the *Collection* was to show the trend of evolution and not merely to state the law prevailing at any given moment, "the collection is not limited to laws, regulations or treaties which are at present in force in or among various States; all such material enacted, issued or concluded during the period under consideration is included".[191]

In addition to neutrality laws proper, the *Collection* contains relevant provisions of penal codes, such as those regarding enlistment in foreign armies, laws and regulations enacted pursuant to the Non-Intervention Agreement of 1937 concerning the Spanish Civil War, and also "laws and regulations enacted or issued by members of the League of Nations for the imposition and enforcement of economic and financial sanctions during the Italo-Ethiopian War".[192] On the other hand, purely belligerent measures, provisions of private law and diplomatic correspondence are excluded in principle. Diplomatic correspondence is included where it is of special value or where it constitutes the only source of information.

[188] E., in *British Year Book of International Law,* vol. 15 (1934), p. 202.

[189] *A Collection of Neutrality Laws, Regulations and Treaties of Various Countries.* Edited and Annotated by Francis Deak and Philip C. Jessup. 2 vols. 1939. Carnegie Endowment for International Law.

[190] *Ibid.,* p. xi.

[191] *Ibid.,* p. xii.

[192] *Ibid.,* p. xiv.

The material is classified in two parts. Part I comprises laws and regulations and part II provisions from 151 treaties relating to neutral rights and duties. In part I the material for each country is generally divided into two categories: measures of a permanent and measures of a temporary character. "The measures of a temporary character have been usually grouped in three sub-categories: first, neutrality proclamations and declarations; second, laws, decrees and ordinances; third, orders, regulations and instructions of executive or administrative agencies".[193] Both parts I and II include editorial notes on sources, etc.

"A Chronological List of all Treaties covering Neutral Rights and Duties, 1778-1938" gives references to 272 treaties comprising: date, parties, type of treaty, source and number of articles relating to neutrality. There is also an ample analytical index (75 pp).

Although the *Collection* appeared at an unpropitious moment, it was found to be a "monument of painstaking effort and of scholarly discretion", and "indispensable to any serious student of international law and relations".[194] It was also recognized that the documentation "supporting the hotly contested draft convention on the Rights and Duties of Neutral States in Naval and Aerial War is colossal, not to say overwhelming" and that it "must greatly lighten the task of Foreign Offices, shipping boards and the practitioners of maritime law in countries which are still asserting the rights and observing the duties of neutrals".[195] The view was expressed that while "this monumental collection will answer many questions that confront the lawyers of some countries, its most enduring portion may be the remarkably full documentation on the attempt made to enforce collective sanctions against Italy. For if war is ever to be made illegal, these are the precedents that will shine in use".[196]

### (iv) Piracy

The *Collection of Piracy Laws,*[197] prepared in connexion with the work on piracy undertaken by the Harvard Research in International Law, includes "so far as possible, all laws dealing with the suppression and punishment of piracy and robbery on the seas" but "law incidentally referring to piracy" were omitted. On the other hand, material of a border-line nature was "reprinted where it appeared to be of value for illustrative purposes, although some of it perhaps cannot properly be regarded as a part of the laws of piracy". The *Collection* does not contain legal provisions of a general nature which may be

[193] *Ibid.*, p. xv.
[194] H. L., in *Cambridge Law Journal,* vol. 7 (1939–41), p. 428.
[195] P. E. Corbett, *American Journal for International Law,* vol. 34 (1940), p. 753.
[196] *Ibid.*, p. 754.
[197] *A Collection of Piracy Laws of Various Countries.* Ed. by Stanley Morrisson. This collection, unlike the other works discussed above, was not published in a separate volume but forms part V of the volume of the *Research in International Law* published in 1932 and containing the Draft Conventions on Diplomatic Privileges and Immunities . . . and Piracy.

applicable to piracy "although they contain no specific references to the subject in question".[198]

The collection covers some 60 countries, dominions, colonies, etc. Where pertinent legislation is in force, the *Collection* includes it; otherwise a statement is made that no pertinent legislation appears to have been enacted.

In the preparation of this *Collection,* the editor enjoyed "the assistance of the Department of State of the United States, which through its missions aided in procuring the texts of the laws of many countries".[199]

### (v) Legislation for the Defence of American Republics

On 5 November 1943, the Emergency Consultative Committee for Political Defence *(Comité Consultivo de Emergencia para la Defensa Politica)* resolved to publish a series of comparative studies of the emergency legislation enacted or in force in the different American Republics. These appeared in 1947 in two volumes under the title *Legislación para la Defensa Politica en las Repúblicas Americanas.* Although not a collection of legislative texts but rather a series of studies in the field of comparative law, it is believed that this work should be mentioned here on account of its intrinsic importance. Moreover, any student of the problem will find in it numerous references to the laws in force in the different countries. The subjects treated by individual scholars include: control of aliens, prevention of abuse of nationality, entry and exit of aliens including their expulsion, control of media of communications, control of associations, protection of essential installations against sabotage, and repression of acts against the security of other American States.

## L. COLLECTIONS OF DECISIONS AND OPINIONS OF INTERNATIONAL ORGANIZATIONS ON QUESTIONS OF INTERNATIONAL LAW

Opinions and decisions of international organs, other than international tribunals on questions of general international law, have frequently been regarded as evidence of international law. A comprehensive collection of such opinions, particularly with reference to the Assembly and Council of the League of Nations, was planned as part of the series *Fontes Juris Gentium*[200] but failed to materialize. However, one work of an unofficial character on the League of Nations is available and another, official, relating to the United Nations is in process of compilation.

198 All references *ibid.*, p. 891.
199 *Ibid.*
200 See *supra,* p. 47.

## 1. League of Nations

A *Répertoire of Questions of General International Law before the League of Nations, 1920–1940*[201] was prepared by Walter Schiffer and published in 1942 "to facilitate access to the important legal material scattered throughout the volumes of the Official Journal of the League of Nations and thereby to enrich the study of international law and its applications".[202]

Attention was focused on those passages in the Official Journal of the League which deal with questions of general international law as distinguished from the particular international law of the Covenant of the League. The term general international law "includes custom; conventions or draft treaty stipulations have, however, also been taken into consideration when they were found interesting from the point of view of international law or its evolution, and dealt with its fundamental institutions and problems. Efforts made toward unification of the law dealing with certain essential problems have also been included".[203]

For this purpose all documents in the Official Journal and its supplements were analysed and the material classified under six main headings: I. General questions; II. Persons in international law; III. Objects of international law; IV. Legal relations between States; V. International disputes; VI. War and neutrality. Under each main heading there are several sub-headings.

The method of presenting the material was as follows: "All references or groups of references referring to a special legal problem are preceded by a short summary of the contents of the texts referred to. This summary is given in the form of a general title or of a sentence. An interrogative sentence indicates that contradictory opinions were expressed while the legal problem was being discussed. The interrogative form is also used when summing up in a sentence a legal opinion referred to in the document which the author of the document does not approve. The words *Question de* . . . indicate that a legal problem has only been mentioned without a solution having been offered".[204]

References to texts were frequently supplemented by footnotes which "were intended to give the reader information which, though not directly concerned with the legal case involved, is however necessary in order to judge the value of the texts referred to. They show the evolution of the case in which the legal problem was raised. They give information, for instance, on the circumstances which led to the discussion of a problem, on some text referred to during the discussion, on phases of procedure linking up various texts referring to the same question, or to the outcome of some proposal".[205]

The *Répertoire* is in French but the table of contents, the headings and sub-headings,

[201] *Répertoire des Questions de Droit International Général posées devant la Société des Nations 1920–1940. Etabli par Walter Schiffer. Publié sous la direction de A. C. Breycha-Vauthier. (1942).*
[202] Cf. *ibid.*, Editorial note by Pitman B. Potter.
[203] *Ibid.*, p. 21.
[204] *Ibid.*, p. 21.
[205] *Ibid.*, p. 25.

and index are in both French and English. Moreover, all references are to League documents which are available in both languages. The hope was expressed, nevertheless, "that as soon as circumstances permit an English translation may be available".[206] It does not appear, however, that such a translation has yet been published.

The *Répertoire* was recognized as "a book of reference which certainly will become indispensable to any person or institution working in the field of international law".[207] It was stressed that "it is not a mere index. To a large extent it is a digest which enables the reader to form an idea of the nature of the legal rule propounded or accepted. The work covers not only the proceedings of the Assembly and of the Council and of their committees, but also of the special and technical commissions. The classification is altogether admirable and the references are easy to follow. . . . The *Répertoire* is the product of prodigious and conscientious effort and both Dr. Schiffer and the Geneva Research Centre deserve the thanks of the students and of the practitioner for this indispensable instrument of work".[208]

## 2. United Nations

The Secretary-General in his *Annual Report on the Work of the Organization, 1 July 1947–30 June 1948,* stated that the Secretariat had begun to make a systematic collection of opinions and precedents on questions of international law. The relevant portion of the *Report* is as follows:[209]

"Particular importance attaches to the development of those rules of international law which have found expression in the Charter and to the legal precedents which are constantly being built up in the practice of the various organs of the United Nations. Hardly any problem comes before the United Nations which does not raise questions of a legal character and does not require a study of the previous application and interpretation of the Articles of the Charter and of the practice and precedents in the various organs. With the increasing activities of the United Nations, a strong need has thus been felt for a systematic collection of practices and precedents with respect to the application of the provisions of the Charter. To meet this need, the Secretariat has engaged in the preparation of a systematic annotation of the Articles of the Charter as they have been interpreted or applied by the various organs of the United Nations.

"In addition, apart from the Charter, rules of international law are constantly being applied and interpreted in the organs of the United Nations and by the Secretariat. The widespread activities of the Organization are a fertile source of questions which require legal analysis and opinions, and the legal precedents thus established in the day-to-day work of the Organization are an important part of the process of developing international

[206] See *British Year Book of International Law,* vol. 21 (1944), p. 261.

[207] Hans Kelsen, in *American Journal of International Law,* vol. 37 (1943), p. 353.

[208] Cf. *British Year Book of International Law,* vol. 21 (1944), p. 260.

[209] Annual Report of the Secretary-General on the Work of the Organization, 1 July 1947–30 June 1948. General Assembly, Official Records: Third Session, Supplement No. 1 (A/565) 1948, p. 108.

law under the auspices of the United Nations. At present these precedents are scattered through various records of meetings and Secretariat memoranda, but the Legal Department of the Secretariat has begun a systematic collection and arrangement of the legal opinions so as to make more readily available the principles of international law followed in the Organization."

## M. THE HARVARD RESEARCH IN INTERNATIONAL LAW

The *Research in International Law* or the Harvard Research, as it is commonly called, was organized in anticipation but independently of the League of Nations preparatory work for the First Conference on the Codification of International Law. It owes its inception to the initiative of the Faculty of the Harvard Law School which in November 1927 "undertook to organize a Research in International Law for the purpose of preparing a draft of an international convention on each of the three subjects selected by the Eighth Assembly to be dealt with at the First Conference on the Codification of International Law".[210]

The organization of the *Research* included a director, Judge Manley O. Hudson, an advisory committee, an executive committee, a reporter and, in some instances, assistant reporters for each of the subjects dealt with successively by the *Research.* The reporters were assisted by committees of advisers. All the committees were composed of lawyers actively engaged in the field of international law.

The method adopted for the *Research* was that "followed by the American Law Institute, which is very similar to that of the *Institut de droit International*".[211] A draft would first be drawn up by the reporter and submitted to the members of the advisory committees; then meetings of the reporters and advisers were held at which "drafts were discussed and modified".[212]

The work of the first phase of the *Research* was "undertaken with the object of placing before the representatives of the various Governments at the First Conference on Codification of International Law the collective views of a group of Americans specially interested in the development of international law".[213] In the general introduction to the volume containing the fruits of the second phase, after noting that "the publications of the Research were frequently referred to at the Conference at The Hague in 1930", reference was made to a recommendation of the Conference that with a view to placing at the disposal of subsequent conferences for the codification of international law fresh scientific work, "international and national institutions should undertake at a sufficiently early date the study of the fundamental questions of international law, particularly the principles and rules and their application, with special reference to the points which were placed

210 *Research in International Law,* Harvard Law School. Nationality. Responsibility of States. Territorial waters. 1929. p. 3.

211 *Ibid.*

212 *Ibid.*, p. 9.

213 *Ibid.*

on the agenda of such conferences''.[214] As a consequence the drafts resulting from the second, third and fourth phases of work of the *Research* were ''made with the object of stating the collective views of a group of Americans specially interested in the development of international law concerning subjects which may be considered in connexion with the codification of international law. The drafts represent the result of the work of American jurists and scholars after thorough consultation, and as such it is hoped that they may merit the attention of persons interested in the development of international law''.[215]

As appears from the foregoing, the *Research* was continued after the First Conference on the Codification of International Law held at The Hague in 1930, and new subjects were added to the three selected in contemplation of that Conference. Altogether the work of the *Research* comprised four phases and thirteen subjects covering ''the principal aspects of the international law of Peace (and of Neutrality) with the exception of those relating to Recognition and to State Territory and the High Seas''.[216]

In more detail the phases and subjects dealt with were as follows:

The first phase, from 1927 to 1929, devoted to three subjects:

(1) Nationality, with Richard W. Flournoy, Jr., as reporter;

(2) Responsibility of States for injuries to foreigners, with Edwin M. Borchard as reporter; and

(3) Territorial waters, with George Grafton Wilson as reporter.

The second phase, from 1929 to 1932, devoted to four subjects:

(1) Diplomatic privileges and immunities, with Jesse S. Reeves as reporter;

(2) Legal position and functions of consuls, with Quincy Wright as reporter;

(3) Competence of courts in regard to foreign States, with Philip C. Jessup as reporter; and

(4) Piracy, with Joseph W. Bingham as reporter.

The third phase, from 1932 to 1935, devoted to three subjects:

(1) Extradition, with Charles K. Burdick as reporter;

(2) Jurisdiction with respect to crime, with Edwin D. Dickinson as reporter; and

(3) Law of treaties, with James W. Garner as reporter.[217]

The fourth phase, from 1935 to 1939, devoted to three subjects:

(1) Judicial assistance, with James A. Rogers as reporter;

(2) Rights and duties of neutral States in naval and aerial war, with Philip C. Jessup as reporter; and

[214] *Research in International Law,* Harvard Law School, 1. Diplomatic privileges and immunities . . . (1932), p. 10.

[215] *Research in International Law Under the Auspices of the Faculty of the Harvard Law School. I. Judicial assistance* . . .(1939), p. 10.

[216] International Law Association. *Report of the Committee on the Development of International Law, adopted by the Executive Council on 3 May 1947, for presentation to the Prague Conference in September 1947* (1947), p. 27.

[217] *Research in International Law Under the Auspices of the Faculty of the Harvard Law School, I. Judicial assistance; II. Rights and duties of neutral States in naval and aerial war; III. Rights and duties of States in case of aggression. American Journal of International Law,* vol. 33 (1939), supplement, p. 102.

(3) Rights and duties of States in case of aggression, with Philip C. Jessup as reporter.[218]

The executive committee of the *Research* decided to include in the fourth phase the subject of Recognition of States. Work on this subject, however, has not been completed.[219]

The result of the work of the *Research* was published by the Harvard Law School in separate volumes and republished, with the same pagination, as supplements to the *American Journal of International Law*. The results of the first phase thus appeared in 1929, both independently and in a special supplement to volume 23 of the *Journal;* those of the second phase in 1932 and republished as the supplement to volume 26 of the *Journal;* those of the third phase in 1935 and republished as the supplement to volume 29 of the *Journal;* and the result of the fourth phase was published in 1939 and republished as the supplement to volume 33 of the *Journal.*

The presentation of the results of the work of the *Research* was uniformly in the form of draft conventions on each of the subjects "the articles of which were accompanied by extensive comment consisting of notations from and discussions of opinions of writers, of decisions of courts, of national legislation, and of governmental practice. Practically all drafts include appendices giving extracts from and an analysis of municipal laws, treaties, official documents, and the like".[220] The *Research* also supplied exhaustive bibliographies on each of the subjects.

The "wholly unofficial" character of the *Research* was emphasized and the readers were warned that "the drafts must not be taken as in any way representing the views of the Government of the United States".[221]

The great volume of pertinent documentation assembled by the *Research* in the course of its work includes, as noted above, not merely statutory, conventional and jurisprudential elements but also doctrine and State practice. Its value has been generally recognized. Thus the Judicial Committee of the Privy Council, in a judgement delivered in 1934, referred to the "most valuable treatise on the subject of piracy contained in the *Research into International Law* by the Harvard Law School" and declared: "In it nearly all the cases, nearly all the statutes, and nearly all the opinions are set out . . ."[222]

Discussing the results of the first phase of the work of the *Research* as a French international lawyer noted that this volume *"témoigne d'une méthode originale et à ce titre il merite l'intérêt le plus vif"* and pointed out that each article of the draft conventions was the subject *"d'un commentaire approfondi. On trouvera également dans ce recueil une analyse des législations étrangères, le texte des résolutions élaborées par diverses associations doctrinales, ainsi que la reproduction des projets de convention élaborés par le Comité de codification de la S. D. N.*

[218] *Ibid.*, pp. 2–9.
[219] *Ibid.*, p. 9.
[220] International Law Association, *op. cit.*, p. 26.
[221] This statement is to be found in the general introduction to each of the volumes of the *Research.*
[222] In *re* a Reference under the Judicial Committee Act of 1833. In *re* Piracy *Jure Gentium*, (1934), AC. 586; 51 L.T.R. 12. Reprinted in *American Journal of International Law*, vol. 29 (1935), pp. 140–152 (p. 148).

*Au point de vue documentaire et bibliographique, le travail publé par la Research in international law d'Harvard est d'une valeur de tout premier ordre".*[223]

A judge of the Permanent Court of International Justice expressing his admiration "for diligent labour of research" with which the work of the second phase was executed, declared: "The desire expressed by the first Codification Conference at The Hague in the spring of 1930 for further scientific preparation could not be better fulfilled than through labours such as those which have been given permanent form in the present work. Its use has again and again demonstrated that doctrinal writings and all other materials have been gone over with a completeness which astounds the student of the subject". He expressed the hope "that the work will receive the widest possible distribution in professional circles".[224]

Similarly, it was stressed that there can be no difference of opinion regarding the "value of the contribution to international law" made by the *Research*[225] not only from the point of view of students, but also of "those who have to do with the working and the shaping of the international law and procedure".[226]

It may be of interest to recall here that after a careful review of the whole work of the *Research* and after noting that the various drafts "are a production of distinguished scientific merit from both the point of view of analysis and of the material which has been made available", the *Report of the Committee on the Development and Formulation of International Law* (International Law Association), expressed the opinion "that the groups of reporters and advisers whose formation we are about to recommend for the purpose of formulating rules on the various branches of international law should take as a basis of their study the work already produced by the Harvard Research".[227]

The method adopted by the *Research* met with some criticism. Thus one writer, having gratefully acknowledged "the wealth of material which has been unearthed by these teams of research workers" declared "the method of comparative national studies recommends itself as compared with the methods adopted by the Harvard Research drafts".[228]

## N. PREPARATORY WORK FOR THE FIRST CONFERENCE ON THE CODIFICATION OF INTERNATIONAL LAW

It remains to refer, among the existing evidences of customary international law, to the preparatory work for the First Conference on the Codification of International Law which resulted from the efforts of the Preparatory Committee appointed by the Council

[223] Charles Rousseau, in *Revue Général de Droit International Public*, vol. 37 (1930), p. 213.

[224] W. Schücking, in *Harvard Law Review*, vol. 46 (1932–33), pp. 873–874.

[225] A. P. H., in *British Year Book of International Law*, vol. 14 (1933), p. 225.

[226] Warwick Chipman, in *Harvard Law Review*, vol. 53 (1939–40), p. 1069.

[227] International Law Association, *Report of the Committee on the Development and Formulation of International Law, adopted by the Executive Council on 3 May 1947, for presentation to the Prague Conference in Sept. 1947* (1947), p. 27.

[228] G. Schwarzenberger, "The Inductive Approach to International Law", *Harvard Law Review*, vol. 60 (1946–47), p. 564, note 53.

of the League of Nations on 28 September 1927. Pursuant to its terms of reference laid down in the Assembly Resolution of 27 September 1927, the Preparatory Committee requested Governments to supply the necessary information on nationality, territorial waters, and responsibility of States, under these heads:

*(a)* The state of their positive law, national and international, with, as far as possible, full details as to bibliography and jurisprudence;

*(b)* Information derived from the practice at home and abroad;

*(c)* Their views as regards possible additions to the rules in force and the manner of making good existing deficiencies in international law.[229]

In response to this report thirty Governments submitted replies, but as the Preparatory Committee noted, some of the replies did not deal with all the questions on which information was requested. Taking into account the information thus made available on the state of positive international law, the Committee drew up "Bases of Discussion" on Nationality, Territorial Waters and Responsibility of States.[230] These Bases of Discussion are accompanied by the "Complete text of the replies made by the Governments on the schedule of points submitted by the Preparatory Committee".

These Bases of Discussion as well as the replies of the Governments constitute, in the view of one writer, "an authoritative and invaluable source of information on the subjects concerned".[231] In the view of another, the replies of the Governments are "valuable statements . . . as to their practice and as to their views of the concrete rule of international law".[232] It was pointed out, however, that "while the replies . . . constitute a valuable source of information . . . many Governments, being aware that their answers were to be given in connexion with a proposed code on the subject, submitted disputations on what they would like to see adopted, rather than what had actually been the practice of their countries".[233]

## O. WRITERS

The role of writers in connexion with the question of the evidence of international law has been stated in Article 38, paragraph 1 *(d)* of the Statute of the International Court of Justice which directs the Court to apply "subject to the provision of Article 59 . . . the teachings of the most highly qualified publicists of the various nations, as subsidiary means for the determination of rules of law".

The creative contribution of writers of different nations and different schools to the

229 League of Nations, Document C.44. M.21. 1928. v. See also *Historical Survey of Development of International Law and its Codification by International Conferences.* Memorandum prepared by the Secretariat. Document A/AC.10/5. 29 April 1947, p. 68.

230 Respectively Documents C.73. M.38. 1929. V; C.74. M.39. 1939 V; and C.75. M.69. 1929 V.

231 L. Oppenheim, *International Law,* vol. 1 (1947), 6th edition by H. Lauterpacht, p. 59.

232 Sir Cecil Hurst, *A Plea for the Codification of International Law on New Lines.* Read before the Grotius Society, 16 October 1946, p. 6.

233 Yuen-li Liang, "Methods for the Encouragement of the Progressive Development of International Law and its Codification", *The Year Book of World Affairs,* 1948. Vol. 2 (1948), p. 254.

development of international law and to its systemization is too well known to require further discussion here. Illustrative lists of important works on international law have been compiled and published in a number of books.[234]

The works of the early writers have been reproduced and translated into English in the series, *Classics of International Law,* edited by James Brown Scott and published by the Carnegie Endowment for International Peace. This series includes works by Ayala, Bynkershoek, Gentili, Grotius, Legnano, Pufendorf, Rachel, Suarez, Textor, Vattel, Victoria, Wolff, and Zouche.

A comprehensive and classified bibliography of the literature on international law remains to be produced.[235] Perhaps, in this connexion, the *Bibliographie du Droit des Gens et des Relations Internationales* by Karl Strupp, should be mentioned. The first—and so far the only—volume covering the years 1933 to 1936 inclusive appeared in 1938. It lists altogether about 2,800 publications, mostly in the field of international law. As it was intended as a *bibliographie raisonnée* the first part of the volume contains reviews of sixty-one books which were regarded by the editor as the most important for the period. The second part contains, for many countries, lists of treaties, monographic studies, articles and, in some instances, of doctoral dissertations. The third part consists of a systematic list of publications. In the compilation of this, the first and experimental volume, Professor Strupp had the assistance of some fifty contributors from different countries.

The *Bibliographie* was said to fill an "unquestionable" need but it was felt that there "was room for progress in the direction of coming still nearer to what may be considered an ideal bibliography". At the same time, the hope was expressed that this bibliography would become "a regular annual publication covering the literature of the immediately previous year".[236]

There is little doubt that a comprehensive, systematic and objective bibliography on international law published at regular intervals, possibly annually, would contribute greatly to the study and practice of international law. On similar grounds, it has been suggested that leading treatises and monographs should be made available in one or more translations.[237]

[234] E.g. Charles Rousseau, *Principes Généraux du Droit International Public,* vol. I (1944); M. O. Hudson, *Cases on International Law,* 2nd edition (1936), pp. xxii–xxxvii; Oppenheim, *International Law,* vol. 1, 6th edition by H. Lauterpacht (1947), pp. 95–101; Charles G. Fenwick, *International Law,* 3rd edition (1948), pp. xxvi; D. Anzilotti, *Cours de Droit International,* vol. 1 (1929), pp. 2–36; A. S. de Bustamante, *Derecho Internacional Publico,* vol. 1, 2nd edition (1938); D. Antokoletz, *Tratado de Derecho Internacional Publico,* vol. 1 (1928), ch. III.

[235] For existing bibliographies cf. Oppenheim, *loc. cit.,* pp. 108–109. See also *International Legal Bibliography,* 1932 (1938), issued by the *Istituto di Studi Legislativi.*

[236] Josef L. Kunz, in *American Journal of International Law,* vol. 33 (1939), p. 613.

[237] For a suggestion along this line cf. *Proceedings of the Fifth Conference of Teachers of International Law and Related Subjects* (1933), p. 172, remarks by Professor Charles G. Fenwick.

# II. SUGGESTIONS OF ORGANIZATIONS AND PUBLICISTS FOR THE IMPROVEMENT OF DOCUMENTATION OF CUSTOMARY INTERNATIONAL LAW

It is thought useful to end this survey with a brief review of suggestions made from time to time by unofficial organizations and publicists for the improvement of the documentation of customary international law.

## A. THE INSTITUT DE DROIT INTERNATIONAL

At its first session held after the war of 1939–1945, at Lausanne in 1947, the *Institut de Droit International* adopted a resolution on the Codification of International Law in which it is declared that "the most important contribution to the work of codification would consist in carrying out, on the national and international planes, research activities of a scientific character with a view to arriving at an exact statement of the actual condition of international law. This inventory would serve as a basis at once for a scientific effort and also for official action undertaken according to methods deemed best suited to filling the gaps of international law and remedying its imperfections".[238]

In the discussion preceding the adoption of the above resolution, Judge Jules Basdevant, Vice-President of the International Court of Justice, emphasized the importance of adequate documentation as a basis of the "restatement" *(exposé)* of international law, as a scientific activity. He said:[239]

[238] *American Journal of International Law*, vol. 42 (1948), Supplement p. 169; *Annuaire de l'Institut de Droit International*, vol. 41 (1947), p. 262.
[239] *Annuaire*, vol. 41 (1947), p. 239.

*"Par sa nature, l'établissement d'un tel exposé est un travail scientifique. Pour le mener à bien, des recherches nationales devraient être entreprises, recherches comme celles qui ont conduit à la publication du* Digest *de Moore et du* Digest *de Hackworth, ainsi qu'à la publication de* Law of Treaties *de McNair. Ces recherches nationales devraient être coordonnées dans leur objet, leurs méthodes et leurs résultats. Cette coordination ferait passer [l'exposé] du plan national sur le plan international. L'Institut de Droit international pourrait rechercher quelles sont les méthodes les mieux appropriées pour effectuer et coordonner de telles recherches."*

Referring to Judge Basdevant's statement Dr. Max Huber, formerly President of the Permanent Court of International Justice, said:[240]

*"Il faut faire d'abord le statement du droit international tel qu'il est conçu dans chaque pays. Cela a toujours été négligé à cause du désir d'arriver vite à un résultat."*

## B. THE CONFERENCE OF [AMERICAN] TEACHERS OF INTERNATIONAL LAW AND RELATED SUBJECTS

The first Conference of this organization, meeting at Washington, D.C., in April 1914, considered various plans for increasing the facilities for the study of international law and adopted a resolution calling for a detailed bibliography of international law and the publication of all documents, both foreign and domestic, bearing upon international law, including treaties and documents relating to arbitration and diplomatic correspondence. Specifically the resolution called for the publication of a law reporter of international cases.[241]

Noting the inaccessibility of judicial decisions and of the legislation of various countries relating to international law, the second Conference, held in 1925, expressed the hope "that some means may be found for compiling such decisions and legislation and making the compilations generally available".[242]

The third Conference in 1928 urged in particular the publication of a continuing series of decisions of municipal courts on questions of international law. For this purpose the Conference envisaged the creation of an organization having correspondents throughout the world, an editorial board and sufficient funds. The Conference also went on record as favouring the publication of diplomatic correspondence, of official reports of American delegates to international conferences, and of the proceedings of such conferences. The Conference further advocated the publication by the Department of State of the "cases and counter-cases and the oral arguments of all arbitrations to which the United States is or has been a party since the Fisheries Arbitration, 1910, and that this practice be adopted in the future".[243]

240 *Annuaire*, vol. 41 (1947), p. 241 f.

241 *Conference of Teachers of International Law and Related Subjects.* Washington, D.C., 23–25 April 1914, pp. 68–69.

242 *Proceedings of the Second Conference of Teachers of International Law and Related Subjects.* Washington, D.C., 23–25 April 1925 (1926), p. 116.

243 *Proceedings of the Third Conference of Teachers of International Law*, Washington, D.C., 25–26 April 1928 (1928), pp. 154 f. See also *ibid.*, pp. 29, 165–168. It may be noted that in 1929 the Department of State inaugurated its *Arbitration Series.*

At a later meeting, the Conference urged a "comprehensive digest of the awards, and arguments and a bibliography of the cases, counter-cases, and arguments, and perhaps of the critical literature concerning the subject".[244]

Considering the inadequacy of source materials, the Conference suggested that more materials be collected and published in the different countries "according to a preconceived plan". This task "should be done co-operatively, the scholars of each country, or at least of each group of countries or continent, assuming some responsibility for the digesting of their own country or regional material under a plan or system of subheadings agreed upon in advance".[245]

A report on "Research in International Law and Relations in the United States and in Europe" presented at the Fourth Conference concluded:

"The investigation of source material is one of the elementary functions of science, but the inadequacy of the tools and apparatus in our field has greatly hampered its development. . . . It is proposed that in each country there be established scientific organizations, preferably connected with universities, which shall make it their function to deal with the source material of their own country . . . and shall co-operate in their efforts with similar organizations in other countries. By such co-operation and exchange of views, the best ideas and plans are likely to be adopted, systematization will be achieved, and duplication of effort avoided".[246]

The Conference also discussed ways and means of making the source material more readily available at its meetings held in 1933, 1938, 1941 and 1946.[247]

## C. AMERICAN SOCIETY OF INTERNATIONAL LAW

This Society has given attention to the general problem of documentation of international law and made some concrete proposals of interest.

Thus in a resolution adopted at its twenty-first annual meeting in 1927, the Society recognized that "there is great need for an authoritative repository of the decisions of municipal courts of the various countries in matters affecting public international law" and registered "its approval of the publication of the decisions of municipal courts in matters of public international law".[248] The Society, on this occasion, authorized the appointment of a committee to explore the practical aspects involved in constituting and publishing such an "authoritative repository".

The question of collecting and publishing decisions of international tribunals was discussed at some length at the twenty-third annual meeting of the Society. The Society

[244] *Proceedings of the Fourth Conference of Teachers of International Law and Related Subjects.* Briarcliff Lodge, 10–17 October 1929 (1930), p. 184.

[245] *Loc. cit.*, p. 183.

[246] *Proceedings*, 1929, p. 186.

[247] Cf. *Proceedings of the Fifth Conference of Teachers of International Law and Related Subjects*, 26–27 April 1933, pp. 8, 197; *Proceedings of the Sixth Conference* . . . 27–30 April 1938, pp. 5, 311; *Proceedings of the Seventh Conference* . . . 23–25 April 1941, pp. 8, 168; *Proceedings of the Eighth Conference* . . . 24–25 April 1946, pp. 118 f.

[248] *Proceedings of the American Society of International Law at its Twenty-first Annual Meeting*, 28–30 April 1927, p. 121.

adopted a report of its Committee on the enlargement of the scope of the publications of the Department of State in which it expressed the desire for a "regular series of international arbitral decisions in which the United States is concerned either as a party or through the participation of an American official as arbitrator—a series comparable to the reports of the United States Supreme Court".[249] This proposed series was to include awards as well as abstracts of the arguments of the parties and, according to a suggestion, was not to be confined to those arbitrations to which only the United States was a party. It was to include all arbitrations.[250]

## D. COLUMBIA UNIVERSITY RESEARCH IN INTERNATIONAL LAW

The Department of Public Law and Jurisprudence of Columbia University, in a Memorandum circulated in the thirties[251] advocated a realistic approach to the problem of international relations and proposed to seek the solution of such problems "through the aid of unimpeachable evidence", e.g. evidence from governmental archives.

The Columbia Research plan, drafted with two principal objectives in mind: first to elicit conclusions of Foreign Offices on questions of international law, and second to safeguard the inviolability of confidential matter, contained three main points:

(1) "To formulate a fairly comprehensive and detailed inquiry (not to be likened to a questionnaire) as to the views of particular Governments or Foreign Offices on a group of legal questions within a single category (such as Treaties);

(2) "To secure an expert in international law of highest reputation in his own country and enjoying the confidence of its Foreign Office, to make, under its full permission and guidance, an investigation of the evidence of its views which it is prepared to disclose; and

(3) "To publish in the United States under the direction of the Department the fruits of investigation."

The Department of Public Law was aware of the fact "that Foreign Offices may be expected to remain uninterested in a project such as is now contemplated, unless convinced that they will gain more than they will sacrifice through the giving of publicity to their conclusions". On the other hand, the Department fully realized that the ends sought cannot be achieved unless the work is undertaken by investigators who will enjoy the confidence of the Foreign Offices concerned and who, in addition, will be endowed with the necessary skill and tact. In the view of the Department: "By every reasonable means the investigator should aspire to obtain recognition of the research as an unofficial yet easy and responsible channel through which governmental conclusions on the law

[249] *Proceedings of the American Society of International Law at its Twenty-third Annual Meeting,* 24–27 April 1929, pp. 68, 204.

[250] *Op. cit.,* p. 74. Cf. also *Proceedings of the American Society of International Law at its Twenty-fifth Annual Meeting,* 23–25 April 1931, p. 261.

[251] For text of the Memorandum cf. *The Law of Treaties,* by A. D. McNair. (1938), pp. 553–556.

might find accurate expression and exact reflection." For this purpose the Department suggested that the Foreign Offices involved might assign a competent official to furnish the necessary aid to the investigator.

The Columbia Research plan aimed essentially at the gradual and progressive investigation of Foreign Office materials, at present largely inaccessible, with reference to topics where research is most needed. It was also envisaged that such investigations might be carried out simultaneously in a small number of countries which may be disposed to co-operate.

Materials collected by the investigators would be published by the Department. On this point the Memorandum contains the following considerations:

"The primary purpose of the Department would be to reproduce accurately and fully the Governmental views disclosed in whatever form they might be revealed by the investigators. Such views might, in some cases, express themselves in documents which there was a willingness to have published; in others, they might take the form of memoranda indicative of authoritative conclusions. The danger of distortion of views or of critical commentaries distasteful to a contributing Government would be carefully avoided. Each contributing State or Government would, of course, be made the recipient of everything that was printed by the Department."

This Memorandum was discussed by representatives of the Department of Public Law with international lawyers and the Foreign Offices of several countries. One of the results of such discussions was the volume *The Law of Treaties: British Practice and Opinions* by Arnold D. McNair.[251a]

## E. INSTITUTE OF FOREIGN PUBLIC AND INTERNATIONAL LAW

In the preface to the first volume[252] published in the *Fontes Juris Gentium* series the Director of the Berlin Institute of Foreign Public and International Law *(Institut für ausländisches öffentliches Recht und Völkerrecht),* Viktor Bruns, referred to the vast growth of documentation of international law and observed:

"It is far beyond the powers of an individual to gather even so much as a general notion of all the most essential documents and events. The choice of material, therefore, on which a work of international law is based must necessarily be more or less arbitrary or casual. This is also the reason why in international law, more than in any other subject, a dangerous subjectivity has arisen.

"If a greater degree of objectivity is to be gained for research and practice in international law, it is necessary that, first of all, vast, difficult and unselfish preliminary work should be done; the enormous bulk of material must be collected, sifted and systematically arranged, in order that every student of questions of international law should be

[251a] See p. 45.
[252] Series A, *sectio* 1, *tomus* 1, *Digest of the Decisions of the Permanent Court of International Justice,* 1922–1930.

placed in a position enabling him to make a rapid survey of the documents relating to the particular subject of his study . . .

"This programme of work can only be carried out by a larger number of scientifically trained and capable jurists working together according to a uniform method and a uniform system. It, therefore, seemed to the Director of [this] Institute that this undertaking should be one of its principal tasks."[253]

The Institute, whose contribution to the supply of the lack of a survey of documentation alluded to in the statement quoted is embodied in the *Fontes Juris Gentium* series, neither advocated nor followed any particular theory "in regard to the doctrine of juristic sources". It held that "the answer to the doubtful questions . . . as to what documents are to be utilized in ascertaining the rules of international law and what is their importance for this purpose . . . will be different according to the point of view taken by the responsible worker in regard to the basic problems of international law . . ." and confined itself to the making of "a comprehensive survey of international practice" in all its aspects.[254] The scope and content of this work are discussed elsewhere in this paper.[255]

## F. PUBLICISTS

The views of publicists may be summarized conveniently under four or five separate heads. First, general appraisals regarding the availability and sufficiency of documentation on customary international law in the broad sense; secondly, proposals for the collection and publication of documentation illustrating State practice on questions of international law; thirdly, proposals for the collection and publication of awards and decisions of international tribunals and courts; and fourthly, proposals for the collection and publication of decisions of municipal courts on questions of international law.

### 1. General

The late Judge John Bassett Moore whose immense contribution to the study of international law is well known[256] became so impressed with the need for greater availability of the evidences of international law that, in 1911, he urged, in addition to a collection of all treaties, ancient and modern, (1) the preparation and publication of all State papers, both American and foreign, relating to foreign affairs, somewhat after the manner of the *British and Foreign State Papers,* but on a broader basis; and (2) the collection and publication of international judicial decisions designed "to constitute a permanent and continuing source of authority for all international proceedings of a judicial or even of a

[253] *Ibid.,* pp. xv–xxvi.
[254] *Ibid.,* pp. xxi–xxii.
[255] See pp. 47–48.
[256] Cf. e.g. his *History and Digest of the International Arbitrations to which the United States has been a Party,* 6 vols., 1898; *A Digest of International Law,* 8 vols., 1906; and *International Adjudications, Ancient and Modern,* 1929 ff. These three works are discussed *supra.*

mediatorial nature".[257] These collections, in his judgment, would "place at the disposal of tribunals, national as well as international, of administrative officials and of writers and students, the sources of international law in an amplitude and completeness never before essayed".[258]

To turn to more recent writers, one or two statements may be sufficient to illustrate the persisting desire to make the evidence of customary international law more readily available.

One author states that "one of the most important tasks in the field of international law at the present time is to make the source materials of international law more widely and more readily accessible".[259]

Another, writing of the importance of customary international law, declares: "It hardly requires mention that, apart from exceptions . . . the immense material from which 'international custom, as evidence of a general practice accepted as law', may be gathered has hardly yet been touched by international lawyers. . . . It is suggested, therefore, that the most that can be done at this stage is a systematic analysis, country by country, of the attitudes of the subjects of international law to the rules of international customary international law".[260]

Emphasizing the potential role of the United Nations, another writer recently observed: "The materials with which the international lawyer must work are manifold. They exist, and they should be made more accessible. The United Nations can perform an important service and encourage the progressive development of international law by promoting the collection and publication of these materials".[261]

## 2. State Practice

Discussing various sources of international law, Judge Sir Cecil Hurst declared there was general agreement "that the source of international law which is of paramount importance is the practice of States, manifested by the treaties they conclude or by their conduct. It is true that far more material is published by the Governments today than was general in the nineteenth century. It is therefore easier for a student nowadays to be well informed as to the practice of States". He warned, however, that "before the importance from the point of view of building up the science of international law of a Government's conduct on some particular occasion can be appreciated, that conduct has to be viewed and studied in the light of all the surrounding circumstances—why the Government acted as it did; what was the reaction of other Governments and so forth".[262]

[257] *International Adjudication,* Modern Series, vol. I (1929), p. ix.

[258] *Ibid.,* p. x.

[259] Bishop, "Recent American Judicial Decisions Involving International Law", *American Journal of International Law,* vol. 42 (1948), p. 195.

[260] Georg Schwarzenberger, "The Inductive Approach to International Law", *Harvard Law Review,* vol. 60 (1947), p. 563.

[261] Herbert W. Briggs, "Finding International Law", *American Journal of International Law,* vol. 42 (1948), p. 103.

[262] "A Plea for the Codification of International Law on New Lines." Read before the Grotius Society, 16 October 1946, *Transactions,* vol. xxxii, p. 152.

The importance of background material for any attempt to deduce rules of international law from official utterances, has of course been fully realized by Judge John Bassett Moore in preparing his *Digest of International Law.*[263]

Another writer pointed out that "to prove the existence of a principle of international law by means of State practice" was by no means an easy matter. For it was necessary "to prove consistent practice on the part of all Governments in any one field of international law and it is only from such consistent practice that the existence of a generally recognized principle of international law may be concluded". The difficulty, an important one, in proving a consistent practice of several, let alone of all, Governments, stems, it was argued, from the fact "that the spade-work urgently needed for ascertaining international practice is still almost entirely lacking. The example of John Bassett Moore, who, in his *Digest of International Law,* was the first to undertake the task of recording the practice of the United States, has been copied in no other country. In most cases it is not the scientific research workers who are at fault, but the appropriate Government authorities, who refuse to allow the material to be sifted and published".[264]

In a similar vein, having pointed out with regret that no record of the practice of other countries exists comparable to that of the "United States Foreign Relations" and the Digests of Moore and Hackworth,[265] another writer described the resulting situation as follows:[266]

"As it is, the treatment of various questions of international law in monographs and otherwise, tends to be one-sided inasmuch as it is based largely on the practice of the United States. Until the Foreign Offices of Great Britain and France—and also of some of the smaller countries such as Belgium, Holland and Sweden—have followed the lead of the State Department in this matter we cannot hope for a more comprehensive and accurate treatment by writers of questions of international law than is the case at present. It is also clear that from the point of view of the requirements of the staffs of the Foreign Offices and of the diplomatic and consular representatives of the countries concerned, the encouragement of publications of this kind is desirable and, in the long run, highly economical. It would make unnecessary the compilation, amidst some haste, of special memoranda bearing on situations as they arise in particular cases; and there is no doubt that other Government departments would greatly benefit from the existence of a semi-official publication of this nature."

Adverting to the view that the publication of official correspondence—which in any event must be largely the result of official initiative and effort—might adversely affect the interest of the country or Government concerned, the same writer noted that the United States authorities have apparently discarded the idea "that publication of international correspondence may be used against them as a precedent and that, in consequence, it

[263] Cf. Preface to vol. I, pp. iv–v.

[264] *Fontes Juris Gentium,* edited by Victor Bruns. Series B, section I, vol. 1: Digest of the Diplomatic Correspondence of the European States, 1856–1871 (1932), p. xix.

[265] Reference is made to the *Digest of International Law* by Green H. Hackworth, 8 vols. (1940–1944).

[266] H. Lauterpacht, in the *British Year Book of International Law,* vol. 22 (1945), p. 310.

ought to be kept secret as far as possible". He was of the opinion that "the benefits accruing from the publication of the records outweigh decisively any such remote disadvantages".[267]

### 3. International Law Reports

The situation prevailing in the matter of reporting decisions and awards of international tribunals has been graphically summed up as follows:[268]

"Few international tribunals in the past have arranged for a systematic publication of texts of their decisions to make them available for the professional public. The fact presents an awkward handicap to a jurist or a scholar seriously pursuing a study of international jurisprudence. He is forced to delve in a mass of heterogeneous documentation, some of it highly fugitive in character, to discover the materials he needs; and after the discovery he may lack assurance as to their authenticity. Often he must rely on wholly secondary aids. Temporary tribunals frequently become *functus officio* once their decisions are rendered, and the form in which the decisions are published by the parties is sometimes far from satisfactory. The awards given by tribunals of the Permanent Court of Arbitration were published by its International Bureau, but the publications were not given systematic distribution except to Governments.

"Decisions of the Central American Court of Justice were published unsystematically in a periodical which was not entirely official. Some of the numerous decisions of the Mixed Arbitral Tribunals created in 1919 and 1920 were published in an unofficial collection, but so many of them are unavailable for general purposes that it is still difficult to appraise the work of those tribunals. It remained for the Permanent Court of International Justice to set a satisfactory standard for the publications relating to its work, and its success in doing so was due to the genius of its first Registrar. The various series of the Court's publications give, usually in two languages, an almost complete history of each case and they are on sale throughout the world. Still needed, however, is an international council on the reporting of decisions of international tribunals generally, similar to the Incorporated Council of Law Reporting for England and Wales, and it might in time make for international law a contribution second in importance only to that achieved by the publication of treaty texts in the League of Nations Treaty Series. The provision in the Hague Conventions of 1899 and 1907 that all arbitral awards in which the parties to the Conventions were interested should be communicated to the International Bureau might have led to such a development, but unfortunately the opportunity was neglected."

While the need for more ready access to what has been described as "a growing

[267] *Ibid.*
[268] Manley O. Hudson, *International Tribunals—Past and Future* (1944), pp. 119–120.

source of law, not only as evidence of custom, but as precedents for the decision of cases''[269] has been acutely felt for a long time, it appears to be a fact that "a complete collection of international arbitrations, even limited to the nineteenth century and the first quarter of the twentieth, still remains to be undertaken''.[270] Indeed, the suggestion has even been made that we do not as yet possess a definitive list of arbitrations.[271]

It may be apposite to quote here also the author of a recent book on international arbitration who, stressing the needs particularly of the practitioner for a readily accessible and reasonably complete collection of international arbitral decisions, said:[272]

"If we are to have a fully developed system of international jurisprudence for application by international tribunals, we must establish a means for a uniform publication of their decisions. Cases still lie buried in the unpublished archives of Governments, limited and sporadic printings of others are made, with the result that the few repositories of precedents gathered together by scholars such as John Bassett Moore and de La Pradelle become the handbooks of advocates. . . . How can there be a common international law in the full sense of that term when parties labour in ignorance of all its applicable precedents? Under the present system we must look to chance and the industry and learning of counsel and the members of the court as our only surety that the court will be well advised. This is not to deny, but rather to emphasize, the value of the individual efforts that have been made in this direction. The task is, however, more than an individual one."

It will be recalled that it was Judge Moore's intention to furnish in his *International Adjudications* an "intelligible and fully documented report of all judicial decisions of international questions not recorded in the ordinary law reports''.[273] However, this monumental enterprise, like the *Recueil* by de La Pradelle and Politis, was discontinued after the publication of six volumes in the Modern Series and of one volume in the Ancient Series.[274] Reference may also be made to the series *Fontes Juris Gentium* which has met with a similar fate.[275]

Private initiative and effort, it appears, have thus far not been able to fill the gap. It may be pertinent, then, to mention here the proposal that the United Nations should take steps to correct this situation:[276]

"Means should be provided whereby Governments may register copies of arbitral decisions with some international body under the United Nations as they have in the past registered their treaties with the League of Nations."

[269] Edwin M. Borchard, "The Theory and Sources of International Law", *Recueil d'études sur les sources du droit en l'honneur de François Gény*, vol. III (1935), p. 350.

[270] Dionysio Anzilotti, *Cours de Droit International*, vol. I (1929), p. 77.

[271] Denys P. Myers in *American Journal of International Law*, vol. 34 (1940), p. 554.

[272] Kenneth S. Carlston, *The Process of International Arbitration* (1946), p. 263.

[273] J. B. Moore (ed.), *International Adjudications, Ancient and Modern*, 1929. *et seq*.

[274] Discussed more fully above, pp. 50–52.

[275] The *Fontes Juris Gentium* are more fully discussed above, pp. 47–49.

[276] Carlston, *op. cit.*, p. 263.

## 4. Collections and Digests of National Decisions on Questions of International Law

Parallel with the need for a comprehensive and systematic collection and publication of international arbitral awards runs the desire for a similar collection and publication of national decisions on questions of international law. Thus it has been observed that "international law reports on the same or similar lines as the regular reports of national courts published in the various countries have for a long time been considered by many to be a desirable piece of apparatus" both in the academic study as well as in the practice of international law.[277]

The prediction has been made that the study of international law would be revolutionized if a general and global collection of cases, both national and international, were produced.[278] The reason for the persistent demand for making every decision bearing upon international law, whether emanating from a national or international court, promptly available to students and practitioners[279] may be attributed to the belief that municipal court decisions show on certain question of international law a substantial degree of uniformity. To the extent that such uniformity has come about, it has been said, the decisions of municipal courts, which are organs of the State, "may be regarded as evidence of customary international law".[280]

Obviously, in order to ascertain the frequency of decisions of municipal courts on points of international law and, at the same time, the degree of concordance or divergence achieved by courts in the different parts of the world, it is necessary to possess as complete a collection of such decisions as possible. While concordant decisions, it is said, may be regarded as "evidence of practice that has become customary law",[281] decisions which indicate a substantial degree of divergence are "of considerable usefulness as an indication of problems awaiting solution".[282] Hence, it may be said, knowledge of the decisions of municipal courts on questions of international law is likely to encourage the progressive development of customary international law in any case, be it through pointing up matters of substantial agreement between the different jurisdictions, or be it through bringing out points of difference between the courts in the various countries. The view has been expressed that digests and reports of judicial decisions were tools necessary not merely for the "scholarly endeavours" but "perhaps some day for eventual codification".[283]

[277] H. Lauterpacht in preface to *Annual Digest and Reports of Public International Law Cases*, 1933–1934 (1940), p. ix.

[278] M. O. Hudson, "Twelve Casebooks on International Law", *American Journal of International Law*, vol. 32 (1938), p. 455.

[279] Edwin D. Dickinson at the 24th Annual Meeting of the American Society of International Law. Cf. *Proceedings*, pp. 151–152.

[280] International Law Association, *Report of the Committee on the Development and Formulation of International Law, 1947*, p. 9.

[281] Liang, "Methods for the Encouragement of the Progressive Development of International Law and its Codification", *The Yearbook of World Affairs, 1948*, vol. 2 (1948).

[282] International Law Association, *Report, 1947*, p. 10.

[283] W. W. Bishop, Jr., "Recent American Judicial Decisions Involving International Law", *American Journal of International Law*, vol. 42 (1948), p. 195.

# PART THREE

## Ways and Means

# I. THE PRESENT STATE OF THE EVIDENCE OF CUSTOMARY INTERNATIONAL LAW: NEED FOR IMPROVEMENT

The foregoing survey reveals that a substantial body of evidence of customary international law is available. But it is no less clear from it that the existing state of documentation needs to be improved. The practice of some States is documented less adequately than that of others.[284] Whilst there are very detailed publications dealing with the work of the Permanent Court of International Justice and the International Court of Justice, the decisions of other international tribunals are less adequately treated.[285] Though decisions of municipal courts are to some extent available, and though the position as regards the period since the end of the War of 1914–1918 is infinitely better than that for any earlier period so far as concerns such decisions, there is clearly room for some improvement in their treatment.[286] Some effort has indeed been made to collect and publish national legislation bearing on international law,[287] and the decisions and opinions of international organizations on questions of general international law.[288] But, again, much remains to be done.

Amongst the main shortcomings of existing collections is the incompleteness in documentation which results from their compilation on too rigidly selective lines, e.g., from the restriction of a particular collection to "treaties", or to "decisions", or to

[284] See p. 33 f.
[285] See pp. 61–68.
[286] See p. 74 f.
[287] See pp. 82–90.
[288] See pp. 76–79.

"diplomatic documents". The overlapping and duplication between different collections is another obvious defect, as is the frequent omission of so-called "background materials", without which documents very often are of imperfect value. The absence of continuity, too, is a serious defect. The tale of undertakings which have not been completed is very long: Moore's *International Adjudications* ceased to appear after only seven volumes had been published;[289] de La Pradelle's *Recueil général periodique* survived only five years;[290] de La Pradelle and Politis's *Recueil des arbitrages internationaux* was carried up to only 1872;[291] the *Fontes Juris Gentium* also collapsed;[292] and Smith's *Great Britain and the Laws of Nations* did not go beyond the second volume.[293] This is particularly regrettable so far as concerns those works which set out to provide periodical reports of decisions, both international and national, since the lack of up-to-date international law reports is perhaps the most serious which is to be remarked. The *Annual Digest and Reports of Public International Law Cases,* it is true, has continued to appear despite the difficulties which have been occasioned by the war of 1939–1945, but, as has been seen, new copies of the earlier volumes in that series are not at present available.[294]

Upon a consideration of this situation it would seem to follow that in connexion with any project for its improvement by a programme of publication, especial attention should be paid to (1) the need for the systematic planning of publications, especially with a view to the avoidance of duplication and overlapping; (2) the desirability of completeness of presentation, with special regard to the inclusion of so-called "background material"; and (3) the desirability of regularity and continuity in publication, and of publication upon such a scale as to insure general availability.

It would also seem to follow that the problem of current publications ought to be distinguished from plans for the collection or digesting of materials relating to the recent or more recent past.

## II. POSSIBLE METHODS OF PREPARATION OF COLLECTIONS OR DIGESTS

It is apprehended that there are four possible alternative methods whereby evidence of customary international law may be assembled with a view to its being made more readily available. These may be designated respectively, the topical approach, the chronological approach, the approach by countries, and the approach by the category of evidence.

The topical approach involves collecting evidence of international law with refer-

[289] See p. 51.
[290] See p. 56.
[291] See pp. 53–54.
[292] See pp. 47–49, 71–73, 79–82.
[293] See pp. 47–49.
[294] See pp. 68–70.

ence to particular topics, such as diplomatic privileges and immunities, treaties, etc., from every available source, be it treaty, the practice of States, or the opinion of publicists. This was the approach adopted by the Harvard Research in International Law[295] and it is the method indicated to the International Law Commission as appropriate to its task of codifying international law. For, in virtue of article 18 of its Statute, the Commission is to "survey the whole field of international law with a view to selecting topics for codification", and, in pursuance of article 20, the Commission is to "prepare its drafts in the form of articles and [to] submit them to the General Assembly together with a commentary containing: (*a*) adequate presentation of precedents and other relevant data, including treaties, judicial decisions and doctrine; (*b*) conclusions relevant to: (i) the extent of agreement on each point in the practice of States and in doctrine; (ii) divergencies and disagreements which exist, as well as arguments invoked in favour of one or another solution". In view of the latter provision, it would appear that the topical approach is to some extent inherent in the Commission's work, not only in connexion with codification but also in connexion with the progressive development of international law. It may, therefore, be taken that it is unnecessary to examine this approach in any detail in relation to the Commission's responsibilities under article 24 of its Statute.

The chronological approach, involving the collection of evidence of customary international law in respect of certain periods rather than certain topics, is one which has been frequently used in connexion with the collection of judicial decisions and of national legislation and with the compilation of digests or collections of State practice. It would appear that any attempt to implement article 24 of the Statute must involve some use of this method which, however, is not likely by itself to yield entirely satisfactory results.

The method of approach by countries has been employed in such important works as the *Digests* of Moore and Hackworth,[296] in Hyde's *International Law Chiefly as Applied and Interpreted in the United States* (2nd ed., 1947), and in McNair's *Law of Treaties.*[297] Its application is contemplated by article 19 (2)[298] of the Statute of the International Law Commission in reference to the Commission's function of codifying international law. A rigorous application of this procedure would involve the collection of all relevant data from every country, or from a substantial number of countries, and would presumably lead to the separate publication of materials relating to each country treated. But it is open to question whether the method need be strictly applied in all respects. For instance, it is doubtful whether the method is of great utility in connexion with the publication of international awards. Moore's *History and Digest*[299] was indeed limited to "International Arbitrations to which the United States was a Party", but his later work, *International*

[295] See pp. 93–96.

[296] See pp. 43–44.

[297] See p. 46.

[298] This paragraph reads: "The Commission shall, through the Secretary-General, address to Governments a detailed request to furnish the texts of laws, decrees, judicial decisions, treaties, diplomatic correspondence and other documents related to the topic being studied and which the Commission deems necessary."

[299] See p. 43.

*Adjudications,*[300] was not so limited and was intended to embrace all arbitrations, as was also de La Pradelle and Politis's *Recueil des arbitrages internationaux.*[301] On the other hand, the approach by countries may be considered to be more appropriate as respects decisions of municipal courts and was indeed adopted by the editors of the *Fontes Juris Gentium,*[302] though not followed by compilers of the *Annual Digest and Reports of Public International Law Cases.*[303] The same method, it is conceived, is equally appropriate to the national legislation on matters relating to international law. Such collections as have appeared in recent years have, it is true, followed rather the topical approach, but the approach by country, and, in some instances, also the chronological approach, have been adopted as subsidiary principles of classification.[304] However, it is in reference to State practice that the approach by countries has been recommended most strongly, and the frequently expressed desire for more digests of the type of those of Moore and Hackworth, illustrating the application and interpretation of international law by particular States, of course implies an endorsement of this method. At the same time it is to be observed that at least one digest of State practice, the *Digest of the Diplomatic Correspondence of the European States* in the *Fontes Juris Gentium* series,[305] did not follow this method. And it would appear that the choice of method in the preparation of digests of State practice is likely to be largely influenced by the choice of the organ or organs responsible for their preparation. If Governments are to assume responsibility for the compilation of such digests, as possibly they will do in view of the necessity for access to official archives, the method of approach by countries is likely to be that chosen.

There would appear to be ample precedents for the method of approach by categories of evidence. Moore's *International Adjudications,*[306] de La Pradelle and Politis's *Recueil des Arbitrages internationaux,*[307] the *Annual Digest and Reports of Public International Law Cases*[308] and the digests of the *Decisions of the German Supreme Court,*[309] and of the *Diplomatic Correspondence of the European States*[310] in the *Fontes Juris Gentium* series, besides the collections of national law on specific subjects issued under the auspices of the Harvard Research in International Law[311] all exemplify this approach. So also do the *United Nations Reports of International Arbitral Awards*[312] and the *Yearbook of Human Rights.*[313] The existence of these works would indicate that this approach has been found

[300] See p. 49.
[301] See pp. 53–55.
[302] See pp. 75, 80–82.
[303] See pp. 69, 74, 78–79.
[304] See pp. 79–90.
[305] See p. 47.
[306] See p. 49 f.
[307] See pp. 53–55.
[308] See pp. 68–70, 78–79.
[309] See pp. 80–82.
[310] See pp. 47–49.
[311] See pp. 94–95.
[312] See p. 48.
[313] See pp. 83–84.

both adequate and feasible and that it is one likely to suggest itself to the International Law Commission as a basis for the further implementation of article 24 of its Statute.

But the existence of the various methods of approach outlined does not involve the choice of one to the exclusion of the other. It may be advisable to give some consideration to different combinations of the various approaches in connexion with the several categories of evidence of customary international law. Thus, in the preparation of collections of decisions of municipal courts or of digests of State practice the approach by countries might well be combined with the approach according to the category of evidence, whilst the latter, combined with the chronological approach, would be appropriate to the compilation of a collection of international judicial decisions.

## III. POSSIBLE METHODS OF PROCURING THE PUBLICATION OF MORE COMPLETE COLLECTIONS OF EVIDENCE OF CUSTOMARY INTERNATIONAL LAW

The International Law Commission has, under its Statute, considerable latitude as regards both methods and objections to be recommended for the making of evidence of customary international law more readily available. Conceivably it could confine its deliberations to the question of making available *current* State practice and of collecting *current* judicial decisions and legislation. In this connexion it is to be noted that the *United Nations Treaty Series* comprehends only current treaties. It may be a matter for consideration whether efforts should not be made to collect in the first instance the evidence of State practice and other relevant material for the period beginning with the end of the War of 1914–1918, the point of departure chosen for the *United Nations Reports of International Arbitral Awards.*[314] A still broader approach might involve going back still further—perhaps to the beginning of the century, or to 1800, or to 1794. This comprehensive approach would also involve consideration as to whether or not projected collections should be planned in more than one stage. For instance, in view of the urgent need for easier access to current materials, it might be considered desirable to issue two series of a compilation covering a considerable period of time, as were issued the Modern and Ancient Series of Moore's *International Adjudications.*[315] Alternatively, it might be thought best to put in hand as soon as possible the collection of contemporary materials in several series which would move not only forward but also backward, until ultimately the whole period contemplated was covered.

One possible method within the scope of article 24 of the Statute which the Commission might wish to consider is the continuation, and perhaps the expansion, of an existing publication, such as the *Annual Digest and Reports of Public International Law*

[314] See p. 49.
[315] See p. 49 f.

*Cases,* which might be developed, in accordance with the declared policy of its editorial committee, into "international law reports appearing at annual intervals",[316] or even, as its editor hopes, extended backwards so as to cover the whole period from the time of the Jay Treaty of 1794 to the present days.[317] The revival of some of the collections which have been discontinued, such as Moore's *International Adjudications*[318] or the *Fontes Juris Gentium* series,[319] might also be considered. Similarly, the possibility of expanding *United Nations Reports of International Arbitral Awards,*[320] so as to make these the standard source of international arbitral awards, both past and contemporaneous, might be examined.

In the alternative, the Commission might consider it best to recommend the undertaking of a completely new *Corpus Juris Gentium,* derived from all the different categories of evidence of customary international law. The paragraphs next following indicate briefly some possible ways of approaching such a task.

## IV. THE ORGANIZATION OF THE PREPARATION OF A SYSTEMATIC AND COMPREHENSIVE COMPILATION OF EVIDENCE OF CUSTOMARY INTERNATIONAL LAW

If, under the auspices of the International Law Commission, the preparation of what has been termed a *Corpus Juris Gentium* is to be undertaken, it would seem that the following alternatives would present themselves:

(*a*) All or part of the work might be undertaken and carried out by the Secretariat of the United Nations under the direction of the International Law Commission; or

(*b*) All or part of the work might be undertaken and carried out by Governments; or

(*c*) All or part of the work might be undertaken and carried out in the existing unofficial scientific institutions in different countries; or

(*d*) All or part of the work might be undertaken and carried out by individual experts, persuant to a plan laid down by the International Law Commission and under the direction of the Secretariat of the United Nations.

Each of these methods would obviously possess both advantages and disadvantages and very probably a combination of more than one of them would be desirable. Thus, whilst the first method may be regarded as quite acceptable for the compilation of collections or digests of decisions of national and international tribunals, and possibly of legislative materials on questions of international law, it would be neither appropriate nor satisfactory for the preparation of digests of State practice. Governments are in a pecul-

[316] See pp. 69–70.
[317] *Annual Digest 1941–1942,* p. x.
[318] See p. 49.
[319] See pp. 47–49, 75, 80–82.
[320] See p. 49.

iarly favourable position as respects the publication of digests of State practice and the works of Moore and Hackworth indicate that Governments are not only in a position to undertake so complex a task, but that they are capable of doing so in conformity with the highest standards of scholarship. It remains, of course, still to be explored how far Governments, assuming their willingness for the task, could be induced to accept such a uniform method of compilation and classification as would be desirable, and perhaps essential, in order to ensure that such digests might be of the greatest possible use.

Whilst methods (*c*) and (*d*), taken by themselves, might appear to be less serviceable than the others outlined, they might be of more utility when adopted in combination with methods (*a*) and (*b*). Thus, individual experts might be of considerable assistance to the Secretariat. For instance, they might be attached temporarily to the Secretariat in order to facilitate the collections of decisions of municipal courts and of national legislation on questions of international law. Again, scientific institutions might assist not only the Secretariat but also Governments. Thus, Governments willing to have digests of their practices prepared, but unable to undertake the work themselves, might be willing to grant access to their archives to national bodies or national specialists selected by themselves. And national bodies, already existing or created *ad hoc,* might assist the Secretariat by furnishing materials needed for such compilations as may be entrusted to it. Some possible combinations of the alternatives outlined are discussed below.

## A. THE SECRETARIAT AS CENTRAL ORGAN

A strong case, it is believed, can be made out in favour of constituting the Secretariat of the United Nations, acting under the direction of the International Law Commission, the central organ for discharging the task contemplated by article 24 of the Statute. Some degree of centralization is clearly needed in order to secure uniformity and completeness. And the Secretariat is equipped to provide the translations necessary for producing texts in the three working, and five official, languages of the United Nations.

So far as concerns digests of State practice, Governments could furnish the Secretariat with relevant materials—abstracts of diplomatic correspondence, Foreign Office minutes, diplomatic and consular instructions, and opinions of law officers, etc.—and the Secretariat could then, in accordance with instructions of the International Law Commission, assume responsibility for editing, translating and publication. In regard to decisions of international tribunals, it might be desirable for Governments to assume responsibility for furnishing the Secretariat with copies of all past arbitral decisions to which they may have been parties, and also to undertake for the future to file with the Secretariat copies of such awards in much the same manner as they register treaties in accordance with article 102 of the Charter. Alternatively such awards might be deposited with the Registry of the International Court of Justice, which is responsible for the editing of the *United Nations Reports of International Arbitral Awards.*

Decisions of municipal tribunals could perhaps be more easily collected by the Secretariat in collaboration with individual experts or national scientific organizations than by the agency of Governments; though in respect of such countries as do not possess published reports the assistance of Governments might have to be sought.

The somewhat more difficult task of collecting legislative materials on matters of international law would be much assisted by Governmental co-operation, though it is perhaps not indispensable. Legislative enactments are commonly published and the Secretariat could well undertake the task of collecting pertinent acts and decrees if it had access to complete sets of official publications of Governments. Failing this, the assistance of individual experts or national bodies might be enlisted, or Governments might be prevailed upon to undertake the regular communication to the Secretariat of relevant texts. And it may finally be noted that the *Legislative Series* of the International Labour Office[321] might well serve as a model for any projected publication by the Secretariat.

## B. INDIVIDUAL UNDERTAKINGS BY GOVERNMENTS

The co-operation of Governments, it has been indicated already, would be essential to the proper functioning of the Secretariat of the United Nations as a central organ for the production of compilations of customary international law, and particularly for the preparation of digests of State practice. As an alternative to this scheme, the main responsibility might be placed on the shoulders of Governments, the part of the Secretariat being limited to such auxiliary services as translation and publication. Whilst such a system might have many advantages, it would not be free from drawbacks unless steps were taken to ensure a minimum of uniformity, for instance by means of detailed instructions, perhaps dealing separately with each category of material, for the guidance of compilers.

## C. DIVISION OF LABOUR BETWEEN GOVERNMENTS AND THE SECRETARIAT

A *via media* between the two methods already discussed might lie in entrusting to Governments the compilation of State practice and in assigning to the Secretariat the function of preparing other compilations. If this plan were adopted, it would clearly be desirable to place at the disposal of Governments an outline of suggestions regarding classification and annotation of material etc.; and it might also be desirable to have translations of texts completed by Governments prepared and published by the Secretariat. In this connexion some thought might be given to the question as to whether or not some assistance from a central source, be it technical or otherwise, could not be furnished to those Governments with comparatively limited resources.

321 See p. 83.

## D. UTILIZATION OF NATIONAL INSTITUTIONS OR COMMITTEES

Governments favourable to the idea of preparation of digests, but not willing to assume responsibility for work of this nature immediately, might be disposed to entrust the task to national institutions or committees. Whether such bodies should be official or unofficial in character would clearly depend on national practice and traditions. In some cases a suitably qualified institution might be found already to exist. In others it might be expedient to create *ad hoc* an official research body. There are many precedents for the latter course. Thus, in 1897 the Netherlands Government set up a Royal Commission for the Codification of Private International Law in connexion with the Hague Conferences for the Unification of Private International Law. The Seventh International Conference of American States called for the creation of national committees of jurists specially qualified in international law with a view to preparing for the codification of international law, which bodies have been transformed into standing committees by article 71 of the charter of the Organization of American States adopted at the Conference of Bogota on 30 April 1948. In connexion with the plan under consideration here, such committees would be concerned not so much with matters of codification as with the preparation of digests of international law. This would involve their furnishing the research workers required. Possibly the necessary funds could be provided by Governments, or by private foundations. In some cases these funds might cover also the cost of publication.

The question of co-ordination between the different national committees would be a serious one. It would seem that it might be solved in one of two ways. Either the International Law Commission might work out an outline to be submitted to the national bodies for their guidance or the committees themselves might form an international co-ordinating committee.

## E. ENLISTMENT OF THE SERVICES OF INDIVIDUAL EXPERTS

So far as concerns the compilation of digests of international law, it is the virtually unanimous opinion of writers that the work is now beyond the powers or resources of any one individual. Whilst the need for the initiative and supervision of a competent scholar is conceded, experience goes to show that the co-operation of a substantial number of assistants is indispensable. But it is clearly open to Governments who are willing to prepare such digests to make individual scholars rather than officials generally responsible for them. This presupposes resort to the methods outlined under paragraphs (*b*) and (*c*) above and is not therefore an alternative solution. In other words, there being a widespread belief that Governments alone are fitted to undertake the task of preparing comprehensive digests of international law, individual experts cannot be expected to assume this important task of their own initiative.

As respects compilations or digests of international arbitral awards, a distinction should perhaps be made between the publication of past awards and the official publication of contemporary decisions. The suggestion has been made above that Governments should undertake to communicate to the Secretariat or the Registry of the International Court of Justice documents relating to current arbitral proceedings to which they may be parties.[322] But in so far as concerns past arbitral awards there would appear to be ample scope for individual initiative and effort. In fact, as is well known, several existing collections of such awards are owed to such initiative and effort, e.g., Moore's *International Adjudications* and de La Pradelle and Politis's *Recueil des arbitrages internationaux.*[323] On the other hand, Moore's *History and Digest of International Arbitrations,* whilst very largely an individual production, was compiled and published under Governmental auspices.[324]

But though the contribution of individual students may be very large, it may well be that other methods are more suitable for the execution of a comprehensive programme in a reasonably short space of time. If such a programme is inaugurated, it might be necessary to consider the organization of teams of experts working in collaboration with each other under the direction of the Secretary-General.

The same considerations apply equally to the compilation of collections or digests of decisions of national courts involving issues of international law, a task for which individual scholars are well suited provided their efforts are guided by a common plan. But the task is perhaps one which is insufficiently attractive to any large number of qualified international lawyers to permit the expectation that it will be undertaken privately within any reasonable time without encouragement and support from some central source such as either the Secretariat or national committees or institutions might provide.

Individual experts are likewise qualified to compile collections of national legislation bearing on international law and might perform this function even with respect to current material, if the Secretariat does not assume this task with the co-operation of Governments. But here again some central co-ordination of methods of selection and editing would be highly desirable.

The question would obviously arise as to the most appropriate method for the recruitment of individuals for the tasks outlined. Two ways would appear open: appointment by Governments or by the Secretary-General. There is perhaps no particularly persuasive reason for burdening Governments with the function unless they are prepared to provide assistance, financial or otherwise, for the projects to be undertaken, in which case they would probably wish to exercise some measure of control. It would probably simplify co-ordination of appointments if these were to be made by the Secretary-General.

## V. SOME SECONDARY SUGGESTIONS

One or two other points seem likely to be worthy of the attention of the International Law Commission in connexion with article 24 of its Statute. The first is the ques-

[322] See p. 119.
[323] See pp. 49, 53.
[324] See p. 43.

tion of access to Governmental archives which, as is well known, is not always easy. It is not in every case even possible to obtain information in advance as to what archives are open and what they comprise. A general inquiry into the situation prevailing in Europe was undertaken by the Institute of Intellectual Co-operation and some information of interest to international lawyers is to be found in the *Guide international des archives—Europe* published by that body in 1934. Amongst other surveys extant may be mentioned that in the *Guide to the History of the United States, 1775-1921,* by S. F. Bemis and G. B. Griffin (1935), and Temperley and Penson's *Survey of British State Papers (A Century of Diplomatic Blue Books, 1814-1914,* (1938)). Recent monographic literature indicates that there is a growing trend towards an inductive approach and that greater reliance is being placed on materials illustrating State practice. It would clearly be very useful if Governments would be more liberal in giving permission to scholars to use such materials. And the International Law Commission might be disposed to consider how Governments could be encouraged to this end.

Again, the possibility may be considered of promoting the wider distribution of existing collections of evidence of international law. One step in this direction would be the obtaining of precise information as to what is actually in the libraries in the different capitals and other national research centres. If, as appears very possible, such a survey should reveal important gaps, the provision of nuclear collections, possibly deposited with the various national libraries, might be considered. The supply of photostatic copies of works now out of print would be another possibility which might be explored, as also would be the enlistment of the co-operation of Governments and of private foundations with a view to the establishment and maintenance of standard libraries of international law in different parts of the world.

# INTERNATIONAL LAW AND PEACE

## I

It is common ground, I believe, that the future of international law has come to be regarded as inextricably bound up with the progress of international organization. Lacking its own organs, the international legal order needs the props offered by institutions created by States for the accomplishment of a variety of political, social and economic purposes. In the layman's view, however, international law of itself and by itself is expected to exercise a decisive influence on the policies of States. The layman and often the jurist forget that international law cannot exert any influence by itself but only through the organs of States. Whenever States resort to force or war in pursuit of their objectives, the layman is prone to conclude that international law has failed to prevent war and maintain peace rather than that the States have failed to maintain peace and prevent war. It was commonly assumed that the prevention of war and the preservation of peace were a, if not the, function of international law just as prevention of violence and preservation of domestic peace constitute a function of municipal law. This has not been so and even if it had been international law would still of and by itself neither prevent war nor preserve peace any more than municipal law could prevent revolutions or civil disorders without the apparatus of government which on the domestic plane is taken for granted. When international violence flares up, there are those who call for an improved, expanded, modernized even institutionalized law without going so far as to advocate the establishment of world government to administer a world law just as national States administer national law. On the other hand there have always been scholars who denied that international law could preserve peace, or that law without government could ever be effective and who accordingly pursuaded themselves that in order to establish peace among sovereign States it was necessary first to abolish the sovereign States and then replace international law with international government. Be that as it may, the preservation of peace has not always been a function of international law.

## II

The nineteenth century positivist was content to take international law as he found it, as a body of precepts based on customs or treaties, derived from the free will of States, as the Permanent Court of International Justice was to say in the Lotus case, and intended to facilitate the co-existence of a plurality of States sharing a certain civilization thus leaving a substantial part of mankind outside the pale of law. Resort to force in peace time was carefully circumscribed by the doctrine of reprisals but the law did not presume to prohibit recourse to war as an instrument of national policy or as a means of obtaining redress for an injury or as a crude procedure for the settlement of inter-state disputes. The law of peace was limited in scope and the area of domestic jurisdiction, the reserved domain, was extensive. The law of war was equally limited in scope and the discretion of belligerents correspondingly extensive subject to some humanitarian principles which in turn were hedged in with escape clauses for the convenience of the belligerents. Law and the sovereign State could easily co-exist because the law made no excessive demands upon the States either in the choice of their objectives or in the choice of means for the attainment of the same. As the Permanent Court observed in the Lotus case, since international law proceeds from their own free will "restrictions upon the independence of States cannot, therefore, be presumed." This dictum caused some annoyance to progressive international lawyers but, I believe, it was then and still is substantially a correct statement of the law.

Still, we can trace to the 19th century, the beginning of a deliberate effort of governments to develop international law by extending it geographically, *ratione personae,* to non-European States, and substantively, *ratione materiae,* by means of conventions to new areas of concern to the evolving business community whose interests, spurned by the technological revolution in industrial production and communications, have become increasingly transnational in scope. This development of the material scope of international law took two forms: first, what might be called the law of international cooperation, which would include the law of international rivers, postal, telegraph, telephone, and ultimately radio communications, copyright, trade marks, and related matters and secondly what might be called the law of restraint upon the use of force best exemplified by the conventions resulting from the two Hague Peace Conferences of 1899 and 1907. Thus, international law was launched deliberately though hesitatingly on its new career as an instrument of control of the use of force in international relations in order to reduce the recourse to war and establish a stable international legal order, an order of peace.

A factor in this process was no doubt the peace movement although its significance may be subject to differing appraisals. A number of hopeful assumptions about the nature of man and of international relations contributed to the new activity of States such as the belief in the rationality and perfectibility of the human species, in the harmony of interests, the conviction that war was an irrational, wasteful and uncivilized method for settling international controversies, that was was neither inevitable nor desirable, that arbitration and other procedures for peaceful settlement of disputes should take the place of war in an increasingly interdependent, prosperous and civilized world, that, in short, an international community was already in existence and needed only some improvements, some institutional props in order to become transformed from a primitive, decentralized order into a more perfect centralized legal order which would guarantee peace.

Thus two fallacies were born and they are still with us: One is that wars originate in controversies about legal rights and second that conflicts which lead to war that is political conflicts between governments could be depoliticized and rendered amendable to peaceful procedures such as negotiation, good offices, inquiry, mediation and ultimately arbitration. The Hague Conferences gave expression to all this in the Convention concerning the peaceful settlement of disputes and lent official governmental sanction to the idea of peace through law or more precisely peace through arbitration, that is, through law applied objectively by impartial tribunals, preferably a permanent tribunal.

A perfect example of this essentially legal conception of international relations is the following statement by Hans Kelsen. Writing in 1943 he said that

> "The next step on which our efforts must be concentrated is to bring about an international treaty concluded by as many states as possible—victors as well as vanquished—establishing an international court with compulsory jurisdiction . . . To eliminate war, the worst of all social evils, from interstate relations by establishing compulsory jurisdiction, the juridical approach to an organization of the world must precede any other attempt at international reform. Among the two aspects of the postwar problem, the economic and the legal, the latter has a certain priority over the former . . . It is not true that war is the consequence of unsatisfactory economic condition; on the contrary, the unsatisfactory situation of world economy is the consequence of war. If the history of the last thirty years has taught us anything, it is the primacy of politics over economics. Hence the elimination of war is our paramount problem. It is a problem of international policy and the most important means of international policy is international law."[1]

## III

The League of Nations was not merely the first experiment in collective security, it was, more importantly, the first experiment in transforming the primitive, rudimentary, decentralized international community into an international community organized on the basis of international law. This dominant idea was expressed in the Preamble of the Covenant that it was the purpose of the League to achieve international peace and security, *inter alia,* "by the firm establishment of the understandings of international law as the ac-

[1] Hans Kelsen, "Compulsory Adjudication of International Disputes", 37 *American Journal of International Law* 397–406 (1943) at pp. 397–398.

tual rule of conduct among governments," and "by the maintenance of justice and a scrupulous respect for all treaty obligations in the dealings of organized peoples with one another". The idea was further expressed by the distinction between licit and illicit wars, by the obligation to respect and preserve against external aggression the territorial integrity and political independence of all members, by stipulating an agreement to submit any dispute to arbitration which the members recognize as suitable and which cannot be settled by diplomacy, by providing for the establishment of a Permanent Court of International Justice competent to hear and determine any dispute of an international character, by stipulating the duty of members to submit to the Council any dispute likely to lead to rupture and which has not been given over to arbitration and, finally, by providing sanctions in Article 16 against a State which resorted to war in violation of these undertakings.

This experiment in an organization of the international community on the basis of law backed by a Permanent Court and by sanctions, and supplemented by the Kellogg-Briand Pact and various other agreements such as the Locarno Pact, failed within less than twenty years.

To be sure, the League was by no means a total failure. The law of international cooperation, grew from infancy to adolescence, through a process described as international legislation, and the League in more ways than one stimulated the development of this law to minister to the many requirements of an increasingly interdependent community of nations characterized by an unprecedented mobility of persons, goods and capital.

However, as an instrument of the law of restraint, the law designed to limit recourse to force for whatever purpose and to channel the resolution of inter-State conflicts into peaceful procedures, both political and judicial, on the basis of law, the League was a failure. True, it settled or was helpful in the settlement of many conflicts including some outbreaks of armed hostilities, but in a larger perspective it failed. According to a widely-held though not necessarily altogether accurate opinion, it failed primarily because it tended to be "legalistic" in its procedures and in its outlook, because, relying on an inflexible concept of international law, it attempted to freeze international relations into a permanent and immutable mold; because, viewed from another angle, it put a premium on stability and deprecated the dynamic character of international relations and the corresponding needs for peaceful change and revision not merely of the peace treaties but of international law itself which gave them the sanction and legitimacy of an established order.

It appears, furthermore, from this point of view at any rate, that the League precisely because it favored and relied on the techniques of law and specifically of international law, was incapable of dealing with the ideological conflicts, the clash of different and hostile social, economic and political systems, and the rival claims of the haves and the have-nots. Such novel conflicts were not amenable to regulation and resolution by the impartial application of the norms of international law which knew nothing and still knows very little about such non-legal differences.

As to the role of the Permanent Court of International Justice, one of its members, Judge Manley Hudson, wrote in 1944:

> "The perseverance of the effort which led to the establishment of the Court was possible only because it was closely linked with a desire to safeguard the maintenance of the world's peace. The effort had been kept alive during many years by men whose preoccupation was not so much with the administration of justice according to law as with the prevention of war. The Court was conceived of, therefore, as a great bulwark of peace, and popular support was enlisted for it on that basis. On the record of its eighteen years of useful service, however, some doubt may be entertained with reference to the Court's fulfillment of such a role. Its jurisdiction was quite limited, and in the cases which came before it for judgment the Court was called upon to decide juridical differences which usually depended on the construction of treaty provisions too complicated to excite popular agitation . . . It would be difficult to say that any of the cases threatened to become a *casus belli,* though some of them related to differences which, if the Court had not been available and if they had been allowed to fester, might have led to serious complications. The Court's bolstering of the structure of peace was accomplished through its advisory opinions, through the confidence which it inspired, and through the encouragement which it gave to the extension of the law of pacific settlement, rather than through its disposition of particular disputes."[2]

## IV

The second experiment in organizing the community of nations, the United Nations started out by minimizing the role of international law and maximizing the responsibility of the Great Powers for maintaining or restoring international peace and security. The story of the UN is too well-known to require recapitulation. Suffice it to recall that in the Dumbarton Oaks Proposals, the first official draft of the Charter, there was no reference to international law. This omission was made good at San Francisco, where some provisions relating to international law notably in the Preamble and in Art. 13 were included but the spirit remained indifferent to law. Within the first few years, it became evident how greatly the UN differed in this respect from the League. Where the League tried—often vainly—to depoliticize political differences and may have been guilty of an excess of zeal in this endeavor, the UN from the start evinced a powerful drive to politicize legal conflicts—one has only to recall the debates in the 1946 General Assembly on the questions of Indians in South Africa and of domestic jurisdiction—so much so that as early as 1949 the British Attorney General, Sir Hartley Shawcross, speaking in the Sixth Committee, was moved to say that his Government "deplored the fact that some States . . . denied international law and the International Court of Justice their proper place in the community of nations."[3] And two years later, his successor, Attorney General Heald, warned that "an organization which dealt with legal matters in a cavalier manner . . . would tend to subordinate the rule of law to considerations of expediency and convenience."[4]

[2] Manley Hudson, *International Tribunals, Past and Future* (1944), p.238.
[3] *General Assembly Official Records,* 4th Session, Sixth Committee (October 12, 1949), p.105.
[4] *General Assembly Official Records,* 6th Session, Sixth Committee (November 21, 1951), p.27.

The picture has not changed with the passage of time and one can say without exaggeration that neither the rule of law nor, as recent events demonstrate, due process of law have been among the chief preoccupations of the Assembly. It would be tempting to point the finger at the Great Powers and say, with Professor Kunz, that according to their political interests, they invoke the revolutionary purposes (Art. 1) or the traditional principles (Art. 2, par. 1 & 7)[5]; but this would minimize the politics of the rank and file of the UN membership, particularly of what is commonly called the Afro-Asian bloc, and its adverse influence on the role of international law in the UN and in international relations generally.

If the League could be charged with undue partiality to stability, the UN has exhibited, with a vengeance, a dynamic conception of international politics which has been facilitated by the prolonged absence of peace treaties, of agreed settlements at crucial points of East-West contacts, and the resulting political fluidity. While this dynamism may have been beneficial in speeding the liquidation of colonial holdings by European Powers without undue regard to what is sometimes contemptuously called "legal technicalities", it may also explain the failure of the UN to follow through on cease-fires with stable political settlements. Preoccupied with its fire-brigade function of peace-keeping with the glaring exception of Vietnam, the UN has, as the Secretary-General U Thant pointed out recently, neglected peace-making, as the periodic flare-ups in Palestine and Kashmir vividly demonstrate. The fault in my view is not with international law but with the UN which declines to apply it to the controversies brought before it. There may be wisdom in refraining from premature settlements but surely it is poor statesmanship to allow those differences to fester and poison the international atmosphere.

However, the UN is anything but a simple organization. If it does not suffer from split personality, one may say that it operates on several levels. Though paying little or no heed to law in its political activities, the work of the UN in promoting the progressive development of international law and its codification has been nothing short of spectacular. There is no space to recite in detail the conventions, among them the Genocide Convention, which were drafted by the Assembly and its Committees. Nor is it possible here to enumerate the results of the work of the International Law Commission which surely must be regarded as surprisingly successful in view of the forebodings voiced by authorities when it embarked upon its functions. The four Geneva Conventions on the Law of the Sea and the two Vienna Conventions on Diplomatic and Consular Relations are surely a rich harvest by any standard. And to this must be added the completed draft articles on the Law of Treaties which, it is expected, will be submitted to a diplomatic conference in 1968. The articles on the Law of Treaties may fairly be regarded as a contribution of first magnitude for the development of international law.

This aspect of the activities of the ILC the significance of which must not be underestimated is, however, not directly concerned with the maintenance of peace and security.

[5] Josef L. Kunz, "The United Nations and the Rule of Law", 41 *American Journal of International Law* 504–508 (1952) at p. 506.

In the work undertaken at the behest of the General Assembly and which was intended to strengthen the foundations of the new legal order initiated in the UN Charter, the Commission was successful in the sense that it delivered to the Assembly the Draft Declaration on Rights and Duties of States, the articles formulating the Nuremberg Principles, the Draft Code of Offenses against Peace and Security of Mankind, including a definition of aggression, and the Draft Code of Arbitral Procedure. All these drafts would have contributed substantially and were originally intended to contribute to the further evolution of the law of restraint which is, of course, of crucial importance for a stable international legal order. But the Assembly failed utterly and completely to continue the work of the Commission and bring it to a successful conclusion.

It is ironical to say the least that the Assembly which exhibits so much dynamism in its political activities and which attempts to further the progressive development of international law in many new fields including outer space by means of resolutions, should have censured the draft of arbitral procedure on the ground that the Commission

> had exceeded its terms of reference by giving preponderance to its desire to promote the development of international law instead of concentrating on its primary task (i.e.) the codification of custom.[6]

What the Assembly and its members, both old and new, wanted to express was that the traditional freedom of arbitral procedure with its manifold opportunities for frustrating the undertaking to arbitrate was deemed preferable to the procedure designed by the Commission to ensure that an undertaking to arbitrate should be carried out in good faith. Thus in this area the idea of liberty prevailed over the need for restraint.

While the contributions of the International Law Commission remain on the shelf, the Soviet Union, in the UN as well as in the International Law Association, raised the question of making the restraints on the use of force and intervention more explicit and more emphatic under the heading "Peaceful Co-existence". The title of the item was changed to "Consideration of Principles of International Law concerning Friendly Relations among States in accordance with the Charter of the United Nations", and a Special Committee, frankly political in character, was established in 1963 and has met twice with inconclusive results. It is obvious that any attempt to add to the restraints on the use of force already laid down in the law of Charter and which to a large extent have been nullified by practice, supported by teleological or "major purpose" methods of interpretation, would meet with determined political opposition. Thus it has been reported that at the Mexico City Conference of the Committee in 1964 the United States representative had provisionally approved a consensus paper one paragraph of which reads as follows:

> "Every State has the duty to refrain from the threat or use of force to violate the existing boundaries of another State."

[6] *Year Book of the International Law Commission*, vol. II (1958), p.80.

The United States representative was overridden by the Department of State which feared that this paragraph, which on its face appears to state an elementary principle of international law, might prejudice "any future application of the doctrine of hot pursuit in the Vietnam struggle".[7] It would seem that in a conflict, whether real or merely apparent, between the *raison d'état* and international law, international law is the loser. Put in a different way, short-term interests prevail over the long-term interests of States and of mankind.

In the field of the law of cooperation it would be difficult to find a comparable twenty-year period of such luxuriant growth. Established functional organizations have been continued and new agencies created some of which, such as the International Monetary Fund, operate in extremely sensitive areas of what was traditionally regarded as the reserved domain. Although we may still be far from realizing some of the ultimate objectives of the functional school, namely, the complete depoliticization of inter-state relations and the establishment of a stable peaceful order by the back door as it were, Governments and the elites in various countries have become acutely aware of the necessity of placing economic and social interdependence on solid institutional foundations. It has become evident, I believe, that the nation-States precisely because they are sovereign only in a limited territory, are incapable of regulating individually relationships which are essentially and increasingly trans-national in scope.

However, one of the fondest postulates of the functionalists, namely the elimination of politics from international cooperative agencies has come to grief. The relentless policy of the United States to exclude Communist China from the stream of international relations has penetrated every functional organization and every conference held under the auspices of the United Nations. More recently the Afro-Asian bloc has raised the issue of apartheid in functional organizations, aimed at the exclusion of South Africa and has scored some success. In so doing it has resorted to pressure tactics the constitutionality of which is a matter of some doubt.

## V

A discussion of "Peace and International Law" would be incomplete without a consideration of the International Court of Justice, the principal judicial organ of the United Nations. For better or worse the Court was made an integral part of the machinery of the United Nations serving its various purposes including peace and security. No substantial improvement was made in its jurisdiction. Proposals to make it compulsory were rejected in San Francisco. Thus, all members of the United Nations became automatically parties to the Statute of the Court, but this is only a matter of form. Jurisdiction remains optional and out of 122 members only 42 States Members, including twelve States "born" after 1945 and two non-members of the UN, have accepted the jurisdic-

[7] Edward McWhinney, "The 'New' Countries and the 'New' International Law", 60 *American Journal of International Law* 1–33 (1966) at p.15.

tion of the Court as compulsory. Much has been written about the decline of the compulsory jurisdiction of the Court and the regressing quality of the declarations by means of which States have signified their acceptance of the jurisdiction as obligatory for certain types of legal disputes.[8] Self-judging reservations of the Connally type and reservations *ratione temporis* permitting termination by notice to the Secretary-General and taking effect immediately are indicative of the cautious attitude of some States.

The relevant statistics are well-known. Since 1946 the Court was seised of 37 cases of which 8 were in the nature of a unilateral invitation to the other party to accept the jurisdiction of the Court. Of the remaining 29 cases, 13 were based on Art. 36, par. 2 of the Statute, 12 involved compulsory jurisdiction based on other instruments, three came by way of a special agreement and one case involved the interpretation of a previous judgment. The Court rendered 28 judgments of which only 13 were on merits including the Judgment of July 18, 1966, in the South West Africa cases, which, however, was officially called 'Second Phase', the Court having declined to rule on the merits. There are only two cases, the Barcelona Traction Company (Belgium-Spain) and the Continental Shelf cases (Denmark/Germany; and Netherlands/Germany) pending. The present Court's predecessor, the Permanent Court of International Justice was seised of 66 cases and gave 32 judgments.

If the reduction in the number of judgments may not be a cause of concern, the decline in the advisory jurisdiction is most remarkable. The Permanent Court received 28 requests whereas the International Court received only 12 requests, 10 from the General Assembly, and one each from the ILO and IMCO. No request has been made since 1961. In order to appreciate the drastic deterioration it is necessary to bear in mind that in the case of the Permanent Court only two organs, the Assembly and the Council of the League, were entitled to request advisory opinions, whereas in the case of the present Court, 27 organs of the United Nations, Specialized Agencies and the International Atomic Energy Agency are empowered to request advisory opinions. It may also be pointed out that whereas in the League, rightly or wrongly, unanimity in the Council was required, in the organs of the United Nations and Specialized Agencies only a qualified majority is required. And finally, during the life-time of the old court all requests came from the Council of the League but the Security Council of the UN has never requested an opinion.

All this may be taken as indicative of the role of international law in the work of the United Nations. Although the Security Council is reminded in Art. 36, par 3 of the Charter that "legal disputes should as a general rule be referred by the parties to the International Court of Justice", the Council only once, in the Corfu Channel dispute, made such a recommendation.

The explanations for the stagnation or perhaps, more correctly, retrogression of the judicial functions are legion. Some writers trace it to prevailing tensions, others to the

[8] H. Waldock, "Decline of the Optional Clause", 32 *British Year Book of International Law* 244 (1955–1956).

lack of confidence in the composition of the Court and the law that it applies. Somewhat along the same line is the view of some writers that the law which the Court applies is static and a protector of the *status quo,* that the law is obsolete in that it fails to take into account social and economic factors, and that what some States, particularly the new States, desire is a change in the law and not the application of existing law. Still another group of writers point out that recourse to the Court may be regarded as an unfriendly act, and that the prohibition of the use of force by the Charter has removed an incentive, particularly for smaller States, to seek the protection of the Court. In this connection it will be recalled that the Institute of International Law adopted in 1959 a resolution declaring that inasmuch as resort to force has been outlawed, recourse to the Court constitutes a normal method for the settlement of legal disputes and that, consequently, such recourse must never be regarded as an unfriendly act toward the respondent State.

Whatever the correct explanation may be—and there is an element of truth in each of them—, there is no point, I feel, in gainsaying the fact that States, by and large, old and new, prefer to rely on negotiations or on the political and highly politicized procedures of the United Nations or of regional organizations as the forum for handling disputes in which they happen to be involved or in which they happen to have a stake. In the United Nations the risk is limited: the worst that can happen is an unfavorable resolution which is not legally binding and which can be challenged on the ground that it is not based on the applicable law; but more often the result of the proceedings is a stalemate. And Governments seem to prefer stalemate rather than run the risk of an unfavorable judgment by the Court which is final, legally binding and based on the impersonal criteria of law. As long as Governments seek security from law rather than security through law, no improvement in the situation is to be expected.

Thus the contribution which the Court was enabled to make to the maintenance of peace through law has been very limited. In spite of this, its role in the development of international law has been substantial and its jurisprudence does not bear out the charge that it applies static law or that it is impervious to economic or social factors. Anyone who seriously studies the jurisprudence of the Court cannot help but be impressed with the boldness of the Court as an innovator. Suffice it to recall its Advisory Opinions in the Reparation for Injuries and Genocide cases, and its judgments in the Corfu Channel, the Anglo-Norwegian Fisheries, and the Nottebohm cases. In some instances the Court preferred judicial caution to judicial boldness. Its recent judgment in the South-West Africa cases which has been violently attacked in some quarters may be seen as an example of judicial caution and in the view of some of its critics as an example of misplaced judicial abstention. If the Court ever is given an opportunity to rule in a similar case, there is enough material in the seven dissenting opinions for the Court to change or modify its judgment. In any event its weight as a precedent is not likely to be great. However, whether one agrees or disagrees with the Court's judgment, it required, in my view, boldness, deep conviction and a sense of duty to decide the case against the applicants. And it is open to question whether the Court made a greater contribution to peace and the eventual solution of the problem, presented to it, by deciding the way it did rather by deciding it the way preferred by an equal number of judges.

For the Court was faced with fundamental questions of policy. This may not be apparent from a reading of the judgment but it is revealed, I believe, in some of the dissenting opinions. And that question related to the weight to be given—with a degree of retroactivity—to the changes in the attitude of States manifested chiefly in the General Assembly with respect to human rights including *apartheid* and the many problems of colonialism, in construing the terms of the mandate, its jurisdiction clause and Article 22 of the Covenant which were all drafted by another generation imbued with different values.

## VI

And this brings me to my last point, which is the role of the General Assembly in shaping and developing international law as part of its function to promote peace and security. While only few Governments and scholars would be prepared to go so far as to claim that the Assembly currently fulfils the role of an international legislature, there is no unanimity at all about the weight to be attached to the resolutions of the Assembly as an element in the formation of international law. It is by resolutions which are generally regarded as legally not binding that the Assembly expresses its view or policy with respect to such matters as human rights, colonialism, economic development, outer space, etc. Some would like to see in such resolutions, particularly when they are repeated over and over again, a sort of abbreviated process for the development of customary international law, while others are not prepared to modify their view on the traditional sources of law. This cleavage can be seen even in the recent judgment. While the decision of the Court in the South West Africa cases sharply distinguished between law and policy as evidenced in the relevant resolutions of the General Assembly, among the dissenters there are judges who would go so far as to say that the latter were evidence of a new norm of international law binding upon the Mandatory while others would go no further than construe them as evidence of an international standard to be applied in determining whether the Mandatory has fulfilled its obligations under the Mandate and the 'sacred trust' principle of the Covenant.

It is by no means self-evident, I submit, that the proliferating pronouncements made by majorities of the General Assembly should receive or are entitled to receive from the Court a judicial imprimatur as norms or standards of international law, in the light of the fact that these products of "parliamentary diplomacy" are the result of *mariages de convenance* and a trading of voting favors carried on with perfect *insouciance* by the delegations precisely because they themselves attribute no such significance to their bargains and the ensuing resolutions. A vote cast for a resolution is neither necessarily the manifestation of a conviction that it is in conformity with the law of the Charter or that it is productive of a rule or norm or standard of international law or any sort of obligation whatever. They are moves in the checkered game of pressure politics so characteristic of the United Nations, although some resolutions, by their origin, scope and purpose are entitled to be appreciated as elements in the formation of new or the weakening of old rules of law.

Whatever view one takes of the law-making role of the General Assembly—and we are still far from a consensus—it is encouraging to note that international lawyers have shown a growing disposition to re-examine the traditional sources of international law. The Court may well have a contribution to make to the formation of such a consensus in this twilight area between politics and law.

## VII

What then are the conclusions to be drawn from the preceding analysis as to the future role of international law in preserving peace? About 50 years ago, Elihu Root, in the second year of World War I, addressed himself to the problem and said:

> "Law cannot control national policy, and it is through the working of long-continued and persistent national policies that the present war has come . . . But law, if enforced, can control the external steps by which a nation seeks to follow a policy, and rules may be so framed that a policy of aggression cannot be worked out except through open violation of law which will meet protest and condemnation of the world at large, backed by whatever means shall have been devised for law enforcement."[9]

Since then some progress has been made in formulating the rules Mr. Root had in mind which I have here called the law of restraint. In some instances involving even powers of the first rank, as in the 1956 Suez crisis, it has been possible to make the restraint effective. But when a Super-power becomes directly involved in hostilities, as the Soviet Union in Hungary in 1956, or as the United States currently in Vietnam, the processes devised by States for enforcing restraint upon States are ineffective or paralysed. The law of restraint in such cases which fortunately have been infrequent will be enforced by self-restraint or not at all. Put in another way, unless and until there is a revolutionary change in international relations, the law of restraint will, in the case of the Super-powers, depend on self-restraint. As international law cannot operate by and of itself, it can be effective only to the extent that Governments can be induced to make it effective, in response to outside pressure, whether it takes the more tangible form of action by the United Nations, or the less tangible manifestation of an aroused public opinion. But public opinion needs to have a guide and a base in an objective determination of the facts. This requirement for public opinion as a sanction of international law has been known at least since 1899 when the Hague Conference gave prominence to the procedure of fact-finding. Never has such a process been more needed than at present. The Charter makes provision for investigations but this provision has not been activated. The recent British initiative in putting the problem of fact-finding on the agenda of the General Assembly is to be welcomed but it would be unreasonable to expect spectacular results. The last thing which

[9] *Proceedings of the American Society of International Law,* vol. 9, 2–11 (1915) at p.7.

Governments seem to want when they resort to substantial violence is an objective determination of the facts. They prefer that public opinion feed on the facts as they appear to them as interested parties, that is, on their version of the truth.

More recently, only ten years ago, an eminent scholar, Charles de Visscher, raised the question:

> "Is the pessimism at present exhibited by certain scholars with regard to current prospects of international law completely reasonable? More particular, is it really justifiable to speak of a deterioration in the judicial methods of settling disputes?"[10]

In his opinion the pessimism is not justified in so far as international law and the judicial method *per se* are concerned. It is the external factors which are responsible for the deterioration of both law and the judicial function. These factors include the absence of peace treaties and their stabilizing role, the increased politicization of international relations and the resulting tensions, all of them in different ways, concludes Prof. de Visscher, "weigh heavily upon the attitude of governments, which are already naturally little inclined to divest themselves of the settlement of their disputes in favor of international tribunals. They fear both the effect of the process and the repercussions however distant, of the judgment."[11] And he agrees with Politis that justice will not bring peace but that peace will bring justice.[12] In short, international law takes its place behind statecraft, it is led but does not lead.

This may be so, but behind the statesmen are the people, at least in democratic societies. And, to conclude on a hopeful note, it may be reasonable to assume that as the peoples gradually and progressively become more assertive and aware of their interests, they will steer their governments away from the traditional preoccupation with power toward new goals. Political modernization, economic development and social welfare have become the chief and urgent objectives of domestic policy. It must and will be realized that these goals cannot be achieved on the internal, domestic plane unless they also become the objectives of foreign policy on the international plane. It has been said that a society cannot be half free and half slave. In the same vein it may be said that we cannot have a "great society" at home and international anarchy abroad.

The functional approach has suffered some setbacks, but the development of the international law of cooperation has been steady, impressive and by and large responsive to the needs of an interdependent world. The law of restraint must continue to be based on self-restraint, a precarious but in the foreseeable future at any rate, the only foundation on which a law for sovereign States can be based. But the law of international cooperation holds promise of future growth and ultimately of a stable international order.

Finally, I submit, it is as unrealistic to expect international law by itself to usher in

[10] Charles de Visscher, "Reflections on the Present Prospects of International Adjudication", 50 *American Journal of International Law* 467–474 (1956) at p.467.
[11] Loc., cit., at p.474.
[12] Politis, *La Justice Internationale* pp.253–254.

an era of peace as it is misleading to attribute the outbreak of war to a breakdown of international law. In truth, it is not international law that breaks down but statesmanship. Just as in domestic life it is the task of statecraft to anticipate revolution, that is, the breakdown of law and order, by a timely process of peaceful change and adjustments in the law, so in the international society it is the task of statesmen to anticipate violence and war by a process of peaceful change and adjustment in international law. Law and adjudication are but tools of diplomacy and recourse to violence and war are indicative of a breakdown of diplomacy. The formula that war is diplomacy by other means was coined by a general and adopted by Governments to conceal their own short-comings. International lawyers should reject the proposition that war is due to a breakdown of the law; the opposite, I believe, is true: international law breaks down because Governments responding to elitist pressures and guided by unrealistic assumptions choose to pursue their objectives by other means, that is, by recourse to force and war.

# SOURCES OF UNIVERSAL INTERNATIONAL LAW

It may be useful to ask at the outset what meaning is intended to convey by the words "universal international law." It is a relatively new phrase which has come into vogue in the last few years, probably as a result of more intensely perceived ideological division in the world, the insistence on a common set of values as a precondition for a viable legal order, and, more recently, the challenge to the traditional body of doctrine and precept emanating from new States in Asia and Africa. It may be a matter of judgement whether the various controversies are of greater importance to scholars or to state practice. To be sure, the world is ideologically divided; the existence of common values among the different States and cultures is a matter of doubt, and jurists in various countries are preoccupied with the attitude, or more concisely, attitudes of new States toward international law. The actual impact of these factors on international law is not so easily perceived. Surely, international law is evolving, as it has in the past, in response to new needs, to technological developments, to the family of nations. No one in his right mind would want to have it otherwise. But clearly the forward movement of the law has not been the same in all its branches.

Leaving aside the law of warfare, it may be useful to distinguish three branches of international law: constitutional law, the law of cooperation and the law of restraint. Constitutional law is what one finds in most text-books—subjects of international law, recognition, succession, jurisdiction and its limitations, territory, high seas, treaties, responsibility, diplomatic and consular relations and such. This branch of the law is largely common or customary international law although it has been possible, through the efforts of the United Nations, to formulate in conventions a substantial body of this law—high seas, territorial seas, fisheries, continental shelf, consular and diplomatic relations. The law of treaties is on its way towards conferences of plenipotentiaries and, hopefully, a convention. Other items such as succession and responsibility of States are soon to be taken up by the International Law Commission.[1] Also, the Commission decided to put in hand the study of the most-favoured-nation clause in the law of treaties, a topic of substantial interest to new States.[2] The topics of state responsibility and succession of States and Governments in respect of treaties and in respect of rights and duties resulting from sources other than treaties have been of great interest to the new States and, if one may say so, their prime targets of criticism. Their viewpoints and interests in those subjects will now be expressed and formulated in the proper forum.

In this branch of the law it is well to recall that there is generally "a common basis of agreement on principle" but "a wide divergence of practice in the matter of its detailed application."[3] Hence there is some opportunity for codification but an even larger need for progressive development.

The law of cooperation, which started in the 19th century and has come to regulate an impressively large segment of transnational relations, is based essentially on conventions. Some of them in the area of communications, established permanent institutions in which nearly all existing States, whether new or old, participate. They are the translation into law of convergent interests. As far as one can determine, these instruments have met with general acceptance by the new States.

The third branch of international law, the law of restraint, is rather novel and may be said to be still in an experimental stage. Concerned as it is with limitations upon the use of force as an instrument of national policy, it obviously may come into conflict with that policy. Beginning with the Hague Peace Conferences of 1899 and 1919, through the League of Nations, the Kellogg-Briand Pact, the law of restraint was believed to have found a solid framework in the United Nations. But the relevant Charter provisions have been eroded through facile interpretations, and acute conflicts of interest have contributed to the undermining of its social foundation. There may be some consolation in recalling the indictment of the unilateral use of force by the International Court of Justice in the *Corfu Channel* case:

> The Court can only regard the alleged right of intervention as the manifestation of a policy of force, such as has, in the past, given rise to most serious abuses and such as cannot, whatever be the present defects in international organization, find a place in international law.[4]

To make this pronouncement effective is a task for the future. But the impotence of the United Nations in the face of latent conflicts between Member States and of open warfare in Vietnam suggests the inference that the law of restraint will not work without self-restraint on the part of old and new States.

The question of universality of international law, in the contemporary discussion

[1] Report of the International Law Commission on the work of its nineteenth session, 8 May–14 May 1967. *GAOR* 22nd Sess., Supp. No. 9 (A/C 709/Rev.1), p. 24 f.

[2] *Ibid.*, p. 25.

[3] Survey of International Law. Memorandum submitted by the Secretary-General, Doc. A/CN. 4/1, 5 November 1948. Sales No. 1948, Vol. 1, p. 7.

[4] I.C.J. *Reports*, 1949, pp. 4, 35.

can now be concretely examined with respect to these three branches of the law. No doubt all States have an interest in the law of restraint, and there does not appear to be any particular reason why this law, whatever its weakness, should not be acceptable to new as well as old States. From the formal point of view they are all bound by the Charter which currently is the principal source of that law. The law of co-operation appears to offer no particular target for criticism. Any State which finds it against its interest can opt out and shift for itself. However, this branch of the law, in the view of many jurists, does not go far enough in promoting the socio-economic interests of the new States. A law of social welfare may be highly desirable, and no doubt some progress has been made along multilateral and bilateral lines. Much more needs to be done but the obstacles are many and progress is impeded by divergent political goals. The 1964 UNCTAD Conference has brought into the open the demands of the developing nations and the resistance of some of the developed countries to majority rule. A reconciliation of goals and means for their achievement will not be brought about by an accumulation of voting victories. Patient and persistent confrontation of reasoned arguments may well be a slow but promising path to progress. The contingency that if, in this area, no universally acceptable rules can be created by a process of compromise and adjustment of the interests involved "regional systems of international law would tend to develop among the emerging states, on the one hand, and the western States, on the other,"[5] is hardly a realistic alternative. This may not be a promising segment of international relations for the growth of universal international law, but it is even less so for a regional system of emerging States, most of which share a lack of capital in order to develop whatever natural and human resources they may have.

In the past, capital exporting countries could invoke rules alleged to be rules of universal or general international law according to which expropriation of foreign private property was improper unless it was for a public purpose, non-discriminatory, and the owner received prompt, adequate, and effective compensation. The standard of compensation was stated somewhat differently in the Hickenlooper Amendment to the United States Foreign Assistance Act of 1961: "speedy compensation for such property in convertible foreign exchange, equivalent to the full value thereof, as required by international law."[6] But is this sort of compensation really required by international law and, if so, is this standard one of general or universal compensation? In the *Sabbatino* Case Justice Harlan speaking for the Supreme Court, found that:

> certain representatives of the newly independent and underdeveloped countries have questioned whether rules of state-responsibility toward aliens can bind nations that have not consented to them and it is argued that the traditionally articulated standards governing expropriation of property reflect "imperialist" interests and are inappropriate to the circumstances of emergent States.[7]

[5] S. Prakash Shinha, *New Nations and the Law of Nations* (Leyden: Sijthoff 1967), p. 145.

[6] U.S.C. 2370

[7] *Banco Nacional de Cuba v. Sabbatino*, U.S. Supreme Court, 23 March 1964, 376 U.S. 396, *AJIL* (Washington), Vol. 58 (1964), p. 792, pp. 779–814.

It may not have been necessary to argue that the standards reflect "imperialist" interests, for it stands to reason that no investment would have been or will be made without suitable guarantees against seizure by arbitrary fiat of Governments. It may have been sufficient to say that these standards appeared now to be inappropriate to the circumstances of emergent States generally—as if they constituted a separate class of States—or of some of them or to some of the investments, namely, those reflecting imperialist interests of exploitation rather than genuine participation in promoting economic development.

In any event, it will be a matter for consideration whether and to what extent there are many sources of law which could be mobilized to maximize the interests of developing countries without sacrificing the legitimate interest of investors.

This leads us to the third branch of the law, the constitutional part of it. Indeed, the rules concerning expropriation, while extremely relevant in the context of economic cooperation, have traditionally formed part of this branch of the law. So do the rules regarding succession referred to above. The developing countries have concentrated their attacks on the constitutional branch of international law, for here rather than in connection with the other two branches, the argument seemed to have a degree of plausibility that traditional international law reflected essentially or exclusively the interests of Western States and could not automatically be assumed to apply to the new States. A variant of the same attack is derived from the theory of consent: if international law derives its binding force from the consent of States, it cannot be held binding on new States which have never consented to it, and, moreover, would not find it to their advantage to do so.

It is not necessary to argue this point in the context of this paper but it may be helpful to point out: first, the new States do not reject all of this branch of international law.[8] Secondly, assuming the validity of the principle that new States are bound by common or customary international law, it is by no means evident whether all or only a part of it can be deemed to be of such generality as to become automatically binding on new States; thirdly, as noted earlier, there is much less "hard" law than one might be led to believe on the basis of textbooks, though there may be agreement on broad principles; and finally, a good deal of the constitutional branch of international law has the character of dispositive law, that is, it lays down guidelines for the action of States but does not compel or require action. Thus the rules concerning statehood, recognition, treaties, diplomatic relations, do not require States to establish or recognize States. They do not require States to enter into treaties or establish diplomatic relations; if States want to do any of these things, they ought to be done in conformity with certain procedures and principles.

Representatives of new States have occasionally criticized positivism and its reliance

[8] See the excellent paper by R.P. Anand, "Role of the 'New' Asian-African Countries in the Present International Legal Order," *AJIL*, Vol. 56 (1962), p. 388, pp. 383–406: Sinha on the other hand, while admitting that new States have, generally speaking, "these existing principles of international law which are helpful in promoting their national interests," they have "rejected or criticized those which tend to obstruct realization of their national interests," *loc. cit.*, pp. 80 and 137. It may be observed that such a selective approach to the precepts of international law on the part of new States may justify a similar selective approach on the part of the old States, and that it is by no means self-evident that this would be to the advantage of new States.

on the practice of States, which has been, sometimes, identified with the practice of the Great Powers. Positivism has also been attacked by those who wish the International Court of Justice to play a more creative part in the application of law to concrete disputes.[9] It is true, of course, that the positivist approach values highly the practice of States, not merely the practice of the Great Powers, but "the concerdant and recurring action of numerous States in the domain of international relations," it also requires proof that in each case "such action was enjoined by law."[10] The International Court of Justice, in particular, has, in conformity with Article 38 of its Statute, affirmed the need of *opinio juris,* that is, of the conviction of respecting a legal norm.[11] In at least three cases the Court has made clear its conception of customary international law in conformity with the positivist approach—the *Asylum,* and *Anglo-Norwegian Fisheries,* and the *Rights of United States Nationals in Morocco* cases.[12] To quote the pronouncements of the Court on this subject in only one case, the *Asylum* case, the Court said:

> The party which relies on a custom of this kind must prove that this custom is established in such a manner that it has become binding on the other party. The Colombian Government must prove that the rule invoked by it is in accordance with a constant and uniform usage practised by the States in question, and that this usage is the expression of a right appertaining to the States granting asylum and a duty incumbent on territorial States.[13]

This could be interpreted as confined to the particular facts of the case, were it not for the immediately following sentence:

> This follows from Article 38 of the Statute of the Court, which refers to international custom "as evidence of the general practice accepted as law."[14]

This puts the Court's pronouncement on a broad base and vouchsafes for it the nature of a construction of Article 38 insofar as it relates to international custom. The positivist approach, thus conceived and applied, hardly offers a profitable target for criticism on the part of new States. If it should cause unhappiness to anybody, it would be to the old States whose pretensions of law are thus thrown into jeopardy. It may well be that a good deal of that which has been presented as law in the textbooks and invoked by Governments in political discourse may have to be eliminated when subjected to the close scrutiny of the court.

After the preliminary observations, the problem of the sources of universal international law will be examined. Potentially, treaties, custom, general principles of law, and judgments of the International Court of Justice and arbitral tribunals may be regarded as

[9] Jenks C. Wilfred, *The Prospects of International Adjudictaion* (London, 1964), p. 217 ff.

[10] Manley O. Hudson, *The Permanent Court of International Justice, 1920–1942.* (New York, 1934), p. 609; See also Clive Parry, *The Sources and Evidence of International Law* (Manchester, 1965), p. 62 ff.

[11] Charles de Visscher, *Theories et Realities on Droit International Public* (3rd ed), p. 480.

[12] I.C.J. *Reports* (1950), pp. 266, 276–7; 1951, pp. 106, 131, and 1952, p. 176, at 200.

[13] I.C.J. *Reports,* 1950, p. 266.

[14] *Ibid.,* pp. 276–7.

sources. This selection is made without entering into the doctrinal debate whether Article 38 of the Statute of the Court represents a general statement of the sources of international law or merely a specific directive to the Court on how to adjudicate upon disputes submitted to it. It is also considered unnecessary in the present context, to express any view of the meaning or meanings of the term "source." Finally, the potential of the General Assembly of the United Nations for law-making shall be considered.

## TREATIES

There is a record of many treaties which, though concluded between a limited number of States, has contained or produced principles which have found universal acceptance. Thus the Paris Convention of 13 October 1919, relating to the Regulation of Aerial Navigation, which never counted more than 37 parties, proclaimed in Article 1: "The High Contracting Parties recognize that every Power has complete and exclusive sovereignty over the air space about its territory . . . and the territorial waters adjacent thereto." This rule was confirmed by the Chicago Convention of 7 December 1944, on International Civil Aviation. There is no doubt that this rule has become part of universal international law regardless of the number of States which have actually become parties to either Convention. The Soviet Union, for instance, is party to neither Convention but is entitled to sovereignty over its air space.

Further examples are the Conventions on the Law of the Sea of 1958. Apart from the fact that some of the rules formulated in these Conventions, particularly those on the High Seas and on the Territorial Sea, may claim to be in force for all States as part of customary international law, the Convention on the Continental Shelf lays down a principle which must now be regarded as having the character of universal international law. Article 2(1) states: "The coastal State exercises over the continental shelf sovereign rights for the purpose of exploring it and exploiting its natural resources." It is not necessary, in this context, to examine the Vienna Conventions on Diplomatic Relations of 1961 and on Consular Relations of 1963. Both Conventions affirm in the Preamble 'that the rules of customary international law should continue to govern questions ("matters" in the 1963 Convention) not expressly regulated by the provisons of the present Convention." Whatever the reasons may have been for inserting this "saving" clause, it is clear that in matters regulated expressly the Conventions shall prevail over customary international law.

The draft Articles on the Law of Treaties have already been mentioned. If and when embodied into a formal convention, they will clarify such controversial matters as reservation, error, fraud, coercion of the State or its representative, *jus cogens,* impossibility of performance, *rebus sic stantibus, pacta sunt servanda,* and many others of interest to both the old and new States. In an area where there has hardly been either time or opportunity for the evolution of customary international law, the General Assembly by resolution 2222 (XXI) of 19 December 1966, adopted the text of the Treaty Governing the Activities of States in the Exploration and Use of Outer Space, including the Moon and Other Celestial Bodies. No doubt the rules laid down in this Treaty will come to be regarded as having the character of universal international law regardless of the number of contracting parties.

The work of the International Law Commission on succession of States and Governments and on state responsibility, to which reference has been made earlier in this paper, will provide many opportunities for discussing concrete proposals from new States concerning the law in these uncertain and controversial areas.

The treaty process, then, may be said to offer a useful approach to the universalization of international law in certain areas of transnational relations.

In conclusion it may be observed that a treaty, though formulating principles intended for universal application, will not achieve this objective unless it is supported by the essential States. Essential States, in this context, refers to States without whose consent and acceptance the Treaty is not likely to achieve its intended purpose. Thus, a convention along the lines of the principles adopted by the 1964 UNCTAD Conference, even if accepted by a very large number of States, will not be productive unless it is also accepted by the very small number of economically developed countries. Law and politics can never be completely divorced.

## CUSTOM

Frequently regarded as the prime source of universal international law, custom has come to be looked upon as inadequate to cope with the rapidly evolving needs of an expanding society of nations. It has, for a time at least, been rejected by writers in the Soviet Union, although their position seems to have undergone a change.[15] On the other hand, custom by its very nature is slow in emerging from the practice of States accepted as law. By comparison, the treaty process appears more rapid, even if often extremely slow, and more flexible in meeting concrete requirements of States. However, the process of creating rules of customary international law needs to be examined in connection with the functioning of international organizations.

## GENERAL PRINCIPLES OF LAW

The clause in Article 38(1*c*) of its Statute directing the Court to apply "the general principles of law recognized by civilized nations" was understood to emphasize "the creative role to be played by the Court," and "has been widely hailed as a refutation of the extreme positive conception of international law, and even as revolutionary."[16] In actual

[15] Lissitzyn, *loc. cit*, pp. 46 ff. The textbook *International Law*, issued by the Institute of State and Law, Academy of Sciences of the U.S.S.R., in 1960, refers at p. 12 to international law although it gives priority to treaties and states: "Neglect for International Treaty Law and an exaggeration of the importance of international custom is characteristic of many bourgeois jurists. This is in line with the policy of certain imperialist circles, a policy of violating treaty obligations and giving legal form to illegal international practices under the label of 'international custom'."

[16] Hudson, *loc. cit.*, at p. 611.

the General Assembly. Throughout the years the Assembly may be said to have tried, first, to revitalize international law and to deal with the fundamentals of a new international legal order. Secondly, it has contributed to the development and codification of traditional law and, thirdly, to the formulation of principles in areas not yet governed by international law. In order to achieve or promote these objectives the Assembly has proceeded pragmatically, using a variety of media, including the International Law Commission or *ad hoc* committees or conferences, and has embodied the results in conventions or resolutions. A few selected examples will illustrate the pertinent activities of the United Nations.

Within the third field of its endeavors, the General Assembly, by Resolution 1962 (XVIII) of December 13, 1963, adopted the "Declaration of Legal Principles Governing the Activities of States in the Exploration and Use of Outer Space" and by Resolution 1963 (XVIII) of the same day formulated the legal principles involved in "International co-operation in the peaceful uses of outer space."[14] These basic resolutions in a new field of concern to Members emanated from the Committee on the Peaceful Uses of Outer Space which was established by the Assembly and which reported to the First (Political and Security) and not the Sixth (Legal) Committee. The legal significance of these resolutions in the formulation of international law will be discussed later. Insofar as Resolution 1962 (XVIII) is concerned, it proposed no further steps. By contrast, Resolution 1963 (XVIII) recommended that consideration should be given "to incorporating in international agreement form" legal principles governing the exploration and use of outer space. The Assembly considered, then, that these principles needed, in order to become fully binding, to be incorporated in a treaty, the classic medium of international legislation. The same medium was considered, in the same resolution, necessary for formulating principles concerning liability for damage caused by objects launched into outer space and assistance to and return of astronauts and space vehicles. The Assembly's Committee on the Peaceful Uses of Outer Space was charged with the necessary preparatory work. Resolutions 1721 D (XVI) of December 20, 1961, and 1802 IV (XVII) of December 14, 1962, on satellite communications have already been implemented by the "Agreement Establishing Interim Arrangements for a Global Commercial Communication Satellite System" of July 24, 1964, which entered into force on August 20, 1964.[15]

## The Work and Contributions of the International Law Commission

For purposes of codification and progressive development of international law the Assembly has relied chiefly on the International Law Commission, an autonomous body established by Resolution 174 (II) of November 21, 1947, which incorporates the Statute

[14] The Assembly dealt in Resolutions 1802 (XVII) of December 14, 1962, 1721 (XVI) of December 20, 1961, and 1472 (XIV) of December 12, 1959, with the problem of the peaceful uses of outer space.

[15] *United States Treaties and Other International Acts Series,* No. 5646 (Washington, D.C.: U.S. Government Printing Office, 1964). See also, James Simsarian, "Interim Arrangements for a Global Commercial Satellite System," *The American Journal of International Law,* April 1965 (Vol. 59, No. 2), pp. 344–351.

As already noted, both Courts, the Permanent Court and the International Court, have made only sparing and occasional use of Article 38(1*c*). One or two pronouncements will be recalled. In the *Chrozow (Merits)* case, the Court observed:

> It is a principle of international law, and even a general conception of law, that any breach of an engagement involves an obligation to make repartion.[24]

It may be noted that, strictly speaking, the reference to "a general conception of law" was unnecessary. In the same case the Court stated another general principle:

> It is, moreover, a principle generally accepted in the jurisprudence of international arbitration, as well as by municipal courts, that One party cannot avail himself of the fact that the other has not fulfilled some obligation or has had recourse to some means of redress, if the former Party has, by some alleged act, prevented the latter from fulfilling the obligation in question, or from having recourse to the tribunal which would have been open to him.[25]

Here, too, the reference to "municipal courts" may be regarded as unnecessary.

In the *German Settlers* case the Court held without any reference to general principles: "Private rights acquired under existing law do not cease on a change of sovereignty."[26]

In a later judgement, in the *Polish Upper Silesia* case, the Court was more explicit in saying:

> . . . this follows from the principle of respect for vested rights, a principle which, as the Court has already had occasion to observe, forms part of generally accepted international law.[27]

It would seem unnecessary to quote the propositions from separate and dissenting opinions on such principles as *res judicata* and others. It may be more relevant to recall some of the cautionary statements which tend to indicate limits upon the capacity of the Court to draw upon general principles of law. Thus Judge Read, in his Dissenting Opinion in the *Nottebohm* case, stated:

> The Court cannot determine 'generally recognized principles' or decide cases on the basis of such principles. Its competence is limited by the peremptory and mandatory provisions of Article 38 of the Statute, to decisions 'in accordance with international law.'[28]

On the other hand, Judge Moreno Quintana, in his Separate Opinion in the *Guardianship* case, sought to overcome the apparent tension between these two mandatory provisions:

[24] P.C.I.J., Series A, No. 17, p. 29.
[25] *Ibid.*, p. 31.
[26] Advisory Opinion No. 6, 10 September 1923, Series 3, No. 6, p. 36.
[27] P.C.I.J., Series A, No. 7, p. 42.
[28] I.C.J. *Reports*, p. 37.

> *Ordre public* is indissolubly bound up with the general principles of law recognized by civilized nations which, under Article 38, paragraph 1(*c*) of the Statute, the Court is required to apply as a main source of law in discharging its function of deciding in accordance with international law such disputes as are submitted to it.[29]

Still on the same theme, the statement by Judge Chagla, in his Dissenting Opinion in the *Right of Passage* case, is apposite:

> A principle of international law may also be imported from municipal law where the principle is universally recognized and when that principle is not in conflict with any rule of international law itself.[30]

Finally, concerning the method of applying a general principle of law, Judge Lauterpacht, in his Separate Opinion in the *Guardianship* case, stated:

> Clearly, it is not the Swedish notion of *ordre public* which can provide the exclusive standard in this connection. The answer is that, the notion of *ordre public*—of public policy—being a general legal conception, its contents must be determined in the same way as that of any other general principle of law, in the sense of Article 38 of the Statute, namely, by reference to the practice and experience of the municipal law of civilized nations in that field.[31]

Enough has been said that drawing upon general principles of law can never be a simple matter. It is one thing to invoke some general maxims of law as both Courts have done on rare occasions; it is another to make systematic use of them. It will also be noted that many, if not most or all, of the maxims relate to the adjective rather than substantive law.[32] However, in spite of Judge Lauterpacht's injunction that general principles of law would have to be applied "by reference to the practice and experience of municipal law", a task of staggering proportions, the possibility cannot be excluded that in the future, and under appropriate circumstances, recourse may be had to such principles as a source of universal international law.

In the context of the controversy concerning compensation for expropriated property of an alien individual or corporation, it may be permitted to refer to the principle of "unjust enrichment" which Lord McNair suggested could be one "of the rules of law likely to be recognized as 'general principles'."[33] This principle was applied in the *Lena Goldfields Arbitration* in 1930, but as Lord McNair points out, the Soviet Government "as the result of negotiations, finally agreed to pay a sum very much less than the amount awarded against it."[34] Apart from this, the principle of unjust enrichment hardly offers a

29 I.C.J. *Reports* 1958, p. 107.
30 I.C.J. *Reports* 1957, p. 177.
31 I.C.J. *Reports* 1958, p. 92.
32 Parry, *loc. cit.*, p. 87.
33 *Ibid.*, p. 15 f.
34 *Ibid.*, at p. 12. The Soviet Government withdrew its arbitrator from the tribunal of arbitration which nonetheless made the award.

definite or precise yardstick for measuring the quantum of compensation. Would it be unreasonable, for instance, for the tribunal to consider the benefits which the state or country concerned derived from the operation of, say, a concession along with the benefits which the foreign company derived from it, and fix the amount of compensation accordingly? What is the practice and experience of municipal law and courts in this matter? Or, along the lines of Judge McNair's statement quoted above, what is the underlying policy of that principle which could usefully be adopted by international tribunals? Speaking generally of concession or as he prefers to call them, "economic development agreements", Lord McNair makes the following observation which seems to bear on the above point:

> In practice it is generally found that the company which undertakes the task of developing the resources of a foreign undeveloped country finds it either desirable or necessary to engage in a very considerable social programme for the purpose of securing decent conditions of life for its employees, including the provision of hospital, education and other social facilities.[35]

This must be considered a wise counsel for foreign investors and, it is submitted, should be a factor in determining "unjust enrichment." But would it be in accordance with principles of justice and fair dealing to go beyond that and inquire whether and what the holder of an "economic development agreement" has contributed to the development of the economy of the country concerned in determining whether the taking country has enriched itself in offering to pay no compensation or what may appear on its face as only a modest compensation?

The principle of unjust enrichment, properly understood and refined in the context of principles of economic development, may well commend itself for consideration as a principle of universal international law.

## INTERNATIONAL COURT OF JUSTICE

It seems almost unnecessary to discuss the question whether the jurisprudence of international tribunals and particularly that of the two World Courts can be or has been a source of universal international law. However, a few observations of a general nature may be useful.

It is obvious from a study of the major works on international law, that great importance is attached by jurists to pronouncements of international tribunals, and to their function as expositors of international law. A proposition of law is deemed to rest on secure foundations if it is based on an award or judgment. Insofar as the present Court is concerned, it is directed "to decide in accordance with international law" disputes submitted to it. Unless the Opinion of the Court can be based on a treaty or convention

[35] *Ibid.*, p. 2.

or another act which is found by the Court to be binding upon the parties to the dispute, it will be based on international law. In determining the applicable rule the Court may draw on a wide variety of materials including general principles of law. As Elihu Root argued in the 1920 Committee of Jurists which drafted the Statute of the Permanent Court, "the world was prepared to accept the compulsory jurisdiction of a Court which applied the universally recognized rules of international law" but not "of a Court which would apply principles, differently understood in different countries."[36]

The Permanent Court had occasion to expound its conception of international law in the *Lotus* Case which was submitted to it not by way of the Optional Clause, but by way of a special agreement between France and Turkey. The Court was concerned with the interpretation of Article 15 of the Convention of Lausanne of 24 July 1923 which provided that "all questions of jurisdiction shall . . . be decided in accordance with principles of international law." Addressing itself to the question of the meaning of the words "principles of international law", the Court states:

> Now the Court considers that the words 'principles of international law,' as ordinarily used, can only mean international law as it is applied between all nations belonging to the community of States. . . . In these circumstances it is impossible—except in pursuance of a definite stipulation—to construe the expression 'principles of international law' otherwise than as meaning the principles which are in force between all independent nations and which therefore apply equally to all the contracting Parties.[37]

As indicated earlier, the Court has essentially adhered to this conception of law in pursuing a positivist approval and requiring strict proof of what is claimed to be applicable law. The Court may have gone too far in that direction but that is essentially a matter of opinion. Perhaps the Court has erred on the side of caution, but as long as the prevailing pattern of international relations does not change, caution may be the better part of judicial behaviour.

The nature of the cases which came before both Courts determined and confined, it is believed, the contribution which the Courts have been enabled to make to the development of the law. There is not very much of substantive law though there is a great deal on adjective law and principles of interpretation.[38] In several well known instances, the Courts have stimulated the progressive development of international law. The rule of the *Lotus* case can be included here. It was changed in the 1958 Geneva Convention on the High Seas. The judgement in the *Corfu Channel* case relating to passage through international straits was influential in the same Convention. The judgements of the Court in the *Anglo-Norwegian Fisheries* case contributed to the rules concerning the drawing of base lines and the width of bays. The Advisory Opinion in the *Reservations* case was applied by the International Law Commission in its Draft Articles on the Law of Treaties. The

[36] Quoted in Hudson, *loc. cit.*, p. 195.

[37] P.C.I.J. Series A. No. 10. pp. 16–17.

[38] It may be sufficient to refer as authority to H. Lauterpacht's, *The Development of International Law by the International Court* (1958), *passim.*

or even more precise law, but they may still be potent enough to unsettle what previously passed for established though uncertain customary rules of international law. This could be so in spite of the fact that all of the conventions have been approved by two-thirds majorities at the Geneva and Vienna Conferences and that virtually all the then existing states participated in them with the notable exception of Communist China. Thus, the new states, which sometimes express the view that traditional customary international law has developed without their collaboration and fails to reflect their interests and aspirations, have had an opportunity to participate in the codification of large portions of the law.[41] The pessimists may yet be right,[42] but the progress achieved so far cannot be regarded as less than encouraging although some sticky problems still lie ahead.

## Formulating the Bases of a New Legal Order

The activities of the Assembly relating to the fundamentals of a new international legal order cover a very wide field and are difficult to survey and even more difficult to evaluate. A beginning might be made with the interest of the Assembly in formulating in an up-to-date fashion the basic principles of such an order. In accordance with this aim, the Assembly requested and the Commission drafted the declaration on the rights and duties of states mentioned above. In fourteen articles the Commission set out some principles already contained in the Charter, e.g., in Article 2, paragraphs 2 and 5, and Article 51, as well as some principles which have frequently been referred to as fundamental rights of states. These included the rights to independence, jurisdiction, and equality, and some duties, such as the duty to refrain from intervention, fomenting civil strife, resorting to war as an instrument of national policy, and, as corollary thereto, recognizing any territorial acquisition in violation of the prohibition. Finally, Article 14 stated the duty to act in accordance with international law and "the principle that the sovereignty of each State is subject to the supremacy of international law."[43] Obviously the drafting was open to criticism as were some of the proposed articles.[44] The last mentioned article was attacked as a reactionary attempt to enslave certain states. And yet, if there is to be a viable "new international order," which the preamble of the resolution proclaims as already established, it is difficult to see how this principle could be excluded. As for the rest, some ground rules need to be established and accepted if there is to be any meaningful order among states at all. Be that as it may, the Assembly's request to governments for comments and suggestions on the draft articles and any further action went unheeded,

[41] A substantial number of recently emerged states ratified the conventions mentioned above. See also Rosenne, *British Year Book of International Law, 1960,* Vol. 36, p. 159.

[42] For a reserved opinion, see Julius Stone, "On the Vocation of the International Law Commission," *Columbia Law Review,* January 1957 (Vol. 57, No. 1), pp. 16–51.

[43] General Assembly Resolution 375 (IV) of December 6, 1949.

[44] Hans Kelsen, "The Draft Declaration on Rights and Duties of States," *The American Journal of International Law,* April 1950 (Vol. 44, No. 2), pp. 259–27.6

and in 1951 the Assembly postponed the matter until a majority of Members had transmitted their replies.[45]

The attempt at a wholesale reconstruction of the underpinnings of the new order was then discontinued in favor of a piecemeal approach in the course of which a number of related projects were undertaken which will be discussed presently. The Assembly, however, was to be led back to the consideration of fundamentals in consequence of a Soviet proposal to consider principles of peaceful coexistence. The term "peaceful coexistence" being anathema to the free-world segment of the United Nations membership, General Assembly Resolution 1815 (XVII) of December 18, 1962, bears the properly sanitized title "Consideration of principles of international law concerning friendly relations and co-operation among States in accordance with the Charter of the United Nations." The preamble is long and full of reaffirmations of certain statements which have become current in discussions within United Nations organs. The resolution recognized "the paramount importance, in the progressive development of international law and in the promotion of the rule of law among nations" of seven principles already embodied in the Charter,[46] resolved, pursuant to Article 13 of the Charter, to study these principles and decided to place four of these principles, (a), (b), (c), and (f), on the agenda of its eighteenth session. At that session the Assembly adopted Resolution 1966 (XVIII) on December 16, 1963, and decided to entrust the study of these principles to a Special Committee on Principles of International Law Concerning Friendly Relations and Cooperation Among States, to be appointed by the President.[47] Thus, the Assembly decided to bypass the International Law Commission and to work with a political committee. To be sure, the Special Committee was to be representative of the principal legal systems, it would be based on the principle of equitable geographic distribution, and Members were invited to appoint jurists as their representatives.

The Special Committee was fully aware of the importance of its task. It considered the four principles as constituting "cornerstones of peaceful relations among States" and as going "to the very root of peaceful relations among States." As to the wisdom of undertaking the task assigned to it, the Committee was divided. On the one hand, some members thought it was necessary to bring the Charter principles up to date by taking into account "the evolution that had occurred in international law during the past twenty years, both in the practice of States and of the United Nations." On the other hand some members

[45] General Assembly Resolution 596 (VI), December 7, 1951.

[46] To wit: (a) This principle is identic with Article 2(4); (b) this is identic with Article 2(3); (c) "The duty not to intervene in matters within the domestic jurisdiction of any State, in accordance with the Charter"; (d) "The duty of States to co-operate with one another in accordance with the Charter"; (e) "The principle of equal rights and self-determination of peoples"; (f) "The principle of sovereign equality of States"; and (g) "The principle that States shall fulfil in good faith the obligations assumed by them in accordance with the Charter." By General Assembly Resolution 1966 (XVIII) it was decided to place principles (d), (e), and (g) on the agenda of the nineteenth session, which was, however, paralyzed by the controversy over the application of Article 19 of the Charter.

[47] General Assembly *Official Records* (18th session), Supplement No. 15, p. 70. The President appointed 27 Members to serve on the Special Committee, including a small number of new states. As Cameroun was unable to attend, the Special Committee, which met at Mexico City from August 27 to October 2, 1964, consisted of 26 members.

And finally, a passage may be quoted which provides the necessary jurisprudential background for Judge Tanaka's approach and conclusion:

> Briefly, the method of the generation of customary international law is in the stage of transformation from being an individualistic process to being a collectivistic process. This phenomenon can be said to be the adaptation of the traditional creative process of international law to the reality of the growth of the organized international community. It can be characterized, considered from the sociological view-point, as a transition from traditional custom-making to international legislation by treaty.[48]

Although the question-begging nature of Judge Tanaka's reasoning must appear obvious—is the reality of the growth of the organized international community in fact a reality or an overly sanguine gloss on it?—it was appreciated, and rightly so, as "an historic dissenting opinion," as augmenting "the trend toward substituting consensus for consent as the basic law-creating energy in international society," and as an indication of a transformation "from a sovereignty-centered international system to a community-centered international system."[49]

It should be conceded that such a transformation may appear to be overdue, and that the law and the lawyers have for far too long consciously or unconsciously been imbued with Vattel's individualistic approach to international law, but the real question is: has the state-system, as we know it today, abandoned sovereignty-centrism for community-centrism? Have the Members of the United Nations indicated through their actual behaviour and not merely through their rhetoric, that they have accepted subordination to the community-process of the General Assembly of their "sovereign equality" which is vouchsafed to them in Article 2(1) of the Charter?

Obviously, there is room here for different evaluation of the United Nations in action and as an experience in the behaviour of States. However, insofar as the record of the United Nations goes, there has been no transformation from a state-centered to an organization- or community-centered system. Therefore, Judge Tanaka's view may indicate the development of the future but is not convincing as an appraisal of the actual developments in and out of the United Nations. Judge Jessup's argument in favour of a standard based on consensus rather than consent—for obviously South Africa never consented—is more realistic and probably would have prevailed had he and his dissenting colleagues been in the majority.

It is clear from the statements of these two judges that both reject the proposition that individual resolutions or declarations have a legislative character. This, in the present submission, is the correct view.[50] It was the view of the Secretary-General of the United Nations, the late Dag Hammarskjold, who was thoroughly familiar with the operations

48 *Ibid.*, p. 294.

49 Richard A. Falk, "The South-West Africa Cases: An Appraisal," *International Organization* (Boston), Vol. 29, (1967), pp. 1–24, at p. 23.

50 See Leo Gross, "The United Nations and the Role of Law," *International Organization*, (1965), pp. 537–61, 555–8; see also Johnson, *loc cit.*, at pp. 121–2, Parry; *loc. cit.*, p. 21. See also *supra*.

of the Organization and advocated for it the character of a "dynamic instrument," but looked upon the Charter as "a first step in the direction of an organized international community."[51] On the subject under discussion he expressed himself as follows:

> However, the decisions of the Assembly have, as regards Member States, the character of recommendations (except for financial assessments and certain other types of organizational action) so that obligations like those arising out of an agreement, coming into force after a conference, do not normally flow from them. But although the decisions, legally, are only recommendations, they introduce an important element by expressing a majority consensus on the issue under consideration.[52]

The same view was put forward by the Office of Legal Affairs of the United Nations.[53] After reviewing the use and meaning of the terms recommendation and declaration, the Office of Legal Affairs concludes:

> Consequently, insofar as the expectation is gradually justified by State practice, a declaration may by custom become recognized as laying down rules binding upon States.

In other words, resolutions and declarations are not of and by themselves law-creating agencies but State practices culminating in custom. They may well be starting points for the development of customary international law or of conventional international law. For, in many instances, resolutions and declarations were followed by conventions. Thus the various resolutions and declarations, particularly Resolutions 1962 (XVIII) and 2130 (XX) on legal principles governing the activities in outer space, was followed by Resolution 2222 (XXI) promulgating the Treaty on Principles Governing the Activities of States in the Exploration and Use of Outer Space. Another example is the Universal Declaration of Human Rights of 1948 which was followed by Resolution 2200 (XXI) promulgating the International Convenant on Economic, Social and Cultural Rights, the International Covenant on Civil and Political Rights, and the Optional Protocol to the latter Covenant.[54] These examples could be multiplied. In any event, this two-stage procedure of the Assembly confirms the view that the declarations and resolutions were not *per se* legally binding. Had they been legally binding, the drafting of formal instruments, which in the case of the Human Rights Covenants consumed eighteen years, would have been quite unnecessary. Saying that resolutions are not legally binding is not the same as saying that they were not effective. They may well be effective but this is a matter for the Member States and their responsiveness to General Assembly action.

Of special interest to new States has been Resolution 1803 (XVII) of 14 December

[51] Introduction to the Annual Report of the Secretary-General on the Work of the Organization 16 June 1960—15 June 1961, GAOR: 16th Sess., Supp. No. 1A (A/4800/Add. 1), p. 1.

[52] *Ibid.*, p. 3.

[53] Memorandum on the "Use of the Terms 'Declaration' and 'Recommendation'," Doc. E/CN. 4/L. 610, 2 April 1962.

[54] GAOR: 21st Sess., Supp. No. 16 (A/6316), at pp. 12 and 49 ff.

1962, on Permanent Sovereignty Over Natural Resources. As is well known this resolution in paragraph 4 declares that in case of expropriation, nationalization, or requisitioning, the owner shall be paid "appropriate compensation in accordance with the rules in force in the State taking such measures in the exercise of its sovereignty and in accordance with international law."

This clause is clearly not even a compromise between different schools of thought on the subjects; rather it may be viewed as an undigested juxtaposition of the position held by these schools. In spite of this, it has been suggested by this writer, that the Resolution "may be deemed to have administered the *coup de grace*" to the claimed "prompt, adequate and effective" rule. Could one go a step further along judge Jessup's line of reasoning and regard it as setting a standard based on a very wide consensus? There has been, in this matter, no accumulation of resolutions comparable to that on social discrimination. That is a strike against it. On the other hand, there has been so much and so widespread a controversy about it—as acknowledged by the U.S. Supreme Court in the *Sabbatino* case referred to above—that the Resolution could be deemed to be in the mainstream of legal thinking on the subject.

A more troublesome question is whether a standard based on consensus rather than consent could be held to be effective and binding upon the dissenting minority, even if that minority consisted of only one State. Judge Jessup seems to have assumed that it could be applied to the interpretation of the Mandate even though South Africa openly and consistently opposed it. In the cases cited earlier, the *Asylum,* the *Fisheries,* and the *U.S. Nationals in Morocco* cases, the Court seemed unwilling to apply as a universal international law a rule or principle to which the State concerned had objected or to which it had not agreed. In the present submission it would seem to be the better view that in appropriate cases it would perhaps be justifiable to apply the standard concerning compensation and probably the standard concerning social discrimination. In the *South West Africa* cases the Court never reached the point, and the Court has not yet faced the issue of compensation for expropriated property as an issue of customary international law.

Having said all this, it may be appropriate to suggest that the potential of the General Assembly as a law-making institution, through the medium of resolutions and declarations, has yet to be tested. But the potential is there, and if wisely used, could become a significant source of universal international law.

As noted earlier, resolutions or declarations of the General Assembly need not be legally binding in order to be effective. What is necessary, above all, is to mobilize the resources of the United Nations in order to make them effective.

# II

# DEVELOPMENT OF INTERNATIONAL LAW BY THE UNITED NATIONS

# THE UNITED NATIONS AND THE ROLE OF LAW

Legal controversy within the United Nations has resulted from the confrontation of the Organization's purposes with the specific rules set forth in the Charter for their implementation. Two sections of the Charter stand out as having produced yet unresolved legal tangles: One is the provision relating to the maintenance of international peace and security through effective collective action; the other is the group of provisions relating to self-determination and human rights. The Cold War and the attempts of the Great Powers to use the UN to attain or defend their policy objectives have shaped the attitude of Members toward the law and the role of law in the more clearly political activities of the UN. Consequently, politico-legal controversy has arisen with respect to the allocation of competences and powers between the General Assembly and the Security Council, the manner of operation of these two bodies, and the distribution of responsibility for "enforcement action" between the UN and regional organizations.

In addition, controversy has developed between Members anxious to implement speedily the purposes relating to human rights and racial equality or nondiscrimination and Members resisting such policies as impinging on domestic jurisdiction. The clash between the commitment of the Organization to the promotion of human rights and the sweeping reservation in Article 2, paragraph 7, has also shaped in large measure the attitude of Members with respect to the role of law in this area of UN activities. For these differences in interpretation did not remain restricted to issues relating directly to human rights, as in the South African questions, but came soon to embrace other issues as well, such as self-determination and control over natural resources—in fact, all aspects of colonialism including economic development.

These problems, however, except for a few general remarks in the following section, must remain outside the scope of the present analysis, which is concerned with the deliberate efforts of the United Nations to contribute to the development and codification of international law. The world Organization has attempted to fulfill this task directly through resolutions, declarations, and draft conventions and indirectly through the International Law Commission. This is a vast and challenging area which this study will try to describe briefly.

## THE CHARTER AND LIVING LAW

With respect to the general problem of the role of law in the United Nations, some theoretical observations may be made. It has been argued that the United Nations is essentially a political and dynamic institution and therefore cannot be held to a strict observance of the law. To this writer such a view is not persuasive. There is no contradiction between the essentially political character of the United Nations as an international institution and its obligation to respect applicable rules. As the International Court of Justice said in the first membership case:

> The political character of an organ cannot release it from the observance of the treaty provisions established by the Charter when they constitute limitations on its powers or criteria for its judgment. To ascertain whether an organ has freedom of choice for its decisions, reference must be made to the terms of its constitution.[1]

The Charter is not exclusively or even predominantly concerned with purposes; as well as setting forth the objectives of the United Nations, it formulates principles and even detailed rules with respect to the manner in which the Organization's goals can be achieved. Certainly, the UN can best attain its aims by respecting the law, by acting so as to give effect to its purposes and principles and yet not breach its Charter in any way.[2]

The United Nations is indeed a political and dynamic institution, but it does not follow, as sometimes suggested, that it operates in a politico-legal vacuum. Politically it operates within the system of sovereign states competing and cooperating; legally it operates within the framework of the Charter. Rules of interpretation are abundant, and a skillful interpreter can easily "prove" the compatibility of almost any resolution with the applicable rules.[3] It should not be forgotten, however, that the often quoted San Francisco statement on interpretation which declares that each organ of the UN "will interpret such parts of the Charter as are applicable to its particular functions" also says:

> It is to be understood, of course, that if an interpretation made by any organ of the Organization or by a committee of jurists is *not generally acceptable* it will be *without binding force.* In such circumstances, or in cases where it is desired to establish an authoritative interpreta-

[1] Admission of a State to the United Nations (Charter, Article 4), Advisory Opinion of May 28, 1948: I.C.J. Reports 1948, p. 64.

[2] See the joint dissenting opinion of Judges J. Basdevant, B. Winiarski, Sir Arnold D. McNair, and John E. Read in *ibid.*, pp. 85, 92.

[3] Leo Gross, "Problems of International Adjudication and Compliance with International Law: Some Simple Solutions," *The American Journal of International Law,* January 1965 (Vol. 59, No. 1), pp. 48–59. See infra.

tion as a precedent for the future, it may be necessary to embody the interpretation in an amendment to the Charter.[4]

Since amendments are hard to come by, particularly when they would impose further limitations upon the sovereignty of the Members,[5] the first sentence quoted should be regarded as the correct statement of principle: The organs of the United Nations have no power of authoritative interpretation except, of course, where finality attaches to their decisions, as in the cases of Assembly resolutions admitting states to membership or Security Council action to which Article 25 applies.[6] As a consequence, it follows as a working rule that for an interpretation to acquire binding force it must be "generally acceptable." This condition may be regrettable, but those who wish to disregard it will have either to change the state system or trust that through such extralegal methods as diplomatic pressure the dissenting Members will be brought to acquiesce. Bowing to such pressure does not, however, necessarily signify a change in the Member's legal position. Resolutions of both the General Assembly and the Security Council need not be legally binding in order to be effective; they may be effective even though their legality is doubtful. The Charter, however, probably reflects the maximum rather than the minimum of consensus that could have been reached at San Francisco. Going beyond the San Francisco consensus has proved extremely difficult although, as in the instance of decolonization, not impossible. Decolonization, however, was far more the result of political forces, not necessarily connected with the UN, than of the acceptance of increased legal authority for the UN.

It has also been argued that the United Nations is a "living" institution and that the Charter is more like a constitution than an ordinary treaty. According to this view, allowance must be made for change and adaptation of the law, and the possibility should be recognized of the growth of a "common law" arising from the practice of the organs in applying, adjusting, modifying, supplementing, and even supplanting provisions of the Charter.[7] This approach to the Charter goes back to the earliest years of the UN[8] and

[4] Report of the Rapporteur of Committee IV/2 (Judicial Organization, Legal Problems) to Commission IV (Judicial Organization), Document 933, June 12, 1945, in *Documents of the United Nations Conference on International Organization, San Francisco, 1945* (New York: United Nations Information Organization, 1945), Vol. 13, p. 710. Italics added.

[5] By Resolution 1991 (XVIII) of December 17, 1963, the General Assembly, in accordance with Article 108, adopted amendments to the Charter providing for an increase in membership of the Security Council from eleven to fifteen and an increase in the requisite majority from seven to nine; the membership of the Economic and Social Council (ECOSOC) would be enlarged from eighteen to 27. These amendments, if entered into force, will change the "balancing power" between various groups of Members but will not impose new obligations upon the Members.

[6] D. H. N. Johnson, "The Effect of Resolutions of the General Assembly of the United Nations," *British Year Book of International Law, 1955–1956* (London: Oxford University Press, 1957), Vol. 32, pp. 97–123.

[7] One example of this kind of evolution is the practice of the General Assembly of electing two Members for one nonpermanent seat on the Security Council in disregard of the "mandatory" provision of Article 23, paragraph 2. Another is the general long-standing practice of taking lightly the "mandatory" provision in Article 23, paragraph 1, that in electing nonpermanent members due regard should especially be paid "in the first instance to the contribution of Members of the United Nations to the maintenance of international peace and security. . . ." One wonders whether the Members which participate in these elections believe they are acting in accordance with the "good faith" principle in Article 2, paragraph 2.

[8] Benjamin V. Cohen has pointed out that on October 30, 1946, the United States representative, Warren R. Austin, declared in the General Assembly: "Under the broad and flexible construction of the Charter which the United States wishes to develop, we foresee a great and expanding area of operations for the General Assembly." (*The United Nations: Constitutional Developments, Growth and Possibilities* [Cambridge, Mass: Harvard University Press, 1961], p. 16.)

has come to be used as an instrument for fulfilling a variety of aims. It has been sustained by a desire, even a sense of duty, on the part of many UN Members to reach out for solutions or some manifestation of authority unhampered by "legalistic" considerations; a feeling that the law was inadequate for the task at hand; a general distrust of international law by some Members; a sense of frustration over the abuse of the veto and a corresponding determination to prevent the extension of the veto by refusing to admit a sort of "absentee ballot" in the Security Council, or a financial veto in the Assembly, or any kind of veto in the operation of regional organizations; and a determination to eliminate all vestiges of colonialism.

Like the liberal interpretation of the Charter, however, the successful use of the so-called "common law" and even of customary international law requires broad acceptance of the resulting legal formulas—practice alone will not suffice. As Judge Sir Percy Spender put it, "Unless it is of a peaceful, uniform and undisputed character accepted by all current Members . . .," practice has no probative value.[9] While, as noted above, each organ has the right to interpret the Charter, "the majority has no power to extend, alter or disregard the Charter."[10] To be sure, those who regard practice, pure and simple, as a source of the "common law" of the United Nations may draw comfort from the opinion of the Court in the *Expenses* case to the extent that it relied on practice[11] without the qualification suggested by Judge Spender. But the melancholy proceedings at the nineteenth session of the General Assembly and its failure either to apply Article 19 or to find a solution acceptable to all should dampen the faith of the more exuberant interpreters in the ability of the United Nations to operate without a broad consensus. The truth of the matter is that in 1964–1965 the United Nations was not yet ready to implement this forward-looking advisory opinion of the Court. The minority in opposition was small and determined. Its ranks would, however, soon swell to include all the economically developed Members[12] if the Assembly were to include in the budget of the Organization an item of, say, $5 billion for economic development, surely a major purpose of the United Nations, and assess those Members accordingly. Pursuant to the advisory opinion this could be regarded as a "reasonable" exercise of the powers recognized by the Court to be vested in the General Assembly.

What has been said about practice as a source of the "common law" of the United Nations applies in principle to the alleged growth of customary international law. Strictly speaking, there is an aggravating factor. Even if the time element is excluded from con-

[9] *Certain Expenses of the United Nations (Article 17, paragraph 2, of the Charter), Advisory Opinion of 20 July 1962: I.C.J. Reports 1962, p. 195.*

[10] *Ibid.*, p. 197.

[11] *Ibid.*, p. 160.

[12] The distinction between "economically less developed countries" which includes all Members other than 26 listed by name has been made by the General Assembly in recent resolutions relating to the financing of the UN Operation in the Congo (ONUC) and the UN Emergency Force (UNEF). See, for instance, Resolutions 1885 (XVIII) of October 18, 1963, and 1983 (XVIII) of December 17, 1963.

sideration, according to prevailing doctrine consistent and uniform practice must be supplemented by its acceptance as law. Proof of such acceptance is extremely difficult and, in the absence of a judgment by a commonly accepted authority, almost always a matter of controversy. No doubt certain practices have developed in the United Nations, but have they been accepted as law? The mere fact that Members support by their vote certain resolutions does not necessarily imply that they do it out of a sense of legal obligation rather than in a spirit of accommodation nor even that they regard the resolution as constitutional. Members are responsive to certain moods and pressures, and the Organization itself can become an outstanding "pressure group" defying the application of the legal yardstick. As Judge Spender pointed out, the majority rule which prevails in the Assembly and the Council "may enable action to be taken which is beyond power" but when legal considerations are invoked, "*de facto* extension of the Charter must be disregarded."[13] In short, the growth of customary international law within the framework of the Charter is not excluded, but assertions that such growth has occurred should be treated with caution unless there is reliable evidence that there is not merely consensus as to practice but that this practice has become a matter of law.

## LAW AS AN OBJECTIVE OF THE UN SYTSEM

From the beginning of its existence the United Nations has been concerned with the development of international law. The Covenant of the League of Nations, in its preamble, declared that the High Contracting Parties intended to promote international peace and security "by the firm establishment of the understandings of international law as the actual rule of conduct among Governments. . . ." The Charter, on the other hand, refrained from committing the United Nations to such an objective, which after the cataclysm of the Second World War may have struck its founders as premature. A more cautious attitude seemed to be indicated. It was reflected in the preamble and in Article 13, paragraph 1 (a), of the Charter. The preamble recognized that conditions had to be established under which respect for international law could be maintained. Article 13, paragraph 1 (a), directed the Assembly to initiate studies and make recommendations for the purpose of "encouraging the progressive development of international law and its codification." This task the Assembly has discharged in a variety of ways, directly or through one of its subordinate committees or commissions, principally the International Law Commission. In addition to the Assembly, the contribution to the development of law of other principal organs, namely, the Economic and Social Council (ECOSOC), the Secretary-General, the United Nations Administrative Tribunal, and the International Court of Justice, should be noted.

Rather than taking up separately the contributions made by these agencies, this analysis will attempt to make some generalizations regarding the objectives pursued by

[13] *I.C.J. Reports 1962*, p. 197.

the General Assembly. Throughout the years the Assembly may be said to have tried, first, to revitalize international law and to deal with the fundamentals of a new international legal order. Secondly, it has contributed to the development and codification of traditional law and, thirdly, to the formulation of principles in areas not yet governed by international law. In order to achieve or promote these objectives the Assembly has proceeded pragmatically, using a variety of media, including the International Law Commission or *ad hoc* committees or conferences, and has embodied the results in conventions or resolutions. A few selected examples will illustrate the pertinent activities of the United Nations.

Within the third field of its endeavors, the General Assembly, by Resolution 1962 (XVIII) of December 13, 1963, adopted the "Declaration of Legal Principles Governing the Activities of States in the Exploration and Use of Outer Space" and by Resolution 1963 (XVIII) of the same day formulated the legal principles involved in "International co-operation in the peaceful uses of outer space."[14] These basic resolutions in a new field of concern to Members emanated from the Committee on the Peaceful Uses of Outer Space which was established by the Assembly and which reported to the First (Political and Security) and not the Sixth (Legal) Committee. The legal significance of these resolutions in the formulation of international law will be discussed later. Insofar as Resolution 1962 (XVIII) is concerned, it proposed no further steps. By contrast, Resolution 1963 (XVIII) recommended that consideration should be given "to incorporating in international agreement form" legal principles governing the exploration and use of outer space. The Assembly considered, then, that these principles needed, in order to become fully binding, to be incorporated in a treaty, the classic medium of international legislation. The same medium was considered, in the same resolution, necessary for formulating principles concerning liability for damage caused by objects launched into outer space and assistance to and return of astronauts and space vehicles. The Assembly's Committee on the Peaceful Uses of Outer Space was charged with the necessary preparatory work. Resolutions 1721 D (XVI) of December 20, 1961, and 1802 IV (XVII) of December 14, 1962, on satellite communications have already been implemented by the "Agreement Establishing Interim Arrangements for a Global Commercial Communication Satellite System" of July 24, 1964, which entered into force on August 20, 1964.[15]

## The Work and Contributions of the International Law Commission

For purposes of codification and progressive development of international law the Assembly has relied chiefly on the International Law Commission, an autonomous body established by Resolution 174 (II) of November 21, 1947, which incorporates the Statute

[14] The Assembly dealt in Resolutions 1802 (XVII) of December 14, 1962, 1721 (XVI) of December 20, 1961, and 1472 (XIV) of December 12, 1959, with the problem of the peaceful uses of outer space.

[15] *United States Treaties and Other International Acts Series,* No. 5646 (Washington, D.C.: U.S. Government Printing Office, 1964). See also, James Simsarian, "Interim Arrangements for a Global Commercial Satellite System," *The American Journal of International Law,* April 1965 (Vol. 59, No. 2), pp. 344–351.

of the Commission. Originally composed of fifteen and since 1962 of 25 experts[16] elected by the Assembly in their individual capacities, the Commission has become representative of the membership and of the world's principal legal systems. The Commission's members serve only part-time, which has its drawbacks—the inevitably slow pace of its work—as well as its advantages—to wit the availability of first-rate lawyers who could not accept a full-time appointment. It seems to be the fact that although the members serve in their individual capacity and therefore independently of governments, an increasingly large number, now about two-thirds, nevertheless hold official positions.

The Commission's Statute, like Article 13, paragraph 1 (a), of the Charter, distinguishes between codification and progressive development.[17] In practice, however, the distinction has become blurred, and "a single consolidated procedure has been made applicable to both types of work."[18] This practice did not affect the provision in the Statute stating that the General Assembly and other agencies, but not the Commission, had the power to initiate projects which were wholly or predominantly concerned with progressive development.

The Commission during its first ten sessions concluded work on sixteen projects.[19] Since then, it has completed the draft articles on consular intercourse and immunities[20] and finished the last section of its draft on the law of treaties,[21] which it has now submitted to governments for their observations. The completion of this draft constitutes a major achievement in view of the significance of treaties in interstate relations. The Commission will at a later stage, presumably after reexamination of all the draft articles in the light of the observations received from the governments, consider whether the three parts of the law of treaties should be amalgamated to form a single draft convention or whether they should be embodied in a series of related conventions.[22] The Commission's program of work provides for completion of the study of the law of treaties and of

[16] Membership was increased to 21 by General Assembly Resolution 1103 (VI) of December 18, 1956, and to 25 by General Assembly Resolution 1647 (XVI) of November 6, 1961.

[17] Article 15 of the Statute reads as follows:

> In the following articles the expression "progressive development of international law" is used for convenience as meaning the preparation of draft conventions on subjects which have not yet been regulated by international law or in regard to which the law has not yet been sufficiently developed in the practice of States. Similarly, the expression "codification of international law" is used for convenience as meaning the more precise formulation and systematization of rules of international law in fields where there already has been extensive state practice, precedent, and doctrine.

[18] Shabtai Rosenne, "The International Law Commission," *British Year Book of International Law, 1960* (London: Oxford University Press, 1961), Vol. 36, p. 142.

[19] 1) Draft declaration on rights and duties of states; 2) ways and means for making the evidence of customary international law more readily available; 3) formulation of the Nuremberg Principles; 4) question of international criminal jurisdiction; 5) draft code of offenses against the peace and security of mankind: 6) question of defining aggression; 7) reservations to multilateral conventions; 8) draft on arbitral procedure; 9) draft convention on the elimination of future statelessness; 10) draft convention on the reduction of future statelessness; 11–14) draft convention on the law of the sea, comprising territorial waters, the high seas, fishing and conservation of the living resources of the high seas, and the continental shelf; 15) draft on diplomatic intercourse and immunities; and 16) revision of 1958 draft on arbitral procedure. (*Yearbook of the International Law Commission, 1958* [UN Document A/CN.4/SER.A/1958/Add. 1], Vol. II, p. 109, footnotes 39 and 40.)

[20] General Assembly *Official Records* (16th session), Supplement No. 9, p. 2.

[21] General Assembly *Official Records* (19th session), Supplement No. 9, p. 7.

[22] *Ibid.*, p. 9.

special missions[23] and for work on the question of relations between states and intergovernmental organizations, in that order. The Commission then will deal with questions of succession of states and governments and state responsibility.[24]

Of the topics studied by the Commission several have been submitted to international conferences and cast in the form of regular conventions open for signature and notification. The United Nations Conference on the Law of the Sea, held in Geneva in 1958, adopted four conventions on the law of the sea and an Optional Protocol on Compulsory Settlement of Disputes. The Conference failed to agree on the width of the territorial sea, a matter on which the Commission has refrained from submitting a proposal.[25] The second Geneva Conference on the Law of the Sea, which met in 1960, again failed to reach agreement on this extremely controversial question by a very narrow margin.[26] The United Nations Conference on Diplomatic Intercourse and Immunities of 1961 adopted the Vienna Convention on Diplomatic Relations, and the United Nations Conference on Consular Relations of 1963 adopted the Vienna Convention on Consular Relations.[27] The 1959 United Nations Conference on the Elimination or Reduction of Future Statelessness which considered the Commission's draft conventions on the elimination of future statelessness and on the reduction of future statelessness adjourned without accomplishing its task (although the 1961 New York Conference did adopt the Convention on the Reduction of Statelessness). No action has been taken so far by the Assembly with respect to the draft code of offenses against the peace and security of mankind. The 1953 draft on arbitral procedure was not acceptable to the General Assembly largely for two reasons: first, because the Assembly deemed that the Commission

> had exceeded its terms of reference by giving *preponderance* to its desire to promote the development of international law instead of concentrating on its *primary* task, [*i.e.*] the codification of custom

and secondly, because it was felt "the Commission's draft would distort traditional arbitration practice, making it into a quasi-compulsory jurisdictional procedure."[28] The Commission at its tenth session adopted a set of model draft articles from which, in the words of the rapporteur, Professor Georges Scelle, *"every trace of obligation has been eliminated."*[29] This draft did not, however, fare better than the first, as the Assembly merely

[23] At its 1964 session the Commission adopted sixteen draft articles on the subject of special missions. (*Ibid.*, pp. 98–142).

[24] *Ibid.*, p. 143.

[25] The Commission had also omitted articles on the question of access to the sea of landlocked states. This subject was, after a preliminary conference convened by the Swiss government, part of the agenda of the Geneva Conference.

[26] See Arthur H. Dean, "The Second Geneva Conference on the Law of the Sea: The Fight for Freedom of the Seas," *The American Journal of International Law*, October 1960 (Vol. 54, No. 4), pp. 751–789.

[27] At both Conferences optional protocols on acquisition of nationality and compulsory settlement of disputes were also adopted.

[28] *Yearbook of the International Law Commission, 1958*, Vol. II, p. 80.

[29] *Ibid.*, p. 3. Italics added.

took note of it.[30] The rapporteur probably came close to the truth when he analyzed the reasons for the negative attitude of governments as follows:

> As the number of States Members of the United Nations increases, so the majority hostile to the Commission's draft seems bound to increase, for the more recently the new Members have acquired their sovereignty the greater will be their desire to maintain it whole and entire.[31]

This resolution must have been a personal disappointment to the rapporteur who had devoted his life to the promotion of the rule of law. The episode is merely one more evidence of the intractability of the environment.

The report of the Commission on reservations to multilateral conventions[32] was adopted by the General Assembly in Resolution 598 (VI) of January 12, 1951. The Assembly recommended that organs of the United Nations, specialized agencies, and states

> should, in the course of preparing multilateral conventions, consider the insertion therein of provisions relating to the admissibility or nonadmissibility of reservations and to the effect to be attributed to them.

None of the conventions resulting from the work of the Commission contains such provisions.

The Commission's draft declaration on rights and duties of states was deemed by the Assembly

> a notable and substantial contribution towards the progressive development of international law and its codification and as such commends it to the continuing attention of the Member States and of jurists of all nations.[33]

The work of the Commission on the Nuremberg principles and the draft code of offenses against the peace and security of mankind will be discussed later.

There has been a good deal of controversy about the work of the Commission and the desirability of codifying international law. The principal target of complaints has been the slowness of its progress.[34] The Commission has been sensitive to this criticism and in defense it has pointed out that the record was far from discouraging. The Commission noted that for the first ten years it presented on the average one completed piece of work to the Assembly each year; it responded to several requests of the Assembly which did not

[30] General Assembly Resolution 1262 (XIII) of November 14, 1958.

[31] *Yearbook of the International Law Commission, 1958,* Vol. II, p. 2.

[32] General Assembly *Official Records* (6th session), Special Supplement No. 9, pp. 2–8.

[33] General Assembly Resolution 375 (IV) of December 6, 1949.

[34] See the debate on the work of the Commission in the Sixth Committee at the fifteenth session in General Assembly *Official Records . . . Sixth Committee* (15th session, Part I), pp. 9–115. H. Lauterpacht expressed the view that the work of codification would require several generations in his "Codification and Development of International Law," *The American Journal of International Law,* January 1955 (Vol. 49, No. 1), p. 42. J. Robinson found the balance sheet of the Commission discouraging in "The Metamorphosis of the United Nations," *Recueil des Cours de l'Académie de Droit International,* 1958 (Leyden: A. W. Sythoff, 1959), Vol. II, p. 575.

call for draft articles but only for a report or opinion; the quality of the work was more important than the rate of speed with which it was turned out; and finally, at a time when

> the whole of international law and international relations was now going through a period of adjustment . . . speed was not necessarily the most important consideration.[35]

The Commission, in order to work more efficiently, has in recent years established a drafting committee to which have been referred

> not merely pure drafting points, but also points of substance which the full Commission had been unable to resolve, or which seemed likely to give rise to unduly protracted discussion.[36]

Private meetings of this sort have been immensely useful in expediting agreement. The Commission has also extended its regular annual session, held short winter sessions in 1962 and 1963, and has proposed to hold a four-week winter session in 1966 in order to complete its current program of work before the expiration of its term of office in 1966.[37] But delays attributable to such political factors as the Cold War and the emergence of new states[38] are beyond the control of the Commission and may in fact have been less potent in the work of the Commission in the last few years than is sometimes assumed. The crucial test for the Commission will come in connection with the codification of the law of state succession and responsibility of states.

In spite of what, in the present view, must be regarded as an impressive record of achievement, the question is still open of how effective the work of the Commission will be. A good though not conclusive gauge for measuring this is the progress in ratifying the conventions mentioned above. The conventions resulting from the recent Vienna Conferences may not offer an adequate test although the Convention on Diplomatic Relations received 33 ratifications as of November 1964, that is, within three years.[39] By January 1, 1965, that is, after a lapse of close to seven years, the various Geneva conventions had been ratified by numbers ranging between fourteen and 29 states.[40] Conventions which fail to receive a substantial number of ratifications may not be heralds of new

[35] *Yearbook of the International Law Commission, 1958,* Vol. II, pp. 109–110.

[36] *Ibid.,* p. 108.

[37] General Assembly *Official Records* (19th session), Supplement No. 9, p. 51, paragraphs 37, 38.

[38] Rosenne, *British Year Book of International Law, 1960,* Vol. 36, pp. 155–156.

[39] UN Document ST/LEG/SER.A/213, p. 19. The Convention came into force on April 24, 1964 (UN Document ST/LEG/SER.A/208, p. 14).

[40] The Convention on the Territorial Sea and the Contiguous Zone was ratified by 23 states including the Soviet Union, the United Kingdom, and the United States; the Convention on the High Seas by 29 states including the same Great Powers; the Convention on Fishing and Conservation of the Living Resources of the High Seas by fourteen states including the United Kingdom and the United States; and the Convention of the Continental Shelf by 24 states including the Soviet Union, the United Kingdom, and the United States. (*Treaties in Force: A List of Treaties and Other International Agreements of the United States in Force on January 1, 1965* [Department of State Publication 7817] [Washington, D.C.: U.S. Government Printing Office, 1965], p. 263). The Optional Protocol of Signature concerning the Compulsory Settlement of Disputes received only one ratification (Haiti)! (UN Document ST/LEG/3, Rev. 1, pp. 26–28).

or even more precise law, but they may still be potent enough to unsettle what previously passed for established though uncertain customary rules of international law. This could be so in spite of the fact that all of the conventions have been approved by two-thirds majorities at the Geneva and Vienna Conferences and that virtually all the then existing states participated in them with the notable exception of Communist China. Thus, the new states, which sometimes express the view that traditional customary international law has developed without their collaboration and fails to reflect their interests and aspirations, have had an opportunity to participate in the codification of large portions of the law.[41] The pessimists may yet be right,[42] but the progress achieved so far cannot be regarded as less than encouraging although some sticky problems still lie ahead.

## Formulating the Bases of a New Legal Order

The activities of the Assembly relating to the fundamentals of a new international legal order cover a very wide field and are difficult to survey and even more difficult to evaluate. A beginning might be made with the interest of the Assembly in formulating in an up-to-date fashion the basic principles of such an order. In accordance with this aim, the Assembly requested and the Commission drafted the declaration on the rights and duties of states mentioned above. In fourteen articles the Commission set out some principles already contained in the Charter, e.g., in Article 2, paragraphs 2 and 5, and Article 51, as well as some principles which have frequently been referred to as fundamental rights of states. These included the rights to independence, jurisdiction, and equality, and some duties, such as the duty to refrain from intervention, fomenting civil strife, resorting to war as an instrument of national policy, and, as corollary thereto, recognizing any territorial acquisition in violation of the prohibition. Finally, Article 14 stated the duty to act in accordance with international law and "the principle that the sovereignty of each State is subject to the supremacy of international law."[43] Obviously the drafting was open to criticism as were some of the proposed articles.[44] The last mentioned article was attacked as a reactionary attempt to enslave certain states. And yet, if there is to be a viable "new international order," which the preamble of the resolution proclaims as already established, it is difficult to see how this principle could be excluded. As for the rest, some ground rules need to be established and accepted if there is to be any meaningful order among states at all. Be that as it may, the Assembly's request to governments for comments and suggestions on the draft articles and any further action went unheeded,

[41] A substantial number of recently emerged states ratified the conventions mentioned above. See also Rosenne, *British Year Book of International Law, 1960,* Vol. 36, p. 159.

[42] For a reserved opinion, see Julius Stone, "On the Vocation of the International Law Commission," *Columbia Law Review,* January 1957 (Vol. 57, No. 1), pp. 16–51.

[43] General Assembly Resolution 375 (IV) of December 6, 1949.

[44] Hans Kelsen, "The Draft Declaration on Rights and Duties of States," *The American Journal of International Law,* April 1950 (Vol. 44, No. 2), pp. 259–276.

and in 1951 the Assembly postponed the matter until a majority of Members had transmitted their replies.[45]

The attempt at a wholesale reconstruction of the underpinnings of the new order was then discontinued in favor of a piecemeal approach in the course of which a number of related projects were undertaken which will be discussed presently. The Assembly, however, was to be led back to the consideration of fundamentals in consequence of a Soviet proposal to consider principles of peaceful coexistence. The term "peaceful coexistence" being anathema to the free-world segment of the United Nations membership, General Assembly Resolution 1815 (XVII) of December 18, 1962, bears the properly sanitized title "Consideration of principles of international law concerning friendly relations and co-operation among States in accordance with the Charter of the United Nations." The preamble is long and full of reaffirmations of certain statements which have become current in discussions within United Nations organs. The resolution recognized "the paramount importance, in the progressive development of international law and in the promotion of the rule of law among nations" of seven principles already embodied in the Charter,[46] resolved, pursuant to Article 13 of the Charter, to study these principles and decided to place four of these principles, (a), (b), (c), and (f), on the agenda of its eighteenth session. At that session the Assembly adopted Resolution 1966 (XVIII) on December 16, 1963, and decided to entrust the study of these principles to a Special Committee on Principles of International Law Concerning Friendly Relations and Cooperation Among States, to be appointed by the President.[47] Thus, the Assembly decided to bypass the International Law Commission and to work with a political committee. To be sure, the Special Committee was to be representative of the principal legal systems, it would be based on the principle of equitable geographic distribution, and Members were invited to appoint jurists as their representatives.

The Special Committee was fully aware of the importance of its task. It considered the four principles as constituting "cornerstones of peaceful relations among States" and as going "to the very root of peaceful relations among States." As to the wisdom of undertaking the task assigned to it, the Committee was divided. On the one hand, some members thought it was necessary to bring the Charter principles up to date by taking into account "the evolution that had occurred in international law during the past twenty years, both in the practice of States and of the United Nations." On the other hand some members

[45] General Assembly Resolution 596 (VI), December 7, 1951.

[46] To wit: (a) This principle is identical with Article 2(4); (b) this is identical with Article 2(3); (c) "The duty not to intervene in matters within the domestic jurisdiction of any State, in accordance with the Charter"; (d) "The duty of States to co-operate with one another in accordance with the Charter"; (e) "The principle of equal rights and self-determination of peoples"; (f) "The principle of sovereign equality of States"; and (g) "The principle that States shall fulfil in good faith the obligations assumed by them in accordance with the Charter." By General Assembly Resolution 1966 (XVIII) it was decided to place principles (d), (e), and (g) on the agenda of the nineteenth session, which was, however, paralyzed by the controversy over the application of Article 19 of the Charter.

[47] General Assembly *Official Records* (18th session), Supplement No. 15, p. 70. The President appointed 27 Members to serve on the Special Committee, including a small number of new states. As Cameroun was unable to attend, the Special Committee, which met at Mexico City from August 27 to October 2, 1964, consisted of 26 members.

> expressed doubts about the utility of hasty declarations or statements which proclaimed in a non-binding fashion principles already binding upon States under the Charter

and were of the opinion that failures on the part of the United Nations "had not been due to lack of clarity of Charter principles . . . but to the fact that certain States were not resolved to support any international system of law." As to the procedure to be followed it was said that

> resolutions of the General Assembly did not in themselves constitute international law, but they might represent an important step in the process of making international law

and that "the most important element in the process of evolving international law was universality." The Special Committee's function then was seen as ascertaining "the area in which there was a consensus among delegations."[48]

The results of the Special Committee's labors were perhaps necessarily and predictably disappointing. On the first three principles no consensus was reached,[49] and the Special Committee achieved unanimity only on the principle of equality. The agreed statement contained the four points already accepted at the San Francisco Conference[50] and these additional understandings: Each state has the duty to respect the personality of other states, and each state has the right freely to choose and develop its political, social, economic, and cultural systems.[51]

Thus, the second attempt of the United Nations to formulate more precisely some basic principles of the international legal order largely miscarried, so far at any rate. Once again the high hopes in some quarters that a fresh approach by a body on which developing states were adequately represented offered "an opportunity to rethink problems and to establish rules which can be utilized to eliminate the cause of tensions and of threats to the peace"[52] have been dashed. The elimination of tensions may well be the basic precondition. But this is a task for high-level statesmen and not for jurists.

## RESPONSIBILITY OF INDIVIDUALS FOR ACTS CONTRARY TO INTERNATIONAL LAW

In another effort to infuse new principles into the old international order, the Assembly was concerned with the formulation of individual and criminal responsibility of

[48] Report of the Special Committee on Principles of International Law Concerning Friendly Relations and Cooperation Among States (UN Document A/5746, November 16, 1965), pp. 15–18.

[49] *Ibid.*, pp. 60, 67, 104, 141.

[50] Document 944, *Documents of the United Nations Conference on International Organization, San Francisco, 1945* (New York: United Nations Information Organization, 1945), Vol. 6, p. 457, and Vol. 1, p. 614.

[51] Report of the Special Committee, UN Document A/5746, p. 163, paragraph 339.

[52] John N. Hazard, "New Personalities to Create New Law," *The American Journal of International Law*, October 1964 (Vol. 58, No. 4), p. 959. For a recent study of coexistence, see Edward McWhinney, " 'Peaceful Coexistence' and Soviet-Western International Law," *The American Journal of International Law*, October 1962 (Vol. 56, No. 4), pp. 951–970.

individuals for acts contrary to international law. Various tribunals both national and international, notably the International Military Tribunal in Nuremberg, have recognized such responsibility. The General Assembly, by Resolution 95 (I) of December 11, 1946, affirmed "the principles of international law recognized by the Charter of the Nürnberg Tribunal and the judgment of the Tribunal." At the same time the Assembly instructed the Committee on the Codification of International Law, the forerunner of the International Law Commission,

> to treat as a matter of primary importance plans for the formulation, in the context of a general codification of offences against the peace and security of mankind, or of an International Criminal Code,

of those principles.[53] In another resolution the Assembly affirmed that genocide, as defined therein,

> is a crime under international law which the civilized world condemns, and for the commission of which principals and accomplices—whether private individuals, public officials or statesmen,. . .—are punishable.

It directed the Economic and Social Council to study the preparation of a draft convention on genocide.[54] The stage was thus set for a major effort at lawmaking in a relatively uncharted and highly controversial field.

The Economic and Social Council produced and the Assembly adopted in due course the Convention on the Prevention and Punishment of the Crime of Genocide.[55] This entered into force on January 12, 1951, and was ratified by a large number of states. It is surely a landmark in the legal protection of national, ethnic, racial, and religious groups and therefore of individuals belonging to such groups. As stated in the preamble, the object of the Convention is "to liberate mankind from such an odious scourge." Whether this has been achieved may be doubtful. The efficiency of enforcement by national tribunals is open to question, and the international penal tribunal referred to in Article VI of the Convention has not been established. But by Resolution 260 B (III) of December 9, 1948, the Assembly requested the International Law Commission to study "the desirability and possibility of establishing an international judicial organ for the trial of persons charged with genocide or other crimes."

The Commission was divided but decided by a majority vote that the establishment of an international criminal jurisdiction was both desirable and possible. In the rapporteur's view, "the rule of law in the community of States could only be ensured" by such a jurisdiction vested with power to try and punish persons "who disturbed international public

[53] Resolution 95 (I), contained in UN Document A/64/Add. 1, p. 188.

[54] General Assembly Resolution 96 (I), December 11, 1946 contained in *ibid.*, p. 189.

[55] General Assembly Resolution 260 A (III) of December 9, 1948. For an analysis, see Josef L. Kunz, "The United Nations Convention on Genocide," *The American Journal of International Law*, October 1949 (Vol. 43, No. 4), p. 738.

order."[56] The Assembly established a committee[57] which submitted a draft statute for an International Criminal Court in 1951.[58] Like the Commission, this committee was divided on both the desirability and possibility of establishing such a court.[59]

In the meantime the International Law Commission pursued the formulation of the substantive law to be applied by the proposed Criminal Court or another tribunal. It adopted the text of the Nuremberg principles without, however, expressing an opinion on whether or not "the principles contained in the Charter [of the International Military Tribunal] and judgment constituted principles of international law." It was thought to be precluded from doing so by the affirmation of those principles in General Assembly Resolution 95 (I).[60] The Commission then took up work on the draft code of offenses against the peace and security of mankind. It submitted a draft to the sixth session of the Assembly,[61] but the Assembly failed to take it up either at that or the seventh session. The Commission then, in the light of comments received from governments, completed its task at its sixth session and submitted the draft code to the Assembly.[62] The draft code included the Nuremberg principles and the provisions of the Genocide Convention, as well as additional offenses and a makeshift open-ended definition of aggression.[63]

## THE PROBLEM OF DEFINING AGGRESSION

It may be recalled that in 1950 the Assembly had referred to the Commission a Soviet proposal concerning a definition of aggression.[64] The Commission, however, did not furnish a separate definition of aggression but included it in the draft code of offenses.[65] The Assembly was not satisfied with this approach. It considered a definition "possible and desirable, with a view to ensuring international peace and security and to developing international criminal law" and decided to study the matter itself at the seventh session.[66] At that session it established a special committee of fifteen members for this purpose.[67] The special committee met in 1953 and submitted a report which was discussed at the

[56] General Assembly *Official Records* (5th session), Supplement No. 12, paragraphs 135, 140. The Assembly in Resolution 260 B (III) referred to the above and requested the International Law Commission to pay attention to the possibility of establishing a criminal chamber in the existing International Court of Justice; the Commission expressed no view on the subject.

[57] General Assembly Resolution 489 (V) of December 12, 1950.

[58] UN Document A/AC.48/4.

[59] See Quincy Wright, "Proposal for an International Criminal Court," *The American Journal of International Law*, January 1952 (Vol. 46, No. 1), pp. 60–72, and Yuen-li Liang, "Notes on Legal Questions concerning the United Nations," *ibid.*, pp. 73–88.

[60] General Assembly *Official Records* (5th session), Supplement No. 12, Part III, paragraph 96.

[61] General Assembly *Official Records* (6th session), Supplement No. 9, p. 10.

[62] General Assembly *Official Records* (9th session), Supplement No. 9, Chapter III, pp. 9–12.

[63] To wit, Article 2, paragraph 1, states:

> Any act of aggression, including the employment by the authorities of a State of armed force against another State for any purpose other than national or collective self-defence or in pursuance of a decision or recommendation of a competent organ of the United Nations.

[64] General Assembly Resolution 378 B (V) of November 17, 1950.

[65] General Assembly *Official Records* (9th session), Supplement No. 9. See footnote 63 above.

[66] General Assembly Resolution 599 (VI) of January 31, 1952.

[67] General Assembly Resolution 688 (VII) of December 20, 1952.

ninth session of the Assembly.[68] At this session the Assembly decided to reconstitute the special committee and instructed it to report to the eleventh session.[69] At the same time the Assembly decided to postpone further consideration of the draft code and of the question of an international criminal jurisdiction in order to be able to take these matters up together with the question of defining aggression.[70] Consideration of the three questions was again postponed in 1957;[71] the committee on the question of defining aggression met in 1965 but without result.

Thus ended another attempt to remedy some of the weaknesses of the international legal order. There is obviously room for different views as to the immediate importance of the draft code and a definition of aggression.[72] They may not be the most urgent tasks confronting the United Nations and even if they were—and the Assembly must have thought the tasks at least worthwhile—they may not have been feasible in the current state of international affairs. Certainly the decision to search for a definition of aggression and other serious breaches of international law is eminently political. Any addition to the law of the United Nations would necessarily be in the nature of a serious limitation on the freedom of action of the Members. Such limitations may seem undesirable unless and until the United Nations becomes capable of providing effective security and effective procedures for the peaceful settlement of disputes.

The fate of the Commission's draft on arbitral procedure and the nonuse of the International Court of Justice by both the United Nations and its Members bear eloquent testimony to the fact that neither the Organization nor its Members are prepared to entrust matters of vital concern to them to such depoliticized procedures. The decision to depoliticize such matters is itself a political decision. The question of security has become closely linked with the issue of arms control and disarmament, the achievement of which is not yet in sight. The momentum for a radical transformation of the international legal order, which impelled the Assembly to tackle the definition of aggression in the context of the draft code, has been lost. As a result of the Cold War and the ever present threat of thermonuclear destruction, the search for security through fundamental reforms of a structural character gave way to the search for security through more readily available and familiar patterns. In such familiar surroundings insecurity seems to have become bearable.

## FORMULATING THE BASES OF A NEW SOCIO-ECONOMIC ORDER

The Assembly's concern for the advancement of a new international political and socio-economic order has taken the form primarily of passing resolutions, sometimes sol-

[68] General Assembly *Official Records* (9th session), Supplement No 11.

[69] General Assembly Resolution 895 (IX) of December 4, 1954. For the report of the 1956 session of the Special Committee on the Question of Defining Aggression, October 8–November 9, 1956, see UN Document A/AC.77/L.13.

[70] General Assembly Resolutions 897 (IX) of December 4, 1954, and 898 (IX) of December 14, 1954.

[71] General Assembly Resolutions 1181 (XII) of November 29, 1957, and 1186 (XII) and 1187 (XII) of December 11, 1957.

[72] See Julius Stone, *Aggression and World Order. A Critique of United Nations Theories of Aggression* (London: Stevens & Sons Limited, 1958).

emnly called "declarations." The following come readily to mind as they surely constitute landmarks in this line of endeavor: the Universal Declaration of Human Rights (General Assembly Resolution 217 A [III] of December 10, 1948), the Declaration on the Granting of Independence to Colonial Countries and Peoples (Resolution 1514 [XV] of December 14, 1960), the Declaration on the Elimination of All Forms of Racial Discrimination (Resolution 1904 [XVIII] of November 20, 1963), and Resolution 1803 (XVII) of December 14, 1962, on "Permanent sovereignty over natural resources." In a sense these resolutions are concerned with the same or closely related matters that were involved in the more formal procedures discussed above. Thus, the Universal Declaration is concerned with the rights of individuals which may be regarded as a counterpart to the duties implicitly assumed in the draft code of offenses against the peace and security of mankind. The resolution on permanent sovereignty, like the draft declaration on rights and duties of states, is concerned with an "inalienable right" of states.[73] The Declaration on Colonialism is concerned as is the Declaration on Racial Discrimination with fundamental human rights and the former, in addition, proclaims an "inalienable right" of peoples.[74]

It would be extremely difficult to provide a representative sample of the efforts of the Assembly to promote economic development. Reference may be made to the 1964 United Nations Conference on Trade and Development (UNCTAD) which in a sense capped the concern of the United Nations with the developing nations and brought into focus some of the guiding principles. The Conference adopted fifteen general principles and thirteen special principles by very large majorities with the United States as the lone dissenter with respect to some of them. They range from relatively innocuous statements often made before in other forums in the same or similar formulation[75] to controversial ones on which the future economic relations between different socio-economic systems and between developing and developed countries should be based.[76] The principles in their entirety disclose an intent to formulate a Magna Charta for economic relations with a bias frankly in favor of the developing countries.[77]

[73] In the preamble the Assembly speaks of "the recognition of the inalienable right of all States freely to dispose of their natural wealth and resources in accordance with their national interests."

[74] In the preamble of General Assembly Resolution 1514 (XV) the Assembly expresses the conviction "that all peoples have an inalienable right to complete freedom, the exercise of their sovereignty and the integrity of their national territory."

[75] E.g., General Principle One:

> Economic relations between countries, including trade relations, shall be based on respect for the principle of sovereign equality of States, self-determination of peoples, and non-interference in the internal affairs of other countries.

This was adopted by 113 in favor, 1 against (United States), with 2 abstentions. (*Proceedings of the United Nations Conference on Trade and Development, Geneva, 23 March–16 July 1964*, Vol. I: *Final Act and Report* [UN Document E/CONF.46/141, Vol. I], p. 18.)

[76] Thus General Principle Four reads in part:

> All countries pledge themselves . . . to help promote, in developing countries, a rate of growth consistent with the need to bring about a substantial and steady increase in average incomes, in order to narrow the gap between the standard of living in developing countries and that in developed countries.

The vote on this was 98 in favor, 1 opposed (United States), with 17 abstentions. (*Ibid.*)

[77] For a concise summary and evaluation, see Oscar Schachter, "Legal Problems" in Richard N. Swift (ed.), *Annual Review of United Nations Affairs, 1963–1964* (Dobbs Ferry, N.Y: Oceana Publications, 1965), pp. 125–127.

## UN RESOLUTIONS AS A SOURCE OF LAW

The resort to the medium of resolutions as a vehicle for the progressive development of international law does not imply that the United Nations has abandoned the medium of the treaty or convention, or in more colloquial terms that the formulation of "hard" law (treaty) has been set aside in favor of "soft" law (resolution or declaration). The United Nations is pragmatic about its choice of media, and sometimes "soft" law is only considered a precursor of "hard" law. Thus, in the field of human rights, pending the completion of the covenants on human rights, the General Assembly adopted several conventions on some specific subjects such as slavery, political rights of women, and consent to marriage.[78] On the other hand, the Assembly adopted the Declaration on the Elimination of All Forms of Racial Discrimination and at the same time requested the Economic and Social Council to give "absolute priority" to the preparation of a draft convention on the same subject.[79]

There are differences of opinion on the significance or role of resolutions or declarations of the General Assembly as sources of international law. It may be observed first of all that where the Assembly has chosen a two-stage approval—first a declaration or resolution, followed by a convention—it has drawn a distinction between the traditional and accepted source of legal obligation, the convention, and the novel and controversial form, the resolution or declaration. The distinction is of vital significance and, it is submitted, should be maintained.

This is not to suggest that the traditional sources of international law should not be kept under continuous review and that their adequacy need not be tested in the light of contemporary developments. There is room for a number of intermediate positions between the two extremes: At one pole of a continuum is the proposition that the General Assembly has a legislative or quasi-legislative function,[80] and at the other pole is the proposition that resolutions of the Assembly are legally not binding. The former view assumes and must assume that where the Assembly adopts resolutions such as those relating to human rights, self-determination, etc., it is merely elaborating principles already accepted as binding by the Members; and, in turn, it assumes further that the Assembly has the

[78] Supplementary Convention on the Abolition of Slavery, the Slave Trade, and Practices Similar to Slavery of September 4, 1956 (UN Document E/CONF.24/23 or UN Sales No. 57.XIV.2) (the Convention came into force on April 30, 1959, upon the deposit of the second ratification; by July 1963, 49 states were parties); Convention on the Political Rights of Women of 1953, to which 39 states are parties; and Convention on Consent to Marriage, Minimum Age for Marriage and Registration of Marriages (General Assembly Resolution 1763 A [XVII] of November 7, 1962). On the current state of the work of the United Nations on human rights, see Myres S. McDougal and Gerhard Bebr, "Human Rights in the United Nations," *The American Journal of International Law,* July 1964 (Vol. 58, No. 3), pp. 603–641; and Richard B. Bilder, "The International Promotion of Human Rights: A Current Assessment," *ibid.,* pp. 728–734.

[79] General Assembly Resolutions 1904 (XVIII) and 1906 (XVIII) of November 20, 1963. It may be noted that the Assembly has been preparing a draft declaration on the right of asylum and a draft declaration and draft convention on freedom of information (General Assembly Resolutions 1839 [XVII] and 1840 [XVII] of December 19, 1962).

[80] Jorge Castañeda, "The Underdeveloped Nations and the Development of International Law," *International Organization,* Winter 1961 (Vol. 15, No. 1), pp. 38–48.

power of authentic and binding interpretation.[81] As was pointed out earlier, this view has not been generally accepted,[82] and it is doubtful whether it would be desirable to accept it. The latter position adheres to the original conception of the Assembly as a deliberative body endowed with limited powers and certainly, by design and not by omission, not endowed with legislative prerogatives. The two-stage approach followed by the Assembly and mentioned earlier is a clear and incontrovertible evidence that the Assembly shares this view of its own powers.

The significance of the resolutions of the Assembly is primarily political. Many are designed to give direction to the Members and the Organization as well. Some resolutions, such as those dealing with outer space, may derive especial significance from the fact that they represent the consensus of the two powers which have a virtual duopoly in that virginal field.[83] Where there is or is claimed to be law, as, for instance, with respect to compensation for the expropriation of property owned by aliens, a resolution of the Assembly, such as that on "Permanent sovereignty over natural resources" may have sufficient force to create or increase uncertainty as to the claimed law without being sufficiently persuasive to create a new rule. In this particular case the international standard according to which the state taking such measures must pay "prompt, adequate and effective" compensation has been under attack for so long and by so substantial a number of states that it could be fairly doubted whether that standard ever was or still is a rule of customary international law. This being so, the resolution of the Assembly proposing merely "appropriate compensation"[84] may be deemed to have administered the *coup de grâce* to the alleged international standard. This conclusion is based not on any assumption of the resolution's having an obligatory character. It may be based more simply on the traditional concept of customary international law according to which a rule requires practice and the *opinio juris,* that is, the manifestation of conviction that the practice has been accepted as binding or obligatory. The debates in the Assembly stretching over a period of years would indicate that this conviction was lacking, that there was no supporting consensus.[85] Thus, as a convenient index for determining the existence or absence of consensus, the debates in the Assembly and the resolutions which it adopts may serve a useful purpose. But consensus without state practice is not productive of a rule of law.

There is a long way from the birth of an idea to its consummation in a rule of law, be it conventional or customary. Resolutions of the Assembly purporting to be of a law-

[81] *Ibid.,* p. 47; and Manfred Lachs, "The Law in and of the United Nations," *Indian Journal of International Law,* 1960–1961 (Vol. I), p. 438.

[82] See pp. 170–171 above for Mexico City statement of the Special Committee on Principles of International Law Concerning Friendly Relations and Cooperation Among States.

[83] See Oliver J. Lissitzyn's remarks in Swift, p. 128. Additional factors are the absence of a competing doctrine or consensus.

[84] Operative paragraph 4 of General Assembly Resolution 1803 (XVII) of December 14, 1962.

[85] In the *Sabbatino* case the United States Supreme Court held that consensus was lacking for the old standard and referred specifically to the long-standing opposition of the Communist countries, the declared opposition of many new countries, and the actual practice of states which accepted less than full compensation. (*Banco Nacional de Cuba v. Sabbatino,* in *United States Reports* [Washington, D.C: U.S. Government Printing Office, 1964], Vol. 376, pp. 398 ff.)

making character are certainly "an important link in the continuing process of development and formulation of new principles of international law."[86] It has been suggested that the traditional statement of sources of international law in Article 38 of the Statute of the International Court of Justice and the distinction between binding and nonbinding sources "was becoming increasingly irrelevant and unrealistic."[87] This is perhaps too extreme a view, although it may serve a useful purpose to reexamine Article 38, which had been part of the Statute of the Permanent Court of International Justice and was adopted in 1945 without change in the Statute of the new Court, and perhaps to arrange for a reexamining of the sources of international law generally by a committee of governments.[88] Until this is done, however, it may be proper to regard debates in and resolutions of the General Assembly not so much as sources but, in the words of Article 38, paragraph 1 (d), of the Statute "as a subsidiary means for the determination of rules of law." They might rank with, or even ahead of, "the teachings of the most highly qualified publicists" but below judicial decisions.

To close this analysis on a slightly ironical note: The Sixth Committee held a far-ranging debate in which it frequently expressed dissatisfaction with the state of international law, its own modest role in the United Nations, the slow progress of the work of the International Law Commission, and its near starvation in having had referred to it only three out of about 90 items on the agenda of the General Assembly; it noted the attitude of new states toward traditional international law which, having grown up without their participation, has failed to reflect their interests; yet finally, it adopted unanimously a Ukranian amendment to the pending draft resolution which called for the "strict and undeviating observance [of international law] by all Governments."[89]

## CONCLUSION

There will be no disposition to quarrel with the estimate that while

> since the Second World War remarkable advances have been made in virtually every sector of international organization . . . there has been no comparable advance in international adjudication.[90]

[86] Wolfgang Friedmann, *The Changing Structure of International Law* (New York: Columbia University Press, 1964), p. 139.

[87] Lissitzyn, in Swift, p. 127.

[88] This proposal was made by Mr. Castañeda "in order to take into account numerous resolutions and decisions produced by a vast array of international organizations." (General Assembly *Official Records . . . Sixth Committee* [15th session], November 9, 1960, p. 79, paragraph 13.)

[89] *Ibid.*, p. 115. The full text of the preambular paragraph in which the Ukrainian amendment was incorporated reads as follows:

> Considering that the conditions prevailing in the world today give increased importance to the role of international law—and its strict and undeviating observance by all Governments—in strengthening international peace, developing friendly and co-operative relations among nations, settling disputes by peaceful means and advancing economic and social progress throughout the world.

(General Assembly Resolution 1505 [XV] of December 12, 1960.)

[90] C. Wilfred Jenks, *The Prospects of International Adjudication* (Dobbs Ferry, N.Y: Oceana Publications, 1964), p. 1.

To this may be added the almost pathetic appeal made in the International Court of Justice by the President, Judge Sir Percy Spender, on the opening of its hearings on the merits of the *South West Africa Cases* in 1965:

> This unique and permanently constituted judicial means of implementing a vital Charter purpose stands ever ready at the service of the members of the world community.[91]

This reminder could not be more timely as there will be only one case left on the Court's general list after the judgment in these cases. Important and substantial as have been the contributions of the Court in adjudicating contentious cases, these or the advisory opinions will not be discussed herein inasmuch as they are dealt with elsewhere in this volume.[92]

One observation, looking to the future, may be submitted. As the UN gains in stature and comes increasingly to play a significant part in international affairs, disputes of a legal character may well arise between it and its Members. Article 34, paragraph 1, of the Court's Statute which states that "only states may be parties in cases before the Court" may have been fully justified in 1920 when it was drafted and the League of Nations was quite new. It cannot be foreseen what expansion international organization will take in the years to come. Today this provision has become an anachronism pure and simple and should be removed. The United Nations, at least, "at present the supreme type of international organization" as the Court said in the *Reparation* case,[93] should no longer be denied active and passive capacity in contentious cases. To confer this capacity on the United Nations will require the solution of many incidental problems such as which organ of the United Nations should have the capacity to institute proceedings,[94] but these problems are not beyond the ingenuity of lawyers.

The United Nations started out in an uncharted political situation. Settlements have been made in some areas. But other parts of the political map of the world remain only provisionally marked out. The ideological conflict has lost little of its virulence, and periods of "thaw" and "freeze" have alternated. Deeply felt emotions over the last but hard remnants of colonialisn and racial discrimination have characterized the debates of the Assembly almost since the beginning. The rapid increase in the membership has made the United Nations more nearly universal and representative of the international society; it has also made it rather more unwieldy. The forum for the annual discussion of the arms race, while it has shifted from the Assembly to the Eighteen-Nation Committee on Disarmament in Geneva, continues to cast a shadow over the Organization. In these circumstances the wonder is that the United Nations has been able to accomplish as much as it

[91] ICJ Communiqué No. 65/3, March 15, 1965.
[92] See Shabtai Rosenne, "The Court and the Judicial Process," "International Organization," Vol. XIX, No. 3, 1965.
[93] *Reparation for Injuries Suffered in the Service of the United Nations, Advisory Opinion: I.C.J. Reports 1949*, p. 179.
[94] Jenks, pp. 210 ff.

has in promoting the growth of law and in laying the socio-economic as well as the political foundations for further growth.

Yet it may be fair to suggest that more could be done in using the standard of law in the day-to-day work of the United Nations. There is virtue in promoting solutions by accommodation or compromise rather than on the basis of law if that serves the purpose.[95] But which and how many disputes, one may ask legitimately, have been actually settled in this fashion? To be sure, the hostilities in Indonesia, Kashmir, Palestine, and Suez have been effectively brought under control, but have any of the underlying disputes—Indonesia, apart, which was a special case—been settled? This is not to imply that they could or would have been settled by the resort to law or to the Court. But perhaps they might have been brought nearer to a settlement. The same observation might be made for matters such as the question of Indians in South Africa or *apartheid.* There was a risk inevitably in referring a situation involving Article 2, paragraph 7, of the Charter to the Court for an advisory opinion, but even if the Court had denied the competence of the General Assembly the result would not have been disastrous as without it the Assembly failed anyhow to make any headway. Moreover, it is not unreasonable for a Member which claims that its vital interests are affected to ask that the legal issue of competence be judicially clarified. This is said without reference to any particular dispute or situation and without reference to any particular Member or Members.

The experience of the first two decades has demonstrated that the United Nations, particularly the General Assembly, has frequently through its far-ranging activities affected vital interests of the Members and no doubt may increasingly do so in the next decade. Accordingly it stands to reason that some means, some procedure, will have to be provided to resolve conflicts. A Member that desires to have legal issues clarified should be afforded an opportunity to have them so clarified by the advisory procedure of the Court. It may not be unreasonable to expect, as a counterpart, that the Member as well as the requesting organ agree in advance to abide by the advisory opinion. There are ways and means for the United Nations to protect itself against abuse, against purely obstructionist proposals to refer a host of questions to the Court. Moreover, the Court itself can be relied upon to insist upon the integrity of the judicial function.

One need not naïvely expect that a judicial clarification of questions of competence or similar legal issues will set all conflicts at rest as legal issues rarely comprise the whole controversy. But it may be expected that, without departing from the advisory opinion, the Member and the United Nations or the Members concerned will be able to move ahead on the political level where interests can be composed and conciliated. What seems to be required in the years to come is that both the Organization and the Members free themselves from a certain antijudicial bias which seems to have been prominent in the first

[95] Oscar Schachter, "The Quasi-Judicial Rôle of the Security Council and the General Assembly," *The American Journal of International Law,* October 1964 (Vol. 58, No. 4), pp. 960–965.

two decades of the United Nations and that resort to legal arguments be not confined merely to the debates.

Law can and should play a more vigorous part in resolving legal controversies without contesting the role which politics must inevitably play in the activities of the United Nations. But it is simply not enough to brush aside the law on the ground that the issue in question is also political. No doubt this will be so in most cases which arise in the United Nations but if all legal issues have political angles, so have political issues a legal angle.

As the President of the International Court, Judge Sir Percy Spender, said recently:

> It is, of course, self-evident that all disputes between nations are not susceptible of resolution by judicial means. It is, however, equally evident that the functions of this Court may be invoked more frequently than they are, if not in final settlement of all the issues in disputes between nations, at least, on the judicial level, in clarification of certain issues involved, so rendering disputes more amenable to complete and final settlement. It is to be observed that the Charter enjoins the settlement by peaceful means, of disputes the continuance of which is likely to endanger the maintenance of international peace and security, and lays it down that legal disputes between States should be referred, as a general rule, to this Court to be dealt with in accordance with international law.[96]

Just as an advisory opinion will rarely empty a controversy of all its contents, so a judgment will not necessarily set at rest all the underlying political or socio-economic issues. Parties may be more willing to compromise their interests than their legal stands. The risk is, of course, unavoidable that a judgment or an advisory opinion may stiffen a party's position with respect to the underlying conflicts of interest. This risk is unavoidable. It requires a political decision to depoliticize a dispute or parts of it just as it requires a political decision to politicize the whole of the dispute.

[96] ICJ Communiqué No. 65/3, March 15, 1965, p. 3.

# THE DEVELOPMENT OF INTERNATIONAL LAW THROUGH THE UNITED NATIONS

## INTRODUCTION

It is proposed to focus attention in this essay on the contribution of two of the six principal organs of the United Nations to the development of international law—the General Assembly and the International Court of Justice. This is done for reasons of economy, and there is no intention to imply that the other principal organs would not have to be considered if a more comprehensive treatment of the subject were attempted. Certainly, the practice of the Security Council is a rich mine for legal exploration, but in principle and given its limited jurisdiction, the Council's contribution would be chiefly in the area of the interpretation and application of the Charter. The work of the other two councils, the Economic and Social Council and the Trusteeship Council, has largely been channeled to the General Assembly. The Secretariat, through the legal opinions of the secretary-general, has made a notable contribution to the interpretation of the Charter and is also relevant from the point of view of general international law. But it is the General Assembly which is charged by Article 13(1) of the Charter with the task of initiating studies and making recommendations for the purpose of "encouraging the progressive development of international law and its codification." The inclusion of the Court hardly needs explanation or justification as traditionally international lawyers have looked to tribunals or arbitration and the predecessor of the Court of the United Nations, the Permanent Court of International Justice of the League of Nations, for substantial contributions to the development of the law.

Before discussing the work of the Assembly and the Court, it may be useful to trace briefly the development of international law prior to the establishment of the United Nations. The final section will be concerned with the prospects for the future.

## THE DEVELOPMENT OF INTERNATIONAL LAW PRIOR TO THE UNITED NATIONS

The development of modern international law may be conveniently related to the final stage of the wars against Napoleon in 1814–1815. During the preceding period the doctrine of the classical writers including Vitoria, Suarez, and Grotius, and the practice of states were concerned with laying the foundations of the law of nations, the problems arising from the age of discoveries, and the emergence, following the settlement of Westphalia of 1648, of a multiplicity of sovereign states which recognized no common superior authority other than that of the fledgling law of nations. It seems fitting, therefore, that the era of legal positivism and continuous technological progress marked initially by the Industrial Revolution was ushered in by two significant acts of deliberate law creation: the provision in the Final Act of the Congress of Vienna of June 9, 1815, concerning freedom of navigation on international rivers, and the regulation signed at Vienna on March 19, 1815, concerning the classification of diplomatic agents. The latter was designed to clarify the ranking of diplomatic officials through which the official business between states is conducted, their immunities and privileges having been based on customary international law. The former was intended, as the Permanent Court of International Justice was to say a hundred years later in its advisory opinion in the *Jurisdiction of the European Commission of the Danube* case, to do away with monopolistic controls by the riparian states which "not only hampered the development of commerce but also tended to prevent the growth of international relations appropriate to a state of peace."[1] It may be noted in passing that international regulation of the navigation on international rivers such as the Rhine and the Danube was continued at several interstate conferences, including the Paris Peace Conference of 1919 following World War I, and, insofar as the Danube is concerned, at the Peace Conference of Paris in 1947 following World War II. The Statute on the Regime of Navigable Waterways of International Concern adopted at Barcelona in 1921 is a landmark in the efforts of liberalizing navigation from oppressive national control. It may also be noted that the work begun in Vienna in 1815 concerning diplomatic agents was substantially completed at the United Nations conference held in Vienna in 1961, which on April 16 adopted the Convention on Diplomatic Intercourse and Immunities. This convention, declares the preamble, is to contribute "to the development of friendly relations among nations, irrespective of their differing constitutional and social systems."[2] The 1815 regulation was adopted by eight monarchical powers (Austria, France, Great Britain, Portugal, Prussia, Russia, Spain, and Sweden) which in-

[1] Publications of the PCIJ Series B, No. 14 (1927), p. 38; also in Manley O. Hudson, *World Courts Reports* (Washington, D.C.: Carnegie Endowment for International Peace, 1935), II, 164.

[2] Ian Brownlie (ed.), *Basic Documents in International Law* (Oxford: Clarendon Press, 1967), p. 112.

vited "the representatives of other crowned heads to adopt the same regulations," whereas the 1961 conference was attended by representatives of eighty-one (seventy-five members of the United Nations) states with widely differing political systems.

International lawmaking continued throughout the nineteenth century at an impressive pace. Relative political stability in Europe, the center of the then prevailing international system, may well have been a factor in the process but probably no more than that. The technological exploitation of scientific discoveries and the expanding commerce involving movement of goods and persons and communications of all sorts across national boundaries called for international regulation by means of treaties. The sovereign state, then as now, knows of no other way for transcending its own limitation—namely, that its writ runs only as far as its national boundaries and that any movement of persons, goods, or communications across its boundaries required the cooperation of its neighbors and its neighbors' neighbors. Customary international law relating to traffic across the seas solved the problem when it gradually gave scope and some precision to the principle of freedom of the high seas. But a more comprehensive and explicit regulation was achieved only in 1958 when the United Nations Conference on the Law of the Sea, attended by eighty-five states, adopted four conventions, two of which, the Convention on the High Seas and the Convention on the Territorial Sea and the Contiguous Zone, deal with various aspects of navigation.[3] However, the pressing demands for freer movement of goods, persons, and communication across the land, later across the air, and in the future across outer space could not and can not wait for principles and rules to develop through the usually slow process of customary law. An alternative method had to be adapted and adopted. The method of negotiating and adopting multilateral conventions—that is, treaties binding on more than two states—was selected. Bilateral treaties, treaties binding on two states only, have been used prior to and along with multilateral conventions but their usefulness as a tool of regulation in an increasingly interdependent world is limited. Where general problems require general regulation, the multilateral treaty is the instrument chosen by governments. As a supplement to such a treaty or where specific matters affecting the interests of and intercourse between two states are concerned, the bilateral treaty will continue to be used.

An example or two will illustrate the process. Postal communications had been the subject of numerous bilateral agreements which came to exhibit certain common features. A conference held in 1863 did not succeed in framing a multilateral convention but a conference of twenty-two states held in Berne in 1874 did and created the General Postal Union which in 1878 was expanded into the Universal Postal Union which is now one of the specialized agencies of the United Nations. It counts 135 participating states, more than any other international instrument and organization. The discovery and practical application of the telegraph led first to bilateral arrangements, but very soon the states responded to the need for a more comprehensive and uniform regulation by concluding the

[3] See Brownie, *Basic Documents*, pp. 70, 80.

International Telegraph Convention in Paris in 1865. Initially, the treaty and the organization based on it comprised twenty states. As new discoveries were made—telephone and broadcasting—they too were brought under an international regime. A series of treaties led in 1932 to the creation of the International Telecommunications Union which has become a specialized agency of the United Nations and has a membership of 133 states.

During the fifty-year period 1864 to 1914, the year of the outbreak of World War I, numerous multilateral conventions were concluded on topics of relevance to the growing volume of transactions such as weights and measures, trademarks, copyrights, patents, and others where uniformity of law appeared desirable. To borrow a term from the United Nations International Law Commission, the states engaged on an unprecedented scale in the progressive development of international law.[4] During the same period states also attempted to codify certain aspects of customary international law, particularly the law of war and neutrality. This is a process which had its start with the Paris Declaration of 1856, which formulated four rules on naval warfare and which continued at several conferences, the latest of which is the Geneva Conference of 1949, which adopted four conventions.[5] The most important of these conferences were the first and second Hague Peace Conferences of 1899 and 1907, respectively, which, in addition to several conventions dealing with the law of war, also produced the Convention for the Pacific Settlement of International Disputes of 1899, revised in 1907. This convention provided for establishment of the still existing Permanent Court of Arbitration.[6] The Hague conferences mark the beginning of periodic conferences for both the codification and the progressive development of international law.[7] One of the most ambitious attempts at codification was the London Naval Conference of 1908–1909, growing out of The Hague Conference of 1907. This conference was remarkable for three reasons: first, it was intended to formulate the law of naval warfare and thereby make possible the establishment of the International Prize Court; second, it was the first major conference which had the benefit of thorough preparation; and, third, it was confronted with the problem of distinguishing between the codification of the "common law of nations" and its development.[8] Thorough preparation has come to be accepted as prerequisite for the subsequent activities of the League of Nations and the United Nations. The separation of codification

[4] M. O. Hudson, *International Legislation,* I (1931), IX (1946), counted 257 multilateral conventions for the period 1864–1914 (I, p. xxxvi) and 670 for the period 1919–1945 (IX, p. xvi). However, not all of these instruments entered into force.

[5] These are: Convention for the Amelioration of the Condition of the Wounded and Sick in Armed Forces in the Field; Convention for the Amelioration of the Condition of Wounded, Sick and Shipwrecked Members of Armed Forces at Sea; Convention Relative to the Treatment of Prisoners of War; and the Convention Relative to the Protection of Civilian Persons in Time of War. *U.S. Treaties and Other International Acts Series* 3362–3365.

[6] J. B. Scott (ed.), *The Hague Conventions and Declarations of 1899 and 1907* (New York: Oxford University Press, 1915).

[7] For a survey see this writer's study prepared for the Division for the Codification of International Law of the Secretariat of the United Nations and distributed as UN Document A/AC.10/5, April 29, 1947; republished in 41 AJIL Suppl. 29–111 (1947). This study is entitled "Historical Survey of the Development of International Law and its Codification by International Conferences" (Henceforth cited: "Historical Survey").

[8] *Ibid.,* p. 44f.

from development has been accepted in principle, but abandoned in practice, by both the League and the United Nations.

The establishment of the League of Nations provided the first opportunity for a sustained effort for both the development and codification of international law. Unlike the conventions of the nineteenth century which were linked to functional organizations with a single purpose, like the postal and telegraph agencies, the League was a multipurpose institution with an elaborate infrastructure including a highly efficient and sophisticated Secretariat. The League provided the auspices for many conferences which resulted in over one hundred twenty international instruments covering a wide array cf subjects: arbitration and security, unification of commercial law, agricultural credit, counterfeiting currency, customs, bones, hides and skins, unification of river law, railways, road traffic, humanitarian and social questions (traffic in women and children, obscene publications, slavery), and narcotics. Many of these instruments failed to enter into force, others merely served as models, and some continue in force, and the secretary-general of the United Nations has taken over the depository function with respect to them.[9]

Several League treaties which are still in force were amended by protocols or were further developed by additional treaties concluded under United Nations auspices. This was the case in the fields of control of narcotics and other dangerous drugs,[10] traffic in persons,[11] obscene publications,[12] economic statistics,[13] and slavery.[14] Partly as a result of the war in Vietnam, the United Nations gave prominence to the Geneva Protocol for the Prohibition of the Use in War of Asphyxiating, Poisonous or other Gases and of Bacteriological Methods of Warfare of June 17, 1925, which resulted from the work of the League in the field of security. The General Assembly on December 16, 1969, adopted Resolution 2603 (XXIV), in which it noted that (1) a majority of the states existing in 1925 adhered to the protocol; (2) since then further states have become parties to it; (3) other states have declared that they will abide by its principles and objectives; (4) those principles and objectives have commanded broad respect in the practice of states; and (5) the General Assembly, in its Resolution 2162B (XXI) of December 5, 1966, "without any dissenting vote, has called for the strict observance by all States of the principles and objectives of the Geneva Protocol."[15]

The League of Nations, after what seemed to be very careful preparation, failed in its one and only effort to codify substantial and controversial parts of customary interna-

[9] See *Multilateral Treaties in respect of which the Secretary-General Performs Depository Functions.* List of Signatures, Ratifications, Accessions, etc., as at December 31, 1969. UN Pub. Sales No.: E. 70.V.3. Document ST/LEG/SER.D/3 (1970). Part II of this publication lists twenty-seven League of Nations multilateral treaties. (Will henceforth be cited: *Multilateral Treaties.)*

[10] *Ibid.*, chap. VI.

[11] *Ibid.*, chap. VII.

[12] *Ibid.*, chap. IX.

[13] *Ibid.*, chap. XII.

[14] *Ibid.*, chap. XVIII.

[15] General Assembly, *Official Records* (24th sess.), Suppl. 30 (A/7630), p. 16. The General Assembly reiterated its call for strict observance of the protocal in Resolution 2662 (XXV) which was adopted by a vote of 113:0:2. *Ibid.* (25th sess.), Suppl. 28 (A/8028), p. 14.

tional law. The topics selected were nationality, territorial waters, and responsibility of states for damage to the persons and property of aliens. A diplomatic conference of forty-seven governments, members and nonmembers of the League, was held at The Hague in 1930. No agreement was reached on territorial waters and responsibility of states. With respect to nationality, no agreement was reached on the main question, the principles which govern the acquisition of nationality. The delegates were able, however, to draft instruments relating to certain conflicts of nationality laws, to military obligations in certain cases of double nationality, and to certain cases of statelessness.[16] One of the factors generally believed to have caused difficulties was disagreement as to what the law actually was as well as the desire of certain governments to modify existing law which they considered unsatisfactory.[17] However, the "bases of discussion" drawn up by the Preparatory Committee for the conference enriched the literature on the subjects concerned. A by-product of the League's officials effort was the unofficial Harvard Research on International Law, organized by Professor Manley O. Hudson, which resulted in several draft conventions, the first three of which were devoted to the topics selected for The Hague conference.[18] Used all over the world by scholars and tribunals, the Harvard Research continues to serve as a standard work on the subjects with which it dealt and as a monument to Manley O. Hudson.

Even a short survey of the League's activities in the development of international law would be incomplete without mentioning the International Labor Organization which up to 1946 formed an integral though autonomous part of the League. Since then it has become an independent institution and a specialized agency of the United Nations which in 1971 had 121 members. The mission of the organization is to promote international peace through social justice and improvement of conditions of labor. During the period of its connection with the League, it adopted 67 International Labor Conventions and, since 1946, 63 more conventions were adopted. The organization also addressed 134 recommendations to the member states which were intended to influence their domestic legislation in the direction of social welfare. While the International Labor Conventions enter into force when ratified by two member states, some have received a very large number of ratifications: thus the Forced Labor Convention of 1930 was ratified by 106 members, the Freedom of Association and Protection of the Right to Organize Convention of 1948 by 77 members, and the Right to Organize and Collective Bargaining Convention of 1949 by 89 members. Altogether, the International Labor Conventions received 3,500 ratifications.[19] The United States of America is the champion nonratifier of International Labor Conventions, having ratified 2 out of some 130 conventions: the

[16] "Historical Survey," p. 82.

[17] *Ibid.*, pp. 84–86.

[18] For a list of the topics covered by the Harvard Research, see "Note on the Private Codification of Public International Law," 41 AJIL Suppl. 138–147 (1947), pp. 146–147.

[19] See Summary of Reports on Ratified Conventions: International Labor Conference, 53rd sess., 1969, 3rd item on the Agenda (Report III, Part I), Nos. 29, 87, 98; and C. Wilfred Jenks, *Social Justice in the Law of Nations* (New York: Oxford University Press, 1970).

Minimum Age (Sea) Convention (Revised) of 1936, and the Certification of Able Seamen Convention of 1946.[20]

## THE UNITED NATIONS

### Concern with the Fundamental Bases of a New International Legal Order

The contributions of the United Nations to the development of international law have exceeded all expectations. Beginning with its first session in 1946, there has been a steady stream of resolutions, declarations, and conventions adopted by the General Assembly or by diplomatic conferences convened under its auspices. While there can be no doubt, after five and twenty years, about the Assembly's enthusiasm amounting almost to a passion for the progressive development of international law and through it of branches of municipal law, there has been and there remains a lingering doubt about its consistency and methodology in pursuing this task. It would seem that the Assembly selected whatever organ appeared most serviceable for a particular purpose or created a new one as convenience dictated, and cast the results of its work in whatever form—resolution, declaration, convention—was acceptable to its members. This process was bound to create problems—if not for the Assembly then at least for scholars who felt the need for evaluating, from the legal point of view, the significance of the new forms in which a good deal of the Assembly's contribution was cast, namely, resolutions and declarations, in preference to or in anticipation of the traditional form of conventions.

The first actions of the Assembly at the second part of its first session appear, in retrospect, to have set the pattern. Recognizing that the Charter in Article 13, paragraph 1 (a) laid an obligation upon it to initiate studies and make recommendations for "encouraging the progressive development of international law and its codification," the Assembly adopted on December 11, 1946, Resolution 94 (I) instituting a Committee of Seventeen Members to study the methods for carrying out this obligation.[21] However, without awaiting the recommendations of the committee, the assembly proceeded at once to the adoption of two resolutions which were neither in the nature of studies nor explicitly in the nature of recommendations as laid down in paragraph 1 (a) of Article 13. In Resolution 95 (I), adopted on the same day, the Assembly "*affirms* the principles of international law recognized by the Charter of the Nürnberg Tribunal and the judgment of the Tribunal."[22] In Resolution 96 (I) of the same day, the Assembly "*affirms* that genocide is a crime under international law . . . for the commission of which principals and accomplices . . . are punishable." The Assembly perceived no inconsistency in pro-

[20] Summary Report, *ibid.,* Nos. 58, 74. In fairness it should be pointed out that in many matters legislation in the United States is up to the standards of the ILO conventions.

[21] Resolutions adopted by the General Assembly (1st sess.), Part II, Document A 64/Add. 1, p. 187.

[22] *Ibid.,* p. 188.

ceeding to request the Economic and Social Council, one of the principal organs of the United Nations, to undertake the necessary studies with a view to drawing up a draft convention on the crime of genocide.[23] The Council discharged its task and the Assembly two years later, on December 9, 1948, approved the Genocide Convention or, to give its full title, Convention on the Prevention and Punishment of the Crime of Genocide, by Resolution 260 (III).[24] Some seventy-five states have ratified or acceded to the convention in the usual manner, some with reservations, and some governments made objections to some of the reservations.[25] Here the Assembly affirmed the crime by resolution and in anticipation of the adoption of the convention. What was the legal significance of the resolution prior to the adoption of the convention? Suppose that for one reason or another the convention would never have been drafted or, if drafted, failed of adoption in the Assembly?

The further course of the Nuremberg principles is illustrative of the relevance of the latter question.

Having first committed itself to the affirmation of the principles of international law recognized by the Charter and the Judgment of the International Military Tribunal, the Assembly on November 21, 1947, adopted Resolution 177 (II) in which it entrusted the International Law Commission, whose members were to be elected in 1948, with the

> formulation of the principles of international law recognized in the charter of the Nürnberg Tribunal and in the judgment of the Tribunal.[26]

The International Law Commission itself was established by Resolution 174 (II), adopted on the same day, and it did not begin to function until April 12, 1949, when it held its first session. The commission first debated the question "whether or not the Commission should ascertain to what extent the principles contained in the Charter and in the judgment constituted principles of international law."[27] Had the commission, some of whose members were out of sympathy with the post-World War II war crimes trials, particularly the crimes against peace, embarked on ascertaining what, if any, the principles of customary international law were which had found expression in the Charter and Judgment of the Tribunal, the result would have been in doubt. A finding supported only by a majority of the commission might well have been regarded as disavowing the Assembly's confident affirmation that there were indeed some principles of customary international law contained in the Charter and in the judgment. Some jurists may have been tempted to point out that the Assembly *appeared* to say one thing but meant another. What the Assembly appeared to declare and what the resolution was generally understood to imply, was that in the Assembly's view the Charter and the judgment were

[23] *Ibid.*

[24] General Assembly, *Official Records* (3rd sess.), Part I, Resolutions (A/810), p. 174.

[25] *Multilateral Treaties*, pp. 61–67.

[26] General Assembly, *Official Records* (2nd sess.), Resolutions (A/519), pp. 111–112. In the same resolution the Assembly also directed the commission to prepare a draft code of offenses against the peace and security of mankind.

[27] *The Work of the International Law Commission*, UN Pub. 67.V.4 (1967), p. 21. Henceforth cited as: *Work of the ILC*.

based on principles of customary international law; that, in other words, the 1945 Charter in formulating some principles which were highly controversial—such as individual responsibility for crimes against peace and humanity, denial of immunity for acts of state or acts done in conformity with national law, and others—merely gave expression to existing law. Others may have been inclined to interpret the resolution as implying that *if or to the extent that* the Charter and the tribunal contained principles of customary international law, they were affirmed by the Assembly. The decision of the commission, in the light of these alternatives, was becomingly diplomatic, namely that "since the Nürnberg principles had been unanimously affirmed by the General Assembly in Resolution 95 (I) of 11 December 1946, the task entrusted to the Commission was not to express any appreciation of those principles as principles of international law but merely to formulate them."[28]

The subsequent course taken in the Assembly with regard to the Nuremberg principles was anticlimactic. The commission formulated seven principles in 1950 and transmitted them to the Assembly.[29] The Assembly, having lost its initial fervor, neither adopted nor rejected them. Instead, it decided by Resolution 488 (V), adopted on December 12, 1950, to send them to the member states for comments and instructed the commission to take such comments into account in drafting the Code of Offences against the Peace and Security of Mankind.[30] Thus the Nuremberg principles became linked with the major project of the code which still gathers dust in the archives of the United Nations because this code in turn was linked with yet another project—namely, that of defining aggression—which is still under the active consideration of a committee of the Assembly.

Pursuant to Resolution 488 (V), referred to above, the commission submitted a draft in 1951, a draft Code of Offences against the Peace and Security of Mankind, but this was not considered at the 1951 session nor was it considered at the 1952 session of the Assembly. In the meantime, the Assembly by Resolution 378 (V) of November 17, 1950, had, at the behest of the Soviet Union, requested the commission to define the concept of aggression. The commission, after some hesitation, included a definition in the draft code which it submitted to the Assembly in 1954 in the following terms:

> The following acts are offences against the peace and security of mankind:
>
> (1) Any act of aggression, including the employment by the authorities of a State of armed forces against another State for any purpose other than national or collective self-defence or in pursuance of a decision or recommendation of a competent organ of the United Nations.
>
> (2) Any threat by the authorities of a State to resort to an act of aggression against another State.[31]

It is certainly not surprising that the Assembly was not satisfied with this definition. It proceeded, beginning in 1952, with the establishment of special committees which

[28] *Ibid.*
[29] *Ibid.*, pp. 63–64.
[30] *Ibid.*, p. 21.
[31] Article 2 of the draft code, the text of which is reproduced *ibid.*, pp. 64–65.

were charged with the task of defining aggression. None of them succeeded in reaching a consensus on the definition of this elusive concept.[32] The latest Special Committee, established in 1967, was urged to submit a definition to the twenty-fifth anniversary session. This the committee failed to do, but it did report that "it did not have sufficient time to complete its task" and recommended to the Assembly that it be invited "to resume its work as early as possible in 1971."[33] No doubt the Assembly will accept the Special Committee's recommendation. It remains to be noted that by Resolution 1186 (XII) of December 11, 1957, the General Assembly transmitted the 1954 draft code of offences to the member governments for comment. Since then the draft code did not appear on the agenda of the Assembly.[34]

To round out the picture of the several interlocking efforts of the Assembly stemming from its 1946 affirmation of the Nuremberg principles, mention should be made of the work on the question of an international criminal court. This was initiated by Resolution 260B (III) adopted by the Assembly on December 9, 1948. In it the Assembly requested the International Law Commission

> to study the desirability and possibility of establishing an international judicial organ for the trial of persons charged with genocide or other crimes over which jurisdiction will be conferred upon that organ by international conventions.[35]

The Assembly also requested the commission to consider the possibility of establishing "a Criminal Chamber of the International Court of Justice." Fortunately, the commission did not pursue this idea and generally did not manifest much enthusiasm for the project. Accordingly, a committee was established, by Resolution 489 (V) of December 12, 1950, which produced a draft statute for an international criminal court. Consideration of it, however, was postponed in 1954 and again in 1957 since this project related to the draft Code of Offences and the task of defining aggression.[36] Thus, nearly twenty-five years after the adoption of the initial resolution affirming the Nuremberg principles, the Assembly has failed to carry out the several projects to which it was impelled by a certain internal logic. It was certainly logical for the Assembly to want to be sure what the principles were to which it had subscribed, although if logic had been the guide of the Assembly in the first place it would have considered the formulation of the principles before affirming them. However, having reversed the order of formulation and affirmation, it was logical to want to place the principles in the larger framework of a Code of Offences against the Peace and Security of Mankind including, as the 1954 draft does, the crime of

[32] On the history of attempts by the League of Nations to define the concept and for a thorough analysis of the problems involved in working out a definition, see Julius Stone, *Aggression and World Order* (London: Stevens & Sons, 1958) and my review of it in 34 *British Year Book of International Law* (1958), pp. 421–425.

[33] General Assembly, *Official Records* (25th sess.), Suppl. 19 (A/8019), *Report* of the Special Committee on the Question of Defining Aggression, July 13–August 14, 1970, p. 4.

[34] For a short history of the draft code, see *Work of the ILC*, pp. 26–28.

[35] *Ibid.*, p. 21.

[36] *Ibid.*, pp. 21–22.

genocide. The desire for a definition of aggression and the statute for a permanent international criminal court already envisaged in the 1948 Genocide Convention[37] was a logical outgrowth of the related projects. In a larger sense, so was the project for a formulation of a draft declaration on the rights and duties of states, which the International Law Commission was instructed to prepare by Resolution 178 (II) of November 21, 1947. The draft elaborated by the commission at its first session in 1949 consists of fourteen articles, some of which are restatements of principles contained in the Charter of the United Nations and the 1928 Kellogg-Briand Pact, or generally found in textbooks on international law. The most remarkable and therefore probably the most objectionable principle is contained in Article 14:

> Every State has the duty to conduct its relations with other States in accordance with international law and with the principle that the sovereignty of each State is subject to the supremacy of international law.[38]

This principle is as elementary as it is self-evident, and the wonder is that the commission found it necessary to make it explicit. Any normative conception of international law as a law governing relations between states can settle for no less but the General Assembly, which obviously had second thoughts about this matter as about the Nuremberg principles, the draft Code of Offences, and international criminal jurisdiction was quite willing to settle for the rather lame statement in Resolution 375 (V) of December 6, 1949, in which it deemed the draft declaration

> a notable and substantial contribution towards the progressive development of international law and its codification and as such commends it to the continuing attention of Member States and of jurists of all nations.[39]

If the project of a draft declaration of the rights and duties of states needs to be excused and explained, it can be excused and explained by the relative immaturity of the Assembly and perhaps of the commission as well. The Assembly cannot invoke this ground, however, when it embarked on a somewhat analogous project in 1962 by resolving

[37] Article 6 of the convention provides for trial of persons charged with genocide by national tribunals "or by such international penal tribunal as may have jurisdiction with respect to those Contracting Parties which shall have accepted its jurisdiction." For an analysis of the crime of genocide, see the article "Genocide as a Crime under International Law" by the "father" of the Genocide Convention, the late Raphael Lemkin, in 41 AJIL 145–151 (1947).

[38] *Report* of the International Law Commission to the General Assembly on the work of the 1st sess., Document A/CN.4/13, June 9, 1949, p. 21; also in *Work of the ILC*, p. 62.

[39] General Assembly, *Official Records*, Resolutions (A/1251), p. 66. The reaction of one jurist, Hans Kelsen, was a textual critique "The Draft Declaration on Rights and Duties of States," 44 AJIL 259–276 (1950), and that of another, Herbert W. Briggs, the editor of a rightly highly regarded case book, was as follows: "The utility of manifestoes like the Draft Declaration . . ., which appears to reflect the natural law approach of inherent ('basic') rights of States, seems doubtful to many international lawyers, including the Editor." *The Law of Nations, Cases, Documents, and Notes*, 2nd ed. (New York: Appleton-Century-Crofts, 1952), p. 15. Such an attitude overlooks the enormous debt which positive international law owes to natural law.

> to undertake, pursuant to Article 13 of the Charter, a study of the principles of international law concerning friendly relations and co-operation among States in accordance with the Charter with a view to their progressive development and codification, so as to secure their more effective application.[40]

For all except one of the seven principles eventually selected for study, progressive development and codification, are contained in the Charter[41] and several of them were included, albeit in a somewhat different form, in the draft Declaration of Rights and Duties of States. Nonetheless, in 1963 the Assembly established a Special Committee on Principles of International Law concerning Friendly Relations and Co-operation among States which labored for six years. Under continuous prodding of the Assembly, the Special Committee finally submitted in 1970 a draft Declaration on Principles of International Law concerning Friendly Relations and Co-operation among States "as expressing the consensus of the delegations' members of the Drafting Committee."[42] This draft declaration "on" rather than "of" principles—a subtle nuance—reached the twenty-fifth anniversary session of the United Nations in the nick of time. By Resolution 2625 (XXV) adopted on October 24, 1970, the "draft declaration" became simply the "declaration" in which the Assembly declared *inter alia:*

> *Deeply convinced* that the adoption of the Declaration on Principles of International Law concerning Friendly Relations and Co-operation among States in accordance with the Charter of the United Nations on the occasion of the twenty-fifth anniversary of the United Nations would contribute to the strengthening of world peace and constitute a landmark in the development of international law and of relations among the States, in promoting the rule of law among nations and particularly the universal application of the principles embodied in the Charter,
>
> Considering the desirability of the wide dissemination of the text of the Declaration,
>
> 1. *Approves* the Declaration on Principles of International Law concerning Friendly Relations and Co-operation among States in accordance with the Charter of the United Nations, the text of which is annexed to the present resolution;
> 2. *Expresses its appreciation* to the Special Committee . . . for its work resulting in the elaboration of the Declaration;
> 3. *Recommends* that all efforts be made so that the Declaration becomes generally known.[43]

Thus came to end another effort to come to grips with fundamental problems of international law and relations. The very title of the declaration represents a victory for the

[40] Resolution 1815 (XVII) of December 18, 1962, noted in *Report* of the Special Committee on Principles of International Law concerning Friendly Relations and Co-operation among States. General Assembly, *Official Records* (25th sess.), Suppl. 18 (A/8018), p. 3.

[41] The exception being the principle numbered (c): "The duty not to intervene in matters within the domestic jurisdiction of any State, in accordance with the Charter." The reference to the Charter is somewhat misleading as there is no directly analogous clause in the Charter. Article 2(7) of the Charter is concerned with intervention by the United Nations and not with intervention by states in matters essentially within the domestic jurisdiction of any state.

[42] See *Report* of the Special Committee (*supra,* n. 40), p. 62, paragraph 83.

[43] General Assembly, *Official Records* (25th sess.), Suppl. 28 (A/8028), p. 121.

United States and its supporters who were determined to sidetrack the original Soviet proposal for a codification of the principles of peaceful coexistence. The action of the Assembly in 1970 closely parallels its action in 1949 with respect to the draft Declaration of the Rights and Duties of States: it approves the declaration and it recommends that it become generally known. More innocuous words could not have been chosen. Whatever intrinsic merit the declaration of 1970 may have was further diminished by the words "in accordance with the Charter of the United Nations" which did not appear in the title given to the declaration by the Special Committee.[44] Thus the principles of international law must be read in conformity with the Charter as the overriding law. That this is so appears from the formulation of some of the principles themselves. Thus the principle on the nonuse of force—Article 2(4) of the Charter—is elaborated in several paragraphs, the last of which reads:

> Nothing in the foregoing paragraphs shall be construed as enlarging or diminishing in any way the scope of the provisions of the Charter concerning cases in which the use of force is lawful.[45]

The second and third principles on the settlement of disputes and nonintervention in matters of domestic jurisdiction, respectively, contain similar clauses safeguarding the law of the Charter.[46]

To make doubly sure that the protracted labor of the Special Committee has no impact upon the Charter, the 1970 resolution, in a section entitled "General Part," declares:

> Nothing in this Declaration shall be construed as prejudicing in any manner the provisions of the Charter or the rights and duties of Member States under the Charter or the rights of peoples under the Charter, taking into account the elaboration of these rights in this Declaration.

The Assembly further declares:

> The principles of the Charter which are embodied in this Declaration constitute basic principles of international law, and consequently appeal to all States to be guided by these principles in their international conduct and to develop their mutual relations on the basis of the strict observance of these principles.[47]

[44] That title was, it may be recalled, Draft Declaration on Principles of International Law concerning Friendly Relations and Co-operation among States. *Report* of the Special Committee, p. 62. paragraph 83.

[45] *Supra*, n. 43, p. 123.

[46] *Ibid.* The final clause in the formulation of the non-intervention principle reads as follows: "Nothing in the foregoing paragraphs shall be construed as affecting the relevant provisions of the Charter relating to the maintenance of international peace and security." This is a curious statement inasmuch as the maintenance of peace and security is the business of the organization and not of individual states, and the exception from Article 2(7) is contained in the final clause in that provision.

[47] *Ibid.*, p. 000.

It is obvious that the declaration is the product of contradictory policies with respect to the Charter and its elaboration by means other than the formal amendment provided for in Article 108. Hence the ambiguity in the formulation of the principle of interpretation and the paradoxical proposition that, on the one hand, the Charter principles are principles of international law and that, on the other hand, these principles should guide all states in their conduct. One may legitimately wonder whether the description for the Charter principles as "guides" was intended to raise or diminish their binding force as principles of international law.

To return to the starting point of this necessarily brief and incomplete analysis of one phase of the efforts to promote the development of international law, what is the nature of the contribution in legal terms? I suggest the affirmation of the Nuremberg principles by the Assembly, the further resolutions of the Assembly, the work of the International Law Commission on the draft Declaration of Rights and Duties of States and the draft code of Offences against the Peace and Security, and finally the work of the Special Committee on Principles of International Law and its qualified endorsement by the General Assembly have enriched the legal literature on some basic problems of international law and relations. The hesitant attitude of the Assembly, reflecting the divergent policies of members, rules out any confident statement that the various principles, other than those embodied in the Charter itself, are legally binding. They may become legally significant, even legally binding, but that will depend on the conduct of the member states.

We would be living in a different world if the various projects dealing with fundamental aspects of a new legal order had been brought to fruition, but it seems that we shall have to live in a different world in order to be able to bring them to fruition.

## The Development of International Law through International Conventions

On the more mundane level of the work of the International Law Commission there has been impressive progress indeed. Created in 1947 with a membership of 15, raised to 21 and 25 in 1956 and 1961, respectively, the commission's mandate has been both progressive development and codification of international law.[48] Broadly representative of the membership of the United Nations, of old and new states, of the main forms of civilization, of the principal legal system and geographic regions, the commission's members are elected and serve for terms of five years in their individual capacities. Nonetheless, several members of the commission are officials of their governments, while others are

[48] As stated in Article 15 of the commission's statute, "the expression 'progressive development of international law' is used for convenience as meaning the preparation of draft conventions on subjects which have not yet been regulated by international law or in regard to which the law has not yet been sufficiently developed in the practice of States. Similarly, the expression 'codification of international law' is used for convenience as meaning the more precise formulation and systematization of rules of international law in fields where there already has been extensive State practice, precedent and doctrine." *Work of the ILC*, p. 57.

selected from law faculties and the bar. Far from detracting from the efficiency of the commission, this mixture of independent and official experts has been regarded as one of its assets, along with the fact that members of the commission serve only in a part-time capacity. The commission usually holds one session annually, lasting for several weeks. The latter feature has been regarded as a shortcoming by those who found the pace of work disappointingly slow and therefore advocated that the commission be transformed into a full-time body. On the other hand, the part-time character of the commission, in the words of one of its members,

> seems to have encouraged the type of professional representation which has been found in the Commission almost since its initiation—academic lawyers working harmoniously alongside professional diplomats with some general legal training and much practical experience, a goodly number of experienced legal advisers of Ministries for Foreign Affairs, and some experienced general lawyers, including national judges. This has provided the Commission with sufficient expertise on the specific topics of international law which it was considering at a given moment, an adequate leavening of impractical legal philosophizing, and a similar adequate leavening of the chronic impatience of the shrewd practical lawyer and diplomat at scholasticism, pedantry and mere academic brilliance.[49]

Apart from its composition, the method of work adopted by the commission deserves a great deal of credit for its accomplishments. The statute of the commission lays down the general guidelines for both progressive development and codification. The feature common to both is the provision for submission of draft articles to the governments directly for their comments as well as to the General Assembly. There is a degree of overlapping here as the governments may make their comments directly to the commission in response to its request but they also, and much more frequently, comment on the draft articles and the underlying conceptions in the Legal (Sixth) Committee of the General Assembly, which is composed of all members of the United Nations. The result has been a "marriage of governmental reaction and professional expert investigation by the International Law Commission" and an awareness of the political as well as juridical implications of the commission's work at various stages.[50] This process ensures the success of the diplomatic conferences which were convened by the Assembly to adopt the draft articles prepared by the commission with a minimum of amendments. The formulation of the draft articles accompanied by extensive commentaries reflects the opinion of governments as expressed in comments and debates in the Assembly. Although the commission appoints one of its members as rapporteur for each of the projects, who is responsible for the research and the initial drafting, the result is probably as much due to his scholarship, drafting skill, and tact as to the collective wisdom of the commission. Further refinements of the commission's method of work have been to entrust a large measure of re-

[49] Shabtai Rosenne, "The Role of the International Law Commission," *Proceedings of the American Society of International Law*, 24–37 (1970), p. 27.

[50] *Ibid.*, p. 29. The commission's draft articles on the law of treaties have been debated at five sessions of the Assembly between 1962 and the opening of the Vienna Conference on the Law of Treaties in 1968.

sponsibility for the substantive formulation of the draft articles to a Drafting Committee, to shun formal voting, and to seek consensus instead.[51] It was a simplification if not a refinement of its work for the commission to gradually emancipate itself from the distinction laid down in the statute, as noted earlier, between progressive development and codification of international law. That distinction had already complicated the work of the London Naval Conference of 1908[52] and of the League of Nations Codification Conference of 1930.[53] Only one of the products of the International Law Commission, the Geneva Convention on the High Seas, of April 29, 1958, declares in the preamble that the parties to that convention desired "to codify the rules of international law relating to the high seas."[54] The other conventions are silent on this point, although the last three conventions contain language which may be construed as an indirect reference to codification.[55] There are certainly good reasons for minimizing the distinction between progressive development and codification, no matter how sound the distinction may be on theoretical grounds, in the practice of the commission. Any statement which the commission or a convention may make about the nature of the rules would certainly not be conclusive, although it would be relevant. The evaluation of the conventions drafted by the commission as progressive development or codification is best left to the writers, the practitioners, and the courts.[56]

In discussing the work of both the International Law Commission and the General Assembly in the development of international law, it is essential not to lose sight of an imponderable by-product: namely, the participation of new states. Many of them entered the international community with a negative or, at the very least, highly critical attitude with respect to the inherited body of customary international law. The view has often been expressed by their spokesmen that this body of law reflected not their interests but the interests of the dominant colonialist powers and that, in any event, it was not attuned to the needs of a changed and still changing international society, a society multiracial in character and exhibiting different constitutional and social systems. Through participation in the debates in the commission, particularly since its enlargement to twenty-five members in 1961, in the General Assembly and its Sixth Committee, and finally in the

[51] For further analysis of the commission's organization and method of work, in addition to the article by Rosenne, see the book by a former member of the commission, Herbert W. Briggs, *The International Law Commission* (Ithaca, N.Y.: Cornell University Press, 1965); and Luke T. Lee, "The International Law Commission Re-Examined," 59 AJIL 545–570 (1965).

[52] See *supra*, p. 186.

[53] See *supra*, p. 187.

[54] *Work of the ILC*, p. 104.

[55] Thus in the preamble to the Vienna Convention on Diplomatic Relations of April 18, 1961, the parties affirm "that the rules of customary international law should continue to govern questions not expressly regulated by the provisions of the present Convention," *Ibid.*, p. 121. The Vienna Convention on Consular Relations of April 24, 1963, *ibid.*, p. 142, and the Vienna Convention on the Law of Treaties of May 23, 1969, 63 AJIL 875 (1969) contain substantially identical language.

[56] The complexity of the problem is well illustrated by the recent judgment of the International Court of Justice in the *North Sea Continental Shelf* case of February 20, 1969. In that case the Court had to examine the argument of the Netherlands and Denmark that the equidistance principle in Article 6(2) of the Geneva Continental Shelf Convention of 1958 was or has become a principle of customary international law; and that, consequently, it was binding on the Federal Republic of Germany even though the latter had not become a party to the convention. ICJ *Reports* (1969), p. 3, at 28ff.

diplomatic conferences on the law of the sea in Geneva in 1958 and 1960, on diplomatic relations, consular relations, and the law of treaties in Vienna in 1961, 1963, and 1968–1969, respectively, they have had a full opportunity to state their positions, defend their interests, and make the weight of their votes felt. Statistical evidence of their participation in debates on international law questions may not be a reliable indication of their interests. Other governments friendly and sympathetic to their views may have taken up the cudgel for them. Moreover, dissatisfaction with the law is by no means limited to new states. And, finally, some of the new states may still be short of qualified personnel both at home and abroad.

The topics selected by the commission, it must fairly be noted, were not of especial interest to the new nations. The year 1960 was the year in which a substantial number of formerly colonial territories were admitted to membership in the United Nations. Prior to that the commission was engaged in drafting articles on the law of the sea, a project which is of considerable interest to a number of new states, but the diplomatic conference on the law of the sea took place in 1958, that is, before their admission. The second and unsuccessful Law of the Sea Conference took place in 1960 for the purpose of defining the extent of the territorial sea and thus to complete the work of 1958. That conference, however, also was held prior to their admission. The subsequent topics—diplomatic and consular relations and the law of treaties—are of general interest and the new states took a particularly active part in the elaboration of the law of treaties. The subjects of the responsibility of states and succession of states and governments may offer a better test of the interest and participation of new states. In the meantime, it is natural that they should concentrate their resources on matters such as decolonization and economic development which are "bread and butter" issues to them.[57]

At its first session in 1949, the sense of the commission was "that while the codification of the whole of international law was the ultimate objective, it was desirable for the present to begin work on the codification of a few of the topics, rather than to discuss a general systematic plan, which might be left to later elaboration."[58] This has, so far remained the policy of the commission. However, at its 1969 session the commission confirmed "its intention of bringing up to date in 1971 its long-term programme of work, taking into account the General Assembly recommendations and the international community's current needs."[59] At its first session the commission reviewed twenty-five topics and drew up a provisional list of fourteen topics for codification. Five of these topics have so far not been dealt with and some or all of these may be discarded in 1971.

[57] David A. Kay, *The New Nations in the United Nations, 1960–1967* (New York: Columbia University Press, 1970), pp. 49, 182. For statistics on speeches made by new nations during the fifteenth to twenty-first sessions in plenary and committee meetings see pp. 191–199. On p. 48 Kay writes: "Similarly, 69.7% of the new nations did not speak on any of the international law topics before the 15th Assembly, and at the 21st session 32.6% of these nations did not speak on this subject." Insofar as topics are concerned which were actively under consideration of the International Law Commission and of the Assembly at those sessions, the statement must be read in the light of the observations made in the text above.

[58] *Report* of the ILC to the General Assembly on the Work of its First Session, A/CN.4/13, p. 6.

[59] *Report* of the ILC on the Work of its twenty-second Session, General Assembly, *Official Records* (25th sess.), Suppl. 10 (A/8010/Rev. 1), p. 40.

These are recognition of states and governments, jurisdictional immunities of states and their property, the right of asylum, the treatment of aliens, and jurisdiction with regard to crimes committed outside national territory. Of the nine topics selected for codification three were given priority—the law of treaties, arbitral procedure, and the regime of the high seas—and rapporteurs were appointed. The remaining six topics were succession of states and governments; the regime of territorial waters; nationality, including statelessness; diplomatic intercourse and immunities; consular intercourse and immunities; and state responsibility. The result of the commission's work on these nine topics can be summarized briefly.

It may be convenient to begin with a topic which was not crowned with success—namely, arbitral procedure. In 1953 the commission submitted to the General Assembly a draft on arbitral procedure which received a largely hostile reception. This was due in substance to the basic conception of the draft—namely, that once states have voluntarily agreed to submit a dispute to arbitration they were legally bound to take all the subsequent steps required for the arbitration to take place (appointment of arbitrators and of an umpire, etc.), and that if either party failed to take any of those steps they would be taken by a third party. As interpreted by the Rapporteur, the Assembly rejected what it considered an attempt to deprive traditional arbitration of its diplomatic character and transform it into a "quasi-compulsory jurisdictional procedure."[60] A revised draft was prepared and adopted by the commission in 1958, and the Assembly took note of it. This is known as "Model Rules on Arbitral Procedure" and no further action was taken by the commission or the Assembly.[61]

The commission's work on nationality, including statelessness, fared somewhat better. No work was done on nationality as another organ of the United Nations, the Commission on the Status of Women, took in hand the question of the nationality of married women which had already appeared on the agenda of the League of Nations 1930 Codification Conference. Accordingly, the Commission on the Status of Women drafted a Convention on the Nationality of Married Women which was adopted by the General Assembly in 1957.[62] With respect to statelessness, the commission prepared two drafts, one on the elimination and another on the reduction of future statelessness. The drafts were based on what turned out to be an erroneous impression, that the object in view was elimination and reduction of future statelessness. Since statelessness is the product of autonomous and conflicting national legislations and practices, changes in such legislations and practices were required in the drafts. The governments, however, seemed not disposed to make the necessary modifications in their legislation.[63] The Assembly, by Reso-

[60] *Yearbook of the ILC* (1958), II, 80.

[61] *Ibid.*, pp. 83–88. The text of the model rules is also printed in *Work of the ILC*, p. 69. See also Leo Gross, "The United Nations and the Role of Law," 19 *International Organizations* 537–561 (1965), at 545. *Supra*, at 166.

[62] *Work of the ILC*, p. 28. The Commission on the Status of Women was also responsible for two other conventions: the Convention on the Political Rights of Women adopted by the Assembly in 1952 and the Convention on Consent to Marriage, Minimum Age for Marriage, and Registration of Marriages adopted by the Assembly in 1962. All three conventions are in force. See *Multilateral Treaties*, pp. 305, 311, 313.

[63] *Work of the ILC*, p. 29.

lution 896 (IX) of December 4, 1954, left the door open for a diplomatic conference if at least twenty states expressed an interest in it. The United Nations Conference on the Elimination or Reduction of Future Statelessness was eventually held in Geneva in 1959 and thirty-five states participated. It adopted the commission's drafts as bases of discussion. This conference failed to reach agreement and another conference was held in New York City in 1961 which adopted the Convention on the Reduction of Statelessness on August 30, 1961. It may be noted that if in the interval no progress was made on the reduction of statelessness, progress was achieved on reducing the number of interested states. Only thirty states were represented at the second conference, only five states signed it, and only one of those (United Kingdom) ratified, and one (Sweden) acceded to it.[64]

The means for reduction of future statelessness are essentially two in number. According to Article I (1) of the convention, "a Contracting State shall grant its nationality to a person born in its territory who would otherwise be stateless." And, according to Article 8 (1), subject to stated exceptions, "a Contracting State shall not deprive a person of its nationality if such deprivation would render him stateless."[65] Unrelated to the International Law Commission are three instruments with respect to refugees and statelessness in the making of which the General Assembly or one of its subsidiary organs was involved.[66]

The work of the International Law Commission on the law of treaties and the regime of the high seas, given priority in 1949, was crowned with success. The work on the law of the high seas was expanded to include the regime of territorial waters, which was selected for codification without being accorded priority. In drawing up articles on these topics, the commission had the benefit of the advice of outside groups of experts.[67] The final report of the commission—covering, along with the traditional law of the high seas and territorial waters, the continental shelf and conservation of living resources of the sea—served as a basis of discussion of the United Nations Conference on the Law of the Sea held in Geneva in 1958, pursuant to General Assembly Resolution 1105 (XI) of February 21, 1957. It was attended by eighty-six states, including seventy-nine members of the United Nations. The conference adopted four substantive instruments: the Convention on the Territorial Sea and the Contiguous Zone, the Convention on the High Seas; the Convention on Fishing and Conservation of the Living Resources of the High Seas, and the Convention on the Continental Shelf. The conference also adopted an Optional Protocol of Signature concerning the Compulsory Settlement of Disputes.[68] The ques-

[64] *Multilateral Treaties,* p. 101.

[65] For text of the convention see *Work of the ILC,* p. 135.

[66] The Convention relating to the Status of Refugees of 1951 was adopted by a conference convened pursuant to Assembly Resolution 429 (V) of December 14, 1950. *Multilateral Treaties,* p. 83; The Convention relating to the Status of Stateless Persons of 1954 was adopted at a conference held pursuant to a resolution of April 26, 1954, of the Economic and Social Council; *ibid.,* p. 94; the Protocol relating to the Status of Refugees of 1967 was approved by ECOSOC in 1966 and transmitted to interested states in virtue of Assembly Resolution 2198 (XXI) of December 16, 1966, p. 103.

[67] For a brief history of the commission's work on this topic, see *Work of the ILC,* pp. 31–35.

[68] For text of these instruments see *Work of the ILC,* pp. 97–121.

tion of the free access to the sea of landlocked countries was before the conference but not fully resolved. In 1965 the United Nations Conference on Transit Trade of Land-Locked Countries was held, and it adopted a convention under the same title.[69]

All four conventions of 1958 as well as the optional protocol entered into force. Thirty-seven states are parties to the Convention of the Territorial Sea, forty-four to that on the high seas, twenty-eight to that on fisheries, and forty to that on the continental shelf. Many states attached reservations to their ratifications and many states objected to some or all of them.[70] It will be recalled that only one of the conventions, that on the high seas, purports to codify the existing rules of international law. The rather low proportion of ratifying states to the number of states which had a hand in the drafting of the four conventions could be interpreted as an indication that the conventions are not fully responsive to the needs of many states. The optional protocol is binding on only twenty states which have ratified one of the four conventions and signed or ratified the optional protocol.[71]

As noted earlier, the 1958 Conference on the Law of the Sea was unable to agree on the breadth of the territorial sea. Therefore, a second conference was held in 1960 which was attended by eighty-two states. This conference failed by a narrow margin to adopt a proposal to fix the width of the territorial waters at six miles and the width of exclusive fishing rights at twelve miles.[72] The 1960 conference merely confirmed the existence of a firmly held position on the width of the territorial sea which first came into the open at the League of Nations Conference of 1930. Since then the international community has been functioning under the regime of what might be called "free-floating" boundaries of the territorial waters and fishing rights. A somewhat similar regime was adopted by the 1958 conference with respect to the delimitation of the continental shelf. As stated in Article 1 of the Convention on the Continental Shelf:

> For the purpose of these articles, the term "continental shelf" is used as referring (a) to the seabed and subsoil of the submarine areas adjacent to the coast but outside of the area of the territorial sea, to a depth of 200 metres, or, beyond that limit, to where the depth of the superjacent waters admits of the exploitation of the natural resources of the said areas; (b) to the seabed and subsoil of similar submarine areas adjacent to the coasts of islands.

The convention thus lays down a fixed limit—a depth of 200 meters—and a "moving" or "creeping" limit determined by the technological feasibility of exploitation. Inasmuch as by Article 2, "the coastal State exercises over the continental shelf sovereign rights for the purpose of exploring it and exploiting its natural resources," the "creeping" limit

[69] *Ibid.*, p. 34, n. 26.
[70] For ratifications, reservations, and objections see *Multilateral Treaties*, pp. 345–362.
[71] *Ibid.*, p. 363. The interlocking provision is in Article V of the optional protocol.
[72] For a first-hand account by the chairman of the U.S. delegation to the conference see Arthur H. Dean, "The Second Geneva Conference on the Law of the Sea: The Fight for Freedom of the Seas," 54 AJIL 751–790 (1960); for a comment on this by the chairman of the Mexican delegation to that conference see Alfonso Garcia Robles, "The Second United Nations Conference on the Law of the Sea—a Reply," 55 AJIL 669–675 (1961); and a response by Mr. Dean, *ibid.*, pp. 675–680.

appeared to offer a privileged position to states with advanced technology and to penalize the so-called developing nations. At the very least, it seemed to deprive them of the benefits of the last source of mineral and other resources and a share in the produce of the exploitation of the seabed and the subsoil.

Thus the absence of agreement on the limit of the territorial sea and the "creeping" limit for the continental shelf[73] become entwined with the new problem of a politically acceptable legal regime for the seabed. In 1968 the Assembly established a committee with the somewhat long-winded title Committee on the Peaceful Uses of the Sea-Bed and the Ocean Floor beyond the Limits of National Jurisdiction. As a result of the committee's work and further debates in the Assembly's Political Committee, the General Assembly in 1969 adopted four resolutions. Only the first of these, Resolution 2574A (XXIV), is relevant in this context. It was adopted on December 15, 1969, by 65 votes to 12, with 30 abstentions, and requests the secretary-general

> to ascertain the views of Member States on the desirability of convening at an early date a conference on the law of the sea to review the regimes of the high seas, the continental shelf, the territorial sea and contiguous zone, fishing and conservation of the living resources of the high seas, particularly in order to arrive at a clear, precise and internationally accepted definition of the area of the sea-bed and ocean floor which lies beyond the limits of national jurisdiction, in the light of the international regime to be established for that area.[74]

The terms of the projected conference are very comprehensive indeed. The regime to which reference is made, as described in another resolution adopted on the same day, is to ensure the exploitation of the resources of the seabed and ocean floor "for the benefit of mankind, irrespective of the geographical location of States, taking into account the special interests and needs of the developing countries, whether land-locked or coastal."[75] As guideline for the conference which is scheduled for 1973, the Assembly adopted at its 1970 session a declaration according to which the resources of the seabed and ocean floor are "the common heritage of mankind" and their exploitation "shall be carried out for the benefit of mankind as a whole." And the president of the Assembly, Dr. Edvard Hambro (Norway), was quoted as having observed at the conclusion of the twenty-fifth session that "the seabed is being decolonized before it is colonized."[76] As a forecast for the projected conference, this does not sound unlikely at all given the present composition of the United Nations. The vast majority of its 127 members consists of new states, a large number of which were admitted since the 1958 Conference on the Law of the Sea and therefore had no share in its outcome.

[73] There may be some limit to the "creeping" limit but this depends on how narrowly or how broadly the term "adjacent" in Article 1 will be interpreted in practice. Louis Henkin, "The United Nations and the Rules of Law," 11 *Harvard International Law Journal* 428–436 (1970), p. 432. See *ibid.*, p. 443, n. 4.

[74] General Assembly, *Official Records* (24th sess.), Suppl. 30 (A/7630), p. 10.

[75] General Assembly Resolution 2574B (XXIV), *ibid.*, at 11.

[76] *New York Times*, December 18, 1970, p. 1. Resolution 2749 (XXV), December 17, 1970, General Assembly, *Official Records* (25th sess.), Suppl. 28 (A/8028), p. 24.

In this context it may be conveniently noted that the 1970 session of the General Assembly, by 104 votes to 2, with 2 abstentions, adopted by Resolution 2660 (XXV) the Treaty on the Prohibition of the Emplacement of Nuclear and Other Weapons of Mass Destruction on the Sea-Bed and Ocean Floor. This treaty was drafted in substance by the United States and the Soviet Union and was submitted to the Assembly by the Geneva Conference of the Committee on Disarmament. Under its terms

> States which become parties would undertake not to place nuclear or other weapons of mass destruction on the floor of the sea outside of a zone beginning 12 miles off shore. Facilities for storing, testing or using such weapons would also be prohibited from that area. The Treaty contains provisions for verification under which any party may observe the activities of any other party carried out on the sea-bed.[77]

Surely this treaty marks a milestone in the efforts of the United Nations to ensure that the seabed and ocean floor are used essentially, though not exclusively, for peaceful purposes. Under the terms of the treaty not all military uses of the seabed and ocean floor are excluded. In this respect there is some analogy with the regime for outer space.[78]

The third topic accorded priority in 1949 by the International Law Commission, the law of treaties, was successively in the hands of four rapporteurs. The completion of work on this topic will probably rank as one of the great accomplishments of the commission. The draft articles with expert commentaries were discussed at two diplomatic conferences in Vienna in 1968 and 1969, convened pursuant to resolutions of the General Assembly of 1966 and 1967. In the same resolutions the Assembly had also decided that the results of the work of the conferences should be embodied in an international convention.[79] The Vienna Convention on the Law of Treaties of May 23, 1969, is the first comprehensive though not exhaustive "codification and progressive development of the law of treaties."[80] Some aspects of the law which have not been included in the Vienna Convention will be handled by the commission separately. One of them is the succession in respect of treaties and the other is the question of treaties concluded between states and international organizations or between two or more international organizations.[81] The Vienna conference itself adopted a resolution recommending that the General Assembly refer the latter question to the International Law Commission inasmuch as the Vienna Convention's scope is limited to treaties between states.

The Vienna Convention on the Law of Treaties is the product of an impressive collaboration between a very substantial number of states—103 attended the first and 110 the second session of the conference—of different social, political, and economic systems and varying stages of development. Success was made possible by the very thorough ex-

[77] United Nations Press Release WS/480, December 11, 1970, p. 3, and *ibid.*, pp. 11, 12.

[78] See *infra*, p. 210.

[79] General Assembly, *Official Records* (22nd sess.), Suppl. 16(A/6716), p. 80.

[80] Preamble of the convention, the text of which is reproduced in 63 AJIL 875–903 (1969). The Final Act of the UN Conference on the Law of Treaties is in Doc. A/Conf./39/26.

[81] *Report* of the ILC on the Work of its Twenty-second Session, May 4–July 10, 1970, *supra*, n, 59, pp. 31, 41.

pert work of the commission and several consultations with governments and discussions in the Assembly's Sixth Committee. Since treaties are and will remain in the foreseeable future the main tool for conducting business between states and for developing international law, the importance of the Vienna Convention can hardly be overestimated. As Rosenne put it: "With the law of treaties the codification effort is entering the core of the law."[82] The Convention in its eighty-five articles represents a consensus and accommodation of a large variety of viewpoints for "no part of the Vienna Convention of 1969 was adopted by a bare two-thirds majority, but always by one well in excess of two-thirds."[83] Any attempt by the majority to dictate to the minority would obviously have jeopardized the ratification of the Convention by important states.

It is not possible within the scope of this essay to provide more than a very brief reference to some of the more significant features of the convention. First of all, it must be noted that the convention is not retroactive; that is, it applies only to treaties concluded after its entry into force (Article 4). It includes both the *pacta sunt servanda* rule[84] and an elaborate formulation of the controversial *rebus sic stantibus* doctrine (Article 62). With regard to the relation between treaties and municipal law, the convention provides that "a party may not invoke the provisions of its internal law as justification for its failure to perform a treaty." This makes explicit one of the implications of the supremacy of international law over municipal law. With respect to the controversial question of the relevance of internal law regarding the competence of governments to conclude treaties, the convention reflects clearly the position of the internationalists although it makes allowance for the constitutionalists.[85] The desire for a more incisive formulation had to be compromised by the desire for accommodation.

The use of force against a state in procuring its consent to a treaty (duress) has traditionally *not* been regarded as vitiating its validity. In accordance with the prevailing trend to eliminate the use of force in international relations, the convention provides that "a treaty is void if its conclusion has been procured by the threat or use of force in violation of the principles of international law embodied in the Charter of the United Nations" (Article 52). To many of the new states, and others as well, this did not go far enough. To them any use of force, even in the more subtle form of economic coercion, is unacceptable. In a spirit of accommodation, the conference adopted a declaration included in its Final Act, in which it "solemnly condemns the threat or use of pressure in any form, whether military, political, or economic, by any State in order to coerce another State to perform any act relating to the conclusion of a treaty in violation of the principles of the

[82] Rosenne, "Role of International Law Commission," p. 33.

[83] *Ibid.*, p. 34.

[84] Article 26: "Every treaty in force is binding upon the parties to it and must be performed by them in good faith."

[85] Article 46: "1. A State may not invoke the fact that its consent to be bound by a treaty has been expressed in violation of a provision of its internal law regarding competence to conclude treaties as invalidating its consent unless that violation was manifest and concerned a rule of its internal law of fundamental importance. 2. A violation is manifest if it would be objectively evident to any State conducting itself in the matter in accordance with normal practice and in good faith."

sovereign equality of States and freedom of consent."[86] The declaration as such is not legally binding but it is relevant as an expression of international public policy.

Probably the most controversial and in a sense perhaps progressive principle incorporated in the Convention is that of the so-called *jus cogens*. Traditionally, states enjoy a virtually unlimited autonomy in entering into treaties insofar as their subject matter is concerned. In the future, this autonomy is to be curtailed by the following principle in Article 53 of the Vienna Convention:

> A treaty is void if, at the time of its conclusion, it conflicts with a peremptory norm of general international law (i.e., *jus cogens*). For the purpose of the present Convention, a peremptory norm of international law is a norm accepted and recognized by the international community of States as a whole as a norm from which no derogation is permitted and which can be modified only by a subsequent norm of general international law having the same character.[87]

The inclusion of this new principle was strongly resisted by some states, particularly France. Article 53 does not contain a substantive definition of *jus cogens* norms, although the commission's commentary provides examples of what is sometimes thought to be a peremptory norm.[88] The inclusion of Articles 53 and 64 was made acceptable to a powerful minority only by providing a measure of compulsory settlement with regard to disputes concerning their application or interpretation. If a dispute is not settled through the means indicated in Article 33 of the Charter of the United Nations,[89] any one of the parties of the dispute may, in virtue of Article 66(a), submit it to the International Court of Justice by a written application. They may also by common consent agree to submit the dispute to arbitration. Article 66(a) is not free from ambiguity as it does not stipulate that the Court shall have compulsory jurisdiction if a unilateral application is made by one of the parties to the dispute.

The prevailing reluctance to accept the compulsory jurisdiction of the Court can also be seen in Article 65 which lays down the procedure to be followed with respect to invalidity, termination, withdrawal from or suspension of the operation of a treaty on any of the grounds stated in the convention including fundamental change of circumstances (*rebus sic stantibus*). If a party invokes any of these grounds and the other party

[86] Final Act, UN Conference of the Law of Treaties (A/Conf./39/ii/Add. 2), p. 285.

[87] Another article, Article 64, deals with the contingency of the emergence of *jus cogens* in the future: "If a new peremptory norm of general international law emerges, any existing treaty which is in conflict with that norm becomes void and terminates."

[88] In one place the commentary refers to "the hypothesis that in international law today there are a certain number of fundamental rules of international public order from which no State may derogate even by agreement with another State." In another, reference is made to suggested examples such as treaties "contemplating or conniving at the commission of acts such as trade in slaves, piracy or genocide," or "treaties violating human rights, the equality of States or the principle of self-determination," or treaties "contemplating an unlawful use of force contrary to the principles of the Charter," or treaties "contemplating the performance of any other act criminal under international law." General Assembly, *Official Records* (21st sess.), Suppl. 9 (A/6309/Rev.1), *Report* of the ILC on the second part of its 17th sess. January 3–28, 1966, and on its 18th sess. May 4–July 19, 1966, p. 77, paragraph 3, and p. 89, paragraph 1.

[89] These include negotiations, inquiry, mediation, conciliation, arbitration, judicial settlement, resort to regional agencies or arrangements, or other peaceful means chosen by parties.

raises objections within three months, the parties are bound to seek a solution through the means indicated in Article 33; that is, through mutual consent or unilaterally, by setting in motion the procedure for conciliation specified in an annex to the convention. The Commission of Conciliation shall first seek an amicable settlement of the dispute and, failing that, make a nonbinding recommendation for consideration of the parties. The convention is silent about the consequences of a failure of the parties to settle the dispute amicably with or without the assistance of the Conciliation Commission, thus leaving a gap in the progressive development of international law.

Of the other six topics selected in 1949 for codification without being accorded priority, two more have been completed: diplomatic intercourse and immunities and consular intercourse and immunities. Held in Vienna in 1961, the United Nations Conference on Diplomatic Intercourse and Immunities was attended by eighty-one states of which seventy-five were members of the United Nations.[90] On April 18, 1961, the conference adopted the Vienna Convention on Diplomatic Relations which entered into force in 1964, and to which ninety-one states have become parties.[91] This convention is concerned only with regular diplomatic relations, as was the 1815 Vienna regulation.[92] The question of "*ad hoc* diplomacy" was on the agenda of the conference but work on it was not completed. At the recommendation of the conference, the General Assembly referred the topic back to the International Law Commission which completed its work in 1967. The draft articles prepared by the commission on "*ad hoc* diplomacy" or "special missions" were discussed in the Assembly's Sixth Committee, and the Assembly itself adopted the Convention on Special Missions by Resolution 2530 (XXIV) of December 8, 1969. In Article 1 this convention defines *special missions* as follows:

> A "special mission" is a temporary mission, representing the State, which is sent by one State to another State with the consent of the latter for the purpose of dealing with it on specific questions or of performing in relation to it a special task.[93]

In view of the rapid increase of ad hoc diplomacy since the end of World War II, the clarification of the status, immunities, and privileges of such special missions will be welcomed by both the sending and receiving states. The Vienna Convention on Diplomatic Relations and the Convention on Special Missions emphasize in their respective preambles that the "purpose of such privileges and immunities is not to benefit individuals but to ensure the efficient performance of the functions of diplomatic (special) missions as rep-

[90] It is the standing practice of the General Assembly to invite to conferences held under its auspices members of the United Nations or of specialized agencies or of the IAEA or parties to the Statute of the Court. By means of this formula, Communist China and the Communist regimes of North Korea, North Vietnam, and East Germany are excluded from participation in the codification and progressive development of international law. See, for example, par. 3 of Resolution 2166 (XXI), December 5, 1966, General Assembly, *Official Records* (21st sess.), Suppl. 16 (A/6316), p. 95.

[91] *Multilateral Treaties*, p. 44.

[92] See *supra*, p. 185.

[93] General Assembly, *Official Records* (24th sess.), Suppl. 30 (A/7630), p. 99.

resenting States."[94] Both conventions have thereby pronounced themselves in favor of the functional theory of immunities and privileges.

The Vienna Conference on Diplomatic Relations also adopted an Optional Protocol concerning the Compulsory Settlement of Disputes arising from the application or interpretation of the convention. Only thirty-eight states are parties to this protocol as compared with ninety-one parties to the convention itself. A similar protocol was adopted by the General Assembly with respect to the Convention on Special Missions.

The draft articles on consular relations prepared by the International Law Commission formed the basis of discussion at the United Nations Conference on Consular Relations held in Vienna in 1963. It was attended by ninety-five states. The work of this conference of plenipotentiaries resulted in the Vienna Convention on Consular Relations and an Optional Protocol for the Compulsory Settlement of Disputes of April 24, 1963.[95] The convention has become binding on thirty-eight states and the optional protocol on fifteen states.[96]

The three instruments, the conventions on diplomatic and on consular relations and on special missions, are an important contribution to both the codification and the progressive development of international law governing the intercourse between states. They should facilitate peaceful relations between members of the international community which has grown so much in number and in diversity. There remains one gap to fill, namely, the law applicable to representatives of states to international organizations. In connection with its work on diplomatic relations, the International Law Commission considered the question of the "relations between States and international organizations and the privileges and immunities of such organizations."[97]

While some aspects of this matter are covered by existing conventions,[98] the General Assembly requested the commission to continue its work on the legal position of representatives of states to international organizations. The commission expects to complete work on this topic in 1971. The draft articles will also cover permanent missions of member states to international organizations; their conduct, facilities, privileges, and immunities; and permanent observers of nonmember states.[99]

[94] For the text of the Vienna Convention on Diplomatic Relations, see *Work of the ILC,* p. 121, and the text of the Convention on Special Missions, the annex to the resolution referred to above in n. 93. A similar clause is included in the Vienna Convention on Consular Relations. See *infra,* p. 207.

[95] Text in *Work of the ILC,* p. 142. It may be noted that the Vienna Conferences of 1961 and 1963 also adopted optional protocols relating to the acquisition of nationality. See *ibid.,* pp. 132, 164. The purpose of these protocols is to exclude the acquisition of nationality by members of the mission or the consular post solely by the operation of the law of the receiving states. This applies to those members who are not nationals of the receiving states.

[96] *Multilateral Treaties,* pp. 53, 57.

[97] *Work of the ILC.* p. 28.

[98] The chief instrument is the Convention on the Privileges and Immunities of the United Nations which was adopted by Resolution 22A(1) of February 13, 1946. The host country of the United Nations, the United States, acceded to this convention only in 1969, subject to some reservations. Altogether, 102 states are parties to the convention. General Assembly, *Official Records* (25th sess.), Suppl. 1 (A/8001), *Report of the Secretary-General on the Work of the Organization,* June 16, 1969–June 15, 1970, p. 229f. On November 21, 1947, the General Assembly adopted the Convention on the Privileges and Immunities of the Specialized Agencies, to which seventy-two states are parties. *Ibid.,* p. 230. In 1947 the United Nations concluded the Headquarters Agreement with the United States.

[99] Permanent observer missions to the headquarters of the United Nations are maintained by the Federal Republic of

Two of the six subjects selected for codification in 1949 are still on the agenda of the International Law Commission: responsibility of states and state succession. Active work on state responsibility was started in 1955 and continued until 1961. As the special rapporteur who was in charge of the subject was not reelected, a new special rapporteur was appointed in 1963. The original intention was to deal with the traditional subject of responsibility of states for injury to the person or property of aliens. The resumed work started from a "fresh viewpoint," namely, the responsibility of states for "internationally wrongful acts," in which, the commission agrees, "progressive development would be particularly important."[100] This topic is of special interest to new states and, in spite of several resolutions of the General Assembly urging the commission to try to achieve results, progress to date has been exceedingly slow, even making allowance for a change in the direction and the preoccupation during the sixties with the law of treaties. Whichever way the topic is approached, it is likely to prove highly controversial. If the commission's codification work entered "the core of the law," with the law of treaties, it will complete, with the law of state responsibility, "this hard core of obligational law, and thus provide the trunk from which all other branches of the law will draw their strength."[101] However, the trunk needs roots and the roots need a fertile soil and in 1971 the election of members of the commission will take place.

In connection with the succession of states and governments, the work proceeded very slowly but since 1967 it has been receiving more active consideration. It was decided to deal with the topic under three headings: (1) succession in respect of treaties, (2) succession in respect of matters other than treaties, and (3) succession in respect of membership of international organizations. Active work was started on the first two topics; the third was deferred.[102] Members of the commission

> stressed the importance which State succession had at the present time for new States and for the international community in view of the modern phenomenon of decolonization, and agreed . . . that special attention should be given in the study to the problems of concern to new States.[103]

A report on the second topic (succession of states in respect to matters other than treaties) ran into trouble because it proposed to deal first with the question of acquired rights, a well-known but always controversial principle of customary international law.[104] Progress may well be expected on the first topic (succession in respect of treaties)

Germany, the Holy See, the Republic of Korea, Monaco, Switzerland, and the Republic of Vietnam. *Report* of the ILC on the Work of its Twenty-second Session, Document A/8018, p. 5.

[100] *Ibid.*, p. 36, paragraph 64, p. 37, paragraph 66(b), and p. 38, paragraph 71.

[101] Rosenne, "International Law Commission," p. 33.

[102] Report of the ILC, *supra,* n. 99, p. 29.

[103] *Work of the ILC,* p. 50.

[104] As reported, in the view of most members of the commission, "the topic of acquired rights was extremely controversial and its study, at a premature stage, could only delay the Commission's work on the topic as a whole. The efforts of the Commission should, therefore, be directed to finding a solid basis on which to go forward with the codification and progressive development of the topic, taking account of the different legal interests and current needs of States." *Report* of the ILC (supra, n. 99), p. 30, paragraph 33.

because the initial proposal supported unanimously by members of the commission is designed to take it out of the context of succession—namely, the transmission of rights and obligations from the old to the new state—and to consider it "as a particular problem within the general framework of the law of treaties."[105] As provisionally defined, succession means "the replacement of one State by another in the sovereignty of territory or in the competence to conclude treaties with respect to territory." The provisions of the Vienna Convention on the Law of Treaties of 1969 will be taken "as an integral part of the legal foundations of the law relating to succession in respect of treaties."[106] The principle on which the provisional draft articles are based that there is no "general obligation on a new State to take over the treaties of its predecessor" found support among members of the commission[107] and will appeal to the new states generally.

Currently, in addition to the topics just discussed, the commission's agenda includes the question of treaties concluded between states and international organizations or between two or more international organizations, and the study of the most-favored-nation clause.[108] It has already been noted that at its 1971 session the commission intends to bring up to date its long-range program.[109] There is every hope that the partnership between the Assembly and the commission will continue to be fruitful but progress in the core and controversial areas of international law may be slow.

To round out the survey of the progressive development of international law by the General Assembly by means of conventions, two areas must be mentioned: outer space and human rights. By Resolution 1721 (XVI) of December 20, 1961, the Assembly established the Committee on the Peaceful Uses of Outer Space. The first result of the committee's work was Resolution 1962 (XVIII), entitled Declaration of Legal Principles Governing the Activities of States in the Exploration and Use of Outer Space, which was adopted unanimously on December 13, 1963. This was followed by the Treaty on Principles . . . Outer Space, including the Moon and Other Celestial Bodies, which was negotiated outside the United Nations but "commended" by the Assembly in Resolution 2222 (XXI) of January 25, 1967, to which the text of the treaty was annexed. The third major step was the Agreement on the Rescue of Astronauts, the Return of Astronauts and the Return of Objects Launched into Outer Space, which was "commended" by Assembly Resolution 2345 (XXII) of December 19, 1967.

The treaty follows generally the Declaration of Legal Principles. It provides for peaceful exploration of celestial bodies "on a basis of equality"; it lays down the principle of nonappropriation;[110] and bars the use of nuclear and other kinds of weapons of mass

[105] *Ibid.*, p. 32, paragraph 38, and p. 34, paragraph 49.

[106] *Ibid.*, p. 32, paragraphs 38 and 39.

[107] *Ibid.*, p. 34, paragraph 54.

[108] *Ibid.*, p. 41.

[109] *Ibid.*, p. 40. In the meantime the General Assembly adopted Resolution 2669 (XXV) recommending that the commission take up the study of the law relating to the non-navigational uses of international watercourses, with a view to codification and progressive development. General Assembly, *Official Records* (25th sess.), Suppl. 28 (A/8028), p. 127.

[110] Article 2: "Outer space, including the Moon and other celestial bodies, is not subject to national appropriation by claim of sovereignty, by means of use or occupation, or by any other means." Brownlie, *Basic Documents*, p. 106.

destruction in space or on celestial bodies.[111] This treaty, like the seabed treaty, does not, however, exclude all military activity in outer space such as reconnaissance. The treaty also provides for mutual inspection.[112]

While it is possible to arrive at agreement on the principles applicable to distant celestial bodies, no agreement has yet been reached on such down-to-earth matters as a delimitation of outer space and a convention "to establish international rules and procedures concerning liability for damage caused by the launching of objects into outer space and to ensure, in particular, prompt and equitable compensation for damage."[113] This is of direct concern to all people whereas the exploration of outer space is of direct interest to a handful of states. It may be noted that the preparatory work with respect to outer space is carried out in the Committee on the Peaceful Uses of Outer Space, its legal subcommittee, and the First (Political) Committee of the Assembly.

In the field of human rights, the General Assembly has from the outset manifested profound concern and has engaged in continuous and far-ranging activities. Reference has already been made to the 1948 Genocide Convention.[114] The basic act is the Universal Declaration of Human Rights, adopted without a dissenting vote by the Assembly in Resolution 217 (III), of December 10, 1948. It was proclaimed, as stated in the preamble, "as a common standard of achievement for all peoples and all nations." The declaration did not claim and does not have binding character. It contains, along with the usual political and civil rights, social and economic rights such as the right to social security, to work, to education, and others which have become associated with the social welfare state and have already been outlined in Article 55 of the Charter. Work on human rights was continued in the Economic and Social Council, in its Human Rights Commission, in the Assembly's Third Committee (Social, Humanitarian, and Cultural Questions), and, of course, in plenary meetings of the Assembly itself. The Assembly voiced its concern with human rights in innumerable resolutions, sometimes called declarations, some of which achieved the stage of conventions.

The most important achievement of the United Nations is without a doubt the two human rights covenants—the International Covenant on Economic, Social and Cultural Rights and the International Covenant on Civil and Political Rights—and the optional protocol to the latter. All three instruments were adopted by Resolution 2200 (XXI) of

[111] Article 4: "States Parties to the Treaty undertake not to place in orbit around the Earth any objects carrying nuclear weapons or any other kind of weapons of mass destruction, install such weapons on celestial bodies, or station such weapons in outer space in any other manner." *Ibid.* There is no corresponding provision in the declaration of the General Assembly.

[112] Article 12: "All stations, installations, equipment and space vehicles on the Moon and other celestial bodies shall be open to representatives of other States Parties to the Treaty on a basis of reciprocity. Such representatives shall give reasonable advance notice of a projected visit, in order that appropriate consultations may be held and that maximum precautions may be taken to assure safety and to avoid interference with normal operations in the facility to be visited." *Ibid.*, p. 109. There is no corresponding provision in the Assembly declaration.

[113] Paragraph 5 of General Assembly Resolution 2061B (XXIV) of December 16, 1969. This resolution recalls the Assembly resolutions since 1961 relating to the question of liability. Resolution 2601A (XXIV) refers to the definition of outer space. General Assembly, *Official Records* (24th sess.), Suppl. 30 (A/7630), pp. 12–13.

[114] See *supra*, p. 190. For conventions on rights of women, see *supra*, p. 198, and refugees and stateless persons, see *supra*, p. 199.

December 16, 1966.[115] Neither of the two covenants has yet entered into force. They have become binding on eight states (Colombia, Costa Rica, Cyprus, Ecuador, Libya, Syria, Tunisia, and Uruguay); they will enter into force after the deposit of the thirty-fifth ratification or accession. The optional protocol had been ratified by four states (Colombia, Costa Rica, Ecuador, and Uruguay) and will enter into force three months after the deposit of ten ratifications or accessions.[116]

It is impossible to indicate even in outline the substantive content of the covenants. Both instruments provide in Article 1 for the right of political and what is sometimes called economic self-determination.[117] The paucity of acceptances of the covenants indicates that although the members were able and willing to accept compromise formulas to accommodate different political and socioeconomic systems, they are reluctant to adjust their domestic systems to the rights included in the covenants. This reluctance accounts also for the weakness of the procedures for international supervision. In the Covenant on Economic, Social and Cultural Rights, they have been reduced to reports which the contracting parties agree to submit, in Article 16, "on the measures which they have adopted and the progress made in achieving the observance of the rights recognized herein." In this fashion the "rights" have become indistinguishable from the standards of achievement formulated in the 1948 Universal Declaration.

The procedures laid down in the Covenant on Civil and Political Rights are more explicit. They also include for the parties the duty to make reports on measures taken to give effect to the various rights. In addition, the parties have the option of conferring upon the Human Rights Committee provided for in Part IV of the convention the competence to receive complaints from a state party that another state party "is not fulfilling its obligations under the present Covenant" (Article 41[1]). The committee shall, under certain conditions, "make available its good offices to the State Parties concerned with a view to a friendly solution" (Article 41 [1] [e]). Failing this, the committee shall make a report without any recommendation. The Optional Protocol to the Covenant on Civil and Political Rights opens up the possibility for individuals to address communications to the Human Rights Committee in cases in which they "claim to be victims of a violation by that State Party (i.e., the State Party which has ratified the Protocol or has acceded to it) of any of the rights set forth in the Covenant" (Article 1). The procedure before the committee is limited to written communications which shall be examined in closed meetings. The committee "shall forward its views to the State Party concerned and to the

[115] General Assembly, *Official Records* (21st sess.), Suppl. 16 (A/6316), p. 49. The text of the three instruments is annexed to the resolution. They are reproduced along with the Universal Declaration in Brownlie, *Basic Documents*, pp. 132–175.

[116] General Assembly, *Official Records* (25th sess.), Suppl. 1 (A/8001), *Report of the Secretary-General on the Work of the Organization*, June 16, 1969–June 15, 1970, p. 112.

[117] Article 1: "1. All peoples have the right of self-determination. By virtue of that right they freely determine their political status and freely pursue their economic, social and cultural development. 2. All peoples may, for their own ends, freely dispose of their natural wealth and resources without prejudice to any obligations arising out of international economic co-operation, based upon the principle of mutual benefit, and international law. In no case may a people be deprived of its own means of subsistence."

individual'' (Article 5). How much all these enforcement procedures lag behind an acceptable model can be gleaned by comparing them with those established under the European Convention on Human Rights of 1950. These include the right of individual and group petition, a commission, and a Court of Human Rights.[118] The European convention, like the international covenant, contains escape clauses which permit the imposition of restrictions in the interest of national security or public order or other overriding considerations. However, the factual justification of the invocation of such contingencies is subject to judicial control in case of the former, whereas in the case of the latter it does not seem to be subject to any review whatever.[119]

The United Nations, from its inception, has been concerned particularly with one human right: the right not to be subjected to racial discrimination. One of its chief preoccupations has been the policy of racial discrimination, known as apartheid, practiced in South Africa and by South Africa in the former mandate of South-West Africa.[120] On the general level the Assembly adopted, by Resolution 1904 (XVIII) of November 20, 1963, the United Nations Declaration on the Elimination of All Forms of Racial Discrimination, in which it affirmed the necessity of speedily eliminating racial discrimination throughout the world. This was followed by the International Convention on the Elimination of All Forms of Racial Discrimination, adopted by the Assembly in Resolution 2106A (XX) of December 21, 1965.[121] This is a very elaborate instrument with enforcement procedures which appear much stronger than those included in the covenant discussed above. The convention is in force for thirty-eight states.[122] A draft convention on the elimination of all forms of intolerance and discrimination based on religion or belief is on the agenda of the Assembly.[123]

The consideration of the Nuremberg principles by the General Assembly may appropriately be recalled in the context of human rights inasmuch as crimes against humanity are punishable as crimes under international law.[124] An issue which pertains to this matter relates to the application of national statutes of limitation to the prosecution of war criminals. The issue arose concretely in the Federal Republic of Germany and was generally discussed in the Economic and Social Council. Acting on its recommendation, the General Assembly by Resolution 2391 (XXIII) of November 26, 1968, adopted the Convention on the Non-Applicability of Statutory Limitations to War Crimes and Crimes against Humanity. The convention has been ratified by ten socialist states and has

[118] For text and literature see Brownlie, *Basic Documents*, p. 194.

[119] For a case before the European Court of Human Rights, see the *Lawless* case, 56 AJIL 171–211 (1962), Judgments of November 14, 1960 and July 1, 1961.

[120] The practice of racial discrimination in South-West Africa was the very issue in the case between *Ethiopia and Liberia v. South Africa* before the International Court of Justice. The Court's judgment of July 18, 1966, rejected the claims of the applicant governments on the ground that they failed to establish "any legal right or interest appertaining to them in the subject-matter of the present claims." ICJ *Reports* (1966), p. 6, at 51.

[121] For text see Brownlie, *Basic Documents*, pp. 178–192.

[122] General Assembly, *Official Records* (25th sess.), Suppl. 1 (A/8001), *Report of the Secretary-General on the Work of the Organization*, June 16, 1969–June 15, 1970, p. 106.

[123] *Ibid.*, p. 112.

[124] On the Nuremberg principles, see *supra*, p. 190.

entered into force on November 11, 1970.[125] The preamble of the convention recalls the resolutions of the Assembly relating to war criminals, including Resolution 95 (I) of December 11, 1946, in which it affirmed the Nuremberg principles. Article I provides that "no statutory limitation shall apply to the following crimes, irrespective of the date of their commission," namely, war crimes and crimes against humanity "as they are defined in the Charter of the International Military Tribunal, Nürnberg, of 8 August 1945, and confirmed by resolutions 3(I) of 13 February 1946[126] and 95(I) of 11 December 1946 of the General Assembly of the United Nations, particularly the 'grave breaches' enumerated in the Geneva Conventions of 12 August 1949 for the protection of war victims."

It is interesting to note that, in the context of this convention, the possibility of establishing an international criminal court has again come up for consideration.[127] This was to be accomplished by means of an optional protocol to the convention. A draft optional protocol was submitted to the Assembly, but the Assembly decided by Resolution 2392 (XXIII) of November 26, 1968, to defer its consideration until "it resumes consideration of the question of international criminal jurisdiction." Thus the Assembly continues to be involved in the consideration of the bases of a new international legal order.

Numerous instruments relating to special activities of the United Nations, such as control of traffic in narcotic and other dangerous drugs, traffic in persons, and other areas, need not be discussed here.[128]

## The Development of International Law by the General Assembly through Resolutions and Declarations

Having considered the progressive development of international law by means of conventions or treaties adopted by the General Assembly or plenipotentiary conferences held under its auspices or convened at its behest, it remains to consider its contribution to the growth of law through resolutions. It is universally recognized that conventions or treaties are a source of international law or a source of legal obligation. There is no agreement but a good deal of controversy with respect to the question whether resolutions, even if called declarations, are a source of law or of legal obligation. The fact that international conventions are specifically listed in Article 38 (1) of the Statute of the International Court of Justice, which is usually regarded as a statement of sources of international law, and resolutions of organs of the United Nations are not, is certainly not of critical importance as this article was inherited from the Statute of 1920 of the Permanent Court of International Justice and antedates contemporary developments. International custom, however, is listed in Article 38 (1) and it was natural that those who are inclined to the

[125] *Report of the Secretary-General* (*supra*, n. 122), p. 112.

[126] This resolution is concerned with the extradition and punishment of war criminals. For Resolution 2391 (XXIII), see General Assembly, *Official Records* (23rd sess.), Suppl. 18 (A/7218), p. 40.

[127] For earlier consideration see *supra*, p. 192.

[128] For a listing of such instrument see *Multilateral Treaties*, passim.

view that resolutions have legal significance tend to look upon them as a means, a new means, of creating customary international law.

Probably the strongest endorsement of the latter view came from the pen of Judge Tanaka. In his dissenting opinion in the *South-West Africa* case, Judge Tanaka stated that individual resolutions or declarations "have no binding force upon the members of the organization"; that they must be repeated frequently since "what is required for customary international law is the repetition of the same practice"; and that with respect to the issue at hand—the existence of a rule of equality of treatment or nondiscrimination—"the accumulation of authoritative pronouncements such as resolutions, declarations, decisions, etc., concerning the interpretation of the Charter by the competent organs of the international community can be characterized as evidence of the international custom referred to in Article 38, paragraph 1 (b)."[129] Judge Jessup, on the other hand, in his dissenting opinion in the same case, rejected the argument "that the so-called norm of non-discrimination had become a rule of international law through reiterated statements in resolutions of the General Assembly, of the International Labor Organization, and of other international bodies." He based this rejection on the ground that "since these international bodies lack a true legislative character, their resolutions alone cannot create law."[130] Elsewhere, he stated the view that "the accumulation of expressions of condemnation of apartheid . . . as recorded in the resolutions of the General Assembly of the United Nations are proof of the pertinent contemporary international community standard."[131]

There are some flaws in Judge Tanaka's proposition. If individual resolutions have no binding force for the members, this must be due to the absence of legislative authority. If this is so, then how can it be explained that an accumulation of such nonbinding resolutions results in a binding norm of international law? To say that this results from practice, which is an element of customary international law, is to confuse the practice of organs with the practice of members of the United Nations. The accumulation of the resolutions is evidence of the former and not of the latter. Customary international law is the product along with *opinio juris* of the practice of states and not the practice of organs. Moreover, there is the open question, how large the accumulation must be, and the further question of the size of the majority, its composition, and so on.

Another flaw seems to be the attribution of resolutions to the members instead of to the United Nations. It is universally recognized that the United Nations has an interna-

[129] ICJ *Reports* (1966), p. 292. Judge Tanaka explained this process saying: "Briefly, the method of the generation of customary international law is in the stage of transformation from being an individualistic process to being a collectivistic process. This phenomenon can be said to be the adaptation of the traditional creative process of international law to the reality of the growth of the organized international community. It can be characterized, considered from the sociological viewpoint, as a transition from traditional custom-making to international legislation by treaty." *Ibid.*, p. 294. Judge Tanaka did not explain how the highly individualistic "international legislation by treaty" can result, seen sociologically or otherwise, from the new collectivistic customary law-creating process.

[130] *Ibid.*, p. 432. Judge Jessup also invoked another consideration which is not material here.

[131] *Ibid.*, p. 441. In this context he declared that this conclusion "does not rest upon the thesis that resolutions of the General Assembly have a general legislative character and by themselves create rules of international law."

tional legal personality;[132] it acts through its various organs in a corporate capacity. Therefore, the resolutions which it adopts are resolutions of the corporate body, the United Nations, and not of the members, although they may be and usually are addressed to them.

Still another flaw appears in the attribution to the General Assembly of the power or competence to give authentic interpretations of the Charter.[133] The Charter has deliberately conferred no such authority on the Assembly, not even on the Court.[134] It is, to put it no higher, doubtful whether such an authority has been acquired by the Assembly though there is no doubt that the General Assembly often seems to have claimed this authority or proceeded on the assumption that it was indeed endowed with it. It is another but, in the present submission, relevant question whether it would be wise or desirable to attribute the competence of authentic—that is, binding—interpretation to so highly political and politicized a body as the Assembly.[135]

To accept Judge Tanaka's conclusions would be tantamount to accepting the Assembly as a world legislature, operating on the basis of the one-state-one-vote principle, and promulgating binding acts by a two-thirds majority which a simple majority could conceivably reduce to a simple majority.[136] The circumstances that a single act would not be binding but would have to be repeated—how many times?—is of some but minor significance. Considering that in the *Expenses* case, the Court attributed to the Assembly a virtually unlimited power with respect to expenditure which can be imposed upon the members,[137] the United Nations would seem to be possessed of some powers of a world government. It is scarcely conceivable that the members or even the organs of the United Nations intended this to happen.

If the major proposition, that the Assembly has competence to create "customary" international law by the process of the reiteration of resolutions, must be rejected, the minor proposition that the Assembly may play a role in the development of customary international law is unobjectionable. It is a factual proposition and depends merely upon proof that, in fact, this or that resolution initiated the process culminating in the emergence of a new rule of customary international law.[138] To be sure, the adoption of a reso-

[132] See the advisory opinion of the International Court of Justice in the *Reparation for Injuries* case. ICJ *Reports* (1949), p. 174, at 179.

[133] See Judge Tanaka's dissenting opinion, *supra*, n. 129, p. 294. Judge Tanaka surely overshot the mark when he attributed retroactive effect to the authentic interpretation.

[134] See Gross, "Role of Law," p. 160f.

[135] This argument is of a general character and does not address itself to the question of the powers of the Security Council under chap. VII of the Charter.

[136] See Article 18(3) of the Charter.

[137] ICJ *Reports* (1962), p. 151. See also Leo Gross, "Expenses of the United Nations for Peace-Keeping Operations: The Advisory Opinion of the ICJ," 17 *International Organization* 1–35 (1963). See infra.

[138] This seems to be the view of the memorandum of the Office of Legal Affairs of the United Nations Secretariat. Commenting upon the distinction between "recommendation" and "declaration," the memorandum states that "in view of the greater solemnity and significance of a 'declaration,' it may be considered to impart, on behalf of the organ adopting it, a strong expectation that Members of the international community will abide by it. Consequently, insofar as the expectation is gradually justified by State practice, a declaration may by custom become recognized as laying down rules binding upon States." Document E/CN.4/L. 610, April 2, 1962, pp. 1–2.

lution or declaration may create, may indeed be based on, the expectation that the members generally or particular members will act in accordance with the resolution or declaration. But this is a far cry from saying that they are legally bound to do so or that expectations as to the conduct of states are identical with legal norms governing the conduct of states in the particular subject matter.[139] It is trite to say that many expectations, whether expressed in international conventions or in resolutions of international or national assemblies, have remained unfulfilled.

However, if it is right to say that resolutions may be the initial step in the formation of custom, its existence would still depend upon the usual requirements: practice of states (objective element) and sense of legal obligation (*opinio juris,* the subjective element). This has been confirmed many times by the International Court of Justice, most recently in the *North Sea Continental Shelf* case. Referring to the *opinio juris* requirement, the Court said that two conditions must be fulfilled:

> Not only must the acts concerned amount to a settled practice, but they must also be such, or be carried out in such a way, as to be evidence of a belief that this practice is rendered obligatory by the existence of a rule of law requiring it. The need for such a belief, i.e., the existence of a subjective element, is implicit in the very notion of the *opinio juris sive necessitatis.* The States concerned must therefore feel that they are conforming to a legal obligation. The frequency, or even habitual character of the acts, is not in itself enough.[140]

The Court's concept and application of customary international law has been criticized,[141] and obviously there is room for differences of opinion, but the Court, like other organs of the United Nations, is dealing with sovereign states and states do not easily assume legal obligations.

In any event, the reiteration of resolutions setting forth certain goals may say something about the attitude of the organ, but the real question is whether or not the member states—not merely in words spoken in the General Assembly and in votes—respond to the resolution and, in particular, whether in responding they do so out of a sense of legal obligation and not merely because they find it convenient or inevitable to bow to public opinion or to pressures in and out of the United Nations. There are benefits to be reaped in conforming to Assembly resolutions and costs are involved in opposing them. Thus conduct conforming to resolutions may be the outcome of a "costs-benefits" calculation and, apart from the rhetoric of law so popular in the Assembly, there need be no reason to

[139] With reference to numerous resolutions of the Assembly calling for the termination of colonial situations, Dr. Rosalyn Higgins said, "I would have thought that cumulatively, even if individually they are not 'binding' on these countries (viz., Portugal and South Africa), they do create a community expectation about what is and is not lawful behavior." "The United Nations and Law-making: The Political Organs," *American Society of International Law, Proceedings,* 64 AJIL 37–48 (1970), at 42. In the absence of an independent norm of conventional or customary international law, the conduct of the states concerned cannot be qualified as lawful or unlawful unless it is assumed that the relevant resolutions cumulatively have created the norm requiring states to divest themselves of their colonial holdings. This is Judge Tanaka's line of reasoning which I cannot accept.

[140] ICJ *Reports* (1969), p. 3, at 44.

[141] C. Wilfred Jenks, *The Prospects of International Adjudication* (Dobbs Ferry, N.Y.: Oceana, 1964), p. 237.

analyze such conduct in terms of law.[142] However, if such an analysis is attempted, it would have to be not in terms of expectations but along the lines of the usual concept of customary international law—that is, practice of states and sense of legal obligation. Since writers concerned with the legal effect of Assembly resolutions usually start out by attributing such effect to them, there has not been sufficient analysis of specific resolutions or declarations to determine whether they have "by custom become recognized as laying down rules binding upon States."[143] In a study which offers such an analysis, Resolution 1514 (XV) of December 14, 1960, entitled Declaration on the Granting of Independence to Colonial Countries and Peoples, one of the most frequently reiterated resolutions, it is concluded that it "is as much a part of our international law as any of the familiar traditional doctrines."[144] This conclusion is based on the "confirmed re-citation" of the resolution, the "fixed and universal expectation" that colonialism will be terminated, and that "no State could be unaware of this expectation or that the resolution was merely a 'recommendation' with no normative force as an authoritative interpretation of the United Nations Charter, and few colonial Powers have attempted to permanently obstruct decolonization."[145] No doubt, a few colonial powers have so far, at any rate, held on to their colonial territories or their "overseas" metropolitan territories. That the resolution has created expectations is hardly open to doubt, though the expectation seems—so far, at any rate—less than universal. That the resolution *in toto* or some of its parts constitutes an authoritative interpretation rather than a revision of the Charter is by no means clear, even if it were granted, for the sake of the argument, that the Assembly has the competence to make such interpretations.[146] Be that as it may and granted that many dependent and colonial territories were given independence both before and after the adoption of Resolution 1514 (XV), no evidence has been offered that the states concerned have done so out of a sense of legal obligation. Decolonization and the application of the principle of self-determination to colonial and other peoples have been a continuing process for several decades and owe their dynamics to forces of nationalism rather than to law.

[142] Professor R. Falk is very close to this position when he says: "The degree of authoritativeness that the process of law-creating by Assembly action comes to enjoy depends upon the extent to which particular resolutions influence behavior and gain notoriety in legal circles and the extent to which this process is incorporated into the developing framework of an evolving system and science of international law." "On the Quasi-Legislative Competence of the General Assembly," 60 AJIL 782–791 (1966), p. 786. The difference is that Professor Falk starts out by positing the process of "law-creating" by the Assembly whereas in my view it would be appropriate to speak of the process of "resolution-creating." To speak of "law-creating" anticipates the outcome which depends upon the states and, to a much lesser degree, the science of international law.

[143] See the memorandum of the Office of Legal Affairs, n. 138.

[144] Samuel A. Bleicher, "The Legal Significance of Re-Citation of General Assembly Resolutions," 63 AJIL 444–478 (1969) at 475. For the frequency of the citation of this and a few other resolutions, see *ibid.*, pp. 455–456.

[145] *Ibid.*, p. 475.

[146] A more discriminating view will be found in Hanna Bokor-Szegö, *New States and International Law* (Budapest: Akademiai Kiado, 1970). In her opinion the declaration interprets the Charter in defining the right of self-determination but in several respects, "when it condemns all forms of colonial rule," disregards the distinction between trust and non-self-governing territories and when it "demands the immediate granting of independence to all dependent territories," it goes beyond the Charter. "These provisions of the Declaration . . . cannot be considered interpretation of the Charter. They amend and develop it in a progressive sense. As, however, amendments to the Charter are governed by its provisions in Chapter XVIII, the Declaration in question could not validly modify the appropriate articles of the Charter." *Ibid.*, pp. 28–29.

Looking at the practice of states, one finds that forty-five territories with approximately 28 million people still remain under colonial rule, despite the reiteration "of their fundamental and inalienable right to self-determination and independence,"[147] and the assiduous activity of the Special Committee which was set up by the Assembly in 1963 to speed up the implementation of the 1960 declaration. As before, it is the administering authority and not the Assembly which determines when its obligations under Chapter XI are satisfied and its obligation to transmit information has come to an end. To be sure, this is deplored by the Special Committee. Thus the United Kingdom has simply informed the Assembly's Fourth Committee that certain territories under its administration "having achieved the status of Associated States, they had achieved 'a full measure of self-government' and that information on them would not be transmitted in the future." This occurred in 1967 and the attitude of the United Kingdom has not changed since then.[148] France seems to have taken a similar attitude with two of its remaining territories.[149]

If, then, some members take the attitude that they and not the Special Committee or the Assembly determine the fulfillment of their obligations under the Charter, Portugal rejects the authority of the Assembly to determine that its overseas possessions are non-self-governing territories within the meaning of Chapter XI of the Charter and that it is bound to transmit information with respect to them. For this it has been repeatedly condemned.[150] Still less does Portugal admit that these territories are entitled to self-determination and independence. The conditions in southern Africa are bleak indeed, but the secretary-general is probably right in saying that Portugal must be convinced by the members "of the wisdom of acknowledging the right to freedom and independence of the peoples of the Territories under its administration."[151] It will be particularly necessary not merely to convince Portugal that these territories have a right to independence but it will be even more imperative to change the factors in its "costs-benefits" calculations.

Finally, it would seem that even the General Assembly itself does not consider that it has authority to create what has sometimes been called "instant" international law by means of resolutions or declarations. In several cases the passage of a declaration—as in connection with human rights, outer space, and racial discrimination—was merely a first step. This was followed by the elaboration and adoption of international conventions along similar or identical lines—that is, the normal procedure for the creation of norms of international law. Such conventions are, however, binding on the contracting states. If

[147] *Supra*, n. 122, Suppl. 1A (A/8001/Add. 1), *Introduction to the Annual Report of the Secretary-General*, p. 14, paragraph 113.

[148] *Report* of the Special Committee on the Situation with Regard to the Implementation of the Declaration on the Granting of Independence to Colonial Countries and Peoples (covering its work during 1970), Document A/8023/Add. 8, Annex, p. 5. On pp. 6–8 there is a list of non-self-governing territories, the total number of which is somewhat less than forty-five.

[149] *Ibid.*, p. 6. The last territory, New Hebrides, is a condominium with the United Kingdom.

[150] *Ibid.*, p. 4.

[151] See *surpa*, n. 147, *Introduction to the Annual Report of the Secretary-General*, p. 15, paragraph 122.

the preceding resolution or declaration had already binding legal character for the members, why incorporate the same or essentially similar content in an international convention which is binding only on the contracting states?[152] The inference seems inescapable that the declarations have not created new international law. Referring to the 1966 Covenants on Civil and Political and on Economic, Social and Cultural Rights, the secretary-general of the United Nations stated that their ratification "will *complement* the Universal Declaration of Human Rights with *legally binding provisions,* including measures of implementation, and it will give a much firmer basis to the role of the United Nations in the protection of human rights."[153] This, it is submitted, seems an accurate perception of the relation between declarations and resolutions, on the one side, and international conventions, on the other. This leaves open the question which is beyond the scope of this essay, whether some resolutions have or have not entered into the process from which customary law emerges.

## The Contribution to the Development of International Law by the International Court of Justice

The contribution of the International Court of Justice to the progressive development of international law has been very modest but significant. The Court had very few cases to decide—only twenty-four contentious cases—and even fewer requests for advisory opinions—only thirteen, of which one is pending.[154] Several cases and requests were of a very narrow compass, requiring perhaps no more than the interpretation of a contested clause in a treaty. It is, incidentally, in this area that the Court made a decisive contribution inasmuch as the rules concerning the interpretation of treaties in the Vienna Convention on the Law of Treaties (Articles 31 and 32) are based on the jurisprudence of the Court as well as of its predecessor, the Permanent Court of International Justice. In some cases the Court made pronouncements of a general character which were incidental to the contested issue. Some examples will illustrate the point.

In several cases the Court had occasion to express its views on the nature of customary international law. The Court's pronouncement in the *North Sea Continental Shelf* case was referred to above. The Court expressed a similar view in the *Asylum* case.[155] In the *Right of Passage* case, the Court recognized the existence of a local custom binding on only two states.[156] These pronouncements clarified the concept substantially and stimulated scholarly discussion.

More directly, the Court made contributions to the progressive development of international law in the *Corfu Channel* and *Fisheries* cases. In the former case, the Court held

[152] See Gross, "Role of Law," p. 160f. Supra.

[153] See *supra,* n. 147, *Introduction to the Report of the Secretary-General,* p. 12, paragraph 103. Italics supplied.

[154] This is the request of the Security Council of July 29, 1970, for an opinion on the "Legal Consequences for States of the Continued Presence of South Africa in Namibia (South West Africa) notwithstanding Security Council Resolution 276 (1970)." ICJ *Yearbook* (1969–1970), p. 5.

[155] *Asylum* case (Colombia/Peru) ICJ *Reports* (1950), p. 266, at 276, 277.

[156] Case concerning *Right of Passage over Indian Territory (Portugal v. India),* ICJ *Reports* (1960), p. 6, at 39.

"that States in time of peace have a right to send their warships through straits used for international navigation between two parts of the high seas without the previous authorization of a coastal State, provided that the passage is innocent."[157] This holding facilitated the work of the International Law Commission on the law of the high seas and was incorporated in the 1958 Geneva Convention on the Territorial Sea and Contiguous Zone (Article 16[4]).

In the *Fisheries* case, the Court found that the drawing of straight base lines for the delimitation of the territorial sea was not contrary to international law and that the traditional ten-mile rule for the closing line of bays "has not acquired the authority of a general rule of international law."[158] Again, the Court cleared the way for the International Law Commission, and the relevant articles in the 1958 Geneva Convention on the Territorial Sea and Contiguous Zone are based on the Court's holdings (Article 4).

Still another contribution to the development of international law was made by the Court in the advisory opinion concerning *Reservations to the Genocide Convention.* In this case the Court rejected both the "absolute integrity" theory—namely, that a reservation to a multilateral convention must be accepted by all states in order to permit the reserving state to become a party to it—as well as the sovereignty theory—namely, that a reserving state, in virtue of its sovereignty, may become a party to the convention without the consent of other controlling parties. Instead, the Court held that a state "which has made . . . a reservation which has been objected to by one or more of the parties to the Convention but not by others, can be regarded as being a party to the Convention if the reservation is compatible with the object and purpose of the Convention."[159] The International Law Commission initially preferred, in opposition to the Court, the integrity theory but it reversed itself in connection with its work on the law of treaties, and the Vienna Convention on the Law of Treaties incorporated the Court's holding in its Articles 19–23 on reservations.

Several cases may be included here because they contain significant pronouncements which clarify contested points of law although they have not contributed directly to its codification. In the *Reparation* case, the Court not merely affirmed the international legal personality of the United Nations but also developed a theory of the functional protection by the United Nations of its agents and of the implied powers of the organization.[160] In the hotly contested issue of the status of *South-West Africa,* the Court laid the juridical foundations for its subsequent consideration in the General Assembly by holding that the mandate survived the dissolution of the League of Nations, that the supervisory function of the League Council passed to the United Nations General Assembly, and that South Africa as the mandatory was under the continuing obligation to administer the mandate in accordance with Article 22 of the Covenant of the League, and to transmit petitions

[157] *Corfu Channel* case (*United Kingdom/Albania),* ICJ *Reports* (1949), p. 4, at 28.
[158] *Fisheries* case (*United Kingdom v. Norway*), ICJ *Reports* (1951), p. 116, at 129 and 131.
[159] ICJ *Reports* (1951), p. 15, at 24, 29.
[160] Advisory opinion: ICJ *Reports* (1949), p. 174, at 179, 182, 184.

from the inhabitants of the territory. The Court, however, also held that South Africa was under no obligation to place the territory under the trusteeship system of the United Nations.[161] This being an advisory opinion, it was legally not binding upon South Africa. Attempts to obtain from the Court a binding judgment, the execution of which could ultimately be enforced by the Security Council, failed. The Court, "by the President's casting vote—the votes being equally divided," decided "to reject the claims of the Empire of Ethiopia and the Republic of Liberia."[162] The judgment provoked strong, almost intemperate criticism in and out of the United Nations, and it was gratifying that the secretary-general of the United Nations rose to the defense of the Court against political pressures.[163]

In the *Nottebohm* case, the Court recognized that international law leaves it to the state to determine who are its nationals, but the state "cannot claim that the rules it has thus laid down are entitled to recognition by another State unless it has acted in conformity with this general aim of making the legal bond of nationality accord with the individual's genuine connection with the State which assumes the defence of its citizens by means of protection as against other States."[164] This "genuine bond" or "genuine link" theory has aroused much discussion in the literature. However, in spite of it, the theory was adopted into Article 5 of the 1958 Geneva Convention on the High Seas. It provides that "each State shall fix the conditions for the grant of its nationality to ships . . . and for the right to fly its flag," but "there must exist a genuine link between the State and the ship." The provision is intended to curb the use of so-called "flags of convenience."

This brief survey is by no means exhaustive of the contribution which the jurisprudence of the Court has made to the development of international law. A more extensive analysis would be of interest primarily to specialists.

## CONCLUSION

By all criteria, the contribution of the United Nations to the progressive development of international law has surpassed all expectations. It would be surprising if the pace set in the first twenty-five years of the United Nations will be matched by that of the next quarter of a century. As indicated above, the International Law Commission has some very difficult topics on its agenda. The interest of the members of the United Nations seems increasingly concentrated on economic development, abolition of racial discrimination, and decolonization. The problem of the exploitation of the seabed for the general welfare rather than for the exclusive benefit of technologically highly developed states re-

[161] Advisory opinion: ICJ *Reports* (1950), p. 128, at 143–144.

[162] *South West Africa* Cases (*Ethiopia v. South Africa; Liberia v. South Africa*), Second Phase, Judgment, ICJ *Reports* (1966), p. 6, at 51.

[163] General Assembly, *Official Records* (22nd sess.), Suppl. 1 (A/6701/Add. 1), *Introduction to the Annual Report of the Secretary-General on the Work of the Organization,* June 16, 1966–June 15, 1967, p. 19, par. 155.

[164] *Nottebohm* case (*Liechtenstein v. Guatemala*), ICJ *Reports* (1955), p. 4 at 23.

mains to be solved. The treaty on liability for damage caused by space objects remains to be drafted. The question of direct broadcast satellites has been on the agenda of the United Nations for some years. Problems of human environment will require for their solution technical skill and statesmanship in order to safeguard the interests of the developing countries. The growing interdependence in trade will require regulation by international conventions. For this purpose the General Assembly, by Resolution 2205 (XXI) of December 17, 1966, established the United Nations Commission on International Trade Law.[165]

The role of science and technology in the development of nations is and will be a major problem. The Assembly requested the secretary-general, by Resolution 2658 (XXV) of December 7, 1970, to undertake a study of the ways and means for strengthening international cooperation in the new applications of science and technology.

In all of these fields one may expect some action by the United Nations. It may take the form of international convention or of declarations and resolutions. So far the energies of the United Nations have been focused on substantive law. The field of adjective or remedial law to ensure that the substantive law is properly applied and enforced has been sorely neglected. The optional protocols to the Geneva and Vienna conventions have not been widely ratified. None has been ratified by the Soviet Union and the United States. The remedies provided for in the Human Rights Covenants are merely halting steps in the right direction. A proposal for the creation of the post of United Nations High Commissioner for Human Rights was on the agenda of the 1969 and 1970 sessions of the General Assembly but it was not adopted.[166] The General Act for the Pacific Settlement of International Disputes, originally adopted by the League of Nations in 1928 and revised by the General Assembly of the United Nations in 1949, has been entirely accepted by five members (Belgium, Norway, Denmark, Luxembourg, and Upper Volta) and partially by one (Sweden).[167] This act provides for the settlement of political and legal disputes by conciliation, adjudication (the International Court of Justice), and arbitration. The disappointing fate of the work of the International Law Commission on a draft Code of Arbitral Procedure may be recalled in this context as further evidence of the neglect of remedial procedures by the United Nations.

The use, or perhaps the nonuse, of the International Court of Justice has already been indicated. There is no contentious case pending before the Court and since 1961 there has been only one request for an advisory opinion. Only forty-six states—forty-four members and two nonmembers—have accepted the jurisdiction of the Court as compulsory under Article 36 (2) of its statute.[168] The reasons for this neglect of the principal judicial organ of the United Nations by its organs and its members are too complex to be

[165] For the history of the commission, its functions, and composition, see General Assembly, *Official Records* (22nd sess.), Suppl. 1 (A/6701), *Annual Report of the Secretary-General on the Work of the Organization,* June 16, 1966–June 15, 1967, pp. 180–182.

[166] For a brief history of the proposal, see *supra*, n. 122, *Annual Report of the Secretary-General,* p. 115.

[167] *Ibid.*, p. 229.

[168] ICJ *Yearbook* (1969–1970), p. 51.

discussed here.[169] Fortunately, there have been some indications lately of concern about the future of the Court. At the 1970 session of the General Assembly, several members submitted a proposal entitled "Review of the Role of the International Court of Justice." In their view such a review "is urgently needed." And they proposed the study "of obstacles to the satisfactory functioning of the International Court of Justice, and ways and means of removing them." They also proposed that the Assembly authorize an *Ad Hoc* Committee to undertake this study.[170] The General Assembly did not adopt this proposal. It decided, however, by a resolution adopted on December 15, 1970, to begin with a request to the members for their comments and suggestions concerning the future role of the Court, an invitation to the Court to state its views, and a request to the secretary-general for a comprehensive report.[171] It is to be hoped that this will mark the beginning of a new era in the fortunes of the Court and in the elaboration of procedures designed to secure the application of substantive law. Substantive and remedial law are interdependent, there is no need to further one at the expense of the other, for if the states and their peoples are to reap the benefits of the substantive law they need to have at their disposal adequate means for obtaining redress. It is time to restore a balance between the two interdependent branches of the law.

[169] For a brief analysis, see Leo Gross, "The International Court of Justice and the United Nations," Hague Academy of International Law, *Recueil des Cours,* I, 1967 (Leyden: Sijthoff, 1968), 319–435, particularly 422–435. See infra.

[170] Document A/8042, August 14, 1970, p. 3.

[171] Resolution 2723 (XXV), in General Assembly, *Official Records* (25th sess.), Suppl. 28 (A/8028), p. 128.

# FAMILY PLANNING AS A HUMAN RIGHT: SOME JURISPRUDENTIAL REFLECTIONS ON NATURAL RIGHTS AND POSITIVE LAW*

## 1. INTRODUCTION

The persistent rhetoric of inalienable or inherent rights of man in a substantial segment of its activities suggests that the United Nations has committed itself to a revival of natural law, certainly of its language and possibly of its spirit as well. In this respect it differs radically from its predecessor, the League of Nations, which was very much attached to positive international law. One of its objectives, as stated in the Preamble of the Covenant, was "the firm establishment of the understandings of international law as the actual rule of conduct among Governments" and another was "the maintenance of justice and a scrupulous respect for all treaty obligations." It is true that the League was credited with the revival of one of the main concepts of natural law, namely the distinction between just and unjust war. But that was a misunderstanding. Having committed itself to the scrupulous respect of *pacta sunt servanda,* a norm of customary international law, the Covenant distinguished in Articles 12, 13, and 15 between legal and illegal, not just or unjust, resort to war and provided in Article 16 for sanctions against the Member which resorted to war in violation of these legal obligations.

The Charter, by contrast, begins with an ambiguity ("We the peoples of the United Nations"),[1] and after committing itself, not to abolish tyrannical governments,

* A talk delivered at the Indian Law Institute on 8.2.1974, Reprinted from Human Rights and Population: From the Perspectives of Law, Policy and Organization. Originally published in "Human Rights and Population," by the Law and Population Programme of the Fletcher School of Law and Diplomacy, Tufts University. Law and Population Book Series, No. 5, 1973, pp. 25–35.

[1] This ambiguity is resolved in the final paragraph of the Preamble, the so-called "establishment" clause in which the Governments come into their own, relieve the peoples of any further responsibility and establish the organization to be known as the United Nations.

but rather to "save succeeding generations from the scourge of war which twice in our lifetime" was started by tyrannical governments, proceeds "to reaffirm faith in fundamental human rights . . .", that is in natural law. For whenever there is an appeal to such rights, to "the dignity and worth of the human person," there is an appeal to natural law and *vice versa.*[2] The natural law aspect of the Charter is expressed and elaborated in a series of declarations, resolutions and conventions: in the 1948 Universal Declaration of Human Rights and the 1966 International Covenants, one on Economic, Social and Cultural Rights, and the other on Civil and Political Rights. It singles out a specific human right as in the Declaration on the Elimination of All Forms of Racial Discrimination of November 20, 1963, and the companion Convention of the same title of March 7, 1966. The United Nations also singles out a particular category of human beings, namely women, for particular attention and devoted both conventions and resolutions in order to secure for them a status of equality. One of the most recent and important steps in that direction was taken at the 1968 United Nations International Conference on Human Rights. First, the Proclamation of Teheran in paragraph 15 calls for elimination of "the discrimination of which women are still victims in various parts of the world." It then declares that "an inferior status for women is contrary to the Charter of the United Nations as well as the provisions of the Universal Declaration of Human Rights," and finally that "the full implementation of the Declaration on the Elimination of All Forms of Discrimination Against Women is a necessity for the progress of mankind." The Proclamation goes on to say, in paragraph 16, that "parents have a basic human right to determine freely and responsibly the number and the spacing of their children" and, adds in Conference Resolution XVIII adopted on May 12, 1968, "a right to adequate education and information in this respect." Thus, after some years of gestation, a new basic human right, the right of family planning, was born. It shares with other basic human rights in their character as natural rights. Unlike the political and civil rights of man, it is not rooted in the classic doctrine of natural law although it could be read into it either as an aspect, albeit a modern one, of the dignity of man or as a *sine qua non* for the enjoyment by women of political rights and to some extent of civil rights. No doubt it is a precondition for the equal enjoyment by women of economic, social and cultural rights. As a basic human right, family planning derives its strength and authority from the United Nations as a forum for the proclamation of what might be called modern natural law. What is the object of the frequent, almost perennial appeals to natural law in the United Nations?[3]

[2] H. Lauterpacht, *An International Bill of the Rights of Man* (New York: Columbia University Press, 1945), pp. 26, 31, 35.

[3] This essay is limited to some aspects of human rights including family planning. The appeal to natural law in other areas of United Nations activity, such as decolonization, must therefore be left out of account here.

## 2. NATURAL LAW AS A SOURCE AND CENSOR OF POSITIVE LAW

Natural law has been understood in different ways and invoked for different purposes. According to one definition, "the essence of the natural law movement has been to deduce from human nature or, for that matter, from human reason, ready-made legal precepts, which, because of their source in the universally identical human nature, claim validity for all times and for all parts of the world."[4] In another version, natural law was presented as divine law, as flowing from "the eternal law of God" and has survived in this form particularly in the Catholic Church and some Christian writers.[5] However, the dominant form of natural law has been secular, and Grotius is generally given credit for having separated the law derived from reason from God's command.[6] It is, of course, assumed that this immutable and universal law must be deduced from "true" or "uncorrupted" and not from "depraved" reason.[7] Moreover, only if a "correct conclusion" is drawn from the law of nature is it a rule of natural law and not merely one of positive law.[8] Whatever may be the subtleties of the differences between the various schools of natural law on the one hand and positive law on the other, they are of no consequence here. The important point is that all normative systems, be they derived from a divine source or from nature or from reason, or whether they be, like positive law, enacted by authority, are mediated by prophets and men. Priests transmit divine or revealed law, and laymen derive precepts from reason or nature, and men, be they kings or legisla-

[4] G. Radbruch, *Grundzüge der Rechtsphilosopie* (Leipzig : Quelle & Meyer, 1914), p. 3 (author's translation).

[5] Frede Castberg, "Natural Law and Human Rights : An idea-Historical Survey," in *International Protection of Human Rights* (Proceedings of the Seventh Nobel Symposium, Oslo, Sept. 25-27, 1967 ; ed. by Asbtörn Eide and August Schon (New York : John Wiley & Sons, 1968)), pp. 15, 26, and literature there cited. See also Kotaro Tanaka, "Some Observations on Peace, Law and Human Rights," in : *Transnational Law in a Changing Society* ed. by W. Friedmann, L. Henkin and O. Lissitzyn (New York : Columbia University Press, 1972), pp.242–259, at 250–255, and R. Stammler, *Wirtschaft und Recht* (Leipzig : Veit & Co., 1896), p. 170.

[6] Castberg, *supra*, no. 5, pp. 16–17 ; Lauterpacht, *supra* note 2, p. 34; Julius Stone, *Human Law and Human Justice* (Stanford : Stanford University Press, 1965), pp. 74–75. The references to Grotius are to his *De Jure Belli ac Pacis*, (1925), Prolegomena, par. 11 and Book 1, Chap. 1, sex. X, par. 5, where it is said : "The law of nature is unchangeable—even in the sense that it cannot be changed by God. Measureless as is the power of God, nevertheless it can be said that there are certain things over which that power does not extend;. . . . Just as even God, then, cannot cause that two time two shall not make four, so He cannot cause that which is intrinsically evil be not evil." *The Classics of International Law*, ed. by J.B. Scott (Oxford : The Clarendon Press, 1925), p. 40. Stammler in his book, *The Theory of Justice* (New York : Macmillian, 1925), p. 78–79, offers a *reductio ad absurdum* of the theory of natural law as derived from reason: "If then the theory of the law of nature is to be discredited because it is based upon reason, the latter must be assumed to be a power which imports empirical matters (in this case concrete legal principles) from a sphere lying outside of reality. How, indeed, reason can do any such thing, and what sort of unknown land it is from which, independently of experience, it is to introduce intelligible ideas, is a matter which remains entirely dark. He who thinks of 'reason' as a magic power by which we conjure something from an unknown sphere into the world of experience has, scientifically speaking, reached a deadpoint. For if we think of reason as divorced from all experience, then no man possesses any such magic power. Nor is it true, as some have supposed, that this power of reason arises in every individual "de novo." The idea of a psychic quality of this nature existing in the individual is a chimerical fancy and an obscure word which has no clear meaning. A faculty of reason which stands with one foot in the world of experience and with the other outside, and carries over legal principles from the latter into the former, does not really represent any intelligible idea, no matter how extensive and how fine this fantastic image is conceived to be. Such a faculty could not even (as the opponents of the law of nature have expressed it) 'furnish knowledge that is true subjectively but not objectively.' For it is no faculty at all and has no reality either subjective or objective."

[7] Stone, *Supra* note 6, pp. 76, 78.

[8] *Id.* at 75.

Mr. D. K. Ghosh, Director of Research welcoming
Dr. Leo Gross

tive assemblies, proclaim or enact positive law. Between the original source and the formulated precepts, man always plays a mediating role.

Natural law has been the target of frequent criticism from lawyers concerned with positive law and philosophers concerned with the purity of method. Lawyers would deny that natural law was law in any meaningful sense of the word. With this criticism, we are not concerned. From the philosophical standpoint, the claim of natural law to immutability and universality has been attacked. Adherents of Kantian philosophy, in particular, have contended that it was impossible to present the contents of a particular legal precept as an immutable ideal and that there were no such precepts with *a priori* validity.[9] While the category of "right law" or "just law" may claim universal validity, no particular precept may make such a claim as to its content. Therefore, there is only a "natural law with a changing content,"[10] since all content is contingent and derived from experience. We are not here concerned with the philosophical question whether Stammler correctly or incorrectly understood Kant's distinction between form and substance.[11] For even he claimed that there was a universally valid goal of social life and that it was possible to determine whether legal norms under given empirical conditions were conducive to that goal.[12] Thus his concept of "natural law with a changing content" was to be understood as "legal precepts which, under given empirical condictions, contain a theoretically correct law."[13] It has been pointed out that by introducing the concept of a universally valid social ideal, Stammler has returned to the old concept of a universally valid natural law.[14]

From the point of view of strict positivism there is no "natural law" in any meaningful sense of the term "law". What is formulated, proclaimed and defended as natural law is merely a subjective view of individuals or collectives such as the United Nations General Assembly with respect to what law, the "right" law ought to be. For the positivist there is a fundamental distinction between the *lex lata* (the given law) and the *lex ferenda* (the law which ought to be), and he takes normally to notice of natural law until it has been transformed into positive law: on the domestic plane through enactment or on the international plane through a convention or another recognized law-making procedure.

Be that as it may, natural law of the old as well as of the new style has served several purposes: as a source and censor of positive law, as a defender of the existing order and as a principle of action. The first function is simple: natural law is seen as a sort of model for legislation, that is, it comprises precepts which should be incorporated into positive law.[15] There is little doubt that positive law, both national and international law, incorporated many precepts which were first postulated as natural rights, such as civil and po-

[9] Stammler, *supra* note 5, p. 184.
[10] *Id.* at 185 ("ein Naturrecht mit wechselndem Inhalt").
[11] Stone, *supra* note 6.
[12] Stammler, *supra* note 5, p. 185.
[13] *Id.* at 181–183 of the second edition (1906).
[14] Radbruch, *supra* note 4, p. 23. This social ideal is a "community of free men." ("Gemeinschaft frei wollender Menschen").
[15] Paul Roubier, *Théorie Générale du Droit* (Paris : Sirey, 2nd ed., 1951), p. 187; Lauterpacht, *supra*, no. 2, p. 34; Stammler, *supra* note 6, p. 78.

litical rights, and the positive law of some countries incorporates natural law by reference[16] for the purpose of filling gaps or resolving apparent contradictions between rules intended in the code. Properly understood, natural law, as a source, does not claim to have validity in positive law; what it does claim is that the law-making authorities amend the law in accordance with its precepts.[17] Natural law can then be conceived as a sort of water table from which water flows into the mainstream of positive law. Legislatures, judges and jurists influence that flow, accelerating it at some times and closing it off at others.

In the United Nations the appeals to natural law[18] have often been cast in the form of a source or model for positive law. They comprise all the standard-setting declarations[19] and conventions on human rights. The latter, in particular, are invitations to the Governments to transform the standards into positive law, both domestic and international. The fact that the declarations have been repeated time and again and that the 1966 International Covenants have not yet entered into force indicates that the appeals have not met with a satisfactory response.

The function of "natural law as a censor of the positive legal order"[20] is more difficult to describe. Here the immutable and eternal principles of natural law are not a source but the antithesis of positive law. As Roubier put it: "The essential function which has always been attributed to natural law is its political and moral function, a function of supervision (*controle*) pursuant to which a fence is erected against the unjust precepts established by public authorities."[21] The "overriding censorship" and "most dramatic"

[16] See Article 7 of the Austrian Civil Code of 1811 and Article 1 of the modern Swiss Civil Code of 1907. Article 7 provides that in cases which cannot be decided by the usual means of interpretation (grammatical, natural construction of law or analogy), the case "must be decided, with regard to the carefully collected and well considered circumstances, according to the precepts of natural law" ("natürlichen Rechtsgrundsätzen"). (Author's translation.) Article 1 of the Swiss Code empowers the judge, in case of a gap in the law, to apply customary law, and in its absence to decide the case "according to rules which he would establish if he were the legislator." (Author's translation.) About the role of equity in English law, see Stone, *supra* note 6, p. 77.

[17] Stammler, *supra* note 5, p. 185. Elsewhere, Stammler, *supra* note 6, p. 24, characterized the relation between positive and natural law as follows : "All positive law is an attempt to be just law." But natural law is neither the only nor necessarily the final source of justice. Stone says that while "sometimes, no doubt, in the centuries and millennia of discussions of justice, natural law was the preferred way of talking of justice as a criterion of good law", *supra* note 6, p. 294, "the Hebrew prophets have inspired men's dedication to the highest ideals of justice without resorting to a mediating 'natural law'." *Id.* at 293.

[18] Though not necessarily *eo nomine*, as not all members accept the doctrine of natural law. For a Marxist view, see Anita M. Haschitz, "Le Probléme du Droit Natural à la Lumière de la Philosophie Marxiste du Droit," *Revue Roumaine des Sciences Sociales*, Série de Sciences Juridiques, Vol. 10, pp. 19–41 (1966) and Imre Szabò, "The theoretical foundations of human rights," in Nobel Symposium 7, *supra* note 5, pp. 35–45. In Szabó's view, "The socialist concept is sharply opposed to any kind of natural law," and human rights, in particular, "are neither laws nor rights, but moral ideals, or . . . pretensions conceived of as rights, formulated in respect of the law-to-be-created ; accordingly, they should not be called rights at all." *Ibid.*, p. 36. An early clash between the naturalists and the anti-naturalists occurred in 1948 in connection with the text of Article 1 proposed by the Human Rights Commission for the Universal Declaration of Human Rights which was as follows : "All human beings are born free and equal in dignity and rights. They are endowed by *nature* with reason . . ." GAOR : Pt. 1, Third Comm. Annexes, Doc. A/C.3/243, Agenda item 58. Italics supplied. In the debate in the Third Committee several delegations (USSR, Belgium, China, Yugoslavia among them) opposed the words "by nature" and it was decided by a vote of 26:4 with 9 abstentions, to delete them. *Ibid.*, Third Cttee, Summary Records of Meetings, pp. 35–118–125. They do not appear in the final text.

[19] Thus the General Assembly proclaimed the Universal Declaration of Human Rights "as a common standard of achievement for all peoples and all nations . . ."

[20] Stone, *supra* note 6, p. 74.

[21] Roubier, *supra* note 15, p. 188. Author's translation.

characteristic of natural law in "its actual social operations," according to Stone, "is that when the criteria of justice are put into the framework of a system of natural law, and used to test the justice of positive law, the duplication of the word 'law' in both phrases has an additional effect rather independently of the criteria of justice themselves. This effect is that a theory of natural law tends not only to criticize positive law by reference to whether it realizes justice, but also to *deny that its norms are valid at all* unless they are in keeping with certain norms of natural law."[22] The conflict between the two normative orders, that of positive law and that of natural law, can be overcome by the fusion of them into "one governing order" in which natural law is the superior order which "strikes down" positive law when it conflicts with it.[23] Alternatively, the conflict remains and in that case, like justice, natural law precepts appear as "a demand on the law maker, and an appeal to all members of the society to do whatever is necessary to bring about the repeal or other withdrawal of the impugned law."[24]

If "striking down" objectionable positive law has rarely been attempted by the United Nations,[25] it appeals to member States to transform the proclamations and declarations of inalienable rights into positive national and international law, as the case may be, by adding to or reforming existing law have been very frequent and urgent. Although repeated with almost ritualistic regularity in session after session, these invocations of the two functions of natural law as source and censor of positive law have not been notably successful.

## 3. NATURAL LAW AS A PRINCIPLE OF ACTION

As a defender of the established order, natural law has been invoked to legitimize some ideal order such as the divine right of kings to rule autocratically against those who would advocate or who did advocate the sovereignty of the people or constitutional government. It tends to sanctify the personal rule of heads of state against the rule of law. More specifically, in connection with family planning, natural law is invoked as sanctifying life from its conception against those who would or do advocate a right of abortion. The sanctity of life is invoked against the right of privacy which has come to be recognized in some countries, including the United States, as including the right of women to have an abortion, at least during the early period of pregnancy.

What then may be regarded as the proper or more promising function of natural law in the framework of the United Nations? The fourth function, it is submitted, is one which combines its function as a source of law with its censorial function with regard to positive law into a principle of action. "Natural law," it has been said, "can dispense with reason, for all reasons marshalled in its support are nothing but constructs of the

[22] Stone, *supra* note 6, pp. 76, 291. Italics in original.

[23] *Id.* at 292. Elsewhere Stone says: "The assertion of this overriding power is therefore, we believe, better expressed as a separate specific mark of natural law." *Id.* at 295.

[24] *Id.* at 292. Justice in this context is seen as independent of natural law. See no. 17 *supra*.

[25] Such attempts are outside the scope of this paper.

imagination; as a matter of fact it belongs to the field of praxis and of action. Its ideals have no objective existence; what we call natural law is nothing but our own ideal which we hold up against positive law; thus natural law is the reaction of human personality against a positive order which threatens it with destruction. Without any doubt this is the most significant usefulness (*utilité*) of natural law."[26] In this sense, natural law can indeed serve a most useful purpose. Mere appeals to fundamental or inalienable or inherent rights of man will move neither men nor Governments, no matter how solidly they are anchored in the doctrine of natural law and no matter how often they are repeated. Unless the appeals are followed by well-conceived action, they will be of no avail. The field of human rights has the appearance of a wasteland littered with programmatic declarations and resolutions. Their reiteration year after year dulls the sensibilities of men and Governments. The very obvious weakness of remedies in one human rights convention or another illustrates the reluctance of Governments to move from proclaiming programmes to taking action. Even in the few cases where the Assembly has been able to harness the resources of the Security Council, its efforts have not been crowned with success. Perhaps in the present state system, the Westphalian system, based on the sovereignty of territorial states, it would be idle to expect more. But there is no other system in sight.

The time may well have come when the United Nations should review its methods in the pursuit of the ideal of human rights generally and the right to family planning in particular. A proposal to create the post of a High Commission for Human Rights has been shelved from year to year.[27] Perhaps this is where action should be concentrated. The population situation is critical and the demands for economic development become increasingly urgent. Vast sums of money are not likely to be forthcoming, and even if they should, they would not keep up with the dynamics of the world's population. Compared with the staggering proportions of the task of economic development in all countries, rich and poor, family planning looks like a modest beginning and within the grasp of nearly every country. In addition to public funds which would be made available, private philanthropy could be mobilized. In fact it has already made significant contribution in the relevant research.[28]

Family planning, as shown above, is not merely related to human dignity and a condition for many other political, economic, social and cultural rights, it is one vital aspect of the right to information. For reduced to its most basic aspect, it claims the right of families to have access to information. As stated in the Teheran Conference Resolution XVIII, couples have a basic human right "to adequate education and information" in

[26] Roubier, *supra* note 15, p. 186. Author's translation.

[27] The proposal has been on the agenda of the United Nations for a number of years but its consideration was postponed in 1971 until 1973. G.A. Res. 2841 (XXVI) of December 18, 1971. GAOR : 21st Sess. No. 29 (A/8429), p. 88. As outlined in the ECOSOC Resolution 1237 (XLII) of June 6, 1967, the High Commissioner would have several functions. One of these, of special interest in the context of family planning, was to "render assistance and services to any State Member . . . at the request of that State ; he may submit a report on such assistance and services with the consent of the State concerned." E.S.C.O.R.: 42nd Sess., Supp. no. 1, (E/4393), pp. 18–19. See also Roger S. Clark, *A United Nations High Commissioner for Human Rights* (The Hague : Nijhoff, 1972).

[28] See *e.g., The President's Ten-Year Review and Annual Report 1971,* The Rockefeller Foundation, pp. 35–44.

Dr Leo Gross addressing the gathering

respect to the basic human right "to decide freely and responsibly on the number and spacing of their children." The question of a treaty or declaration on freedom of information has been before the General Assembly for nineteen years and was shelved again at the 1971 session.[29] This question of freedom of information has obviously political overtones as it touches upon sensitive matters such as freedom of the press, radio and television programs, etc. There is no reason why the freedom of information should not be tackled in stages and in separate instruments. Top priority could then be given to the right to receive and disseminate information relating to family planning. Similarly, the question of creating the post of a High Commissioner for Human Rights could be approached in stages. Top priority could then be given to his function in the field of family planning, and his competence extended to other human rights in subsequent stages. In this way, an important step would be taken towards achieving one of the primary purposes of the United Nations: the transformation of its "faith in fundamental human rights, in the dignity and worth of the human person, in the equal rights of men and women" into reality on the international plane. Without family planning the faith in equal rights of men and women would be sheer hypocrisy.

However, since contrary to an assumption of the naturalists, human rights are not, and do not become, automatically part of the positive, enforceable law of States, family planning must first be introduced into that law. This has been done in some States, and others can do it on their own or pursuant to a bilateral or multilateral treaty. The action on the national level would have to go in several directions: first, removing existing obstacles; secondly, recognizing the right of families to determine the number and spacing of children; and thirdly, guaranteeing access to information and education. It would be important to ensure the proper observance of these provisions by appropriate remedies. The point need not be labored that access to courts is an essential aspect of these remedies.[30] Rights derived from law may be modified or cancelled by another law of the legislature, and therefore rights based on statutory legislation are not solidly entrenched. Human rights, fundamental human rights, should form part of the constitution, the supreme law of the land, which could be changed only by a constitutional amendment. The individual should have the right to appeal to the courts for a determination of the constitutionality of statutory legislation.[31] This would endow courts with the power of judicial review, the power to declare invalid, because unconstitutional, acts of the legislature and administrative organs. This power exists in some countries and it constitutes an essential cog in the machinery for safeguarding human rights on the national level. The creation of a procedure for individual complaints being channelled to the proposed Human Rights

[29] G.A. Res. 2722 (XXV) of December 15, 1970, GAOR : 25th Sess. No. 28 (A/8028), p. 87, and G.A. Res. 2844 (XXVI) of December 18, 1971, *ibid.*, 26th Sess., Supp. no. 29 (A/8429), p. 90. Reference may be made to the Soviet proposal at the 1972 session of the General Assembly for a treaty on television programmes sent *via* satellites.

[30] Hans Kelsen, *Pure Theory of Law* (Berkley : University of California Press, 1967), pp. 140–145.

[31] As Kelsen explains : "A fundamental right (or liberty) represents a right in the sense of a legal power if the legal order confers upon the individual affected by an unconstitutional statute the legal power to initiate the procedure that leads to the annulment of the unconstitutional statute." *Id.* at 143.

Commissioner of the United Nations or the Human Rights Commission under the European Convention is an essential feature of the machinery for safeguarding human rights on the international level. A Court of Human Rights is the final arbiter in the European system.

As international safeguards must be built on national guarantees, a brief reference may be made to the Basic Law of the German Federal Republic of 1949. Being of fairly recent origin it may serve as a useful model. Article 1(2) declares human rights, listed in subsequent articles, "inviolable and inalienable." These rights "shall bind the legislature, the executive, and the judiciary as directly enforceable law," (Article 1(3) ). The meaning of this is relatively simple: The basic rights can be enforced without the necessity of implementing legislation. However, the Basic Law does provide that details regarding rights may be laid down by law, that is statutory law. In this connection the following provision is important which is intended to protect the stipulated human rights against undue restrictions or erosion by statute. Article 19(1) provides: "Insofar as under this Basic Law a basic right may be restricted by or pursuant to a law, such law must apply generally and not solely to an individual case. Furthermore, the law must name the basic right, including the Article." Of equal, perhaps even greater, importance, is paragraph 2 of Article 19: "In no case may a basic right be infringed upon in its essential content." In paragraph 4, recourse to courts is provided for.[32] Thus, in virtue of positive law, natural law may exercise its supreme censorial power, namely, strike down positive law which conflicts with a precept of natural law incorporated in the positive law of the constitution.[33]

Thus, in conclusion, it may be said that natural law still has its uses, but not in the exaggerated conception of a law hovering above positive law and striking down inconsistent positive law, but as a principle of action purposefully directed towards the modification of old or the creation of new positive law. As a principle of action, its goal should be the enhancement of the quality of life in the pursuit of which men and women should participate on a footing of equality, in law as well as in fact. Equality is not a mechanical concept. As the Permanent Court of International Justice said, the notion of equality in fact "*excludes* the idea of a merely formal equality. . . . Equality in law precludes discrimination of any kind; whereas equality in fact may involve the necessity of different treatment in order to attain a result which establishes an equilibrium between different situations."[34] Women have achieved equality in law with men in many countries. But being in a different situation from men, family planning is an essential ingredient in the establishment of an equilibrium between the sexes in fact. Equality in fact is the necessary precondition for the exercise by women of important political, economic, social and educational rights, formulated by the United Nations and incorporated in the internal law of many States.

[32] Ian Brownlie, *Basic Documents on Human Rights* (Oxford : Clarendon Press, 1971), pp. 18–19, 23–24.

[33] Castberg, *supra* note 5, p. 27.

[34] Minority Schools in Albania, Advisory Opinion of April 6, 1935. Publications of the P.C.I.J., Series A/B, No. 64, p. 19. Emphasis supplied.

# SOME INTERNATIONAL LAW ASPECTS OF THE FREEDOM OF INFORMATION AND THE RIGHT TO COMMUNICATE*

This paper is intended to provide an overview of the legal framework—that is, the principles and rules of international law which may be applicable to the freedom of information, the "free flow" of information, and its postulated evolution from a "one-way" flow to a "balanced" or "two-way" flow in the name of the right to communicate. In the first part some observations will be made on the nature and basic principles of international law, which, although familiar to international lawyers, may provide useful background material for nonlawyers who are interested in the flow of information through the medium of newspapers, radio, or television. Next, the question will be examined whether the freedom of information and its ancillary "rights" are based on principles or rules of international law binding upon States. Finally, it may be helpful to indicate whether, in the absence of any such specific principles or rules concerning the media of information, there are any rules in neighboring areas, such as air and space law, which may be applicable to the flow of information across national boundaries.

## I

International law has traditionally been perceived as regulating relations between States. While this has been, and still is, correct in the sense that States have the capacity to make and unmake international law, it has also been true that, at least in its modern era—which is usually traced to the Peace of Westphalia (1648)—international law has been

* This contribution was commissioned and is copyrighted by the Edward R. Murrow Center of the Fletcher School of Law and Diplomacy, Tufts University, for its Conference on "The Third World and Press Freedom," May 11-13, 1977, Time-Life Building, New York.

concerned with individuals. Freedom of religion is a long-standing concern going back to that Peace. Increasingly, with the onset of the industrial revolution and the rapid increase in the movement of persons and goods across national boundaries, international law was the medium through which States attempted to facilitate such transnational activities. It could not be otherwise, since States have exclusive authority only within their territory. If transactions going beyond the territory of a State are to be regulated at all, the cooperation of two or more States is required. This is also true with respect to activities within the territory of a State, which are intended to produce, or which in fact *do* produce an effect in the territory of another State. Thus, international law develops with, and depends on, the consent of two or more States and takes the form of a bilateral or multilateral treaty that usually requires ratification. This is called conventional international law. However, there is also customary international law, which emerges from the practice of states and their acceptance of such practice as binding.[1] The origin and evolution of customary international law has never been explained satisfactorily. While it may be a matter of controversy whether a certain principle or rule is or is not part of customary international law, there is no doubt that a body of customary international law exists. Thus, in the case of a dispute submitted to the International Court of Justice, the Court, "whose function is to decide in accordance with international law such disputes as are submitted to it," is directed to apply international conventions and "international custom, as evidence of a general practice accepted as law."[2]

It is important to bear in mind that since international law depends upon the consent or practice of two or more States,[3] the agreement of the States concerned is necessary in order to determine the meaning of a written or unwritten (customary) principle or rule and its applicability in a given situation. By common agreement, this function may be conferred by the States at variance on a tribunal of arbitration or the International Court

[1] In a recent judgment (North Sea Continental Shelf, Judgement of February 20, 1969 I.C.J. *Reports,* 1969) the International Court of Justice emphasized these two requirements by stating that mere acts are not sufficient to establish a rule of customary international law. "For in order to achieve this result" said the Court,

> two conditions must be fulfilled. Not only must the acts concerned amount to a settled practice, but they must also be such, or be carried out in such a way, as to be evidence of a belief that this practice is rendered obligatory by the existence of a rule of law requiring it. The need for such a belief, i.e., the existence of a subjective element, is implicit in the very notion of the *opinio juris sive necessitatis.* The States concerned must therefore feel that they are conforming to what amounts to a legal obligation. The frequency, or even habitual character of the acts is not in itself enough. There are many international acts, e.g., in the field of ceremonial and protocol, which are performed almost invariably, but which are motivated only by considerations of courtesy, convenience or tradition, and not by any sense of legal duty. (p. 3, at 44, para. 77)

[2] Article 38(1)b of the Statute of the Court, which is an integral part of the Charter of the United Nations. The Court is also directed to apply "the general principles of law recognized by civilized nations" and, as subsidiary means, the teachings "of the most highly qualified publicists of the various nations."

[3] This aspect of international law was formulated in the *Lotus* case, decided in 1927 by the Permanent Court of International Justice, the predecessor of the present Court, as follows (Publications of the *P.C.I.J.* Ser. A, No. 10)

> International law governs relations between independent States. The rules of law binding upon States therefore emanate from their own free will as expressed in conventions or by usages generally accepted as expressing principles of law and established in order to regulate the relations between these coexisting independent communities or with a view to the achievement of common aims. Restrictions upon the independence of States cannot therefore be presumed. (p. 18)

of Justice, which renders a binding decision. Just as the rules require common consent for their creation, so they require common consent for their interpretation and application. Of course, States do hold views—sometimes very firm views—about their own rights and obligations and those of other States, but such views must be taken for what they are: views of interested parties. As such, they have no binding force for other States, they are autointerpretations. Before a tribunal or the Court they become allegations as to the facts and the law and are treated as such. However, it should be noted that resort to a tribunal or the Court is the exception and that States prefer to seek settlement of disputed facts or principles by diplomatic negotiations or to postpone solutions or, in some cases, to resort to unilateral action that may aggravate or stalemate the dispute.[4]

One of the characteristics of States in modern international law is their independence or sovereignty. This term has been much debated and frequently misunderstood. But as defined by a distinguished jurist (Separate Opinion of Judge Anzilotti in the Austro-German Customs Union case (1931), Publications of the *Permanent Court of International Justice,* Series A/B, No. 41, p. 57), sovereignty means "that the State has over it no other authority than that of international law." States, though sovereign, are not above the law but are bound by it.[5] This may seem like a truism, but in the rhetoric of states one frequently encounters the mistaken notion that the limitations that international law inevitably imposes upon States are somehow contrary to, or incompatible with, their sovereignty. But compliance with the law is inseparable from the very notion of international law. Thus the Charter of the United Nations, which declares, in Paragraph 1 of Article 2, that "the Organization is based on the principle of the sovereign equality of all its Members," also declares in Paragraph 2:

> All Members, in order to ensure to all of them the rights and benefits resulting from membership, shall fulfill in good faith the obligations assumed by them in accordance with the present Charter.

The duty to fulfill obligations in good faith applies, of course, not merely to the Charter but to all conventional and customary international law. The 1969 Vienna Convention on the Law of Treaties incorporates in Article 26 the customary rule of interna-

[4] Sir Gerald Fitzmaurice (1973) provides an explanation that seems very persuasive. Drawing upon his experience as legal adviser, he concludes that "apart from the natural reluctance to litigate felt by almost everyone, governments prefer to deal with disputes by political means rather than by submission to adjudication, and fight shy of the *commitment* involved by going to law: they dislike the loss of control that is entailed over the future of the case, the outcome of which they can no longer influence politically once it is before a court of law, since this will depend upon legal considerations with which they do not find themselves at home" (p. 279). It may well be that this fear of losing control is the most important psychological factor in determining the justiciability of disputes in the *subjective* sense (Gross, 1977, p. 210).

[5] In a document prepared for the General Assembly by the International Law Commission (Draft Declaration on Rights and Duties of States, Article 14, GA Res. 375(IV), of Dec. 6, 1949, Annex), established by the Assembly for the progressive development and codification of international law, this point was formulated as follows: "Every State has the duty to conduct its relations with other States in accordance with international law and with the principle that the sovereignty of each State is subject to the supremacy of international law." Although the Assembly did not adopt the Draft Declaration, it deemed it "a notable and substantial contribution towards the progressive development of international law and its codification" and, as such, commended it "to the continuing attention of Member States and jurists of all nations."

tional law of *pacta sunt servanda:* "Every treaty in force is binding upon the parties to it and must be performed by them in good faith."

In the same vein, Section X of the Declaration on Principles Guiding Relations between Participating States in the Final Act of the 1975 Helsinki Conference on Security and Co-Operation in Europe, provides:

> The participating States will fulfill in good faith their obligations under international law, both those obligations arising from the generally recognized principles and rules of international law and those obligations arising from treaties or other agreements, in conformity with international law, to which they are parties.
>
> In exercising their sovereign rights, including the right to determine their laws and regulations, they will conform with their legal obligations under international law; they will furthermore pay due regard to and implement the provisions in the Final Act of the Conference on Security and Co-Operation in Europe. (Conference on Security and Co-Operation in Europe, p. 82)

It may be both useful and necessary to refer to two additional basic principles that may have a bearing on the freedom of information and the right to communicate. It is generally accepted that States may not invoke provisions of their internal law as justification for their failure to perform their obligations under treaties or under customary international law. This principle is incorporated in Article 27 of the 1969 Vienna Convention on the Law of Treaties with a qualification, which is not material here. The principle hardly needs elaboration or justification. Were it otherwise it would always be open to States to escape their obligations under international law by the simple act of changing their constitution or amending their legislation. This would spell the end of international law and usher in an era of anarchy. It is, therefore, of vital importance for all States who prefer international order to international anarchy to act in accordance with the "generally accepted principle of international law that in the relations between Powers who are contracting Parties to a treaty, the provisions of municipal law cannot prevail over those of the treaty" (The Greco-Bulgarian "Communities" case, Advisory Opinion of the *P.C.I.J.*, 1930. Publications of the *P.C.I.J.*, Series B, No. 17, p. 32).

The other principle of equal importance is known as domestic jurisdiction. In the absence of applicable principles or rules of customary and conventional international law, States are free to exercise their sovereignty within their territory. As the Permanent Court of International Justice stated in the *Lotus* case, cited above, "restrictions upon the independence of States cannot . . . be presumed." The principle of domestic jurisdiction is reinforced by the principle of nonintervention, which found expression in too many instruments to be examined here, including the Final Act of the Helsinki Conference (Conference on Security and Co-Operation in Europe, 1975). It provides in Section VI:

> The participating States will refrain from any intervention, direct or indirect, individual or collective, in the internal or external affairs falling within the domestic jurisdiction of another participating State, regardless of their mutual relations. . . . Accordingly, they will, *inter alia,* refrain from direct or indirect assistance to terrorist activities, or to subversive or

> other activities directed toward the violent overthrow of the regime of another participating State. (p. 80)

It is not clear what is meant by "external affairs falling within the domestic jurisdiction." (For a recent study of domestic jurisdiction, see Watson, 1977.)

It is a frequent error, in the rhetoric of Governments and jurists, to refer to domestic jurisdiction as "inherent" or "indivisible" or "inalienable." There is nothing inherent or indivisible about it. On the contrary, it is a relative principle. As the development of conventional law demonstrates, the area of domestic jurisdiction has been dramatically reduced. Suffice it to recall matters of security and finance, economics and communications, health and sanitation, and finally of human rights, which have become matters of international concern and regulation by treaty and even, as some argue with respect to human rights, by customary international law. The Permanent Court of International Justice, in a landmark case (Tunis-Morocco Nationality Decrees case, Advisory Opinion 1923, *P.C.I.J.*, Series B, No. 4, p. 24), correctly stated the principle saying:

> The question whether a matter is or is not solely within the jurisdiction of a State is an essentially relative question; it depends upon the development of international relations.

What is or is not within the domestic, that is, discretionary, jurisdiction,[6] depends not merely upon the state of development of international relations, but upon the States concerned. Thus, two or more States may enter into an agreement concerning freedom of the press, the gathering and transmission of news through specified media, or the admission or exchange of radio or television broadcasts. Between parties to such an agreement, these matters are no longer within their respective domestic jurisdiction. But the same matters remain within the domestic jurisdiction of States that have assumed no commitments in relation to other States. In short, it is not the nature of the subject matter that is decisive for answering the question whether it is or is not within domestic jurisdiction, but rather the existence or absence of treaty commitments or of a principle or rule of customary law. It may not be amiss to emphasize, since there is some confusion on this point, that in the absence of an obligation derived from customary or conventional international law, the State is "sole judge," even though the subject matter is of concern to other States or of international concern. It is always open to States to enter into agreements that serve their mutual interests. If there is no principle or rule by which a State binds itself in relation to another State, it may admit or exclude reporters or radio or television broadcasts as it may exclude any aliens or books or newspapers or raw materials or manufactured goods.

It may be noted that there were periods in the development of international rela-

[6] In the same case, the Court held that the clause in Article 15(8) of the Covenant of the League of Nations concerning matters "solely within the domestic jurisdiction" relates to "certain matters which, though they may very closely concern the interests of more than one State, are not, in principle, regulated by international law. As regards such matters, each State is sole judge."

tions when freedom of persons and goods prevailed in a substantial part of the world. In such time periods it was not only a fact of international life but one that was regarded as mutually beneficial. But, increasingly, laissez faire gave way to assertions of control and regulations, to what may be called "dirigisme." This has certainly been so since the end of World War I, and has become dominant since World War II, in spite of the unprecedented interdependence between the States and peoples of the world. The freedoms that were once taken for granted have become part and parcel of a continuing bargaining process between pairs of States, between groups of States, and between all States in the international system.

In this process, international organizations play a vital part. They offer a convenient forum for large-scale conferences. This is particularly true of the United Nations and, in matters of culture and education, UNESCO. When deliberations in the United Nations or in UNESCO yield a convention or a treaty, such a convention or treaty will become binding on the States that sign and ratify or accept them in the usual way. But, on occasion, as a first step to a treaty, such as the 1967 Outer Space Treaty, the organization concerned merely adopts, by the requisite majority or unanimously, a resolution or declaration. The question then arises whether such resolutions or declarations are binding on members generally or on those who voted for them. There is also the question whether resolutions, such as the 1948 Universal Declaration of Human Rights, are or have become part of customary international law and therefore binding on all States. This question is of fundamental importance, as Article 19 of the Universal Declaration proclaims the freedom of information and, perhaps, even the right to communicate, and is regarded as the legal basis for the "free flow" of information through all media and across national boundaries.

## II

In the current debate about freedom of information, Article 19 of the 1948 Universal Declaration of Human Rights occupies a central place. It states:

> Everyone has the right to freedom of opinion and expression; this right includes freedom to hold opinions without interference and to seek, receive and impart information and ideas through any media and regardless of frontiers.

Read in its ordinary meaning, this clause establishes one world for the purpose of receiving and imparting information as an individual right. It is clear from the text that there was no intent here to promote a one-way flow of information. On the contrary, flow in all directions and regardless of frontiers was the aim. That the flow of information has become one-sided in some parts of the world, and in relations between a number of States, is not due to Article 19 but to other factors that are well known. Article 19 was not designed to generate information, but merely to ensure its unobstructed flow in accordance with the law of the sending and receiving States. The latter condition, laid down in Article 29 of the Declaration,[7] is frequently overlooked, but it is as much a part of the Declaration as is Article 19.[8] This is not surprising, considering that the text of the Preamble proclaims the Declaration as "a common standard of achievement" and that the rights and freedoms enumerated in the Declaration should be secured "by their universal and effective recognition and observance" among the peoples of the Member States. Thus, the States are to provide for these freedoms, including Article 19, and the individuals enjoy them in virtue of, and within the limits of, national constitutions, laws, and legal traditions.

But did the Declaration impose a legal obligation on the States to adopt its rights and freedoms into their legal systems? If it did not, or if the States failed to enact implementing legislation, can individuals claim these rights directly from the Declaration? The latter question can be answered in the negative, although there were some cases in which it was invoked in a domestic court. But, in principle, such resolutions or declarations are not self-executing, and Article 29 (cited above) would support this conclusion.

The former question has been much debated in the literature, and the Declaration has often been described as binding in the discussions in the United Nations and elsewhere. Much has been made of the fact that the 1948 Declaration was recited in countless subsequent resolutions of the General Assembly. It has also been pointed out that it was adopted in the constitutions and the legislation of many States. Obviously this argument can equally well be turned around: the adoptions would indicate that the States concerned considered them necessary in order to make the Declaration applicable within their territories. It has also been argued that the Declaration implements the general provisions of the UN Charter that are binding on Members. This argument begs the question: do the provisions of the Charter relating to human rights impose obligations or are they, particularly Article 55, merely statements of objectives and purposes for achievements of which

[7] Article 29 reads as follows:
(1) Everyone has duties to the community in which alone the free and full development of his personality is possible.
(2) In the exercise of his rights and freedoms, everyone shall be subject only to such limitations as are determined by law solely for the purpose of securing due recognition and respect for the rights and freedoms of others and of meeting the just requirements of morality, public order and the general welfare in a democratic society.
(3) These rights and freedoms may in no case be exercised contrary to the purposes and principles of the United Nations.

[8] In a recent Soviet textbook, *International Space Law*, edited by A. S. Piradov, (1976), the following view on Article 19 is to be found:

> For over a quarter of a century legal scholars have now been arguing as to whether there is a universally recognized principle of the freedom of information in international law. The main argument of those who claim that there is such a principle is the fact that some declarations and conventions on protecting human rights contain provisions concerning the right of everyone freely "to seek, receive and impart information and ideas through any media and regardless of frontiers."
>
> These provisions, however, have a different meaning than that attributed to them by some legal experts and diplomats. To begin with, human rights are not in the full sense of the word international. The rights of citizens are regulated by the legislation of every state on a sovereign basis and independently of any external authority. Acts of international law relating to human rights merely imply the acceptance by states of certain general principles, which are to be reflected in their national legislation. The degree to which these general principles are taken into account and the form this takes can vary according to national, historical and other features. Article 28 of the Universal Declaration of Human Rights states that "everyone is entitled to a social and international order in which the rights and freedoms set forth in this Declaration can be fully realised." Obviously only each state itself can ensure a proper social order on its territory, and this applies to the mass media too. (p. 190)

the Members, in Article 56, "pledge themselves to take joint and separate action in cooperation with the Organization"? The text supports an affirmative response to the latter.

Moreover, the Charter does not confer a legislative function or competence on the General Assembly. Apart from resolutions relating to the internal functions of the Organization, like admission of States to membership, adoption of the budget, and some similar matters, resolutions, even when they are called declarations in order to underscore their significance, are recommendations which do not bind the Members legally.

The General Assembly recently had occasion to discuss the question whether its resolutions are a distinct source of law which the International Court of Justice should apply in appropriate cases. The Assembly gave what appears to be a clearly evasive answer. It recognized in the Preamble of Resolution 3232(XXIX) of November 12, 1974:

> that the development of international law may be reflected inter alia, by declarations and resolutions of the General Assembly which may to that extent be taken into consideration by the International Court of Justice.

No doubt this is possible, but there must first be a development of international law in the usual way, that is, practice and the conviction that this has become legally binding. As the International Court of Justice pointed out in the *Continental Shelf* case, these two conditions must be satisfied. (See footnote on p. 238.)

Similar views were expressed as early as 1962 in a Memorandum of the Office of Legal Affairs of the UN Secretariat[9] and quite recently by Eric Suy, the Legal Counsel and Undersecretary-General of the United Nations.[10] It is reasonably certain that the Universal Declaration has not yet become part of customary international law.

The 1948 Declaration was intended as the first stage in the process of formulating an obligatory international bill or rights. This process was completed in 1966 by the adoption of two instruments: the International Covenant on Economic, Social and Cultural Rights and the International Covenant on Civil and Political Rights, to which is attached an Optional Protocol. These Covenants and the Protocol entered into force on January 3,

[9] In this Memorandum (U.N. Doc. E/CN.4/L.610, April 2, 1962), it was stated that a declaration "may impart, on behalf of the organ adopting it, a strong expectation that Members of the international community will abide by it. Consequently, insofar as the expectation is gradually justified by State practice, a declaration may by custom become recognized as laying down rules binding upon States" (pp. 1–2).

[10] In a letter to the *New York Times,* dated March 22, 1977, he wrote (Suy, 1977): "While it is clear that a General Assembly declaration does not have the force of law by the mere fact of adoption, it is possible that in the course of time such a declaration, if it reflects the legal conviction of states, may acquire the force of customary international law through state practice." Mr. Suy's letter was a written response to a letter by the former director of the Human Rights Division in the UN Secretariat, Mr. John P. Humphrey, in which he stated (Humphrey, 1977): "Whatever the intention of its authors may have been at the time, this declaration (of human rights) has, in the opinion of the most competent lawyers who have studied the matter, now become (insofar as the norms enunciated in it are justifiable) part of the customary law of nations and is therefore binding on all states, whether they voted for it or not." In support of Mr. Humphrey and disagreeing with Mr. Suy, Mr. K. Venkata Raman wrote to the *Times* (Raman, 1977): "The legal authority of the Universal Declaration rests in its relation to the U.N. Charter, which, as President Carter has rightly pointed out, is legally binding on every member government of the United Nations." For a more elaborate argument along these lines, see Buergenthal (1974) and Lee (1972). The concept of the "right to communicate" was formulated by Jean D'Arcy (1969) and has subsequently been expanded upon by writers such as Harms and Richstad (1975).

1976 and on March 23, 1976, respectively. As of April 1977, forty-two States have become bound by the Economic Rights Covenant and thirty-nine States by the Civil and Political Rights Covenant and Protocol. The Optional Protocol has been ratified by thirteen States and three States, Denmark, Norway, and Sweden, made declarations under Article 41 of the Civil and Political Rights Covenant. Spain ratified both covenants (UN Press Release, W/812, April 29, 1977, p. 2).

The Protocol contains provisions for examining "communications from individuals claiming to be victims of violations of any of the rights set forth in the Covenant." Such communications and comments from the governments alleged to have committed violations will be considered by the Human Rights Committee established pursuant to Article 28 of the Civil and Political Rights Covenant. The Committee is to report on its activities to the General Assembly through the ECOSOC. The oversight provisions under this Protocol do not go very far, and their effectiveness remains to be tested. This Covenant also opens the way to State-to-State complaints for those parties to it that have made a declaration under Article 41. Such complaints are to be considered by the Human Rights Committee which will endeavor to resolve the matter. In case no solution is reached, the Committee may, pursuant to Article 42, and with the prior consent of the States Parties, establish a Conciliation Commission. The Commission shall seek a solution, but if no solution is reached, the Commission shall make a report. This shall include the findings on all questions of fact and the Commission's views "on the possibilities of an amicable solution of the matter" (Article 42, para. 7(c)). It is then open to the parties to accept the contents of the report. The effectiveness of this procedure is yet to be tested.

The Covenant on Economic, Social and Cultural Rights is generally considered the "softer" of the two Covenants for two reasons. First, it lacks any enforcement procedure whatsoever, and, second, it formulates rights that are to be secured by the action of the States Parties. However, in the current discussion on freedom of information, Article 15 should not be overlooked:

Article 15

1. The States Parties to the present Covenant recognize the right of everyone:
   *(a)* To take part in cultural life;
   *(b)* To enjoy the benefits of scientific progress and its applications;
   *(c)* To benefit from the protection of the moral and material interests resulting from any scientific, literary or artistic production of which he is the author.
2. The steps to be taken by the States Parties to the present Covenant to achieve the full realization of this right shall include those necessary for the conservation, the development and the diffusion of science and culture.
3. The States Parties to the present Covenant undertake to respect the freedom indispensable for scientific research and creative activity.
4. The States Parties to the present Covenant recognize the benefits to be derived from

the encouragement and development of international contacts and co-operation in the scientific and cultural fields.

The content of Articles 19 and 29 of the Universal Declaration, in a somewhat modified form, appear in Article 19 of the Civil and Political Rights Covenant, and this article includes some of the content of Article 29 of the Universal Declaration cited above. Article 20 of the Covenant is also relevant, as it appears to qualify the right to freedom of information laid down in Article 19. The text of these two articles is as follows:

Article 19

1. Everyone shall have the right to hold opinions without interference.
2. Everyone shall have the right to freedom of expression; this right shall include freedom to seek, receive and impart information and ideas of all kinds, regardless of frontiers, either orally, in writing or in print, in the form of art, or through any other media of his choice.
3. The exercise of the rights provided for in paragraph 2 of this Article carries with it special duties and responsibilities. It may therefore be subject to certain restrictions, but these shall only be such as are provided by law and are necessary:
*(a)* For respect of the rights or reputations of others;
*(b)* For the protection of national security or of public order *(ordre public)*, or of public health or morals.

Article 20

1. Any propaganda for war shall be prohibited by law.
2. Any Advocacy of national, racial or religious hatred that constitutes incitement to discrimination, hostility or violence shall be prohibited by law.

Two observations are in order. First, the right to freedom of information has now become part of a legally binding treaty for States that have, or will become, parties to the Covenant. Second, like Article 19 of the Universal Declaration, it offers a legal basis for a two-way flow of information. On the other hand, it is to be noted that it establishes the right for individuals, and it is not clear how far, if at all, it confers rights upon the *media themselves;* and also the net of possible legal restrictions (Article 19, para. 3(b) and Article 20) is cast very wide. The fact that a State, like the U.S.S.R., which has not been regarded in the West as a champion of the right to freedom of information, has become a party to the Covenant, may indicate its belief that it can live comfortably with Article 19. On the other hand, this fact may also be seen as a token of willingness to bring the Soviet Union closer to the basic requirements of the right to freedom of information.

Clearly, if nothing else, Article 19 offers a legal basis for promoting the freedom of information on the international plane. How useful it will prove to be depends on the number of States that ratify or accede to the Covenant. If the United States takes the freedom of information and other rights seriously and desires to play a significant role in their application, it must ratify the Covenant and Protocol and also make the optional declaration under Article 41 of the former. President Carter signed the two Covenants on behalf of the United States on October 5, 1977 (*New York Times,* October 6, 1977, p. A2).

The 1966 Civil and Political Covenant was in the works for nearly two decades and does not reflect the emerging concern with one-, two-, or multiple-way flow of information in its wider sense. Notably absent is a specific reference to what is called the "right to communicate." It has already been suggested that this right may conveniently be seen as included in the formulation given to the right to freedom of information in Article 19 of the Covenant.

It is interesting to note that the right to communicate is also absent from the more recent Final Act of the Helsinki Conference. To be sure, there is nothing in the "Third Basket" that could be construed as an endorsement of the one-way flow of information. Nor is there anything that could be construed as an endorsement of the two-way flow. Like the 1948 Universal Declaration the "Third Basket" is a statement of aims and objectives, and as such it lacks the specificity normally associated with legal prescriptions. There is, however, no doubt that Parts 2 and 3 entitled "Information" and "Co-operation and Exchanges in the Field of Culture," respectively, are imbued with the spirit of mutuality and mutual agreement. They offer some guidance for the future collaboration between States represented at the Helsinki Conference, as well as between States in all parts of the world.

## III

The proposition that has been basic to the argument presented so far is that, in principle, States are sovereign under international law. The area of their discretionary jurisdiction depends upon the development of customary and conventional international law. A State does not have to prove that it is free to act in certain matters, but it has to prove that there are no limitations placed upon its freedom to act either by customary international law or by conventions to which it is a party. It is important to recall that a State's view on its legal rights or obligations is not conclusive. Freedom to receive and impart information across national boundaries, even if it were established as a principle of customary international law, would still be subject to State regulation. It has been admitted that the limitations imposed by international law upon a State's regulatory authority are ill defined (see Buergenthal, 1974, pp. 83–84)—so that, in practice, the freedom may be reduced to the vanishing point. Without pretending at a detailed analysis, some general observations may be suggested, especially with respect to radio and television broadcasts.

It has already been said that States are sovereign over their territory. It has to be added now that States are also sovereign in the air space above their territory and their territorial waters.[11] This principle was first formulated by the Paris Convention for the Regulation of Aerial Navigation of October 13, 1919. It provides that "every State has complete and exclusive sovereignty in the air space above its territory and territorial waters." The principle was restated in the Chicago Convention on International Civil Aviation of 1944 as follows:

Article 1

The contracting States recognize that every State has complete and exclusive sovereignty over the airspace above its territory.

Article 2

For the purposes of this Convention the territory of a State shall be deemed to be the land areas and territorial waters adjacent thereto under the sovereignty, suzerainty, protection or mandate of such State.

The effect of these principles has been summed up in a leading treatise (Oppenheim, 1955) as follows:

> The principle of exclusive sovereignty in the air space for the subjacent State, which has received general approval in connection with aerial navigation, enables that State to prohibit the disturbance of the air space over its territory by means of Herzian waves caused for the purpose of wireless communication and emanating from a foreign source. (p. 529)

But this principle has been limited by several telecommunication conventions and by radio regulations of a general and regional character.

Controversies have arisen over the right of a State to "jam" broadcasts emanating from other countries.[12] The United States Department of State considered the jamming of the Voice of America "unlawful" as such, because it is claimed to be contrary to Article 44 of the Atlantic City Telecommunications Convention of 1947 (Article 48 of the 1965 Montreux Convention) and Article 3 of the Radio Regulations, which prohibit "harmful interference" to radio services of Members. However, referring to the U.S.S.R. jamming, the Department stated that "an additional factor enters into the

[11] There is a good deal of controversy about the extent of territorial waters. They range from three to twelve miles and more. The Third Law of the Sea Conference, in progress since 1974, may produce an agreement on this matter.

[12] "Jamming" has been defined as "the deliberate use of interfering radio signals from one or more transmitters to garble legitimate emissions from other transmitters in order to make them unintelligible at reception" (letter by Assistant Chief of Telecommunications Policy Staff (Lebel), Department of State, of August 30, 1950. 13 Whiteman, *Digest of International Law*, p. 1030). In its Draft Convention of 1972 (see p. 253 in this volume), the Soviet Union included Article IX, worded as follows:

> 1. Any State Party to this Convention may employ the means at its disposal to counteract illegal television broadcasting of which it is the object, not only in its own territory but also in outer space and other areas beyond the limits of the national jurisdiction of any State.
>
> 2. States Parties to this Convention agree to give every assistance in stopping illegal television broadcasting.

problem, namely, the nature and the extent of the right of a sovereign government to prevent the broadcasting into its territory of information which, for reasons of its own, that government deems harmful to its national interest." The Department of State went on to say (see Whiteman, cited in fn. 12, p. 248):

> On this question there appears to exist no specific or formal limitations under international law to the action which a sovereign government can take.
>
> Where a government resorts to jamming of incoming radio signals to prevent such "harmful" information from reaching its territory, it is theoretically confined in that process to the use of signals which will cause no harmful interference *outside its territory*. I use the expression "theoretically confined" because it is obviously not possible technically to generate a radio signal which will completely blanket incoming radio broadcasts up to a point coinciding exactly with the national boundaries, and yet will have no appreciable effect immediately beyond that point. But it is possible to limit the geographical range of the jamming radiations to a fairly well defined distance beyond the borders, while accomplishing the desired purpose within the national territory. (pp. 1031–32)

It is unnecessary for the purpose of this paper to examine the technical provisions of the Radio Regulations on "unnecessary transmission" and "harmful interference." It is sufficient to note the admission that there are no "formal limitations" on the action a sovereign government may take against transmissions it deems to constitute "unnecessary transmission" and "harmful interference" or just plain propaganda. It may well be that further technological progress will enable jamming to be carried out by a State in a "theoretically confined" area, that is, within the confines of its territory. In any event, the U.S. was not required to accept the Soviet view on the matter any more than the Soviet Union was required to accept as correct the U.S. view.

In this particular case, the United States found ample support in the United Nations. First, the ECOSOC Sub-Committee on Freedom of Information, then ECOSOC, and finally the General Assembly adopted resolutions in which mention was made of General Assembly Resolution 59(I),[13] Article 19 of the 1948 Universal Declaration, and Article 44 of the Atlantic City Telecommunications Convention. General Assembly resolution 424(V) of December 14, 1950 continued as follows:

[13] This resolution, adopted on December 14, 1946, called for the convocation of a conference on freedom of information. The Preamble, however, is still of interest and is as follows:

THE GENERAL ASSEMBLY,
WHEREAS
Freedom of information is a fundamental human right and is the touchstone of all the freedoms to which the United Nations is consecrated;
Freedom of information implies the right to gather, transmit and publish news anywhere and everywhere without fetters. As such it is an essential factor in any serious effort to promote the peace and progress of the world;
Freedom of information requires as an indispensable element the willingness and capacity to employ its privileges without abuse. It requires as a basic discipline the moral obligation to seek the facts without prejudice and to spread knowledge without malicious intent:
Understanding and co-operation among nations are impossible without an alert and sound world opinion, which, in turn, is wholly dependent upon freedom of information;

*Considering* that the duly authorized radio operating agencies in some countries are deliberately interfering with the reception by the people of those countries of certain radio signals originating beyond their territories, and bearing in mind the discussion which took place in the Economic and Social Council and in the Sub-Commission on Freedom of Information and of the Press on this subject,

*Considering* that peace among nations rests on the goodwill of all peoples and governments and that tolerance and understanding are prerequisites for establishing goodwill in the international field,

1. *Adopts* the declaration of the Economic and Social Council contained in its resolution 306 B (XI) of 9 August 1950 to the effect that this type of interference constitutes a violation of the accepted principles of freedom of information;

2. *Condemns* measures of this nature as a denial of the right of all persons to be fully informed concerning news, opinions and ideas regardless of frontiers;

3. *Invites* the governments of all Member States to refrain from such interference with the right of their peoples to freedom of information;

4. *Invites* all governments to refrain from radio broadcasts that would mean unfair attacks or slanders against other peoples anywhere and in so doing to conform strictly to an ethical conduct in the interest of world peace by reporting facts truly and objectively;

5. *Invites* also Member States to give every possible facility so that their peoples may know objectively the activities of the United Nations in promoting peace and, in particular, to facilitate the reception and transmission of the United Nations official broadcasts.[14]

This vigorous endorsement of the principles of freedom of information is somewhat qualified by Paragraph 4. Who is to judge the contents of the broadcasts? "Unfair attacks or slanders" and "ethical conduct" are rather broad concepts lacking objective definitions. And, as suggested above, General Assembly resolutions do not make law. Moreover, the Assembly, marching to a different drummer, adopted in 1972 Resolution 2916(XXVII) which is greatly more restrictive.[15] Be that as it may, the attempt to base the illegality of jamming on, and to derive support for the free flow of information into the territory of another State without its consent from, telecommunication conventions does not appear persuasive. In the first place, these conventions are designed to ensure the enjoyment of radio broadcasts *within* a State's territory. Second, the reliance on the prohibition of harmful interference which pervades applicable conventions begs the question, for this principle, as defined in Article 35 of the 1973 Telecommunication Convention of Madrid-Torremolinos, protects only States which themselves "operate in accordance with the provisions of the Radio Regulations."[16]

[14] Jens Evensen (1965) commented on this resolution as follows: "Such allegations may admittedly be commendable de lege ferenda; but to maintain that these views express prevailing rules of international law, is probably not tenable" (p. 560). Similar views were expressed more explicity by O'Connell (1965): "There is no duty on a State not to resort to *jamming of radio* broadcasts from other States. Sometimes the right to jam is explained as an act of self-defense, but it is preferable to treat it as an act of sovereignty, unless there is some treaty requirement favorable to free transmission. . . . Various United Nations organs have condemned the practice but this is not law-creative." (p. 331). Views of several writers on the subject will be found in Whiteman, *Digest of International Law,* pp. 265–271.

[15] See p. 253.

[16] Annex 2 of this Convention defines "harmful interference" as "any emission, radiation or induction which endangers the functioning of a radio navigation service or of any safety service, or seriously degrades, obstructs or repeatedly interrupts a radio communication service operating in accordance with the Radio Regulations." In Article 19 of the Convention, Members reserve the right to stop any private telegram and "to cut off any other private telecommunications which appear dangerous to the security of the State or contrary to their laws, to public order or to decency."

The most recent area of international regulation is outer space. This will be briefly examined in order to determine whether the space law provides a new basis for freedom or free flow of information irrespective of state sovereignty and the right of excluding harmful or undesirable messages.

The Treaty on Principles Governing the Activities of States in the Exploration and Use of Outer Space, Including the Moon and Other Celestial Bodies, was adopted by General Assembly Resolution 2222(XXI) on January 25, 1967. Unlike the conventions on air discussed above, the Space Treaty proclaims the freedom of outer space in Article 1(2): "Outer space, including the Moon and other celestial bodies, shall be free for exploration and use by all States without discrimination of any kind, on a basis of equality and in accordance with international law, and there shall be free access to all areas of celestial bodies." Although there is no provision in the Space Treaty relating directly to the current controversy about satellite broadcasting, the reference to international law in Article 1 is probably significant. Of potential significance are several other provisions in Articles 3, 6 and 9.

Article 3 stipulates a duty for States Parties that the use of outer space shall be carried out "in accordance with international law, including the Charter of the United Nations, in the interest of maintaining peace and security and promoting international co-operation and understanding."

Article 6 stipulates the international responsibility of States Parties for the activities carried out "by governmental agencies or by non-governmental entities, and for assuring that national activities are carried out in conformity with the provisions set forth in the present Treaty." The activities of non-governmental entities "in outer space . . . shall require authorization and continuing supervision by the appropriate State Party to the Treaty."

Article 9 requires that all activities in outer space shall be conducted "with due regard to the corresponding interests of all other States Parties to the Treaty." It then goes on to lay down the requirement of consulation in case of harmful interference in these words:

> If a State Party to the Treaty has reason to believe that an activity or experiment planned by it or its nationals in outer space, including the moon and other celestial bodies, would cause potentially harmful interference with activities of other States Parties in the peaceful exploration and use of outer space, including the moon and other celestial bodies, it shall undertake appropriate international consultations before proceeding with any such activity or experiment. A State Party to the Treaty which has reason to believe that an activity or experiment planned by another State Party in outer space, including the moon and other celestial bodies, would cause potentially harmful interference with activities in the peaceful exploration and use of outer space, including the moon and other celestial bodies, may request consultation concerning the activity or experiment.

The provision for consultations does not ensure that agreement will be reached, but if none is reached, the States concerned will act in accordance with their own conception of their rights and obligations. It must, of course, be clearly understood that such autointerpretations have no binding force.

The references to international law and the Charter of the United Nations may include both formal and substantive principles. Insofar as the content of television or radio transmission is concerned, it is well to recall that, under international law, States have the right of self-determination. Pursuant to it, the States are free to adopt political, economic, social, and cultural policies and systems of their own choosing. This is expressly incorporated in Article 1(1) of both International Covenants of 1966.[17] The right of self-determination of States is not to be confused with the controversial right to self-determination of peoples.

The principle of freedom of outer space like the freedom of the high seas has its limits. Just as the freedom of the high seas ends where the territorial sea begins, so freedom of outer space ends where the territorial air space begins. But whereas there is a right of innocent passage through the territorial sea there is no such right through territorial air space. The right of innocent passage does not include, apart from some exceptions, the right for ships to enter ports without the consent of the territorial State. Similarly the use of outer space for satellite broadcasting does not include the right to enter the territorial air space or the territory of the subjacent State. If it is conceded, as in the present submission it must be, that a State may exclude radio transmissions, then it must also be conceded that it may exclude television broadcasts. It is always open to States to negotiate agreements for opening up access to their territories for radio and for television broadcasts. Some States have done so. Other States have not opposed it, but without any sense of legal obligation. There is as yet no general agreement on the subject.

However, the usual procedure of preparing the ground for a binding treaty on satellite broadcasting through nonbinding resolutions has been under way for several years. Without any pretense at comprehensiveness, one or two resolutions will be mentioned. One is the "Declaration of Guiding Principles on the Use of Satellite Broadcasting for the Free Flow of Information, the Spread of Education and Greater Cultural Exchange" adopted on November 15, 1972, by the General Conferences of UNESCO. (UNESCO: General Conference, 17th sess., Paris, 17 Oct.-21 Nov., 1972, Vol. I Resolutions and Recommendations, pp. 67–69.)

The 1972 UNESCO Declaration, while recognizing in Article V "the free flow of information" as the objective for satellite broadcasting and the principle of freedom of information in Article IX, also calls for respect for "the sovereignty and equality of all States." It contains suggestions for greater attention to the culture and degree of development of different countries. Article VI stresses "the right" of each country, "to decide on the content of the educational programmes broadcast by satellite to its people." Article IX(1), not surprisingly, spells out the requirement of consent:

[17] The text is as follows: "All peoples have the right of self-determination. By virtue of that right they freely determine their political status and freely pursue their economic, social and cultural development." It would have been more appropriate to say that "states" have this right, as international law deals with states and not peoples.

> In order to further the objectives set out in the preceding articles, it is necessary that States, taking into account the principle of freedom of information, reach or promote prior agreements concerning satellite broadcasting to the population of countries other than the country of origin of the transmission.

This may be utterly unacceptable to advocates of "freedom of trade" and freedom of competition, but it is merely an application to new technology of a well-settled principle of international law. As noted earlier, since World War I there has been a trend away from free trade toward protectionism and, at most, "freer trade." Protectionism has frequently been justified in terms of the need to protect "infant industries." Today, cultural protectionism may similarly be supported by developing countries in terms of the perceived need to protect "infant cultures." Saying this is not necessarily approving it. It is certainly arguable that all States and peoples stand to gain from a balanced multilevel exchange of programs that respects national susceptibilities, perhaps even idiosyncracies.[18]

In the United Nations, the Soviet Union on August 9, 1972, introduced a "Draft Convention on Principles Governing the Use by States of Artificial Earth Satellites for Direct Television Broadcasting" (Doc. A/8771. GAOR: 27th sess., Agenda items 28, 29, and 37, Annexes, pp. 1–5). The outcome of the debate was Resolution 2916(XXVII) of November 9, 1972, which noted the draft convention and, it its operative part, requested the Committee on the Peaceful Uses of Outer Space to undertake the elaboration of principles for a convention on direct television broadcasting.[19] In the Preamble, the General Assembly expressed its belief that such broadcasting "must be based on the principles of mutual respect for sovereignty, non-interference in domestic affairs, equality, co-operation and mutual benefit." It also considered that satellite broadcasting "could raise significant problems connected with the need to ensure the free flow of communications on a basis of strict respect for the sovereign rights of States." In this connection it is important to note that Article IX of the Soviet Draft Convention extended the protective principle from the air to outer space in providing:

> 1. Any State Party to this Convention may employ the means at its disposal to counteract illegal television broadcasting of which it is the object, not only in its own territory but also in outer space and other areas beyond the limits of the national jurisdiction of any State.
> 2. States Parties to this Convention agree to give every assistance in stopping illegal television broadcasting. Under Article V of the proposed Soviet Convention direct television broadcasting would be illegal if carried out without the consent of the State concerned. Any transmission of television broadcasts would also be illegal if contrary to substantive limitations on content which are indicated in broadly inclusive terms in Article IV and VI.

[18] The case for "cultural protectionism" is examined and rejected by Hargrove (1974). The current demands for the protection of the steel, television, shoe, and garment industries in the United States come inevitably to mind.

[19] A legal unit of the Committee met in New York in March/April 1977. U.N. Press Release WS/806, 18 March 1977, p. 6, and WS/810, 15 April 1977, p. 4.

The United States, which cast the only negative vote against the resolution, insisted in the debate that the resolution "does not put sufficient emphasis on the central importance of the free flow of information and ideas in the modern world," and that "in actual practice the sovereignty of States and the unimpeded flow of information and ideas should complement rather than conflict with one another" (GAOR: 27th sess., Plenary, 2081st mtg., Nov. 9, 1972, p. 5).

The most recent document in this series is the "Draft Declaration of Fundamental Principles Governing the Use of the Mass Media in Strengthening Peace and International Understanding and in Combating War, Propaganda, Racism and Apartheid" submitted to the UNESCO General Conference at its Nineteenth Session in Nairobi in 1976 (Enclosure IV 19C, 19C/91, 1 July 1976). The consideration of this draft declaration was postponed. It is a politicized draft, including pronouncements and cross-references to highly objectionable resolutions of the General Assembly of the United Nations. Its emphasis is particularly strong on national sovereignty, noninterference, "the existing disequilibrium in the circulation of information" from developing countries, and the achievement of "a balanced exchange of information" (Article IV). It also would make it a duty for mass media to promote the realization "of a new international economic order" (Article VII). It calls on "professional organizations in the field of mass communication to define and promote standards of professional ethics on a national and international level" (Article XI). Finally, it declares in Article XII: "States are responsible for the activities in the international sphere of all mass media under their jurisdiction."

Obviously this declaration, even if adopted, would have no binding force (see Opening Address by Mr. John E. Fobes, Deputy Director-General of UNESCO, Annex II, Appendix 1, p. 3 of the document cited), and it may be possible that it is ultra vires the competence of UNESCO. However, while in some parts the draft declaration may reflect, albeit in a somewhat exaggerated form, the principles of international law discussed above, it is indicative of a strong tendency in the direction of "dirigisme," or state control. The principle of State responsibility is well known in international law, and the Space Treaty incorporates it in Article 6, but only with reference to activities by nongovernmental entities. The proposed Article XII would extend it to activities of all media, notably the press, an extension that is bound to meet with strong opposition of the proponents of the free press. The intended objective of the draft declaration may well be the controlled flow of controlled information. States are free to choose the sociopolitical system under which they wish to live, but there is no reason why States attached to the principles of freedom of thought and of expression and the free flow of information should participate in attempts to subvert them. In this context, the following statement by Paradov (1976) is of interest:

> This leads to the conclusion that in international relations there does not exist—and cannot be established in the present circumstances—any universally recognised principle of the freedom of mass information. This being so, the problem of the freedom of information requires a new approach, with due consideration for the changes that have taken place in international law over the past 25 years. It appears that the international community re-

> quires not so much the adoption of a covenant on the freedom of information as criteria defining the rights and obligations of states in the process of their use of the international mass media.
>
> The specific features of direct TV broadcasting require the framing of special legal rules to give more precise definition to the rights and obligations of states in this sphere of activities.
>
> The most important legal aspects of direct TV broadcasting are, in our view, agreement to ban direct TV broadcasts for foreign populations without the explicit consent of the governments of the states concerned; an unconditional ban on the use of direct TV broadcasts for the propaganda of war, militarism, racism, and other ideas condemned by international law, or for interference in the internal affairs of states; recognition of the international responsibility of states for the contents of direct TV broadcasts conducted either by governmental or nongovernmental organizations; the solution of the problems involved in the possible unpremeditated emergence of direct TV broadcast signals beyond the boundaries of the states co-operating in this field; the allocation of sections of the synchronous equatorial (geostationary) orbit, most convenient for deploying broadcasting satellites, and an unconditional ban on the use of subliminal techniques in direct TV broadcasting. (pp. 192ff.)

It is not the purpose of this paper to discuss ways and means for promoting a balanced flow of information in which there is an ample literature. It may well be, as suggested earlier, that a case can be made for protecting "infant industries" in the field of press, radio, and television. Perhaps a more sustained effort in this direction will be made when it is realized that "protectionism" in its widest sense is not at all incompatible with existing customary international law, although, insofar as real goods are concerned, a host of bilateral and multilateral agreements among compatible States have smoothed the rough edges of national sovereignty. It has often been said that national sovereignty is the greatest obstacle to progress. But the radical alternative, a world state, is still beyond the horizon. Thus, there are only palliatives to think about, and one of them is to try to work within the system. Radicals of all States have rejected this approach as unacceptable. But, for responsible governments, there is no other.

## REFERENCES


Buergenthal, T. (1974). The right to receive information across national boundaries. *In* "Control of the Direct Broadcast Satellite: Values in Conflict." (Aspen Institute Program on Communications and Society, in Association with the Office of External Research, Department of State), pp. 73–84. Aspen Institute Program on Communications and Society, Palo Alto, California.

Conference on Security and Co-Operation in Europe. (1975). "Conference on Security and Co-Operation in Europe, Final Act, Helsinki, 1975." U.S. Government Printing Office, Washington, D.C. (Department of State Publication 8826, General Foreign Policy Series 298.)

D'Arcy, J. (1969). Direct broadcast satellites and the right to communicate. *EBU Review* No. 118B, 14f.

Evensen, J. (1965). Aspects of international law relating to modern radio communications. *In* Hague Academy of International Law, "Recueil des Cours," Vol. II, pp. 471–583. Sijthoff, Leyden, The Netherlands.

Fitzmaurice, G. (1973). "The Future of Public International Law and of the International Legal System in the Circumstances of Today." Special Report, Livre du Centenaire 1873–1973, pp. 196–328. Institut de Droit International.

Fitzmaurice, G. (1976). Enlargement of the contentious jurisdiction of the court. *In* "The Future of the International Court of Justice'' (L. Gross, ed.) pp. 461–498. Oceana Publications, Dobbs Ferry, New York.

Gross, L. (1953). States as organs of international law and the problem of autointerpretation. *In* ''Law and Politics in the World Community.'' (G. A. Lipsky, ed.), pp. 59–88. University of California Press, Berkeley, California. See infra.

Gross, L. (1977). On the justiciability of international disputes. *In* ''A Tribute to Hans Morgenthau.'' (K. Thompson and R. J. Myers, eds.). New Republic Book Company, Washington, D.C. See infra.

Hargrove, J. L. (1974). International law and the case for cultural protectionism. *In* ''Control of the Direct Broadcast Satellite: Values in Conflict.'' (Aspen Institute Program on Communications and Society, in Association with the Office of External Research, Department of State), pp. 85–96. Aspen Institute Program on Communications and Society, Palo Alto, California.

Harms, L. S., and Richstad, J. (1975). Human rights, major communications issues, communication policies and planning—and the right to communicate. *In* ''The Global Context for the Formation of Domestic Communications Policy,'' pp. 55–62. International Broadcast Institute, London.

Humphrey, J. P. (1977). Human rights: The ''weak'' U.N. Covenant. *New York Times* March 20, p. E16.

Lee, L. T. (1972). Law, human rights and population: A strategy for action. *Virginia Journal of International Law 12,* 309–325.

O'Connell, D. P. (1965). ''International Law,'' Vol. I. Oceana Publications, Dobbs Ferry, New York.

Oppenheim, L. (1955). ''International Law'' (H. Lauterpacht, ed.), Vol. I, 8th ed. McKay, New York.

Piradov, A. S., ed. (1976). ''International Space Law.'' Progress Publishing, Moscow.

Raman, K. V. (1977). World human rights: The binding declaration. *New York Times* April 7, p. A24.

Suy, E. (1977). A powerful influence. *New York Times,* April 1, p. A28.

Watson, J. S. (1977). Autointerpretation, competence, and the continuing validity of Article 2(7) of the Charter. *American Journal of International Law 71,* 60–84.

# THE RIGHT OF SELF-DETERMINATION IN INTERNATIONAL LAW

This paper is exclusively concerned with the status of the concept or right of self-determination in the sense of the right of an entity—a people or nation or another group—to establish itself as an independent state. Consequently the right of a people already organized into a state to choose its form of government—democracy, autocracy, and so on—or to give itself a political or economic system or to adopt a certain ideology is left out of account. This right is well established in international law although its scope and range have not been precisely defined. The Draft Declaration on Rights and Duties of States prepared by the International Law Commission in 1949 states in Article I: "Every State has the right to independence and hence to exercise freely, without dictation by any other State, all its legal powers, including the choice of its own form of government."[1]

More recently the General Assembly adopted Resolution 2131 (XX) on December 21, 1965 in which this right is recognized. Thus paragraph 1 declares: "No State has the right to intervene, directly or indirectly, for any reason whatever, in the internal or external affairs of any other State. Consequently armed intervention and all other forms of interference or attempted threats against the personality of the State or against its political, economic and cultural elements are condemned."[2]

In view of the general though somewhat imprecise acceptance of this right of self-

[1] Annex to GA Res. 375 (IV), 6 Dec. 1949. UN Doc A/1251, p. 67. See also GA Res. 2625 (XXV) "Declaration on Principles of International Law Concerning Friendly Relations and Co-operation among States in accordance with the Charter of the United Nations," adopted on Oct. 24, 1970. GAOR: Sess., Supp. no. 28 (A/8028), pp. 121, 123.

[2] "Declaration on the inadmissibility of Intervention in the Domestic Affairs of States and the Protection of their Independence and Sovereignty," GA Res, 2131 (XX), Dec. 21, 1965, GAOR: 20th Sess., Supp. no. 14 (A/6014), p. 12 See also Declaration, cited above.

determination in international law, it seems unnecessary to deal with it any further. It may be enough to recall that this right may be limited by the charter of the United Nations, by bilateral treaties, or by policies and principles adopted by intergovernmental regional organizations such as the Organization of American States.

Insofar as self-determination in the first sense is concerned, the questions have frequently been raised by whom the right may be claimed and who has the duty to grant or recognize it. It has been argued that unless a satisfactory answer can be given to these two questions it is not possible to speak of a right, properly so-called, of self-determination. This argument has merit, since usually when a right in the legal sense is created by a proper authority, the bearers of the right and the corresponding duty are ascertained or ascertainable as individuals generally or individuals or corporations belonging to a certain class or category.

The United Nations resolutions and declarations on the subject of self-determination are sometimes general and sometimes addressed to particular states. Thus colonial territories or peoples are referred to or particular governments such as Portugal are singled out. It is submitted that for the purposes of this chapter the questions of the identity of the bearer of the right and of the corresponding obligation are of no importance. The reason for this is that in any event the existence of the alleged right of self-determination in the legal sense will depend upon the authority or competence of the organs of the United Nations, particularly of the General Assembly, to create such a right or obligation. Thus if the General Assembly has no law-making competence it will be lacking this competence regardless of whether the resolution in question proclaims a right of self-determination for peoples or nations generally or for peoples or nations under colonial domination or for particular peoples like the peoples of Portugal or under Portuguese colonial rule.

Attempts are sometimes made to circumvent the question of the law-making competence of the General Assembly by arguing that the right of self-determination is included in the charter and that the relevant resolutions merely interpret the charter in an authoritative or authentic manner, that is, with a binding effect for members of the United Nations.

It is unnecessary to discuss this approach in any detail. There is an abundant literature on the subject. It may be enough to recall that there is not and never has been any consensus on the question whether the seven references to human rights in the charter are binding, singly or together, on the members. The fact that the General Assembly devoted more than 20 years to the elaboration of two Human Rights Covenants which depend for their binding force upon ratification by the members militates against the attribution of binding force to the human rights provision in the charter.

As to the right of authentic interpretation of the General Assembly there is still an unresolved controversy. No such right is conferred upon the Assembly in the charter and no such right can be derived from any relevant document such as the San Francisco Statement on the interpretation of the charter.[3] The Advisory Opinion of the International Court of Justice in the *Expenses* case may be read as a confirmation by the court of the right of an assembly to interpret authentically and with binding force the expenditures of the organization, which fall within the meaning of Article 17 (2) of the charter. Two points, however, need to be made: in the first place this right would be derived, as indeed it was derived by the court, from Article 17 (1), which confers upon the Assembly the power to "approve the budget of the Organization" and from Article 17 (2), which established the obligation of the members to bear "the expenses of the Organization . . . as apportioned by the General Assembly." In the matter of human rights there is no comparable, clear statement of legal obligation. In the second place, the Advisory Opinion of the Court has failed to resolve the conflict with respect to this matter. Members continue to resist what appears to some of them an unwarranted enlargement of the Assembly's power to interpret the charter obligations. If this is so with respect to an undoubted legal obligation, it will be all the more so when there is no solid legal anchor to which an interpretation of human rights could be attached.

The conclusion then emerges, at least provisionally, that the alleged right of self-determination cannot be derived from a simple interpretation of the charter. This aspect of the problem albeit in a somewhat different approach will be discussed in the following section.

Generally it may be said that a right which is claimed to be grounded in international law must be the product of a law-making process. The classic law-creating agencies—the formal sources of international law—are treaties and custom. Article 38 of the Statute of the International Court of Justice adds "general principles of law recognized by civilized nations." It is controversial whether these principles are those of municipal or of international law. Be that as it may, they will be left out of account here for two reasons. First, there is no space to undertake a systematic comparative study of the different systems of municipal law, and second I have a strong suspicion that the results of such an effort are not likely to be productive.

Finally, the question will be raised whether the General Assembly has a law-making competence, in particular whether its resolutions and declarations are legally binding upon the members. It may be said at once that certain resolutions of the Assembly, namely those relating to the internal functioning of the organization such as appointments, admission to membership, and others of this variety are undoubtedly legally binding providing they are in conformity with the charter itself. Political discretion does not mean that the rules of the charter can be disregarded. As Judge Bustamante said in the *Expenses* case, "The real reason for the obedience of States Members to the authorities of the Organization is the conformity of the mandates of its competent organs with the text of the Charter." He went on to say: "It cannot be maintained that the resolutions of any organ of the United Nations are not subject to review: that would amount to declaring

[3] See Leo Gross, "The United Nations and the Role of Law," *International Organization*, 19 (1965), 538f. Supra, at p. 160.

the pointlessness of the charter or its absolute subordination to the judgment—always fallible—of the organs."[4]

In order to avoid confusion between the two meanings of self-determination, I shall use "right to self-determination" in referring to the right of a people or nation to establish itself as a state,[5] and "right of self-determination" in referring to the right of the people of a state to choose its form of government, economic system, and so on.

The charter being a multilateral treaty may be and is the source of legal obligation for its members. "Self-determination of peoples" is referred to in Article 1 (a) of the charter of the United Nations as a "principle." It is mentioned in Article 55 which restates the purposes in more specific language. Paragraph *c* of this article refers generally to "human rights and fundamental freedoms" among the purposes which the United Nations shall promote. Self-determination is not specifically included in the list of objectives in Article 73 relating to non-self-governing territories. Development of self-government is, however, included in Article 73 (b). "Self-government or independence" is one of the basic objectives of the Trusteeship system but its implementation is made dependent, in Article 76 (b), on the terms of the trusteeship agreements.

The members which were responsible for the administration of non-self-governing territories and trust territories have largely divested themselves of their responsibilities.

From the recital of the relevant charter provisions it is *clear that nowhere has a right to self-determination* in the legal sense been established. I have no intention to disparage the potency of self-determination as a principle and a purpose of the United Nations. But no matter how potent it may be in the actual operations of the United Nations, still it is not a right in terms of the charter.

However, treaties may be interpreted and what is known as subsequent conduct of the parties is relevant in this context. Subsequent conduct of the parties may also be considered as a method of amending the treaty apart from any formal procedure for amendment which may be laid down in the treaty. The formal procedure for amending the charter is the subject of chapter 18 (Articles 108 and 109), but this procedure has not been applied in connection with self-determination. To put it in another way, the principle of self-determination has not been converted into a right to self-determination by an amendment of the charter. It remains to be examined whether such a transformation has occurred as a result of subsequent conduct.

The International Law Commission included in Article 27 (3) of its Draft Articles on the Law of Treaties devoted to the "General Rule of Interpretation," the following clause: "There shall be taken into account, together with the context: (b) any subsequent

[4] International Court of Justice *Reports* 1962, pp. 151, 304.

[5] This is in conformity with General Assembly Resolution 1514 (XV) and the Declaration cited above, p. 124.

practice in the application of the treaty which establishes the understanding of the parties regarding its interpretation."[6]

In its commentary the commission pointed out that recourse to subsequent practice as an element of interpretation is well established in the jurisprudence of international tribunals. The question obviously arises how widespread subsequent conduct must be in order to qualify as a tool of interpretation. On this point the commission was quite specific by stipulating in its 1964 draft that the practice must be one which "establishes the understanding of *all* the parties." In the 1966 final draft the word "all" was omitted but the commission stated that:

> By omitting the word "all' the Commission did not intend to change the rule. It considered that the phrase "the understanding of the parties" necessarily means "the parties as a whole." It omitted the word "all" merely to avoid any possible misconception that every party must individually have engaged in the practice where it suffices that it should have accepted the practice.[7]

The clause quoted above was considered by the Vienna Conference on the Law of Treaties in 1968 and the Committee of the Whole recommended its adoption.[8] In the committee the United States proposed an amendment the object of which appears to have been to incorporate in the text the essence of the commission's commentary. This proposal, however, was rejected.[9]

It is relevant to note that the Committee of the Whole modified the text of Article 4 submitted by the ILC to make it clear that the draft articles on the law of treaties do apply to treaties which are constituent instruments of an international organization "without prejudice to any relevant rules of the organization."[10]

As I am not aware of the existence of "any relevant rules" of the United Nations in this matter, Article 5 of the Vienna Convention may be applied to the charter of the United Nations. If this is so it would be necessary to examine whether the "principle of self-determination" has been generally understood or has been understood by all the parties to the charter as constituting a "right to self-determination." The same examination would then have to be made with respect to the human rights provisions. More specifically, it would have to be determined whether the practice established the understanding of all the parties that these provisions on human rights constitute rights and obligations in the legal sense and whether these rights and obligations have come to encompass the "right to self-determination."

[6] Reports of the International Law Commission on the Second Part of its seventeenth session . . . and on its eighteenth session . . . GAOR: 21st Sess., Supp. no. 9 (A/6309/ Rev.1), p. 49. The text is identical with Art. 31(3b) of the 1969 Vienna Convention on the Law of Treaties except for the replacement of "understanding" by "agreement."

[7] Ibid., p. 53. Italics supplied.

[8] Draft Report of the Committee of the Whole on its work at the first session of the Conference, Doc. A/CON. 39/G.I/L.370, p. 141.

[9] Ibid., p. 136. The text of the proposed amendment was as follows: "Any subsequent practice in the application of the treaty which establishes the *common* understanding *of the meaning of the terms as between the parties generally.*"

[10] Ibid., p. 32. The commission's draft made the applicability of the articles to constituent instruments "subject to any relevant rules of the organization." Ibid., p. 26. Same text in Art. 5 of the Vienna Convention.

It seems very doubtful, to put it no higher, whether the subsequent practice is sufficiently consistent to permit a positive conclusion along the lines indicated. There is no question that the oratory in the General Assembly and the resolutions of the Assembly are replete with affirmations of the "right to self-determination." But in testing the application of Article 31 (3b), the subsequent practice of the members, that is, the parties as distinguished from the practice of the organs of the United Nations, it is necessary to evaluate the behavior of the so-called colonial countries, along with the behavior of the parties which have advocated unconditional and speedy decolonization. The negative attitude and behavior of some of the parties would defeat any attempt to attribute to the subsequent practice the degree of universality indicated in the commentary of the International Law Commission. In the present submission subsequent practice as an element of interpretation does not support the proposition that the *principle* of self-determination is to be interpreted as a *right* to self-determination or that the human rights provisions have come to be interpreted as rights with corresponding obligations either generally or specifically with respect to the right to self-determination.

As indicated above, subsequent practice is also relevant as a process for modifying treaties. As formulated in Article 38 of the ILC's draft, it reads as follows: "A treaty may be modified by subsequent practice in the application of the treaty establishing the agreement of the parties to modify its provisions."[11]

This article was deleted by the Committee of the Whole of the Vienna Conference.[12]

However, the clause proposed by the ILC has the support of at least one arbitral tribunal to which the commission refers in its commentary, namely a tribunal between France and the United States which was concerned with the interpretation of a bilateral air transport agreement. In the context of the award of 1963 the tribunal's statement was probably no more than a *dictum*. The commission refers to no other authority. For the purpose of this discussion and subject to Article 5 of the Vienna Convention, let us assume that Article 38 was declaratory of customary international law and not merely an attempt at progressive development of the law. The commission, in its commentary, pointed out that: "In formulating the rule in this way the Commission intended to indicate that the subsequent practice, even if every party might not itself have actively participated in the practice, must be such as to establish the agreement of the parties as *a whole* to the modification in question."[13] Applying the rule as interpreted by the commission to the question of self-determination the conclusion appears inescapable that the practice of the parties as distinguished from the practice of the organs of the United Nations has not been sufficiently consistent and not as widespread as would be necessary to support the

[11] *International Law Commission Report,* p. 65.
[12] *Draft Report of the Committee of the Whole,* p. 154.
[13] *International Law Commission Report,* p. 66

conclusion that the principle of self-determination has been modified and is now to be regarded as a right to self-determination with a corresponding obligation on the part of the colonial or other states involved.

The relevance of the practice of the organs, that is, of the resolutions and declarations adopted by the organs of the United Nations, will be taken up below.

To sum up, the charter does not establish a right to self-determination; the principle of self-determination and the articles of human rights in the charter cannot be interpreted as having been transformed into legal rights with corresponding legal obligation as a result of subsequent practice, and they cannot be construed as having been modified by subsequent practice.

The next formal source of international law to be considered is custom, or in the words of the Statute of International Court of Justice, "international custom, as evidence of a general practice accepted as law" (Article 38[1 b] ). It is generally agreed that in order to constitute a rule of customary international law two elements must be shown to be present. General practice in the first place, and acceptance of this practice as law in the second place. The first element is generally characterized as objective and the second as subjective or psychological. Obviously the first is more easily ascertainable from the behavior of states than the second but in proceedings at law proof of both elements has been required.

The pronouncements on the subject by the Permanent Court of International Justice and the International Court of Justice are infrequent but remarkably consistent. The Permanent Court in the *Lotus* case (1927) had the opportunity to elaborate the distinction between mere usage and usage which is required as a matter of legal obligation. The court held first that the rules of law emanate from the will of states as expressed in treaties or "by usages generally accepted as expressing principles of law," and second that custom must have "the force of law establishing it," and third that the party invoking a rule of law must prove that the states have not merely performed certain acts or abstained from performing them, but that they did so out of a sense of legal obligation. In the *Lotus* case the question related to the exercise of criminal jurisdiction and the agent for the French government referred to a number of judgments to the effect that states have refrained from exercising jurisdiction in certain circumstances. On this point, which is relevant to the present analysis, the court said that the judgments relied upon by the French agent: "would merely show that States had often, in practice, abstained from instituting criminal proceedings, and not that they recognized themselves as being obliged to do so; for only if such abstention were based on their being conscious of having a duty to abstain would it be possible to speak of an international custom."[14] The judgment went against the French government, France having failed to prove the existence of the sense of duty, or what is commonly called, *opinio juris*.

[14] *Permanent Court of International Justice*, Series A. no. 10, p. 28.

In a more recent case, the International Court of Justice had occasion to set forth its view on customary international law. In the *Asylum* case the court stated:

> Finally, the Colombian Government has referred to a large number of particular cases in which diplomatic asylum was in fact granted and respected. But it has not shown that the alleged rule of unilateral and definitive qualification was invoked or . . . that it was, apart from conventional stipulations, exercised by the States granting asylum as *a right appertaining to them and respected by the territorial States as a duty incumbent on them and not merely for reasons of political expediency.* The facts brought to the knowledge of the Court disclose so much uncertainty and contradiction . . . and the practice has been so much influenced by *considerations of political expediency* in the various cases, that it is not possible to discern in all this any constant and uniform usage, accepted as law.[15]

In another context, the court made its position abundantly clear:

> The Party which relies on a custom of this kind must prove that this custom is established in such a manner that it has become binding on the other Party. The Colombian Government must prove that the rule invoked by it is *in accordance with a constant and uniform usage* practiced by the States in question, and that this *usage is the expression of a right appertaining to the State granting asylum and a duty incumbent* on the territorial State. This follows from Article 38 of the Statute of the Court.[16]

The court adhered to this position in the *Fisheries, Rights of Nationals* and the *Continental Shelf* cases, in which the *Lotus* case was expressly confirmed.[17]

If these criteria of customary international law are applied to the right to self-determination the conclusion is inescapable that this right is not or not yet one that can be characterized as based on customary international law. True, self-determination has been granted or conceded to an impressively large number of peoples or nations but it would not be possible to supply the missing element, namely that practice was based on a sense of legal obligation. On the contrary, the practice of decolonization is a perfect illustration of a usage dictated by political expediency or necessity or sheer convenience. And moreover, it is neither constant nor uniform.

It was to be expected that the stand taken by the court on the concept of customary international law and the exacting standards of proof were subjected to a good deal of penetrating criticism. But while it is easy to criticize the court for supporting an excessively rigid position, it is extremely difficult to suggest a concept which, operationally, would be more satisfactory by opening the way to greater flexibility. Only one approach will be discussed here which merits serious consideration by virtue of the great authority supporting it.

The late Judge Lauterpacht while fully aware of the difficulties of proving the *opinio*

[15] Reports 1950, p. 277. The court referred again to political expediency, pp. 285, 286. Italics supplied.
[16] Ibid., p. 276. Italics supplied.
[17] ICJ *Reports* 1969, pp. 3, 44.

*juris* was opposed to dispensing with it altogether on the ground that to do so would be contrary to practice. But he offered an alternative in the following:

> Unless judicial activity is to result in reducing the legal significance of the most potent source of rules of international law, namely the conduct of States it would appear that the accurate principle on the subject consists in regarding *all uniform conduct* of Governments (or, in appropriate cases, abstention therefrom) as evidencing the *opinio necessitatis juris except when it is shown that the conduct in question was not accompanied by any such intention.* The Judgement in the *Asylum* case is not inconsistent with some such approach. The solution may not be altogether satisfactory, but it is probably more acceptable than the alternative method of exacting rigid proof of the existence of international customary law in a manner which may reduce to a bare minimum its part as a source of law. Of this, the decision in the *Lotus* case . . . provides an interesting example. While it is impracticable to demand positive proof of the existence of legal conviction in relation to a particular line of conduct, it is *feasible and desirable to permit proof that in fact the opinio necessitatis juris* was absent.[18]

It is of secondary importance whether Lauterpacht's alternative approach is compatible with the jurisprudence of the court. What is important is to ask whether it really offers an alternative and secondly, whether this alternative would lead to a result different from that based on the jurisprudence of the court. A state which claims the existence of a rule on the ground of "uniform conduct" or "uniform abstention" of governments would be hard put to it to furnish the required evidence. In the second place, it would still have to prove that this conduct has become binding on the other state or, following Lauterpacht's alternative, that the other state was not unaware of the *opinio juris* implied in its conduct. On the other hand, that state would probably be able to show that its conduct was not accompanied by any sense of legal obligation.

It is consequently submitted that in so far as self-determination is concerned the acceptance of Lauterpacht's alternative would not lead to the finding that it has become a rule of customary international law in the sense of creating a right on the one side and a duty on the other. Practice there is but it falls short of "uniform conduct of Governments" and even if it did measure up to it—and there is room here for differences of opinion—it would be easy to argue the absence of the *opinio juris.*

Faced with the difficulty of accelerating the growth of customary international law in an international system subject to accelerating change and the difficulty of invoking or proving rules of that law, governments and writers have taken to argue that certain resolutions and declarations of the General Assembly have law-creating effect. In particular such effect has been claimed for the General Assembly Resolution 1514 (XV) adopted on December 14, 1960.[19]

Whether salvation, or escape from the confinement of the classic law-creating procedures, can be found by attributing law-making competence to the General Assembly

[18] Sir Hersch Lauterpacht, *The Development of International Law by the International Court* (New York, Praeger, 1958), p. 380. Italics supplied.

[19] G.A.O.R.: 15th Sess. Supp. no. 16 (A/4684), p. 66.

generally or in some particular circumstances has become a matter of lively controversy. There is no room to examine this controversy in any detail nor is there any need for it, since the arguments on either side of the fence are well-known. Nonetheless it may be useful to indicate some salient points in the controversy.

At the outset it may be well to recall that the new dispensation has not yet received judicial imprimatur. The relevance of General Assembly resolutions and similar acts of other international organizations was argued extensively in the *South West Africa* cases. The International Court of Justice in its judgement in the Second Phase in 1966 limited itself to its traditional function, that is to apply the law as it finds it and not to indulge in judicial law making. In the dissenting opinions a variety of points of view was expressed ranging from a denial by Judge Jessup that the General Assembly has law-making competence to the affirmation of such competence by Judge Tanaka. The applicants argued: "that the practice of States and the views of the competent international organs are so clear, so explicit, and so unanimous in respect of the policies against discrimination, that such standards have achieved the status of an international rule of law, as a legal conclusion based upon the application of Article 38."[20]

Judge Jessup, while accepting the alternative proposition of the applicants, based on the same grounds, that there is "an international standard as an aid to interpretation," rejected the contention that "the so-called norm of nondiscrimination had become a rule of international law through reiterated statements in resolutions of the General Assembly, of the International Labour Organization, and of other international bodies." Such a contention, he said, would be open to attack on the ground: "that since international bodies lack a true legislative character, their resolutions alone cannot create law."[21]

Elsewhere in his dissenting opinion Judge Jessup repeated that he did "not accept Applicants' alternative plea which would test the apartheid policy against an assumed rule of international law ('norm')," and that it was "therefore not necessary to discuss here whether unanimity is essential to the existence of *communis opinio juris.*" But, said Judge Jessup:

> "the accumulation of expressions of condemnation of apartheid . . ., especially as recorded in the resolutions of the General Assembly of the United Nations, are proof of the pertinent contemporary international community standard . . . This Court is bound to take account of such a consensus as providing the standard to be used in the interpretation of Article 2 of the Mandate."[22]

Judge Tanaka, displaying a remarkable degree of judicial boldness, expressed his views as follows:

> Of course, we cannot admit that individual resolutions, declarations, judgments, deci-

[20] ICJ *Reports* 1966, p. 431.
[21] Ibid., p. 432. In a note, Judge Jessup added: "The literature on this point is abundant."
[22] Ibid., p. 441.

> sions, etc., having binding force upon the members of the organization. What is required for customary international law is the repetition of the same practice; accordingly, in this case resolutions, declarations, etc., on the same matter in the same, or diverse, organizations must take place repeatedly.
>
> Parallel with such repetition, each resolution, declaration, etc., being considered as the manifestation of the collective will of individual participatant States, the will of the international community can certainly be formulated more quickly and more accurately as compared with the traditional method of the normative process. *This collective, cumulative and organic process of custom-generation* can be characterized as the middle way between legislation by convention and the traditional process of custom making, and can be seen to have an important role from the viewpoint of the development of international law.
>
> In short, the accumulation of authoritative pronouncements such as resolutions, declarations, decisions, etc., concerning the interpretation of the Charter by the competent organs of the international community can be characterized as evidence of the international custom referred to in Article 38, par. 1 (b).[23]

In his dissenting opinion Judge Tanaka also said: "the method of the generation of customary international law is in the stage of transformation from being an individualistic process to being a collectivistic process.[24]

Judge Jessup, at the beginning of his Dissenting Opinion, quotes with approval a statement by Charles Evans Hughes, who was a member of the Permanent Court of International Justice and later Chief Justice of the United States. It was also quoted with approval by the late Judge Lauterpacht to whom he pays tribute:

> A dissent in a court of last resort is an appeal to the brooding spirit of the law, to the intelligence of a future day, when a later decision may possibly correct the error into which the dissenting judge believes the court to have been betrayed.[25]

Judge Tanaka's forward-looking reasoning may well belong "to the brooding spirit of the law" but the judicial caution of Judge Jessup is more in tune with current notions about the law-generating process. Indeed if we have already reached the stage where a community-centered process has taken the place of the classic state-centered process, that is, the process of consent, then it would be difficult to understand why the General Assembly itself is still using the method of treaty law as a vehicle for creating and making binding upon the states the political, civil, economic and other human rights, the duty of non-discrimination on racial grounds, and similar matters. If Judge Tanaka's view is accepted as a correct statement of the law then there is no doubt that self-determination has become a right based on customary international law through the repeated resolutions of the General Assembly over a number of years.

However, if Judge Jessup's view is the correct one, and in the present submission it is, then the resolutions and declarations on self-determination would at best be productive of a standard of interpretation. This standard could be used in the interpretation of an

[23] Ibid., p. 292. Italics supplied.
[24] Ibid., p. 294.
[25] Ibid., p. 32/15.

appropriate treaty clause which established an obligation in the matter of self-determination, just as Judge Jessup proposed to use it in order to test the execution by South Africa of its obligation under Article 2 of the mandate. But as has been shown above, there is no such clause in the charter establishing an obligation and none could be found in customary international law.

The International Court of Justice in the *Expenses* case attached some significance to the practice of the General Assembly in interpreting the range of Article 17 (2) of the charter and the resulting scope of the financial obligations of the members.[26] Judge Spender in his Separate Opinion took categorical exception to the view that subsequent practice of organs of the United Nations as evidenced in resolutions and declarations can be used in the same manner as subsequent practice of states for the purpose of interpretation. Judge Fitzmaurice shared this view in his Separate Opinion. The gist of Judge Spender's opinion is that "unless it is of a peaceful, uniform and undisputed character accepted by all current Members" practice of organs has no probative value.[27] The question of the proper role of the practice of organs of international organization while not new is of substantial complexity.[28]

In any event, subsequent practice of organs like subsequent practice of states parties to a treaty could only serve as a tool of interpretation and on condition that it is accepted by all member states. As indicated earlier, subsequent practice, whether of organs or of states, does not lead to the conclusion that the charter established a right to self-determination and a corresponding duty on the part of the member states in question.

It is now necessary to consider the question whether a single resolution such as General Assembly Resolution 1514 (XV) can be said to be legally binding on members of the United Nations, that is, the question of the law-making competence of the General Assembly. That members of the United Nations hold an affirmative view with respect to this question needs no proof. Some statements may be quoted for the purpose of illustration. Thus in the aftermath of the 1966 judgment in the *South West Africa* cases, the Soviet delegate expressed the view that the court "should have rendered a decision consistent with General Assembly resolution 1514 (XV), condemning racism and colonialism." The delegate of Iran stated that "the issue in the present case was that legislation enacted by the United Nations had not been put into effect," whereas the delegate of Pakistan, echoing Judge Tanaka, declared:

> The insensitivity of these Judges to current international standards or legal norms, their disregard of the mode of generation of customary international law, their refusal to apply, in the performance of their functions in accordance with Article 38 of the Statute of the International Court of Justice, directives manifested in the resolutions of the General

[26] See on this Leo Gross, "Expenses on the United Nations for Peace-Keeping Operations: The Advisory Opinion of the International Court of Justice," *International Organization*, 17 (1963), 1–35. See infra.

[27] ICJ *Reports* 1962, p. 195.

[28] For a detailed analysis see Salo Engel, " 'Living' International Constitutions and the World Court (Subsequent Practice of International Organs under their Constituent Instruments)," *International and Comparative Law Quarterly*, 16 (1967), 865–910.

> Assembly, are things which are bound to perturb enlightened public opinion throughout the world.[29]

The issue has thus been squarely raised whether the General Assembly has indeed the competence which some members believe it has.

In this connection, reference may be made to a memorandum by the office of Legal Affairs in the U.N. Secretariat on the "Use of the Terms 'Declaration' and 'recommendation' " of April 2, 1962 appended to this paper.

Paragraph 4 of the memorandum states what I believe to be the correct view on the subject. First, a declaration or recommendation of a UN organ "cannot be made binding upon Member States," and second insofar as the "strong expectation that Members of the international community will abide by it . . . is gradually justified by State practice, a declaration may by *custom* become recognized as laying down rules binding upon States."

In a similar vein, the late Secretary-General, Dag Hammarskjöld, stated that "all international organizations have under their charters or constitutions only very limited powers of imposing legal obligations on Member States without their consent. Thus there can be no question of legislating international law in such organizations."[30]

There is a fairly widespread tendency to accord to resolutions of international organs some relevance in the process of creating new international law without going so far as regarding them as a means of "instant" law. My own view has been that, depending upon the subject of the resolution, the degree of preparation that was devoted to its formulation, the extent to which it is supported and accepted by the relevant members, resolutions represent a stage in the evolution of a new rule of customary international law unless the General Assembly decides to treat such resolutions merely as a step toward an international convention. The latter procedure was followed in connection with human rights, the legal principles governing the activities of states in the exploration and use of outer space, racial discrimination, and other matters. Law creation then follows the traditional pattern of seeking and receiving formal consent through ratification.

In other instances, a resolution or declaration has so far at any rate been the first and last step. This has been so in connection with General Assembly Resolution 1803 (XVIII) on Permanent Sovereignty over Natural Resources of December 14, 1962, and the Resolution 1514 (XV) which is here relevant, the "Declaration on the granting of Independence to colonial countries and peoples," of December 14, 1960. Resolution 1803 (XVII) may have a very potent impact indeed on the *quantum* of compensation to be paid in case of nationalization of alien property. The old formula "prompt, adequate and effective" has been under attack at least since 1930 and the new formula "appropriate compensation" may well be on the road to becoming part of the customary international law. But

[29] G.A.O.R.: 21st Sess., Fifth Committee, 1124th mtg., October 10, 1966, pp. 23–25 (Iran). Ibid., 1414th Plenary mtg., Doc, A/PV. 1409–1431, p. 10.

[30] Andrew W. Cordier and Wilder Foote, eds., *Public Papers of the Secretaries-General of the United Nations,* II, *Dag Hammarskjöld* (New York, Columbia University Press, 1972), 602. See also Tammes, *Decisions of International Organs as a Source of International Law,* 94 Hague *Recueil des Cours,* 265–363 (1958, II).

it is well to bear in mind that *opinio juris* without practice can no more produce a rule of law than practice without *opinio juris.*[31]

In terms of Article 38 (1d) of the statute of the International Court of Justice such resolutions may serve "as a subsidiary means for the determination of rules of law." I suggested that they may rank with, or even ahead of, "the teachings of the most highly qualified publicists" but below judicial decisions.[32]

A somewhat similar intermediate position has been expressed as follows:

> Without having the character of a treaty, with all its constitutional implications, resolutions of this kind unquestionably are an important link in the continuing process of development and formulation of new principles of international law. In some cases they will be preparatory to formal international convenants; in other cases they will serve as highly authoritative statements of international law in certain fields.[33]

I cannot fully subscribe to the last part of the statement though it would be possible to apply it in fields such as cooperation in outer space, where there is little or no settled law at all.

Relevant in this context is the international cooperative effort to produce an impartial and objective textbook on international law, edited by Max Sorensen. According to this, resolutions and declaration of the General Assembly are not in themselves acts creative of new rules of international law because the General Assembly has no legislative power. On the other hand, a unanimous or nearly unanimous resolution may contribute to the formation of customary international law or be evidence of such a rule.[34] In this text book it is also suggested that some resolutions may manifest a recognition of certain legal principles by members voting for them, a possibility which certainly cannot be excluded in some areas such as outer space but it would be a matter of proving that the vote was indeed intended to express acceptance of legal principles by the members concerned.

Finally, this textbook suggests that resolutions may be interpretations of rules or principles in the charter and which are themselves binding. This view has already been discussed. The General Assembly has no power of authentic, that is, binding interpretation. In the area of self-determination there are no binding rules or principles in the charter.

It may be worthwhile to include in this survey the view on self-determination of a distinguished Polish jurist, Manfred Lachs, who has been elected a member of the International Court of Justice. He agrees with the position I have taken that "the relevant provisions of the Charter were not creative of a new rule of international law. All they

[31] On this see Leo Gross, "The United Nations and the Role of Law," Supra, pp. 176–178.

[32] Ibid., p. 177.

[33] Wolfgang Friedmann, *The Changing Structure of International Law* (New York, Columbia University Press, 1964), p. 139. See also S. K. Bailey, "Making International Law in the United Nations" *Proceedings,* American Society of International Law, 61st Annual Meeting (1967), p. 239.

[34] M. Virally, "The Sources of International Law" in Max Sorensen, ed., *Manual of Public International Law* (New York, St. Martin's Press, 1968), p. 162

did was to confirm and lay down a principle which had long been growing and maturing in International Society.''[35] But the issue of self-determination has become a permanent item on the Agenda of the United Nations. Resolution 1514 (XV) should ''be viewed as interpreting the principles of 'self-determination' enunciated in Chapter I'' of the charter. Lachs concludes that ''under the circumstances, there seems no doubt that the interpretation given by the General Assembly is authoritative and binding.''[36]

Writing three years later, Lachs seems to have modified his views or perhaps given them a somewhat more precise formulation. The 1960 Declaration on the ending of colonialism like the 1948 Declaration on Human Rights are from the formal point of view only resolutions but they set in motion a process the political and legal effects of which go far. One cannot but agree with this proposition. Lachs goes on to say that these and other resolutions ''lay solid foundations for obligatory norms, which, in general, constitute the work of those organizations. For this reason they have undoubtedly a part in the formulation of international law.''[37]

I shall make no attempt to weigh the opinions on one side or the other of the argument. The weight of the reasoned argument as distinguished from sheer oratory may well be on the side of those who accord to resolutions of the General Assembly a role in the formation of law. From a legal standpoint all I can say is that I regard this view as a better one and as being more in accord with the prevailing system of international law and the character of the statal environment in which it functions. Both the environment and the system are far from satisfactory but we have to live in and with it.

Before leaving this part of my analysis, two or three factors relating to self-determination may be mentioned briefly. The first factor is that the General Assembly has recently characterized and condemned as ''crimes against humanity'' certain activities in the context of a denial of the right to self-determination. Thus, in Resolution 2184 (XXI) of December 12, 1966, the Assembly ''*condemns* as a crime against humanity, the policy of the Government of Portugal, which violates the economic and political rights of the indigenous population by the Settlement of foreign immigrants in the Territories and by the exporting of African workers to South Africa.''[38]

The General Assembly has also condemned ''the policies of apartheid practiced by the Government of South Africa as a crime against humanity.''[39] Could denial of the

[35] ''The Law In and Of the United Nations,'' *Indian Journal of International Law,* 1 (1961), 432. Along similar lines the following statement is relevant! ''Thus it might seem that it is only within the last generation that it has come to be admitted that there is a principle of self-determination of peoples which must underlie all international law. Yet, as the foregoing analysis of the process of changes in territorial sovereignty and of state succession must sufficiently demonstrate, that principle has always underlain the system of international law,'' Clive Parry, ''The Function of Law in the International Community,'' in Max Sorensen, ed., *Manual of Public International Law,* p. 19.

[36] Ibid., pp. 438, 439.

[37] ''Le Rôle des organizations internationales dans la formation du droit international,'' in *Melanges offerts a Henri Rolin* (1964), p. 166. My translation.

[38] G.A.O.R. 21st Sess., Supp. no. 16 (A/6316), p. 70.

[39] G.A. Resolution 2202 (XXI) of October 16, 1966, ibid., p. 20. Both resolutions were recalled in Res. 2144 (XXI) of October 26, 1966, ibid., p. 47.

right to self-detrmination be characterized as a crime against humanity at some future time?[40]

The second factor is the increasingly strident appeal to assist in the struggle for independence. Thus in the Resolution 2184 (XXI) referred to above, the Assembly *"appeals* to all States to give the peoples of the Territories under Portuguese domination the moral and material support necessary for the restoration of their inalienable rights." If this is not a call to what in other contexts is called "wars of national liberation" it comes close enough to it. It will be noted that the appeal is addressed to "all States" which, conveniently, includes The People's Republic of China.[41]

It is interesting that in the objective and impartial *Manual* Professor K. Skubiszewski considers that Article 2 (4) of the charter does not apply in the relations between a state and its people, that the right of the people to fight the government is deduced "from the principle of self-determination and the political right of revolution," and that the conflict while "formally domestic" in nature is nonetheless a "conflict between armed forces which represent different authorities and different peoples. Fighting by the local people for the independence of their country that is part of the colonial empire of an extraneous power, sometimes referred to as a war of liberation, is lawful."[42] If such fighting is lawful on one side, can it be lawful on the other side as well? Is military or other assistance to the "local people" also lawful?[43]

The third factor is the increasing tendency to enlist the plenary powers of the Security Council for the purpose of achieving the policy objectives formulated in the resolutions of the General Assembly. Suppose that the Council would resort to enforcement action in order to assist a people to achieve self-determination, would such action transform the principle into a right to self-determination? If such an action were to be construed as a sanction in the legal sense then—to use Kelsen's terminology—the denial of

[40] This has indeed been done indirectly by Resolution 2621 (XXV) of October 12, 1970, in which the Assembly declared, "The further continuation of colonialism in all its forms and manifestations is a crime which constitutes a violation of the Charter of the United Nations, the Declaration on the Granting of Independence to Colonial Countries and People and the principles of international law." G.A.O.R.: 25th Sess., Supp. no. 28 (A/8028), p. 2.

[41] See par. 2 of the above resolution, and Resolution 2627 (XXV) of October 24, 1970, ibid., p. 4, Resolution 2708 (XXV) of December 14, 1970, ibid., p. 7, and Resolution 2625 (XXV) of October 24, 1970, ibid., p. 124.

[42] "Use of Force by States, Collective Security, Law of War and Neutrality," in Max Sorensen, ed., *Manual of Public International Law*,. P. 771. The "inalienable right of all colonial peoples to self-determination" and the "legitimacy" of their struggle for freedom "by all appropriate means" or "by all the necessary means" at their disposal has been reaffirmed or recognized in Resolutions 2627(XXV) of October 24, 1970, and 2708 (XXV) of December 14, 1970, ibid. See also Res. 2734 (XXV) of December 16, 1970, ibid., p. 23, par. 18, and Res. 2649 (XXV) of November 30, 1970, ibid., p. 74, par. 2.

[43] In this connection Resolution 3103 (XXVIII) of December 12, 1973 entitled "Basic principles of the legal status of the combatants struggling against colonial and alien domination and racist régimes" is relevant. The resolution confirms that colonialism is a crime (see Res. 2621 [XXV], n. 38a above) and that struggle for self-determination is legitimate, and declares that any attempt to suppress this struggle is contrary to the Charter and various resolutions and "constitutes a threat to international peace and security," that armed conflicts involving such a struggle are to be regarded as "international armed conflicts," and that the Geneva Conventions of 1949 should apply to the combatants carrying on this struggle. In Resolution 3163 (XXVIII) of December 14, 1973, the Assembly urges in par. 7 "all States and the specialized agencies . . . to provide moral and material assistance to all peoples struggling for their freedom and independence in the colonial territories . . . in particular to the national liberation movements of the territories in Africa—in consultation, as appropriate, with the Organization of African Unity."

self-determination would be a delict, that is, an infringement of a people's legal right to self-determination.

The standpoint from which the position of the right of self-determination has been considered so far may be identified as positivistic. It might be of interest to study the problem of self-determination from the point of view of the policy-oriented methodology. Characterized by the employment "of certain processes of thought—a frame of reference, a method of inquiry, a disciplined and contextual mode of analysis,"[44] it prefers to regard international law as part of the world power process,[45] as a result of which the law is drained of its normative character and content. The role of law in the process of power is broken down into seven functional phases of decision making, namely prescription, recommendation, intelligence, invocation, application, appraisal, and termination.[46] Each of these is broken down into a number of tasks. The reader may wish to consider the desirability of applying this multiphased approach to the problem of self-determination. The overriding goal of this policy-oriented approach is an international law of human dignity which is bound to reflect subjective value preferences and judgments.

Self-determination has a place in this mode of thinking as a goal but it is one of several goals:

> While according great deference to the principle of self-determination such international law might, further, balance self-determination with capacity for, and acceptance of, responsibility and seek an organization of government in territorial units large enough to discharge responsibility. Contemporary techniques in community planning might be employed to encourage the establishment of appropriately balanced, economic regional communities. The goal of a law of freedom is not the extreme of anarchy but an ordered, productive, shared liberty and responsibility.[47]

From an impressionistic point of view it would seem that the deference thus accorded to self-determination falls short of the principles embodied in Resolution 1514 (XV). That resolution calls for transfer of "all powers to the peoples . . . without any conditions or reservations" and declares specifically that there must be no "balancing"—"Inadequacy of political, economic, social or educational preparedness should never serve as a pretext for delaying independence." Regional communities might be incompatible with respect for "the integrity of their national territory," that is, the territory of the dependent peoples. To the extent that this approach is policy-oriented the outcome of analysis may depend upon which country's policy is chosen implicitly or explicitly as the overarching goal.

The foregoing analysis suggests the conclusion that the "principle" of self-determination in Article 1(2) of the charter has not been transformed into a right to self-determi-

[44] Myres S. McDougal and Associates, *Studies in World Public Order* (New Haven, Yale University Press, 1960), p. 990.
[45] Ibid., p. 12.
[46] Ibid., p. 14.
[47] Ibid., p. 1010

nation and that, independently of the charter, no such right has become part of customary international law, for the following reasons:

1. The General Assembly has no competence to interpret charter principles with binding force for all or some members;

2. The "principle" of self-determination has not been transformed into a "right" to self-determination by the subsequent practice of the parties as a means of interpretation of treaties or as a means of modifying treaty provisions;

3. The General Assembly has no law-making competence, neither generally nor with specific reference to self-determination;

4. The practice of organs of the United Nations has not become a new method or source of generating rules of customary international law;

5. Resolutions or declarations of the General Assembly may be a step in the formation of customary international law through practice accepted as law.

In my view, the potency of the principle of self-determination depends less upon its characterization as right to self-determination, that is, as a norm of contemporary international law—regardless of the persuasiveness of any particular line of legal reasoning which would permit such a characterization—than upon the effectiveness of the political pressure that can be mobilized in and out of the United Nations in order to make it prevail. For even norms of international law if not complied voluntarily must as a last resort be enforced.

## APPENDIX

Commission On Human Rights
Eighteenth session

### Use Of The Terms "Declaration" And "Recommendation"
### Memorandum by the Office of Legal Affairs

1. At the request of the Commission on Human Rights, the following comments on the use of the terms "declaration" and "recommendation" are submitted by the Office of Legal Affairs.

2. The Shorter Oxford English Dictionary defines a "declaration" *inter alia* as: "The action of setting forth or announcing openly, explicitly or formally: a proclamation as embodied in a document, instrument or public act." It defines a "recommendation" *inter alia* as: "The action of recommending a person or thing worthy and desirable; Exhortation, advice," These definitions may provide the departure point for indicating the differences between a "declaration" and "recommendation."

3. In United Nations practice, a "declaration" is a formal and solemn instrument, suitable for rare occasions when principles of great and lasting importance are being enunciated, such as the Declaration on Human Rights. A recommendation is less formal.

4. Apart from the distinction just indicated, there is probably no difference between

a "recommendation" or a "declaration" in United Nations practice as far as strict legal principle is concerned. A "declaration" or a "recommendation" is adopted by resolution of a United Nations organ. As such it cannot be made binding upon Member States, in the sense that a treaty or convention is binding upon the parties to it, purely by the device of terming it a "declaration" rather than a "recommendation." However, in view of the greater solemnity and significance of a "declaration," it may be considered to impart, on behalf of the organ adopting it, a strong expectation that Members of the international community will abide by it. Consequently, in so far as the expectation is gradually justified by State practice, a declaration may by custom become recognized as laying down rules binding upon States.

5. In conclusion, it may be said that in United Nations practice, a "declaration" is a solemn instrument resorted to only in very rare cases relating to matters of major and lasting importance where maximum compliance is expected. Doc. E/CN.4/L.610, April 2, 1962, pp. 1–2.

# IMMUNITIES AND PRIVILEGES OF DELEGATIONS TO THE UNITED NATIONS

## I. INTRODUCTION

In the sixteen years since the United Nations on the invitation of the United States established its principal headquarters in New York, there have been remarkably few incidents and little publicity in connection with the immunities and privileges of Members' representatives.[1] This is no doubt due not to the clarity or quality of the relevant juridical instruments but to the tact and understanding of all concerned: the United Nations and more particularly its Secretaries-General, the representatives of the Member States and in a very large measure the Department of State and the United States Mission to the United Nations. It was the violent reaction of Chairman N. S. Khrushchev, attending the fifteenth session of the General Assembly as head of the Soviet Union delegation, against the restrictions imposed upon his movements in the United States by the Department of State which drew attention to the question of the rights and privileges of delegations to the United Nations. For the first time the head of the delegation of a great power and a permanent member of the Security Council was subjected to such restrictions. Speaking in the General Assembly, Mr. Khrushchev referred to "the various restrictions of the rights or representatives of States in the United Nations" and the "instances . . . of the representatives of young African and Asian States being subjected to racial discrimina-

[1] The number of members of permanent missions to the United Nations including their families was estimated at approximately 1,000 in 1960. This represents about one-seventh of the total number of persons entitled to diplomatic privileges in the United States. William Barnes, "Diplomatic Immunity from Local Jurisdiction," Department of State *Bulletin*, August 1, 1960 (Vol. 43, No. 1101), p. 173-182 at p. 181.

tion." He raised the question "whether or not thought should be given to the choice of another location for the United Nations Headquarters which would better facilitate the effective work of this international organization."[2] The nature and extent of these restrictions will be discussed below but it may be well to begin with a survey and analysis of the bewildering array of instruments which govern this matter.

As a background for these regulations it may be appropriate to recall that the choice of the present location at Turtle Bay in Manhattan's East Side was imposed upon the United Nations mainly by financial considerations. The five sites contemplated by the Headquarters Commission in 1946 ranged from relatively modest to substantial areas which would have accommodated a sizeable and self-contained United Nations community of some 50,000 persons including the personnel of the Secretariat, the permanent missions, and delegations to meetings of the various organs. Had the United Nations been able to set up shop at such a site many of the difficulties which have in fact arisen would have been avoided. As it is, there is barely room in the present headquarters for the necessary meetings; there is insufficient room for delegates to work efficiently in connection with meetings; and of course there are no facilities for housing the staff or representatives or for providing them with the requisite office space. It may also be recalled that in each of the five sites recommended by the Headquarters Commission, which did not include Turtle Bay, there was "both local opposition and support" with respect to the United Nations.[3]

## II. INSTRUMENTS GOVERNING THE STATUS OF DELEGATIONS

The status, rights and privileges of delegations to the United Nations at its Headquarters are governed by several international instruments:

1. The Charter of the United Nations, in particular Article 105;

2. the General Convention on the Privileges and Immunities of the United Nations adopted by the General Assembly on February 13, 1946; and

3. the Agreement between the United Nations and the United States regarding the Headquarters of the United Nations of June 26, 1947.

In addition there are several United States statutes which bear on the subject:

1. the International Organizations Immunities Act of 1945 as amended in 1952 (Public Law 291); and

2. the Joint Resolution authorizing the President to bring into effect the Headquarters Agreement, approved August 4, 1947 (Public Law 357).

There are also several relevant executive orders and laws of the State of New York and of the City of New York.[4] Principles of customary international law may have to be

[2] Document A/PV. 869, September 23, 1960, p. 101.

[3] Report of the Headquarters Commission, Document A/69, October 1946, p. 7-11.

[4] All these instruments are conveniently available in the United Nations Legislative Series: *Legislative Texts and Treaty Provisions concerning the Legal Status, Privileges and Immunities of International Organizations* 1959 (U.N. Publications Sales No.: 60. v. 2) p. 128-173, 183-193, 204-217. Hereafter referred to as *Legislative Texts.* This work is the source of all references to relevant national and international instruments in this paper.

drawn on to fill gaps, to provide appropriate rules of construction of the applicable instruments, and to determine the relation between the municipal instruments of the United States on the one hand, and the Charter, the General Convention, and the Headquarters Agreement on the other. Concerning the latter point there should be no ambiguity: in case of a conflict between international law and municipal law the former ought to prevail. And there need be no doubt that this would be so if a dispute between the United Nations and the United States were submitted to the arbitral tribunal provided for in Section 21 (a) of the Headquarters Agreement or if the International Court of Justice were asked for an advisory opinion on a legal question relating to such a dispute as provided for in paragraph (b) of Section 21. However, no dispute has ever been submitted to settlement in accordance with this procedure. Such problems as have arisen have been ironed out in negotiations between the Secretary-General and representatives of the United States. These arrangements may well have left unsolved the underlying issues of principle. An issue of this kind has arisen and will illustrate the political and legal complexities involved.

The Joint Resolution, Public Law 357, authorizing the President to bring into effect the Headquarters Agreement contains a reservation which was never brought officially to the notice of the General Assembly and was ignored in the Resolution 169 (II)A of October 31, 1947, by which it approved the Agreement.[5] The Report of the Sixth Committee devoted to an analysis of the Agreement is likewise bare of any reference to the Reservation.[6] Is the Reservation then part of the law governing the Headquarters of the United Nations? The Legal Department in a memorandum on the subject was of the opinion that it was not, whereas the United States Department of State expressed and continues to hold the contrary view. The problem, like so many other problems, was bypassed and remains unsolved.

The multiplicity of instruments is the source of more than one anomaly. The United States International Organizations Immunities Act was enacted on December 29, 1945, well in advance of the General Convention and the Headquarters Agreement, both of which were intended to implement the general principles enunciated in Article 105 of the Charter.[7] The United States legislation was never amended to bring it into line with the instruments adopted by the General Assembly in virtue of its powers under Article 105, paragraph 3.[8] Another anomaly is that the United States which through its Govern-

[5] For the text of Reservation see *infra* note 26 and the discussion on p. 287 ff.

[6] Document A/427, October 27, 1947.

[7] With respect to the timing of this enactment it has been suggested that

> there is some evidence that the Department of State, in sponsoring the present legislation, intended that it should serve to implement completely the future obligations of the United States under the convention to be concluded for the purpose of giving effect to Articles 104 and 105 of the Charter. In fact one of the motives in seeking enactment of the legislation at the particular time may well have been to define the position of the United States in advance of any action by the General Assembly and thus to influence the substantive content of its recommendations or of any convention that might be proposed.

Lawrence Preuss, "The International Organization Immunities Act," 40 *American Journal of International Law,* p. 332-345 (1946) at p. 341 ff.

[8] C. Wilfred Jenks, *International Immunities* (London: Stevens, 1961), p. 11. Jenks notes that the United Kingdom did so amend its legislation.

ment and the Congress invited the United Nations "to locate the seat of the United Nations Organization within the United States"[9] has failed to accede to the General Convention which is the basic instrument concerning the privileges and immunities of the United Nations. It was certainly not anticipated that the host country would persistently decline to accede to the Convention which had been accepted by a majority of Members including the Soviet Union. The interdependence between the General Convention and the Headquarters Agreement was always recognized. Thus in Resolution 259(III) of December 8, 1948, the General Assembly declared that the Headquarters Agreement and the General Convention "are complementary . . . since *these instruments taken together* are intended to define the status of the United Nations in the country where these headquarters are located" and that "if the United Nations is *to achieve its purposes and perform its functions effectively,* it is essential that the States Members should unanimously approve the provisions of the said Convention." Finally, the Assembly invited all Members which had not yet acceded to the convention to do so "at the earliest possible moment."[10]

Similarly, a report of the House Committee on Foreign Affairs stated that

> the general convention is designed to clarify and implement the obligations assumed by member nations in ratifying Articles 104 and 105 of the Charter of the United Nations. The convention is *incorporated by reference in the headquarters agreement* between the United States and the United Nations . . . , as a *coordinate and complementary enactment.*

The Report further stated

> While the headquarters agreement deals with the special relationship of the United States as host to the United Nations headquarters in this country, the convention refers to the general obligations of the United States as a member of the United Nations. Accession to the convention will therefore further define the privileges and immunities in the United States of the United Nations, its personnel, and of member representatives to the United Nations.[11]

The Headquarters Agreement does indeed "incorporate by reference" in Section 13, paragraph (*b*) 3 and paragraph (*d*), the corresponding provisions, specifically and generally, of the General Convention which bear directly upon the subject here under consideration. More importantly still, Section 26 provides explicitly:

> The provisions of this agreement shall be complementary to the provisions of the General Convention. In so far as any provision of this agreement and any provisions of the General Convention relate to the same subject matter, the two provisions shall, wherever possible, be treated as complementary so that both provisions shall be applicable and neither shall narrow the effect of the other; but in any case of absolute conflict, the provisions of this agreement shall prevail.

[9] House Concurrent Resolution 75, inviting the United Nations, passed unanimously by the House and the Senate is expressly mentioned in the Joint Resolution regarding the Headquarters Agreement.

[10] General Assembly *Official Records* (3rd Session), Part I, Resolutions, Document A/810, p. 173. Italics supplied.

[11] United Nations Participation Act. Report of the Committee on Foreign Affairs on H.R. 6802–A Bill to strengthen the United Nations and Promote International Cooperation for Peace. 80th Congress, 2d Session, H.R. No. 2291, 1948, p. 44 ff. Italics supplied. Hereinafter cited as House Report No. 2291.

This clause calls for some observations. First of all it makes abundantly clear that both the United Nations and the United States Department of State assumed that the United States would promptly accede to the General Convention. This accession has not been forthcoming after nearly a decade and a half, apparently for reasons of a political character which have nothing to do with the question of immunities and privileges of representatives.[12] Secondly, the incorporation by reference is unconditional; that is, the General Convention may be regarded as binding upon the United States even without formal accession. Such a construction resting upon the relevant sections of the Headquarters Agreement, particularly Section 26, has not been adopted in practice but is perfectly tenable juridically.[13] Political considerations have probably made the adoption of such a construction both impractical and undesirable. In any event, it is perfectly clear that politically the relationship between the United States and the United Nations is as anomalous as the juridical construction of the Headquarters Agreement is complex, owing to the abstention of the United States from the General Convention.

The rule of construction laid down in Section 26 quoted above is itself by no means free from ambiguity. On the face of it, it is quite unexceptionable; it is a general rule of interpretation that in case of conflict the specific provision prevails over the general. However, in this case this rule would have for a consequence that the Headquarters Agreement must prevail over the Charter to the extent that the General Convention merely spells out in some detail the principles contained in Article 105. It is not for the General Assembly or any other organ of the United Nations to surrender rights or obligations provided for in the Charter itself. Such an act would be *ultra vires* and therefore null and void. Therefore, it would seem to follow that the rule of construction in Section 26 can only be applied where no Charter principles are involved. This proposition is strengthened by another rule of construction formulated in Section 27 of the Headquarters Agreement: "This agreement shall be construed in the light of its primary purpose to enable the United Nations at its headquarters in the United States, fully and efficiently, to discharge its responsibilities and fulfill its purposes."

There is every reason to regard this rule as basic for the political as well as juridical construction of the relations between the United States and the United Nations. It is extremely rare to find a precept of this nature, incorporating as it does the principle of the major purpose interpretation in an international compact. This very rarity attests to the

[12] House Report 2291 refers to three aspects of the General Convention which stirred up controversy: exemption for American nationals serving in the Secretariat from income tax and service obligations and the laissez-passer. P. 16-20.

[13] The juridical basis of the construction suggested above may be found, apart from the text itself, in Article 38 of the Statute of the International Court of Justice. The Court, pursuant to paragraph I(a), shall decide disputes submitted to it in accordance with "international conventions, whether general or particular, establishing rules expressly recognized by the contesting States." The important point here is that the Court is not restricted to conventions binding upon the parties to the dispute by reasons of formal ratification or accession. Such formal acts are no doubt solid evidence of recognition but what is required is evidence of recognition and this can be given in a less formal fashion. The Court might look to the vote in the General Assembly on the General Convention as evidence of United States recognition. However, the references in the Headquarters Agreement would in any event constitute sufficient evidence of recognition if the Court, pursuant to Section 26 (b) of the Agreement, were asked for an advisory opinion on a legal question requiring a construction of a conflict between the Agreement and the General Convention.

will of both the United Nations and the United States to carry forward the Charter objectives and these must be the ultimate guiding principle in giving effect, on the political as well as the juridical plane, to the Agreement. This, in a nutshell, was and is the whole intent and purpose of Article 105 of the Charter. Already at the San Francisco Conference, the Report of the Rapporteur of Committee IV/2 to Commission IV made it very clear that nothing which the Assembly may do in implementing the general principles of Article 105 may impair its first paragraph: "The Organization shall enjoy in the territory of each of its Members such privileges and immunities as are necessary for the fulfillment of its purposes." This paragraph said the Report,

> sets forth a rule obligatory for all members as soon as the Charter becomes operative. In the opinion of the Committee, this rule should apply under any circumstances, its authority being in no way subordinated to the exercise by the Assembly of the power specified in paragraph II.

The Committee deemed it inadvisable to spell out in detail the necessary immunities and privileges but, it declared, "If there is one certain principle it is that no member state may hinder in any way the working of the Organization or take any measures the effect of which might be to increase its burdens, financial or other."[14]

This fundamental principle applies to the Organization but it must equally apply to the Secretariat, the Members, and their representatives, without whom the Organization could not operate at all. Any national restrictions, controls, or administrative rulings, whether general or particular, which would impede the effective and independent functioning of the Organization or any of its organs, would seem to be incompatible with that principle. To be sure, the modern approach to immunities and privileges favors the functional test. But the test must be the free and independent exercise of its functions by the Organization. And this test may be applied by national authorities and by the Organization itself, but ultimately and authoritatively it should be construed by the organs which are entrusted with the international control, that is, the arbitral tribunal and the International Court of Justice in accordance with the provisions of the General Convention and the Headquarters Agreement.

This construction of the primacy of UN objectives clearly raises the issue of national internal security and national interest of the host country. The almost continual influx of representatives of Members, at its peak for General Assembly sessions, and the residence in the territory of the United States of a substantial number of members of permanent missions to the United Nations and of members of the Secretariat inevitably pose a problem of national security for the United States. Are considerations of national internal security of the United States on the same plane as, or even superior to, the principle of the freedom and independence from national control and interference of the United Nations? And there is another question: can the United States as the host country derive any advan-

[14] UNCIO Documents, Vol. XIII, p. 704, Document 933, June 12, 1945.

tage from its position as the grantor of entry visas and residence privileges in order to promote its national interest? May the United States, more precisely, in retaliation for treatment accorded its own national diplomatic representatives in certain Members' countries impose, as it does, corresponding restrictions on the representatives of those Members to the United Nations?

An indication of United States policy can be seen in the following: the United States restricted to a minimum the scope of applicable international regulations by refusing to accede to the General Convention and by attaching a sweeping reservation to the Headquarters Agreement which it did accept. The resulting situation then appears to be as follows: the privileges and immunities of members of the Secretariat of the United Nations are not governed by any international instrument, apart from the Charter, to which the United States is a party. Their status is subject to unilateral United States legislation, notably the International Organizations Immunities Act of December 29, 1945, Public Law 291, and the Immigration and Nationality Act of 1952, Public Law 414.[15] The status, privileges, and immunities of representatives of Members are governed by Public Law 291 as well as Public Law 357 of August 1947 which is the Joint Resolution authorizing the President to bring into force the Headquarters Agreement. Section 6 of Public Law 357 is in the nature of a unilateral reservation of national security and is not part of the arrangement between the United States and the United Nations.[16] Public Law 357, which incorporates the Headquarters Agreement insofar as representatives of Member States are concerned, governs explicitly and subject to the reservation only their transit to and from the Headquarters district but not their privileges and immunities which are provided for in the General Convention to which the United States is not a party. The status, privileges, and immunities of members of permanent delegations to the United Nations are governed by the Headquarters Agreement but subject to the reservation in Public Law 357; they may also be subjected to Public Law 291. The General Convention does not deal specifically with resident representatives but there is no reason why the general principles regarding the representatives of Members should not also apply to resident representatives. The interplay between the several instruments will now be examined.

[15] This Act is relevant insofar as an alien admitted for permanent residence, and employed by an international organization or a foreign mission must, in order to retain his immigrant status and prevent reclassification as nonimmigrant, file a waiver under section 247 of this Act of privileges and exemptions accruing to him under any law or executive order. For further information concerning this see *Legislative Texts*, p. 145 ff.

[16] It is not reprinted in the *Legislative Texts* although it was included in the *Handbook on the Legal Status, Privileges and Immunities of the United Nations*, Document ST/LEG/2, September 19, 1952, p. 292 ff.

## III. SOME SPECIAL PROBLEMS

### I. Acceptance of Members' Representatives

Section 8 *(a)* of Public Law 291 provides:

> No person shall be entitled to the benefits of this title unless he (I) shall have been duly notified to and accepted by the Secretary of State as a representative, officer, or employee; or (2) shall have been designated by the Secretary of State, prior to formal notification and acceptance, as a prospective representative, officer, or employee. . . .

Whatever the meaning of subsection (2) may be, it is clear from subsection (I) that the enjoyment of the privileges and benefits of Members' representatives is conditioned by prior notification to and acceptance by the Secretary of State. Public Law 291 specifies the privileges afforded such representatives with respect to entry into and departure from the United States as well as their immunity from suit and legal process for their official acts. Clearly notification of such persons is a necessary condition for the enjoyment of such privileges and immunities and for inclusion in the "Bluebook" published every two months by the United States Mission to the United Nations in cooperation with the Protocol Division of the United Nations.[17] By analogy to the Diplomatic List issued by the Department of State with respect to the Diplomatic Corps in Washington, inclusion in the Bluebook is *prima facie* evidence of status.

The requirement of acceptance or approval as a condition for the enjoyment of privileges and immunities by representatives of Members is a different matter altogether. Does the entry of such representatives depend upon the approval by the Secretary of State? Clearly the analogy which comes to mind is the procedure of *agréation* provided for diplomatic representatives accredited to the President of the United States. The representatives of Members, however, are not accredited to the government of the United States in any way or in any sense. *Agréation* implies prior approval and national control. It has its traditional place and significance in connection with diplomatic representatives of foreign states who are to transact business with the United States government. Representatives of Members to the United Nations have no business to transact with the United States. Representatives to meetings of the General Assembly or to other organs of the United Nations bear credentials which are scrutinized by those organs. Permanent delegates, although they present their credentials to him, are not accredited to the Secretary-General for this would imply control and the right to reject persons appoined by Members. No such right has been conceded by the sovereign Members to the Secretary-General.

The question of the accreditation of representatives was discussed at the third session of the General Assembly. It was then generally understood that even the term "credentials" was out of place "because it tended to give the impression that the United

[17] See *Handbook*, p. 66

Nations was a State, headed by the Secretary-General."[18] The term is used for want of a better one and representatives are accredited to the United Nations "and any of its organs,"[19] or to specific organs. Following this discussion the General Assembly on December 3, 1948, adopted Resolution 257 (III) on Permanent Missions to the United Nations, recommending that credentials of members of such missions be signed by the head of state or government or the minister of foreign affairs and that they "shall be transmitted to the Secretary-General."[20] The requirement of an *agrément* was thus implicitly ruled out. The reason for this is obvious, for not only is it desired, rightly or wrongly, to avoid enhancing the role of the Secretary-General, but, as a matter of fact, the representatives attached to permanent missions have no powers to bind their government. They maintain liaison between the United Nations and the Member States and fulfill various other functions[21] but, it was pointed out, "relations between the Secretariat and the Member States were maintained, not through the intermediary of permanent mission [sic], but through the Ministries for Foreign Affairs."[22]

It should be noted in this connection that neither the General Convention nor the Headquarters Agreement provides for accreditation to the United Nations or the Secretary-General or the Secretary of State as a condition for privileges and immunities. Accreditation is specifically required as condition of entry only for representatives of the press, radio, film, or other information media. Section II of the Headquarters Agreement provides that such representatives shall be "accredited by the United Nations . . . in its discretion after consultation with the United States." Neither of the international instruments provides for prior approval by the Secretary of State. The Headquarters Agreement, which is in force in the United States as Public Law 357, being more recent must be deemed to have superseded the earlier Public Law 291 which does provide for such approval. But there is no apparent conflict between the two acts; one deals with the subject matter and the other does not. One could argue that the Headquarters Agreement regulates exhaustively the relations between the United Nations and the United States. This indeed would seem to be the proper juridical position for the United Nations under international law but not necessarily for the officers of the United States who are governed by the law of the land and who are bound to administer it. Obviously this difference may well lead to friction which could only be eliminated by resort to the procedure for authoritative interpretation provided for in the Headquarters Agreement or by nego-

[18] Sir Gerald Fitzmaurice (United Kingdom). General Assembly *Official Records* (3d Session). Part I, Sixth Committee, p. 624.

[19] This formula is used by the United States. Cf. remarks by Mr. Maktos (United States), ibid., p. 628. See also John G. Hadwen and Johan Kaufmann, *How United Nations Decisions are Made* (Leyden: A. W. Sijthoff, 1960), p. 26.

[20] General Assembly *Official Records* (3d Session), Part I, Resolutions (Document A/810), p. 171.

[21] Hadwen and Kaufmann, who have served on the permanent missions of Canada and the Netherlands respectively, described these functions as follows: "They maintain contact with the U.N. Secretariat on a continuous basis, report on previous meetings, anticipate coming meetings and act as a channel of communication and centre of information for the relationship of their country with the U.N." *Ibid.*, p. 26. And ". . . the Permanent Representative in New York has a wide and significant representational function to fulfill." *Ibid.*, p. 28

[22] Sir Gerald Fitzmaurice (United Kingdom), General Assembly *Official Records* (3d Session), Part I, Sixth Committee, p. 636. Practice since then has tended to give a greater role to the permanent missions.

tiation between the Organization and the United States. It will be shown below that an opportunity to seek this clarification has not been seized by either side.

From the point of view of the United States the requirement of approval may serve both national interest and internal security. For it is the basis for prior control of the entry into the United States of representatives of Members who on one ground or another are not deemed acceptable to the United States. On the other hand, the requirement would seem to be incompatible with the independence of the Organization which is necessary for the effective exercise of its functions and the fulfillment of its purposes.

2. Access to the United Nations Headquarters

Difficulties have arisen in connection with the admission to the United Nations Headquarters of representatives of non-governmental organizations recognized by the United Nations for the purpose of consultation under Article 71 of the Charter and in at least one case of an official of a specialized agency.[23] They were discussed in the Economic and Social Council at some length. Although they did not concern representatives of Members directly, the arguments pro and con apply equally to them as all categories of persons having business with the United Nations are regulated by the same omnibus clause, Section II of the Headquarters Agreement which provides:

> The federal, state or local authorities of the United States shall not impose any impediments to transit to or from the headquarters district of: (I) representatives of Members or officials of the United Nations, or of specialized agencies . . . (4) representatives of non-governmental organizations recognized by the United Nations. . . .

Two representatives of non-governmental organizations were denied visas for entry into the United States in order to attend the fifteenth session of the Economic and Social Council. The United States representative, Mr. Wadsworth, explained the action of his government as follows:

> . . . The United States Government had been unable to grant Mrs. Luckock and Mr. Dessau the visas which they had requested. In connexion with the case, the United States had exercised the right to safeguard its security, which it had specifically reserved in section 6 of the Joint Resolution (Public Law 357), adopted by the 80th Congress, which authorized the Government to enter into the Headquarters Agreement, and in the United States representative's note of 21 November 1947 which had brought the Agreement into effect. . . .
>
> His Government had decided to refuse the visas only after having carefully considered the matter and in full recognition of its responsibilities towards the United Nations.[24]

The representative of Poland, Mr. Birecki, characterized this denial as "a flagrant violation of the Headquarters Agreement" but the Council adopted the proposal of the Swedish

[23] Mrs. Gunnar Myrdal, a prominent official of UNESCO, who was first denied the necessary visa by United States authorities but was eventually admitted. Remarks by Mr. Sterner (Sweden), ECOSOC *Official Records* (16th Session), p. 249–256.

[24] ECOSOC *Official Records* (15th Session), 679th plenary meeting, April 9, 1953, p. 37.

representative to ask the Legal Department of the Secretariat for an opinion "on the compatibility of the United States Government's decision with the Headquarters Agreement."

The Legal Department concluded first

> that persons falling within the classes referred to in Section II of the Headquarters Agreement are entitled to transit to and from the Headquarters District, and that this right of transit has not been made the subject of any reservation.

The Department's second conclusion was

> should the United States adhere to its position, it is clear that there would then exist a dispute between the United Nations and the United States concerning the interpretation or application of the Headquarters Agreement. The Council will note that Section 21 of the Headquarters Agreement establishes the procedures for handling any such dispute.[25]

The Legal Department pointed out that the Reservation in Section 6 of Public Law 357 had never been made known to, nor considered or accepted by, the General Assembly. The Department conceded that the United States note of November 21, 1947 stated:

> Pursuant to instruction from my Government, I have the honor to inform you that the Government of the United States of America is prepared to apply the above-mentioned Headquarters Agreement subject to the provisions of Public Law 357.

But it's observed that the note made no reference to the Reservation and that "it did not give notice to the Secretary-General that the United States might claim the authority to restrict transit to and from the Headquarters District." Finally, it pointed out that in any case the Reservation would not apply to the case under consideration inasmuch as the Reservation refers "to control by the United States of the entrance of aliens into any territory of the United States *other than* the Headquarters District, its immediate vicinity, and the necessary area of transit."[26]

[25] Document E/2397. ECOSOC *Official Records* (15th Session), Annexes, Agenda item 34, paragraphs 13, 14, p. 3. The text of Section 21 is as follows:

(a) Any dispute between the United Nations and the United States concerning the interpretation or application of this agreement or of any supplemental agreement, which is not settled by negotiation or other agreed mode of settlement, shall be referred for final decision to a tribunal of three arbitrators, one to be named by the Secretary-General, one to be named by the Secretary of State of the United States, and the third to be chosen by the two, or, if they should fail to agree upon a third, then by the President of the International Court of Justice.

(b) The Secretary-General or the United States may ask the General Assembly to request of the International Court of Justice an advisory opinion on any legal question arising in the course of such proceedings. Pending the receipt of the opinion of the Court, an interim decision of the tribunal shall be observed by both parties. Thereafter, the arbitral tribunal shall render a final decision, having regard to the opinion of the Court.

[26] The text of Section 6 of Public Law 357 is as follows:

Nothing in the agreement shall be construed as in any way diminishing, abridging, or weakening the right of the United States to safeguard its own security and completely to control the entrance of aliens into any territory of the United States other than the headquarters district and its immediate vicinity, as to be defined and fixed in a supplementary agreement between the Government of the United States and the United Nations in pursuance of section 13 (*e*) of the agreement, and such areas as it is reasonably necessary to traverse in transit between the same and foreign countries. Moreover, nothing in secion 14 of the agreement with respect to facilitating entrance into the United States by persons who wish to visit the headquarters district and do not enjoy the right of entry provided in

As the representatives in question were not admitted by the end of its session the Council decided to place the question of access to the Headquarters on the agenda of its next session and ask the Secretary-General for a report on his negotiations with the United States. The upshot of the discussion at the Council's sixteenth session seems to have been the maintenance of their respective legal positions by both the Secretary-General and the United States, but there have been no recent denials of access. The United States departed neither then nor since from the stand that the Reservation gave it authority to restrict in the interest of security the transit to and from the Headquarters of the representatives involved in the controversy, i.e. all the persons listed in Section II of the Agreement, including representatives of Members. Neither the Agreement nor the Reservation admits of any differentiation. The Secretary-General, however, while maintaining his stand juridically gave ground practically. This he did in several ways: first, he recognized that under the Agreement and subject to its purpose the United States can protect its security by granting visas valid only for transit to and from the Headquarters District and sojourn in its immediate vicinity, in accordance with Section 13 *(e)* of the Agreement; secondly, he acknowledged that

> cases may arise, the treatment of which under the Agreement will raise questions. I refer to cases in which there is clear and convincing evidence that a representative of a non-governmental organization is coming to the United States purportedly for United Nations business but also, or primarily, for a purpose outside the scope of such activities, and where further the competent authorities of the Government of the United States are satisfied that the admission of that person would be prejudicial to the national security of the United States. In the opinion of the United States representatives, such cases are outside the scope of the Headquarters Agreement, and they therefore hold that in such cases the United States Government is entitled to refuse a visa.

With respect to such persons the United States gave the assurance that their cases will be considered at the highest levels, that timely decisions would be taken, and that the Secretary-General would be consulted and kept informed "in order to assure that the decision made is in accordance with the rights of the parties concerned."

Thirdly and finally, the Secretary-General drew attention to a second category of persons, saying:

> Also from the United Nations point of view it should be recognized that a person should be excluded from the host country if there is clear and convincing evidence that he intends, in bad faith, to use his trip as a cover for activities against that country's security. This particular problem may well not have been studied and resolved when the Headquarters Agreement was drafted. However, I would consider it proper for me to accept a method of application of the Headquarters Agreement which is in accordance with the interpretation put forward by the United States representative only if such a method of application had been explicitly authorized by the competent organ.[27]

section 11 of the agreement shall be construed to *amend or suspend in any way* the immigration laws of the United States or to commit the United States in any way to effect any amendment or suspension of such laws.
61 STAT. 756 at 767. Italics supplied.

[27] Progress Report by the Secretary-General on negotiations with the United States of America concerning the interpretation of the Headquarters Agreement, July 27, 1953, Document E/2482, ECOSOC *Official Records* (16th Session), Annexes, Agenda Item 33, p. I-2, paragraphs 3, 4, 5.

In his oral statement the Secretary-General seemed to go a little further in meeting the United States stand by saying that the Agreement should be construed, under Section 27, in the light of the primary purpose of the United Nations,[28] but

> to use the rights held under the Headquarters Agreement in the manner under discussion would, in fact, represent an abuse; would be contrary to the interests of the United Nations; and would therefore be in fact against the spirit of the Headquarters Agreement.[29]

Anticipating the debate in the Council, he also stated that arbitration might have to be resorted to but he did not think that arbitration "would give him a better basis for his actions or greater safeguards for the United Nations than it already had."[30]

Concerning the first point, Section 13 *(e)*[31] does not confer any substantive rights on the United States. Restrictions of this kind are contemplated in the Agreement only for resident representatives of Members whose governments are not recognized by the United States.[32] However, in practice the United States has issued limited visas to other representatives; in fact, one of the representatives who was on grounds of security denied a visa to attend the Fifteenth Session of the Council but was granted a visa to the Sixteenth Session, was issued a restricted visa on April I, 1954, by the United States Consulate in Vienna as a result of his application of January 27, 1954.[33] It is not easy to

[28] For text of this section see above p. 282.

[29] ECOSOC *Official Records* (10th Session), 743d Meeting, July 31, 1953, p. 249 ff, paragraph 7.

[30] *Ibid.*, p. 250, paragraph 9.

[31] The text is as follows:

> The Secretary-General shall, at the request of the appropriate American authorities, enter into discussions with such authorities, with a view to making arrangements for registering the arrival and departure of persons who have been granted visas valid only for transit to and from the headquarters district and sojourn therein and in its immediate vicinity.

[32] Text of Section 15 (4) last sentence:

> In the case of Members whose governments are not recognized by the United States, such privileges and immunities need be extended to such representatives . . . only within the headquarters district, at their residences and offices outside the district, in transit between the district and such residences and offices, and in transit on official business to or from foreign countries.

[33] Section 13 (*a*) provides that visas "shall be granted without charge and as promptly as possible." The text of the limited visa reproduced from Document E/C.2/386 p. 3 is as follows:

> Mr. Jan Hardwick Dessau, whose admission to the United States is based on the following conditions:
>
> (1) That such alien shall proceed directly from the port of entry to New York City and shall remain continuously in that city during his sojourn in the United States within a certain area on Manhattan Island, to wit:
>
> > On Manhattan Island, bounded on the north by E. 97th St. and transverse road No. 4; bounded on the west by 9th Avenue, between 28th and 49th Streets, 8th Ave. from 49th Street to Columbus Circle; Central Park West from Columbus Circle to transverse road No. 4; bounded on the south by 28th Street, from 9th Avenue to First Avenue; by 26th St. from First Avenue to East River Drive; bounded on the East by East River Drive, and shall depart therefrom only in connection with departure from the United States.
>
> (2)That such alien shall be in possession of a valid visa or other form of valid authority assuring his entry into the country whence he came or to some other foreign country following his sojourn in the United States Headquarters District;
>
> (3) That upon the expiration or cancellation of any invitation by the United Nations he will depart forthwith from the United States; and
>
> (4) That he will not engage in any activities in the United States outside of his official duties with the United Nations District Headquarters."

understand why his coming in April 1953 was incompatible, but his coming in July 1953, and again in 1954, was compatible with United States security. However, strictly speaking, under the Agreement the United States is bound exclusively "not to impose any impediments to transit to or from the headquarters district" of Members' representatives, and it is not bound to permit them to sojourn in the United States. Ideally, from the viewpoint of the United States, representatives to United Nations meetings should reside outside the territorial area of the United States which still extends only three miles from the low-water mark and commute to the meetings in the Headquarters District. From the United Nations viewpoint the ideal solution would be for the representatives to reside within the District, but its very exiguity militates against such a rational solution.

This being so, the United States Reservation appears in a somewhat peculiar light. From the formal juridical point of view the stand taken by the Legal Department is unassailable. The Reservation was not communicated to the United Nations and it does not form part of the Headquarters Agreement. The Secretary-General of the United Nations, however, was rather less than prudent in apparently not taking the trouble to familiarize himself with the terms of Public Law 357 subject to which, as stated explicitly in its formal note, the United States declared its willingness to apply the Agreement. As far as officials of the United States Government are concerned it is valid law and binding upon them. As remarked already, the conflict between the United Nations and the United States positions should properly be submitted to arbitration if it cannot be resolved by negotiation. As the United States declined to modify its position, nothing but arbitration remained unless the United Nations chose to modify its stand. Furthermore, the supplementary agreement pursuant to Section 13 *(e)* envisaged in the Reservation has not yet been concluded. There is, therefore, no agreed definition of the "immediate vicinity" of the District. The delineation given in the limited visa is unilateral.

The basic issue is, however, whether the Reservation modifies the unconditional obligation of the United States with respect to transit to and from the Headquarters District. As the Legal Department construed it, it does not, but as construed by the United States, it does. The text of the Reservation appears sufficiently ambiguous to support either construction. The Secretary-General, however, preferred without formally recognizing the validity of United States security considerations, to accept them pragmatically.

The question of expulsion will be considered later. With respect to preventive control based on evidence of intent to engage in activities prejudicial to the security of the United States or unrelated to United Nations business, several members expressed serious misgivings at the 743rd and 745th meetings of ECOSOC.[34] Thus, the delegate of Poland Mr. Katz-Suchy, termed the Secretary-General's recognition of such grounds "unfortunate, as the reason for the exclusion was nebulous in the extreme and left the door open to exclusion based on the weakest of reasons." The Indian delegate, Mr. B. Sen, feared that if the Council endorsed the Secretary-General's view "the Headquarters Agreement

[34] See ECOSOC *Official Records* (16th Session), 743d meeting July 31, 1953, p. 251–254; 745th meeting August 1, 1953, p. 268–275.

would be gravely weakened,'' while the Yugoslav delegate, Mr. Mates, doubted ''whether a mere intention afforded sufficent justification for depriving a person of his rights.'' Mr. Boris (France) was of the opinion that the United States position ''would have to be approved by the General Assembly,'' which implied that an amendment to the Agreement would be required. In the view of the Soviet delegate, Mr. Arutyunyan, ''actual violations of the Headquarters Agreement had taken place'' and he doubted whether in these cases security considerations were the reason. On the other hand, the United States delegate, Mr. Baker, maintained that ''there had been no violation—merely difficulties of interpretation, which his Government and the Secretary-General were clearing up.'' After this desultory discussion had run its course, a platitudinous resolution was unanimously adopted expressing the Council's trust that ''any remaining questions will be satisfactorily and expeditiously settled within the provisions of the Headquarters Agreement.'' It was obvious that those who felt strongly on the issue did not have the votes for a strong resolution or did not wish to push matters to a head.

One possible course of action seems to have escaped the delegates, and that is the termination of consultative status of non-governmental organizations which chose as their representatives persons whose motivations or intentions could reasonably be suspected. However, as this paper is concerned with representatives of Members, this possible way out of the dilemma is irrelevant. Insofar as representatives of Members are concerned, the dilemma remains, for the concessions offered by the Secretary-General would certainly be of no avail in their case. One part of the dilemma is the security of the United States; the other is the effective functioning of the United Nations free from national control.

### 3. Sojourn in the United States and the Question of Reciprocity

It will be recalled that, strictly speaking, the United States is obligated by the Headquarters Agreement to permit representatives of Members only transit to and from the Headquarters District. With regard to residence or sojourn in the United States a distinction must be made between representatives to meetings such as sessions of the General Assembly, that is, *ad hoc* representatives and resident representatives who form part of permanent missions to the United Nations. Insofar as *ad hoc* representatives are concerned, neither the General Convention nor the Headquarters Agreement contains a specific provision. Section II of the General Convention, in saying that representatives of Members ''shall, while exercising their functions and during their journey to and from the place of meeting'' enjoy certain privileges and immunities, obviously assumes that these representatives will be resident at or near the place of meeting. Similarly, Section 13 of the Headquarters Agreement assumes that representatives to meetings will not merely transit from outside the United States to the meetings but that they will reside in the United States. Furthermore, by indirection, Section 13 *(e)* distinguishes between persons who will not be limited in their sojourn in the United States and persons ''who have been granted visas valid only for transit to and from the headquarters district and sojourn therein and in its immediate vicinity."[35] The Reservation in Public Law 357 envisaged that the "immediate vicinity" of the district would be defined in a supplementary agreement but did not even envisage an agreed list of persons to be limited in their sojourn to the district and its immediate vicinity. The only specific indication of such persons is to be found, as mentioned above, in the clause relating to resident representatives of Members whose governments are not recognized by the United States. In the absence of any agreement on the subject, the matter is left to the discretion of the United States in the exercise of its territorial sovereignty unless one can read into the Headquarters Agreement a limitation upon this sovereignty in favor of unlimited freedom of movement for representatives of Members. It may be that this was taken for granted and that it was deemed unnecessary to include a clause limiting explicitly the territorial sovereignty of the United States in this respect.

It is also possible to argue that *ad hoc* representatives of Members enjoy freedom of movement in virtue of customary international law. The General Convention in Section II provides explicitly that representatives of Members to the organs of the United Nations shall enjoy certain listed privileges and immunities and then provides generally that they shall enjoy "such other privileges, immunities and facilities not inconsistent with the foregoing as diplomatic envoys enjoy. . . ." It is the clear purpose of the Convention to assimilate in this respect the representatives of Members to diplomatic envoys and grant them all those privileges which customary international law has come to include. Freedom of movement and travel within the territory of the receiving states is part of those privileges. It has been reaffirmed by the Vienna Convention on Diplomatic Relations of April 18, 1961.[36] As was pointed out earlier, one of the anomalies in the existing legal relations between the United Nations and the United States is that the latter has not, or not yet, accepted the General Convention, the one and only international instrument which, apart from the Charter itself, regulates the immunities and privileges of the representatives of Members. However, it has also been pointed out that the Headquarters Agreement incorporates, by reference, provisions of the General Convention. Section 13*(d)* of the Agreement appears especially relevant in this context:

> Except as provided above in this section and in the General Convention, the United States retains full control and authority over the entry of persons or property into the territory of the United States and the conditions under which persons may remain or reside there.

In plain language the United States retains full territorial sovereignty unless this is restricted by the Agreement or the Convention. The Agreement is not clearly in point but the Convention is and insofar as freedom of movement and travel in the territory of the United States outside its security zones is concerned, the pertinent provisions of the Convention must be

[35] For full text of this clause see this volume, p. 289, note 31.

[36] The relevant Article 26 reads as follows: "Subject to its laws and regulations concerning zones entry into which is prohibited or regulated for reasons of national security, the receiving State shall ensure to all members of the mission freedom of movement and travel in its territory." 55 *American Journal of International Law*, p. 1070 (1961) and UN Document A/ CONF.20/13, p. 8.

deemed to be incorporated into the Agreement. These provisions which in turn refer to customary international law thus limit the control and authority of the United States regarding representatives of Members having diplomatic privileges and immunities.

The restrictions imposed upon the representatives of the Soviet Union and some other Members prior to the 1960 session of the General Assembly must be viewed against this background. In particular, the United States Mission to the United Nations requested that Chairman N. S. Khrushchev "reside in the closet convenient proximity to the headquarters of the United Nations" and that his "movements other than those connected with arrival and departure be limited to those required by his official mission, not beyond Manhattan Island."[37] The aide-memoire handed to the Soviet mission on September 10, 1960, referred to the problem of security posed for the United States by the unwanted visit of Mr. Khrushchev and states that it "has, of course, been complicated by the hostile public statements of the head of the Soviet Government and by the destruction of an American plane over international waters by Soviet action and the continued illegal detention of two American flyers."[38] On September 13, 1960, the Soviet Ambassador protested against this "unfriendly act" which "can be directed only toward worsening in advance the international atmosphere." He declared that no provision in the Headquarters Agreement gave the United States "the right to act arbitrarily" and that if the United States

> refuses to provide for the unhindered fulfillment by the delegations arriving in New York of the tasks entrusted to them, the question naturally arises how in such a case the United Nations can in the future function normally on the territory of the United States.[39]

The United States mission in reply reaffirmed its stand and concluded: "Travel beyond the limits of Manhattan Island is clearly not essential to the normal functioning of a delegation to a session of the United Nations General Assembly."

The motives of the United States for taking this action are not an issue here nor is the question whether in fact it contributed in any way to the atmosphere in which that session of the General Assembly took place. It may be noted, however, that in limiting Mr. Khrushchev to Manhattan Island the United States government imposed more severe limitations upon his movements than those which are in force for the permanent mission of the Soviet Union.

With respect to the security of *ad hoc* representatives which is involved here in contradistinction to the security of the United States, Section II of the Headquarters Agreement provides that "the appropriate American authorities shall afford any necessary protection to such persons while in transit to or from the headquarters district." Clearly

[37] Department of State *Bulletin*, October 3, 1960 (Vol. 43, No. 1110), p. 521. A similar request was addressed to the Hungarian and Albanian missions to the United Nations. The text of the aide-memoire to the Albanian mission was not released. The United States does not recognize the present government of Albania.

[38] *Ibid* The aide-memoire to the Hungarian mission referred to hostile public statements, denial of human rights and uncooperative attitude toward the UN.

[39] *Ibid.*, p. 523. The Soviet note also expressed the expectation that Mr. Khruschchev be given the possibility of traveling between New York and Glen Cove, the seat of the Soviet Mission. It appears that this request was granted.

this clause imposes an obligation on the United States and even in its absence the United States would probably be obligated by principles of customary international law to afford the necessary protection to visiting diplomats. However, the question is whether this clause can be used as a legal basis for restricting the representatives to Manhattan Island or to any other part of the United States. Strictly speaking, as already noted, Section II of the Agreement is only concerned with transit to and from the Headquarters District. It is certainly correct, as the United States mission pointed out, that travel in the United States is not essential to the functioning of delegates to the General Assembly. In the case of Mr. Khrushchev, however, the United States discriminated between various heads of government who responded to Mr. Krushchev's proposal to hold a summit meeting in connection with the General Assembly. Discrimination may not be contrary to international law but it is always objectionable and certainly Section II contemplated equal treatment for representatives of Members. Furthermore, the treatment accorded Mr. Krushchev was motivated by his "bitterly antagonistic" attitude toward the United States.[40] The United States thus appeared to take advantage of its position as host of the United Nations in order to score a point in its national interest. The temptation to do so may have been very strong, but it may be doubted whether in yeilding to it, it was proper to be oblivious of the interests of the United Nations.[41] Moreover, it may be doubted whether the action of the United States was compatible with Section 12 of the Headquarters Agreement which appears to rule out considerations of the kind relied upon by the United States. According to this clause, "The provisions of Section II shall be applicable irrespective of the relations existing between the Governments of the persons referred to in that section and the Government of the United States."

The status of resident representatives is regulated in Section 15 of the Headquarters Agreement. Here a distinction is drawn between representatives of Members whose governments are recognized by the United States and those which are not. With respect to the former it is laid down that they

> shall, whether residing inside or outside the headquarters district, be entitled in the territory of the United States to the same privileges and immunities, subject to corresponding conditions and obligations, as it accords to diplomatic envoys accredited to it.

It is thus assumed that members of permanent delegations may reside either within the district, which is hardly feasible, or outside of it. Insofar as is known, no restrictions are in force with respect to the area in which they may reside. There were complaints relating indirectly to the location of residences of missions arising from the assessment of real estate taxes upon official residences. Exemption from payment of these taxes was

[40] President Eisenhower's statement of September 17, 1960. Department of State *Bulletin* October 3, 1960 (Vol. 43, No. 1110), p. 523.

[41] ". . . When in 1960 the Pakistani Government declined to issue a visa to enable an Israeli representative to attend a meeting of the Economic Commission for Asia and the Far East which was to have been held in Karachi the meeting was adjourned and subsequently held in Bangkok." Jenks, *International Immunities,* p. 89.

orignally granted only within a certain radius of New York City. This would be construed as a limitation upon the freedom of missions to establish themselves wherever they chose, and it was certainly incompatible with the diplomatic privileges accorded to members of permanent missions. However, all grounds for complaints were removed by a law of the State of New York of April 18, 1961, amending the old laws of 1955 and 1957 on the basis of which the exemption from real estate tax was limited to a certain area.[42]

The freedom of movement in the territory of the United States is limited for resident representatives of the Soviet Union, the Ukrainian SSR, the Byelorussian SSR, Albania,[43] Hungary, Romania, and Bulgaria. They may move freely in the area lying within a twenty-five mile radius of Columbus Circle on Manhattan Island. For travel outside this area they are required to notify the Department of State and obtain its permission. These restrictions are reciprocal in nature and were imposed as a result of restrictions placed on United States diplomatic personnel in the countries of the missions concerned. They are communicated to the missions by formal notes from the Department of State.[44]

The issue to be considered here is that of reciprocity. That this principle prevails in diplomatic practice is not doubted.[45] It applies on a bilateral basis. The relations between the United States and missions to the United Nations are not based on the traditional bilateral relationship. Reciprocity in the application of restrictive measures is intended as a retaliatory measure to induce the state which first imposed restrictions to remove them. By applying retaliatory measures to permanent missions to the United Nations as well as to the diplomatic missions accredited to it, the United States brings to bear additional pressure upon the state concerned, against which that state cannot retaliate. This advantage accrues to the United States from its unique position as host to the United Nations headquarters. But its legal position vis-à-vis missions is regulated by the Charter, the General Convention, and the Headquarters Agreement, and unless a legal basis is found in these instruments, there is none.

The United Nations Charter provides no more support than the General Convention for reciprocal and discriminatory treatment.[46] The Headquarters Agreement does

[42] On this subject see Delson, "Immunity from Taxation on Real Property owned by Delegations to the United Nations," 49 *American Journal of International Law,* p. 555–557 (1955).

[43] The case of Albania will not be considered further as it comes within the ambit of Section 15 concerning representatives of Members whose governments are not recognized by the United States. Insofar as Bulgaria is concerned this restriction applies only to non-diplomatic personnel of the mission.

[44] See "Contemporary Practice of the United States relating to International Law," 56 *American Journal of International Law,* p. 526–539 (1962) at p. 534 ff.

[45] It is recognized specifically in Article 47 of the Vienna Convention on Diplomatic Relations.

[46] A letter from the then Legal Adviser of the Department of State, Mr. Ernest A. Gross, dated May 26, 1948, to the Chairman of Subcommittee No. 6 of the Committee on Foreign Affairs concluded. "(1) The Charter of the United Nations imposes the obligation on member states to grant certain privileges and immunities not conditioned on reciprocity. . . . (3) The Section 9 proviso in the [International Organizations and Immunities] act relates only to privileges, exemptions, and immunities granted under the International Organizations Immunities Act. Even if the proviso were construed to relate to privileges and immunities under the Convention on the Privileges and Immunities of the United Nations and the proviso were regarded as recognizing a power in the Secretary to enforce reciprocity, it would not be operative since the Convention would prevail; the latter instrument does not provide for the making of any conditions of reciprocity." House Report No. 2291, p. 16.

not provide for reciprocity. Section 12 of the Agreement[47] rules out reciprocity insofar as *ad hoc* representatives are concerned by explicitly stipulating that Section II shall be applicable irrespective of the relations existing between the United States and the state of the representatives. Section 15 provides special treatment for resident representatives of governments not recognized by the United States. The same section also provides generally that the resident representatives shall be "entitled in the territory of the United States to the same privileges and immunities, subject to corresponding conditions and obligations, as it accords to diplomatic envoys accredited to it." Whatever the words "corresponding conditions and obligations" may mean, such as noninterference in the domestic affairs of the United States, they do not include reciprocity and discrimination. These are not "obligations or conditions" of envoys. Therefore, this clause does not and cannot support the practice of the United States with regard to reciprocity and discrimination.[48] Thus none of the three applicable international instruments can be involved in this matter. As the Swiss Federal Council, which is host to the European Headquarters of the United Nations and several specialized agencies declared: reciprocity cannot apply with respect to international organizations.[49]

Yet the United States maintains the restrictions. The juridical basis for reciprocal restrictions cannot be sought in principles of international law. For restrictions so based can only be imposed on diplomatic envoys accredited to the United States as a reaction against restrictions imposed on envoys of the United States to the sending state. The juridical relationship which exists between the United States as host country to the United Nations and the resident representatives of Members to the Organization is not at all analogous to the relationship between diplomatic envoys accredited to the United States by states with which the United States maintains diplomatic relations on the basis of international law including the principle of reciprocity.

It remains to consider the International Organizations Immunities Act, Public Law 291. This Act, it will be recalled, was enacted on December 29, 1945, that is, after the Charter entered into force but prior to the adoption of the General Convention and the conclusion of the Headquarters Agreement. Concerning this Act and the question of reciprocity, the Legal Adviser of the Department of State in the letter of May 26, 1948, referred to above, expressed the following conclusion:

> (2) The International Organizations Immunities Act restricts the power of the Secretary of State in managing United States foreign relations, to enforce conditions of reciprocity in

[47] See p. 294 above.

[48] The Legal Adviser of the State Department also concluded: "(4) The headquarters agreement, although it does not provide for making of any requirement of reciprocity in the granting of privileges and immunities by the United States, may empower this Government to require the recall of certain foreign nationals covered by the Convention, if they are regarded as personae non gratae; the agreement prevails over the Convention in case of conflict." House Report No. 2291, p. 16.

[49] Quoted in Cahier, *Etude des Accords de Siège Conclus entre less Organizations Internationales et les Etats où elles Résident,* 1959, p. 198, n. 23. The passage appears in the message of the Swiss Federal Council to the Federal Assembly of July 28, 1955, which after noting that reciprocity applies in the case of diplomatic missions in Berne concludes: «En revanche, la réciprocité ne peut jouer à L'égard des Organisations internationales.»

> the granting of privileges and immunities. To the extent that the act does not restrict the Secretary's power, it nevertheless makes no affirmative grants of power and merely leaves the Secretary with such authority as he may possess apart from the act and in view of the effect of the Charter of the United Nations.[50]

The power left to the Secretary to enforce reciprocity is presumably the power derived from general international law with respect to diplomatic envoys to the United States which is not questioned here. That power is not applicable to resident representatives of Members who in virtue of the Headquarters Agreement enjoy the same privileges and immunities as the United States accords to diplomatic envoys accredited to it. Their status is radically different. They are not envoys accredited to the United States and they derive their privileges and immunities status from the Agreements and Resolutions of the General Assembly and not from customary international law which governs the normal diplomatic relations between sovereign states.

Moreover, there is only one pertinent clause in the Act and this rules out reciprocity. And this clause, even if it should be construed as authorizing the enforcement of reciprocity, does not deal with representatives of Members but with officers and employees of international organizations and might at best sustain reciprocal restriction with respect to such persons but could not be construed extensively to include representatives of Members.[51] It may not be amiss to recall that officers and employees of the United Nations, that is, staff members of its Secretariat, are not governed in the United States by an international instrument except the Charter inasmuch as the United States has so far failed to accede to the General convention. The Headquarters Agreement, curiously enough, is silent on this subject.

The conclusion appears inescapable that the discriminatory treatment of certain resident representatives has no juridical support in any of the applicable international instruments and cannot be supported by Public Law 291 which is the unilateral enactment of the United States. Furthermore, it cannot find a juridical basis in customary international law relating to diplomatic relations. Enough has been said about the United States Reservation to the Headquarters Agreement. Whatever the legal status of this Reservation may be, by its own terms it safeguards only the security of the United States and the disciminatory treatment here under consideration has been based on considerations of reciprocity and not of national security.

[50] House Report No. 2291, p. 16.

[51] Section 9 of Public Law 291, entitled "Benefits not conditioned upon reciprocity—Right reserved" reads as follows:
> The privileges, exemptions, and immunities of international organizations and of their officers and employees, and members of their families, suites, and servants, provided for in this title, *shall be granted notwithstanding the fact that the similar privileges, exemptions, and immunities granted to a foreign government, its officers, or employees, may be conditioned upon the existence of reciprocity by that foreign government: Provided,* that nothing contained in this title shall be construed as precluding the Secretary of State from withdrawing the privileges, exemptions, and immunities herein provided from persons who are nationals of any foreign country on the ground that such country is failing to accord corresponding privileges, exemptions, and immunities to citizens of the United States.

Italics supplied.

## IV. PRIVILEGES AND IMMUNITIES OF REPRESENTATIVES OF MEMBERS

Representatives of Members to organs of the United Nations enjoy functional immunities and privileges in virtue of Article 105, paragraph 2, of the Charter. This applies generally to both *ad hoc* and resident representatives. The General Convention in Section II, again without making any distinction, enumerates certain specific rights such as immunity from arrest, inviolability for all papers and archives, use of codes, exemption from immigration restrictions, facilities in respect of currency restrictions and baggage, and provides generally

> such other privileges, immunities and facilities not inconsistent with the foregoing as diplomatic envoys enjoy, except that they shall have no right to claim exemption from customs duties on goods imported (otherwise than as part of their personal baggage) or from excise duties or sales taxes.

The United States, however, as already repeatedly noted, has not acceded to the General Convention. Unless the suggested "incorporation by reference" construction is adopted, this provision is not applicable in the United States and is not binding upon it. The Headquarters Agreement, apart from transit to and from the headquarters district, and one or two other matters to be discussed in the following section, does not deal with the immunities and privileges of *ad hoc* representatives of Members either generally or specifically. On the contrary, Section 13 *(d)* reserves to the United States all rights not surrendered in the Agreement itself or in the General Convention.[52] It would seem to follow, then, that apart from the limited concessions made in the Agreement and the general proviso in the Charter, the United States retains full control over *ad hoc* representatives. This anomalous situation is the result of the failure of the United States to accede to the General Convention.

Public Law 291, the International Organizations Immunities Act, is the source of such privileges and immunities as the United States unilaterally confers upon *ad hoc* representatives. Excepting entry privileges, Section 7*(b)* recognizes only immunity "from suit and legal process relating to acts performed by them in their official capacity and falling within their functions as such representatives." This is a far cry from normal or full diplomatic privileges and immunities and those specified in the General Convention. And even these exiguous privileges and immunities are dependent upon notification to and acceptance by the Secretary of State.[53] Moreover, as will be shown presently, they can be terminated at will by the Secretary of State.

Resident representatives, by comparison, enjoy normal diplomatic privileges and

[52] "Except as provided above in this section and in the General Convention, the United States retains full control and authority over the entry of persons or property into the territory of the United States and the conditions under which persons may remain or reside there."

[53] See p. 284 ff above. From the point of view of the applicable international instruments it has been maintained that prior notification is not a substantive condition for the enjoyment of the privileges which result automatically from the status of the representative or official; as a procedural requirement it can be satisfied by subsequent notification.

immunities in virtue of Section 15 of the Headquarters Agreement. These would include all those listed in the General Convention for representatives of Members generally and include also those excluded therein, i.e., the exemption from excise and sales taxes. This exemption forms part of the usual privileges accorded diplomatic envoys by customary international law and is recognized in Article 34 of the Vienna Convention on Diplomatic Relations. The omission of *ad hoc* representatives in the provisions of the Headquarters Agreement devoted to immunities and privileges is traceable to the assumption that the United States would, as host country, naturally accede to the General Convention. In view of the resistance of the United States it would seem to be imperative to fill the gap by an amendment of, or an additional protocol to, the Headquarters Agreement. The fact that no incidents have arisen or that their occurrence has not reached the public is no argument against making explicit the privileges and immunities of representatives. To do so would afford protection to the representatives, clarify their status in possible litigation before courts, and safeguard the United States from possible criticism at home and abroad.

## V. TERMINATION OF PRIVILEGES AND IMMUNITIES

Normally persons entitled to diplomatic privileges and immunities begin to enjoy them from the moment they enter the territory of the receiving state. They continue to enjoy them until their mission is terminated by the sending state or by the receiving state. The latter act is performed by declaring the person concerned *persona non grata* and in this case the immunities continue until the expiry of a reasonable period.[54] In the case of representatives of Members to the United Nations it would be reasonable to assume that they begin to enjoy such privileges and immunities as are accorded them from the moment they enter the territory of the United States. The question of termination is one of some complexity. Termination by the sending Member State clearly ends the representative character of the person concerned and, except for the reasonable period to depart, his privileged status. May the United States terminate the privileges and immunities of representatives and cause them to depart?

Analogies to diplomatic envoys are necessarily misleading as there is no analogy of the relation between the host state on the one hand and representatives of Members to the United Nations on the other and the relationship between a sending and receiving state in case of customary diplomatic envoys. This is confirmed by the fact that the General Convention is silent on the subject and accords no right of termination to the state which acts as host to meetings of United Nations organs. Clearly the independent exercise of their functions would be jeopardized if the host state could unilaterally and at its discretion terminate and thereby prevent them from exercising the function entrusted to them by the Member States. That is the meaning of Article 105, paragraph 2, of the Charter. How-

[54] See Articles 9, 39, and 43 of the Vienna Convention on Diplomatic Relations.

ever, absence of an express stipulation does not necessarily prevent or remove misunderstandings.

The Headquarters Agreement accordingly deals with the subject explicitly though not without some ambiguity. The Agreement contains several provisions on the subject. Section 13 *(b)* (I) lays down the general principle:

> No proceedings shall be instituted under such laws or regulations[55] to require any such person to leave the United States except with the prior approval of the Secretary of State of the United States. Such approval shall be given only after consultation with the appropriate Member in the case of a representative of a Member. . . .

The following paragraph, Section 13 *(b)* (2) provides that "a representative of the Member concerned . . . shall have the right to appear in any such proceedings on behalf of the person against whom they are instituted." And, finally, Section 13 *(b)* (3) lays down the rule which is of particular interest here:

> Persons who are entitled to diplomatic privileges and immunities under Section 15 or under the General Convention shall not be required to leave the United States otherwise than in accordance with the customary procedure applicable to diplomatic envoys accredited to the United States.

This wealth of regulation is embarrassing, and it is all the more remarkable as it was not included in the original draft Agreement. The Sixth Committee of the General Assembly considered this addition and declared it acceptable on the explicit understanding, first, that the provision should be invoked only on serious grounds, which would preclude the possibility of unwarranted accusation, and secondly that there would be consultation between the United States government and the government of the Member in cases relating to representatives.[56] Such caution was understandable, for one clause requires consultation prior to the Secretary's decision, whereas another refers to "the customary procedure" regarding envoys accredited to Washington which in accordance with customary international law does not require consultation.[57] In any event the practice of declaring an envoy *persona non grata* cannot be applied to an *ad hoc* representative or a resident representative of a Member who is in the two categories of persons expressly included in Section 13 *(b)* (3), the reason being that such persons are not accredited to the

[55] This refers to the preceding paragraph which states in part:

> In case of abuse of such privileges of residence by any such person in activities in the United States outside his official capacity, it is understood that the privileges referred to in Section II shall not be construed to grant him exemption from the laws and regulations of the United States regarding the continued residence of aliens, provided that:

[56] Report of the Sixth Committee: Agreement between the United Nations and the United States of America regarding the Headquarters of the United Nations, October 27, 1947. Document A/427, p. 4, paragraph 7.

[57] Thus Article 9 of the Vienna Convention correctly states:

> The receiving State may at any time and without having to explain its decision, notify the sending State that the head of the mission or any member of the diplomatic staff of the mission is *persona non grata*. . . . In any such case, the sending State shall, as appropriate, either recall the person concerned or terminate his function with the mission.

United States.[58] The proviso might have, however, an acceptable meaning if it is intended to extend, under customary practice, to representatives having diplomatic immunities and who are required to leave the United States a reasonable period to depart. This would be consistent with the assumption underlying the proviso that they do enjoy diplomatic immunities and privileges. Similarly, the requirement of consultation is consistent with both the security requirement of the United States and the requirement of the Charter that the representatives of Members shall have the immunities necessary for the independent exercise of their functions. The provision in Section 13 *(b)* (2) that a representative of the Member concerned shall have the right to appear in proceedings initiated for the purpose of requiring a person to leave is a further safeguard insofar as it applies to representatives of Members.

In his Report to the Economic and Social Council of July 27, 1953,[59] the Secretary-General of the United Nations, adverting to the security of the United States, declared:

> As provided in section 13 *(b)*, the United States can carry out deportation proceedings under its laws and regulations against persons admitted under the Headquarters Agreement who abuse the privileges of residence in activities in the United States outside their official capacity.[60]

While the Secretary-General was putting forth a general proposition recognizing the right of deportation under Section 13 *(b)*, several speakers referred to this right with respect to representatives of non-governmental organizations and not of representatives of Members.[61] This section does not establish or recognize the right of deportation though this may be the last resort if the representative in question does not leave when required to do so by the United States. But this drastic step, when representatives of Members are involved, is the last resort; it comes conceivably at the end but certainly not at the beginning of the procedure laid down in this section. Deportation of representatives of Members invested with diplomatic immunities and privileges would be a most unusual step, for nothing in the Headquarters Agreement gives the United States the right to deprive such representatives of their diplomatic character; this position is founded upon the Agreement and the General Convention, which for this purpose and in this context, must be regarded as incorporated by reference in the Agreement.

However, the United States reserved the right of unilateral action in Public Law 291, the International Organizations and Immunities Act, Section 8 *(b)* which reads as follows:

[58] "It should be obvious, however, that the principle of *persona non grata* does not apply under the provisions of this section." Yuen-li Liang, "Notes on Legal Questions Concerning the United Nations." 42 *American Journal of International Law*, p. 435-447 (1948) at p. 445.

[59] See p. 287 ff above.

[60] Document E/2492, p. 1, paragraph 3. ECOSOC *Official Records* (16th Session), Annexes, Agenda Item 33.

[61] E.g. the representatives of France, p. 254, paragraph 49, and the Soviet Union, p. 268, paragraph 12. ECOSOC *Official Records* (16th Session), 743d and 745th meetings.

> Should the Secretary of State determine that the continued presence in the United States of any person entitled to the benefits of this title is not desirable, he shall so inform the foreign government or international organization concerned, as the case may be, and after such person shall have had a reasonable length of time, to be determined by the Secretary of State, to depart from the United States, he shall cease to be entitled to such benefits.

This clause is, of course, superseded by the Headquarters Agreement to the extent that it is in contradiction with it. The Agreement requires consultation with the government of the representative, it provides for participation in the proceedings, and it is silent on the cessation of privileges and immunities. But this is, as noted above,[62] a matter of construction.

Section 8 *(b)* if taken literally, leads, moreover, to results which are absurd. It states that persons, including presumably representatives, will forfeit benefits under this title. The benefits, apart from certain facilities regarding entry, and related matters, are specified in Section 7 *(b)* of Public Law 291 as follows:

> Representatives of foreign governments in or to international organizations . . . shall be immune from suit and legal process relating to acts performed by them in their official capacity and falling within their functions as such representatives . . . except insofar as such immunity may be waived by the foreign government. . . .

The combination of Section 7 *(b)* and Section 8 *(b)* leads to the truly remarkable conclusion that representatives of Members could become answerable in the American courts for acts within their functions, that is, within their official capacity. Such a proposition is untenable and quite incompatible with the rules applicable to diplomatic envoys under customary international law.[63] Moreover, under the Headquarters Agreement, the right to require a representative to leave the United States is designed to protect the United States against the abuse of privileges and immunities by a Member's representatives "in activities in the United States *outside* his official capacity,"[64] and not "inside" his official capacity. An interpretation which leads to absurd results must be rejected although it is not at all absurd to imagine a situation where representatives by acts performed in the exercise of their official duties might endanger the security of the United States. However, the Charter, in the interest of the "independent exercise of their function in connection with the Organization" shields them from responsibility and accountability everywhere though regrettably probably not in their own countries. That stage in the development of international organization has not yet been reached. It follows then that

[62] See p. 279 above.

[63] Thus Article 39, paragraph 2 of the Vienna Convention lays down the well-known rule in the following words:
> When the functions of a person enjoying privileges and immunities have come to an end, such privileges and immunities shall normally cease at the moment when he leaves the country, or on expiry of a reasonable period in which to do so, but shall subsist until that time, even in case of armed conflict. However, with respect to acts performed by such a person in the exercise of his functions as a member of the mission, immunity shall continue to subsist.

[64] Section 13 *(b)* quoted above in note 55, p. 300. Italics supplied.

in spite of the sweeping language, Section 8 *(b)* must be construed restrictively and not literally, that is, as depriving a representative only of the privileges or benefits with respect to residence or visit in the United States.

An unlimited right of expulsion, however, might also seriously endanger the independent exercise of the function of both *ad hoc* and resident representatives. That may be the reason for the procedure of consultation and participation in proceedings leading to expulsion expressly provided for in the Headquarters Agreement. It has been suggested that there has already developed a rule of customary international law establishing immunity from coercion for representatives and solid guarantees against expulsion from the territory of the state where they exercise their function.[65] But Public Law 291 provides no such guarantees and having been enacted prior to the Agreement, makes no reference to the procedure provided therin. Far from it, it empowers the Secretary of State in his unfettered discretion, to strip of the benefits of the law "any person" whose "continued presence in the United States is not desirable." To be sure, the Agreement may be deemed to have superseded the earlier Public Law 291, but it is doubtful whether this is so in practice as may be seen from the incident involving M. Miroslav Nacvalac, a member of the permanent mission of Czechoslovakia to the United Nations since July 18, 1958 and its Counselor since June 13, 1961.

## VI. CASE OF MIROSLAV NACVALAC

Mr. Nacvalac was known to the United States government as chief of Czechoslovak Civilian Intelligence Operations in the United States. The record of his activities is immaterial. However, although his "improper activities" were known to this government for some time, "no action was taken to expel Nacvalac from the United States, since during his contacts with American citizens Nacvalac indicated his interest in discussing the possibility of defecting and remaining in the United States." A meeting was held on June 13, 1961, in New York City at which representatives of this government were present "to discuss Nacvalac's alleged interest in remaining in the United States with him since this government is always willing to entertain legitimate requests for political asylum." However, "during the course of this meeting it became unmistakably clear that Nacvalac's motivations and intentions were not genuine and were highly suspect. Subsequent to that meeting a note was delivered to the Czechoslovak United Nations delegation requesting that arrangements be made for Nacvalac's immediate departure from the United States."[66]

The Secretary-General promised to investigate the charges and counter-charges while the Czechoslovak mission claimed that the incident threatened the independence of

[65] Cahier, *loc. cit.*, p. 401.

[66] United States Mission to the United Nations Press Release 3733, June 16, 1961. For the Czechoslovak version, see *The New York Times*, June 17, 1961. According to this, United States intelligence agents tried to hire Nacvalac as a spy and when he refused, the United States took action against him. See also State Department Press Release 415, June 20, 1961, and United States Mission Release 3734 of the same date.

delegates to the United Nations and demonstrated the need to move the headquarters to another country.[67]

The request for his immediate departure, based on the "highly improper activities" of Nacvalac "which had no relationship with his duties as a member of the Permanent Delegation to the United Nations," was deemed by the United States government to be

> clearly authorized under Section 13 (b) of the Headquarters Agreement between the United States and the United Nations, which states that, in the case of abuse of privilege of residence by any member of any permanent delegation, it is understood that the privileges granted elsewhere in this Agreement (Section 11) shall not be construed so that such members shall be exempt from the laws and regulations of the United States regarding the residence of aliens. Mr. Naclavac's (sic!) activities clearly constitute an abuse of his privileges of residence.[68]

When the request was not complied with, the Czechoslovak mission was informed of the following decision taken by the United States government:

> The status accorded Miroslav Nacvalac pursuant to Section 101 (a) (15) (G) of the Immigration and Nationality Act by virtue of his entry into the territory of the United States of America as a member of the Permanent Mission of the Czechoslovak Socialist Republic to the United Nations is herewith revoked. The effect of this revocation of status is to place Miroslav Nacvalac in the category of an alien illegally in the United States of America.
>
> Under the laws and regulations of the United States of American, Miroslav Nacvalac may elect to depart voluntarily or, in lieu of such voluntary departure, be removed.[69]

The case of the United States would have gained strength if the government had acted promptly as soon as it became aware of the "highly improper" activities of Mr. Nacvalac[70] instead of letting him carry on until his alleged interest in defecting was revealed three years later as not motivated "by sincere political convictions." Be that as it may, it seems reasonably clear that the United States, in final analysis, looked for and found a basis for its action not in the Headquarters Agreement but in Public Law 291.

In the absence of full documentation bearing on this incident, it is not possible to formulate definite conclusions. From the press release it would appear that the procedure provided for in the Agreement was not followed. There is no evidence of consultation. Instead the United States addressed a peremptory request to the Czechoslovak mission that arrangements be made for the "immediate departure" of Mr. Nacvalac. Section 13 *(b)* (3) of the Agreement stipulates that persons entitled to diplomatic privileges—and Mr. Nacvalac was one of them—shall not be requested to leave the United States otherwise than in accordance with the customary procedure applicable to diplomatic envoys accred-

[67] *The New York Times,* June 18, 20, 21, and 22, 1961. The text of the notes of June 16 and 19, 1961, to the Secretariat of the United Nations was released by the mission.

[68] Note to the Secretary-General of the United Nations. United States Mission to the United Nations Press Release 3734, June 20, 1961.

[69] United States Mission to the United Nations Press Release 3735, June 21, 1961.

[70] This point was made in the Czechoslovak note of June 19, 1961, to the Secretariat of the United Nations.

ited to the United States. There is no evidence that the customary reasonable period to depart was granted in this case.[71] If Mr. Nacvalac was involved not merely in "highly improper" but illegal activities a request to waive his privileged status might have been made. On the other hand, the procedure actually resorted to in this case, that is the "revocation of status" accompanied by a threat of deportation, seems altogether in accord with Section 8 *(b)* of Public Law 291. It may be noted that deportation implies detention and this is specifically ruled out by the General Convention,[72] to which we must again point out the United States is not a party. We would again submit, nevertheless, that this may be deemed to be incorporated by reference in the Agreement.

It may well be that the action of the United States in this case was within the spirit if not the letter of Section 13 of the Agreement and that no resort was explicitly made and that no resort was necessary to Section 8 *(b)* of Public Law 291. In spite of the fact that the case of Mr. Nacvalac was totally devoid of any appealing features and that it may not have been considered a case on which to take a stand, a question of principle was involved: the extent of the power of the host country to expel a member of a permanent delegation or an *ad hoc* representative of a Member. This and nothing else would have called for clarification by the procedure for arbitration provided for in the Agreement. The person involved was wholly irrelevant, but the issue is not because it goes to the heart of the status of delegates to the United Nations. If the action of the United States was legally correct then indeed there is no international guarantee for the independent exercise of their functions by the representatives of Members to the Organization. On the contrary, in final analysis, the representatives enjoy privileges and immunities at the sufferance of the United States and not as a legal right resulting from a legal obligation.

## VII. SUMMING UP

The arrangements governing the status of representatives, in spite of anomalies, inconsistencies, and ambiguities, have worked satisfactorily in practice, but it cannot be gainsaid that they are in the nature of a "fair weather" *modus vivendi.* The question is whether the United Nations, which has been variously described as our "best hope for peace" and a cornerstone of American foreign policy, does not deserve better treatment, a

[71] When leaving the United States on June 22, Mr. Nacvalac made a statement in which he declared:

> Upon the instructions of my Government I leave this country for reasons of gross pressure and dictate on the part of the United States Government which contrary to the Agreement on the United Nations Headquarters unilaterally decided to revoke my privileges belonging to me as to a member of the Permanent Mission of my country and threatened me by a forcible action if I do not leave this country without delay. . . . My forcible expulsion from this country is a direct consequence of my refusal to become a traitor, which was pointed out by the representatives of the United States espionage institutions.

He also asserted "that Mr. Hammarskjöld, who personally took this case in his hands, as well as the Secretariat of the United Nations, did not take any measures against this arbitrariness of the United States Government." Text released by the Permanent Mission of the Czechoslovak Socialist Republic to the United Nations.

[72] Section II of the General Convention reads as follows: "Representatives of Members . . . shall, while exercising their functions . . . enjoy the following privileges and immunities: (a) immunity from personal arrest or detention. . . ."

"fair deal": fair to it and fair to the United States as the host country. This is essentially a question of policy; the legal formulae exist and can be perfected easily. It will be objected that no matter what formulae are chosen, the United States, when the chips are down, will extract every ounce of advantage from its positions as host country to pursue its policy objectives and, if necessary, to safeguard its security. This may be so, although it need not be so. However, before pursuing this theme a little further it may be well to indicate the problem of policy: in a nutshell it is whether the privileges and immunities accorded the representatives to the United Nations and without whom the United Nations cannot function, are to continue to be "concessions extended by the Nation on its own terms, as in the existing International Organizations Immunities Act," or are to be recognized as "rights to be exercised under international law."[73] The fundamental contrast between a regime based on the Act and a regime based on the General Convention has been accurately described as follows:

> In the case of the former, ultimate control lies within the power of the President, who, with respect to the organizations to be granted privileges under the act, may deprive as well as bestow. Under the convention, however, the status of the United Nations and its agents enters into the field of international law, and differences thereunder become a matter ultimately to be settled only before an international tribunal. This is the all-inclusive development contemplated in the convention.[74]

Until the United States accepts the General Convention the representatives of the Members are, internationally speaking and apart from the Charter, *ex lex,* and even the Headquarters Agreement lacks the essential complement with the view to which it was negotiated and concluded. Whether the United States would sacrifice much in acceding to the General Convention may be debated. The House Foreign Affairs Committee was of the opinion that the decisive step was made when the United States joined the United Nations and subscribed to the principles enunciated in Article 105 of the Charter. As of May 16, 1962, sixty-nine members have accepted the Convention. The House Committee referred to above had already pointed out in 1948:

> To withhold adherence to this convention would gain the United States nothing. It would simply reverse the position this Government has consistently taken in opposition to those member nations who take refuge in rigid adherence to theories of sovereignty in opposing measures to make the United Nations effective as an instrument of security.

This might have been written yesterday for the situation is exactly as set out except that the United States is cheerfully oblivious of the fatal contradiction in its position and continues to preach water and drink wine.

However, acceptance of the General Convention might not be sufficient. Privileges and immunities, as the somewhat analogous situation of the Western rights in Berlin

[73] House Report No. 2291, p. 21.
[74] *Ibid.,* p. 20.

shows, cannot merely be denied outright; they can also be eroded. Anyone who has ever had anything to do with privileges and immunities, whether of diplomats or international civil servants, knows that there is only one way to preserve them and that is to insist scrupulously on the full measure. Otherwise attrition will set in. There is perhaps a suspicion but not much evidence, that the Secretary-General has not always taken that line and that by seeking accommodation he may have impaired some of the very modest privileges to which the Secretariat staff as well as the representatives of Members or non-governmental organizations and others are entitled. It is certainly a fact that the procedure for settling differences through arbitration has never been employed although it might have been more effective than the procedure of negotiation. Here it may again be objected that if the United States feels strongly on a matter, it will disregard the award of the tribunal of arbitration. This might conceivably happen although in practice the cases are fortunately rare in which governments fail to carry out an award or judgment. It is, after all, not very likely that a matter of life or death to the nation will arise in connection with the application of the General Convention or the Headquarters Agreement. However, if either instrument, in the light of experience, should impose an unfair burden on the host country, it might be desirable to negotiate appropriate amendments or additions.

A change in the handling of complaints arising under the General Convention or the Headquarters Agreement might be considered. Heretofore such complaints have been addressed to the organ concerned or to the Secretariat, and the Secretary-General had in his judgement to determine whether or not he should open negotiations with the appropriate authorities of the United States. One wonders whether this solution is a happy one, particularly when representatives of Members are concerned. Representatives of Members should not depend in this matter on the administrative branch of the United Nations. It might be more appropriate for the General Assembly by analogy to national parliaments to establish a small permanent committee on privileges and immunities of representatives. Like all other committees of the General Assembly, this committee would be serviced by the Secretariat, and its work would be subject to review by the General Assembly itself. Complaints would be addressed to this committee and examined on their merits. If any speedy action were required, the chairman of this committee could take up the complaint with the designated authority of the United States. If no solution acceptable to the committee is worked out, the committee would instruct the Secretary-General to initiate the procedure for arbitration. The procedure of arbitration may not always be ideally satisfactory, but there is no reason to condemn it in advance and to avoid it at almost all cost. It is certainly the only alternative to negotiations which might result in whittling down the status of representatives. In any event, a committee of the General Assembly should relieve the Secretary-General of what must have been an unwelcome burden and take over the function of watchdog of the immunities and privileges of Members' representatives.

In the matter of accreditation there is also room for improvement. Representatives of Members should not be and are not accredited to the United States, and their enjoyment of privileges and immunities must not depend upon acceptance by the Secretary of State of the United States. Here there is a policy question for the Members. For reasons of prestige and sovereignty they have refrained from accepting accreditation to the Secretary-General of the United Nations. For similar reasons accreditation to the deliberative organs of the United Nations has become a mere matter of form or of politics. However, if Members persist in appointing as representatives persons who are objectionable to the host country on more grounds than one, a problem arises. What is involved, besides the prestige of Members, is the effectiveness of the United Nations. It does not show much respect for the Organization if Members appoint as representatives persons whose main assignments lie in a field unrelated to the United Nations. The Organization should therefore have the means to protect itself and its integrity. This might be done by the committee mentioned above or by a committee on accreditation established by the General Assembly. Appointments would be notified to the committee and the host country. Any relevant information in the possession of the host country should be communicated to this committee which would have power to accept or reject as representative a person nominated by a Member. The committee might also be given the power to declare a representative *persona non grata* if after appropriate representations the Members concerned refused to recall him. The committee in such a case, would, in consultation with the host country, fix a reasonable period to depart at the expiration of which the privileges and immunities of such a person would end. His capacity to represent the Member in the organ to which he was appointed would come to an end as soon as he was declared *persona non grata.* It is not claimed that this procedure is ideal or that it will always protect the host country. What is urged is that an international process of accreditation is necessary if objections against a national process are to be sustained. Members cannot have it both ways; maintain integrally their own sovereignty and deny it to the United States. Membership in the United Nations imposes restraints on all and presumably the advantages outweigh the sacrifice of a very small measure of traditional sovereignty. Some controls are obviously imperative. The problem is to find ways and means for substituting effective international controls in place of national controls. The United Nations will either control itself or it will be controlled by a Member government.

If an effective international procedure for accreditation could be devised and implemented by the United Nations, the United States would receive all the reasonable guarantees that residence would not be abused by representatives to the detriment of its security. Ideally, the headquarters of the United Nations should have been established in an enclave large enough to accommodate all the representatives of Members as well as representatives of non-governmental and inter-governmental organizations, the Organization's staff, representatives of the press, radio, etc. Anybody wishing to enter the territory of the United States outside the United Nations enclave would have to go through the regular processes provided by United States law and would be wholly subject to it while on its territory. But the ideal solution was not adopted when the question of headquarters was open to deliberation. It could hardly be reopened today. Moving the headquarters to another country or even Berlin would present problems fundamentally not dissimilar from those which have arisen in the United States unless in the process it was possible to secure for the United Nations an extraterritorial area and status.[75] The chances for such an improvement cannot be discussed in the abstract and no country has yet offered an extraterritorial area to the United Nations comparable to, say, the District of Columbia. Governing such an enclave would obviously present financial and administrative problems but no obstacles are insuperable if the Organization is to have the safeguards which will enable it to discharge its function without unilateral governmental interference.[76]

In the present context of international relations the problem of the immunities and privileges of delegates to the United Nations is in final analysis only one aspect, albeit an important one, of the coexistence of the United Nations and the prevailing nation-state system. The International Court of Justice found unanimously that the United Nations "at present the supreme type of international organization" was "a subject of international law" and in "the possession of a large measure of international personality and the capacity to operate upon an international plane."[77] In so doing the United Nations operates on the same plane as and concurrently with the states. It is not essential that all subjects of international law be established on a territorial basis. It is not a question of principle but rather one of functional necessity. The time may not yet have come when the United Nations will be face to face with this necessity, but it is certainly not far off. If it is to function as an effective and reasonably independent actor in the international arena, it will have to get from the Member States the necessary territorial base. Without it, its functional independence and freedom from control or interference by any one Member government will always be precarious.

However, no prediction is ventured, and the United Nations may never advance decisively beyond the stage of an institutionalized diplomatic conference to the stage in which the Organization, conceived "primarily as a dynamic instrument," would "develop forms of executive action."[78] So far governments have behaved in the typical traditional manner: they want to solve the intractable problems of international relations including disarmament, and some have even strongly endorsed the idea of a powerful international executive action through the United Nations. It is moot whether any of these objectives can be achieved without profound structural changes in the state system and whether such transformations would be acceptable to the states. On the other hand, insofar as the problem of the status of delegates to the United Nations is concerned, improvements can be conceived which do not involve a radical transformation of the United Nations or of the state system.

[75] Switzerland recognized the extraterritoriality of the International Labor Organization. Jenks, *loc. cit.*, p. 27.

[76] Jenks considers as one of the foundations of the immunities of international organizations that they "should have a status which protects them against control or interference by any one government in the performance of functions for the effective discharge of which they are responsible to democratically constituted international bodies in which all the nations concerned are represented." *Loc. cit.*, p. 17.

[77] *Reparation for Injuries suffered in the Service of the United Nations*, Advisory Opinion, April 11, 1949; *I.C.J. Reports 1949*, p. 179.

[78] *Introduction to the Annual Report of the Secretary-General on the Work of the Organization 16 June 1960-15 June 1961.* General Assembly *Official Records* (16th Session), Supplement 1A, p. 1. Reproduced in *International Organization*, Autumn 1961 (Vol. 15, No. 4), p. 549-563.

The existing situation is certainly not intolerable. Improvements can be made by fully developing the existing international instruments and utilizing the judicial guarantees already provided for without fundamental or even far-reaching alterations in the existing pattern of relationships between the Organization, the representatives who constitute its deliberative bodies, and the Member governments. Now is the time to think of providing stronger guarantees for immunities and privileges of delegates to the United Nations than is afforded under the prevailing fair-weather arrangements and which would be effective even in seriously strained situations.[79] The clouds which gathered on the international sky in the wake of the U-2 and RB-47 incidents were probably more black than menacing and yet the reaction of the United States on the eve of the 1960 session of the General Assembly was prompt and may well have provided the sparks which set off the oratorical storm in the Assembly.

*The voice of the international community is weak and muffled in comparison with the powerful voices of domestic interests, but where it corresponds with conscience, it is nevertheless a formidable deterrent.*

—Robert E. Asher, in Robert E. Asher, Walter W. Kotschnig, William Adam Brown, Jr., *et al, The United Nations and Economic and Social Cooperation* (Washington: Brookings Institution, 1957).

[79] For the difficulties which the gathering storm of World War II created for the League of Nations and the International Labor Organization in 1939-1940, see Jenks, *loc. cit.*, p. 27-29, and the same author, *The Headquarters of International Institutions* (London: Royal Institute of International Affairs, 1945), p. 48-49.

# III

# INTERNATIONAL LAW AND INDIVIDUAL RESPONSIBILITY

# THE CRIMINALITY OF AGGRESSIVE WAR

The judgment delivered on September 30, 1946, by the International Military Tribunal brought to a close the first prosecution instituted under the London Agreement of August 8, 1945, entered into by the governments of the United States, France, Great Britain, and the U.S.S.R. But the publication of the judgment stirred a new wave of sharp criticism of the moral and legal foundations of the Nuremberg Trial. The charge that the Tribunal itself, as well as the substantive law which it applied, was *ex post facto* was renewed with vigor. So was the charge that no real justice was done at Nuremberg, because vanquished war criminals only were brought before the Tribunal and no attempt was made to try alleged war criminals of the victorious nations.

The latter charge naturally makes a strong appeal to public opinion. It would be difficult to dispute the soundness of this sentiment on any except technical grounds.[1] The ends of a true international legal order in time of peace as well as in time of war would unquestionably be better served if equal justice were meted out to all offenders against the law of nations, irrespective of whether the ultimate fortune of battle placed them in the camp of the victor or of the vanquished.[2] Ideally, victory should confer upon war criminals no immunity nor automatic amnesty.

The charge that from both the procedural and the substantive point of view the Nuremberg Trial was *ex post facto,* or retroactive, goes, of course, to the very heart of the

[1] Sheldon Glueck, *The Nuremberg Trial and Aggressive War* (1946), pp. 98–99, 119–121.

[2] Charles Cheney Hyde, "Punishment of War Criminals," *Proceedings of the American Society of International Law,* Vol. 37 (1943), p. 43 f.; Sheldon Glueck, *War Criminals; Their Prosecution and Punishment* (1944), p. 116.

matter. Counsel for defense urged this point before the Tribunal.[3] The supporters of the legality of the trial concentrated their efforts on disproving the soundness of this defense. To this end, they undertook to prove that by 1939 there had developed a customary rule of international law making the initiation and waging of aggressive war not merely illegal but also a criminal act. If this is assumed to be correct, then the substantive international law applied by the Tribunal was not *ex post facto;* on the contrary, the criminality of aggressive war and of individual responsibility formed part of positive international law at the time of the German attack on Poland on September 1, 1939. However, even if this assumption were made, there would still remain the objection that the adjective law was *ex post facto.* This, by comparison, may appear a relatively minor point. Indeed, the creation of the Tribunal and its rules of procedure is so obviously *ex post facto* that a degree of formal retroactivity seems to be admitted.[4] This leaves for further examination and discussion the assertion that the substantive law of the International Military Tribunal as formulated in Article 6, paragraph (a), of the Charter was *ex post facto.*[5] No attempt will be made here to discuss the question whether war crimes *stricto sensu* and crimes against humanity as defined in paragraphs (b) and (c) of Article 6 of the Charter formed part of international law before or on September 1, 1939, or at any subsequent time prior to the Agreement of October 8, 1945.[5a]

[3] Cf. "Judgment of the International Military Tribunal for the Trial of German Major War Criminals, Nuremberg, 30th September and 1st October, 1946," in *British Parliamentary Papers,* Misc. No. 12 (1946), Cmd. 6964, p. 38. Hereinafter referred to as the *Judgment.*

[4] Thus Glueck, *The Nuremberg Trial and Aggressive War,* p. 91. Sir Hartley Shawcross, Chief Prosecutor for Great Britain and Northern Ireland, argued before the Tribunal: "There is thus no substantial retroactivity in the provisions of the Charter. It merely fixes the responsibility for a crime already clearly established as such by positive law, upon its actual perpetrators." "The Trial of German Major War Criminals," *Proceedings before the International Military Tribunal,* Part 2, p. 57 (Published under the Authority of H.M. Attorney-General by His Majesty's Stationery Office, 1946), hereinafter referred to as *Proceedings.* But even procedural retroactivity is denied by the Tribunal. Arguing *de minore ad majorem,* and relying upon the precedent of the Hague Convention of 1907 respecting the Laws and Customs of War on Land, the Tribunal declared that although the Kellogg-Briand Pact "does not expressly enact that such wars [of aggression] are crimes, or set up courts to try those who make such wars," it was nevertheless possible to try and punish individuals for violations of the Pact just like individuals have in the past been tried and punished by military tribunals for violations of rules of land warfare. *Judgment,* p. 40. The validity of this analogy is not immediately clear.

[5] The relevant text of Article 6 of the Charter is as follows: "The Tribunal established by the agreement referred to in Article 1 hereof for the trial and punishment of the major war criminals of the European Axis countries shall have the power to try and punish persons who, acting in the interests of the Eruopean Axis countries, whether as individuals or as members of organizations, committed any of the following crimes."

The following acts, or any of them, are crimes coming within the jurisdiction of the Tribunal for which there shall be individual responsibility:

(a)Crimes against peace: namely, planning, preparation, initiation, or waging of a war of aggression, or a war in violation of international treaties, agreements or assurances, or participation in a common plan or conspiracy for the accomplishment of any of the foregoing." *Trial of War Criminals.* Department of State, Publication 2420, 1945, p. 16.

[5a] This paper is not concerned with the question whether it was just to try and punish Nazi war criminals or whether the maxim *nullum crimen sine lege, nulla poena sine lege* has a moral or legal, a subjective or objective, significance. These questions are discussed briefly by the Tribunal, *Judgment,* p. 39, and more extensively by Glueck, *op. cit.,* pp. 77 ff., and by Mr. Henry L. Stimson in "The Nuremberg Trial: Landmark in Law," *Foreign Affairs,* Vol 25 (1947), p. 183. Also the extent to which states, and even their nationals, may be punished for engaging in an illegal war falls outside the compass of the present study. But the Tribunal declared that "the undoubted right" of the countries to which the German Reich unconditionally surrendered "to legislate for the occupied territories has been recognized by the civilized world." *Judgment,* p. 38. If international law recognizes the right of conquest, it may be arguable that it is within the power of the victor to impose upon the enemy measures short of total extinction, provided that in so doing the victor does not infringe an established principle of international law. This paper is mainly concerned with the reasoning by which the U.S. Chief of Counsel, Mr. Robert H. Jackson, and Professor Glueck have supported the law set forth in the Charter of the Tribunal. Incidentally, it suggests an alternative approach.

In his capacity as Chief Counsel for the United States in prosecuting the principal Axis war criminals, Mr.Justice Jackson said that we could not deny "that our own day has its right to institute customs and to conclude agreements that will themselves become sources of a newer and strengthened international law." On the other hand, he maintained that "by the time the Nazis came to power it was thoroughly established that launching an aggressive war or the institution of war by treachery was illegal and that the defense of legitimate warfare was no longer available to those engaged in such an enterprise. It is high time that we act on the juridical principle that aggressive war-making is illegal and criminal."[6]

Mr. Justice Jackson developed the thought that "unjustifiable war" is a crime upon the basis of, and in reliance upon, the Kellogg-Briand Pact, the Geneva Protocol of 1924 for the Pacific Settlement of International Disputes, the Resolution of the Eighth Assembly of the League of Nations of 1921, and the Resolution adopted by the twenty-one American Republics at the Sixth Pan-American Conference held at Havana in 1928.[7]

Similarly, Professor Glueck, while affirming the authority of the United Nations "as an act of the will of the conqueror" to frame and adopt the Charter of the International Military Tribunal, undertakes to show "that the time has arrived in the life of civilized nations when an international *custom* has developed to hold aggressive war to be an international crime."[8] If the existence of such a custom could be proved, those lawyers "who insist that it is 'illegal' and *'ex post facto'* to regard aggressive war as a crime and to hold individual members of a Government responsible for such a crime"[9] would be convinced that their apprehensions or charges are without foundation in international law.

Somewhat along the lines of Mr. Justice Jackson's thought, Professor Glueck relies on the Kellogg-Briand Pact, the draft Treaty of Mutual Assistance of 1923, the Geneva Protocol of 1924, the League of Nations Resolution of 1921, the Havana Resolution of 1928, the General Convention of Inter-American Conciliation of 1928, and the Anti-War Treaty of Non-Aggression signed at Rio de Janeiro on October 10, 1933,[10] known as the Saavedra Lamas Pact. In addition, Professor Glueck refers to one or two unofficial statements[11] and to certain of the Hague Conventions of 1899 and 1907 and the Geneva

[6] "Reports of Robert H. Jackson to the President, released by the White House on June 7, 1945," *Trial of War Criminals*, p. 9, and *Proceedings*, Part I, p. 81. The Tribunal also stressed the dynamic character of international law and, adopting the thesis urged upon it by the prosecution, declared "that resort to a war of aggression is not merely illegal, but is criminal." *Judgment*, p. 41. However, whereas Mr. Justice Jackson claims that the principle referred to above had been in existence at the time the Nazis came to power, the Tribunal held that the Charter "is the expression of international law existing at the time of its creation," that is, in 1945. *Judgment*, p. 38. This is a significant discrepancy. As the violation of the Kellog-Briand Pact by Germany occurred in 1939, the existence of the alleged principle should have been traced back to that period.

[7] *Trial of War Criminals*, p. 10. See also *Proceedings*, Part I, p. 81.

[8] Glueck, *op. cit.*, pp. 25, 26. See also *ibid.*, pp. 34, 45.

[9] *Ibid.*, p. 25.

[10] *Ibid.*, pp. 28–32. The Tribunal supports its thesis by the Pact of Paris, the draft Treaty of Mutual Assistance, the Geneva Protocol, the Assembly Resolution of 1927, the Havana Resolution of 1928, the Treaty of Versailles, and the case *Ex Parte* Quirin decided by the United States Supreme Court in 1942. *Judgment*, p. 40 f.

[11] *Ibid.*, pp. 32–34.

Conventions of 1929 relative to the treatment of prisoners of war and for the amelioration of the condition of wounded and sick of armies in the field, respectively.[12]

It goes without saying that the norms of positive international law are derived chiefly from custom as well as from treaty. The only question is whether there is sufficient evidence to prove the existence of a customary norm or principle of international law to the effect that aggressive war is an international crime. Unofficial statements are hardly relevant in this connection. They illustrate at best a trend in professional circles or in public opinion. The Hague and Geneva Conventions were designed to reduce the unavoidable suffering involved in warfare; to that extent, they may be said to have shaped the *ius in bello* without attempting to regulate extensively the *ius ad bellum.*

The Kellogg-Briand Pact, while it condemned recourse to war for the solution of international controversies, fails to make the violation of this declaration a crime under international law. The Pact also contains no evidence that a violation of the self-denying ordinance—not to resort to war as an instrument of national policy—would be considered as a crime under the Pact or under general international law. These two omissions are of some significance, since the draftsmen of the Pact, or at least some of them, must have been conversant with the Assembly Resolution of 1927 and the terms of the draft Treaty of Mutual Assistance of 1923 and of the Geneva Protocol of 1924. Here there was a rare opportunity to establish the rule that henceforth resort to aggressive war, or to war as an instrument of national policy, or as an instrument of solving international controversies, shall be deemed to constitute an international crime. The opportunity was not seized. This solemn treaty, duly signed and ratified or adhered to by the great majority of the members of the family of nations, lends no support to the view that aggressive war is a crime in the precise meaning of the term. On the contrary, far from viewing the violation of the declarations and obligations incorporated in the Pact as an international crime, the High Contracting Parties were content to declare in the preamble of the Pact that "any signatory power which shall hereafter seek to promote its national interests by resort to war should be denied the benefits furnished by this Treaty." This was an important though primarily negative clarification of the status of the treaty-breaking state: such a state could not use the Pact as a shield against appropriate action by the other signatories. In view of the fundamental and unconditional obligation not to use war as an instrument of national policy, such a clarification was useful in removing any possible doubt in the matter.[13] Beyond this, the Pact neither specifies nor limits the sanctions which the opposing signatories may decide to impose upon the violators. They are free to act within the limits of international law.

[12] *Ibid.,* pp. 27, 28. The prosecution in the Japanese War Crimes Trial adopted a similar trend of thought. Cf. "Trial of Japanese War Criminals," Department of State, Publication 2613 (1946), p. 14 f.

[13] See note of the French Ambassador to the Secretary of State, Mar. 30, 1928. *Treaty for the Renunciation of War.* Department of State Publication No. 468, 1933, p. 27; note of the British Secretary of State for Foreign Affairs to the American Ambassador, May 19, 1928, *ibid.,* p. 44; address by M. Aristide Briand, French Minister of Foreign Affairs, delivered at Paris, Aug. 27, 1928, preceding the signing of the Treaty, *ibid.,* p. 314. See also James T. Shotwell, *War as an Instrument of National Policy* (1929), pp. 220–226.

Unofficial proposals for implementing the Kellogg-Briand Pact made by individual writers, and notably by the International Law Association,[14] are not relevant to this context. Moreover, it is conceded that both the responsible statesmen and writers as well "were far from regarding it as an international penal statute."[15] A resort to war in violation of the Kellogg-Briand Pact may properly be regarded as illegal, but not as criminal.[16] If the violation of the Pact cannot be regarded as an international crime, then the Pact must be struck from the list of instruments which have recently come to be construed as having contributed a legal foundation to the formation of a customary or conventional international norm making aggressive war a criminal offense.

On September 29, 1923, the Assembly of the League of Nations unanimously adopted a Resolution requesting the Council "to submit the draft Treaty of Mutual Assistance to the Governments for their consideration, asking them to communicate their views in regard to the aforesaid draft Treaty."[17] Article 1 of the draft reads: "The High Contracting Parties solemnly declare that aggressive war is an international crime and severally undertake that no one of them will be guilty of its commission."[18]

It is not clear whether the term "international crime" was used in the technical sense or as the expression of a general moral reprobation. No evidence has been adduced that the former sense was intended. It is significant, however, that none of the governments which submitted observations on the draft appeared to have been aware that in Article 1 a revolutionary departure from the prevailing attitude of the League towards the consequences of war was intended.[19] It would seem, therefore, that until substantial evidence to the contrary is submitted, the 1923 draft Treaty cannot be of assistance in proving that League Members intended to regard a resort to aggressive war as an international crime in the technical sense of Article 6, paragraph (a), of the Charter of the International Military Tribunal.[20] The fact that the draft never became a binding treaty productive of legal obligations would tend further to reduce its value as a precedent, even if the term "international crime" were shown to have the technical meaning which is apparently attributed to it at the present moment.

The Geneva Protocol for the Pacific Settlement of International Disputes, unanimously adopted by forty-eight delegations present in the Assembly of the League of Na-

[14] Cf. Quincy Wright, "The Meaning of the Pact of Paris," *American Journal of International Law*, Vol. 27 (1933), pp. 39–61; H. Lauterpacht, "The Pact of Paris and the Budapest Articles of Interpretation," *Transactions of the Grotius Society*, Vol 20 (1935), pp. 178–202, particularly at p. 181 f. and p. 186; International Law Association, *38th Report* (1934), p. 66.

[15] Glueck, *op. cit.*, p.19.

[16] Thus Glueck, *ibid.*, p. 21.

[17] League of Nations, *Official Journal*, Sp. Supp. No. 13 (1923), p. 154.

[18] *Ibid.*, p. 403.

[19] "Reduction of Armaments. Treaty of Mutual Assistance. Replies from Governments." Doc. A. 35. 1924. IX. The Finnish government, in its reply of Jan. 18, 1924, observed that "when the Committee describes as an international crime a war which violates the provisions of the Covenant, this is tautology as far as the members of the League are concerned while the states non-members of the League would probably not recognize an act forbidden by the Covenant as an international crime unless it appears as such in the light of the general principles of international law." *Ibid.*, p. 5

[20] But see Glueck, *op. cit.*, p. 28 f.

tions on October 2, 1924, and opened for signature on the same date, [21] asserts in the Preamble "that a war of aggression constitutes a violation of international solidarity and an international crime."[22] Still in the Preamble, the desire is expressed "of ensuring the repression of international crimes." It is said that this Protocol "did express the strong attitude of leading jurists and statesmen of most of the nations of the world regarding both the illegality and the criminalism of aggressive war."[23] The use of the term "international crime" on two occasions, although only in the Preamble and not in any of the articles of the Protocol, is certainly significant. It remains to be seen whether here, any more than in the draft Treaty of 1923, the members of the League intended to attribute to the term "international crime" the technical meaning attributed to it now.

The comments of M. Politis and M. Beneš, two statesmen most intimately involved in the drafting of the Protocol, disclose no such intent. In view of the epochal importance now attributed to the words "international crime, " it is surprising to find that M. Politis in his comment on the Preamble and on the condemnation of aggressive war did not find it necessary to draw the attention of the League members to the new approach to the problem of responsibility for aggressive war.[24] Nor is there any indication in the comments by Mr. Beneš that the punishment of the aggressor should thenceforth be based on the principle of individual criminality rather than, as theretofore, on the principle of collective responsibility. On the contrary, the references in the Protocol itself to the sanctions of Article 16 of the Covenant would seem to confirm the intention of the draftsmen to fit the Protocol into the framework of the Covenant.[25] In commenting upon the sanctions against an aggressor state, M. Beneš stresses Article 15 of the Protocol which introduces the idea that the cost of measures undertaken for the repression of aggression "shall be borne by the aggressor state up to the extreme limit of its capacity."[26] This statement does not permit of any other conclusion than that the Geneva Protocol, in spite of the words "international crime," was not intended to change the collective character of the sanctions provided for in Article 16 of the Covenant. If the latter have sometimes been referred to as "punitive" measures, "punitive" in such a context did not mean "criminal."

In the memorable words of M. Beneš, the purpose of the draftsmen of the Geneva Protocol was "to make war impossible, to kill it, to annihilate it."[27] To this purpose the "gaps" in the Covenant were filled by establishing a comprehensive system of compul-

[21] Assembly Resolution, Oct. 2, 1924, *Official Journal,* Sp. Supp. No. 23 (1924), p. 225. Mr. Justice Jackson's statement that the Geneva Protocol was "signed by the representatives of forty-eight Governments" *(Trial of War Criminals,* p. 10, and *Proceedings,*, Part I, p. 80, is somewhat exaggerated. The Protocol was signed on behalf of nineteen Governments. Cf. "Signatures, Ratifications, and Accessions in respect of Agreements and Conventions Concluded under the Auspices of the League of Nations." Twenty-first List. *Official Journal,* Sp. Supp. No. 193 (1944), p. 155.

[22] The term "international crime" in this context presumably refers to aggressive war. Cf. P. J. Noel-Baker, *The Geneva Protocol* (1925), p. 29.

[23] Glueck, *op. cit.,* p. 30.

[24] Cf. "General Report submitted to the Assembly on behalf of the First and Third Committees by M. Politis, Rapporteur for the First Committee, and M. Beneš, Rapporteur for the Third Committee." Doc. A. 135 (1). 1924. IX. *Official Journal,* Sp. Supp. No. 23, 1924, pp. 479 ff., at p. 482 f.

[25] But cf. Glueck, *op. cit.,* p. 30.

[26] Cf. "General Report," p. 495.

[27] *Ibid.,* p. 497.

sory arbitration and an effective chain of sanctions. But this system included no penalty for individuals, and it certainly failed to implement the notion that aggressive war constitutes an international crime.

The Report of the British Delegates relating to the Geneva Protocol, November 1, 1924, would probably have drawn the attention of the British government to any intended revolutionary changes in the structure of international law and of the Covenant of the League. In the view of the British delegates, however, there was apparently no need for doing so; as for the Geneva Protocol, "so far as it contains anything new, it is to be found in the definition of aggression which follows as a necessary corollary to the limitations inserted in the establishment of a universal system of peaceful settlement. But even here the principle is not new."[28] Here—that is, in Article 10 of the Geneva Protocol—is the new feature; but even this apparent innovation is said to be merely an elaboration of the Covenant. Be that as it may, Article 10 certainly contemplated only states as aggressors, and only states could commit the crime of aggression.[29] The "guilt" of initiating and waging an aggressive war—that is, the guilt of committing the international crime mentioned in the Preamble of the Protocol—would be the guilt of a state. It could not be otherwise. The sanctions elaborated in Article 11 are quite logically conceived as collective measures directed against the "criminal"—that is, the aggressor state.

On the basis of this brief survey of preparatory work and contemporary opinion, it is difficult to accept the proposition that "the signature of the Protocol by the leading statesmen of the world, representing the vast majority of civilized states and peoples, is itself evidence of a strongly entrenched custom to regard aggressive war as an international crime."[30] It seems scarcely compatible with the requirements of sound juristic construction to put forward the mere repetition of the term "international crime" as evidence of a "strongly entrenched custom."

The Resolution adopted by the League of Nations Assembly on September 24, 1927, is regarded as a further link in the chain of events which are said to have contributed to the formation of an international custom to regard aggressive war as an international crime. In this Resolution, the Assembly expressed its conviction "that a war of aggression can never serve as a means of settling international disputes and is, in consequence, an international crime."[31] In the view of Professor Glueck, this Resolution

[28] "League of Nations. Fifth Assembly. Report of the British Delegates relating to the Protocol for the Peaceful Settlement of International Disputes." *British Parliamentary Papers*, Misc. No. 21 (1924), Cmd. 2289, p. 8. Cf. D. H. Miller, *The Geneva Protocol* (1925), pp. 11, 23 f., 106–113. Mr. Miller examined the Geneva Protocol "primarily from the legal viewpoint" *(ibid., p. 3)*, and the fact that he virtually disregarded the condemnation of war as an international crime *(ibid.*, p. 54) may perhaps be interpreted as implying that, from a legal standpoint at any rate, no criminal-law principles have found their way into the Protocol.

[29] Noel-Baker, *op. cit.*, p. 114.

[30] Glueck, *op. cit.*, p. 29, note 14. It may be observed in passing that the Protocol was signed on behalf of no more than nineteen governments, which did not represent the vast majority of civilized states and peoples. It was signed on behalf of Albania, Belgium, Brazil, Bulgaria, Chile, Czechoslovakia, Estonia, Finland, France, Greece, Haiti, Latvia, Liberia, Paraguay, Poland, Portugal, the Kingdom of the Serbs, Croats and Slovenes, Spain, and Uruguay. Cf. "Signatures, Ratifications . . ." p. 155. The Tribunal repeats almost textually Professor Glueck's estimate of the Geneva Protocol *Judgment*, p. 40. It thus repeats his error regarding "the vast majority of civilized states and peoples."

[31] League of Nations, *Official Journal*, Sp. Supp. No. 54, 1927, p. 155.

shows "how strong was the conviction that the time had arrived in the affairs of states and their peoples, to call a spade a spade."[32] If he means thereby that the Assembly Resolution was intended to create a rule of international law making aggressive war an international crime in the technical sense of the word, such an interpretation finds no support in the words of the Rapporteur of the Third Committee, M. Sokal, who introduced the Resolution. M. Sokal reported to the Assembly that the Committee was of the opinion that the Resolution "would have a salutary effect on public opinion and would help to create an atmosphere favorable to the League's future work in the matter of security and disarmament." In order to dispel any possible doubt as to the interpretation to be placed upon the proposed resolution, M. Sokal made the following significant statement:[33] "While recognizing that the draft resolution does not constitute a regular legal instrument which would be adequate in itself and represent a concrete contribution towards security, the Third Committee unanimously agreed as to its great moral and educative value."

As author of the Resolution and as Rapporteur of the Third Committee, M. Sokal was certainly in a position to submit an authoritative interpretation of the Resolution's sense and intent. There is no evidence that the members of the League interpreted the Resolution which they adopted in a different light, e.g., as productive of legal changes in the body of positive international law. On the basis of available evidence, the conclusion seems inevitable that no legal significance can be attached to that Resolution, and that the latter cannot serve to substantiate the far-reaching claims put forth on its behalf. [34] The attribution to the Assembly of legislative powers in the domain of international law would necessarily have to be based on two assumptions: first, that the Assembly was competent to create international law; and secondly, that the Assembly was competent to do so by means of resolutions. For both of these assumptions there is no foundation.[34a]

It remains to consider some instruments adopted by the American Republics. At the Sixth International Conference of American States held at Havana in 1928, a Resolution on Arbitration and Conciliation was adopted in which the American Republics desired "to express that they condemn war as an instrument of national policy in their mutual relations."[35] In another Resolution on Aggression adopted at the same Conference, the American States, considering "that war of aggression constitutes an international crime against the human species," resolved that "all aggression is considered illicit and as such is declared prohibited."[36] It does not appear from the official Report of the American

[32] Glueck, *op. cit.*, p. 31.

[33] League of Nations, *Official Journal,* Sp. Supp. No. 54, 1927, p. 155.

[34] Cf. *ibid.*, p. 83, where M. Sokal explains the motives behind the draft resolution which he submitted to the Assembly. M. Sokal's proposal was discussed in the Third Committee. Cf. Minutes of the Third Committee, *Official Journal,* Sp. Supp. No. 57, particularly pp. 45–47. The statement of the delegate of the Netherlands, M. Loudon, is of special significance because it draws a clear line between the "great moral value" of the Polish proposal and "the outlawry of war in a more legal form." *Ibid.*, p. 46.

[34a] Cf. Dietrich Schindler, "Die Verbindlichkeit der Beschlüsse des Völkerbundes" (1927), *passim.*

[35] James Brown Scott (ed.), *International Conferences of American States, 1889–1928* (1931), p. 437.

[36] *Ibid.*, p. 441 f.

Delegation to that Conference that any particular importance or legal meaning was attached to the condemnation of war or to the declaration that it constituted an international crime.[37]

Pursuant to the Havana Resolution, an International Conference of American States on Arbitration and Conciliation was held in Washington in 1928–29. This Conference adopted the "General Convention of Inter-American Conciliation," the Preamble of which expressed the desire "to demonstrate that the condemnation of war as an instrument of national policy in their mutual relations . . . constitutes one of the fundamental bases of inter-American relations."[38] The Convention, however, deals with arbitration and conciliation and makes no attempt at implementing the condemnation of war. It may be pertinent to refer here to the cogent statement of the American delegate, Mr. Charles E. Hughes, in the Committee on Arbitration.[39] We are not here to add to international law. We are not here to codify international law. We are not here to create, we have no power to create, additional rights under international law. We have no power to impose upon any state additional duties under international law. We are simply providing means for pacific settlement."

Finally, the Anti-War Treaty on Non-Aggression and Conciliation, signed at Rio de Janeiro on October 10, 1933, included in the Preamble a condemnation "of wars of aggression and territorial acquisitions that may be obtained by armed conquest." In Article I, the contracting parties "solemnly declare that they condemn wars of aggression in their mutual relations or those with other states."[40] This treaty, commonly known as the Saavedra Lamas Pact, is the American counterpart to the Kellogg-Briand Pact. Carlos Saavedra Lamas explained the purpose of the proposed Anti-War Pact in these terms: "The Argentine Government wishes thus to contribute to the uniform acceptance of the Kellogg-Briand Pact and, what is of greater importance, to its effective application through the conclusion among the South American Republics of a similar and coinciding agreement, intended to coöperate in the attainment of the same lofty aims."[41] The Saavedra Lamas Pact is thus presented as an improved Kellogg-Briand Pact. The improvement, however, is not sought in the realm of penal sanctions against individuals, but in the realm of methods and procedures for the peaceful settlement of international controversies.[42]

The conclusion drawn by Professor Glueck from the above resolutions, treaties, and draft treaties is as follows:[43] "All these solemn expressions of the conviction of civilized

[37] Cf. "Report of the Delegates of the U.S.A. to the Sixth International Conference of American States." U. S. Govt. Printing Office (1928), p. 26.

[38] Scott, *op. cit.*, p. 455.

[39] "Proceedings of the International Conference of American States on Conciliation and Arbitration," Washington, Dec. 10, 1928–Jan. 5, 1929. U.S. Govt. Printing Office (1929), p. 614.

[40] U.S. Treaty Series, No. 906, 1936.

[41] "The Anti-War Treaty proposed by Argentina and the Brazilian Reply," *Bulletin* of the Pan American Union, Apr., 1933, p. 320 ff., at p. 327.

[42] *Ibid.*, p. 341 f.

[43] Glueck, *op. cit.*, p. 34. Similarly Sir Hartley Shawcross: "Thus there is no doubt that by the time the National Socialist State of Germany had embarked upon the preparation of the war of aggression against the civilized world, and by the

States and statesmen regarding the need for conciliation, for the settlement of international disputes by pacific means only, for the renunciation of war as an instrument of national policy, and, logically, for the recognition that aggressive war is an international crime, greatly reënforce whatever inference to that effect is derivable from the Kellogg-Briand Pact itself. They may be regarded as powerful evidence of the existence of a widely prevalent custom among civilized peoples sufficient to energize a juristic climate favorable to the regarding of a war of aggression as not simply unjust or illegal, but down-right *criminal.*"

Mr. Justice Jackson, having made a somewhat less exhaustive review of the relevant documents, prefers to rely chiefly upon the Kellogg-Briand Pact, and he argues that a violation of this Pact "cannot be regarded as anything less than a crime against the international community." He concludes: "We therefore propose to charge that a war of aggression is a crime, and that modern international law has abolished the defense that those who incite or wage it are engaged in legitimate business."[44] The preparatory work, the intrinsic meaning of the acts in question, and contemporary opinion, it is believed, fail to substantiate any such far-reaching conclusions. The most that may be said is that governments on several occasions have used a terminology which, separated from its context and attending circumstances, can easily be misunderstood. It has indeed been said that "the concepts of crime, culpability, or responsibility" employed in connection with aggressive war "were concepts of national criminal law which could hardly be adapted to international relations."[45] Similarly, several governments expressed the opinion that "the desire to effect an extension of sanctions corresponding to the extension of the prohibitions of resort to war contained in the Covenant arose from pushing too far the analogy with the conception of crime and punishment in municipal law."[46]

It is significant that Count 2 of the indictment against the Nazi defendants is not based upon the charge that they had violated "customary international law."[47] The charges preferred against them do not include the various resolutions and draft treaties which are said to have formed new customary international law in the matter of aggressive war and individual criminal responsibility. They include notably the Kellogg-Briand Pact and several other treaties, agreements, and assurances to which Germany was a party.[48] Under positive international law, a violation of these treaties, agreements, and assurances exposed Germany to such sanctions as the governments concerned should

time it had accomplished that design, aggressive war had become, in virtue of the Pact of Paris, and the treaties and declarations to which I have referred, illegal and a crime beyond all uncertainty and doubt. And it is on that proposition, and fundamentally on that Universal Treaty, the Briand-Kellogg Pact, that Count 2 of this Indictment is principally based." *Proceedings,* Part II, p. 54.

[44] *Trial of War Criminals,* p. 10. See also *Proceedings,* Part I, p. 80 f.

[45] Remarks made by Dr. Cohn, the delegate of Denmark, in the First Committee of the Tenth Assembly, on Sept. 17, 1929, in connection with the proposed amendment of the Covenant in order to bring it into harmony with the Kellogg-Briand Pact. *Official Journal,* Sp. Supp. No. 76 (1929), p. 29.

[46] "Report of the First Committee [Rapporteur M. Henri Rollin] to the Assembly." Doc. A. 86. 1931. V. *Official Journal,* Sp. Supp. No. 93 (1931), p. 220.

[47] But see Glueck, *op. cit.,* p. 36.

[48] *Trial of War Criminals,* Appendix C., p. 82–89.

eventually determine as appropriate with a view to insuring, in the future, a greater degree of respect for international legal obligations.

In the formation of customary international law, the time element is, of course, important, but perhaps not exclusively controlling. A mere practice of states, a habit of doing things in a certain manner, no matter how long or how widely practiced, could not, it is submitted, create by itself new customary international law. The Permanent Court of International Justice, in the Lotus case, rejected the French attempt to derive a rule of positive international law regarding jurisdiction in collision cases from the practice of states by saying that the agent of the French government had merely succeeded in showing "that states had often, in practice, abstained from instituting criminal proceedings, and not that they recognized themselves as being obliged to do so." The Court went on to say: "For only if such abstention were based on their being conscious of having a duty to abstain would it be possible to speak of an international custom. The alleged fact does not allow one to infer that states have been conscious of having such a duty."[49] The same thought, of course, is at the root of Article 38, paragraph 2, of the Statute of the Permanent Court of International Justice, which reads: "International custom, as evidence of a general practice accepted as law.[50] The Statute of the International Court of Justice contains an identic clause in Article 38, paragraph 1 (b). Westlake said: "Custom must not be confounded with mere frequency or even habit of conduct. In any state or society in which customary law is admitted, custom as a part of law means the conduct which is enforced as well as the strict or loose nature of the society allows . . . and which is followed as well from the fear of such enforcement as from the persuasion that the received rule requires such conduct to be followed. In other words, custom is that line of conduct which the society has consented to regard as obligatory."[51] Thus the mere habit of repeating certain formulae must be distinguished from the practice or usage of states which is inspired by a sense of legal obligation. Little, if any, evidence of such practice has been offered in the matter of criminal responsibility of individuals for instituting wars of aggression.

Moreover, it is common ground for a majority of international lawyers that the law of nations is based upon the consent or acquiescence of states.[52] It must be noted that the text of, and the circumstances attending, the resolutions, draft treaties, and treaties discussed above do not disclose on the part of the governments concerned the necessary consent to or acquiescence in the establishment of a new rule of international law making aggressive war a crime in the technical sense of the word.

[49] Permanent Court of International Justice, *Publications*, Series A, No. 10 (1927), p. 28.

[50] Judge Manley O. Hudson, commenting on this clause, said: "The elements necessary are the concordant and recurring action of numerous states in the domain of international relations, the conception in each case that such action was enjoined by law, and the failure of other states to challenge that conception at the time. The appreciation of these elements is not a simple matter, and it is a task for persons trained in law." *The Permanent Court of International Justice, 1920–1942* (1943) p. 609.

[51] John Westlake, *International Law*, Vol. I (1910), p. 14; Charles Cheney Hyde, *International Law* (second ed.), Vol. I, (1945), p. 11.

[52] Green H. Hackworth, *Digest of International Law*, Vol. I (1941), p. 1 ff.; Hyde, *op. cit.*, p. 4 ff.

Without stretching to the breaking-point the accepted notions of custom in international law, it does not seem admissible to deduce such a rule from mere pronouncements that aggressive war is condemned as international crime. Such pronouncements, significant as they undoubtedly are, were made as M. Sokal explains, for their "moral and educative value."[52a] Having regard to the usual circumspection of governments, it appears inconceivable that what may probably become the most revolutionary change in the history of modern international law should have been brought about in a haphazard manner and without thorough preparation or discussion, and without clearly expressed intent on the part of the governments concerned. For this reason, it would seem doubtful whether an international tribunal, displaying the traditional judicial caution in the administration of international law, would have found the Nazi defendants guilty of "crimes against peace" under customary international law.[53] For the same reason, the Charter of the International Military Tribunal cannot be regarded as merely receiving, confirming, or codifying an existing "international custom, as evidence of a general practice accepted as law."

Mr. Justice Jackson's contention "that the London Agreement only recognized an evolution that already had been consummated"[54] does not seem to be supported by sound evidence. It would be more in harmony with the teachings and practice of international law to say that the Charter created, *inter partes,* a new principle for which, this may be admitted, a favorable climate had been prepared in the inter-war period. In doing so, the Charter may be regarded as expressing a profound sense of justice and as adapting the traditional concept of the sanctions in international law to the more refined technique of law-enforcement prevailing in the municipal law of civilized communities. In making individuals responsible for fidelity to fundamental international law, it takes into account a wide-spread postulate that individuals should be made subjects of international law to a larger extent and on a more permanent basis than had been the case heretofore. The Charter may well come to be regarded as having blazed a new trail for "the firm establishment of the understandings of international law as the actual rule of conduct among governments."[55] But until this principle is generally accepted by states, there will be a period of

[52a] The Tribunal, however, finds that the acts in question "may be regarded as strong evidence of the intention to brand aggressive war as an international crime." *Judgment,* p. 40.

[53] The value of the judgment of the International Military Tribunal, unsupported as it is by authority as a precedent in international law is problematic. True it is that certain *dicta* of the Tribunal may be regarded as endorsing the views set forth by Messrs. Jackson and Glueck. It is, however, important to bear in mind that the Tribunal repeatedly declared that it was bound by the law established by the Four Powers in the Charter. Thus, with reference to Article 6 of the Charter, it stated: "These provisions are binding upon the Tribunal as the law to be applied to the case." And in a different context it said categorically that "the law of the Charter is decisive, and binding upon the Tribunal." Of significance is also the following: "The Charter makes the planning or waging of a war of aggression or a war in violation of international treaties a crime; and it is therefore not strictly necessary to consider whether and to what extent aggressive war was a crime before the execution of the London Agreement. But in view of the great importance of the questions of law involved, the Tribunal has heard full argument from the Prosecution and Defence and will express its views on the matter." *Judgment,* pp. 3, 38.

[54] Foreward to Professor Glueck's book, *The Nuremberg Trial and Aggressive War,,* p. x.

[55] Preamble to the Covenant of the League of Nations.

transition from the traditional concept of collective responsibility for illicit conduct of states to the new concept of individual responsibility for crimes against international law.[56]

It was perhaps with the desire to hasten this process that President Truman, in his opening address to the General Assembly of the United Nations on October 23, 1946, recalled that "twenty-three members of the United Nations have bound themselves by the Charter of the Nuremberg Tribunal to the principle that planning, initiating, or waging a war of aggression is a crime against humanity for which individuals as well as states shall be tried before the bar of international justice."[57] While this constitutes a strong endorsement of the Charter of the International Military Tribunal, one may well doubt whether the particular formulation chosen by the President lends support to the thesis advocated by Mr. Justice Jackson. Obviously in contradiction with that thesis, however, appears a statement made by Mr. Trygve Lie, Secretary-General of the United Nations, in his oral supplementary report to the General Assembly: "In the interest of peace and in order to protect mankind against future wars, it will be of decisive significance to have the principles which were employed at the Nuremberg trials, and according to which the German war criminals were sentenced, made a permanent part of the body of international law as quickly as possible."[58] Here the Secretary-General seems to proceed on the theory, which is believed to be correct, that thus far the criminal responsibility of individuals for crimes against peace does not form part of international law. It is to be hoped that a way will be found, by amending the Charter of the United Nations or otherwise, to establish *pro futuro* rather than *pro praeterito,* as is the case in the Charter of the International Military Tribunal, the truly revolutionary principle of individual responsibility for crimes against peace.[59] This is a task of the highest importance, and one which can best be accomplished by that process known as international legislation. It cannot, it is submitted, be the task of international lawyers to attempt to remove "the in-

[56] Hyde, *op. cit.*, p. 8 f. See also H. Lauterpacht, *The Development of International Law by the Permanent Court of International Justice* (1934), p. 103; W. Friedman, "International Law and the Present War," *Modern Law Review*, Vol. 3 (1941), p. 179 f.

[57] *Journal of the United Nations,* No. 13: Supp. A-A/P. V/34, p. 8.

[58] *Journal of the United Nations,* No. 15: Supp. A-A/P. V/35, P. 24.

[59] The General Assembly of the United Nations, on Dec. 11, 1946, adopted unanimously a Resolution proposed by the United States Delegation in which it "affirms the principles of international law recognized by the Charter of the Nürnberg *(sic)* Tribunal and the Judgment of the Tribunal" and "directs the Committee on the codification of international law . . . to treat as a matter of primary importance plans for the formulation, in the context of a general codification of offences against the peace and security of mankind, or of an International Criminal Code, of the principles recognized in the Charter of the Nürnberg *(sic)* Tribunal and in the judgment of the Tribunal." *Journal of the United Nations,* No. 58: Supp. A-A/P. V/55, p. 485. The delegate of Cuba pointed out in the Sixth Committee (Legal Questions) that he could not vote for the proposed resolution "because it affirmed the principles of international law by a mere reference to them, without enumerating them explicitly. The Cuban delegation," he said, "thought that the adoption of principles of such importance should not be based on mere references, but should be the outcome of a thorough study of each of the principles concerned." *Journal of the United Nations,* No. 56: Supp. No. 6-A/C. 6/123, p. 127. For these reasons, the representatives of Cuba, Argentina, and Peru voted against the proposal in the Sixth Committee. *Journal of the United Nations,* No. 58: Supp. No. 6-A/C. 6/127, p. 129. See also Documents A/C. 6/116 and A/236. It should be noted that this Resolution followed the action of nineteen governments of the United Nations which had previously expressed their adherence to the London Agreement. Cf. *Judgment,* p. 1.

consistencies and short-comings of international law . . . by juristic effort, however well-meaning.''[59a]

Is it, then, in the light of the foregoing considerations, necessary, as has been thought by some critics of the Nuremberg Trial, to conclude that the trial was ''illegal'' because *ex post facto?* Illegal from the viewpoint of international law, or from that of the municipal law of one or the other states party to the London Agreement, of which the Charter of the International Military Tribunal forms an integral part? Obviously, the standard of comparison which must be adopted cannot be other than that of international law.

The relevant question then is: Is there in positive international law a rule, comparable to Article I, sec. 9, par. 3, of the Constitution of the United States, prohibiting *ex post facto* legislation? Those who affirm the illegality of the Nuremberg Trial[60] have not taken the trouble to prove the existence of such a restrictive rule. It would indeed be difficult to do so, for, as the Permanent Court of International Justice declared in the Lotus case, restrictions upon the independence of states cannot be presumed.[61]

Starting from this premise, the following line of reasoning might be adopted to justify the legality of the London Agreement. In a primitive society such as the international community, in which there are no centralized institutions for legislation, adjudication, and law enforcement, states must provide for their security as best they can, always acting within the accepted rules and principles of international law. To assert the existence of a prohibition to create new norms and endow them with retroactive effect would be a serious limitation upon the independence of states. Furthermore, such an assertion could be successfully maintained only if it were shown that there are in international law not merely substantive, but also formal, norms having the character of a constitutional or higher law which cannot be changed by the traditional process of treatymaking between independent states. This presupposes an analogy between international law and, e.g., the federal law of the United States, which is based on a written, enacted constitution. For such an analogy there appears to be no foundation in the theory of positive international law or in the practice of states. If an analogy must be drawn, it is suggested that the British constitution lends itself better for this purpose than the American. Although lacking a formal constitution in the American sense, there are in Great Britain principles and norms having constitutional character. But Parliament is supreme. An act of Parliament could not be held unconstitutional even if it materially altered or suspended some of the fundamental norms of the realm.[62]

[59a] Lauterpacht, *The Pact of Paris and the Budapest Articles of Interpretation,* p. 190.

[60] Cf. writers cited in Glueck, op. cit., p. 74, note 3. As mentioned above, Professor Glueck seems to deny substantive, but does not entirely rule out formal retroactivity. *Ibid.,* p. 91.

[61] Permanent Court of International Justice, *Publications,* Series A, No. 9, p. 18.

[62] See Frederic A. Ogg, *European Governments and Politics* (2nd ed., 1945), p. 36 f.: ''Leaving out of account practical and moral restraints which operate powerfully upon it, and thinking only of what may be done under the law, Parliament can alter or rescind any charter, agreement, or statute; it can cause any official of the government to be dismissed and any judicial decision to be made of no effect; it can put an end to any usage and overturn any rule of common law; it can bend the constitution in any direction that it desires. It follows that every parliamentary act is 'constitutional'; if a measure is

A similar situation may be said to prevail in common international law. States are bound by the body of international law. But at the same time they are, like Parliament, supreme law-makers. A treaty may be said to derogate a custom and a later treaty to derogate an earlier treaty between the parties concerned. Thus, even if *ex post facto* norms were prohibited by international law, which has been denied,[63] it could be argued that states may depart from this prohibition by mutual consent without committing an illicit act.

If this line of reasoning were accepted as admissible, a good deal of current criticism might have been avoided if the Four Powers, following the precedent of the Treaty of Versailles, had decided to secure the adherence of the German government to the London Agreement. In the case of Germany, this was not possible because no German government was at the time in existence.[64] The Four Powers could have acted on behalf of Germany.[65] This, they have not done. Could they impose their will upon Germany? This is, in fact, asserted by Professor Glueck,[66] and the International Military Tribunal, declared:[67] "The making of the Charter was the legitimate exercise of sovereign legislative power by the countries to which the German Reich unconditionally surrendered."

In concluding, it may be well to recall the words of Grotius concerning "the duty of the victor toward those who make an unconditional surrender." On the one hand, Grotius observed that "wars are well ended when they terminate with pardoning." But on the other hand, he remarked: ". . . I do not think that it makes any difference whether the one who surrenders says that he surrenders himself to the wisdom, or to the moderation, or to the mercifulness, of the victor. All these words are merely gracious expressions. The fact remains that the victor becomes absolute master."[68] It seems that the passage of three hundred years or so has not materially improved the condition of the enemy that has unconditionally surrendered.

passed which is contrary to the constitution as it has hitherto stood, the constitution simply becomes something different in that regard. One who follows English political discussion even from afar, will now and then hear it charged that a legislative proposal, or even a law, is unconstitutional. But this means only that somebody considers the offending proposal or act to be inconsistent with previously accepted fundamental law, or with an established usage, or with international law, or perhaps only with the accepted standards of morality. An act so regarded is legally quite as valid and enforceable as if no question had been raised. No one can allege that it is *ultra vires.* The word of Parliament, i.e. the *latest* word, is law, however it may cut across existing constitutional arrangements; and as such it will be enforced by the courts."

[63] Hans Kelsen, *Peace Through Law* (1944), p. 87.

[64] In the case of the International Military Tribunal for the Far East, the consent of the Japanese government to the trial of Japanese war criminals is presumed to have been granted in the instrument of surrender signed by Japan on Sept. 2, 1945. Department of State *Bulletin,* Vol. XIV (1946), p. 361.

[65] The basis for this is the Declaration regarding the Defeat of Germany and the Assumption of Supreme Authority with respect to Germany, paragraph 5 of the Preamble, and Articles 11 and 13. *American Journal of International Law,* Vol. 39 (1945), Supp., p. 171 ff.

[66] Glueck, *op. cit.,* p. 25: "There is no question but that, as an act of the will of the conqueror, the United Nations had the authority to frame and adopt such a Charter."

[67] *Judgment,* p. 38.

[68] Grotius, *De Jure Belli ac Pacis,* translated by Francis W. Kelsey. "Classics of International Law," ed. by J. B. Scott, Vol. II (1925), pp. 826, 828.

# THE PUNISHMENT OF WAR CRIMINALS: THE NUREMBERG TRIAL

## I. INTRODUCTION

When the International Military Tribunal on October 1, 1946, pronounced judgment on 22 Germans accused as major war criminals, a truly historic trial came to an end. It was the first such tribunal constituted by a number of Great Powers and in the interests of all the United Nations. Since the beginning of the modern state system, this was the first time that the leaders of a Great Power, its statesmen, soldiers, journalists and propagandists were held accountable for crimes against peace and humanity, which themselves were substantial innovations or developments. Ordinary war crimes, usually within the province of domestic military courts, were also for the first time tried by an international tribunal.

The record of the trial which started on November 14, 1945, comprises, in 42 volumes, not merely an authentic record of the trial itself, but the most remarkable and detailed evidence of the policies and practices of the Nazi regime both before and during World War II. As such it has a unique place in the historic documentation of the policies of a Great Power. Insofar as Germany is concerned, this documentation was substantially amplified by the trials in Nuremberg before American Military Tribunals and elsewhere before British, French and other tribunals of Ministers, diplomats, and high officials in the Foreign Office, of doctors and jurists, of business men and Nazi officials. Altogether 177 Germans were tried by the American Tribunals in Nuremberg.[1] Twenty eight Japanese were tried as major war criminals before the International Military Tribunal for the Far East, the so-called Tokyo Tribunal, which on November 12, 1947, rendered judgment. Altogether a substantial number of major war criminals of the Axis Powers was tried and found guilty by the two international tribunals and many more major and minor war criminals by national tribunals of the various United Nations.[2]

The Nuremberg trial being the first of its kind and the first in a series of trials held by several of the United Nations could not fail to arouse controversy and raise a number of questions such as: was it *ex post facto,* was it contrary to established usage or custom, was it fair and were the defendants accorded the normal privileges, was it in har-

[1] Altogether, the United States War crimes program in all theaters comprised 956 cases in which 3306 defendants were tried. Following is a detailed breakdown of the trials and their results:

| | GERMANY | | | JAPAN | | | | | | |
|---|---|---|---|---|---|---|---|---|---|---|
| | Nuremberg IMT | Nuremberg Other | Dachau | IMT FE | Yokohama and Tokyo | China | Manila | Italy | Navy Pacific Islands | Total |
| No. of Cases | 1 | 12 | 489* | 1 | 321 | 11 | 87 | 9 | 25 | 956 |
| No. of Defendants Tried | 22 | 177 | 1672 | 25 | 998 | 75 | 207 | 14 | 116 | 3306 |
| No. of Defendants Acquitted | 3 | 35 | 256 | 0 | 143 | 8 | 15 | 3 | 8 | 471 |
| No. of Defendants Convicted | 19 | 142 | 1416 | 25 | 855 | 67 | 192 | 11 | 108 | 2835 |
| No. of Death Sentences Adjudged | 12 | 24 | 426 | 7 | 124 | 10 | 88 | 7 | 28 | 726 |
| No. of Death Sentences Executed | 10** | 12 | 260 | 7 | 51 | 6 | 69 | 5 | 11 | 431*** |
| No. of Death Sentences Unexecuted | — | — | — | — | — | — | — | — | — | — |

* Includes 14 Austrian Cases.

** Martin Borman convicted *in absentia*—never apprehended; Herman Goering committed suicide just before time set for execution.

*** Other death sentences commuted, vacated, etc.

[2] It has been estimated that Great Britain held 541 trials, Australia 275, France 271, the Netherlands 35, Poland 25, Norway 11, Canada 5, China 2, and Greece 1. Alan Appleman, *Military Tribunals and International Crimes* (Indianapolis: The Bobbs-Merril Co., 1954), p. 265. As to the Netherlands this estimate appears to be incorrect. According to materials kindly prepared by Professor Verzijl the Netherlands data are:

| | | | | |
|---|---|---|---|---|
| I. Arrested | | | | 489 |
| Released without prosecution | | | 249 | |
| Indicted | 240 | | | |
| Convicted | | 208 | | |
| Acquitted *(vrijspraak, ontslag van rechtsvervolging, niet-ontvankelijk-verklaring)* | | 32 | | |
| | | —— | 240 | |
| | | | —— | 489 |
| II. Convicted | | | | 208 |
| 1 year terms | | 12 | | |
| 1– 5 year terms | | 61 | | |
| 5–10 year terms | | 52 | | |
| 10–15 year terms | | 34 | | |
| 15–20 year terms | | 25 | | |
| life term | | 6 | | |
| death penalty | | 18 | | |
| | | —— | | 208 |
| III. Death sentences | | | | 18 |
| converted into life term through *gratie* (pardon) | | 9 | | |
| executed | | 5 | | |
| default | | 4 | | |
| | | —— | | 18 |

See also *Law Reports of Trials of War Criminals,* Selected and Prepared by the United Nations War Crimes Commission (H.M. Stationary Office, London, 1949, Vol. XV), pp. XVIf.

mony with, or contrary to, international law and justice? Not the least interesting questions are: How was the fateful decision arrived at? What were the alternatives considered and why were some adopted and others rejected?

## II. STATE PRACTICE

According to a still current view regarding the practice of belligerents prior to World War I, peace treaties generally included a so-called amnesty clause according to which nationals of either belligerents, civilians as well as soldiers, were not to be tried and punished for violations of the laws of war.[3]

It is by no means clear what precisely the intent and purpose of such amnesty clauses was. They differ in formulation in different peace treaties. In any event, the meaning of an amnesty is, that a punishment already pronounced is terminated or that a pending trial is stopped by an act of grace of the Government. It surely does not mean that there was no right to try and inflict punishment. The practice of issuing amnesties or pardons of a general or limited nature was moreover criticized on the ground that it was contrary to common sense as all states have an interest in the repression of crimes.[4]

Whether wise or unwise, the pre-World War I practice did not crystallize in a rule of international law *prohibiting* the punishment of war criminals. On the contrary, it may be construed as a recognition of the right of governments to try and punish violators of the rules of war pending hostilities and until the formal termination of war by a peace treaty or otherwise.

It is important to bear in mind that by virtue of international law states are free, within broad limits, to agree to any particular rule which they deem to be in their interest. Thus in the Treaty of Versailles in 1919 the governments concerned insisted on a rule which departed from earlier peace treaties and foreshadowed the war crimes trials connected with World War II. The reason for this departure was, in the first place, the desire to vindicate the respect due to the prescriptions of international law which were so frequently and so flagrantly disregarded in the course of the World War I. Moreover, in earlier wars there may have been some doubt as to what these prescriptions were. Such doubts have been largely removed by the codification of the rules of warfare on land and sea, on the treatment of wounded and prisoners of war which was accomplished at the first and second Hague Conferences in 1899 and 1907.

The Treaty of Versailles provided: (1) (in Art. 227) for the trial of William II, formerly German Emperor, "for a supreme offense against international morality and the sanctity of treaties. . . . with a view to vindicating the solemn obligations of international undertakings and the validity of international law;" (2) (in Art. 228) for the trial and punishment (after the termination of the war) of persons accused of violations of the

[3] Charles G. Fenwick, *International Law* (1924), p. 578; Julius Stone, *Legal Controls of International Conflict* (1954), p. 356; L. Oppenheim *International Law*, Vol. II (7th ed. by H. Lauterpacht, 1952), p. 611.

[4] Coleman Phillipson, *Termination of War and Treaties of Peace*, (1916), p. 246.

laws and customs of war, either (a) before a national military tribunal of the victorious government concerned, or (b) (in Art. 229) before a military tribunal combining several national military tribunals if more than one victorious government was concerned. Germany not merely agreed to these provisions but also undertook to assist in every way by extraditing persons wanted for trial, and by furnishing necessary evidence.

More far-reaching proposals were discussed but not adopted. In some ways, they were to influence the planning for the trials of World War II criminals.

These provisions remained largely on paper, for a variety of reasons, one of which was certainly Germany's obstruction, another, the Netherlands' refusal to hand over William II to the Allies, and, most important, the lack of will to enforce the treaty on the part of the victors. The Versailles experiment taught the Allies at least one lesson, namely, how *not* to set about for trying German war criminals.

From this brief review of State practice prior to World War II, one may conclude: (1) no rule of international law developed which would in any sense militate against the trial of war criminals in the technical sense of the word, *i.e.,* violators of the laws and customs of war; and (2) in actual practice, belligerents have shown neither a strong desire nor any determination to prosecute war criminals once peace was re-established.

## III. WORLD WAR II DEVELOPMENTS

The first formal pronouncement concerning the trial of war criminals was the St. James Declaration of January 13, 1942, in which the governments of Belgium, Czechoslovakia, France, Greece, Luxemburg, the Netherlands, Norway, Poland, and Yugoslavia announced their aim to punish "through the channels of organized justice" crimes committed by Germany in occupied territories. The Declaration referred specifically to "imprisonments, mass expulsions, the execution of hostages, and massacres."[5]

On December 17, 1942, Mr. Anthony Eden, the British Foreign Secretary, stated that the governments of Belgium, Czechoslovakia, Greece, Luxemburg, the Netherlands, Norway, Poland, the United States of America, the United Kingdom, the U.S.S.R., Yugoslavia and the French Committee of National Liberation "condemned in the strongest possible terms this bestial policy of cold-blooded extermination" of Jews. He also affirmed their "solemn resolution to ensure that those responsible for these crimes shall not escape retribution, and to press on with the necessary practical measures to this end."[6]

The most important step along these lines was the Moscow Declaration of October 30, 1943, signed on behalf of President Franklin D. Roosevelt, Prime Minister Winston S. Churchill and Marshall Stalin. The heads of the Big Three in the interests of the 32

[5] War and Peace Aims, Sp. Supp. No. 1 to the *United Nations Review;* January 30, 1943), p. 116; see also *History of the United Nations War Crimes Commission and the Development of the Laws of War* (hereinafter referred to as *"History"*), compiled by the United Nations War Crimes Commission (H.M. Stationary Office. London, 1948), p. 90.

[6] *History,* p. 106

United Nations declared in substance that (1) at the time of the armistice, those German officers and men and members of the Nazi Party who have been responsible for the atrocities, massacres and cold-blooded mass executions will be sent back to the countries in which these crimes were done in order to be punished in accordance with their laws; and (2) major criminals whose offenses have no particular geographical location will be punished by a joint decision of the governments of the Allies.[7]

Following the Moscow Declaration, preparations for warcrimes trials were actively pursued, the initiative resting with the United States. Thus, at the San Francisco Conference which drafted the Charter of the United Nations, an American Draft of Definitive Proposal was submitted to the Foreign Ministers of France, the United Kingdom and the Soviet Union, along with an American Memorandum on prosecution and punishment of certain war criminals.[8] Informal discussion among these delegations, held May 2–10, 1945, resulted in agreement on certain principles. Negotiations with the Great Powers were from then on actively pursued by Mr. Justice Robert H. Jackson, whom President Truman on May 2, 1945, appointed as representative of the United States. On June 11, 1945, the United Kingdom Government invited the United States, France, and the Soviet Union to a conference to be held in London. These invitations were accepted and the conference held from June 26 to August 8, 1945. The discussion, based upon a revised American draft of June 14[9], resulted in an Executive Agreement, signed August 8, 1945, for the Prosecution and Punishment of the Major War Criminals of the European Axis.[10] Annexed to the Agreement was the Charter of the International Military Tribunal which contains the constitution, jurisdiction and functions of the Tribunal.[11] Nineteen United Nations adhered to the London Agreement[12] but they did not in any way participate in the Nuremberg Trial, which was conducted solely by the United States, the United Kingdom, the Soviet Union and France. It is clear from the record that the London Agreement was largely due to the energetic and persistent efforts of the United States. It may be noted that the United Nations War Crimes Commission established at a diplomatic conference of 17 nations held in London on October 30, 1943, did much useful work in surveying the laws of war, compiling lists of war criminals, and proposing draft conventions to ensure their punishment. It might well have become, as perhaps it was intended, the center of the United Nations' endeavor in this important field. The crucial

[7] *History*, p. 107; see also: United Nations, *The Charter and Judgement of the Nürnberg Tribunal. History and Analysis* (hereinafter referred as "*The Charter*"). Memorandum submitted by the Secretary-General (U.N. Publications, Sales No. 1949. V. 7), p. 87.

[8] Report of Robert H. Jackson, U.S. Representative to the *International Conference on Military Trials* (hereinafter referred to as "*International Conference*"), London 1945 (Department of State Publication 3080, 1949), p. 22, Doc. IV, and p. 28, Doc. V.

[9] *International Conference*, Doc. IX, p. 55.

[10] *Ibid.*, Doc. LX, p. 420.

[11] *Ibid.*, p. 422; the English and French texts of Article 6, *para.* c, were amended by Protocol of Oct. 6, 1945, to bring them into harmony with the Russian text, *ib.* Doc. LXI, p. 429.

[12] *Ibid.*, p. VIII. These nations are: Australia, Belgium, Czechoslovakia, Denmark, Ethiopia, Greece, Haiti, Honduras, India, Luxembourg, the Netherlands, New Zealand, Norway, Panama, Paraguay, Poland, Uruguay, Venezuela, and Yugoslavia.

negotiations, however, initiated by the United States took place wholly outside the Commission.

## IV. MAJOR DECISIONS IN PREPARING FOR WAR CRIMES TRIALS

### (1.) *Judicial Trial or Political Disposition?*

Early in their exchanges of views the United Nations were faced with the problem whether to punish some major Axis war criminals by a simple executive or political decision, or whether to bring them for trial before a tribunal. It was recalled that Napoleon I, having been denounced by the Congress of Vienna on March 13, 1815, "as Enemy and Perturbator of the World" who has "incurred liability to public vengeance", was banished to St. Helena by decision of the allied powers of August 2, 1815, following his surrender to the British Government.[13]

The United States Government seems from the first to have been favorably inclined towards a judicial proceeding, as was the Soviet Government[14]. The United Kingdom put forward a reasoned argument against a trial. The British Government took it for granted that Hitler, Mussolini and a number of "sub-criminals" associated with them must "suffer the penalty of death for their conduct leading up to the war and for the wickedness which they have either themselves perpetrated or have authorized in the conduct of the war."[15] While appreciating the arguments in favor of "some form of preliminary trial", the British Government was even more impressed with the difficulties. A trial of Hitler for violating "the international standard" was likely to be "exceedingly long and elaborate"; it might be presented as a "put-up job" to justify a punishment already decided upon, it might result in a change of public feeling as to the justification of trying Hitler at all and be denounced as a farce, and, moreover, Hitler might be expected to take advantage of any opportunity to turn the tables. The British Government also doubted whether Hitler's unprovoked attacks on various countries could properly be regarded as "crimes under international law". In the past, wars of conquest were not regarded as crimes. If the tribunal were to proceed according to international law, the accused might argue "that this part of the indictment should be struck out".[16] The United States, by contrast, as early as January 1945 formulated a view that the punishment without trial of Hitler, Himmler and others, while having "the advantage of a sure and swift disposition", "would be violative of the most fundamental principles of justice, common to all the United Nations".[17] The United States position was further elabo-

[13] *History*, p. 242, footnote 1 (c).
[14] *Ibid.*, p. 94.
[15] *International Conference*, p. 18.
[16] *Ibid.*, p. 19.
[17] Memorandum of January 22, 1945, prepared for President Roosevelt for his guidance at the Yalta Conference, *ibid.*, p. 6.

rated in a memorandum of April 30, 1945, which was delivered to the Foreign Ministers of the United Kingdom, the Soviet Union and France at the San Francisco Conference.[18] After restating that the United States was vigorously opposed to political disposition of the Axis leaders by joint action of the Allies, the following points in support of a trial were developed in some detail: (1) the violation of generally accepted standards of the conduct of nations and individuals during the war, in preparing and starting it, is a criminal violation of international law: (2) recognition of the principle that punishment will be inflicted by judicial action is "historically . . . . the first step in the approach to the democratic standards of liberty under law"; (3) punishment, if it is to lead to progress, cannot be carried out by a political disposition which "may be regarded eventually, and probably immediately, as adoption of the methods of the Axis itself"; rather it should be motivated "primarily by its deterrent effect, by the impetus which it gives to improved standards of international conduct and, if the theory of punishment is broad enough, by the implicit condemnation of ruthlessness and unlawful force as instruments of attaining national ends"; (4)"the method of punishment must not detract from the moral force behind the Allied Cause"; (5) punishment by the judicial method is more likely to commend itself to the judgment of history and to "induce future government leaders to think before they act in a similar fashion".[19]

The United States was not impressed with the arguments that the trial might last almost indefinitely, or that it might offer "an effective sounding board for propaganda and an easy road to martyrdom." It felt that a fair and speedy trial could be devised and "that we should not allow the bug-a-boos of possible embarrassments to hinder us from establishing the principle".[20] Concerning the question raised by the British Government, namely whether international law was applicable to the preparation for war and the launching of aggressive war in violation of Germany's treaty obligations, the United States argued that the very breadth of the offense "is a most important reason for a trial, for it is highly desirable that there be established and declared by actual decision, after adequate hearing and determination of the facts, the principles of international law applicable to the broad, vicious Nazi enterprise. . . . International law must develop to meet the needs of the times just as the common law has grown, not by enunciating new principles but by adapting old ones".[21]

The discussions at San Francisco among the Foreign Ministers of the Big Four ended in a victory for the United States. The four governments agreed to the principle: "Trial of the major war criminals rather than political disposition".[22] The question does not seem to have been seriously raised again in the course of the subsequent negotiations at the London Conference.

[18] *Ibid.*, p. 28.
[19] *Ibid.*, pp. 33–35.
[20] *Ibid.*, pp. 35–36.
[21] *Ibid.*, p. 37.
[22] *Ibid.*, p. 22.

(2). *The Tribunal: Its Establishment and Composition*

The decision having been taken to resort to the judicial method for the punishment of the Axis war criminals, it remained to decide what kind of tribunal or tribunals should be established to reap the full advantages of this method. In the Moscow Declaration, the distinction was made between war criminals whose offenses had a particular geographical location, that is, whose offenses were committed in a particular occupied country such as Norway or France and presumably against nations or residents of those countries, and major criminals whose offenses had no particular geographical location.

In the Memorandum of January 22, 1945, prepared for President Roosevelt to guide him at the Yalta Conference, the Secretaries of State and War and the Attorney General expressed their preference for an international military commission or court to be established either by Executive Agreement of the Heads of States of the interested United Nations, or by the Control Council for Germany.[23] The American draft of April 1945 submitted to the Foreign Ministers of the United Kingdom, France and the Soviet Union at the San Francisco Conference proposed more concretely the establishment by the four Powers of one or more "International Military Tribunals" to try the leaders of the European Axis and their principal agents. In addition it was proposed that the four Powers may establish occupation courts or other tribunals for the trial of other war criminals who would not be sent back to the countries where they had committed their crimes.[24]

There seems to have been no basic disagreement. The Soviet Union in a note of October 14, 1945, declared it essential to hand over the leaders of Fascist Germany to "the courts of the special international tribunal".[25] At San Francisco the four Powers agreed to the principle that an international military tribunal be established to hear the cases of the major war criminals.[26] Implicit in this decision was the decision that the tribunal be a military one, that is, composed of military personnel. It is not clear why the four Powers preferred a military tribunal. The American Memorandum of January 22, 1945, referred to above, expressed the preference of its authors for a military composition on the ground that military personnel was "less likely to give undue weight to technical contentions and legalistic arguments".[27] Whatever the merits of this thought may be, it did not appear to weigh heavily with the Governments concerned, as only the Soviet Union appointed a military man, General I. T. Nikitchenko, as judge of the Nuremberg Tribunal. The others were civilians.[28]

There may have been another reason for planning in terms of a military tribunal. This may be the assumption expressed, for instance, in the American Memorandum of

[23] *Ibid.*, p. 7.

[24] *Ibid.*, pp. 25–26.

[25] *Ibid.*, p. 17; see also the Soviet Aide-Mémoire of June 14, 1945, *ibid.*, p. 61.

[26] *Ibid.*, p. 22. It may be noted that on May 21, 1945, President Truman designated Mr. Justice Jackson as prosecutor of charges before an "international military tribunal". *Ibid.*, p. 21.

[27] *Ibid.*, p. 8.

[28] Lord Justice Lawrence (U.K.), Mr. Francis Biddle (U.S.A.), Professor Donnedieu de Vabres (France).

April 30, 1945, referred to above, that the *emphasis* in the trial will be placed "upon those patent violations of the customs of war which most shock the Allies (e.g., murder of prisoners of war, abuse of populations in occupied territories, deportation of Allied peoples for use as slave labor, etc.)".[29] Actually, there was less emphasis in the trials upon the war crimes peculiarly within the competence of military judges, than upon the crimes against peace and humanity which from the long-range point of view are of transcendent importance. Be that as it may, it appears that in these two decisions, one regarding the establishment of an international tribunal and the other regarding its military character, American initiative clearly prevailed. The agreement reached at San Francisco was adhered to throughout the London Conference, though on one or two occasions it seemed in jeopardy when difficulties arose concerning the seat of the tribunal and the law to be applied by it.[30] The differences of views regarding the seat of the tribunal, mainly between the Soviet and the American representatives, were removed in providing that its permanent seat be in Berlin (as the Russians proposed) and the first trial be held in Nuremberg (as proposed by the Americans).

Having resolved these questions, the four Powers had to decide on two other questions: by whom and how shall the tribunal be established, and how shall it be composed? In the "Yalta Memorandum" of January 22, 1945, referred to above, the Secretaries of State and War and the Attorney General favored an Executive Agreement of the Heads of State of the interested United Nations for the establishment of the Tribunal. They also envisaged, as an alternative, its establishment by action of the Control Council for Germany.[31] In the subsequent draft proposals of April 1945, submitted to the Foreign Ministers at San Francisco, an Executive Agreement of the four Powers was suggested, with the possibility of other members of the United Nations adhering to it. This approach, it was explained, was preferable "because the agreement will be largely a matter affecting the four nations engaged in the occupation of Germany and because of the necessity for speed in reaching agreement".[32] Whatever the merits of the latter argument may be, the first argument betrays a somewhat parochial view of the world-wide and long-run significance of the trials.

The British and Soviet Governments accepted on June 3 and 14, respectively, the American draft as basis of discussion. The British Government at the same time suggested that representatives of the four Powers be appointed, preferably in the person of four prosecuting counsel, for further discussions in London.[33] However, this did not settle the question for on June 14, the United States presented to the other Governments a revised draft of an Executive Agreement. According to this, the International Military Tribunal was to be set up by the Control Council for Germany.[34] The British Government ob-

[29] *Ibid.*, p. 36.
[30] *Ibid.*, pp. 343, 385, 397, 400.
[31] *Ibid.*, p. 7.
[32] *Ibid.*,. pp. 23, 30.
[33] *Ibid.*, pp. 41, 61.
[34] *Ibid.*, p. 56.

jected to this, arguing that the tribunal should be set up by the four Powers and that it "would be a mistake to place it under the Control Council".[35] This idea prevailed. The draft agreement submitted by the American Delegation to the London Conference on June 30, 1945, adopted the British view and provided that the tribunal be set up by the four Powers. A Soviet draft of July 2, 1945, also followed the British lead in this matter.[36] There was no question of associating other members of the United Nations with the establishment of the tribunal though accession to the Agreement was open to them.

The composition of the Tribunal appears as the logical consequence of the method of its establishment. The four Powers which participated in the negotiations and signed the London Agreement also appointed the four judges, each of the signatories one. As this aspect of the Nuremberg Trial attracted much attention it may be worth while to indicate one or two proposals which appeared in the negotiating stage but were not retained. The first American memorandum, the so-called "Yalta Memorandum" of June 22, 1945, suggested that the court consist of seven members, one each to be appointed by each of the four Powers and "three to be appointed by agreement among the other United Nations who become parties to the proposed procedure".[37] The Memorandum of April and its revised draft of June 14, 1945, dropped the additional three members and proposed that the four members be appointed by the Control Council.[38] Following the British objections to the role assigned to the Control Council in the American papers, the revised United States draft of June 30, 1945, provided for direct appointment by the Governments.[39] The Soviet Delegation, however, elaborating on the first American ideas, proposed not merely for the appointment but also for the recall of the members of the tribunal by the Control Council.[40] The Soviet proposals met with rather strong objections of the American representatives[41] and eventually the Soviets agreed to the appointment of members of the Tribunal independently of the Control Council.[42]

The London Conference was unanimous in excluding other members of the United Nations from participating in the trial, while at the same time making the Agreement open to their adherence.[43] Participation of neutral judges in the trial does not appear to have been even mentioned.[44] This may be explained by the temper of the United Nations which brooked no sympathies for neutrals. There was of course no question of German participation in the Tribunal.

[35] *Ibid.*, pp. 86, 97.
[36] *Ibid.*, pp. 121, 128.
[37] *Ibid.*, p. 7, 8.
[38] *Ibid.*, pp. 26, 56.
[39] *Ibid.*, pp. 86, 97, 121.
[40] *Ibid.*, pp. 172, 173.
[41] *Ibid.*, pp. 150, 151.
[42] *Ibid.*, pp. 187, 196.
[43] *Ibid.*, pp. 224–226. In order to avoid any possibility of raising false hopes, the text of the draft Agreement of July 11, 1945, which provided for "accession" was changed in the final text to "adherence".
[44] The inclusion of neutral judges was considered by an unofficial body called the International Commission for Penal Reconstruction and Development. See *History*, p. 95.

## (3). *The Law*

A difficulty of considerable gravity arose in connection with the determination of the law to be applied by the Tribunal. Many of the atrocities committed by the Nazis were begun before and multiplied during the war. It was recognized by the American Secretaries of State and War and the Attorney General in the "Yalta Memorandum" of January 22, 1945, that such atrocities were neither "war crimes" nor offenses against international law.[45] The absence of a generally accepted standard applicable to such atrocities, and unprovoked attacks, was the main reason which led the British Government to think "that execution without trial" was preferable to judicial action.[46]

The problem facing the Four Powers can be reduced to this: either the Tribunal is directed to apply international law and find this law using the traditional methods of international tribunals, or the Tribunal is directed simply to apply the law laid down by the Powers. Almost from the first, the United States inclined to the latter view. Thus the draft presented at the San Francisco Conference to Messrs. Eden, Molotov and Bidault, the Foreign Ministers of Great Britain, the Soviet Union and France, respectively, expressly stated that the defendants cannot challenge the law making criminal the acts set forth in the agreement providing for the trial of major criminals.[47]

The American draft agreement of June 14, 1945, which was submitted to the London Conference, came to grips with the problem in providing that "the tribunal shall be bound by this declaration of the parties to this Agreement that the following acts are criminal: a. Atrocities and offenses against persons or property constituting violations of international law, including the laws, rules and customs of land and naval warfare". It also proposed a very broad definition of international law as including "treaties between nations and the principles of the law of nations as they result from the usages established among civilized peoples, from the laws of humanity, and the dictates of the public conscience".[48] Commenting upon this at the Conference, the United States representative, Mr. Justice Jackson, invited the closest scrutiny "because every word will come back to plague us before we get through with the trial", and declared that "it would be very unfortunate if we were to go into this trial with an argument as to whether the acts were criminal, and it should be left to the court to sift out from the various authorities what the law is".[49] A similar thought was expressed by the British representative Sir David Maxwell Fyfe, who said: "What we want to abolish at the trial is a discussion as to whether the acts are violations of international law or not. We declare what the international law is so that there won't be any discussion on whether it is international law or not".[50]

[45] *International Conference,* p. 5.
[46] *Ibid.,* p. 18.
[47] *Ibid.,* p. 24.
[48] *Ibid.,* pp. 57, 58.
[49] *Ibid.,* p. 82.
[50] *Ibid.,* p. 99; for the British amendment to the American draft see *ibid.,* pp. 86, 87, and the revised American draft, *ibid.,* pp. 121, 169.

The question was discussed at some length at the London Conference, there being a general desire to avoid any language in the Agreement setting up the Tribunal which might conceivably lead to a discussion of the applicable international law, or to devise some means to settle, as Mr. Justice Jackson put it, "what the law is for the purposes of this trial and end the argument". He felt it was "entirely proper that these four powers, in view of the disputed state of the law of nations, should settle by agreement what the law is as the basis of this proceeding".[51] This agreement, he pointed out, "fulfills in a sense the function of legislation".[52] The British and Soviet representatives shared the same preoccupation.[53] The only question which remained was to find the appropriate formula. This was eventually and laboriously accomplished. Insofar as the substantive law was concerned, all references to international law were successively eliminated from a series of drafts.[54] The formula written into Article 6, paragraph 1 of the Charter of the Tribunal reads: "The following acts, or any of them, are crimes coming within the jurisdiction of the Tribunal for which there shall be individual responsibility".[55]

In spite of the labor spent by the London Conference on this formula, it failed to prevent the defendants from challenging the law laid down by the Four Powers. It also failed to restrain the Tribunal itself from delving into this very controversial matter. The Tribunal felt it necessary to argue in its judgment not merely that the law of its Charter was obviously binding upon it, but that it was also "the expression of international law existing at the time of its creation".[56]

### (4). *Defining the Crimes*

The London Conference faced a formidable task in formulating the substantive law, that is, the offenses for the commission of which the major war criminals were to be tried. As the Tribunal was to apply this law and nothing but this law, it was imperative to define it with sufficient precision as well as elasticity. Almost from the first it was proposed by the United States that these criminals should be held responsible for three groups of offenses: one group comprised violations of the rules and customs of war or war crimes in the strict and traditional sense of the word.[57] There was not much difficulty in reaching agreement on this group and in including some of the more doubtful offenses such as deportation to slave labor of civilian populations and killing of hostages.

The second group comprised originally atrocities, mass murders, imprisonments, deportations, torture and inhuman treatment of civilians.[58] It was this aspect of the Nazi

[51] *Ibid.*, p. 329.
[52] *Ibid.*, p. 331.
[53] *Ibid.*, pp. 328, 335, 336.
[54] *Ibid.*, pp. 197, 205, 351, 359, 373, 374, 378, 390–395.
[55] *Ibid.*, p. 423.
[56] Trial of the Major war Criminals before the International Military Tribunal, Vol. I (1947), p. 218.
[57] *International Conference*, p. 24, "American Draft of Definitive Proposal, presented to Foreign Ministers at San Francisco, April 1945."
[58] *Ibid.*, pp. 4, 24.

system, including but not limited to, a policy of the extermination of Jews and of persecutions on religious and political grounds, which aroused the indignation of the civilized world and provoked its condemnation. This group of crimes came to be known as Crimes against Humanity.

The Four Powers were faced with a twofold difficulty in connection with these crimes. One was that they were initiated when the Nazi regime came into power in 1933, that is, well before the outbreak of the Second World War in 1939, and the other, that some of them were committed on German territory in conformity with domestic law or against German nationals. In principle the treatment of nationals it not regulated by international law. The United Kingdom seems to have been well aware of this difficulty which it tried to solve by proposing that the Tribunal be bound to regard as criminal violations atrocities, persecutions and deportations on political, racial or religious grounds committed in pursuance of the common plan to violate rules of war or launch a war of aggression or invade other countries, and regardless of whether or not in violation of domestic law.[59] This was approved by the United States and incorporated in its draft,[60] but it does not seem to have been comprehended by the French and Russian representatives.[61] The point was explained by the British and American representatives, the latter saying that "ordinarily we do not consider that the acts of a government toward its own citizens warrant our interference". But, he said, "we think it is justifiable that we interfere or attempt to bring retribution to individuals or to states only because the concentration camps and the deportations were in pursuance of a common plan or enterprise of making an unjust or illegal war in which we became involved".[62] The French representative felt that such a formulation put on the prosecutors the burden of proving the connection between the Nazi plan against the Jews and the Nazi plan of aggression, and this might be difficult to accomplish. This view was not shared by the British representative.[63] The Soviet representatives raised some point of detail but did not question the link between this group of crimes and the plan of making an illegal war. The title for this group "Crimes against Humanity" appears first in the American draft of July 31, 1945, and was suggested to Mr. Justice Jackson "by an eminent scholar of international law".[64] The final text incorporated in Article 6, paragraph c, of the Charter of the Tribunal reads:[65]

> "Crimes against Humanity: namely, murder, extermination, enslavement, deportation, and other inhumane acts committed against any civilian population, before or during the war, or persecutions on political, racial or religious grounds in execution of or in con-

[59] *Ibid.*, p. 87.
[60] *Ibid.*, p. 170.
[61] See French and Soviet drafts of July 19 and 23, 1945, respectively, *ibid.*, pp. 293, 327. The French proposed the following formula: "The policy of atrocities and persecutions against civilian populations."
[62] *Ibid.*, pp. 329, 333.
[63] *Ibid.*, p. 361.
[64] *Ibid.*, p. 416.
[65] *Ibid.*, pp. 423, 429. The above text is reproduced as amended by the Protocol to Agreement and Charter, October 6, 1945. Prior to the amendment there was a semicolon between "war; or". The semicolon would have divorced the first group of crimes from the connection with the words "in execution of or in connection with any crime . . ."

nection with any crime within the jurisdiction of the Tribunal, whether or not in violation of the domestic law of the country where perpetrated."

There is room for an honest difference of opinion whether from a short-term or long-term viewpoint the Anglo-American or the French formula should have been preferred. Neither formula, it must be admitted, could be based wholly on existing international law, if at all. The Anglo-American formula did prove difficult of application in the main trial, as well as in subsequent trials. It remained a task for the United Nations to carry forward the French formula through the Genocide Convention and the draft covenants on human rights.

The third group became the focal point cf the charges against major war criminals and the subject of vigorous debates at the London Conference. In the American draft of April 1945, presented to Foreign Ministers Eden, Bidault and Molotov at San Francisco, this group consisted of the following "criminal acts:

(b) Invasion by force or threat of force of other countries in violation of international law or treaties.

(c) Initiation of war in violation of international law and treaties.

(d) Launching a war of aggression.

(e) Recourse to war as an instrument of national policy or for the solution of international controversies".[66]

This group of crimes was called in a later American draft "The Crime of War", but the British representative, the Lord Chancellor, Sir William Jowitt, suggested "Crime against Peace", a term used in a work by Professor Trainin, one of the Soviet representatives.[67] This nomenclature was adopted and put into the Charter of the Tribunal.

The original American proposal was subjected to several changes. In accordance with the basic decision already discussed,[68] to avoid any discussion of international law by the Tribunal or the defendants, references to international law had to be eliminated. There was, however, another and weightier reason for this. In the London Conference as well as in other bodies concerned with this problem,[69] doubt was expressed whether aggressive war was a crime under international law. However, Mr. Justice Jackson urged as early as June 6, 1945, that it was "high time that we act on the juridical principle that aggressive war-making is illegal and criminal".[70] At the London Conference, the British representative pointed out that the proposed crime "launching of a war of aggression" "may involve a discussion of different schools of thought as to whether that is an existing offense against international law, and there is the further question whether we are breaking new ground".[71] This was strongly felt by the French representative, Professor Gros,

[66] *Ibid.*, p. 24.
[67] *Ibid.*, pp. 395, 416. A. N. Trainin, *Hitlerite Responsibility under International Law* [London, 1945].
[68] *Supra*, pp. 339–340.
[69] *See History*, pp. 180–187.
[70] *International Conference*, p. 52.
[71] *Ibid.*, p. 98.

who said: "We do not consider as a criminal violation the launching of a war of aggression. If we declare war a criminal act of individuals, we are going further than the actual law". He distinguished criminality of a war of aggression and individual criminal responsibility for launching such a war.[72]

In the discussion of this point, the Soviets took the position that the Conference's task was not to formulate law but merely to formulate the basis for the trial of war criminals who have been "defined" as such in the Moscow Declaration of 1943.[73] The American representative, Mr. Justice Jackson, on the other hand appears to have thought of the future as well as of the past. He pointed out in particular that the United States position since 1939 was based "on the proposition that this was an illegal war from the moment that it was started, and that therefore, without losing our rights as neutrals or non-belligerents, it was our right to extend aid to the nations under illegal attack, and the lend-lease program, the exchange of bases for destroyers, and much of American policy was based squarely on the proposition that a war of aggression is outlawed".[74]

It appears from this that in the first place the Conference was asked by the Soviets merely to implement the Moscow Declaration. As they saw it, "the fact that the Nazi leaders are criminals has already been established. The task of the Tribunal is only to determine the measure of guilt of each particular person and mete out the necessary punishment—the sentences." And the task of the Conference was "to form the basis for the trial not of any criminals who may commit international crimes in the future but of those who have already done so". Therefore, they favored the French draft because it provided for responsibility of individuals and not of States, and also "because the crimes are set forth in such a manner that they are turned only against those who have committed the crimes".[75] On the main points, the French representatives agreed with the Soviets and, subject to some adjustments, were prepared to accept the Soviet draft.[76]

The American representative was conscious, as was the British representative, that international law on the subject, particularly regarding responsibility of individuals, "is indefinite and weak in our support on that, as it has stood over the recent years".[77] Nevertheless, he urged the adoption of a definition of the crime of aggression, one that would not apply to the Axis alone. He admitted that the Four Powers were only dealing with Axis aggressions but he thought that "our definition would sound pretty partial if we are defining an act as a crime only when it is carried out by the Axis powers. . . . If it is a

[72] *Ibid.*, p. 295.
[73] *Ibid.*, p. 298.
[74] *Ibid.*, p. 299.
[75] *Ibid.*, pp. 298, 303; see also pp. 377, 382, and p. 373 for a Soviet draft of definitions of the crime: "Aggression against or domination over other nations carried out by the European Axis Powers in violation of treaties, agreements and assurances."
[76] *Ibid.*, pp. 377 f.
[77] *Ibid.*, pp. 328, 331, 337.

good rule of law, it should bind us all, and if not, we should not invoke it at this trial''.[78] He proposed consequently a general definition of aggression.[79]

Another matter of greatest importance to the American representative was, as mentioned above, the inclusion of ''launching a war of aggression'' in the list of crimes, to show that this war was illegal. In this respect, he emphasized, the American position was different from that of the other Powers. The other Powers were attacked in violation of treaties but the United States ''were acting under the theory that there was an illegal war long before we were attacked''.[80]

The British position was bent on achieving a compromise between the different views of the other three Powers. They agreed with the French and the Soviets that the Conference was ''dealing in accordance with our reference from Moscow''.[81] They did not seem to object to a definition of aggressive war but did not hold out for it, and were quite willing to compromise on the other points.

A compromise then was worked out. A definition of aggression was not adopted. The French and the Russians were opposed to it, partly because drafting a definition was not within the competence of the Conference, and partly because of the complexity of the problem.[82] The British proposed, and the United States accepted, a formula which ''would give a pointer without defining'' aggression by referring to certain treaties to which Germany was a party, such as the Kellogg-Briand Pact of 1928.[83] To satisfy the Americans' insistence on including ''launching a war of aggression'' and the French insistence on initiation of wars in violation of treaties, the British proposed that both be included as crimes. The American representative accepted this.[84] To satisfy the American desire to establish substantive crimes without appearing to limit them to the crimes already committed by the Axis, and the Soviet, French and British views that the Conference was to prepare for the trial of Axis war criminals pursuant to the Moscow Declaration, an introductory paragraph which limits the jurisdiction of the Tribunal to a trial of nationals of the European Axis Powers was placed into the article defining the crimes. The draft for this paragraph was submitted by the Soviet representative and accepted by the others.[85] The American position was thus recognized by defining the crimes themselves without any reference to the European Axis or to the Moscow Declaration. The American stand on this was unyielding for, as Mr. Justice Jackson said: ''I am not willing to charge as a crime against a German official acts which would not be crimes if committed by officials of the United States. I think no one will respect any conviction

[78] *Ibid.*, pp. 336.
[79] *Ibid.*, p. 294; see also pp. 273, 305, 375.
[80] *Ibid.*, pp. 383, 385.
[81] *Ibid.*, p. 386.
[82] *Ibid.*, pp. 303, 304, 305, 307, 308.
[83] *Ibid.*, pp. 307, 308.
[84] *Ibid.*, pp. 386, 387.
[85] *Ibid.*, p. 416; see also pp. 387, 397.

that rests on such a legal foundation''.[86] The American proposal on this point was accepted,[87] and the article on ''Crimes against Peace'' finally adopted.

One more point arose in connection with the definition of crimes. As this is a matter of some complexity, it will be dealt with very briefly. It concerned making the common plan or conspiracy for the accomplishment of the Crimes against Peace a distinct crime. In the American Plan of April 1945, presented to the Foreign Ministers of France, Great Britain and the Soviet Union, there was only a very general indication of this specific interest.[88] Great emphasis was put on this point by the United Kingdom delegation in its plan of June 28, 1945, submitted to the London Conference, where it was stated that ''the chief crime of which it is alleged that the leaders in Germany are guilty is the common plan or conspiracy to dominate Europe, and it is therefore most desirable to include this crime specifically in the statutes of the Court''.[89] In some of their drafts, the Soviets referred to ''organizers, instigators and accomplices'' who were to be held responsible for the crimes along with the perpetrators, and the Americans to the ''general rule of liability that those who participate in the formulation or execution of a criminal plan involving multiple crimes are liable for each of the offenses committed and responsible for the acts of each other''.[90] But these references occurred in connection with the extent of liability and not, as in the British draft, as part of the listing of crimes. The drafting subcommittee of the Conference, however, in its outline of July 11, 1945, included the common plan among the crimes within the jurisdiction of the Tribunal.[91] The French, to whom the concept of ''conspiracy'' was foreign, attempted to achieve the same objective as the British by different means.[92] The Soviets, in this matter, followed the French lead.[93] The United States representative looked upon the ''common plan'' or ''conspiracy'' stipulation ''as a means by which we hope to reach a great number of persons who are deserving of trial and punishment but against whom specific acts, other than joining in the plan and promoting the plan, might be very difficult to prove. And we see no acceptable substitution for that article as a means of reaching any large number of persons''.[94] Apart from the differences in outlook revealed in the discussion of this point between the Anglo-American and the Continental conceptions of law,[95] there was also a difference of views whether the common-plan liability should include all three groups of crimes or be limited to Crimes against Peace. Agreement was finally reached on including the crime of ''participation in a common plan or conspiracy'',[96] to make it spe-

[86] *Ibid.*, p. 394.
[87] *Ibid.*, p. 395, 416.
[88] *Ibid.*, p. 24; see also pp. 51, 58, 65.
[89] *Ibid.*, p. 87; see also p. 99.
[90] For Soviet plan, see *ibid.*, p. 181, and for American plans, see pp. 58, 124, 181.
[91] *Ibid.*, p. 197; see also p. 205, the British draft of July 11, 1945, which is identical on this point with the subcommittee draft.
[92] *Ibid.*, p. 296.
[93] *Ibid.*, p. 327, 328.
[94] *Ibid.*, p. 332.
[95] *Ibid.*, p. 387.
[96] *Ibid.*, pp. 381, 382, 388.

cifically applicable to Crimes against Peace, and to include a broad principle of responsibility applicable to "leaders, organizers, instigators and accomplices participating in the formulation or execution of a common plan or conspiracy to commit" Crimes against Peace or Humanity or War Crimes. Acceptance of these provisions appears largely to be due to the perseverance and skill of Mr. Justice Jackson.

### (5). *The Criminals*

It was understood from the outset that the trials would be limited, in accordance with the Moscow Declaration, to a number of the highest-ranking Nazi leaders and their principal accomplices. It was proposed by the United States in the draft of April 30, 1945, presented to the Foreign Ministers of France, Great Britain and the Soviet Union, that the trial comprise also "the principal Nazi organizations and their members, through whom the most bestial of the Nazi cruelties have been put into effect".[97] According to this draft, the defense of superior orders shall not absolve the accused from responsibility but may be considered, if justice so requires, in mitigation of punishment. Nor shall an accused be able to escape the trial on the ground that he was the head or principal officer of a state[98]. Offenses against the armies of the United Nations would be punished by the appropriate national tribunals. Perpetrators of atrocities in territories occupied by Germany during the war as well as traitors such as Quisling, Laval, "Lord Haw-Haw", would be dealt with in a similar manner.[99]

A tentative list of defendants prepared by the British delegation to the London Conference on July 17, 1945, was as follows: Göring, Hess, Ribbentrop, Ley, Keitel, Kaltenbrunner, Rosenberg, Hans Frank, Frick and Streicher. All of these, and several others, were actually tried by the Nuremberg Tribunal.[100] It was the duty of the chief prosecutors appointed by the Four Powers to select the defendants.

The proposal to deny immunity to Heads of State and high governmental officials does not seem to have created any difficulty at the London Conference. The position of the American representative, Mr. Justice Jackson, as stated even before the opening of the Conference, was that the "obsolete doctrine that a head of state is immune from legal liability" should not be recognized. He suspected this doctrine to be "a relic of the doctrine of the divine right of kings", and deemed it inconsistent with the principle of responsible government. Similarly, he rejected the immunity of those who carry out orders from an official superior, on the ground that "society as modernly organized cannot tolerate so broad an area of official irresponsibility". The defendants may plead superior orders but it is for the tribunal to determine what weight to attach to it.[101]

It may well be that the Conference refrained from discussing the merits of both

[97] *Ibid.*, pp. 23, 25, 29, 47.
[98] *Ibid.*, pp. 24.
[99] *Ibid.*, p. 43.
[100] *Ibid.*, p. 259.
[101] *Ibid.*, pp. 46–47; see also pp. 367–368.

these proposals because it was beyond its power to do so. The decision to punish the major war criminals was taken at Moscow at the highest level and could not be undone by subordinates. Moreover, it is clear from the record that the Allies contemplated the trial of Hitler, the head of the German State, Göring and others who held the highest positions in Germany.[102] These facts became of the greatest importance in connection with the discussion of Crimes against Peace,[103] when the French representative, in a manner which is by no means clear, argued against Mr. Justice Jackson that there was no legal basis to say that launching of a war of aggression shows criminal responsibility of the people who launched that war, "and that it may be a crime to launch a war of aggression on the part of a state that does so, but that does not imply the commission of criminal acts by individual people who have launched a war". He proposed instead to "define their crimes according to their practical results, if you show that the Germans have been breaking treaties, and as a result of that have annexed populations, run concentration camps, and violated international law by criminal acts against people, what you will condemn are those acts which in fact are criminal in all legislation, and you will condemn them for having directed those acts".[104] To declare such acts to be criminal violations of international law, would be "*ex post facto* legislation". The Soviet representative, Professor Trainin, suggested that personal responsibility should be emphasized and that "the four countries may, for the purposes of *this* trial, declare certain acts to be criminal; and for the purpose of *this* trial the laws declared by the Four Powers should be sufficient".[105] A compromise along these lines was eventually worked out as discussed above.[106] However, the question of the legal basis for the individual or personal criminal responsibility of the Nazi leaders for the Crimes against Humanity remained obscure. It is probably a fair statement that the representatives of the Four Powers had doubts about basing this responsibility on international law.[107] It is obvious that no basis could be found in the national legislation of any of the Four Powers or of Germany for attributing personal and criminal responsibility to those acts or crimes. Moreover, relations between States are governed by international law and not by the national legislation of any particular country or group of countries. If there was no basis in international law for the Crimes against Peace, then, regrettably, there was no basis at all. It was one thing to direct the Tribunal to adjudicate, as suggested by Professor Trainin, in accordance with the law laid down by the Four Powers which created it, and another to base this law on, or to derive it from, existing principles of international law. Be that as it may, this aspect of the Nuremberg Trial was destined to become a matter of controversy both during and after the trial.

The responsibility of the principal Nazi organizations such as the Gestapo, the S.S. and others, was much debated at the London Conference. It was stated in the American

[102] *Ibid.*, pp. 6, 61, 69.
[103] *See Supra*, Vol. II (1955), pp. 15–19.
[104] *Ibid.*, p. 297
[105] *Ibid.*, p. 335. Italics supplied.
[106] *Supra*, Vol. II (1955) p. 17–18.
[107] *International conference*, pp. 329, 331, 333, 334, 337.

Memorandum of April 1945 that the tribunal should adjudicate the criminal character of certain organizations, and such adjudication should be binding on all military tribunals established by the occupation powers. In such subsequent trials, membership in these organizations should be the "only necessary proof of guilt of any particular defendant" but evidence should be admitted of "the nature and extent of the individual's participation".[108] More precisely, the individual was to be allowed "to plead only personal defenses or extenuating circumstances, such as that he joined under duress".[109]

At first, the Soviet representative raised an objection to the inclusion of organizations, on the ground that these Nazi organizations had already been declared "to be illegal and criminal and therefore should be utterly destroyed". He insisted that "the line taken here follows the decisions of the Three Powers in the Crimean (Yalta) Agreement".[110] Following the Soviet position already indicated in connection with other crimes, the Soviet representatives pointed out again that "organizations such as the S.S. or the Gestapo have already been declared criminal by authorities higher than the Tribunal itself, both in the Moscow and the Crimeo Declarations, and the fact of their criminality has definitely been established. We cannot imagine any position arising in which the Tribunal might possibly bring out a verdict that any one of these organizations was not criminal when it has most definitely been labeled so by the governments".[111]

Mr. Justice Jackson explained that the trial of organizations in combination with the conspiracy theory constitutes "the heart" of the American proposal and "the means through which . . . a large number of people can be reached with a small number of long trials—perhaps one main trial".[112]

The difference between the Soviet and the American positions as seen by the former was that Americans would put organizations on trial and deduce from their criminality the guilt of members whereas the Soviets would conclude from the criminality of individual members of organizations "that the whole organization to which they belong is in effect a criminal organization".[113] Having emphasized the difference of approach the Soviets were quite willing to compromise if an acceptable text could be worked out.[114] And Mr. Justice Jackson admitted that the difference on this point was not as serious as it had appeared to be.[115] He agreed to the following statement made by the Soviet representative:

"The question of the guilt of the organization cannot be reopened once the criminality of that organization has been established. The only question we are emphasizing is that each individual member of an organization should not be subjected to punishment as soon as his connection has been discovered, and that as and when such individuals are

[108] *Ibid.*, pp. 32–33.
[109] *Ibid.*, p. 48.
[110] *Ibid.*, p. 72; see also pp. 93–94.
[111] *Ibid.*, p. 107
[112] *Ibid.*, p. 129.
[113] *Ibid.*, p. 134.
[114] *Ibid.*, p. 136.
[115] *Ibid.*, pp. 137, 140.

found they must nevertheless be given an opportunity to bring forth a defense, and that the punishment to be meted out to them will be according to the part taken".[116]

In this fashion it was believed, that the main principle of the trial, namely individual responsibility, can be reconciled with the notion of collective responsibility underlying the trial and conviction of organizations. The decision to try organizations was largely due to the efforts of the American representatives.

## V. THE JUDGMENT OF THE INTERNATIONAL MILITARY TRIBUNAL

The Tribunal constituted pursuant to the London Agreement and Charter of August 8, 1945, tried twenty-two individuals and seven groups of organizations.[117]

The indictment charged the individual defendants with one or more crimes:

Count I, the common plan or conspiracy;

Count II, crimes against peace;

Count III, war crimes;

Count IV, crimes against humanity.

The defendants pleaded not guilty. After an exhaustive and fair trial in which the defendants were given opportunity of rebuttal, the Tribunal acquitted Hjalmar Schacht, Franz von Papen and Hans Fritzsche. The others were found guilty on the counts indicated below and sentenced as follows:

Hermann Göring: all four counts; sentence: hanging
Rudolf Hess: counts I and II; sentence: life imprisonment
Joachim von Ribbentrop; all four counts; sentence: hanging
Wilhelm Keitel: all four counts; sentence: hanging
Ernst Kaltenbrunner: counts III and IV; sentence: hanging
Alfred Rosenberg: all four counts; sentence: hanging
Hans Frank: counts III and IV; sentence: hanging
Wilhelm Frick: counts II, III and IV; sentence: hanging
Julius Streicher: count IV; sentence: hanging
Walter Funk: counts II, III and IV; sentence: life imprisonment
Karl Doenitz: counts II and III; sentence: ten years
Erich Raeder: counts I, II and III; sentence: life imprisonment
Baldur von Schirach: count IV; sentence:twenty years
Fritz Sauckel: counts III and IV; sentence: hanging
Alfred Jodl: all four counts; sentence: hanging

[116] *Ibid.*, pp. 141 f; see also pp. 238–242, 246–248, 369–371, 383.

[117] The following groups were indicted: the Reich Cabinet, the Leadership Corps of the Nazi Party; the *Schutzstaffeln*, known as the "SS"; the *Sicherheitsdienst*, known as the "SD"; the *Geheime Staatspolizei*, known as the "Gestapo"; the *Sturmabteilungen*, known as the "SA"; the General Staff and High Command of the Armed Forces, known as the "OKW".

Martin Bormann[118]: counts III and IV; sentence: hanging
Arthur Seyss-Inquart: counts II, III and IV; sentence: hanging
Albert Speer: counts III and IV; sentence: twenty years
Constantin von Neurath: all four counts; sentence: fifteen years[119]

The Tribunal also found that the following organizations were criminal: the Leadership Corps of the Nazi Party, the "SS", the "SD" and the "Gestapo". The judgment was unanimous, excepting the dissent of the Soviet Judge with respect to the acquittal of Schacht, Von Papen and Fritzsche, the sentence for Hess and the acquittal of the Reich Cabinet, the General Staff and the O.K.W. (Oberkommando der Wehrmacht). In his view, all of these individual defendants and organizations should have been found guilty as charged and Hess should have been sentenced to hanging.[120] The sentences were executed, with the exception of the sentence against Göring, who committed suicide.[121]

It will be observed that only two defendants were found guilty of crimes against humanity alone. No defendant was found guilty of conspiracy alone, and only one was found guilty of the crime of conspiracy and the crime against peace. Of those who were found guilty of the crime against peace, all were also guilty of war crimes. From these findings as well as from its reasoning, it may be deduced that the Tribunal adopted a restrictive interpretation of the somewhat novel crime of conspiracy. The Tribunal decided to disregard the charge of conspiracy to commit war crimes and crimes against humanity and to "consider only the common plan to prepare, initiate, and wage aggressive war". On the other hand, the Tribunal rejected as "unsound" the plea of the defense that "such common planning cannot exist where there is complete dictatorship". In the opinion of the Tribunal, "Hitler could not make aggressive war by himself. He had to have the co-operation of statesmen, military leaders, diplomats, and business men". If they knowingly assisted him, they were responsible, for, as the Tribunal said: "the relation of leader and follower does not preclude responsibility here any more than it does in the comparable tyranny of organized domestic crime".[122] The Tribunal also held that "the conspiracy must be clearly outlined in its criminal purpose" and "must not be too far removed from the time of decision and of action".[123] This restrictive view of the charge of conspiracy limited its applicability to those defendants who belonged to the core of the Hitler clique, Göring, Hess, etc.

The crimes against peace, which formed the subject of prolonged discussions at the London Conference were not elaborated by the Tribunal. The London Conference as well as the Tribunal failed to define "aggression". The Tribunal did, however, give an

[118] Bormann was tried and sentenced *in absentia*; see *Trial of the Major War Criminals Before the International Military Tribunal*, (published at Nuremberg, Germany, 1947), Vol. I, p. 6 (hereinafter referred to as "Trial").

[119] *Trial*, p. 365.

[120] *Ibid.*, pp. 342–364.

[121] Those sentenced to prison sentences were jailed in the Spandau prison in Berlin, which continues to be under the control of the Four Powers.

[122] *Ibid.*, p. 226.

[123] *Ibid.*, p. 225.

indication of its interpretation of this concept by distinguishing "agresssive acts", *i.e.*, the seizure of Austria and Czechoslovakia, from "aggressive wars" against twelve nations beginning with the war against Poland on September 1, 1939.[124]

No distinction, however, was made by the Tribunal between "aggressive wars" and "wars in violation of international treaties, agreements, or assurances". Having found some of the defendants guilty of planning and waging aggressive wars against twelve nations, the Tribunal deemed it "unnecessary to discuss the subject in further detail, or even to consider at any length the extent to which those aggressive wars were also 'wars in violation of international treaties, agreements, or assurances' ".[125] The initiation of a war of aggression is in the opinion of the Tribunal not only an international crime but "the supreme international crime".[126] Of the accused, however, none was found guilty of initiating an aggressive war. Hitler presumably alone was considered as the initiator of the twelve aggressive wars.[127]

Of all the defendants convicted on count II, only Dönitz, who on May 1, 1945, succeeded Hitler as the Head of State, was found "active in waging aggressive war".[128] Others like Raeder, however, were found to have "participated in the planning and waging of aggressive war".[129] Findings of planning and preparing aggressive war were made against Göring, Keitel, Raeder and Jodl in the military, Göring, Von Ribbentrop and Rosenberg in the diplomatic, and Funk in the economic field.[130]

The Tribunal accepted the comprehensive definition of war crimes laid down in the London Agreement and declared that they "were already recognized as War Crimes under international law" and that it was too well settled to admit of argument "that violations of these provisions constituted crimes for which the guilty individuals were punishable".[131]

In the matter of crimes against humanity, the Tribunal adopted a restrictive interpretation in declaring that although the policy of persecution, repression, and murder of civilians, including Jews, before 1939, was ruthlessly carried out, it was of opinion "that revolting and horrible as many of these crimes were, it has not been satisfactorily proved that they were done in execution of, or in connection with, any" crime against peace or war crime. Therefore, the Tribunal would not make a "general declaration that the acts before 1939 were Crimes against Humanity within the meaning of the Charter, but from the beginning of the war in 1939 War Crimes were committed on a vast scale, which were also Crimes against Humanity; and insofar as the inhumane acts charged in the In-

124 *Ibid.*, p. 186.
125 *Ibid.*, p. 216.
126 *Ibid.*, p. 186.
127 United Nations, *The Charter and Judgment of the Nürnberg Trial,* History and Analysis (1949, sales No. 1949, V, 7), p. 58 (hereinafter referred to as "*Charter*").
128 Trial, p. 311.
129 *Ibid.*, p. 316; similar findings were made against Göring, Keitel, Jodl, Seyss-Inquart, and Frick; see *Charter,* pp. 59-60.
130 *Charter,* pp. 56-58.
131 *Trial,* p. 253.

dictment, and committed after the beginning of the war, did not constitute War Crimes, they were all committed in execution of, or in connection with, the aggressive war, and therefore constituted Crimes against Humanity."[132] This indicates clearly the Tribunal's approach to crimes against humanity. Apart from Streicher and von Schirach who were found guilty of this type of crime alone, all other defendants convicted of this crime were also convicted of war crimes. Von Schirach participated in the deportation of Jews from Vienna after he became Gauleiter, and the Tribunal assumed that he could not have been unaware of the extermination to which they were vowed. Of Streicher, the Tribunal said that his "incitement to murder and extermination at the time when Jews in the East were being killed under the most horrible conditions clearly constitutes persecution on political and racial grounds in connection with War Crimes, as defined by the Charter (of the Tribunal), and constitutes a crime against Humanity".[133]

The Tribunal approached the problem of organizations with deliberate caution. It stressed that the trial of organizations was "a far-reaching and novel procedure", and that the theory of "group criminality" was new and in opposition to the well-settled legal principle that guilt was personal, and that care must be taken lest innocent persons be punished.[134] Using the discretion conferred upon it by the London Agreement and Charter, the Tribunal declined to make a finding of guilt against the Reich Cabinet, the General Staff, the High Command and the "SA". The latter, the Tribunal declared, has been since the purge of 1934 a group of "unimportant Nazi hangers-on." The former were either not groups at all, or did not function as groups or were so small in number that their members could be tried individually. The Tribunal found that not a single meeting of the Reich Cabinet was held after 1937, and the Secret Cabinet Council never met at all.[135] The Tribunal's findings with respect to the other organizations, encompassed in no case the entire membership. In each case, the Leadership Corps, the "Gestapo", the "SD" and the "SS", the Tribunal characterized the group of members in position of responsibility, excluded those who ceased to hold positions of responsibility before September 1, 1939, and limited the finding of criminality to the former group. Emphatically, the Tribunal declared that membership alone was not enough, and those who had no knowledge of the criminal purposes or acts should not be held responsible.[136]

In connection with crimes against peace, it is to be noted that the Tribunal decisively rejected the plea of the defendants that Germany acted in self-defense.[137] The Tribunal also rejected the plea of the defendants that the law of the London Charter was *ex post facto,* that there could be no punishment without pre-existing law, that aggressive war was not a crime at the time when the acts charged were committed, that no penalty had been established for their commission and no court had been created for the trial and

[132] *Ibid.,* p. 254.
[133] *Ibid.,* pp. 304, 319.
[134] *Ibid.,* p. 256.
[135] *Ibid.,* pp. 275–279.
[136] *Ibid.,* pp. 256–273.
[137] *Ibid.,* pp. 280 ff.

punishment of offenders. It had been foreseen at the London Conference that such pleas amounting to a total challenge of the Tribunal's jurisdiction would be made. The Tribunal's law was accordingly formulated in such a fashion as to obviate the need for giving any reasons or justification for the trial and the underlying legal principles. The Tribunal was fully aware of this but impressed with the great importance of the issues raised, it proceeded to express its own views. In doing so, the Tribunal's reasoning itself became subject of much subsequent discussion.

The Tribunal observed that the principle of "no punishment without a pre-existing law" was not a limitation upon sovereignty but a principle of Justice. The defendants at bar must have known that attacking neighboring nations was a violation of international law and treaties. To punish them, in these circumstances, could not be unjust and the principle had no application in the present case.

Rejecting the plea that aggressive war was not a crime in 1939 when Germany attacked Poland, the Tribunal referred to the General Treaty for the Renunciation of War of August 27, 1928 (also known as the Kellogg-Briand Pact) and expressions of opinion in the League of Nations on the subject. The Tribunal concluded that "resort to a war of aggression is not merely illegal, but is criminal".[138] The Tribunal was not impressed with the arguments of the defendants that neither the Kellogg-Briand Pact nor any other instruments established a court and laid down the punishment. Said the Tribunal: "Such international agreements as the Pact of Paris have to deal with general principles of law, and not with administrative matters of procedure".[139]

Rejecting the defendants' plea that international law is concerned with states and not individuals and their punishment, the Tribunal declared: "Crimes against international law are committed by men, not by abstract entities, and only by punishing individuals who commit such crimes, can the provisions of international law be enforced".[140] Answering the contention of the accused that as high officials of the German State they acted on behalf of Germany, that their acts had the character of acts of State, and that therefore they were not personally responsible, the Tribunal while admitting that under certain circumstances State representatives enjoyed immunity for their official acts, held: "The authors of these acts (which are condemned as criminal by international law) cannot shelter themselves behind their official position in order to be freed from punishment in appropriate proceedings." And it went on to lay down what may well be the pivotal point of the judgment:

> ". . . the very essence of the Charter is that individuals have international duties which transcend the national obligations of obedience imposed by the individual state. He who violates the laws of war cannot obtain immunity while acting in pursuance of the authority of the state if the state in authorizing action moves outside its competence under international law".[141]

[138] *Ibid.*, pp. 219–222.
[139] *Ibid.*, p. 221.
[140] *Ibid.*, p. 223.
[141] *Ibid.*, p. 223.

This principle may be construed as affirming the superiority of international law over domestic or municipal law and the duty of individuals to obey international law rather than carry out domestic law or orders which are violative of international law. It is probably needless to point out that the Tribunal has thus laid down a principle of the greatest significance for the individual and the traditional framework of modern society, the nation-state.

The Tribunal, rejecting the plea of superior orders, that is the argument of the defendants that they were acting under Hitler's orders and could not be held responsible for carrying them out, relied on "the law of all nations". According to this the superior order may be urged in mitigation of the punishment. "The true test," said the Tribunal, "which is found in varying degrees in the criminal law of most nations, is not the existence of the order, but whether moral choice was in fact possible".[142] In so doing the Tribunal gave expression to a restrictive interpretation of the law laid down in the London Charter.

Speaking of the basis of its own jurisdiction, the Tribunal acknowledged that it rested on the London Agreement and Charter and that "the law of the Charter is decisive, and binding upon the Tribunal". However, the Tribunal, instead of resting content with this statement which was both correct and sufficient, went on to argue that

> "the making of the Charter was the exercise of sovereign legislative power by the countries to which the German Reich unconditionally surrendered; and the undoubted right of these countries to legislate for the occupied territories has been recognized by the civilized world. The Charter is not an arbitrary exercise of power on the part of the victorious Nations, but in the view of the Tribunal, as will be shown, it is the expression of international law existing at the time of its creation: and to that extent is itself a contribution to international law".[143]

The contentions of the Tribunal, obviously intended to answer the doubt of the defendants regarding the legal basis of the trial, raise several issues. The German Reich did not surrender to the victorious nations. The Act of Military Surrender of May 8, 1945, was signed on behalf of the German Supreme Command. It was a military and not a political act. Paragraph 4 provided that "this act of military surrender is without prejudice to, and will be superseded by, any general instrument of surrender imposed by, or on behalf of, the United Nations and applicable to *Germany* and the German armed forces as a whole." It does not appear that such a general instrument applicable to Germany as a whole was ever executed. It is true by the Berlin Declaration of June 5, 1945, that Allied Powers assumed "supreme authority with respect to Germany, including all the powers possessed by the German Government", without thereby affecting the annexation of Germany. In virtue of this assumption of authority the Allied Powers could and did legislate for Germany. The Tribunal, however, was not established by a law of the Allied

[142] *Ibid.*, p. 224.
[143] *Ibid.*, p. 218.

Control Council, but by an executive agreement between the Four Powers and without Germany's consent. It will be recalled that the United States suggested to have the Tribunal set up by the Control Council for Germany and that the Soviet representative at the London Conference proposed that the members of the Tribunal be appointed by the Council but this was not agreeable to the other participants..

The statement of the Tribunal, that its Charter was "the expression of international law existing at the time of its creation", goes beyond the Charter itself. The Charter laid down the law for this particular trial of major war criminals of the Europen Axis. The Tribunal thus implies that the law of the Charter was "an authoritative expression of general international law".[144] In so doing, the Tribunal adopted substantially the point of view expounded at the London Conference by Mr. Justice Jackson.

## VI. CONCLUSIONS

It may be well to state at the outset the belief that substantial justice was done at Nuremberg. Crimes defying human imagination on an incredibly large scale have been committed and some of those bearing a large share of responsibility were punished. The issues or controversies of a rather technical character relating to the trial pale in significance compared with the larger ethical issues involved in this historical attempt to let punishment follow the crime. Nonetheless these technical issues are important and deserve consideration.

The legal basis for the trial has not been satisfactorily explained. International tribunals are established by agreement of the States concerned. In the case of the Nuremberg Tribunal Germany did not consent to its establishment nor to the law to be applied by it. By contrast, Japan agreed in the Peace Treaty of 1951 to the Tokyo trials.[145] This defect in the creation of the Nuremberg Tribunal extends to all the specific points at issue with respect to the applicable law. That resort to aggression or to war in violation of treaties constituted not merely an illegal but also a criminal act, either in 1939 or in 1945, continues to be debated in spite of the Nuremberg judgment.[146] The Charter of the United Nations adopted prior to the London Agreement and Charter neither defines aggression nor makes resort to it a criminal act. There is no prohibition in international law against *ex post facto* creation of law or against the creation of law having retroactive effect.[147] If Germany consented, as Japan did, to the law of the Nuremberg Tribunal there would be no ground to criticize it on that score. The same observation applies to individual responsibility for crimes against peace. In international law individual liability is the exception,

[144] *Charter*, p. 38.

[145] Article II of the Treaty of Peace with Japan, 8 September 1951 (entered into force 28 April 1952) reads as follows: "Japan accepts the judgments of the International Military Tribunal for the Far East and other Allied War Crimes Courts both within and outside Japan, and will carry out the sentences imposed thereby upon Japanese nationals imprisoned in Japan . . ."

[146] See this writer, "Criminality of Aggressive War", *American Political Science Review*, Vol. XLI 1947, pp. 205 ff and *supra*, p. 313; Stone, *Legal Controls of International Conflict*, 1954, p. 302.

[147] This writer, *ibid.*, pp. 223; Stone, *ibid.*, 302, 360, 368.

and collective liability the rule. Even the Charter of the United Nations provides for enforcement action against the aggressive state and not for punishment of those instigating or waging aggressive war. The London Charter departed from a well established principle of international law. In so doing it may well have pointed the direction for the development of international law.

The law of the London Charter also breaks new ground in denying the defendants the protection of the act of state. This may be a salutary departure from traditional concepts of international law. Even under these concepts the plea of act of state does not constitute a good defense before a properly constituted international tribunal. A state is responsible for its own acts or acts attributable to it. The flaw here again lies in establishment of the tribunal and not in its law.

The attempt made by the Tribunal and also by writers[148] to find a legally sound basis for the Nuremberg proceedings in the unconditional surrender rests on debatable grounds. It has already been pointed out that the surrender which actually took place was tendered by the German High Command and that a general instrument of surrender applicable to Germany was never executed. The Tribunal also said that in creating it and defining the law it was to administer, the Four Powers "have done together what any one of them might have done singly".[149] This may apply to war crimes and possibly to crimes against humanity but can hardly apply to crimes against peace if their novelty is accepted. One might perhaps find a legally more satisfactory basis in construing the London Agreement as a treaty which imposes a burden upon a third state, that is a state which is not a signatory to the agreement. As a rule, treaties establish principles of law or obligations only for the contracting parties, in accordance with the basic premise that without consent treaties have no binding force. However, exceptions are not unknown and the London Agreement might be regarded as a treaty falling into this exceptional category.

The Nuremberg proceedings have sometimes been criticized on the ground that they were unilateral in the sense that the victor tried the vanquished. This criticism, which may be taken to be directed primarily against crimes against peace, has been denied legal or moral force.[150] On the other hand, the gravity of the unilateral character of the proceedings has been stressed as a precedent for the future, for if the charge of aggressive war "is to be employed in future as a general rule of international law, the question must be faced: 'Can we conceive of any war in which the victorious powers will allow the defeated to establish or participate in tribunals to try the leaders of the victors, however clear their aggressive intent and acts?' If, as is believed, this is inconceivable, and if history does not permit the assumption that an aggressor can never be victorious, the rule created at Nuremberg must be seen as placing in the hands of aggressors a powerful new instrument, not only of oppression of men, but of the fabrication of history".[151]

[148] Stone, *ibid.*, pp. 302, 359.
[149] Trial, p. 218; see also Stone *ibid.*, p. 359.
[150] Stone, *ibid.*, p. 326
[151] Stone, *ibid.*

The Tribunal in rejecting the plea of superior orders pointed out that the true test is not the existence of the order but whether a moral choice was in fact possible. It is suggested that this consideration is vitally relevant to the whole concept of individual responsibility. Is there any sound ground for holding individuals responsible for acts in conformity with domestic but in violation of international law unless a moral choice was in fact possible? This question is raised not so much with reference to those individuals condemned in Nuremberg but with reference to the future. Do individuals as a matter of practical experience and not of theory, possess the necessary knowledge to make an intelligent and accurate choice, and do they have the moral or legal right to refuse their co-operation in the achievement of national objectives which they consider either immoral or illegal? This might involve a conflict between the private view of the individual and the official view of the Government. The individual, as a result of the Nuremberg proceedings and judgment, has been placed in the unenviable position of having conceivably to choose between obedience to national law, with the possible consequence of making himself responsible before an international tribunal, and obedience to international law as he sees it, with the almost certain consequence of rendering himself responsible before a domestic tribunal. The uncertainty of international law tends to intensify the difficulty confronting the individual as well as his state.

The General Assembly of the United Nations on December 11, 1945, adopted a resolution in which it affirmed the principles of international law recognized by the Charter of the Nürnberg (sic) Tribunal and in the judgment of the Tribunal. Further work on the formulation of these principles was done by the International Law Commission of the United Nations. This Commission also drafted a code of offenses against the peace and security of nations, which is largely based upon the Nuremberg principles. This draft code has been considered by the General Assembly and by the Member Governments but has not been accepted as yet. No doubt its adoption would go a long way towards clarifying the law in which the individual has a vital interest. Unilateral trials might be avoided in the future if a permanent and truly international criminal court were established. The United Nations has embarked upon the ambitious scheme of drafting the statute for such a court. If established, this court would apply the projected code of criminal offenses against the peace and security of mankind which is based throughout on the responsibility of individuals.

It is expected in some quarters that the post-World War II war crimes trials will exercise a detering effect upon would-be aggressors. This, of course, remains to be seen. The acts of aggression which have occurred since the end of World War II do not support this expectation. Nor do they support the expectation that the war crimes trials would be a precedent for the future.[152] It is freely admitted, however, that these events and the experience based upon them are far from conclusive. It is, of course, not clear whether those who refer to the Nuremberg trial as a precedent for the future have in

[152] Whitney R. Harris, *Tyranny on Trial*, p. 560; but see Hans Kelsen, "Will the judgment in the Nuremberg trial constitute a precedent in international law?", International Law Quarterly Vol. 1 (1944), pp. 153–171.

mind international trials for the prosecution of the crimes against peace or the war crimes or the crimes against humanity, although it has been affirmed "if Nuremberg stands for anything" it stands for the proposition that those "who, through the instrumentality of a state subservient to their commands, engage in aggressive war" should be prosecuted and punished.[153]

Undoubtedly there is truth in the statement "that no effective international machinery is available to reach victorious aggressors" and that "successful aggression, like succesful treason, is a crime for which the perpetrators, while they prevail, will not be punished".[154] It might be added that it is not likely that such an effective machinery will be devised in any forseeable future for the trial and punishment of victorious aggressors. The debates in the United Nations on the subject of the proposed international criminal court and the draft code of offenses against the peace and security of mankind certainly do not encourage any fond hopes. But this, it is submitted, has no bearing upon the problem whether the victorious aggressors or the victorious opponents of aggression will have the resolution and courage to bring before the bar of international tribunals those members of their own armed forces or of their own civilian populations who may be alleged by either side to have committed war crimes or crimes against humanity. Yet, if the Nuremberg principles are to be a precedent for the future, can it be gainsaid that this is precisely what would have to happen in all countries involved in armed conflict? It would appear, therefore, that unless belligerents surrender to international justice their own offenders against the laws of war and of humanity, no decisive contribution will be made towards the effective and objective establishment of the Nuremberg principles as a precedent for the future. Only in this manner, it is suggested, can the claim be vindicated that herceforth, at any rate, the Nuremberg principles will apply to all nations everywhere in the world and regardless whether the offenders belonged to the victorious or the vanquished nations.

The war crimes trials after World War II may be seen in a still broader frame of reference. One of the chief characteristic developments of the 20th century has been the rise of totalitarian States which claim the undivided and unconditional allegiance of their nationals. As individuals they are exhorted and indeed expected on pain of penalty to subscribe without reservation to the prevailing ideology as dispensed by the State or Party; they are, by the same token, bound to subordinate their own as well as the traditional concepts of right and wrong as formulated in the Western civilization to the values propounded by the State or Party. International law as it developed over the centuries in Western Europe, incorporated and reflected the basic values of this civilization as they applied to international relations. According to a widely accepted view regarding the relation between international law and the individual (the view of the 19th century positivists), the State was the immediate and the individual the mediate subject of international law. The modern view, on the other hand, has been to regard the individuals or at least

[153] Harris, *ibid.*,.
[154] Harris, *ibid.*, p. 562.

some of them—the heads of State, the ministers, and others—as being the direct subjects of international law without any mediation by the State. This view has been denounced as reactionary by the totalitarians along with its theoretical foundation which is the supremacy of international over municipal law. The intent and purpose of the totalitarian States, this was demonstrated in Nuremberg, has been, on the other hand, to cut the individual off from any rapport with any law or morality distinct from or superior to national law or morality. It is against this context that it is possible and perhaps even necessary to place the Nuremberg trials. For these trials were in a profound sense a demonstration against the totalitarian subjection of the individual to ''nationalized'' truth; they were a protest against the erasure of the individual as a subject, mediate or immediate, of international law, and as a responsible member of the international community. For the very essence of the law laid down in the London Charter as interpreted by the International Military Tribunal has been

> that individuals have international duties which transcend the national obligations of obedience imposed by the individual state.

This proposition must appear as sheer heresy to the totalitarian States. Thus the war crimes trials may be regarded as a plea for the autonomy of the individual as a moral person, and in a profound sense, as a plea for his relatedness to a higher law which no State is in a position to obliterate. Those who launched the war crimes trials and enacted their law as well as those who regard them as a precedent for the future must accept the view that States are limited in their competence to requiring the individual to do only those things which are in conformity with international law and are bound to regard the individual as a responsible member of the international community.

# INTERNATIONAL TERRORISM AND INTERNATIONAL CRIMINAL JURISDICTION

When the League of Nations, following the assassination of King Alexander I of Yugoslavia and French Prime Minister Louis Barthou, took up in 1934 the question of defining more precisely the rules of international law concerning the repression of terrorist activity, its committee of experts drew up and a conference adopted on November 16, 1937 two Conventions, one for the Prevention and Punishment of Terrorism and another for the Creation of an International Criminal Court.[1] The fact that only one state—India—ratified the former and none ratified the latter is not a conclusive argument against the soundness of the League approach which was thorough and coherent,[2] concerned with both the substantive law and its impartial and uniform application by an international tribunal. A High Contracting Party to the Convention was entitled to commit the accused for trial to the International Criminal Court if it did not wish to try them before its own courts or to grant extradition in accordance with the principle *aut dedere aut judicare.*

When the United Nations embarked on the ambitious project to formulate the Nuremberg principles it followed to some extent the model of the League. The International Law Commission submitted in 1954 a revised Draft Code of Offenses against the Peace and Security of Mankind[3] and another organ of the General Assembly drafted the statute for an International Criminal Court. The Draft Code is a comprehensive document in-

[1] HUDSON, INTERNATIONAL LEGISLATION, 862–78, 878–93 (1941).

[2] It included even what is currently called a "gun control law" in Article 13 and dealt in Article 14 with the use of forged passports and the issue of passports to persons not entitled to them "with the object of assiting any activity contrary to the purpose of this Convention."

[3] ILC: Report covering the work of its 6th Session, 3 June–28 July 1954. GAOR: 9th Sess., SUPP. No. 9 (A/2693), 9–12.

cluding the Nuremberg crimes,[4] genocide, and even a paragraph on terrorism.[5] Both drafts shared a similar fate. Consideration of the draft Code and draft Statute was postponed in 1957 and again in 1968 until the Assembly completed its work on the question of defining agression.[6]

Since the elaboration of the Draft Code, the work of the United Nations on terrorism in its various manifestations has been in response to events and consequently piecemeal. This has been so whether one considers the three hijacking conventions or the draft articles on the Prevention and Punishment of Crimes against Diplomatic Agents and other Internationally Protected Persons prepared by the International Law Commission,[7] or the U.S. Draft Convention for the Prevention and Punishment of Certain Acts of International Terrorism, submitted to the 1972 session of the General Assembly.[8] This latter project fared very badly in the Sixth Committee where it was submerged in the boundless problem of the underlying causes of terrorism and never surfaced again.[9]

In any event, it is doubtful whether this piecemeal approach will add up to a comprehensive system for the prevention and punishment of terrorist activites. Certainly without a tribunal to give a degree of coherence and consistency to the several international instruments, their application by national tribunals may well fall short of the objectives of certainty and impartiality.

It is gratifying, therefore, to note that an unofficial organization, The Foundation for the Establishment of an International Criminal Court, is devoted to the study of the problem of terrorism in the broad framework of the League and the Draft Code of Offences against the Peace and Security of Mankind rather than in the current response-to-events manner of the United Nations. Under the direction of its President, Professor Robert K. Woetzel, the Foundation continued work on drafting a convention on international crimes and a statute for an international criminal court. Two conferences in 1972, one at the Villa Serbelloni[10] and the other at Wingspread[11] were attended by experts from the United States and abroad.[12] The drafts which emerged from the discussions have no official standing but they will be available to governmental officials who

[4] Report of the 1953 Committee on International Criminal Jurisdiction, 27 July–20 August 1953. GAOR: 9th Sess., SUPP. No. 12 (A/2645).

[5] Article 2, par. 6 lists among the offences against the peace and security of mankind: "The undertaking or encouragement by the authorities of a state of terrorist activities in another state, or the toleration by the authorities of a state of terrorist activities in another state, or the toleration by the authorities of a state of organized activities calculated to carry out terrorist acts in another state."

[6] GA Res. 1186 (XII) and 1187 (XII), Dec. 11, 1957 and UN Doc. A/7250, Sept. 26, 1968, at 3, par. 10.

[7] ILC: Report on the work of its 24th Session. A/8710, at 225, 232–57. 67 AJIL 98 (1973).

[8] UN Doc. A/C. 6/L. 850, Sept. 25, 1972.

[9] GA Res. 3034 (XXVII), Dec. 18, 1972. It was adopted by a vote of 76 for, 35 against, with 17 abstentions. The resolution, however, reaffirmed the inalienable right to self-determination of all peoples under colonial and racist regimes and condemned "the continuation of repressive and terrorist acts" by such regimes in denying self-determination and independence to such peoples.

[10] Rockefeller Foundation Study and Conference Center, Bellagio (Italy).

[11] Johnson Conference Center, Racine, Wisconsin.

[12] The Serbelloni meeting was attended by three jurists from Bangladesh concerned with the preparation of war crimes trials: Kamal Hossain, Minister for Law and Parliamentary Affairs, Serajul Huq, Chief Counsel, War Crimes Tribunal, and S. R. Pal, Chief Council, War Crimes Tribunal.

will find it very worthwhile to study them and draw upon them when the appropriate stage is reached on the official level.[13]

The draft on international crimes has been made more comprehensive than the 1953 Draft Code by the inclusion of hijacking, kidnapping of public officials, acts of violence against internationally protected persons, international acts of terrorism, illicit traffic in drugs, and finally international pollution of the environment "causing substantial harm to the health, safety and welfare of mankind." The substantive convention is linked to the proposed criminal court in the same fashion in which the League of Nations linked the International Criminal Court to its Convention on Terrorism: each party undertakes to prosecute the alleged offender or to extradite him or to surrender him to the International Criminal Court. There is a difference in the formulation. The Foundation draft establishes an obligation to prosecute or to extradite or to surrender him whereas the League Convention in Article 2 provided that a party instead of prosecuting the accused before his own courts or extraditing him shall be entitled to commit him for trial to the International Court. In either case, the government concerned has a choice which it may find to its advantage to exercise. In neither case is any choice offered to the accused.

The former Secretary-General of the United Nations, U Thant, was reported to have suggested the creation of an international tribunal to deal with hijacking of airplanes because such crimes were "directed against an international service affecting a diversity of nations, men and interests." They were in a different category from other crimes and therefore "could not be dealt with by national courts defending the interests of one particular people or nation."[14] The Foundation, like the League of Nations and the United Nations in its earlier phase, is concerned with at least offering the possibility of an international proceeding for what are substantially international crimes, that is, crimes affecting more than one state or an international service. The Foundation has performed and it will continue to perform a useful function in educating jurists of different countries in a vital problem area of an evolving body of international law, in both its substantive and procedural aspects.

[13] The drafts have been published with the assistance of the Johnson Foundation under the title: "The Establishment of an International Criminal Court, 1st and 2nd International Criminal Law Conference" (1973). Copies may be obtained from the Johnson Foundation, Racine, Wisconsin 53401.

[14] New York Times, Sept. 15, 1970, at 17.

# IV

# PROBLEMS OF INTERPRETATION

# STATES AS ORGANS OF INTERNATIONAL LAW AND THE PROBLEM OF AUTOINTERPRETATION

## INTRODUCTION

KELSEN's epochal contribution to the study of international relations consists in the theoretical conception of international law as the law above the states, as "law in the same sense as national law,"[1] and in the practical proposals for making this law a more effective instrument of social control than it had been in the unhappy past.[2] Thus, at the end of his fundamental study on sovereignty, written during and published almost immediately after World War I, he expressed the hope that the concept of state sovereignty will give way to the development of the present primitive society of nations toward a genuine *civitas maxima* in the substantive and political sense.[3] Indeed, in my view, Kelsen's theory of international law furnished the ideal foundation for the peace movement, that is, for all efforts directed at the substitution of international order for international anarchy and its instrument, imperialism.[4] Thus, many years later in discussing the

[1] Hans Kelsen, *General Theory of Law and State* (Cambridge: Harvard University Press, 1946), p. 328; *Law and Peace in International Relations* (Cambridge: Harvard University Press, 1942), pp. 61 ff., particularly pp. 78 ff.

[2] Hans Kelsen, *Peace through Law* (Chapel Hill: The University of North Carolina Press, 1944), *passim*.

[3] Hans Kelsen, *Das Problem der Souveränität und die Theorie des Völkerrechts* (Tübingen: J. C. B. Mohr, 1920), p. 320: "Denn die Vorstellung von der Souveränität des eigenen Staates ist bisher—ob mit Recht oder Unrecht—allem im Wege gestanden, was auf eine Ausgestaltung der Völkerrechtsordnung zu einer arbeitsteiligen Organisation, was auf die Einsetzung von besonderen Organen zur Fortbildung, Anwendung und Durchsetzung des Völkerrechts, was auf eine Weiterentwicklung der Völkerrechtsgemeinschaft aus ihrem Zustande der Primitivität zu einer civitas maxima—auch im politisch-materiellen Sinne dieses Wortes—abzielt. Als unendliche Aufgabe aber muss solcher Weltstaat als Weltorganisation allem politischen Streben gesetzt sein."

[4] Leo Gross, *Pazifismus und Imperialismus* (Leipzig und Wien: F. Deuticke, 1931), pp. 430–453.

theory of *bellum justum,* while claiming that the role of force, particularly of war, in international law and relations, admits of two interpretations equally possible from the scientific viewpoint, Kelsen declared that "it is not a scientific, but a political decision which gives preference to the *bellum justum* theory." He explained that his preference was justified "by the fact that only this interpretation conceives of the international order as law, although admittedly primitive law, the first step in an evolution which within the national community, the State, has led to a system of norms which is generally accepted as law. There can be little doubt that the international law of the present contains all the potentialities of such an evolution; it has shown a definite tendency in this direction. . . . We choose this interpretation (that is, *bellum justum*), hoping to have recognized the beginning of a development of the future and with the intention of strengthening as far as possible all the elements of present-day international law which tend to justify this interpretation and to promote the evolution we desire."[5]

Similarly, when discussing the alternatives of comprehending all legal phenomena as parts of a single system, namely the hypotheses of the primacy of national law and that of international law, Kelsen, while affirming that only a monistic construction is scientifically possible, denies that the science of law can impose the choice between those two equally possible epistemological hypotheses. The choice can be made, however, on ethical and political grounds.[6]

In appraising Kelsen's contribution to international law—outstanding in its theoretical as well as practical political aspects—it appears advisable to bear in mind his deep-seated desire to guide the development of international law toward a more centralized and therefore more effective legal order. Whenever scientifically two conceptions appear to him to be equally possible, he invariably declares his preference in favor of that likely to promote that objective. The intimate *rapport* between Kelsen's theoretical and political thinking is frequently overlooked by critics of the Vienna School who refer to it as "magnificently logical and barrenly abstract" and who believe that the "transfer of concepts and terms from the State environment, where they are native, to the profoundly different context of international relations," has thrown "legal theory into a confusion from which it can only emerge by violent distortions of the phenomena which it seeks to unify."[7] Kelsen has subjected traditional presentations of international law to a rigorous critique and has without question introduced into international law such concepts as monopoly of force, sanctions, delict, centralization, decentralization and, above all, a concept of law itself. It is proposed to examine in this paper some of these concepts in the hope of clarifying the issue of whether it is theory which is responsible for the "damaging repercussions on the practical plane,"[8] or whether these are rather due to the shortcom-

[5] Kelsen, *Law and Peace,* pp. 54 ff.

[6] Kelsen, *General Theory,* p. 388: "A person whose political attitude is one of nationalism and imperialism will naturally be inclined to accept the hypothesis of the primacy of national law. A person whose sympathies are for internationalism and pacifism will be inclined to accept the hypothesis of the primacy of international law. From the point of view of the science of law, it is irrelevant which hypothesis one chooses. But from the point of view of political ideology, the choice is important since tied up with the idea of sovereignty."

[7] Percy E. Corbett, *Law and Society in the Relations of States* (New York: Harcourt, Brace and Company, 1951), p. 10.

[8] *Loc. cit.*

ings of international law itself which Kelsen could certainly not be accused of glossing over. It may then be possible to determine whether it appears desirable to adjust somewhat the theory to the facts of international relations and what the necessary qualifications may be. It is commonly agreed that theory cannot be to any appreciable degree in advance of international law nor can it afford to lag behind. The inquiry will concentrate on one of Kelsen's principal theses, namely, that the international, like the national, society is characterized by a monopoly of force, that sanctions are applied by states as organs of the society, and consequently are to be constructed as the reaction of the society against the delict. This will lead to a brief analysis of one of the central problems of international law, that of autointerpretation. As the sanction is the key to Kelsen's concept of law, it may be useful to introduce the inquiry with a brief discussion of this concept and its application to international law.

## LEGAL RULES AND VALIDITY OF INTERNATIONAL LAW

The starting point of Kelsen's theory of international law is the question whether international law is law in the same sense as national or municipal law, the prototype of all law. The basic unit of law is the legal rule or norm which Kelsen defines as a hypothetical judgment: "If A is, B ought to be" or, more specifically: "If someone steals, he ought to be punished."[9] The order of law being a coercive order, a sanction ought to take place when a delict occurs. The delict, far from being a negation of law, "is the fundamental condition for the application of the law, for the execution of the sanction established by law. . . . Only by the fact that a sanction is attached to certain conduct does this conduct become a delict in the juristic sense. . . . Delict and sanction are correlative ideas."[10] Law, by providing and socially organizing sanction, is distinguished from other normative orders such as religion and morality.[11] Kelsen distinguishes between primary and secondary norms. Thus the sentence "One shall not steal; if someone steals, he shall be punished" can be separated into the primary norm: If somebody steals, he shall be punished; and the secondary norm: one shall not steal. The secondary norm is contained in the primary norm, "which is the only genuine legal norm."[12] While the secondary norm addresses itself to the subjects and is "valid" for them, the primary norm addresses itself to the organ which ought to execute the sentence, and is "valid" for it. Consequently, "only the organ can, strictly speaking, 'obey' or 'disobey' the legal norm, by executing or not executing the stipulated sanction."[13] The efficacy of law can be subdivided into primary and secondary: primary efficacy refers to the application of the law by the organ; secondary efficacy refers to the subject's obedience to the law.[14] According to

[9] Kelsen, *General Theory*, p. 46.
[10] Kelsen, *Law and Peace*, p. 24.
[11] *Ibid.*, p. 9.
[12] Kelsen, *General Theory*, p. 61.
[13] *Loc. cit.*
[14] *Ibid.*, p. 62.

Kelsen, "law is efficacious if it is applied by the organ—if the organ executes the sentence. And the organ has to apply law precisely in the case where the subject 'disobeys' law: this is the case for which the sanction is stipulated. There is, however, a certain connection between factual obedience and the factual application of law. If a legal norm is permanently disobeyed by the subjects, it is probably no longer applied by the organ either. Therefore, though the efficacy of law is primarily its being applied by proper organs, secondarily its efficacy means its being obeyed by the subjects."[15]

There remains the question whether the organ is in duty bound to execute the sanction in case a subject disobeys the law, the norm in the secondary sense. In Kelsen's theory, the law-applying organ is

> legally obligated to execute the sanction . . . only if there is a further norm which attaches a further sanction to the nonexecution of the first sanction. . . . The organ of the second norm may in turn be obligated by a third norm to execute the sanction stipulated by the second norm, and so on and so forth. However, this series of norms cannot be extended indefinitely. There must be a last norm of the series such that the sanction which it stipulates is not a legal duty in the sense defined. If the meaning of this norm is also expressed by saying that under certain conditions a sanction 'ought to' be enacted, then the concept of 'ought' does not coincide with the concept of legal duty. An organ which 'ought' to enact a sanction may, or may not, be obligated to do so.[16]

It may be recalled here that Verdross, like Kelsen, also argued that in any legal order we arrive sooner or later at a "marginal" organ *(Grenzorgan)* which also ought to execute the law but whose failure to do so is not the condition of a legal sanction. Unlike Kelsen, however, Verdross derives from this phenomenon support for the view that the ultimate sanctions of law are moral in character—the marginal organ is in conscience morally bound to respect fully the law and to execute it to the best of its ability.[17] While Kelsen insists on a thorough separation of law and morality, Verdross on the contrary conceives the validity of law as dependent on morality, and far from being separated from other norms, law appears as interwoven with other categories of norms into a "normative carpet" *(normativer Teppich).*[18]

How is this general theory of law applied to international law? International law is law in the same sense as national law, says Kelsen, "if it is possible to describe the material which presents itself as international law in such a way that the employment of force by one state against another can be interpreted only either as delict or sanction."[19] As according to "a commonly accepted view . . . there exists in international law such a thing as a delict,"[20] it remains for Kelsen to show that there is also a sanction. It being generally agreed that reprisals namely, a "limited interference in the sphere of interests of

[15] *Loc. cit.*
[16] *Ibid.*, p. 59 f.
[17] Alfred Verdross, *Völkerrecht* (2d ed., Berlin und Wien: J. Springer, 1950), p. 26.
[18] *Ibid.*, p. 26.
[19] Kelsen, *General Theory*, p. 328.
[20] *Ibid.*, p. 329.

one State by another" are "only admissible as a reaction against a wrong . . . there is nothing to prevent our calling a reprisal a sanction of international law."[21] However, in addition to the "limited" there is also the "unlimited" forcible interference in the spheres of interest of the states, which is known as war. The problem then arises whether it is "*possible* to interpret war . . . as either a delict or a reaction against a delict, a sanction."[22] This problem is fundamental because the characterization of international law as "true law" depends "upon whether it is *possible* to interpret international law in the sense of the theory of *bellum justum* or whether, in other words, it is possible to assume that, according to general international law, war is in principle forbidden being permitted only as a sanction, that is, as a reaction against a delict."[23] Kelsen's solution of this problem is well known. On the one hand, he admits that "the technical inadequacies of general international law do indeed to a certain extent justify the interpretation of the opponents of *bellum justum.*" But, consistently, these opponents "must not regard international law as true law." On the other hand, the theory of *bellum justum* namely, "that war is in principle a delict and is permitted only as a sanction" is also possible. Scientifically, both theories are possible, and each will choose between them according to his political preference.[24]

The theory of *bellum justum* is intimately linked to the view of "general international law as an order turning the employment of force into a monopoly of the community." Whether or not the international community is endowed with or characterized by a monopoly of force will be discussed below. It may be useful at this point to examine briefly some of the other aspects of Kelsen's general theory of law as applied to international law. Assuming for the sake of argument that both reprisal and war are sanctions of international law, can the material traditionally known as international law be reduced to propositions of the type "if A is, then B ought to be"? This is not possible. In general international law, the "ought" must be replaced by "may."[25] International law authorizes but does not require states to execute sanctions against a wrong-doing state. The "organs" of international law or international community, the states, like the "organs" in primitive legal orders, are under "no legal duty . . . to execute the legal sanctions. . . . If the legal norm is expressed by saying that when certain conditions are fulfilled the organ ought to order and execute the sanction, then the word 'ought' only denotes the specific sense in which the sanction is 'stipulated,' 'provided,' 'determined,' in the norm."[26]

It will be recalled that, as stated above, an organ is under a duty to execute a sanction if its conduct is made the content of another superior norm, and that, finally, one arrives at a last norm, the sanction of which is not a legal duty of the "marginal organ."

[21] *Ibid.*, p. 330.
[22] *Ibid.*, p. 330; italics mine.
[23] *Ibid.*, p. 340; italics mine.
[24] *Ibid.*, p. 341.
[25] Verdross, *op. cit.*, p. 26.
[26] Kelsen, *General Theory*, p. 60.

While municipal law, the prototype of "true law," is generally characterized by a hierarchy of organs, beginning with the "first" and ending with the "marginal" organ, general international law on the contrary is characterized by the coincidence between the first and the marginal organ: the "injured" state is generally the first and at the same time the marginal organ.[27] The organ of international law, however, has been said to be bound by the moral maxim of *bona fides*.[28]

The distinction between primary and secondary norms applies to international law (that is, states shall not break a treaty; if a state breaks a treaty, it shall be punished), provided it is borne in mind that the "ought" or "shall" in the primary norm of international law does not carry the meaning which, but for the marginal organ, it does carry in municipal law, namely, that of the legal duty. However, some difficulty is encountered in connection with what has been called above primary and secondary efficacy. The secondary norm is efficacious if it is obeyed by the subjects. The primary, what Kelsen calls the "genuine," norm, on the other hand, would be efficacious "if it is applied by the organ—if the organ executes the sanction; and the organ has to apply law precisely in the case where the subject 'disobeys' law: this is the case for which the sanction is stipulated."[29] Now, while it is commonly accepted that states by and large obey international law, that is, the secondary norms of which they are the addressees, the primary, genuine norm, that which provides for the application of the sanction, by the "organ" of the international community, is rarely applied. The cases of breaches of international law or, one ought to say more properly, perhaps, of alleged breaches of international law, which remain "unpunished" are many indeed. It is arguable, therefore, that the primary norms of international law are characterized by a lack of efficacy and that the international legal order on the whole is not efficacious. Whether a primitive legal order with which Kelsen frequently compares international law is or is not on the whole an efficacious order does not seem to be material in this context. It also appears unnecessary to examine here the question whether the international legal order may properly be called a primitive community or compared with primitive communities.[30]

[27] There may be exceptional cases of what might be called devolution of the right or duty to take action. This seems to be the notion underlying Professor C. H. M. Waldock's interpretation of the British action in the *Altmark* incident; see his article "The Release of the Altmark's Prisoners," *British Year Book of International Law* (London: Oxford University Press, 1947), pp. 216–238, at p. 236.

[28] Verdross, *op. cit.*, p. 28. Along somewhat similar lines see the observation of the French representative, Joseph Barthélemy, in the Assembly of the League of Nations with reference to the perennial question quis custodem custodiet: "Le droit existe et s'impose, mais, lorsqu'on arrive à certaines hauteurs, le droit n'a plus la sanction matérielle." Records of the Fourth Assembly, Plenary, p. 82.

[29] Kelsen, *General Theory*, p. 62.

[30] George Schwarzenberger, *Power Politics* (2d ed., New York: Frederick A. Praeger, 1951), p. 255 says on this subject: "International society has been described as a primitive community. It may be implied in this classification that, in due course, there will be an automatic progress towards a fully developed international community. . . . Such a diagnosis is meaningless unless its basic proposition, the conception of the primitive community, is used in a technical sense. In this case, it is fallacious to assume that primitive communities live in a state of anarchy. . . . In reality, the inter-State system is not a primitive community, but an extreme type of society relations." Corbett, *op. cit.*, p. 12 observes: "An excuse frequently offered for the weakness of international law in times of crisis is that it is a primitive system. . . . But the excuse is misleading. Primitive communities are commonly marked by a social solidarity and a dependence upon tradition which, with the scantiest organization, secure a high degree of law-observance."

The essential question is whether the international legal order is a valid one. Validity and effectiveness are sharply distinguished by Kelsen: "Validity of law means that the legal norms are valid, that men ought to behave as the legal norm prescribes; that men ought to obey and apply the legal norms. Efficacy of law means that men actually behave as, according to the legal norms, they ought to behave, that the norms are actually applied and obeyed."[31] Nevertheless, although conceptually validity is distinguished from efficacy and "the specific existence of a legal order, or of a system of norms, is not its efficacy but its validity," Kelsen admits an interdependence between validity and efficacy: "The efficacy of a legal order—the fact that its norms are really obeyed and applied—is of a certain importance for the validity of the legal order. Only a legal order the norms of which are generally obeyed and applied is considered valid. It is not necessary that all the norms of this order be always and without exception obeyed or applied; but it is necessary that it be on the whole efficacious."[32] It may be difficult to agree upon the meaning of the phrase "on the whole efficacious." If we continue to apply the distinction between primary and secondary norms, upon the efficacy of which of them does the validity depend? That international law is "on the whole" obeyed, that is, that the secondary norms are efficacious, is a proposition which has already been advanced. The norms of morality and religion, however, are also obeyed, perhaps even more consistently than those of international law. If validity depends also upon the efficacy of the primary, the "genuine" norms, that is, upon the execution of the sanction by the organ, then indeed it may be doubted whether international law is a valid order. The doubt is enhanced by the fact that owing to the decentralized character of international law, particularly with respect to the law-applying function, it may be debatable whether reprisals or war, when resorted to by one state against another, are actually used as a reaction against a wrong. If, furthermore, there is no certainty in particular cases whether an alleged rule is a rule of positive international law, and if there is no certainty whether in a given situation a state is not merely alleged to have violated it but has actually acted contrary to it, then obviously there is room for doubt whether the use of force should be construed as sanction or as delict. This chain of doubts, of which Kelsen is fully aware, has led some writers to deny that international law is positive or valid law in the same sense as national law.[33]

## THE CONCEPT OF THE MONOPOLY OF FORCE OF THE INTERNATIONAL COMMUNITY

In order that there be a state of law, it is deemed necessary that there be a sphere of interests protected by law, which means that force be permitted only as a sanction against

[31] Kelsen, *General Theory*, p. 39.

[32] Kelsen, *Law and Peace*, p. 15.

[33] E.g., Walther Burckhardt, *Die Organisation der Rechtsgemeinschaft* (Basel: Helbing und Lichtenhahn, 1927), pp. 164 ff., 374 ff.

a delict and that moreover the sanction itself be conceived as "the reaction of the legal community against the delict."[34] This is the theoretical basis of Kelsen's concept of just war. If international law is to be described in the terms of the rule of law discussed above, then it must be possible to interpret the sanction—reprisal or war—as "a reaction of the international legal community."[35] In the primitive community, according to Kelsen,

> the man avenging the murder of his father upon one whom he considers to be the murderer is himself regarded not as a murderer but as an organ of the community. . . . The distinction between murder, as a delict, and homicide, as a fulfillment of a duty to avenge, is of the greatest importance for the primitive society. It means that killing is only permitted if the killer acts as an organ of his community, if his action is undertaken in execution of the legal order. The coercive action is reserved to the community and is, in consequence, a monopoly of this community.[36]

To be sure, a social order based on the principle of self-help

> leaves much to be desired. Nevertheless, it is possible to consider this state a legal state and this decentralized order a legal order. . . . History teaches that evolution everywhere proceeds from blood revenge toward the institution of courts and the development of a centralized executive power, that is toward steadily increasing centralization of the coercive social order. We are entirely justified in calling the still decentralized coercive order of primitive society 'law,' in spite of its rather crude techniques such as self-help; for this decentralized order constitutes the first step in an evolution which ultimately leads to the law of the State, to a centralized coercive order. As the embryo in the mother's womb is from the beginning a human being, so the decentralized coercive order of primitive self-help is already law, law *in statu nascendi.*[37]

The transition from a prestate community to the state, that is, from embryonic to full-fledged law is marked by the establishment of centralized judiciary.[38]

Is it possible to apply the concept of force monoply to the international community? Is it possible, in other words, to construe the materials known as international law in such a manner that the sanction appears as the reaction of the international community against a delict? From the point of view of the just war theory, this appears to be possible, whereas from the vantage point of those who reject it, it is not. According to a theory of *bellum justum,* war is forbidden in general international law and "is permitted only as a reaction against an illegal act, a delict, and only when directed against the State responsible for this delict."[39] Kelsen is, of course, fully aware of the objections against the *bellum justum* theory, such as the absence of any organ competent to determine whether a state and which state has violated "the sphere of interests of a State, normally protected by

[34] Kelsen, *General Theory,* p. 22.
[35] *Ibid.,* p. 328.
[36] *Ibid.,* pp. 338 f.
[37] *Ibid.,* p. 339.
[38] *Ibid.,* p. 325.
[39] *Ibid.,* p. 331.

international law."[40] This question, given the absence of a tribunal in general international law, cannot be decided by the science of law but "only and exclusively" by the governments at variance. And they, as Kelsen notes, "may decide the question in different ways."[41] Similarly, as indicated above, science cannot decide that the ***bellum justum*** is the only possible theory but it can and does show that it is a possible one.[42] Having for political reasons opted in favor of the just war theory, Kelsen concludes that "the difference between national and international law is only a relative one; it consists, in the first place, in the degree of centralization or decentralization. National law is a relatively centralized legal order. . . . International law, compared with national law, is a more decentralized order. It represents the highest degree of decentralization occurring in positive law."[43] As a consequence of its decentralized character, general international law "leaves it to the parties to a controversy to ascertain whether one of them is responsible for a delict, as the other claims, and to decide upon, and execute, the sanction. General international law is in this respect, too, a primitive law. It has the technique of self-help. It is the state violated in its right that is authorized to react against the violator by resorting to war or reprisals."[44]

The state that is thus authorized by international law to apply force "acts as an organ of the international community. Put in another way, it is the international legal community itself that reacts against the violator of the law through the medium of the State resorting to reprisal or waging a just war."[45] Admitting that from the sociotechnical point of view the difference in degree of centralization is important, Kelsen contends that the existence of a monopoly of force is even more important as "between an order that reserves to the community the use of force and one that does not, there exists a much greater difference than between two coercive orders both of which monopolize the use of force, but one of which is centralized and the other decentralized. If international law can be counted as an order which monopolizes the use of force—and such, as we have seen, is the case—then it is similar to national law in a decisive point."[46] Thus Kelsen has "answered the question whether so-called international law is law in the same sense as national law by saying that it is possible, though not necessary, to regard the material called international law as true law."[47]

Granted Kelsen's premise, then the statement that it is possible to regard international law as true law may be qualified to mean that international law like primitive law itself is an embryonic law, a law *in statu nascendi (werdendes Recht)*. Accordingly, the community constituted by such a law would appear as a prelegal order or as an embryonic community, just as the order constituted by primitive law was characterized by Kelsen as a "pre statal legal order." And finally, if the concept of force monopoly is to be applied

[40] *Ibid.*, p. 330.
[41] *Ibid.*, p. 337.
[42] *Ibid.*, p. 341.
[43] *Ibid.*, p. 325.
[44] *Ibid.*, p. 327.
[45] Kelsen, *Law and Peace*, p. 57.
[46] *Ibid.*, p. 61.
[47] *Ibid.*, p. 56.

to the international community, then it would seem that in the present embryonic stage of the development of the international community, it is only imperfectly realized. The international community may be said to possess a force monopoly *in nuce.* Such qualifications should be acceptable to those who share Kelsen's estimate that international law even in the present state "contains all the potentialities" for an evolution which "within the national community, the State, has led to a system of norms which is generally accepted as law."[48]

## THE SANCTION AS A REACTION OF THE INTERNATIONAL COMMUNITY AGAINST A DELICT

It appears from the foregoing that the starting point for Kelsen's argument is the concept of a force monopoly which characterizes national law. The concept of force monopoly means that all "forcible interference in the sphere of interests of one subject to the order must be regarded as either a delict or a sanction."[49] In opposition to this view, it has been pointed out that English law, for instance, "recognizes the use of force in several ways that are neither delict nor sanction," and that "in dictatorial States the sphere of 'extra-legal' force that is neither delict nor sanction is even greater."[50] The weight of Kelsen's theory, however, would seem to be not so much the concept of force monopoly, but its underlying idea that acts of force in a community must be construed as acts of force of the community. Such a presentation would have the virtue of avoiding the controversy as to whether or not, in fact, municipal law systems—all of them or at least the majority of them—permit the use of force exclusively as a sanction against a delict. Thus, the question may be restated in this form: When a state resorts to reprisals or war, is it acting as an organ of the international community? Is it possible to regard reprisal or war as reaction of the international community against a delict? Without going into the controversy as to whether there exists a genuine international community, which is denied by some writers,[51] the answer to the question may be sought on the norm-logical plane or on the plane of positive international law. As the pure theory of law is also a theory of positive law and in this context of positive international law,[52] the latter approach seems to commend itself. Now, the materials considered as constituting international law scarcely support the contention that war or reprisals constitute a reaction of the international community against a delict. On the contrary, in a dispute between two states, one alleged to be the wrong-doing state and the state alleged to be the injured state, states not involved directly in the dispute are normally considered as strangers to the dispute; there is

[48] Kelsen, *General Theory,* p. 341

[49] Kelsen, *Law and Peace,* p. 56.

[50] Glanville L. Williams, "International Law and the Controversy concerning the Word 'Law,' " *British Year Book of International Law* (London: Oxford University Press, 1945), pp. 146–163, at p. 157.

[51] Corbett, *op. cit.,* pp. 40 ff.

[52] Kelsen, *General Theory,* p. xv: ". . . the pure theory of law seeks to attain its results exclusively by an analysis of positive law. Every assertion advanced by a science of law must be based on a positive legal order or on a comparison of the contents of several legal orders."

no obligation on the part of the states at variance to consult with, or seek the agreement, of third states before resorting to war or reprisals. Nor have, for that matter, strangers to the dispute normally the right to interfere or intervene in the dispute. This is precisely the reason why Articles 2 and 3 and Articles 27 and 48, respectively, of the Hague Conventions of 1899 and 1907 for the Pacific Settlement of International Disputes were considered as important innovations and improvements in international law and relations.[53] Under these provisions a modest measure of community interest in avoiding recourse to arms was affirmed. An important further step in developing community interests in preventing war is represented by Article 11 of the Covenant. Mr. Elihu Root, commenting on Colonel House's original draft covenant for a League of Nations, said with reference to the clause which later evolved into Article 11:

> The view now assumed and generally applied is that the use of force by one nation towards another is a matter in which only the two nations concerned are primarily interested, and if any other nation claims a right to be heard on the subject, it must show some specific interest of its own in the controversy. That burden of proof rests upon any other nation which seeks to take part if it will relieve itself of the charge of impertinent interference and avoid the resentment which always meets impertinent interference in the affairs of an independent sovereign State. . . . The requisite change is an abandonment of this view, and a universal formal and irrevocable acceptance and declaration of the view that an international breach of the peace is a matter which concerns every member of the Community of Nations—a matter in which every nation has a direct interest, and to which every nation has a right to object. . . . It is the gradual growth and substitution of this idea of community interest in preventing and punishing breaches of the peace which has done away with private wars among civilized peoples.[54]

Similarly, though independently, Lord Parker proposed, in the House of Lords on March 19, 1918, to introduce in international affairs the "hue and cry" and as a consequence to recognize that "war, from whatever cause, is a danger to our common civilization."[55] Professor Jessup pointed out, as did Mr. Root, that international law "resembles tort law rather than criminal law in the national legal system" and suggested

[53] Carnegie Endowment for International Peace, James Brown Scott ed., *The Hague Conventions of 1899 and 1907* (New York: Oxford University Press, 1915).

Article 2: "In case of serious disagreement or dispute, before an appeal to arms, the contracting Powers agree to have recourse, as far as circumstances allow, to the good offices or mediation of one or more friendly Powers."

Article 3: "Independently of this recourse the contracting Powers deem it expedient and desirable that one or more Powers, strangers to the dispute, should, on their own initiative and as far as circumstances may allow, offer their good offices or mediation to the States at variance. Powers strangers to the dispute have the right to offer their good offices or mediation even during the course of hostilities. The exercise of this right can never be regarded by either of the parties in dispute as an unfriendly act."

Article 27 of the 1899 convention (Article 48 in the 1907 convention): "The contracting Powers consider it their duty, if a serious dispute breaks out between two or more of them, to remind these latter that the Permanent Court is open to them. Consequently, they declare that the fact of reminding the parties at variance of the provisions of the present Convention, and the advice given to them, in the highest interest of peace, to have recourse to the Permanent Court, can only be regarded as friendly actions."

[54] Mr. Root's letter to Colonel House, August 16, 1918, printed in Charles Seymour, ed., *The Intimate Papers of Colonel House* (Boston: Houghton Mifflin, 1928), IV, 43. Also in Sir Alfred Zimmern, *The League of Nations and the Rule of Law 1918–1935* (London: Macmillan, 1939), p. 231.

[55] *Parliamentary Debates (Lords), Fifth Series,* XXIX, 506.

that "the significance of this comparison is that under the traditional international legal system, a breach of international law is considered to be a matter which concerns only the States whose rights are directly infringed; and no other State, nor the community of states, is entitled to remonstrate or object or take action."[56] Although more could be said on this subject, it would seem unnecessary to labor the point. Traditional international law normally does not consider reprisal or war resorted by one state against another as a reaction of the international community against a delict. To overcome this deficiency is precisely the *raison d'être* and the principal task of international organizations such as the League of Nations and the United Nations. Apart from special arrangements, international law furnishes no basis for the imputation of the sanctions to the international community.

## STATES AS ORGANS OF THE INTERNATIONAL COMMUNITY

It is commonly agreed that the international community has no centralized and specialized organs for the creation, application and enforcement of law. Kelsen has consequently formulated two propositions: First, that the international community is a decentralized community, and, second, that states act as organs of this community. Along somewhat similar lines is Georges Scelle's concept of the *"dédoublement fonctionnel."* Starting, as does Kelsen, from the *"carence institutionnelle"* of international law, Scelle considers that organs created by the national states, such as heads of states, act in a dual capacity: as organs of the national as well as organs of the international community.[57] This he calls *dédoublement fonctionnel,* and the insight into this dual function of state organs has been said to be of the greatest importance for the understanding of international law.[58] The basic concept for Kelsen is the unity of national and international law, and "an aspect

[56] Philip C. Jessup, *A Modern Law of Nations* (New York: Macmillan, 1948), p. 10.

[57] Georges Scelle, *Manuel de Droit International Public* (Paris: Domat-Montchrestien, 1948), pp. 21 f: "Cependant, c'est la tare originelle et persistance de l'ordre juridique international que sa carence institutionnelle. Apparemment, il n'y a pas dans la Société internationale d'organes législatif, judiciare, exécutif. . . . Et pourtant, il faut bien que les trois fonctions essentielles de réglementation, de contrôle, de l'utilisation des compétences et de réalisation matérielle du Droit soient accomplies. Elles le sont, mais de façon imparfaite et précaire. Elles le sont à la façon dont elles l'étaient dans les milieux féodaux et quasi-anarchiques ou le pouvoir, au lieu d'être centralisé et hierarchisé, restait sporadique et partagé. Ce sont les gouvernements nationaux ou étatiques qui, chacun pour son compte en même temps que pour le compte de la collectivité internationale, accomplissent, dans la limite de leurs possibilités d'action locale et matérielle, les trois fonctions indispensables: création du droit; vérification juridictionnelle; exécution. Tantôt il s'associent à cette fin et avisent d'un commun accord (congrès, conférences, Concert européen); tantôt, au contraire, ils agissent unilatéralement, et, de ce chef, entrent en compétition ou en conflit. Cet unilatéralisme peut aller jusqu'à la guerre, emploi de la force pour imposer la conception juridico-politique d'un gouvernment étatique à un autre, à plusieurs autres, ou à la totalité des autres gouvernements de la communauté internationale (impérialisme mondial). . . . La loi du dédoublement fonctionnel est le succédané *dangereux* de l'organisation institutionnelle défaillante des ordres juridiques internationaux. C'est un pis-aller, dans le stade actuel de l'inter-étatisme. Si on ne l'admet pas, il devient impossible d'expliquer la technique des fonctions sociales dans le milieu international. Mais cette technique traditionnelle doit progressivement faire place à une hiérarchie des institutions *correspondant à la loi de la hiérarchie des ordres juridiques.* See also Lazare Kopelmanas "La Théorie du dédoublement fonctionnel et son utilisation pour la solution du problème dit des conflits de lois," *La Technique et les principes du droit public,* Etudes en l'honneur de Georges Scelle (Paris: Librairie Générale du Droit et de Jurisprudence, 1950), II, 753 f.

[58] Verdross, *op. cit.,* p. 69.

of this unity is the fact that the States as acting persons are organs of international law, or of the community constituted by it. The creation and execution of an order are the functions of its organs, and the international legal order is created and executed by States. It is especially the creation of international law by treaty that clearly reveals the States as organs of the international community."[59] By virtue of international law, "when two States conclude a treaty, they function as organs of international law. The representatives of the two contracting parties together form the composite organ that creates the contractual norm. . . . Of this composite order, the representatives of the contracting States are part organs. It is the international legal order which leaves it to each national order to determine the individual who, as a representative of the State, is competent to conclude treaties with the representative of another State. Hence, the representative of a contracting State is primarily a (partial) organ of the international community, and only secondarily an organ of his own State."[60]

For the following discussion of the role of states as organs for the application and enforcement of international law, it is important to bear in mind that it is not a single state but at least two states that constitute an organ for the creation of international law, this organ being conceived as a composite of which the participating states constitute part organs. However, this clear and, as I believe, correct interpretation of the process by which conventional international law is created is somewhat obscured by Kelsen's concluding words in the subchapter entitled: The State as Organ of the International Legal Order (The Creation of International Law): " 'The State as an organ of international law'—this is only a metaphorical expression of the fact that the legal order of each State, each national legal order, is organically connected with the international legal order and through this order with every other national order, so that all legal orders merge into one integrated legal system."[61] This indeed may be so if one speaks of one state as an organ of international law but then the metaphor becomes misleading, for few are the cases where one state, as single state, acts as an organ of general international law. Piracy may be used as a case in point. When a state captures and punishes a pirate, according to Kelsen's interpretation of piracy, that state may be said to act as an organ of the international community.[62] Here a single state acts as an organ of the international community. By stretching the point somewhat, one might also mention in this connection the prize courts. Belligerents that establish prize courts in case of maritime war may be regarded as organs of the international community, at least to the extent that they apply international and not the national law of the belligerents themselves.

Returning now to the application and enforcement of international law, the question arises whether one or the other state involved in a controversy may be considered as

[59] Kelsen, *General Theory*, p. 351.
[60] *Ibid.*, p. 354.
[61] *Ibid.*, p. 354.
[62] *Ibid.*, p. 344.

an "organ of the international legal order." As pointed out, Kelsen, in conformity with the decentralized character of international law, claims that it is the "injured State," that is "the State, violated in its right, which is authorized to react against the violator by resorting to war or reprisals."[63] The injured state thus is supposed to act as an organ of the international community. Kelsen, of course, is fully aware of the difficulties involved in his efforts to revive the *bellum justum* theory, of which the point here under consideration is an integral part. The medieval defenders of the theory of just war as well as its modern proponents face the difficulty: who determines what is a just cause of war? Which state is injured in its rights and therefore entitled to resort to war against a delinquent state? As long as emperor and pope enjoyed a position of preëminence in the family of nations, there may have been some support, however slight, for the doctrine of *bellum justum* in the actual conduct of international affairs. As soon as this preëminence vanished, there disappeared also the concrete basis for the *bellum justum* doctrine.[64] States which recognize no common superior may and, indeed, will use the doctrine of *bellum justum* as an ideology. History is replete with illustrations. Theories, however, die hard, and the theory of *bellum justum* continued to find proponents who developed subtle distinctions between "invincible ignorance," "excusable ignorance" and, presumably, downright bad faith. Who was to judge? Obviously, in the absence of a common superior, the state itself. And it has been said indeed that in place of the just-war doctrine there came "the idea that the Sovereign was to make war as an accuser and as a judge."[65] Now, if no self-evident criterion can be found for determining which state was just or wrong, the distinction might have conveniently been dropped, as was done by the positivists or it might be maintained in a diluted form, as was done by the eclectics including Vattel.

In the end result there would seem to be no basic difference between the view of the positivists that states may go to war for any reason or no reason, and the surviving view of the eclectics, shared by some positivists,[66] that states may go to war only if they are injured in their rights, but leave it to the states directly concerned to determine, in good faith, of course, whether they are injured, by which states, and what action to take. In either case states are considered to have the right to autodecision *(Recht der Selbstentscheidung)* and the right of autoenforcement *(Recht der Selbstdurchsetzung),* and this view supposedly prevailed from the classic period of international law down to World War

[63] *Ibid.,* p. 327. See also Josef L. Kunz, "The 'Vienna School' and International Law." Reprinted from the *New York University Law Quarterly Review,* XI (March, 1934), 48: "Of course, war is a primitive means; the State entitled to a right is itself the judge and the sheriff in its own cause, which must easily lead to abuses; its ultimate success does not depend so much on its right, but on its force; but exactly the same is true of blood-feud or vendetta. But a State going to war—authorized by international law to do so—is nevertheless acting as an organ of international law, as well as men taking their recourse to blood-feud under the law are acting as organs of this law."

[64] William Ballis, *The Legal Basis of War* (The Hague: M. Nijhoff, 1937), p. 107.

[65] *Ibid.,* p. 103.

[66] Professor Charles Cheney Hyde in *International Law* (Boston: Little, Brown and Co., 1945), II, 1655 says that "a State which resorts to force in order to obtain a desired form of redress from another, and by such process to settle a controversy through ways of its own devising, asserts the right not only to be the sole judge of its own cause, but also to be the enforcer by its own strong arm of demands which in its judgment are not unwarranted," and in III (1945), 1686 he says: "It always lies within the power of a State to endeavor to obtain redress for wrongs or to gain political or other advantages over another, not merely by the employment of force, but also by direct recourse to war."

I.[67] The problematic character of this doctrine is by no means resolved by saying that states ought to exercise the right of autodecision and autoenforcement in good faith, because in the absence of a common superior the interested state will determine whether it acted in good faith or not.

Although Kelsen's theory avoids the obvious pitfalls of the theory of autodecision and autoenforcement, it has not been preserved from misunderstanding. Responsible for this may have been two aspects of Kelsen's writings.

On the one hand, Kelsen affirms that "general international law leaves it to the *parties* to the controversy to ascertain whether one of them is responsible for a delict, as the other claims, and to decide upon, and execute, the sanction."[68] It will be noted that here the parties are considered empowered by international law to determine the facts, the applicable law, and the sanction. True enough, in accordance with the principle or technique of self-help prevailing in international law the injured state is left with the choice of executing the sanction or refraining from it. In any case, the injured state, however, is that state which, in accordance with the foregoing, has been determined by the states at variance.

As Kelsen points out, on the other hand, in the absence of a tribunal competent to decide the questions whether a state has been injured, and by whom, this all-important question can only be decided by "mutual agreement between the parties. But this would be the exception inasmuch as a State would hardly admit having violated the rights of another State."[69] So far, there has been no deviation from the sound line of reasoning that in accordance with the decentralized character of international law the organ competent to decide the question of a violation is, like the organ competent to create conventional international law, a composite organ. The component parts of this organ are the states at variance, and perhaps other states, if they have a *locus standi* in the affair. Whether this composite organ can be established and will be in the position to reach a decision is, of course, open to question, although it may be noted in passing that cases where questions of alleged violations of international law have been decided by agreement between the parties are not so rare as might appear from Kelsen's statement. Cases of apologies and damages for injury done to other states as the result of mediation or arbitration are, in fact, quite frequent, though perhaps not as frequent as one would like them to be.

Had Kelsen left his analysis at this point, he would have remained within the framework of international law, but there would have been but scant basis for the *bellum justum* theory. To find that basis, Kelsen continued to argue that in the absence of an agreement between the parties at variance, no uniform solution can be reached, that the question of fact and law cannot be decided by the science of law or by jurists, and that "only and exclusively the Governments of the States in conflict are authorized to decide this question; and they may decide the question in different ways. . . . Thus, the distinction be-

[67] Verdross, *op. cit.*, p. 36.
[68] Kelsen, *General Theory*, p. 327; italics mine.
[69] *Ibid.*, p. 337.

tween war as a sanction and war as a delict would become highly problematic."[70] If Kelsen, in spite of the problematic nature of the distinction between just and unjust war which, to be sure, is "grounded primarily in the technical insufficiency of general international law,"[71] maintains the just-war doctrine and regards the "injured" state as an organ of the international community, then this is due to his desire to present international law as "true" law, as law in the same sense as national law. This amounts to affirming a distinction between just and unjust war, and consequently the nature of international law as true law *in abstracto,* while *in concreto* it would appear from Kelsen's premise that neither the distinction nor the character of interntional law as true law can be maintained. This being so, is there any sound basis or any compelling reason for considering individual states as organs of international law? This question will be discussed presently.

## AUTOINTERPRETATION IN INTERNATIONAL LAW

It will be readily appreciated that the phrase "the creation and execution of an order are a function of its organs and the international legal order is created and executed by States" and similar statements emphasizing the capacity of states as enforcement organs of international law as well as the doctrine of *bellum justum* itself lends itself easily to misunderstanding. Thus, it has been said that since there is no authority competent to determine alleged violations of international law a war is always "just" if the interested party pretends that an interest had been infringed; the state which determines the law and the delict is always the interested party.[72] Another writer believes that according to general international law and the theory of Kelsen in particular, each state has the exclusive right to determine the law, the fact, and the sanction; as each state has the same right there are two contradictory norms of international law opposed to each other and canceling each other out. The result then is that there is no international law above the states.[73] In the

[70] *Loc. cit.* See also Kelsen, *Peace through Law,* p. 13.

[71] Kelsen, *General Theory,* p. 338.

[72] Georges Vlachos, "Quelques considerations sur le droit et la sanction," *La Technique et les principes du droit publique,* Etudes en honneur de Georges Scelle (Paris: Librairie Générale du Droit et de Jurisprudence, 1950), II, 608, says:

". . . dès qu'il y a 'délit,' la guerre est 'juste,' elle est 'juste' même si l'on y recourt pour se faire justice à soi-même. Et, puisque le contrôle et la vérification des situations juridiques subjectives, des prétendus 'droit subjectifs' des Etats, sont quasi inexistants, dans un droit 'primitif' comme le droit international normatif, la guerre serait toujours 'juste' si, de l'avis des intéressés eux-mêmes, il y avait une intervention délictueuse de leurs intérêts. Prétendre que ce sont les normes qui déterminent ce qui est un 'droit' et ce qui est un 'délit,' c'est changer seulement les mots, puisque en tout état de cause le sujet qui juge et applique la norme est celui-là même qui en réclame l'avantage."

[73] Panayis A. Papaligouras, *Théorie de la Société Internationale* (Zürich: Les Editions Polygraphiques, 1941), p. 174: "Selon la conception traditionnelle—et selon celle de Kelsen—chaque Etat est l'instance compétente qui décide librement dans chaque cas particulier, sans qu'il existe aucune possibilité juridique de contrôle. *Il y a donc un grand nombre d'instances parallèles, d'instances ayant la capacité de poser des normes et forcées, chaque fois qu'il y a un conflit, de poser des normes contradictoires les unes aux autres.* Selon le droit international général l'Etat A est seul compétent pour décider si une norme concrète est juridiquement valable, si un fait est existant, s'il droit être qualifié comme guerre, comme intervention, comme nul . . . Si l'Etat A prend une quelconque de ces décisions, s'il affirme une norme, sil qualifie, etc., il pose une règle juridique, une norme appartenant au droit international. Mais l'Etat B est également compétent pour trancher ces mêmes questions et sa décision, elle aussi, pose une norme. Toutes les fois qu'il y aura un conflit international, la norme posée par l'Etat A sera contradictoire a celle posée par B, si non il n'y aurait pas conflit. Par conséquent, toutes les fois qu'il y aura la moindre divergence, il y a deux normes contradictoires qui s'opposent

opinion of the same writer, a supranational legal order does not exist and is, in fact, logically impossible.[74] Instead of one supranational legal order, there are several state orders each having for its basic norm the rule that each state is the creator of law.[75] International law then may be regarded as positive morality or as the sum total of rules of a state order which attaches to certain facts the juridical consequence of war or of reprisals. The choice between these two views is regarded as a matter of personal preference or opinion.[76] If a state is the creator of law, domestic as well as international, then it may also freely change the rules, provided it has the power to guarantee their effectiveness.[77] A powerful state could even abolish the norm *pacta sunt servanda.*[78] A weak state, on the other hand, could not create international law because it lacks the power to enforce it by war or reprisals; but then in reality a weak state is not at all a state, only a "fictional" state.[79] This is the result, which may well be regarded as absurd, of an attempted *reductio ad absurdum* of Kelsen's theory of international law.

However, in fairness to the opinions mentioned above, it must be pointed out that they are by no means isolated. Efforts to explain the technical deficiency of international law by relying directly or indirectly on the prototype of law and organization, namely the law and organization of states, have paradoxically enough led sometimes to a denial of international law rather than to its vindication as law. It may be enough to recall Georg Jellinek's theory of autolimitation to show the legal character of international law, and his conclusion that in the absence of organization, international law is an "anarchical" law, and the international society has an anarchical character.[80] Similarly, Georges Scelle, in consequence of his theory of *dédoublement fonctionnel,* is moved to affirm that now as in the classic theory of international law, every government "possesses and possessed the competence to declare and enforce the law, and to act as an organ of international legal order. One should not fail to see the elements of anarchy inherent in this."[81] Professor Brierly contends that owing to the absence of a "central organ for the enforcement of

et qui s'annulent mutuellement. Le fonctionnement d'un droit superétatique est impossible, logiquement exclu. Dans ce sens, un droit international superétatique est inexistant."

[74] *Ibid.*, p. 186.

[75] *Ibid.*, p. 176.

[76] *Ibid.*, p. 179, 181.

[77] *Ibid.*, p. 183.

[78] *Ibid.*, p. 184.

[79] *Ibid.*, p. 185.

[80] George Jellinek, *Allgemeine Staatslehre* (3d ed., Wien und Berlin: J. Springer, 1921), p. 379: "Die Staatengemeinschaft ist daher rein anarchischer Natur, und das Vöklkerrecht, weil einer nichtorganisierten und daher keine Herrschermacht besitzenden Autorität entspringend, kann füglich als ein arachiches Recht bezeichnet werden, was zugleich seine Unvollkommenheiten und Mängel erklärt."

[81] Scelle, *op. cit.*, p. 22: "Quoiqu'il en soit, en droit international classique et même dans l'état actuel des choses, tout gouvernement étatique possédait et possède compétence pour dire et réaliser le droit et agir ainsi comme organe de l'ordre juridique international. On ne saurait se dissimuler ce que cela comporte d'anarchie. Mais il n'y a d'autre remède a cet état de chose que l'institutionnalisme superétatique, tel qu'il se réalise par le fédéralisme. C'est pourquoi l'ordre juridique international ne peut faire de progrès qu'en se rapprochant d'un ordre juridique supranational."

See also Alf Ross, *Textbook of International Law* (London: Longmans, Green, 1947), p. 54, who speaks of the anarchical character of international law, and Lazare Kopelmanas, *L'Organsation des Nations Unies* (Paris: Labrairie du Recueil Sirey, 1947), I, 241 who refers to the "système anarchique du droit international dans lequel chaque Etat détermine, en ce qui le concerne, la valeur des obligations internationales qu'il a contractées."

international legal rights as such . . . each State remains free subject to the limitations on the use of force . . . to take such action as it thinks fit to enforce its own rights.''[82] It stands to reason that if a state is free to enforce ''its rights,'' it presumably has also the implied competence of determining what the applicable law is, and what its rights are under it.[83] This is substantially the same position which led Papaligouras to deny that there is such a thing as international law.

Of great interest is the work of Professor Burckhardt who also denies that international law is a valid order because it lacks organization. He criticizes the prevailing view that there is customary international law because taken by itself the application of rules by the subjects of the law cannot create binding customary law. Customary law must be declared as such by a competent organ, for instance, by a tribunal. In the international society, however, international tribunals have authority to declare the law only for the parties, and therefore do not create objective law.[84] In a polemic against Kelsen, Burckhardt argues that it is not enough to say that ''in virtue of the law which is also his law, it is the State illegally violated in its rights which is called upon to enforce the law against the violator. And for this reason it acts as organ of the legal order.''[85] For to say that the injured state is called upon to enforce its right is to anticipate the decision that the rights of this particular state were in fact violated, whereas it is the task of a legal order first to determine the injury before it can be known which state was injured.[86] Moreover,

[82] J. L. Brierly, *The Law of Nations* (4th ed., Oxford: The Clarendon Press, 1949), p. 92.

[83] See Lazare Kopelmanas, *L'Organisation des Nations Unies,* (Paris: Librairie du Recueil Sirey, 1947), I, 259: ''. . . le droit international classique ne connait pas la séparation des fonctions. Les Etats y conservent aussi bien le monopole de création que celui d'application des règles de droit. Il en résulte la concentration entre leurs mains des pouvoirs d'interprétation authentique, correspondant à la fonction législative, en même temps que des pouvoirs d'interprétation individuelle, correspondant à la fonction exécutive. La distinction entre les deux ne semble vraiment pas possible, car, en déterminant à propos d'une difficulté précise le contenu de son obligation internationale, au delà du cas particulier l'Etat fixe par son attitude également sa conception officielle du texte impliqué.''

[84] Walther Burckhardt, *Die Organisation der Rechtsgemeinschaft* (Basel: Helbing und Lichtenhahn, 1927), p. 377: ''Eine weitverbreitete Meinung lehrt nun aber, dass es ein internationales Gewohnheitsrecht gibt, nämlich im Sinne eines positiven Rechtes. Unsere Ausführungen über das Gewohnheitsrecht zeigen jedoch, dass das nicht richtig sein kann. Durch die Uebung der Rechtsgenossen allein kann verbindliches Gewohnheitsrecht nicht entstehen; es entsteht nur durch die massgebende Mitwirkung der rechtsanwendenden Behörden, als der amtlichen Organe der positiven Rechtsordnung. Nicht was die Rechsunterworfenen unter sich befolgen, ist von Rechts wegen gültig, sondern was von der eingesetzten Vertretung der Rechtsordnung (ausdrücklich durch die Rechtssetzung oder stillschweigend durch die Anwendung) als objektives Recht anerkannt wird. Eine solche Vertretung gibt es aber im Völkerrecht nicht, weil die Staatengemeinschaft nicht objektiv rechtlich organisiert ist. Es gibt wohl *vertraglich* eingesetzte Gerichte (und andere Instanzen); aber sie handeln alle nur kraft rechtsgeschäftlichen Auftrages der Staaten, die sie eingesetzt haben, und ihre Entscheidungen haben demgemäss auch nur vertragliche Verbindlichkeit; sie begründen subjektive Rechtsverhältnisse, nicht objektives Recht. Die Verbindlichkeit ihrer Sprüche ist beschränkt auf die Parteien des Schiedvertrages; sie ist bedingt, nämlich quoad titulum durch die Verbindlichkeit dieses Vertrages, quoad materiam, dem Inhalte nach, durch den Willen der Parteien; wenn die Parteien über das anzuwendende Recht übereinkommen, wie im Alabamafalle, ist das internationale Gericht daran gebunden; es ist nicht die selbständige Stimme des Rechts, wie es das Gericht im primitiven Staat (ohne gesetzgebende Behörde) ist, wo der Richter das Recht zu finden, d.h. zugleich mit der Entscheidung des konkreten Falles festzustellen hat. Wenn die positive Geltung des Rechts davon abhängt, dass eine organisierte Macht es handhabt, können vertraglich eingesetzte Behörden nicht dieses Recht schaffen: denn die Zuständigkeit der Behörden hängt selbst von einem Rechtsgeschäft ab das schon im geltenden Recht begründet sein muss, um gültig zu sein.''

[85] Kelsen, *Das Problem der Souveränität und die Theorie des Völkerrechts,* p. 259. See also his *General Theory,* p. 327, where substantially the same view is expressed. P. 339, n. 68, above.

[86] Burckhardt, *op. cit.,* p. 128: ''Begrifflich ist es gewiss denkbar, dass die Rechtsordnung jeweilen eine vor dem Streit nicht dazu berufene Person berufe, den Streit zu entscheiden; aber nicht in der Weise, dass sie 'den Verletzten' zum Richter einsetze. Denn um was handelt es sich? Was ist die Aufgabe der Organisation? Die Entscheidung darüber, was

as abstract legal norms can be enforced only *in concreto,* it is incumbent upon the legal order to provide for an authoritative declaration whether a certain rule of law is still binding. In order to say that a certain conduct is legal or illegal, it is imperative to know not merely what the law may have been at any time, but what law is currently in force. It is the task of organizations to perform this function.[87] A legal order cannot depend on the individual conviction or the good faith of every state; a legal order must be binding as it is, regardless of the conviction of the individual subject of law.[88]

To regard international law as a decentralized legal order or to affirm that international law lacks central organs for its creation, application, and execution is by no means tantamount to saying that each and every state acts as an organ of the international community. Whether states act as organs of international law is not a question which can be answered without reference to positive international law. It may also be well to remember that Kelsen uses the phrase "the State as an organ of international law" as a metaphorical expression for the unity of law, national as well as international. Kelsen, it is submitted, does not minimize the significance of the very real difference in the type or extent of organization prevailing in the national states and in the international society. While admitting the significance of this difference, as one of the contents of the national and international legal orders, he does not consider it essential from the point of view of

rechtens ist und die Durchsetzung dieses als Recht Erkannten; hier die Entscheidung eines Streites nach dem geltenden Recht und die Vollstreckung der Entscheidung. Wenn die Rechtsordnung dazu *eine* Person (oder eine einheitlich beschliessende Mehrheit) beruft, deren Entscheidung verbindlich sein soll, mag es auch eine Privatperson sein, oder besser: eine Person, die *bisher* kein Amt hatte und kein *ständiges* Amt erhält; aber es muss bestimmt sein, welche; und wenn die Rechtsordnung sagen würde: der Verletzte ist der Richter, so würde sie den Streit als entschieden voraussetzen, bevor ein Richter da war; denn um zu wissen, wer verletzt ist, muss man den Streit entschieden haben, was eben die Aufgabe des Organes sein soll. . . . Darüber muss sich eine vollständige Rechtsordnung aussprechen; nicht nur, welches die Normen des Verhaltens der Rechtsgenossen sind, sondern auch wer diese Normen anwende und die rechtsanwendende Entscheidung erzwinge, ja auch wer über die Verbindlichkeit der Grundsätze selbst entscheide. Man kann sich Verhaltungsregeln *denken* ohne diese Zuständigkeitsordnung, die Organisation; aber man kann sie sich nicht als *geltendes* Recht denken ohne solche Ordnung, und zwar nicht ohne die durch Menschen betätigte, verkörperte Organisation."

[87] Burckhardt, *op. cit.*, pp. 125 f.: "Jede Rechtsordnung muss bestimmen, wer den Zwang anzuordnen hat und in welcher Weise er anzuordnen ist. Da aber die Norm nicht in ihrer Abstraktheit erzwungen werden kann, sondern nur in ihrer konkreten Anwendung auf den einzelnen Fall, muss der Erzwingung notwendigerweise die Entscheidung vorausgehen, dass die betreffende Norm auf den vorliegenden Fall anzuwenden ist. Die Erzwingung des Rechts setzt also die verbindliche Anwendung des abstrakten Rechtssatzes auf den konkreten Tatbestand voraus: die Rechtsordnung muss daher, um erzwingbar zu sein, auch diese Zuständigkeit vorsehen; die Instanz, die in verbindlicher Weise entscheidet, dass der Rechtssatz in concreto anwendbar ist, und das Verfahren, nach dem es zu geschehen hat. Und endlich muss auch eine Instantz da sein, um die Regeln selbst zu bestimmen. Wir sind vorhin von der Voraussetzung ausgegangen, die Regeln seien gegeben und für einmal ausser Frage; das mag zu gewissen Zeiten zutreffen, wenn nämlich eine Autorität sie früher schon bestimmt hat; aber grundsätzlich kann von der Aufgabe nicht abgesehen werden, auch die Rechtsnormen selbst, die gelten sollen, zu bestimmen. Ist das früher schon entschieden worden, so sind die damals angenommenen Normen doch nur deshalb *heute* verbindlich, weil die Autorität, die sie aufgestellt hat, noch heute anerkannt wird (was auch eine Entscheidung ist), bzw. weil die heute zuständige Behörde nichts anderes entscheidet. Es muss stets jemand entscheiden, welche Normen gelten; die Entscheidung darüber ist logisch ebenso unentbehrlich wie die Entscheidung darüber, wo die geltende Norm anzuwenden und wie die Entscheidung zu vollstrecken ist. Denn gleich wie die Rechtserzwingung die Entscheidung voraussetzt, dass das zu erzwingende konkrete Verhalten rechtmässig ist, so setzt die Entscheidung, dass ein Verhalten rechtsmässig (ein anderes rechtswidrig) ist, einen Rechtssatz voraus, an dem dieses konkrete Verhalten gemessen wird. Diese Aufgabe, die jede Rechtsordnung stellt, lediglich weil sie ein *rechtliche* Ordnung ist, ist die Aufgabe der Organisation."

[88] *Ibid.*, p. 124: "Denn das wäre keine Rechtsordnung mehr, die Ordnung, die grundsätzlich auf die freiwillige Befolgung ihrer Vorschriften abstellte, auf die persönliche Ueberzeugung und Gewissenhaftigkeit jedes einzelnen; die also nicht gelten wollte, so wie sie einmal lautet, ohne Rücksicht auf die individuelle Ueberzeugung der Rechtsgenossen, wie es eben zum Wesen des Rechtes gehört."

the Pure Theory of Law insofar as its aim is to discover norm-logical relations.[89] Thus, absence of an organ empowered to determine objectively the violation of law as the condition of a sanction is seen as a serious practical and political shortcoming, and not as an obstacle to the theoretical construction of the lawful war as an international sanction.[90] But how far can a theory go in discounting practical difficulties and still remain a theory of positive international law? What modifications are necessary to restore harmony between theory and practice?

The technical organizational insufficiency of international law may, and in fact does, make it difficult to determine whether a state acts in accordance with, or contrary to, international law. It is one thing to admit the insufficiency and, I submit, quite another thing to exploit its existence to the point of contending that every state has a right of autodecision and autoenforcement. It is generally recognized that the root of the unsatisfactory situation in international law and relations is the absence of an authority generally competent to declare what the law is at any given time, how it applies to a given situation or dispute, and what the appropriate sanction may be. In the absence of such an authority, and failing agreement between the states at variance on these points, each state has a right to interpret the law, the right of autointerpretation, as it might be called. This interpretation, however, is not a "decision" and is neither final nor binding upon the other parties. In consequence of the technical insufficiency prevailing in general international law, we may never know, or, in some cases, we may not know for a time, which autointerpretation was correct. A controversy, in other words, may remain unsettled forever or for a long time. This is, for better or worse, the situation resulting from the organizational insufficiency of international law. Neither victory nor defeat in war are objective tests of the legal issues involved, if indeed the causes of war were differences of a legal and not of a political nature.

It can be shown, I believe, that states have the right of autointerpretation but not the right to decide questions of inernational law, that is, to make binding decisions for others. It may be well to remind ourselves that in general international law there is no duty for states to submit disputes to third-party decisions. Resort to all or any procedure for the settlement of disputes, be it a decisional or nondecisional procedure, is voluntary and not compulsory.[91] The decentralized character of international law in this matter manifests itself in the absence of a duty to submit disputes to any of the procedures and in the need for the parties to the dispute to collaborate in reaching an agreed solution as well as in the restriction of the solution reached to the parties concerned. The agreed interpretation of the rule of general international law resulting from negotiation or arbitration or adjudication, while binding upon the parties, is not authoritative for strangers to the dispute nor for any other tribunal which may be seized of the same or a substantially iden-

[89] Kelsen, *Das Problem der Souveränität,* p. 258.
[90] *Ibid.,* p. 266.
[91] Eastern Carelia case, Permanent Court of International Justice, Advisory Opinion of July 23, 1923, *Series B, No. 5,* p. 27.

tical question. This explains the lack of uniformity in the jurisprudence of international tribunals on such subjects as the Calvo clause and others. It does not follow from the principle of voluntary submission to procedures for pacific settlement nor does it follow from the doctrine of sovereignty "that the State is in principle the sole judge of the existence of any individual rule of law, applicable to itself."[92] On the contrary, more than a hundred years ago Chief Justice Marshall said that it was a consequence of the principle of "the perfect equality of nations . . . that no one can rightfully impose a rule on another. . . . As no nation can prescribe a rule for others, none can make a law of nations."[93] Equality and sovereignty are sometimes used as synonyms; even if this were not so, sovereignty in the sense indicated would obviously be incompatible with the sovereignty of any other state, and the state which claims to be "the sole judge of the existence of any individual rules of law" would thereby subject other states to its judgment. Regardless of the pretensions of writers and even of governments, "the well-known rule that no one can be judge in his own suit holds good."[94] Far from acting as disinterested organs of international law, let alone as objective judges, individual governments as subjects of international law are interested parties. Probably every arbitral proceeding would show that rather than act as the expounders of international law, they act as advocates for themselves. A few illustrations, it is hoped, will substantiate the point that attempts of governments to arrogate to themselves the right to decide questions of international law were emphatically rejected.

In its recent judgment in the Colombian-Peruvian asylum case, the International Court of Justice had occasion to pass on the right of a diplomatic representative to make a provisional qualification of an offense alleged to have been committed by the refugee seeking asylum and the right of the territorial state to contest the qualification. The court found that the Colombian government "has not claimed the right of qualification for the sole purpose of determining its own conduct," but "its claim must be understood in the sense that Columbia, as the State granting asylum, is competent to qualify the offense by a unilateral and definitive decision binding on Peru." The court held that "the principles of international law do not recognize any rule of unilateral and definitive qualification by the State granting asylum."[95] With reference to the facts, namely, whether or not on January 3–4, 1949, there existed in Peru a case of urgency within the meaning of Article 2, paragraph 2, of the Havana Convention on Asylum and the belief of the ambassador of Colombia in the existence of such urgency, the court declared: "But this subjective appreciation is not the relevant element in the decision which the Court is called upon to take concerning the validity of the asylum; the only important question to be considered here is the objective existence of the facts, and it is this which must determine the decision

[92] H. Lauterpacht, *The Function of Law in the International Community* (Oxford: The Clarendon Press, 1933), p. 3.

[93] Case of the *Antelope* (1825), 23 U.S. 30, in Herbert W. Briggs, *The Law of Nations* (New York: F. S. Crofts and Co., 1944), p. 15.

[94] "Frontier between Turkey and Iraq," Permanent Court of International Justice, Advisory Opinion of November 21, 1925, *Series B, No. 12,* p. 32.

[95] Judgment of November 20, 1950, International Court of Justice, *Reports 1950,* p. 274.

of the Court." And the court held that the grant of asylum was not made in conformity to the convention.[96] The judgment of the court clearly draws a line between the subjective appreciation of the facts made by the interested parties, and the objective appreciation made by the court. It also distinguishes sharply the right of a party to interpret international law and treaties "for the sole purpose of determining its own conduct," and the competence to decide the question of law with binding force for the other party. The right of autointerpretation is thus affirmed, as a limited right, and the right of autodecision is rejected.[97]

It may be useful to refer to some cases in which the resort to force against another state was put to the test of an arbitral or judicial decision. In the Naulilaa case between Germany and Portugal, the Mixed Arbitral Tribunal, in its award of July 31, 1928, found that the German aggression of October–December, 1914, against the frontier of Angola was not to be considered as licit reprisal in the absence of a proper cause, of a prior summons, and of a proportionality between the alleged offense and the reprisal.[98] Germany, having satisfied herself presumably that resort to reprisals was legitimate in the circumstance, acted at her own peril. She certainly did not act as an organ of the international community and her aggression could not be interpreted as the reaction of the international community against Portugal. More recently, in the Corfu Channel case, the International Court of Justice had occasion to consider resort to intervention and other methods of self-help. Following the explosions of October 22, 1946, in the Corfu Channel which caused damage to, and loss of human life on, British men-of-war passing through the channel, the United Kingdom government ordered a mine-sweeping operation in the channel ("Operation Retail") which took place without Albania's consent on November 12–13, 1946. Having rejected the British defense based on "the alleged right of intervention," the court, referring to the second justification of the United Kingdom, which "classified 'Operation Retail' among methods of self-protection or self-help," held:

> The Court cannot accept this defense either. Between independent States, respect for the territorial sovereignty is an essential foundation of international relations. The Court recognizes that the Albanian Government's complete failure to carry out its duties after the

[96] *Ibid.*, pp. 287–288.

[97] See also arbitral award by G. Kaeckenbeeck in the dispute between Poland and Germany regarding the nationality rights of minorities of German extraction in Poland. Poland claimed the right unilaterally to determine *(constater)* whether in virtue of the Treaty of Versailles Polish nationality was acquired and that "cette constatation sera considerée comme reconnue par l'Allemagne." The arbitrator held: "Du fait que l'acquisition de la nationalité polonaise est reglée dans l'article 91 du Traité de Versailles, qui fait partie d'un groupe de dispositions relatives à la cession de territoire faite par l'Allemagne à la Pologne, résulte que cette question présente un caractère qui n'est purement unilatéral, mais qui intéresse au contraire les deux Etats contractants. . . . Mais ce caractère international, qui du fait des obligations contractées implique une certaine limitation de l'autonomie de deux Etats, n'implique nullement pour cela une co-souveraineté des deux Etats en ce qui concerne l'application. Chaque Etat agit et décide souverainement; mais, dans la mésure où il a contracté des obligations, il est tenu d'agir et de décider conformément à ces obligations. Les enfreint-il, le caractère international de la question se révèle par le fait que le co-contractant a le droit d'exiger le respect du Traité. Tant que l'infraction n'a pas eu lieu, le caractère international de la question reste pour ainsi dire latent." *Actes et Documents de la Conférence Germano-Polonaise* tenue à Vienne du 30 avril au 30 août 1924, p. 386.

[98] *Recueil des décisions des tribunaux arbitraux mixtes,* VIII (Paris: Librairie du Recueil Sirey, 1928), 425.

> explosions and the dilatory nature of its diplomatic notes, are extenuating circumstances for the action of the United Kingdom Government. But to ensure respect for international law, of which it is the organ, the Court must declare that the action of the British Navy constituted a violation of Albanian sovereignty.[99]

Whether the court's decision should be understood "as a condemnation of all intervention involving the use or display of force, and as a rejection of the view that self-help . . . can ever be a legitimate means of redressing international wrongs" or as relating merely to the particular instance of self-help before the court, is of course a question which merits reflection and study.[100] What is immediately clear, however, is that put to the test of a judicial determination, the action of the United Kingdom government appeared not as a proper use of force, not as self-help resorted to as an organ of international law, nor as a reaction of the international community against a delict, but rather as an illegal act applied unilaterally by an interested party against another state, and without the latter's consent. Not the United Kingdom but the International Court of Justice, by agreement between the United Kingdom and Albania, fulfilled the functions of an organ of international law.

It will be recalled that before the signing of the Treaty for the Renunciation of War in Paris on August 27, 1928, the United States note of June 23, 1928 declared that the proposed treaty did not in any way restrict or impair the right of self-defense: "That right is inherent in every sovereign State, and is implicit in every treaty. Every nation is free at all times and regardless of treaty provisions to defend its territory from attack or invasion, and it alone is competent to decide whether circumstances require recourse to war in self-defense."[101] The United States may thus have conveyed the impression that the contracting parties have not merely the right of autointerpretation, but the right of autodecision as well. The International Military Tribunal, however, considering the question of whether the invasion of Denmark and Norway by Germany was an act of self-defense, declared: "It was further argued that Germany alone could decide, in accordance with the reservations made by many of the Signatory Powers, at the time of the conclusion of the Kellogg-Briand Pact, whether a preventive action was a necessity, and that in making her decision, her judgment was conclusive. But whether action taken under the claim of self-defense was in fact aggressive or defensive must ultimately be subject to investigation and adjudication if international law is ever to be enforced."[102] Thus what appeared to be a right of making a unilateral decision regarding the applicability of the inherent right of self-defense was found by the International Military Tribunal to be no more than the right of autointerpretation subject to objective investigation and conclusive adjudication.

[99] Corfu Channel case, Judgment of April 9, 1949, International Court of Justice, *Reports 1949*, p. 35.

[100] G. G. Fitzmaurice, "The Law and Procedure of the International Court of Justice: General Principles and Substantive Law," *British Year Book of International Law* (London: Oxford University Press, 1950), p. 5.

[101] Reprinted in Denys P. Myers, *Origin and Conclusion of the Paris Pact* (Boston: World Peace Foundation, 1929), p. 355.

[102] International Military Tribunal, *Trial of the Major War Criminals* . . . (Nuremberg: 1947), I, 208.

It is interesting to note that Sir Hartley Shawcross, chief prosecutor for the United Kingdom, before the International Military Tribunal, when discussing the question of self-defense in connection with the Kellogg-Briand pact, had this to say:

> Neither the Pact of Paris nor any other treaty was intended to—or could—take away the right of self-defense. Nor did it deprive its signatories of the right to determine, in the first instance, whether there was danger in delaying and whether immediate action to defend themselves was imperative; and that only is the meaning of the express proviso that each State judges whether action in self-defense is necessary. But this does not mean that the State thus acting is the ultimate judge of the property and of the legality of its conduct. It acts at its peril. Just as the individual is answerable for the exercise of his common law right of defense, so the State is answerable if it abused its discretion, if it transforms 'self-defense' into an instrument of conquest and lawlessness, if it twists the natural right of self-defense into a weapon of predatory aggrandizement and lust. The ultimate decision as to the lawfulness of action claimed to be taken in self-defense does not lie with the State concerned, and for that reason, the right of self-defense, whether expressly reserved or implied, does not impair the capacity of a treaty to create legal obligations against war.[103]

It may be noted in passing that the judgment of the International Military Tribunal followed the reasoning of Sir Hartley Shawcross and confirmed Professor Lauterpacht's interpretation of the Kellogg-Briand pact, namely that, although recourse to self-defense "must, in the first instance, be a matter for the judgment of the state concerned" and although the state has "the provisional right to act . . . the question of the right of recourse to war in self-defense is in itself capable of judicial decision."[104]

As international law in its conventional and customary form is not the product of the will of one state but emanates from the free will of two or more states, so is the competence of authentic or authoritative interpretation vested in the community of nations or in the states parties to the treaty. In the advisory opinion on the Jaworzina case, the Permanent Court of International Justice referred to the "established principle that the right of giving an authoritative interpretation of a legal rule belongs solely to the person or body who has the power to modify or suppress it."[105] This is so, it is submitted, because, as Kelsen pointed out, an "authentic interpretation . . . is a law-creating act."[106] An authentic interpretation, being binding, is within the competence of the norm-creating body. In a dispute regarding the interpretation of a bilateral treaty, the competent authority is the composite organ formed by the two contracting parties, or a tribunal instituted by the parties with the power to settle the dispute. To attribute to one party alone the capacity of an organ, that is, the right to decide the meaning of a treaty, would amount to conferring on it the right to create a norm binding on the other state, that is, juridically speaking, subordinate the other state to the jurisdiction of the former. If no other principle of international law then certainly the principle of equality militates against such an

[103] *Ibid.*, XIX, 461.
[104] Lauterpacht, *op. cit.*, p. 179 f.
[105] Advisory Opinion of December 6, 1923, *Series B, No. 8*, p. 37.
[106] Kelsen, *The Law of the United Nations* (New York: Frederick A. Praeger, 1951), p. xv.

attribution. Obviously, autointerpretation has no binding character. In autodecision, such a character is implied, but without any justification in general international law. Thus, in the David J. Adams case, the Anglo-American arbitral tribunal declared: "The fundamental principle of the juridical equality of States is opposed to placing one State under the jurisdiction of another State. It is opposed to the subjection of one State to an interpretation of a Treaty asserted by another State. There is no reason why one more than the other should impose such a unilateral interpretation of a contract which is essentially bilateral."[107] It may be apposite to refer here to the note of September 19, 1949, from the United States to Rumania and the substantially identical notes to Bulgaria and Hungary in the dispute relating to the application of provisions regarding human rights under peace treaties entered into with those countries. In its note to Rumania, the United States stated:

> The United States Government considers that the Rumanian Government has no grounds for declaring unilaterally that a dispute over Rumania's execution of Article 3 of the Peace Treaty does not exist. Since the interpretation placed by the United States Government on the acts of the Rumanian Government with reference to the latter's treaty obligations respecting human rights and freedom does not correspond with the interpretation advanced by the Rumanian Government, the existence of a dispute is self-evident.[108]

It thus appears to be contrary to positive international law for one state to impose its interpretation of a treaty upon the other.

The same consideration applies in multilateral treaties. Each contracting party has a right of autointerpretation, but not of autodecision. The right of authentic interpretation is vested in the composite organ formed by all the contracting parties. Unless the treaty provides for an alternative procedure, an authoritative interpretation can result from negotiations leading to an agreement, or from arbitration or adjudication. The London Protocol of January 17, 1871, signed by the representatives of Great Britian, Austria-Hungary, France, Germany, Italy, Russia, and Turkey, expressly recognized "that it is an essential principle of the law of nations that no Power can liberate itself from the engagements of a treaty, nor modify the stipulations thereof, unless with the consent of the Contracting Powers, by means of an amicable arrangement."[109] This protocol is

[107] The tribunal continued: "The fact that this interpretation is given by the legislative or judicial or any other authority of one of the Parties does not make that interpretation binding upon the other Party. Far from contesting that principle, the British Government did not fail to recognize it. . . . For that reason the mere fact that a British Court, whatever be the respect and high authority it carries, interpreted the treaty in such a way as to declare the *David J. Adams* had contravened it, cannot be accepted by this Tribunal as a conclusive interpretation binding upon the United States Government. Such a decision is conclusive from the national British point of view; it is not from the national United States point of view. . . . Then the duty of this international Tribunal is to determine, from the international point of view, how the provisions of the treaty are to be determined and applied to the facts, and consequently whether the loss resulting from the forfeiture of the vessel gives rise to an indemnity." Decision given December 9, 1921. American and British Claims Arbitration, *Report* of Fred K. Nielsen (1926), p. 524, at p. 530. Quoted in G. H. Hackworth, *Digest of International Law,* V (Washington, D.C.: U.S. Government Printing Office, 1943), p. 268.

[108] U.S. Department of State, *Bulletin,* XXI, No. 534 (October 3, 1949), 514. The existence of a dispute was confirmed in the Advisory Opinion of March 30, 1950, International Court of Justice, *Reports 1950,* p. 65.

[109] Edward Herstlet, *The Map of Europe by Treaty,* III, 1904. The principle of 1871 was restated in the Text of Proposals drawn up by the representatives of Belgium, the United Kingdom, and Italy on March 19, 1936, in connection with the remilitarization of the Rhineland by Germany. League of Nations, *Official Journal,* 17th year (April 1936), 348.

usually referred to in connection with the *clausula rebus sic stantibus* doctrine. However, the principle of the sanctity of treaties recognized by the great powers applies equally to modifications of treaties which may be brought about by interpretation. It is part of the principle of *pacta sunt servanda* that the right of authentic interpretation belongs to the composite organ which created the treaty and not to any of the states members of that organ. The prohibition is directed against unilateral interpretation amounting to modification of a multilateral treaty. The decentralized character of international law makes itself felt even here. For under general international law two state parties to a multilateral treaty may, to the extent that this does not prejudice the rights of others, make modifications derogating from the general treaty. Similarly, two or more states may submit a dispute concerning the interpretation of a multilateral treaty to arbitration or adjudication. The interpretation laid down by a tribunal or court is binding upon the parties and upon the parties to the proceedings alone. Article 59 of the statute of the International Court of Justice, in providing that "the decision of the Court has no binding force except between the parties and in respect of that particular case," constitutes an emphatic recognition of the decentralized character of international law.

The principle enunciated in the London Protocol rejecting unilateral interpretations which may be characterized as modifications of multilateral treaties lays down the procedure by dint of which a binding interpretation can be secured. That procedure is implied in the requirement of the consent of the contracting parties. A treaty, however, may establish, again with the consent of the contracting parties, alternative procedures for interpretation and formal modifications or amendments. Thus, the constitution of the International Labor Organization lays down in Article 36 the procedure for amendments, that is, for formal modifications, and in Article 37 a procedure for an interpretation by decision of the International Court of Justice.[110] The constitution of the International Civil Aviation Organization, in Article 94, provides for amendments, in Article 84, for interpretations by decision of the United Nations Council, from which an appeal may be taken to an *ad hoc* tribunal or to the International Court of Justice. The articles of agreement of the International Bank for Reconstruction and Development and of the International Monetary Fund, in Articles 8 and 17 respectively, provide for amendments and, in Articles 9 and 18 respectively, for binding decisions on questions of interpretation by the executive directors and for final decision by the board of governors. Such decisions are binding on all members. According to Article 75 of the constitution of the World Health Organization, disputes concerning application or interpretation may be settled by negotiation or by the Health Assembly or by the International Court of Justice, or another mode of settlement agreed to by the parties. There being no cut-and-dried difference between interpretation and modification, it would seem that in all cases in which a treaty provides for binding decisions on questions of interpretation by an organ of the organization, as well as for a formal amending procedure, there are in fact two possibilities or pro-

[110] See also Arts. XVII and XX of the constitution of the Food and Agricultural Organization, and Arts. XIII and XIV of the United Nations Educational, Scientific and Cultural Organization.

cedures for modifying the treaty—one through authoritative interpretation and another through amendment.

If a treaty fails to provide a procedure for settling questions of interpretation but includes provisions for amendment, the latter procedure or the agreement of all contracting parties is required to settle such questions. This situation exists in the United Nations. Any organ of the United Nations may interpret those parts of the Charter as are applicable to its particular function. In principle, such interpretations, however, are not authentic or authoritative, that is, they lack binding force. States at variance on the correct interpretation of the Charter may submit the dispute to the International Court of Justice, as in the case of any other treaty. The decision of the court, while binding upon the parties, would not *ipso facto* be binding upon the other members of the organization. In other words, so far as the other members are concerned, the interpretation of the court would not be authentic or authoritative. This was so understood by Committee IV/2 of the United Nations Conference on International Organization which declared: "If an interpretation made by any organ of the Organization or by a committee of jurists is not generally acceptable, it will be without binding force. In such circumstances, or in cases where it is desired to establish an authoritative interpretation as a precedent for the future, it may be necessary to embody the interpretation in an amendment to the Charter. This may always be accomplished by a recourse to the procedure provided for amendment."[111] The considerations set forth above seem to be entirely in harmony with the view adopted by the committee.

The principles applicable to the interpretation and modification of treaties are substantially identical with those governing the interpretation and modification of customary international law. If customary international law is considered as the product of the family of nations, then the family of nations alone is competent to interpret or modify rules of customary international law. There being no formal, institutionalized procedure to declare or formulate the will of the family of nations, its view may be ascertained through diplomatic channels or by means of a general conference leading to a resolution or treaty. In keeping with the decentralized character of the international society, any group of two or more states may agree on an authoritative or authentic interpretation with binding force for that group. Negotiation, conference, arbitration, or adjudication are among the procedures available for such purposes. The interpretation thus arrived at may find general acceptance by states not parties to the original proceedings.

Arbitration and adjudication appear to be among the classic methods for seeking and obtaining an authoritative interpretation on questions arising from the autonomous application and interpretation of international law. Usually, arbitration and adjudication are advocated as means to prevent war or as alternative to war, the "arbiter of nations." This has been so particularly since the first Hague conference, and has become a stock in trade in the writings of the peace movement. This approach assumes that wars arise out of dif-

[111] Report on the Interpretation of the Charter approved by Committee IV/2 on June 2, 1945. UNCIO, Doc. 887, Annex II.

ferences regarding the interpretation of international law. As a by-product of this line of thought there developed a controversy regarding the distinction between so-called justiciable and nonjusticiable disputes. The upshot of this controversy has been to clarify the issue to the extent of dispelling any doubt there may have been as to the suitability of arbitration and adjudication for deciding questions of international law, that is, questions concerning the interpretation and application of existing, positive international law. On the other hand, it brought into sharp focus the still prevailing reluctance, nay unwillingness, of states to submit such disputes to compulsory arbitration, that is, to a decisional procedure. Finally, and perhaps unwittingly, it revealed that many disputes ostensibly about questions of interpretation and application of international law are in fact controversies about claims for more or less far-reaching changes in the distribution of territories as elements in the struggle of power, or for other revisions of the existing treaty structure. Kelsen has been one of the most consistent opponents of the distinction between the so-called justiciable and nonjusticiable disputes, and an advocate of a comprehensive system of compulsory adjudication. These views were predicated on the ground that acceptance of compulsory adjudication and relinquishment of the untenable division of disputes into justiciable and nonjusticiable would materially contribute to a durable peace.[112] This no doubt is true, but only to the extent that disputes about international-law questions cause wars. Such a view, however, is perhaps an oversimplification of political realities. The legal arguments aired by governments on suitable occasions may in fact be legal cloaks for political ends. What causes war in such a situation is not the legal cloak but the clash of seemingly irreconcilable political ends. To expose the legal argument for what it is may serve a useful purpose, provided the governments concerned are willing to avoid or postpone the clash. Arbitration and adjudication are not particularly suitable for resolving political claims. Their role in the international society, like that of courts in national societies, is more modest. It is to settle disputes regarding interpretation and application of international law. Much would be gained if such disputes were regularly submitted to a decisional procedure. International law would gain greatly in stature and precision and many an international controversy would be reduced to size if submitted to arbitration. Theoretically as well as practically, the gain would consist in making autointerpretation not the final but, as it should be, the preliminary stage in disputes between states. Autointerpretation is easily presented, or rather misrepresented, as autodecision for want of a compulsory procedure leading to a heteronomous and binding decision. But appearances are misleading; they harden public opinion on one side or the other. States sometimes act as if they were organs of international law or as if they were authorized spokesmen for the international society, or as if they resorted to war in a just cause whereas in fact they are interested parties without any mandate or competence from the international society; and what is represented as a just cause of war or as a war in self-

[112] Kelsen, *Peace through Law*, p. 13: "As long as it is not possible to remove from the interested States the prerogative to answer the question of law and transfer it once and for all to an impartial authority, namely, an international court, any further progress on the way to the pacification of the world is absolutely excluded."

defense may, if put to the test of a judicial tribunal, turn out to have been nothing but an unjust war or war of aggression. Such is the lesson of the post-World War II trials. It cannot be the function of the theory of international law to lend color to the pretension that this or that state acts as an organ of the international society.

Moreover, the fact that in international relations recourse to a heteronomous procedure for the interpretation and application of international law is still the exception rather than the rule, and the further fact that negotiations often lead to deadlock rather than to an agreed solution render it extremely difficult to determine whether controversial rules of international law are still part of positive international law or have ceased to be so. The basic norm that states ought to behave as they have customarily behaved,[113] gives no indication concerning the content of positive international law. The empirical material which presents itself as international law contains inconsistencies and contradictions: States themselves have not followed and do not always follow the same line of conduct. The rule enunciated in the London Protocol which, it has been said, "was honored more in the breach than in the observance,"[114] is perhaps as good an example as any. Does it countenance the modification or termination of treaties by less than the agreement of the contracting parties? Is a modification contrary to that rule a violation of international law pure and simple, or a challenge to the basic norm, that is, an attempt at a revolutionary creation of international law?[115] If the revolution fails, the state which attempted the revolution is considered as a law breaker and, as the Nuremberg trial has shown, can be punished for defying the law. When, however, can it be said that a revolution, a challenge to the basic norm, has succeeded? Assuming that the post-war conduct of some states were put to the test of judicial determination, it is scarcely open to doubt that an uninstructed tribunal[116] would put that conduct to the test of traditional international law. As long, however, as allegation stands against allegation—and in international law and relations such allegations (autointerpretations) stand pitted against each other for long periods—it may be difficult to determine whether that conduct should be tested in the light of traditional international law or of the very principle on which it claims to be based. This problem is encountered in customary as well as in conventional international law. One may well ask whether the members of the United Nations, for instance, still adhere to the basic norm that they should behave in conformity with the Charter as adopted at San Francisco, or whether the basic norm is assumed to be that members should behave in conformity with the Charter as interpreted at any given moment by a two-thirds majority of the members. As the Charter of the United Nations, in contradistinction to the constitution of some of the specialized agencies mentioned above, does not confer upon

[113] Kelsen, *General Theory*, p. 369.

[114] Jessup, *op. cit.*, p. 144.

[115] See Josef L. Kunz, "Revolutionary Creation of Norms of International Law," *American Journal of International Law*, XLI (1947), 119-126, to the effect that it is possible to conceive an illegal but not a revolutionary creation of norms of international law.

[116] The International Military Tribunal was an instructed tribunal as its charter contained the law to be applied in the trial. The tribunal was not free to "find" the applicable law.

the General Assembly the power to interpret the Charter authoritatively, the practice of the General Assembly amounts to an autointerpretation having the appearance and practical effect of an autodecision for as long as it is not submitted to the test of judicial investigation and determination. The conflict between East and West, to use the current and somewhat simplified formula, subjects customary as well as conventional international law to the strains and stresses characteristic of a period of transition in international law and relations.

## CONCLUSION

Traditional international law, evolved gradually in the wake of the cataclysmic dismemberment of the hierarchical order of the Middle Ages, has been and still is characterized by a substantial degree of autonomy preserved by the states which form the international society. Autointerpretation is the result and principal manifestation of this autonomy. The establishment of an international tribunal with compulsory jurisdiction for all states and all disputes would inject into international law and relations a degree of heteronomy which would enhance the stature of international law as law. It was advocated by some as a guarantee against war. Others demanded it on the ground that without a modicum of organization it was premature to consider international law as true law, or as valid law, or as law at all. It was shown above that the practice of autointerpretation rooted in international law makes it difficult indeed to regard states as organs of international law and to maintain the *bellum justum* theory in any but a metaphorical sense. The absence of a modicum of institutionalized community interests is also an obstacle to the position that in its present stage the international society possesses a force monopoly.

Thus, for a variety of mutually complementary reasons, the development of institutions operating in the entire family of nations for a long time has been regarded as a desirable and indeed a feasible method to make international law an effective order without sacrificing its character as a law regulating the conduct of states on the basis of equality. This is, however, not necessarily the only method. World government or world federation are frequently praised and propagated as the more effective alternatives. Moreover, some observers claim to discern in the transitional period—the struggle between two agglomerations of states and power—the trend to a new hierarchial pattern within each of the two groups. This trend is characterized by the emergence of hegemonial or leading states. The effective establishment of the hegemony of one state or of a restricted concert of states might provide international law with the necessary degree of executive power, as, to some extent, it did in the nineteenth century. The present subordination of the states to the impersonal and unorganized authority of international law would be superseded by the subordination of the majority of states to the personal and organized authority of the leading state or states. This apparently has already happened in the group of states led and organized by the Soviet Union. For the "free world" it may not be too late to arrest the trend if it desires to remain free. States so far have been manifestly reluctant to subordinate themselves to collectively administered institutions for the creation, interpretation, and application of international law. The sacrifice in autonomy, particularly in the cherished right of autointerpretation involved in such an organization of the society of states, was deemed too great. The diminution inevitably involved in a hierarchical pattern may very likely be vastly greater. The choice seems no longer to be, as it has been in the past, between autonomy and heteronomy, but between different patterns of heteronomy.

# EDITORIAL COMMENT

## PROBLEMS OF INTERNATIONAL ADJUDICATION AND COMPLIANCE WITH INTERNATIONAL LAW: SOME SIMPLE SOLUTIONS

The present writer had the opportunity of attending discussions relating to the concern widely held about the prospects for the settlement of international disputes through judicial procedures and, more particularly, through the International Court of Justice. Participants included leading scholars and practitioners. The group seemed more impressed with the difficulties than the possibilities of making the Court a more effective instrument or, in the words of the Institute of International Law, of considering reference of disputes to the Court or another adjudicative instance as "a normal method of settlement of legal disputes."[1] The participants certainly did not see any easy solution for what has been described as the crisis of confidence in the Court.[2]

The American Society of International Law at its 1964 Annual Meeting approached the problem in a wider perspective by exploring a variety of ways and means for "Causing Compliance with International Law." Professor Richard Falk, in opening the debate, stressed the limited rôle of international adjudication and, as to the future, was of the opinion that "the rôle of courts will remain marginal as long as the nation state continues to be the pre-eminent center of power and loyalty in world politics."[3] In discussing the

[1] Resolution adopted at the Neuchâtel Session in 1959, 54 A.J.I.L. 136 (1960).

[2] For some constructive suggestions for opening up a wider range of procedures and remedies, see Jenks, The Prospects of International Adjudication, Ch. 3.

[3] 1964 Proceedings, American Society of International Law 3.

rôle of experts in providing authoritative guidance, he seemed to deplore the display, in connection with the United States quarantine in the crisis over Soviet missiles in Cuba in the fall of 1962, "of national patriotism at the expense of scholarly detachment."[4] Professor Julius Stone formulated nine canons of realism and urged, among other things, that low-level disputes with respect to which reasonably certain rules of international law exist or are believed to exist, should be steered in the direction of the International Court of Justice or some other judicial institutions.[5] Professor Louis Sohn submitted suggestions for "fractionating the obligation to go to the Court" by permitting and persuading states to be more discriminating in accepting the compulsory jurisdiction of the Court pursuant to Article 36 of the Statute. The point of his proposal was that states might not wish to expose themselves to an unlimited range of legal disputes but might be more inclined to take the risk in specified areas, of which he listed 30, beginning with recognition of states and ending with expulsion of aliens. The list was, of course, tentative and by no means exhaustive.[6] This proposal requires no change in the Statute but merely a rational use of the faculty open to states under Article 36 to formulate reservations *ratione materiae.* Professor Stone doubted that there was "much to be gained by a kind of 'supermarket' selling approach."[7] As other approaches have not met with overwhelming success so far, there can be no harm in suggesting or, more correctly, calling the attention of the states to the flexibility which is inherent in the present system of Article 36. In any event, Professor Stone was unfair in attributing to Professor Sohn a "supermarket" mentality; Professor Sohn described his approach as the "smörgasbord" approach, hoping that states might be tempted to "nibble here and there."[8] *Bon appétit!*

A sort of break-through was achieved by Professor Roger Fisher. He proposes a "post-decisional veto," that is, the right, to be defined and circumscribed, to refuse or suspend or postpone—it is not clear which—the execution of a judgment of the Court as an inducement for accepting the compulsory jurisdiction of the Court. In the case of the United States, the Connally Amendment might be repealed and in its place the United States might reserve the right to suspend the binding force of the judgment.[9] A reservation of this sort "appears less damaging than the Connally Amendment," and it seems clear, to Professor Fisher at any rate,[10] that "some such reservation would make third-party settlement more acceptable both to the United States and to other governments as well."[11] This is an unverified and, one must add hopefully, unverifiable proposition. The Connally Amendment did not produce any bene-

[4] *Ibid.* at 5. He expressed a similar sentiment in "The Adequacy of Contemporary Theories in International Law—Gaps in Legal Thinking," 50 Virginia Law Review 231–265, at 236 (1964). The essays to which he referred appeared in the July, 1963, issue of the American Journal of International Law.

[5] Proceedings at 28.

[6] *Ibid.* 131–136.

[7] *Ibid.* at 141.

[8] *Ibid.* at 136.

[9] *Ibid.* at 129, where the rough draft of the proposed reservation will be found.

[10] And to Professor Stone as well, who commented: "when paper promises of compliance could not in the nature of things be enforced, we might well promote organic growth of procedural solutions by admitting the right of veto." *Ibid.* at 141.

[11] *Ibid.* at 129.

fits for the United States; it backfired on the one occasion when the United States appeared before the Court as plaintiff against Bulgaria,[12] as it had backfired against France in the *Norwegian Loans* case. If its purpose was to close the Court to the United States, it achieved this end extremely well. As to the proposed veto with respect to the binding force of the Court's judgment, there can be little doubt that it would operate in the same way and with the identic effect: to close the Court to the United States. For it can hardly be imagined that any state would go to the trouble of accepting the challenge of the United States or of challenging it to have the Court adjudicate a dispute, to the expense and formidable effort of preparing the memorials and plead orally, if the end result, the judgment, could be vetoed by the United States. The principle of reciprocity, moreover, would operate here as it does with respect to other reservations.

The foregoing assumes that a reservation of the sort proposed by Professor Fisher could validly be made. This point, and it is a crucial one, is not elaborated beyond asserting that an amendment to the Statute might be required "to give the defendant government some residual immunity if the *(sic!)* worst came to the worst" or the attachment of a reservation to the jurisdiction of the Court. The veto, however, could surely not be regarded as a reservation to the jurisdiction of the Court. It would have no connection with Article 36 of the Court's Statute, unless the concept of jurisdiction were to undergo drastic surgery. Nor could the desired result be achieved by an amendment of the Statute, although, if the binding force of judgments were to be abolished, consequential changes might have to be made in the wording of some articles, notably Articles 59 and 60 of the Statute. This observation leaves aside the problem of extending the post-decisional veto to the execution of judgments. Here again, consequential changes would be required. The proposed reservation would have to be attached, it is submitted, to Article 94, paragraph 1, of the Charter. This purpose could be achieved only by the process of amendment, since the procedure of making reservations to the Charter even under the assumption that it could have been validly effected, is, of course, no longer available to Members of the United Nations.

As indicated above, it is not clear what precisely Professor Fisher has in mind. In several passages he argues that it would be easier for the United States to accept the compulsory jurisdiction of the Court, if it were given "some kind of veto over decisions of the Court *after* they had been made,"[13] that other governments would be in the same position if each nation were given "a legal 'out' if it finds itself confronted with a decision that it then considers unacceptable,"[14] and that "giving governments a right of some kind to *reject* an international decision is not a drastic step."[15] This writer believes that it would be a very drastic step indeed, for it would involve an attack on a firmly established principle of customary as well as conventional international law. Tampering

[12] See this writer's "Bulgaria Invokes the Connally Amendment," 56 A.J.I.L. 357–382 (1962). See also *infra*.
[13] *Ibid.* at 124. Italics supplied.
[14] *Ibid.*
[15] *Ibid.* Italics supplied.

with the binding force of judgments would undermine the foundation on which the whole structure of international adjudication rests.

Assuming that what is proposed relates not to the validity of judgments but to their execution, one is forced to ask whether the reservation is necessary. The execution of judgments belongs to what Rosenne calls the "post-adjudicative phase"[16] of the judicial process and finds its place in the political realm. In the system of the United Nations the execution of judgments is entrusted to a political organ, the Security Council, pursuant to Article 94(2). Insofar as the United States is concerned, it is fully in position to prevent any action, whether recommendatory or decisional, which it considers inimical to its interests by the exercise of its veto power.[17] If the question of the non-execution of a judgment were raised in another organ, say, the General Assembly,[18] the situation might be different, as no veto would protect the United States there. The Security Council, given the deliberate ambiguity of Article 94, paragraph 2, is not limited to recommending or deciding automatically action to enforce the judgment, if not barred by a veto, but may, without casting doubt on the *res judicata,* make recommendations or decisions which "at most have a suspensive or moratory effect on the judgment."[19] Thus, if no more than a suspension were the object, it could well be achieved without an amendment to the Charter. But it would be the international community acting through the Security Council which would have to be convinced that a suspension or moratorium is in the general interest rather than in the particular interest of a Member.

A recommendation or decision under Article 94, paragraph 2, could be frustrated by any of the permanent members of the Security Council, though it could not be so frustrated in the General Assembly. In the latter case there might be the difficulty of securing the necessary majority, which may not be an easy task. The object of the proposed reservation thus becomes clear: to secure for the United States or for all Members a unilateral veto regardless of the general interest in the execution or suspension of the judgment. This would be as self-judging a reservation as is the Connally Amendment and, since it could conceivably be invoked for self-seeking interests, it might be detrimental to the moderate degree of stability and order which exists currently, and resisted on this ground. In this writer's view it should be resisted. Surely the United States is not in need of more protection from international law than it already enjoys. Be that as it may, the proposed post-judgment veto, contrary to the view that it "should increase the normal pattern of compliance,"[20] seems irrelevant to the problem of compliance with international law.

The rationale behind this veto, however, is relevant. "Providing a legal right of rejection," argues Professor Fisher, "in large part simply confirms the practical power of

[16] Rosenne, The International Court of Justice at 73 f. and 108; and Jenks, *op. cit.* at 667.
[17] This point is considered in greater detail by Rosenne, *ibid.* at 107 f.
[18] *Cf.* Rosenne, *ibid.* at 108.
[19] Rosenne, *ibid.* at 109.
[20] Fisher, *loc. cit.* at 126.

non-compliance that already exists."[21] The thought is to reduce "the gap between the rules about power and the power itself," for

> As long as national governments have an undoubted physical power of frustration of an international decision, we will, I believe, develop more effective legal machinery if we recognize that fact and define substantive and procedural limits upon that power of frustration than if we pretend it did not exist. The power of words is great, but not so great as to abolish the power of political review of judicial decisions.[22]

As has been shown, the power of political review of the consequences of judicial decisions is available, but the postulated power of political review of the judicial decisions is something else, for it deprives such decisions of their legal character as *res judicata.* There is, however, for anyone concerned with securing compliance with law or, more especially, international law, a clear indication of the way to handle this problem.

Clearly by reducing the gap between what individuals or states can actually do and what the law requires them to do or prohibits them from doing, the problem of compliance could be simplified or totally eliminated. This has not been the path of the law. For, as reported in Scriptures, Cain was punished for the slaying of Abel. If there were no law at all, there would be total compliance, a condition usually described as anarchy. And if there were very little law, there would be some compliance and, hopefully, a little less anarchy, and so on until the point is reached where the creation of more law would become counterproductive. In other words, compliance appears as a function of the quantity and quality of law in society, be it national or international, and of the number, character and quality of decision-makers. It is also a function of the organization for the application, enforcement and change of law, all of which are rudimentary in the extreme in the international society. Since the prospects for making this organization more effective are very slim indeed, those who are preoccupied with the problem of compliance must concern themselves with the quantity and quality of existing international law. The prospects for improving its quality are not very bright, and they become dimmer with the reduction in the use of the judicial function. The contribution which the United Nations has made or may make is not negligible but insufficient. More and speedier progress could be made by reducing the quantity of law: less law, less violation of law, more compliance. This could be done by outright repeal of those parts of the Charter where the gap between norm and performance has become conspicuous or by the more tortuous path of interpretation. Progress in this direction has been quite remarkable.

As Professor Sohn said, we would be more realistic and wiser if we would "elevate our sights a little lower."[23] The practical way to accomplish this is to beat a retreat from the Charter to the 19th century, which was wise enough to let the states have the freedom to use force, war or arbitration as interchangeable instruments of national policy.

[21] *Ibid.* at 124.
[22] *Ibid.* at 129.
[23] *Ibid.* at 131.

The attempts to limit this freedom through the League of Nations Covenant, the Kellogg-Briand Pact and currently the United Nations Charter, have largely failed and there is some pressure to argue the limitation away. Professor Stone, agreeing with Dean Acheson, said that surely "the survival of states is not a matter of law."[24] This sounds realistic enough but, in the context in which Dean Acheson used these words, they may have related to Article 51 of the Charter, which safeguards the right of self-defense against armed attack. But in the Cuban crisis there was no armed attack and yet the survival of the United States was believed to be at stake. Dean Acheson and Stone then read the Charter, including Articles 2, paragraph 4, and 51, as not limiting the "residual power" of Members to take any measures in self-defense if and when their survival, in their judgment, of course, is at stake. This seems entirely plausible in the context of the Cuban crisis, and is good 19th-century doctrine. But how about other contexts? Should a state, a weaker and smaller state, subordinate its political, economic and social well-being to the observance of those rules of international law which deal with the use of force, expropriation or state succession? Why should they be expected to be temperate and "promote by example a spirit of compliance with international law"?[25] Should not rather the well-established, well-to-do and well-protected state set this example? Should not compliance with international law, like charity, begin at home?

The result so easily obtained by Dean Acheson and Stone can be achieved slightly more laboriously, but only slightly so, by a suitable method of interpretation. Thus, Professor McDougal, in the context of the Cuban crisis, contends that

> nothing in the "plain and natural meaning" of the words of the Charter requires an interpretation that Article 51 restricts the customary right of self-defense. The proponents of such an interpretation substitute for the words "if an armed attack occurs" the very different words "if, and only if, an armed attack occurs."[26]

The principle of interpretation applied by Professor McDougal, which might be called the "negative plain meaning" principle, opens up old vistas—the 19th century—as well as new ones. It could be applied to many articles of the Charter as well as to treaties generally and precepts of customary international law. However, it may be questioned whether the "fallacy of word-juggling"[27] is within the reserved domain of the proponents of the "positive plain meaning" principle, for it would seem that the "negative plain meaning" method involves some word-juggling too. This will be seen from the following comparisons of the two versions of Article 51 in which A refers to the former, and B to the latter method:

A: if, "and only if," an armed attack occurs.
B: if, "but not only if," an armed attack occurs.

[24] *Ibid.* at 27. Mr. Acheson's remarks will be found on p. 14 of the 1963 Proceedings.
[25] Stone, 1964 Proceedings, American Society of International Law at 31.
[26] "The Soviet-Cuban Quarantine and Self-Defense," 57 A.J.I.L. 597–604, at 600 (1963).
[27] *Ibid.*

Some other comparisons may illustrate the versatility of the method:

Article 51.
A: if an armed attack occurs "only" against a Member.
B: if an armed attack occurs "but not only" against a Member.
Article 1, par. 1.
A: to take "only" effective collective measures.
B: to take "not only" effective collective measures.[28]
Article 2, par. 3.
A: settle international disputes "only" by peaceful means.
B: settle international disputes "not only" by peaceful means.
Article 2, par. 4.
A: All members shall "always" refrain . . . from the threat or use of force.
B: All members shall "not always" refrain. . . .
Article 53, par. 1.
A: But no enforcement action shall be taken without the "prior" authorization . . .
B: But (no) enforcement action shall be taken "with or without" "prior or subsequent or no" authorization . . .

Examples could be multiplied, but it is hoped the usefulness and versatility of the "negative plain meaning" method has been sufficiently demonstrated. Insofar as the particular case of the Soviet-Cuban quarantine is concerned, the difference between Stone, Acheson and McDougal seems to boil down to this: Stone and Acheson simply deny that there was any applicable law or that Article 51 governed the situation, whereas McDougal accepts the applicability of Article 51 and maintains that the action was in conformity with, or, at the very least, not contrary to Article 51 as interpreted in accordance with the "negative plain meaning" canon.

In case there should be precepts of customary or conventional law which are quite intractable and resistant to any of the above methods, still another more dependable and comprehensive principle or canon could be envisaged. It could be formulated, quite tentatively, as follows: Every precept shall mean what it plainly says ("positive plain meaning" principle), what it plainly does not say ("negative plain meaning" principle), as well as its opposite ("opposite plain meaning" principle), and no precept shall be deemed to curtail the residual power of a state to take limited, moderate and necessary measures which in its judgment ("autointerpretation" principle) are best calculated to promote or ensure its national survival ("survival" principle). This comprehensive rule could, naturally, be refined and improved. It would, of course, be understood that every state acts at its peril and, therefore, smaller and weaker states should use it with caution lest they be accused of flouting international law and punished to boot. There is still a good deal of vitality in the Roman adage: *Quod licet Jovi non licet Bovi.* The recognition of the power factor might thus appear to run counter to the principle of sovereign equality enshrined in the Charter. But every student knows that this principle has been and continues to be a

[28] "Only" and "not only" may modify "collective" or "effective" as desired.

legal fiction and, moreover, the problem here is no problem in reality, if the "negative plain meaning" principle is applied.

Another example will illustrate the use to which this principle can usefully be put. The Test Ban Treaty, which Professor Fisher commends as an example of legal regulation and therefore limitation of the power of states to frustrate a treaty,[29] provides in Article IV:

> Each Party shall in exercising its national sovereignty have the right to withdraw from the Treaty if it decides that extraordinary events, related to the subject matter of this Treaty, have jeopardized the supreme interests of its country. It shall give notice of such withdrawal to all other Parties to the Treaty three months in advance.

Now, the "positive plain meaning" principle yields the obvious results: There must be extraordinary events, there must be a jeopardy to the supreme interests—a rather awkward substitute for the well-known vital interests—and there must be three months' notice. This reading interpolates the word "only" in the first sentence thus: "Each Party . . . only if it decides." It is plain that "only" is not in the text and therefore the right to withdraw from the Treaty cannot be limited to the stated circumstances ("negative plain meaning" principle), and can be exercised in other circumstances as well. The second sentence could be considered as somewhat intractable. But the "opposite plain meaning" principle clearly eliminates the requirement of three months' notice. Q.E.D. Moreover, this requirement is nonsensical in any event and falls to the ground simply when subjected to the venerable principles that an "absurd" meaning should not be attributed to a treaty provision, that every provision should be interpreted in the context in which it appears, and that the major purpose should be effectuated. It is absurd to assume that a party will know three months in advance that "extraordinary events" are about to occur, as it is in the nature of such events that they arrive habitually unheralded; the provision clearly recognizes that the "supreme interests" of the party must be safeguarded; the treaty should, then, be so interpreted as to carry forward this objective, and, therefore, the requirement of three months' notice is no requirement at all, but plainly a drafting error. One might end this little but instructive exercise with the query: To what do the words "in advance" refer? To the extraordinary events? Or to the withdrawal? A good draftsman was obviously conspicuous by his absence in the drafting of this treaty. Or was the English text of this clause penned by a Russian?

The principles briefly sketched above present, it is believed, an attractive smörgasbord for experts eager to interpret international law. It must be conceded, however, that they lend themselves to abuse. Consequently, in order to prevent nibbling by unauthorized persons such as, for instance, Soviet experts, some precautions will

[29] Fisher, 1964 Proceedings, American Society of International Law at 125.

have to be taken. This matter, fortunately, appears to be outside the purview of the present paper.

It has so far been assumed that by dint of one principle of interpretation or another, it will be possible to arrive at a clear-cut conclusion whether, given a certain set of facts and the validity of the applicable rule, a state's conduct has or has not complied with the posited rules. However, scholars do not necessarily have to assume the rôle of judges sitting in adversary proceedings who must uphold or reject the contentions of the parties. They might be better off to play a more discreet rôle. This has indeed been proposed by Professor Falk, who suggested that, rather than to "dichotomize inquiry," it would be

> better to think of compliance as a position on a spectrum, rather than as a two-way switch that is either on or off; it we adopt the idea of a spectrum, then legality is a matter of degree varying with the circumstances of the case.[30]

Leaving on one side the "two-way switch" in view of the present writer's complete ignorance of electronics, Professor Falk's proposal is entirely in line with modern trends in theorizing about international relations to think in terms of a continuum or spectrum. It is certainly proper for experts, as suggested above, to refrain from formulating conclusions and to present, as Professor Falk suggests, arguments pro and con, to dispense praise for restraint, moderation, *et cetera.* All this, it is felt, is no argument in favor of the spectrum approach. Presumably at one side of the spectrum would be compliance and at the other, non-compliance, and the conduct of states, whether in a crisis or not, would be placed at or somewhere between the poles, in the grey area. But, unfortunately, legality like virtue is not a matter of degree. One can sympathize with the fallen damsel and stress the "unfortunate misfortune" in which she found herself when she fell, but fall she did. So, *mutatis mutandis,* it is with state conduct. If the United States quarantine is considered as a reprisal, it must be tested for its legality in the light of the applicable law. Leaving out of consideration the question whether reprisals are or are not compatible with the Charter, it would be relevant to consider the question of summation, proportionality, et cetera, as was done in the *Naulilaa* case. But the condition *sine qua non* of compliance with international law would be a prior illegal act on the part of the Soviet Union. What this act was, has never, to this writer's knowledge, been clearly stated, and it is at least doubtful whether President Kennedy construed the Soviet Union's conduct as illegal rather than dangerous to the security of the United States.

On the other hand, if the United States quarantine is regarded as a measure of self-defense, its conformity with international law must be tested in the light of the Charter, or if the Charter does not apply, in the light of customary international law. If the Charter did not prohibit self-defense in circumstances other than armed attack, the United States' conduct *ab initio* was lawful. This initial lawfulness might have been marred by

[30] *Ibid.* at 5.

excessive action, *et cetera.* Here all the aspects of the United States' action, such as moderation, proportionality, *et cetera,* become relevant if, according to customary international law, these factors are relevant. If they are relevant, then the action was lawful initially as well as throughout. The second hypothesis would be that the Charter intended to prohibit resort to self-defense except in case of armed attack. In view of the abuses committed in the name of self-defense or self-help,[31] and in view of the plain meaning of Article 2, paragraph 4, and Article 51 ("positive plain meaning" principle), a strong argument could be made in favor of the second hypothesis. For proponents of this construction the spectrum is no help. They must make up their minds. And considerations of moderation, *et cetera,* may sweeten the pill, but they have no other choice but to swallow it. Apart from an exegesis of the Charter, past precedents, including the Anglo-French action in Suez in 1956, would have to be examined to discover any light which they might shed for the proper construction of the Charter.

Loyalty to this country may cloud the expert's impartiality. Even in a free society this may be so. The government's rôle as a dispenser of awards and the society's mark of approval or disapproval are factors which may or may not be relevant. But in a free society, at any rate, silence is an acceptable option. There is no reason to assume, however, that "neutral experts"[32] are in fact more impartial than national experts. They may be free from bias where interests of their own country are not directly involved. But in this age of interdependence this cannot be taken for granted. And surely there is no reason to assume that they are better versed in international law than national experts. It all hinges on the quality of their legal opinion.

Preoccupation with legal issues carries with it the risk of overlooking the need for weighing political actions and conceivable alternatives, of concentrating on the issue at hand and disregarding its political or economic antecedents. It may be inevitable to consider the legal aspects of the Bay of Pigs operation or the Cuban quarantine or the incidents in the Gulf of Tonkin, but the political factors and motivations may be just as relevant even for international lawyers. They cannot be divorced from the perennial confrontation known as the Cold War and its corrosive impact on compliance with international law.

In any event, it may be safely suggested, whatever experts think or say or, according to Professor Falk, should think or say about compliance, does not alter the legal aspects of a case. Experts do not pronounce authoritative interpretations of international law, even though they may flatter themselves of so doing. The attitude of the state or states involved is decidedly more relevant for determining compliance or non-compliance. Unless they reach an agreement, there is a stand-off: one auto-interpretation faces the other and neither is authoritative for or binding upon the other. Acquiescence in a political claim does not produce a rule of law any more than the formulation of a political claim is necessarily evidence of a stand on the relevant rules of law. And currently experts and govern-

[31] See Corfu Channel case, [1949] I.C.J. Rep. 4, at 35.

[32] Falk, *Ibid.* at 8.

ments seem to have at least one position in common, namely, that it is more prudent to keep a dispute out of court than to run the risk of an authoritative but perhaps unfavorable interpretation.

It has been noted above that compliance is a function of the quantity and quality of law, of the capabilities of decision-makers, *et cetera.* Governments in their lawmaking activities sometimes display excessive concern with the problem of compliance, as for instance in connection with the "self-enforcing" Test Ban Treaty. On other occasions they seem to respond with almost excessive abandon to pressures of interest groups or of public opinion. The desire to banish war and the use of force and even the threat of force was no doubt one of those "idealistic" motifs in drafting the Charter and other instruments as well. But are the states and their citizens ready for a warless world? Or will they have to pass through a lawless world before they start building a warless world? If Articles 2, paragraph 4, 51 and 53 had not been written into the Charter, there would have been less controversy and less pressure to find compliance with the law. There is some international law which, even under optimistic assumptions, can hardly be made to work in contemporary international politics.

Compliance with international law is also, though to a lesser extent, a function of the experts. At this point of history, experts may do more harm than good to international law as a form of, or stage in, the regulation of international relations, if they formulate in universal terms propositions intended to deal with particular situations. They may produce nothing but a boomerang effect, and add a dubious case of compliance with the law to another. The cause of compliance is not likely to be advanced by doctrines which achieve no more than to plaster over instances of non-compliance. Nor will it be promoted by proposals for "planned non-compliance" or "built-in non-compliance" with judgments of international tribunals. It is far better, in this writer's view, to let international adjudication advance at the current snail's pace than to attempt to speed it forward by such means. The result could only be a setback. The existing procedures and remedies as indicated above are a sufficient political protection against an abuse of the judicial power, which moreover is wholly speculative. If governments feel insufficiently protected, let them set up an appeals tribunal to give them the desired judicial guarantees. It is illusory in the extreme to pretend that compliance with international law by one skillful device or another can be made a painless affair, like the promise of the school book, *French Without Tears,* or of its French equivalent, *Rire et Apprendre.* Governments may try to get something for nothing but they know that such gains are apt to be short-lived. In the long run they will be as they have been in the past, inimical to progress in developing the modicum of order and stability that is compatible with an international law built on and around the sovereignty of states.

Consistency need not be a virtue in national decision-makers, but independent experts may do more harm than good in throwing consistency to the winds. What is argued on behalf of one country in the form of a general statement on international law must apply equally to all countries. Rules of interpretation used by one expert may obviously be used by another. To argue complementarity of rules in international law is hardly tenable. International law would not deserve even the courtesy title of "system" if it accommodated at one and the same time rules and their opposites. Unfortunately, in the art of interpretation this complementarity has been achieved: for any or many principles there is an opposite principle and moreover there is no agreement as to which rule applies and when. The danger is not to be ruled out that, by the manipulation of these principles, the experts may successfully interpret international law away and find themselves face to face with *Le Néant.*

# TREATY INTERPRETATION: THE PROPER RÔLE OF AN INTERNATIONAL TRIBUNAL

## I

The proper rôle of an international tribunal "is to decide in accordance with international law such disputes as are submitted to it" (Art. 38 (1) of the Statute of the I.C.J.). Its "primary function" is "to administer justice based on law."[1] The interpretation of relevant treaties and other materials on which the contentions and submissions of the parties to the dispute are based is a means to an end, a means to reach a decision, and not an end in itself. International tribunals are not research institutes and they are not equipped with a staff of legal clerks or experts in the sciences of logic, semantics, communications or psychoanalysis. They are usually empowered to call witnesses and experts, to establish a commission of inquiry into the facts or the tribunal may itself conduct such an inquiry or on-the-spot inspection. The tribunal's function is to reach a decision as expeditiously and efficiently as possible. A tribunal may not decline to render a judgment on the ground of *non liquet,* although the International Court of Justice may refuse to adjudicate the dispute on the ground of judicial propriety.[2]

[1] Joint Dissenting Opinion of Judges Lauterpacht, Wellington Koo and Spender in the Aerial Incident Case, I.C.J. Reports 1959, p. 127, at 191.

[2] The Cameroons Case, I.C.J. Reports 1963, p. 15, at 38. See Leo Gross, "Limitations upon the Judicial Function," 58 A.J.I.L. 415–431 (1964). See also *infra.*

## II

The first step to be taken by a tribunal in the process of adjudication is to satisfy itself that it has jurisdiction; "jurisdiction," said Lauterpacht, "must be proved up to the hilt."[3] The last step is the formulation of the judgment. The question is asked whether a tribunal should concern itself with the consequences or effect of its judgment. This is not a matter which pertains properly to interpretation, but it has been raised by Professors McDougal, Lasswell and Miller in that context.

The doctrine is divided on the subject. In the *Cameroons* case the Court declined to give judgment on the ground that

> The Court's judgment must have some practical consequence in the sense that it can affect existing legal rights or obligations of the parties, thus removing uncertainty from their legal relations. No judgment on the merits in this case could satisfy these essentials of the judicial function. ([1963] I.C.J. Rep. at 34).

Lauterpacht was of the opinion that an international tribunal should not "be guided by the desire to avoid solutions which may have no prospect of being acted upon in practice." ( *Op. cit.* at 290, note 13.) Jenks seems to lean to the view that a tribunal might be concerned with the enforceability of its judgment.[4] Quite explicitly Professors McDougal, Lasswell and Miller include among their "recommended principles of content . . . the principle of *enforceable decision,* or the expectation that authoritative outcomes will be put into effect." In their view

> In estimating post-outcome response to the applier-interpreter's decision the calculation must include the prospects of compliance and noncompliance, and of the generalization of noncompliance to the point of destroying current institutions of public order. We recommend an early start on the operation of *estimating the effect of decision.*[5]

I do not believe that a tribunal should be influenced by considerations of this sort in the process of interpretation. Such considerations introduce political elements into the process which would better remain outside of it. In the case where a dispute is brought before the International Court of Justice by special agreement or before an *ad hoc* tribunal by special agreement, the parties clearly want a judgment. In contrast, when the Court is seised by means of a unilateral application, it is not equally obvious that both parties desire a judgment, although technically and legally they are committed to comply with the decision (Art. 94, paragraph 1, of the Charter). Moreover, if one considers the adjudicative process as a stage in the process of resolution of conflicts between states, it must be left to the parties and not to the tribunal to determine by mutual agreement what use they will make of the judgment. A case of *fiat justicia pereat mundus* is not likely to arise.

[3] The Development of International Law at 91 (1958).

[4] The Prospects of International Adjudication at 666–667 (1964). See also I Rosenne, The Law and Practice of the International Court at 118–119, and 310, note 1; and II *ibid.* 606–607 (1965).

[5] The Interpretation of Agreements and World Public Order at 384 (1967).

Finally, and hypothetically, suppose the International Court of Justice had declined in 1966 to give a judgment on the merits in the *South West Africa* cases on the ground that a judgment in favor of the Applicants would have been unenforceable. True enough, the Security Council of the United Nations has a general mandate under Article 94, paragraph 2, of the Charter, to recommend or decide "upon measures to be taken to give effect to the judgment." But this clause is so uncertain in its formulation and the constellation of forces in the Security Council so unpredictable, that the Court might have inclined to the view that enforcement was most unlikely to be forthcoming and that its judgment might plunge the United Nations into a fatal crisis. What would have been the reception accorded to such a decision? Hardly more favorable than that which was actually accorded to the judgment of the Court in 1966.

In the *Haya De La Torre* case the Court, faced with the question in what manner its judgment in the *Asylum* case should be executed by Colombia and Peru, declared:

> The Court observes that the Judgment confined itself . . . to defining the legal relations which the Havana Convention had established between the Parties. It did not give any directions to the Parties, and entails for them only the obligation of compliance therewith. ([1951] I.C.J. Rep. 71 at 79.)

To define the legal relations between the parties on the basis of the applicable law is, as Mr. Rosenne observed, "the limit of the Court's judicial functions and apparently of its official interest as well." (*Op. cit.* at 119.)

## III

The judgment of a tribunal will normally include a review and analysis of the contentions and conclusions submitted by the parties, and the dispositive or operative clause. The connecting link between the analysis and the operative clause is the reasoning of the tribunal. How explicit should a tribunal be in developing the reasons for its decision? With respect to the pronouncements of the International Court of Justice

> there has been strong criticism—too persistent to be ignored—that too often the major decisions of the Court have been marred by the brevity of their language, so that the successive logical steps cannot easily be followed, at least without most careful scrutiny of all the pleadings.[6]

Along similar lines, Professors McDougal, Lasswell and Miller have recommended "the principle of *explicit rationality,* affirming the importance of making explicit the principles of interpretation and application that influence the decision reached by the applier-interpreter."[7]

This is a counsel of perfection, more appropriately addressed to a single judge than

[6] Rosenne, note 4 above, at 607.

[7] *Op. cit.* note 5 above, at 390; see also pp. 64, 265, 270.

to a tribunal of several judges. Representing as they do different legal cultures, they can more easily reach an agreement on the disposition of the dispute than on the grounds for the disposition. As the proliferation of separate opinions in the International Court of Justice often indicates, there are more ways than one for arriving at a decision.[8] The function of a tribunal, after all, is to decide the controversy and not to attempt to unify the doctrinal differences of its members. It may well be that in some cases a judgment "does not so much represent the joint opinion of the judges as the common denominator of their divergent views." (Rosenne, at 618.) In some cases, and they need not necessarily be "acutely controversial" in character, "a laconic unanimity may be more impressive and serviceable than a wealth of legal reasoning." (Jenks, at 315.)

## IV

The function of interpreting treaties is always a creative one in the sense that the judicial process is one of the concretization of more or less general principles to a particular set of circumstances. In that limited sense it is possible to speak of "judicial legislation." However, the term is also used in a broader sense by those who advocate a creative rôle for international tribunals. This attitude is often expressed by the plea that when interpreting treaties tribunals should give preference to the principle of effectiveness or purpose-oriented interpretation as against the so-called restrictive or strict interpretation, or by the plea that tribunals should be guided by principles of "international public policy," by overriding goals of a public order of human dignity, or simply community policies. There are significant differences of attitude and emphasis between these positions, but for the sake of brevity they will be discussed together.

A convenient starting point for a discussion of these positions may be the proposition that when states agree to submit a dispute to an international tribunal, they expect the adjudication to be based on the impersonal criteria of the law, be it conventional or customary. That is the law which they have freely accepted or consented to. It is true today as it was at the time of the judgment in the *Lotus* case that they will not be bound without their consent. The principle of consent may not be immutable, but I suggest that it has not undergone a drastic mutation yet. The potency of the *Lotus* case can be seen in the prominent place given to it in the recent judgment of the International Court of Justice in the *Continental Shelf* cases: practice and *opinio juris,* that is, consent to be bound, are still the ingredients of customary law.[9]

It is also important to recall that the pleas for judicial creativeness and judicial legislation appeared at a time when, in the absence of an effective international legislature, international tribunals appeared as the most promising institutions for the progressive de-

[8] A good example of this is the Guardianship case in which Judge Lauterpacht arrived at the operative clause by quite a different reasoning than the Court. I.C.J. Reports 1958, p. 55, at 79. In this connection the Membership case may be mentioned in which two judges voted for the conclusion of the Court but showed in their separate opinions that they disagreed not only with the reasoning but with the conclusion as well. See Leo Gross, "Election of States to United Nations Membership," 1954 Proceedings, American Society of International Law 37–59, at 45. See also *infra.*

[9] I.C.J. Reports 1969, p. 3, at 44; 63 A.J.I.L. 591 (1969).

velopment of international law. Assuming this to be true, several comments may be made. First, the last few decades, particularly since World War II, have been an era of enormous legislative innovation by states. Whether one looks at international organizations, the Charter for the International Military Tribunal, the fields of space, sea, including the continental shelf, and air or human rights—everywhere there have been significant innovations. All of them were introduced by states. Secondly, an international tribunal has clearly a more promising opportunity for judicial creativity in the field of customary than in that of conventional international law. Several judgments of the International Court come to mind: the *Corfu Channel* case, the *Fisheries* case, the *Nottebohm* case. There have been some notable innovations in advisory opinions, as in the *Reservations, Reparation* and *Expenses* cases. However, only the first two were accepted in practice, for they did not impose any new obligations upon the Members of the United Nations. The opinion in the *Expenses* case was ineffective because it was not acceptable to a group of significant Members. One could even argue that it turned out to be unacceptable to the United States.[10]

The opinions and the 1962 judgment relating to *South West Africa* provide another instructive example of "judicial legislation." The first basic opinion of the Court on the *Status of South-West Africa* was described by Judge McNair as *"a piece of legislation"* that amounted "to imposing a *new* obligation upon the Union Government" of South Africa.[11] What possible incentive could there be for a state to comply with a "piece of legislation"? Lauterpacht welcomed the opinion precisely on the ground that it represented an instance of "judicial legislation" and as no more than "an example of the legitimate application of the principle of effectiveness to basic international instruments." ( *Op. cit.* 124, 280). But Lauterpacht, as judge, reminded the Court that, in holding that the United Nations succeeded to the supervisory functions of the defunct League of Nations, "it did so although the Charter contained no express provision to that effect and although the United Nations and the League of Nations were different institutions."[12] It seems not unreasonable to suggest that in that case the Court misapplied the principle of effectiveness in interpreting the Charter.

The Court itself is of course aware of the limits of the effectiveness principle. In the *Peace Treaties* (Second Phase) case the Court declared that it was its duty—as it is the duty of all international tribunals in the present submission—"to interpret the Treaties, not to revise them," and that

> . . . the rule of effectiveness, cannot justify the Court in attributing to the provisions for the settlement of disputes in the Peace Treaties a meaning which . . . would be contrary to their letter and spirit. ([1950] I.C.J. Rep. 221 at 229.)

[10] See Ambassador Arthur Goldberg's statement of August 16, 1965, 53 Department of State Bulletin 454 at 456 (1965); 60 A.J.I.L. 104 (1966).

[11] I.C.J. Reports 1950, p. 128, at 161–162 (italics supplied). See also Leo Gross, "The International Court of Justice and the United Nations," 120 Hague Academy of International Law, Recueil des Cours at 385–387 (I, 1967). *Infra.*

[12] Joint Dissenting Opinion of Judges Lauterpacht, Wellington Koo and Spender in the Aerial Incident case (Preliminary Objections), I.C.J. Reports 1959, p. 127, at 173.

The Court recalled this ruling on the limitation of the effectiveness principle in its 1966 judgment in the *South West Africa* cases, and declared that this principle

> can have no application in circumstances in which the Court would have to go beyond what can reasonably be regarded as being a process of interpretation, and would have to engage in a process of rectification or revision. ([1966] I.C.J. Rep. 6 at 48.)

There is obviously no clear-cut way to distinguish once and for all between reasonable interpretation and the filling of gaps, removal of ambiguities and more obvious methods of revising an instrument. Lauterpacht correctly emphasized the relativity of the distinction and pointed out that it is often controversial "which of the opposing views interprets the treaty and which revises it?" (*Op. cit.* at 287, note 10.) However, every doubt disappeared in the *Aerial Incident* case. In a Joint Dissenting Opinion with Judges Wellington Koo and Spender, Judge Lauterpacht argued cogently and convincingly, in my view, that the Court has not merely rewritten Article 36, paragraph 5, of the Court's Statute but has also added extraneous conditions to it.[13]

It may be noted in passing that the Court in that case virtually by-passed the text of Article 36, paragraph 5 and started its reasoning with the object of that clause. (*Loc. cit.* at 136.) The Court also applied the *restrictive* principle, saying that "thus to restrict the application of Article 36, paragraph 5, to the States signatories of the Statute is to take into account the purpose for which this provision was adopted." (*Ibid.* at 139.) The Court was rightly concerned with the question of consent and unwilling to subject Bulgaria to the operation of the clause without its consent. However, as the Joint Dissenting Opinion persuasively argued, Bulgaria's consent was supplied when she applied and was admitted to membership in the United Nations.[14]

It may be fitting to conclude this section with the warning of one of the strongest and most persistent advocates of judicial creativity in connection with the interpretation of treaties:

> An international court which yields conspicuously to the urge to modify the existing law—even if such action can be brought within the four corners of a major legal principle—may bring about a drastic curtailment of its activity. (Lauterpacht, *op. cit.* 76.)

Professors McDougal, Lasswell and Miller seem to share Lauterpacht's view by agreeing that "the tribunal should be modestly hesitant to impose new policies, especially in derogation of apparently expressed genuine shared expectations." (*Op. cit.* at 264–265.) On the other hand they also seem to recommend that the interpreter be guided in his task by policy considerations which are expressed in a variety of formulations that

[13] I.C.J. Reports 1959, p. 127, at 156, 168, 178, 183, 184, 191.

[14] *Ibid.* at 170. For an analysis of this case see Leo Gross "The Jurisprudence of the World Court: Thirty-Eighth Year (1959)," 57 A.J.I.L. 751–780, at 753–766 (1963). See also *infra*.

do not seem to be necessarily consistent. Thus, "The most general objective of claimants . . . is of course to secure an application of general community policies—including that of giving the highest possible deference, compatible with overriding community goals, to the genuine shared expectations of the parties about commitment—in the resolution of such controversies." (*Ibid.* at 22.) Having first ascertained "the genuine shared expectations of the particular parties to an agreement," the second goal of interpretation is, in case of gaps, contradictions or ambiguities, to supplement the expressions of the parties "by making reference to the basic constitutive policies of the larger community which embraces both parties and decision-maker. It would appear that no conceivable alternative goal is in accord with the aspiration to defend and expand a social system compatible with the overriding objectives of human dignity." (*Ibid.* at 40–41.)

The third and final goal, the "policing" goal, stipulates "that when grave contradictions are found between the explicit expectations of the parties to an agreement and the requirements of fundamental community policy, decision-makers should refuse to give effect to the expectations of the parties." *(Ibid.)*

The "policing" goal is, of course, very radical indeed. Words or concepts such as "general" and "fundamental" community policy, "genuine shared expectations," "overriding community goals," "basic constitutive policies," "overriding objectives of human dignity," are pregnant with ambiguity far greater than ever confronted an international tribunal in interpreting the words and concepts in a treaty. Reference is apparently made to communities of various orders ranging from a relatively compact community comprising the parties and the tribunal—which at a minimum would be three communities but which in the case of a dispute brought before the International Court of Justice would comprise seventeen communities—to a world-wide community.

It would be a task of staggering magnitude for any tribunal to define with the necessary degree of precision the relevant community policies, to determine which are basic, fundamental or constitutive, and which are not, and to give some meaning, considering this diversity of the communities, to the concept of "overriding objectives of human dignity." A tribunal would have to be very sure of its ground if it were to refuse to give effect to the expectations of the parties as formulated in an otherwise valid international instrument. Even so, its career is likely to be short-lived for want of clients.

It is useful to compare this approach with that of a very persistent advocate of "international public policy." Jenks lays down eight canons governing recourse to public policy by international tribunals. First he recommends that the concept be accepted with caution; next he makes clear that "public policy is the policy of the law and not of any individual judge or of any government, organization or school of thought which claims to be above the law," and on the particular point here under consideration, he states

> that public policy operates within the limits of the law. In international matters it cannot override a treaty obligation or well established custom, but it may be of great assistance in determining the intent or extent of a treaty obligation, its effect on pre-established custom, or the degree of proof of custom which should be regarded as necessary. (*Op. cit.* 458–459.)

In this reduced sense international public policy may be of some, probably marginal, utility for an international tribunal in interpreting treaties, provided that the tribunal remains ever mindful that what the parties seek is a judgment which is squarely based on law and not on policy, and that the most they are likely to accept is a judgment based on law infused with a sense of policy.

To lawyers who are accustomed to see their courts function regularly as instruments of social policy, this may be quite unsatisfactory. But then domestic courts function in a community whereas international tribunals function irregularly in a community which is only a "civilizing idea": the international community in which they operate "is a potential order in the minds of men; it does not correspond to an effectively established order."[15]

To ascribe to such a community policies and goals is to address oneself to the future and not to the present, to an ideal but not to the real world. In any event it is not to be assumed that states would expose themselves to the adjudication of their disputes on the basis of policies not of their own choosing, if they have shown themselves so remarkably reluctant to submit themselves to adjudication on the basis of law.

Having said this, it must be admitted that an international tribunal may and often does find guidance in the preamble of a treaty which sets forth the agreed objectives of the parties, in the principles of international law and the general principles of law. The International Law Commission in its "General Rule of Interpretation" recognized the legitimacy of recourse to such means of interpretation by providing that treaties shall be interpreted "in good faith" and "in the light of its object and purpose" and in accordance with "any relevant rules of international law applicable in the relations between the parties."[16] In this rule for the guidance of interpreters the Commission intended to include what is serviceable with respect to major purpose interpretation or the principle of effectiveness as well as restrictive interpretation. (I.L.C. Report at 351, par. 6.) The rules dealing with *rebus sic stantibus* (Articles 59 and 62), with peremptory norms (*jus cogens*, Articles 50 and 61), impossibility of performance (Article 58), and other rules relating to the invalidity, termination and suspension of the operation of treaties govern the application of treaties but not their interpretation. It is, of course, a matter of interpretation how and when they apply.[17]

[15] De Visscher, Theory and Reality in Public International Law at 99 (1957).

[16] Report of the International Law Commission on the Work of the Second Part of its Seventeenth Session, General Assembly, 21st Sess., Official Records, Supp. No. 9 (A/6309/Rev.1), reproduced in 61 A.J.I.L. 248, at 271–272 (1967). (Hereinafter cited as I.L.C. Report.)

[17] For the text of these articles as adopted by the Committee of the Whole of the U.N. Conference on the Law of Treaties, see Doc. A/Conf. 39/C.1/L.370/Add. 1–7. Arts. 50 and 61 were adopted in a modified form. For the texts of Arts. 27 and 28 (renumbered 31 and 32) adopted by the Vienna Conference on May 23, 1969, see Doc. A/Conf. 39/27, pp. 16–17.

## V

A tribunal in search of guidance for the interpretation of treaties is faced with an *embarras de richesses.* There is available to it, in addition to the Harvard Research on the Law of Treaties, the resolution of the Institute of International Law of 1956, the *Restatement,* the articles on the Law of Treaties drafted by the International Law Commission[18] and the "check-list" elaborated by Professors McDougal, Lasswell and Miller. A tribunal may select those principles which appear most useful and practical to it. I would recommend, if I had to select a single set of principles, the Articles (27 and 28) of the International Law Commission, although I regard the *Restatement* as quite acceptable with one exception: Paragraph 1 (g) of Section 147 and Section 153, which deal with change of circumstances or the rule of *rebus sic stantibus,* is not a principle of interpretation but, as stated earlier, one of several principles relating to the validity and application of treaties.[19] Furthermore, by attributing binding force to a unilateral invocation of the changed circumstances rule by an interested state (in Section 153), the *Restatement* contradicts paragraph 2 of Section 148 which correctly formulates a general principle of international law:

> An interpretation of an international agreement made by a national authority, whether judicial or otherwise, is not binding under international law upon a party that has not agreed to accept it.

This is an accurate statement of the limits of unilateral, that is, autointerpretation, and by implication it reveals that only an authentic interpretation, that is, one that is accepted by both parties, has binding character: *ejus est interpretare legem cujus condere.* The Permanent Court of International Justice observed with reference to that maxim:

> that it is an established principle that the right of giving an authoritative interpretation of a legal rule belongs solely to the person or body who has power to modify or suppress it.[20]

Of course the parties to a treaty may, by mutual consent, confer upon a tribunal the power to give an authoritative interpretation.

Articles 27 and 28 (on interpretation) of the International Law Commission have been most carefully considered by its members, the governments had two opportunities to comment on them, they also had several occasions to discuss them at the Sixth Committee of the General Assembly, and they were adopted unanimously by the Committee of the Whole of the U.N. Conference on the Law of Treaties.[21] The Committee rejected

[18] The relevant texts are conveniently reproduced with comments in Rosenne, "Interpretation of Treaties in the Restatement and the International Law Commission's Draft Articles: A Comparison," 5 Columbia J. of Transnat. Law 205–212 (1966).

[19] Rosenne, *loc. cit.* at 226–229.

[20] Delimitation of the Czechoslovak-Polish Frontier (Question of Jaworzina), Advisory Opinion No. 8, Dec. 6, 1923, Series B, No. 8, pp. 6–57 at 37. See also De Visscher, Problèmes d'Interprétation Judiciaire en Droit International Public at 20 (1963).

[21] See Doc. A/CONF.39/C.1/L.370 at 140, par. 10. See also Rosenne, note 18 above, at 212 ff.

an American proposal to combine the two articles into one and to make some alterations in the text.[22] There would have been some advantage to follow the pattern of the *Restatement* and to incorporate the supplementary means of interpretation, including the preparatory work, into Article 27. However, a tribunal is not likely to be deterred from using such means of interpretation by the fact that they are mentioned in a separate article. Certainly the practice of the International Court is not likely to be changed, as the two articles are largely based on its jurisprudence. The Commission itself stressed "the unity of the process of interpretation."[23]

There is no room to discuss in any detail the contents of Articles 27 and 28. It may be preferable to indicate their contents in the light of the critical objections urged against them.

The Commission's draft has been criticized because it "insists" on "establishing a hierachy among the elements [of interpretation] to which recourse is authorized . . ."[24] This is an inference drawn from the Commission's distinction between Article 27 and Article 28. The Commission emphasized merely that the supplementary means of interpretation, compared with the text, context, and other means included in Article 27, are not "alternative, autonomous, means of interpretation" but only an aid to them. The Commission was also concerned "not to weaken unduly the authority of the ordinary meaning of the terms." (I.L.C. Report at 360, par. 19.) Therefore, the Commission without limiting the scope of the supplementary means to preparatory work, and the circumstances of the conclusion of the treaty, did not wish to make recourse to such means "automatic." In accordance with prevailing jurisprudence it stated that recourse may be had to such means for the purpose of confirming the meaning derived from Article 27, or of determining it when the interpretation, according to Article 27, "(a) Leaves the meaning ambiguous or obscure; or (b) Leads to a result which is manifestly absurd or unreasonable." (I.L.C. Report at 354, par. 10.) That this approach is in accordance with the practice of the International Court is probably not open to doubt. In its most recent judgment the Court said:

> A review of the genesis and development of the equidistance method of delimitation can only serve to confirm the foregoing conclusion. . . .[25]

Of course, the Court in this case as in all other cases was fully aware of this genesis as the parties probably included it in their pleadings. It makes sense and it makes for economy of effort not to start with history or preparatory work without first having an idea of what one is looking for.[26] Furthermore, as the practice of international tribunals indicates, a

[22] Doc. A/CONF.39/C.1/L.370 at 139, par. 8.

[23] I.L.C. Report at 354, par. 10. Rosenne prefers the arrangement of the Restatement; see note 18 above, at 222.

[24] McDougal, "International Law Commission's Draft Articles upon Interpretation: Textuality *Redivivus*," 61 A.J.I.L. 992–1000, at 995 and 998, note 30 (1967).

[25] North Sea Continental Shelf Cases, I.C.J. Reports 1969, p. 3, at 32.

[26] Lauterpacht, note 3 above, at 130–134.

search of preparatory work does not necessarily yield only one result. The Commission very wisely, I believe, left some discretion to the good judgment of the tribunal.

For the same reason the Commission did not wish to make recourse to the principles of interpretation obligatory as supposed by Professor McDougal.[27] It stated that "recourse to many of these principles is discretionary rather than obligatory and the interpretation of documents is to some extent an art, not an exact science." (I.L.C. Report, at 350, par. 4.) The eventual inclusion of these principles in a convention on the law of treaties, while not indispensable, is no more likely to become a strait jacket for the International Court than Article 38 of its Statute. As the Commission was fully aware, many of the principles of interpretation

> are, for the most part, principles of logic and good sense valuable only as guides to assist in appreciating the meaning which the parties may have intended to attach to the expressions that they employed in a document. *(Ibid.)*

The principal argument against the Commission's approach centers on paragraph 1 of Article 27 entitled "General Rule of Interpretation":

> A treaty shall be interpreted in good faith in accordance with the ordinary meaning to be given to the terms of the treaty in their context and in the light of its object and purpose.

The three authors of the New Haven study have insisted throughout on their recommendations being "understood as implementing our overriding concern for context as against text; or, rather, for the location of a text, if any, in a valid configuration of past, present, and future events."[28] If the implication of the words after the semi-colon is that an international tribunal should disregard the text of a treaty about the meaning of which the parties are at variance, and adjudicate on another text described as "a valid configuration of past, present and future events," then the authors propose a task which no tribunal, present or future, could or should wish to undertake.

It would be a fundamental misconception to present the difference between the approaches of the Commission and of the New Haven study respectively in the form of a dichotomy of text *v.* context. Rather it is a question of more or less context, as will be shown presently. The Commission's deliberate emphasis on the text as the starting point of interpretation is not directed against the contextual interpretation, which in fact is specifically included in Article 27 in some illustrative but not exhaustive detail, but against the "extra-textual approach of Sir Hersch Lauterpacht, strongly advocating a process of interpretation based upon investigation into the presumed or ascertainable intentions of the parties *ab initio.*"[29] One may, as Professor McDougal does, oppose the Commission's

[27] Note 24 above, at 999.

[28] *Op. cit.* note 5 above, at 390. Professor McDougal wrote: "The great defect, and tragedy, in the International Law Commission's final recommendations about the interpretation of treaties is in their insistent emphasis upon an impossible, conformity-imposing textuality." *Loc. cit.* note 24 above, at 992.

[29] Rosenne, note 18 above, at 229.

reliance, in the first but not in the last place, on the proposition "that the text must be presumed to be the authentic expression of the intentions of the parties; and that, in consequence, the *starting point* of interpretation is the elucidation of the meaning of the text, not an investigation *ab initio* into the intentions of the parties."[30]

It will be noted that the Commission used the word "presumed" and that presumption is rebuttable, as Lauterpacht pointed out in reference to "plain meaning," but that is a matter of proof. (*Op. cit.* at 59.) As the Commission also makes clear, the text is the "starting point" of interpretation. Whether it will become its "end point" depends upon other elements of interpretation.

This leads to the consideration of the context. One may dispute the selection of elements of the context, but, as pointed out earlier, Article 27 is not exhaustive but illustrative. The "checklist" recommended by the authors of the New Haven study (*op. cit.* at 385) for scanning the context may be more inclusive, but, as Professor Metzger suggested, it may also involve the tribunal in "exhaustive and exhausting inquiries where every conceivable 'participant,' or 'value,' or 'interest,' or 'objective,' or other conceivable checkpoint on a checklist, has to be examined minutely, though its relative significance is small or quite obvious."[31]

The order in which elements of the context appear in Article 27 do not imply, as Professor McDougal recognizes,[32] any hierarchy. As the Commission, repudiating the imputation that it was "laying down a hierarchical order," pointed out,

> the application of the means of interpretation in the article [27] would be a single combined operation. All the various elements, as they were present in any given case, would be thrown into the crucible, and their interaction would give the legally relevant interpretation. (I.L.C. Report at 352, par. 8, and 353, par. 9.)

Whether all or only some will be thrown into the hopper, conceivably along with some of the items in the "checklist" of the New Haven study, will depend upon the complexities of the case and the pleadings of the parties. The judicial process represents an intimate and sometimes prolonged interaction between the tribunal and the parties. It is for the parties, in the first place, to develop arguments relating to facts and law. They do it in the form of contentions and conclusions, supported by evidence. It is for the tribunal to review and analyze, rationally and economically, their contentions and conclusions and evaluate the evidence. This is no easy matter in a dispute such as the *Barcelona Traction Company* case, in which the printed materials run over 12,000 pages.[33] Rules of interpre-

[30] I.L.C. Report at 354, par. 11 (italics added). See also De Visscher, note 20 above, at 53, and Max Huber's remarks there quoted in note 1.

[31] Metzger, "Treaty Interpretation and the United States-Italy Air Transport Arbitration," 61 A.J.I.L. 1007 at 1011 (1967). In that case the tribunal started with the text and continued with the context, the subsequent practice and related factors bearing on the situation of the parties, all of which supported the analysis of the "ordinary meaning" of the text. *Ibid.* at 1009.

[32] Note 24 above, at 998, note 30.

[33] Report of the International Court of Justice, Aug. 1, 1967–July 31, 1968, General Assembly, 23rd Sess., Official Records, Supp. No. 17 (A/7217), p. 3.

tation are useful guidelines for a tribunal in finding its way through a maze of arguments to a disposition of a case. If the parties have any "genuine shared expectations" or only divergent expectations they will have expressed them in words, in the treaty text and their pleadings. If the words they used or use have meaning different from the ordinary meaning, it is for them to adduce the necessary evidence which in turn will be couched in words. To be sure some words are a means of communication which may be full of uncertainties, but it is the principal means in the relations between states. Signs and gestures may be significant depending upon the circumstances of the case. They were significant in the *Temple* case, as they routinely are in all disputes relating to sovereignty based on historic titles, occupation, etc. In some cases a concept such as "innocent passage" may have essentially a contextual meaning as in the *Corfu Channel* case. Generalizing, one can say that a tribunal will cast its contextual net as wide, in space as well as in time, as is required by the nature of the dispute.

It is unrealistic to assume that states, in entering into agreements, are blind instruments of an "invisible hand" which prompts them to use language which does not or does not fully express their intentions or "genuine shared expectations." In some cases, as in the recent Fisheries Agreement between Japan and New Zealand,[34] the agreement is accompanied by several exchanges of notes. States may at any time enter into supplementary agreements modifying the earlier one. They may make reservations. They may include in the agreement clauses providing for termination and modification. All these and others are legitimate means for ensuring that expectations will be honored. But an international tribunal cannot engage in a process of psychoanalysis or administer a Rorschach test to extract from the parties expectations or objectives which have not been externalized in some fashion before, during or after they entered into an agreement. Articles 27 and 28 of the I.L.C. draft make it entirely possible for any externalized objective, expectation or intention to be considered by a tribunal. It is up to the parties to furnish the tribunal with sufficient evidence that they had indeed such objectives, expectations or intentions and that they were or had become, through a supplementary agreement or subsequent conduct, as Article 27, paragraph 3(a) and (b), expressly provides, part of their contractual or legal relationship which forms the substance of the dispute.

The principle of *anticipated solution* included by the authors of the New Haven study, seems highly speculative. It reads as follows:

> The principle of *anticipated solution* recommends giving priority to solutions that were anticipated, and not rejected, during the agreement process, yet were not incorporated in a final text. (*Op. cit.* at 386.)

I am tempted to recommend that diplomats who enter into this sort of deal should be fired. One wonders how an international tribunal could use this principle and how the parties to a dispute would present their case on the basis of anticipated solutions, which

[34] Signed at Wellington, July 12, 1967. 6 Int. Legal Materials 736 (1967).

apparently were not only not rejected but were not adopted. For if they had been adopted or were in any significant degree linked to the agreement, why were they not incorporated in the final text or in an additional protocol, or an exchange of notes? How would the United States Senate give its "advice and consent" to the ratification of a treaty which consisted in part of a text and in part of unrecorded and unsubmitted anticipated solutions?

As admitted earlier, words may not be an ideally precise method of communication and I, for one, would be unwilling to exclude the possibility that the sciences of logic, semantics and communication may in due course furnish important new insights which, along with the established rules of interpretation, will enable the draftsmen of international agreements to express their intentions and objectives in a more precise manner.[35] But we should not overlook altogether the fact that the modern treaty-making process involves many opportunities for control. The prospect of a treaty with a certain state is carefully considered in many government departments before being taken up with it; it may go through several drafts before it is incorporated in a final text; this text is again carefully scrutinized in several government departments, in hearings before the Senate (in this country) or Parliament, by the Senate itself and finally it is still open to the states to withhold ratification or attach reservations.

The treaty text is not the haphazard product of a casual get-together of diplomats but the product of experts and lawyers. An international tribunal seems, therefore, entirely justified in assuming that the treaty means what it says and says what it means. This is, of course, a rebuttable presumption. Therefore, as Professor Metzger pointed out, the "rejection of 'ordinary meaning in context' as the starting point of analysis, is quite unreal and impractical." (*Loc. cit.* at 1009.) A tribunal does not display "cadaver-like obedience to the textualist command"[36] if it starts with the ordinary meaning in context and ends there because the parties have failed to submit sufficient evidence that the text is not a reliable guide to their intentions. It may be, of course, "that the parties to any particular treaty may have a common intent quite different from that expressed by ordinary means and may communicate to each other by many different signs and acts of collaboration."[37] If they have and if they did, their signs and communications would fall somewhere within the four corners of Articles 27 and 28, or they would produce a suitable piece of evidence to the tribunal. Professor McDougal also argued that

> To impose upon such parties certain alleged "ordinary" meanings and an artificial, preclusionary hierarchy in the relevance of modes of communication may amount to clumsy and arbitrary deformation, completely contrary to the basic policies of a free world order. (*Loc. cit.* 1025–1026.)

[35] As the Commission stated: "In addition the establishment of some measure of agreement in regard to the basic rules of interpretation is important not only for the application but also for the drafting of treaties." I.L.C. Report, par. 5, at 351. This expectation is shared by the authors of the New Haven study, note 5 above, at 393.

[36] Note 5 above, at 363.

[37] Professor McDougal's Statement on behalf of the United States Delegation, to the Committee of the Whole, April 19, 1968, 62 A.J.I.L. 1021–1027 at 1025 (1968).

Enough has been said to show that the Commission did not intend and did not establish any "preclusionary hierarchy." But if there is any danger of deformation, it could work both ways and not necessarily to the detriment of a free world order. It may be that some policies and actions of the United States may have appeared contrary to the ordinary meaning of the United Nations Charter or other relevant instruments to which the United States is a party. Such cases have not come, and are most unlikely to come, before an international tribunal. But if such a case came before a tribunal, and if that tribunal, after studying the pleadings, finally but not easily concluded that one or the other party was at fault, is it really reasonable to expect such a tribunal to espouse an "interpretation of survival" in favor of that party which belongs to the free world? Could such a tribunal be regarded as "impartial"? And, finally, is it impartial when it is partial to the free world?

# V

# PROBLEMS OF VOTING

# VOTING IN THE SECURITY COUNCIL: ABSTENTION FROM VOTING AND ABSENCE FROM MEETINGS

THE action of the Security Council in the Korean affair, instituted by the note of the United States of June 25, 1950,[1] stirred up interest in some of the unresolved questions concerning the interpretation of Article 27 of the Charter. The questions to be considered are those arising from the abstention of a permanent member from voting on a matter of substance and those arising from the absence of a permanent member from a meeting of the Security Council in the course of which matters of substance, and more particularly matters falling under Chapter VII, are submitted to vote.

## I. ABSTENTION FROM VOTING

The second part of Article 27, paragraph 3 makes abstention from voting mandatory in case a member, whether permanent or elected, is a party to the dispute. This provision is clear and need not be further discussed here. It is also unnecessary in this context to go into the question of whether this mandatory rule includes the duty to abstain on preliminary decisions such as whether a matter is a dispute or a situation, whether the dispute is of a certain gravity as indicated in Articles 33 and 34, and whether a state is party to a dispute.

Before going further it may be useful to recall the text of the first part of paragraph 3 of Article 27: "Decisions of the Security Council on all other matters shall be made by an affirmative vote of seven members including the concurring votes of the permanent members." This text has sometimes been said not to require the concurring vote of all the permanent members other than those bound by the mandatory rule in the second part of paragraph 3 of Article 27. Interpretation of the requirement, however, need give rise

[1] Document A/1495. Department of State, *United States Policy in the Korean Crisis,* Publication 3922 (1950), p. 11.

to no serious differences of opinion in view of the legislative history of Article 27 and the insistence both before and after the San Francisco Conference on the principle of unanimity of the permanent members of the Security Council.[2] Any remaining doubt might be set at rest by reference to the equally authentic French text of that paragraph which speaks of "un vote affirmatif de sept de ses membres dans lequel sont comprises les voix de tous les membres permanents", the equally authentic Spanish text which speaks of "el voto afirmativo de siete miembros, incluso los votos afirmativos de todos los miembros permanentes", the equally authentic Russian text which uses the word "bcex" meaning "all," and finally the Chinese text which uses the word "ch'unan t'i" meaning "all." There is scarcely any room for doubt, therefore, that in matters other than those falling under Article 27, paragraph 2 and under the mandatory rule of abstention under the second part of paragraph 3 of Article 27, the affirmative vote of all the five permanent members is required in addition to the affirmative vote of two elected members.[3]

In practice, the Security Council has adopted a somewhat different view of the voting requirements which should govern its action. Beginning with the resolution of April 29, 1946 concerning the establishment of a sub-committee to examine certain aspects of the Spanish question,[4] permanent members of the Security Council abstained from voting on what appeared to be matters of substance. In such cases the resolutions, although they did not receive the affirmative vote of all the permanent members of the Council, were considered to be legally valid. The soundness of this practice has been questioned.[5] And it has not always been accepted without reservation. It has not always been clear whether the resolution referred to a matter of substance or of procedure. On the Spanish question, for example, there was some doubt whether the sub-committee was established under Ar-

[2] "In the consultations among delegations of the sponsoring Governments and France at San Francisco a strict view was taken of this requirement, and the agreement reached among these delegations was that the concurrence of the five permanent members should take the form of affirmative votes of all of them in favor of the decision. This agreement was not, however, put down in writing, nor was it ever communicated to the other delegations at San Franciso." Yuen-li Liang, *The Settlement of Disputes in the Security Council: The Yalta Voting Formula*, 24 BRITISH YEAR BOOK OF INTERNATIONAL LAW 358 (1947).

[3] See, however, HANS KELSEN, THE LAW OF THE UNITED NATIONS 240 (1950). Kelsen suggests that Article 27, paragraph 3 allows two different interpretations. According to one, no valid decision can be taken on non-procedural matters if one of the permanent members is absent from the meeting or abstains from voting: "A permanent member may exercise his veto by being absent or by abstaining from voting." This interpretation, he believes to be supported also by the Statement of the Four Sponsoring Powers. According to the other interpretation, absence of or abstention by a permanent member does not prevent valid decisions on non-procedural matters since Article 27, paragraph 3, only requires "the concurring votes of the permanent members" and does not require the concurring vote of "all" the permanent members, whereas Articles 108 and 109 require ratification by all the permanent members of the Security Council. The second interpretation, in his view, prevails in the Security Council. This interpretation, based as it is on discrepancies in the wording of different articles of the Charter, is not supported by the wording of Article 27, paragraph 3, in the other equally authentic texts. *Cf.* also statement by Mr. Edward R. Stettinius before the Senate Committee on Foreign Relations: "A majority of seven members which includes all five of the permanent members is required in any decision by the Council for dealing with disputes either by peaceful means or by enforcement action, except that a party to a dispute must abstain from voting in the peaceful settlement stage." The Charter of the United Nations, *Hearings before Senate Committee on Foreign Relations*, 79th Cong., 1st Sess. 211 (hereinafter referred to as *Hearings*).

[4] See Security Council, *Official Records* (1st year), no. 2, p. 244.

[5] Liang, *supra* note 2, says that "it is not certain that voluntary abstention by one of the permanent members is compatible with the literal language of Article 27, paragraph 3. . . ." See also PAUL HASLUCK, WORKSHOP OF SECURITY 137 (1948): ". . . the practice of abstention from voting which has been already recognized on several occasions in the Council (although it would appear to be inconsistent with the strict letter of the Charter) could become standard."

ticle 29, in which case the vote of any seven members was sufficient, or under Article 34 in which case the affirmative vote of all the permanent members was required.[6]

### 1. Practice of the Security Council

In view of the uncertainty frequently surrounding the nature of any resolution put to a vote and in view of the practice adopted in reporting votes in the Official Records of the Security Council, it is difficult to provide the correct number of votes on matters of substance in which one or more permanent members abstained but where the requisite majority of seven votes was present to carry the resolution. Mr. Zaydin (Cuba) in the *Ad Hoc* Political Committee of the General Assembly declared on May 4, 1949, that there had then been "twenty-six resolutions of the Security Council in which one or more of the five permanent members had abstained from voting [which] had been considered legal and valid, and had been adopted without protest or hindrancce."[7] He also pointed out[8] that in the majority of cases the abstention had been on the part of the delegation of the Soviet Union. The Department of State has listed ten "of the more important precedents involving action by the Security Council on substantive matters taken without the concurrence of an affirmative vote by the Soviet Union," and three cases in which the Soviet Union "voted with the majority but on which other permanent members of the Council abstained" without questioning the legality of the action taken by the Council.[9]

Although Mr. Zaydin's statement apparently was not based on an official document of the United Nations, it is possible to draw up a list of at least twenty-six resolutions in which one or more of the permanent members abstained from voting and which were considered substantive rather than procedural in character. Taking the annual reports of the Security Council to the General Assembly as a basis and following their topical arrangement these resolutions seem to fall into that category:

#### A. Period from 17 January 1946 to 15 July 1947

*The Spanish Question*

1. Resolution of April 29, 1946, appointing a sub-committee.[10]
Abstained: USSR

[6] A participant in the meeting of the Security Council on this question, the representative of Australia, said in retrospect:

> "No one had been absolutely sure whether it was appointed under Article 29 or Article 34, but most of us had felt that, to save argument about voting procedures, it might be better to assume that it came under Article 29."

HASLUCK, *op. cit. supra* note 5, at 104. See also remarks of Mr. van Kleffens (Netherlands) in *Official Records* (1st year), no. 2, p. 244.

[7] *Official Records*, 3d session of the General Assembly, part II, *Ad Hoc* Political Committee, p. 207.

[8] *Id.* at 209.

[9] Department of State, *United States Policy in the Korean Crisis*, Publication 3922 (1950), p. 62.

[10] *Report of the Security Council to the General Assembly*, Document A/93, p. 94.

*The Corfu Channel Question*

2. Resolution of April 9, 1947, recommending reference of dispute to the International Court of Justice.[11]

Abstained: USSR

*General Regulation and Reduction of Armaments*

3. Resolution of February 13, 1947, providing for the establishment of the Commission for Conventional Armaments and its terms of reference.[12]

Abstained: USSR

B. Period from 16 July 1947 to 15 July 1948

*The Indonesian Question*

4. Resolution of August 1, 1947, calling upon parties to cease hostilities.[13]

Abstained: France, the United Kingdom and the USSR abstained on parts of the resolution; the resolution as a whole was not put to a vote.

5. Resolution of August 25, 1947, providing for the establishment of a consular commission.[14]

Abstained: USSR and the United Kingdom

6. Resolution of August 25, 1947, tendering the good offices of the Council to the parties.[15]

Abstained: USSR

7. Resolution of November 1, 1947, calling upon the parties to consult and interpret the resolution of August 1, 1947.[16]

Abstained: USSR

8. Resolution of February 28, 1948, noting the signing of the Truce Agreement.[17]

Abstained: USSR

*The India-Pakistan Question*

9. Resolution of January 17, 1948, calling upon parties to refrain from aggravating the situation.[18]

Abstained: USSR

10. Resolution of January 20, 1948, establishing a Commission of Three and laying down terms of reference.[19]

Abstained: USSR

[11] *Id.* Document A/366, p. 108.
[12] *Id.* at 131.
[13] *Id.* Document A/620, p. 30; Security Council, *Official Records, 2nd* year, no. 68, p. 1700.
[14] *Id.* at 33.
[15] *Ibid.*
[16] *Id.* at 42.
[17] *Id.* at 49.
[18] *Id.* at 56.
[19] *Id.* at 57.

11. Resolution of April 21, 1948, laying down a comprehensive plan for the settlement of the dispute.[20]

Abstained: France and China abstained on some parts of the resolution and the USSR on every part of it.

12. Resolution of June 3, 1948, reaffirming previous resolutions.[21]

Abstained: China and USSR

*The Palestine Question*

13. Resolution of March 5, 1948, calling upon the permanent members of the Council to consult.[22]

Abstained: United Kingdom

14. Resolution of April 17, 1948, calling upon parties to cease all military activities.[23]

Abstained: USSR

15. Resolution of April 23, 1948, establishing a truce commission.[24]

Abstained: USSR

16. Resolution of May 22, 1948, calling upon parties to issue a cease-fire order.[25]

Abstained: USSR

17. Resolution of July 15, 1948, determining that the situation in Palestine constitutes a threat to the peace within the meaning of Article 39 of the Charter and ordering the parties, pursuant to Article 40 of the Charter, to desist from further military action.[26]

Abstained: USSR

C. Period from 16 July 1948 to 15 July 1949

*The Indonesian Question*

18. Resolution of July 29, 1948, calling upon parties to observe the "Renville" truce agreement.[27]

Abstained: USSR

19. Resolution of December 24, 1948, calling upon parties to cease hostilities.[28]

Abstained: France and USSR

20. Resolution of December 28, 1948, calling upon the Netherlands Government to set free political prisoners.[29]

[20] *Id.* at 70.
[21] *Id.* at 71.
[22] *Id.* at 78.
[23] *Id.* at 84.
[24] *Id.* at 85.
[25] *Id.* at 92.
[26] *Id.* at 111.
[27] *Id.* Document A/945, p. 2.
[28] *Id.* at 8.
[29] *Id.* at 11.

Abstained: France and the United Kingdom

21. Resolution of January 28, 1949, calling upon the Netherlands Government to discontinue all military operations and recommending negotiations on the basis of principles laid down in the Resolution.[30]

Abstained: France on all paragraphs of the Resolution and the USSR on some parts of it.

*The Palestine Question*

22. Resolution of November 4, 1948, calling upon parties to withdraw troops and establish permanent truce lines.[31]

Abstained: USSR

23. Resolution of November 16, 1948, calling upon the parties, as a further preliminary measure under Article 40 of the Charter, to seek agreement with a view to establishment of the armistice.[32]

Abstained: USSR

24. Resolution of December 29, 1948, calling upon parties to order an immediate cease-fire.[33]

Abstained: USA and USSR

25. Resolution of March 4, 1949, recommending to the General Assembly the admission of Israel to membership in the United Nations.[34]

Abstained: United Kingdom

*Respective Functions of the Security Council and the Trusteeship Council with regard to Strategic Trust Areas.*

26. Resolution of March 7, 1949, providing for the implementation of Article 83, paragraph 3, of the Charter.[35]

Abstained: USSR

No report of the Security Council to the General Assembly is available at this writing for the period from July 16, 1949 to July 15, 1950. It is possible, however, to cull from the official records of the Security Council three resolutions on what appear to be matters of substance adopted between July 16 and December 29, 1949:

27. Resolution of July 27, 1949, recommending to the General Assembly the acceptance of Liechtenstein as a Party to the Statute of the International Court of Justice.[36]

Abstained: USSR

[30] *Id.* at 22.
[31] *Id.* at 46.
[32] *Id.* at 49.
[34] *Id.* at 89.
[35] *Id.* at 91.
[36] Security Council, *Official Records* (4th year), 432d Meeting, no. 35, p. 6.

28. Resolution of August 11, 1949, adopting the Franco-Canadian proposals (S/1367) concerning Palestine.[37]

Abstained: USSR

29. Resolution of September 27, 1949, concerning retroactive reimbursement of travelling expenses of alternates on certain commissions.[38]

Abstained: USSR

This list, which includes all of the resolutions enumerated by the Department of State in the White Paper on Korea, makes no pretense at completeness. Any such claim would be hazardous in view of the lack of clarity concerning criteria determining matters of substance or procedure. The resolutions included above provide, however, at least a useful sample of decisions of substance in which one or more of the five permanent members abstained from voting. Several preliminary conclusions may be drawn from this list. First, it may be said that the resolutions cover a fairly wide range of subjects; secondly, that some of the resolutions referred explicitly to Articles 39 and 40 of the Charter, which concern only problems of substance; thirdly, that every one of the five permanent members of the Council has abstained from voting on one or more resolutions, and that in some cases two or more permanent members abstained from voting on parts or on the whole of the same resolution; fourthly, that in some cases members explained their abstention while others reserved their position; and finally, that in at least one case—the admission of Israel—doubt was expressed as to the legality of the vote in the Security Council in which one permanent member, the United Kingdom, abstained from voting.

### 2. Explanation of Abstention and Reservation

#### a. The Spanish Question

In connection with the vote on the appointment of a sub-committee to deal with the Spanish question, the representative of the USSR, Mr. Gromyko, explained his vote as follows:[39]

> "Bearing in mind, however, that some members of the Council declare that they are still unsatisfied with the information at the disposal of the Council regarding the question raised by the representative of Poland, and bearing in mind, in this connexion, that my voting against the Australian draft resolution would make its adoption impossible, I shall abstain from voting.
>
> "I consider it necessary to draw the attention of the Security Council to the fact that my abstention from voting on this matter may in no way be regarded as a precedent capable

[37] *Id.* no. 38, p. 13.

[38] *Id.* no. 44, p. 10.

[39] *Id.* (1st year), no. 2, p. 243.

of influencing in any way the question of the abstention of permanent members of the Security Council."

While the representative of the Netherlands, Mr. van Kleffens, reserved his position regarding the nature of the matter,[40] Mr. Stettinius, the representative of the United States, declared:[41]

"I wish to reserve the position of the United States of America on the statement the USSR representative has just made. With that understanding, I am prepared to agree that Mr. Gromyko's abstention should not create a precedent for the future."

### b. The Indonesian Question

The representatives of France and of the United Kingdom abstained on almost all parts of the resolution of August 1, 1947, on the Indonesian Question. The respresentative of the United Kingdom, Mr. Lawford, after referring to Article 27, paragraph 3, explained his vote saying:[42]

"The United Kingdom has abstained; but in view of the fact that everybody here clearly wishes this war to stop, the United Kingdom does not wish its abstention to be treated as a veto, invalidating the resolution which has otherwise secured the necessary majority."

Following this statement, the President of the Security Council, Mr. F. El-Khouri (Syria) declared:[43]

"I think it is now jurisprudence in the Security Council—and the interpretation accepted for a long time—that an abstention is not considered a veto, and the concurrent votes of the permanent members mean the votes of the permanent members who participate in the voting. Those who abstain intentionally are not considered to have cast a veto. That is quite clear."

In spite of this statement by the President, the representative of France, Mr. Parodi, felt it necessary to[44]

"add that, as representative of a permanent member of the Council, I was careful not to vote against the resolution, although I was opposed to it, but merely abstained, in order to facilitate the general progress of our work."

This, it is suggested, is a very relevant incident in evaluating the legal significance of abstention by a permanent member from voting in the Security Council. The abstaining

[40] *Id.* at 244.
[41] *Id.* at 245.
[42] *Id.* (2nd year), no. 68, 173d Meeting, p. 1711.
[43] *Id.*
[44] *Id.* at 1713.

permanent members did not wish to impede the work of the Security Council by casting a "veto"; on the contrary, their abstentions were designed to make it possible for the Security Council to function along the lines indicated by the majority. The words of the President—"those who abstain intentionally"—may be especially significant, though it was hardly possible to speak of the "the interpretation accepted for a long time" since the practice had been inaugurated by the Soviet Union barely fifteen months earlier.

### c. The India-Pakistan Question

At the 230th meeting, January 20, 1948, the Security Council voted on a draft resolution providing for establishment of a Commission of Three and designation of the scope of its duties. The vote was nine in favor, none against and two abstentions, one of the abstaining members being the USSR. The President declared the resolution adopted.[45] Mr. Arce (Argentina) at the 232nd meeting, January 23, 1948, made the following statement:[46]

> "The resolution which was voted at the meeting of January 20, 1948 . . . did not obtain the favorable vote of the five permanent members of the Security Council. Nevertheless, the vote was considered valid and the Security Council has agreed to carry out this resolution without further observation.
>
> "We have here a decision of substance, and it falls under paragraph 3 of Article 27 of the Charter. The Argentine delegation voted in favor of this resolution and these words do not modify our way of thinking in this connection.
>
> "I consider it my duty, however, to place on record that this decision is invalid legally. I am aware that this is not the first time that this has occurred. It is, however, the first time that it has occurred since Argentina has been elected as a member of the Security Council. . . .
>
> "I wish to place on record, however, that I do not oppose the permanent members of the Security Council renouncing the use of their privilege if they consider it desirable, but when they do so, it should be done publicly."

In reply to this strong statement, which, however, was not a formal challenge to the President's ruling, Mr. Noel-Baker (United Kingdom), said:[47]

> "Hitherto, as I understand it, the abstention by a permanent member of the Security Council in a vote on a matter of substance is, by practice and precedent in the Security Council, not considered a negative vote by that member, and I hope and trust that that understanding and practice will be adhered to."

Mr. de la Tournelle (France) associated himself fully with the remarks made by the representative of the United Kingdom,[48] and no further action appears to have been taken on this occasion.

[45] Document S/PV. 230, p. 71.
[46] Document S/PV. 232, p. 2.
[47] *Id.* at 11.
[48] *Id.* at 12.

### d. Application of Israel for Membership in the United Nations

At the 414th meeting, May 4, 1949, the Security Council discussed and voted upon the application of Israel for admission to the United Nations. Before the voting took place, Sir Terence Shone (United Kingdom) declared:[49]

> "In the circumstances, my delegation has no alternative but to abstain from voting if the question of Israel's admission comes to a vote. We shall not vote against Israel's admission. We have said in the past that we do not intend to use our privileged vote to block the admission of any State which obtains the requisite majority."

The vote on the United States resolution recommending admission was as follows: in favor: 9, against: 1, abstaining: 1 (the United Kingdom). The Official Records sums up the vote in these words: "The resolution was adopted by 9 votes to 1, with 1 abstention."[50] Immediately after the vote, the President, Mr. A. Alvarez (Cuba), stated:[51]

> "In accordance with the principle established by the Security Council on resolutions subject to the unanimity rule, abstention by a permanent member of the Council does not render the Council's decision invalid. I therefore declare the United States draft resolution to be adopted."

These references to "the unanimity rule" and the "established" method of avoiding it did not pass unnoticed. After the President's ruling, Mr. Arce (Argentina) who voted in favor of the resolution, said:[52]

> "I do not wish to comment on the President's statement that the Council, having adopted the draft resolution by more than seven votes required by the Charter, has decided to recommend Israel's admission to membership in the United Nations. I wish, however, to go on record as stating that, contrary to the view held by some, if not by practically all the permanent members of the Council, this resolution has not been supported by the five permanent members of the Council as required in Article 27, paragraph 3, of the Charter. While the President has referred to an established principle, I do not believe that the Security Council can establish principles to modify the Charter whenever it thinks fit."

Speaking after Mr. Arce, Mahmoud Fawzi Bey (Egypt), who voted against the resolution, said:[53]

[49] Security Council, *Official Records* (4th year), no. 17, p. 2.

[50] *Id.* at 14.

[51] *Ibid.*

[52] *Ibid.* Norway may also have held doubts as to the validity of the ruling. Mr. Sunde, who expressed the intention of voting in favor of the application of Israel, concluded: "In this connexion, I should also like to point out that we do not think that a decision which the Security Council might now take to recommend the admission of Israel should be taken as a precedent in respect of the legal questions involved." *Id.* at 4. It is not clear from this statement what "legal questions" Mr. Sunde had in mind. Reference may have been made to the preceding declaration of the representative of the United Kingdom.

[53] *Id.* at 14.

"For reasons similar to those expounded by the representative of Argentina, I wish to express my doubt as to certain interpretations of the way in which Article 27, paragraph 3, of the United Nations Charter should be applied."

Neither speaker, however, formally challenged the ruling of the President. The final word, by Mr. Malik (USSR), was in support of the ruling:[54]

"I would merely like to draw the Council's attention to the fact that, in accordance with the established practice of the Security Council, when a permanent member of the Council abstains from voting, such action is not interpreted in the way that some are now endeavouring to interpret it."

This cryptic remark closed the discussion. It was re-opened in the *Ad Hoc* Political Committee of the General Assembly at the second part of its third session and subsequently in the plenary meetings of the General Assembly itself. The application of Israel was discussed in Committee at the 42nd and subsequent meetings. Some representatives doubted the validity of the Security Council's recommendation and challenged it as defective. Some considered it to be valid. As will appear below, the merits of the issue were never decided, since it was ruled that the General Assembly had not the power to question a decision of the Security Council. While it is therefore not necessary to reproduce all the pertinent statements, it is desirable to quote one or two which received special attention. The practice of the Security Council was submitted to a careful scrutiny by Sir Mohammed Zafrulla Khan (Pakistan) who raised a preliminary question officially reported as follows:[55]

"The Committee was proceeding on the assumption that the Security Council had recommended the admission of Israel to membership in the United Nations. The record of the voting in the Security Council, however, disclosed that one of the permanent members, the United Kingdom, had registered an abstention. Accordingly, the provision of Article 27 of the Charter had not been observed. . . .

"He was aware that the Security Council had proceeded on the basis of a practice it was trying to establish whereby the abstention of a permanent member in decisions of a substantive nature was not to be treated as a veto. Paragraph 3 of Article 27, however, did not mention the veto; it merely stipulated that the concurring votes of the permanent members must be included in the seven or more affirmative votes necessary for the adoption of substantive decisions. Moreover, regardless of the interpretation placed by the Security Council in its own practice on the abstention of a permanent member, the General Assembly was not bound by any action taken by the Council which failed to comply with the explicit terms of Article 27.

"The record of the Security Council's proceedings further revealed that when the vote had been taken, the President had stated that although the decision was governed by the rule of unanimity, the abstention of a permanent member did not invalidate it, inasmuch as it had obtained more than the seven affirmative votes required by

[54] *Ibid.*

[55] *Official Records* of the 3rd session of the General Assembly. Part II, *Ad Hoc* Political Committee, Summary records of the Meetings, April 6–May 10, 1949, p. 181.

the Charter. Two members of the Council had taken exception to that interpretation. . . .

"Moreover, the United Kingdom, which had abstained from voting in favour of the Council's recommendation to admit Israel to membership, had both generally and specifically made it clear that its abstention could not be construed as an affirmation. . . . Clearly, the United Kingdom had not concurred in the decision of the Security Council on the admission of Israel because it had not been satisfied that the applicant State fulfilled the conditions laid down in Article 4 or that the merits of the case warranted an affirmative vote.

"In view of those considerations, the Committee had before it no Security Council decision which had been taken in accordance with the conditions laid down in the Charter. Should any member of the Committee not agree with him on that subject, it would be necessary to clarify the interpretation of Article 27. That could be done either by referring the matter to the International Court of Justice with a request for an advisory opinion, or by sending the recommendation back to the Security Council in accordance with rule 126 of the rules of procedure. Surely, the General Assembly could take no decison until it had dispelled all doubt concerning the regularity of the Council's recommendation to admit Israel to membership."

At the subsequent meeting, the 43rd, on May 4, 1949, Sir Terence Shone (United Kingdom)[56]

". . . recalled the argument advanced at the preceding meeting by the representative of Pakistan to the effect that the Security Council's recommendation on the admission of Israel was invalid because it failed to comply with the terms of paragraph 3 of Article 27. While he did not wish to debate the legal interpretation of that Article, Sir Terence did wish to emphasize certain other considerations which should be borne in mind.

"In addition to the laws and rules which governed the conduct of the various United Nations organs, they had established certain practices which had acquired great force. Since July 1946, a practice had been created in the Security Council whereby a permanent member could, by abstaining from the vote, permit the Council to take action which that member did not affirmatively support, provided that such action had been approved by the affirmative votes of seven members. That procedure had been explicitly sanctioned by all five permanent members on various occasions.*

"On 14 April 1949, the General Assembly had sanctioned that practice by adopting a resolution based on the conclusions contained in the report of the Interim Committee relating to the voting procedure in the Security Council.** By a vote of 43 to 6, with 2 abstentions, it had recommended *inter alia* to the permanent members that they give favourable consideration to the possibility of forbearing from exercising their veto when seven affirmative votes had already been cast in favour of certain decisions, among them, recommendations to the Assembly on the admission of new Members.

"Irrespective of the strictly legal position, it was unwise to abandon a practice whereby the permanent members of the Council were attempting to avoid hampering decisions by exercising their veto. However, the United Kingdom delegation was not anxious to prevent the Assembly from examining the whole question. Its position had been made clear when it had abstained from voting on the Security Council's recommendation to admit Israel to the United Nations. It had abstained on the grounds that it did not wish to use

[56] *Id.* at 200.
*Discussion of Indonesian question, p. 9.
**See *Official Records* of the 3rd session of the General Assembly, Part II, 195th plenary meeting.

its privileged vote to block the admission of any State which obtained the requisite majority. . . ."

The validity of the Security Council's resolution was formally challenged by Mr. Abbas (Iraq) who submitted a draft resolution which referred to Article 27, paragraph 3, of the Charter and continued as follows:[57]

> "Considering that it is difficult to consider an abstention by one of the permanent members of the Security Council as an affirmative vote of concurrence,
>
> "The General Assembly resolves that:
>
> "1. An inquiry should be sent to the Security Council seeking further explanation for the validity of the vote taken with regard to the application of Israel to membership in the United Nations, and,
>
> "2. Aside from any explanation which might be forthcoming from the Security Council, and without prejudice to the discussion of the merits of the case, find it necessary to seek an advisory opinion from the International Court of Justice upon whether a vote of abstention by a permanent member of the Security Council can be considered a vote of concurrence or whether such a vote can be consonant with the provisions of paragraph 3 of Article 27 of the Charter of the United Nations and therefore this Committee instructs the Secretary-General of the United Nations to take the necessary measures to obtain the advisory opinion of the International Court of Justice on this matter at the earliest possible date and to forward such information as might be obtained to the Committee concerned with this matter."

When the issue had been first raised in the Political Committee, the Chairman, General Carlos P. Romulo (Philippines), had ruled that "It was beyond the competence of the Committee to question the regularity of the vote in the Security Council and the validity of the decisions taken."[58] Under this ruling, the merits of the Abbas resolution could not have been reached. The Chairman therefore declared his willingness to put the ruling to vote.[59] Mr. Abbas stated that he was not challenging the ruling, and the question was dropped temporarily. It arose again, however, at a later stage of the discussion, at the 44th meeting, May 4, 1949, when General Romulo, on his own behalf, recalled his ruling, this time in more specific terms:[60]

> "On the previous day he had ruled the Iraqi draft resolution (A/AC.24/64) out of order because it challenged the validity of the Security Council resolution recommending the application of Israel for admission to membership in the United Nations. That ruling still held [but] would be put to the vote if the Iraqi representative insisted on his proposal."

The Iraqi representative did not insist but reserved his right to raise the point in the Committee or in the General Assembly at a later date.[61] Thereupon,[62]

[57] Document A/AC.24/64.4, May 1949.

[58] *Official Records* of the 3rd session of the General Assembly. Part II, *Ad Hoc* Political Committee, Summary records of the Meetings, April 6–May 10, 1949, p. 183.

[59] *Id.* at 189.

[60] *Id.* at 203.

[61] *Id.* at 206.

[62] *Id.* at 209.

"The Chairman said that since the Iraqi delegation had withdrawn its draft resolution, while reserving its right to present it at a later date, a discussion of that draft resolution or any reference to it would henceforth be declared out of order."

The issue was raised again a week later at the 207th Plenary Meeting of the General Assembly, held May 11, 1949. The Iraqi representative "reiterated his request that the General Assembly should consult the International Court of Justice on the matter of the Security Council's recommendation and remarked that, by rejecting that request, the Assembly would tacitly admit that its course of action was illegal."[63] Before putting the question of the admission of Israel to a vote, the President of the General Assembly, Dr. H. V. Evatt (Australia), explained the manner in which it had come before the General Assembly and said:[64]

"In accordance with the provisions of Article 4, of the Charter, the Security Council had formally recommended the admission of Israel to membership in the United Nations (A/818). Referring to the suggestion that the General Assembly might discuss the question of the vote which had taken place in the Security Council, the President ruled that the manner in which the recommendation of the Security Council had been adopted concerned the internal government and procedure of the Security Council and must be accepted by the General Assembly as a recommendation of the Security Council within the meaning of the Charter. The President did not doubt that the ruling of the Chairman of the Ad Hoc Political Committee was correct."

The President's ruling was not challenged.

### e. Application of Portugal for Membership in the United Nations

On September 13, 1949, at the 443rd meeting of the Security Council the application of Portugal was put to the vote and received nine votes in favor and two votes against. One of the negative votes was that of the Soviet Union. Mr. Arce (Argentina) made a statement after the vote in which he said:[65]

"that four permanent members voted in favor, exactly as in the vote on the application for the admission of the state of Israel which was submitted for consideration by the General Assembly.

"I know that it will be objected that while, in the one case there was an abstention—that of the United Kingdom—in the other case there was an opposing vote by the Soviet Union.

"The Charter, however, does not distinguish between abstentions and negative votes. It says simply that the concurring votes of the five permanent members are necessary. In the voting on Portugal there were only four, as in the voting on Israel."

[63] *Official Records* of the 3rd session of the General Assembly. Part II, p. 310.
[64] *Id.* at 330. See also observations by Mr. Nisot (Belgium), *id.* at 190, and Mr. Fawzi Bey, *id.* at 191.
[65] Security Council, *Official Records* (4th year), no. 41, p. 29.

## 3. Conclusions

What conclusions, then, may be drawn from the practice of the Security Council regarding abstention? Any even tentative conclusion must, of course, be tempered by the fact that United Nations practice is ambiguous and brief. And it may be premature to speak of a "common law" which has developed in the Security Council on the basis of or in opposition to the Charter. Nevertheless, the following remarks seem in order.

One conclusion stands out: no substantive resolution in the voting of which a permanent member abstained but which received the requisite majority of seven, has been held invalid or illegal. Some members of the Security Council and some other members of the United Nations have, however, raised direct or indirect questions as to both.[66] In fact, there is some basis for criticism. As has been pointed out above,[67] the practice of treating an abstention as in result an affirmative vote, is not in literal conformity with the mandatory requirement of Article 27, paragraph 3. It therefore also technically violates the Provisional Rules of Procedure of the Security Council. Under Rule 40 "voting in the Security Council shall be in accordance with the relevant Articles of the Charter and of the Statute of the International Court of Justice."[68] This rule incorporates the requirements of Article 27, paragraph 3, into the structure of the Provisional Rules. It is a mandatory rule, directing the Council to vote in accordance with the Charter, and provides for no exception and no mitigation of its rigor. There is, of course, no legal duty for a permanent member to vote in the negative.[69] But if he does not vote in the affirmative, the effect should at least theoretically be the same. The literal requirement for adopting valid substantive decisions in Article 27, paragraph 3, reinforced by Rule 40 of the Provisional Rules of Procedure, is not satisfied by abstention.[70]

Despite the force of these arguments, it is the opinion of the writer that the practice of abstention, although not in conformity with Article 27, paragraph 3 and Rule 40, nevertheless may be deemed to be in accordance with the principle of unanimity of the permanent members. It is this principle which underlies Article 27, paragraph 3, and which forms the basis of the agreement reached at the Yalta Conference on the voting formula to govern the Security Council. It will also be recalled that at the San Francisco Conference the Four Sponsoring Governments and France attached the greatest importance to

[66] See pages 438–42 *supra*. It should be repeated, however, that the General Assembly never really attempted to pass on the validity of resolutions of the Security Council. The ruling of the President of the General Assembly, Mr. H. V. Evatt, in connection with the application of Israel, was explicit and was not challenged.

[67] See pages 429–30 *supra*.

[68] Provisional Rules of Procedure of the Security Council. Document S/96/Rev. 3, January 27, 1948.

[69] It has been said that "there was no principle laid down in the Charter, nor did any precedent exist to the effect that a country which had the right of veto was obliged to vote in the affirmative or in the negative." Mr. Zaydin (Cuba) in the *Ad Hoc* Political Committee. *Official Records loc. cit.*, p. 207.

[70] There have been attempts to read Article 27, paragraph 3, as if it said that decisions shall "be made by an affirmative vote of seven members including the concurring votes of the permanent members *present and voting*." The phrase "present and voting," however, was not only omitted from the text, but was specifically rejected at the San Francisco conference. See pages 466–7 *infra*. For specific use of the phrase, see Articles 18, 67, and 89 of the Charter, and Rules 86 and 125 of the Rules of Procedure of the General Assembly.

the principle of unanimity. In the "Statement of the Delegations of the Four Sponsoring Governments on Voting Procedure in the Security Council," these Governments, arguing that beyond a certain point "decisions and actions by the Security Council may well have major political consequences and may even initiate a chain of events which might, in the end, require the Council under its responsibilities to invoke measures of enforcement," declared,[71]

> "This chain of events begins when the Council decides to make an investigation, or determines that the time has come to call upon states to settle their differences, or to make recommendations to the parties. It is to such decisions and actions that unanimity of the permanent members applies, with the important proviso . . . for abstention from voting by parties to the dispute."

The compatibility of abstention with the principle of unanimity, which is argued here, may be demonstrated by reference to the Covenant and the practice of the League of Nations.

Article 5 of the Covenant, with some exceptions, required in both the Assembly and the Council "the agreement of all the Members of the League represented at the meeting." In the practice of the League Assembly and Council, abstention was not regarded as a negative vote and, consequently, was not considered incompatible with the principle of unanimity laid down in Article 5. Article 19, paragraph 5, of the Rules of Procedure of the Assembly[72] and Article IX, paragraph 3 of the Rules of Procedure of the Council provided accordingly. Article IX, paragraph 3, recognizing a practice of long standing in the Council, stated explicitly: "In counting the votes, abstentions from voting shall be disregarded."[73] In accordance with Article 5, paragraph 1, of the Covenant, however, this clause could not prevail over exceptions expressly provided in the Covenant such as in Article 16, paragraph 4, concerning expulsion. This Article was one of the exceptions to the principle of unanimity enunciated in Article 5, paragraph 1, in the sense that it required not merely "the agreement of all the members of the League represented at the meeting," but a "vote of the Council concurred in by the Representatives of all other members of the League represented thereon," *i.e.* of all members represented on the Council other than the member to be expelled.[74] This special voting requirement was more stringent than the general rule of unanimity in Article 5 of the Covenant.

It might be argued that Article 27, paragraph 3, being closer in its wording to Article 16, paragraph 4, than to Article 5, paragraph 1, of the Covenant, should be interpreted in the same manner. It must be borne in mind, however, that Article 16, paragraph 4, was an exception to the general principle of unanimity. On the other hand, it was specifically stated in the Statement of the Four Sponsoring Powers referred to

[71] UNCIO Documents, Vol. XI, p. 712.
[72] RULES OF PROCEDURE OF THE ASSEMBLY. Rev. Ed., April 1937. C.144.M.92.1937.
[73] RULES OF PROCEDURE OF THE COUNCIL. June 1938. C.197.M.106.1938. Paragraph 3, quoted above was added to the Rules adopted in 1920.
[74] Leo Gross, *Was the Soviet Union Expelled from the League of Nations?* 39 AM. J. OF INT'L. LAW 36 (1945). See also *infra*.

above that there was "no question under the Yalta Formula of investing [the permanent members] with a new right, namely the right of veto, which the permanent members of the League Council always had." So far as the permanent members of the Security Council are concerned, therefore, the Charter, like the League Covenant, with only explicit exceptions, simply incorporated the principle of unanimity as it is established in international law and relations. On this ground, the analogy to Article 5, paragraph 1, and to the practice of the League thereunder seems defensible. If this reasoning is admitted, the abstention of the permanent members is not inconsistent with the principle of unanimity embodied in Article 27, paragraph 3 of the Charter. The controlling consideration is agreement even if it be no more than tacit agreement to the action which the Security Council, supported by the requisite majority of seven, proposes to take. As long as this agreement is there, the Security Council may act.

Moreover, as Sir Terence Shone pointed out in his important statement quoted above,[75] the General Assembly itself, in paragraph 3 of its Resolution 267 (III) adopted April 14, 1949, seemed to encourage the practice of abstention. "In order to avoid impairment of the usefulness and prestige of the Council through excessive use of the veto," the General Assembly recommended that the permanent members consult on important decisions. In particular, in paragraph 3(c), it recommended that: "If there is not unanimity, [they] exercise the veto only when they consider the question of vital importance, taking into account the interest of the United Nations as a whole, and to state upon what ground they consider this condition to be present."[76] At a meeting held October 18, 1949, all permanent members agreed to paragraph 3 of Resolution 267 (III).[77] It will be noted, no doubt, that according to that paragraph abstention is considered compatible with unanimity.

Some consideration should be given to the circumstance that on several occasions noted above, members of the United Nations either voiced doubt as to the validity of the practice of abstention or declared that their acceptance or toleration of that practice should not serve as a precedent. This may have been deemed necessary in order to safeguard the integrity of Article 27, paragraph 3. It seems clear, however, that this abundance of caution was superfluous, since no mere practice could change the strict requirement of Article 27, paragraph 3. In other words, abstention is not a fatal defect as long as there is agreement in the Security Council, and particularly among its permanent members, not to regard it as such.[78] This is perhaps another way of saying that the prac-

[75] See page 440 *supra*.

[76] *Official Records* of the 3rd session of the General Assembly, Part II; Resolutions. Document A/900, p. 7.

[77] Security Council, *Official Records* (4th year), no. 48, p. 2.

[78] Liang, *supra* note 2, at 359, says: "In spite of the uncertainty of the legal consequences of the abstention of the Soviet representative in the Spanish question, there is reason to believe that, in the practice of the Security Council, abstentions by permanent members will not be counted as negative votes, just as before the adoption of Article 9 of the Rules of Procedure by the League Council in 1933 the practice was to disregard, in the counting of votes, abstentions from voting. This development will probably be based upon the theory that a permanent member who has the opportunity to exercise its veto power but chooses to refrain from exercising it should not be obliged to have its abstention counted as a negative vote—a development which may be accepted by the permanent members themselves as a means to mitigate the rigours of the 'veto.' "

tice of abstention rests on suffereance rather than on a rule of the Charter, or a binding precedent, or an explicit and formal agreement of the permanent members of the Council. In short, it presupposes the continued disposition of those members not to regard abstention as failing to satisfy the mandatory requirement of Article 27, paragraph 3. It cannot be presumed or enlarged without their consent. On the contrary it must be indicated in each case, explicitly as by an explanation of the vote, which was the case in connection with some resolutions, or tacitly as was also the case in several instances. This type of agreement, tenuous as it may appear to be in the light of the literal provisions of the Charter, has been manifested in a variety of cases falling under different provisions of the Charter including limited resolutions under Articles 39 and 40.

It should be noted at this point, however, that the usefulness of agreement by sufferance has its limits. There is no case on record where the Security Council has adopted a resolution under Article 39 or otherwise recommending or deciding the use of armed force, and where a permanent member agreed by abstaining. This is as might be expected. It seems inconceivable that a permanent member would abstain from voting if a resolution looking to the use of force were put to the vote. It may be well to recall in this connection the Statement of the Four Sponsoring Powers which is most explicit on this point:[79]

> "In view of the primary responsibilities of the permanent members, they could not be expected, in the present condition of the world, to assume the obligation to act in so serious a matter as the maintenance of international peace and security in consequence of a decision in which they had not concurred."

The Statement is the only interpretation of the Yalta voting formula on which the five permanent members were able to agree at San Francisco. Agreement there was dictated by reality. Conviction, not mere sufferance, is needed to enforce measures for the maintenance of international peace and security. It is for this reason that the Sponsoring Powers did not refer to unanimity as in other parts of the Statement, but to unanimity qualified in a way which throws into prominence the need for concurrence of each permanent member.

Commentators without exception have realized and pointed up the need for this extension of the unanimity principle. For example, Dr. Pasvolsky, commenting on the Statement before the Senate Committee on Foreign Relations stated:[80]

> "When [a permanent member] is not a party to the dispute, then the action taken by the Security Council may lead to a chain of measures in which [that member] would have to participate, and since that claim may end up with the use of force, it was thought that the countries which would have the primary responsibility for the action to be taken in the

[79] UNCIO Documents, vol. XI, p. 713.

[80] *Hearings* 283. The Chairman, Senator Tom Connally, said: "Since unanimity is going to be required in the final analysis on the use of force, we had better maintain that same principle from the beginning of the dispute." *Id.* at 284.

maintenance of international peace and security should be in a position to concur or not to concur in the steps which might lead to that action."

The quoted passage is typical. Implicit in its explanation is recognition of the fact of force. It is due to this fact that, although the so-called "veto" has been the object of frequent criticism, no proposal for ameliorating its use and obviating its consequences has denied that the veto should be maintained in cases under Chapter VII of the Charter, involving enforcement measures.[81] The reason for this is not obscure. As the use of force to prevent or repel aggression is one of the fundamental objectives of the United Nations, and the principle that responsibility should be commensurate with power one of its basic assumptions, so is the use of force linked with responsibility and power. As the head of the United States Delegation to the San Francisco Conference pointed out in his Report to the President:[82]

"The Council is to use the power of the member states in accordance with the realities of the distribution of power. The voting procedure of the Security Council is expressive of the actualities of the possession and the exercise of power in the modern world. The five principal military powers of our time are made permanent members of the Council. *Furthermore, in order that their possession of power and their use of power may be made to serve the purpose of peace, it is provided that they shall exercise their power only in agreement with each other and not in disagreement.*"

## II. ABSENCE FROM THE SECURITY COUNCIL

There are not many cases on record where a permanent or a nonpermanent member of the Security Council was absent from a meeting of the Council in the course of which resolutions were put to the vote. It is possible, however, to find in the records of the Security Council some such instances preceding the prolonged absence of the Soviet Union from the Council from January 13 to August 1, 1950.

### 1. The Iranian Question

In the course of the debate on this question, Mr. Gromyko (USSR) declared at the 27th meeting of the Security Council, March 27, 1946, after the rejection of his proposal to postpone the consideration of this question until April 10:[83]

". . . I am not in a position as the representative of the USSR, to take part in a discussion of the Iranian question after the rejection of my proposal. For these reasons I am unable to take part in the Council meeting and I am leaving the Council chamber."

[81] See *Official Records* of the 2d part of the 1st session of the General Assembly, First Committee, p. 84–127, and specifically the Australian proposals of November 8, 1946, p. 323.
[82] *Hearings* 41 (Italics supplied). See also the British Commentary on the Charter of the United Nations, Misc. No. 9 (1945), Cmd. 6666, nos. 85, 87.
[83] Security Council, *Official Records* (1st year), no. 2, p. 58.

He thereupon left the Council Chamber. The Soviet Union was not represented at the 28th, 29th and 30th meetings, and was not included in the list of those "present" in the Official Records of the Security Council. Its absence was not otherwise recorded. The Security Council meanwhile continued its business without Mr. Gromyko.[84] At the same meeting as that of the walkout, its 27th on March 27, 1946, the Council put to a vote and adopted an Egyptian proposal to invite the Iranian representative to come to the Council table. Before putting this to a vote, the President of the Council, Mr. Quo Tai-chi (China), said:[85]

> "I understand that, since this is a purely procedural question, a decision can be taken even in the absence of the USSR representative. If that interpretation is correct, we shall proceed with the voting."

No formal vote was taken at the 28th and 29th meetings, but at its 30th meeting, April 4, 1946, the Security Council adopted a United States draft resolution "by 9 votes." This resolution, taking note of certain statements by the Soviet and Iranian governments, provided in its operative part for deferment of further proceeding on the Iranian appeal until May 6. In a letter to the President of the Council, dated April 6, 1946, Mr. Gromyko, argued that the Security Council should not have considered the Iranian question and that this question should be removed from the agenda of the Council:[86]

> "The Soviet Government, moreover, cannot ignore the resolution adopted by the Security Council on 4 April. Under this resolution the Security Council decided to continue the consideration of the Iranian question on 6 May despite the fact that on 3 April the Soviet Government stated that the question of the evacuation of Soviet troops had been settled by an understanding reached between the Soviet and Iranian Governments. Such a resolution of the Security Council might have been well-founded if the position in Iran had threatened international peace and security, as provided in Article 34 of the Charter of the United Nations.
>
> "Under the Charter, the Security Council may investigate any dispute or any situation which might endanger the maintenance of international peace and security. It is, however, quite obvious that in fact such a position did not and does not now exist in Iran, so that the Security Council had no reason to give further consideration to the Iranian question on 6 May.
>
> "Accordingly, the above-mentioned resolution of the Security Council of April 4 is incorrect and illegal, being in conflict with the Charter of the United Nations."

At the 32nd meeting, April 15, 1946, Mr. Gromyko amplified somewhat his arguments why the April 4 resolution was "contrary to both the meaning and to the letter of the Charter." The situation on Iran, he stated, was not a threat to the peace within the

[84] *Id.* at 58 *et seq.*
[85] *Id.* at 60. Sir Alexander Cadogan (United Kingdom) thereupon noted that the proposal "still requires seven unqualified votes." This remark, however, seems to have been made purely for purposes of clarification.
[86] Documents S/30, April 8, 1946.

meaning of Article 34. Moreover, the Security Council had failed to hear both parties directly concerned in the dispute, and also failed to decide that the question constituted a dispute or a situation justifying Council consideration.[87]

The Soviet position met with opposition. In the ensuing discussion, Mr. van Kleffens (Netherlands) observed that[88]

> "The veto right of the great Powers is a limited right and therefore cannot be extended beyond the terms of the Charter by the great Power which is a party to a question before the Council, simply by absenting itself from the Council's deliberations."

He wanted to "make it quite clear that the Council never took up the Iranian case on its merits but only the question as to whether the examination of the merits of the case should or should not be postponed." Sir Alexander Cadogan (United Kingdom) pointed out that the April 4 resolution "merely resolved that the Council defer further proceeding" for certain purposes and said:[89]

> "That is the point of the Council's resolution, and I maintain that it could be held that that was hardly more than procedural."

And Colonel Hodgson (Australia) stated:[90]

> "As to the view that the action taken by this resolution was illegal, incorrect and contrary to the Charter, whatever we may individually think about the resolution, whether we think it right or wrong, wise or unwise, it was a decision properly taken with the requisite majority by this Council. It conflicts with no rules of procedure and we are bound by it. Further, I can find nothing in the Charter which shows that it does so conflict."

It would seem to follow from this exchange of views that the Soviet representative did not attack the April 4 resolution on the ground that it was adopted in his absence but on other grounds. The validity of the resolution, moreover, was defended on the same level. By both sides, the resolution was considered to be procedural in character and therefore one that merely required the vote of any seven members of the Council. Mr. van Kleffens's remarks are not entirely clear but they may be understood to mean that by absenting itself from the Council the permanent member acquired no additional rights—that is, it could not thereby in effect veto procedural action so as to prevent the Council from carrying on its business and adopt resolutions of a procedural character.

At the 36th meeting, April 23, 1946, the Council having rejected a French draft resolution proposing in fact to remove the Iranian question from its agenda, Mr. Gromyko (USSR) declared that he considered the decision to retain the question on the agenda to be "contradictory to the United Nations Charter" and he felt that the Soviet

87 Security Council, *Official Records* (1st year), no. 2, p. 124.
88 *Id.* at 128.
89 *Id.* at 130.
90 *Id.* at 132.

delegation "cannot in the future take part in discussions of the Iranian question by the Security Council."[91] As a consequence, the Soviet Union was absent from the 40th meeting, May 8, 1946, in the course of which the problem of the legal effect of the absence of a permanent member upon the ability of the Council to function was discussed at some length. Emphasizing the gravity of the problem, a problem "which goes right to the foundations of the working of the Security Council," Mr. Hasluck (Australia) stated:[92]

> "It seems to us that if a member of the Council absents himself from the Council, he is establishing a situation which affects not only his own position as a member, but also the functioning of the Council, and we should like to reach some clearer idea of what is the exact consequence of such action.
>
> "It is obviously not a matter which the Council can resolve this afternoon, but we suggest it is a matter which the Council must resolve in the very near future. When a member so absents himself, does that mean that he has voluntarily surrendered for the time being his powers and responsibilities as a member of this Council? . . .
>
> "It seems to us that if a member refuses to participate, or fails to participate, in the work of this Council, then for the time being he abandons the special powers which accrue to him as a member, and has no powers greater than those of any other Member of the United Nations. . . .
>
> "The Australian delegation does not admit that the absence of a member affects the voting procedure. That is a matter on which we make no pronouncement at the present time; but that the Council should ever be asked to entertain the idea that by absenting himself one of its members can bring into question its ability to function or take any action does seem to us to be most dangerous and the beginning of a system which would rapidly prove unworkable. Even if we adopt so simple a resolution as the one before us today, it may be that the constitutionality of that resolution will, rightly or wrongly, be called into question because of the absence of a member."

And he suggested that "the first step towards resolving this question must be to obtain from the absent member a clearer idea of what he claims is the effect of his absence." Sir Alexander Cadogan (United Kingdom) did not think that the problem was quite so grave and said:[93]

> "The absence of one of our number from this table does not halt the Council's work. We sit here and function. As regards a quorum, I believe we have no rule relating to a necessary quorum, unless you could infer something from the voting rule which requires that any actual resolution or decision requires an affirmative vote of at least seven members."[94]

[91] *Id.* at 214.

[92] *Id.* at 248–250.

[93] *Id.* at 251.

[94] The question of the quorum is not discussed further here since Sir Alexander furnished the proper answer. Whereas Article VIII of the League Council's Rules of Procedure required a quorum of the majority of members, the Provisional Rules of Procedure of the Security Council are silent on the matter. Hence, the presence of at least seven members is required for decisions of a procedural nature, and the presence of at least two non-permanent members and five permanent members is required for decisions on all other matters. This follows from Article 27, paragraph 3. See, however, KELSEN, *op. cit. supra* note 3, at 244: "Since there is no special rule concerning the quorum for decisions of the Security Council, the presence of all members of the Council is required for the adoption of a resolution. However, in the practice of the Security Council absence of a member, even of a permanent member, does not prevent this body from adopting a resolution." See discussion page 461, *infra*.

Absence, in his view,

> "may be considered to a certain extent to amount to an evasion of that responsibility [*i.e.*, to all the Members of the United Nations]. Well, that is a matter which any member of the Council must settle with his own conscience. But, as regards the effect of his absence upon the action of the Council or upon the voting, I cannot see that there is really any difference between absence from this table or presence at the table and abstention from a vote. It seems to me that the general effect is the same. There is a difference in some ways; that is to say, the absence certainly does imply some sort of evasion of responsibility or obligations, and may in some cases reduce the authority of the Council, but I cannot see that it has any actual effect upon the ability of the Council to take a decision, any more than has sitting in a chair and abstaining from voting."

Mr. van Kleffens (Netherlands) brought the discussion from the level of abstract or general argument to that of the concrete question before the Council and said:[95]

> "When I read the draft resolution presented by the representative of the United States, I thought that in spite of the absence of the representative of the USSR we could legitimately adopt this resolution because it is clearly a matter of procedure, so that the affirmative vote of seven members, whether permanent or not, is sufficient."

Referring to Mr. Hasluck's statement, Mr. van Kleffens observed

> "It seems to me that we must give an answer to one of the questions which he raised—although I hardly thought myself that it was or could be a question at all—namely, whether the Council can legitimately adopt a resolution on a matter of procedure in spite of the fact that one member of the Council has chosen to be absent. . . .
>
> "It cannot be the intention of the Charter to give to any member of the Council, whether a permanent or not, the power to prevent a resolution from being adopted by the simple expedient of absenting himself.
>
> "I therefore think that we can quite legitimately adopt a resolution on the matter of procedure; and may I recall that without this question being explicitly raised, we implicitly took that point of view on a previous occasion. As to the possibility of taking a decision on the question of a permanent member's right to absent himself, I should like to reserve my opinion. It seems to me that we need not go into that point this afternoon."

The United States resolution to defer further proceedings on the Iranian matter "was adopted without objection" and, of course, without formal note that the Soviet representative did not participate in the voting.[96] At the 43rd meeting, May 22, 1946, again in the absence of Mr. Gromyko, the Security Council adopted the President's proposal to adjourn the discussion of the Iranian question.

This was the first time that the Security Council was faced with the absence of one of its permanent members. It is important to observe first that the Security Council continued to discuss the Iranian question; second that it adopted resolutions which seem to have been regarded as procedural and not as substantive; third that although it was in-

[95] Security Council, *Official Records* (1st year), no. 2, p. 251.
[96] *Id.* at 252.

vited to give attention to the serious problem created by the absence of a permanent member, the Seucrity Council as a body did not do so; and fourth, that the Security Council made no effort "to obtain from the absent member a clear idea of what he claims is the effect of his absence," although that seemed to Mr. Hasluck to be "the first step towards resolving this question."[97] Thus the question of principle raised by the absence of the Soviet representative, the question which, as Mr. Hasluck put it "goes right to the foundation of the working of the Security Council," was left undecided by the Council. The Council was content to deal with the question at hand, namely its competence to adopt procedural resolutions. This was answered in the affirmative; not explicitly, to be sure, but as Mr. van Kleffens suggested, implicitly.

The absence of the Soviet Union from some meetings of the Security Council on the Iranian question prompted some writers to deductions which are by no means consistent with the record or with each other. According to one view[98]

> "In the practice of the Security Council absence of a member, even of a permanent member, does not prevent this body from adopting a resolution. Absence of a permanent member is considered to be equivalent to abstention from voting."

Similarly, it has been said:[99]

> "While the question has thus arisen but once, it would appear, on the basis of the Council's action in the Iranian case, that an absence is regarded as having the same legal effect, so far as voting is concerned, as an abstention. It would thus appear that the absence of a permanent member does not prevent the Security Council from taking a decision on a substantive question."

The contrary view has been expressed as follows:[100]

> "In view of the fact that on matters of substance the concurring votes of the permanent members is required, the Soviet Delegate by thus absenting himself cast a blanket veto over all substantive decisions which the Council might have decided to take."

None of these statements, it is believed, are well founded. The last view, while it expresses a widely held interpretation of Article 27, paragraph 3, reads into the Security Council treatment of the Iranian question a precedent which does not exist. The Council was not faced with any decision or resolution on the merits of the case. The former views appear to be unfounded for the same reason. It appears from the Official Records of the Council that merely procedural decisions were adopted,[101] that is, resolutions intended to

[97] *Id.* at 250.

[98] KELSEN, *op. cit. supra* note 3, at 244.

[99] LELAND M. GOODRICH & EDVARD HAMBRO, CHARTER OF THE UNITED NATIONS: COMMENTARY AND DOCUMENTS 223 (rev. ed. 1949).

[100] WELLINGTON KOO, JR., VOTING PROCEDURES IN INTERNATIONAL POLITICAL ORGANIZATIONS 291, n. 4 (1947).

[101] B. A. Wortley, *The Veto and the Security Council Provisions of the Charter,* 23 BRITISH YEAR BOOK OF INTERNATIONAL LAW 97 (1946).

defer and finally to adjourn the consideration of the Iranian question, or to invite the representative of Iran to come to the Council table. While it may be tempting to regard at least certain parts of the April 4 resolution as being substantive in character linked to a procedural operative part, it would seem to be the better part of wisdom to accept the view of those representatives who argued that the resolution was altogether procedural and who professed to have voted accordingly.

### 2. The Indonesian Question

The representative of the Ukrainian Soviet Socialist Republic, a nonpermanent member of the Security Council, was absent from the 388th, 389th, 390th, 391st and 392nd meetings. In the course of the 392nd meeting, December 24, 1948, a draft resolution submitted by the delegations of Colombia, Syria and the United States was put to the vote. The draft resolution was of a substantive character. The Council first voted separately on the different paragraphs, the amendments thereto, and then on the draft resolution as a whole. Although the Ukrainian SSR was not included in the list of those "present" in the Official Record for that meeting or the four previous meetings, neither was its absence specifically noted. The vote on the first paragraph was recorded as for adoption, 7 to none, with 4 abstentions. Those abstaining were listed as follows: Belgium, France, Ukrainian Soviet Socialist Republic, and the Union of Soviet Socialist Republics. Mr. Jessup (USA) requested some information after this vote and asked: "Is an absent member counted as having abstained?" The President Mr. F. van Langenhove (Belgium) replied:

> "It seems to me that he must be counted as having abstained. I do not see how we could act otherwise. Are we agreed on this point?"

Thereupon Mr. Munoz (Argentina) desired "some clarification from the President regarding the counting of the votes," and the President said:[102]

> "There are four abstentions, the Ukrainian SSR being among the States which have abstained. Is the representative of Argentina satisfied with this explanation?"

The representative of Argentina was apparently satisfied. Mr. Malik (USSR) explained the absence of the Ukrainian delegate and the voting proceeded. Throughout the voting on the different paragraphs, the amendments thereto, and the resolution as a whole the Ukrainian SSR was listed in the Official Record among the abstaining members. Mr. Tarasenko (Ukrainian SSR) was present at the 393rd meeting, December 27, 1948, and there explained the reasons for his absence, but seems to have raised no question regarding his Government being recorded as abstaining on the resolution adopted on December 24, 1948.

[102] Security Council, *Official Records* (3rd year), no. 134, p. 30 ff.

Here there appears to be for the first time in the annals of the Security Council a vote on a substantive resolution taken in the absence of a member of the Council in connection with which the absent member was reported as abstaining. The President went on record as treating the representative of a member Government who in fact was absent as if participating and abstaining in the long succession of votes. He might have suggested that an absent member should be recorded as absent, which was the fact, rather than as abstaining, which was not the fact, but was at best a theory regarding absence and at worst a piece of fiction. He did not. Sir Alexander Cadogan's view that there is not "any difference between absence from this table and presence at the table and abstention from vote" was put to use and neither contested by any member present, nor attacked by the absent member after he became a present member.

It will be noted, however, that the absent member was one of the non-permanent members of the Council, whose vote according to Article 27, paragraph 3, was not essential for the adoption of a resolution which otherwise received the requisite number of votes. The value of the incident as a precedent is thereby placed in doubt, since what the Ukraine did—support or vote against the resolution, abstain or withdraw completely—could have had no effect on the outcome. Neither the presence nor the affirmative and concurring vote of this member was required by Article 27. The issue was in effect moot before it could arise at all.

### 3. Admission to Membership of the United Nations

At its 445th meeting, September 15, 1949, the Security Council voted on the Soviet draft resolution (S/1340/Rev.2) concerning the admission *en bloc* of all states whose application for membership was then pending in the Security Council. Sir Alexander Cadogan (United Kingdom) presided. The Council first voted on parts of the draft resolution and then on the draft resolution as a whole. The analysis of the latter vote and its result, taken by show of hands, is reported in the Official Records as follows: "In favor: Ukrainian Soviet Socialist Republic, USSR. Against: Canada, etc. Abstaining: China, etc.; Argentina did not participate in the voting. The draft resolution was rejected by 4 votes to 2, with 4 abstentions. One member of the Council did not vote."[103]

What actually happened at this meeting of the Security Council is not entirely clear. Argentina is listed in the Official Records as "present" and also is listed in the breakdown of the votes taken on parts of the Soviet draft resolution.[104] There is no explanation of Argentina's non-participation in the vote on the draft resolution as a whole. Apparently either the representative of Argentina somehow arranged to be present at the meeting yet not participate in the final vote, or was temporarily absent from the Council chamber when the final vote was taken. In either case, the method of recording the result of the vote in this particular case, indicating as it clearly does that Argentina did not in

[103] Security Council, *Official Records* (4th year), no. 42, p. 45.
[104] *Id.* at 30, 40–41.

any way participate in the voting, appears preferable to that adopted in the preceding case involving the absence of the Ukrainian Soviet Socialist Republic.[105]

4. January 13 to July 31, 1950

At the 461st meeting, January 13, 1950, after the Security Council rejected a motion to unseat the representative of China, Mr. Malik (USSR) declared that[106]

> "As regards the Soviet Union, its position in this question is one of principle and is entirely consistent. It will not sit on the Security Council until the representative of the Kuomintang group, who is now illegally occupying a seat in that organ of the United Nations, has been removed from membership of the Council. His presence here is undermining the prestige and authority of the Security Council and of the United Nations as a whole. As a result, the Security Council itself is being transformed into an organ the decisions of which cannot be considered legal in these circumstances.
>
> "In the light of the above, I, as representative of the Soviet Union in the Security Council, have to state that the USSR delegation will not sit on the Security Council as long as the representative of the Kuomintang group has not been excluded from the Security Council.
>
> "At the same time, the USSR delegation wishes to announce that the USSR will not recognize as legal *any* decision of the Security Council adopted with the participation of the representative of the Kuomintang group, and will *not* be guided by any such decisions."

After Mr. Malik had left the Council chamber, Mr. Chauvel (France) formally challenged the "right of the USSR delegation to do what it has just done, namely to refuse to co-operate with the Council" and said: "It does not seem possible to recognize that it has the right totally to paralyse the work of the Council."[107] He was answered by Mr. Gross (U.S.A.):[108]

> "The United Nations is strong enough to withstand such tactics as these. The absence of the Soviet Union representative will not prevent us from conducting the business to which we are pledged. It is the view of my Government that the absence of a permanent member from a meeting of the Security Council in no way diminishes its powers or its authority to act. The Charter provides in Article 28 that 'The Security Council shall be so organized as to be able to function continuously.' We cannot permit the arbitrary action of our Soviet Union colleagues to prevent us from fulfilling our obligation to the Charter."

Between January 13 and June 25, 1950, the Security Council held several meetings at which a number of votes were taken, some clearly procedural in character, some clearly

[105] This incident is particularly significant as it occurred under the presidency of Sir Alexander Cadogan, who, it will be recalled, in connection with the absence of the Soviet Union in the Iranian case propounded the view that he really could see no difference between absence and abstention. It would seem that in this instance Sir Alexander Cadogan did not follow his earlier view and it would also seem that he did not feel it necessary to adhere to the view expounded by Mr. van Langenhove at the 392nd meeting.

[106] *Id.* (5th year), no. 3, p. 10.

[107] *Id.* at 13.

[108] *Id.* at 14.

substantive, and some where there may be room for doubt. The Official Records for all these meetings omit the Soviet Union from the list of those "present" but fail to note its absence. On the other hand, the breakdown of the votes as well as their conclusion or summary refer to the absence of the Soviet Union in a formula which varies only slightly. Thus at the 462nd meeting, January 17, 1950, Mr. T. F. Tsiang (China) presiding, the result of the vote on the Yugoslav proposal regarding the agenda is recorded as follows:[109]

In favor: Yugoslavia
Against: China, etc.
Abstaining: Ecuador, etc.
Absent: Soviet Union

Then follows the summary: "The proposal was rejected by 7 votes to 1, with 2 abstentions, one member being absent." At the same meeting a vote on the French draft resolution calling upon the Security Council to transmit to the Commission for Conventional Armament General Assembly Resolution 300 (IV) was reported as follows:[110]

In favor: China, etc.
Not voting: Yugoslavia
Absent: Soviet Union

The summary: "The resolution was adopted by 9 votes in favor, one member not voting and one member of the Council being absent." It may be noted here that the Yugoslav delegate, Mr. Bebler, having declared: "I cannot take part in the vote on this question" was correctly reported as "not voting" rather than as abstaining. It may also be noted that Mr. Gross (USA) replying to Mr. Bebler, referred to the absence of a permanent member "which clearly is an absence volunteered by the representative himself and which, I think, the Council has clearly indicated it will not take as a deterrent to its proceeding in an orderly manner with its business."[111] It is not clear, however, when, where and how the Council as an organ, distinct from the members composing it, gave the indication to which Mr. Gross referred.

At the same meeting the Security Council voted on the Yugoslav draft resolution to forego the application of Rule 18 of the Council's Provisional Rules of Procedure. The members voting were again classified into "in favor," "against," "abstaining" and "absent." The summary was accordingly: "The paragraphs were rejected by 6 votes to one with 3 abstentions, one member of the Council being absent."[112]

At the 463rd to 469th meetings the India-Pakistan question was discussed. At the

[109] *Id.* no. 4, p. 3.
[110] *Id.* at 9.
[111] *Id.* at 10.
[112] *Id.* at 15.

468th meeting, February 28, 1950, the Indian proposal to amend Rule 13 of the Council's Provisional Rules of Procedure was adopted. The Official Records merely report that the proposal was adopted, and contain no breakdown of the vote.[113] At the 470th meeting, March 14, 1950, Mr. H. Viteri Lafronte (Ecuador) presiding, draft resolution S/1461 was put to the vote. The Official Records classify the members voting into "in favor," "abstaining" and "absent" and summarize: "The draft resolution was adopted by 8 votes in favor, with 2 abstentions, one member of the Council being absent."[114] This resolution called upon the Governments of India and Pakistan, *inter alia* to prepare and execute within a period of five months a program of demilitarization. It also envisaged the appointment of a United Nations representative to perform certain functions described therein. The appointment of the representative, Sir Owen Dixon (Australia) took place at the 471st meeting, April 12, 1950, and the Official Records report the Soviet Union as absent in the breakdown of the vote, no summary of the vote being given.[115]

At the 472nd meeting, May 24, 1950, Mr. J. Chauvel (France) presiding, the Council voted on a French draft resolution taking note of the General Assembly Resolution 268 B (III), and deciding "should an appropriate occasion arise, to base its action upon the principles contained therein." In the breakdown of the vote the Soviet Union is reported as absent and the conclusion is: "The draft resolution was adopted unanimously, one member of the Council being absent."[116] Before the vote, Mr. Viteri Lafronte (Ecuador) referred to the absence of the Soviet Union and said:[117]

> "It is a matter of concern to all the members of the Council that we are not working with the full membership provided under the Charter at the time when it was drafted. This is not the occasion for us to discuss whether the writers of the Charter were right or wrong in providing that there should be five permanent members of the Security Council. That provision is, however, contained in the Charter, and we find that there is some irregularity in our activity when one of the permanent members does not participate and when the question of the representation of one of the other permanent members is so controversial that it cannot perhaps be said that we have the full hundred per cent representation which we would like to have."

This statement is rather significant, revealing as it does a certain awareness of "irregularity" in the activities of the Council under the circumstances. It also reflects somewhat less assurance than was voiced by Mr. Gross a short time before.

The next meeting of the Security Council, the 473rd, convened on June 25, 1950, at the urgent request of the United States, considered the "Complaint of Aggression upon the Republic of Korea." The Council, under the presidency of Sir Benegal N. Rau (India), adopted a resolution noting the armed attack on the Republic of Korea by forces from North Korea, determining this action to constitute a breach of the peace, calling for

[113] *Id.* no. 10, p. 11.
[114] *Id.* no. 12, p. 4.
[115] *Id.* no. 13, p. 5.
[116] *Id.* no. 14, p. 16.
[117] *Id.* at 12.

the immediate cessation of hostilities, calling upon the authorities of North Korea to withdraw their forces to the thirty-eighth parallel, etc. It also called upon all members to render every assistance to the United Nations in the execution of this resolution and to refrain from giving assistance to the North Korean authorities. The resolution was voted first in several parts and then as a whole. The members were again classified in the Official records as "in favor," "abstaining" and "absent" (USSR), and the result formulated as follows: "The resolution as revised was adopted by 9 votes in favor, with one abstention, one member of the Security Council being absent." Similarly the vote on the Yugoslav draft resolution calling for cessation of hostilities, withdrawal of forces and inviting the Government of North Korea to state its case before the Council, was reported as rejected "by 6 votes to one, with 3 abstentions, one member of the Council being absent."[118]

The vote at the 474th meeting, June 27, 1950, on the United States draft resolution recommending that members of the United Nations furnish such assistance to the Republic of Korea as might be necessary to repel the armed attack and to restore international peace and security in the area, was reported in a like manner, indicating clearly the absence of the Soviet Union, and concluding: "The resolution was adopted by 7 votes to one, two members of the Council not voting and one member being absent."[119] Before the vote, the representative of Egypt, Mahmoud Fawzi Bey said: "If the Council desires to vote, I shall not be able to participate. I ask that my position be considered as non-participation in voting, and trust that this will be inscribed in the record."[120] The President, Sir Benegal N. Rau, then said: "Like the representative of Egypt, I shall not participate in the voting." Again the members were classified in the vote as follows: in favor, against, not voting, and absent. A similar breakdown of the voting appears in the Official Records on the Yugoslav draft resolution proposing to initiate a procedure of mediation between the parties, etc., which was rejected at the same meeting. Egypt and India were reported as "not voting" and the Soviet Union as "absent."[121] By this time it seems to have become an established practice in the Council to consider "not voting" as a position distinct from abstention.

At the 475th meeting, June 30, 1950, no votes were taken. The Security Council was informed of various communications relating to its previous resolution. Among these was a cablegram of June 29, 1950 (S/1517) from the Soviet Union stating that the Security Council resolution of June 27 had no legal basis. Another cablegram from the Minister of Foreign Affairs of the Korean People's Democratic Republic was received stating that his Government did not consider the discussion and decisions of the Council on the Korean question as lawful in view of the fact[122]

[118] *Id.* no. 15, p. 18.

[119] *Id.* no. 16, p. 17.

[120] *Id.* at 15. Note that the Yugoslav representative had followed the same procedure at the 462nd meeting. See page 456 *supra*.

[121] *Id.* at 16.

[122] Document S/1527 and Document S/1527/Corr.1. See also Cablegram dated July 2, 1950, from the Minister of Foreign Affairs of the Korean People's Democratic Republic, Document S/1554.

"1. that the Korean People's Democratic Republic was not brought into consultation on the matter and the question of Korea was decided without the participation of the Government of the Korean People's Democratic Republic,

"2. because the representatives of a power such as the Soviet Union were absent from the Security Council and representatives of the great Chinese power were not admitted."

The cablegram from the Soviet Deputy Minister of Foreign Affairs, A. Gromyko, referred to the June 27, 1950, resolution and declared:[123]

"As is known, moreover, the above resolution was passed in the absence of two permanent members of the Security Council, the USSR and China, whereas under the United Nations Charter a decision of the Security Council on an important matter can only be made with the concurring votes of all five permanent members of the Council, viz. the United States, the United Kingdom, France, the USSR and China. In view of the foregoing it is quite clear that the said resolution of the Security Council on the Korean question has no legal force."

The representative of France, Mr. Chauvel, discussing the Soviet arguments recalled his reasoning relating to Article 24, paragraph 1, at the 460th and 461st meetings, and said:[124]

"The delegation of the Soviet Union, by abandoning the Council, has abandoned the Charter. When it returns to the one and to the other, it will find again its right of speech, of criticism, of vote and veto. So long as it has not done so, the USSR Government has no legal or moral basis for contesting the action of the United Nations."

Mr. Austin underscored the fact[125]

"that the freedom-loving people of the world have overcome every obstacle that has been erected in their minds or in their policies in order to take a strong, clear and definite position. By these acts they have overcome timidity, they have overcome the fear that they might perhaps violate some technicality or some strict construction raised solely for the purpose of paralysing or even killing collective action by the United Nations to attain its noble purposes."

At the 476th meeting, held July 7, 1950, the President, Mr. Arne Sunde (Norway), drew attention to the cablegram dated July 6, 1950 (S/1579) from the Soviet Union reiterating the arguments contained in the earlier cablegram of June 29, referred to above. Speaking in this connection, Mr. Alvarez (Cuba) stated:[126]

"The Cuban delegation takes this opportunity to place on record its disagreement with the interpretation given by the Soviet Union in its communication to the Secretary-General (S/1517), regarding the validity of the decisions taken by the Security Council on

[123] Document S/1517. See also Document S/1523 and Document S/1545 for communications from the Governments of Czechoslovakia and Poland respectively.

[124] Security Council, *loc. cit.*, no. 17, p. 8.

[125] *Id.* at 11.

[126] *Id.* no. 18, p. 7. It should be noted that the Cuban representative here arbitrarily equated absence with abstention, without regard to the application of the principle of unanimity.

25 and 27 June, since it is an established practice in the Council, and one that the USSR has accepted on many occasions, that the abstention of a permanent member from participation in decisions of the Council does not constitute a veto."

At this meeting the Security Council discussed a United Kingdom-French draft resolution for the establishment of a unified command and other matters. Speaking on this, Sir Gladwyn Jebb (United Kingdom) made some observations concerning the character of the action taken so far. These remarks, although not directly linked with the problem of absence, have some bearing on the argument to be developed in the concluding part of this paper. Sir Gladwyn said:[127]

> "Had the Charter come fully into force and had the agreement provided for in Article 43 of the Charter been concluded, we should, of course, have proceeded differently, and the action by the Security Council to repel the armed attack would no doubt have been founded on Article 42. As it is, however, the Council can naturally act only under Article 39, which enables the Security Council to recommend what measures should be taken to restore international peace and security. The necessary recommendations were duly made in the resolutions of 25 and 27 June, but in the nature of things they could only be recommendations to individual members of the United Nations. . . .
>
> "In any event, since we believe the Security Council is acting under Article 39 of the Charter, its function is not an operative one; all it should do is to make sure that the individual efforts of the members concerned are properly coordinated."

The United Kingdom-French draft resolution was put to the vote and adopted. The Official Records do not list the Soviet Union as absent in the breakdown of the vote but the summary follows the established pattern: "The resolution was adopted by 7 votes to none, with 3 abstentions, one member of the Council being absent."[128]

At the 479th meeting, July 31, 1950 the last meeting of the Security Council held before the return of the Soviet Union representative, draft resolution S/1652 concerning Korean relief submitted by the representatives of France, Norway and the United Kingdom was put to the vote and the result reported in the usual way, to wit: "In favor: China, etc. Abstaining: Yugoslavia. Absent: Soviet Union. The resolution was adopted by 9 votes in favor with one abstention, one member of the Council being absent."[129]

## 5. Conclusions

As the preceding survey shows, the Official Records of the meetings of the Security Council from January 13 to July 31, 1950, with one or two insignificant exceptions,[130]

[127] *Id.* at 3. See discussion pages 469–70 *infra*.
[128] *Id.* at 8.
[129] *Id.* no. 21, p. 7.
[130] Except for votes on non-controversial adoptions of the agenda, there are only two exceptions. One is the vote on the Indian proposal at the 468th meeting to amend Rule 13 of the Provisional Rules of Procedure. There the *Official Records* merely report that the Council adopted the proposal. The other is the vote on the United Kingdom-French resolution adopted at the 476th meeting, where the Soviet Union is not listed as absent in the breakdown of the vote, although the conclusion contains the words "one member of the Council being absent."

reported the absence of the Soviet Union in the analysis of every vote. The Official Records contain no indication that the Security Council pronounced on the question whether the absence of the Soviet Union was analogous or equivalent to abstention from voting, although this view was occasionally expressed by individual representatives of the member Governments comprising the Security Council. Yet, in spite of the officially noted absence of the Soviet Union, a permanent member of the Council, and in spite of the failure of the Council to clarify explicitly the legal effect of such an absence, the various resolutions of a substantive character were reported as "adopted" in the Official Records. How can this remarkable performance be explained, if it can be explained?

It may be useful, before proceeding further, to discuss briefly the question of the quorum in the Security Council, that is whether the Council is properly constituted and is able to take valid decisons if one or more members are absent from its meetings.

There is no explicit provision for a quorum in the Charter. The Provisional Rules of Procedure of the Security Council, unlike those of the General Assembly,[131] or of the Council of the League of Nations,[132] are silent on the subject. This being so it may be possible to argue that in the absence of a rule to the contrary the Security Council is properly constituted, and can make valid decisions, only in the presence of all of the eleven members. Under this interpretation, the Security Council could not function, in the absence of one or more members, as a corporate body deriving its existence and competence from the Charter. However, in the Iranian case involving the absence of a permanent member, and in the Indonesian case involving the absence of a non-permanent member, the Security Council did in fact continue to function. In the former case it considered itself competent to adopt procedural decisions, while in the latter case it adopted substantive decisions. This indicates that until the prolonged absence of the Soviet Union from January to August 1950, the Security Council did not deem the presence of all of its members necessary to constitute a quorum. But it will be noted that prior to that time the Council always included those members whose presence was required for the adoption of procedural or substantive resolutions in accordance with Article 27, paragraphs 2 and 3. With this proviso, the practice of the Council would seem to support the view expressed at the 36th meeting by Sir Alexander Cadogan that the quorum might be deduced from the voting requirement in that article of the Charter.[133]

Such an interpretation is not without force. A close link between voting and quorum requirements is not at all unknown in international organization. Such a tie-up, for example, was explicitly provided in Article 19 of the Inter-American treaty of Reciprocal Assistance, signed at Rio de Janeiro on September 2, 1947, which reads:[134]

[131] Rule 68: "A majority of the Members of the General Assembly shall constitute a quorum." Rules of Procedure of the General Assembly. A/520/Rev.1. 1 January 1950. P.12.

[132] Article VIII: "The Council shall not discuss or decide upon any matter unless the majority of its members are present." Rules of Procedure of the Council. Doc.C.197.M.106, 1938 p. 4.

[133] See page 450 *supra*.

[134] *Inter-American Conference for the Maintenance of Continental Peace and Security, August 15–September 2, 1947*, Department of State Publication 3016, p. 63.

"To constitute a quorum in all the meetings referred to in the previous Articles, it shall be necessary that the number of States represented shall be at least equal to the number of votes necessary for the taking of the decision."

The position of the members of the Security Council since January 1950, however, cannot be understood in the light of either Sir Alexander's interpretation or the more stringent view that the presence of all members is needed for a quorum. The view sometimes expressed in the Council that by absenting itself from the Council the Soviet Union had violated its obligation under the Charter to participate in the work of the Council has no bearing under either of the two interpretations. The first can properly be said to go no further than to say that any member whose vote is not required may be absent without invalidating Council decisions. As to all questions of substance, therefore, the absence of a permanent member would have the same result under this less stringent test as under the complete membership test—namely, absence of a quorum and accordingly inability on the part of the Security Council to function as a corporate body deriving its powers and competence from the Charter.[135]

No other interpretation can result in any rational stopping place. If the absence of one permanent member is not a fatal defect, as the members of the Council seem to have assumed since January 1950, is there any reason why it should not be argued that the absence of two or more members would similarly not prevent the Council from functioning and taking "binding" decisions? Such consequences, which may well be deemed absurd, are not altogether excluded if the recent practice of the Security Council is continued. As long as, disregarding the mandatory requirement of Article 27, paragraph 3, the Security Council is exclusively concerned in interpreting a vote with finding a majority of seven and no "veto," a vote on matters of substance taken in the absence of four permanent members but concurred in by the remaining one plus the six non-permanent members might be interpreted as a valid vote. This rather surprising result is no more in contradiction with the Charter than the present practice. It is indeed possible to interpret the Charter in more ways than one. However, as far as the voting rule and the quorum in the Security Council is concerned, there is at best a choice between two alternatives, neither of which is capable of supporting the recent practice.

Officially as well as unofficially it is argued in justification of the recent Security Council practice that "the voluntary absence of a permanent member . . . is clearly ana-

[135] Said Ambassador Jessup: "The Soviet Union had the legal power to attend the meeting of the Security Council and, by taking the responsibility before the world, to cast a veto to block Security Council action. The USSR did not have the power to block action by staying away from the meeting in violation of its obligations under Article 28." Jessup, *The United Nations and Korea,* 23 DEP'T STATE BULL. 86 (1950). If Ambassador Jessup had in mind that under Article 28 the Soviet Union had the legal duty to attend meetings of the Security Council, then, under Article 28, there would appear to be required a quorum consisting of all of the eleven members of the Council. This is Kelsen's point. See note 94 *supra.* Then in the absence of one member, that is in the absence of a quorum, the Council would not be properly constituted and could not validly discharge any of its functions. It could not even determine that absence is equivalent to abstention, as this could be done only by a properly constituted Council. This in turn would require unanimity of the five permanent members of the Council and the affirmative vote of two other members. Neither of these conditions was present in the Council between January and August 1950.

logous to abstention."[136] Such a view is at best based on the one precedent in the Indonesian case, which involved a non-permanent member whose absence was involuntary. It will be recalled that at the 392nd meeting of the Security Council, the absent member, the Ukrainian Soviet Socialist Republic, was recorded by the President, Mr. van Langenhove (Belgium), as having abstained from voting despite the fact that that member was in fact absent. Whether this was correct procedure may be left to one side. The important point is that this precedent, if one may properly call it so, was not followed in any other case. In the earlier Iranian case, the Soviet Union, although absent from several meetings in the course of which resolutions were put to the vote, was not reported as having abstained from voting. In the case involving Argentina at the 445th meeting of the Council, Sir Alexander Cadogan as President of the Council did not apply his rather tentative view that there was no difference between absence and abstention. Argentina was correctly reported as not participating in the vote, rather than as abstaining. Moreover, as the votes at the 462nd and 474th meetings of the Council indicate, a member which does not vote is so reported and not classified as abstaining. The Council would thus seem to have recognized a difference between abstention and "not voting".

In the light of this practice and in the absence of any formal pronouncement, it is not easy to see how the argument that absence equals abstention can be attributed persuasive or convincing force. There is an obvious inconsistency: a member which is present and "not voting" is considered as not participating in the vote and not as abstaining, whereas a member obviously not present and not participating in the vote is supposed to have participated in the vote and abstained even though, in the case of the Soviet Union, its opposition to the proposed action was conveyed to the Council in unmistakable terms ruling out any attribution of intent to abstain. If the Security Council as a corporate organ has been of the opinion that absence is tantamount to abstention, this fact should have been noted in the Official Records. So important a matter should not be left to inference. Instead, the Official Records consistently reported the Soviet Union as absent during the entire period under consideration. This being so, it is difficult to see how, in the light of the mandatory requirement of Article 27, paragraph 3, the resolutions in question could have been declared "adopted".

This conclusion that the requirement laid down in Article 27, paragraph 3, is not met when one permanent member is officially reported as absent from the meetings and the votes, rather than as abstaining, has been called a "technicality," to use the words of the United States representative (Mr. Austin) at the 475th meeting. It is submitted that this "technicality" is certainly a very important one since Article 27 deals with technical rules governing voting in the Security Council, reinforced by the mandatory Rule 40 of

[136] Department of State Publication 3922, *United States Policy in the Korean Crisis*, p. 63. See also Philip C. Jessup, *The United Nations and Korea*, 23 DEP'T STATE BULL. 86 (1950): "Clearly it can make no difference in terms of the application of the Charter on this point whether the representative of a permanent member sits at the table and abstains or whether he fails to come at all."

the Council's Provisional Rules of Procedure. Neither the rule nor the requirements of Article 27, paragraph 3, lose any of their overriding political and legal significance by being called "technical." Explicit exceptions are provided in the Charter and in the annexed Statute of the International Court of Justice. And, as has been pointed out, an exception by sufferance has grown up where the Security Council, and more particularly the permanent members, have in effect agreed to let a proposal carry in accordance with the principle of unanimity. But abstention is itself an exception to Article 27, paragraph 3, not provided for in the Charter. It cannot be used as a lever to justify a further exception by an analogy unsupported by all the permanent members of the Council, and, on the contrary, hotly contested by one of them.

That Article 27, paragraph 3 does not lend itself to extensive interpretation has been recognized. At the hearings on the Charter before the Senate Foreign Relations Committee, Senator Tom Connally, speaking as Chairman, said:[137]

> "The construction of this paragraph was that this proviso [*i.e.* the second part of paragraph 3] is an exception to the general rule, and where a party to the dispute is a member of the Security Council, that there are then only four permanent members of the Security Council, excluding the party to the dispute, that vote; in that case the votes of any other three nonpermanent members can be counted to make up the number of seven. In all other cases, however, the votes of five permanent members are required."

Thus any attempt at a broadening interpretation of the voting order in the Security Council appears contrary to the unambiguous terms of Article 27, paragraph 3, and unjustifiable in view of its history. It finds a certain explanation, however, in the penchant of members of the Council to regard as adopted any substantive resolution which has received seven affirmative votes and has not been "vetoed" by any of the permanent members. This overlooks the patent fact that Article 27, paragraph 3, does not require a "veto" in order to defeat a nonprocedural action but, on the contrary, requires the affirmative and concurring votes of all permanent members in order to adopt such an action. For this reason the formula which generally is used in the Official Records in reporting the acceptance of resolutions on nonprocedural matters is incorrect. In laying down the voting rule "on all other matters," Article 27, paragraph 3, makes a clear distinction between the votes of permanent and the votes of non-permanent members. This distinction should not be overlooked in announcing and reporting the result of a vote. By merely noting that a resolution was adopted by seven or more votes in favor, "one member of the Council being absent," the Official Records do not distinguish between permanent members and non-permanent members. This is contrary to the explicit requirement of

[137] *Hearings* 265. Senator Connally added: "I wanted to make that clear before we got involved in a lot of questions on the subject." The point seems clear enough, but clarity has not helped matters much. The Security Council is nonetheless "involved in a lot of questions on the subject" of voting.

See also the observation of Mr. van Langenhove (Belgium) as President of the Council: "In so far as it sanctions an exception to the voting order, Article 27, paragraph 3, must, where applicable, be interpreted strictly; it cannot be stretched to cover cases which are not mentioned in Chapter VI of the Charter." Security Council, *Official Records* (2d year), No. 21, p. 426.

Article 27, paragraph 3, whenever votes "on all other matters" are involved. In so doing the Official Records to some extent help to maintain the current fiction.

Some members of the Security Council seem to justify the action in the Korean crisis on the ground that by absenting itself from the Council the Soviet Union violated obligations derived from Article 24, paragraph 1, or Article 28, paragraph 1.[138] This contention may or may not be well-founded. It must be noted, however, that while it has been advanced on different occasions by individual members of the Council, it has never been adopted by the Council as an organ of the United Nations. Even if it is assumed, for the sake of argument, that the Soviet Union by absenting itself from the Council violated obligations contained in or derived from those articles of the Charter, it would still appear doubtful whether the conclusion is well-founded that the Security Council is in the position to consider as valid resolutions of a substantive character which do not conform to the mandatory requirement of Article 27, paragraph 3. Whatever be the merits of the international law version of the "clean hands" doctrine *(inadimplenti non est adimplendum)* in case of a bilateral treaty, its application to the interpretation of the Charter of the United Nations would lead to the extremely curious results pointed out above.

International case law points up the difference when multilateral rather than bilateral agreement is involved. For example, the Advisory Opinion of the International Court of Justice of July 18, 1950 on the Interpretation of Peace Treaties (second phase) is pertinent. Speaking of the power of the Secretary-General of the United Naitons to appoint a third member of the Commission for the settlement of disputes in accordance with Article 36 of the Treaty of Peace with Bulgaria, and corresponding provisions in the Treaties of Peace with Hungary and Romania, the Court[139] made it clear that one party's failure to fulfill its obligations did not mean that the intent of the multilateral agreement could be by-passed:

> "As the Court has declared in its Opinion of March 30th, 1950, the Governments of Bulgaria, Hungary and Romania are under an obligation to appoint their representatives to the Treaty Commissions, and it is clear that refusal to fulfil a treaty obligation involves international responsibility. Nevertheless, such a refusal cannot alter the conditions contemplated in the Treaties for the exercise by the Secretary-General of his power of appointment. These conditions are not present in this case, and their absence is not made good by the fact that it is due to the breach of a treaty obligation. The failure of machinery for settling disputes by reason of the practical impossibility of creating the Commission provided for in the Treaties is one thing; international responsibility is another. The breach of a treaty obligation cannot be remedied by creating a Commission which is not the kind of Commission contemplated by the Treaties. It is the duty of the Court to interpret the Treaties, not to revise them."

[138] See page 456 *supra*.
[139] I.C.J. Reports 221-28 (1950).

The Court went on to discard as irrelevant another maxim *(ut res magis valeat quam pereat),* which might be used to bolster the argument for the recent Security Council action. The Court declared that this maxim[140]

> "often referred to as the rule of effectiveness, cannot justify the Court in attributing to the provisions for the settlement of disputes in the Peace Treaties a meaning which, as stated above, would be contrary to their letter and spirit."

Finally, the Court did not feel justified "in exceeding its judicial function on the pretext of remedying a default for the occurrence of which the Treaties have made no provision."

It is clear from the opinion of the International Court of Justice that neither the alleged violation of the Charter by the Soviet Union nor the rule of effectiveness sometimes evoked in the Security Council can justify an interpretation of Article 27, paragraph 3, which is contrary to its letter and spirit. This article, as generally understood, embodies the principle of unanimity of the permanent members of the Security Council. Whether the permanent members were wise in making it the sheet anchor of the Security Council is not the issue here. The error, if there was one, consisted, in the first place, in assuming that unanimity among the great powers would be forthcoming on major political issues in the post-war world, rather than in accepting the fact that without this unanimity the organization could not function as an effective organ for the maintenance of international peace and security. In the second place, it was an error of the first magnitude to overlook the necessity of providing for the contingency that unanimity might not be forthcoming in cases in which, politically, inaction of the Council would not be acceptable. As the opinion of the International Court of Justice shows, this is not the only case in which necessary precautions, political or juridical, have been omitted. The opinion of the Court also shows that such defects cannot easily be glossed over by strained interpretation.

The seriousness of these shortcomings in the Charter were early realized, but left uncorrected. At the drafting stage at the San Francisco Conference a number of governments expressed their misgivings at the obvious faults of the Yalta voting formula. For example, the Canadian delegation specifically proposed in Committee III/1 to amend the Yalta voting formula in such a manner that on substantive matters "an affirmative vote of at least two-thirds of the members present and voting, including the concurring votes of the permanent members present and voting" would be required and sufficient. In explaining this proposal the Canadian delegate declared that[141]

> "since the Yalta voting formula required an affirmative vote of seven out of eleven members of the Council, absence or abstention would be equivalent to a negative vote and the chances of a deadlock would thus be greatly increased."

[140] *Id.* at 229.

[141] Document 1105/III/1/48(2). UNCIO Documents, vol. XI, p. 534.

The Canadian delegate concluded by saying that "if such a change were not made now . . . practical reasons would soon lead to a demand for the amendment of the Charter in this respect." In the ensuing discussion the delegate of New Zealand suggested that "the word 'concurring' in paragraph 3 had to be looked into in order to determine what would happen when a permanent member was absent." And the Australian delegate "believed that 'concurring' meant that each permanent member must be present and must vote." The delegate of the Soviet Union, however, "thought that the introduction of the Canadian proposal at this meeting would lead to difficulties," and the Canadian delegate "withdrew his amendment but urged that the sponsoring governments take the matter under consideration."[142] This apparently has not been done and the consequences are now upon us.

France also noted the possibility of long deadlock in the Security Council, and also made an abortive attempt to provide against it. The French proposal was in essence this:[143]

> "Should the Council not succeed in reaching a decision, the members of the Organization reserve to themselves the right to act as they may consider necessary and in the interest of peace, right and justice."

But France also was forced to withdraw her proposal. What she had in mind was clearly inspired by the experience of the League of Nations, and more particularly Article 15, paragraph 7 of the Covenant. However, no reference to the experience of the League, explicit or implicit, could prevail over the stubborn determination of the Four Sponsoring Governments, in which France finally concurred, to have the Yalta voting formula in the Charter or to have no Charter at all. Characteristic of this is the following statement of the United States delegate in Committee III/1 at the June 12, 1945, meeting:[144] The US Delegate

> "requested the delegates to cast their votes in favor of the present voting provisions and to do so in the knowledge that they were creating one of the greatest documents drawn by the hand of man. He was aware of the discouragement which had been voiced by certain delegates, but this was not the first time in history that cynicism had presided at the birth of great events. He hoped that certain statesmen here would prove to be as wrong as those who had voiced doubts and apprehensions at the time of the framing of the United States Constitution."

The powers were warned of the consequences. Those who so grandiloquently proclaimed the virtues of the Charter and who urged upon a sceptical conference the acceptance of the Yalta voting formula, now invoke the unworkability of that formula as an excuse for departing from it by less than five-power agreement. In thus availing themselves of the obvious shortcomings of the voting rule laid down by themselves for the

[142] *Id.* at 516.
[143] Document 1102/III/1/62. UNCIO Documents, vol. XI, p. 696.
[144] Document 956/III/1/47. UNCIO Documents, vol. XI, p. 490.

Security Council, they are bound to admit the general weakness of the conception upon which they based the main pillar and guardian of the post-war security system. Many of the other governments participating in the San Francisco Conference share the responsibility. For the "veto fixation" which got hold of so many delegates and which resulted in incessant attacks on the great power "veto," resulted merely in making "the definition and use of the veto more rigid and restrictive than it might otherwise have been. Article 27 was stiffened and toughened by the blasts of small-power eloquence."[145] This may account in part for the omission of exploring fully the implications of the Yalta voting formula on the Council's functions for preserving peace and security.

The second main defense of present Security Council practice—the attempted analogy between absence and abstention—is also untenable, because it fails to do justice to the notion or meaning of abstention which, as developed elsewhere in this paper, is a manifestation of consent in disguise. Abstention is not, of course, consent in disguise or otherwise to the resolution in question; rather it is consent to the action which is to result from the resolution. Such a manifestation, disguised or implied, cannot be said to exist if the permanent member in question, in official statements and communications has made the imputation of such consent impossible. Mr. Malik, before leaving the Security Council on January 13, 1950, announced on behalf of the Soviet Union that it would "not recognize as legal any decision of the Security Council adopted with the participation of the representative of the Kuomintang group, and will not be guided by any such decision." It is true that he did not specifically say then that the Soviet Union would not recognize as legal and would not be guided by decisions adopted in its absence. But if this ommission is significant, it was remedied in subsequent written communications and in statements before the Security Council at the meetings held since August 1, 1950.

Another point should be made here. The General Assembly Resolution 267 (III) of April 14, 1949, accepted by all the five permanent members of the Security Council, provided for consultation among the permanent members before voting.[146] There is no evidence available to the public as to whether such consultations took place before the June 25 or the June 27, 1950, resolutions. If they had taken place, it would have been possible perhaps to ascertain what the view of the Soviet Union was regarding the consequences of its own absence and its attitude to the proposed resolutions. Its argument concerning the presence of the "Kuomintang group" representative might well have been disregarded, as that question had been disposed of in the only manner in which the Security Council could resolve such matters. It would not have been possible to dispose with equal ease of the point of view of the Soviet Union about the consequences which it attached to its own absence.

It is of course true that strict application of Article 27, paragraph 3, may result in deadlock or "paralysis" of the Security Council. But that is what was intended. The great powers meant by their adoption of the Yalta voting rule that the Security Council

[145] HASLUCK, *op. cit. supra* note 5, at 131.
[146] Security Council, *Official Records* (4th year), no. 48, pp. 1, 2.

should take no action unless each of the big five agreed to it. The Council was infected from birth with the virus of paralysis. Under the Yalta rule, the Council can act if its five main limbs and at least two others move in the same direction, otherwise it cannot act at all. This was foreseen at the San Francisco Conference. It was precisely for this reason that extended powers were then conferred upon the General Assembly of the United Nations—powers which went well beyond anything contemplated at Dumbarton Oaks. This being so, what difference can or does it make whether the paralysis of the Security Council is the result of an obstructionist veto or of an equally obstructionist absence? The Charter is not at all concerned with the "veto." The Charter does require the concurring vote of the five permanent members, and is not concerned with the manner or circumstances which prevent the fulfilment of this requirement. It might have been drafted otherwise. As the Canadian and French proposals referred to above indicate, different and in many ways sounder solutions to the voting problem in the Security Council were before the San Francisco Conference. The great powers, however, were unwilling to change the Yalta voting formula in any way. That formula represented not the minimum but the maximum of agreement that could be reached by them then as well as now.

The Security Council is not identical with the United Nations, and a "paralysis" of the former need not extend to the General Assembly and its clearly stated powers to direct the activities of the United Nations even in matters affecting international peace and security.[147] Legally and politically, action by the General Assembly could have produced in the Korean crisis substantially the same results as those achieved by means of Security Council resolutions without being open to the criticism to which the latter is exposed. At the 476th meeting of the Security Council, Sir Gladwyn Jebb suggested that the resolutions adopted by the Council since June 25 were in the nature of recommendations pursuant to Article 39 of the Charter. They were therefore legally not binding even if they were in conformity with Article 27, paragraph 3, and their execution depended upon the will of the individual members of the United Nations. Similar results would have been achieved by resolutions of the General Assembly. Having declared the impossibility of the Security Council to function owing to the absence of one of the permanent members, the Assembly could have called upon the member governments to lend assistance to the Republic of Korea, etc.

With reference to Article 2, paragraph 5, the results of such General Assembly action would have been substantially the same as if there had been a Security Council resolution. The positive obligation (to "give to the United Nations every assistance in any action it takes in accordance with the present Charter") would come into play in the case of action taken by the General Assembly as well as in the case of action taken by the Security Council. On the other hand, the negative obligation (to "refrain from giving assistance to any state against which the United Nations is taking preventive or enforcement action") would not arise in either case. In the first place, the authorities of Northern Ko-

[147] Cf. KELSEN, *op. cit. supra* note 3, at 266.

rea have not been regarded as a "state" by the Security Council and probably would not have been so regarded by the General Assembly; and secondly the action contemplated in the Security Council resolutions cannot be regarded, any more than would be resolutions of the General Assembly, as "preventive or enforcement action,"—terminology generally taken to refer only to action pursuant to Articles 41 and 42, not to resolutions based on Article 39.

Moreover, it is at least arguable, though perhaps doubtful, that members of the United Nations were in the position to carry out the measures envisaged in the Council resolutions under reference even if it were admitted that formally they did not conform to the mandatory requirement of Article 27, paragraph 3. They may not have felt bound to carry them out any more than they would if the Council had taken a formally valid recommendation; they may none the less have felt it desirable or even imperative to carry them out. Such was the case in the Syria-Lebanese question before the Security Council in 1946. A draft resolution on this question was put to the vote at the 23rd meeting, February 16, 1946, and "vetoed" by the Soviet representative. Mr. Bidault (France) then said:

> "from a legal standpoint, this vote does not create an obligation.
>
> "However, I should like to add in the name of France that, having signified my agreement to the text submitted to us, without, however, taking part in the voting, I shall not now withdraw my consent on purely formal grounds, and I shall stand by my decision."

Similarly, Mr. Bevin (United Kingdom) declared:[148]

> "We will, as a party to this conflict, carry out the majority decision of the Council as expressed in the vote."

In like manner, the 53 members of the United Nations who are said to support in one way or another the measures recommended in the Korean affair might have been equally active in their support without contending that the June 25 and 27 resolutions were adopted by the Council in conformity with Article 27, paragraph 3, since in any event, as Sir Gladwyn Jebb suggested at the 476th meeting, the function of the Security Council in the Korean affair is not an operating one.[149]

It is characteristic of the extent to which members of the Security Council as well as others have become victims of the "veto complex" that nearly all the arguments in favor of the "absence equals abstention" thesis revolve around an interpretation of Article 27,

[148] Security Council, *Official Records* (1st year), First Series, no. 1, p. 368.

[149] At least one of the 53 member governments appears to have taken this view of the Security Council resolutions. Mr. Osten Unden, Minister of Foreign Affairs of the Government of Sweden, in his cablegram of July 3, 1950, to the Secretary-General, said: "By the resolution of June 25th the members of the Security Council who voted for the resolution called upon all members of the United Nations to refrain from giving assistance to the North Korean Authorities"; and again "as far as the Resolution of June 27th is concerned the members of the Security Council who have voted for it have recommended. . . ." Document S/1564. This indicates that the Swedish Government at least considers the resolutions and recommendations contained therein as resolutions accepted by those members of the Security Council who voted "in favor" rather than as resolutions formally adopted as such by the Security Council.

paragraph 3, which finds almost no support in its text or history. The principle expressed therein is that of unanimity of the five permanent members, and not that of the veto. The paragraph does not say that a substantive resolution is lost or rejected when one permanent member votes against it, which is the notion underlying the "veto" approach. It does say, on the contrary, that decisions on all matters other than of procedure shall "be made by an affirmative vote of seven members including the concurring votes of the permanent members." It is consequently the duty of the President of the Security Council to declare the result of a vote in those terms. That is the expression of the principle of unanimity and of the traditional principle of consent in international law as applied to voting in international organizations. This principle is satisfied, of course, by an affirmative and concurring vote—that is by express consent to the proposed Security Council action. It is also satisfied by abstention—that is by tacit consent to the Council action. It is not satisfied when there is neither express not tacit consent to the proposed Council action. The precedents of abstention are many and supported, as they must be, by all of the permanent members of the Security Council and encouraged by the General Assembly itself. The same cannot be said of absences.[150]

Whether the recent conduct of the Security Council in the Korean affair in particular has created or will create precedents accepted by all of the permanent members of the Council remains at this writing in the realm of doubt. The legal effect of absence is, after all, a question of the interpretation of the Charter, even though in this respect the Charter, like many other international instruments, is expressive of a political agreement. This agreement was formalized at the Yalta Conference, in the Statement of the Four Sponsoring Governments in which France concurred, and finally in the Charter itself. While the validity and binding force of the Statement, or certain parts of it, have been the subject of different interpretations on different occasions in the Security Council and elsewhere, it still remains an important piece of evidence regarding the meaning attached to the principle of unanimity by the five permanent members of the Security Council and expressed in Article 27, paragraph 3, of the Charter. In spite of its political and ideological overtones, the controversy regarding the legal effect of the absence of a permanent member from the Security Council reduces itself thus to a question of the proper interpretation of one of the fundamental clauses in the Charter; like other such questions which have arisen in the past, this one is believed to be susceptible of objective and judicial determination.

[150] At the second part of the First Session of the General Assembly, Mr. Noel Baker (United Kingdom) expressed in the First Committee the hope that "it could be agreed that, as a customary practice, neither absence nor abstention should count as a veto." Official Records of the Second Part of the First Session of the General Assembly, First Committee, p. 115. See also *Suggestions regarding voting in the Security Council laid before the permanent members by the United Kingdom Secretary for Foreign Affairs on 15 November 1946*, Document A/C.1/95, *id.* at 327. Suggestion 7 reads: "It would be of great advantage if it were possible to provide, by some means, that a permanent member could abstain from voting without automatically vetoing the proposal. Similarly, that mere absence of a permanent member should not have the effect of a veto." This official British proposal made as it was after the Iranian incident involving the first "walk-out" of the Soviet Union, came to naught. This is no doubt significant as is Mr. Noel Baker's reference to "customary practice" growing out of agreement. Obviously, the Iranian incident created no such "customary practice" which would have a bearing for the future. And no "customary practice" in this matter can grow out of disagreement between the five permanent members of the Security Council. Agreement there is regarding abstention; there is none regarding absence.

# THE DOUBLE VETO AND THE FOUR-POWER STATEMENT ON VOTING IN THE SECURITY COUNCIL

Under Article 109, Section 3, of the United Nations Charter, the question of the Charter's revision is automatically placed on the agenda in 1955, and a general conference must be called on the vote of a majority of the General Assembly and any seven members of the Security Council. In view of this, it becomes especially important to examine certain of the problems which the United Nations has faced under its present Charter with a view to determining whether change in any provision is necessary. One problem which has bedeviled the Security Council almost from its inception is what procedure to follow in deciding the preliminary question whether a given proposal is a matter of procedure requiring a simple majority of seven members, or a matter of substance requiring a qualified majority of seven members, including the votes of the five permanent members.[1] If it is decided that the preliminary question is governed by the principle of unanimity of the five permanent members, then any permanent member may establish the non-procedural character of a given proposal by use of the veto and then may veto the proposal itself. This has come to be called, in and out of the Security Council, the double veto. If the veto itself is unpopular among members and commentators on the Charter, the double veto is

[1] The procedure for voting in the Security Council is found in Article 27:

1. Each member of the Security Council shall have one vote.
2. Decisions of the Security Council on procedural matters shall be made by an affirmative vote of seven members.
3. Decisions of the Security Council on all other matters shall be made by an affirmative vote of seven members including the concurring votes of the permanent members . . . .

Throughout this paper the term unqualified majority will be used to represent a vote on which a majority of any seven members is required, that is, the vote on a procedural issue; the term qualified majority will be used to represent a vote requiring a majority of seven, including the concurring vote of the permanent members, that is, the vote on a substantive issue.

even more so. Resolution of the question is made more difficult by the prevailing tendency to restrict the application of the veto by a liberal interpretation of the so-called Yalta voting formula in Article 27 of the Charter.[2]

To elucidate the problem of the double veto it will be necessary to examine the range and binding character of the Statement by the Delegations of the Four Sponsoring Governments on Voting Procedures in the Security Council, the practice of the Security Council in answering the preliminary question, and finally the presidential rulings on this subject. An examination of the experience of the League of Nations will place our inquiry in a better perspective.[3]

## I. THE DOUBLE VETO IN THE LEAGUE OF NATIONS

Unlike the recent history of the United Nations, there were only one or two instances when the Assembly or the Council of the League was confronted with the preliminary question, which under the Covenant involved deciding whether a proposal required the unanimous vote provided for matters of substance in Article 5, paragraph 1, or the majority vote provided for matters of procedure in Article 5, paragraph 2.[4]

The first discussion of this problem was in a report of the committee on the election of the four non-permanent members of the Council, which recommended geographical distribution and adopted by a majority vote the view that the provisions of the proposed resolutions be deemed matters of procedure within Article 5, paragraph 2. In the ensuing debate the President of the Assembly, Mr. Hymans (Belgium), referring to this draft resolution, said: "As a matter of fact these provisions are not simply matters of procedure . . . . [T]hey must be passed unanimously,"[5] Mr. Schanzer (Italy) took a similar position and pointed out that the provision concerning geographical distribution "constitutes an amendment . . . of the Covenant, and as such it is a question of principle."[6] Some members supported and others opposed this view, but the reporter of the Committee,

[2] Resolution 267 (III), GEN. ASSEMBLY OFFICIAL RECORDS, 3d Sess., Pt. II (Resolutions) 7 (1948), is evidence of this tendency, as is also the practice of the Security Council in not considering abstention of even a permanent member as a negative vote. But see Gross, *Voting in the Security Council*, 60 Yale L.J. 229–37 (1951). See also *supra*, pp. 429–471. Even more radical is Resolution 377 (V), the Acheson Plan. GEN. ASSEMBLY OFFICIAL RECORDS, 5th Sess., Supp. No. 20 at 10 (1950).

[3] Some commentators have objected to comparison on the ground that what is substantive under the Charter is a residual concept, that is, determined by reference to what is procedural, while under the Covenant a majority vote for questions of procedure was the exception to the general rule of unanimity. This distinction, it is argued, makes discussions of the Covenant irrelevant in interpretation of the Charter. See JIMENEZ DE ARECHAGA, VOTING AND THE HANDLING OF DISPUTES IN THE SECURITY COUNCIL 9 (1950).

[4] COVENANT OF THE LEAGUE OF NATIONS ART. 5, ¶ 1:

Except where otherwise expressly provided in this Covenant or by the terms of the present Treaty, decisions at any meeting of the Assembly or of the Council shall require the agreement of all the Members of the League represented at the meeting.

¶ 2:

All matters of procedure at meetings of the Assembly or of the Council, including the appointment of Committees to investigate particular matters, shall be regulated by the Assembly or by the Council and may be decided by a majority of the Members of the League represented at the meeting.

[5] LEAGUE OF NATIONS RECORDS OF FIRST ASSEMBLY (Plenary Meetings) 423 (1920).

[6] *Id.* (Plenary Meetings) at 427.

Mr. Balfour (British Empire), suggested that the provision regarding geographical distribution be made a recommendation to the members rather than a substantive proposal so that the legal validity of the committee's resolutions could not be challenged. This suggestion was accepted and adopted by a vote of 27 to 4.[7]

Commentators, citing the above incident, have concluded that resolution of the preliminary question was itself a substantive question and could be decided only by a unanimous vote.[8] Some writers, however, relying on an incident which occurred during the Council's debates on the Japanese invasion of Manchuria, seem to incline to the view that the preliminary question could be considered as procedural and could therefore be decided by majority vote.[9] The Council had authorized its President, Mr. Briand (France), to forward the minutes of the Council together with documents relating to this question to the United States Government for its information. The President then proposed United States representation at the Council table. The Japanese representative raised the preliminary question and submitted a memorandum expressing the Japanese government's opinion as follows:

> In the present case, two things have to be distinguished — namely, the question of substance arising in regard to the invitation of a State not a Member of the League, and the question of the sending of the actual invitation after the question of substance has been settled. As regards the question of substance . . . the decision . . . can only be taken by a unanimous vote. The only question on which a majority vote is allowable is the question of the sending of the invitation, for this is a question of procedure.[10]

Preceding the vote on the proposed invitation to the United States, the President pointed out that there was a misunderstanding, that there was no question of issuing an invitation but merely of "prolonging" by more continued contact a form of cooperation with the United States which already existed and had been decided upon unanimously. Lord Reading (British Empire) argued along similar lines and, referring to the Japanese memorandum quoted above, "felt justified in assuming that the Japanese representative himself admitted that the question was one of procedure."[11] Other members associated themselves with the statements made by the President and Lord Reading who emphasized that the constitutional question of the vote required to resolve the preliminary question would be "strictly reserved."[12] The proposal was then put to the vote and adopted by 13 votes to 1 (Japan).[13] In these circumstances the view of the President prevailed that

[7] *Id.* (Plenary Meetings) at 433–35. The whole discussion of this problem may be found in *id.* (Plenary Meetings) at 418–35.

[8] *E.g.*, JOHN F. WILLIAMS, CHAPTERS ON CURRENT INTERNATIONAL LAW AND THE LEAGUE OF NATIONS 439, 443 (1929); I SCHÜCKING AND WEHBERG, DIE SATZUNG DES VÖLKERBUNDES 457–58, 517 (3d ed. 1931). See also Burton, who points out that in practice, however, the question was usually left open "in the hope, usually justified, that agreement on its procedural nature may later become possible." M. E. BURTON, THE ASSEMBLY OF THE LEAGUE OF NATIONS 182 (1941).

[9] Stone, *The Rule of Unanimity: The Practice of the Council and Assembly of the League of Nations*, 14 BRIT. Y.B. INT'L LAW 18, 40 (1933); RICHES, MAJORITY RULE IN INTERNATIONAL ORGANIZATION 24 n.56 (1940).

[10] 12 LEAGUE OF NATIONS OFFICIAL JOURNAL 2325 (1931).

[11] 12 *id.* at 2327.

[12] *Ibid.* But see RAY, LA POLITIQUE ET LA JURISPRUDENCE DE LA SOCIÉTÉ DES NATIONS 30 (1932).

[13] 12 LEAGUE OF NATIONS OFFICIAL JOURNAL 2329 (1931).

since the principle of cooperation with the United States had been adopted unanimously, a majority vote was deemed sufficient to decide the form of this cooperation. Moreover, the President declared that "it was, of course, understood that note was taken of the reservations made by the Japanese representative, and that the constitutional question remained intact and could not be settled by the vote which had been given."[14] This incident then, far from supporting the construction placed upon it, shows adherence to the principle that the constitutional question could not be settled by a majority vote.[15]

To sum up: the experience of the League, though far from extensive, indicates that, pursuant to Article 5 of the Covenant, resolution of the preliminary question whether a matter was one of procedure or substance was treated in both the Council and the Assembly as constituting a substantive question and was therefore subject to the unanimity rule.

## II. STATEMENT BY THE DELEGATIONS OF THE FOUR SPONSORING GOVERNMENTS ON VOTING PROCEDURE IN THE SECURITY COUNCIL

### A. Contents

During the San Francisco Conference there was much debate concerning Article 27, and the subcommittee on clarification of the voting formula addressed a formal questionnaire concerning exercise of the veto in the Security Council to the sponsoring powers—Russia, Great Britiain, China, and the United States.[16] These four delegations then prepared a joint statement "designed to interpret the formula *officially,* insofar as such an interpretation of a basic constitutional provision could appropriately be made in advance of its adoption and without any practical experience as to the operation of the Organization or the Security Council."[17] This joint Statement, with which France associated herself, clarified to some extent the Yalta voting formula. In Part I, it gave several examples of decisions to be governed by the unqualified majority vote of any seven members and of other decisions to be governed by a qualified majority. The latter are those decisions which, according to the Statement, may well initiate a "chain of events which might, in the end, require the Council under its responsibilities to invoke measures of enforcement" under Chapter VII. The first link in the chain of events is the ordering of an investigation. For at that time "the Council has to consider whether the investigation—which may involve calling for reports, hearing witnesses, dispatching a commission of inquiry,

[14] 12 *id.* at 2330.

[15] See Koo, Voting Procedures in International Political Organizations 101 (1947). Discussion on the whole question is in 12 League of Nations Official Journal, 2272–2454 (1931).

[16] 11 U.N. Conf. Int'l Org. Docs. 699 (1945).

[17] Report of the Chairman of U.S. Delegation to the President in *Hearings before the Senate Committee on Foreign Relations on the Charter of the United Nations, 79th Cong.* 1st Sess. 44 (1945) (emphasis supplied). The Statement is reprinted in 11 U.N. Conf. Int'l Org. Docs. 710 (1945).

or other means—might not further aggravate the situation."[18] This is obviously a very general standard which leaves many decisions[19] to the judgment of the Council, since the Charter itself is silent as to the specific vote required. Therefore in Part II of the Statement the sponsoring governments answered the question of the subcommittee which they felt had not been answered in Part I. As this question and the official answer to it are of importance for the following analysis, they are here reproduced in full.

In case a decision has to be taken as to whether a certain point is a procedural matter, is that preliminary question to be considered in itself as a procedural matter or is the veto applicable to such preliminary question?

1. In the opinion of the Delegations of the Sponsoring Governments, the Draft Charter itself contains an indication of the application of the voting procedures to the various functions of the Council.

2. In this case, it will be unlikely that there will arise in the future any matters of great importance on which a decision will have to be made as to whether a procedural vote would apply. Should, however, such a matter arise, the decision regarding the preliminary question as to whether such a matter is procedural must be taken by a vote of seven members of the Security Council, including the concurring votes of the permanent members.[20]

No formal action was taken by the Committee or the San Francisco Conference concerning the Statement.[21] The practice of the Security Council reveals a divergence of opinion on the binding character and range of the Statement, and particularly on the nature of the vote required and the applicability of presidential rulings to resolve the preliminary question.

### B. Its Binding Character

In the discussions of the Security Council, a distinction has been made with respect to the binding force of the Statement for the Council or the United Nations in general, for the non-permanent members, and for the permanent members. As far as the first question is concerned Mr. Evatt (Australia) expressed the views of many when he stated: "What was placed in a document at San Francisco does not govern the interpretation of the Charter. It is not contained in the Charter. It does not bind the Security Council . . . . Those of us who opposed the veto principle in certain respects at San Francisco carefully guarded lest that should be held as authoritative and binding."[22] On the other

[18] Statement, Pt. I, ¶ 5.

[19] For a list of such matters, see Koo, *op. cit. supra* note 15, at 193.

[20] II U.S. Conf. Int'l Org. Docs. 707, 713–14 (1945). The inclusion of this last paragraph was part of a general compromise with the Soviet Union concerning the range of application of the Statement. See p. 487 *infra*.

[21] For a detailed discussion of the drafting of the Statement see Koo, *op. cit. supra* note 15, at 147–52, 159–95.

[22] Security Council Official Records, 1st Year, 1st Ser., No. 2 at 416 (1946).

hand, Mr. Tarasenko (Ukranian S.S.R.) criticized attempts to disregard the Statement as quite illegal, contrary to its spirit, and "the spirit of the Charter itself since the Declaration is an inseparable part of the Charter."[23]

It has often been declared in the Security Council that the Statement was not binding on non-permanent members. This would seem to reinforce the position of those who deny that it is binding on the Council as such. Even the Soviet Union, the strongest and most vocal protagonist of the Statement, has not contended that it was binding on the Council or the non-permanent members,[24] maintaining in this respect a position less extreme than Mr. Tarasenko's. Obviously non-permanent members of the Council who denied that the Statement was binding on the United Nations or the Security Council also denied that it had any binding effect on themselves.[25] Commenting on this attitude, however, Mr. Gromyko observed that "it would be a very poor sample of cooperation were the smaller Powers to ignore a document which embodies and supplements the obligations assumed by the Great Powers under the United Nations Charter."[26]

There has been more discussion concerning the binding effect of the Statement on the *permanent* members. The Soviet government has never wavered in its position that it was binding on the permanent members and castigated the other permanent members when it thought they were failing to live up to the declaration made at San Francisco.[27] Great Britain also regarded the Statement as binding on the permanent members but on more than one occasion referred the Soviet Union to paragraph 8 of Part I of the Statement which declared that it was not to be assumed "that the permanent members, any more than the non-permanent members, would use their veto power wilfully to obstruct the operation of the Council."[28] On the other hand, Mr. Arce (Argentina) challenged the binding character of the Statement on the ground that the United States and the United Kingdom were "forgetting the rule of international law according to which even treaties formally signed and ratified by the parliaments concerned may be revoked when the conditions under which agreement was reached have changed. How can it be maintained that a mere statement which was not even in the form of an agreement should not now be revoked?"[29]

This implied invitation to the permanent members to apply the doctrine of *rebus sic stantibus* (changed circumstances) to revoke the Statement has not been accepted. It is interesting, however, to compare Mr. Arce's position with the developing position of the

[23] *Id.*, 3d Year, No. 73 at 3–4 (1948).

[24] See remarks of Mr. Gromyko, *id.*, 2d Year, No. 89 at 2398, 2401 (1947).

[25] See remarks of Mr. Muñoz (Argentina), *id.*, 3d Year, No. 71 at 38 (1948); General McNaughton (Canada), *id.*, 3d Year, No. 71 at 40; Mr. El-Khouri (Syria), *id.*, 3d Year, No. 73 at 4. Mr. van Kleffens (Netherlands) expressed an isolated view when he stated: "The most we can say about . . . [the Statement], although some may express reservations, is that it was to a greater or lesser extent acquiesced." But he did distinguish the Statement from the Charter. *Id.*, 1st Year, 1st Ser., No. 2 at 423 (1946); *id.*, 1st Year, 1st Ser., No. I at 129.

[26] *Id.*, 3d Year, No. 73 at 9 (1948).

[27] See *id.*, 1st Year, 1st Ser., No. 2 at 424 (1946); *id.*, 2d Year, No. 89 at 2398 (1947).

[28] *Id.*, 3d Year, No. 71 at 38 (1948); *id.*, 3d Year, No. 73 at 22.

[29] *Id.*, 3d Year, No. 73 at 12–13.

United States. Mr. Dulles, speaking to a committee of the General Assembly in 1947, stated that since the Statement rested on several unwarranted assumptions, the United States would feel free to seek better voting procedures, but would not abandon the Statement until the matter were further explored.[30] This view, however, was not immediately put forth in the Security Council debates by the United States. When Mr. Gromyko declared a United States draft resolution rejected because he had voted in the negative both on the resolution and the preliminary question, Mr. Herschel Johnson (United States) protested against the frustration of "the will of this Council" but declared that the Soviet delegate was "within his technical rights in deciding that this matter was, from his point of view, not a question of procedure."[31]

In a debate in the Security Council in 1948, Mr. Austin quoted Mr. Dulles' statement but concluded: "You may call it what you like: if it is an agreement, we stand by the agreement; if it is a statement, we stand by the statement."[32] Later, however, he clarified his earlier remarks:

> I did not say that the United States considered itself bound by the statement made in San Francisco . . . but I said exactly the opposite. . . . I said that we had not changed our attitude. We feel free, however, to do so. . . . and I reserve the right of my Government to do so whenever that course seems advisable.[33]

The foregoing statements demonstrate that the permanent members of the Security Council, for the present time at any rate, have accepted the Statement as binding,[34] though there appeared differences of opinion as to its proper use. To be sure, there is a sharp difference in emphasis. Whereas the Soviet Union regarded the Statement as binding, even constituting an integral part of the Charter obligations,[35] the United States reserved its position for the future and the United Kingdom warned the Soviet Union that abuse might undermine the Statement.

There was much discussion in 1950 as to the binding character of the Statement in the debate on the Chinese Communists' complaint of armed invasion of Formosa. Here an attempt was made to use the "double veto" and apparently defeated. As this case has been described as a "radical departure from all previous precedents on the double veto,"[36] and one in which "the practice of a presidential ruling to prevent a double veto was applied for the first time,"[37] it merits some attention. On September 29, 1950, the President of the Council, Sir Gladwyn Jebb (United Kingdom), submitted to vote an

[30] Quoted by Mr. Austin in *id.*, 3d Year, No. 73 at 5, 6 .The assumptions which Mr. Dulles referred to were: it was unlikely that the veto would be used wilfully; investigations would be apt to lead to active measures; it was unlikely that there would be matters of great importance on which the preliminary vote would have to be taken.

[31] *Id.*, 2d Year, No. 89 at 2401 (1947).

[32] *Id.*, 3d Year, No. 73 at 6 (1948).

[33] *Id.*, 3d Year, No. 73 at 29.

[34] The French representative expressed this view in *id.*, 5th Year, No. 48 at 8 (1950) and the Chinese representative in *id.*, 3d Year, No. 73 at 27 (1948) and *id.*, 5th Year, No. 48 at 6 (1950).

[35] *Id.*, 3d Year, No. 73 at 32-33.

[36] Rudzinski, *The So-Called Double Veto*, 45 AM. J. INT'L L. 443, 456 (1951).

[37] JIMÉNEZ, *op. cit. supra* note 3, at 16.

Ecuadorean resolution to invite a representative of Communist China to attend meetings of the Council during the discussion of the complaint.[38] In its preamble the resolution referred to the Council's powers under Rule 39[39] of its rules of procedure. Before the vote Mr. Tsiang (China) stated that "a preliminary determination as to the nature of the vote is absolutely essential."[40] The President ruled this request out of order and suggested that he raise the question after the vote, which was 7 in favor, 3 against (China, Cuba, United States), and 1 abstention (Egypt). In the President's opinion the resolution was adopted.[41] Mr. Tsiang disagreed, referring to the Statement as well as three earlier cases in which the "double veto" was cast, and claimed "that because of the lack of my concurrence in the vote, the resolution has not been adopted."[42]

In the ensuing debate, Mr. Chauvel (France) said: "The French delegation has no intention of questioning the San Francisco Declaration, to which it subscribed" but he did not think that the resolution was "in fact a question of substance."[43] Mr. Malik (Soviet Union) delivered a lengthy refutation of Mr. Tsiang's reference to the three earlier cases and concluded that his attempt to have his vote counted as a veto was "without the least admissible basis."[44] Mr. Gross (United States) expressed the view that "The Charter of the United Nations and the Four Power Declaration of San Francisco and the precedents of the Security Council themselves seem to us solidly to support the conclusion that a motion of this kind is procedural" and referred to three invitations which had been accepted as valid although in two cases the Soviet Union had cast negative votes and in one the United Kingdom and France had done likewise.[45]

Mr. Bebler (Yugoslavia) then noted the right to insist on a qualified majority to decide the preliminary question but regarded the Chinese position as amounting to a reversal of the practice of the Council since that right "is confined to questions the procedural nature of which is in doubt. But the question of inviting States parties to a dispute is expressly mentioned as a question of procedure."[46] Mr. Tsiang nevertheless insisted on the preliminary question being put. The President, however, asked the Council to vote whether it regarded the vote on the Ecuadorean resolution as procedural. After this vote the President said: "The proposal is therefore adopted; there were 9 votes in favor, 1 against and 1 abstention."[47] Of course, it will be noted that there was no proposal before the Council and therefore none could be adopted unless one regards the confirmation of

[38] SECURITY COUNCIL OFFICIAL RECORDS, 5th Year, No. 48 at 2 (1950).

[39] "The Security Council may invite members of the Secretariat or other persons, whom it considers competent for the purpose, to supply it with information or to give other assistance in examining matters within its competence." Rule 39, Provisional Rules of Procedure, SECURITY COUNCIL DOC. NO. S/96 (1946).

[40] SECURITY COUNCIL OFFICIAL RECORDS, 5th Year, No. 48 at 3 (1950).

[41] *Id.*, 5th Year, No. 48 at 5.

[42] *Id.*, 5th Year, No. 48 at 5–7. He referred to the discussions in the Spanish, Greek, and Czechoslovak questions. See pp. 487–488, and 490 *infra*.

[43] SECURITY COUNCIL OFFICIAL RECORDS, 5th Year, No. 48 at 8 (1950).

[44] *Id.*, 5th Year, No. 48 at 10.

[45] *Id.*, 5th Year, No. 48 at 12–13.

[46] *Id.*, 5th Year, No. 49 at 1.

[47] *Id.*, 5th Year, No. 49 at 5.

the vote taken previously as a proposal. The Chinese representative claimed that his vote was a veto as provided for in the Statement, but the President ruled that "notwithstanding the objection of our Chinese colleague, the vote which the Council took this morning on the Ecuadorean resolution is procedural."[48] Thereupon, Mr. Tsiang said he had "a point of order" which, it is submitted, was perhaps a fatal mistake. He thought that the ruling of the President was ultra vires; he protested and suggested that the President's ruling be referred to the International Court of Justice for an advisory opinion.[49] The President interpreted a further intervention by Mr. Tsiang as a challenge to his ruling and submitted it to a vote under Rule 30 of the provisional rules of procedure in spite of Mr. Tsiang's observation that everybody in the Council knew that "a matter of this kind is not subject to a Presidential ruling."[50] The vote on the President's ruling was probably unique in the annals of the Security Council as no member voted in favor or against. The President interpreted this remarkable vote quite properly when he said that his ruling stood, but in Mr. Tsiang's opinion the President's ruling was arbitrary and the decisions were "illegal and therefore invalid."[51]

Whether or not resort to rulings under Rule 30 is proper in such matters will be discussed elsewhere.[52] It may be remarked here that Mr. Tsiang, having made a point of order, could not very well complain if it was disposed of under Rule 30. Moreover, in Part I of the Statement this type of question had been specifically declared to be procedural. It will be observed that no member of the Council doubted the continued validity of the Statement, although the United States, at least, took its stand as much on General Assembly Resolution 267 (III)[53] as on the Statement. Mr. Gross accepted the ruling of the President even though it ran counter to United States interest, the invitation therefore was issued, and Communist China participated in the discussion on Formosa.[54] The Statement survived this test in which it was believed to have been improperly invoked.

## C. Range of Application of the Statement

One of the most important points in defining the range of application of the Statement is to determine where it goes beyond the Charter provisions and where it merely makes them explicit. In much of the debate concerning the preliminary question it has been assumed that the requirement of a qualified majority depended on the Statement rather than on Article 27 of the Charter.[55] The practice and interpretation of the Cove-

[48] *Ibid.*

[49] *Id.*, 5th Year, No. 49 at 5–6.

[50] *Id.*, 5th Year, No. 49 at 7. The possibility of raising some substantive question which if raised might have prevented the Council from going any further with the Formosa question was suggested by Mr. Chauvel (France). *Id.*, 5th Year, No. 48 at 8. But see Mr. Tsiang's comment, *id.*, 5th Year, No. 49 at 2.

[51] *Id.*, 5th Year, No. 49 at 7–8.

[52] See pp. 489–492 *infra.*

[53] See pp. 484, 493 *infra.*

[54] See Security Council Official Records, 5th Year, No. 49 at 8–10 (1950) and *id.*, 5th Year, No. 67 at 19–20.

[55] See, *e.g.*, remarks of Mr. van Kleffens (Netherlands) and Mr. Gromyko, *id.*, 1st Year, 1st Ser., No. 2 at 422–24; Koo, *op. cit. supra* note 15, at 193.

nant of the League discussed above and analysis of the text of Article 27 shows this view to be erroneous. Although Article 27 of the Charter differs in words from Article 5 of the Covenant, it is essentially the same in meaning. A simple majority of seven members under Article 27, paragraph 2 is required for procedural matters, whereas a qualified majority of seven members under paragraph 3 is required for all other matters. Resolution of the question whether a matter is procedural should not itself be considered procedural. Whether paragraph 2 or 3 applies involves an interpretation of the Charter, and it can hardly be argued that interpretation of the Charter is "intrinsically" procedural or that it belongs to that category of matters usually deemed procedural.[56]

But this does not resolve the further question whether the preliminary question can be raised indiscriminately or only with reference to genuinely doubtful matters. Three views have been propounded concerning the use of the preliminary question. According to one, identified with the Soviet position, the preliminary question can be raised with respect to any vote. According to another equally extreme position, it may not be raised with respect to any. The intermediate position would limit its use to doubtful cases.

Certain remarks of the Soviet representaitve are relied upon to support the first view. In connection with the admission of Albania to membership, Mr. Gromyko reminded the Council of the Statement and said, "the representatives of all the States who are permanent members of the Security Council cannot fail to agree that if any one of the permanent members of the Security Council objects to any particular proposal being regarded as procedural, no positive decision can be made."[57] This remark is consistent with the intermediate position if an objection is required to be bona fide.[58] If the Soviet government had espoused the extreme view that under the Statement it had discretionary power to transform *any* procedural matter into a substantive one, it exercised this power with remarkable restraint considering its free use of the veto and its violent opposition to certain questions and proposals. It may be remarked that every time the Soviet Union exercised the double veto, it was supported by one or more of the permanent members in the vote on the preliminary question: in the Spanish question, by France; in the Albanian question, by China, France, and Great Britain. In the Greek question, no one voted with the Soviet Union, but the United States representative believed it to be acting within its technical rights; and in the Czechoslovak question, the Soviet Union was materially sup-

[56] See KELSEN, THE LAW OF THE UNITED NATIONS 248, 258 (1950). Mr. Lange (Poland) has said: "Obviously, whether the matter is procedural or not is not a procedural matter. Consequently, paragraph 3 of Article 27 applies, and I think there is *no need to invoke in any way, or even discuss* the agreement among the five permanent members." And Mr. Johnson (United States) at the same meeting said: "I think there is no doubt that under the existing agreements and *under the Charter* the President has been within his technical rights in deciding that this matter was, from his point of view, not a question of procedure." SECURITY COUNCIL OFFICIAL RECORDS, 2d Year, No. 89 at 2401 (1947) (emphasis supplied in both quotations).

[57] *Id.*, 1st Year, 2d Ser., No. 5 at 130 (1946). Mr. Gromyko spoke in Russian and the French translation of these words is *"une proposition donnée"* which should be rendered "a" rather than "any" particular proposal.

[58] Mr. Vishinsky's remarks in 1946 to the same effect were directed solely to the particular resolution that was before the Council. Moreover, both Mr. Wellington Koo (China) and Mr. Riaz (Egypt), whose delegation had submitted the resolution, agreed with Mr. Vishinsky that the matter was clearly one of substance. *Id.*, 1st Year, 1st Ser., No. 1 at 129–31 (1946).

ported by the abstention of France, Great Britain, and the United States. The radical view of the powers accruing to the permanent members under the Statement was indeed formulated by Mr. Evatt[59] and its use was attempted by China, unsupported by any member, in the Formosa question.

The opposite extreme was developed by some writers evaluating the lessons of the Formosa case. It is true that Mr. Tsiang's attempt to raise the preliminary question was defeated. But Part I of the Statement had specifically declared this type of question to be procedural. The underlying presumption of the Statement is, of course, that matters not considered as procedural by the Statement or the Charter are, in principle, substantive, but this presumption can be overcome by the qualified majority. Thus, though the end result in the Formosa case—in effect a rejection of the attempt by the Chinese Government to invoke the Statement—appears justified in terms of the Statement itself, attempts to read into it the rather far-reaching implication that the preliminary question may never be raised seem unjustified.[60]

There remains then the middle way, the way indicated by the Statement as well as by the Charter, that the preliminary question cannot properly be raised and subjected to the qualified vote where there is merely a difference of opinion and not a reasoned doubt as to the interpretation of the Charter.[61] Consideration of the Chilean resolution on the Czechoslovak case[62] offers an instructive example of the procedure to be used in determining whether there is a genuine doubt or merely a difference of opinion. The President, after careful review of the Statement, viewed the resolution as involving an "investigation."[63] "Therefore . . . it seems . . . that the question [whether this is a matter of substance or procedure] may appear doubtful and that, in the circumstances, the final provision of the Declaration, according to which the concurring vote of the five permanent members is necessary to decide whether a question is a matter of procedure, retains its importance."[64]

Also in the Formosa case, Mr. Gross (United States) made the point that "part II of

[59] Discussing a ruling upholding, in effect, the double veto, he stated "the permanent member, according to that ruling, can say, not only 'I can veto the decision of the Council,' but, 'I can determine the question which I will veto.' " *Id.*, 1st Year, 1st Ser., No. 2 at 425 (1946). Mr. Evatt's view has been restated by Mr. El-Khouri (Syria) and Mr. Austin (United States). *Id.*, 3d Year, No. 63 at 23, 25 (1948) and *id.*, 3d Year, No. 73 at 17, 30.

[60] See pp. 491–492 *infra* for views of one commentator who sees far-reaching implications in the Formosa case. The most remarkable interpretation of the Charter and Statement provisions for answering the preliminary question was given by Mr. El-Khouri (Syria), as President of the Council, during the discussion concerning the procedural or substantive character of the resolution authorizing transmission of the first three reports of the Atomic Energy Commission to the General Assembly. Mr. El-Khouri, conceding that the permanent members were bound by the Statement, stated that if the permanent members agreed that a resolution were procedural, then the preliminary question would be so decided, presumably on the ground that there would not be more than six votes opposed. But Mr. El-Khouri implied that if the permanent members were divided and if there were seven votes in favor of the view that the draft resolution was procedural, he would so rule. See Security Council Official Records, 3d Year, No. 88 at 19 (1948). Mr. Gromyko, arguing that the resolution was substantive, nevertheless refrained from pressing matters to a vote, presumably anticipating certain defeat if he did. The resolution was adopted by nine votes in favor with two abstentions, one of which was Russia.

[61] See Rudzinski, *supra* note 36, at 456.

[62] See pp. 490–491 *infra*.

[63] He was referring to that part of the Statement giving examples of the type of decision to be governed by vote of a qualified majority. See pp. 476–477 *supra*.

[64] Security Council Official Records, 3d Year, No. 73 at 20–21 (1948).

the San Francisco Declaration cannot be taken as altering or rendering illusory part I of that statement,"[65] and that it "was never intended, and cannot properly be construed, as giving the five permanent members of the Security Council the right to use the device of the double veto to determine unilaterally as non-procedural, matters which according to the Charter, or by agreement contained in part I of the San Francisco Declaration, are procedural."[66] By the same token, it is submitted, matters which according to the Charter and the Statement are non-procedural cannot by the device of a simple presidential ruling be turned into procedural matters or points of order. To steer a middle course is admittedly difficult, but, as the practice of the Security Council has shown, not impossible. General Assembly Resolution 267 (III) offers a further guide in steering the difficult middle course.[67] Unfortunately it was not accepted by all the permanent members of the Council although Mr. Gross stated that his delegation had been guided by it in the Formosa question.[68] But the General Assembly did not say, as the United States representative suggested in 1950,[69] that the thirty-five decisions listed in the annex of the Resolution fell into a procedural category. The General Assembly merely recommended that "the decisions set forth in the attached annex *be deemed* procedural and that the members of the Security Council conduct their business accordingly."[70] To recommend that certain decisions be deemed procedural is obviously quite different from saying that they are procedural. Whatever the value of the General Assembly recommendation in this field, it might conceivably be argued that the General Assembly rendered a disservice to the development of sound voting procedures in the Security Council in merely "deeming" certain decisions to be procedural which, in the practice of the Council and pursuant to the Statement, have been treated as procedural decisions. This is particularly true of the invitation to parties to a dispute irrespective of whether they be members or non-members of the United Nations. If such invitations are procedural decisions, the Council was right in the Formosa case. If, on the other hand, they are merely deemed procedural, then the representative of China was right in asking for a substantive vote to resolve the doubt and the President was wrong in his "ruling" that, despite the negative vote of China, the decision was procedural in character.

## D. Present Validity

> If the Four-Power Declaration is regarded by the permanent members as in some sense constituting an international agreement, then surely the obligations under the Charter, of the permanent members of the Security Council shall, as stated in Article 103, prevail over any obligations assumed under the Four-Power Declaration or "any other international agreement."[71]

[65] *Id.*, 5th Year, No. 48 at 13 (1950).
[66] *Id.*, 5th Year, No. 49 at 9–10.
[67] Gen. Assembly Official Records, 3d Sess., Pt. II (Resolutions) 7 (1948).
[68] Security Council Official Records, 5th Year, No. 49 at 8 (1950).
[69] *Id.*, 5th Year, No. 49 at 9.
[70] Gen. Assembly Official Records, 3d Sess., Pt. II (Resolutions) 7 (1948) (emphasis supplied).

Mr. Gromyko characterized this novel argument by General McNaughton (Canada)—which, it would appear, has not been used before or since—as "wrong and erroneous" and said: "The San Francisco Declaration. . . . is not an agreement under which the Five Powers have assumed obligations in addition to those assumed under the Charter. The Declaration is an interpretation of the provisions of the Charter. It would therefore be altogether unjustifiable to set the obligations assumed under the Five Power Declaration against those assumed under the Charter."[72] It is submitted that even if the Statement were an agreement in the sense of Article 103 of the Charter, that article does not lay down the procedure for determining the compatibility or incompatibility between obligations under the Charter and those under any other international agreement. Assuming that the Security Council were competent to determine the existence of a conflict, the decision appropriate in a matter of such gravity would probably be considered to be non-procedural in character and therefore subject to a qualified majority vote. However, as has been argued, the final paragraph of the Statement dealing with the preliminary question is quite compatible with the Charter and merely makes specific what is implicit in Article 27.

The validity of the final paragraph of the Statement has been attacked on at least three other grounds: the doctrine of *rebus sic stantibus*; the doctrine of abuse of right; and abrogation by persistent violation of Part I of the Statement. It is common to these lines of argument that they assume the Statement to be in the nature of an agreement among the five permanent members. Some members of the Security Council have indeed made allusion to the doctrine of *rebus sic stantibus*.[73] However, the permanent members have not yet argued that because of changed conditions the Statement has lost its validity. Nevertheless the United States and the United Kingdom indicated the possibility of some such development. There is no room here to discuss the doctrine. Suffice to say that its place in international law is controversial.

Somewhat akin to the preceding argument is that based on another controversial doctrine, that of the abuse of right. Paragraph 8 of Part I of the Statement furnishes the starting point for this line of argument.[74] It is possible to argue that this paragraph expresses no more than assumption and does not constitute an obligation not to use the veto wilfully. On the other hand, one might advance the proposition that no rights under international law, and particularly no rights under the Charter, should be used arbitrarily or capriciously. In any event, it has been quite common both in and out of the United Nations to charge the Soviet Union with abuse of the right of veto. General Assembly Resolution 267 (III) recommended to the permanent members certain measures in order "to avoid impairment of the usefulness and prestige of the Council through exces-

[71] Security Council Official Records, 3d Year, No. 71 at 40 (1948); see also Jimenez de Arechaga, Voting and the Handling of Disputes in the Security Council 10 (1950).

[72] Security Council Official Records, 3d Year, No. 71 at 42 (1948).

[73] See remarks of Mr. Arce, p. 478 *supra*; remarks of Mr. Dulles, p. 479 *supra*; remarks of Mr. Austin, pp. 479–80 *supra*; see also Jiménez, *op. cit. supra* note 71, at 42–45.

[74] See p. 478 *supra* for text.

sive use of the veto."[75] And General Assembly Resolution 337 (V), the so-called Acheson Plan, goes much further in providing for emergency sessions of the General Assembly "if the Security Council, because of lack of unanimity of the permanent members, fails to exercise its primary responsibility for the maintenance of international peace and security . . . ."[76]

The widespread belief that the Soviet Union abused its veto power and therefore violated the self-denying ordinance expressed in the Statement not to use the veto "wilfully" has led to the suggestion that such a violation might cause the whole agreement to be terminated by the other parties to it.[77] But which organ of the United Nations would be competent to determine whether circumstances have changed, rights have been abused, or an agreement violated? It would be difficult to make the General Assembly the competent organ in view of the coordinate status of these principal organs of the United Nations. The Security Council itself might be regarded as competent, but it could hardly arrive at a decision, for could a decision on such a matter be any other than non-procedural in character and therefore governed by a qualified majority vote? The competence of the International Court of Justice to interpret the Charter has been established, and conceivably it might give an opinion on a particular case involving the application of Article 27.[78] One wonders, nevertheless, whether the Court would wish to give what might easily be regarded as a political evaluation of the general problem of the operations of the Security Council. How the permanent and non-permanent members use their voting power is essentially a question of judgment, though whether a question is procedural or non-procedural is not a political but a juridical question and susceptible of judicial determination.

All four grounds for invalidating the Statement raise serious legal and political difficulties. Moreover, it is suggested that those who advocate the annulment of the Statement overlook substantial benefits which would be lost by the lapse of the Statement. It is proposed to turn our attention now to those advantages.

## E. Benefits

The negotiations leading to the formulation of the Statement resulted in the reluctant acceptance by the Soviet Union of the insistent claim of the United States and especially of the United Kingdom that the veto should not prevent a party to a dispute from being heard and should not prevent the Council from considering and discussing a dispute brought before it in accordance with the provisions in the Charter.[79] The Soviet Union,

[75] Gen. Assembly Official Records, 3d Sess., Pt. II (Resolutions) 7 (1948).

[76] *Id.*, 5th Sess., Supp. No. 20 at 10 (1950).

[77] See Jiménez, *op. cit. supra* note 71, at 14.

[78] See U.N. Charter Art. 92; see also p. 481 *supra*. Mr. Tsiang, discussing the Formosa question, suggested that the International Court of Justice be asked for an advisory opinion on the question whether he was justified in claiming a right to veto the Ecuadorean resolution, but he also stated that in general "the veto is not subject to any judicial review." Security Council Official Records, 5th Year, No. 49 at 6 (1950).

[79] Koo, Voting Procedures in International Political Organizations 166–95 (1947). See also Report of the

on the other hand, is reported to have desired to include in the Yalta voting formula, that is, in Article 27 of the Charter, a specific provision that the preliminary question whether or not a matter was procedural or substantive be governed by a qualified majority including the concurrent votes of the permanent members.[80] This was thought unnecessary by the United States and the United Kingdom, but in a spirit of compromise this provision was included in the Statement along with the provision concerning vetoless consideration and discussion of disputes and hearing of parties to the disputes.[81] As the Charter does not explicitly provide that an individual member alone cannot prevent consideration and discussion of a dispute or a situation, it could well be argued that the decision to consider and discuss a dispute or a situation is determined by a qualified majority vote. What is procedural depends upon treaty regulation, state practice, or generally on agreement of the states concerned. Therefore, if the Statement were considered invalid *ab initio* or if it were abandoned, it would be uncertain whether "consideration and discussion" was governed by a qualified or an unqualified majority.

What is believed to be true of "discussion and consideration" may also be true of some of the other decisions listed in paragraph 2 of Part I of this Statement.[82] In the absence of the Statement, some of these decisions might be construed as not coming within the usual meaning of procedural matters. It is to be noted that the Statement itself fails to classify these decisions as procedural but merely provides that they would be governed by a procedural vote, that is, by an unqualified majority of any seven members. The Statement then is of great importance. It removes these decisions from the realm of controversy and the necessity of solution by a qualified majority and places them securely under the rule of the unqualified majority of any seven members. The simple voting rule for these questions rests on the Statement and not on the Charter. To remove or renounce the Statement, it is felt, would be extremely unwise and would complicate the business of the Security Council.

## III. PRACTICE OF THE SECURITY COUNCIL FOR RESOLVING THE PRELIMINARY QUESTION

Having defined the range of the application of the Statement and the proper legal basis for the substantive character of the decision on the preliminary question, the next question to be determined is whether in the practice of the Security Council, resolution of the preliminary question has actually been governed by the substantive vote. This practice

Chairman of the U.S. Delegation to the President in *Hearings before the Senate Committee on Foreign Relations on the Charter of the United Nations*, 79th Cong., 1st Sess. 44 (1945).

[80] Koo, *op. cit. supra* note 79, at 189. Article 18 of the Charter contains a specific provision for resolving such problems in the General Assembly. Mr. Arce (Argentina) has contended that an unqualified majority should govern the preliminary question "so that there may be some conformity between the provisions governing the Security Council and these governing the General Assembly." SECURITY COUNCIL OFFICIAL RECORDS, 3d Year, No. 63 at 27 (1948). But as Kelsen rightly observes, there is no basis in the Charter for this analogy. THE LAW OF THE UNITED NATIONS 253 n.3 (1950).

[81] That the latter provision was a concession can be seen from Koo's account of the drafting history of the Statement, *op. cit. supra* note 79, at 159–95, especially 182–83.

[82] See KELSEN, *op. cit. supra* note 80, at 254: "The procedural character of all the decisions referred to in paragraph 2 of Part I of the Statement is at least doubtful."

is by no means uniform or clear. It may be best to examine several incidents and then see whether any general inferences may be drawn.

The problem first arose in 1946 in connection with discussion on the advisability of severing diplomatic relations with Spain. The vote on a subcommittee draft resolution was 9 in favor and 2 against (Poland, USSR). The President, Mr. Nájera (Mexico), obviously assuming the resolution to be of a procedural nature, declared it adopted. Mr. Gromyko objected that the draft resolution had a substantive character and that it was rejected because one of the permanent members had voted against it. He asked for a vote on the preliminary question. The preliminary question—raised here after the resolution was ruled procedural by the President—was put to the vote, treated as substantive, and the Soviet veto prevailed. There was no formal challenge.[83] The preliminary question was raised again in 1946 in connection with the postponement of Albania's application for membership to the United Nations. The substantive vote was again applied and prevailed, there being no formal challenge.[84]

In the discussion of the border incidents between Greece and her northern neighbors in 1947, the President, the representative of the Soviet Union, raised the preliminary question. Owing to his own negative vote, he declared the matter to be substantive. The draft resolution itself was then put to the vote and ruled rejected by the President because of his own negative vote; Mr. Johnson (United States) declared that there was no doubt that under the existing agreements and under the Charter the President had been within his technical rights in declaring that the matter was not procedural.[85] The preliminary question was voted upon again in 1948 at the meeting to discuss the seizure of power by the Communists in Czechoslovakia. The President (the representative of France), interpreting the vote, ruled that the draft resolution was one of substance because a permanent member, the Soviet Union, had cast a negative vote. The ruling was challenged, and the President asked those who objected to his interpretation to raise their hands. Six members did so and the President declared that his ruling stood as the motion for its rejection failed to obtain the affirmative vote of seven members. This ruling was not challenged. The resolution was treated as substantive, put to the vote, and declared not adopted because one of the negative votes was that of a permanent member.[86]

The question of inviting a representative of the Communist Government of China has already been discussed.[87] In this case the Statement was applied, though not the final paragraph of Part II, but rather paragraphs 2 and 3 of Part I. Therefore, the final paragraph of Part II being improperly relied upon, the Council, over the dissenting voice of Mr. Tsiang, proceeded by a series of procedural votes, including one under Rule 30 of the rules of procedure.

[83] Security Council Official Records, 1st Year, 1st Ser., No. 2 at 413–32 (1946).
[84] *Id.*, 1st Year, 2d Ser., No. 5 at 124–34.
[85] *Id.*, 2d Year, No. 89 at 2397–2401 (1947). Mr. Johnson's statement is quoted at p. 479 *supra*.
[86] *Id.*, 3d Year, No. 73 at 19–27 (1948).
[87] See pp. 479–81, 483 *supra*.

## IV. PRESIDENTIAL RULINGS AND THE PRELIMINARY QUESTION

The Charter does not provide for a ruling by the President on the result of a vote; neither do the Council's provisional rules of procedure. According to Rule 30[88] the President is bound to state his ruling whenever a point of order is raised by a representative. The rules of procedure do not define a point of order. Presumably it relates to the conduct of business pursuant to those rules.[89] As voting on a presidential ruling has been regarded in the practice of the Security Council as a procedural matter, this lends additional support to the view that points of order relate to procedural matters.[90] Could then the method of voting and the interpretation of the result of the vote be regarded as the proper subject of a point of order and accordingly of a presidential ruling? And if so, is a presidential ruling on this issue subject to a procedural vote under Rule 30? The first question has sometimes been denied in theory but seemingly affirmed in practice. As to the second question, perhaps no more than an inference can be derived from the practice of the Security Council.

Both the Soviet Union and China have emphatically claimed that the application of the Statement is beyond the range of a presidential ruling.[91] In practice, presidential rulings on the preliminary question were not infrequent, though in some cases proceedings in the Council were such as to lend themselves to different and perhaps conflicting interpretations. In the discussion on the Spanish question the President was understood to have ruled that the subcommittee resolution was procedural, and he submitted his ruling to the vote. However, he did not consider the ruling adopted, although nine members voted for it, because of the negative vote of two permanent members.[92] The ruling here was apparently deemed subject to a *substantive* vote. In view of this, it might be better to say that the President did not submit his ruling but rather the preliminary question to the vote and drew his conclusion from the vote in accordance with the final paragraph of the Statement and Article 27, paragraph 3, of the Charter.

The proceedings involving Albanian application for membership were by no means clear. The President, Mr. Lange (Poland), said he had made a ruling that the draft resolution before the Council was a matter of procedure. As Mr. Gromyko objected, Mr. van Kleffens (Netherlands) asked the President to apply Rule 30 and submit his ruling to the Council for immediate decision. Mr. Lange said he was in full agreement with Mr. van

[88] Rule 30, Provisional Rules of Procedure, SECURITY COUNCIL DOC. NO. S/96 (1946): "If a representative raises a point of order, the President shall immediately state his ruling. If it is challenged, the President shall submit his ruling to the Security Council for immediate decision and it shall stand unless overruled."

[89] See Report of the Special Committee on Methods and Procedures, GEN. ASSEMBLY DOC. NO. A/937 at 30–32 (1949).

[90] It may be noted, however, that in the Corfu Channel dispute, the President, Mr. Langenhoven (Belgium), believed himself justified in making a ruling under Rule 30 on the question whether or not the United Kingdom as a party to the dispute should abstain from voting under Article 27, paragraph 3, and whether the establishment of a subcommittee was among the matters mentioned in Chapter VI of the Charter. SECURITY COUNCIL OFFICIAL RECORDS, 2d Year, No. 21 at 426 (1947). But it is doubtful whether such questions are "points of order" to be settled by the ruling of the President, or whether they concern interpretation of the Charter.

[91] *Id.*, 2d Year, No. 21 at 427; *id.*, 2d Year, No. 89 at 2394; see p. 481 *supra*.

[92] SECURITY COUNCIL OFFICIAL RECORDS, 1st Year, 1st Ser., No. 2 at 413–22 (1946); see p. 488 *supra*.

Kleffens; as a matter of fact, he submitted not his ruling but the preliminary question by asking "all those who believe that it is a matter of procedure to raise their hands."[93] As four permanent members voted in the negative and there were only five affirmative votes, there was no majority of seven to support the belief that this was a procedural matter. Therefore, the President's emphasis after the vote that "[f]our permanent members voted against the ruling"[94] seems significant. In the first place, he had ingeniously omitted putting his ruling to the vote under Rule 30, and in the second place, in the absence of even a procedural majority against his ruling, the reference to the negative vote of four permanent members indicates that in the President's view a substantive vote was required. The Official Records of this meeting convey the impression that some members were not fully aware of the President's maneuver.[95]

Of considerable significance were the proceedings at the meeting on the Greek question concerning the procedural or substantive character of the United States draft resolution.[96] The President, Mr. Gromyko, ruled the resolution substantive because of his use of the double veto. When the United States representative challenged this ruling, the President did not submit his ruling to a vote but asked for a vote "upon the proposal that the question is one of procedure," that is upon the preliminary question. There being 8 votes in favor, 2 against (Poland, USSR) and 1 abstention, the President said: "I consider that the proposal is rejected since one of the permanent members . . . voted against it. I ask the Council to consider my statement as a ruling of the President." And he added: "Until I am overruled, this ruling stands."[97] The President's "ruling" was not challenged and could not very well be challenged since he merely interpreted the result of the vote while quite erroneously, it is submitted, referring to it as a ruling. Had his "ruling" been challenged, would Rule 30 and a procedural vote have applied? This possibility was excluded because of the acceptance by the United States of the result of the vote.

In the Czechoslovak case, there was again a difference of opinion as to whether the Chilean draft resolution was procedural or substantive. The President, Mr. Parodi (France), asked the Council to vote on the preliminary question. The result was 8 in favor, 2 against (Ukrainian SSR, USSR), and 1 abstention (France). The President, referring to the final paragraph of the Statement, interpreted the vote "as a decision to consider the vote on the resolution as one of substance" and called this interpretation a "ruling."[98] This met with the objection of the Canadian representative, who suggested that the ruling should be submitted to the decision of the Council.[99] The representatives

[93] SECURITY COUNCIL OFFICIAL RECORDS, 1st Year, 2d Ser., No. 5 at 132 (1946). Mr. Rudzinski in *The So-Called Double Veto*, 45 AM. J. INT'L LAW 443, 451 (1951), states that the President had asked "those who agree with the *ruling* that. . . ." (emphasis supplied). This is not supported by the report of the meeting in the Official Records. Hence Mr. Rudzinski's deduction, 45 *id.* at 452, that the Statement was applied to a vote under Rule 30 is not well founded.

[94] SECURITY COUNCIL OFFICIAL RECORDS, 1st Year, 2d Ser., No. 5 at 133 (1946).

[95] The whole discussion is in *id.*, 1st Year, 2d Ser., No. 5 at 130–35.

[96] See p. 488 *supra*.

[97] SECURITY COUNCIL OFFICIAL RECORD, 2d Year, No. 89 at 2400–01 (1947).

[98] *Id.*, 3d Year, No. 73 at 21 (1948).

[99] *Id.*, 3d Year, No. 73 at 22.

of Belgium, Colombia, Syria, Argentina, and the Soviet Union spoke along similar lines, but the reference by the Soviet representative to the desirability of a ruling under Rule 30 was quite inconsistent with previous emphatic assertions by the Soviet Union that questions of voting were not subject to presidential ruling.[100] The President then asked the Council: "Will those who object to my interpretation raise their hands?" It will be noted that the President avoided putting his ruling to the vote. Instead he called for a vote on his interpretation of the preceding vote. As there were only six votes to reject—one short of a majority—the "ruling" stood.[101]

Therefore it is not possible to say whether the President and the Council would have considered a simple majority of seven members sufficient to affirm the procedural character of the draft resolutions in question. Nor is it entirely clear that the vote took place under Rule 30, although numerous references to that rule were made in the discussion preceding the vote. Moreover, the President did not submit a ruling on a point of order to a vote but, on the contrary, called for a vote on his interpretation.[102] The proceedings in this meeting as in that which considered Albanian application for membership do not support the view that the term "ruling" was used in the sense of a Rule 30 ruling. Nor was such a "ruling" overruled by a simple majority vote in either case.

There remains for consideration the Formosa case. As noted previously it is not correct to regard the Statement as having been applied to the evaluation of the vote taken under Rule 30.[103] As no member of the Council took part in the last vote, the only vote directly under Rule 30, there was nothing for the President to evaluate. Moreover, there was and there can be no difference of opinion that when a point of order is raised and the decision of the President with regard thereto is challenged, a procedural vote applies. For these reasons, it is believed that the Formosa case does not warrant the conclusion that "the Council may, by a *procedural* vote of seven of its members . . . decide that the double veto does not apply to the matter under consideration, *thus denying to a permanent member the exercise of the veto*" and that as a consequence "the unlimited anarchical right of the double veto was restricted to its proper place and put under the control of the Council's majority."[104]

The far-reaching conclusions drawn from the Formosa case are unwarranted because the point at issue was settled in the Statement as one subject to a procedural vote, and there was no more reason to start a series of votes on this point than there would have been on a motion of adjournment. What is subject to a procedural vote by the Charter and the Statement can be decided by a procedural vote. The point of order, if raised, is another such matter which is subject to a procedural vote. The President may not have

[100] See note 91 *supra*.

[101] SECURITY COUNCIL OFFICIAL RECORD, 3d Year, No. 73 at 27 (1948). As to a discrepancy between the verbatim minutes and the Official Records see Rudzinski, *supra* note 93, at 454 n.35. The French text refers to the "interpretation" of the President.

[102] Consequently the conclusions drawn from this incident by Mr. Rudzinski, *id.* at 455–56 do not seem to be well founded.

[103] As did Rudzinski, *id.* at 455.

[104] *Id.* at 457.

conducted the meeting in the best of form, but the end result does not lend itself to deductions beyond the point actually decided.

Such unwarranted deductions, as already pointed out, might also lead to attempts, in contravention of the Charter, to eliminate the use of the veto even from decisions where, at least until now,[105] there has been no doubt that the principle of the unanimity of the permanent members applied. To set up a simple majority as arbiter of when Article 27, paragraph 3, and the veto apply and when they do not would, in theory as well as in practice, run counter not merely to the Statement but also the Charter itself the root of the evil—if one chooses to regard it as such—of the veto as well as of the double veto.

## V. CONCLUSION

After this survey of the practice and problems of the Security Council with respect to the Statement, it may now be in order to suggest some conclusions. It is hardly necessary to point to the absurdity of proposals, whether they be seemingly inspired by the proceedings in the Formosa case or not, to substitute Rule 30 for the law of the Charter and in particular for Article 27. Juridically speaking, it is quite elementary that rules of procedure cannot supersede the law of the Charter.[106] It may be permissible to resort to rules of procedure as "illustrative of a common practice on the part of the parties to an international instrument, which may be evidence as to its correct meaning."[107] The rules of procedure of the Council, however, which after six years are still provisional and rudimentary, unlike the Statement, afford no such evidence with respect to voting. Rule 40 refers back to the Charter and to the Statute of the International Court of Justice.[108] Alternatively, it might be argued that Rule 40 incorporates by reference and without any modification not based on such common practice as abstention, the voting rules of the Charter and of the Statute. But if fails completely to elucidate their application. On either reading, then, it follows that voting in the Security Council is and remains under the sway of the Charter, and the Charter cannot lawfully be modified by resort to Rule 30 of the rules of procedure, but only by the amendment procedure laid down in Chapter XVIII of the Charter.

The Formosa incident, rather than inspiring far-flung ideas about exorcising the veto from the Charter, should convince all members of the United Nations and particularly those represented on the Security Council of the usefulness of the Statement as a

[105] *Id.* at 460.

[106] See Fitzmaurice, *The Law and Procedure of the International Court of Justice: Treaty Interpretation and Certain Other Treaty Points*, 28 BRIT. Y.B. INT'L LAW 22 (1951):

It is of course in one sense quite true that the rules of procedure of an organ such as the General Assembly of the United Nations cannot be employed to contravene or enlarge the constitutive instrument under which they are made, and must themselves be consistent with it. It may be argued, therefore, that they can equally not be made use of to *interpret* such instruments since they are dependent and consequential on them, and it is on the correct interpretation of the relevant instrument in the first place, that the correctness of the rules may depend, rather than the reverse.

[107] *Ibid.*

[108] Rule 40, Provisional Rules of Procedure, SECURITY COUNCIL DOC. NO. S/96 (1946): "Voting in the Security Council shall be in accordance with the relevant Articles of the Charter and of the Statute of the International Court of Justice."

means of facilitating the functioning of the Security Council. To achieve this, it is necessary to free oneself from the unfounded notion that the double veto has its basis in that document and in it alone. The double veto is a logical and, in a sense, inevitable consequence of the voting rule embodied in Article 27 of the Charter just as it was the logical and inevitable consequence of Article 5 of the Covenant of the League of Nations. On the other hand, the advantages of the Statement are considerable. To be sure they do not constitute a maximum, or perhaps from an idealistic point of view the minimum, of what may appear desirable in the interest of peace. General Assembly Resolution 267 (III) contains a more comprehensive list of decisions recommended as subject to an unqualified majority of seven members. However, that resolution has not been accepted by the Soviet Union, whereas the advantage of the Statement is that it represents the common view of the five permanent members. In the circumstances, it offers a by no means negligible alleviation from the rigors of the voting rules of the Security Council. The Formosa incident should serve as a warning. Had the Statement been accepted as probative of the interpretation to be placed upon Article 27[109] instead of being assailed, it would have offered an agreed guide to deciding whether a procedural or a substantive vote was required to invite a representative of the Chinese Communist Government.

The Statement has been considered by the permanent members as binding on them though not on the non-permanent members. Both the permanent and also the non-permanent members have relied, the latter somewhat inconsistently, upon paragraphs 2 and 3 of Part I of the Statement, particularly with regard to invitation of parties to the dispute and the vote governing consideration and discussion of disputes and situations. The final paragraph of Part II of the Statement has been the main target of debate. But this paragraph is unnecessary since it merely reflects the voting rules incorporated in Article 27 of the Charter. In other words the substantive vote on the preliminary question whether a given proposal is procedural in character is anchored in the Charter and not in the Statement, whereas the vetoless discussion and consideration of disputes and situations and to a lesser degree perhaps, the hearing of parties to such disputes is provided for in the Statement and not in the Charter. The danger faced by the Security Council then is: if the Statement is rendered inoperative by resort to the doctrine of changed circumstances or abuse of right, the advantages of the Statement might be jeopardized without compensating benefits in the form of abolition of the substantive vote for the preliminary question.

The practice of the Security Council tends to show that the preliminary question can be raised only when there is reasonable doubt as to the nature of the vote required, and that whenever it was raised, it was treated as a substantive issue. The Statement offers useful guidance in determining whether there is reasonable doubt, at any rate until Gen-

[109] In the *South-West Africa* case, the International Court of Justice declared "Interpretations placed upon legal instruments by the parties to them, though not conclusive as to their meaning, have considerable probative value when they contain recognition by a party of its own obligations under an instrument. International Status of South-West Africa, [1950] I.C.J. Rep. 128, 136 (Advisory Opinion).

eral Assembly Resolution 267 (III) is accepted by all the permanent members of the Security Council or detailed rules of procedure are adopted.

The Council's practice, it is suggested, does not support the view that results of voting or determination of the kind of vote applicable to a given case is subject to presidential rulings in the sense of Rule 30 of the rules of procedure. To interpret this practice otherwise would imply that a ruling by the President on the preliminary question, though handled under Rule 30, was subject to a substantive vote, whereas presidential rulings, under the same rule, on other matters were subject to a procedural vote. The Formosa case does not invalidate the interpretation here suggested. On the other hand, this case in no way supports the extreme view that the exercise of the veto has been placed under the curatorship of a simple majority of the Council. No matter how desirable such a curatorship might be, it is believed to be juridically impossible to replace the authority of the Charter with rules of procedure which, moreover, do not and cannot abrogate but can merely supplement the law of the Charter. The tools of interpretation have not been fashioned for this purpose.[110] The movement in favor of liberating the Security Council from the veto has overlooked altogether the fundamental principle that "[t]he political character of an organ cannot release it from the observance of the treaty provisions established by the Charter when they constitute limitations on its powers or criteria for its judgment."[111] It may be important to recall here Article 25 of the Charter, the significance of which cannot be underestimated: "The members of the United Nations agree to accept and carry out the decisions of the Security Council in accordance with the present Charter." The members are bound to carry out decisions of the Council which are in accordance with the Charter and not those which are rather dubiously, one suspects, in accordance with its rules of procedure. It is also well to remember that as envisaged by the final paragraph of the Statement only questions of some gravity require decisions by a substantive vote, and such matters, involving as they do interpretations of the Charter and of the Council's powers under it, cannot easily be settled by less than a substantive vote. At this point there is a confluence of the law of the Charter and practical politics.

Efforts to make the Security Council "work" in disregard of the limitations on its power and the constitutional conditions for its exercise are bound to create grave dangers for the continuance of the United Nations. In the General Assembly of the United Nations "resolutions" were all too often substituted for "solution" of the grave problems on its agenda. There is every reason to think that if the well-meaning opponents of the veto had their way, they would force the Soviet Union and her satellites out of the United Nations or else the Security Council too would fall into the General Assembly pattern of passing resolutions to cover up the failure of statesmanship to seek and ulti-

[110] A thoughtful and experienced student and friend of the United Nations, Mr. A. H. Feller, who no doubt was an advocate of the "broad construction" of the Charter, reminded us that "the process of adaptation through interpretation and usage has its defined limits. The United Nations is a legal order and it cannot tear itself loose from the specific restrictions of the Charter, irksome though they may be from time to time to one interest or another. The veto cannot be excised by interpretation." UNITED NATIONS AND WORLD COMMUNITY 43 (1952).

[111] Admission of a State to the United Nations (Charter, Art. 4), [1948] I.C.J. Rep. 57, 64 (Advisory Opinion).

mately to find solutions. One reason for the requirement of unanimity of the Great Powers was precisely to force the Security Council to seek effective solutions. To rest content with ineffective resolutions adopted without the support or, worse, over and against the opposition of one or more of the Great Powers will neither promote nor in the end preserve peace. Lawyers who pretend to have found a way to eliminate the principle of unanimity of the Great Powers by dint of a "broad construction" of the Charter are bound to engender dangerous illusions. Far from bridging, they will merely further widen the gulf which divides the Great Powers. The veto is not the cause but the reflex of the pattern of international politics which has prevailed for centuries. Trying to get rid of the veto is like trying to get rid of politics.

# THE QUESTION OF LAOS AND THE DOUBLE VETO IN THE SECURITY COUNCIL

The Security Council, which for many years has been remarkable as the most inactive among the principal organs of the United Nations, adopted on September 8, 1959, a draft resolution jointly sponsored by the United States, the United Kingdom and France, the text of which is as follows:

> The Security Council
> Decides to appoint a sub-committee consisting of Argentina, Italy, Japan and Tunisia, and instructs this sub-committee to examine the statements made before the Security Council concerning Laos, to receive further statements and documents and to conduct such inquiries as it may determine necessary and to report to the Security Council as soon as possible.[1]

The vote on the resolution was 10 in favor, 1 against, and no abstentions. The President of the Council, the representative of Italy, declared "therefore the draft resolution is adopted."[2]

Preceding and following the vote, which the Soviet delegate considered as invalid because it was contrary to the Charter, the Four-Power Declaration of June 7, 1945,[3] and the practice of the Security Council, there was a debate on procedural matters relating to the agenda item before the Security Council and the nature of the resolution. In the latter connection the question of the "double veto" was aired extensively for the first time since the Council on September 29, 1950, voted on a proposal to invite Communist

[1] U.N. Doc. S/4216, Sept. 8, 1959.

[2] Security Council, Doc. S/P.V. 848, Sept. 7, 1959, p. 78. Voted in favor: Argentina, Canada, China, France, Italy, Japan, Panama, Tunisia, United Kingdom, United States; voted against: U.S.S.R. *Ibid.*

[3] For the Four-Power Declaration on Voting Procedure in the Security Council, with which France subsequently associated herself, see 11 U.N.C.I.O. Docs. 711. This document will be cited hereinafter as the Four-Power Statement.

China to be represented in the discussion of its complaint of armed invasion of Formosa (Taiwan).[4] This case will be briefly discussed below.

## QUESTION OF THE AGENDA

The procedural debate relating to the agenda was concerned with the question whether the Council was properly seized of a matter and by whom. The Security Council was convened "urgently" by its President at the request of the Secretary General for the consideration of an item entitled "Report by the Secretary-General on the letter received from the Minister for Foreign Affairs of the Royal Government of Laos, transmitted by a note from the Permanent Mission of Laos to the United Nations, 4 September 1959."[5] The letter under reference requested the Secretary General "to take appropriate procedural action" on the Laotian Government's request, of which the text was as follows:

> Since 16 July 1959, foreign troops have been crossing the frontier and engaging in military action against garrison units of the Royal Army stationed along the northeastern frontier of Laos. These garrison units have been obliged to evacuate several posts and to engage in numerous defensive actions. It is obvious that these attacks would not have taken place if the attackers had not come from outside the country and would not have continued if the attackers had not been receiving reinforcements and supplies of food and munitions from outside. As a result of these attacks, losses have been suffered by the Royal Army. On 30 August a new attack, more violent than the previous ones, was launched against the posts of Muong and Xieng Kho. Elements from the Democratic Republic of Viet-Nam took part in the attack, which was supported by artillery fire from the other side of the frontier. In the face of this flagrant aggression, full responsibility for which rests with the Democratic Republic of Viet-Nam, Laos requests the assistance of the United Nations, of which it is a Member; it is doing so under Article 1, paragraph 1, and Article 11, paragraph 2, of the Charter. In particular, the Royal Government requests that an emergency force should be dispatched at a very early date in order to halt the aggression and prevent it from spreading.[6]

The item on the Council's Agenda at its 847th Meeting was then the "Report by the Secretary-General" referred to above.[7] After a brief explanation by the President, the Secretary General stated that he "does not introduce formally on the agenda of the Council anything beyond his own wish to report to the Council"; that his request to report "is not based on the explicit rights granted to the Secretary-General under Article 99 of the Charter"; that to do so "would have meant the inscription by the Secretary-General of a substantive issue on the agenda"; and, finally, that

> In this latter respect it would necessarily also have involved a judgment as to the facts for which, in the present situation, I have not sufficient basis.[8]

[4] See Security Council, 5th Year, Official Records, Nos. 48 and 49 (1950).
[5] U.N. Doc. S/4213, Sept. 5, 1959.
[6] U.N. Doc. S/4212, Sept. 5, 1959.
[7] U.N. Doc. S/Agenda 1847.
[8] U.N. Doc. S/P.V. 847, Sept. 7, 1959, p. 6.

The Soviet representative drew attention to "a certain procedural inconsistency" in convening the Council, and pointed out that none of the applicable rules of the Council's Provisional Rules of Procedure had been or could be involved, and that, in particular, neither the Government of Laos nor the Secretary General had submitted for the Council's consideration the question raised in the Laotian Government's letter of September 4, 1959.[9] The Secretary General, after the adoption of the agenda by a vote of 10 in favor and 1 against, proceeded to review the history of his own diplomatic negotiations or consultations in and with the Government of Laos, the Co-Chairmen of the 1954 Geneva Conference and Members of the Security Council. In view of the Laotian Government's request "to take the appropriate procedural action," he had "to report to the Security Council on the request received for such consideration and such initiatives as the Council may find called for."[10]

In view of this and the fact that the item on the agenda was the "Report from the Secretary-General," the Security Council might have indicated to the Secretary General the "appropriate procedure" for bringing the complaint made by Laos before the Council. This the Members of the Council were not disposed to do, although the Soviet representative repeatedly indicated that, in his government's view, Laos should have addressed itself to the International Commission established by the Geneva Conference. Instead of giving procedural advice in response to a request for indication of the appropriate procedure, the Security Council addressed itself to the substance of the Laotian note of September 4, 1959, as if this note had been addressed to it with a request for action. This indeed was the initial and decisive result of the opening statement by the representative of the United States:

> I shall speak briefly to the report by the Secretary-General, which, as we all know, includes and transmits the communication from the Government of Laos and *which communication is accordingly now officially before us.*[11]

In this simple fashion a metamorphosis of the agenda was accomplished. From then on, the Laotian communication, not the Secretary General's Report, was the subject of the Security Council's consideration as, one might suspect, it was intended to be from the very outset.

One can only speculate why the Laotian Government did not, or was not advised to, submit a complaint to the Security Council as it should have done, and why, instead, a somewhat peculiar if not devious method was determined upon to bring it on the Council's agenda. Surely, there could not have been any apprehension of the majority's ability to put it on the agenda, had it been addressed to the Council. In fact it was not addressed

[9] *Ibid.* 8–10.
[10] *Ibid.* 37–40.
[11] *Ibid.* 41 (italics supplied).

to the Council but to the General Assembly. The reference to Article 11, paragraph 2, made this abundantly clear.[12]

The action of the Secretary General may well have been no more than a somewhat awkward correction of the Laotian error. On the other hand, it might be that the Laotian Government did not wish to appear in the Council and argue its case, including the bypassing of the International Commission. Clearly, had it appealed to the Council, it would have been invited to participate in the discussion. Possibly, its adversary, the Democratic Republic of Viet-Nam, might have also been invited to sit in the Council and thus been given an opportunity to offer arguments and possibly evidence in rebuttal of the Laotian charges.[13] At the very least, the Soviet Union could have been counted upon to propose such an invitation and this might possibly have provoked a discussion involving questions of recognition and other matters. In any event, there might have been delay and even some difficulty in confining the scope of the proposed subcommittee's inquiry to Laos, when logically its inquiry should have encompassed the area of disturbance on both sides of the frontier. The initiative of the Secretary General avoided all these possible complications and opened the way for a streamlined, if utterly superficial, treatment of the Laotian complaint.

Finally, one might suppose that the Laotian appeal to the General Assembly was less than felicitous, and for two reasons. It might have had to face some delay in calling a special session, even if a majority of the Members had consented to call it, and it may have seemed doubtful whether the information available to the Secretary General would have been deemed sufficient to request a special session so close to the regular annual session. Secondly, even if a special session had been convened, it certainly would have been more difficult to mobilize the necessary majority in favor of an investigation in the area, let alone the sending of a non-existing emergency force there. All these uncertainties and even risks were dexterously avoided by channeling the Laotian note to the more manageable forum of the Security Council.

## THE TERMS OF REFERENCE OF THE SUBCOMMITTEE

The documentation regarding the Laotian complaint consisted exclusively of the text of the complaint itself. The Secretary General's report shed no light on the substance of the allegations made by Laos, confined as it was, more or less, to the diplomatic ante-

[12] It was only the representative of Tunisia who pointed out this defect, saying: "My delegation would like to note its regret that the Government of Laos did not see fit to address its complaint to the Security Council and that it did not itself request a meeting of the Council. Article 11, par. 2, of the Charter, which it invokes, seems to cover rather the action on the part of the General Assembly. Nevertheless, the request for assistance against aggression and specifically the request for the dispatch of an emergency force are both sufficiently grave so as to come within the purview of the Security Council." *Ibid.* 81.

[13] Both the President of the Council and the representative of Tunisia referred to a letter from the Prime Minister of the Democratic Republic of Viet-Nam which rejected the allegations of the Laotian Government. *Ibid.* 4–5, 81. This letter was distributed by the President for the information of the members of the Council but was not part of the documentation before the Council.

cedents of the complaint. On the substance, the Secretary General, it will be recalled, reserved judgment, admitting that for a "judgment as to facts" he had "not sufficient basis." The Soviet delegate went more extensively than any other member of the Council into the facts. There was no difference of opinion that the situation was serious. In the view of the Soviet representative it was due to the failure of the Laotian Government to abide faithfully by the Geneva Agreements of 1954 and the Vientiane Agreements of 1956 and 1957 between the Laos Government and the Pathet Lao armed forces. In consequence of these breaches "there appeared the threat of a civil war."[14]

The United States representative, on the other hand, had "no doubt at all that aggression is being committed. The newspapers are full of it. It is common knowledge. . . . The telegram from the Foreign Minister of Laos, in and of itself, is *prima facie* evidence of the need for the Security Council to act, and to act quickly."[15] It is difficult to recall an instance in which a responsible Member Government has committed itself to so lighthearted a view of what constitutes *prima facie* evidence. Only one other Member of the Council, China, seems to have shared the United States view that the situation constituted, or was the result of, "armed invasion from outside."[16] The British representative, after noting the difficulty of being "certain about the borderline between civil strife and foreign interference," was of the opinion that Laos exercised its right to appeal to the United Nations in the belief "that its integrity is now in peril and . . . that the peril has been contrived by its neighbors."[17] Other Members appreciated the situation in varying degrees of seriousness.

It is necessary to view against this background the joint draft resolution submitted by the United States at the 847th Meeting. The text of this draft is identical in every respect with the text of the adopted resolution quoted earlier. What strikes one is the remarkable and obvious disparity between the deliberately innocuous language of the draft resolution and the situation as pictured by Laos and one of the sponsors of the resolution, the United States. What insights could the subcommittee gain from a study of the record of the Council debate? Clearly, the language of the draft was designed to support the majority argument that it was merely a procedural and not a substantive matter and did not disclose the real intent of the sponsors. Contemporary reports in the press, which the United States representative invoked, gave some indication of the intended function of the subcommittee, namely, to move as speedily as possible to Laos and investigate the situation. However, there is even in the record of the Security Council sufficient disclosure of the purposes of the committee and its nature. Thus, the representative of Japan desired

[14] *Ibid.* 26.
[15] *Ibid.* 41. See also letter dated Sept. 24, 1959, from the Permanent Representative of the United Kingdom addressed to the Secretary General. U.N. Doc. S/4223, p. 3.
[16] U.N. Doc. S/P.V. 847, p. 76.
[17] *Ibid.* 56.

> to make it clear, first, that we are especially interested in having full information collected on the developments in the areas concerned; second, that in our opinion, therefore, it is at this time premature to discuss the substance of the matter; and, third, that we hope that the United Nations presence in the area in the form of such a sub-committee will contribute to easing the tension which seems to exist.[18]

Thus United Nations presence in the area, *i.e.*, in Laos, and collecting information were regarded as the objectives of the subcommittee by one of its designated Members. That this was indeed so was expressed in varying forms of precision by other Members of the Council. France, one of the co-sponsors of the draft resolution, stressed the need to "seek further information," whereas, in the view of the United Kingdom, another co-sponsor, the members of the subcommittee "should make themselves specialists in this problem," and "they could hear evidence submitted from all sides and report on the facts to the Council, thus providing a sound basis for any action which might subsequently be necessary."[19]

This concept of the subcommittee's nature and purpose was echoed by other Members.[20] It was indeed shared by the Soviet Union, whose representative agreed that the subcommittee was to be a "fact-finding" body. It was to receive from the Council a "black-check; it can do anything it chooses." And since a charge of aggression had been made by Laos, it "would have to go into charges. It would have to ascertain whether such aggression occurred, whether the charges are justified."[21]

The model of reticence set by the representative of the United States in moving purely and simply the adoption of the draft resolution was not emulated by the other Members. The natural propensity of diplomats to talk prevailed, and the result was the emergence of a remarkable consensus regarding the function of the subcommittee: it was to conduct an investigation into the situation in Laos' disturbed border region and thus furnish the Council with the facts which might or might not support the Laotian charge of "flagrant aggression" by the Democratic Republic of Viet-Nam. However, on the question of the vote required for the adoption of the resolution the Council split 10 to 1, as was to be anticipated.

[18] *Ibid.* 62.

[19] *Ibid.* 51 and 57.

[20] The Canadian delegate declared: "Some properly impartial report on the facts of the situation would, therefore, appear to be necessary before the Council could usefully deal with the substance of the communication to the Secretary-General." *Ibid.* 63–65. The delegate of Argentina said: "Can we do less than investigate the facts on the spot?" *Ibid.* 67–70. In the opinion of China the subcommittee was "to gather information." *Ibid.* 77–80. The delegate of Tunisia noted the absence of "sufficient elements of information" and the need for the subcommittee to contribute "to a fair and objective study of the situation." *Ibid.* 82–85, 86. The delegate of Panama declared that the subcommittee "would bring the moderating influence of the United Nations into the picture" and "confine itself to submitting the facts to the full Council." U.N. Doc. S/P.V. 848, p. 16. The President, speaking as the representative of Italy, stated that the draft resolution's "purport is the collecting of information on the situation developing in Laos." *Ibid.* 26.

[21] U.N. Doc. S/P.V. 848, pp. 32, 33–35.

## VOTING ON THE DRAFT RESOLUTION AND THE QUESTION OF THE DOUBLE VETO

In submitting the draft resolution to the Council, the delegate of the United States laid out clearly the guide lines for the anticipated debate on the voting rule, saying:

> Now, the language of this resolution is virtually identical with language which has been used before, notably in the action under Article 29 of the Charter, in the Spanish case in 1946. In that case the vote in the Security Council was 10 for, none against, and 1 abstention; and the member who abstained was the then representative of the Soviet Union, Mr. Gromyko, who is now the Foreign Minister of the Soviet Union. This resolution is squarely within the provisions of Article 29 of the Charter. It is a step which is necessary for the Council in the performance of its functions in this case. It is a subsidiary organ—that is, when it is created it will be a subsidiary organ—which will in effect provide for the continuation of the Council's consideration on this subject.[22]

This concept was shared explicitly or tacitly by other Members of the Council, although at least one of them, the Argentine delegate, made a valiant attempt to distinguish investigation from investigation which is so disarmingly simple in nature that it bears quotation:

> Chapter VI of the Charter provides for such investigations. This is a solemn step which implies that the investigating body undertakes a solemn commitment.
>
> Our purpose here is a more modest one. All that is suggested is that a small sub-committee of the Security Council should undertake what would indeed be very difficult for the Council itself to do as a body, namely to investigate matters on the spot and to see exactly what is happening. The sub-committee is an extension of the Council itself and, as such, its establishment is clearly within the procedural powers vested in the Council under Article 29.[23]

This attempt to draw a distinction without a difference, as well as the reference to the Spanish case, failed to impress the Soviet delegate, who insisted that the draft resolution was "a substantive proposal on the issue before the Council" and, as such, "subject to the uniformity [*sic*] rule, Article 27," in accordance with the constant practice of the Council.[24]

The reference to the Spanish case proves nothing. Indeed, if it proves anything at all, it is that a draft resolution, identical in language with the pending one, was considered as subject to the unanimity rule under Article 27. For on that occasion, the first involving abstention by a permanent Member of the Council, the Soviet delegate explicitly declared that, bearing in mind the desire of some Members of the Council for further information, "and bearing in mind, in this connection, that my voting against the Australian draft resolution would make its adoption impossible, I shall abstain from voting."[25]

[22] U.N. Doc. S/P.V. 847, pp. 42–45.
[23] *Ibid.* 71.
[24] U.N. Doc. S/P.V. 848, pp. 27–30, 31.
[25] Security Council, 1st Year, Official Records, No. 2, p. 243. See also Leo Gross, "Voting in the Security Council: Abstention from Voting and Absence from Meetings," 60 Yale Law Journal 209–257, at 215 (1951). See also *supra*, pp. 429–471.

He thus clearly indicated his views regarding the nature of the Australian draft resolution and only the Netherlands delegate expressly reserved his position on this point.[26] If the Spanish case was invoked as precedent, then the pending resolution was not so much "squarely within the provisions of Article 29" as it was within the meaning of Article 27, paragraph 3.[27] In spite of the similarity of language between the Spanish resolution and the present one, there are significant differences in intent and background: in the Laotian case there was a charge of flagrant aggression and the subcommittee was to bring the "presence" of the United Nations and inquire into facts in Laos. None of these elements was present in the Spanish case. As regards the vote required for the Laotion draft resolution, these elements cannot but have an important bearing.

The Soviet delegate invoked several cases in support of his contention that the draft resolution was subject to the voting rule of Article 27, paragraph 3, and also to the Four-Power Statement of June 7, 1945. He emphasized particularly the "chain of events" which begins with an investigation and which, according to paragraph 5 of the Statement, "may involve calling for reports, hearing witnesses, dispatching a commission of inquiry or other means." To decisions relating to investigation, the principle of unanimity of the permanent Members applies.[28] The Soviet delegate also pointed out that, according to Part II of the Statement, in case of doubt as to which vote applies, a non-procedural vote is required to resolve it.[29] He requested the President to put first to the vote the preliminary question: "Should the vote on this draft resolution be regarded as a procedural vote or not?"[30] No Member of the Council intervened at this point to interrupt the dialogue between the President and the Soviet delegate and urge that the "preliminary" question be decided after the vote on the draft resolution. From the tactical point of view of the majority, it is submitted, this was a grave error. The President, left to his own devices, agreed to put to the vote the motion: "Should the vote on the draft resolution submitted in Doc. S/4214 be considered a procedural one?"[31] The result of the vote was 10 in favor and 1 against (U.S.S.R.), and the President declared:

> Therefore, the resolution should be considered procedural. It is the interpretation of the chair, shared by the overwhelming majority of the members, that the draft resolution falls

[26] *Ibid.* 244.

[27] It should be noted that the Australian delegate at the 37th Meeting on April 25, 1946, submitted a revised text to "cut out the idea of a formal investigation under Article 34 of the Charter so as to enable the proposed body to be brought in under Article 29 as a subsidiary organ." Repertoire of the Practice of the Security Council 1946–1951, p. 203 (1954).

[28] See note 3 above.

[29] The relevant portion of Part II of the Four-Power Statement reads: "1. In the opinion of the Delegations of the Sponsoring Governments, the Draft Charter itself contains an indication of the application of the voting procedures to the various functions of the Council.

"2. In this case, it will be unlikely that there will arise in the future any matters of great importance on which a decision will have to be made as to whether a procedural vote would apply. Should, however, such a matter arise, the decision regarding the preliminary question as to whether or not such a matter is procedural must be taken by a vote of seven members of the Security Council, including the concurring votes of the permanent members."

[30] U.N. Doc. S/P.V. 848, p. 41.

[31] *Ibid.* 42.

clearly under Article 29 of the Charter . . . .[32] Since this Article appears under the heading of "Procedure", this cannot mean anything but that all matters included in it are of a procedural nature. The Charter itself declares, consequently, that this is a procedural question and must be voted accordingly under Article 27, paragraph 2. In the previous practice the Security Council has always considered the establishment of subsidiary organs as a matter of procedure. The Chair can act only in accordance with the Charter and the rules of procedure, and this is my ruling.[33]

The Soviet delegate disagreed with this declaration and stated:

Your interpretation, Mr. President, is altogether illegal; it is at variance with the Charter and it is at variance with the Declaration of the Four Powers to which France adhered. Moreover, it is at variance with the unvaried practice of the Security Council hitherto. Consequently, it is null and void.[34]

The Soviet delegate recalled various votes in the Security Council, as did several other Members. The representative of the United Kingdom referred to that part of the Four-Power Statement which provides that a procedural vote shall apply to the establishment of such bodies as the Council may deem necessary for the performance of its functions, to paragraph 1 of Part II of the Statement,[35] and concluded:

The second paragraph of part II[36] on which the Soviet representative relied was therefore clearly intended to apply only when the Charter did not give any guidance; it was intended to apply to those cases where there was a genuine doubt as to whether a matter was procedural or substantive. In the present case, Article 29 of the Charter gives a clear indication, namely, that, as a matter of procedure and administrative convenience, the Security Council can appoint sub-committees of its members as is now proposed.[37]

Positions were restated but not varied, the draft resolution put to the vote, in which there were 10 in favor and one (U.S.S.R.) against, and the resolution was considered adopted by the President and the majority of the Council, but not, of course, by the dissenting Member.[38] The arguments invoked in support of the legality of the resolution and for overriding the Soviet "double veto" will now be examined.

The Four-Power Statement was discussed by several Members. The question whether or not it is binding and on whom is not material,[39] nor is the President's view "that this document cannot be interpreted in a way inconsistent with the Charter."[40] It

[32] Art. 29 reads: "The Security Council may establish such subsidiary organs as it deems necessary for the performance of its functions."

[33] U.N. Doc. S/P.V. 848, pp. 42, 43–45.

[34] *Ibid.* 47–50.

[35] See note 29 above.

[36] See *ibid.*

[37] U.N. Doc. S/P.V. 848, p. 68.

[38] *Ibid.* 78. The Soviet position and alternative proposals for handling the Laotian complaint were reiterated in the letter dated Sept. 15, 1959, from the Permanent Representative of the U.S.S.R. to the Secretary General, U.N. Doc. S/4222.

[39] On this point see Leo Gross "The Double Veto and the Four-Power Statement in the Security Council," 67 Harvard Law Review 251–280, at 256 ff. (1953). See also *supra*, pp. 473–495, at 477.

[40] U.N. Doc. S/P.V.848, p. 77.

would be more plausible to say that the Charter should not be interpreted in a way inconsistent with the Statement, for that would reflect the precise intent and purpose of the Statement. However, as was pointed out elsewhere, it is a common error to believe that the double veto is rooted in the Statement. It is the very essence of the voting rule laid down in Article 27 of the Charter.[41] Article 27, paragraph 2, provides that decisions on "procedural matters" shall be made by a vote of seven Members, whereas, according to Article 27, paragraph 3, "decisions on all other matters" shall be governed by a qualified majority of seven Members, including the concurring votes of the permanent Members. It follows from this arrangement, it is submitted, that the majority of seven applies to matters which incontrovertibly are "procedural" by agreement or precedent. The qualified majority which embraces "all other matters" includes by necessary implication the question whether a matter is procedural. The President having put to the vote the preliminary question, that is, the question *whether* the vote should be considered "a procedural one," placed the vote on this question squarely within the range of Article 27, paragraph 3. He was therefore, it is submitted, not at liberty to declare, as he did, *after* the vote, that the resolution should be considered procedural. In so doing he put himself into the indefensible position of implying that the vote on the preliminary question, that is, on *whether* the matter was a procedural one, was governed by Article 27, paragraph 2, which applies exclusively to matters which *are* procedural. There is no warrant for the President's position in Article 27 or anywhere else in the Charter.

The "ruling" by the President was not challenged and, it is submitted, rightly so. Nothing in the Charter nor in the Council's Provisional Rules of Procedure confers upon the President the power to make a ruling on the question of voting in the Security Council. Rule 40 merely refers to the Charter.[42] To have challenged the ruling of the President would, in the light of past practice, have been unprofitable and might have implied acknowledgment of his power to make rulings on the applicability of Article 27 of the Charter. Whether this omission was due to an oversight or astuteness on the part of the Soviet delegate is immaterial. In any event, the President's power to make rulings is confined by the Provisional Rules to the "conduct of business," and the range of matters coming under this head is indicated in Chapter VI of the Rules. Moreover, according to Rule 30, the President's ruling "shall stand unless overruled." This can be done by a majority of seven Members, as it is a procedural matter. To concede to the President the power to make rulings on the question whether a matter shall be voted on under paragraph 2 or 3 of Article 27 of the Charter would be tantamount to replacing Article 27 of the Charter by Rule 30 of the Rules of Procedure.[43] Such a consequence appears as unthinkable as it is undesirable.

The President's claim, supported by Members of the Council, that the proposal to

[41] See Gross, *loc. cit.* note 39, at 277, and *supra* 492.

[42] Rule 40 of the Provisional Rules reads: "Voting in the Security Council shall be in accordance with the relevant Articles of the Charter and of the Statute of the International Court of Justice." U.N. Doc. S/96/Rev. 4, p. 11.

[43] On this point see Gross, *loc. cit.* note 39 above, at 272, 277 ff., and *supra* 489, 492.

set up a subcommittee fell under Article 29 of the Charter is uncontested and incontestable. To admit this is, however, to admit merely the obvious. But surely, neither the President nor the majority of the Council desired to commit themselves to the doctrine that in appointing a subsidiary organ its terms of reference are of no consequence whatsoever. In the case of Laos the terms of reference were innocuous enough, as probably they were calculated to be. However, it is submitted, neither the complaint by Laos with respect to which the draft resolution was offered[44] nor the intended function of the proposed subcommittee can be ignored. Its function was amply, if perhaps indiscreetly, described by several Members.[45] In the light of these indications, it cannot be gainsaid that it was intended to be a fact-finding or investigating committee and that it was to ensure United Nations "presence" in the area where Laos charged a "flagrant aggression" had occurred. These functions and objectives can obviously not be considered as merely procedural, and accordingly the establishment of a subsidiary organ charged with such functions and serving such objectives can scarcely be regarded as a mere procedural matter. The reference to the Spanish case was not in point insofar as the requisite majority vote was concerned. The United Kingdom delegate admitted that the second paragraph of Part II of the Four-Power Statement "was intended to apply to those cases where there was a genuine doubt as to whether a matter was procedural or substantive."[46] The view of the President and the majority that here there was no case of "genuine doubt" fails to carry conviction and to remove the doubt that necessarily surrounded this matter. The doubt was precisely due to the link between the draft resolution, its context, its terms of reference and their revealed real meaning. This link was well recognized in the Czechoslovak case in 1948. The then President of the Council correctly interpreted the Soviet vote on the preliminary question as a veto.[47]

In support of his ruling the President relied on past practice and especially on "a case similar to the one to which my ruling applies." He referred to the 507th Meeting, when the President of the Council

> asked the Council to vote on whether the Ecuadorian draft resolution voted upon that morning was a procedural matter. There were 9 votes in favor, 1 against and 1 abstention, the vote against being that of a permanent member, and the President declared adopted the proposal to consider the matter procedural.[48]

The reference is obviously to the Formosa case. It is neither possible nor necessary to examine here in detail that instance of a frustrated attempt on the part of the delegate of

[44] See p. 499 above, the statement by the United States representative that the Laotian note of September 4 "is accordingly now officially before us."

[45] See p. 502 above.

[46] See p. 505 above. See also Gross, *loc. cit.* note 39 above, at 264, 278: See also *supra* 483, 493: "The practice of the Security Council tends to show that the preliminary question can be raised only when there is *reasonable doubt* as to the nature of the vote required, and that whenever it was raised, it was treated as a substantive issue."

[47] See Repertoire of the Practice of the Security Council 1946–1951, Cases 49 and 98, pp. 149 and 160.

[48] U.N. Doc. S/P.V. 848, p. 76. The President quoted the above passage from 2 Repertory of the Practice of United Nations Organs.

China to invoke the double veto.[49] Suffice it to recall that the Ecuadorean draft resolution, under Rule 39 of the Council's Rules of Procedure, proposed to invite a representative of Communist China to attend the Council meetings during its discussion of the complaint of aggression upon Formosa (Taiwan). Pursuant to this rule, the Council may invite members of the Secretariat or other persons to supply it with information. The Chinese delegate requested a vote on the preliminary question, basing his action on the Four-Power Statement. This request was denied by the President, the representative of the United Kingdom, and the resolution was put to the vote. The vote being 7 in favor, 3 against (China, Cuba, United States), and 1 abstention (Egypt), it was declared adopted.[50] Then followed the episode on which the President relied in the Laos case. The Formosa case, however, is not a case in point at all. In the first place, the "preliminary question" followed the vote on the principal motion and, moreover, it is dubious whether it really was put in the correct manner. Secondly, the invitation to a state to participate in the discussion relating to the dispute is provided for in Article 32 of the Charter and is especially listed in the Four-Power Statement as one of the decisions governed by a procedural vote.[51]

The invitation to a state to participate in discussions of the Council is a separate and distinct step in the procedure designed solely to give it a fair hearing. The establishment of a subcommittee is not. It cannot be separated from its context. It cannot be separated organically from its terms of reference, although it might be separated for purposes of voting, and even the various functions might be put to the vote separately, as some of them may be procedural and others substantive in nature. It is therefore imperative to evaluate the functions to be carried out by the Council through the instrumentality of a subsidiary organ. Article 29 makes this abundantly clear in providing that the Council "may establish such subsidiary organs as it deems necessary for the performance of *its functions.*" The proposed subcommittee, being a subsidiary organ of the Council, would perform the Council's functions, and, logically as well as legally, the voting rule which governs the Council's performance of certain functions must also be deemed to govern the performance of the same functions by a subsidiary organ.

The Council may investigate not merely under Article 34, but presumably in connection with any of its specific functions. Investigation is surely not a procedural matter solely because it is a step, albeit an essential one, in the Council's procedure or process of solving an issue brought before it. In this case the Council had been confronted, not with a trivial issue, but nothing less than the complaint of "flagrant aggression." That in itself should have had the effect of bringing it within the range of Chapter VII. The Laotian request "that an emergency force should be dispatched at a very early date in order to halt

[49] For an analysis of this case see Gross, *loc. cit.* note 39 above, at 259 ff. and 275. See also *supra* 478ff. and 491. See also Rudzinski, "The So-called Double Veto," 45 A.J.I.L. 443 (1951).

[50] Security Council, 5th Year, Official Records, No. 48, p. 5 (1950).

[51] The relevant passage is as follows: ". . . the Council will, by a vote of any seven of its members . . . invite any State when it is a party to a dispute being considered by the Council to participate in the discussion relating to that dispute." See note 3 above.

the aggression and prevent it from spreading'' should remove any doubt as to which chapter of the Charter applied, although this matter was never clarified in the Council's handling of the Laotian affair. In any event, under whatever chapter the Council acts, investigation is a serious turning point in the Council's consideration of a complaint. Quite logically, therefore, from both a political as well as a juridical point of view, the Four-Power Statement laid down the principle that the ''chain of events begins when the Council decides to make an investigation, the Council has to consider whether the investigation—which may involve calling for reports, hearing witnesses, dispatching a commission of inquiry, or other means—might not further aggravate the situation.''[52]

As the discussion in the Security Council perhaps unwittingly revealed, the proposed subcommittee was to perform such functions. Therefore, the Soviet objection, unlike that of the Chinese representative in the Formosa case, rested solidly on the Four-Power Statement and on the Charter as well, inasmuch as the former is merely a comment on the latter. Furthermore, whereas the Chinese delegate attempted to resort to the double veto in order to veto a procedural action, the Soviet delegate attempted to use the same instrument in order to induce the Council to apply a non-procedural vote to a non-procedural matter in accordance with the Four-Power Statement, which simply makes explicit the applicable rules of the Charter. To be sure, the establishment of a subcommittee is a procedural matter, but the entrusting of certain Security Council functions to it is not necessarily so. This must depend on the nature of the functions. Investigation is not and has not been considered in the Council as a procedural matter, regardless of the mantle under which it was proposed.[53]

[52] See note 3 above, at 712.

[53] The subcommittee declared in its report that it regarded its task as that of an ''inquiry'' rather than ''investigation,'' the distinction implying ''that it must receive information on the facts from the government concerned, rather than seek facts itself on its own initiative.'' Report of the Security Council Sub-Committee under resolution of Sept. 7, 1951, Doc. S/4236, Nov. 5, 1959, p. 7, par. 15. The committee nevertheless visited the sites of the alleged aggression and heard numerous witnesses (civilian officials, military personnel, peasants and civilian population, prisoners and wounded). *Ibid.*, pp. 21–27. The committee concluded ''that although there were actions of different scope and magnitude, all of them—throughout the four periods (from 16 July to 11 October) were of a guerilla character. From the statements of the Laotian authorities, and from those of some witnesses, it appears, however, that certain of these hostile operations must have had a centralized co-ordination. Practically all witnesses (forty out of forty-one) stated that the hostile elements received support from the territory of the D.R.V.N. (Democratic Republic of Viet-Nam) consisting mainly of equipment, arms, ammunition, supplies, and the help of political cadres. The same emerges from the official Laotian documents submitted and from some of the material exhibits. Hostile elements seemed centred around former members of the U.C.P.L. (Unité Combattantes du Pathet Lao—Pathet Lao Combat Units) previously integrated in 1957, the 2nd Battalion of Pathet-Lao, which deserted from the Plaine des Jarres on 11 May 1959, and sections of the frontier minorities (Thais, Meos and a few Khas). According to a document presented to the Sub-Committee by the Laotian Government, participation of regular D.R.V.N. army units were reported during the attacks on the River Ma area on 30 August. The Laotian Government states in another document presented to the Sub-Committee on 15 October 1959, that after 15 September 1959, the D.R.V.N. units re-crossed the border into North Viet-Nam, excepting those who occupied the section of Laotian territory between the left bank of the River Ma and the frontier. Witnesses reported that in certain cases there had been participation of armed elements with ethnic Viet-Namese characteristics, but they did not identify them as belonging to North Viet-Namese regular army units. The ensemble of information submitted to the Sub-Committee did not clearly establish whether there were crossings of the frontier by regular troops of the D.R.V.N.'' *Ibid.*, p. 31, pars. 95–98. It appears with clarity from the committee's report that the situation in Laos was vastly more complicated than could be gauged from the debates in the Security Council.

## CONCLUSION

It has been argued elsewhere that the Four-Power Statement has substantial advantages.[54] It would therefore appear worthy of respect, regardless of the question of its binding force. In the Laos case it was not merely the Statement but the Charter itself that suffered a setback. It is not by disregarding the law of the Charter that the Security Council will promote the rule of law in international relations. What the Laos case demonstrated is the persistent attempt of Members of the United Nations to substitute rule by majority for the rule of law. It also demonstrated another and futile effort to liquidate the cold war by majority voting of sorts. Such simplism has failed in the past and is not likely to succeed in the future. The issues of the cold war are altogether too intractable to yield to parliamentary diplomacy, no matter what amount of stagecraft is bestowed upon it.

[54] See Gross, *loc. cit.* note 39 above, p. 269. f. See also *supra* p. 486.

# VOTING IN THE SECURITY COUNCIL: ABSTENTION IN THE POST-1965 AMENDMENT PHASE AND ITS IMPACT ON ARTICLE 25 OF THE CHARTER

## I

The amendments to the Charter adopted by General Assembly Resolution 1991 (XVIII) A of December 17, 1963, relating to the Security Council entered into force on August 31, 1966.[1] As a result, the number of the non-permanent members was raised from six to ten, bringing the total of members of the Council to fifteen and the word "seven" in paragraphs 2 and 3 of Article 27 was replaced by the word "nine." The rest of paragraph 3 of Article 27 was left unchanged and the affirmative and concurring votes of the permanent members continue to be required for decisions of the Council "on all other matters," that is, on all matters other than procedural ones. It is clear from the debates preceding the adoption of the amendments that there was no intention to tamper with this requirement which confers on each of the permanent members the power to cast a "veto," that is, a negative vote.[2] No attempt has been made to clarify the effect of the absence of a permanent member from the Council upon the adoption of decisions re-

[1] General Assembly, 18th Sess., Official Records, Supp. No. 15, at 21–22, 59 A.J.I.L. 985–986 (1965); for a discussion, see Schwelb, "Amendments to Articles 22, 27 and 61 of the Charter of the United Nations," *ibid.* 834–856; and *idem,* 60 *ibid.* 371–378 (1966); regarding the entry into force see "Protocol of Entry into Force of the Amendments to Articles 22, 27 and 61 of the Charter of the United Nations . . . ." Doc. A/6019, Sept. 27, 1965.

[2] As the delegate of Pakistan, Mr. Hasan, observed in the Special Political Committee, the proposed change "related only to a matter of form, namely, the composition of the Council, and not to the substantive aspect represented by the position of the permanent members and their veto power." General Assembly, 18th Sess., Official Records, Special Political Committee, Summary Records, p. 249, par. 18.

lating to non-procedural matters or the effect of the abstention by a permanent member in the vote on such a decision.[3] Presumably, by tacit accord, it was deemed wiser to leave the proverbial Pandora's box locked.

What effect the amendments will have on the position of the permanent members[4] or on the operations and effectiveness of the Security Council as the principal organ of the United Nations, having the primary responsibility for the maintenance of international peace and security, remains to be seen. The intent of the amendments, as stated in the Preamble of Resolution 1991 (XVIII) A was, first, to provide "for a more adequate geographical representation of non-permanent members,"[5] and, secondly, to make it "a more effective organ for carrying out its function under the Charter of the United Nations." One of the effects of the amendments is the possibility that resolutions and decisions can be adopted by a vote of ten or nine non-permanent members if the five permanent members abstain from voting, and provided the practice is continued and accepted that an abstention by one or more permanent members shall not be regarded as contrary to the requirement of Article 27(3). Whether this practice shall be continued was questioned by Portugal and South Africa.

## II

On April 9, 1966, the Security Council adopted Resolution 221 (1966) by a vote of 10 in favor, none against and 5 abstentions (Bulgaria, France, Mali, U.S.S.R., Uruguay) on the subject of Southern Rhodesia. Concerned about reports that substantial supplies of oil may reach Rhodesia, the Council determined "that the resulting situation constitutes a threat to the peace," called upon the Portuguese Government not to receive at Beira oil destined for Rhodesia, or other oil to be pumped through the pipeline from Beira to Rhodesia; called upon "the Government of the United Kingdom to prevent by the use of force if necessary the arrival at Beira of vessels reasonably believed to be carrying oil destined for Rhodesia"; and empowered it "to arrest and detain the tanker known as the Joanna V upon her departure from Beira in the event her oil cargo is discharged there."[6] The resolution refers to no article of the Charter, but one could surmise that it was adopted pursuant to Chapter VII, and more specifically Articles 39, 41, 42 and/or 48(2).

On April 27, 1966, the Minister for Foreign Affairs of Portugal addressed a letter to the Secretary General commenting upon Council Resolution 221 and formulating certain reservations. It requested that these reservations be "submitted to the Office of Legal Affairs of the United Nations" and its replies be communicated to it "so that the Portu-

[3] Gross, "Voting in the Security Council: Abstention from Voting and Absence from Meetings," 60 Yale Law Journal 209–257 (1951) and *supra* pp. 429–471.

[4] Schwelb, *loc. cit.* at 847.

[5] In order to achieve this a pattern for the election of such members is laid down in the resolution: (a) five from African and Asian states; (b) one from Eastern European states; (c) two from Latin American states; (d) two from Western European and other states. On the legal effect of this provision see Schwelb, *loc. cit.* at 852–855.

[6] Doc. S/RES/221(1966), 60 A.J.I.L. 925 (1966); Report of the Security Council July 16, 1965—July 15, 1966, General Assembly, 21st Sess., Official Records Supp. No. 2 (A/6302), p. 62, par. 581, and p. 67, par. 612.

guese Government will be able to be better informed in the matter." The Portuguese Government raised several issues relating to the legality and purpose of the resolution which do not relate to the issue here under consideration. With reference to the vote in the Security Council in which two permanent members—France and the Soviet Union—abstained, it referred to the text of Article 27(3), the "jurisprudence" of the Council "according to which the abstention of a permanent member is not equivalent to a veto," the fact that as long as the Council was composed of eleven members, it could not adopt a resolution "against the simultaneous abstention of the five permanent members," the contingency that in the new Council of fifteen members it was possible to "adopt a resolution against the abstentions of the five permanent members," and asked for clarification of three questions which appeared to it "exremely serious, and to affect the very constitutional structure and political balance of the Council." These questions are:

> (a) If the abstention of a permanent member of the Security Council is understood not to be equal to a veto, must it then be considered that a resolution under Chapter VII, involving the use of force, can be deemed to be adopted even when all the permanent members have abstained?
>
> (b) If this conclusion is wrong, how many and which of the permanent members of the Council may abstain without such abstention causing the rejection of a draft resolution?
>
> (c) If the conclusion is correct, is it to be understood that the non-permanent members of the Council have the right, or the practical opportunity, to take decisions concerning peace, war and world security, and to formulate and have a policy implemented which affects the entire community of nations, without the votes of all or some of the permanent members?[7]

The doubts expressed by Portugal were also entertained by the Republic of South Africa. In a *note verbale* of June 22, 1966, South Africa reserved its position "regarding the validity of the said resolution and of the procedure whereby the Security Council purported to adopt it."[8]

The Secretary General informed the Portuguese Minister on June 21, 1966, that "in the first instance for my own information, a detailed study of the points raised by you was prepared by the Office of Legal Affairs"; that "it has never been the practice that the Office of Legal Affairs gives advice, on the sole request of a Member State, on questions of the nature raised in your letter"; and that while "only the Security Council is in a

[7] Docs. S/7271, April 28, 1966, and S/7271/Corr. 1. The letter contained also the following statement: "The Portuguese Government, which represents a country not a member of the Security Council, has a point of view of its own which is certainly very similar to that of many countries Members of the United Nations; but it considers that, when action under Chapter VII is sought for the first time in the fifteen-member Council, and force is resorted to in the face of the abstention of some permanent Members, the entire problem needs urgent examination under the new conditions prevailing in that important organ of the United Nations."

[8] Doc. S/7392, July 1, 1966. That Government stated also that it has "given consideration to the legal aspects of this matter particularly as this is the first occasion since the amendment of Article 27 of the Charter on which the Security Council purported to give a decision involving enforcement measures in terms of Chapter VII, and as the validity of this action has been widely questioned on various grounds including the fact that two permanent members abstained from voting on the draft resolution in question."

position to give an authoritative interpretation of its resolution 221 (1966), of the Charter Articles on which it is based, and the procedures followed in adopting it," he felt that he "should take at least the responsibility, on this occasion, of informing you that the detailed study prepared for my information does not, in its conclusions, support any of the reservations advanced by the Government of Portugal."[9]

The Portuguese Minister of Foreign Affairs addressed, on July 29, 1966, a communication to the President of the Security Council repeating the previous question. The reply of the President of August 6, 1966, stated that the subject would be brought to the attention of members of the Council for consideration.[10] It does not seem, however, that the Council ever considered the Portuguese reservations. These were restated in a letter dated February 3, 1967, from the Portuguese Minister to the Secretary General in connection with Resolution 232(1966) adopted on December 16, 1966.[11] Resolution 232(1966) was adopted by the Security Council by a vote of 11 in favor, none against and 4 abstentions (Bulgaria, France, Mali, U.S.S.R.).[12] This resolution imposed "mandatory sanctions" against Southern Rhodesia. The Council acted explicitly "in accordance with Articles 39 and 41 of the United Nations Charter"; determined that "the present situation in Southern Rhodesia constitutes a threat to international peace and security"; decided that all States Members shall apply a selective embargo on trade with Southern Rhodesia and other measures; called upon all Members "to carry out this decision of the Security Council in accordance with Article 25 of the United Nations Charter"; and, finally, reminded the Members "that the failure or refusal by any of them to implement the present resolution shall constitute a violation of Article 25 of the Charter."[13]

The position of the Portuguese Government appears to be that, unless and until the questions relating to the voting procedures in connection with both resolutions—Resolution 232(1966) was adopted with two permanent members (France, U.S.S.R.) abstaining—and others relating to substantive aspects receive authoritative replies, it will not comply with them.[14] The position of South Africa seems substantially the same. Whatever may have been the motivation, the questions raised by the two governments revive the old issue about the voting rules in the Security Council and require consideration.

## III

The reply given by the Secretary General was crisp and to the point. There will be general agreement with his proposition that the Security Council is entitled to give an

[9] Doc. S/7373, June 21, 1966; the Secretary General maintained his position in his letter of Feb. 17, 1967, to the Minister for Foreign Affairs of Portugal, in which he acknowledged letters of Feb. 3, 1967, addressed to him by the Portuguese Minister. Doc. S/7798, March 1, 1967.

[10] The President's reply was never circulated in document form but its substance was stated by the Portuguese Government in its letter of Feb. 3, 1967, Doc. S/7735/Rev. 1, p. 3.

[11] Doc. S/7735/Rev. 1, Feb. 14, 1967.

[12] Doc. S/P.V. 1340th meeting, Dec. 16, 1966, pp. 76–80.

[13] Doc. S/RES/232(1966); 61 A.J.I.L. 654 (1967).

[14] Doc. S/7735/Rev. 1, p. 4, par. 6.

authoritative interpretation. Certainly, the procedure of the Security Council could not be questioned by the General Assembly. The tenor of the Advisory Opinion of the International Court of Justice in the *Competence of the General Assembly* case would discourage any attempt by the Assembly to question the validity of any resolution which the Council itself considers validly adopted.[15] Moreover, there is the case of the admission of Israel to the United Nations in 1949. On that occasion the validity of the Security Council recommendation to admit Israel was challenged in the General Assembly on the ground that one permanent member, the United Kingdom, had abstained. The then President of the Assembly, Mr. H. E. Evatt (Australia) ruled

> that the manner in which the recommendation of the Security Council had been adopted concerned the internal government and procedure of the Security Council and must be accepted by the General Assembly as a recommendation of the Security Council within the meaning of the Charter.[16]

It is certainly true, as suggested by the Secretary General, that the Security Council was in a position to give an authoritative interpretation of its Resolution 221(1966). But there is not reason why the Council or the Assembly as well should not be legally able to ask the International Court of Justice for an advisory opinion on the constitutionality of the voting on that or any other resolution. In addition to the Advisory Opinion referred to above, there is another precedent, namely, the request of the Assembly for an opinion in the *Membership* case.[17] In that matter the voting practice in the Security Council was in controversy, and the Court did not see any reason for declining to give the requested opinion on the ground that it came from the Assembly and not from the Security Council.

Furthermore, there is the well-known San Francisco Statement on interpretation which recognizes the right of each organ to interpret those parts of the Charter which are "applicable to its particular functions." It also recognizes the right of the Court to interpret the Charter, a right which, moreover, the Court itself has affirmed on several occasions.[18] The Statement also pointed out "that if an interpretation made by any organ of the Organization . . . is not generally acceptable it will be without binding force," and that in such circumstances it may be necessary "to embody the interpretation in an amendment to the Charter."[19]

The report incorporating the statement on interpretation of the Charter was unanimously adopted by Commission IV on June 15, 1945,[20] and the Plenary Session adopted the report of Commission IV on June 25, 1945.[21] The rule enunciated by the Conference

[15] [1950] I.C.J. Rep. 4, particularly at 10: ". . . nowhere has the General Assembly received the power to change, to the point of reversing, the meaning of a vote of the Security Council."

[16] General Assembly, 3rd Sess., Official Records, Pt. II, at 330, and Gross, *loc. cit.* note 3 above, at 223. And *supra.*

[17] [1948] I.C.J. Rep. 57.

[18] See Membership case, [1948] I.C.J. Rep. 57 at 61, and Expenses case, [1962] *ibid.* 151 at 156.

[19] Doc. 933, June 12, 1945, in 13 U.N.C.I.O. Docs. 703, at 710.

[20] Doc. 1153, IV/12(1), June 22, 1945, *ibid.* 105.

[21] Doc. 1210, P/20, June 27, 1945, 1 *ibid.* 627.

"would seem still to hold good."[22] If one were to stop at this point, the reservations formulated by South Africa and Portugal could be maintained unless and until the practice of the Security Council with respect to abstentions by permanent members were incorporated in an amendment to the Charter. This conclusion would seem to derive added strength from the rules of interpretation adopted by the International Law Commission. In Article 27(2a) of its Draft Articles on the Law of Treaties, the Commission included in the context of a treaty for the purpose of interpretation "any agreement relating to the treaty which was made between all the parties in connexion with the conclusion of the treaty."[23] If there is any doubt as to the character of the Statement as an "agreement," it would certainly qualify as part of the preparatory work to which, pursuant to Article 28 of the Draft Articles, recourse may be had under certain circumstances.

The position taken by the two governments may, however, be also examined more specifically from the point of view of the nature of Resolutions 221 (1966) and 232 (1966). The former was presumptively taken on the basis of Chapter VII but it is not couched in the language of a "decision." It would therefore be doubtful whether it would come within the range of Article 25 of the Charter. The latter, on the other hand, explicitly invokes Articles 39 and 41 of the Charter, it "decides" what the Members shall do or refrain from doing, and twice reminds the Members of their obligations under Article 25 of the Charter. The binding force which Article 25 confers upon decisions of the Security Council would seem to rule out any reservations by individual Members: once adopted by the Council, decisions are *ipso facto* binding and ought to be carried out. Any other interpretation, it could be argued, would undermine the maintenance of international peace and security. From this standpoint Article 25 would appear as the natural and logical corollary of Article 24. Ambassador Arthur J. Goldberg seems to have espoused this view when he said with reference to Resolution 232(1966): "This determination by the Council in the exercise of its charter powers is conclusive and may not be contested by any member."[24]

This categorical statement notwithstanding, another difficulty has to be faced at this point. Article 25 qualifies the decisions of the Council and presumably the duty of Members to accept and carry them out by the words "in accordance with the present Charter." While different interpretations of this clause are possible, the chief point is that, far from ruling out challenges of the constitutionality of the decisions of the Council, it invites them. Grounds for such challenges may be of two kinds: formal and substantive. The South African Government limited its reservation to the voting procedure, that is, to the formal validity of Resolution 221(1966). The Portuguese Government, on the other hand, challenged not merely the voting procedure, the formal validity of Resolutions

[22] Dissenting Opinion of Judge Winiarski in the Expenses case, [1962] I.C.J. Rep. at 229.

[23] I.L.C. Reports on the Second Part of Its 17th Sess., Jan. 3–28, 1966, and on Its 18th Sess., May 4–July 19, 1966. General Assembly, 21st Sess., Official Records, Supp. No. 9 (A/6309/Rev. 1), p. 49; 61 A.J.I.L. 348 (1967) (hereinafter cited as "I.L.C. Rep.").

[24] "International Law in the United Nations," 56 Dept. of State Bulletin 140–145, at 143 (1967).

221(1966) and 232(1966), but also their substantive validity.[25] Leaving out the substantive aspect as outside the scope of this paper, the formal challenges may be examined from two points of view: Is their validity to be determined in terms of the "present" Charter or in terms of the Charter as interpreted in practice?

From the former standpoint the answer could hardly be in doubt. The reservations expressed by members of the Security Council when the Soviet Union first abstained in 1946 in connection with the Spanish Question would support the interpretation that, strictly speaking, abstention was not compatible with Article 27(3).[26] This approach would not commend itself on the ground that it puts the problem in too narrow and rigid a framework. It is also one which has not been contended for by South Africa and Portugal. Portugal seemed primarily concerned with the rôle of abstentions in decisions involving the use of force and more generally in the post-amendment era.

Turning to the second alternative, that is, the validity of the resolutions in terms of the Charter as interpreted in practice, two approaches suggest themselves. According to one, the practice since 1946 would be construed as amounting to a rule of customary international law modifying the "present" Charter, whereas, according to the other, the practice would be just that—the practice of an organ the probative value of which is far from clear. In case the former approach is adopted, the reservations of South Africa and Portugal would appear as clearly untenable. But it is by no means evident that the practice of the Council has hardened into a rule of law with the effect of superseding the rule laid down in the Charter.

Assuming that what we have is merely a practice the legal effect of which is doubtful, the two governments would be justified in raising the issue, particularly with respect to the effect of that practice in the post-amendment phasc and with respect to Chapter VII decisions, and asking for a clarification.

## IV

The Secretary General, in his communication referred to above, rejected the reservations on the basis of the study prepared for him.[27] A detailed study of the subject was published by the Legal Counsel of the United Nations, Dr. Stavropoulos.[28] His conclusion is that the consistent practice of voluntary abstention in voting on non-procedural matters has been accepted by the permanent members and "acquiesced in by other Members of the Organization, and can now be considered a firm part of the constitutional law of the United Nations."[29] This is derived from the fact that since 1946, permanent mem-

[25] See pars. 5–7 of its letter of April 27, 1966, Doc. S/7271, and also its letter of July 29, 1966, addressed to the President of the Security Council, Doc. S/7445, Aug. 3, 1966, and its letter to the Secretary General dated Feb. 3, 1967, Doc. S/7735/Rev. 1, Feb. 14, 1967.

[26] See Gross, *loc. cit.* note 3 above, at 215 ff. See also *supra*, pp. 429–479.

[27] P. 513 above.

[28] Constantin A. Stavropoulos, "The Practice of Voluntary Abstentions by Permanent Members of the Security Council under Article 27, paragraph 3, of the Charter of the United Nations," 61 A.J.I.L. 737–752 (1967).

[29] *Ibid.* at 752.

bers of the Council have voluntarily abstained "at least 264 times in connection with the vote on part or the whole of various non-procedural decisions of the Council which were declared to be adopted."[30] With respect to abstentions in votes relating to Chapter VII, the evidence is less copious. Apart from the two resolutions the validity of which has been questioned, Dr. Stavropoulos refers to Resolution 54 of July 15, 1948, in the Palestine question which invoked Article 39, and other resolutions which in the view of one or more permanent members fell under that chapter.[31] His conclusion on this part of the issue, based in part on preparatory work, is emphatic:

> . . . there is no basis in the text of the Charter or in the practice of the Security Council to distinguish between the effect of a voluntary abstention by a permanent member when the Council is acting under Chapter VII of the Charter and when it is acting under other chapters and articles.[32]

As to that part of the Portuguese reservation which questioned the continuation of the practice of the Council in the current post-amendment phase, Dr. Stavropoulos is, of course, well aware that resolutions can be adopted on non-procedural matters even if all five permanent members of the Council abstain. He sees no reason why, in an event which, to be sure, is not likely to occur, the old practice of not treating abstentions as a negative vote, should not continue.[33] In his view the implementation of a resolution calling for major enforcement measures would "require the active co-operation of all or some of the permanent members and it is difficult to believe that some members would be prepared to commit themselves, through abstention, to taking measures with which they did not fully agree when negative votes on their part could free them of such a commitment."[34] It is, of course, more likely that a resolution which elicited a massive abstention on the part of the permanent members would have become so emasculated as to be fairly meaningless politically precisely in order to avoid a veto. On the other hand, in connection with some issues it may be politically difficult for a permanent member to oppose head-on what seems to be the prevailing current of opinion. In such a case would that

[30] *Ibid.* at 743.

[31] *Ibid.* at 749–750.

[32] *Ibid.* at 750.

[33] The possibility of such an event occurring, while remote, must not be excluded. Dr. Stavropoulos refers (p. 752) to one instance, Resolution S/RES/202(1965) adopted on May 6, 1965, by a vote of 7 to none, with 4 abstentions, the abstainers being four of the five permanent members, namely, France, U.S.S.R., United Kingdom, and the United States. The resolution (Doc. S/6329/Rev. 1) was concerned with Southern Rhodesia. In the explanation of the vote, the representatives of France and the United Kingdom stated that they were concerned about the question of the competence of the Council. The representative of the United States shared these doubts, although he had "no trouble endorsing the principles set forth in the first six operative paragraphs." The Soviet representative considered the resolution "obviously inadequate, although it contained some positive elements." Security Council, 20th Year, Official Records, 1202nd Meeting, p. 17, par. 90; p. 19, par. 96; p. 20, par. 100; and p. 21, par. 109. The representative of the Ivory Coast suggested that the compromise had to be accepted to avoid the "notorious veto," and "that in the light of the present circumstances, the great Powers themselves will in the end understand why the smaller Powers oppose the idea of concentrating all powers in the hands of the Security Council, and since we have just seen the kind of resolutions we may expect in that case." *Ibid.* p. 25, par. 137.

[34] *Loc. cit.* at 752.

member or those members be legally committed to do what the resolution purported to require?

## V

In assessing the significance of the practice of the Security Council in connection with abstentions by permanent members on non-procedural issues, one consideration, it is submitted, could be eliminated. Dr. Stavropoulos is concerned with the effect which acceptance of the reservations formulated by Portugal and South Africa would have on past resolutions on non-procedural matters in which one permanent member or more abstained.[35] There is no compelling reason for assuming that a contrary practice of the Council, namely, treating abstention by a permanent member as failing to satisfy the requirement laid down in Article 27(3), would have or need to have retroactive effect.

The long-standing practice of the Council in the matter of abstention is no doubt impressive, but what precisely is its significance? If it continues, the next question to be considered is whether resolutions adopted with one or several abstentions have the same legal validity and the same binding force as resolutions concurred in by all the permanent members. The increase in membership of the Council and the consequent possibility for all permanent members to abstain in the vote on a non-procedural matter, possibly involving enforcement action, is a factor which may have some bearing in sifting alternative answers.

With respect to the first question—the legal significance of practice—three views require attention: practice of organs, subsequent practice of contracting parties as an element of interpreting a treaty clause, and subsequent practice of contracting parties as a procedure for modifying provisions of a treaty.

The International Law Commission examined these three aspects of practice. It decided to exclude practice of organs from the scope of its Draft Articles on the Law of Treaties on the ground that "this special problem appears to relate to the law of international organizations rather than to the law of treaties, and the Commission did not consider that it would be appropriate to deal with it in the present articles."[36] The Commission correctly, it is believed, pointed out that

> The problem of the effect of the practice of organs of an international organization upon the interpretation of its constituent instrument raises the question how far individual Member States are bound by the practice. Although the practice of the organ as such may be consistent, it may have been opposed by individual Members or by a group of Members which have been outvoted.[37]

[35] *Ibid.* at 744–745, where a list of such resolutions is printed.
[36] 1964 I.L.C. Rep. (16th Sess.) (Doc. A/5809, Oct. 8, 1964), p. 86, par. 14.
[37] *Ibid.* at 85, par. 14.

On the other hand, and consistently with its decision of 1964, the Commission in its final draft included Article 4, which admits and recognizes the autonomy of international organizations with respect to their costituent instruments.[38] This raises, then, the question whether within the juridical framework of the United Nations there have developed any rules governing the legal significance of the practice of organs, particularly in relation to the binding force of such practice upon individual Members. There are no such express rules generally and there is no rule specifically with respect to the practice in connection with Article 27(3). The interpretative statement adopted by the San Francisco Conference could be regarded as constituting a general rule. According to this rule the practice of an organ would not be binding upon dissenting or opposing Members.[39]

The International Court of Justice in the *Expenses* case made liberal use of the practice of organs in connection with relevant articles of the Charter, particularly Articles 17 and 11(2).[40] But apart from the circular nature of the Court's reasoning[41] the real question in connection with the practice of organs is whether it is binding at all and if so whether it is binding upon Members voting in favor of certain resolutions but not upon dissenting Members. This aspect of the problem was considered by Judges Spender and Fitzmaurice in their Separate Opinions and Judge Bustamante in his Dissenting Opinion. While Judge Fitzmaurice appeared to emphasize consent or tacit recognition as an independent and necessary requirement of the binding force of practice, he concluded that, while the practice of the United Nations "cannot be less than very material," it was impossible to regard it "as conclusive in the matter." This is particularly so if, as was the case in connection with the expenses of the United Nations, that very practice "is put in issue."[42]

Judge Bustamante pointed out that "the real reason for the obedience of States Members to the authorities of the Organization is the conformity of the mandates of its competent organs with the text of the Charter." Whereas there is

> a legal presumption that each of the organs of the Organization is careful in its actions to comply with the prescriptions of the Charter; but when, in the opinion of one of the Member States, a mistake of interpretation has been made or there has even been an infringement of the Charter, there is a right to challenge the resolution in which the error has been noted for the purpose of determining whether or not it departed from the Charter.
>
> It cannot be maintained that the resolutions of any organ of the United Nations are

[38] Art. 4 reads as follows: "The application of the present articles to treaties which are constituent instruments of an international organization or are adopted within an international organization shall be subject to any relevant rules of the organization." 1966 I.L.C. Rep. (17th and 18th Sess.), General Assembly, 21st Sess., Official Records, Supp. No. 9 (A/6309/Rev. 1), p. 11.

[39] P. 515 above.

[40] The following are deemed representative statements: "It is a consistent practice of the General Assembly to include in the annual budget resolutions, provision for expenses relating to the maintenance of international peace and security." "The practice of the Organization throughout its history bears out the foregoing elucidation of the term 'action' in the last sentence of Article 11, paragraph 2." [1962] I.C.J. Rep. 151, at 160 and 165.

[41] Leo Gross, "Expenses of the United Nations for Peace-Keeping Operations: The Advisory Opinion of the International Court of Justice," 17 Int. Organization 1–35 at 14 ff. (1963). See also *infra.*

[42] [1962] I.C.J. Rep. at 201.

> not subject to review: that would amount to declaring the pointlessness of the Charter or its absolute subordination to the judgment—always fallible—of the organs.[43]

A presumption of validity of resolutions of the organs of the United Nations, whether from the material viewpoint as contended by the Court and Judge Fitzmaurice,[44] or from the formal point of view, as would be the case with the conformity with the voting requirement in Article 27(3), is always rebuttable; it is not, it is submitted, in the nature of a presumption *juris et de jure.* Where the presumption could rely, as in connection with voluntary abstention of permanent members in votes on non-procedural matters, on a long-continued and consistent practice, the rebuttal may be more difficult but it cannot be excluded *a limine.*

This, in substance, is the essence of Judge Spender's closely reasoned argument against equating "subsequent conduct of the *parties* to a treaty" with "the practice followed by an *organ* of the United Nations."[45] There is no basis for this in the jurisprudence of the present Court or of its predecessor, the Permanent Court of International Justice.[46] A practice cannot be relied on against Members which decline to accept it expressly or tacitly. As Judge Spender put it:

> Apart from a practice which is of a peaceful, uniform and undisputed character accepted in fact by all current Members . . . I accordingly entertain considerable doubt whether practice of an organ of the United Nations has any probative value either as providing evidence of the intentions of the original Member States or otherwise a criterion of interpretation. As presently advised I think it has none.[47]

In short, the views of Judges Spender, Fitzmaurice and Bustamante, each in its own manner, consider consent in one form or another as prerequisite for practice of organs to have legal effect upon Members of the United Nations. This, it will be recalled, is the nub of the San Francisco Statement on the interpretation of the Charter. As Judge Spender put it:

> Each organ of the United Nations, of course, has an inherent right to interpret the Charter in relation to its authority and functions . . . their right to interpret the Charter gives them no power to alter it.[48]

In its second aspect practice appears as a factor in the interpretation of treaties. Subject to Article 4, referred to above, the International Law Commission's Article 27, paragraph 3(b) of the general rule of interpretation is relevant. In connection with the context of a treaty there shall be taken into account

[43] *Ibid.* at 304.
[44] *Ibid.* at 168 and 204.
[45] *Ibid.* at 195. Italics in the original.
[46] See *Ibid.* at 192–195, for a refutation of alleged precedents one of which was invoked by the Court, *ibid.* at 157.
[47] *Ibid.* at 195.
[48] *Ibid.* at 197. For a different view which, however, is not free from ambiguity, see Oscar Schachter, "The Relation of Law, Politics and Action in the United Nations," 109 Hague Academy, Recueil des Cours 169–256, at 187 (1963, II).

> Any subsequent practice in the application of the treaty which establishes the understanding of the parties regarding its interpretation.[49]

In the present context it is only necessary to establish the meaning of the words "the understanding of the parties." In its Comment the Commission states as follows:

> . . . The text provisionally adopted in 1964 spoke of a practice which "establishes the understanding of *all* the parties." By omitting the word "all" the Commission did not intend to change the rule. It considered that the phrase "the understanding of the parties" necessarily means "the parties as a whole." It omitted the word "all" merely to avoid any possible misconception that every party must individually have engaged in the practice where it suffices that it should have accepted the practice.[50]

This statement appears to be in accord with what has been said in connection with the practice of organs. In order to be able to consider subsequent practice of parties to a treaty as an authentic means of interpretation, the practice or conduct must be comprehensive, that is, embracing all parties. It could be argued that insofar as the practice to consider abstention of the permanent members as being in conformity with the requirement of Article 27(3), there was, indeed, such an all-embracing understanding before the coming into force of the amendment changing the composition of the Security Council. Query No. 1: Has the practice acquired such a degree of acceptance that it could not be called in question now as it has been by Portugal and South Africa? Query No. 2: Is the amendment of the Charter sufficiently important to justify the view that beginning with its entry into force a new phase in the functioning of the Council has started in which the previous understanding does not automatically continue? In other words, has the practice of the parties acquired binding force so that it is not open to any member, whether permanent or not, of the Council or to any Member of the Organization not represented on the Council to challenge it?

There does not seem to be any clear-cut answer to any of these queries. The Commission stressed the point that the practice must be "consistent" and that it must establish "the understanding of all the parties" in order to qualify as an authentic means of interpretation. It seems obvious that, even if the practice continues to be consistent, it no longer establishes the understanding of all the parties, that is, of all the Members of the United Nations. Furthermore, it is not at all clear from the Commentary of the Commission whether this rule of interpretation is applicable in case of a practice which is clearly *contra legem.* The reservations of some members of the Council on the occasion of the first abstention by the Soviet Union in 1946 would be evidence of their common understanding that abstention was incompatible with the text of Article 27(3). Analogies to the League

[49] I.L.C. Rep., *op. cit.* at 49.

[50] *Ibid.* at 53, par. 15. Italics supplied. In the same sense the comments by the Government of the United States, 61 A.J.I.L. 1123–1161 at 1159 (1967), on the 1964 draft.

of Nations practice in the matter of abstention are misplaced, as the voting rule for the Council of the League was different from the voting rule for the Security Council.[51]

It remains to consider the third aspect of practice, namely, practice as a process for modifying provisions of a treaty. Again it may be appropriate to recall at the outset Article 4 of the Commission's final Draft Articles on the Law of Treaties. Are there any relevant rules of the United Nations on this subject? There appear to be none[52] except the Statement on the interpretation of the Charter, which emphasizes the requirement of general consent. This requirement, however, is, as will be seen presently, consistent with the view of the Commission.

The Commission in Article 38 states as follows:

> A treaty may be modified by subsequent practice in the application of the treaty establishing the agreement of the parties to modify its provisions.[53]

In the Commentary two points are made which are relevant: first, that the practice to modify a treaty just as the practice to interpret a treaty in a certain way "must be such as to establish the agreement of the parties as a whole to the modification in question";[54] and secondly, that a consistent practice establishing the common consent of the parties "to the application of the treaty in *a manner different from that laid down in certain provisions,* may have the effect of modifying the treaty."[55]

These specific comments suggest two conclusions: first, that the consent of the parties or their acquiescence is required for a practice modifying the provisions of a treaty. The practice of the Security Council over a period of twenty years and covering a wide range of non-procedural matters meets this test. Secondly, that the practice in the application of a treaty does not purport to be in the nature of an interpretation but is frankly in the nature of a modification of treaty provisions. The practice of the Security Council would easily satisfy this requirement. It would be extremely strained, even by means of a teleological interpretation which may in certain circumstances be appropriate to constituent instruments of international organizations,[56] to maintain that abstention by a permanent member in the voting on a non-procedural matter is compatible with the text of Article 27(3). The International Law Commission gave priority to the "ordinary meaning" of the terms of a treaty and, referring to the jurisprudence of the International Court of Justice, it declared in the Commentary that "the textual approach to treaty interpretation is regarded by it (the Court) as established law."[57] Having regard to the

[51] See Gross, *loc. cit.* note 3 above, at 215 f., and p. 227 for a statement by Dr. Liang which draws such an analogy. See also *supra*, pp. 429–471.

[52] And none was cited by Dr. Stavropoulos.

[53] I.L.C. Rep., *op. cit.* 66.

[54] *Ibid.* at 66, par. 2.

[55] *Ibid.* at 65, par. 1 of Commentary to Art. 38. Italics supplied.

[56] Rosenne, "Is the Constitution of an International Organization an International Treaty? Reflections on the Codification of the Law of Treaties," 12 Comunicazioni e Studi (Milan, Instituto di Diritto Internazionale e Straniero) 23–89, at 77 ff. (1966).

[57] I.L.C. Rep., *op. cit.* at 52, par. 11.

equally authentic texts of the Charter in the French, Spanish, Russian and Chinese languages, and accepting the Commission's Article 29 regarding the interpretation of treaties in two or more languages,[58] there is hardly any doubt left that abstention by a permanent member in the voting on a non-procedural matter is incompatible with Article 27(3).

The construction of the practice as modifying rather than as interpreting Article 27(3) of the Charter would meet the necessity of stability in the operation of the Security Council. It may be true, as the Commission declared, that "the line may sometimes be blurred between interpretation and amendment of a treaty through subsequent practice," but it is also true that "legally the processes are distinct."[59] The practical results may also be quite distinct.[60]

As suggested above,[61] a practice is always precarious, as it requires the common consent of the parties and it very probably could not be relied upon in relation to dissenting Members such as Portugal and South Africa. It might be necessary to invoke the doctrine of estoppel or preclusion to overcome their opposition. In any event it is pertinent to recall the pronouncements of the International Court of Justice in the *Peace Treaties* (Second Phase) case on "the natural and ordinary meaning of the terms" of the treaties and that "it is the duty of the Court to interpret the treaties, not to revise them."[62]

In the case of a treaty modified by practice, a tribunal would interpret it

> as revised and . . . give effect to any revision arrived at by the parties. In the last analysis, it seems to be a matter chiefly of the nature and weight of the evidence required to establish the existence of such a revision, whether it results from writing or from practice.[63]

The distinction between these two functions of practice—practice in the sense of subsequent conduct of the parties as a means of interpreting, and practice as a process for modifying provisions of a treaty—lies precisely in the fact that the latter is an independent principle and the former is not. As the Arbitral Tribunal between the United States and Italy declared in 1965:

> The conduct of the parties in their application of the 1948 Agreement is not, of course, in itself decisive for the interpretation of the disputed text; it can however serve as

[58] *Ibid.* at 54–56; see also Gross, *loc. cit.* note 3 above, at 210. See also *supra.*

[59] *Ibid.* at 66, par. 1 of Commentary to Art. 39.

[60] But see Stavropoulos, *loc. cit.* at 741; "Whether the example of voluntary abstentions under Article 27, paragraph 3, of the Charter is considered as a case of interpretation or a case of modification through subsequent practice—the practical if not the legal effects being the same . . ."

[61] See p. 522 above.

[62] [1950] I.C.J. Rep. 221 at 227 and 229.

[63] Sir Gerald Fitzmaurice, "The Law and Procedure of the International Court of Justice 1951–4: Treaty Interpretation and Other Treaty Points," 33 Brit. Yr. Bk. Int. Law 203–293 at 225 (1957); see also pp. 212 and 252. Sir Gerald (at p. 225) links the principle of revision by conduct with the doctrine of "Emergent Purpose." Such connection may indeed exist in some cases but not in others. As an independent principle, revision by conduct may stand on its own feet.

> *additional evidence* as regards the meaning to be attributed to the text on the basis of the objective sought and the intentions of the parties.[64]

Distinguishing practice in this sense from practice which results in a rule of customary international law, the Tribunal stated:

> . . . the matter at issue is not to deduce a legal standard from the practice followed but merely to reveal the interpretation the parties gave to the provisions in dispute, which can serve as additional evidence in ascertaining the intentions of the parties and illustrate their intent as of the time the Agreement was concluded.[65]

The practice of the Security Council concerning abstention could hardly qualify as "additional evidence" of the intent of the parties "as of the time" the Charter was drafted and initially implemented.

On the other hand, the 1963 Arbitral Tribunal, in the dispute between France and the United States regarding air transport services, admitted practice as a process for modifying treaty provisions in a passage quoted by the International Law Commission in support of Article 38:

> This course of conduct may, in fact, be taken into account not merely as a means useful for interpreting the Agreement, but also as something more: that is, as a possible source of a subsequent modification arising out of certain actions or certain attitudes having a bearing on the juridical situation of the parties and on the rights that each of them could properly claim.[66]

It may be concluded, then, that if it is desired to explain juridically the practice of the Council in the evaluation of abstention of permanent members, and if this practice is to be placed on a firm legal foundation, then the construction of this practice as a rule of customary international law modifying *pro tanto* Article 27(3)[67] of the Charter is indicated.[68] If the practice is construed as customary international law, the reservations of Portugal and South Africa must be regarded as untenable.[68a] However, this does not, it is believed, conclude the matter.

[64] Italy-United States Air Transport Agreement. Advisory Opinion of Tribunal, July 17, 1965, 4 Int. Legal Materials 974–984 at 983 (1965); also in 60 A.J.I.L. 413–418 at 418 (1966). Italics supplied.

[65] *Ibid.*

[66] I.L.C. Rep., *op. cit.* at 65, par. 1 of Commentary on Art. 38; 58 A.J.I.L. 1023 (1964). The Italo-American Tribunal distinguished this holding from its own view regarding practice. *Ibid.*

[67] The text of Art. 27(3) would then read as follows: "Decisions of the Security Council on all other matters shall be made by an affirmative vote of nine members and without the negative vote of any of the permanent members; . . ." or: "Decisions of the Security Council on all other matters shall be made by an affirmative vote of nine members including the concurring votes of the permanent members provided that abstention shall not be construed as a negative vote; . . ."

[68] This is the view of Professor G. I. Tunkin in the passage from his book, Droit International Public 94–95 (1965), quoted by Stavropoulos, *loc. cit.* at 746. Tunkin, however, derives the custom from "the interpretation of paragraph 3 of Article 27 of the Charter which has been followed by the Security Council." His view is not shared by this writer for the reasons developed in this paper.

[68a] It is assumed, of course, that the process of modification of a treaty by subsequent practice applies even in case of a multilateral treaty which, like the Charter, provides a specific method for amending it. See I.L.C. Rep., p. 62, par. 4, and p. 66, par. 3 of Commentary to Art. 38.

## VI

It is suggested that a distinction may be drawn between the validity of resolutions on non-procedural matters, such as Resolutions 221(1966) and 232(1966), declared adopted with some of the permanent members abstaining, and their binding force for the Members of the United Nations. Assuming the correctness of the above construction, the resolutions ought to be regarded as formally valid. But validity is one thing, binding force is another. This is clearly and easily seen in connection with resolutions of the General Assembly. Resolutions relating to the internal economy of the Organization, such as admission to membership, appointment of the Secretary General, budget and many other matters, have legally binding force if they are formally valid. Resolutions relating to the maintenance of international peace and security calling for some action by the Members have no legally binding force even if they are formally valid.

A similar distinction could be made with respect to resolutions of the Security Council. Generally, resolutions under Chapter VI have no legally binding force for Members even if they are formally valid. On the other hand, decisions under Chapter VII have, pursuant to Article 25 of the Charter, legally binding force if they are also formally valid.[68b] The distinction is juridically and politically highly relevant and, as a matter of fact, the reply to be given to one of the questions raised by Portugal depends on this distinction.[69] Fitzmaurice examined the question whether a resolution of the General Assembly, "though not obliging member States to take certain action, may act as an authority to them to do so . . . and how far such a resolution can operate to release a member State from a pre-existing obligation." His answer is as follows:

> . . . as regards decisions of the Security Council—since Members have an obligation under the Charter to carry them out, they would be justified for this purpose in breaking a pre-existing treaty, and indeed bound to do so, so far as the Charter goes. But, as they are not under any direct legal obligation to carry out Assembly resolutions, they could not plead any conflict of *obligations* . . . . The pre-existing obligation would therefore prevail, in law.[70]

This, it is believed, is a correct statement of the principle. Accordingly, assuming Resolutions 221(1966) and 232(1966) to be not merely valid but also legally binding, Members, including Portugal, would be justified as well as obligated to carry them out even if pre-existing obligations stood in the way.

[68b] The question of the substantive validity of General Assembly and Security Council resolutions is not considered here.

[69] The Portuguese Government noted that Res. 221(1966) "constitutes a clear denial of the principle of freedom of the seas and the principle of free access to the sea by landlocked countries. As these principles have been embodied in conventions which have the status of international law, the Portuguese Government does not believe that the Security Council can legislate against international law as now in force. Otherwise, it must be asked whether international law is to be regarded as repealed. If the reply should be in the negative, the resolution of 9 April will have to be regarded as invalid. If it should not be possible to give an absolute reply, the question would then be when can the Council violate international law and when can it not do so?" Doc. S/7271, April 28, 1966, p. 3, par. 5. The answer to this question will be given in the text. It may be observed here that, in the apparent contemplation of the Portuguese Government, Southern Rhodesia is a state or that it otherwise qualifies for the right of access to the sea as a landlocked country.

[70] Sir Gerald Fitzmaurice, "The Law and Procedure of the International Court of Justice, 1951–4: Questions of Jurisdiction, Competence and Procedure," 34 Brit. Yr. Bk. Int. Law 1–161 at 5 (1958). Italics in the original.

The question which, in the present submission, needs to be faced is whether Security Council decisions adopted pursuant to Article 27(3) as modified by practice having the character of custom, are still to be considered as imposing legal obligations upon the Members pursuant to Article 25, or whether in consequence of the modification of Article 27(3) there are compelling reasons for considering Article 25 as having been modified or as requiring modification. The change in the composition of the Security Council and the possibility created thereby that decisions calling for action under Chapter VII may be validly adopted even if all permanent members abstain, is certainly a factor, though perhaps not a decisive factor, which requires consideration. The factor which is decisive in this context is that abstention by permanent members in voting on such decisions may change or, to use a stronger word, frustrate the political basis for the action by the Security Council, particularly if abstention is followed by inaction by the permanent members.

There is hardly any room for doubting the political assumptions on which the United Nations as a security organization was established. It was the continued cooperation of the great Powers which, as permanent members of the Security Council, would enjoy, by reason of their power and their political responsibilities, a special, dominant position on that body. This political assumption found legal expression in Articles 24, 25, 27(3) and 106 of the Charter. In matters of major political consequence the great Powers were to act in concert and not to shirk their responsibility by abstaining. The juridical expression of the political concert of power was a guarantee for the rank and file of the membership of the United Nations first, that they would not be called upon to involve themselves in any type of enforcement measures unless the power and prestige of the great Powers were solidly behind them; and secondly, that, because of voting requirement, such measures would be taken only in exceptional cases. Abstention by permanent members amounting to a consistent and continued practice thoroughly undermines these reasonable expectations. This in itself could appear to justify the conclusion that decisions of the Security Council particularly under Chapter VII should be regarded as permissive rather than as legally binding.

Another factor which should be taken into account is the selection of the non-permanent members. The Charter in Article 23(1) laid down two criteria for their election: a special one, the "contribution of Members . . . to the maintenance of international peace and security" and an additional one, "equitable geographical distribution." For many years the second criterion has tended to be dominant and the first, the special criterion, to be practically disregarded. This practice could only have a detrimental effect on the rôle and responsibility of the Council as the organ entrusted with primary responsibility for the maintenance of international peace and security. Now this practice has been reinforced by General Assembly Resolution 1991 (XVIII) A on the amendment of Article 23(1). In operative paragraph 3 that Resolution "decides" the geographical pattern which shall govern the election of non-permanent members of the Council. It is legally correct to say that this decision is "not part of the Charter amendments and, therefore, not part of the Charter."[71] However, the election which took place following the entry into force of the Amendments would indicate that, even though not part of the Charter, the decision of the Assembly and not the law of the Charter governed the election of non-permanent members. No useful purpose will be served, it is felt, in preserving the fiction that the Security Council in its composition is equipped to discharge effectively its primary responsibility. This should not be taken as a criticism of the importance which geographical distribution has come to occupy in the election of non-permanent members. It is merely suggested that decisions of a Security Council which is *not* the Security Council intended by the Charter, should not automatically have the legal significance which Article 25 attributes to the decisions of the Security Council intended by the Charter.

It is not possible within the scope of this paper to investigate the practical political consequences of decisions of the Security Council which were validly adopted, although without the concurring votes of the permanent members. In many instances it is a matter of controversy under what article or chapter resolutions were adopted by the Council. For this reason alone it would be difficult to carry out such an investigation into the actual behavior of Members generally and of the permanent members of the Security Council in particular. But there is another and even more subtle difficulty. Members may appear as carrying out decisions or supporting Security Council action or as refraining from doing so without it being possible to determine whether their behavior is motivated by a sense of legal obligation or of political interest or of sheer opportunism.

In the *Expenses* case the Court, after reciting various Security Council resolutions relating to the operations in the Congo, and finding that they were adopted unanimously or without a dissenting vote, concluded:

> In the light of such a record of reiterated consideration, confirmation, approval and ratification by the Security Council and by the General Assembly of the actions of the Secretary-General in implementing the resolution of 14 July 1960, it is impossible to reach the conclusion that the operations in question usurped or impinged upon the prerogatives conferred by the Charter on the Security Council . . . .[72]

Yet some Members of the United Nations and even members of the Security Council reached the opposite conclusion and acted upon it. Judge Koretsky in his Dissenting Opinion, referring to the conclusion of the Court cited above, pointed out that the unanimity was more apparent than real. He referred particularly to the objection of the Soviet representative "against entrusting the Secretary-General with the implementation of the suggested measures" and stated:

> Therefore, any kind of vote on the resolution (and especially abstention from voting) does not mean that *all* the paragraphs of the resolution were approved by all those who did

[71] Schwelb, *loc. cit.* at 852.
[72] [1962] I.C.J. Rep. 151, at 176–177.

> not cast a dissenting vote. Such reservations are often made, even while voting "for" a resolution.[73]

If this is the real situation as distinguished from the apparent situation, does it make sense, legally speaking, to attribute more than permissive authority to resolutions of the Council?

The resolution of May 6, 1965, referred to above[74] was adopted by seven votes to none, with four abstentions, all four being permanent members of the Council. Three of them explained their abstention on the ground that they had doubts about the competence of the Council to adopt it. Strictly speaking, such a resolution would be of doubtful legal validity. Relying more on the apparent than the real vote, it could be, as it has been, considered as formally valid, but should it be legally binding? The resolution, dealing with Southern Rhodesia, was particularly addressed to the United Kingdom. Its representative spoke as follows after its adoption:

> The fact that we have abstained from the vote on this resolution must certainly not be held in any way to mean that we accept the competence of the Security Council in the situation before us.[75]

It may in any event be doubtful whether this resolution fell under Chapter VII and consequently under Article 25 of the Charter, but on its face the representative's statement would seem to reject the attribution of any binding force to the resolution.

It is not intended to argue here that, as a consequence of the actual behavior of Members of the United Nations, resolutions relating to Chapter VII measures are invariably and without exception of permissive rather than legally binding character if not concurred in by the permanent members. The practice may neither be consistent nor continue to serve as an authentic means of interpretation of, or as modifying, the relevant Charter provisions. But it is believed that there are sufficient reasons militating against any confident assumption that these provisions have retained their pristine integrity and offer a reliable basis for predicting the conduct of Members when called upon to take action pursuant to such resolutions. This conclusion is, moreover, in harmony with the whole trend in the United Nations from coercive and legally binding enforcement measures to permissive and voluntary peacekeeping operations. The Charter has set before the Members a pattern of collective security which experience has shown to be unattainable. The obstacles, all of them political in character and some of them transcending the United Nations, may be temporary. But this is a matter for hope and not for prediction.

It may be objected that the suggested transition from obligatory to permissive measures may undermine the effectiveness of the Security Council as the primary guardian of international peace and security and that the Security Council is reduced to the level of the

[73] *Ibid.* at 279.
[74] P. 518 above.
[75] Security Council, 20th Year, Official Records, 1202nd meeting, May 6, 1965, at 18, par. 90.

General Assembly. This is not so, for the undermining has been performed by the Security Council with the assistance of the rank and file Members of the United Nations.

What then should be the answers to Portugal's questions? In answer to the first question it is suggested that resolutions under Chapter VII are deemed valid even when all permanent members of the Council abstain in the vote. The second question therefore does not arise. The third question, insofar as it relates to the right of non-permanent members to have a policy implemented which affects the entire community of nations, may be answered as follows: Resolutions under Chapter VII are legally valid if adopted by nine non-permanent members without the opposing vote of any of the permanent members, but they are permissive and not legally binding; they may be implemented by Members willing to do so; however, assuming the above to be correct, Members would not be justified in breaking pre-existing obligations. Finally, if a state, whether a Member of the United Nations or not, should complain that such a pre-existing obligation had been violated, the matter could, by mutual consent, be referred to an arbitral tribunal or to the International Court of Justice for a judicial determination.

# VOTING IN THE SECURITY COUNCIL AND THE PLO

## I. INTRODUCTION

The United States and some other members of the United Nations have been concerned in recent years about the substance of some resolutions of the General Assembly and the procedures by which they were adopted. Their concern was intensified by certain actions at the twenty-ninth session, when the Assembly sustained a ruling of its President with respect to the representation and participation of South Africa in that and future sessions,[1] when it curbed the right of Israel to participate in the debate on the question of Palestine, when it accorded to the representative of the PLO (Palestine Liberation Organization) a treatment usually reserved to the head of a member state, and when it declared by Resolution 3210(XXIX) of October 14, 1974, "that the Palestinian people is the principal party to the question of Palestine" and invited the PLO "to participate in the deliberation of the General Assembly on the question of Palestine in plenary meetings."

However questionable some or all of these actions may be from a constitutional

[1] The text of the ruling was as follows:

> On the basis of the consistency with which the General Assembly has regularly refused to accept the credentials of the delegation of South Africa, one may legitimately infer that the General Assembly would in the same way reject the credentials of any other delegation authorized by the Government of the Republic of South Africa to represent it, which is tantamount to saying in explicit terms that the General Assembly refuses to allow the delegation of South Africa to participate in its work

UN Doc. A/PV.2281, Nov. 12, 1974 at 76. Also in Resolutions of Legal Interest Adopted by the General Assembly at its Sixth Special Session and Twenty-Ninth Regular Session 21 (1974). *See also* 29 GAOR, Supp. 31, at 10–11, UN Doc. A/9631 (1974), where the text of the ruling is, however, not reproduced.

point of view, they could not have been prevented by a group of members which is in the minority in the Assembly. Nor could this group prevent the Assembly from adopting at the thirtieth session, Resolution 3379(XXX) in which it "determines that Zionism is a form of racism and racial discrimination."[2]

One would have been justified in expecting that the United States and other minority members, particularly those which are permanent members of the Security Council, would have been on their toes to prevent the contagion of unbridled majoritarianism from infecting that principal organ of the United Nations. This, regrettably, has not been the case.

## II. VOTING IN THE SECURITY COUNCIL ON NOVEMBER 30, 1975

On November 30, 1975, the Security Council, by a vote of 13 to 0, with China and Iraq not participating in the vote, adopted Resolution 381(1975),[3] prolonging the mandate of the UN Disengagement Observer Force (UNDOF) for six months and linking this third extension with the decision "to reconvene on 12 January 1976, to continue the debate on the Middle East problem including the Palestine question, taking into account all relevant United Nations resolutions."

There is no harm, following the precedent of the Council's Resolution 338(1973), in linking peacekeeping with peacemaking. In the case of Resolution 381(1975), however, there is a deliberate attempt, which could have been prevented, to introduce into the debate in the Council resolutions of the General Assembly which had been opposed by a minority including the United States. As interpreted by the United States, for instance, "all relevant United Nations resolutions" meant "only Security Council resolutions 242(1967) and 338(1973)."[4] The Soviet Union understood the words to include "first and foremost Security Council resolution 338(1973) and General Assembly resolution 3236(XXIX)."[5] If the debate was to be based on Security Council resolutions alone, the United States and possibly the United Kingdom and France should have voted against the resolutions unless the controversial terms were eliminated. This might but not necessarily would have prevented the extension of the mandate of UNDOF, but in the circumstances

[2] G.A. Res. 3379(XXX), Nov. 10, 1975. Resolutions of Legal Interest Adopted by the General Assembly at its Seventh Special Session and Thirtieth Regular Session 68 (1975).

At the close of the thirtieth session on December 17, 1975, the U.S. representative to the United Nations declared:

> None will learn with surprise that for the United States, at very least, the 30th General Assembly has been a profound, even alarming disappointment. This splendid hall has, since the opening of the Assembly, been repeatedly the scene of acts which we regard as abominations. We have not sought to conceal this view. Nor is it our view alone. Throughout the world individuals and governments have observed this General Assembly with dismay.

74 DEPT. STATE BULL. 139 (1976).

[3] UN Doc. S/PV.1856, Nov. 30, 1975, at 16.

[4] *Id.* at 12–15. *See also* similar statements by Costa Rica, Japan, France, the United Kingdom, Italy, and Sweden, *id.* at 31, 33–35, 37, 41, 44–45, and 56.

[5] *Id.* at 64–65. The Soviet representative also referred to G.A. Res. 3375 (XXX) (see *infra* note 40), as did the representative of Tanzania. *Id.* at 58.

this might have been the lesser evil. In any event the cease-fire and disengagement of forces do not depend upon the stationing of the Force.[6]

It is not suggested that the extension of UNDOF is automatic. It is up to the Security Council to renew the mandate or let it lapse. What is suggested is that the cease-fire is not legally dependent on the stationing of UNDOF but on Security Council Resolution 338(1973) of October 22, 1973, and the above-mentioned Agreement signed on May 31, 1974, under the terms of which Israel and Syria committed themselves to observe scrupulously the cease-fire on land, sea, and air and refrain from all military actions in implementation of Resolution 338(1973). As to the stationing of the Force, it has to be observed that the Security Council in Resolution 350(1974) of May 31, 1974, welcomed the Agreement and decided: "the Force shall be established for an initial period of six months, subject to renewal by further resolution of the Security Council."[7] There are no conditions attached to it. In particular, there does not seem to exist any sort of "good faith" agreement with respect to the current United Nations Emergency Force (UNEF) in Sinai or UNDOF which would make this operation dependent on the continuing consent of either Egypt or Syria, as was the case in connection with UNEF established in 1956. The "good faith" agreement was incorporated in the "*Aide-mémoire* on the basis for the presence and functioning of the United Nations Emergency Force in Egypt" of November 20, 1956, negotiated by Secretary-General Dag Hammarskjöld and Egypt[8] and approved by the General Assembly in Resolution 1121(XI) of November 24, 1956.[9]

The *aide-mémoire* derived from the Secretary-General's understanding that UNEF would be functioning under the terms of the "Uniting for Peace" resolution and "would be limited in its operations to the extent that the consent of the parties concerned is required under generally recognized international law. While the General Assembly is enabled to *establish* the Force . . . it could not request the Force to be *stationed* or *operate*

[6] The contractual underpinnings of the disengagement were recalled by the representative of Costa Rica:

> The action that it [the Security Council] has taken today cannot be separated from the background which caused it to be taken. The preceding action concerned the Agreement on Disengagement between Israeli and Syrian forces, on which the Secretary-General submitted a report to the Council . . .
>
> The Agreement itself, which is not restricted by any deadline, was the result of the sovereign will of the signatory parties and represents a commitment to be observed by both parties. In this connexion, let us recall the final paragraph of Annex B of that Agreement, which reads:
>
> > "Israel and Syria will support a resolution of the United Nations Security Council which will provide for the UNDOF contemplated by the agreement. The initial authorization will be for six months subject to renewal by further resolution of the Security Council . . ."
>
> This implies that the Disengagement Agreement was not conditioned by any given deadline, that the renewal of the mandate is something to which the Security Council must agree, although such decisions cannot jeopardize the Agreement nor subject it to conditions. This emerges clearly from the very text of the Agreement.

*Id.* at 29–30. For the Secretary-General's report, see UN Doc. S/11302/Add. 1, May 30, 1974. The quoted paragraph is at *id.* 4.

[7] 29 SCOR Res. and Dec. 4 (1974).

[8] 11 GAOR, Annexes, Agenda Item 66, UN Doc. A/3375 (1956).

[9] 11 GAOR, Supp. 17, at 61, UN Doc. A/3572 (1956).

on the territory of a given country without the consent of the Government of that country."[10] The *aide-mémoire* was the basis for Egypt's unilateral termination of UNEF on May 18, 1967, and for Secretary-General U Thant's acquiescence.[11] The current UNEF was established by Security Council Resolution 341(1973) of October 27, 1973[12] on the basis of the report of the Secretary-General on the implementation of Resolution 340(1973).[13] The report does not refer to any prior agreement with Egypt,[14] and UNDOF does not seem to be contingent on Syria's continuing consent, although politically the withdrawal of consent may well spell the end of UNDOF if the Council so decides or fails otherwise to deal with the situation.[15]

After the adoption of Resolution 381(1975), the President of the Council, on the basis of informal consultations, read a statement "regarding the agreement of the majority of the Security Council as an opinion of that majority":

[10] Second and final Report of the Secretary-General on the plan for an emergency UN Force, Nov. 6, 1956. Italics in original. GAOR, 1st Emerg. Spec. Sess., Annexes, Agenda Item 5, UN Doc. A/3302 (1956). The Secretary-General indicated that the situation might be different if the Security Council were to use the force "within the wider margins provided under Chapter VII" of the Charter. The present UNEF was established, as was UNDOF, by the Security Council but whether under Chapter VII is a matter of construction.

[11] Spec. Report of the Secretary-General, May 18, 1967. 22 GAOR, Annexes, Agenda Item 21(b), UN Doc. A/6669 (1967); and Report of the Secretary-General on the withdrawal of the emergency force, June 26, 1967, GAOR, 5th Emerg. Spec. Sess., Annexes, Agenda Item 5, UN Doc. A/6730 (1967). For relevant excerpts from these reports, as well as those cited *supra* notes 8 and 10, see R. HIGGINS, UNITED NATIONS PEACEKEEPING 1946–1967 (1969), particularly at 263, 337, 339, 342–43, 355. Reviewing the constitutional basis of the 1956 UNEF, Higgins disagrees with the view that "Egypt was legally completely unfettered in demanding UNEF's withdrawal." She states:

> There are strong grounds for arguing that Egypt voluntarily tempered reliance on "sovereign consent" by acknowledging that good faith would be relevant if ever she wished UNEF to withdraw before its tasks were completed. Its tasks were not yet completed, and in May 1967 it would have been legally appropriate to call the good faith of Egypt in question.

*Id.* 367.

[12] 28 SCOR RES. AND DEC. 11 (1973).

[13] *Ibid.* For the Secretary-General's report, see 28 SCOR Supp. for Oct.–Dec. 1973, at 91, UN Doc. S/11052/Rev. 1, Oct. 26, 1973.

[14] After the vote on Resolution 341(1973), the representative of Egypt announced that his government had "accepted Security Council resolution 340(1973) as a first step in the implementation of the decisions adopted by the Security Council" and declared the readiness of his government "to co-operate with the United Nations in the implementation of Security Council resolutions 338(1973), 339(1973) and 340(1973)." He also stated that:

> In giving its consent to the entry and presence of the United Nations Emergency Force on Egyptian territory, the Government of Egypt is exercising its sovereign rights to enable the United Nations to proceed with this first step and temporary measure towards putting an end to the aggression committed against Egypt since 1967.

UN Doc. S/PV.1752, Oct. 27, 1973, at 36. *See also* UN Doc. S/PV.1750, Oct. 25, 1973 and the Egyptian statement in UN Doc. S/11055, Oct. 27, 1973, 28 SCOR Supp. Oct.–Dec. 1973, at 92. The legal significance of the Egyptian statement is not clear. It was not endorsed by the Security Council.

[15] This seems to have been the understanding of the United States and the Soviet Union in their statements before the adoption of Resolution 350(1974) *supra* note 7. The former declared: "the general principles which guided the United Nations Emergency Force clearly apply to all aspects of the United Nations Disengagement Force, including the assurances of its continued effective functioning for the duration of the mandate established in the draft resolution." UN Doc. S/PV.1774, May 31, 1974, at 4–5. The Soviet representative noted his government's approval of the statement of the Secretary-General "to the effect that the United Nations Disengagement Observer Force will be created on the basis of the general principles which were presented by the Secretary-General" in his previous report. *Id.* at 11. The report referred to is UN Doc. S/11052/Rev. 1, *supra* note 13.

> It is the understanding of the majority of the Security Council that when it reconvenes on 12 January 1976 in accordance with paragraph (a) of resolution 381(1975) the representatives of the Palestine Liberation Organization will be invited to participate in the debate.[16]

In accordance with the prior agreement no vote was taken on this statement,[17] although some members of the Council declared that they were not part of the majority.[18] France, although not objecting to the President's statement, correctly pointed out that this was "a procedural step which could have been settled, in accordance with normal practice, when the debate planned for January is taken up."[19] The Italian representative made the additional point that it was not "in conformity with the rules of procedure and normal practice to anticipate a decision which belongs to the Security Council to take when it meets on 12 January, the more so since from 1 January 1976 its composition will not be the same as at present."[20] The President, the representative of the USSR, wishing "to make a clarification" stated: "A decision taken by one membership of the Council is binding upon the next membership of the Council."[21] This is a dubious proposition at best although it is true, of course, that a resolution of the Council validly adopted remains in force until amended or abrogated by a subsequent resolution. In this case there was no formal resolution. A "standing decision" to participate in the Council's consideration of certain agenda items is not unknown in the practice of the Council. Reference may be made to the invitation of June 25, 1950, under rule 39 of the Council's Provisional Rules of Procedure, to the Government of the Republic of Korea "to sit at the Council table during the consideration" of the complaint of aggression upon the Republic.[22] Although it was claimed to be "binding," the President of the Council, the representative of the Soviet Union, during the month of August 1950, insisted that in accordance with rule 39 "the Security Council decides in each separate meeting whether to invite 'members of the Secretariat or other persons' "[23] and, practicing the filibuster technique for which he became notorious at the time, he declined to rule on the following point of order raised by China:

> Does the President consider it obligatory upon him to carry out the decision of the Security Council of June 25 by inviting the representative of the Republic of Korea to take his place at the Council table?[24]

16 UN Doc. S/PV.1856, Nov. 30, 1975, at 16.

17 *See* UN Doc. S/11889, Nov. 30, 1975.

18 Thus, Costa Rica, Italy, and the United States. UN Doc. S/PV.1856, Nov. 30, 1975, at 31, 46, and 53.

19 *Id.* at 37. Similarly the United Kingdom considered "that in accordance with the established procedures and rules of the Council the question of participation in any meetings of the Council is a matter which has to be decided at the time of those meetings themselves." *Id.* at 41.

20 *Id.* at 46.

21 *Ibid.*

22 Repertoire of the Practice of the Security Council 1946–1951, UN Doc. ST/PSCA/1 (1954), Case 53, at 114. *See also* Case 64, *id.* at 119.

23 Case 93, *id.* at 131–32.

24 *Ibid.*

As will be shown, consistency in the interpretation and application of the Charter and rules of procedure is a rare virtue in the practice of the organs of the United Nations.

## III. VOTING IN THE SECURITY COUNCIL ON DECEMBER 4, 1975

The next step relating to the participation of the PLO occurred on December 4, 1975, when the Council met pursuant to a letter of December 3, 1975 from Lebanon concerning Israeli attacks directed at Palestinian refugee camps on Lebanese territory. The Council had also received a letter of the same date from Egypt, requesting the participation of the PLO in the discussion of the Lebanese complaint. At the outset, the President of the Council (the representative of the United Kingdom) made the following statement:

> In the course of the informal consultations that have taken place prior to this meeting , the representatives of Guyana, Iraq, Mauritania, the United Republic of Cameroon and the United Republic of Tanzania have put forward the same proposal. I have been asked by those five members of the Council to record that this proposal is not being put forward under rule 37 or rule 39 of the provisional rules of procedure of the Security Council, but, if it is adopted by the Council, the invitation to the Palestine Liberation Organization to participate in this debate will confer on it the same rights of participation as are conferred when a Member State is invited to participate under rule 37.[25]

In response to a question by the French representative, the President affirmed that "the representatives of the Palestine Liberation Organization would not be invited under rule 39 of the provisional rules of procedure."[26] The representative of France then stated "that this invitation can be extended only on the basis of rule 39," that "in fact, the only persons who have so far been heard by the Council outside the context of rule 39 have been representatives of Member or non-Member States of the Organization," and that

[25] UN Doc. S/PV.1859, Dec. 4, 1975, at 3.
Rule 37 reads:

> Any Member of the United Nations which is not a member of the Security Council may be invited, as a result of the decision of the Security Council, to participate, without vote, in the discussion of any question brought before the Security Council when the Security Council considers that the interests of that Member are specially affected, or when a Member brings a matter to the attention of the Security Council in accordance with Article 35(1) of the Charter.

Rule 39 reads:

> The Security Council may invite members of the Secretariat or other persons, whom it considers competent for the purpose, to supply it with information or to give other assistance in examining matters within its competence.

Since rule 38 lays down the rights of a member invited under rule 37, it may be useful to quote its text.

> Any Member of the United Nations invited in accordance with the preceding rule or in application of Article 32 of the Charter to participate in the discussions of the Security Council may submit proposals and draft resolutions. These proposals and draft resolutions may be put to a vote only at the request of a representative of the Security Council.

[26] UN Doc. S/PV.1859, Dec. 4, 1975, at 3.

"since the formula envisaged for hearing the representatives of the Palestine Liberation Organization is different from that laid down in rule 39 of the rules of procedure, my delegation will, to its regret, be unable to associate itself with the decision that it is proposed this Council should take."[27] The delegate of Italy considered that the invitation could only be based on rule 39 and that the proposal raised "serious doubts and reservations as to its acceptability and its conformity with the provisions of the Charter, the rules of procedure and the spirit of this Organization."[28] In the view of Japan, rule 39 was "applicable to the present case."[29] The strongest statement on the proposal, from the legal point of view, was made by the President of the Council speaking as the representative of the United Kingdom:

> That proposal contemplates conferring on the Palestine Liberation Organization a right to participate in the proceedings of the Council in this debate going far beyond what has customarily been accepted as appropriate in such a case. The granting to the PLO of this exceptional status in the Council's proceedings would, in the view of my Government, constitute an undesirable and unnecessary departure from the established practice of the Security Council. The provisional rules of procedure of the Council provide only for Member States of the Organization to enjoy such treatment. We see no sufficient reason to depart from that position. We certainly do not regard it as appropriate to accord such exceptional treatment to a body which is not merely not a Member State of this Organization, but which does not claim to be a State at all, nor to be the government of a State. The Palestine Liberation Organization has been accorded a certain status by the General Assembly, but it does not, in our view, have the same status as those States which have been recognized as permanent observers to this Organization.[30]

Clearly what was involved was not merely a procedural issue and respect for precedent. What was involved was a constitutional issue of the first magnitude. There was also a political issue, namely the question whether the PLO should be invited at all. The United States representative spoke primarily to the latter issue when he urged "all who share the hope for a just peace in the Middle East to withhold their support from this egregious attempt to use this body to deal with an amorphous, terrorist organization as though it were a concrete entity with the attributes of a sovereign Government."[31]

The supporters of the proposal skirted the consitutional issue presented by the words "the invitation . . . will confer on it the same rights . . ." and argued either that

[27] *Id.* at 6.

[28] *Id.* at 11–12. He explained his doubts and reservations saying:

> First of all, no one can fail to take for granted that so far this Organization is an organization of sovereign States. The rights, duties and privileges and responsibilities set and conceived within the United Nations are linked to the very essence of statehood. Whatever feelings, consideration or sympathy we may have for a given organization, whenever some form of relationship is being established between that organization and the United Nations we must accept the fact that there is an inherent difference between it and a sovereign State, to the extent that it lacks statehood.

*Id.* at 12.

[29] *Id.* at 14–15.

[30] *Id.* at 38, 39–40.

[31] *Id.* at 8–10.

the invitation should be made without reference to rule 39, as did Iraq and the USSR, or that the observer status of the PLO conferred a special privilege on it which justified the proposal.[32] At the end of his speech the representative of the USSR said: "No juridical casuistry can in any way justify opposition to the adoption of such a decision by the Council."[33]

The proposal was put to the vote and the result was nine votes in favor, three against (Costa Rica, the United Kingdom, and the United States of America), with three abstentions (France, Italy, and Japan). And the President declared: "Accordingly, the proposal has been adopted."[34] This was perhaps not unexpected, but the President should have declared that the proposal had not been adopted, as two permanent members of the Council, the United Kingdom and the United States of America, had voted against it.

Clearly the proposal presented a procedural and a substantive constitutional issue. The procedural issue was that part of it which accorded an invitation to the PLO. According to the practice of the Security Council going back to its beginnings, invitations to members, states non-members, and individuals or representatives of organizations have been considered as matter falling under paragraph 2 of Article 27 of the Charter. In some of the cases the question was left open under which article of the Charter or which rules of procedure the invitation was adopted.[35] In some cases the invitation was supported by invoking "the spirit of the Charter or 'equity.' "[36] In some cases the invitation was restricted to making "a partial statement";[37] in other cases it was of a general nature like the invitation to the Republic of Korea mentioned above.[38] In one case, the invitation to the Republic of Indonesia in 1947, the President (Syria) stated that the invitation to the Republic "to appear before the Security Council during the discussion of this question, [was] without any definition or determination of the sovereignty of that Republic."[39] As the debate preceding and following the adoption of the invitation to the PLO shows, members of the Council, including the USSR, were no strangers to "juridical casuistry." It would seem that the invitation to the PLO "to participate in this debate" was a matter governed by the Council's provisional rules of procedure and fell to be decided under rule 39, whether or not this rule was invoked.[40]

[32] *Id.* at 17, 21, 22–25.

[33] *Id.* at 26.

[34] *Id.* at 41.

[35] *See* Repertoire, *supra* note 22, at 116–18.

[36] *Id.* at 102 and Case 55 at 115, Case 56 at 116.

[37] *Id.* Case 56 at 116. *See also* Case 52 at 114.

[38] Text at *supra* note 22. Repertoire, Case 52 at 114 and Case 64 at 119. In Case 55 (*id.* at 115) it was debated whether a "general invitation" should be extended to the People's Republic of China.

[39] Case 59, *id.* at 117–18.

[40] In the Security Council the representative of Iraq argued that rule 39 which refers to "other persons" could not be applied inasmuch as the PLO had been "granted an official status within the United Nations—namely, the status of permanent observers, as the sole legitimate representative of the Palestinian people," that the rules of procedure did not provide for this category, and that in the only analogous case, the invitation to the permanent observers from South and North Vietnam, the invitation "was extended to them to come and appear before the Council without reference to any rule of the provisional rules of procedure." UN Doc. S/PV.1859, Dec. 4, 1975, at 16, 17. The United States representative rejected

The second part of the proposal, namely that the invitation "will confer upon it [the PLO] the same rights as are conferred when a Member State is invited to participate under rule 37," poses a constitutional question of the first magnitude. Rule 37, along with rule 38, refers exclusively to members of the United Nations as does Article 31 of the Charter, and rule 38 refers to Article 32. Both articles of the Charter stipulate the conditions under which members of the United Nations which are not members of the Security Council or states which are not members of the United Nations may be invited to participate in the discussion of any question in case of the former and of any dispute to which they are parties in case of the latter. The Council never determined whether the item on its agenda was a "question" or a "dispute." As it must have been obvious to all members of the Council that the PLO was neither a member nor a state non-member of the United Nations, and that the PLO itself, as pointed out by the United Kingdom, made no claim to be a state or the government of a state,[41] rule 37 could not be applied.

There is no provision in the Charter or in the rules of procudure for "as if" decisions or actions by the Council, that is for the tretament of a body as if it were a member state. It follows that the action of the Security Council was *ultra vires* the powers of the Council under the Charter as well as the procedure laid down in the rules of procedure. The action of the Council was, legally speaking, null and void.

It was within the rights and, indeed, the responsibilities of the permanent members to prevent the intrusion into the Council of the sheer majoritarianism cultivated in the General Assembly. Even if the argument of *ultra vires* is not accepted, the second part of the proposal would have to be decided in accordance with Article 27(3) of the Charter and not, as the President seems to have assumed, in accordance with paragraph 2 of Article 27. It seems unconscionable that the United States, which so strongly criticized certain actions of the Assembly, should have acquiesced in this obvious violation of the Charter.

It may be farfetched, but the possibility cannot be excluded that the United States was deterred from invoking the veto and possibly the double veto by the precedent it cre-

the analogy on three grounds: first, the invitation was limited to making statements and "not to participate fully"; secondly, the invitation was "extended on a 'no-objection' basis," there were no objections in the case of the two Vietnams whereas "there are objections in this case"; and thirdly, there was no reason to refer to any rule because "we knew under what rule we acted—the fact is that the legal basis of the invitation was rule 39." *Id.* at 27. This provoked comments from the representatives of Iraq, the Soviet Union, and Mauritania, which held the presidency at the time of the Vietnam invitation, and a clarification by the United States. *Id.* at 32–38.

The allergy of the Security Council to the citation of specific articles of the Charter or rules of procedure is too well known to require comment. All that needs to be said is that the observer status of the PLO was completely irrelevant. General Assembly Resolution 3237(XXIX), November 22, 1974, invited the PLO "to participate in the session and the work of the General Assembly in the capacity of observer," and in all international conferences held under the auspices of the Assembly and other organs of the United Nations. Resolution 3375(XXX), November 11, 1975, to which the Soviet Union referred (*id.* at 21), called for the invitation of the PLO "to participate in all efforts, deliberations and conferences on the Middle East which are held under the auspices of the United Nations, on an equal footing with other parties, on the basis of resolution 3237(XXIX)." Whatever the intention of the Assembly may have been, it could not possibly have intended to amend the Charter or to dictate to the Security Council how to conduct its business which is governed by the Charter and its rules of procedure.

[41] At the end of his speech, the representative of the PLO said to the absent U.S. representative that he wanted "to assure him that the so-called terrorists of today will be tomorrow the rulers, with their Jewish brothers, of liberated Palestine—a Palestine for both Arabs and Jews, free of ethnic or religious discrimination, a Palestine free of racist Zionism." UN Doc. S/PV.1859, Dec. 4, 1975, at 79.

ated in the Laotian question. On that occasion, there was likewise before the Council a mixed proposal, one part of which was clearly of a procedural nature and the other equally clearly was not. On that occasion it was the Soviet Union which argued that the vote should be in accordance with Article 27(3) and invoked the double veto. With the assistance of a conniving President (Italy), the resolution was declared adopted in spite of the negative vote of the USSR.[42]

The Lebanon case also included a feature which may be seen as raising the issue of the propriety, if not of the constitutionality, of the invitation to the PLO. The issue was raised by the Italian representative who pointed out that the Israeli bombing raid was directed against Lebanon and that "Lebanon is the only subject of international law which is entitled to make its point, to present its claim, in response to the Israeli act of infringement of its national sovereignty."[43] Referring to the duty of the members of the United Nations "to defend respect for the provisions of the Charter," he considered it "incongruous and incompatible with the very essence of international law that two different entities—to use very simple words—the Lebanese State and the Palestine Liberation Organization, should be granted the same right to act in the international sphere, namely, within this Council, with regard to the same complaint and in connexion with a clear act of violation of territorial integrity." He also wondered "how many Member States of the United Nations would claim that this Council can indeed go beyond its powers and prerogatives by allowing such a radical change, which can certainly not be described as procedural inasmuch as it raises a very substantive matter of crucial importance for world order; a problem, to my mind, which goes much beyond the specific case under consideration."[44] As it turned out, all fifteen members of the Security Council supported this radical change, including the United Kingdom, which, although sharing the preoccupation of Italy,[45] failed along with the United States to characterize its negative vote as a veto and which, by virtue of its positon as President of the Council, it was fully capable of

[42] *See* L. Gross, *The Question of Laos and the Double Veto in the Security Council,* 54 AJIL 118 (1960) see also *supra,* pp. 497–510; and *infra* p. 547.

[43] UN Doc. S/PV.1859, Dec. 4, 1975, at 13. It may be objected that Italy's contention is too narrow and categorical in view of the dictum of the International Court of Justice in *Barcelona Traction* (Second Phase). In the context of a state's obligations with respect to foreign investments and foreign nations, the Court observed:

> These obligations, however, are neither absolute nor unqualified. In particular, an essential distinction should be drawn between the obligations of a State towards the international community as a whole, and those arising vis-à-vis another State in the field of diplomatic protection. By their very nature the former are the concern of all States. In view of the importance of the rights involved, all States can be held to have an interest in their protection, they are obligations *erga omnes.*

[1970] ICJ Rep. 3, at 32, para. 33. Apart from other considerations, this dictum is qualified by the words "all States" and is therefore inapplicable here as the PLO neither is nor claims to be a state. In so far as states are concerned, Articles 31 and 32 lay down the conditions for their participation in the Security Council when it is seized of questions or disputes affecting their interests.

[44] UN Doc. S/PV.1859, Dec. 4, 1975, at 13.

[45] "There is a further consideration," stated the representative of the United Kingdom, "to which we attach considerable weight, that the essence of the complaint which is now before the Security Council is that of a complaint concerning the infringement of the territorial sovereignty of a Member State, Lebanon, which will itself be taking full part in our proceedings." *Id.* at 39–40.

making effective. By failing to do so, the President can be seen as contributing to the making of the Council into what on another occasion he had said it was not, namely the "O.K. Corral."

On the substance of the Lebanese complaint, the violation of Lebanese sovereignty and territoral integrity and the nature of the Israeli raid, a striking light was shed by the Soviet Union and, to a significant extent, the PLO. In defending the invitation to the PLO, the Soviet representative argued that the PLO was "not only an equal party in the Middle East conflict but, in this case, it is also the *principal victim* of aggressions, because the act of international piracy by Israel was perpetrated not only in the territory of Lebanon but in areas where Palestinian refugee camps were situated. This was a dual crime committed by Israel: a violation of territorial integrity and an unprovoked attack on a sovereign State and an attack which caused a great many casualties on the site of a camp of refugees who had been driven from their homes as a result of Israeli aggression."[46] In short, as the representative of the Byelorussian SSR put it, "the aggressive acts of Israel were directed *in* Lebanon *against* the Arab people of Palestine and against a Palestinian refugee settlement."[47] Thus these two members of the Security Council in effect supported the Israeli claim that while the attack took place *in* Lebanon it was not directed against Lebanon but against refugee camps which have been widely regarded as camps of the military arm of the PLO.

That the targets of the raid were the camps and not Lebanese settlements was confirmed by Lebanon in detailing the casualties.[48] According to the Lebanese representative bombs were dropped, "some of which were time-bombs."[49] The PLO representative also furnished details about the raid and casualties and also, perhaps unwittingly, offered this information: "The *enemy* [presumably Israel] also used timed explosive bombs, intended to explode one hour after the attack. These bombs were, however, *all dismantled by our forces*."[50] Thus, it would seem, the target of the "enemy" was not Lebanon but camps with refugees including "our forces," that is, forces of the PLO. The pity is that unlike Jordan, which expelled these "forces" in 1970 and has enjoyed peace since then, Lebanon does not have the will or the means to assert its sovereignty in and over its territory.[51] It is also a pity that it did not occur to any member of the Security Council to recall the 1970 Declaration on Principles of International Law concerning Friendly Relations and Co-operation among States in accordance with the Charter which provides, *inter alia:*

[46] *Id.* at 22–25. Italics supplied.

[47] *Id.* at 31. Italics supplied.

[48] According to the Lebanese representative, "8 Lebanese and 78 Palestinians were killed in northern Lebanon; 2 Lebanese and 106 Palestinians were injured . . . In Nabatiyeh in the south, 4 Palestinians are known to have been killed along with 12 Lebanese. Nine Lebanese and 11 Palestinians were injured." *Id.* at 46.

[49] *Ibid.*

[50] *Id.* at 76. Italics supplied.

[51] In this context, reference may be made to a dispatch from Beirut entitled *Lebanese Christians Seize Palestinian Refugee Camp,* by J. Markham in N.Y. Times, Jan. 15, 1976, at 3. It is reported that "the rightists were 'sorting out' the camp's residents. Its registered inhabitants would be permitted to stay, a spokesman said, but 'foreign' guerrillas would be 'disarmed and sent back where they came from."

> Every State has the duty to refrain from organizing or encouraging the organization of irregular forces or armed bands, including mercenaries, for incursion into the territory of another state.
>
> Every State has the duty to refrain from organizing, instigating, assisting or participating in acts of civil strife or terrorist acts in another State or acquiescing in organized activities within its territory directed towards the commission of such acts, when the acts referred to in the present paragraph involve a threat or use of force.[52]

Had these principles along with others been considered, there might have been a chance of a more fruitful analysis of the respective rights and duties of Israel and Lebanon. In any event, the Soviet Union made an important contribution to the clarification of the situation by lifting the screen of Lebanese sovereignty to reveal the real party in interest, the PLO. Regrettably, but not surprisingly, the debate in the Council ignored this important point, as it has done on previous occasions with respect to Lebanon's complaints against Israel.[53]

Finally, a word on the observer status of the PLO, which was strongly emphasized by supporters of the invitation with the rights of a member state.[54] Invitations to organizations to attend General Assembly sessions as observers are nothing new. The O.A.S. was so invited by General Assembly Resolution 253(III) and the League of Arab States by Resolution 477(V). At the same session at which the PLO was invited as observer, the Assembly also invited, by Resolution 3208(XXIX), the European Economic Community and, by Resolution 3209(XXIX), the Council for Mutual Economic Assistance "to participate in the sessions and work of the General Assembly in the capacity of observer." As explained long ago by the Secretary-General: "Observer status in the General Assembly simply means the right to attend without participation in debate or in voting and, on invitation, to participate in debate."[55] Such invitations are extended to organizations without in any way modifying or enhancing their status. To be sure, in Resolution 3375(XXX), the General Assembly called on unspecified conferences on the Middle East to invite the PLO "on an equal footing with other parties."[56] Even this language changes nothing in the status of the PLO and it remains to be seen which conferences will heed the call of the Assembly. There are conferences and conferences, and some may be more flexible than others in inviting nongovernmental bodies on a footing of equality

[52] G.A. Res. 2625(XXV), Oct. 24, 1970. 25 GAOR Supp. 28, at 121, UN Doc. A/8028 (1970). The two quoted paragraphs are in the section entitled: "The principle that States shall refrain in their international relations from the threat or use of force against the territoral integrity or political independence of any State, or in any other manner inconsistent with the purposes of the United Nations."

[53] There is never a perfect analogy but the Eichmann case may be recalled in which the Security Council pursued a rational course in distinguishing form from substance. In that case, the Council on June 23, 1960 adopted Resolution 138 (1960) in which it declared that the infringement of the sovereignty of a member state caused "international friction" and "may, if repeated, endanger international peace and security," and called on Israel "to make appropriate reparation" but did not ask for the return of Eichmann, as requested by Argentina. 15 SCOR RES. AND DEC. 4 (1960).

For an analysis of this case, see H. Silving, In Re Eichmann, 55 AJIL 307 (1961).

[54] *E.g.*, the Soviet Union, UN Doc. S/PV.1859, at 21, 22–25, 33–35.

[55] Report of the Secretary-General on "Question of Invitations to Certain Regional Organizations Invited to Attend Previous Session of the Council (ECOSOC)," UN Doc. E/2028, June 20, 1951, at 3.

[56] *See supra* note 40.

with states and governments. In any event, the Security Council is not a conference "held under the auspices of the United Nations," and therefore Resolution 3375(XXX) is applicable.

## IV. VOTING IN THE SECURITY COUNCIL ON JANUARY 12, 1976

The third stage relating to the participation of the PLO in the Security Council started on January 12, 1976, when the Council met to discuss the Middle East problem in conformity with the Council's Resolution 381(1975) of November 30, 1975. In accordance with the President's statement on that occasion, the representatives of the PLO were to be "invited to participate in the debate."[57] However, having recalled the statement, the President of the Council (United Republic of Tanzania) proceeded to say:

> This proposal is not being put forward under rule 37 or rule 39 of the provisional rules of procedure of the Security Council, but, if it is adopted by the Council, the invitation to the Palestine Liberation Organization to participate in this debate will confer on it the same rights of participation as are conferred when a Member State is invited to participate under rule 37.[58]

This formula is identical with that put forward on December 4, 1975,[59] and declared adopted over the negative votes of two permanent members of the Security Council, the United States and the United Kingdom. It may be assumed that the majority of the Council, emboldened by its success of December 4, 1975, had decided to press its advantage, and to enhance the stature of the PLO, notwithstanding the President's statement of November 30, 1975, to the contrary, by assimilating it to a "Member State."[60] The majority may have assumed that the opponents of the formula would contest it again on procedural rather than on constitutional grounds and that they would not insist on having their negative votes evaluated as vetoes. In this, the majority turned out to be right. In the vote the United States cast the only negative vote, whereas the United Kingdom joined France and Italy in abstaining.[61]

The supporters of the formula could base their arguments this time not merely on the observer status of the PLO but on the "precedent when at one of its previous meetings it [the Council] invited the representatives of the Palestine Liberation Organization to participate as full representatives in a debate of the Security Council from beginning to

[57] *See* text at *supra* note 16.

[58] UN Doc. S/PV.1870, Jan. 12, 1976, at 11.

[59] *See supra* p. 536.

[60] The "rights" of a "Member State" invited under rule 37 specifically do not include the right to vote. Under rule 38, a member state "may submit proposals and draft resolutions" but they "may be put to a vote only at the request of a representative on the Security Council." *See supra* note 25.

For a concise statement of "important differences" between Article 32 of the Charter and rule 39, see E. Kerley, *The Powers of Investigation of the United Nations Security Council*, 55 AJIL 892, at 917, n. 88 (1961). One of these differences is that: "persons invited under Rule 39 attend as sources of information rather than as participants." *Ibid.*

[61] UN Doc. S/PV.1870, Jan. 12, 1976, at 57. Owing to the changed composition of the Council the vote was eleven to one, with three abstentions.

end of that debate."[62] Among the opponents, the United States stressed the need to safeguard "the integrity of Security Council procedures and . . . the future effectiveness of this body," and that if members "take liberties with those procedures and, under the influence of immediate political positions with respect to a given question before this Council, establish or reaffirm unwise precedents, this will come back to haunt us." The United States also, correctly, it is believed, argued: "For the most elemental of reasons, only Member States can participate in our proceedings as Member States,"[63] but as on December 4, 1975, it failed to draw the correct consequence from this most elemental reason. The United Kingdom, while recalling its earlier opposition to the "undesirable and unnecessary departure from our established practice" and that its earlier "procedural objections . . . were not shared by the majority" of the Council, announced that it did not "think it right to press these procedural objections to the point of voting against the proposal, and therefore we will abstain."[64] The third permanent member of the Council, France, insisted after the vote that outside of rule 39 "only representatives of States, whether Members or non-members of the Organization, may be heard by the Security Council" and that its abstention "can be explained by the status which the Council, contradicting its rules of procedure, is attempting to confer upon the PLO in our work."[65] Thus, of three permanent members which were opposed to the proposal, two surrendered to the majority and one—the United States—cast a negative vote without invoking Article 27(3) of the Charter.[66] Thus the unprincipled majoritarianism[67] of the Soviet and

[62] *Id.* at 27 (the representative of the USSR).

[63] *Id.* at 13–15, 16.

[64] *Id.* at 43, 44–45.

[65] *Id.* at 59–60.

[66] There is no question that the United States was fully aware of the gravity of the matter. Thus at one point its representative wondered whether the matter was one of procedure or of substance but while conceding that it was one of procedure considered it to be a case of "erosion of procedure" and "of fundamental concern to us." *Id.* at 51, 52. At another point he said:

> What we may very well have to come to judge and are seeing here today is the commencement of an effort to subvert the open and public proceedings of the Security Council and replace them by the rule of an extra-legal, semi-secret *Apparat*, which is inaccessible to the membership of the United Nations and inaccessible to the processes of inquiry. There is a term for this: the term is "totalitarianism."

*Id*. at 52. He also recalled that his "Secretary of State has spoken of the prospect that this institution will end as an empty shell." *Id.* at 53–55.

[67] This was aptly characterized by the representative of the United Kingdom in the debate on the credentials of South Africa at the twenty-ninth session of the General Assembly on November 12, 1974. Addressing himself to those who "suggested that the delegation of South Africa should be excluded from participating in our future proceedings," he stated:

> Let me start by making the fundamental, if obvious, point that this Organization is governed by the Charter. It cannot, consistently with itself and with the role which it is designed to play in international affairs, disregard that Charter. We are either a law-abiding, law-respecting body or we are nothing, a mere talking shop. If we put aside the Charter whenever its provisions may seem to a majority of us—even, indeed, to a preponderant majority of us—inconvenient, then we lose all claim to authority and to credence. In short, the Charter is and must be the constitutional foundation for all that we do. Respect for the Charter must permeate all our decisions. That much, I trust, is common to all of us here today.

UN Doc. A/PV.2281, Nov. 12, 1974, at 23–25. As the ruling of the President of the Assembly (see *supra* note 1) demonstrates, this "trust" was clearly misplaced.

Third World blocs which all too often has come to prevail in the Assembly has found a second home in the Security Council.

## V. CONCLUDING OBSERVATIONS

Could this outcome have been prevented? Obviously no categorical answer is possible. It is possible, however, to indicate briefly alternatives which were open to those permanent members of the Council which opposed the objectionable part of the invitation, namely that it would confer upon the PLO "the same rights of participation as are conferred when a Member State is invited to participate under rule 37."

The motion to invite the PLO consisted of two parts: the first part was the invitation, and the second part was the status of the PLO if invited. Under rule 32 of the Council's Provisional Rules of Procedure, "Parts of a motion or of a draft resolution shall be voted on separately at the request of any representative, unless the original mover objects." It is not clear who the "original mover" was at the January 12, 1976, meeting. The President seemed to be the mover.[68] Leaving aside the question whether the President is empowered to make such proposals, it may be assumed that he could and should have made it in his capacity as representative of Tanzania. Had he objected, there would have been no separate vote on the two parts of the motion. Had he raised no objection, there would have been a clear indication of which members favored the invitation and which objected to the controversial second part. The vote on the invitation pure and simple is procedural; the vote on the second, in the present submission, is not.

It seems just possible, though no more than that, that if the motion had been voted in two parts at the December 4, 1975, meeting the first part would have been adopted by more than the requisite majority, but the second part might not have been adopted. Sweden, which was in favor of inviting the PLO, might have abstained in the separate vote on the second part, but as it was given no choice Sweden cast the crucial vote with the Soviet and Third World bloc in the vote which took place on December 4.

An attempt to separate the vote on the motion was the first possibility which was missed. The second possibility, which was also missed, was to argue the impermissibility of the second part on constitutional or, to adopt the usual language, on substantive grounds. As indicated earlier, to invite a state or an organization to participate in the Council debate is one thing, to confer upon such a state or organization the rights of a member state is another. No matter how strongly the United States, the United Kingdom, and France deplored a departure from established practice or the erosion of the rules of procedure, they put their arguments on the plane of procedure. This was, in the present submission, a fundamental error. The pretended assimilation of the PLO to a member state or the conferral of rights of a member state raises a question of the constitutional law of the United Nations and not of procedure. There is nothing in the Provisional Rules of

[68] He said: "With this background in view, I should like to put forward the proposal . . ." UN Doc. S/PV.1870, Jan. 12, 1976, at 11.

Procedure to permit the Council to assimilate a state or, still less, an organization to a member state. Nor could there be any such thing in these rules which are solely concerned with the conduct of proceedings in the Council. They supplement the applicable articles of the Charter and do not and cannot supplant them. This is seen particularly clearly in rule 40 which deals with the delicate question of voting: "Voting in the Security Council shall be in accordance with the relevant Articles of the Charter and of the Statute of the International Court of Justice."[69]

Assuming that the objecting permanent members of the Council, or the United States alone, had taken a stand on the constitutional grounds of the law of the Charter, what might have been the outcome? On December 4, 1975, these members or the United States alone could have argued that the proposed invitation was not adopted because two permanent members voted against it. Alternatively, the United States could have raised the preliminary question whether the proposed invitation was procedural. If, as suggested above, the motion had been separated into two parts, the preliminary question would relate only to the contested second part. The possibility of raising the preliminary question is explicitly laid down in the Four-Power Statement of June 7, 1945, with which France associated itself, on voting in the Security Council. The relevant part of it reads:

> 1. In the opinion of the Delegations of the Sponsoring Governments, the Draft Charter itself contains an indication of the application of the voting procedures to the various functions of the Council.
>
> 2. In this case, it will be unlikely that there will arise in the future any matters of great importance on which a decision will have to be made as to whether a procedural vote will apply. Should, however, such a matter arise, the decision regarding the preliminary question as to whether or not such a matter is procedural must be taken by a vote of seven members of the Security Council, including the concurring votes of the permanent members.[70]

As the Charter contains no indication whatever by what vote the Council could confer the rights of a member state on a nonstate entity, the preliminary question was in order. In view of the fact that the United Kingdom, a party to the Statement, held the presidency in December 1975, it appears possible that the President would have called for a vote on the preliminary question and then for a vote on the question itself, and if the United States had not concurred in either vote, the President would have declared that the motion was not adopted in view of the negative vote of a permanent member. If the motion had been voted in parts, the same procedure could have been followed with respect to the second part of the motion and the results would have been the same with respect to that part.

A further point may be made. In the past there was controversy as to the binding

[69] Article 10(2) of the Statute provides the only exception to the voting rule in Article 27(3) of the Charter. On the subordination of the rules of procedure to the Charter, see Fitzmaurice, *The Law and Procedure of the International Court of Justice: Treaty Interpretation and Certain Other Treaty Points,* 28 BRIT. Y.B.I.L. 1, at 22 (1951) and P.C. Jessup, *Parliamentary Diplomacy,* 89 HAGUE, REC. DES COURS 201, at 204 (1956-I).

[70] Doc. 852, III/1/37(i), 11 UNCIO Docs 713 (1945).

force of the Four-Power Statement.[71] There is no need to review this controversy for the simple reason that the preliminary question and the resulting so-called double veto have their legal basis in Article 27, paragraphs 2 and 3. As the Soviet delegate, Mr. Gromyko, rightly it is believed, pointed out, the Four-Power Statement "is an interpretation of the provisions of the Charter."[72] Article 27(2) applies only to procedural matters, whereas, according to paragraph 3 of Article 27, "decisions on all other matters," and this obviously includes the question whether a matter is procedural, "shall be made" by a qualified majority of seven—since the entry into force of the amendment to Article 27 on August 31, 1965, nine-members including the concurring votes of the permanent members. The so-called double-veto procedure has a solid basis in the Charter itself.[73] Still, whether and how it will be applied depends to a substantial degree on the President of the Council. It might have been applied successfully in December 1975 for the reason stated above. In any event, those who were concerned about preventing the contamination of the Security Council by the majoritarianism of the Assembly had the obligation, it is submitted, to use the available legal and constitutional procedure in order to forestall the adoption of an unconstitutional motion.

On January 12, 1976, the situation in the Council was different from that of December 1975 because the presidency was in the hands of a Third World state. Still, for the reason stated, the United States, alone if necessary, should have called for a vote on the separate and separable parts of the motion and if this failed should have called for the preliminary question on the whole motion. If the United States had done so, the President could have called for a vote on the preliminary question and announced that, owing to the negative vote of a permanent member, the motion was not procedural. He would then call for a vote on the motion itself and announce that it was not adopted owing to the negative vote of a permanent member. This would be the correct procedure in conformity with the Four-Power Statement and/or Article 27(3) of the Charter.

Alternatively, the President could have gone half-way, as did the President of the Council in the question of Laos. The then President (Italy) called for a vote on the preliminary question proposed by the Soviet Union: "Should the vote on the draft resolution submitted in Doc. S/4214 be considered a procedural one?"[74] After the vote which was

[71] *See* L. Gross, *The Double Veto and the Four-Power Statement on Voting in the Security Council*, 67 HARVARD L.R. 251, particularly at 256–62 (1953). See also *supra*, pp. 473–95.

With reference to the Statement, Stone observed: "Insofar as it was an unrepudiated basis of the drafting of [Article 27], it is a proper, and indeed virtually authoritative, means of interpretation." J. Stone, LEGAL CONTROLS OF INTERNATIONAL CONFLICT 213 (1954). But *see* Fitzmaurice that "minutes, declarations, resolutions . . ., having the character of an *agreed* interpretation should be regarded, if not as part of the treaty itself, then as ancillary thereto, and as part of the complex of instruments produced by the conference in connection with the treaty it drew up." *Supra* note 69, at 12–13. Italics supplied. *Quere:* agreed by whom? *See also* S. D. BAILEY, VOTING IN THE SECURITY COUNCIL 18 (1969) and B. V. COHEN, THE UNITED NATIONS 11 (1961).

[72] 3 SCOR, No. 71, at 42 (1948), quoted in Gross, *supra* note 71, at 226 in H.L.R. and *supra* at 485.

[73] *See* Cohen, *supra* note 71, at 12, who disagreed with the proposition in the text.

[74] 14 SCOR, 848th meeting 12 (1959).

The draft resolution sponsored by the United States, the United Kingdom, and France read:

> The Security Council decides to appoint a sub-committee . . . and instructs this sub-committee to examine the

ten to one (USSR), the President, contrary to the Four-Power Statement and Article 27(3), declared: "Therefore, the resolution should be considered procedural. It is the interpretation of the Chair, shared by the overwhelming majority of the members, that the draft resolution falls clearly under Article 29 of the Charter."[75] The Soviet delegate, correctly it is believed, observed:

> The President's interpretation of the vote is illegal. It is at variance with the Charter, it is at variance with the four-Power declaration to which France subscribed, and it is at variance with the practice of the Security Council. For these reasons, it is null and void.[76]

In the circumstances nothing more could be done, there being no provision in the Charter for a judicial review of acts of the organs of the United Nations. If the President of the Council on January 12, 1976, had followed this precedent, the United States would have found itself in the same position as was the Soviet Union on September 7, 1959.

Still another alternative open to the President on January 12, 1976, would have been to make a ruling, before or after the vote[77] on his motion, that the motion was procedural whether or not the United States called for a vote on the preliminary question. There are some precedents for presidential rulings in connection with voting in the Security Council,[78] but they are not free from ambiguity. In the present submission, it is inadmissible to subject voting in the Security Council to a ruling by the President for two reasons. Rule 40 quoted above[79] simply refers to the Charter and the Charter does not provide for a resolution of a controversy as to the applicable voting rule. The preliminary-question procedure is the only one available to the Council but its application depends upon the good faith of the President and of the members of the Council and that is, as the Laotian incident shows, not always forthcoming. The dissenting member may protest, as did the Soviet Union, but no effective judicial remedy is available.

The second reason is that the "parliamentary" remedy which is available is unconstitutional. This remedy consists in a ruling by the President and a challenge to that rul-

> statements made before the Security Council concerning Laos, to receive further statements and documents and to conduct such inquiries as it may determine necessary and to report to the Security Council as soon as possible.

UN Doc. S/4214, Sept. 7, 1959. Text the same as adopted, *see* 14 SCOR, Supp. July–Sept. 1959, UN Doc. S/1416, Sept. 8, 1959. *Also cited* in Gross, *supra* note 42, at 118, and *supra* at 497.

While the setting up of a sub-committee was a procedural matter, the conduct of inquiries was, in the Soviet view, not a procedural matter and therefore the whole draft resolution was not procedural. *See id.* at 122–24.

[75] 14 SCOR, 848th meeting 13 (1959).

[76] *Id.* at 13–14. *Cited in* Gross, *supra* note 42, at 118, and *supra* at 497.

For a defense of the procedure in the Laos case, See Kerley, *supra* note 60, at 216–18. He distinguishes between investigation under Article 34 for the sole purpose of determining the Council's competence which is subject to Article 27(3) and the Council's "general procedural capacity to receive information from persons willing to provide it as part of its consideration of a question," which is governed by Article 27(2) of the Charter. *Id.* at 218. This "general procedural capacity" appears to be derived from the Council's powers of discussion and consideration as well as from rule 39 of the Council's rules of procedure. *Id.* at 205–07.

[77] It may be noted that in the practice of the Security Council the preliminary question may be raised before or after the vote on the contested draft resolution or motion.

[78] *See* Gross, *supra* note 71, at 270–76 in H.L.R. and see also *supra* 487–492.

[79] *See* text at footnote 69 *supra*.

ing. The Provisional Rules of Procedure of the Council provide for a ruling by the President but, according to rule 30, only on a point of order.[80] By no stretch of imagination can questions relating to voting on draft resolutions or motions be subsumed under the admittedly vague rubric "point of order." Moreover, in the practice of the Council, a procedural, that is unqualified, majority is required for overruling the President's ruling. Thus if the President had ruled on January 12, 1976, that the motion to invite the PLO with the rights of a member state was procedural, this ruling would have stood as there was no requisite majority to overrule. The consequence of admitting presidential rulings would be that a majority of any nine members could overrule the President's ruling that a matter was not procedural and a minority of any seven members could prevent overruling the President's ruling that the matter was procedural.[81] It would be both politically undesirable and constitutionally inadmissible to place Article 27(3) of the Charter under the sway of presidential rulings under rule 30 of the rules of procedure.[82] To do so would be to open the door once and for all to the sort of majoritarianism which even in the General Assembly is highly undesirable and unconstitutional when it is relied upon to override the applicable provisions of the Charter.[83] It would reduce the Security Council to "a mere talking shop."

The United States, like the Soviet Union in 1959, would have had no effective remedy to challenge the President's ruling, but it could and should have made it quite clear that it stood for the application of the Charter and that Article 27(3) was not subject to parliamentary devices. No matter what the attitude of the United States may have been in and out of the United Nations during the cold war, there can be no doubt that it has an abiding interest in the observance of international law and the Charter of the United Nations.[84] Law and the rule of law are basic values to free societies even, and especially so, in

[80] Rule 30 reads:

> If a representative raises a point of order, the President shall immediately state his ruling. If it is challenged, the President shall submit his ruling to the Security Council for immediate decision and it shall stand unless overruled.

[81] It is unnecessary to consider here Article 18(3) of the Charter which refers to a different body, with a different composition, and above all with different functions.

[82] *See* Gross, *supra* note 71, at 279 in H.L.R. and also at *supra* p. 494.

Cohen disagrees with this view and welcomed the procedure in the Laotian question as a means "to limit any abuse in the exercise of the so-called double veto." *Supra* note 71, at 13. In Stone's view:

> the truth is that the approach via the Four Power Statement sanctifying the double veto, and that via Rule 30 excluding it, are competing legal starting points . . . . These competing starting points might, of course, yield opposite results on a particular matter if both were simultaneously applied to it. In fact both will not be attempted to be applied simultaneously: the effect of the competition of starting points is merely that the choice between them is determined by politics, not by law. It is for this reason that the disposition of such matters in the future will depend on which Member of the Security Council is President at the time. It is this officer who makes the choice and his choice will be determined by the political position of his State.

*Supra* note 72, at 226. While there is truth in Stone's last sentence, in the present submission, the starting points are not both legal: one based on Article 27 is legal, the other based on rule 30 is not. As to Cohen's position it may be observed that it was presumably based on the comfortable assumption that the liberation of the Council from the double veto was in the interest of the United States. This is certainly not so, if it ever was so, in a long-range calculation of the national interest.

[83] *See* statement by the representative of the United Kingdom, *supra* note 67.

[84] A change in the U.S. attitude as exhibited on the Laotian question is implied in the text.

It may be pointed out that the attitude of the United States is not unchangeable. Thus in connection with voting in the critical times, and it is a worthy effort to stand up for them. The United States was right in warning on September 12, 1975, against the "erosion of procedure."[85] It would have been even better and more to the point to warn against the "erosion of the Charter" and use all the constitutional means available to it as a member of the Council in defense of the Charter. The scenarios outlined above indicate that the best chance for a successful defense was in connection with the proceedings of December 4, 1975. An attempt to resort to the preliminary-question procedure on January 12, 1976, would probably have been unsuccessful but it would have laid the basis for opposing sheer majoritarianism via rule 30 in the future.

The voting rules in Article 27 of the Charter were and remain an essential condition for the creation and continued existence of the United Nations. More than that they were and remain an essential condition of United States and Soviet membership in the United Nations. If that condition is eroded, the continued membership of the United States, at any rate, may well become doubtful.

Security Council on the admission of the two Vietnams, the United States adopted a stand which at best is only linguistically different from the stand of the Soviet Union prior to 1955 on the simultaneous admission of Western and Soviet backed candidates for membership in the United Nations. The International Court of Justice ruled in 1948 that a member "is not juridically entitled to make its consent to the admission dependent on conditions not expressly provided by paragraph 1 of said Article" (Article 4 of the Charter). [1948] ICJ Rep. 57, at 65. Yet when the Security Council rejected the inclusion in its agenda of the application of the Republic of Korea, the United States vetoed the applications of the two Vietnams. Its representative stated that the United States "would have voted for the admission of the Republic of South Korea, the Democratic Republic of Viet-Nam, and the Provisional Revolutionary Government of South Viet-Nam" but that it would "have nothing to do with selective universality, a principle which in practice admits only new members acceptable to the totalitarian States." UN Doc. S/PV.1836, Aug. 11, 1975, at 58–60; see also UN Doc. S/PV.1834, Aug. 6, 1975, at 41 and UN Doc A/PV.2354, Sept. 19, 1975, at 87–91.

At a later meeting of the Security Council, the U.S. representative recalled the Court's ruling that "package deals" were not in order but applied it to the other side which linked the admission of the Republic of Korea "to the case of North Korea." He expressed the view that the Security Council is not "entitled, authorized or wise in linking these two matters in the face of the judgment of the Court and, indeed, of our recent well-established practice." UN Doc. S/PV.1842, Sept. 26, 1975, at 53–55. The United States then vetoed again the applications of the two Vietnams. UN Doc. S/1868, Sept. 30, 1975, at 23.

[85] *See supra* note 66.

# VI

# SOME PROBLEMS OF ORGANIZATION IN THE UNITED NATIONS

# WAS THE SOVIET UNION EXPELLED FROM THE LEAGUE OF NATIONS?

In the discussion of current problems of international organization frequent reference is being made to the action taken by the Council of the League of Nations in 1939 with reference to the membership of the Soviet Union.[1] While the matter may be thought to have interest chiefly for historians, it might serve a useful purpose to reëxamine the action taken in 1939 from a legal point of view. It is conceivable that a conclusion on the legal points involved might serve as a basis for removing some of the untoward features of the existing situation.

The Covenant of the League of Nations provides in paragraph 1 of Article 5 that

> except where otherwise expressly provided in this covenant or by the terms of the present Treaty, decisions at any meeting of the Assembly or of the Council shall require the agreement of all the Members of the League represented at the meeting.

Express provision otherwise is contained in paragraph 4 of Article 15 of the Covenant, to the effect that

> any Member of the League which has violated any covenant of the League may be declared to be no longer a Member of the League by a vote of the Council concurred in by the representatives of all the other Members of the League represented thereon.

[1] The Soviet publication "War and the Working Class" was reported to have made the following comment in discussing the Soviet Union's insistence on a unanimous vote of the Great Powers for dealing with any alleged case of aggression: "It is difficult to forget that the League of Nations did not find it necessary to expel Poland for seizing Vilna or Italy for invading Ethiopia, but voted for expulsion of the Soviet Union when it deprived Germany of a springboard prepared for invasion." See dispatch from Moscow in *The New York Times*, October 20, 1944, p.6.

Before analyzing these two provisions of the Covenant it may be useful to recall certain provisions of the Rules of Procedure of the Council adopted by that body on May 26, 1933.[2] Article VIII of the Rules provides that "the Council shall not discuss or decide upon any matter unless the majority of its members are present."[3] Article IX, paragraph 1, of the Rules restates with some changes the fundamental principle of paragraph 1 of Article 5 of the Covenant quoted above. The last sentence of paragraph 3 of Article IX of the Rules states that "in counting the votes, abstentions from voting shall be disregarded."[4]

It is obvious from a comparison of the provisions of the Covenant that the wording of paragraph 4 of Article 16 differs from that of paragraph 1 of Article 5. Whereas the latter requires the agreement of all Members of the Council present at the meeting,[5] the former requires the concurrence of all Members of the League represented on the Council other than the Member which has been found to have violated a covenant of the League. It is generally admitted that Article 16, paragraph 4, departs from the unanimity rule of Article 5, paragraph 1, by excluding the vote of the interested State if that State is represented on the Council.[6] On the other hand, it would seem to require, first, the presence in the Council of all Members of the League represented on the Council and, secondly, the affirmative concurrence in the vote of the Council of all Members represented on the Council. This interpretation of Article 16, paragraph 4, has been stressed by several students of the Covenant.[7]

It has been urged against this interpretation that the wording of Article 16, paragraph 4, is not definite enough "to exclude the necessity of reading it subject to Article 5,

[2] League Doc.C.197.M.106.1938.

[3] This provision was included in substance in Art. 6 of the Rules of Procedure of the Council adopted at Rome on May 17, 1920: Hudson, M.O., *International Legislation*, Washington, 1931—, Vol. I, p. 127.

[4] This addition to the Rules of 1920 has apparently been overlooked by Cromwell A. Riches, *Majority Rule in International Organization*, Baltimore, 1940, p. 23, note 53.

[5] D. H. Miller, *The Drafting of the Covenant*, New York, 1928, Vol. I, p. 285: "It was at first suggested to leave out the words 'at the meeting,' but after some consideration it was thought that they had better remain so as to prevent one State from stopping the holding of a meeting, or to cover the case when one Member might not find it possible to be represented."

[6] Schücking, W., and Wehberg, H., *Die Satzung des Völkerbundes*, Berlin, 1931 (3d ed.), Vol. I, p. 521; same, 1924 (2d ed.), p. 637. Sir John Fischer Williams, "The League of Nations and Unanimity," in A.J.I.L., Vol. 19 (1925), p. 486, argues that this exception depends "not only on the language of the Covenant but also on the general principles that no one is a judge in his own cause." See also the Treaty of Lausanne Case, Permanent Court of International Justice, *Publications*, Series B, No. 12, p. 32.

[7] Schücking and Wehberg, work cited, Vol. I, p. 510: *Bei der Ausschliessung eines Mitgliedes wegen Verletzung der Bundespflichten müssen gemäss Article 16, Abs. 4, der Satzung* alle *im Rate vertretenen Bundesmitglieder (mit Ausnahme des Auszuschliessenden) sich an der Abstimmung beteiligen. Es genügt hier also kein Beschluss des Rates, wenn in dessen Sitzung nicht alle Mitglieder (mit Ausnahme des Auszuschliessenden) vertreten sind.* See also second edition, p. 637; Cromwell A. Riches, *The Unanimity Rule and the League of Nations*, Baltimore, 1933, p. 49: "In one case the Covenant clearly requires that more than a majority of the members be present for taking a decision . . . . It would seem, therefore, that, to exclude a member from the League, all members of the Council except the representatives of the state to be excluded would have to be present and cast affirmative votes while in all other cases the Council could act with only a majority present." Georges—Tibère Èles, *Le Principe de l'unanimité dans la Société des Nations et les Exceptions à ce Principe,*" Paris, 1935, p. 188: *Une telle exclusion ne peut être prononcée que par le vote de tous les Membres de la Société, autres que l'État à exclure, représentés au Conseil. Une réunion qui prononcerait l'exclusion d'un Membre devrait donc être au complet. D'autre part, comme le texte exige expressément* "le vote de tous les autres Membres" etc., *il semble difficile d'appliquer, dans ce cas, la règle d'après laquelle les abstentions n'empêchent pas l'unanimité.* Also J. Ray, *Commentaire du Pacte de la Société des Nations*, Paris, 1930, p. 536.

paragraph 1."[8] This view, it is said, is based on "legal interpretation" as well as "upon the undesirability of ever preventing the Council from taking necessary decisions, even if by chance or by design a state entitled to be represented is not so represented."[9]

It is true that in general the practice of the Council, even before it crystallized in paragraph 3 of Article IX of the Rules of Procedure of the Council adopted in 1933, was based on the assumption that "abstention did not prevent unanimity from being secured."[10] It is equally true that the practice of the Council even before it crystallized in Article VIII of the Rules of 1933 did not support the view expressed by the Brazilian representative at the Meeting of the Council held on June 10, 1926, that whereas the presence of all its Members is not necessary for a meeting of the Council, the Council could not take any action or any decision if it were deprived of the presence of one of its Members either owing to resignation or owing to a final severance from the League.[11]

If this view were accepted then indeed the Council, in exercising its power under Article 16, paragraph 4, would be justified in applying Article VIII of the Rules of Procedure of the Council concerning the quorum and also Article IX, paragraph 3, last sentence, concerning abstentions from voting. That such a view would not adequately interpret the conditions laid down in Article 16, paragraph 4, follows from Article 5, paragraph 1, of the Covenant and from Article IX, paragraph 1, of the Rules, both of which provide for exceptions from the general principle of unanimity which they formulate. This part of Article 5, paragraph 1, must be given the weight that is due to it. Otherwise what would be the purpose of providing for exceptions if every exception had to be negatived by reference to the general principle? It is submitted that if the wording of Article 16, paragraph 4, is deemed sufficiently definite to exclude the State against which the proceedings are directed from the vote of the Council, and this has not been contested, then there is no reason to believe that the remainder of this paragraph is couched in less definite language. These exceptions of Article 16, paragraph 4, to the general principle of unanimity of Article 5, paragraph 1, stand together. If one is admitted there is equal reason to admit the other.

This interpretation finds support in the preparatory work bearing on the history of paragraph 4 of Article 16. This provision was introduced in the Drafting Committee of the Commission on the League of Nations which on April 1 and 2, 1919 discussed the Hurst-Miller text of the Covenant.[12] It was apparently intended by the Drafting Committee that it should constitute a separate article numbered XVII A.[13] The incorporation

[8] Julius Stone, "The Rule of Unanimity: the Practice of the Council and Assembly of the League of Nations," in 14 *British Year Book of International Law* (1933), p. 31.

[9] Same.

[10] *Committee on the Composition of the Council. Part I. Report on the Work of the First Session.* Doc.C.299.M.139.1926.V, p. 26. The words quoted above were spoken by M. Motta, Chairman of the Committee. Similar views were expressed by other Members of the Committee, in particular by M. Scialoja. Same, p. 26.

[11] League of Nations, *Official Journal* 1926, p. 888. See same, p. 890, for the views of M. Scialoja and M. Paul-Boncour.

[12] Miller, work cited, Vol. II, Docs. 28 and 30, pp. 658 and 672.

[13] "Changes made by Drafting Committee," Memorandum of Mr. Baker intended to show the changes made by the Drafting Committee in the English Text before them (in Doc. 656). D. H. Miller, *My Diary at the Conference of Paris*, n.p., n.d., Vol. VII, Doc. 678, p. 404; see also same, Doc. 679, p. 409.

of this new Article XVII A into Article 16 of the Covenant as paragraph 4 of that Article was presumably done by Messrs. Miller and Hurst.[14] It may not be immaterial to recall in this connection that according to contemporary comment the provision introduced in the Drafting Committee was intended "to meet the case of a State which after breaking its covenant still claims to vote on the Council or in the Assembly."[15] A similar reason is advanced by Florence Wilson[16] and the British Commentary on the Covenant.[17]

While the preparatory work with reference to the English text of paragraph 4, Article 16, contains no clue to the proper interpretation of this provision, some light is shed by the history of the French text. In the first French translation of the English text a State which has violated any of its obligations resulting from the Covenant could be excluded from the League *par un vote du Conseil émis a l'unanimité des voix, moins la sienne, s'il y est représenté.*[18] The word "unanimité" is maintained in the Lapradelle text of April 16th and 17th and in the Larnaude text, agreed to by Mr. Miller, of April 18, 1919.[19] However, in the "French print of April 21, 1919" the word "unanimité" was eliminated and a new formula substituted for it which reads as follows: *L'exclusion est prononcée par le vote de tous les autres Membres de la Société représentés au Conseil.*[20] This new formula, which is not a perfect rendering of the English Text,[21] is maintained in the French print of April 23, 1919[22], in the French Report of the Commission of the League of Nations of April 28, 1919,[23] and in the final French text of the Covenant.

The changes in the successive French translations of paragraph 4, Article 16, are significant. Mr. Miller assures us that "each French print had to be gone over from beginning to end, word for word, to see if and where it had been changed,"[24] Referring specifically to the formula employed in the French print of April 21, 1919, mentioned above, he says: "The new translation of that paragraph is not a very literal rendering of the English, but its legal effect, I think, is exactly the same."[25] This statement constitutes a substantial corroboration of the interpretation of paragraph 4, Article 16, suggested above. There would hardly have been a valid reason for changing the *unanimité* employed in three successive French texts to the present wording if the English text had been understood to establish merely the conventional unanimity. The conclusion seems

[14] Same, Doc. 679, p. 406, note a and Doc. 681, p. 413, note a; see also text of the *Diary,* Vol. I, p. 219, note b.

[15] "Note by the British Delegation on the Redraft submitted by the Drafting Committee": Miller, *Drafting of the Covenant,* Vol. I, p. 417. See also C. W. Jenks, "Expulsion from the League of Nations," in *British Year Book of International Law,* 1935, p. 156; *Message from the Federal Council of Switzerland to the Federal Assembly of Switzerland concerning the Question of the Accession of Switzerland to the League of Nations, August 4, 1919,* Cambridge, England, 1919, p. 130.

[16] Miller, *Diary,* Vol. XIX, p. 30.

[17] "The Covenant of the League of Nations with a Commentary Thereon," in *British Parliamentary Papers,* Misc. No. 3 (1919), Cmd. 151, p. 17.

[18] "French Text of April 7, 1919," Miller, *Drafting,* Vol. II, Doc. 36, p. 768.

[19] Same, Doc. 37, p. 783, where the Lapradelle Text is printed in the left and the Larnaude Text in the right column.

[20] Same, Doc. 38, p. 797.

[21] Sir John Fischer Williams, "The League of Nations and Unanimity," in A.J.I.L., Vol. 19 (1925), p. 483, note 28.

[22] Miller, *Drafting,* Doc. 39, p. 810.

[23] Same, Doc. 40, p. 825.

[24] Same, Vol. I, p. 522.

[25] Same, p. 523.

inevitable that the English text was not so understood and that not *unanimité* but only the precise words *le vote de tous les autres Membres de la Société représentés au Counseil* express the correct legal meaning of Article 16, paragraph 4.

No useful purpose would be served by denying that, assuming the above interpretation to be correct, the Council could under certain conditions be prevented from taking necessary decisions under Article 16, paragraph 4. This may be regrettable, but it would seem that the precise wording of paragraph 4, Article 16, leaves no room for the introduction of "legal correctives."[26] If a state which is entitled to be represented on the Council is, by design, not so represented, and thus prevents the Council from declaring a Covenant-breaking state to be no longer a Member of the League, the consequence is the same as if that state had exercised the veto power to which it is entitled. The same is true of states which are represented on the Council but which refrain from taking part in the vote. On the other hand, the accidental absence of a State represented on the Council from a meeting of the Council could cause but a temporary delay.

It may be useful to recall that, prior to its decision of December 14, 1939, the Council had never exercised the power conferred upon it by Article 16, paragraph 4. Its possible application was, however, discussed on various occasions. It was considered in 1921 as a sanction in the case of states which failed to pay the contributions due from Members under Article 6, paragraph 5, of the Covenant.[27] It was stated in 1934 by Mr. Eden that in the view of the United Kingdom Government, Liberia had so grossly failed to observe the undertaking of Article 23, paragraph b, of the Covenant that the League would be quite entitled to consider her expulsion under paragraph 4 of Article 16.[28] Writers on the subject emphasized the general nature of the sanction of Article 16, paragraph 4, which could consequently be applied to the violation of any obligation resulting from the Covenant.[29] It was also pointed out that Article 16, paragraph 4, could be resorted to in order to overcome the deadlock resulting from the opposition of a Member to the application of measures which require a unanimous decision in the Council and which are directed against a Covenant-breaking state.[30]

[26] *Committee on the Composition of the Council. Part I. Report on the Work of the First Session.* C.299.M.139.1926.V, p. 15.

[27] "Report of the Subcommittee of the Committee on Amendments to the Covenant presented to the Plenary Committee," Doc. A.C.13.1921. See also "Legal Position of States which do not pay their Contribution to the League," Report by the Secretary-General submitted to the Council on March 9, 1927: Doc.C.36.1927.V. League of Nations *O.J.*, 1927, p. 505. Ray, work cited, p. 273, 535.

[28] League of Nations, *O.J.*, 1934, p. 511.

[29] Ray, p. 536; Schücking-Wehberg, 2nd ed., p. 636; Göppert, Otto, *Organisation und Tätigkeit des Völkerbundes*, Stuttgart, 1938, pp. 95, 198.

[30] Precisely with a view to avoiding the difficulty indicated above the Assembly adopted the following amendment to Article 16 of the Covenant on October 4, 1921: "It is for the Council to give an opinion whether or not a breach of the Covenant has taken place. In deliberations on this question in the Council the votes of Members of the League alleged to have resorted to war and of Members against whom such action was directed shall not be counted." On the other hand it was pointed out by M. de Brouckère in his Report on Point 1 (b) of the Proposal laid before the Preparatory Commission for the Disarmament Conference by the French Delegation, that "if Article 16 is only resorted to in cases to which it properly applies, the amendment proposed in 1921 with regard to the calculation of unanimity loses much of its impor-

For the purpose of this analysis it seems unnecessary to state in detail the circumstances in which the Finnish Appeal of December 3, 1939, was received, and dealt with, by the League.[31] The decisive stage in the League procedure was reached on December 14, 1939. Meeting at 10 A.M. on that day, the Assembly of the League of Nations discussed the Report provided for in Article 15, paragraphs 4 and 10, of the Covenant, submitted by the special Committee of the Assembly,[32] and adopted a resolution the relevant parts of which read as follows:

The Assembly:

I

WHEREAS, by the aggression which it has committed against Finland, the USSR has failed to observe not only its special political agreements with Finland but also Article 12 of the Covenant of the League of Nations and the Pact of Paris;

AND WHEREAS, immediately before committing that aggression, it denounced, without legal justification, the Treaty of Non-aggression which it had concluded with Finland in 1932, and which was to remain in force until the end of 1945:

Solemnly condemns the action taken by the USSR against the State of Finland;. . .

II

WHEREAS, notwithstanding an invitation extended to it on two occasions, the USSR has refused to be present at the examination of its dispute with Finland before the Council and the Assembly;

AND WHEREAS, by thus refusing to recognize the duty of the Council and the Assembly as regards the execution of Article 15 of the Covenant, it has failed to observe one of the League's most essential covenants for the safeguarding of peace and the security of nations;

AND WHEREAS it has vainly attempted to justify its refusal on the ground of the relations which it has established with an alleged Government which is neither *de jure* nor *de facto* the Government recognized by the people of Finland in accordance with the free working of their institutions;

AND WHEREAS, the USSR has not merely violated a covenant of the League, but has by its own action placed itself outside the Covenant;

AND WHEREAS the Council is competent under Article 16 of the Covenant to consider what consequences should follow from this situation:

Recommends the Council to pronounce upon the question.[33]

tance. In cases where a state has shown its definite intention to disturb the peace, to defy the whole of the League, and, furthermore, to break the most solemn of undertakings which it has given to its fellow Members, expulsion, as contemplated in Article 16, seems inevitable and the votes which it will no longer be called upon to cast are surely not a matter of great concern. But the diffculty pointed out in 1921 may recur in a fresh form when Article 11 of the Covenant comes to be applied." "Reports and Resolutions on the Subject of Article 16 of the Covenant." Doc. A.14.1927.V, pp. 42, 70, 71.

[31] The relevant documents will be found in League of Nations *O.J.*, 1939, p. 509.

[32] On December 11, 1939, the Assembly, having heard the statement of the Delegate of Finland, decided to set up a Special Committee to study the appeal of the Finnish Government. *Records of the Twentieth Ordinary Session of the Assembly, Plenary Meetings,* p. 11, The Committee had referred to it a number of written and verbal proposals and declarations including that of the Argentine delegation at the plenary meeting on December 13th. The delegate of the Argentine Republic in his address of December 13, 1939, stated that the Soviet Union had "placed itself outside the Covenant" and, demanding "the expulsion of the Soviet Union from the League of Nations," he concluded by voicing his "Government's unalterable decision, that the Argentine Republic can no longer consider itself a Member of the League of Nations as long as the Soviet Union is able to claim that title." Same, pp. 14, 16, 17. The *Report of the Special Committee,* dated December 13, 1939, Doc.A.46.1939.VII, will be found in League of Nations *O.J.*, 1939, pp. 531–541.

[33] *Records of the Twentieth Ordinary Session of the Assembly, Plenary Meetings,* p. 53.

This resolution was adopted unanimously although several Members represented at the meeting refrained from voting.[34]

The Council, meeting in the afternoon of the same day, adopted a Resolution reading as follows:

> The Council,
> having taken cognisance of the resolution adopted by the Assembly on December 14, 1939, regarding the appeal of the Finnish Government;
> 1. Associates itself with the condemnation by the Assembly of the action of the USSR against the Finnish State; and
> 2. For the reasons set forth in the resolution of the Assembly,
>
> In virtue of Article 16, paragraph 4, of the Covenant,
>
> Finds, that, by its act, the USSR has placed itself outside the League of Nations. It follows that the USSR is no longer a Member of the League.[35]

At the end of the discussion the President spoke as follows:

> The Council will take note of the statements that have just been made and, as abstentions do not count in establishing unanimity, if there are no other observations, I shall take it that the draft resolution has been adopted.[36]

The resolution of the Council gives rise to several questions. In the first place was the resolution adopted in accordance with Article 16, paragraph 4, of the Covenant? At the time of the vote fourteen states Members of the League were represented on the Council. Seven Members appear to have assented to the resolution, viz., France, Great Britain, Bolivia, Belgium, the Dominican Republic, South Africa and Egypt. Several states represented on the Council and present at the Meeting, viz., China,[37] Finland, Greece, and Yugoslavia abstained from voting. Two states represented on the Council, apart from the USSR, viz., Iran and Peru, were not represented at the Meeting.

Having regard to the circumstances attending the vote of the Council, it seems necessary to conclude that the Council's resolution of December 14, 1939, did not have the legal effect of terminating the membership of the USSR in the League of Nations. The Council's resolution was not an exercise of the power conferred upon the Council by paragraph 4, of Article 16. Owing to the absence of Iran and Peru[38] from the Meeting, all

[34] Paragraph 5 of Rule 19 of the Rules of Procedure of the Assembly provides: "For the purpose of this Rule, representatives who abstain from voting shall be considered as not present." Rules, Revised edition, April 1937. Doc.C.144.M.92.1937.

[35] League of Nations *O.J.*, 1939, p. 506.

[36] League of Nations *O.J.*, 1939, p. 508. Before submitting for the Council's approval the draft resolution the President reminded the delegates of the provision of Article 16, paragraph 4. Having quoted verbatim the text of that paragraph, he then said: "Article 16, paragraph 4, of the Covenant, which I have just read to you, provides for a vote by the Members of the League represented on the Council." Same, p. 506.

[37] The Delegate of China declared that in the absence of final instructions from his Government he would abstain from the vote to be taken on the resolution before the Council. Same, p. 508.

[38] Peru withdrew from the League on April 9, 1941, having given notice of withdrawal on April 8, 1939, in accordance with Article 1, paragraph 3, of the Covenant. League of Nations *O.J.*, 1939, p. 204.

states Members of the League which were at the time represented on the Council were not represented at the Meeting, and, owing to the abstention of China, Finland, Greece, and Yugoslavia all states represented on the Council other than the USSR did not affirmatively concur in the vote of the Council. For these two reasons the conditions laid down in Article 16, paragraph 4, appear not to have been fully satisfied. The Council has never met since December 14, 1939, and the legal effect of the resolution of that date has not been examined by the Council itself.

With reference to the substance of the Council's resolution it may be recalled that the first part of the finding "that, by its act, the USSR has placed itself outside the League of Nations," was subject to some criticism. Indeed it was pointed out by the Representative of the Netherlands in the course of the discussion on the Assembly resolution, which contains the same statement, "that the Netherlands Government does not greatly favor this expression, which has no basis in the articles of the Covenant."[39] This is of special importance as the second part of the Council's finding is deduced from the first. It may be argued that if the premise is open to doubt, the conclusion is necessarily also open to doubt. According to the Covenant a state Member of the League does not cease to be a Member *ipso facto* and does not lose its rights and duties as a Member as a consequence of the violation of its obligations under the Covenant.[40] On the contrary, in its capacity of Member it becomes subject to such sanctions as may be decided upon by the competent organs of the League. As several precedents convincingly demonstrate, the wrong-doing state continues to be a Member of the League until the termination of its Membership in accordance with one of the three modes established in the Covenant.[41]

The resolution of the Assembly which is incorporated by reference in the resolution of the Council is not sufficiently precise in stating the covenant which the USSR had violated and on the basis of which it should be declared to be no longer a Member of the League. The application of paragraph 4 of Article 16 is clearly limited to the violation of a covenant of the League. The Assembly resolution, however, refers to the Pact of Paris and to the Russo-Finish Treaty of Non-aggression of 1932. In addition the resolution charges the USSR in the first part to have failed to observe Article 12 and in the second part to have failed to observe one of the League's most essential covenants for the safeguarding of peace and the security of nations by refusing to recognize the duty of the Council and the Assembly as regards the execution of Article 15 of the Covenant. And yet in the operative part of the Assembly resolution it is stated that the USSR has violated "a covenant" of the League and in the finding of the Council it is stated that "by its act" the USSR has placed itself outside the League. It is difficult to decide which of the two or more failures to observe international engagements set forth in the Assembly resolution was the basis for the action of the Council.[42] It will be recalled that, according to the

[39] *Records of the Twentieth Ordinary Session of the Assembly,* Plenary Meetings, p. 35.
[40] Göppert, p. 94.
[41] *The Rules and Procedure Governing Admission to and Loss of Membership in the League of Nations. Report of the Special Committee set up to study the Application of the Principles of the Covenant.* Doc.A.7.1938.VII, p. 59.
[42] Oppenheim, L. *International Law,* Vol. II, London, 1940 (6th ed., by Lauterpacht), p. 137, note 2.

preparatory discussions, the purpose of including Article XVIIA, which later became the fourth paragraph of Article 16, in the Covenant was "to meet the case of a state which after breaking its Covenant still claims to vote on the Council or in the Assembly."[43] The USSR made no such claim. Having informed the Secretary-General on December 5, 1939, that it would be unable to take part in the meetings of the Assembly and of the Council,[44] the USSR was not represented at these meetings. While the USSR for reasons stated in its communications of December 5 and 12, 1939,[45] felt unable to take part in the proceedings instituted by Finland, it made no attempt to interfere with the discharge of the tasks incumbent upon the Assembly and the Council of the League under Article 15 of the Covenant.

[43] Above, p. 555. Mr. Jenks expresses the view that "it may well become one of the constitutional traditions of the League never to have recourse to the clause except in the type of case for which it was originally intended"; work cited, p. 157.

[44] Doc.C.375.M.288.1939.VII. League of Nations *O.J.*, 1939, p. 512.

[45] Same, p. 532.

# THE CHARTER OF THE UNITED NATIONS AND THE LODGE RESERVATIONS

## I. INTRODUCTION

The prompt adoption of the Charter of the United Nations by the United States stands in bold relief against the failure to ratify the Covenant of the League of Nations twenty-five years ago. The causes responsible for the success of the Charter and the failure of the Covenant are probably diverse in character and varying in importance. The indorsement of the Charter by a virtually unanimous vote in the Senate was probably due in no small measure to the decision of the Roosevelt Administration to place the issue of American participation in an international security organization, almost from the very beginning, on a non-partisan basis.[1] The issue, however, was not one of joining an international organization of the Woodrow Wilson type. The vote in the Senate, accordingly, does not necessarily represent a belated conversion to the idealism of Wilson. It would seem, on the contrary, that the Roosevelt Administration, drawing on the rich experience of international coöperation during the interwar period, and more particularly during World War II, had taken care to keep from the Charter all the important matters to which the majority of the Senate, in voting on the Covenant with the Lodge Reservations on March 19, 1920, had taken exception. It may be that this policy was merely part of an over-all strategy aiming at bringing the United States into some sort of international security organization rather than running the risk of a repetition of the 1919/1920 drama. It may be, on the other hand, that the Roosevelt Administration, together with

[1] *Report to the President on the Results of the San Francisco Conference*, Department of State, Publication 2349, Conference Series 71, 1945, p. 24

the other sponsoring governments, had become genuinely convinced that the League Covenant represented a type of international organization which, under the prevailing circumstances, was unattainable or undesirable or unworkable in practice.

These are questions which are here posed without any attempt to answer them. Without entering into the merits of the Wilson-Lodge controversy, this paper will examine the extent to which, in several of its essential aspects, the Charter actually conforms to the pattern of international organization discernible in the Lodge Reservations, taken in conjunction with the Covenant to which they relate. The avowed over-all objective of Senator Henry Cabot Lodge was to make the League "safe" for the United States.[2] The Charter of the United Nations was apparently also devised so as to make it safe for the United States to participate therein. This at any rate was acknowledged by Mr. John Foster Dulles when he urged upon the Senate's Committee of Foreign Relations the view that: "Actually, the document before you charts a path which we can pursue joyfully and without fear. Under it we remain the masters of our destiny."[3] Senator Vandenberg expressed a similar view when he assured the President of the Senate that "the flag stays on the dome of the Capitol."[4] As space limitations make it impossible to review the Charter in the light of all the relevant Reservations, the drawing up of a "safe" international security organization will be illustrated by reference to the more important and apparently still relevant reservations, namely those bearing upon voting strength, the Monroe Doctrine, domestic jurisdiction, the right of withdrawal, and the preservation of territorial integrity and political independence.[5] For the same reason emphasis will be placed upon the international aspects of the reservations under consideration rather than upon their domestic implications.

## II. VOTING STRENGTH AND THE PEACEFUL SETTLEMENT OF DISPUTES

The fourteenth Lodge Reservation related to the voting strength of the British Empire and the Dominions in the League. Senator Lodge apparently assumed that the vote of the four British Dominions and of India which were to become Members of the League in their own right would be controlled by the Empire and that as a consequence England

[2] Henry Cabot Lodge, *The Senate and the League of Nations,* 1925, p. 209.

[3] *The Charter of the United Nations,* Hearings before the Committee on Foreign Relations, U.S. Senate, Seventy-Ninth Congress, First Session on the Charter of the United Nations for the Maintenance of International Peace and Security, Submitted by the President of the United States on July 2, 1945, p. 641.

[4] See Congressional Record, 79th Congress, First Session, Vol. 91, No. 147, July 23, 1945, p. 8089; but see Senator Fulbright, at p. 8095. The following is the context: "The United States retains every basic attribute of its sovereignty. We cannot be called to participate in any sort of sanctions, military or otherwise, without our own free and untrammeled consent. We cannot be taken into the World Court except at our own free option. The ultimate disposition of enemy territory which we have captured in this war is dependent solely upon our own will so far as this Charter is concerned. Our domestic questions are eliminated from the new organization's jurisdiction. Our inter-American system and the Monroe Doctrine are unimpaired in their realities. Our right of withdrawal from the new organization is absolute, and is dependent solely upon our own discretion. In a word, Mr. President, the flag stays on the dome of the Capitol."

[5] The text of the reservations will be found in 59 Congressional Record, Part V, March 19, 1920, p. 4599.

would dispose of six votes in the League as against one vote of the United States. It would have made little difference in the Council of the League whether the Empire disposed of one or six votes since, under Article 5, paragraph 1, all decisions required the agreement of all the Members and the United States was to be a permanent member of the Council. With reference to cases submitted to the Council or the Assembly under Article 15 of the Covenant it has been said "that Reservation 14 covers certain cases which conceivably might happen, but which are so remote in probability as to be nearly impossible."[6] It was believed accordingly that this reservation was "of almost no practical importance."[7]

The question raised by the Lodge Reservation with regard to the voting strength of the British Empire in the League might conceivably have been raised again in connection with the voting strength of the U.S.S.R. in the United Nations. It is true, of course, that, pursuant to Article 18, paragraph 1, each Member of the General Assembly, and, pursuant to Article 27, paragraph 1, each Member of the Security Council, has one vote. Following the Yalta Conference two constituent republics of the Soviet Union, namely the Ukrainian and the Byelorussian Soviet Socialist Republics, were admitted to the San Francisco Conference and consequently to membership in the United Nations.[7a] The question might well be asked whether in their conduct of foreign affairs these two Soviet Republics possessed a "free will" of their own comparable to that possessed by other states of like magnitude. By the Soviet Law of February 1, 1944, all of the Union Republics were given "the right to enter into direct relations with foreign states, to conclude agreements with them, and exchange diplomatic and consular representatives with them." But, according to Article 14, paragraph (a), of the Constitution of 1936, as amended, the jurisdiction of the U.S.S.R. extends to: "The representation of the Union in international relations, conclusion and ratification of treaties with other states, the establishment of the general procedure in the mutual relations between the Union Republics and foreign states."[8]

Aside from considerations arising from the structure and the role of the Communist Party in the Soviet Union it may be doubted whether, having regard to the above quoted article of the Soviet Constitution, the Union Republics are endowed with complete independence in the exercise of the powers conferred upon them by the Law of February 1, 1944. It remains to be seen, of course, to what extent the Ukrainian and Byelorussian Soviet Republics will conduct themselves, within the framework of the United Nations, independently from the U.S.S.R.

It is rather interesting to note that no apprehension comparable to that of Senator Lodge was voiced in view of the potential unequal voting strength of the U.S.S.R. and

[6] Miller, D. H., *My Diary at the Conference of Paris*, n. d., Vol. XX, p. 591.

[7] Miller, p. 592.

[7a] See Sohn, L. B., "Multiple Representation in International Assemblies," in A.J.I.L., Vol. 40 (1946), p. 71.

[8] Constitution (Fundamental Law) of the Union of Soviet Socialist Republics as amended and supplemented by the First, Second, Third, Sixth, Seventh and Eighth Sessions of the Supreme Soviet of the USSR. Published by Information Bulletin, Embassy of the USSR, Washington, D. C. December, 1945.

the U.S.A. This may be explained, at least partially, by the structure of the United Nations. Under the Charter the Security Council has no power to take decisions binding on any of the five Great Powers except in matters of procedure. The situation is somewhat different in the General Assembly where decisions may be made by a simple or by a two-thirds majority. This would seem to give to the Soviet Union an advantage over the other Members. In some matters of political consequence, however, such as the admission of new Members, suspension of the right and privileges of membership, and expulsion of Members, the General Assembly cannot act without the Security Council where the Great Powers are in a controlling position under the principle of unanimity. In others, such as those concerning maintenance of international peace and security, the decisions of the General Assembly will be in the form of recommendations which are not legally binding upon Member States. The powers of the Economic and Social Council may be exercised by a simple majority vote but they are generally speaking of a preparatory, advisory or scientific character. Similarly, the powers of the Trusteeship Council are narrowly circumscribed although exercisable by a majority vote. Furthermore, the position of the administering authorities will be largely defined and safeguarded in the Trust Agreements entered into pursuant to Article 29 of the Charter.

In the matter of procedures for the pacific settlement of disputes which were a prime concern to Senator Lodge in the fourteenth Reservation the position of the United States is fully protected and that is so irrespective of the voting strength of any Member. For under the Charter the Security Council or the General Assembly can at best formulate recommendations which are not legally binding. They do not, moreover, produce the limited legal effect attributed to recommendations of the Council and the Assembly of the League under Article 15, paragraph 6 and 10, respectively. In the Security Council it is a moot point whether the operative provision of Chapter VI could be applied without the prior voluntary admission by a permanent Member (a) that it was involved in a dispute rather than a situation or (b) that it was a party to the alleged dispute or (c) that the dispute was of the nature defined in Article 33 of the Charter.[9] It is also open to discussion, at present, whether the Security Council can be validly seized under Article 37, paragraph 1, without prior and voluntary agreement between both parties to the dispute.[10] It may well be that the self-denying ordinance of Article 27, paragraph 3, cannot begin to display its beneficial effect until some vital preliminary questions are cleared up by the affirmative vote of all the permanent, and of at least two other, Members of the Security Council. Such a result would, of course, deprive Chapter VI of a good deal of its apparent strength though by no means of all its usefulness. It would also reveal that at the bottom, though not on the surface, the Charter represents a less radical departure from the voluntary character of peaceful procedures for the settlement of international disputes which prevails in

[9] *Proceedings of the American Society of International Law,* 1946, p. 79: remarks by Judge Hudson, Mr. Wilcox and Professor Quincy Wright. See also Clyde Eagleton "The Jurisdiction of the Security Council over Disputes," A.J.I.L., Vol. 40, 1946, p. 528.

[10] Goodrich. L. M., and Hambro, E. *Charter of the United Nations,* 1946, p. 152.

general international law than was the case in the League of Nations. Whether this is so the future practice of the Security Council may reveal. In any case, the essentially advisory nature of the Security Council's function under Chapter VI obviated, presumably, any need for special safeguards for the United States in case the Byelorussian or the Ukrainian Soviet Republics were to be among the elected Members of the Security Council and thus perhaps increase the voting power of the U.S.S.R.

## III. THE MONROE DOCTRINE

The fifth Reservation related to Article 21 of the Covenant which was intended to safeguard "the validity of international engagements such as treaties of arbitration or regional understandings like the Monroe Doctrine, for securing the maintenance of peace." Although this article was inserted at the urgent request of President Wilson,[11] it was apparently construed by Senator Lodge as submitting the Monroe Doctrine to the jurisdiction of the League. This danger the fifth Reservation was intended to remove. It is unnecessary to make a detailed examination of Article 21 or of the fifth Reservation. It was said that Article 21, on the one hand, "neither weakens nor limits any of the safeguards provided in the Covenant," and that, on the other, "it cannot have the effect of giving them (viz. the engagements referred to in Article 21) a sanction or validity which they did not previously possess."[12] The interpretation was also advanced that while Article 21 could not completely eliminate the jurisdiction of the League in disputes involving the Monroe Doctrine, the League was bound to grant to the United States a free hand as soon as it determined that the dispute in question was related to the Monroe Doctrine.[13]

With such interpretations the Lodge Reservation was not inconsistent. It may be doubted whether it was necessary.[14] The League of Nations could not pass upon policies. The League was concerned, in Articles 10, 11, and 15, with external aggression, any threat or danger of aggression, any war or threat of war, and disputes likely to lead to rupture. Neither Article 21 nor presumably the fifth Reservation, if accepted, would have precluded the League from the application of Articles 10 and 11.[15] In the case of Article 15 a situation might have arisen in which the United States or another member would invoke Article 21. In that case, as submitted above, Article 21 might have produced a situation similar to that produced by Article 15, paragraph 8, of the Covenant relating to disputes arising out of a matter which by international law is solely within the domestic jurisdiction of one of the parties. In actual practice, however, Article 21 constituted no impediment to the procedure under Article 15 in disputes relating to or between Latin

[11] Miller, *The Drafting of the Covenant*, 1928, Vol. I, p. 444.
[12] Telegram from the President of the Council of the League to the Government of Costa Rica, September 1, 1928, *Official Journal*, 1928, p. 1608.
[13] Schücking, W., and Wehberg, H., Die Satzung des Völkerbundes, 1924 (2d ed.), p. 679; Göppert, Otto, *Organisation und Tätigkeit des Völkerbundes*, Stuttgart, 1938, pp. 60, 314.
[14] Miller, *My Diary*, Vol. XX, p. 580; Fleming, D. F., *The United States and the League of Nations*, 1918–1920, 1932, p. 425.
[15] Fleming, D. F., *The United States and the League of Nations, 1918–1920*, 1932, p. 424.

American Republics members of the League. In support of this conclusion it is possible to refer to the Tacna Arica dispute between Bolivia, Chile, and Peru, 1920, the Leticia dispute between Columbia and Peru, 1933, and the Chaco dispute between Bolivia and Paraguay, 1934.[16]

No explicit reference to the Monroe Doctrine has been included in the Charter of the United Nations. In recent years, however, the Monroe Doctrine has frequently been defined as a doctrine or policy of self-defense or self-protection.[17] Now the Charter of the United Nations recognizes in Article 51 the right of individual and collective self-defense. To the extent that it expresses no more than the right of self-preservation or self-defense, the Monroe Doctrine, it has been said, is implicitly recognized in Article 51. The same has been said of "the hemispheric policy of self-defense against non-American powers" as voiced in the Declaration of Lima of 1938, the Act of Havana of 1940, and the Act of Chapultepec of 1945.[18] It was so explained in the Senate Foreign Relations Committee where the Chairman, Senator Tom Connally, insisted that "the Monroe Doctrine survives in its entirety, unless the Charter somewhere specifically limits it, and (that) the purpose of the Charter is to strengthen the Doctrine rather than to weaken it."[19] Similarly, Mr. Dulles maintained that "there is nothing in the Charter which impairs a nation's right of self-defense" and "that there is nothing whatsoever in this Charter that impairs the Monroe Doctrine as a doctrine which has been proclaimed, sustained, and recognized by the world as a doctrine of self-defense."[20]

In spite of the determined effort made in San Francisco to obtain for the Monroe Doctrine complete recognition[21] and thus to realize to the fullest extent the idea which animated Senator Lodge in the fifth Reservation, there remains some doubt whether this was really achieved. As Article 51 of the Charter now stands, it provides (a) for the inherent right of individual or collective self-defense if an armed attack occurs against a member and (b) for a procedure subordinating, in a sense, the exercise of this right to the authority of the Security Council under Chapter VII of the Charter. Self-defense, as widely understood, is "that form of self-protection which is directed against an aggressor or contemplated aggressor."[22] In the same order of ideas, the Act of Chapultepec of March 3, 1945, envisages the use of armed force and of measures short of force "to prevent or repel aggression."[23] It would seem therefore that traditionally, and particularly

[16] Hackworth, Green Haywood, *Digest of International Law,* Vol. I, 1940, p. 752; Vol. V, 1943, p. 455; Vol. VI, 1943, pp. 50, 51.

[17] See statements quoted in Hackworth, work cited, Vol. V, pp. 440–462.

[18] Report to the President, p. 107.

[19] Hearings, p. 307. Senator Milliken expressed the view "that that Doctrine goes much further than self-defense against an actual act of aggression": same, p. 304.

[20] Hearings, p. 650.

[21] Statement by Mr. Dulles, *Hearings,* p. 650.

[22] Hyde, C. C., *International Law,* 1945 (2d ed.), Vol. I, p. 237.

[23] See Part I, paragraph 6 and Part II of the Act of Chapultepec. Inter-American Conference on Problems of War and Peace, Pan-American Union, Congress and Conference Series, No. 47, 1945, p. 33. See also the Declaration of Lima of 1938 and the Declaration of Habana of 1940 referred to in the Preamble of the Act.

within the American system, the right of self-defense is regarded as being applicable in cases of actual as well as of potential aggression.

The Charter of the United Nations, in Article 51, accepts the right of self-defense but only in case an armed attack occurs against a Member State. This may be construed as excluding resort to self defense against contemplated or impending aggression.[24] In this sense Article 51 may be deemed to limit somewhat the Monroe Doctrine even if it were understood to cover no more than the policy of the United States to resort to self-defense whenever the peace and integrity of the new world is threatened.[25] On the other hand, even if the United States invoked properly the right of self-defense under the Monroe Doctrine—and perhaps under an extended Act of Chapultepec—but did so improperly under Article 51 or any other pertinent provision of the Charter, no action could be taken against it on account of its veto in the Security Council. It is owing to this circumstance, it is believed, rather than because of Article 51 that the Monroe Doctrine may be said to survive "in its entirety."[26] And that as a further consequence the "Doctrine is to be interpreted by the United States alone" as postulated in the fifth reservation.[27]

## IV. DOMESTIC JURISDICTION

The fourth reservation of Senator Lodge related to Article 15, paragraph 8, of the Covenant. Its purpose was to take the determination of the domestic character of a dispute to which the United States was a party out of the hands of the Council and the Assembly and to reserve to the United States "exclusively, the right to decide what questions are within its domestic jurisdiction."[28] While this Reservation was deemed merely to reiterate "the antagonism to international arbitration which exists in the Senate" and while it was recognized that "the language used is logically indefensible," it was believed at the time that "it sounds much worse than it will prove to be in operation."[29] It may well be that this judgment would have been borne out had the United States joined the League of Nations. Perhaps the Reservation did not go far enough in order to achieve complete protection for the domestic affairs of the United States. This can hardly be said of the sweeping reservation which found its way into Article 2, paragraph 7, of the Charter. Before discussing this clause it may be useful to recall briefly the meaning of the corresponding provision of the Covenant to which Senator Lodge took exception.

The right of a party to a dispute to claim that the Council or the Assembly of the League lacked jurisdiction because of the domestic character of the substance of the dis-

[24] Hans Kelsen, "Organization and Procedure of the Security Council of the United Nations," 59 *Harvard Law Review* (1946), p. 1114; Goodrich and Hambro, work cited, p. 173.
[25] See Secretary Hull's statement quoted in Hackworth, work cited, Vol. V, p. 458.
[26] Senator Tom Connally's statement, *Hearings*, p. 307.
[27] Goodrich and Hambro, p. 180.
[28] Lodge, work cited, p. 185.
[29] Miller, *My Diary*, Vol. XX, pp. 577, 578–580; Fleming, pp. 422–424.

pute was limited by the Covenant to the procedure under Article 15. This exception, therefore, did not affect the powers conferred upon the Council or the Assembly or the corresponding duties imposed upon Members by other Articles of the Covenant. It did, in particular, not apply to Articles 10, 11, 12, or 16. Thus the Council's mediatorial mission under Article 11 and the Members' obligation under Article 12 to submit disputes likely to lead to a rupture to arbitration or to judicial settlement or to inquiry by the Council was in principle unaffected by the exception contained in Article 15, paragraph 8.

Furthermore, the exception of domestic jurisdiction in Article 15, paragraph 8, related by its terms to the power of the Council or the Assembly to make recommendations in regard to the dispute. As the making of recommendations was only one aspect of the Council's powers and only one part of the Council's report under Article 15, the exception could not be said to apply to the mediatorial action of the Council under Article 15, paragraph 3, and to the inquiry into the facts of the dispute made by the Council under paragraph 4 of Article 15. Correspondingly, Members were not exempt from the duty laid down in Article 15, paragraph 2, to communicate to the Council "as promptly as possible statements of their case with all the relevant facts and papers."

Moreover, the Covenant limited the exception in several ways. It could validly be raised only with reference to a matter which was solely within the domestic jurisdiction, which, secondly, was so by international law and which, thirdly, was found to be so by the Council. All these questions were strictly questions of international law which lent themselves to juridical determination. It was in this spirit that the Council interpreted the exception laid down in Article 15, paragraph 8, in disputes which came before it. Thus in the dispute between Finland and Sweden relating to the Aaland Islands the Council referred the question to a committee of jurists and in two other cases—the Franco-British dispute concerning the Nationality Decrees in Tunis and Morocco and the Greco-Turkish dispute relating to the Expulsion of the Ecumenical Patriarch—the Council referred the question to the Permanent Court of International Justice. In the first two cases the objection founded in Article 15, paragraph 8, was overruled. In the third case the dispute was settled through negotiations between the parties.

By contrast, the reservation of domestic jurisdiction as formulated in Article 2, paragraph 7 of the Charter, with one exception to be noted later, embraces the whole of the field of action of the United Nations. It may be said to restrict the power of all organs of the United Nations and to limit the duties assumed by the Members. In particular, it relieves the Members from the duty "to submit such matters to settlement under the present Charter." They would seem to be released not merely from their duty under Article 37 to submit a dispute to the Security Council for action under Article 36 or for recommendation of terms of settlement but also from the basic duty assumed in Article 33, to "seek a solution by negotiation, inquiry, mediation, conciliation, arbitration, judicial settlement, resort to regional agencies, or arrangements, or other peaceful means of their own choice." The Security Council, on the other hand, it may be argued, is restrained in the exercise of the powers conferred upon it by Article 33, paragraph 2, and of the basic power conferred upon it by Article 34 to investigate any dispute for the purpose of determining whether a certain dispute or situation "is likely to endanger the maintenance of international peace and security." These are some of the significant inroads of the traditional sovereignty of states into the security system established by the Charter. They do not, however, exhaust the import of Article 2, paragraph 7. It has been pointed out[30] that Article 2, paragraph 7, differs from Article 15, paragraph 8, of the Covenant in the omission of international law as the yardstick of domestic questions, in the omission of the Security Council as the organ competent to determine the validity of an objection founded on Article 2, paragraph 7, and in the substitution of the adjective "essentially" for "solely."

The elimination of international law was justified on the ground that it was "indefinite and inadequate" and "antiquated."[31] This view stands in marked contrast to the current notion that international law is a growing and expanding body of law. It stands, in particular, in contradiction with the extremely dynamic conception of international law relied upon by Mr. Justice Jackson in his defense of the United States' position with reference to the Nuremberg War Crimes Trial.[32] The dynamic concept was stressed by the Permanent Court of International Justice in the Franco-British nationality dispute when the Court declared that "the question whether a certain matter is or is not within the jurisdiction of a state is an essentially relative question; it depends upon the development of international relations."[33] Those who advocated the deletion of a reference to international law may be disappointed in actual practice. As the domestic character of a question can hardly be justified in terms of the municipal law of either party to the dispute, international law as the legal order common to both parties in fact must be resorted to in order to resolve the controversy.[34]

The reason advanced for the substitution of the word "essentially" for "solely" disclosed the great desire for a flexible and wider interpretation of domestic matters.[35] The Permanent Court of International Justice held, on the other hand, that while the question was a relative one, the exception of Article 15, paragraph 8, did not lend itself to extensive interpretation. The existence of a conventional or of a customary rule of international law was deemed sufficient to overrule the contention that a matter was "solely" within the domestic jurisdiction of a state.[36] In the future a party to a dispute, without denying the existence of a pertinent norm of international law, may nevertheless be in the position to deny the applicability of the procedures for the settlement of international dis-

[30] Goodrich and Hambro, work cited, p. 72.

[31] Report to the President, p. 45.

[32] Mr. Justice Jackson's remarks in his Report to the President of June 7, 1945, "Trial of War Criminals," Department of State Publication 2420, 1945, p. 9; also statements quoted in Hackworth, Vol. I, pp. 39–43.

[33] Permanent Court of International Justice, *Publications*, Series B, No. 4, p. 24.

[34] Preuss, Lawrence, "The International Court of Justice, the Senate, and Matters of Domestic Jurisdiction," A.J.I.L., Vol. 40, 1946, p. 724.

[35] "A Commentary on the Charter of the United Nations," in *British Parliamentary Papers*, Misc. No. 9 (1945), Cmd. 6666, paragraph 20 at p. 6.

[36] Permanent Court of International Justice, *Publications*, Series B, No. 4, p. 24.

putes laid down in the Charter. All it has to do is to maintain that in spite of existing international obligations the matter is one that falls "essentially" although perhaps not "solely" within its domestic jurisdiction.

The extension by comparison with the Covenant of the sphere within which states may claim unfettered freedom of action and avoid essential obligations flowing from the Charter is still further emphasized by the absence of a named organ competent to decide whether Article 2, paragraph 7, was properly invoked by a Member Government. Admittedly such an organ would have been faced with a difficult though by no means impossible task. Its mere existence, however, would probably have operated as a restraint upon member governments in making use of Article 2, paragraph 7. It has been contended that in spite of the absence of a reference to a specific organ in Article 2, paragraph 7, each organ of the United Nations and notably the International Court of Justice would be competent to decide whether it had jurisdiction.[37] On the other hand the view has also been advanced that each member would decide for itself whether, having regard to Article 2, paragraph 7, it could decline to accept the jurisdiction of an organ of the United Nations.[38] It was perhaps with a view to avoiding all future controversy that the United States in accepting the compulsory jurisdiction of the International Court of Justice under Article 36 of the Statute made the reservation that it and it alone would determine whether a dispute concerned a matter which was essentially within its domestic jurisdiction.[39] Such would have probably been the result of the operation of Article 2 paragraph 7. For this reason this reservation, assuming that it is a valid exercise of the powers conferred upon states by Article 36 of the Statute, was said to have added little to the broad exception already contained in Article 2 paragraph 7 of the Charter.[40]

The view that it is for each state to determine in appropriate circumstances whether the exception of Article 2, paragraph 7, applies may be supported by the following reasoning: (1) The Organization, according to Article 2, paragraph 1, is based on the principle of the sovereign equality of all its Members. One of the elements of sovereignty included in that principle is "that each state enjoys the right inherent in full sovereignty."[41] One of the rights inherent in full sovereignty is the right of each state to interpret for itself the nature, extent, and meaning of the obligations assumed in the Charter insofar as this right has not been explicitly surrendered.[42] It may be apposite to recall here the dictum of the Permanent Court of International Justice in the Lotus Case that "restrictions upon the independence of states cannot . . . be presumed."[43] (2) The Charter

[37] Statement of the Belgian Delegate, M. Dehousse, in Commission I of the San Francisco Conference, UNCIO, Documents, Vol. VI, p. 112.

[38] Statement of the Uruguayan Delegate, M. Payssé, in same, p. 110. See also Clyde Eagleton, "Covenant of the League of Nations and Charter of the United Nations: Points of Difference," 13 *Department of State Bulletin* (1945), at p. 268.

[39] 15 *Department of State Bulletin* (1946), p. 452.

[40] Wilcox, Francis O., "The United States Accepts Compulsory Jurisdiction," A.J.I.L., Vol. 40, 1946, p. 710.

[41] Report of Rapporteur of Committee 1 to Commission I, Doc. 944 (E) I/1/34 (1). UNCIO, Documents, Vol. VI, p. 457.

[42] Lauterpacht, H., *The Development of International Law by the Permanent Court of International Justice,* 1934, p. 34; Goodrich and Hambro, p. 64.

[43] Permanent Court of International Justice, *Publications,* Series A, No. 10, p. 18.

confers upon no organ of the United Nations the general competence to interpret the Charter authoritatively, that is with binding effect upon all member governments as well as organs of the United Nations. It has been said that each organ will interpret for itself those parts of the Charter which are applicable to its functions.[44] This presumes, of course, that all Members will accept such an interpretation. On the other hand, "it is to be understood, of course, that if an interpretation made by any organ of the Organization or by a committee of jurists is not generally acceptable it will be without binding effect."[45] Thus if a member state objected to the action of any organ of the United Nations including, presumably, the International Court of Justice, on the ground that it constituted an infringement of Article 2, paragraph 7, as interpreted by itself, it could refuse to be bound thereby. The only legal method by which to invest an interpretation with binding force is the procedure of amendment laid down in Chapter XVIII of the Charter. However, in virtue of an accepted understanding a Member may withdraw from the Organization if it disapproves of an amendment.[46] It would seem therefore, that ultimately each state member of the United Nations may interpret for itself the scope and applicability to a given dispute of the exception contained in Article 2, paragraph 7. (3) This view finds further support in the deliberate departure from the precedent of Article 15, paragraph 8, of the Covenant and the resulting omission of an organ competent to decide whether a Member properly invoked the exception of Article 2, paragraph 7. (4) A possible exception might be construed for disputes brought before the International Court of Justice. According to Article 36, paragraph 6, of the Statute, the Court has power to determine whether it has jurisdiction. In passing upon the preliminary objection to its jurisdiction the Court, it is believed, would have to consider the provisions of the Charter including notably Article 2, paragraph 7, along with the Statute and applicable treaties and declarations. A party to a dispute which disagrees with the Court's interpretation of Article 2, paragraph 7, may find some justification in the conclusions of the Committee referred to above for refusing to submit to its jurisdiction and for regarding any action taken by the Court as exceeding the scope of its authority. It seems doubtful whether any ruling of the Court could be properly construed as an "intervention" within the meaning of Article 2, paragraph 7. It may be, however, that in the absence of a clarifying interpretation of this ambiguous term each member state, unless willing to submit to the Court's jurisdiction, will deem itself warranted in adhering to its own view of Article 2, paragraph 7, and notably of the meaning of the term "intervention" which did not appear in Article 15, paragraph 8, of the Covenant of the League.

The exception of domestic jurisdiction, pursuant to the explicit terms of Article 2, paragraph 7, cannot be invoked in case of the application of enforcement measures under Chapter VII. The phrasing of this provision was, of course, deliberate. It was intended to exclude, in the first place, the use of the power conferred upon the Security Council in

[44] Report of the Rapporteur of Committee IV/2. UNCIO, Documents, Vol. XIII, p. 709.

[45] Same, p. 710.

[46] Report to the President, p. 48.

Article 39 to make recommendations. This was an important concession made at San Francisco to the view held by the Australian delegation.[47] Thus the Security Council's power to deal preventively by way of recommendations with threats to the peace would seem to be seriously curtailed. In the second place, the use of the power conferred upon the Security Council by Article 40 seems also to be excluded. It was made clear at the San Francisco Conference that the exception in favor of enforcement measures should be interpreted strictly.[48] As the provisional measures which the Security Council may enjoin upon the parties cannot, strictly speaking, be classified as enforcement measures within the meaning of Articles 41 and 42, they may become inapplicable whenever a party claims that the matter falls essentially within its domestic jurisdiction. This interpretation cannot, it is believed, be ruled out in case of a threat to the peace as distinguished from a breach of the peace or an act of aggression.[49] By comparison with the League's broad powers under Articles 10 and 11, to deal preventively with a threat or danger of aggression and a threat of war, the Security Council's powers in similar cases appear significantly limited.

In conclusion it may be said that whereas the Covenant, in Article 15, paragraph 8, attempted to strike a balance between the legitimate claims of state sovereignty and the minimum requirement of collective security to restrict the discretionary element inherent in that sovereignty, the Charter, in Article 2, paragraph 7, appears, by contrast, to safeguard that discretionary element at the expense of restrictions which are essential to any workable system of international security. By placing the domestic jurisdiction clause among the Principles of the Organization, which constitute, in a sense, its fundamental law, the Charter gives expression to the desire of the member governments to extend the application of this clause "to the activities of the Organization as a whole."[50] By eliminating the yardstick of international law, by substituting "essentially" for "solely," by neglecting to name an organ with power to determine the applicability of the exception of domestic jurisdiction in international disputes, the Charter may be said to be fully in line with the principle of Senator Lodge's fourth Reservation. It was Senator Lodge who objected to the term "solely" by stating that domestic or political questions "relating wholly or in part to its internal affairs" should be considered "solely" within the jurisdiction of the United States. It was Senator Lodge who desired that the United States and not the Council of the League should have the right to determine what these questions were. It was Senator Lodge who desired that all questions so determined should be withdrawn from the basic obligation to submit disputes likely to lead to a rupture to arbitration or judicial settlement or inquiry by the Council or the Assembly. Article 2, paragraph 7, fulfills all these desires and goes beyond them by seriously curtailing the range and effectiveness of the Security Council's preventive activities in discharging its

[47] Report to the President, p. 44.

[48] Statement of the Rapporteur of Committee I/1 to Commission I. UNCIO, Documents, Vol. VI, p. 487.

[49] "A Commentary on the Charter of the United Nations," in *British Parliamentary Papers,* Misc. No. 9 (1945), Cmd. 6666, paragraph 34 at p. 8.

[50] Report to the President, p. 44; *Hearings,* p. 310.

chief responsibility for the maintenance of international peace and security. For all of these reasons it may be difficult to disagree with Mr. Payssé of Uruguay who observed in the First Committee of the San Francisco Conference that with Article 2, paragraph 7, as adopted, "a great jump backwards will be taken."[51]

## V. THE RIGHT OF WITHDRAWAL

The first Lodge Reservation related to Article 1, paragraph 3, of the Covenant which provided for the right of withdrawal after two years notice and subject to the fulfillment of certain obligations. Under the Covenant the right of withdrawal, made explicit at the insistence of President Wilson,[52] was not to be exercised lightly nor was it to be exercised in such a manner as to bring about sudden changes in the legal relations between the Members of the League.[53] The first Lodge Reservation would have excluded any jurisdiction by the League and established the United States as "the sole judge as to whether all of its obligations under the said Covenant have been fulfilled." It has been said that this Reservation "was as correct as it was unnecessary,"[54] for Article 1, paragraph 3, conferred upon every Member of the League "an absolute right of withdrawal."[55] Although the intended purpose of Article 1, paragraph 3, was to confer no such absolute right upon the Members and, in particular, to make "withdrawal attempted in spite of unfulfilled obligations ineffective,"[56] in actual practice Members exercised the right of withdrawal without any effective control by the League.[57]

The Charter of the United Nations, unlike the Covenant contains no regulations in respect of withdrawal. The San Francisco Conference after an exhaustive discussion approved a commentary on withdrawal included in the Report of Commission I. According to this statement Members may withdraw from the Organization (a) if exceptional circumstances occur; (b) if the Organization reveals itself unable to maintain peace or if it could do so only at the expense of law and justice; (c) if a Charter amendment were adopted changing the rights and obligations of Members and (d) if an amendment, adopted by the General Assembly or a General Conference, failed to enter into force because of lack of the required number of ratifications.[58]

Assuming that this interpretation will actually guide the Organization and the Members desirous of withdrawing from it, it must be said that the right of withdrawal is

[51] UNCIO, Documents, Vol. VI, p. 110.
[52] Miller, *The Drafting of the Covenant*, Vol. 1, pp. 293, 296, 305, 342–348.
[53] "Question of the Universality of the League: Participation of all States in the League," Report by Lord Cranborne. Doc. A.7.1938. VII, p. 60. See also "The Covenant of the League of Nations with a Commentary Thereon" in *British Parliamentary Papers*, Misc. No. 3 (1919), Cmd. 151, p. 13.
[54] Fleming, p. 421.
[55] Miller, *My Diary*, Vol. XX, pp. 480, 482, 569–571; but compare Miller, *The Drafting of the Covenant*, Vol. I, p. 343.
[56] Lord Cranborne's Report, p. 60. See also Engel, S. *League Reform*, 1940, pp. 74–74.
[57] Cranborne *Report*, p. 60.
[58] "Report of the Rapporteur of Commission I to Plenary Session," Doc. 1179, I/9 (1), p. 5, UNCIO, Documents, Vol. VI, p. 249; "Verbatim Minutes of the Ninth Plenary Session," 1210, P/20, in same, Vol. I, pp. 616, 620; Report to the President, p. 49; *Hearings*, p. 232.

absolute with the possible qualification that the withdrawing Member will be expected to state its reason.[59] It was so explained and understood in the Senate's Foreign Relations Committee.[60] It was particularly underscored that each Member remained judge of the circumstances motivating its withdrawal[61] and that no sanctions could be employed against a withdrawing Member.[62] The only penalty said Senator Vandenberg, could be an "adverse public opinion."[63]

The Charter thus legalized, tacitly, the practice of League Members in the matter of withdrawal. In this respect it goes to the full extent of the first Lodge Reservation. It should be noted, however, that it goes beyond that Reservation and the League Covenant and practice in two ways. First, it fails to make withdrawal conditional upon the fulfillment of Charter and other international obligations. Senator Lodge did not object to this aspect of the Covenant although he desired it to be clearly understood that the United States would alone "determine as to the fulfillment of its obligations."[64] Secondly, both the Charter and the Committee statement fail to lay down a time interval for the withdrawal to become legally effective. Senator Lodge did not object to the requirement of a two years' notice. In the absence of a rule to the contrary, withdrawal from the United Nations will become presumably effective immediately, that is, even if it were announced on the eve of crucial decisions in the Security Council in connection with the settlement of a dispute or the employment of preventive or enforcement measures. No protection is afforded to the Members of the United Nations against sudden changes in the membership and the attendant changes in the burdens and benefits of membership. This is hardly an improvement on the Covenant. Thus in connection with the right of withdrawal as in the matter of domestic jurisdiction the principle of sovereignty has prevailed over and against what many would regard as the minimum requirements of an international security organization.

## VI. PRESERVATION AND TERRITORIAL INTEGRITY AND POLITICAL INDEPENDENCE

The second Lodge Reservation, the most controversial of all, related primarily to Article 10, the "cornerstone" or the "heart" of the Covenant as conceived by Woodrow Wilson. As to the meaning of Article 10, there was hardly ever a general agreement beyond the statement that it contained two distinct obligations, first, the negative duty to respect, and secondly, the positive duty to preserve as against external aggression the territorial integrity and the political independence of member states. The first duty was hardly open to discussion and it should be noted that Senator Lodge raised

[59] Report to the President, p. 49; statements by Mr. Dulles, *Hearings*, p. 649, and by Dr. Pasvolsky, p. 235.
[60] *Hearings*, pp. 234 f., 240, 246, 324, 348, 646, 647, 648.
[61] Statements by the Chairman, Senator Tom Connally, *Hearings*, p. 649, and by Mr. Dulles, p. 648.
[62] Statements by the Chairman, *Hearings*, p. 234, and Dr. Pasvolsky, pp. 235, 236.
[63] *Hearings*, p. 237; also statements by the Chairman, pp. 234, 649; Senator George and Dr. Pasvolsky, p. 235.
[64] Lodge, work cited, p. 173.

no objection on this score.[65] It was the positive duty which almost from the very beginning had become the center of controversy. In the view of some writers it implied an absolute, automatic, and unlimited obligation to assist the victim of aggression and to reëstablish the *status quo.*[66] Others denied that it had any legal meaning at all.[67] Some decried it as a guarantee of existing territorial alignments,[68] while others contended that, far from "freezing" the territorial situation resulting from the Paris Peace Treaties, Article 10 merely had the legal effect of making wars of conquest illegal.[69]

The prevailing sentiment within the League was opposed to the Canadian proposal made at the very first meeting of the Assembly to simply strike out Article 10 from the Covenant.[70] But the overwhelming majority of the League Members in 1923 supported an interpretation which was designed to adjust the weight and scope of obligations assumed under Article 10 to the situation created by the absence of the United States from the League. Accordingly, Members remained bound by the basic obligation of Article 10, but it was for the constitutional authorities of each Member to decide in what degree it was bound to assure the execution of this obligation by the employment of military forces. The Members also agreed to take into consideration the recommendations of the Council. On the other hand, the Council, in recommending military measures, was to be bound to take into account the geographical location and the special conditions of each member state.[71] It may be said that the League followed the line of thought developed by the Committee of Jurists of 1920. This Committee, it may be recalled, for the first time laid down the view that in Article 10 the Covenant incorporated a principle the implementation of which was to be sought for in the following Articles and notably in Article 16.[72] As Article 16 was not understood to create an obligation to apply military sanctions, there appeared no valid reasons for assuming that the draftsmen of the Covenant intended to lay down so far reaching an obligation in Article 10. Although lacking support in the actual language of Article 10, the restrictive view prevailed in the practice of

65 Miller, *My Diary*, Vol. XX, p. 573.

66 M. Scialoja (Italy) in the Second Assembly, 1921, First Committee, *Minutes*, p. 111.

67 Sir John Fischer Williams, *Some Aspects of the Covenant of the League of Nations*, 1934, p. 122; Kelsen, Hans, *Legal Technique in International Law*,, 1939. p. 70.

68 Memoranda submitted by the Canadian Government in support of the proposal of the Canadian Delegation at the Assembly to strike out Article 10. Doc. C. 215. M. 154. 1921 (A.C. 28). Memorandum of Sir Robert Borden of March 13, 1919, p. 8.

69 M. Rolin in the Second Assembly, First Committee, *Minutes*, p. 110; Belgian Memorandum of May 28, 1923, Doc. A.17.1923, V, p. 2; Kunz, J. L., "L'Article 11 du Pacte de la Société des Nations," *Recueil des Cours de l'Académie de Droit International*, 1932, Vol. I, p. 707. The Draft Treaty of Mutual Assistance of 1923 stipulated in Article 1 that even in case of a legitimate war the political independence and territorial integrity of the opponent must not be violated. Similarly Article 15, paragraph 2, of the Geneva Protocol for the Pacific Settlement of International Disputes.

70 League of Nations. The Records of the First Assembly, Plenary Meetings, p. 275.

71 Assembly, 1923, Plenary Meetings, Text of Debates, p. 77.

72 "Report of the Committee of Jurists addressed to the Committee on Amendments to the Covenant," June 28, 1921, Doc. 24 (1). 1921. V. (A.C. 40 (a) ), Annex I, pp. 10–14; "Report of the Committee on Amendments to the Covenant," September 7, 1921, pp. 3–4. Both reports are reprinted in Doc. C.S.P. 26, pp. 43–47. See also "Article 10 of the Covenant. Report submitted to the Committee by M. Nasrollah Entezam." Doc. A.7.1938. VII, p. 96: "It would appear, however, that, in practice, Article 10 has hardly been treated as other than a general rule of principle, for the application of which resort has been had to the procedure provided by other articles."

the League.[73] In no small measure the absence of the United States from the League may be credited with this result.

The second Lodge Reservation was far from clear.[74] It could be interpreted as simply restricting the commitment of the United States to those means for enforcing Article 10 which were not specifically reserved to Congress.[75] It could also be interpreted as denying the binding character of the Council's action under Article 10. This was a position which was taken by all but one Member of the League in 1923. But the Lodge Reservation could also be understood as simply denying any obligation to take appropriate, that is military, measures for the purpose of upholding the sanctity of the political independence and territorial integrity of member states. The acceptance of this duty has rightly been regarded as the most far-reaching single step yet taken in the development of collective security. If it were Senator Lodge's intent to eliminate "any opportunity of charging the United States with bad faith"[76] then certainly the way to do so was to refuse from the outset to accept the affirmative duty of Article 10 and this is precisely what the second Reservation declares in its opening words. On this vital point no compromise appeared possible. Even under the 1923 interpretation the Members of the League were bound to take into consideration the recommendations of the Council. Moreover, it was made quite clear at the time that while the Members had the right to decide upon the method of implementing their duty under Article 10, there could be no tampering with the duty itself.[77] It would seem, therefore, that the chief objective of the second Lodge Reservation must have been the nullification of the basic duty to preserve League Members against aggression. The excision of the positive duty from Article 10 would have wrought an important transformation of the League of Nations although it may be doubted that it would have deprived the League of all its usefulness as an instrument of collaboration.

The Charter of the United Nations contains no single provision comparable to Article 10 of the Covenant. Insofar as the first duty of Article 10 is concerned it has been said that such a duty to respect the territorial integrity and political independence of states was implicit in Article 2, paragraph 1.[78] Efforts aiming at the inclusion in the Charter of a specific statement "emphasizing respect for territorial integrity and political independence of states" failed at the San Francisco Conference. Agreement was reached, however,

[73] M. Nasrollah Entezam's Report quoted above, p. 96.

[74] Fleming, p. 435.

[75] Miller, *My Diary*, Vol. XX, p. 572.

[76] Lodge, work cited, p. 174.

[77] "Application of the Principles of the Covenant. Article 10. Memorandum prepared by the Secretariat," Doc. C.S.P. 26, p. 33. See also statement by M. Rolin, Rapporteur of the First Committee, in the 1923 Assembly, Plenary Meetings, p. 77.

[78] Official British Commentary on the Charter of the United Nations, paragraph 19 at p. 6; Report to the President, p. 40; Congressional Record, 79th Congress, First Session, Vol. 91, No. 147, July 23, 1945, p. 8096; "Report of the Rapporteur of Committee 1 to Commission I," Doc. 944, I/1/34 (1) p. 12, UNCIO, Documents, Vol. VI, p. 457; Doc. 1123, I/8, pp. 5–6, "Verbatim Minutes of Second Meeting of Commission I; "Report of the Rapporteur of Commission I to the Plenary Session," Doc. 1179, I/9 (1), p. 2, UNCIO, Documents, Vol. VI, p. 246; also UNCIO, Documents, Vol. VI, pp. 69, 70.

on Article 2, paragraph 4.[79] Presumably, there is a difference between the positive duty to respect in Article 10 of the Covenant and the negative duty in Article 2, paragraph 4, of the Charter to "refrain . . . from the threat or use of force against the territorial integrity or political independence of any state, or in any other manner inconsistent with the purposes of the United Nations." Perhaps if disrespect for the integrity and independence of states can be shown in some other manner or in a manner not inconsistent with the purposes of the Charter, then the Members may pursue such policies.

Several attempts were also made at San Francisco to introduce into the Charter the idea of protection or preserving the existence of member states against aggression. The Charter is, of course, quite explicit in stating the chief purpose of the Organization, the maintenance of international peace and security. This has been described as the "overriding and unqualified purpose" of the Charter.[80] And so it is. All attempts to attach some condition or qualification to this purpose have been systematically defeated.[81] Attempts were made, for instance, to add after "security" in Article 1, paragraph 1, the word "justice" or the words "in conformity with the principles of justice and international law." Both proposals carried in Committee by a majority failed to obtain the necessary two-thirds vote. It was said that justice and international law should wait until peace and security were restored.[82] Law and justice, of course, constitute the indispensable basis of a sound international organization. Unfortunately, however, the Organization under the present Charter is neither bound, nor equipped with sufficient power, to restore or maintain law and justice in all circumstances.

Another proposal sought to insert after "security" in Article 1, paragraph 1, the words "and to preserve as against external aggression the territorial integrity and political independence of every member of the Organization." This proposal was defeated, ostensibly on the ground that it would have overloaded the text of the Charter and that a similar idea was expressed in Article 2, paragraph 4.[83] The New Zealand delegation moved to add to Article 2, paragraph 4, the following clause: "All members of the Organization undertake collectively to resist any act of aggression against any member."[84] This motion was lost as it fell short by a few votes of the necessary two thirds majority. The chief purpose of the New Zealand amendment like that of the other proposals was to qualify the overriding purpose of the Organization and to limit the discretionary powers of the Security Council. But the Great Powers were opposed to any amendment which would have qualified the purpose and limited their freedom of action under Chapter VII.

[79] Report to the President, p. 41.

[80] Same, p. 39.

[81] Same, p. 36.

[82] "Report of Rapporteur of Committee 1 to Commission I," Doc. 944, I/1/34 (1), p. 8, UNCIO, Documents, Vol. VI, p. 453; "Report of Rapporteur of Commission I to Plenary Session," Doc. 1179, I/9 (1), p. 1 f, UNCIO, Documents, Vol. VI, p. 245 f; and "Report of Rapporteur of Subcommittee I/1/A to Committee I/1," Doc. 723, I/1/A/19, p. 7, UNCIO, Documents, Vol. VI, p. 702.

[83] "Report of Rapporteur of Subcommittee I/1/A to Committee I/1," Doc. 723, I/1/A/19, p. 7, UNCIO, Documents, Vol. VI, p. 702.

[84] "Report of Rapporteur of Committee 1 to Commission I," Doc. 944, I/1/34 (1), p. 14, UNCIO, Documents, Vol. VI, p. 459. The delegation of Panama submitted a similar proposal.

It was fully realized at the San Francisco Conference that some of the Great Powers would have refused to accept a Charter which imposed upon them a duty comparable to that contained in Article 10 of the Covenant.[85] The battle over Article 10 was fought this time on the floor of the San Francisco Conference rather than on the floor of the Senate. The price for the entry of certain of the Great Powers into an international security organization, now as then, is the elimination of what is widely believed to be the basic notion of collective security from its constitution.

The deliberate rejection of all proposals to impose upon the Organization and its Security Council the duty to preserve against aggression the integrity and independence of member states, does not, however, constitute as radical a departure from the League as may appear from this verbal comparison. Obviously, there is a great discrepancy between the Covenant and the Charter. But the practice of the League was not always in harmony with its Covenant. The practice of the League gradually came to be characterized by the disinclination of member governments to execute their far-reaching obligations under the Covenant and particularly under Article 10 in cases "not directly affecting their own immediate interests."[86] Thus in practice the member governments while paying lip service to the Covenant, have shown themselves extremely reluctant to abandon their liberty of action in examining each case on its merits. The Charter, it will be said, takes note of this attitude and wisely abstains from imposing limitations upon the liberty of governments which they were unwilling to assume again. This, at any rate, seems true of the Great Powers. Theirs is a great responsibility. But it is not part of their responsibility to preserve the integrity and independence of their fellow members. They did not wish to assume such a great responsibility. At least it cannot be said that they create illusions about collective security.

## VII. CONCLUSIONS

Both the Covenant of the League and the Charter of the United Nations belong to the same genus of international organization. They are conceived within the framework of the existing state system. They are based on the principle of state sovereignty. They provide for collaboration in the maintenance of peace. Within this genus it is possible to distinguish different types of organizations. Taking the objective as criterion, multi-purpose organizations may be distinguished from single-purpose organizations and political organizations may be distinguished from non-political organizations and so on. According to membership, universal and non-universal, regional and global organizations may be distinguished. With reference to the problem of enforcing peace three types of organizations have been distinguished: the coercive, the non-coercive, and the intermedi-

[85] Same, p. 3; "Report of Rapporteur of Subcommittee I/1/A to Committee I/1," Doc. 723, I/1/A/19, p. 5, UNCIO, Documents, Vol. VI, p. 700; and Fox, William T. R., "Collective Enforcement of Peace and Security," 39 *American Political Science Review* (1945), p. 970.

[86] Lord Cranborne's report on the "Participation of all States in the League of Nations," Doc. A.7.1938.VII, paragraph 27 (2) at p. 48.

ate type.[87] In the coercive type of international organization there are definite obligations to apply sanctions; in the non-coercive type there are no such obligations; and in the intermediate type there is no more than the obligation to consult but sanctions are possible as a result of consultation.

The League was conceived as an international organization of the coercive variety: Articles 16 and 10 were originally intended to impose upon the Members the obligation to employ force in certain cases. The Lodge Reservations, if generally adopted, would have transformed the League into a non-coercive or an intermediate type of international organization. But President Wilson refused to have his League reduced to "an influential debating society."[88] It is a moot point whether had the United States joined the League with the Lodge Reservations the League would have turned into a mere debating society. It is an historical fact, however, that in the absence of the United States and owing to some other factors, the League did degenerate into a debating society and not a very influential society at that. Whereas Senator Lodge opened the attack on the coercive features of the League on the floor of the Senate, the Canadian proposal in 1920 to strike out Article 10 of the Covenant was the next major step in whittling down the League's collective security system and the first made on the floor of the League Assembly. This was followed in 1921 by the adoption of certain "Resolutions Concerning the Economic Weapon" and other "Resolutions for the Amendment of Article 16."[89] The Council of the League declared in 1921 that it would be guided by these resolutions which had never formally come into force.[90] The long-drawn process of whittling down collective security alternated with efforts to strengthen it. Among the latter, the Draft Treaty of Mutual Assistance, the Geneva Protocol, and others are worthy of note. In the end, however, the Copenhagen Declaration of July 24, 1938, by the states of the Oslo Group, and the United Kingdom Declaration of September 28, 1938,[91] clearly indicated that the unconditional undertaking to apply sanctions had given place to a system of consultation. No change, to be sure, was made in the terms of the Covenant. But in fact by the unilateral action of individual governments and groups of governments, the League had been transformed from a coercive into a non-coercive or perhaps an intermediate type of security organization. Indeed in 1938 the majority of the Members were of the opinion that the League had acquired an intermediate character.[92] Thus the Members themselves under pressure of circumstances brought about that change in the League structure which

[87] Same, p. 41.

[88] U.S. Congress. Senate. Foreign Relations Committee. *Treaty of Peace with Germany, Report of Conference between Members of Senate Committee on Foreign Relations and President of the United States at White House, Aug. 19, 1919;* presented by Mr. Lodge, 1919. Senate Document 76, 66th Congress, 1st Session, p. 6; also Lord Grey's letter to the *London Times* published in *The New York Times,* February 1, 1920, in which he urged the acceptance of the Lodge Reservations. The letter is reprinted in Fleming, work cited, p. 411.

[89] "Reports and Resolutions on the Subject of Article 16 of the Covenant," Doc. A.14.1927.V. p. 42.

[90] Same, p. 44.

[91] "Questions Relating to Article 16 of the Covenant," Doc. C. 444. M. 287. 1938. VII. p. 2, 15; Engel, work cited, p. 147.

[92] "Report Submitted by the Sixth Committee to the Assembly," Doc. A.74.1938. VII; Engel, work cited, p. 154.

Senator Lodge in the interest of the security of the United States had deemed necessary from the outset.

It will be argued that the fatal course of events has vindicated the basic philosophy of the Lodge reservations, that the member states of the League were unprepared for the Wilsonian Covenant, and that, in practice, the idealism of Wilson gave place to the realism of Lodge. Judgments on these matters are not attempted here, for what happened at Geneva took place in an atmosphere far different from that which presumably would have prevailed if American membership in the League and Wilsonian leadership had materialized. It should be noted, however, that if the realism of Lodge is admitted, nothing is granted save the impossibility of establishing a coercive-type league, and this admission does not deny the realism of Wilson that an intermediate or a non-coercive type league would not be sufficient to prevent aggression and to preserve peace. Confining the discussion, therefore, to events that occurred, no matter for what causes and with what disastrous results, it is true that the Geneva League largely adopted in practice the limitations advocated by Lodge. In this sense, and possibly in this sense only, it may be said that the "realism" of Lodge prevailed.

Viewed against the background of the League experience, characterized as it was by a sharp dualism between theory and practice, the United Nations seem to have adjusted at San Francisco the "law in the books" to the "law in action." There are no automatic obligations to apply sanctions. There is, however, an obligation for Members of the Security Council to consult. In the event that as a result of consultation seven Members of the Security Council, including all five permanent members agreed to apply force, the obligations of Chapter VII become operative and Members are bound to participate in enforcement or preventive action to the extent limited in the Charter and in the military agreements. Thus the United Nations on the whole appears to conform closely to the intermediate type of security organization. One important qualification is called for at this point. The consultation required by the Charter and the principle of unanimity in the Security Council exclude all possibility of enforcement or preventive action being decided upon against a Great Power. The Great Powers are subject of course, to the obligations of membership on a footing of equality with all the other Members. But they are beyond the pale of enforcement action; nor can they be subjected to milder forms of disciplinary action such as expulsion or suspension. In short, there is no obligation to employ sanctions against any of the Great Powers. To that extent it appears that the United Nations partakes of the non-coercive type of security organization.

The partly intermediate and partly non-coercive character of the United Nations explains, of course, the high degree of universality which has already been achieved. Faced with the choice between a universal security organization with limited powers and a limited security organization with unlimited powers the delegates at the San Francisco Conference, admittedly exposed as they were to some pressure from the Great Powers, including the United States, voted for the former. In so doing they followed unwittingly, it may be presumed, the pattern of international organization broadly outlined in the course, or as the byproduct, of a political controversy of the first order by Senator Henry

Cabot Lodge, in his fourteen Reservations to the Covenant. His price for the participation of the United States in the League was the scrapping of some of the League principles in order to secure for the United States a greater measure of liberty of action and a lighter load of committments. President Wilson, rightly or wrongly, refused to pay the price. It is a matter of historical record, however, that the League Members themselves in order to maintain a degree of universality have found it imperative to neglect in practice many an important League principle. The separation of the Covenant from the Peace Treaties, a futile gesture, in the interest of universality, may, however, be mentioned here.

When the delegates met at San Franciso they found that in spite of the declared willingness of all the nations to participate in an international security organization, there was still a price to be paid for inducing the essential powers, that is, the Great Powers, to join the Organization as Members. It was the old price and they paid it. By sacrificing some of the principles on which the League was founded and by thus removing the chief obstacle to the participation of some of the essential powers including the United States, at any rate, they secured an impressive degree of unanimity and universality. It is too early yet to say that Litvinov was wrong when he said that a League without universality was better than universality without League principles. It would be premature also to say that the establishment of a League without League principles, of which Senator Lodge was one of the earliest champions, will secure peace for a longer span of time than did the first League.

An organization so constituted presents no dangers to its members. It is safe. It neither guarantees security nor does it endanger security. This at any rate would seem to hold true for the five great powers. The Charter does not commit the members to preserve the territorial integrity and political independence of any state, and it should create no dangerous delusions on this score. It imposes no onerous obligations on peace-loving states, members of the United Nations. It encroaches to no dangerous degree on the liberty of action of the Great Powers while it confers upon them the right to act under certain conditions. The overriding commitment is to consult. If the Great Powers fail to agree they remain free to act inside and perhaps even outside the scope of the Principles and Purposes of the Charter.

As Mr. Dulles stated before the Foreign Relations Committee of the Senate, the Charter "engages our Nation to honorable cooperation for peace and justice and, at the same time, protects those precious American traditions of which the Senate is our principle custodian." "That is why," Mr. Dulles said, "this Charter can be, and I hope will be approved by the Senate without reservation and without dissent."[93] Without going into the question of custodianship, it is possible to believe that many Senators would have welcomed a different type of Charter, but it is scarcely possible to doubt that Mr. Dulles correctly indicated the reasons why the Senate approved the Charter without reservations and almost without dissent.

[93] *Hearings*, p. 645.

# ELECTION OF STATES TO UNITED NATIONS MEMBERSHIP

## A. INTRODUCTION

The question of admission of states to membership in the United Nations, hardened by the "cold war," has been from the very beginning one of the important issues in both the Security Council and the General Assembly. It involves the relation between, and the respective rôles of, these two principal organs of the United Nations in the procedure of admission; the applicability of the "veto" and the double veto; it led to two requests to the International Court of Justice for advisory opinions; and it has provoked an impressive array of juridical arguments to break the deadlock over the admission of a substantial number of states and thus promote the universality of the United Nations.

At its Seventh Session the General Assembly adopted on December 21, 1952, a resolution establishing a Special Committee of 19 Member States to make a detailed study of the question of admission of states to membership in the United Nations, to examine all proposals which have been or may be made and report its conclusions to the Eighth Session.[1] The Special Committee, on which Czechoslovakia, India and the U.S.S.R. declined to serve,[2] held 11 meetings from March 31 to June 15, 1953, unanimously adopted a report and agreed "that no specific recommendations would be submitted to the General Assembly."[3] At its Eighth Session the General Assembly, after a further discussion of

[1] Memorandum on the Historical Background of the Question of the Admission of New Members (hereinafter referred to as Memorandum), U.N. Doc. A/AC.64/L.1, p. 110.

[2] *Ibid.*, p. 109.

[3] Report of the Special Committee on Admission of New Members (hereinafter referred to as Report), U.N. Doc. A/2400, p. 17.

the question, decided to establish a Committee of Good Offices, consisting of the representatives of Egypt, The Netherlands and Peru, and "empowered to consult with members of the Security Council with the object of exploring the possibilities of reaching an understanding which would facilitate the admission of new Members in accordance with Article 4 of the Charter."[4] The Good Offices Committee did not report to the Eighth Session,[5] but will presumably do so at the forthcoming Ninth Session. The Special Committee having failed to agree on a juridical solution, the General Assembly is apparently now exploring the possibilities of a solution along political lines through the mechanism of the Good Offices Committee.

Before discussing some of the specific problems which have arisen, it may be well to recall briefly the pertinent articles of the Charter and their history.

The United Nations Conference on International Organization at San Francisco discussed the question of membership in considerable detail. The Conference rejected universality as an immediate objective in favor of selected and limited membership. The Organization was made open to states which satisfied certain requirements. The committee charged with the task of formulating those requirements "did not feel it should recommend the *enumeration* of the elements which were to be taken into consideration," and believed that the text adopted has become more flexible and "sets forth more clearly than the Dumbarton Oaks Proposals those qualifications for membership which the delegates deemed fundamental, and provides a more definite *guide* to the General Assembly and Security Council on the admission of new Members."[6] The requirements of membership, stated as a *guide,* are found in Article 4, paragraph 1, of the Charter which reads:

> Membership in the United Nations is open to all other peace-loving States which accept the obligations contained in the present Charter and, in the judgment of the Organization, are able and willing to carry out these obligations.

The procedure for the admission of states was also considered in some detail. Unsuccessful attempts were made to confer upon the General Assembly the exclusive power to admit states; to require the recommendation of the Security Council only for the admission of ex-enemy states; and to give the Security Council merely advisory functions.[7] The text which was eventually adopted, incorporated in the Charter as paragraph 2 of Article 4, reads:

> The admission of any such State to membership in the United Nations will be effected by a decision of the General Assembly upon the recommendation of the Security Council.

In support of this procedure, "several delegates emphasized that the purpose of the Charter is primarily to provide security against a repetition of the present war and that, there-

[4] Resolution 718 (VIII) adopted Oct. 23, 1953. General Assembly, 8th Sess., Official Records, Supp. No. 17 (A/2630), p. 5.

[5] United Nations Bulletin, Vol. XVI, Jan. 15, 1954, p. 64.

[6] Memorandum, p. 11. Italics supplied.

[7] *Ibid.,* p. 13.

fore, the Security Council should assume the initial responsibility of suggesting new participating States."[8]

On the other hand, the final authority of the General Assembly was also stressed in the committee which drafted this paragraph. It was agreed that its text should be interpreted as *not* weakening the "right of the Assembly to accept or reject the recommendation for the admission of a new Member, or a recommendation to the effect that a given State should not be admitted to the United Nations."[9] This interpretation is the basis for the so-called Argentine thesis, which will be developed presently.

## B. ARE THE CONDITIONS OF ARTICLE 4 EXHAUSTIVE OR ILLUSTRATIVE?

The United Nations which started out with 51 original Members, received from 1946 to April, 1953, 30 applications for admission to membership. Of these 9 were accepted.[10] Undeniably, the United Nations has made some progress towards universality. However, 21 applicants were not admitted because they have not been recommended by the Security Council.[11] Of these 14 have secured seven or more affirmative votes in the Security Council but were opposed by the negative vote or veto of the U.S.S.R.[12] All of the 14 have been found by the General Assembly to be qualified for membership in the United Nations.[13] The remaining 7 applicants have received less than seven affirmative votes in the Security Council.[14] All of these were supported by the Soviet Union.

As a consequence of Soviet opposition, the questions arose whether a Member in the Security Council or in the General Assembly may base its vote on grounds other than the five conditions specified in Article 4, paragraph 1, namely, that the applicant be (1) peace-loving, (2) a state, (3) that it accept the obligations of the Charter, and (4) that it be able and (5) willing to carry out these obligations. This question was submitted to the International Court of Justice for an advisory opinion along with the further question whether a Member, while recognizing these conditions as fulfilled, could nevertheless subject its affirmative vote to the additional condition, that is, that other states be admitted to membership together with that state, as done by the Soviet Union with respect to the admission of Italy.[15]

[8] *Ibid.*, p. 15.

[9] *Ibid.*, p. 17. The Report of Committee II/1, Doc. 1092 (UNCIO VIII, p. 495), which included this statement, was adopted by Commission II, Docs. 1151, 1180 (UNCIO VIII, pp. 193, 265), and by the Plenary Conference on June 25, 1945, at its ninth meeting, UNCIO Doc. 1210, Vol. I, p. 623.

[10] In chronological order: Afghanistan, Iceland, Sweden, Thailand, Pakistan, Yemen, Burma, Israel, Indonesia. Memorandum, Annex I.

[11] *Ibid.*

[12] Jordan, Ireland, Portugal, Italy, Austria, Finland, Ceylon, Republic of Korea, Nepal, Viet-Nam, Libya, Japan, Cambodia, Laos.

[13] Japan, Viet-Nam, Cambodia, Laos, Libya, Jordan, by General Assembly Resolution 620 (VII) B-G adopted on Dec. 21, 1952. *Ibid.*, pp. 111–113.

[14] Albania, Mongolian People's Republic, Hungary, Rumania, Bulgaria, Democratic People's Republic of Korea, Democratic Republic of Viet-Nam. As of April, 1953, the application of the Democratic People's Republic of Korea had not been voted upon by the Security Council. *Ibid.*, Annex I.

[15] General Assembly Resolution 113 (II)B, adopted Nov. 17, 1947. *Ibid.*, p. 40.

The Court concluded from the "natural meaning of the words used" that the five conditions "constitute an exhaustive enumeration and are not merely stated by way of guidance or example" and by a vote of 9 to 6 replied in the negative to both questions.[16] The Court, however, observed that the exhaustive character of Article 4, paragraph 1, "does not forbid the taking into account of any factor which it is possible reasonably and in good faith to connect with the conditions. . . . no relevant political factor . . . is excluded."[17] In a joint dissenting opinion, which, as Judge Hudson put it, "introduces a note of reality not to be found in the opinion of the majority,"[18] Judges Basdevant, Winiarski, Sir Arnold McNair, and Read noted that the framers of the Charter, having "rejected the principle of universality," were wise in taking the view "that it was impossible to do more than to prescribe certain preliminary and essential qualifications for membership and to leave the question of admission to the good faith and the good sense of the Security Council and the General Assembly, and particularly the former by reason of the special responsibilities laid upon it."[19] After a careful scrutiny of the preparatory work, these four judges gave an affirmative answer to the questions. In so doing they stressed that a Member, in voting on the admission of a state,

> is participating in a political decision and is therefore legally entitled to make its consent to the admission dependent on any political considerations which seem to it to be relevant. In the exercise of this power the Member is legally bound to have regard to the principle of good faith, to give effect to the Purposes and Principles of the United Nations and to act in such a manner as not to involve any breach of the Charter.[20]

The joint dissenting opinion also declared that "if a Member of the United Nations is legally entitled to make its refusal to admit depend on political considerations," that was exactly what it would be doing if it desired "that the admission of the State should involve the contemporaneous admission of other States."[21]

## C. MEANING OF THE CONDITIONS OF ADMISSION

The majority opinion and the joint dissenting opinion on at least one or two points are perhaps not as far apart as they may appear. It is common ground that Members are bound to act in good faith but are not bound to state the reasons for their vote or veto. It is also commonly accepted that the five conditions in Article 4, paragraph 1, are pretty broad and lend themselves to different interpretations. None of them have ever been defined by the General Assembly or the Security Council, and it could be therefore that it does not matter very much whether they are considered elastic and exhaustive or elastic

[16] I.C.J. Reports, 1948, p. 57, at p. 62.
[17] *Ibid.*, at p. 63.
[18] "The Twenty-Seventh Year of the World Court," *American Journal of International Law*, Vol. 43 (1949), p. 8.
[19] I.C.J. Reports, 1948, at pp. 90, 91.
[20] *Ibid.*, at p. 92.
[21] *Ibid.*, p. 93.

and illustrative. Equally unhelpful is a classification of the five conditions into questions of fact or objective conditions. (Is the applicant a state, is it peace-loving and does it accept the obligations of the Charter?) and questions of judgment and appreciation, that is, subjective conditions (Is the applicant able and willing to carry out these obligations?), as even the determination of facts, apart from the formal acceptance of the obligations, involves a substantial degree of appreciation and judgment. More appropriately the conditions should be classified into those which are susceptible of a juridical or legal definition, such as statehood and acceptance of Charter obligations and those which are not, namely, peace-loving, able and willing; the latter are inevitably matters for evaluation along historico-political lines. A question which does not appear to have been faced squarely is what standards should be applied to this sort of evaluation. Moreover, in the heat of the controversy it has been overlooked that it might be useful to have a definition of the Charter obligations which the applicant accepts and is judged to be able and willing to carry out.

It would be futile to attempt to define the term "peace-loving." It has been noted already at San Francisco that no "nation has ever professed any other sentiment."[22] It has also been clear since the Potsdam Declaration that participation in World War II on the side of the Axis or neutrality during that war was not a bar to admission. This has since been confirmed by the admission of Sweden, and the endorsement by the General Assembly and by a majority of members of the Security Council of the admission of Finland and Japan. The exclusion of Spain of the regime of General Franco may be based on other grounds; in fact, it may well be based on grounds not enumerated in Article 4, paragraph 1.

The term "state" has not been defined and, as the experience of the International Law Commission in its work on the Draft Declaration of Rights and Duties suggests, it is not a term which lends itself easily to definition. It is certainly not clear whether the term as used in the Charter refers to independent and sovereign states or to any self-governing community. The original membership of two constituent Soviet republics and the endorsement by the General Assembly and by ten members of the Security Council of the applications of Viet-Nam, Cambodia and Laos serve to suggest that the test of statehood should be applied with a substantial degree of flexibility.

The same observation may be made with reference to the admittedly subjective conditions of the applicant's ability and willingness to fulfill the obligations of the Charter. It is certainly proper, as suggested by the United States, to examine the "international behavior" of applicants in order to ascertain whether they are willing to do so.[23] But such an examination may cover a very large area indeed. This appears to have been even further enlarged by the resolution adopted by the General Assembly on February 1, 1952, in which the Assembly considered

[22] Memorandum, p. 11.
[23] Report, p. 16.

> that the judgment of the Organization that they [all states not original Members] are willing and able to carry out these obligations and are otherwise qualified for membership ought to be based on facts such as: the maintenance of friendly relations with other States, the fulfillment of international obligations and the record of a State's willingness and present disposition to submit international claims or controversies to pacific means of settlement established by international law.[24]

The consideration of these facts may indeed complicate and delay the admission of many states. For example, the Soviet Union opposed the admission of certain states (Ireland, Portugal) on the ground that there were no diplomatic relations between her and those states. Now a Member may vote against the admission of applicants for the simple reason that the relations between the two countries are not friendly. By this resolution the Assembly may, despite itself, have broadened the grounds for the exclusion of certain states.

Somewhat inconsistently, the Assembly in the same resolution reaffirmed its adherence to the Advisory Opinion of the Court that a Member "is not juridically entitled to make its consent to admission dependent on conditions not *expressly* provided by paragraph 1 of Article 4 of the Charter."[25] One may ask: Is the "fulfillment of international obligations" which indeed was a condition of admission to the League of Nations,[26] expressly provided by paragraph 1 of Article 4? Or is "the maintenance of friendly relations," or "the record of a State's willingness and present disposition to submit international claims or controversies to pacific means" expressly provided? The Assembly, while accepting the Court's majority opinion, seems to be moving towards the view expressed in the joint dissenting opinion.

What are the "obligations" of the Charter which an applicant state agrees to carry out? If the term is used in a broad sense, there are many obligations in the Charter. Presumably one has to look to the Principles in Chapter I, Article 2, to find the basic obligations such as the undertakings to settle disputes by peaceful means, to refrain from the threat or use of force in international relations, to support the United Nations in any action it takes in accordance with the present Charter, and to refrain from giving assistance to any state against which the United Nations is taking preventive or enforcement action. It may be possible to regard those undertakings as obligations to the extent to which the disregard of them is subject to sanctions. And indeed the consequence of a persistent violation of the Principles may be expulsion from the Organization. In case such violation constitutes a threat to the peace, a breach of the peace or an act of aggression, the consequence, according to the scheme of the Charter, may be enforcement action. Moreover, in Article 25, the Members "agree to accept and carry out the decisions of the Security Council in accordance with the present Charter." From a realistic standpoint it has been shown that, in view of the paralysis of the Security Council, enforcement action is unlikely in the extreme. This has been recognized by the "Uniting for Peace" Resolution

[24] Resolution 506 (VI)A. General Assembly, 6th Sess., Official Records, Supp. No. 20 (A/2119), p. 4.
[25] *Ibid.* Italics supplied.
[26] Art. 1, par. 2, of the Covenant.

adopted by the General Assembly on November 3, 1950. But pursuant to this resolution the General Assembly cannot take binding decisions; it can only make recommendations which create no obligations for the Member States. The result of these developments then appears to be that the Principles of the Charter either no longer constitute legal obligations because they cannot be enforced or that their significance has been substantially reduced. It is also necessary to recall the virtual abandonment of the fundamental obligation, assumed by all Members and fulfilled by none, to make available to the Security Council armed forces and other facilities necessary for the purpose of maintaining international peace and security.[26a] As long as this duty is unfulfilled the Organization remains under the transitional security arrangements provided for in Articles 106 and 107. In these circumstances it may be open to question whether it is wiser to continue to insist on selective and limited admission or to take a long step towards achieving universality. For the question of membership, as Mr. Ernest Gross pointed out recently, is one which involves "a rather basic difference of view within the free world itself. This is sometimes lost sight of because of the more newsworthy impact of the Soviet vetoes."[27]

Having thus briefly analyzed the conditions of membership, the conclusion may be suggested that Article 4, paragraph 1, simply furnishes the elements for determining the *eligibility* of states for membership in the United Nations, whereas paragraph 2 of Article 4 lays down the procedure to effect admission. Membership then is "open" to states which are eligible for membership in the sense that states which, in the judgment of the Organization, satisfy the five conditions become *eligible*[28] for admission, but the admission must be the result of the *two decisions* provided for in paragraph 2 of Article 4: the *decision* of the Security Council to *recommend* the admission and the *decision* of the General Assembly to pronounce the admission. From this point of view the question whether the five conditions are exhaustive or not become one of secondary importance for three reasons: first, in either case there is a large area for individual evaluation; secondly, even if it is admitted that the conditions are exhaustive, this does not entail a right of the eligible state to admission nor a duty to admit; and thirdly, the decision to admit an eligible state may depend upon considerations which are not, or are not necessarily, connected with the conditions for eligibility. This has been explicitly recognized by Judge Alvarez who, although concurring with the majority, declared that

> cases may arise in which the admission of a State is liable to disturb the international situation, or at all events the international organization, for instance, if such admission would give a very great influence to certain groups of States, or produce profound divergencies between them. Consequently, even if the conditions of admission are fulfilled by an appli-

[26a] Art. 43.

[27] Ernest A. Gross, "Revising the Charter," Foreign Affairs, January 1954, pp. 203–216, at p. 211.

[28] G. G. Fitzmaurice, "The Law and Procedure of the International Court of Justice: International Organizations and Tribunals," 29 British Year Book of International Law (1952) 1–62, at 23.

> cant, admission may be refused. In such cases, the question is no longer a legal one; it becomes a political one and must be regarded as such.[29]

This concession is the more interesting because Judge Alvarez went so far as to hold "that all States fulfilling the conditions required by Article 4 of the Charter have a *right* to membership in that Organization."[30]

The General Assembly adopted the Advisory Opinion of the Court by Resolution 197 (III) of December 8, 1948, in the sense that it recommended to Members of the General Assembly and of the Security Council that in voting on the admission of new Members they should act in accordance with the opinion of the Court.[31] The response to this recommendation was bound to be disappointing. In the first place, both the Advisory Opinion of the Court and the recommendation of the General Assembly lack binding force for the Members of the United Nations. Even if advisory opinions could not be disregarded by the organ which requests them, they have at best only a persuasive force for the individual Members.[32] In this case the reasoning of the joint dissenting opinion seemed more persuasive than that of the majority of the Court. Furthermore, it was pointed out by the Registrar of the Court that of the nine judges who constituted the majority, "two members filed individual Opinions, stating in effect that they agreed with the minority on the most important point and this actually means that the majority of nine in reality was turned into a minority of seven, which led the delegate of the Soviet Union, Mr. Vyshinsky, to state that 'there was in fact no advisory opinion of the International Court of Justice.' "[33] Be that as it may, the Soviet Union, while conceding their eligibility, continued to object to the admission of Italy and perhaps other states on grounds other than those enumerated in the first paragraph of Article 4.

## D. PROPOSALS TO END THE IMPASSE OVER ADMISSIONS

The impasse resulting from the use of the veto by the Soviet Union led to several proposals designed to eliminate this obstacle. These proposals fall into three groups: (1) those which would reduce the rôle of the Security Council in the admission process; (2)

[29] I.C.J. Reports, 1948, p. 57, at p. 71.

[30] *Ibid.* Judge Azevedo expressed a similar view. He too concurred with the majority and argued that an aplicant which satisfies all the required qualifications has a right to have his application accepted. He concluded, nevertheless, by saying his answer "will not hinder the political activity of the organs that are responsible for the maintenance of peace; for elements of expediency, manifest or hidden, can always be considered when reasonable use is made of the wide possibilities opened by Article 4 of the Charter. Respect for law must never constitute a reason for disturbing international harmony, nor cause an upheaval in the life of any society." *Ibid.*, p. 81.

[31] Memorandum, p. 53.

[32] Fitzmaurice, *loc cit.*, pp. 54, 55: ". . . advisory opinions are authoritative in the sense that their legal correctness cannot be officially or formally questioned by the organ to which they are rendered, acting in its corporate capacity. . . . Since . . . advisory opinions are sought by and rendered to the international organs entitled to request them, it can be argued that no individual state is obliged to regard them as having even an authoritative character legally. Nevertheless . . . whatever be their formal authority, their persuasive character and substantive authority must be great."

[33] Edvard Hambro, "The Authority of the Advisory Opinions of the International Court of Justice," 3 International and Comparative Law Quarterly (January, 1954) 2–22, at 21.

those which would eliminate the use of the veto over admission or, at the very least, deny the validity of a veto illegally cast; and (3) the so-called "package" proposals

### 1. The Argentine Thesis

In the first group is the so-called Argentine thesis propounded at every session of the General Assembly. The Argentine Delegation starts from the interpretation accepted at San Francisco, according to which the new text of Article 4, paragraph 2, "did not, in the view of the Advisory Committee of Jurists, weaken the right of the Assembly to accept or reject a recommendation for the admission of a new Member, or a recommendation to the effect that a given State should not be admitted to the United Nations." In the view of the Argentine Delegation, the Security Council's failure to decide on the admission of an applicant, is *equivalent to a recommendation of non-admission;* the General Assembly could then reject this negative recommendation and decide favorably on its admission to membership.[34]

When, at the Fourth Session of the General Assembly, the Argentine Delegation developed this line of reasoning, it proposed reference of several questions to the International Court of Justice for an advisory opinion. Since a majority of representatives supported Argentina, though some reservations and amendments were made, the Assembly resolved to ask the Court for an opinion on the single question:

> Can the admission of a State to membership in the United Nations, pursuant to Article 4, paragraph 2, of the Charter, be effected by a decision of the General Assembly when the Security Council has made no recommendation for admission by reason of the candidate failing to obtain the requisite majority or of the negative vote of a permanent Member upon a resolution so to recommend?[35]

The Court answered the question in the negative by a vote of 12 to 2 and rejected the Argentine thesis, saying:

> The Court cannot accept the suggestion . . . that the General Assembly . . . could treat the absence of a recommendation as equivalent to . . . "an unfavourable recommendation," upon which the General Assembly could base a decision to admit a State to membership.[36]

Referring to the document which forms the basis of the Argentine position, the Court said that "such a recommendation has never been made in practice. In the opinion of the Court, Article 4, paragraph 2, envisages a favourable recommendation of the Security

[34] *Ibid.*, p. 3. "Whatever the vote in the Security Council, whether with or without the veto, when a recommendation was not approved, whatever the reason might be, that decision signified only that the Council did not wish to recommend the candidate. Thereafter, that decision must be transmitted to the General Assembly for final decision by the latter." General Assembly, 3rd Sess., Pt. I, Official Records, *Ad Hoc* Political Committee, p. 121.

[35] Memorandum, p. 76. Resolution 296 (IV)J, adopted Nov. 22, 1949.

[36] I.C.J. Reports, 1950, p. 4, at p. 9.

Council and that only. An unfavourable recommendation would not correspond to the provisions of Article 4, paragraph 2." The Court went on to say that

> nowhere has the General Assembly received the power to change, to the point of reversing, the meaning of a vote of the Security Council.
>
> In consequence, it is impossible to admit that the General Assembly has the power to attribute to a vote of the Security Council the character of a recommendation when the Council itself considers that no such recommendation has been made.[37]

Undismayed by the rejection of its position, which it failed to defend in the oral proceedings before the Court, the Argentine Delegation in the Special Committee on Admission of New Members continued to press its point,[38] supported by El Salvador,[39] but opposed by the Union of South Africa, Egypt, the Philippines, Greece, China, The Netherlands, New Zealand, France,[40] the United Kingdom and the United States. The United States representative pointed out that even if the Assembly had the power to reject an unfavorable recommendation, this did not constitute "a power to admit a State which the Security Council had rejected."[41] The United Kingdom representative, noting that the Security Council contingency of an unfavorable decision has never arisen, commented: "Nor was it likely to arise since, whenever agreement could not be reached in the Council on an application, the result was not an unfavourable recommendation, but no recommendation at all."[42] The support given by Argentina,[43] El Salvador[44] and Peru[45] to the Court's Advisory Opinion in the first admissions case contrasts sharply with their disregard of the Court's Advisory Opinion in the second admissions case.[46]

### 2. Does the Unanimity Rule in the Security Council Apply to the Vote on Admission to the United Nations?

Looking to the same end as the Argentine thesis, but based on a different line of reasoning, are the proposals advanced by the Latin American Republics such as Peru, Cuba, Costa Rica, El Salvador, Honduras and Nicaragua. It is common to them that, unlike the Argentine approach, they do not altogether eliminate but merely reduce the

[37] *Ibid.*, at pp. 9 and 10.

[38] Report, pp. 5–6.

[39] *Ibid.*, p. 5.

[40] *Ibid., pp. 8, 10–12.*

[41] *Ibid.*, p. 8. See also Fitzmaurice, *loc. cit.*, p. 33, who after considering the different senses in which the term "decision" or "recommendation" is used in the Charter, concludes: "But on the actual language of paragraph 2 of Article 4 as interpreted by the Court, the position is that the Security Council either recommends admission or it fails to recommend admission. In the latter event, it is not the case that there is *a recommendation not to admit.* There is simply no recommendation at all. Since the Assembly can only admit an applicant for membership 'upon the recommendation of the Security Council', it follows that it cannot admit in such a case; it can discuss or disapprove, but it has no power to admit, because the essential basis is lacking. This was the real essence of the Court's finding."

[42] Report, p. 9.

[43] General Assembly, 3rd Sess., Pt. I, Official Records, *Ad Hoc* Political Committee, pp. 60, 62.

[44] Report, p. 4.

[45] *Ibid.*

[46] *Ibid.*, p. 4 (Peru), p. 5 (El Salvador), p. 5 (Argentina), p. 7 (Cuba).

rôle of the Security Council in the admission process. They also have this in common, that for a variety of reasons they invite, and indeed are predicated on, a reappraisal of the principle of unanimity which from the beginning has been applied in the Security Council to the voting on the admission of states to membership.

The Peruvian draft resolution is based largely on the ground first, that "the unanimity rule, being an exception, should only be applied restrictively and hence only in the cases which involve the functions exclusively vested in the Security Council," and second, that in the matter of admission, "the final decision lies with the Assembly, and that accordingly the Security Council's recommendation, though necessary, is from the legal point of view a previous step or a procedural stage which, by its nature and according to the spirit and letter of the Charter, does not require the application of the unanimity rule." The Peruvian Delegation accordingly proposed that the Assembly, disregarding the veto, accept the majority votes in the Council as signifying that the applicants "are unanimously recognized as fulfilling the conditions required for membership."[47]

The proposal of the Central American Republics, framed more explicitly than the Peruvian, would have the Assembly decide that the vote in the Security Council be evaluated in conformity with Article 27, paragraph 2, of the Charter, that is, in conformity with the vote prescribed in that paragraph for procedural matters. This proposal is based on the San Francisco Four-Power Statement of June 7, 1945, on Voting Procedure in the Security Council, with which France associated herself. As interpreted by the Central American Republics, the Statement means that the permanent members may use the veto only in cases relating to the maintenance of international peace and security, that is, "*exclusively* in cases in which the Security Council has to make decisions which involve its taking direct measures in connexion with settlement of disputes, adjustment of situations likely to lead to disputes, determination of threats to the peace, removal of threats to the peace and suppression of breaches of the peace." The Central American Republics concluded that other decisions, though connected with the maintenance of peace and security, such as decisions on admission, are to be taken by a "procedural vote" of any seven members of the Council.[48] Regardless of what the Security Council itself may think about its own voting rules, these republics would have the Assembly interpret voting on admission cases in accordance with *their* interpretation of the Four-Power Statement and in conformity with paragraph 2 instead of paragraph 3 of Article 27 of the Charter.

These proposals for a liberal interpretation, so called, of the voting formula, though variously supported, met with strong opposition in the Special Committee on Admission of New Members. Representatives of the Union of South Africa, Egypt, the Philippines, the United States, Belgium, the United Kingdom, Greece, France, Canada, China, Norway, The Netherlands and New Zealand, argued decisively against both the Peruvian and Central American proposals. Counter-arguments were based, in the first place, on the Advisory Opinion in the second admissions case, where the Court held that the Char-

[47] U.N. Doc. A/AC.61/30. Also reproduced in Doc. A/AC.64/L.4, pp. 2–3.

[48] U.N. Doc. A/AC.61/L.31; reproduced in Doc. A/AC.64/L.4. Italics supplied.

ter did not place the Security Council in a subordinate position to the Assembly and did not confer upon the Assembly "the power to change, to the point of reversing, the meaning of a vote of the Security Council."[49] It was not contested that the Assembly had final authority and could reject a favorable recommendation, but the inference was denied that the Assembly could act in the absence of such a recommendation from the Security Council.

In the second place it was pointed out by the United Kingdom Delegation that the Security Council had always considered that decisions on the admission of new Members were subject to the veto rule and that the General Assembly had never contested that interpretation, although the veto power had been abused by the U.S.S.R.; and the United States representative "was not at all sure that the responsibility for interpreting the voting procedures of the Security Council could rest outside that body."[50] Both the Interim Committee studies on the veto in 1948 and the Assembly resolution endorsing proposals made by this Committee implied, in the opinion of the United States Delegation, that membership recommendations are substantive and not procedural. Similarly, when the Assembly in 1949 requested the permanent members of the Council "to refrain from the use of the veto in connexion with the recommendation of States for membership,"[51] it had "evidently recognized that the right" to use the veto existed.[52]

With regard to the rather peculiar interpretation of the Four-Power Statement which is the basis of the Central American proposal, the United States Delegation observed that neither the questionnaire nor the Statement was concerned with the question of admission. For this reason, in the view of the United States, "it could not . . . be assumed that the sponsoring Powers had been addressing themselves to that question or that they had agreed in their Statement that it should be governed by a procedural vote."[53]

In the face of these objections, the representative of El Salvador claimed to find some support in the actual practice of the Security Council. He argued that "contrary to the literal meaning of Article 27, paragraph 3," the Security Council and the General Assembly "had admitted that the absence or abstention of permanent members did not invalidate decisions which included the affirmative votes of at least seven other members of the Council." He noted that this practice, which included the June, 1950, decisions concerning the aggression in Korea, "had been hailed as a step forward in the procedure of the Organization," and urged that a similar development "would be legitimate in the case of the voting procedure followed by the Security Council in regard to the admission of new Members." The delegate of El Salvador was not satisfied with the point made by the representative of France that the practice of abstention, though it might appear "as not totally consistent with the letter of Article 27, paragraph 3," was in fact established by

[49] See, for instance, the arguments of Egypt, the United States and United Kingdom, Report, pp. 8–9.
[50] *Ibid.*, p. 9.
[51] General Assembly Resolution 296 (IV)K, adopted Nov. 22, 1949. Memorandum, p. 76.
[52] Report, p. 9.
[53] *Ibid.*

agreement of the five permanent members and "the general consent of the other Members of the United Nations,"[54] and countered with the question whether, in the case of abstention and absence, the requirement of the concurring votes of the permanent members "was really fulfilled."[55] This question seems to have remained unanswered. The representative of El Salvador with infinite tact refrained from asking the representative of France the obvious question whether the five permanent members had also agreed to regard a substantive vote taken in the *absence* of a permanent member as consistent with the clear requirement of Article 27, paragraph 3.

In their search for supporting arguments some of the Latin American delegations also invoked the "Uniting for Peace" Resolution of November 3, 1950. Thus the Peruvian proposal maintained that this resolution, approved almost unanimously by the General Assembly, "has laid down the doctrine that the exercise of the veto by a Power cannot paralyze the Organization or relieve the General Assembly of its responsibilities under the Charter."[56] Cuba also harnessed the "Uniting for Peace" Resolution in support of its efforts to liberate the Council from vetoes on admissions, and argued that

> if the Assembly had, in spite of Article 12 of the Charter, gone so far as to take up a question involving international peace and security . . . it could surely deal with a matter within its competence when there was no provision in the Charter precluding it from doing so.[57]

This line of reasoning was also rejected. The United Kingdom correctly pointed out that under the "Uniting for Peace" Resolution the General Assembly could only make recommendations which Member States could adopt or reject, whereas a decision on admission "would have binding force on all Members of the Organization, and the Assembly consequently could not, without violating the Charter, take such decisions in the absence of a recommendation of the Council."[58] The position of the United Kingdom seems unexceptionable, for it has been affirmed that admission to the United Nations constitutes general or "indirect" recognition as distinguished from diplomatic or "direct" recognition.[59] It would seem also that Members are bound to consider each other as states not merely within the United Nations but outside the United Nations as well.

The Cuban Delegation, in its working paper before the Special Committee on Admission of New Members, adopted a somewhat different approach. In order to secure the transformation of the substantive vote on admission into a procedural vote, it proposed to invoke the so-called double veto. The Delegation of Cuba, like the Central American del-

[54] *Ibid.*, p. 10.
[55] *Ibid.*, p. 4.
[56] U.N. Doc. A/AC.61/30, also reproduced in Doc. A/AC.64/L.4, p. 3.
[57] Report, p. 7.
[58] *Ibid.*, p. 9. See also the argument of the Netherlands representative to the same effect, *ibid.*, p. 12.
[59] Quincy Wright, "Some Thoughts about Recognition," *American Journal of International Law*, Vol. 44 (1950), p. 552. See also P. O. Humber, "Admission to the UN," 24 British Year Book of International Law (1947) 101–102; Herbert W. Briggs, "Community Interest in the Emergence of New States: The Problem of Recognition," PROCEEDINGS, AMERICAN SOCIETY OF INTERNATIONAL LAW, 1950, p. 179.

egations, relied first of all on Part I of the Four-Power Statement in order to show that the unanimity rule should not apply to voting on admissions. Should the question arise, however, whether a substantive or a procedural vote applies, the Cuban Delegation proposed that, in accordance with Part II of the Statement, the preliminary question be put to the vote. In the usual practice of the Security Council and in accordance with Part II of the Statement, the vote on the preliminary question is a substantive vote. As a consequence a permanent member may by its veto prevent a matter from being considered as procedural and then veto the matter itself. The Cuban Delegation, however, at this point abandoned the Statement and invoked as precedent the proceedings in the Security Council on the question of inviting the Peking authorities to take part in the consideration of the "Complaint of armed invasion of Taiwan (Formosa)." In this, the "Formosa Case," the Chinese representative raised the preliminary question, that is, the question whether the invitation was subject to a substantive vote. As interpreted by the Cuban Delegation, the proceedings in this case reveal that "in the vote the majority decided that it (the invitation) was a procedural question and, as the permanent representative of China vetoed the decision, the President of the Security Council (the United Kingdom representative) ruled that the veto of that permanent member was invalid; he applied rule 30 of the rules of procedure and his ruling was upheld by the Council." This isolated incident, which is elevated to the rôle of "the practice established by the Council," and past declarations made by four permanent members of the Council that they would refrain from using the veto regarding admissions, hold out, in the view of the Cuban Delegation, "considerable hope of success in eliminating the veto in connexion with the admission of new Members if, in accordance with its provisional rules of procedure, the Council takes decisions in this respect by the affirmative vote of *any* seven of its members."[60]

As the question of the range and applicability of the double veto is not germane to the problem of admission, and as the proceedings in the Formosa case were of some complexity,[61] it may be sufficient to note that, referring to the Cuban working paper, the United States representative "was far from certain that sufficient support would be obtainable in the Security Council for a determination that a recommendation to admit a State was a procedural decision."[62] The representative of the United Kingdom simply observed that in the Formosa case "the question had incontestably been a procedural one and part II of the Statement could not be used to override part I,"[63] thus reducing to its proper dimension the range and significance of the Formosa incident.

[60] U.N. Doc. A/AC.64/L.3, also reproduced in Report, pp. 17–19. Italics supplied.

[61] See Leo Gross, "The Double Veto and the Four-Power Statement on Voting in the Security Council," 67 Harvard Law Review (1953) 259, 262, 275, 276. See also *supra*. See also Alexander W. Rudzinski, "The So-Called Double Veto," *American Journal of International Law*, Vol. 45 (1951), pp. 454, 456, 459, 461.

[62] Report, p. 9.

[63] *Ibid.*, p. 10.

### 3. Is an "illegal" vote a valid vote?

The Peruvian Delegation, in order to bolster its proposal for breaking the deadlock over admissions, and relying on the Court's Advisory Opinion in the first admissions case, also contended that

> even if the unanimity rule were applicable to the Security Council's recommendation it would be inadmissible in cases in which it involved a violation of the Charter, such as would be constituted by accepting a veto to the admission of new members which had been acknowledged, by the Power exercising the veto in the Security Council, as eligible within the meaning of Article 4.[64]

In the Special Committee this contention was opposed by the United Kingdom, The Netherlands and Egypt. The United States had no hesitation in agreeing that "the negative votes of a permanent member had been cast on illegal grounds" and that the policy of the USSR was contrary to the Advisory Opinion of the Court of 1948. But in the view of the United States it was doubtful "whether the USSR votes were, in effect, null and void." The Court did not suggest this and "the Council had considered those negative votes to be effective, since it had not submitted to the Assembly favourable recommendations on applications which the USSR delegation had voted against on grounds contrary to the Charter." Moreover, "he was not sure whether the General Assembly could reach a conclusion contrary to that of the Council," as suggested by Peru, "since such a contention might give the Assembly authority which the Charter did not recognize."[65]

The United Kingdom Delegation agreed that the Soviet Union had abused the veto power, but in its view, "it did not automatically follow that the veto exercised under those conditions was invalid."[66] The Netherlands representative pointed out that "the Charter did not provide for a Court which could invalidate the Council's decisions on the grounds of illegal use of the veto, nor did it grant the General Assembly the right to take substantive action in such cases."[67] Similarly the Egyptian representative agreed that "there is no means whereby a juridically unjustified vote can be rendered 'null and void' " and concluded that the Court's "Injunction" in the first admissions case "is merely a moral precept and not a legal prohibition."[68]

### 4. The "Package" Proposals or Proposals for *En Bloc* Admission

None of the Latin American proposals have been accepted so far as they offer no solution for the existing deadlock compatible with the Charter. All of them are based upon strained interpretations of the voting rules in the Security Council, of the powers of the General Assembly, of the practice of the Security Council in the matter of absten-

[64] U.N. Doc. A/AC.61/30, also reproduced in Doc. A/AC.64/L.4, p. 3.
[65] Report, p. 9.
[66] *Ibid.*
[67] *Ibid.*, p. 12.
[68] Report, p. 20.

tions, and of the implications of the "Uniting for Peace" Resolution. This is not said as a criticism, which might appear to be out of place in view of the "liberal" or "effective" interpretation invoked and practiced by the United Nations on different occasions in the past. The Latin American governments, in an endeavor to apply "broad" principles of interpretation to the problem of admission, simply found themselves faced with unwillingness of the great Powers to go along. They seem to have overlooked that

> the problem of international organisations is essentially political in character and can only be solved on a political basis; to assume that lawyers as such could solve the political problems which lie at the heart of our current difficulties is sheer escapism.[69]

The working paper submitted by Egypt and the Philippines frankly abandoned the juridical approach. It suggested a realistic solution which perhaps is a trifle too realistic. Since there is no way to "by-pass" the unanimity principle in the Security Council, and as the Soviet Union is unwilling to follow the other permanent members in declaring a disposition to refrain from the use of the veto, which is called the "great equalizer" in the working paper, there remains as the only possibility the so-called "package proposal" offered by the Soviet Union. According to this, the Security Council would consider the simultaneous admission of fourteen states: Albania, the People's Republic of Mongolia, Bulgaria, Rumania, Hungary, Finland, Italy, Portugal, Ireland, Jordan, Austria, Ceylon, Nepal and Libya.[70]

"Package proposals" have a history which goes back to 1946. In fact the first three applicants for membership, namely, Afghanistan, Iceland and Sweden, were admitted *en bloc* by the General Assembly on November 9, 1946.[71] In 1946, when the Security Council discussed applications from the first nine states, the United States delegate favored a broad and far-sighted action in conformity with Article 4, and, although his government had misgivings about some applications such as those from Albania and the Mongolian People's Republic, he proposed the admission of all the applicants in order to accelerate advancement of universality of membership.[72] This, the first "package" proposal ever made in the United Nations, was supported by the Secretary General, by Brazil, Mexico, Egypt, China and The Netherlands,[73] and opposed by the Soviet Union and Australia, which advocated individual examination of each application.[74] The proposal was then withdrawn by the United States Delegation. It was reintroduced by Mexico and again withdrawn.[75]

In August, 1947, the representative of Syria, supported by the Secretary General,

[69] C. Wilfred Jenks, "The Impact of International Organisations on Public and Private International Law," Grotius Society Transactions for the Year 1951, Vol. 37 (1952), p. 59.

[70] Report, p. 20.

[71] General Assembly Resolution 34 (I), Resolutions adopted by the General Assembly during the First Part of its First Session from 10 January to 14 February, 1946, U.N. Doc. A/64/Add.1, p. 61.

[72] Memorandum, p. 20; and Security Council. Official Records, First Year, 2nd Ser., No. 4, pp. 41–43.

[73] Memorandum, *ibid.;* Security Council, Official Records, *loc. cit.*, pp. 43–52.

[74] Memorandum, pp. 20–21; Security Council, Official Records, *loc. cit.*, pp. 47–50.

[75] Memorandum, p. 21; Security Council, Official Records, *loc. cit.*, p. 53, and No. 5, pp. 114–124.

proposed the collective admission of all thirteen applicants, including Italy, "with a view to making the United Nations a universal organization comprising all peace-loving democratic nations of the world."[76] This proposal was opposed by China and readily dropped by Syria.[77] In September, 1947, Poland, supported by the Soviet Union, submitted the proposal for the admission of Hungary, Italy, Rumania, Bulgaria and Finland, and argued "that this method of collective admission would correspond with the intentions of the framers of the peace treaties."[78] This time, however, the majority of the Council opposed the idea of an *en bloc* admission. The United States and the United Kingdom argued in particular that the Potsdam Declaration and the Peace Treaties contained merely clauses enabling them to support the admission of these ex-enemy states without creating any obligation.[79] From this time on, the position and the arguments of the proponents and the principal opponents of collective admission remained substantially frozen. The Soviet Union and Poland never tired of re-introducing the proposal, which gradually came to include fourteen applicants, without scoring any important success. This came only at the Sixth Session of the General Assembly, when the Soviet proposal for the first time was adopted in the First Committee by a majority of 21 to 12, with 25 abstentions. It was lost in the plenary session, where it was decided that the proposal required a two-thirds majority. In the voting, the Soviet proposal was supported by 22 Members, opposed by 21, with 16 Members abstaining.[80] At the Seventh Session the Soviets fared somewhat worse, their package proposal being supported in committee by 20 Members and in plenary session by 9 only.[81]

This brief history of the "package" proposals may explain why they were offered in the Special Committee as a possible solution. To be sure, the Philippine-Egyptian version assumed that the fourteen states in question were eligible for membership, but emphasized very strongly that in spite of the collective admission in the Security Council it "will be open to anyone in the General Assembly to oppose the inclusion of certain States in the package." Even the "affirmative vote of the permanent members," said the representative of Egypt, "would in no way prejudge the final position of their delegation in the Assembly." A permanent member could, therefore, support the admission of the five Communist applicants in the Security Council and reverse itself and vote against their admission in the General Assembly. To top off their proposal, the Philippine-Egyptian delegations quoted the following statement made by Mr. John Foster Dulles before he became Secretary of State:

> I have now come to believe that the United Nations will best serve the cause of peace if its Assembly is representative of what the world actually is, and not merely representative of the part which we like. Therefore, we ought to be willing that all the nations should be

[76] Memorandum, p. 29.
[77] *Ibid.*, pp. 29–30.
[78] *Ibid.*, p. 33.
[79] *Ibid.*, pp. 33–34.
[80] *Ibid.*, p. 89.
[81] *Ibid.*, pp. 109–110.

> Members without attempting to appraise closely those which are "good" and those which are "bad." Already the distinction is obliterated by the present membership of the United Nations.[82]

The Philippine-Egyptian proposal was criticized as immoral and as sacrificing principle to expediency. Defending it against this reproach, the representative of Egypt argued "that what was really immoral was to keep applicants waiting, not because they were unqualified but because of ideological differences between two groups of States."[83] Some Members such as The Netherlands, China, Greece, Cuba, New Zealand, the Union of South Africa, and the United States, expressed the view that it would be contrary to the letter and the spirit of the Charter and also contrary to the Advisory Opinion of the Court in the first admissions case to vote *en bloc* for the admission of certain states.[84]

The United Kingdom representative distinguished between collective admission which was not contrary to the Charter, provided all applicants were qualified, and the "bargain" which would be contrary to the Charter as well as the Court's opinion. He also insisted that "it would be most irresponsible for the permanent members of the Security Council to vote differently in different organs of the United Nations in such an important matter, and he did not think that they would do so."[85] The Egyptian delegate's counter-argument, that in the past Members have voted against proposals in the Assembly which they had supported in committee, was obviously not a complete answer.[86] The United States representative, while opposing the "bargain," nevertheless drew attention to the fact that the package did not include five states which had been found qualified by the Assembly and asked whether those in favor of the package proposals "felt that they could, after their adoption, prevail upon the U.S.S.R. to withdraw its vetoes against the applicants which it refused to include in its 'package' deal."[87] A cynical observer might suspect that a delegation which rejects bargains for reasons of principle might be tempted to surrender principle to expediency if in so doing it could secure better terms of trade. Be that as it may, it was the French representative, it is believed, who put his finger on the vulnerable aspects of the Egyptian-Philippine proposal when he said that the Soviet Delegation would agree "only if it had full assurance that its own candidates would be accepted not only by the Council, but also by the General Assembly, for which the other permanent members of the Council were of course unable to vouch."[88]

[82] Report, pp. 13, 20. The quotation is from Mr. Dulles' book, War and Peace (1950), p. 190.
[83] Report, p. 13. See Philippine statement, *ibid.*, p. 14.
[84] *Ibid.*, pp. 14–16.
[85] *Ibid.*, p. 15.
[86] *Ibid.*, pp. 13–14.
[87] *Ibid.*, p. 15.
[88] *Ibid.*, p. 16.

## E. Conclusions

The foregoing analysis of the different proposals may be summed up as follows:

Proposals which are based on the notion that the General Assembly may admit states without the favorable recommendation of the Council are considered, rightly it is submitted, as contrary to the Charter. The Peruvian, the Central American, and the Cuban proposals which would allow the General Assembly to determine which vote applies in the Security Council and in the voting on admissions, are also contrary to the Charter and to the constant practice of the Security Council in this matter. Closer analysis of these proposals reveals that they are not substantially different from the Argentine thesis, for they too would have the General Assembly decide on the admission of states to membership without a recommendation of the Security Council, or perhaps more accurately, without a recommendation adopted by a substantive vote in the Security Council. It is clear from the discussion in the Special Committee and in the General Assembly that a substantial number of Members believe that a recommendation of admission requires a substantive, and not merely a procedural, vote in the Security Council.

The proposals for the collective admission of certain applicants, the so-called "package" proposals, were also opposed as contrary to the Charter although, as the vote in the First Committee of the Sixth Session of the General Assembly indicated, a majority was willing to go along. Assuming for the sake of argument that all applicants included in the "package" satisfy the conditions of Article 4, paragraph 1, then, as the representative of the United Kingdom in the Special Committee said, "the manner in which the applicant States were admitted to membership did not matter."[89] Indeed if, and assuming further that, the distinction suggested earlier between *eligibility*, dealt with in paragraph 1 of Article 4, and *decisions on admission*, dealt with in paragraph 2 of Article 4, is sound, then there would be no reason why the decision on admission, essentially a political function, should not encompass a group of states. As was shown, there is a precedent for this in the very first decision of the General Assembly on admission.

The remaining difficulty would seem to be twofold: one is to develop a technical solution for collective admission; and the other relates to the standard of eligibility. The first difficulty, it will be recalled, was pointed up by the French representative in the Special Committee. It might be met if, first, a substantial number of Members negotiated and accepted a slate of applicants, and if, secondly, the procedure were initiated in the General Assembly in the form of a resolution adopted by a two-thirds vote recommending to the Security Council the simultaneous admission of the agreed slate or, perhaps, admitting the slate subject to the Security Council's recommendation. It would then be up to the Security Council to vote on the slate.

Unquestionably the most serious difficulty consists in the standard to be employed in determining eligibility. As suggested earlier, the standard is sufficiently flexible to permit the admission as well as the exclusion of many states. Upon the choice of the standard

[89] Report, p. 15.

depends whether or not the United Nations will achieve greater universality than it has at the present moment.

At this point it is well to recall that the United Nations was established as a heterogeneous organization including different ideologies and different systems of government. It would seem, therefore, that in aiming at universality, the goal cannot be other than heterogeneous universality. This needs to be taken into account in judging eligibility. There may be some tendency in the free world to regard admission "as something like a reward for meritorious conduct,"[90] and to use non-admission as a sanction or punishment for failure of the applicant state to live up to its international obligations. It is questionable whether this was the intention of the framers of the Charter and whether non-admission is a proper sanction. It may certainly be argued that admission to the United Nations implies no approval of the conduct of an applicant state or of its governmental or economic system. But there is some feeling that a Communist state cannot qualify for membership unless it changes its character and objectives, and "it cannot change its character and objectives until it ceases to be Communist."[91] Carried to its logical conclusion this school of thought would aim at substituting for the present United Nations an organization from which Communist states are excluded, inasmuch as there is no way to expel them from the existing Organization.

The vital question seems to be whether any existing tensions and conflicts can be lessened or altogether eliminated by excluding certain states from the United Nations or whether their exclusion intensifies the tensions and aggravates the conflicts. Desirable as universality may be, it would be unwise in the extreme to expect any substantial lessening of the prevailing tensions from any further steps towards it. Nor is the fear justified that such steps would aggravate the situation within the United Nations. The free world cannot hope to escape the problems which exist today by the simple device of keeping a group of states out of the United Nations. It would be equally unrealistic to assume that the admission of Italy and other states, no matter how desirable, would materially advance the solution of any of the major problems which are the by-product of the existence of groups of power and of their substantive policies. The fact of the matter is that if important states are not in the United Nations, solutions will have to be sought outside rather than inside the Organization.

It may have been this thought which moved the Secretary General recently to declare that "it is inherent in the United Nations approach that the Western world and the Communist world meet regularly around the conference table." And in Sir Gladwyn Jebb's view the proven usefulness of the United Nations as a forum for peaceful settlement showed "the unwisdom of those who maintain[ed] that the United Nations would

[90] See Ernest A. Gross, *loc. cit.*, p. 210.

[91] Special Study Mission to Southeast Asia and the Pacific. Report by Hon. Walter H. Judd, Chairman, submitted to the Committee on Foreign Affairs, 83rd Cong., 2nd Sess., Committee Report, pp. 100–101.

be better off without the Communists."[92] In this context it is useful to recall a statement made in January, 1954, by the Secretary of State of the United States that

> universality inevitably means bringing together nations whose governments may strongly disagree. This has disadvantages. But such an organization maintains contacts between potential enemies, affords opportunities to dispel unnecessary misunderstandings, and, as President Eisenhower said in his State of the Union Message of January 7, 1954, it provides "the only real world forum where we have the opportunity for international presentation and rebuttal." This process tends, though slowly, to bring about conformity to a common standard.

The Secretary of State also pointed out that nations sharing security or regional interests may organize themselves into collective self-defense or regional arrangements.[93] From this viewpoint the United Nations would serve as the over-all organization within which there is room for more intimate associations of like-minded states.

Universality has become an article of faith with many people in and out of the United Nations. I have attempted to show some of the difficulties which stand in its way and to stress the need for discarding false hopes which its advocates may have engendered. A further and final argument may be made in favor of universality, once the idea is rejected that it will ensure the solution of major problems of international politics, and as soon as a more sober value is placed upon the benefits which it could conceivably bestow upon the United Nations as a mirror of a divided and troubled world. Universality obviously has great significance for the development of international law. For if it is true, as I believe it is, that the development of international law is bound up with that of international organization, the achievement of universality would mean the transformation of the present decentralized and rudimentary society of nations into a relatively more centralized society, and equally, the transformation of the United Nations into organs of that society. While this falls far short of some expectations, it is a real, although limited, gain to be derived from universality and one that is worth striving for. But a lessening of tensions and a period of peace appear as the conditions of both a more effective international organization and of the growth of a stronger international law. Universality of membership is an important, but not a decisive, element in this process.

[92] The New York Times, March 19, 1954, p. 3, and March 21, 1954, Sec. 4, p. 2. Also London Times, March 19, 1954, p. 3.

[93] "United Nations Charter Review." Statement by Secretary Dulles made before the Charter Review Sub-Committee of the Senate Foreign Relations Committee on Jan. 18, 1954. Dept. of State Bulletin, Vol. XXX, No. 762 (Feb. 1, 1954), p. 171.

**Batch number: 10824482**

Printed by Printforce, the Netherlands

# ESSAYS ON
# INTERNATIONAL LAW
# AND ORGANIZATION

## VOLUME II

BY

LEO GROSS

Springer-Science+Business Media, B.V.

**Library of Congress Cataloging in Publication Data**

Gross, Leo, 1903–
Essays on international law and organization.

Includes index.
1. United Nations. 2. International law. 3. International agencies. I. Title.
JX1977.G759 1983 341 83-9136

**ISBN 978-0-941320-15-3 978-94-017-7048-4 (eBook)**
**DOI 10.1007/978-94-017-7048-4**



Originally published by Transnational Publishers, Inc. in 1984.
Softcover reprint of the hardcover 1st edition 1984

# SUMMARY OF CONTENTS

## VOLUME 1



## VOLUME 2

# CONTENTS

## VOLUME I



### I. Development of International Law



### II. Development of International Law by the United Nations

## III. International Law and Individual Responsibility



## IV. Problems of Interpretation



## V. Problems of Voting

## VI. Some Problems of Organization in the United Nations



# VOLUME II



## VII. Settlement of Disputes by the International Court of Justice

## VIII. Settlement of Disputes by the Political Organs of the United Nations: Some Aspects of the Arab-Israel Dispute

## IX. Domestic Jurisdiction and Peace-Keeping Operations

# VI

# SOME PROBLEMS OF ORGANIZATION IN THE UNITED NATIONS (Continued)

# PROGRESS TOWARDS UNIVERSALITY OF MEMBERSHIP IN THE UNITED NATIONS

## I. INTRODUCTION

The resolution of the General Assembly of December 14, 1955, to admit 16 countries to membership in the United Nations, marked "an event second only to the foundation of the United Nations itself,"[1] and a decisive step towards achieving universality of membership. As the President of the Tenth Session of the Assembly, Mr. José Maza (Chile) put it:

> By the adoption of this resolution the General Assembly has given life to a deep desire which has existed within it for several years, namely, the overcoming of the obstacles which have impeded the development of the United Nations into a real international Organization, representing all the peoples of the world and enjoying true universality.[2]

The actual accomplishment, however, falls short of this somewhat exaggerated statement, for six applicant states: Japan, the Mongolian People's Republic, the Republic of Korea, the Democratic People's Republic of Korea, the Democratic Republic of Viet-Nam and the Republic of Viet-Nam have not yet been admitted. The obstacles towards achieving universality have at the Tenth Session of the General Assembly been overcome

[1] Mr. Martin (Canada), in the Ad Hoc Political Committee, General Assembly, 10th Sess., Dec. 1, 1955. A/AC.80/P.V.25, at 43–45. Since then the Security Council recommended the admission of three new states, the Sudan on Feb. 6, 1956, Morocco on July 20, 1956, and Tunisia on July 26, 1956. See United Nations Review, Volume 3, No. 3, p. 1. There is no doubt that the General Assembly will admit these states at its 11th session, thereby raising the membership to 79 states.

[2] A/P.V.555, at 23–25.

but not removed and a solution to the long-standing problem of admission to membership remains to be found. Before analyzing the method which has been fashioned to secure the admission of sixteen countries it may be appropriate to recall briefly the stages which led to a temporary though substantial denouement.

## II. EARLY EFFORTS TO SOLVE THE PROBLEM OF MEMBERSHIP

Since the inception of the United Nations, thirty-one states, including Spain,[3] have applied for admission to membership. Of these, nine states had been admitted between 1946 and 1950,[4] fourteen had not been recommended by the Security Council as they had not received the concurring votes of all the permanent members, although they had been found eligible for membership by the General Assembly,[5] and seven had failed to secure seven affirmative votes in the Security Council.[6]

Various efforts were made after 1946 to overcome the deadlock resulting from the fact that certain applicants were supported by the Western group of Members and opposed by the Soviet bloc, while others were supported by the latter and opposed by the former. One of the first methods, proposed by the United States and later espoused by the Soviet bloc, envisaged the *en bloc* or simultaneous admission of a group of nine applicants.[7] Other efforts centered around the text of Article 4 and the proper method for its interpretation. In particular, the question was discussed whether admission of an applicant could be made dependent upon conditions other than those listed in paragraph 1 of Article 4, such as the existence of diplomatic relations or the simultaneous admission of other states. The debate on this matter came to a head at the second session of the General Assembly with the result that a request for an advisory opinion was addressed to the International Court of Justice.[8] The Court held that the conditions in Article 4, paragraph 1, were exhaustive and that it was inadmissible to make admission dependent upon extraneous requirements.[9]

The General Assembly by Resolution 197A(III) of December 3, 1948, recommended "that each member of the Security Council and of the General Assembly, in exercising its vote on the admission of new Members, should act in accordance with the

[3] Spain applied in the course of the Tenth Session by letter dated Sept. 23, 1955. Docs. A/2984 and S/3441/Rev. I.

[4] Afghanistan (Nov. 19, 1946), Burma (March 17, 1948), Iceland (Nov. 19, 1946), Israel (May 11, 1949), Pakistan (Sept. 30, 1947), Sweden (Nov. 19, 1946), Thailand (Dec. 16, 1946), Yemen (Sept. 30, 1947), and Indonesia (Sept. 28, 1950). Summary statement by the Secretary General on Matters of which the Security Council is Seized and on the Stage Reached in their Consideration, Doc. S/2310, p. 23.

[5] Jordan, Portugal, Ireland, Italy, Austria, Finland, Ceylon, Republic of Korea, Nepal, Libya, Japan, Viet-Nam, Cambodia and Laos. The General Assembly expressed itself in favor of the admission of these states in Resolutions 113 (II), 197 (III), 296 (IV), and 620 (VII).

[6] Albania, Mongolian People's Republic, Hungary, Rumania, Bulgaria, Democratic People's Republic of Korea and Democratic Republic of Viet-Nam.

[7] Security Council, Official Records, First Year, 2nd Ser., No. 4, pp. 41–43. Memorandum on the Historical Background of the Question of the Admission of New Members, U.N. Doc. A/AC.64/L.1, p. 20.

[8] General Assembly Resolution 113B(II), adopted Nov. 17, 1947.

[9] [1948] I.C.J. Reports 57 at 65; see also A.J.I.L., Vol. 50, 1956, p. 822.

foregoing opinion of the International Court of Justice."[10] The Soviet bloc, however, chose not to accept the opinion of the Court. Far from removing the difference of views which impeded the admission of a large number of states, the opinion of the Court seemed to have the effect of merely stiffening the opposing views and making compromise more difficult. This much may be said without taking sides in the controversy regarding the binding effect of advisory opinions.[11]

Efforts were made in and out of the United Nations to prevail upon the permanent members of the Security Council to forego the use of the veto in voting upon applications for membership. The United States Senate adopted unanimously the so-called Vandenberg Resolution on June 11, 1948. This informed the President of the sense of the Senate that the Government, by constitutional process, should pursue certain objectives within the United Nations Charter, including particularly "voluntary agreement to remove the veto . . . from the admission of new members."[12] The General Assembly, after an exhaustive study by its Interim Committee ("Little Assembly"), adopted on April 14, 1949, Resolution 267(III) on "The Problem of Voting in the Security Council" recommending to the permanent members of the Council, in the sense of the Vandenberg Resolution, that they "seek agreement among themselves upon what possible decisions by the Security Council they might forbear to exercise their veto, when seven affirmative votes had already been cast in the Council." The Assembly, in particular, referred, among others, to recommendations on the admission of a state to membership in the United Nations.[13] Absence of agreement to forego the "veto" in the circumstances indicated in Resolution 267(III), strengthened the position of those delegations which, by means of more or less strained constructions of Article 4, attempted to by-pass the Security Council or, at the very least, the "veto" right of the permanent members. A case in point is the so-called Argentine thesis as expounded by the delegations of that country to various sessions of the Assembly. According to it, the General Assembly may admit a state in case its application is supported by the requisite majority as well as in case it is rejected, or, more correctly, not supported by the requisite majority. The substance of the Argentine thesis was submitted to the International Court of Justice for an advisory opinion on November 22, 1949.[14] The Court's opinion of March 3, 1950, was to the effect, that according to the "natural and ordinary" meaning of Article 4, "the recommendation of the Security Council is the condition precedent to the decision of the Assembly by which the admission is effected," and that paragraph 2 of Article 4, "envisages a favorable recommendation of the Security Council and that only."[15]

Far from removing the difficulty which impeded the admission of states on the

[10] General Assembly, 3rd Sess., Official Records, Pt. 1, Doc. A/810, p. 30.

[11] On this point see G. G. Fitzmaurice, "The Law and Procedure of the International Court of Justice; International Organizations and Tribunals," 29 British Year Book of International Law 1–62 (1952) at 53.

[12] S. Res. 239, 80th Cong., 2d Sess.

[13] General Assembly, 3rd Sess., Official Records, Pt. II, Doc. A/900, p. 7.

[14] General Assembly Resolution 296(IV)J.

[15] [1950] I.C.J. Reports at 10; see also Leo Gross, "Election of States to United Nations Membership," Proceedings, American Society of International Law, 1954, pp. 37–59 at p. 47, and *supra*, pp. 585–605, at p. 594.

waiting list of the United Nations, the Assembly's request for the Court's opinion could have no other effect than to place a legal ban on all other attempts to get around the requirements of Article 4. Thus the Court's opinion was to stand in the way of the Peruvian proposal that the General Assembly, acting on the view that the principle of unanimity did not apply to Security Council votes on recommendations regarding membership, should admit a state if it received a majority of seven votes in the Council. It also was invoked by Members who opposed a related proposal advocated by a group of Central American republics that the Assembly should evaluate a Security Council vote on membership application in the light of Article 27, paragraph 2, rather than on the basis of paragraph 3 of that article. Both these proposals were opposed by a large number of Members, including the permanent members of the Security Council.[16] Inasmuch as the Security Council has always considered recommendations on admission to be subject to the qualified majority vote laid down in Article 27, paragraph 3, the Assembly was barred by the Court's opinion from changing "to the point of reversing, the meaning of a vote of the Security Council."[17]

The drive in favor of universality, however, was gaining momentum. The Secretary General expressed himself strongly in favor of universality of membership[18] and his plea was endorsed by the heads of the specialized agencies.[19]

It is to be noted, however, that whereas the Secretary General and the heads of the specialized agencies expressed themselves in favor of universality without any qualification, the General Assembly in its pronouncements emphasized at the same time that the applicants must satisfy the conditions of admission, that is, they must be eligible for membership in accordance with the requirements laid down in Article 4, paragraph 1. In so doing the General Assembly based itself on the Advisory Opinion of the Court in the first admission case referred to above.[20]

[16] See Report of the Special Committee on Admission of New Members, Doc. A/2400, pp. 8–9, and Leo Gross, *loc. cit.*, 44 ff. See also *supra* at 591.

[17] [1950] I.C.J. Reports 10.

[18] "Memorandum of points for consideration in the development of a twenty-year programme for achieving peace through the United Nations" submitted by the Secretary General on July 26, 1950, Doc. A/1304, par. 5. See also General Assembly Res. 494(V) of Nov. 20, 1950, in which the Secretary General was commended for his initiative. General Assembly, 5th Sess., Official Records, Supp. No. 20, p. 79.

[19] "We re-affirm the validity of this principle of universality. The United Nations system makes ample room for diversity within a universal framework. We believe it would be a disaster if efforts to realize the principle of universality in practice were to be abandoned now. We believe that the greatest efforts should, on the contrary, be directed towards achieving in fact true universality in the membership and programmes of the United Nations and of those of the specialized agencies which are founded on that principle." Seventh Report of the Administrative Committee on Coordination to the Economic and Social Council, Doc. E/1682, May 11, 1950, pp. 2–3.

[20] See above, p. 608. Typical is Res. 506(VI) adopted on February 1, 1952: "The General Assembly, considering that the Charter of the United Nations provides that membership is open to all States not original Members of the Organization and that this universality is subject only to the conditions that they be peace-loving and accept the obligations contained in the Charter and, in the judgment of the Organization, are able and willing to carry out these obligations, "Considering that the judgment of the Organization that they are willing and able to carry out these obligations and are otherwise qualified for membership ought to be based on facts such as: the maintenance of friendly relations with other States, the fulfilment of international obligations and the record of a State's willingness and present disposition to submit international claims or controversies to pacific means of settlement established by international law, "Considering that, according to the advisory opinion of the International Court of Justice of 28 May 1948, a Member of the United Nations voting on the application of a State for membership in the United Nations is not juridically entitled to make its consent to admission

Taking into account the increasingly urgent demands for solving the deadlock, and perhaps also impressed with the fact that a substantial number of Members seemed to support Soviet proposals for *en bloc* admission of a group of selected applicants,[21] the General Assembly at its Seventh Session decided to establish a Special Committee to look into the membership problem. The Committee of 19 Members[22] was instructed to take into account "the principles of international law" and "the other antecedents of the question." The fact is no doubt striking that this decision of the Assembly, compared with Resolution 506(VI) adopted only a few months earlier, is couched in flexible language and is characterized by a weakening of its earlier insistence on the exclusive character of the conditions in Article 4 and the opinion of the Court which ruled out any other.

The Special Committee reported to the Eighth Session of the Assembly but failed to formulate any specific recommendations.[23]

The delegations of Egypt and the Philippines argued in the Special Committee for the abandonment of the juridical and in favor of a frankly political approval. By the juridical method, in connection with the membership problem, the United Nations, far from extricating itself out of the *cul de sac* in which it finds itself, has driven itself even deeper into it. The way out, in the submission of the Egyptian and Philippine governments, should lead through some form of a "package deal."

At the Eighth Session of the Assembly, to which the Special Committee's Report was submitted, a Committee of Good Offices was established by Resolution 718(VII) adopted on October 23, 1953. Under its terms of reference, the Committee of Good Offices was "empowered to consult with members of the Security Council with the object of exploring the possibilities of reaching an understanding which would facilitate the admission of new Members in accordance with Article 4 of the Charter." In the preamble of this resolution it is also declared "that universality in the United Nations is subject only to the provisions of the Charter."[24] As pointed out by Mr. James F. Byrnes

dependent on conditions not expressly provided by paragraph 1 of Article 4 of the Charter; and that this opinion excludes the possibility that, consistently with the letter and spirit of the Charter, Members can base their votes on motives which are outside the scope of Article 4 of the Charter. . . ." General Assembly, 6th Sess., Official Records, Supp. No. 20, p. 4. It seems to have escaped the Assembly that there may well be a contradiction or incompatibility between the first and third "considering" on the one hand, and the second on the other. On this point, see Gross, *loc cit.* at 42, and *supra* at 589.

[21] At the Sixth Session the Soviet proposal for the admission of fourteen states was adopted in the First Committee of the Assembly by a majority of 21 to 12, with 25 abstentions, and in the plenary meeting by 22 to 21, with 16 abstentions. Official Records, 6th Sess., First Committee, p. 257, Plenary, p. 469. At the Seventh Session a similar Soviet move was supported by 20 members in the Committee and by 9 in the plenary meeting. Official Records, 7th Session, *Ad Hoc* Political Committee, p. 317, Plenary, p. 480.

[22] The 19 Members were: Argentina, Belgium, Canada, China, Colombia, Cuba, Egypt, El Salvador, France, Greece, Lebanon, Netherlands, New Zealand, Norway, Peru, Philippines, Union of South Africa, United Kingdom, the United States of America. Under its terms of reference the Special Committee was "to make a detailed study of the question of the admission of States to membership in the United Nations, examining the proposals and suggestions which have been made in the General Assembly and its Committees or which may be submitted to the Special Committee by any Member of the United Nations, such study to be conducted in the light of the relevant provisions of the Charter of the United Nations, the discussions in the General Assembly and its Committees, the debates in the Security Council, the advisory opinions of the International Court of Justice, the other antecedents of the question and the principles of international law." General Assembly Res. 620A(VII) of Dec. 21, 1952, 7th Sess., Official Records, Supp. No. 20, p. 10.

[23] Report of the Special Committee on Admission of New Members, Doc. A/2400, p. 17.

[24] 8th Sess., Official Records, Supp. No. 17, p. 5.

(U.S.A.), the Committee had "no authority to negotiate a package deal."[25] It is significant, however, that the resolution fails to refer to the advisory opinion of the Court interpreting Article 4 in a restrictive sense, on which the Assembly appeared to insist in its earlier resolutions on the subject. Thus it may be regarded as indicative of a weakening of the Assembly's position in this respect.

## III. COMMITTEE OF GOOD OFFICES

The Committee of Good Offices, composed of Egypt, The Netherlands and Peru, nevertheless was guided by Article 4 as interpreted by the Advisory Opinion of the Court. The chairman of the Committee, Mr. Victor A. Belaunde (Peru), had a number of informal consultations with various members of the Security Council which indicated "that there is no fundamental change in the general position on the question such as would make it possible at this juncture to reach an understanding which would facilitate the solution of the problem." The Committee reported to the Assembly that all possibilities of reaching an understanding had not been exhausted, that the Assembly should continue its efforts and was confident that "different views may eventually be harmonized within the spirit of the Charter."[26]

The Assembly accepted the hint that an accommodation might be found within the "spirit" of the Charter if not within the terms of Article 4 as interpreted by the Court, and on November 23, 1954, adopted unanimously a four-Power draft resolution submitted by Argentina, Cuba, El Salvador and India. The assembly noted

> the growing general feeling in favour of the universality of the United Nations, membership in which is open to all peace-loving States which accept the obligations contained in the Charter and, in the judgment of the Organization, are able and willing to carry out those obligations,

and decided to send back to the Security Council "the pending applications for membership," that is, *all* the pending applications and not merely those which it had supported previously by large and repeated majorities. The Assembly also suggested that the Council "consider the desirability of invoking the provisions of paragraph 2 of Article 28 of the Charter to help resolve the problem" and requested the Committee of Good Offices to continue its efforts without laying down any terms of reference, thus conferring upon it the greatest possible latitude.[27]

While no periodic meeting was held,[28] the Committee's Chairman, Mr. Belaunde,

[25] 8th Sess., Official Records, *Ad Hoc* Political Committee, p. 15.

[26] Doc. A/2720, Sept. 3, 1954. General Assembly, 9th Sess., Official Records, Annexes, Agenda item 21, pp. 3–4.

[27] Res. 817(IX) General Assembly, 9th Sess., Official Records, Supp. No. 21 (A/2890), p. 8. For the vote on the draft resolution (Doc. A/AC.76/L.11/Rev.1) in the *Ad Hoc* Political Committee see *ibid.*, Annexes, Agenda Item 21, p. 15, and in the General Assembly, *ibid.*, Verbatim Records of Meetings, p. 330.

[28] The Security Council had not held any meetings on the membership question since September, 1952. Doc. S/3410, p. 24.

took advantage of the meetings held in San Francisco commemorating the first decade of the United Nations, in the course of which statements favoring universality of membership were made,[29] to meet with the foreign ministers of various Powers. The Committee, encouraged by their response, reported to the Assembly that the permanent members of the Council, "although continuing to adhere to their positions on the question of admission, conveyed the impression that such adherence was *not necessarily immutable* in view of the current evolution of the international atmosphere."[30] It thus appeared that by marrying—without benefit of clergy—the "spirit of Geneva" with the "spirit of the Charter," a solution of the long-standing problem of membership might be found and a long step taken towards achieving universality.

In a supplementary report to the *Ad Hoc* Political Committee Mr. Belaunde stressed that the Assembly had given the Committee a "unanimous mandate" with broader powers. As a consequence the Committee after noting that "the greatest effort in Hermeneutics" expended on Article 4 belonged to "a past which we left behind us," was of the opinion that it "was established in the conviction that it was necessary to find a *political* solution of the problem without prejudice to the juridical positions we had taken and for the purpose of securing a rapprochement between the Soviet Union and the Western Powers."[31] Mr. Belaunde also reported that Mr. Molotov proposed the admission of sixteen applicants excluding Japan, with which the Soviet Union had no peace treaty, and North and South Viet-Nam as well as North and South Korea "pending the solution of the problem of unification."[32] The absence of "the problem of unification" suggested by the Soviet Union was to become the decisive criterion for the admission of states to membership.

Mr. Belaunde concluded the report of the Committee of Good Offices saying that following receipt of Spain's application for admission on September 27, 1955,[33] he told Mr. Molotov that "the Soviet Union might, in conformity with the principle of universality which Mr. Molotov himself had invoked at San Francisco, consider the admission of eighteen applicants including Japan and Spain."[34]

[29] In Commemoration of the Tenth Anniversary of the Signing of the Charter of the United Nations in the City of San Francisco on June 26, 1945, Proceedings of the Commemorative Meetings (U.N. Publication, Sales No.: 1955 I.26), pp. 61, 65, 67, 83, 85, 121, 135, 136, 162, 178, 180, 196, 199, 213, 250, 259, 266, 296.

[30] Preliminary Report of the Committee of Good Offices on the Admission of New Members. Doc. A/2973, Sept. 19, 1955, pars. 5, 6 (emphasis supplied).

[31] *Ibid.* at 12 (emphasis supplied).

[32] A/AC.80/P.V.25, at 12, 14–15. The 16 applicants were: Albania, the Mongolian People's Republic, Bulgaria, Rumania, Hungary, Finland, Italy, Portugal, Ireland, Jordan, Austria, Ceylon, Nepal, Laos, Cambodia, Libya. Doc. A/AC.80/P.V./25, at 46 f.

[33] Docs. S/3441/Rev. 1 and A/2983.

[34] A/AC.80/P.V.25, at 17–20, 21.

## IV. THE JOINT DRAFT RESOLUTION OF 28 MEMBERS

On November 16, 1955, a draft resolution, initially sponsored by Canada and 24 other Members, and subsequently by 28 Members altogether, was submitted, the text of which was as follows:

> The General Assembly,
> Having noted the general sentiment which has been expressed on numerous occasions in favour of the widest possible membership of the United Nations. . . . 2. Requests the Security Council to consider, in the light of the general opinion in favour of the widest possible membership of the United Nations, the pending applications of all those *countries about which no problem of unification arises;* 3. Requests further that the Security Council make its report on these applications to the General Assembly during the present session.[35]

Canada, which had taken the initiative in the consultations[36] resulting in the joint draft resolution, introduced it in the *Ad Hoc* Political Committee on December 1, 1955. It was debated on December 1, 2, 5, 6 and 7 when nearly all delegations explained their positions on the underlying assumptions, as well as the merits of the draft resolution.

The Soviet Union supported the draft resolution of 28 but suggested that, in order to give it a clearer meaning, the eighteen countries be enumerated, and introduced an amendment to this effect.[37]

Several Members opposed the Soviet amendment. The New Zealand Delegation feared that

> public discussion of the individual applicants at this stage would only serve to harden differences of view which we know exist, and might thus prejudice the possibility of reaching a satisfactory solution.[38]

In the meantime the sponsors of the original draft resolution accepted what must have appeared to them the essential part of the Soviet amendment, namely, the figure eighteen. Thus amended, the operative paragraph 2 of the draft resolution of 28 read:

> 2. Requests the Security Council to consider, in the light of the general opinion in favour of the widest possible membership of the United Nations, the pending applications *for membership* of all those *eighteen* countries about which no problem of unification arises.[39]

[35] Docs. A/AC.80/L.3, A/AC.80/L.3/Add. 1 and 2, and A/AC.80/L.3/Add. 2/Rev.1. (emphasis supplied). The original 25 sponsors were: Afghanistan, Argentina, Australia, Brazil, Burma, Canada, Colombia, Costa Rica, Denmark, Iceland, India, Indonesia, Iran, Iraq, Lebanon, Liberia, New Zealand, Norway, Pakistan, Saudi Arabia, Sweden, Syria, Thailand, Yemen and Yugoslavia. The three additional co-sponsors were: Chile, Ecuador, Ethiopia.

[36] China was not consulted. See Mr. Tsiang's remark, Doc. A/AC.80/P.V.26 (Dec. 2, 1955) at 2–5.

[37] The amendment proposed to replace the words "of all those countries about which no problem of unification arises" by the following: "of eighteen States (Albania, the Mongolian People's Republic, Jordan, Portugal, Ireland, Hungary, Italy, Austria, Romania, Bulgaria, Finland, Ceylon, Nepal, Libya, Cambodia, Japan, Laos, and Spain)." Doc. A/AC.80/L.5, Nov. 18, 1955. See also Doc. A/AC.80/P.V.25, at 54–55.

[38] For comparable comments of Netherlands, Burma, Philippines, Australia, Pakistan, Yugoslavia, Turkey, Docs. A/AC.80/P.V.25 (Dec. 1, 1955) at 61, A/AC.80/P.V.26 (Dec. 2, 1955) at 42, 54–55, A/AC.80/P.V.28 (Dec. 5, 1955) at 37, 53, 77–78, 79.

[39] Doc. A/AC.80/L.3/Rev.1, Dec. 2, 1955. The added words are emphasized.

The effect of this partial concession to the Soviet viewpoint was that several delegations found the Soviet amendment superfluous.[40]

The Soviet Delegation, taking into account the "clarification" made in the draft resolution, and desiring to reach unanimity, decided accordingly "not to press for a vote on its amendment."[41] The debate had clearly shown that the enumeration of the applicants had become unnecessary because "there cannot be any doubt about what is meant by the eighteen States."[42]

The Delegation of Cuba, which opposed the joint draft resolution of 28, recalled "a document which is very often forgotten," namely, the Charter of the United Nations, and introduced various amendments to that draft resolution and a sub-amendment to the amendment presented by the Soviet Union.[43] The over-all objective of the amendments was "to redeem an omission" by the 28 Members. The Cuban sub-amendment[44] to the Soviet amendment provided for replacing the word "eighteen" by "twenty" and adding the Republic of Korea and the Republic of Viet-Nam to the list of applicants. The Cuban amendment found some support in the *Ad Hoc* Committee but not much. China, which for a variety of reasons opposed the joint draft resolution of 28, supported it as did France.[45] The Belgian Delegation deemed the Cuban amendment "indispensable" because it "specifically recalls the constitutional requirements" and declared it would vote for it.[46]

The opposition was strong and voiced by many delegations. The delegations of Poland, Yugoslavia, Indonesia, Afghanistan, U.S.S.R., Canada, Mexico, United Kingdom, El Salvador, and Colombia, declared either that they would oppose or that they could not support the Cuban amendments.[47] The Cuban Delegation withdrew its sub-

[40] Thus Indonesia, Doc. A/AC.80/P.V.30 (Dec. 6, 1955) at 21; Guatemala, *ibid.* at 53; India, Doc. A/AC.80/P.V.31 (Dec. 7, 1955) at 86; Canada, Doc. A/AC.80/P.V.32 (Dec. 7, 1955) at 13; Mexico, *ibid.* at 17; United Kingdom, *ibid.* at 21.

[41] *Ibid.* 26. A change in the Soviet attitude was intimated earlier in the day; see Doc. A/AC.80/P.V.31 (Dec. 7, 1955) at 63–65.

[42] Mr. Krishna Menon (India), *ibid.* at 86.

[43] Docs. A/AC.80/L.7, A/AC.80/L.8 and Doc. A/AC.80/P.V.27 (Dec. 5, 1955) at 22. The text of the Cuban amendment (A/AC.80/L.7) is as follows: 1. Delete the first paragraph of the preamble and insert the following: "*Having noted* the general sentiment which has been expressed on numerous occasions that the United Nations should have the widest possible membership of States possessing the qualifications required by Article 4 of the United Nations Charter,". 2. Delete the fourth paragraph of the preamble and insert the following: "Believing that a broader representation in the membership of the United Nations will, provided that the Members possess the qualifications required by Article 4 of the Charter, enable the Organization to play a more effective role in the current international situation,". 3. Delete paragraph 2 of the operative part and insert the following: "2. *Requests* the Security Council, in the light of the general opinion that the United Nations should have the widest possible membership of States possessing the qualifications required by Article 4 of the Charter, to consider the pending applications for membership in accordance with the principles established by the advisory opinion of the International Court of Justice of 28 May 1948;". 4. Delete paragraph 3 of the operative part and insert the following: "3. *Requests further* that the Security Council, in accordance with the principles established by the International Court of Justice in its advisory opinion of 28 May 1948, make its report on these applications to the General Assembly during the present session."

[44] Doc. A/AC.80/L.8.

[45] Doc. A/AC.80/P.V.31 (Dec. 7, 1955) at 47; Doc. A/AC.80/P.V.32 (Dec. 7, 1955) at 11.

[46] *Ibid.* at 17, 18–20.

[47] Docs. A/AC.80/P.V.27 (Dec. 5, 1955) at 69 (Poland); A/AC.80/P.V.28 (Dec. 5, 1955) at 76 (Yugoslavia; the Yugoslav Delegation opposed both the Cuban amendment and the sub-amendment); A/AC.80/P.V.30 (Dec. 6, 1955) at 22 (Indonesia); *ibid.* at 42 (Afghanistan); A/AC.80/P.V.31 (Dec. 7, 1955) at 62 (U.S.S.R.); A/AC.80/P.V.32 (Dec. 7, 1955) at 13 (Canada); *ibid.* at 17 (Mexico; Mexico considered that the amendments to the joint draft resolution of 28 "would destroy the very delicate balance in the wording of the draft resolution."); *ibid.* at 21 (U.K.); *ibid.* at 22 (El Salvador); *ibid.*

amendment to the Soviet amendment when this was dropped, but maintained its amendment to the joint draft resolution of 28.[48]

## V. DEBATE ON THE JOINT DRAFT RESOLUTION OF 28 MEMBERS

Delegations of forty odd Members expressed themselves in the *Ad Hoc* Committee with varying degrees of warmth for the solution of the "deadlock confined in a deadlock"[49] offered by the joint draft resolution. Some of them experienced a measure of difficulty in rationalizing their positive attitude, involving as it did a revision of attitudes adopted on earlier occasions, and in reconciling the joint draft resolution with the Charter.[50]

### 1. Universality of Membership

An often recurring theme was the desirability for the United Nations to achieve universality of membership. That it was desirable to aim at this objective was not doubted at the San Francisco Conference. The decision then taken and incorporated in Article 4 of the Charter was, however, in favor of membership open to such states as satisfied certain requirements. In the last few years universality has acquired a rare degree of urgency which was voiced by many a delegation at the Tenth Session of the General Assembly. Mr. Martin (Canada), in introducing the joint draft resolution, urged all Members

> not to allow divergencies of interpretation and disputes over detail or extraneous issues to stunt the expansion of the United Nations and to prevent it from achieving at last its intended and natural world-wide character.[51]

The delegate of Brazil argued that without universality the United Nations "would never represent an integration on a world-wide scale and of a juridical character," and claimed that although Article 4 of the Charter implied a limitation, nevertheless the principle of universality

> by virtue of its own strength, receives full application in paragraph 6 of Article 2, according to which the Charter places non-Member States on the same footing as Member States in everything connected with the maintenance of international peace and security.[52]

at 27 (Colombia). The delegate of Colombia stated that his delegation "has never been in agreement with nor has it accepted, the advisory opinion of the International Court of Justice, in 1948, which, as we all know, is not binding in character." See also the statements by the delegates of Greece, A/AC.80/P.V.28 (Dec. 5, 1955) at 12, and Thailand, A/AC.80/P.V.30 (Dec. 6, 1955) at 37.

48 Doc. A/AC.80/P.V.32 (Dec. 7, 1955) at 31. See *infra* for decision on Cuban amendment.

49 Mr. Shukairy (Syria), A/AC.80/P.V.28 (Dec. 5, 1955) at 38.

50 For rationalizations of the inevitable change of attitude, see remarks by Mr. Martin, Doc. A/AC.80/P.V.25 at 31, 32, and the delegations of Australia, Doc. A/AC.80/P.V.28 at 32–36, Panama, Doc. A/AC.80/P.V.30 at 11, and India, Doc. A/AC.80/P.V.31 at 66.

51 Doc. A/AC.80/P.V.25 (Dec. 1, 1955) at 43–45.

52 Doc. A/AC.80/P.V.26 (Dec. 2, 1955) at 68. The delegate of Pakistan invoked Art. 3 in support of Art. 4 to demonstrate that the authors of the Charter intended the Organization to be universal. Doc. A/AC.80/P.V.28 (Dec. 5, 1955) at

Other delegations bolstered their pleas for universality by reference to the Bandung Conference of April, 1955, where twenty-nine African and Asian states were represented.

Several delegates adopted a somewhat more cautious attitude. Thus the delegate of Israel reminded the Committee that in bridging the gap between the principle of universality and Article 4, the main concern should be "to preserve the integrity of the Charter—this irreplaceable foundation of our Organization."[53] And the delegate of France, which has always supported the principle as "implicit in the foundations of our Charter," did not believe "that we should sacrifice other very explicit rules set forth in the Charter to that principle."[54] The delegate of China, recalled that his delegation had always been ready "to cooperate with other delegations in approaching universality of membership," but declared that in this case "a few delegations have tried to exploit the principle of universality to justify package deals."[55] Sir Percy Spender with remarkable bluntness, summed up the problem as follows:

> The real matter before us—whatever be the words with which we clothe our thoughts—is whether we do or do not support the "package deal" to admit eighteen nations—all or none, irrespective of the terms of the Charter.
>
> I prefer to put the issue before us in that way because this is what I think the issue really is. I am not prepared to coin fine and high-sounding phrases to disguise this unfortunate fact. Nor shall I invoke any high principle—such as the so-called principle of universality, which if it means anything means that a nation is entitled to be admitted to the United Nations irrespective of whether it does or does not comply with the relevant Article, which is Article 4, of the Charter.[56]

This debate is all the more remarkable as the principle of universality is not one which can be found in the Charter. Thus, existing and explicit principles were subordinated to one which is non-existent, and at best, implied.

## 2. Political v. Legal Solution

Several Members underscored the political nature of the problem which demanded a political solution. The delegate of Indonesia told the *Ad Hoc* Committee: "We all have realized that the basic problem at issue is political rather than legal or juridical, and that the persistent deadlock was due primarily to the severe political and ideological controver-

52. The principle of universality was also supported by The Netherlands, Doc. A/AC.80/P.V.25 (Dec. 1, 1955) at 58–60; Egypt, *ibid.* at 57; Burma, Doc. A/AC.80/P.V.26 (Dec. 2, 1955) at 46; Iraq, *ibid.* at 56; Greece, Doc. A/AC.80/P.V.28 (Dec. 5, 1955) at 6; Ukranian S.S.R., *ibid.* at 13–15; Lebanon, *ibid.* at 56; Iceland, *ibid.* at 66; Argentine, *ibid.* at 81; Dominican Republic, *ibid.* at 89; Thailand, Doc. A/AC.80/P.V.38 (Dec. 6, 1955) at 36; Afghanistan, *ibid.* at 41; Liberia, *ibid.* at 43; Saudi Arabia, *ibid.* at 47; Guatemala, *ibid.* at 52; Yemen, *ibid.* at 61; Ecuador, *ibid.* at 73; Uruguay, *ibid.* at 78; Mexico, Doc. A/AC.80/P.V.32 (Dec. 7, 1955) at 16; Colombia, *ibid.* at 26; Bolivia, *ibid.* at 32.

53. Doc. A/AC.80/P.V.30 (Dec. 6, 1955) at 57.

54. Doc. A/AC.80/P.V.32 (Dec. 7, 1955) at 2–10.

55. Doc. A/AC.80/P.V.26 (Dec. 2, 1955) at 6. Mr. Tsiang noted, however, "that there are a goodly number of delegations which, while believing in the principle of universality, reject the package deal."

56. Doc. A/AC.80/P.V.28 (Dec. 5, 1955) at 23–25.

sies in the 'cold war,' " and he called for a compromise "to bridge the controversies by interpreting the meaning and purpose of Article 4 of the Charter . . . in a broad, liberal and impartial sense."[57] In the opinion of the Bolivian delegate, "the legal arguments and procedural arguments put forth cannot be recognized as valid as compared to the important political considerations."[58]

As events were to show, it was premature to hope that acceptance of the compromise would prevent the further application of the veto. It is more remarkable that in spite of frequent references to the Advisory opinion of the International Court of Justice of May 28, 1948, the following holding of the Court was totally ignored:

> The political character of an organ cannot release it from the observance of the treaty provisions established by the Charter when they constitute limitations on its powers or criteria for its judgment. To ascertain whether an organ has freedom of choice for its decisions, reference must be made to the terms of its constitution. In this case, the limits of this freedom are fixed by Article 4 and allow for a wide liberty of appreciation. There is therefore no conflict between the functions of the political organs, on the one hand, and the exhaustive character of the prescribed conditions, on the other.[59]

The political solution was "nothing but an attempt to justify the non-application of the existing law,"[60] the application of which seemed in conflict with the dominant interest of promoting universality of membership at a price.

### 3. A "Package Deal"

The joint draft resolution of 28 deliberately omitted listing by name the applications "of all those countries about which no problem of unification arises." The Soviet amendment which would have made good this omission was opposed and eventually withdrawn. The discretion of the 28 sponsors did not altogether prevent discussion of individual applications, which perhaps was unavoidable, seeing that everybody knew who the nameless "countries" were.[61] On the other hand it did stimulate the criticism that the joint draft resolution proposed a "package deal" or, what appeared to some to be substantially the same, the simultaneous or contemporaneous admission of a group of applicants without individual examination of the eligibility of each of the applicants. There is no necessary connection between these two lines of criticism as there may be a "pack-

[57] Doc. A/AC.80/P.V.30 (Dec. 6, 1955) at 12, 13–15.

[58] Doc. A/AC.80/P.V.32 (Dec. 7, 1955) at 33–35, 36. See also Burma, Doc. A/AC.80/P.V.26 (Dec. 2, 1955) at 47; Australia, Doc. A/AC.80/P.V.28 (Dec. 5, 1955) at 24–25, Greece, *ibid.* at 2–5; Argentina, *ibid.* at 84–85; Ecuador, A/AC.80/P.V.30 (Dec. 6, 1955) at 67; Honduras, *ibid* at 84.

[59] [1948] I.C.J. Reports 57, at 64.

[60] Hans Kelsen, Principles of International Law viii.

[61] It may be noted that the joint draft resolution referred to the applications of countries, whereas Art. 4 of the Charter refers to "states." The Soviet amendment (A/AC.80/L.5) used the term "states." The sponsors of the joint draft resolution did not accept this rather obvious correction. It is a matter of speculation why the term "country" was preferred. It has no legal significance in international law. It may be that this curious terminology was designed to avoid a discussion of whether Outer Mongolia, one of the eighteen "countries," would technically and strictly qualify as "state" in the international law sense of this term or, at the very least, in the Charter sense of the term.

age deal'' combined with individual examination and a contemporaneous admission of a group of states without a ''package deal.''

Several Members, having accepted the need for a political compromise, were also prepared to accept the joint draft resolution, whether it involved a ''package deal'' or not. Mr. Martin (Canada), speaking in the plenary meeting of the General Assembly, admitted that ''we all have the greatest reservations'' with respect to the proposed ''honest compromise,'' but he claimed it was ''not a compromise of principle.''[62]

Sir Percy Spender (Australia), with what must appear as brutal frankness, admitted that the choice was between supporting or rejecting the ''package deal,''[63] and claimed that ''each of us in his heart knows that we officiate at the burial of Article 4 of the Charter.''[64] The will of the overwhelming majority of Members having been frustrated by the veto, and in view of the unwillingness of the permanent members to waive the veto in the Security Council, and of the Council ''to recommend to the General Assembly in face of any veto from a permanent member, we either have to accept the package deal before us or keep excluded from the United Nations indefinitely—perhaps for another decade or more—many nations without whom the Organization has no claim to be called a world organization, whose admission would enrich our deliberations and whose right to sit together with us is and has been for a long time beyond dispute.''[65] The Afghanistan Delegation believed ''that there is nothing in the Charter of the United Nations against collective admission of new Members.''[66] While it is true that there is nothing in the Charter against collective admission, this is not the whole truth. Thus the Venezuelan delegate declared:

> . . . it is an open secret that the draft resolution was proposed on the basis of an understanding that there be an over-all or *en bloc* admission; that is to say, it seeks a solution as a result of prior negotiation rather than on the basis of the appliction of well-known principles. It is precisely this which leads many to ask to what extent the political considerations—that is to say, what is agreed upon in the Organization—may be allowed to overshadow juridical considerations, that is to say, what results from established rules.[67]

And the Soviet Union's position was frankly based ''on the idea that the solution proposed by the twenty-eight States is consistent with the requirements of world public opinion and of the overwhelming majority of States represented here.''[68]

[62] Doc. A/P.V.552 (Dec. 8, 1955) at 58–60, 62.

[63] Doc. A/A.C.80/P.V.28 (Dec. 5, 1955); see *infra*, p. 624.

[64] *Ibid.* at 27.

[65] *Ibid.* at 31, 32. Other delegations also explained their favorable attitude towards the ''somewhat abnormal'' or, from a juridical point of view, the less than perfect procedure by the use or abuse of the veto. See Turkey, *ibid.* at 29, Argentina, *ibid.* at 86.

[66] *Ibid.* at 42.

[67] A/AC.80/P.V.31 (Dec. 7, 1955) at 3.

[68] *Ibid.* at 61. Mr. Krishna Menon, *ibid.* at 71, based his views regarding the joint draft resolution on the equivalence of majority and minority opinions of members of the International Court of Justice in the first admission case (Advisory Opinion of May 28, 1948). In their joint dissenting opinion Judges Basdevant, Winiarski, Sir Arnold McNair and Read declared: ''But it would be a strange interpretation which gave a Member freedom to base its vote upon a certain consideration and at the same time forbade it to invoke that consideration in the discussion preceding the vote. Such a result would

Be that as it may, a large number of Members probably felt without any feeling of exuberance as the Syrian delegate did when he said: "A wholesale admission is the only way open before us. If we do not like it, we must like it."[69]

On the other hand the delegate of China reminded his colleagues that since the Advisory Opinion of the International Court of Justice in the first admissions case, "all delegations, with the exception of the Soviet bloc, have held any package deal to be unconstitutional."[70] The delegate of Cuba regarded the joint draft resolution as "a great triumph for the Soviet Union because we are admitting the principle of a 'package' or '*en bloc*' admission, against which the great majority of Member States—and above all the permanent members of the Security Council—have been protesting."[71]

The delegate of Israel did not interpret the joint resolution as requesting the *Ad Hoc* Political Committee or the Security Council "to renounce—something it could not do—Article 4 of the Charter."[72]

Mr. Nisot, speaking for Belgium, recalled the "overriding postulate" that treaties, particularly the Charter, "should be scrupulously observed." The deliberations in the *Ad Hoc* Committee

> have shown quite clearly that the dominant intention here is to bring about the realization of a kind of deal, a compromise, as a result of which all eighteen applicants would, without distinction as to their merits, be admitted *en bloc,* in a "package deal", to the United Nations.[73]

The French delegate warned that although universality was desirable, "it would be a mistake for the United Nations, and one pregnant with all sorts of consequences, to bring it about by violating the Charter," to reject legality and opt for arbitrariness as the supporters of the joint draft resolution appeared to be doing. "It is not by violating the provi-

not conduce to that frank exchange of views which is an essential condition of the healthy functioning of an international organization. *It is true that it is not possible to fathom the hidden reasons for a vote* and there exists no legal machinery for rectifying a vote which may be cast contrary to the Charter in the Security Council or the General Assembly. But that does not mean that there are no rules of law governing Members of the United Nations in voting in either of these organs; an example is to be found in paragraph 1 of Article 4 *prohibiting* the admission of a new Member which does not fulfill the qualifications specified therein. This distinction, which it has been attempted to introduce between the actual vote and the discussion preceding it, cannot be accepted; it would be inconsistent with the actual terms of the question submitted to the Court, and its recognition would involve the risk of undermining that respect for good faith which must govern the discharge of the obligations contained in the Charter (Article 2, paragraph 2)." [1948] I.C.J. Reports 47, at 29–30 (emphasis supplied).

[69] Doc. A/AC.80/P.V.28 (Dec. 5, 1955) at 46.

[70] Doc. A/AC.80/P.V.26 (Dec. 2, 1955) at 11.

[71] Doc. A/AC.80/P.V.27 (Dec. 5, 1955) at 16, 61. The Cuban delegate also blamed the veto for "the package or the cocktail that international public opinion is being asked to swallow." Doc. A/P.V.552 (Dec. 8, 1955) at 23–25.

[72] Doc. A/AC.80/P.V.30 (Dec. 6, 1955) at 57–61. Speaking two days later in the plenary meeting of the Assembly, the delegate of Israel stated: "We are told, either you admit eighteen States in a package or else you admit none, either you recognize that according to the provisions of the Charter all eighteen of the applicant States are peace-loving and accept and are able to carry out the obligations of the Charter and are willing to do so, or else the doors of the United Nations will be closed to all eighteen States without exception." Doc. A/P.V.552 (Dec. 8, 1955) at 37.

[73] Doc. A/AC.80/P.V.32 (Dec. 7, 1955) at 17, 18–20. See also the observations of the Greek Delegation, Doc. A/AC.80/P.V.28 (Dec. 5, 1955) at 6 ff.; the Dominican Delegation, *ibid.* at 89; and the Paraguayan Delegation, Doc. A/P.V.552 (Dec. 8, 1955) at 41.

sions of the Charter," he insisted, "even in what may appear to be the best interests of the world, that the United Nations will ever achieve" the purpose stated in its Preamble of establishing "conditions under which justice and respect for the obligations arising from treaties and other sources of international law can be maintained."[74]

The United States representative, Mr. Henry Cabot Lodge, Jr., after the fiasco in the Security Council, declared:

> Whether you like it or not, our position has been perfectly clear all the way through. We did not support the package deal. We did not support Outer Mongolia. In fact, we think we heard a sigh of relief when Outer Mongolia did not get in.[75]

## 4. The Vandenberg Resolution

The position of the United States, said Mr. Henry Cabot Lodge, Jr., was guided by three basic principles:

> First, to bring into membership all qualified States which apply. Secondly, to follow the provisions of the Charter as to judging the qualifications of the applicants. Third, to avoid thwarting the will of a qualified majority by the use in the Security Council of the veto—a voting privilege given to five nations in the expectation that it would only be used in exceptional circumstances.[76]

Elaborating the last principle, he recalled "that the Vandenberg resolution expressed the view that there should be agreement never to use the veto to prevent the admission of new Members."[77] In accordance with the first and second principles the United States would support six European and seven Asian applicants. On account of the same principles, the United States could "not support in any form the applications made for Albania, Bulgaria, Hungary, Outer Mongolia and Romania" as these states "are not now independent." On the other hand, the United States recognized "that the issues before us are those about which there can be honest differences of opinion." Mr. Lodge went on to say:

> For this reason, among others, it is not our intention to use the veto in the Security Council to thwart what may be the will of a qualified majority in the Security Council and in the General Assembly in relation to the subject-matter of the joint resolution. Should this bring before the Security Council resolutions on admission which, in our opinion, *involve infractions of the Charter,* we shall, in accordance with the spirit of the Vandenberg resolution, abstain from voting, so as not to exercise—on this question of admissions—the veto power. We shall abstain from voting on the joint resolution now before us, because, while in form this resolution only requests the Security Council to consider certain applica-

[74] A/P.V.552 (Dec. 8, 1955) at 42, 43-45; see also Doc. A/AC.801/P.V.32 (Dec. 7, 1955) at 2-10 for the French position in the *Ad Hoc* Committee.

[75] Doc. S/P.V.708 (Dec. 21, 1955) at 28, 29.

[76] Doc. A/AC.80/P.V.31 (Dec. 7, 1955) at 51.

[77] *Ibid.* at 52.

> tions, some practical applications of that resolution are such that we hesitate to vote for it lest that might seem to involve us in a departure from our principles enumerated above.[78]

Speaking the following day at the 552nd meeting of the General Assembly, Mr. Martin, referring to Mr. Lodge's statement, said: "I think that yesterday the United States delegation gave a great lead."[79] He obviously was satisfied that the United States would not bring to naught his carefully laid plan, although Mr. Lodge was fully aware that a "package deal" was involved, which the United States neither favored nor approved.[80]

Dr. Belaunde declared that the Vandenberg Resolution "established a *legal obligation,* on a reciprocal basis of course, for the United States, which enunciated a high moral principle and which provided a political solution to the impasse created by successive vetoes, an impasse which could have no juridical solution." He added:

> in my view, aside from the *legal obligation contracted* by the United States which was to abstain in order to leave the decision to the General Assembly and not to place obstacles in the form of judgment or prejudices with regard to any applicant, that appeal obviously imposed a *moral obligation* upon all the great Powers either to vote in favour of the admission of the applicants or, in cases of doubt, to follow the Latin principle of abstaining, and thus to facilitate the Assembly's task.[81]

This interpretation of the Vandenberg Resolution appears quite untenable. It created no unilateral and still less a bilateral obligation, legal or moral, international or municipal, for the United States to abstain. Nor is it possible to base the position of the United States on the Vandenberg Resolution as Mr. Lodge attempted to do. The Vandenberg Resolution was a formulation of certain policy objectives for the United States to pursue in the circumstances prevailing at the time. One of these policy objectives is to seek agreement among the permanent members of the Security Council to remove the veto from the admission of new members. There is no evidence in the proceedings that the United States either sought or was successful in achieving agreement along these lines. Moreover, it is difficult to see how the admission of states which in the opinion of the United States would involve "infractions of the Charter" can be reconciled with, let alone based upon, the Vandenberg Resolution. Surely, it was in the spirit of the Vandenberg Resolution that only qualified states would be considered for admission. It is difficult to accept the view that any Member would see its way to supporting the admission of states in violation of the Charter explicitly by an affirmative vote or implicitly by abstention. It is one thing to adopt a broad or compassionate interpretation of the criteria governing the eligibility of states and yet another to make the admission of states possible in disregard of

[78] *Ibid.* at 52, 53–55 (emphasis supplied). Mr. Lodge repeated the substance of this statement at the 701st and 704th meetings of the Security Council. Dec. 10 and 13, 1955. Docs. S/P.V.701 at 35 f. and S/P.V.704 at 40–42.

[79] Doc. A/P.V.552 at 63–65.

[80] Doc. S/P.V.708 (Dec. 2, 1955) at 28, 29.

[81] Doc. A/AC.80/P.V.25 at 14–15, 16 (emphasis supplied). It is not clear on what grounds Mr. Belaunde claims the principle of abstention as a "Latin" principle.

these criteria. There is no support in the Vandenberg Resolution for acquiescence in infractions of the Charter.

## 5. The Joint Draft Resolution of 28 and Article 4 of the Charter

It is obvious that the changing attitude of Members and of the General Assembly with respect to the problem of admission necessitated a reinterpretation of Article 4 in more ways than one. The vast majority of Members was prepared to depart from the established practice of the General Assembly to deal with each application on its merits. Likewise indicative of the radical departure from established practice is the omission of any reference to the fulfilment by the applicants, individually or as a group, of the requirements of Article 4 as interpreted by the International Court of Justice in its Advisory Opinion of May 28, 1948. In the decisive voting in the *Ad Hoc* Committee on the Cuban amendment,[82] which would have made good the omission, only seven Members, namely, the United States, Belgium, China, Cuba, France, Luxembourg and The Netherlands, voted in favor of it, while 37 and 38 voted against it and 14 and 15 respectively abstained.[83] Nevertheless Article 4 and the Court's Advisory Opinion were very much in evidence in the discussions of the *Ad Hoc* Committee.

Mr. Martin, leading off, was at pains to reassure the delegates that the proposed action "does no violence to these principles" of the Charter. However, he requested the delegates to recognize that there "may be legitimate differences in the interpretation given to the Charter,"[84] and that an interpretation shall be preferred which will promote rather than impede "the intended world-wide nature of our membership."[85] Applying some such standard, Mr. Martin suggested for instance, that all of the eighteen nations are peace-loving because none of them, in the age of the hydrogen bomb, is "war-loving," in the sense of "seeking war as an objective or instrument of national policy."[86] It was admittedly a matter of controversy whether all of the eighteen were fully qualified as "States." Mr. Martin pleaded for willingness to compromise in applying this test.[87] Members generally indicated that they had no great difficulty in accommodating themselves to the views expounded by Mr. Martin.[88] Admittedly the terms of Article 4, para-

[82] See *supra*, p. 615.

[83] Doc. A/AC.80/P.V.32 (Dec. 7, 1955) at 52–58. The delegate of France, however, speaking in the plenary meeting of the General Assembly on the following day, said that only six Members, namely, Cuba, Belgium, The Netherlands, Israel, France and the United States had voted in favor of the Cuban amendment (see Doc. A/P.552 (Dec. 8, 1955) at 42). This does not correspond to the verbatim record of the *Ad Hoc* Political Committee referred to above.

[84] Doc. A/AC.80/P.V.25 (Dec. 1, 1955) at 37.

[85] *Ibid.* at 41.

[86] *Ibid.* at 37 ff.

[87] *Ibid.* at 38–40; see also A/AC.80/P.V.32 (Dec. 7, 1955) at 14–15.

[88] See, for example, New Zealand, Doc. A/AC.80/P.V.26 (Dec. 2, 1955) at 36; Greece, Doc. A/AC.80/P.V.28 (Dec. 5, 1955) at 8 (but see A/P.V.552 at 11 for reservations regarding Albania and Outer Mongolia); Syria, *ibid.* at 42: "This language (Membership in the United Nations is open . . .) establishes a presumption of admissibility, and not a presumption of prohibition"; Lebanon, *ibid.* at 57; Iceland, *ibid.* at 66; Indonesia, Doc. A/AC.80/P.V.30 (Dec. 6, 1955) at 13–15; Thailand, *ibid.* at 37; Afghanistan, *ibid.* at 42; Liberia, *ibid.* at 43; Costa Rica, *ibid.* at 85; India, Doc. A/AC.80/P.V.31 (Dec. 7, 1955) at 69–70 f.; Mexico, Doc. A/AC.80/P.V.32 (Dec. 7, 1955) at 16; El Salvador, *ibid.* at 22.

graph 1, are far from clear and were in any event intended to be no more than a "guide."[89] However, there is nothing to be gained from glossing over the fact that the Advisory Opinion of the International Court of Justice of May 28, 1948, aggravated the problem. Thus Sir Percy Spender declared:

> Let it be said, without any reservation, that what we propose to it [sic]—and what the Australian delegation both intends to do and urges other countries to do—is contrary to that Advisory Opinion.[90]

He went on to argue that advisory opinions do not bind the General Assembly or the Security Council, which is at best a debatable proposition.[91] And, proclaiming in effect the majority of Members sovereign, he advanced the somewhat disturbing proposition that if the Court's advisory opinions "happen to coincide with the views of the majority of Members, they acquire of course a special sanctity of their own. If they do not, they can be disregarded—and in the world in which we live they will be disregarded—where political exigencies in accordance with the will of the majority demand that they shall."[92]

Some Members, China and Cuba, agreed with Sir Percy Spender. But the delegate of Ecuador denied that "we are . . . burying Article 4 of the United Nations Charter,"[93] and the United Kingdom delegate was "satisfied that the draft resolution itself is not in conflict with Article 4 of the Charter, or with the rulings of the International Court."[94]

## 6. Appeals to China

As the debate in the *Ad Hoc* Political Committee indicated the virtually certain passage of the joint draft resolution of 28 in the General Assembly, several Members addressed urgent appeals to China to exercise tolerance, as the United States proposed to do,

[89] Gross, *loc. cit.* 39 ff. See also *supra* 586 ff.

[90] Doc. A/AC.80/P.V.28 (Dec. 5, 1955) at 28.

[91] Sir Gerald Fitzmaurice, "The Law and Procedure of the International Court of Justice: International Organizations and Tribunals," 29 British Year Book of International Law 1–62 (1952) at 54 ff.; Gross, *loc. cit.* at 45. See also *supra* 592.

[92] Doc. A/AC.80/P.V.28 (Dec. 5, 1955) at 28. Sir Percy was apparently also of the opinion that in adopting the joint draft resolution of 28, the United Nations was doing something in the nature of an amendment to the Charter or laying a precedent for the future. He said: "I gain some satisfaction from the fact that, if what we are doing is, as I think it to be, contrary to the express provision of the Charter, it will be done by the expression of an overwhelming body of opinion within this Assembly—endorsed, I hope, in the Security Council. An amendment of the Charter would, after all, require no more—for Article 108 provides that amendment may be affected by two-thirds of the Assembly—and that will truly be forthcoming for this resolution—and a majority of the Security Council including the permanent members. . . . We are, in truth, taking a far-reaching step in this resolution. We are laying down a new practice; for it will be a bold man who, in the future, will call in aid Article 4 and its requirements that an applicant shall be a 'peace-loving State' and one which accepts the obligations contained in the Charter and is, in the opinion of the Organization, able and willing to carry out those obligations. I do not seek to place any interpretation upon these important words. It is sufficient for me, however, to say that I do not agree with the somewhat nebulous rules of construction which I have heard referred to in this debate and which reduce them to a meaningless collection of letters." *Ibid.* at 36, 37.

[93] Doc. A/AC.80/P.V.30 (Dec. 6, 1955) at 67. This delegate, however, was willing to concede that "we are making a new political rule in the interpretation of this Article." See statements by Chinese delegate, Doc. A/AC.80/P.V.31 (Dec. 7, 1955) at 41 ff.; and Cuban delegate, Doc. A/P.V.552 (Dec. 8, 1955) at 31.

[94] Doc. A/AC.80/P.V.32 (Dec. 7, 1955) at 21.

and not to prevent by its negative vote the adoption of a favorable recommendation in the Security Council. Sir Percy Spender appealed to Mr. Tsiang not to exercise his vote in such a way as would obstruct the will of the great majority of nations on this matter.[95] Mr. Tsiang was willing to be tolerant where there was a legitimate doubt, but he thought "we must see that Outer Mongolia does not pass the test."[96] No argument would cause Mr. Tsiang to change his attitude, and, in the Security Council, he opposed the admission of the Mongolian People's Republic. This was a "veto" against one of the eighteen states proposed for admission in the joint draft resolution of 28, and thus, in effect, a veto against breaking the deadlock on the basis of this joint draft resolution. It is not material here to assess responsibilities. Suffice it to note that in Mr. Tsiang's judgment the shoe was on the other foot, that is, the "dictatorial stand of eighteen or none" adopted by the Soviet Union was responsible for the failure of the Security Council to adopt positive recommendations.[97]

### 7. Effect on Position of Latin American Members in the United Nations

The Latin American Republics Members of the United Nations, with the exception of Cuba, supported the joint draft resolution of 28, although some of them voiced concern about the possible or probable repercussions which so substantial an increase in membership would produce on their position. In an organization of 60 states, the Latin American Republics had a virtual "veto" on important questions requiring a two-thirds majority of Members present and voting.[98] They were also assured of substantial representation on all organs of the United Nations.

The delegate of Ecuador deemed it necessary that "we maintain the present proportion of representation on the various United Nations organs," with the exception of the Trusteeship Council, where the representation "will always be on an equitable basis between those countries which are Administering Authorities and those which are not."[99] Speaking on behalf of the Latin American group, he suggested revising the Charter in order to increase the membership of various organs by one third, *i.e.*, the Security Council from eleven to thirteen or fourteen (for the benefit of those who believed thirteen to be an

[95] Doc. A/AC.80/P.V.28 (Dec. 5, 1955) at 38. Similar appeals were made by Iraq, Doc. A/AC.80/P.V.26 (Dec. 2, 1955) at 61, Thailand, Doc. A/AC.80/P.V.30 (Dec. 6, 1955) at 37, Saudi Arabia, *ibid.* at 51, Ecuador, *ibid.* at 77, and Peru, Doc. A/AC.80/P.V.31 (Dec. 7, 1955) at 27. The Peruvian delegate quoted the following statement from a confidential document which he did not further identify: "Mr. Tsiang . . . said that he sticks to the rules of every case according to its own merits; but, at the same time, his judgment will be impartial, and, in any case of reasonable doubt, the doubt will be interpreted to the profit of the applicant. He has some suggestions, and will be delighted to speak to us at any time."

[96] *Ibid.* at 47. Mr. Tsiang offered to submit evidence that Mongolia had participated in aggression in Korea. *Ibid.* Since it is not the purpose of this paper to examine the eligibility of the eighteen states, it is sufficient to refer to comments made by delegates in the debates concerning Outer Mongolia.

[97] Doc. S/P.V.704 (Dec. 13, 1955) at 44.

[98] Sir Carl Berendsen (New Zealand), in General Assembly, 2nd Sess., Official Records, Plenary, p. 695.

[99] Doc. A/AC.80/P.V.30 (Dec. 6, 1955) at 68–70. According to this delegate the Latin American group was represented by two of its members on the Security Council, by four on the Economic and Social Council, and by five on the International Court of Justice. *Ibid.* 71.

unlucky number), the Economic and Social Council from eighteen to twenty-four and the International Court of Justice from fifteen to twenty.[100]

The admission of Italy had the immediate effect of increasing to fourteen the number of Members which compose the Trusteeship Council.[101] The proposed increase in the membership of the other organs of the United Nations does not appear unreasonable, although it would, if carried out mechanically, make the Court rather unwieldy. Moreover, the membership of the Court is to reflect "the main forms of civilization and of the principal legal systems of the world"[102] and not the membership of the United Nations. Raising the issue of representation on the other two organs may well provoke an inquiry into such matters as whether or not the Latin American group has been over-represented and whether some method could or should be found to ensure a more adequate representation of regional, political or economic groupings among the Members of the United Nations. The unusually protracted contest between the Philippines and Yugoslavia during the Tenth Session of the Assembly for election to the Security Council may well induce Members to ponder the problem in the context of wider total membership. Representation based merely upon numerical proportionality, as envisaged by the delegate of Ecuador, would not necessarily reflect accurately the economic or political strength of existing groupings and may not be desirable from the point of view of greater effectiveness of the United Nations.[103]

## VI. THE PROCEDURE FOR ACHIEVING THE OBJECTIVE OF THE JOINT DRAFT RESOLUTION OF 28

The procedure for effectuating the objective of the joint draft resolution of 28, namely, the collective admission of a group of eighteen states, five of which have heretofore faced a solid front of opposition, was bound to present a delicate problem.

The Greek representative in the *Ad Hoc* Political Committee observed that if "the permanent members of the Security Council desire to have the guarantee that the candidates that they favour are not likely to lose in the Assembly the required majority of two-thirds, then the draft resolution, as now drawn up, does not seem to offer that guaran-

[100] *Ibid.* See also statements by the delegate of Bolivia, Doc. A/AC.80/P.V.32 (Dec. 7, 1955) at 37, and Chile, Doc. A/557 (Dec. 15, 1955) at 62.

[101] Burma was elected to balance its composition between administering and nonadministering nations. 2 United Nations Review 6 (March, 1956); see also Docs. T/1224 and T/L.633 for suggested consequential revision of the Council's Rules of Procedure.

[102] Art. 9 of the Statute.

[103] Senator Alexander Wiley, Chairman of the Senate Committee on Foreign Relations, observed that, if any substantial number of applicants are admitted to the United Nations, "their votes could have 'a drastic effect' on the present voting which 'has worked well for us.' " Preface to Representation and Voting in the United Nations General Assembly, Staff Study No. 4 (September, 1954), Committee Print, 83rd Cong., 2d Sess., p. iii. This Staff Study concluded that, on the one hand, if the organization continues to expand, "a reconsideration of the voting provisions in the General Assembly might become a more pressing issue," and on the other hand, while "theoretically, there may be logical reasons for supporting a system of weighted voting for the General Assembly," from a practical point of view "it might be better to let well enough alone." *Ibid.* pp. 6, 23.

tee."[104] The compromise agreed to by both the Soviet Union and the 28 sponsors of the joint draft resolution—the inclusion of the figure eighteen—was not deemed satisfactory in view of the reservations which many Members expressed regarding the qualifications of the Communist states. The delegate of the Soviet Union therefore reminded the Committee

> that it is necessary to provide for such a voting procedure as would eliminate any fortuitous circumstances, any unexpected phenomena,[105] which might arise, both in the Assembly and in the Security Council.[106]

The matter was not pressed, perhaps because of the conviction that the deadlock could not be broken in any other way, and of the prevailing sentiment "that the degree of support for the twenty-eight Power draft resolution is a sufficient and powerful indication of the Assembly's views."[107]

The *Ad Hoc* Committee proceeded to vote on the draft resolution paragraph by paragraph, the corresponding Cuban amendment being put to the vote first. The Cuban amendments were rejected one by one, and the paragraphs adopted.[108] The draft resolution as a whole was then adopted by 52 votes to 2 (China, Cuba), with 5 abstentions (the United States, Belgium, France, Greece, Israel).[109] Thus a decisive victory was scored by the joint draft resolution in the first stage.

The second stage in the General Assembly's plenary meeting was almost a mere formality. The joint draft resolution was put to the vote and adopted by 52 votes to 2 (China, Cuba), with 5 abstentions (France, Greece, Israel, United States, Belgium).[110] The President expressed the hope "that the Security Council will receive this manifestation of the will of the General Assembly with the greatest understanding and that, in the discharge of its high functions, the Council will give the most serious attention to the resolution of the General Assembly as promptly as present circumstances require."[111]

The third stage was opened in the Security Council on December 10, 1955.

Three draft resolutions were submitted to the Security Council. First a set of thirteen draft resolutions was submitted by China, proposing the admission, in alphabetical order, of thirteen states; as this was the first initiative, China claimed priority for

[104] Doc. A/AC.80/P.V.28 (Dec. 5, 1955) at 11.

[105] Earlier in his speech Mr. Malik referred to the phenomenon of an abstention "of a mass nature."

[106] Doc. A/AC.80/P.V.31 (Dec. 7, 1955) at 62.

[107] The U. K. delegate, Doc. A/AC.80/P.V.32 (Dec. 7, 1955) at 21.

[108] The amendment to the first paragraph of the preamble was rejected by 38 votes to 7, with 14 abstentions; the first paragraph was adopted by 48 votes to 2, with 4 abstentions; the second and third paragraphs of the draft resolution were adopted by 53 votes to none, with 6 abstentions; the Cuban amendment to the fourth paragraph of the preamble was rejected by 37 votes to 7, with 15 abstentions; the fourth paragraph was adopted by 53 votes to 2, with 4 abstentions; paragraph 1 of the operative part was adopted by 51 votes to none, with 8 abstentions; the Cuban amendment to paragraph 2 of the operative part was rejected by 38 votes to 7, with 14 abstentions, and the paragraph adopted by 52 votes to 2, with 5 abstentions; the Cuban amendment to paragraph 3 of the operative part was rejected by 37 votes to 7, with 15 abstentions, and the paragraph adopted by 52 votes to 2, with 4 abstentions. The United States, France and China voted in favor of all Cuban amendments, the Soviet Union opposed them all, and the United Kingdom abstained. *Ibid.* at 52–58.

[109] *Ibid.* at 59–60.

[110] A/P.V.552 (Dec. 8, 1955) at 71. For text of resolution, see Doc. A/3079, at 7, and S/3467.

[111] *Ibid.* at 72.

it.[112] Next the Soviet Union, referring to the abstention of two permanent members of the Council in the earlier voting in the Assembly, and desiring ironclad "guarantees against any accidents or surprises in the consideration of the admission of new Members, both in the Security Council and in the General Assembly," proposed that (a) applications be examined in the chronological order in which they were received; (b) that meetings of the General Assembly and the Security Council be held simultaneously; (c) that the recommendations of the Council concerning the first state be transmitted immediately to the Assembly; (d) that the Assembly immediately notify the Council of the action taken; (e) that after receipt of the Assembly notification the Council should proceed with the second state, and so on until the list was exhausted.[113]

The third draft resolution, co-sponsored by New Zealand and Brazil, was worded as follows:

> The Security Council,. . .
> Having considered *separately* the applications for membership of Albania, the Mongolian People's Republic, Jordan, Ireland, Portugal, Hungary, Italy, Austria, Romania, Bulgaria, Finland, Ceylon, Nepal, Libya, Cambodia, Japan, Laos and Spain,
> Recommends to the General Assembly the admission of the *above-named* countries.[114]

Sir Leslie Munro, introducing this joint draft, stated:

> We cannot ignore the fact that the General Assembly expects the members of the Council to reach an *understanding* which would permit the immediate admission of *all* eighteen applicants. Still less can we ignore the fact, that in the *absence of such an understanding, no candidate is likely to be admitted.* Therefore, while the procedure my delegation contemplates is one of a separate vote on each applicant, we believe that there must be a vote on the group.[115]

Recognizing that the existence of pressure cannot be denied, he asked for priority to be given to the joint draft resolution.

The Chinese delegate, conceding that by providing for a separate vote on each of the eighteen applicants, the joint draft resolution "managed to keep within the letter of the law," opposed it strongly as "a total surrender" to the Soviet Union stand of "eighteen or none," and formally moved an amendment to the joint draft resolution adding Korea and Viet-Nam to the list of eighteen states.[116] By that time it had become apparent that

[112] Doc. S/P.V.701 (Dec. 10, 1955) at 33–34; the draft resolutions were Docs. S/3468–3480.

[113] *Ibid.* at 28. The text of the Soviet proposal was as follows: "The Security Council, Bearing in mind the General Assembly resolution A/RES/357 of 8 December 1955 on the admission of new Members to the United Nations, Resolves to examine the applications for admission to the United Nations of the eighteen States referred to in the said General Assembly resolution in the chronological order of their receipt, on the understanding that the Council shall take a separate decision on each application and will begin to consider each application after the General Assembly has completed its consideration of the Security Council's recommendation on the preceding application; Empowers the President of the Security Council to reach agreement with the President of the General Assembly concerning the above-mentioned procedure for the examination of applications." *Ibid.* at 29–31.

[114] *Ibid.* at 38 (emphasis supplied).

[115] *Ibid.* at 37 (emphasis supplied).

[116] Doc. S/P.V.703 (Dec. 13, 1955) at 7, 8–9, 10, 26–27, and Doc. S/3506.

there was no hope for the set of draft resolutions submitted by China to obtain priority over the joint draft resolution,[117] and moving the amendment to the New Zealand-Brazilian draft must have seemed a convenient method, as subsequent events were to show, for eliciting two more Soviet vetoes prior to Mr. Tsiang's veto of Mongolia.

The Soviet proposal was opposed on various grounds, but substantially for the reason that the distrust which inspired it was misplaced. The President of the Council could not conceive that the Assembly "will do otherwise than promptly endorse the Council's recommendation by an overwhelming majority" and assured the worried Soviet representative that "the twenty-eight sponsors of the resolution adopted by the General Assembly on 8 December will work wholeheartedly to achieve the objectives desired by the vast majority of the United Nations Members."[118] The Soviet delegate remained unconvinced and the meeting was adjourned over the weekend to allow him time to realize, as the President put it, "the genuineness and advantages of our proposals."[119]

At the opening of the Council meeting on December 13 Mr. Sobolev no longer insisted on priority for his own proposals, thus withdrawing them for all practical purposes, and accepted the joint Brazilian-New Zealand draft resolution on this understanding:

> It is the understanding of the Soviet delegation that this draft resolution represents a *single entity, a single recommendation, which is to be considered by the General Assembly in that sense.* We understand the draft resolution to mean that if the General Assembly amends the recommendations in any way, the Security Council's recommendation would be amended accordingly because it would *lose its meaning as an entity and as a single recommendation, and would consequently have to be referred back to the Security Council for reconsideration.*[120]

The Security Council was then able to proceed to vote on the question of priority. The Iranian proposal to give priority to the Brazilian-New Zealand draft resolution was adopted. The vote was 8 in favor, 1 opposed (China) and 2 abstentions (Belgium, United States).[121] The Council then adopted a Turkish proposal to adjourn until the afternoon, in order to "think over" the Chinese amendment, already referred to,[122] to add Korea and Viet-Nam to the list of eighteen applicants.[123]

The pause in the proceedings failed to yield any changes in the position of the Council's members. New Zealand and the Soviet Union declared themselves against the Chi-

[117] Sir Pierson Dixon was first in objecting to the Chinese draft resolutions and said "it would be quite wrong to begin" with them. Doc. S/P.V.701 (Dec. 10, 1955) at 24.

[118] S/P.V.702 (Dec. 10, 1955) at 2. Similar statements were made by Mr. Entezam, Sir Pierson Dixon and Mr. Belaunde, *ibid.* at 18, 23 f., 26 f.

[119] *Ibid.* at 29 ff. Mr. Sobolev based his adamant position on the argument that "according to a preliminary estimate, some twenty delegations have either not stated their positions, or have made express reservations to the effect that they would not support all eighteen countries. I would therefore ask Sir Pierson Dixon whether he could guarantee that all the fifty-two delegations which voted for the draft resolution will support all eighteen States without exception."

[120] Doc. S/P.V.703 (Dec. 13, 1955) at 3 (emphasis supplied). For background speculation see William R. Frye, "18-17-16 and Why We Lost the Game," The Reporter (Jan. 28, 1956) at 17.

[121] *Ibid.* at 28.

[122] See *supra,* p. 628.

[123] *Ibid.* at 28.

nese amendment.[124] Mr. Tsiang indicated again his disapproval of Outer Mongolia.[125] The United States, the United Kingdom, France and Turkey spoke in favor of the Chinese amendment.[126] The Soviet delegate strongly desired postponing his vetoing the admission of Korea and Viet-Nam until after the vote on the eighteen applicants or, at the least, to have the Council vote on the whole slate, including Korea and Viet-Nam, in the chronological order of their applicants. A formal proposal to this effect was not adopted, there being only one vote in favor (the U.S.S.R.), eight against and two abstentions (Iran, Turkey).

The historic moment was then at hand for voting on the Brazilian-New Zealand proposal. The first paragraph was adopted by 8 votes to none, with 3 abstentions (Belgium, China, United States), and the opening words of paragraph 2 ("Having considered separately the applications for membership of") was adopted by 9 votes to none, with 2 abstentions (China, United States).[127] It is curious that the incongruity of this procedure does not seem to have struck any of the delegations. As a factual statement, which it purports to be, these words are inaccurate. The Council had not yet considered, that is, voted on, any of the applications; as a matter of fact, it was about to embark upon a long and tedious exercise in voting. The President next put to the vote the inclusion of Korea. It was not included, the vote being 9 in favor, 1 against (U.S.S.R.), and 1 abstention (New Zealand). The result of voting on Viet-Nam was identic. Albania was included by a vote of 7 in favor, none against, and 4 abstentions (Belgium, China, France, United States). The dreaded bombshell fell in the voting on Outer Mongolia: there were 8 votes in favor, 1 against (China), and 2 abstentions (Belgium, United States).[128] At this point, Mr. Lodge (U.S.A.) asked the President:

> Is it not possible that, in spite of the omission of the Mongolian People's Republic from the list, the Council could well propose to the General Assembly the admission of seventeen new Members?

This attempt to substitute one "package" for another failed; the President turned it down as he could not accept any proposals while voting was in progress.[129] From then on voting became a mechanical process and the axe fell inexorably. The Soviet Union vetoed all applicants except its own candidates, all of which, it should be noted, received the necessary majority.[130] The President then put to the vote the second paragraph as a whole as

[124] S/P.V.704 (Dec. 13, 1955) at 3–4, 10.

[125] *Ibid.* at 8. "This is a difficult moment for me," he admitted, "and a very important moment for me. In replying to you, Sir, I have to fall back on the words of a great historical figure in European history, 'Ich kann nicht anders,' 'I cannot do otherwise.' " Mr. Sobolev's comment may be noted: "Actually, nothing else was to be expected from a person whose days, perhaps even hours, in the United Nations are numbered."

[126] *Ibid.* at 6, 8, 9, 10.

[127] *Ibid.* at 23.

[128] *Ibid.* at 24.

[129] *Ibid.* at 25.

[130] The result of voting was as follows: Jordan 10:1 (U.S.S.R.); Ireland 10:1 (U.S.S.R.); Portugal 10:1 (U.S.S.R.); Hungary 9:0:2 (China, United States); Italy 10:1 (U.S.S.R.); Austria 10:1 (U.S.S.R.); Rumania 9:0:2 (China, United States); Bulgaria 9:0:2 (China, United States); Finland 10:1 (U.S.S.R.); Ceylon 10:1 (U.S.S.R.); Nepal 10:1 (U.S.S.R.); Libya 10:1 (U.S.S.R.), Cambodia 10:1 (U.S.S.R.); Japan 10:1 (U.S.S.R.); Laos 10:1 (U.S.S.R.); Spain 9:1 (U.S.S.R.): 1

amended: "Having considered separately the applications for membership of Albania, Hungary, Romania, and Bulgaria." As there was one vote in favor (U.S.S.R.), four against (Brazil, China, Peru, Turkey), and six abstentions, the President correctly announced that the paragraph was "not carried," and continued:

> There is nothing to recommend to the General Assembly. Accordingly, I will not put to the vote the last paragraph of the draft resolution. The resolution as a whole falls to the ground.[131]

This was a curious turn in the proceedings. It could hardly be denied that the Council had considered separately the applications of these four states. This was a fact which could not be undone by the vote taken. Nor would there have been any harm in affirming this fact. Having voted for the second paragraph as amended, the President should have put to the vote the third paragraph: "Recommends to the General Assembly the admission of the above-named countries," namely, Albania, Hungary, Rumania and Bulgaria. This paragraph would then have failed to receive the requisite majority and would not have been adopted.

Be that as it may, the carefully planned and expertly piloted proposal to end the deadlock over admission failed. There was from the outset some apprehension lest the maneuver flounder on the position of China. This was quite as inflexible as was the Soviet's "18 or none." Moreover, the Chinese representative could not have been unaware of the likely, if not, in the circumstances, inevitable consequences of his action. He, more than anyone else, was satisfied that the joint draft resolution represented nothing but a "package deal," that it was "18 or none,"[132] and that the majority—whether it involved a sacrifice of principles and possibly of Article 4 of the Charter or not—was prepared to bow to Soviet intransigeance in order to promote a higher principle, that of universality. The United States, too, had it in its power to oppose the "deal" actively but opted in favor of a position of "no support" and apparently of "no opposition" as well.

In the debate the President pointed out, correctly, it is felt, that the problem's solution

> depends, as it has depended in the past, on the great Powers. Our present failure does not, of course, rest on all the great Powers. It rests on those which have incurred a great respon-

(Belgium). *Ibid.* at 26–32. It is remarkable that throughout the voting the President never used the term "veto" or "rejected" but correctly stated: "As the negative vote was cast by a permanent member of the Security Council, the name of . . . is not included." It would be most desirable if this example were emulated by other Presidents of the Security Council.

131 *Ibid.* at 33.

132 Speaking in the Security Council on Dec. 13, 1955, only a few hours before the voting, Mr. Tsiang, summing up his position in an eloquent and moving address, said: "The Soviet Union stand is: eighteen or none. According to the speeches here on Saturday, I understand that the sponsors and the supporters of this draft resolution answer: yes, all eighteen. Therefore, in the substance of this matter, the sponsors and the supporters again made a total surrender to the dictates of the Soviet Union. There is no compromise, there is no consideration of the viewpoint of the other delegations; that is the naked nature of this paragraph." Doc. S/P.V.703 at 8-9.

sibility and which have adopted rigidly negative attitudes in the consideration of this problem. I hope and pray that those attitudes will be modified.[133]

Sir Leslie Munro's prayer was answered with surprising promptness. On the day following, December 14, 1955, the Soviet Union requested an urgent meeting of the Council. The Council met in the afternoon to receive from Mr. Sobolev a statement to the effect that

> the Soviet Union withdraws its negative vote with respect to a number of States and will vote for their admission, but not for that of Japan, on the understanding and the expectation that the question of the admission of Japan and the Mongolian People's Republic, for which no positive solution was provided yesterday by a recommendation of the Security Council, will be referred to the next session of the General Assembly.[134]

On the instructions of the U.S.S.R. Government, he submitted the following proposal:

> The Security Council, . . .
>
> Having considered separately the applications for membership of Albania, Jordan, Ireland, Portugal, Hungary, Italy, Austria, Romania, Bulgaria, Finland, Ceylon, Nepal, Libya, Cambodia, Laos and Spain,
>
> Recommends to the General Assembly the admission of the above-named countries to the United Nations.[135]

After a brief recess, the Council resumed and Mr. Lodge moved that Japan be added to the list. The representatives of the United Kingdom, Brazil, Turkey, Peru, France and China declared at once that they would support the United States amendment and Mr. Sobolev announced that he would vote against it.[136] The President put the various parts of the resolution to the vote. The first paragraph was adopted by 8 votes in favor, none against and 3 abstentions (Belgium, China, United States); the introductory words of paragraph 2 were adopted by 9 votes in favor, none against, and 2 abstentions (China, United States); as the vote on the American amendment concerning Japan was 10 votes in favor, 1 (U.S.S.R.) against, it was not adopted, the negative vote having been cast by a permanent member. The rest of the voting on the 16 applicants was routine;[137] the second paragraph as a whole was carried by 8 votes in favor, none against and 3 abstentions

[133] Doc. S/P.V. 704, at 45. Like Sir Leslie Munro, Sir Pierson Dixon (United Kingdom) was of the opinion that both permanent members, in casting vetoes, have abused the veto. *Ibid.* at 46. Mr. Sobolev, defending the Soviet Union against the charge of rigidity and inflexibility, pointed out that in fact the Soviet Union had not maintained an uncompromising attitude. At the beginning of the Tenth Session of the Assembly the Soviet Union proposed the admission of sixteen states. In the course of the session, it agreed to support the additional candidacy of both Japan and Spain. *Ibid.* 46 f.

[134] Doc. S/P.V.705 (Dec. 14, 1955) at 3.

[135] *Ibid.* at 4–7.

[136] *Ibid.* at 4–7–9–10.

[137] The vote on Albania was 8:0:3 (Belgium, China, U.S.); on Jordan, Ireland, and Portugal unanimous; Hungary 9:0:2 (China, U. S.); Italy and Austria unanimous; Rumania and Bulgaria 9:0:2 (China, U. S.); Finland, Ceylon, Nepal, Libya, Cambodia, and Laos unanimous; Spain 10:0:1 (Belgium). *Ibid.* at 12–21.

(Belgium, China, United States); the last paragraph was adopted by the same vote; the draft resolution as a whole received the identic votes.[138]

Before any of the members of the Council had an opportunity to explain their vote, the United States representative introduced a resolution recommending to the General Assembly the admission of Japan at its eleventh regular session and asked for immediate consideration.[139] The President of the Council promptly and in writing informed the President of the Assembly of the decision of the Council, and Sir Pierson Dixon urged the "quickest possible endorsement of the sixteen whose admission we approved this afternoon."[140] Consideration of the new American proposal was therefore postponed.

The General Assembly meeting within hours after the decisive vote in the Security Council proceeded with unusual dispatch, perhaps even some haste. The business before the Assembly was a draft resolution proposed by 30 Members and 11 additional co-sponsors, that is, by altogether one more than the required two-thirds majority.[141] The text was as follows:

> The General Assembly,
>
> Having received the recommendation of the Security Council of 14 December 1955 that the following countries should be admitted to membership in the United Nations: . . .
>
> Having considered the application for membership of each of these countries,
>
> Decides to admit the above-mentioned sixteen countries to membership in the United Nations.[142] At the request of Cuba, the President, who apparently had no intention of so doing, said that a vote could be taken on each of the applicants separately.[143] No vote was taken on the first part of paragraph 1 of the draft resolution. As each of the applicants received more than the required two-thirds majority,[144] the President suggested that "if the Assembly agrees, we must avoid a vote on the draft resolution as a whole." Since there was no objection, he declared that "the draft resolution as a whole is adopted, note being taken of the abstention of Cuba."[145]

[138] *Ibid.* at 22.

[139] *Ibid.* at 23.

[140] *Ibid.* at 39–40, 41.

[141] Afghanistan, Argentina, Brazil, Burma, Canada, Chile, Colombia, Costa Rica, Denmark, Ecuador, Egypt, El Salvador, Ethiopia, India, Indonesia, Iran, Iraq, Lebanon, Liberia, New Zealand, Nicaragua, Norway, Panama, Peru, Philippines, Saudi Arabia, Sweden, Syria, Uruguay, Yugoslavia, Bolivia, Byelorussian Soviet Socialist Republic, Czechoslovakia, Iceland, Honduras, Pakistan, Poland, Thailand, Ukrainian Soviet Socialist Republic, Union of Soviet Socialist Republics and Yemen.

[142] Doc. A/P.V.555 at 3.

[143] *Ibid.*

[144] The result of voting was as follows: Albania 48:3 (Cuba, Greece, China): 5 (Dominican Republic, Netherlands, Philippines, United States, Belgium); Jordan 55:0:1 (Israel); Ireland, Portugal: unanimous; Hungary 49:2 (China, Cuba): 5 (Greece, Netherlands, Philippines, United States, Dominican Republic); Italy, Austria: unanimous; Rumania 49:2 (China, Cuba): 5 (same as in case of Hungary); Bulgaria 50:2 (China, Cuba): 5 (same as in case of Hungary); Finland, Ceylon, Nepal; unanimous; Libya 56:0:1 (Israel); Cambodia, Laos: unanimous; Spain: 55:0:2 (Belgium, Mexico). *Ibid.* at 4–22.

[145] *Ibid.* at 23–25. South Africa, Paraguay and Haiti were absent during the voting; Ethiopia was absent during the voting on the first eight applicants. However, Paraguay and Haiti requested subsequently that their votes be "registered." Paraguay desired to "register" its abstention with regard to Albania, Hungary, Rumania and Bulgaria; the delegates of Haiti and Ethiopia declared that they supported all 16 applicants. The General Assembly "decided" to "record" the votes of these three delegations. A/P.V.556 (Dec. 15, 1955) at 3–5, 52, 61. It is difficult to see how the Assembly, in view of the fact that there was no vote on the draft resolution as a whole, could decide to "record" abstentions except in a purely

It is unnecessary to review in detail the explanations of votes which the delegate of Ethiopia properly called "a parade of jubilation."[146] Regrets were, of course, frequently voiced that Japan was still outside the fold; the Soviet Union, on the other hand, bestowed her regrets equally upon Japan and Outer Mongolia. With a sense of humor, rare in these debates of the Assembly, Mr. Palamas (Greece) noted that one of the results of the "large admissions of today is that the number of observers to the United Nations will be greatly reduced." He added:

> Perhaps the day is not very far off when the role of observer will be left to our dear friend, Mr. Lindt, the Swiss observer. Mr. Lindt is in fact the only observer who is satisfied with his role and who is not discouraged in observing us.[147]

This tribute to the wisdom of the Swiss representative may well raise the question of the Swiss admission to the United Nations. As Article 43 of the Charter has so far remained unfulfilled, and in view of the broad-minded interpretation of Article 4 which has been adopted by the Security Council and the General Assembly, there would seem to be no reason why Switzerland should not be invited to the United Nations. A truly broad-minded construction of Article 4 need not even exclude a recognition of the special services which Switzerland has traditionally rendered to mankind during its worst crises and of her status which made such services possible. As host to so many activities of the United Nations and international conferences generally, Switzerland well deserves such an invitation.

## VII. WHEN IS A "PACKAGE DEAL" A "PACKAGE DEAL"?

The United States initiative regarding Japan, already referred to, was to lead to a re-opening of the debate in the Security Council on the package deal. The immediate cause of this was the Soviet counter-proposal that the Security Council should recommend to the Assembly "that it admit the Mongolian People's Republic and Japan to the United Nations at its eleventh regular session."[148] In the debate it was pointed out by several delegates that the latter was in the nature of a new "package deal" in that it made the admission of Japan contingent upon the simultaneous admission of Outer Mongolia, and that for this reason it was unconstitutional, being contrary to Article 4.[149] The repre-

formal sense "for the record." On the other hand, it is interesting to note that China, Belgium and the United States, which had abstained, did not request that they be registered as abstaining on the draft resolution as a whole.

146 Doc. A/P.V.556 (Dec. 15, 1955) at 36. It is interesting to note that in the list of those who were regarded as instrumental in steering the organs of the United Nations towards the "solution" of the problem of membership the names of Messrs. Martin (Canada), Belaunde (Peru), Maza (Chile), Sir Leslie Munro (New Zealand), and Dag Hammarskjöld, the Secretary General of the United Nations, were frequently included.

147 *Ibid.* at 12.

148 Doc. S/P.V.706 (Dec. 15, 1955) at 5–10, and Doc. S/3512.

149 See observations by Peru, Doc. S/P.V.706 (Dec. 15, 1955) at 33, 44–45, Belgium, at 39, France at 41, Iran at 46, U.K., Doc. S/P.V.708 (Dec. 21, 1955) at 4–5 f. Neither of the resolutions was adopted by the Council. The American draft resolution received 10 votes in favor, 1 against (U.S.S.R.), and the Soviet draft received 1 vote in favor (U.S.S.R.), while 10 abstained. Doc. S/P.V.706 at 50. A very similar discussion was provoked by a British proposal declaring Japan to be fully qualified for membership and a Soviet amendment declaring both Outer Mongolia and Japan to be fully qualified and expressing the hope that both would soon be admitted. *Ibid.* at 51–55, and Doc. S/P.V.708 at 2. The "unequal" package deal was opposed by France, *ibid.* at 11; the U.S., *ibid.* at 12–13; Belgium, *ibid.* at 14; Turkey, *ibid.* at 21; Iran, *ibid.* at 23. Later in the proceedings the Soviet amendment was voted upon, but received only one vote in favor (U.S.S.R.),

sentative of Brazil declared that his country was "determined not to accept a package deal every time an application is submitted" and that

> A package deal has been accepted once, with our support, though a separate vote was nevertheless taken on each application. That is enough. In future, only one application must be considered at a time, and there must be no bargaining.[150]

This admission is most revealing. Brazil was certainly in a key position to appreciate the nature of the recent negotiations. Mr. Tsiang hoped that "the 'package deal' is over," and Mr. Belaunde stated that the General Assembly resolution "was based on a friendly agreement" which had been partially broken.[151] Sir Leslie Munro, speaking as the representative of New Zealand, who was as familiar with the background of the negotiations as was the representative of Brazil, had a different version of the events:

> I must make it clear that New Zealand's readiness to vote individually for the eighteen candidates can in no way be construed as implying agreement with the view that a permanent member of the Security Council may legally make its favourable vote on one applicant depend on the simultaneous admission of another. It is quite a different matter to assert, as we do, that a solution of the new members problem depends primarily on the reaching of an understanding among the great Powers. Such an understanding, this year, proved possible in respect of sixteen, but not eighteen applicants.[152]

Sir Leslie's distinction is perhaps too subtle to be perceived. For, was the understanding among the permanent members, if there was one, not in the nature of an agreement to admit a group of states and to make the admission of one sub-group dependent on the admission of the numerically larger sub-group? This seems to have been the understanding of Mr. Sobolev, when he reminded his colleagues that the majority of the members of the Council "not only regarded the resolution as a single whole, but acted accordingly." He specifically reminded them that after the so-called people's democracies received the requisite majority, "the Security Council did not stop there but continued the proceedings and annulled its earlier decisions by voting on the resolution as a whole."[153]

As in the opinion of Mr. Lodge a "package deal" had been involved which the United States "did not support," it was therefore left to Sir Pierson Dixon to refute the Soviet assertion of an "understanding," and that the United Kingdom had been a party to a "package deal." A package deal, as he defined it, was "making the admission of one applicant contingent on the admission of another." The mere inclusion of "a number of applicants for admission . . . in the same resolution does not . . . constitute a package

while 10 members abstained. The consideration of the British proposal was postponed by the Council, with the Soviet Union abstaining. *Ibid.* at 34, 36.

150 *Ibid.* at 15.

151 *Ibid.* at 17, 19–20.

152 *Ibid.* at 24.

153 *Ibid.* at 26. The Soviet representative was in error in stating that the resolution was voted as a whole. This was not the case, though it is true that in effect the affirmative decisions taken individually were annulled or more correctly voted as not having taken place. See above, p. 633.

deal. If such a resolution is presented, it is still possible for each member of the Council to consider each applicant on its merits and it is possible to take a separate vote on each applicant. This in fact is what happened on the occasion to which the Soviet Union referred," namely the admission of the 16 applicants. That the United Kingdom Delegation was not party to any "deal" or arrangement is shown by the fact, argued Sir Pierson, that his delegation and other delegations "voted for Bulgaria and the other Communist applicants *after* the Soviet vetoes had started to fall. Was his attitude consistent with a package deal? No, Mr. President."[154]

It is immaterial, it is submitted, that the majority of the Security Council members continued to vote for the Communist applicants after the Soviets began to veto the Western candidates. The decisive fact and probably conclusive evidence of a "package" though not necessarily of a "deal" was the vote following the voting on the individual applicants. It was this vote which wiped out the favorable votes given separately to each of the four Communist applicants. It was by this vote that the majority of the Security Council demonstrated that the admission of this group of states which it had declared qualified for membership, was made contingent upon the simultaneous admission of the larger Western-supported group of states. The majority meant to hold the Soviet Union to its position of all or none, or as it turned out to be, sixteen or none. The admission of the sixteen was no doubt a "package" admission as defined by Sir Pierson even if perhaps it was not a "deal," in the sense of a preconceived and formalized arrangement.[155]

## VIII. CONCLUSION

It remains to consider whether the "package" admission was contrary to the Charter. At this point it is well to make a distinction between Article 4 of the Charter and the interpretation placed upon it by the International Court of Justice in the first Admission Case on the one hand, and the decisions regarding eligibility and admissibility on the other. Regarding the former[156] the Court held that

> The provisions of Article 4 necessarily imply that every application for admission should be examined and voted on separately and on its own merits; otherwise it would be impossible to determine whether a particular applicant fulfils the necessary conditions.[157]

This was done. The eligibility of each of the candidates for admission was voted on separately in both the Security Council and the General Assembly, even though the standard for determining eligibility was reduced to the lowest possible level. It is true that the joint resolution of 28 was adopted as such in both the *Ad Hoc* Political Committee and

[154] *Ibid.* at 30 (emphasis supplied).

[155] But see above, p. 617 ff., and below, p. 638, for statements which indicate the existence of some sort of arrangement or deal.

[156] See Gross, *loc. cit.* at 44, 57. See also *supra* 591, 603.

[157] [1948] I.C.J. Reports 65.

the General Assembly, and without a separate vote on each of the eighteen applicants. However, this resolution was merely a preliminary though essential step in steering the "package" through the Security Council and committing in a sense a large majority of Members to this particular procedure for breaking the deadlock over admissions. It neither determined eligibility nor admissibility in any final or formal sense. This was clearly understood. It was, if the term be permitted, a "trial run" or "dry run" and no more.

How about the decision to admit? The Court held:

> To subject an affirmative vote for the admission of an applicant State to the condition that other States be admitted with that State would prevent Members from exercising their judgment in each case with complete liberty, within the scope of the prescribed conditions. Such a demand is incompatible with the letter and spirit of Article 4 of the Charter.

The Court accordingly was of the opinion that

> a Member of the Organization cannot, while it recognizes the conditions set forth in that provision to be fulfilled by the State concerned, subject its affirmative vote to the additional condition that other States be admitted to membership in the United Nations together with that State.[158]

This, however, is precisely what happened in the Security Council. It is unnecessary to examine the question whether there was "a demand" to subject the vote on admission of one state to the condition that other states be admitted contemporaneously. This pertains to the issue whether there was "a deal" in addition to the "package." The issue largely escapes objective determination.[159] It is scarcely open to doubt, however, that the members of the Security Council, although recognizing that the criteria governing the eligibility of the applicants were satisfied, subjected their admission to the further condition that they be admitted *en bloc* or not at all. This was the position of the Soviet Union, which in effect vetoed the admission of all but the Communist applicants after China had vetoed the admission of Outer Mongolia. This was also the position of the members of the Council, both permanent and non-permanent, which, by their affirmative votes or abstention (China, United States), expressly or tacitly affirmed[160] the eligibility of the

[158] *Ibid.*

[159] Commenting upon the Advisory Opinion of the Court, Charles De Visscher, who was a member of the Court at the time and voted with the majority, observed: "Bien que la question fût en soi une question juridique et que l'Assemblée générale ait par la suite recommandé aux Etats membres de se conformer à la réponse que la Cour y a faite, l'expérience a démontré qu'une consultation ayant un tel objet est dénuée d'intérêt pratique. Rien, en effet, n'oblige les Etats à motiver leurs votes, et les mobiles non exprimés échappent à tout contrôle. En définitive, les données du problème envisagé dans sa réalité totale débordaient le cadre de la question posée." Théories et Réalités du Droit International Public 409 (1953).

[160] The author has argued elsewhere that in cases in which there is the majority required for non-procedural decisions in the Security Council, the abstention by a permanent member has the character of tacit consent. See Gross, "Voting in the Security Council: Abstention from Voting and Absence from Meetings," 60 Yale Law Journal 209–257 at 226 (1951). See also *supra* 429–471. This view has been adopted by Julius Stone, Legal Controls of International Conflict 207 (1954), and Sir Gerald Fitzmaurice, *"Inter Arma Silent Leges,"* 1 Sydney Law Review 332–343 (1955), at 338, note 16: "The practice which has grown up in the Security Council of regarding a resolution as adopted provided no Permanent Member votes against it—i.e. contents itself with an abstention (and this despite the fact that Article 27, paragraph 3, requires a *concurring* vote of the Permanent Members)—is based on the view that silence implies consent."

Communist candidates, but in the end annulled this decision by voting against their admission or by abstaining *en masse* as they were not prepared to see the four Communist states alone admitted to the United Nations while the other applicants remained outside. Thus, in effect, the second injunction formulated by the Court as inherent in Article 4 of the Charter was not observed in the Security Council.

Insofar as the General Assembly is concerned there is strong evidence that at least many of the supporters of the joint resolution of 28 regarded the "solution" as a package which should stand or fall as a whole. Statements to this effect were made by several delegates who endorsed the solution in spite of the fact, if not perhaps because, it was a "package."[161] There is also some evidence that there was a "deal" although it is not possible, for the reason already given, to determine precisely how many or which delegations were involved. Suffice it here to recall the very frank statement made by Sir Percy Spender in the *Ad Hoc* Political Committee:

> Let me emphasize that the intention of the draft resolution is that all eighteen countries should be included. *No one need entertain any apprehension that the sponsors*—who represent a significant proportion of the voters in this Committee, *will fail to honour their commitment in this matter.*[162]

It would seem to follow from this revealing pledge that for many Members, certainly the 28 sponsors for whom Sir Percy spoke, there was a "deal" as well as a "package" involved. In giving it their emphatic support and soliciting that of other Members, they acted contrary to Article 4 of the Charter as interpreted by the International Court of Justice.

The interpretation of the Court, however, is not the only possible one. The text of Article 4 can certainly be understood as involving a separate vote on the eligibility of individual candidates for admission in conformity with paragraph 1 of Article 4. If it is accepted that the process of effectuating the admission of a candidate involves first the determination of its eligibility for, and secondly the decision to admit it to, membership—a process which in the practice of the United Nations is usually not so broken down but telescoped into one decision—then there is no reason to challenge the legality of the procedure adopted for the admission of 18 or 16 applicants in December, 1955.[163] There is nothing in the language of Article 4 which would support the contrary view. Paragraph 1 of Article 4 lays down the criteria governing "the judgment of the Organization" in determining whether a state is eligible for membership. Paragraph 2 of Article 4 lays down the decision by means of which the admission of any state deemed eligible is to be consummated. There are no conditions laid down for this second decision. One or more states may be found to be eligible and yet admission may not take place unless and until the requisite decisions have been made. The practice of the United Nations bears out

[161] See above, pp. 616 ff.
[162] Doc. A/AC.80/P.V.28 (Dec. 5, 1955) at 37 (emphasis supplied).
[163] Gross, *loc. cit.* 57. See also *supra* 603.

the distinction here suggested. Not only has the General Assembly on numerous occasions declared certain states to be fully eligible, but the Security Council has been asked to declare Japan eligible.[164] If it did not do so, it was due to considerations other than the unconstitutionality of such a step. The line of reasoning here suggested would in no way be affected by the view advanced sporadically that a state which is deemed eligible has a right to admission. No such right can be read into Article 4, paragraph 2. However, if so strained an interpretation were preferred, it would not alter the situation in the least, because the admission would still depend on the decisions of the General Assembly and the Security Council. A state which in these circumstances is not admitted has no recourse to a judicial tribunal in order to obtain redress and force its entry into the Organization.

Further support for the view here advanced is to be found in the joint dissenting opinion of Judges Basdevant, Winiarski, Sir Arnold McNair and Read, and even in the separate opinions of Judges Alvarez and Azevedo in the first admission case.[165] The element common to these opinions is that the decision to admit a state to membership is a political decision and therefore subject to political considerations. The interpretation suggested above does not rest upon this ground. On the contrary, it agrees with the view of the majority that neither the political character of the organs affecting admission nor the political character of the decision itself can release these organs from the limitations on their powers and the criteria for their judgment established by the Charter. Rather the interpretation is derived solely from the fact that although paragraph 1 of Article 4 established limitations upon, and criteria for determining, the eligibility of a state, paragraph 2 of Article 4 established no limitations upon, or criteria for decision of, the organs of the United Nations with respect to admission. It is true that the Court considered and rejected this interpretation on the ground that Article 4, paragraph 2, was concerned solely with the "procedure" of admission, while paragraph 1 laid down the "substantive law." In the opinion of the Court it is this substantive law which governs both the determination of eligibility as well as the admission of a state to membership.[166] This construction is clearly not based upon the text of Article 4, paragraph 2, but rather upon the view that this provision is solely concerned with "procedure." However, decisions on procedure do not exclude substantive consideration as the Court seems to assume. Moreover, the decision to admit a state is legally not a procedural but a substantive decision governed by voting rules relating to "important questions" or non-procedural decisions under Articles 18, paragraph 2, and 27, paragraph 3, respectively. It may be useful to point out that both the question addressed to the Court by the Assembly and the operating part of the Court's holding were in terms on paragraph 1 of Article 4.[167] Thus the Court's opinion is authoritative for the interpretation of this part of Article 4 and not for the interpretation of paragraph 2.

[164] See above, p. 634, the United Kingdom proposal of Dec. 15, 1955, that the Security Council take note "that Japan is fully qualified for membership of the United Nations. . . ." Doc. S/P.V.706 (Dec. 15, 1955) at 51–55.

[165] [1948] I.C.J. Reports 57, 91 ff., 71, 81.

[166] *Ibid.*64.

[167] *Ibid.* 58, 65.

These considerations suggest the conclusion that a "package" or *en bloc* admission, that is, the admission of one state or of a group of states on condition that another state or group of states be admitted contemporaneously, is not contrary to Article 4 of the Charter. This view of the legal aspects of the matter does not, of course, dispose of the moral issues involved nor is it concerned with the political wisdom of the action.

It remains to point out a totally different problem posed by the admission of the group of sixteen states to membership. For the first time the United Nations admitted to membership states which are "enemy States" within the meaning of Articles 53 and 107 of the Charter. Hungary, Italy, Rumania, Bulgaria, and Finland, by virtue of he Peace Treaties made with them, certainly fall into this category. Both clauses permit as exception notably to Article 2, paragraph 4, action against any enemy state or action "directed against renewal of aggressive policy on the party of any such State." On the other hand, Article 2, paragraph 1, declares that "the Organization is based on the principle of the sovereign equality of all its Members." There appears to emerge a conflict between these three clauses which it would be highly desirable to resolve and thus to remove any shadow of doubt regarding the status of the "enemy States" as full-fledged Members of the Organization.[168] This is certainly technically possible with regard to Article 53, paragraph 1, for according to this the exceptional regime which it establishes for "enemy States" shall continue "until such time as the Organization may, on request of the Governments concerned, be charged with the responsibility for preventing further aggression by such a State." There is no comparable provision for terminating the applicability of Article 107. And even Article 53, paragraph 1, fails to name the organ which is to assume the aforementioned obligation on behalf of the Organization. Short of an amendment to the Charter clarifying the meaning of both Articles 53, paragraph 1, and 107, as regards enemy states admitted as "peace-loving" states to the United Nations, it would seem most desirable for the General Assembly to express the sense of the Organization on this issue. The large reservoir of competence bestowed upon the General Assembly by Article 10 of the Charter would amply provide the constitutional foundation for such a resolution.

The Tenth Session of the General Assembly took a long step towards achieving universality, even though some essential states like Germany and Japan remain outside. Europe and Asia will be more adequately represented in numbers though not necessarily in spirit. An additional sixteen states have been brought formally under the rule of the law of the Charter. In particular, the admission of Italy and Portugal puts an end to the controversy over the constitutionality of NATO, inasmuch as there is no need any longer

[168] Hans Kelsen, The Law of the United Nations 813 (1951), argues that "the ex-enemy states are, in principle, outside the law of the Charter. This outlawry is permanent; for, according to the wording of Article 107, it is not terminated by the admission of an ex-enemy state to the Organization. The definition of the term 'enemy state' in Article 53, paragraph 2, applies also to states after they have become Members of the United Nations." The learned author adds that this probably was not intended by the draftsmen of the Charter. But see the ambiguous statements in the official British Commentary on the Charter, Misc. Cmd. 6666, p. 9, and the Hearings before the Committee on Foreign Relations, U. S. Senate, 79th Cong., 1st Sess., on the Charter of the United Nations (1945), pp. 302 ff.

to stretch the applicability of Article 51 to include armed attack upon states non-Members of the United Nations. Further and perhaps decisive progress has been made towards the institutional centralization of the largest segment of the otherwise decentralized society of nations. All these gains, however, do not by themselves portend a lasting lessening of tensions. A great deal of statesmanship on all sides will be required if the United Nations is to grow into an effective instrument for the maintenance of international peace and security as well as for the maintenance of law and justice.

# THE UNITED NATIONS AND THE UNITED STATES

## I.

The direction and the process of United Nations activities since the late '60s have been a matter of concern to the United States. A good deal has been written about the circumstances which resulted in the loss of United States leadership in the United Nations and about the new "tyrannical" majority, its ideological motivations,[1] its scant regard for the law of the Charter and the accepted rules of procedure, the desire of the Third World, in particular, for a greater share in the decision-making process and for real, not merely nominal, equality. There are also prescriptions for adapting United States policy to the changed circumstances and building a new world order.[2] They range from suggestions, based presumably on the old adage: vox populi vox dei, that the United States should get along with the Third World to suggestions that the United States should go into opposition and take its stand on the rule of law and in defense of the values of liberal democracy against totalitarianism.[3]

It is not the purpose of this essay to evaluate any particular analysis of the present

[1] Thus, for instance, *Stanley Hoffmann*, in his recent book Primacy or World Order (New York: McGraw/Hill, 1978) observed that since about 1967/68 "Washington has lost control of the General Assembly. The resolutions adopted by it under the leadership of the Group of 77 underdeveloped countries are more remarkable for their ideological effervescence than for their capacity to create a balanced world order." *Ibid.*, p. 86.

[2] See for example *David A. Kay* (ed.), The Changing United Nations. Options for the United States (New York: Praeger, 1977); *Seymour M. Finger* and *Joseph R. Habert* (eds.), U.S. Policy in International Institutions: Defining Reasonable Options in an Unreasonable World (Boulder, Col., Westview Press, 1978); *Cyril E. Black* and *Richard A. Falk* (eds.), The Future of the International Legal Order, Volume IV, The Structure of the International Environment (Princeton, N.J., Princeton University Press, 1972).

[3] *D. P. Moynihan* with *Suzanne Weaver*, A Dangerous Place (Boston: Little Brown & Co., 1978).

condition or any specific policies. Rather it is to suggest some points for consideration about the course of events which, in the view of some authors, transformed the United Nations into "a dangerous place".[4]

II.

In preparing for the future international organization, the overriding concern of the United States was to prevent the debacle of 1919. Accordingly, the restrictive provisions which characterized the League of Nations Covenant and to which the Senate objected had to be omitted.[5] Thus, automatic military and political commitments had to be avoided, the domestic jurisdiction exception had to be clarified, the functions of the assembly and the council had to be separated, and since some sort of majority vote in these organs seemed unavoidable, it was necessary that all politically and militarily relevant action be concentrated in the council where the United States, along with some other great powers, would have the right to veto any action inimical to its interests.

Thus, unlike Article 15(8) of the Covenant of the League, Article 2(7) of the Charter contains no reference to international law, it refers to matters "essentially" and not "solely" within domestic jurisdiction, it was made applicable to the whole Charter by being placed among the "Purposes and Principles" and above all, contrary to the Covenant, it omitted to designate an organ as qualified to decide whether the exception was well-founded in law. Instead, it includes the qualification that "nothing contained in the present Charter . . . shall require the Members to submit such matters to settlement under the present Charter.". The interpretation of these words by the United States was promptly made explicit in the so-called Connally amendment to the Declaration of August 14, 1946, whereby the United States accepted the compulsory jurisdiction of the I.C.J. The Declaration shall not apply to matters essentially within the domestic jurisdiction of the United States "as determined by the United States of America". Clearly the United States assumed that it could unilaterally and peremptorily determine which matters fell essentially into its reserved domain.[6]

Finally, Article 2(7) exempts from its scope "the application of enforcement measures under Chapter VII". This text originated in an Australian proposal. Its purpose was, and still is, to prevent the Security Council from making recommendations regarding a dispute under the pretext or in the guise of a threat to the peace.[7]

The Charter is quite consistent in separating the functions of the General Assembly

[4] *A. Yeselson* and *A. Gaglione*, A Dangerous Place: The United Nations as a Weapon in World Politics (New York: Grossmann Publishers, 1974).

[5] For more detailed analysis, see *Leo Gross*, "The Charter of the United Nations and the Lodge Reservations,", AJIL, Vol. 41 (1947), pp. 531–554. See also *supra* at 563–583.

[6] For more detailed analysis, see *Leo Gross*, "Bulgaria Invokes the Connally Amendment", AJIL, Vol. 56 (April 1962), pp. 357–382. See also *infra*.

[7] As stated by the Australian Delegation, the aim was to discourage States from using or threatening force "in any dispute arising out of a matter of domestic jurisdiction, in the hope of inducing the Security Council to extort concessions from the state that is threatened". Doc. 969, I/1/39, June 14, 1945, UNCIO Documents, Vol. 6, p. 438.

and the Security Council. Chapter VII "Action with Respect to Threats to the Peace, Breaches of the Peace, and Acts of Aggression" was entrusted exclusively to the Security Council. And it is the Council's primary responsibility to take "prompt and effective action", as stated in Article 24(1) for the maintenance of international peace and security. The scope of the Assembly's competence is as wide as the Charter, but when questions relating to the maintenance of international peace and security are concerned "on which action is necessary", such questions shall be referred to the Council in accordance with Article 11(2). The separation of functions is also recognized in Article 12(1) which enjoins the Assembly from making any recommendation with regard to disputes or situations of which the Council is seized unless requested to do so by the Council. It seems that the Council has never exercized this option.

Quite clearly, there is nothing "automatic" about the Council's action. There must be an appropriate resolution or decision and this requires, in accordance with Article 27(3), as amended in 1965, the vote of a qualified majority of 9 members, including the concurring votes of the permanent members on all non-procedural matters. It follows from the wording of this clause that the question whether a matter is procedural requires the same qualified majority. *Ex abundante cautela* this was made explicit in the Four Power Statement on voting in the Security Council with which France associated itself.[8] Thus the voting requirement is as stringent as the action of the Council is politically important. This is as it should be because in Article 25 the Members of the United Nations undertook the unprecedented commitment "to accept and carry out the decisions of the Security Council in accordance with the present Charter". However, it was "safe" for the United States to accept this commitment because there could be no decision to which it objected. The practice not to regard the abstention by a permanent member as contrary to Article 27 (3) was certainly unconstitutional but has become no threat to the United States, although it may have weakened the prestige and effectiveness of the Council.[9]

By contrast, the voting requirement for the General Assembly is relatively easy and is in keeping with its functions to discuss any matter and make recommendations thereto. Article 18 (2) provides for a two-thirds majority of the Members present and voting for important questions generally and for certain specifically listed questions. Unlike in the Council the question whether a two-thirds majority is required may be decided in accordance with Article 18(3) by a majority of the Members present and voting. To be sure, in some matters—such as admission, suspension and expulsion of members—the resolution of the Assembly is legally conclusive but in all these matters a recommendation by the Council is required as a prior condition. The recommendation in turn demands a qualified majority. The most significant exception to this general arrangement is the decision in the budget, and this was to lead to a serious crisis in the '60s.

It is indicative of the spirit in which the United Nations embarked on its career of

[8] Doc. 852, III/1/37/(1) in *UNCIO* Documents, Vol. 11, June 8, 1945, p. 714.

[9] *Leo Gross*, "Voting in the Security Council: Abstention in the Post-1965 Amendment Phase and Its Impact on Article 25 of the Charter." AJIL, Vol. 62 (1968), pp. 315–334. See also *supra*, pp. 511–530.

majoritarianism that even the easy voting rules in Article 18 paragraphs 2 and 3 were found too confining. Accordingly, in order to make the adoption of resolutions even easier, the Assembly included in its Rules of Procedure of 1947, Rule 88, which reads: "For the purpose of these rules, the phrase 'Members present and voting' means Members casting an affirmative or negative vote. Members which abstain from voting are considered as not voting." There can be no question that this rule is unconstitutional, being clearly contrary to the text of Article 18(1): "Each member of the General Assembly shall have one vote." By not counting the votes of the abstaining members, Rule 88 deprives them of their vote. In practice, this did not make any difference since the resolutions were not binding in any event and most frequently were adopted by more than a two-thirds majority. However, Rule 88 could make a difference in marginal cases. Thus in two recent cases in which the United States made efforts of Homeric proportions to prevent the adoption of the resolutions, they were adopted only because of Rule 88. Thus resolution 2758 (XXVI) of October 21, 1971 on the "Restoration of the lawful rights of the People's Republic of China" which ended 21 years of American maneuvers to keep it out of the United Nations, was adopted by a vote of 76 in favor, 35 against, and 17 abstentions. If the abstentions had been counted as provided for in the Charter, the necessary two-thirds majority would have been 84 and not 76.

The other, and more recent case, occurred on November 10, 1975, when the Assembly adopted resolution 3379 (XXX) in which it determined "that Zionism is a form of racism and racial discrimination".[10] The vote on this resolution was 72 in favor, 35 against, and 32 abstentions. If the abstentions had been counted, the required majority would have been 92 and the resolution would have been declared rejected.

However, no matter how the voting rules are manipulated there can be no doubt that, first, there is no trace in the Charter apart from the above mentioned exceptions, of any intention to depart from or modify the principle of international law that a State cannot be bound without its consent. If any confirmation were needed for this proposition, it is provided for in Article 2(1). Second, there is nothing in the Charter to support the attribution of legislative authority to the General Assembly. A proposal to this effect was made and rejected at the San Francisco Conference. The practice of the United Nations in this realm has been altogether too controversial and too issue-oriented to warrant the proposition that some kind of rule of customary international law developed in this matter.[11] Generally speaking, the resolutions of the Assembly—over four thousand—

[10] On the diplomatic background of this resolution, see *Moynihan* and *Weaver*, loc. cit., pp. 169–200.

[11] The above may seem to be contradicted by certain *dicta* of the International Court of Justice in the *Namibia*, and recalled in the *Western Sahara* cases. I.C.J. *Reports* 1971, p. 31, 1975, p. 32, para. 56. Referring to the development of international law in regard to non-self-governing territories since the League of Nations, the Court declared in the *Namibia* case that it "must take into consideration the changes which have occurred in the supervening half-century, and its interpretation cannot remain unaffected by the subsequent development of law, through the Charter of the United Nations and by way of customary law". In his Separate Opinion in the *Western Sahara* case, Judge Dillard called "attention to the fact that the present Opinion is forthright in proclaiming the existence of the 'right' (to self-determination) in so far as the present proceedings are concerned". *Reports* 1975, p. 121. See also Separate Opinion of Judge de Castro *ibid.*, pp. 169–171.

received from the variegated audiences to which they were addressed, the consideration which they deserved.

## III.

The Charter was certainly a blueprint for action but its scope and procedures were circumscribed not merely because it was necessary to protect the minority against the majority but because it was imperative not to encroach upon the sovereign equality of any Members. If the Charter had been applied the Organization might well have become more static than dynamic, but the United States and its allies were determined to make it work in order to achieve its purposes, even at the expense of its principles. To understand the process fully, it would be necessary to discuss the legal training of American representatives and their peculiar experience with the evolution of the American Constitution and the New Deal. This is not possible here and it must simply be posited that they transferred this experience from the domestic to the international arena without much thought to the profound difference between them. The Charter was not to be interpreted as a multilateral treaty, which it still is, but as the constitution of an institution designed to accomplish lofty purposes.[12] Of these, the maintenance of international peace and security was the most important and was invoked in the Iranian question, the first case to come before the Security Council.It was brought before the Council on March 18, 1946, pursuant to Article 35(1) as "a dispute between Iran and the USSR, the continuance of which was likely to endanger the maintenance of international peace and security". The Soviet representative stated that the situation in Iran could not be regarded as a threat of this nature, and that the conditions "necessary for the inclusion of the Iranian question in the agenda had not been satisfied".[13] The Soviet representative thus seemed to call for a decision on the preliminary question whether the Council was competent to deal with the Iranian complaint. Moreover, in order to resolve this question, it would have been necessary to resolve the pre-preliminary question whether the mandatory abstention provision in Article 27(3) applied to the vote on the preliminary question.[14]

The Council, neither then nor in subsequent cases, was inclined to resolve preliminary, let alone the pre-preliminary, questions. A Soviet request to postpone consideration

Whether these *dicta* have resolved the difficult problem of self-determination cannot be discussed any further in this essay. They certainly are indicative of the degree to which the Court acclimatized itself to the rhetoric prevailing in the political organs of the United Nations.

[12] It was natural, therefore, for Americans to invoke the great landmark cases, such as *McCulloch v. Maryland*, 3 Wheaton 406 (1819) and *Missouri v. Holland*, 252 U.S. 430, 433 (1920). In the former, the opinion was written by Chief Justice Marshall, the great architect of the Constitution, and in the latter by Mr. Justice Oliver Wendell Holmes, regarded as a great liberal jurist. Typically, both cases were cited by the Legal Adviser in the Department of State, Professor A. Chayes, in his oral statement in the *Expenses* case. I.C.J. *Pleadings* (1962), June 21, 1962, p. 425, 426.

See also *Leo Gross*, The United Nations and The International Court of Justice, Recueil des Cours, Vol. 120 (I-1967), pp. 319–439, at pp. 401–404. See also *infra*.

[13] *Yearbook of the United Nations* 1946–1947, p. 330.

[14] This reads as follows: "provided that, in decisions under Chapter VI, and under paragraph 3 of Article 52, a party to a dispute shall abstain from voting".

of the matter was rejected and the Soviet representative "left the Council Chamber". The Council proceeded to adopt some temporizing resolutions, thus implicitly affirming its competence. On April 15, 1946, the Iranian Government informed the Council that in view of Soviet assurances for unconditional evacuation of Iranian territory, it "withdraws its complaint from the Security Council".[15] Normally this should have put an end to the matter. Instead, a major constitutional debate ensued on the question whether the Council, under the Charter, could keep an item on the Agenda without exercizing its authority. The Secretary-General argued that it could not but the majority of the Council thought it could. Here was the first clash between a strict and liberal method of interpretation. This became clear from the discussion in the Committee of Experts in which two arguments were put forward which came to dominate Council debates to this day: the first is that the Council was not a court of justice and the second that the "problem should not be regarded from a purely legalistic point of view".[16] Thus the barrier between legality and arbitrariness, so vital in an international institution, was broken down.

But this was not the end of the matter. A French proposal to remove the item from the agenda was rejected, the Soviet representative walked out again, and the Council adopted, on May 22, 1946, a resolution whereby it adjourned, but remained seized of, the Iranian question. The Iranian question became No. 1 on the list of matters of which the Security Council was seized from 1946 to 1976, when, at the request of Iran, dated September 16, 1976, it was at long last removed from the list.[17]

As stated earlier, a strong protection of the reserved domain was a *conditio sine qua non* for the United States as well as for other Members of the Organization. However, the process of dismantling the procedural safeguards built into the Charter, which started with the Iranian question, continued with the Article 2(7). Of all the articles of the Charter, 111 in all, Article 2(7) was probably more often invoked than any other and usually, unless backed up by the veto, without success.

On June 22, 1946, India introduced in the Assembly the question of the treatment of Indians in the Union of South Africa. India complained that, contrary to the Capetown Agreement concluded in 1927 between India and South Africa, which was renewed in 1932, an Act of the South African Government passed in 1946 "the result of which was the complete segregation of Indians as regards both trade and residence".[18] This was the first time that the issue of *apartheid* was raised in the United Nations. South Africa responded that the Indians were subjects of South Africa, that the Charter imposed no specific obligations regarding fundamental human rights, and that, in any event, the matter was within its domestic jurisdiction. "In view of the fact that the present case would form a precedent for the future",[19] South Africa proposed that the Assembly re-

[15] *Yearbook,* loc. cit., p. 332.
[16] *Ibid.*, p. 333.
[17] See Summary Statement by the Secretary-General on Matters of which the Security Council is seized . . . Doc. S/12269, January 5, 1977, para. 4.
[18] *Yearbook,* loc. cit., p. 144.
[19] *Ibid.*, p. 146.

quest the I.C.J. for an advisory opinion on the question whether the matter was, under Article 2(7), essentially within the domestic jurisdiction of South Africa.

Those who opposed this proposal argued then, as was to be argued many times in future debates, that the political aspects of the question were weightier than the legal ones, that the Members were obligated by the Charter to refrain from discrimination on grounds of race and, to clinch the argument that

> "to treat the Indian question as a *legal* matter would weaken the prestige of the United Nations, one of whose noblest tasks it was to promote respect for human rights and fundamental freedoms".[20]

Those who supported the proposal "stressed the importance of the preliminary legal question of the General Assembly's competence".[21] No doubt, in any organization based on the principle of sovereign equality and endowed with broad yet limited competences, the question of competence must be decided prior to any action on the merits. The United States, France, the United Kingdom, Sweden and Mexico were among the members which favored a judicial ruling on the preliminary question.

After a lengthy debate the proposal for a judicial ruling was not adopted. The Assembly adopted instead a resolution in which the Assembly expressed its opinion that the treatment of Indians should be in accordance with existing agreements and the relevant provisions of the Charter.[22]

From a constitutional point, the adoption of the resolution meant first, that the Assembly resolved the preliminary question of competence in its favor and, second, that the Charter contained provisions applicable to the case.

The question of Indians in South Africa remained on the Agenda of the General Assembly for several years. An item entitled "Treatment of People of Indian and Indo-Pakistan origin in the Republic of South Africa" appeared on every General Assembly agenda from 1946 until 1961. In 1962 it was replaced by a more general item entitled "The policies of *apartheid* of the Government of the Republic of South Africa" which has appeared on every General Assembly agenda since then.

In the Indonesian question, Article 2(7) appeared for the first time in the Security Council in the context of decolonization and its handling set a precedent. In July 1947, Australia and India informed the Council of the hostilities in Java between the Netherlands and the Republic of Indonesia. Australia introduced a resolution calling for a cease-fire under Article 40 of the Charter and argued that the matter was "one of international concern".[23] Having invoked Article 2(7), without avail and after the Council in-

[20] *Ibid.*, italics supplied.

[21] *Ibid.*

[22] Resolution 44 (I) of December 6, 1946. The vote was 32:15:7. If all votes were counted the necessary majority would have been 36 and the resolution would not have been adopted.

[23] Security Council Official Records II, No. 67, p. 1622. The phrase that a matter is of international concern acquired widespread acceptance in the United Nations and served to override objections based on domestic jurisdiction. It is elementary, of course, that many matters essentially within domestic jurisdiction, e.g. armaments, may be, and often are, of international concern.

vited an Indonesian representative, the Netherlands declared that "the Council (is) being led step by step toward an assertion of full jurisdiction which it so manifestly does not possess".[24]

In spite of the challenge to its competence, the Council on August 1, 1947, adopted a cease-fire resolution without reference to any article of the Charter and called upon the "parties" to settle their dispute by peaceful means. Thus, without resolving the preliminary question, the Council proceeded on its way and the Republic of Indonesia was elevated to the status of a "party" to the dispute on a footing of equality with the Netherlands. As the President of the Council stated: "The vote on that (Australian-USSR draft) proposal will, after all, reveal the views of the members on the question of competence".[25]

In the debate on the Indonesian question in the Council, as in the debate on the question of Indians in South Africa, the proposal was made to ask the International Court of Justice for an advisory opinion on the question of competence. The United States was prepared to support such a request but, in its view, such a request "must not prevent or delay action by the Security Council and the question should be referred to the Court only when hostilities had ceased, the *status quo ante* had been restored, and the peaceful methods which the Charter enjoined had been resumed".[26] This is a very curious reasoning: if that procedure had been followed it would have assumed competence by the Council and put the Court in the difficult position of either ratifying what had already been done or declaring that the Council lacked competence to do what it did. But how could then the Netherlands be restored to the *status quo ante* the cease-fire resolution?

At a later stage of the Indonesian question, in 1949, the question of the competence of the Council to deal with the matter was raised again by the Netherlands and again the Council was urged to submit the question of competence to the Court for an advisory opinion.[27] This was not done and another resolution on substance (S/1234) was submitted. In that context the Netherlands representative declared:

> If this Resolution (S/1234) is adopted this provision (Article 2 (7), which is one of the cornerstones of the United Nations Charter, will from now on be a dead letter.[28]

As it tuned out, these were prophetic words. An essential part of the Charter system was dismantled improvidently. The Charter was never given a chance to prove itself as the cold war became a dominant factor.[29]

[24] *Ibid.*, No. 77, p. 2012.
[25] *Ibid.*, No. 68, p. 1667.
[26] *Philip C. Jessup*, The Birth of Nations (New York: Columbia University Press, 1974), p. 80.
[27] Security Council Official Records, IV, No. 9, p. 11.
[28] *Ibid.*
[29] See *Jessup*, loc. cit., p. 50: "Throughout (the Indonesian question), the cold war was a dominant factor, and one of the principal motivations was the felt need to 'contain' communism". *Jessup* concludes as follows: "The United Nations proved its value. It would have been inconceivable for the United States to have promoted the evolution of Indonesian independence through unilateral diplomacy. It was only with the aid of United Nations mechanism that Indonesia was born in 1949." *Ibid.*, p. 92.

The veto provision, without which there would have been no Charter, has not become a victim of the cold war, though attempts were made to limit its scope through manipulations of the double veto without which the veto itself would be in jeopardy. The question of the double veto has been debated since 1946. The principal issue was whether the result of a vote in the Security Council was subject to a ruling of the President which stands unless overruled by a procedural vote under Rule 30 of the Provisional Rules of Procedure of the Security Council.[30] The practice of the Council with the possible exception of one case,[31] shows instances of rulings or statements by the President but, by and large, the veto and the double veto survived all attacks until 1959 when the Council decided to send a sub-committee to carry out inquiries in Laos regarding Communist, that is, North-Vietnamese activities. Although the establishment of a sub-committee is clearly a matter of procedure under Rule 29 of the Council's Rules of Procedure, the terms of reference when they involve an investigation, are clearly not procedural. But as the United States argued strongly that the whole resolution was procedural and not subject to the veto, the Soviet delegate asked for a vote on the preliminary question: "Should the vote on the draft resolution submitted in Doc. S/4214 be considered a procedural one?"[32] The vote on the preliminary question was 10 to 1. Since the negative vote was cast by the Soviet Union, the non-procedural character of the proposal was established and the President (the representative of Italy) should have so stated. However, the President declared that the resolution could be considered procedural and was therefore adopted. The Soviet delegate declared his interpretation illegal, null and void.[33] He did not, wisely, challenge the ruling of the President, thus carefully avoiding a precedent which might become undesirable in the future in connection with more important matters. As it turned out, 15 years later, the United States had set a precedent which prevented it from taking a stand on the double veto in connection with the PLO, which will be discussed below.

It remains to review briefly what happened to the separation of functions between the General Assembly and the Security Council. Here, too, the dismantling process started in 1946. When the Security Council failed to reach agreement on the question of Franco Spain, it dropped the matter from its agenda to clear the way for the General Assembly. After a wide-ranging debate, the Assembly, in resolution 39 (I), adopted on December 12, 1946, recommended "that all Members of the United Nations immediately recall from Madrid their ambassadors and ministers plenipotentiary accredited there". The practical impact of the resolution was minimal, as most Members either had no ambassadors (19) or had no diplomatic relations with Franco Spain (30).[34] But did the reso-

[30] Rule 30 reads as follows: "If a representative raises a point of order, the President shall immediately state his ruling. If it is challenged, the President shall immediately submit his ruling to the Security Council for immediate decision and it shall stand unless overruled."

[31] The case concerned the proposal to invite representatives of Communist China in 1950. For a discussion of this incident see *Leo Gross*, "The Double Veto and the Four-Power Statement on Voting in the Security Council", Harvard Law Review Vol. 67 (1953), pp. 259 ff. and 275 f. See also *supra*, pp. 473 ff. and 491 f.

[32] Security Council Official Records, Vol. 14 (1959), 848th meeting, p. 12.

[33] *Ibid.*, pp. 13–14.

[34] *Yearbook of the United Nations 1946–1947*, p. 130.

lution constitute an invasion of the exclusive competence of the Security Council under Article 41 of the Charter? This article includes among the measures short of force "the severance of diplomatic relations" which is usually accomplished by the recall of chiefs of mission. On the other hand, if Article 41 was not violated, did the Assembly disregard the injunction against "action" in Article 11(2)? Surely some action was taken even if one argues that it would have been pointless to refer the question back to the Security Council which had already shown its incapacity for action. Be that as it may, a precedent was established which was recalled in 1950 in connection with the constitutional debate on the Uniting for Peace resolution.

That resolution was the brain-child of the United States which, on the one hand was gratified by the voluntary response of many Members to the nonbinding resolution of the Security Council of June 27, 1950,[35] and on the other was exasperated by the liberal use of the veto by the Soviet Union. Resolution 377 (V) was adopted on November 3, 1950, and, in the view of some commentators, had the effect of shifting the center of gravity from the veto-ridden Security Council to the veto-free Assembly. This resolution is too well-known to require elaboration. But the debate about its constitutionality still continues. The essence of the controversy is whether the Charter confers upon the Council in Article 24 primary but not exclusive authority for the maintenance of international peace and security, and whether the General Assembly may exercise secondary or residual authority in case the Council is paralyzed by a veto. The United States denies and the Soviet Union affirms that the Council's responsibility is exclusive.

The American interpretation of the Charter was supported by the International Court of Justice in the *Expenses* case. Without referring to the Uniting for Peace Resolution, the Court found that the responsibility of the Council was "primary" but not exclusive; that the action prohibited to the Assembly was "coercive or enforcement action" which only the Council may take; and that, accordingly, the Assembly may by way of recommendations organize peacekeeping operations with the consent or at the request of the States concerned.[36]

This was a major victory for the United States and its efforts over time to enhance the stature of the Assembly beyond the intention of the founding fathers of the United Nations. But it turned out to be a Pyrrhic victory as soon as the majority support on which the United States had come to rely disappeared.[37] The General Assembly accepted the Advisory Opinion of the Court but was unwilling for Article 19 of the Charter to be applied against the Soviet Union whose refusal to pay its assessed share of the peacekeeping operations in the Sinai and the Congo had brought it within the ambit of

[35] The Council recommended "that Members furnish such assistance to the Republic of Korea as may be necessary to repel the armed attack (by North Korea) and to restore international peace and security in the area".

[36] I.C.J. *Reports* 1962, pp. 163, 164.

[37] Reliance on majority votes rather than on the law of the Charter was the gist of Professor Chayes' oral statement before the Court in the *Expenses* case when he said: "Member States do not find their protection . . . —if protection is needed—in legal strictures of the Charter, but in the political requirement of a two-thirds majority in the General Assembly both to initiate the action and to make the necessary financial arrangements." I.C.J. *Pleadings* 1962, p. 424.

this article. There followed the non-voting session of the Assembly and in 1965 the U.S. drew the consequences from the fact that it had lost control of the majority, that it had become the minority and that some protection of its unwonted status had become necessary. This was the reason for the so-called Goldberg reservation.[38] It will be noted that the United States reserved its position not merely with respect to peacekeeping operations but "any activities" of which it disapproved. This was necessary because the Court had placed no limits on the budgetary power other than to declare that the expenses must serve the purposes of the Charter which are very comprehensive indeed.[39] The White House has, so far, made no use of the Goldberg reservation but the Congress of the United States did by adopting the so-called Helms amendment which prohibits the use of any funds appropriated for international organizations "for the furnishing of technical assistance by the United Nations or any of its specialized agencies".[40] Unless the Helms amendment is repealed, there may be another financial crisis in the offing for there can be no doubt that technical assistance to developing countries serves the purposes of the United Nations.

It would serve no useful purpose to try to determine precisely when the leadership of the majority passed from the United States to the Third World but the transition certainly occurred on the heels of the financial crisis and the June 1967 war between Israel and Arab States.

## IV.

The new majority took over a severely damaged Charter, enfeebled veto and a greatly enhanced General Assembly. Whether consciously or not, the last limitation on the Assembly's competence derived from Article 12 was removed. The Security Council resolution 242 (1967) laid down the framework for the solution of the Palestine question. On December 10, 1969, the Assembly adopted resolution 2535 B (1967) which clearly encroached on Council resolution 242 (1967) in reaffirming "the inalienable rights of the people of Palestine". Subsequent resolutions, some of which would have failed of adoption if Article 18(2) of the Charter, instead of Rule 88 of the Rules of Procedure, had

[38] At the meeting of the Special Committee on Peace-keeping Operations held on August 16, 1965, the representative of the United States (Ambassador Goldberg) referred to the Advisory Opinion of the ICJ on the *Expenses* case and declared: ". . . on the basis of the entire history of the problem of the financing of peace-keeping operations, the United States had regretfully concluded that, at the present stage in the development of the United Nations, the General Assembly was not prepared to carry out the relevant provisions of the Charter, that is, to apply the loss-of-vote sanction in Article 19 . . . It is agreed that the Assembly must proceed with its work. At the same time, if any Member State could make an exception to the principle of collective financial responsibility with respect to certain United Nations activities, the United States reserved the same option to make exception if, in its view, there were strong and compelling reasons to do so. There could be no double standard among the Members of the Organization". GAOR: 19th Sess., Annexes, Annex 21, Doc. A/5916/Add. 1, Annex, P. 86, para. 7.

[39] I.C.J. *Report* 1962, p. 167. The Court declared that "such expenditures must be tested by their relationship to the purposes of the United Nations in the sense that if an expenditure were made for a purpose which is not one of the purposes of the United Nations, it could not be considered an 'expense of the Organization' ".

[40] Appropriation Act, 1979, Public Law 95-431, 92 Stat. 1021-1022. According to a Bill pending in Congress. H. R. 3363, 96th Congress, 1st Session, section 102 (b), no funds appropriated by the United States may be used for the Committee on the Exercise of the Inalienable Rights of the Palestinian People and the Special Unit on Palestinian Rights established pursuant to Part B of General Assembly Resolution 32/40 adopted on December 2, 1977.

been followed, made increasingly clear that the Assembly had become an advocate of the Arabs against Israel and, since Israel was supported by and large by the United States, against the United States. In 1974, the General Assembly in open defiance of the Security Council and of Article 12, placed "The Question of Palestine" on its Agenda, and adopted on November 22, 1974, resolution 3236(XXIX) setting forth its own plan for the solution of the problem which totally departed from resolution 242(1967).

The "legal strictures of the Charter", already weakened, were now completely disregarded. One or two examples will illustrate the point. By resolution 3210 (XXIX) of October 14, 1974, the Assembly invited "the Palestine Liberation Organization, the representative of the Palestinian people, to participate in the deliberation of the General Assembly on the question of Palestine in plenary meetings". According to Article 9(1) the Assembly consists of Members of the United Nations and they, through their representatives, participate in its deliberations. There is no constitutional basis for an invitation of this sort. It may be recalled that Pope Paul IV was invited to address the General Assembly but not to participate in its deliberations.[41]

Acting perhaps on the motto that nothing succeeds like success, the Third World majority, including the two members from the socialist bloc, proposed in 1975 that the P.L.O. be invited to the discussion of the Middle East problem in the Security Council. The President insisted that the invitation would not be under Rule 39 of the Council's Provisional Rules of Procedure[42] which would be legally unobjectionable but that "the invitation to the P.L.O. to participate in this debate will confer on it the same rights of participation as are conferred when a Member State is invited to participate under Rule 37"[43] which applies to Members of the United Nations which are not members of the Council. Despite strenuous objections of a procedural and even constitutional character, the resolution was adopted on December 4, 1975,[44] by a vote of 9 in favor, 3 against (Costa Rica, the United Kingdom, the United States), and 3 abstentions (France, Italy, Japan). On January 12, 1976, an invitation in identical terms was extended to the P.L.O., but this time the United States, in splendid isolation, cast the only negative vote whereas the United Kingdom switched to abstention. The United States could, and in the present submission, should have challenged the declaration of the President of the Council that the two resolutions were adopted, and invoked the double veto procedure. For if anything was clear, it was that the resolutions were not procedural and raised a constitutional issue. But having scuttled the double veto in the Laotian question, the Department of State felt it could not call it to its rescue now.[45]

[41] GAOR: 20th sess., 1347th Plenary Mtg., October 4, 1965, p. 2, para. 14. Non-statal entities and individuals have been granted the opportunity to state their views in committees of the Assembly.

[42] This reads as follows: "The Security Council may invite members of the Secretariat or other persons, whom it considers competent for the purpose, to supply it with information or to give other assistance in examining matters within its competence."

[43] Doc. S/PV.1859, December 4, 1975, p. 3.

[44] *Ibid.*, p. 41.

[45] For a more detailed analysis, see *Leo Gross*, "Voting in the Security Council and the PLO", *The American Journal of International Law*, Vol. 70 (1976), pp. 470–491. See also *supra*, pp. 531–550.

However, the question of Palestine apart, the Third World was primarily active in advancing its own interest through resolutions establishing a Charter of the Economic Rights and Duties of States[46] and the New International Economic Order which, whatever their objectives and effectiveness, raise no constitutional issues. The activities of the Third World and its sympathizers devoted to the eradication of *apartheid,* racism, and the remnants of colonialism by endorsing liberation movements may be briefly mentioned because they do seem to involve such issues.

The resolution equating zionism and racism has been mentioned already, and the less said about it the better. It speaks for itself and Members who voted for it. Resolution 32(40) of December 2, 1977, has also been mentioned. It is surely an illustration of the excessive politicization of the United Nations. It requested the Secretary-General "to establish within the Secretariat of the United Nations a Special Unit on Palestinian Rights" which would undertake certain tasks on behalf of the Palestinian people and thus on behalf of the P.L.O. which was recognized by the Assembly as the representative of the Palestinian People. Never before has the Secretariat been asked to perform what may best be described as a public relations job on behalf of an organization which is bent on the destruction of a Member of the United Nations,[47] and is in the meantime engaged in terrorist attacks on Israel and moderate Arabs.[48]

*Apartheid* has for many years been a focal point of interest of the Third World and particularly of the African Members. The legal issues involved here are well-known; the Assembly adopts even more strident resolutions and South Africa continues to seek shelter behind Article 2(7).[49]

Of interest are more recent efforts of the Third World to drive South Africa from the United Nations and bring *apartheid* to an end by violent means.

At its 1970 session, an attempt was made to suspend South Africa from participation in the work of the General Assembly by refusing to accept the credentials of the South African delegation. This attempt came to naught when the President of the Assembly, the late Edvard Hambro (Norway), relying on a statement by the United Nations Legal Counsel, on the scope of the "credentials" in Rule 27 of the Assembly's Rules of

[46] But the new majority, no more than the old majority, is interested in reviving the Draft Declaration of the Rights and Duties of States of the International Law Commission which has been gathering dust since 1949.

[47] The Palestinian National Charter, 1968, in: *J. N. Moore,* The Arab-Israel Conflict. Readings and Documents (Princeton: Princeton University Press, 1977), pp. 1086–1091.

[48] Resolution 32 (40) is to be distinguished from General Assembly resolution 32 (43) of December 7, 1977, which was adopted without a vote and requested the Secretary-General to disseminate information about the work of the United Nations in the field of decolonization.

[49] Judge Sir Percy Spencer in his Separate Opinion in the *Expenses* case made a statement which lends legal support to the position of South Africa. He said: "So, if the General Assembly were to 'intervene in matters which are essentially within the domestic jurisdiction of any State' within the meaning of Article 2 (7) of the Charter, whatever be the meaning to be given to these words, that intervention would be the entering into a field prohibited to it under the Charter and be beyond the authority of the General Assembly. This would continue to be so, no matter how frequently and consistently the General Assembly had construed its authority to permit it to make intervention in matters essentially within the domestic jurisdiction of any States. The majority has no power to extend, alter or disregard the Charter." I.C.J. *Reports* 1962, pp. 196–197.

Procedure, considered that such a suspension would be unconstitutional.[50] The Legal Counsel cited the requirements for suspension of the rights and privileges of membership in the General Assembly (preventive or enforcement action against a Member, recommendation by the Security Council, and a two-thirds vote in the Assembly in accordance with Article 18, para. 2) and concluded:

> The participation in meetings of the General Assembly is quite clearly one of the important rights and privileges of membership. Suspension of this right through the rejection of credentials would not satisfy the foregoing requirements and would therefore be contrary to the Charter.[51]

The Third World, undaunted by this failure, made a fresh approach, this time aiming at the expulsion of South Africa, was made in the Security Council in accordancee with Assembly Resolution 3207 (XXIX) of September 30, 1974. However, this effort failed as the draft resolution recommending the expulsion in accordance with Article 6 of the Charter was not adopted. In the voting on October 30, 1974, the draft resolution received 10 votes in favor, 3 against (France, the United Kingdom, the United States), and 2 abstentions (Austria, Costa Rica). As legal grounds for expulsion, the draft resolution cited violations by South Africa of Articles 1, 2, 6, 55 and 56.[52]

The matter returned to the General Assembly whose President was the representative of Algeria, a leading and radical Third World Member. The device used on this occasion was a ruling by the President, a device used by the old majority on other occasions. The President was asked to give a ruling on the meaning of the repeated rejection of the credentials of South Africa. Predictably, he gave the ruling in the following words:

> On the basis of the consistency with which the General Assembly has regularly refused to accept the credentials of the delegation of South Africa, one may legitimately infer that the General Assembly would in the same way reject the credentials of any other delegation authorized by the Government of the Republic of South Africa to represent it, which is tantamount to saying in explicit terms that the General Assembly refuses to allow the delegation of South Africa to participate in its work.[53]

As under Rule 73 of the Rules of Procedure of the General Assembly, a Presidential ruling (on a point of order) stands unless overruled and as the opposing States lacked the votes to overrule, the ruling was allowed to stand. It matters little to the new majority if the Charter is violated, provided it accomplishes its higher aims. Under Rules 27 and 28, the Credentials Committee has authority to examine only the

[50] For a brief summary of the discussion, see *Yearbook of the United Nations 1970*, pp. 143–145.
[51] Doc. A/8160, November 11, 1970, GAOR: 25th session, Annexes, Agenda item 3, pp. 3–4.
[52] *Yearbook of the United Nations 1974*, pp. 111, 115.
[53] Doc. A/PV.2281, November 12, 1974, p. 76.

formal validity of credentials (whether issued by the Head of State or Government or by the Minister for Foreign Affairs) and has no authority to inquire into the legitimacy of the Government.[54]

Much as the violation of the Charter in the credentials issue is to be deplored, the persistent advocacy of wars of national liberation and recent incitement to civil war in a Member State are not merely unconstitutional but constitute retrogressive steps in international law as it developed in the last 300 or 400 years. Contrary to its primordial purpose of maintaining peace through collective action, the Organization has become committed to promote a new kind of "just war" to a degree that some of the resolutions read like communiqués from the battlefront.[55] One or two examples will illustrate the point.

In resolution 33/44 of December 13, 1978, entitled "Implementation of the Declaration on the Granting of Independence to Colonial Countries and Peoples", the Assembly, in operative paragraph 4, "affirms once again its recognition of the legitimacy of the struggle of the peoples under colonial and alien domination to exercise their right to self-determination and independence by all the necessary means at their disposal". In the operative paragraph 2, the Assembly goes on to urge "all States, directly or through their action in the specialized agencies and other organizations within the United Nations system, to provide all moral and material assistance to the oppressed peoples of Namibia and Zimbabwe . . .".[56] The adoption of resolutions under this title has been an annual rite for a long time and it is unnecessary to cite them as their text has remained virtually identical.[57]

However, resolution 32/105J of December 14, 1977, one of fifteen resolutions adopted at that session on the subject of *apartheid*, is rather unique in the annals of the United Nations, for it addresses itself not merely to the liberation movement but directly to the people of South Africa. For this reason it may be worthwhile to quote the four operative paragraphs of this resolution entitled "Assistance to the National Liberation Movement of South Africa". After recognizing in the Preamble "that the policies and action of the racist regime of South Africa have aggravated a threat to the peace in southern Africa and that their continuation would lead to a wider conflict", the Assembly:

1. *Strongly reaffirms* the inalienable right of the people of South Africa as a whole, irrespective of race, colour or creed, to determine, on the basis of majority rule, the future of South Africa;

2. *Further reaffirms* the legitimacy of the struggle of the oppressed people of South

[54] At the resumed 33rd session of the Assembly on May 23, 1979, South African delegates were present. Their presence was challenged and they were again excluded. UN Press Release WS/920, May 25, 1979, p. 1. Western delegates again questioned the legal basis for rejecting the credentials of the South African delegation. *Ibid.*

[55] Thus, in paragraph 4 of resolution 393 (1976) adopted on July 30, 1976, by 14 votes to none, with 1 abstention (the United States), the Security Council "*commends* the Republic of Zambia and other 'front-line' States for their steadfast support of the people of Namibia in their legitimate struggle for the liberation of their country from illegal occupation by the racist régime of South Africa".

[56] See also companion resolution 33/41 of December 13, 1978.

[57] See e.g. resolution 32/42 of December 7, 1977.

Africa and their national liberation movement for the eradication of *apartheid* and the exercise of the right of self-determination by the people of South Africa as a whole;

3. *Declares* that, in view of the intransigence of the racist régime, its defiance of resolutions of the United Nations and its continued imposition of the criminal policy of *apartheid,* the national liberation movement has an inalienable right to continue its struggle for the seizure of power by all available and appropriate means of its choice, including armed struggle;

4. *Further declares* that the international community should provide all assistance to the national liberation movement of South Africa in its legitimate struggle and exercise all its authority, under the provisions of the Charter of the United Nations, including Chapter VII, to facilitate the transfer of power from the minority racist régime to the genuine representatives of all the people of South Africa.

In order to appreciate the gravity of such pronouncements, which, if heeded, are bound to "lead to a wider conflict" it may be helpful to recall that under the Charter's prohibition of the use of force, force can only be used in self-defense under Article 51 or pursuant to appropriate action by the Security Council under Chapter VII. Moreover, the 1970 resolution 2525 (XXV) on Peaceful Coexistence[58] which has been hailed by some as a codification of modern international law, provides in connection with decolonization that certain peoples in their resistance to forcible action aimed at depriving them of their right to self-determination, "are entitled to seek and to receive support in accordance with the purposes and principles of the Charter". Recent resolutions, including the one cited above, do not contain this restriction. The Charter, as the standard of legality, is thus eliminated, although in its General Part the Coexistence resolution unambiguously recognized the primacy of the Charter.

Furthermore, the Coexistence resolution provides that "every State has the duty to refrain from organizing or encouraging the organization of irregular forces or armed bands, including mercenaries, for invasion into the territory of another State". It is fair to suggest that what is illicit for States cannot, by means of Assembly resolutions, be made licit for the Organization. Incursions of this kind have always been illegal under international law. In fact, it is so fundamental a principle that without it we would lapse into a state of anarchy. In international law, States victims of armed bands could and did resort to self-help, usually in the form of reprisals, admittedly crude and somewhat controversial measures to vindicate respect for law in a decentralized legal order.[59] However, this carefully balanced system of rights and obligations has been upset by the inclusion in the Coexistence resolution of the principle: "States have a duty to refrain from acts of reprisal involving the use of force." Of course, if States would respect their duty to prevent incursions into another State's territory, there would be no need for reprisals. But if States

[58] Its full title is: Declaration on Principles of International Law concerning Friendly Relations among States in accordance with the Charter of the United Nations. It was adopted by consensus on October 24, 1970, the 25th anniversary of the coming into force of the Charter.

[59] Reference should be made to the *Naulilaa* case which confirmed the right of reprisal. *Recueil des Decisions des Tribunaux Arbitraux Mixtes,* Vol. 8, p. 409.

do not—and some of them particularly in the Middle East and in southern Africa do not—then what can the victim State do seeing that constitutionally the Security Council has no authority to enforce international law and that politically it is supportive of such States and condemns self-help action on the part of the victim State.[60] Is it seriously expected by the Third World for the target state to suffer armed attacks passively and forego the right of self-defense, *vim vi repellere?*[61]

The consensus Definition of Aggression adopted by Assembly resolution 3314 (XXIX) of December 14, 1974 is so ambiguous as to permit a variety of interpretations.[62] On the one hand it qualifies as an act of aggression "the sending by or on behalf of a State of armed bands . . . which carry out acts of armed force against another State of such gravity as to amount" to the other acts listed in Article 3. On the other hand, it exempts from this definition the right of peoples forcibly deprived of the right to self-determination "to struggle . . . and receive support, in accordance with the principles of the Charter and in conformity" with the 1970 Coexistence resolution. Surely, liberation forces are not sent "on behalf of a State" unless one regards the "frontline" Members of the United Nations as such States. But how can liberation struggles "receive support" in accordance with the Charter unless the Security Council, and not individual States, takes enforcement measures under Chapter VII and pursuant to the exemption in Article 2(7)?

One of the most significant stages in the pacification of Europe has been the elimination of private wars waged by feudal barons and princes and of privateering at sea and the acceptance of public war waged by sovereign States as the only permissible armed contest. Legal positivism put an end to the doctrine of just war and the law of war governed exclusively wars between States.[63] To be sure it would have been better, if it were possible, to abolish war altogether. Attempts in that direction were made at the 1899 and 1907 Hague Peace Conferences, in the 1919 Covenant of the League of Nations, in the 1928 Kellogg-Briand Pact, and the Charter of the United Nations. But the practical results were meager. All the same, however, restricted, public war remained an attribute of sovereignty, a right of last resort or, in the words of Article 51 of the Charter, a right "of

[60] Suffice it to cite Security Council resolution 403 (1977) of January 14, 1977, concerning a complaint by Botswana of violations of its sovereignty by Rhodesia. Instead of condemming Botswana for giving succor to national liberation movements operating from its territory, the Council strongly condemned "all acts of provocation and harrassment . . . committed against Botswana by the illegal régime in Southern Rhodesia". As further evidence for the loss of contact with the real world, one may refer to the statement in the Preamble in which the Council reaffirmed "the legal responsibility of the Government of the United Kingdom . . . over Southern Rhodesia, in accordance with the relevant resolutions".

[61] It has been suggested that this is indeed a consequence of the recognition of a right to self-determination. Traditionally, internal rebellion for whatever cause was not a matter with which international law concerned itself. But if there is now in international law "a right to rebel for certain specified 'causes', racial in nature" then "such a 'right' in international law places a correlative 'duty' upon the State concerned not to resist the exercise of such right of self-determination by force". This would be contrary to Articles 2 (4) and 51 of the Charter and would imply an amendment of the Charter "in a manner which had no vestige of legality". See *G. I. A. D. Draper*, "Wars of National Liberation and War Criminality", in *Michael Howard* (ed.), Restraints on War (Oxford University Press, 1979), p. 157 f.

[62] See *Julius Stone*, "Hopes and Loopholes in the Definition of Aggression", *American Journal of International Law*, Vol 71 (1977), pp. 224-246, particularly pp. 233 and 238.

[63] See *Draper*, loc. cit., p. 136.

individual or collective self-defense if an armed attack occurs against a Member of the United Nations''.

By calling upon all and sundry to aid and abet wars of national liberation[64] and by affirming their ''legitimacy'' the political organs of the United Nations, impelled by the Third World, seem determined to turn the clock back to the turbulence of the Middle Ages and nullify the modest progress that international law has achieved in the pacification of the world.

In a short span of time the legal securities of the Charter were largely dismantled to the point where the will of the majority reigns supreme and undermines the very foundations of international law without which neither the traditional legal nor the new economic order, so dear to the Third World, is possible. What Mr. Justice Holmes said in Missouri v. Holland about the constitution of the United States applies, *grosso modo,* to the Charter of the United Nations: the Charter called into life a being, the development of which could not have been foreseen by the most gifted of its American founders.

[64] On the discriminatory character of such wars which in itself is a throw-back to earlier times, *Draper* writes: ''There has been during the last decade a modified recrudescence of the idea that the 'cause' for which an armed struggle has been initiated by one participant ought to determine whether such struggle is an international armed conflict to which the modern *jus in bello,* i.e. the Humanitarian Law of Armed Conflicts, is applicable. This movement is, upon analysis, not towards a discrimination in the application of that law of armed conflict. It is a move for a discriminatory basis upon which struggles for selective 'causes' should be considered as international armed conflicts. It is, in effect, a double discrimination, as to the identity of a new belligerent 'entity', and as to the 'cause' for which it resorts to armed force.'' *Ibid.,* p. 139.

# ON THE DEGRADATION OF THE CONSTITUTIONAL ENVIRONMENT OF THE UNITED NATIONS

## I

Manipulating constituent instruments of international organizations in order to punish selectively unpopular member states is not a new phenomenon. Of the states which resorted to war in violation of their obligations under the Covenant of the League of Nations—Japan, Italy, the Soviet Union—only one, the Soviet Union, was expelled from the League when on November 30, 1939 it invaded Finland. On December 14, 1939, the Council, in virtue of Article 16(4) of the Covenant found "that by its act, the Union of Soviet Socialist Republics has placed itself outside the League of Nations. It follows that the Union of Soviet Socialist Republics is no longer a Member of the League."[1] However, the specific voting rule in Article 16(4) was not complied with on this occasion.[2] While the League insisted "on a strict application of the unanimity requirement; . . . in a period of moral indignation, niceties of procedure are not likely to be observed."[3] But where was moral indignation when Japan attacked China and Italy attacked Ethiopia and Germany attacked Poland and thus started World War II? The members of the League and the members of the United Nations now seem to be moved to moral indignation only in selected cases which deprives indignation of its

[1] *League of Nations*, O.J., 1939, p. 506.

[2] See Leo Gross, "Was the Soviet Union Expelled From the League of Nations?", 39 *AJIL* 35–44 (1945) at p. 42. See also *supra*, pp. 553–561, at p. 559. For a contrary view see Nathan Feinberg, "L'Exclusion d'un Membre de la Societé des Nations et le principe de l'unanimité," in *Studies in International Law. With Special Reference to the Arab-Israel Conflict* (Jerusalem, The Magnes Press) 1979, pp. 3–16. See also Louis B. Sohn, "Expulsion or Forced Withdrawal from an International Organization," 77 *Harv. L.R.* 1381–1425 (1964), at 1387–1391.

[3] Sohn, *supra*, n. 2, at 1390.

moral basis. Insofar as the expulsion of the Soviet Union is concerned, a more persuasive explanation has been given by the historian of the League F.P. Walters:

> "If no move had been made to submit to the League the issues which had led to war between Germany and Poland, France, and Great Britain, what result could be expected from its intervention in this new conflict? But the Soviet aggression had loosed a storm of anger from one end of the world to the other. All those States whose policy had been affected by fear and hatred of Communism denounced the perfidy of Stalin in language which none of them used about Hitler."[4]

Thus the drive to score an ideological victory prevailed over the traditional concern for constitutional propriety. However, coming as it did in the final phase of the League, it could not produce any lasting harm and did not prevent the forging of the Grand Alliance including the Soviet Union, against Hitler which was transformed into the United Nations.

In the United Nations strong antagonisms developed in the 1960s as groups of States, many of which had been only recently admitted to membership, set out to impose their views on a dissenting minority of individual states such as Portugal over the colonial question and South Africa over the question of Namibia and apartheid.[5] More recently in the context of the Middle East problem, Israel became the target of intense attempts to isolate, suspend or expel it. The earlier incidents are of no particular consequence except the patently unconstitutional "suspension" of South Africa from the General Assembly in 1974. Departing from the so-called Hambro formula according to which South Africa was permitted to sit in the Assembly from 1970 to 1973 although the credentials of its representative were rejected, a conniving President of the Assembly, Ambassador A. Bouteflika (Algeria), disregarding precedent and the opinion of the Legal Counsel of the United Nations[6], gave a ruling interpreting the rejection of credentials as follows:

> "On the basis of the consistency with which the General Assembly has regularly refused to accept the credentials of the delegation of South Africa, one may legitimately infer that the General Assembly would in the same way reject the credentials of any other delegation authorized by the Government of the Republic of South Africa to represent it, which is tantamount to saying in explicit terms that the General Assembly refuses to allow the delegation of South Africa to participate in its work."[7]

[4] *A History of the League of Nations,* 2 vols. (London: Oxford U.P., 1952), Vol. II, pp. 804–05.

[5] Sohn, *supra.* n. 2, pp. 1409–1416; see pp. 1412–1416 concerning the forced withdrawal of South Africa from the ILO in 1964.

[6] "Scope of 'credentials' in rule 27 of the rules of procedure of the General Assembly: statement by the Legal Counsel to the President of the General Assembly at his request," Doc. A/8160, Nov. 11, 1970; also in UN Juridical Year Book pp. 169–70 (1970). The relevant part of the opinion is as follows: "Should the General Assembly, where there is no question of rival claimants, reject credentials satisfying the requirements of rule 27 for the purpose of excluding a Member State from participation in its meetings, this would have the effect of suspending a Member State from the exercise of the rights and privileges of membership in a manner not foreseen by the Charter. . . . The participation in meetings of the General Assembly is quite clearly one of the important rights and privileges of membership. Suspension of this right through the rejection of credentials would not satisfy the foregoing requirements and would therefore be contrary to the Charter." *Ibid.* para. 6. The Legal Counsel distinguished the case of Hungary from 1956 to 1963 and the case of South Africa in 1970 as in both cases the representation of these Members were seated and exercised rights of membership. *Ibid.,* para. 5. He also distinguished the cases of the Congo in 1960, Yemen in 1961, and China. *Ibid.,* para. 4.

[7] Nov. 12, 1974. U.N. Doc. A/PV. 2281, at 76. GAOR: 29th sess. Plenary.

The representative of the United States, Mr. Scali, challenged the ruling on the ground that it violated Articles 5 and 6 of the Charter, dealing respectively with suspension and expulsion. In the circumstances the result was predictable: by a vote of 91 to 22 with 19 abstentions, the ruling was upheld.[8] This is not the place to consider further the constitutionality of the exclusion of South Africa from the General Assembly. As the Legal Counsel pointed out "participation in the meetings of the General Assembly is quite clearly one of the important rights and privileges of membership."[9] It is solidly anchored in Article 9 of the Charter.[10] South Africa was, and continues to be, a Member of the United Nations. There is no rival government, and no manipulation of the rules of procedure can prevail over the explicit terms of the Charter without serious degradation of the organization and the rule of law.[11]

The credentials issue relates to the question whether the delegates are properly authorized—Rule 27 of the Rules of Procedure of the General Assembly—to represent the government, and not to the question whether the government of the Member represents the people of the state or a particular ideology. The Charter does not require a representative or democratic form of government as a condition of admission to the United Nations, nor does loss or lack of a representative or democratic character constitute a ground for suspension or expulsion of Members.

When the General Assembly on March 2, 1981 resumed its 35th session for the sole purpose of tackling the question of Namibia, a West European, Rüdiger von Wechmar (FRG) was in the chair. As the Government of the Federal Republic had voted against President Bouteflika's ruling in 1974, one might have expected President von Wechmar to make at least an effort to revive the Hambro formula.[12] However, for reasons that

[8] *Ibid.*, pp. 71–86. The scenario for this meeting of the Assembly might have been written by Professor Sohn. Using an "imaginative" interpretation, he suggested that exclusion of a recalcitrant Member might be achieved through a challenge of the credentials on the ground that the Government was not a "true" but a totalitarian government or a foreign puppet. This method could be applied even to expel a permanent member of the Security Council, if necessary under the 1950 Uniting for Peace Resolution of the General Assembly. *Supra*, n. 2, pp. 1422–23 and n. 202 on p. 1423. However, the device to invoke a presidential ruling in order to override the Charter was invented by the United States and applied in the question of Laos. See Leo Gross, "The Question of Laos and the Double Veto in the Security Council," 54 *AJIL* 118–131 (1960), at p. 127. See also *supra*, pp. 497–510, at p. 506.

[9] *Supra*, n.6.

[10] Article 9 reads: "1. The General Assembly shall consist of all the Members of the United Nations. 2. Each Member shall have not more than five representatives in the General Assembly."

[11] Concerning the legality of the "suspension" of South Africa see Farrokh Jhabvala, "The Credentials Approach to Representation Questions in the U.N. General Assembly," 7 Cal. Western. I.L.J. 615–638 (1977), and Dan Ciobanu, "Credentials of Delegations and Representation of Member States at the U.N." 25 ICLQ 351–381 (1976). Jhabvala concluded at p. 637, "the decision on South Africa was legal." Ciobanu concluded "that the General Assembly properly exercised its power to inquire into the representation of South Africa in the United Nations, and that its decision of September 30, 1974, to reject the credentials of the delegation appointed by the Government of that State was valid. The same cannot be said of its interpretation of that decision, at the 2281st meeting on November 12 of the same year. . . ." At p. 380. See also Edward McWhinney, "Credentials of State Delegations to the U.N. General Assembly: A New Approach to Effectuation of Self-Determination for Southern Africa," 3 Hastings Const. L.Q. 19–35 (1976). Approving the ruling concerning South Africa McWhinney said: "In considering the issue of representation, the General Assembly and its Credentials Committee may properly be guided by new international law principles, such as the principle of the self-determination of peoples developed or extended since the adoption of the Charter, and also, *inter alia*, by relevant World Court opinions, such as the 1971 ruling on the Namibia question." *Ibid.* at 34 (footnotes omitted). It is beyond the scope of this paper to examine the reasoning which led Jhabvala, Ciobanu and McWhinney to their respective conclusions.

[12] On that occasion, speaking for his Government, Baron von Wechmar referred to the opinion of the Legal Counsel of November 11, 1970, and declared: "In the opinion of my Government, the credentials of the South Africa delegation met

hardly seem convincing, the President chose to play the game according to the rules of the Third World rather than the rules of the General Assembly and the rules of the Charter.[13]

## II

In the cases discussed above the opponents of unconstitutional proceedings were content to register their reasoned protest but took no further action to stop the degradation of the constitutional foundations of the United Nations. Such verbal protests have been without avail. When Israel became the target of prevailing majorities, the United States manifested its protest in words as well as in deeds.

Thus, on November 21, 1974, the General Conference of UNESCO rejected an Israeli request to be included in UNESCO's European regional group. As a result, Israel became the only Member of UNESCO excluded from its regional group. This action followed an earlier resolution in which the General Conference had condemned Israel for "its persistence in altering the historical features of the City of Jerusalem and by undertaking excavations which constitutes a danger to its monuments." The United States objected to this saying that:

> [T]he essential objective of this resolution is not . . . the preservation or protection of historical sites and monuments. Whatever the claimed intentions of those who sponsored it might be, the resolution in fact imposes a completely unjustified sanction upon a Member State of this Organization for reasons that seem to us to be largely motivated by political considerations.[14]

the requirements of Article 27 of the rules of procedure; therefore there were and continue to be no legal grounds for excluding the South African delegation from the General Assembly. . . . We can only hope that this dangerous precedent will remain the only case of its kind, and that the Organization will find its way back to the strict observance of its rules." GA: 29th sess., Doc. A/P.V.2281, November 12, 1974, pp. 93–95. As a matter of fact he not only repeated the dangerous precedent but made it worse by declaring even before the Credentials Committee had made its report on South Africa's credentials: "I shall not recognize requests for participation in this debate until the General Assembly receives a report from the Credentials Committee." Doc. A/35/P.V. 102, March 2, 1981. The request to which he referred was apparently made by South Africa under rule 71 of the Assembly's Rules of Procedure: "During the discussion of any matter, a representative may rise to a point of order, and the point of order shall be immediately decided by the President in accordance with the rules of procedure." This incident is summarized in 18 UN *Monthly Chronicle,* April 1981, at p. 7.

[13] The discussion at the 102nd Plenary Meeting is summarized in 18 *UN Monthly Chronicle* April, 1981, pp. 5–8. The President's explanation is on p. 7. Among those who opposed the Assembly action were the Netherlands on behalf of the 10 members of the EEC, Canada, Austria, Turkey, Iceland on behalf of Denmark, Finland, Norway and Sweden, the United Kingdom, the Federal Republic of Germany, New Zealand, France, Chile, Australia and the United States. The United States was reported as saying: "On so fundamental a question as the rights of membership, the passing of time had not given the Assembly a better legal basis for doing in 1981 what it did improperly in 1974. No one has shown that South Africa's credentials failed to meet the requirements of the rules of procedure. To refuse to consider those credentials as required by the rules was to use the guise of credentials to try to accomplish a suspension that lay beyond the powers of the General Assembly." *Ibid.,* at p. 6. In the view of the Federal Republic of Germany "[I]t was inconsistent with the provisions of the Charter to evaluate the legitimacy and policy of Governments which issued such credentials." *Ibid.,* at p. 8. France "felt that an organization which did not respect its fundamental laws rendered itself vulnerable." *Ibid.* Chile "was sorry that it had to stray from the majority of the Latin American countries and its friends from Asia and Africa, but if firmly believed that the sole hope for respect for the small and medium-sized countries was support for the rules of law—and that was the principle which guided Chile in its vote." *Ibid.*

[14] *1974 Digest of United States Practice in International Law,* p. 45. For a rebuttal of the alleged danger to monuments see statement of the American Jewish Congress quoted in Frederic L. Kirgis, Jr., *International Organizations in their Legal Setting* (West Publishing Co. 1977), p. 550. Concerning the exclusion of Israel from the European Group, it was reported in *The New York Times,* Nov. 22, 1974, col. 1 at 6 that [A]ccording to one UNESCO official, 'the Arab and Socialist-bloc countries did a full time job' in gathering their support, and non-left-leaning African delegations had voiced resentment about

The Congress on December 30, 1974 voted to withhold the American contribution to the budget of UNESCO.[15] This "counter-sanction" was effective. The General Conference of UNESCO admitted Israel to the European regional group in 1976 and Congress lifted the financial embargo.[16]

A different and stronger sanction was applied by the United States against the International Labour Organization. It is apparent from the formal notice of intention to withdraw from the ILO given by Secretary of State Henry Kissinger to the Director General on November 5, 1975 that an accumulation of grievances rather than a single incident motivated it. They were grouped under four heads: (1) The erosion of tripartite representation, which has a long history; (2) Selective concern for human rights, which is found to an even greater degree in the United Nations; (3) disregard of due process, of which "[T]he most blatant example was the 1973 [International Labour] Conference's treatment of Israel"[17]; and (4) The increasing politicization of the Organization.[18] The admission of the PLO to participation in the General Conference of the ILO may well have been regarded as a significant illustration of politicization.[19] However, more or most important may have been the condemnation of Israel by the General Conference in 1974 for "racist" practices in the West Bank in utter disregard of the procedures for which the ILO was justly highly respected.[20]

Pursuant to the notice, President Carter terminated United States membership in the ILO on November 1, 1977, and the reasons for this step including condemnation of members without due process, were outlined by the Secretary of Labor F. Ray Marshall.[21] Three years later, on February 18, 1980, after remedial action was taken by the ILO, the United States resumed membership.[22]

anti-Israeli pressures, 'with much talk of blackmail'." Quoted in Gordon Lang, "UNESCO and Israel," 16 *Harv. I.L.J.* 676–682 (1975) at 681.

[15] *Supra*, n. 14, at 47.

[16] *1976 Digest of United States Practice in International Law*, pp. 49–50. President Ford on Dec. 29, 1976, informed the Congress "that sufficient progress had been made at the recently concluded UNESCO General Conference toward reversing the anti-Israel actions of the 1974 conference to justify a resumption of U.S. funding." *Ibid.*, at p. 50. It may be noted that the United States National Commission for UNESCO in a statement approved on December 5, 1974, opposed the withholding of funds for UNESCO. *1974 Digest*, pp. 46–47.

[17] William P. Alford, "The Prospective Withdrawal of the United States from the International Labor Organization: Rationales and Implications," 17 *Harvard I.L.J.* 623–38 (1976), at 630.

[18] *1975 Digest of United States Practice in International Law*, pp. 70–73.

[19] Kirgis, *supra*, n. 14, at 207. A particularly ugly incident of politicization of the ILO by the United States occurred in 1970 in connection with the appointment of a Soviet citizen as Assistant Director General. See Stephen M. Schwebel, "The United States Assaults the I.L.O.," 65 *AJIL* 136–142 (1971). On that occasion the U.S. Congress voted to block payment of assessment due to the I.L.O.

[20] Alford, supra, n. 17, at 630–31. At the same time the General Conference also discarded standard procedure in condemning Chile for its labor practices.

[21] *1977 Digest of United States Practice in International Law*, pp. 39–40.

[22] Marian L. Nash, "Contemporary Practice of the United States Relating to International Law," 75 *AJIL* pp. 363–368 (1981). In announcing on November 13, 1980, that the United States would rejoin the ILO, President Carter stated: "Since [the U.S. withdrawal], a majority of the ILO members—governments, workers, and employers—have successfully joined together to return the ILO to its original purposes. Through their efforts, steps have been taken to strengthen the independence of employer and worker delegates, undertake investigations of human rights violations in a number of countries, including the Soviet Union, reinforce the principle of due process, and generally reduce the level of politicization in the ILO." *Ibid.*, at 363.

In the wake of the destruction of an Iraqi nuclear installation by Israel, the International Atomic Energy Agency suspended Israel from membership in a manner which provides another example of the degradation of the constitution of a specialized agency and its rules of procedure.

The Security Council on June 19, 1981 adopted resolution 487(1981) in which, after referring to Article 2(4) of the Charter, it:

> 1. *Strongly condemns* the military attack by Israel in clear violation of the Charter of the United Nations and the norms of international conduct;
> 2. *Calls upon* Israel to refrain in the future from any such acts or threats thereof;
> 3. *Further considers* that the said attack constitutes a serious threat to the entire IAEA safeguards régime which is the foundation of the non-proliferation Treaty;
> 4. *Fully recognizes* the inalienable sovereign right of Iraq, and all other States, especially the developing countries, to establish programmes of technological and nuclear development to develop their economy and industry for peaceful purposes in accordance with their present and future needs and consistent with the internationally accepted objectives of preventing nuclear-weapons proliferation;
> 5. *Calls upon* Israel urgently to place its nuclear facilities under IAEA safeguards;
> 6. *Considers* that Iraq is entitled to appropriate redress for the destruction it has suffered, responsibility for which has been acknowledged by Israel;. . . .[23]

The General Conference of IAEA at its 25th session adopted a resolution, GC (xxv) Res. 381, on September 26, 1981, in which it decided by a vote of 51 to 8 with 27 abstentions to consider at its next session the suspension of Israel if it failed to comply with the Security Council resolution.[24] The Agency's Statute provides for suspension of a member by a two-thirds majority vote of the General Conference upon the recommendation of the Board of Governors.[25]

The draft resolution for suspension of Israel invoked, *inter alia,* the "persistent violation of the Statute and the purposes and principles of the Charter of the United Nations"[26] and Israel's failure to comply with Security Council Resolution 487 (1981).[27] As the United States representative Mr. Davis pointed out, there had been no recommendation from the Board of Governors,[28] and the Israeli "attack did not violate any specific Article of the Statute or any agreement entered into pursuant to the Statute. Nor could a one-time action qualify as 'persistent'."[29] Israel maintained that "[t]here could be no greater damage to the international non-proliferation regime than a politicized IAEA"[30] and that

[23] 2288th meeting, UN Doc. S/RES/487 (1981); 75 *AJIL* 724–25 (1981).

[24] UN Dept. of Public Information, Press Release WS/1043, October 2, 1981, pp. 6–7.

[25] Article XIX. B reads: "A member which has persistently violated the provisions of this Statute or of any agreement entered by it pursuant to this Statute may be suspended from the exercise of the privileges and rights of membership by the General Conference acting by a two-thirds majority of the members present and voting upon recommendation by the Board of Governors." *U.S. Treaties and other International Acts Series* 3873, p. 19.

[26] IAEA Doc. GC (XXVI)/OR. 245, October 4, 1982, para. 5. (Tunisia)

[27] *Ibid.,* para. 19. (Zambia)

[28] *Ibid.,* para. 12.

[29] *Ibid.,* para. 9.

[30] *Ibid.,* para. 28.

> "[T]o invoke Security Council resolution 487 or any other resolution as grounds for considering the suspension of Israel's rights and privileges of membership was both artificial and illegal. If such political requirements existed, many States represented at the Conference, in particular Iraq, would be in violation of the Statute and therefore subject to suspension."[31]

The United States representative recalled that "[h]is Government had consistently opposed proposals to expel or suspend Israel illegally in the past, and continued to do so;" that "[t]he Agency's Statute gave no mandate to attempt to enforce resolutions of the Security Council or other United Nations organizations;" that "[b]ecause the Security Council had not imposed sanctions, suspension by the Agency would run counter to the considered judgment of the United Nations organ specifically charged with responsibility for the maintenance of international peace and security;" that "after 30 years marked by military action in virtually every region of the globe, no Member State had ever been suspended" and concluded that "the suspension of Israel from any United Nations body would jeopardize continued United States support for that body and would have grave consequences for its continued participation in it. The illegal suspension of Members would be the dangerous first step toward the unravelling of the whole United Nations system."[32]

In the roll-call vote on the draft resolution to suspend Israel "[t]here were 43 votes in favor and 27 against, with 16 abstentions. The required two-thirds majority being 47, the draft resolution was rejected."[33]

The reasons for the opposing votes were stated by the United States before, and for the abstentions, by Venezuela after the vote.[34] Since the substantive flaws of the defeated draft resolution could not be excised, its proponents fell back upon the credentials route which has worked so well in the case of South Africa, both in the United Nations and in the International Atomic Energy Agency.[35] At the subsequent meeting, September 24, 1982, the delegate of Iraq recalled that in the Credentials Committee seven delegates had rejected Israel's credentials and six had accepted them. He therefore proposed to amend the operative paragraph of the draft resolution of the committee by adding the words "with the exception of the credentials presented by Israel" on the ground that Iraq "refused to consider Israel to be the legal representative of the region" meaning the Golan Heights, Jerusalem, the West Bank and the Gaza strip.[36]

The representative of the United States argued that the rejection of the credentials "would constitute a violation of Article V[37] to the extent that it would be equivalent to

[31] *Ibid.*, para. 27.

[32] *Ibid.*, paras. 8, 10, 11, 13, 14.

[33] *Ibid.*, para. 41. The opposing votes were cast mainly by Western States: the abstentions came from a cross-section of groups other than the Socialist and Arab blocs.

[34] *Ibid.*, para. 42.

[35] See IAEA Doc. GC (XXIII) (Dec. 16, 1979).

[36] IAEA Doc. GC (XXVI)/OR. 246, October 13, 1982, para. 16.

[37] The text of Article V. A reads: "A General Conference consisting of all members shall meet in regular annual session. . . ." Paragraph B of Article V reads: "At such sessions, each member shall be represented by one delegate who may be accompanied by alternates and by advisers. . . ." There is no provision in the Statute for the expulsion of a member.

suspending the privileges and rights of a Member,'' and that suspension required two-thirds majority. He ''deplored the attempt to impose political sanctions on Israel on the occasion of a purely technical question, namely that of determining whether delegations' credentials conformed with the rules laid down'' and issued the warning that:

> ''His delegation wished it to be clearly understood that, in the event of de facto suspension of the exercise by Israel of the rights and privileges of membership, which would be illegal, it would withdraw from the current session of the General Conference and that the Government of the United States would reconsider its participation in the Agency's work.''[38]

The result of the roll-call vote on the amendment proposed by the delegation of Iraq was as follows: ''There were 40 votes in favor and 40 against, with 6 abstentions. In accordance with Rule 78 of the Rules of Procedure, the amendment proposed by the delegation of Iraq was not adopted.''[39]

What followed was somewhat like the theater of the absurd such as has rarely, if ever, been witnessed at a diplomatic conference. The key roles were played by the President, Mr. Siazon (the Philippines) and Mr. Herron, the Director of the Legal Division of the Agency. As reported, the representative of Madagascar ''explained that he had been present at the time of the vote and that he wished his vote to be recorded. His delegation voted 'yes'.''[40]

At request of the President, Mr. Herron

> ''recalled that a similar situation had occurred at a meeting of the Board the previous year. One Governor had returned to the room *before* the end of the ballot. His advice on that occasion had been that the Governor's vote should be recorded, so as not to deprive a delegation of its sovereign right to vote and in accordance with the principle of international law whereby a defect of form—in that case the late recording of a representative's vote—should not invalidate substance, in other words the vote of the representative in question. In the United Nations Organization, the practice was also based on the desire not to deprive a delegation of its right to vote. The vote of the Malagasy delegation should, therefore, be recorded.''[41]

[38] *Ibid.*, paras. 17, 18.

[39] *Ibid.*, para. 25.

[40] *Ibid.*, para. 26.

[41] *Ibid.*, para. 27. Emphasis supplied. The legal expert could apparently not distinguish between registering a vote before or after the announcement of the result of the ballot. The delegate of the Netherlands asked the Director of the Legal Division twice ''up to what time a delegation could still have its vote recorded after the closure of a ballot'' (*ibid.*, paras. 30, 38) only to be told *after* the Iraqi amendment had been adopted that his question ''was purely academic.'' *Ibid.*, para. 39. Changes in a recorded vote are often requested and noted in the record of the meeting but no changes in the announced result of the ballot are made. Sydney D. Bailey, *The General Assembly of the United Nations: A Study of Procedure and Practice.* (New York: Praeger, 1964 Revised ed.), p. 151. In connection with the principles of international law regarding defects of form invoked by Mr. Herron, the Judgment (Jurisdiction) of August 30, 1924, the case of the *Mavrommatis Palestine Concessions* (Greece v. Great Britain) comes to mind. The Permanent Court of International Justice, referring to defects in the Greek Application, declared: ''The Court, whose jurisdiction is international, is not bound to attach to matters of form the same degree of importance which they might possess in municipal law.'' Publication of the PCIJ, Series A, No. 2, pp. 6–93, at 34. In his separate opinion in the *Barcelona Traction Co. Case,* Judge Wellington Koo put the point more explicitly saying: ''International law, being primarily based upon the general principles of law and justice, is unfettered by technicalities and formalistic considerations which are often given importance in municipal law.'' *Barcelona Traction Company* (Preliminary Objections) Judgment of July 24, 1964, ICJ Reports 1964, pp. 60–61 at para. 32. However, it is not clear how those statements could relate to voting in the IAEA. One may wonder whether the Director of Legal Division satisfied the requirements ''of the highest standard of efficiency, technical competence, and integrity'' laid down in VII.D of the Statute for employment in the Agency. See also the statement by the United States delegate, *infra,* n. 47, at 670.

The representative of the United States observed, correctly it is believed, that "the present situation was different because the results of the vote had already been announced," and that "the recording of an additional vote amounted to a reconsideration of the ballot which had already taken place, and a decision to hold a fresh ballot required a two-thirds majority."[42] But as the ballot had shown, the advocates of the *"de facto"* suspension did not have the votes to follow the *de jure* road. The President, after noting that "whichever way the decision went, the rights of one State would be affected," decided to affect the right of Israel rather than the "rights" of Madagascar and to follow, without being aware of it, the Bouteflika way by declaring "that the vote of the Malagasy delegation was valid."[43]

The delegate of the United States challenged the President's ruling and by a vote of 37 to 40, with 9 abstentions, "[t]he appeal against the President's ruling was rejected."[44] As a consequence, the result of the first ballot was amended as follows: "In accordance with the President's ruling, the amendment proposed by the delegation of Iraq to the draft resolution . . . was adopted by 41 votes to 40, with 6 abstentions," and thus once again the law was defeated.[45]

The amended resolution was put to the vote and declared adopted by 41 to 39, with 5 abstentions.[46] The British delegate observed "that he was disquieted by the use of procedural means to achieve political ends, by the ruling of the President and by the opinion given by the Director of the Legal Division. . . . In the circumstances, his delegation could not participate further in the General Conference and was obliged to leave."[47] The United States delegate

> declared that he deplored the President's ruling and was appalled by the opinion rendered by the Director of the Legal Division. The credentials of the delegation of Israel should be accepted as they were absolutely in accordance with the established rules. An item such as the examination of delegates' credentials must not be used as a pretext for re-opening a debate which had already been closed by the decision of the General Conference to reject a draft resolution on the suspension of Israel from the exercise of the privileges and rights of membership. The extent to which the Agency has become politicized, as evidenced by the resolution just adopted, was wholly unacceptable to his Government. The Agency had been founded as a technical body to promote the peaceful uses of atomic energy. Instead, it has become a forum for political debates. The persistent abuse of the United Nations system for the pursuit of political vendettas was an exceptionally dangerous course. The politicization of the Agency must cease. In the circumstances, his delegation must withdraw from the General Conference. His Government would reassess its policy regarding United States support for and participation in the IAEA and its activities.[48]

42 *Ibid*, para. 28. See also the observation of the British delegate, *ibid.*, para. 44, and of the French delegate, *ibid.*, para. 49.

43 *Ibid.*, para. 31.

44 *Ibid.*, paras. 32, 36.

45 *Ibid.*, para. 37.

46 *Ibid.*, para. 43. The total vote on the ruling was 86 and 85 on the amended resolution. Mexico abstained on the ruling but voted for the resolution. Ecuador and Venezuela abstained on the ruling but voted against the resolution. Sri Lanka abstained on the ruling and did not participate in the vote on the resolution.

47 *Ibid.*, para. 44. The delegate of Italy also declared that he "was obliged to leave the meeting." *Ibid.*, para. 48.

48 *Ibid.*, para. 45. Views, critical of the proceedings were also expressed by Japan, Canada, France, Australia, Denmark, Ireland, Greece, and Chile, *ibid.* paras. 46, 47, 49, 50, 51, 53, 54, 55. It may be noted that McWhinney would not have

What effect the action of Great Britain, Italy and the United States will have on the Agency, the specialized organizations, and the United Nations remains to be seen. The United States has decided to suspend payment of its dues to the Agency,[49] as it did in the case of UNESCO mentioned above. The legality of such financial countermeasures is doubtful despite the Goldberg reservation[50] and the failure of other members to pay their dues for peacekeeping operations.[51] There may be some truth in the old saw to fight fire with fire, but there may be some who will blame the politicization of international institutions on those who oppose it instead of on those who were and are its proponents.[52] In order to break this vicious circle one might consider referring the constitutionality of politicizing proposals or actions to the International Court of Justice, but it is unlikely that the majorities that are responsible for such actions would be willing to vote in favor of a request for an advisory opinion. Still less promising in spite of its apparent attractiveness is the proposal to establish the compulsory jurisdiction of the Court by means of a declaration by the United States pursuant, presumably, to Article 36(2) of the Statute of the Court, that the United States accepts such jurisdiction "in all legal disputes hereafter arising concerning the interpretation or application of the Charter of the United Nations."[53] One may doubt the need for such a declaration additional to that made by the United States on August 14, 1946.[54] It provides for the compulsory jurisdiction of the Court "in all legal disputes hereafter arising concerning (a) the interpretation of a treaty." It is well established that the Charter is a multilateral treaty and therefore the

approved of the President's ruling in the case. For "infringements of the Charter or rejections of General Assembly or Security Council resolutions, not directly related to the issue of the representativeness of the delegation seeking accreditation, do not, prima facie, seem to bear upon decisions of the General Assembly and its credentials Committee in this context." *Supra,* n. 11, at 34.

[49] See Judith Miller "Head of World Arms Agency Sees Peril in U.S. Curbs." p. A3. The dues amount to $8.5 million, about 26 percent of the budget. In the same article Dr. Hans Blix, Director General of the Agency, was reported as saying that a prolonged reassessment "could cripple" the operations of the Agency. Mr. Gerard C. Smith, a former representative of the United States, stated on his own behalf and on behalf of three other former representatives to the IAEA, that they opposed withdrawal from the Agency and refusal (after the current suspension) to pay the assessed contributions. On the other hand they deplored "the patently illegal action" taken at the General Conference. *The New York Times,* October 26, 1982, p. A 29.

[50] See Schwebel, *supra,* n. 19, at 140, n. 26. The reservation was made by Ambassador Goldberg on August 16, 1965 in the UN Special Committee on Peacekeeping Operations. He made it "crystal clear that if any member can insist on making an exception to the principle of collective financial responsibility with regard to certain activities of the Organization, the United States reserves the same option to make exceptions if, in our view, strong and compelling reasons exist for doing so. There can be no double standard among the Members of the Organization." U.N. Doc. A/AC. 121/PV. 15, pp. 3–15, and 60 *AJIL* 104 at 106 (1966).

[51] See Bernard D. Nossiter, "U.N. Chief Chides U.S. on Funds," *The New York Times,* January 4, 1983, p. A 2. According to Nossiter the United States owes the UN $612,000 "because Congress has forbidden the use of any funds for the Palestine Liberation Organization and the South-West Africa People's Organization."

[52] For a sample of views see Charles W. Maynes, "American Policies in the United Nations," in Seymour M. Finger and Joseph R. Harbert (eds.) *U.S. Policy in International Institutions. Defining Reasonable Options in an Unreasonable World* (Boulder, Col.: Westview Press, 1978 pp. 403–418; "A New U.S. Policy Toward the United Nations. Ad Hoc Group on United States Policy Toward the United Nations," *ibid.* pp. 449–463; and Philip M. Klutznick, "American Goals in a Changing United Nations," *ibid.* 464–472. See also Lyons, Baldwin and McNemar, "The Politicization Issue in the UN Specialized Agencies" in David A. Kay (ed.), *The Changing UN: Options for the United States* (Praeger, 1977), pp. 81–92.

[53] Sohn, "Enabling the U.S. to contest 'Illegal' UN Acts." 69 *AJIL* 852–854 (1975); the trial balloon launched by Professor Sohn was promptly deflated by Dan Ciobanu in "Could the Use of the Contentious Procedure of the International Court of Justice Have Any Significant Impact upon the Practice of the United Nations? A Reply to Professor Louis B. Sohn.", 70 *AJIL* 328–338 (1976).

[54] *ICJ Yearbook 1946–1947,* pp. 217–218.

proposed declaration would do nothing more than clarify, if that were necessary, the range of the term "treaty" in the original declaration. Moreover, the members who are pressing for illegal acts in and out of the United Nations have not accepted and are not likely to accept the compulsory jurisdiction of the Court. Even if the United States could find a willing adversary, and even if the Court would give a judgment, which is doubtful on grounds of standing,[55] its impact on the practice of the United Nations is even more doubtful for the reasons developed by Dr. Ciobanu.

Be that as it may, the reaction of the United States to the illegal proceedings in the IAEA may well have produced a sobering effect[56] on the attempts to expel Israel at the first part of the 37th session of the General Assembly, from September 21 to December 21, 1982.[57] While the session was in progress, Secretary of State George P. Shultz was reported to have "warned that the United States will walk out of any United Nations body that expels Israel, and will halt its contribution to that unit."[58] It may well be that what was afoot was not an attempt at "expulsion," which pursuant to Article 6 would require a prior recommendation of the Security Council, but at a challenge to the credentials of Israel followed by a "Bouteflika" ruling that might deprive Israel, contrary to Article 9 of the Charter, of its right to participate in the work of the General Assembly.[59] Whatever the aim and the strategy may have been, the attempt was called off and the upshot was a letter to the President of the General Assembly Imre Hollai (Hungary), in which 43 members, including the Soviet bloc and a majority of the Arab or Islamic group, expressed their "reservation on the credentials of the delegation of Israel."[60]

This, however, may not be the end of the unconstitutional drive to "unseat" Israel. For the same group and its allies in the other groups have also been trying another approach, namely to "de-legitimize" Israel by contending that it has failed to satisfy the

[55] See South West Africa Cases, Second Phase, Judgment of July 18, 1966, *I.C.J. Reports* 1966, p. 6 at p. 42, para. 73, and p. 51, para. 99.

[56] Since the United States walked out from the General Conference of the IAEA, President Reagan signed on December 21, 1982, P.L. 97-377, which provides in Sec. 159, for suspension of funds to the Agency until its Board of Governors certifies that Israel may fully participate in the Agency. In his address to the General Assembly on September 30, 1982, Secretary of State Schultz referred to the IAEA and said: "As our action last week in Vienna should make clear, we will not accept attempts to politicize—and, therefore, emasculate—such vital institutions." 82 *Dept of State Bulletin* pp. 1-9 (No. 2068, November 1982) at 9.

[57] The writer has been informed that the United States reaction in the IAEA also had a sobering effect on the International Telecommunication Union, whose Plenipotentiary Conference, in October, 1982, was faced with similar maneuvers concerning Israel and which were thereupon promptly shelved.

[58] Bernard D. Nossiter, "Iran Challenges Israel's Right to Seat at UN," *The New York Times,* October 26, 1982, p. A 15.

[59] It may be recalled that like Secretary Schultz, Resolution 214 (adopted by the U.S. Senate on July 18, 1975) refers to expulsion rather than to the illegal suspension *via* the credentials route. The Resolution states that the Senate "looks with disfavor and concern over persistent attempts by some nations among the so-called nonaligned nations of the Third World to expel Israel from membership in the United Nations; and . . . That if Israel is expelled from the United Nations the Senate will review all present United States commitments to the Third World nations involved in the expulsion, and will consider seriously the implication of continued membership in the United Nations under such circumstances." *1975 Digest of United States Practice in International Law,* at 65. At the 1975 session of the General Assembly Libya, Saudi Arabia and Syria opposed unsuccessfully the acceptance of Israel's credentials. *Ibid.,* p. 66 and U.N.Doc. A/10270, September 29, 1975.

[60] Nossiter, supra, n. 56. UN Doc. A/37/563, October 22, 1982; six more Members added their signatures. Doc. A/37/563/Add. 1, October 25, 1982. For the Israeli response see Doc. A/37/565, October 25, 1982.

conditions of membership laid down in Article 4(1) of the Charter. Aside from the question by dint of what authority the General Assembly may claim the right of "legitimizing" or "de-legitimizing" Member States, reference may be made to General Assembly Resolution 37/123A, adopted on December 16, 1982 as part of the by now habitual omnibus resolution on "the situation in the Middle East," as evidence of this approach. After noting in the Preamble "that Israel's record and actions established conclusively that it is not a peace-loving Member State and that it has not carried out its obligations under the Charter of the United Nations," the Assembly, in operative paragraph 12, *[d]etermines once more* that Israel's record and actions confirm that it has persistently violated the principles contained in the Charter and that it has carried out neither its obligations under the Charter nor its commitment under General Assembly resolution 273(III) of 11 May 1949.[61] In operative paragraph 14, the Assembly "*[r]eiterates* its call to all Member States to cease forthwith, individually and collectively, all dealings with Israel in order totally to isolate it in all fields."[62]

The call for isolating Israel is not new. In the wake of the 1973 Yom Kippur War and an OPEC-imposed rise in oil prices, in other words, since the oil weapon entered international politics, many states, particularly in Africa, have broken diplomatic relations with Israel. The goal of paragraph 12, however, is nothing else but the exclusion of Israel from the United Nations. Constitutionally, this would require the application of Article 6 of the Charter, specifically a recommendation of the Security Council, which is not likely to be forthcoming. The Soviet and Arab blocs and their allies may have other tactics à la Bouteflica in mind and it will be interesting to see what they will be.

Resolution 37/123A was adopted by a vote of 87 to 23, with 31 abstentions; 16 members were recorded as absent.[63] The long-standing practice of the General Assembly to disregard abstentions in calculating the requisite majorities in Article 18 paragraphs 2 and 3 of the Charter has been based on the Rules of Procedure. Rule 86, entitled "Meaning of the phrase 'members present and voting' in Article 18 of the Charter," reads as follows: "For the purposes of these rules, the phrase 'members present and voting' means members casting an affirmative or negative vote. Members which abstain from voting are considered as not voting." This is not the place to argue that Rule 86 is not an interpretation but a constitutionally doubtful amendment of the Charter. It may have served a use-

[61] The same text appeared first in GA res. ES9/1 of February 5, 1982. By virtue of Resolution 273 (III) the General Assembly, acting upon a recommendation of the Security Council, admitted Israel to membership of the United Nations. In the Preamble Resolution 273 (III) refers to resolutions of November 29, 1947 and December 11, 1948. The resolution of November 29, 1947, numbered 181 (III) provides for the "Future Government of Palestine," and the resolution of December 11, 1948, numbered 194 (III) is entitled "Palestine—Progress Report of the United States Mediator." The reference to these resolutions resulted from a lengthly discussion in the *Ad Hoc* Political Committee in the course of which delegates asked the representative of Israel Aubrey Eban to clarify the future policy of Israel concerning refugees, the status of Jerusalem and other matters. Some delegates may have desired to obtain commitments. However, such efforts turned out to be without result other than the incorporation of references to the resolutions in question. See GAOR: 3rd sess. Part II, *Ad Hoc* Political Committee, SR, pp. 179–360. See also Admission of a State to the United Nations, 16 *I.C.J. Reports 1948,* p. 57. The Court found that the conditions prescribed in Article 4 of the Charter are of an "exhaustive character." *Ibid.,* at 64.

[62] UN Press Release GA/6787, January 4, 1983, pp. 56–58.

[63] *Ibid.,* at 62.

ful purpose when the membership was small and it seemed necessary to get on with the business of the Assembly. Nowadays, with a membership of 157 and a large corps of permanent delegations at the headquarters of the United Nations who prepare drafts of resolutions, line up supporters, and actively bargain for votes, there seems no reason why the adoption of resolutions should not be made a little more difficult and more in conformity with Article 18 of the Charter. This could be accomplished by simply eliminating Rule 86 and applying the text of Article 18. The abstaining members certainly participate in the vote and they are recorded accordingly, as are the members that are absent or did not participate in the vote.[64]

A return to the Charter would not prevent the adoption of partisan or ideologically motiviated resolutions but would make their adoption more difficult. Resolution 37/123A would not have been adopted by the required two-thirds majority if the abstentions had been included. The total of votes cast was 140 and the required majority would have been 94, that is, 7 votes more than the 87 favorable votes. It may be of interest to recall that the infamous resolution 3379 (XXX) of November 10, 1975, determining "that Zionism is a form of racism and racial discrimination," would not have been adopted if abstentions had been counted. The vote was 139 and the required majority 93.[65] One need have no illusion about stemming the tide towards majoritarianism in the General Assembly. The reform suggested here would merely put a bridle on it and stimulate the permanent delegations to work a little harder. However, it is well to bear in mind that the two-thirds majority requirement of Article 18(2) can be easily bypassed by the simple majority rule of Article 18(3) combined, if necessary, with a ruling of the President. It would therefore seem that if the United States and other Members are serious about preserving the rule of law and preventing a further degradation of the constitutional environment of the United Nations and its agencies such as occurred last year in the IAEA, they will have to vote, regretfully perhaps, more often "with their feet," as the saying goes, and with their purse, and not merely with their voices or hands.

[64] In this context it may be worth while to recall the reply by the United States to resolution 2925 (XXVII) of November 29, 1973 inviting Member States to make proposals "for enhancing the effectiveness of the decisions and resolutions adopted by United Nations organs." The United States suggested that "the General Assembly might consider modifying its rules so that adoption of resolutions would require an appropriate majority of *all* votes cast, counting those who abstain as present and voting. If this change were made, Assembly resolutions would better express the views of a majority of the Assembly, rather than as now on occasion, of a minority whose views prevailed because of a large number of abstentions." *1973 Digest of United States Practice in International Law*, pp. 52–53. Emphasis in the original. At the next session of the Assembly the representative of the United States said on November 29, 1973, that "recent voting patterns within the United Nations lead us to consider whether or not bloc voting is now too often being used in a manner which raises serious questions for the future effectiveness of this organization. One concern is with the inclination of many U.N. members to support one-sided or simplistic resolutions on complicated or contentious issues, resolutions which do not necessarily represent the weight of world opinion, and which, worse still, have not the slightest chance of being effectively implemented. The United Nations is not an instrument for wish fulfillment. Rather it should be a catalyst for effective action on world problems." *Ibid.*, at 54.

[65] See Leo Gross "The United Nations and the United States," in Völkerrecht und Rechtsphilosophie, edited by Peter Fischer, H. F. Köck and Alfred Verdross (Duncker and Humblot, Berlin, 1980) 403–424, at 406 (footnote omitted). See also *supra*, pp. 643–660, at 646.

## POSTSCRIPT

After finishing this paper, I was informed that in response to the question "Has any action been taken by the Board of Governors [of the IAEA] to certify Israeli participation in the Agency in conformance with the Kasten/McClure Amendment to the continuing resolution?",[66] the Department of State spokesman stated on February 22, 1983: "I understand . . . that action has been taken which will meet the provision of U.S. law known as the Kasten/McClure Amendment and permit the resumption of U.S. financial contributions."[67] This is further evidence of the effectiveness of the suggested "voting" method.

Moreoever, on the same day, at the 600th meeting of the Board of Governors of the IAEA, the Director General, Dr. Blix.

> expressed his gratification that the United States Government, following its reassessment of the Agency's activities, had decided to resume its participation. He recalled that, in a letter of 14 October 1982 sent to all Members of the Board, he had described the factual and legal situation pertaining to Israel's position in the Agency—namely, that Israel remained a fully participating Member of the Agency.[68]

The delegate of India (Mr. Singh) seemed to express some reservation about the legal aspects of the matter, saying that "the Statute [of the Agency] clearly provided that a measure adopted by the General Conference could not be annulled by the Board of Governors."[69] The delegate of the United States (Mr. Kennedy), "after congratulating the Director General on his statement," referred to the decision of his Government to suspend its participation in the activities of the Agency, and warned that "all Member States would pay a high price if the viability and effectiveness of the Agency were threatened, as they had been, by a tendency to accord increasing importance to political issues extraneous to the Agency's work." Finally, he

> hoped that the organization would put behind it the unfortunate political wrangling of the recent past and return whole-heartedly to the mission conferred upon it by its Statute. The United States was thus prepared to renew its commitment to the Agency within the constraints of the country's laws, but that commitment would depend also on the degree to which other Member States were prepared to respect the principles set forth in the Statute.[70]

LEO GROSS

[66] This amendment refers to the provision in Pub. L. No. 97-377 in note 56 *supra*.
[67] Dep't of State Press Guidance, Feb. 22, 1983, at 1-2.
[68] IAEA Doc. GOV/OR.600, at 3 (March 14, 1983).
[69] *Id.* at 11-12.
[70] *Id.* at 12-14

# VII

# SETTLEMENT OF DISPUTES BY THE INTERNATIONAL COURT OF JUSTICE

# SOME OBSERVATIONS ON THE INTERNATIONAL COURT OF JUSTICE

## I

The International Court of Justice, the principal judicial organ of the United Nations, unquestionably has made important contributions to the development of international law, though perhaps not on a scale that was optimistically assumed or, at any rate, hoped for at the time of its founding. Nor has the rôle which it has played in the actual functioning of the organization come up to these expectations. It may be well to recall at the outset what they were. In the words of the Report of the Rapporteur of Committee IV/1 at San Francisco:

> On the basis of the texts proposed for the Charter and for the Statute, the First Committee ventures to foresee a significant role for the new Court in the international relations of the future. The judicial process will have a central place in the plans of the United Nations for the settlement of international disputes by peaceful means. An adequate tribunal will exist for the exercise of the judicial function, and it will rank as a principal organ of the Organization. It is confidently anticipated that the jurisdiction of this tribunal will be extended as time goes on, and past experience warrants the expectation that its exercise of this jurisdiction will command a general support.
>
> A long road has been travelled in the effort to enthrone law as the guide for the conduct of states in their relations one with another. A new milepost is now erected along that road. In establishing the International Court of Justice, the United Nations hold before a war-stricken world the beacons of Justice and Law and offer the possibility of substituting orderly judicial processes for the vicissitudes of war and the reign of brutal force.[1]

[1] Report of the Rapporteur of Committee IV/1 to Commission IV, Doc. 913 (June 12), 13 U.N.C.I.O. Docs. 381, at 393.

In espousing the view that international adjudication of disputes might become a substitute for war and force, the report merely adopted what has virtually become the *leitmotif* of the peace movement, of the advocates of arbitration, since the turn of the century. As will be shown presently, this view no longer predominates, though it has by no means been abandoned. With respect to the hope or expectation that law would be enthroned as a guide for the conduct of states or that the Court would play a significant rôle in the United Nations, there is hardly a difference of opinion; neither has the Court played such a rôle nor has international law significantly expanded its moderating and regulatory influence in the relations of states.

## II

Arbitration or adjudication as an alternative to war for the settlement of disputes is a theme which runs from the Hague Convention for the Pacific Settlement of International Disputes of 1899 through the Covenant of the League of Nations to the Charter of the United Nations. The inspiration for this link was probably provided by the *Alabama Arbitration* of 1872 which, it was widely believed, averted a war between the parties, the United States and the United Kingdom.[2] It is made explicit, along with the still current notion of the limitation of armaments as a means of ensuring peace, in the Russian Circular Note proposing the program of the First Conference of December 30, 1898,[3] and in several articles of the Hague Conventions for the Pacific Settlement of International Disputes of 1899 and 1907.[4]

Characteristically, the governments, while affirming on the one hand the desirability of seeking solutions of differences by methods other than force, are careful, on the other hand, to hedge this commitment in such a way as to leave the door open for war.[5] However, the peaceful settlement of the 1904 Dogger Bank incident involving Russia and Great Britain with the assistance of a commission of inquiry confirmed the belief in the power of public opinion and the efficacy of new devices of diplomacy for the settle-

[2] Sir Arnold D. McNair, The Development of International Justice, p. 3: "But without question the most important, from the point of view of both the danger it averted and the influence it exerted upon the future, is the Alabama Claims arbitration between the United States and Great Britain, which took place in Geneva in 1872. . . . The feature of this arbitration which captured the public imagination and was significant for the future was that two states were prepared to submit to a tribunal . . . disputes which were regarded as affecting their honor and vital interests and as being of such a character that, I think I can say, had never been submitted to arbitration before and had often led to war." See also Percy E. Corbett, Law in Diplomacy 152–156 (1959).

[3] The Hague Conventions and Declarations of 1899 and 1907 (ed. by James Brown Scott, 1915), p. xvii: "Acceptance, in principle, of the use of good offices, mediation, and voluntary arbitration, in cases where they are available with the purpose of preventing armed conflicts between nations."

[4] *Ibid.* 41 ff. Art. 1 of the 1899 Convention reads: "With a view of obviating, as far as possible, recourse to force in the relations between States, the signatory Powers agree to use their best efforts to insure the pacific settlement of international differences." See also Arts. 2, 8, and 15.

[5] See Art. 9: "In differences of an international nature involving neither honor nor vital interests . . ."; and Art. 16: "In questions of a legal nature, and especially in the interpretation or application of international conventions, arbitration is recognized by the signatory Powers as the most effective, and at the same time the most equitable, means of settling disputes which diplomacy has failed to settle." *Ibid.* 45, 55.

ment of issues involving national honor, if not vital interests.[6] The so-called Bryan Treaties of 1913–1914 reinforced the idea that wars can and would be avoided by skillful manipulation of international devices combined with a cooling-off period.[7] This, together with the 1907 proposal for the creation of a permanent judicial Arbitration Court,[8] completes the elements on the basis of which the Covenant of the League of Nations erected a coherent pattern of peaceful settlement. Without eliminating resort to war altogether, Article 12 provided, and the Members agreed, that disputes "likely to lead to a rupture" should be submitted to arbitration or judicial settlement or to inquiry by the Council. Here, without drawing a distinction between legal and political disputes which is shown in Article 13, and confirming the belief of the Hague Peace Conference that wars can be avoided by new devices of diplomacy, a choice is offered between political—inquiry by the Council—and judicial procedures—arbitration and adjudication. The drive for such alternatives to war led, between 1918 and 1928, to the conclusion of well over one hundred and fifty bilateral treaties creating permanent institutions for the settlement of disputes.[9]

The Geneva Protocol for the Pacific Settlement of International Disputes, adopted by the Assembly of the League in 1924, though it never entered into force, is a further stage in the invention of new, and the combination of existing, devices to maintain peace and security and to eliminate war.[10] A similar effort at consolidation and systematization is represented by the General Act for the Pacific Settlement of International Disputes, adopted by the League Assembly in 1928 and adapted to changed conditions by the General Assembly of the United Nations in Resolution 268A(III) of April 28, 1949.[11] The link between some form of peaceful settlement and the elimination of war is particularly striking in the Locarno Agreements of 1925[12] and the Treaty for the Renunciation of War of August 27, 1928, commonly known as the Pact of Paris or the Kellogg-Briand Pact. In the latter the parties "condemn recourse to war for the solution of international controversies," and consequently agree that the solution of all disputes or conflicts of whatever origin or nature "shall never be sought except by pacific means."[13]

In addition to offering a combination of procedures for settling disputes, the Covenant provided for, and the League of Nations established, the Permament Court of International Justice and the enforcement of its judgments as well as of awards rendered by arbitral tribunals.[14] The Court gave, during the period of its existence (1922–1946)

[6] For arbitration in the period between the First Hague Peace Conference and World War I, see Corbett, *op. cit.* 136–186.

[7] See 2 Oppenheim, International Law 14 (7th ed. by H. Lauterpacht, 1952); and 2 Hyde, International Law 1570 (2nd ed., 1945).

[8] Scott, *op. cit.* 31.

[9] Max Habicht, Post-War Treaties for the Pacific Settlement of International Disputes xix (1931). For the period 1929–1941 a similar number of treaties is listed in Systematic Survey of Treaties for the Pacific Settlement of International Disputes, 1928–1948, pp. 1180 ff. (U.N. Pub. Sales No. 1949.V 3).

[10] For text, see Habicht, *op. cit* 929.

[11] General Assembly, 3rd Sess., Official Records, Pt. 2, Resolutions, pp. 10–11 (Doc. A/900).

[12] 54 League of Nations Treaty Series 291.

[13] 94 *ibid.* 59.

[14] Art. 13, par. 4, and Art. 14 of the Covenant.

thirty-two judgments and twenty-seven advisory opinions.[15] Of the latter, twenty opinions were requested by the Council of the League in connection with disputes or situations of international concern which were pending before it.[16]

In spite of this impressive record of fence-building to contain war, minor and major hostilities were fought, and finally the second World War broke out. Did the governments then conclude that the various devices incorporated and developed thoughtfully and systematically in an unprecedentedly large number of bilateral and multilateral instruments were based on a fundamental misconception? By no means. The Charter of the United Nations, which was fashioned before the war was over, resumes the *leitmotif* and declares in new ways the old theme that peaceful procedures should supersede resort to force.[17] It is expressed in Article 1, paragraph 1, in Article 2, paragraphs 3 and 4, and it pervades all of Chapter VI with the solitary exception of Article 38. Contrary to the reaction which had developed in doctrine against the belief in the effectiveness of procedures for peaceful settlement of state differences which are rooted in political tensions or clashes of national interests, the Charter with remarkable consistency pursues one large object: the elimination of war, with the exception of limited self-defense and collective enforcement action, exceptions which are not relevant in this context. Even Article 36, paragraph 3, which directs the Security Council "to take into consideration that legal disputes should as a general rule be referred by the parties to the International Court of Justice," is concerned exclusively with disputes "the continuance of which is likely to endanger the maintenance of international peace and security" or with situations of like nature. These are precisely the sort of disputes or situations which the dominant doctrine today tends to single out as peculiarly unsuitable for decision by the Court. It is worthy of note that in the one and only case in which the Council, acting under Article 36, paragraph 3, recommended that the parties refer their dispute to the Court—in the *Corfu Channel* Case—the United Kingdom brought the dispute to the Council under Article 35, which, like Article 36, deals with what might be called political disputes.[18] The Court had no difficulty in deciding the legal issues involved in the dispute, and awarded damages to the United Kingdom which, regrettably, have not yet been paid by

[15] Manley O. Hudson, The Permanent Court of International Justice, 1920–1942, p. 779 (1943). For a brief analysis of the Court's jurisprudence, see C. Wilfred Jenks, "The Compulsory Jurisdiction of International Courts and Tribunals," Preliminary Report, 24ᵉ Commission, 47 Annuaire, Institut de Droit International 119–132 (1957, I) (referred to hereinafter as Jenks, Preliminary Report).

[16] Jenks, Preliminary Report 121.

[17] It may be noted in passing that this theme was received in the systems of major treaties on international law. Suffice it to refer to Oppenheim, *op. cit.* note 7 above. Part I is entitled "Settlement of State Differences," Chapter I, "Amicable Settlement of State Differences," Chapter II, "Compulsive Settlement of State Differences." In Hyde, *op. cit.*, Part VI is entitled "Differences between States. Modes of Redress other than War," and Vol. 3, Part VII, "Differences between States. War."

[18] Report of the Security Council to the General Assembly covering the period from July 16, 1946, to July 15, 1947. General Assembly, 2nd Sess., Official Records, Supp. No. 2, pp. 51, 61 (Doc. A/366). In the debate the Soviet Union contended that the dispute did not constitute a threat to peace and security and that presumably for this reason it fell outside the competence of the Council. The United Kingdom submitted that it might be hard to define what constituted such a threat. The Council, by placing the item on its agenda and issuing the recommendation, presumably considered itself competent and the dispute as one constituting an actual or potential threat to peace. See also statements by Sir Hartley Shawcross before the Court on Feb. 28 and March 1, 1948. 3 Corfu Channel Case, Pleadings 51–59, at 53 (1948).

Albania.[19] This case, isolated as it is, does not necessarily invalidate the doctrine; nor does it bear out the thesis that adjudication offers an alternative to war. Its contribution, modest though it is, by no means should be belittled, for it does lend support to the often advanced proposition that even so-called political issues can be broken down into legal and political components, and that the former are amenable to adjudication. This separability of the legal and political issues has been recognized by the governments parties to the Brussels Pact of March 17, 1948. They agree to refer to the Court all disputes falling within the scope of Article 36, paragraph 2, of its Statute and to submit to conciliation all disputes outside the scope of this clause. But they also agree

> In the case of a mixed dispute involving both questions for which conciliation is appropriate and other questions for which judicial settlement is appropriate, any Party to the dispute shall have the right to insist that the judicial settlement of the legal questions shall precede conciliation.[20]

The Charter prohibition of the use of force as an instrument for the settlement of disputes leaves to the Members of the United Nations the choice between stalemate and submission to a procedure designed to produce a solution accepted as binding. Whatever one may think about arbitration as an alternative to war, on the juridical plane there are few choices left to governments today. That this is so has been recently recognized in one of the resolutions adopted by the Institute of International Law on September 11, 1959. The Institute,

> Convinced that the maintenance of justice by submission to law through acceptance of recourse to international courts and arbitral tribunals is an essential complement to the renunciation of recourse to force in international relations;

resolved:

[19] [1949] I.C.J. Rep. 4 and 244.

[20] Systematic Survey of Treaties . . . pp. 1160 ff. The full title of this instrument is: Treaty of Economic, Social and Cultural Collaboration and Collective Self-Defense between the United Kingdom of Great Britain and Northern Ireland, Belgium, France, Luxembourg, and The Netherlands (Brussels Pact). The accession of the Federal Republic of Germany and the Italian Republic to this Pact was accomplished through Protocol No. I, Modifying and Completing the Brussels Treaty, Paris, October 24, 1954. Disarmament and Security, A Collection of Documents 1919–1955. Subcommittee on Disarmament, 84th Cong., 2d Sess. (Committee Print, 1956), p. 504. The divisibility of disputes into their legal and political components has been suggested on several occasions by the U.N. Secretary General. Thus, in his Annual Report on the Work of the Organization 1954–1955, he said: "It is apparent that there are a number of controversies between Governments which continue to be sources of tension but which are suitable, in whole or in part, for judicial settlement through the Court." General Assembly, 10th Sess., Official Records, Supp. No. 1, p. xiii (Doc. A/2911); in his Report for 1956–1957 he stated: "Even in the present state of international society there are many disputes which would be closer to settlement if the legal issues involved had been the subject of judicial determination." *Ibid.*, 12th Sess., Supp. No. 1 A, p. 5 (Doc. A/3594/Add.1); and in his Report for 1958–1959 he declared: "It should also be recognized that there are many international disputes which involve legal questions along with the political elements and that submission of such questions to the Court for judicial determination would clear the ground for processes of peaceful negotiation in the political organs of the United Nations. Neglect of the legal elements in international conflicts, and of the means by which they may be clarified, thus stands in the way of progress in the political field and, in the long run, may tend to weaken the weight of law in international affairs." *Ibid.*, 14th Sess., Supp. No. 1 A, p. 3 (Doc. A/4132/Add.1).

> In an international community the members of which have renounced recourse to force and undertaken by the Charter of the United Nations to settle their international disputes by peaceful means in such a manner that international peace and security, and justice, are not endangered, recourse to the International Court of Justice or to another international court or arbitral tribunal constitutes a normal method of settlement of legal disputes as defined in Article 36, paragraph 2, of the Statute of the International Court of Justice.

In a following paragraph the Institute felt it necessary and expedient to add:

> Consequently, recourse to the International Court of Justice or to another international court or arbitral tribunal can never be regarded as an unfriendly act towards the respondent State.[21]

Nothing could express better the prevailing conditions of international adjudication than this paragraph. That so distinguished and well-informed a body of scholars and practitioners found it necessary to plead forbearance for a state which referred a dispute to the Court indicates so clearly how little real progress has been achieved in the sixty years since the First Hague Peace Conference, which deemed it necessary to stipulate that the exercise of the right of third states to offer their good offices or mediation to states at variance "can never be regarded by one or the other of the parties in conflict as an unfriendly act." Similarly, in connection with arbitration, that Conference provided

> The Signatory Powers consider it their duty, if a serious dispute threatens to break out between two or more of them, to remind the latter that the Permanent Court is open to them.
>
> Consequently, they declare that the fact of reminding the conflicting parties of the provisions of the present Convention, and the advice given to them, in the highest interest of peace, to have recourse to the Permanent Court, can only be regarded as friendly actions.[22]

One may be tempted to suggest that sixty years ago governments, acting perhaps under the influence of the widespread peace movement and of public opinion generally, gave official sanction to a fallacy which has two faces: first, that wars arise from disputes suitable for solution by resort to arbitration or other devices, and secondly, that for this reason arbitration or some other devices are desirable and indeed practical alternatives and substitutes for war. In spite of the official sanction of this *leitmotif* and in spite of the proven worth of arbitration and mediation and commissions of inquiry for relieving tensions and actually solving disputes, governments made explicit their determination not to entrust to any of these procedures disputes likely to be sources of war, such as those involving vital interests, independence and honor. The more arbitration becomes generalized and institutionalized, the more sweeping, if less explicit, become the reservations,

[21] 48 Annuaire, Institut de Droit International 381 (1959, II). Reproduced in 54 A.J.I.L. 136 (1960).

[22] Arts. 3 and 27 of the 1899 Convention for the Pacific Settlement of International Disputes. Scott, *op. cit.* 43, 61. *Cf.* also Charles De Visscher, Théories et Réalités en Droit International Public 460 (3rd ed., 1960) (hereinafter cited as De Visscher, Théories).

of which trend the Connally Reservation has rightly come to be regarded as a symbol. As a consequence of these conflicting tendencies—towards and away from arbitration and adjudication as a substitute for war—the institutionalized tribunals, the Permanent Court of Arbitration, the Permanent Court of International Justice and the International Court of Justice, have not been used by governments in a manner commensurate with the expectations aroused by the governments themselves.

The institutions were created for the avowed object of facilitating recourse to third-party judgment, but governments have made, and continue to make, very sparing use of the facility which they maintain at their own expense. The compulsory jurisdiction of the Permanent Court of International Justice was prudently limited to a stated list of four "classes of legal disputes" in the classic sense. A still higher degree of prudence was manifest at the San Francisco Conference in redrafting the Statute of the Court. While the list was left in its original form, the new version of the optional clause contains the further limitation "in all legal disputes."[23] This may well mean that, even if a dispute concerns any of the four stated types, it is open to the respondent state to object to the jurisdiction of the Court on the ground that, even though the dispute relates to the interpretation of a treaty, it is nonetheless not a "legal dispute."[24] Yet in spite of this apogee of prudence, the new Court's business has not grown appreciably over that of its predecessor. It has been contended that the function of the Court should be regarded "as part of the general diplomatic machinery at the disposal of States."[25] This may be so in more senses than one. It is certainly correct to maintain that governments at variance have the choice be-

[23] *Cf.* Art. 36, par. 2, of the Statute of the I.C.J., with the text of Art. 36 of the Statute of the P.C.I.J.

[24] The distinction between justiciable disputes (in the phraseology of the Locarno Treaties, disputes in which the parties are in conflict as to their respective rights) which are in fact regarded as justiciable, and disputes which, although regarded as justiciable in law, are not regarded as justiciable in fact, was made by the British Government in Reservation V of its Declaration of April 18, 1957, accepting the jurisdiction of the Court as compulsory pursuant to Art. 36, par. 2, of the Statute of the Court. 1957–1958 I.C.J. Yearbook 211. This Declaration was somewhat modified by the Declaration of Nov. 26, 1958. 1959–1960 *ibid.* 254. The motivations for such a distinction may be found in the British Observations on the Programme of Work of the Committee on Arbitration and Security of the Preparatory Commission for the Disarmament Conference:

"4. . . . Arbitration treaties impliedly, if not explicitly, impose upon the parties the obligation loyally to accept the decision of the tribunal. An arbitration treaty which goes beyond what the public opinion of a country can be counted on to support when the interests of that country are in question and when a decision unfavourable to those interests is pronounced is a treaty which is useless. It is merely calculated to deceive the public. In a moment of grave importance it may fail to achieve a solution of a dispute even if the dispute is arbitrated in accordance with its terms. . . . 5. It is because it is so generally felt that there are some questions—justiciable in their nature—which no country could safely submit to arbitration that it has been usual to make reservations limiting the extent of the obligation to arbitrate. These limitations may vary in form, but their existence indicates the consciousness on the part of Governments that there is a point beyond which they cannot count on their peoples giving effect to the obligations of the treaty. . . . 12. . . . Disputes legal in their nature may arise between two States with regard to matters falling exclusively within the domestic jurisdiction of one of them. No State can agree to the submission to an international tribunal of matters falling exclusively within the range of its national sovereignty. Similarly, there are some political questions even of a justiciable nature as to which a country feels that for the reasons indicated in paragraph 4 the stage has not yet been reached when it can agree unreservedly in advance to submit them to an arbitration tribunal." League of Nations Official Journal, May, 1928, pp. 695–697.

The logic of this reasoning appears to establish public opinion of the moment as the criterion of the justiciability of a dispute and to lead to the sort of self-judging reservation made by the United States in the so-called Connally Amendment and by the United Kingdom in the Declaration referred to above, excluding from the compulsory jurisdiction disputes "relating to any question which, in the opinion of the Government of the United Kingdom, affects the national security of the United Kingdom or of any of its dependent territories." This exclusion was maintained in the Declaration of Nov. 26, 1958.

[25] Shabtai Rosenne, The International Court of Justice 118 (1957).

tween more than one device for seeking a solution. In this sense the Court may well be conceived as part of the diplomatic arsenal. But of the devices among which they choose some are more "diplomatic" than others. One criterion by which various procedures for the peaceful settlement of disputes may be classified divides them into two categories: the decisional and the non-decisional. The former includes arbitration and adjudication;[26] the latter comprises negotiations, good offices, mediation and conciliation. Commissions of inquiry or other devices designed to elucidate the facts relating to a dispute are by their nature and object auxiliary procedures[27] that may and have been used to advantage in connection with any of the others. The essential difference between these two categories is obvious: procedures in the former are bound to lead to a decision on the points with respect to which the governments are at variance, and the decision is accepted in advance as binding.[28] Procedures in the latter, by contrast, may or may not lead to a resolution of the conflict. The decision on this point is reserved by governments. This is perfectly clear in the case of diplomatic negotiations, and it is equally clear in the case of good offices and mediation.[29] Basically this observation holds good in the case of conciliation commissions, which enjoyed in the interwar period a phenomenal popularity on paper, though not in practice. They were to be particularly suitable for handling political disputes. Be that as it may, the conciliation commissions are not empowered to decide a dispute or conflict of interests. Their task is to seek an amicable settlement acceptable to the parties.[30] The governments reserve the decision.

Generalizing, it seems possible to suggest the rôle which law and power or politics play in these two categories. In the case of the non-decisional procedures there is the greatest opportunity for power and politics. International law need not be excluded and may indeed offer a useful starting or bargaining position, but law is not the dominant factor in the process. The object is a settlement acceptable to the parties. It should be noted that the rôle of politics may be strongest and that of law weakest in negotiation, and this may well be the reason why great Powers show a penchant for this procedure. Among the great Powers this preference is most marked in the Soviet Union, which has been known as a champion of state sovereignty, though not of law. In the other procedures of this category the rôles of politics and law are progressively reversed until they reach something of an equilibrium in the conciliation commission. Here the face-to-face collaboration of three or five distinguished individuals may cushion the impact of politics and enhance the part of fair play and justice, *i.e.,* the elements which make up law, if not *the* law applicable to the case. In this sense it is correct to say that the conciliation commis-

[26] Instruments like the General Convention on the Privileges and Immunities of the United Nations of Feb. 3, 1946 (Doc. A/43), according to which an Advisory Opinion given by the Court "shall be accepted as decisive by the parties" (Art. VIII, Sec. 30), are left out of account here.

[27] See Art. 9 of the 1899 Hague Convention for the Pacific Settlement of International Disputes in Scott, *op. cit.* 45.

[28] The question of a *non liquet* is not material in the present context.

[29] Good offices and mediation, says Art. 6 of the 1899 Hague Convention, "have exclusively the character of advice and never have binding force." Scott, *op. cit.* 44.

[30] De Visscher, Théories 433.

sion represents a "partial depoliticization" in the settlement-seeking procedures.[31] And it is probably this depoliticization, partial though it be, which may be the reason why governments have so rarely activated the commissions which, pursuant to treaties, they so frequently have established.[32]

In the case of the decisional procedures the depoliticization is complete, for here the parties agree to a decision based on law and not on politics.[33] It may be possible to distinguish even in this category degrees of depoliticization between arbitration and adjudication by the International Court of Justice. The distinctions, rather subtle in nature, would relate to the influence the parties exercise on the composition of a tribunal of arbitration, on the law and procedure to be applied, and finally to the perennial problem, on which doctrine is not of one mind, whether arbitral tribunals act as "amiables compositeurs" or as *ad hoc* tribunals of law.[34]

Some of these political elements cannot be eliminated even from the Court: the judges have to be elected by political bodies, special agreements have to be drawn up by states at variance, etc. But once the Court is seized, politics are minimized in the work of the Court as completely and as fully as they can be in any human institution, whereas the rôle of law is maximized. Here the surrender of sovereign states to third-party decision is consummated and this is one among several factors which account for the still prevalent reluctance of states to take their disputes to the Court. The completely depoliticized procedure, however, has compensating virtues which the partially depoliticized procedure lacks. One cannot be sure in the absence of reliable statistics, but it seems fairly safe to contend that governments prefer the completely depoliticized to the partially depoliticized procedures, yet they prefer—and for this statement no precise statistics are needed—the diplomatic and fully politicized procedures to the judicial procedure.

## III

Between 1946 and 1960 the International Court of Justice was seized in 34 contentious cases and received 11 requests for Advisory Opinions.[35] Nine Advisory Opinions

[31] *Ibid.* 431.

[32] For example, *cf.* United Nations Systematic Survey of Treaties for the Pacific Settlement of International Disputes, 1928–1948, pp. 130 ff.

[33] See De Visscher, Théories 442, and Rosenne, *op. cit.* 118.

[34] This distinction goes back to Arts. 15 and 37 of the 1899 and 1907 Hague Conventions for the Pacific Settlement of International Disputes, which define arbitration as follows: "International Arbitration has for its object the settlement of disputes between States by judges of their own choice and on the basis of respect for law." Scott, *op. cit.* 55. See also Corbett, Law in Diplomacy 136 ff. On the fate of the draft on arbitral procedure prepared by the International Law Commission, see 1958 I.L.C. Yearbook (II) 1–15, Doc. A/CN.4/Ser. A/1958/Add. 1, and De Visscher Théories 438 f. This draft, as originally conceived by Georges Scelle, Special Rapporteur, aimed at virtually eliminating completely the discretionary element from the arbitral procedure which De Visscher argues is inherent in it and which the majority of Members of the United Nations were determined to preserve. Reversing gears, the Rapporteur submitted a draft from which, as he put it, "*every trace of obligation has been eliminated.*" (Italics in the original.) 1958 I.L.C. Yearbook (II) 3, par. 6.

[35] This information is culled from the Yearbook of the Court. In the case instituted on Nov. 4, 1960, separately by Liberia and Ethiopia against the Union of South Africa on the basis of Art. 7 of the Mandate for South West Africa of Dec. 17, 1920, and Art. 37 of the Statute, the Court, by order of May 20, 1961, after finding that the submissions of the Applications and Memorials by the applicant governments were *mutatis mutandis* identical and that, accordingly, the Govern-

were given at the request of the United Nations General Assembly, and one each at the request of UNESCO and IMCO, respectively. Of the contentious proceedings three were instituted by special agreement.[36] In one case, the *Corfu Channel* Case, proceedings were instituted by the United Kingdom by means of a unilateral application which in the Court's judgment was accepted by Albania. The Court, rejecting Albania's plea to its jurisdiction, found that these two acts constituted a sufficient basis for affirming its jurisdiction. However, by order of March 26, 1948, the Court placed on record the Special Agreement concluded between the parties on March 25, 1948, and declared that this "now formed the basis of further proceedings before the Court."[37] In eight cases the applicant states—the United States in six and the United Kingdom in two—did not invoke any juridical basis for instituting proceedings such as the Optional Clause or a jurisdictional clause in a treaty. The applications were in the nature of offers or invitations addressed to the adverse party to accept the jurisdiction of the Court. In all cases the adverse party declined such offer or invitation. The American applications related to aerial incidents,[38] and the British cases to Antarctica.[39] In two cases, *Aerial Incident of 27 June 1955, United States* v. *Bulgaria* and *United Kingdom* v. *Bulgaria,* the applications relied on the acceptance in 1921 by Bulgaria of the jurisdiction of the Court under the Optional Clause. In the principal litigation arising out of this aerial incident between Israel and Bulgaria the Court found that Article 36, paragraph 5, of its Statute was not applicable to the Bulgarian Declaration of 1921, and that consequently the Court lacked a basis for its jurisdiction to deal with the case.[40] Following this judgment the proceedings against Bulgaria were discontinued at the request of the United Kingdom and the United States.[41] However, the reasons which motivated the action of the United States were totally unrelated to that judgment.[42]

In one instance, the Case concerning the *Compagnie du Port, des Quais et des Entrepôts de Beyrouth and the Société Radio-Orient (France* v. *Lebanon),* the proceedings were discon-

ments of Ethiopia and Liberia were in the same interest, joined the proceedings instituted against the Union of South Africa, [1961] I.C.J. Rep. 13. On May 30, 1961, the Republic of Cameroun filed an Application instituting proceedings against the United Kingdom, General List No. 48; 1960–1961 Yearbook 91. This case is included in the total of 34.

[36] The Asylum Case (Colombia-Peru), the Minquiers and Ecrehos Case (France-United Kingdom) and the Case concerning Sovereignty over Certain Frontier Land (Belgium-Netherlands), 1960–1961 Yearbook 32. In one case, the Case concerning the Arbitral Award Made by the King of Spain on Dec. 23, 1906 (Honduras *v.* Nicaragua), the parties had made an Agreement governing the procedure for submitting the dispute to the Court. 1957–1958 Yearbook 228.

[37] [1947–1948] I.C.J. Rep. 15 at 27 ff. and [1949] *ibid.* 6 ff. See also Rosenne (The International Court of Justice 292), who refers to this case as an instance of jurisdiction "conferred upon the Court by an informal agreement between the parties, reached by successive acts."

[38] See Nos. 22, 23, 25, 28, 40, 44 of the Court's General List, 1960–1961 Yearbook 62 ff. Replying to the Soviet statement that, in filing an application without Soviet consent, the United States "acted in disaccord with the Statute of the International Court of Justice," the Agent for the United States, in a note of Nov. 25, 1958, addressed to the Registrar of the Court, declared: "It is now well settled that any government qualified to appear before this Court may file its application without prior special agreement." 1958–1959 Yearbook 91. The United States appears thus to have relied implicitly upon the *forum prorogatum* doctrine. See Rosenne, *op. cit.,* 284–302.

[39] See Nos. 26 and 27 of the Court's General List, 1960–1961 Yearbook 64.

[40] Aerial Incident of July 27, 1955 (Preliminary Objections) (Israel *v.* Bulgaria), [1959] I.C.J. Rep. 127. For a discussion of this case see Lucius C. Caflisch, in 54 A.J.I.L. 855–868 (1960).

[41] 1959–1960 Yearbook 85, 93.

[42] *Cf.* [1960] I.C.J. Rep. 146.

tinued at the request of the Agent for the applicant state, who informed the Registrar that, "as the result of conversations between the Government of the Republic of Lebanon and the French Embassy in Beirut, satisfactory arrangements had been concluded, and that the Government of the French Republic considered that the conclusion and execution of new undertakings by the Government of the Republic of Lebanon put an end to the disputes."[43] It is not possible to say to what extent the pendency of the dispute before the Court facilitated the amicable settlement arrived at by the parties. In three other instances the proceedings were discontinued at the request of the applicant state.[44] In fourteen cases objections to the jurisdiction were raised. Three cases were withdrawn before the Court could make a ruling.[45] In one case the preliminary objection was withdrawn.[46] Preliminary objections were overruled in five cases[47] and sustained in five cases.[48] However, a distinction may be made between objections to the Court's jurisdiction pure and simple, and objections contesting the admissibility of the case. If this is done, then it must be said that preliminary objections were sustained in three cases and pleas to the admissibility were sustained in two cases: in the *Nottebohm* Case on the ground of the non-opposability of Nottebohm's nationality, and in the *Interhandel* Case on the ground of the non-exhaustion of local remedies.[49] In one case, that of the *Monetary Gold,* the jurisdiction of the Court was challenged by the applicant state, which the Court found to be unusual but, having regard to special circumstances of the case, compatible with Article 62 of the Rules of Procedure of the Court.[50]

The Court gave judgments on the merits in eleven cases.[51] In addition, the Court

[43] Order of the Court of Aug. 31, 1960, [1960] I.C.J. Rep. 186 at 187. It may be noted that the Lebanese Government transmitted to the Registrar the documents establishing these arrangements. *Ibid.*

[44] Case concerning the Barcelona Traction, Light and Power Company, Ltd. (Belgium *v.* Spain), Order of April 10, 1961, [1961] I.C.J. Rep. 9; Case concerning the Protection of French Nationals and Protected Persons in Egypt (France *v.* Egypt), 1959–1960 Yearbook 52; and "Electricité de Beyrouth" Company Case (France *v.* Lebanon), *ibid.* 65.

[45] Aerial Incident of July 27, 1955 (United States *v.* Bulgaria), Barcelona Traction, Light and Power Company, Ltd. (Belgium *v.* Spain), and Compagnie du Port, des Quais et des Entrepôts de Beyrouth and Société Radio-Orient (France *v.* Lebanon).

[46] In the Case concerning Rights of Nationals of the United States of America in Morocco (France *v.* United States), the United States filed a preliminary objection on June 21, 1951, and withdrew it on Oct. 22, 1951. 1960–1961 Yearbook 53.

[47] The Corfu Channel Case (United Kingdom *v.* Albania), 1960–1961 Yearbook 44; Ambatielos Case (Greece *v.* United Kingdom), *ibid.* 55; Nottebohm Case (Liechtenstein *v.* Guatemala), *ibid.* 58; Case Concerning Right of Passage over Indian Territory (Portugal *v.* India), *ibid.* 68; Case Concerning the Temple of Preah Vihear (Cambodia *v.* Thailand), Judgment of May 26, 1961, *ibid.* 79, 88.

[48] Anglo-Iranian Oil Co. Case (United Kingdom *v.* Iran), *ibid.* 56; Case of the Monetary Gold Removed from Rome in 1943 (Italy *v.* France, United Kingdom and United States), *ibid.* 60; Case of Certain Norwegian Loans (France *v.* Norway), *ibid.* 65; Interhandel Case (Switzerland *v.* United States), *ibid.* 70; and Aerial Incident of July 27, 1955 (Israel *v.* Bulgaria), *ibid.* 71.

[49] [1955] I.C.J. Rep. 4, at 26, and [1959] *ibid.* 6, at 30.

[50] [1954] I.C.J. Rep. 19, at 28–29.

[51] Corfu Channel Case (Merits) (United Kingdom *v.* Albania), [1949] I.C.J. Rep. 4; Fisheries Case (United Kingdom *v.* Norway), [1951] *ibid.* 116; Asylum Case (Colombia/Peru), [1950] *ibid.* 266; Case Concerning Rights of Nationals of the United States in Morocco (France *v.* United States), [1952] *ibid.* 176; Haya de la Torre Case (Colombia *v.* Peru), [1951] *ibid.* 71; Ambatielos Case (Greece *v.* United Kingdom), [1953] *ibid.* 10; Minquiers and Ecrehos Case (France/United Kingdom), [1953] *ibid.* 47; Case Concerning Right of Passage over Indian Territory (Portugal *v.* India), [1960] *ibid.* 6; Case Concerning the Application of the Convention of 1902 Governing the Guardianship of Infants (Netherlands *v.* Sweden), [1958] *ibid.* 55; Case Concerning Sovereignty over Certain Frontier Land (Belgium/Netherlands), [1959] *ibid.* 209; Case Concerning the Arbitral Award Made by the King of Spain on Dec. 23, 1906 (Honduras *v.* Nicaragua), [1960] *ibid.* 192.

gave one judgment in response to a request for an interpretation of an earlier judgment,[52] and one judgment assessing exclusively the amount of damages.[53]

In two cases the Court was requested to issue interim measures of protection. The request was granted in one[54] and denied in the other.[55]

To dispose of the contentious cases and requests for advisory opinions the Court held 334 public meetings between April 18, 1946, its official opening, and November 21, 1960. Not counting the formal meeting in 1946, the Court held, on average, approximately 25 public meetings per year between January 1, 1948, and November 21, 1960. The number of public meetings devoted to cases and advisory opinions runs from a minimum of one in the question of the *Judgments of the Administrative Tribunal of the I.L.O. upon Complaints Made Against UNESCO,*[56] to 52 in the case of the *Right of Passage over Indian Territory*. The number of public meetings held per year varied from three in 1956 to 57 in 1959.

| CASE | NUMBER OF PUBLIC MEETINGS |
|---|---|
| Conditions of Admission of a State to Membership in the United Nations | 4 |
| The Corfu Channel Case | 46 |
| Reparation for Injuries Suffered in the Service of the United Nations | 4 |
| Competence of the General Assembly for the Admission of a State to the United Nations | 2 |
| Interpretation of Peace Treaties with Bulgaria, Hungary and Romania | 7 |
| International Status of South-West Africa | 7 |
| Asylum Case | 11 |
| Haya de la Torre Case | 4 |
| Reservations to the Convention on the Prevention and Punishment of the Crime of Genocide | 6 |
| Fisheries Case | 25 |
| Case concerning Rights of Nationals of the United States of America in Morocco | 9 |

[52] Request for Interpretation of the Judgment of Nov. 20, 1950, in the Asylum Case (Colombia/Peru), [1950] I.C.J. Rep. 395.

[53] The Corfu Channel Case (Assessment of the Amount of Compensation) (United Kingdom *v.* Albania), [1949] *ibid.* 244.

[54] Anglo-Iranian Oil Company Case (United Kingdom *v.* Iran), Order of July 5, 1951, [1951] *ibid.* 89.

[55] Interhandel Case (Switzerland *v.* United States), Order of Oct. 24, 1957, [1957] *ibid.* 105.

[56] In this case the Court dispensed with oral hearings altogether and the one public meeting was devoted to the reading of the opinion. See Leo Gross, "Participation of Individuals in Advisory Proceedings before the I.C.J.: Question of Equality of Parties," 52 A.J.I.L. 16 ff. (1958). See also *infra*, pp. 705–726.

| CASE | NUMBER OF PUBLIC MEETINGS |
|---|---|
| Anglo-Iranian Oil Co. Case | 14 |
| Ambatielos Case | 12 |
| The Minquiers and Ecrehos Case | 17 |
| Effect of Awards of Compensation made by the United Nations Administrative Tribunal | 5 |
| Case of the Monetary Gold Removed from Rome in 1943 | 6 |
| Nottebohm Case | 20 |
| Voting Procedure on Questions Relating to Reports and Petitions Concerning the Territory of South-West Africa | 1 |
| Admissibility of Hearings of Petitioners by the Committee on South-West Africa | 2 |
| Judgments of the Administrative Tribunal of the International Labour Organization upon Complaints Made against the United Nations Educational Scientific and Cultural Organization | 1 |
| Case of Certain Norwegian Loans | 12 |
| Case concerning the Application of the Convention of 1902 Governing the Guardianship of Infants | 8 |
| Interhandel Case | 11 |
| Constitution of the Maritime Safety Committee of the Inter-Governmental Maritime Consultative Organization | 8 |
| Aerial Incident of 27 July 1955 (Israel *v.* Bulgaria) | 12 |
| Frontier Land Case | 8 |
| Right of Passage Case | 52 |
| Honduras-Nicaragua Case | 19 |
| *Total:* | 333 |

| YEAR | NUMBER OF PUBLIC MEETINGS |
|---|---|
| 1946 | 1 |
| 1948 | 41 |
| 1949 | 13 |
| 1950 | 27 |
| 1951 | 35 |
| 1952 | 27 |
| 1953 | 27 |
| 1954 | 11 |
| 1955 | 19 |
| 1956 | 3 |

| | |
|---|---|
| 1957 | 29 |
| 1958 | 16 |
| 1959 | 57 |
| 1960 | 28 |
| *Total* | 334 |

These figures do not of course give an accurate idea of the time devoted by the Court to official business, as no information is available on the number of private meetings. No information is available on the amount of time devoted by members of the Court to the drafting of opinions, orders, and judgments handed down by the Court or on the amount of time spent by members of the Court on their individual or dissenting opinions. While the length of these opinions is not necessarily an index of the time or energy required, some of the detailed and wide-ranging opinions must have required a prodigious amount of energy and a rare devotion to the duties of an international judge. Still, with all these reservations in mind, the figures given below may provide at least a partial indication of the time devoted to the active consideration of a case or a request for an advisory opinion as distinguished from the necessarily substantial time required for the study of the frequently very voluminous written pleadings. This consideration, beginning with the oral hearings, if any, and ending with the delivery of the judgment or advisory opinion, runs from seven days in the case of the *Request for Interpretation of the Judgment in the Asylum Case* to two hundred and five days in the *Case Concerning the Right of Passage over Indian Territory.*

JUDGMENTS

| | Public Sittings | Judgment | Time Elapsed* |
|---|---|---|---|
| Corfu Channel Case (Preliminary Objection): 1947–1948 I.C.J. Rep. 15 | Feb. 26–28, March 1, 2, 5, 1948 | March 25, 1948 | 29 days |
| Corfu Channel Case (Merits): 1949 I.C.J. Rep. 4 | Nov. 9–12, 15–19, 22–26, 28, 29, Dec. 1–4, 6–11, 13, 14, 17, 1948 Jan. 17–22, 1949 | April 9, 1949 | 153 days** |
| Corfu Channel Case (Assessment of the Amount of Compensation): 1949 I.C.J. Rep. 244 | Nov. 17, 1949 | Dec. 15, 1949 | 28 days |
| Asylum Case (Colombia/Peru): 1950 I.C.J. Rep. 266 | Sept. 26–29, 3, 6, 9, 1950 | Nov. 20, 1950 | 25 days |
| Request for Interpretation of the Judgment of Nov. 20, 1950, in the Asylum Case: 1950 I.C.J. Rep. 395 | None | Nov. 27, 1950 | 7 days*** |
| Haya de la Torre Case: 1951 I.C.J. Rep. 71 | May 15, 16, 17, 1951 | June 13, 1951 | 30 days |

* Including the first day of hearings and the day on which judgment was given.

** This total does not take into consideration possible judicial holidays.

*** The time elapsed has been calculated from Nov. 20, date on which the Court received the request for interpretation. Final written observations were made on Nov. 24.

| | Public Sittings | Judgment | Time Elapsed* |
|---|---|---|---|
| Fisheries Case: 1951 I.C.J. Rep. 116 | Sept. 25–29, Oct. 1, 5, 6, 8–13, 15, 17–20, 24–27, 29, 1951 | Dec. 18, 1951 | 85 days |
| Ambatielos Case (Preliminary Objection): 1952 I.C.J. Rep. 28 | May 15, 16, 17, 1952 | July 1, 1952 | 48 days |
| Anglo-Iranian Oil Co. Case (Preliminary Objection): 1952 I.C.J. Rep. 93 | June 9–11, 13, 14, 16–19, 21, 23, 1952 | July 22, 1952 | 44 days |
| Case concerning Rights of Nationals of the U.S.A. in Morocco: 1952 I.C.J. Rep. 176 | July 15–17, 21–24, 26, 1952 | Aug. 27, 1952 | 44 days |
| Ambatielos Case (Merits: Obligation to Arbitrate): 1953 I.C.J. Rep. 10 | March 23–28, 30, 1953 | May 19, 1953 | 58 days |
| The Minquiers and Ecrehos Case: 1953 I.C.J. Rep. 47 | Sept. 17, Oct. 8, 1953 | Nov. 17, 1953 | 62 days |
| Nottebohm Case (Preliminary Objection): 1953 I.C.J. Rep. 111 | Nov. 10, 1953 | Nov. 18, 1953 | 8 days |
| Case of the Monetary Gold Removed from Rome in 1943 (Preliminary Question): 1954 I.C.J. Rep. 19 | May 10–14, 1954 | June 15, 1954 | 37 days |
| Nottebohm Case (Second Phase): 1955 I.C.J. Rep. 4 | Feb. 10, 11, 14–19, 21–24, March 2–4, 7, 8, 1955 | April 6, 1955 | 56 days |
| Case of Certain Norwegian Loans: 1957 I.C.J. Rep. 9 | May 13–15, 17, 20–25, 28, 1957 | July 6, 1957 | 55 days |
| Interhandel Case (Switzerland *v.* United States of America), Request for the Indication of Interim Measures of Protection: 1957 I.C.J. Rep. 105 | Oct. 12, 14, 1957 | Oct. 24, 1957 | 13 days |
| Case concerning Right of Passage over Indian Territory (Preliminary Objections): 1957 I.C.J. Rep. 125 | Sept. 23–27, 30, Oct. 1–3, 5, 7, 8, 10, 11, 1957 | Nov. 26, 1957 | 65 days |
| Case concerning the Application of the Convention of 1902 governing the Guardianship of Infants (Netherlands *v.* Sweden): 1958 I.C.J. Rep. 55 | Sept. 25, 26, 29, 30, Oct. 1, 3, 4, 1958 | Nov. 28, 1958 | 65 days |
| Interhandel Case (Preliminary Objection): 1959 I.C.J. Rep. 6 | Nov. 5, 6, 8, 10, 11, 12, 14, 17, 1958 | March 21, 1959 | 137 days** |
| Aerial Incident of July 27, 1955 (Israel *v.* Bulgaria), (Preliminary Objection): 1959 I.C.J. Rep. 127 | March 16–19, 23–26, April 1–3, 1959 | May 26, 1959 | 72 days |
| Case concerning Sovereignty over Certain Frontier Land: 1959 I.C.J. Rep. 209 | April 27–29, May 1, 2, 4, 5, 1959 | June 20, 1959 | 55 days |

* Including first day of hearings and day of judgment.
** This total does not take into consideration judicial holidays.

| | Public Sittings | Opinion | Time Elapsed* |
|---|---|---|---|
| Case concerning Right of Passage over Indian Territory (Merits): 1960 I.C.J. Rep. 6 | Sept. 21–16, 28–30, Oct. 1–3, 5, 6, 9, 10, 12–17, 19–21, 24, 26–31, Nov. 3–6, 1959 | April 12, 1960 | 205 days*** |
| Case concerning the Arbitral Award made by the King of Spain on 23 December 1906: 1960 I.C.J. Rep. 192 | Sept. 15–17, 19–24, 27–30, Oct. 1, 3, 4, 6, 7, 10, 11, 1960 | Nov. 18, 1960 | 65 days |
| Case concerning the Temple of Preah Vihear (Cambodia *v.* Thailand) (Preliminary Objections): 1961 I.C.J. Rep. 17 | April 10, 11, 12, 14, 15, 1961 | May 26, 1961 | 47 days |
| ADVISORY OPINIONS | | | |
| Conditions of Admission of a State to Membership in the United Nations (Art. 4 of the Charter): 1947–1948 I.C.J. Rep. 57 | April 22, 23, 24, 1948 | May 28, 1948 | 37 days |
| Reparation for Injuries Suffered in the Service of the United Nations: 1949 I.C.J. Rep. 174 | March 7, 8, 9, 1949 | April 11, 1949 | 36 days |
| Competence of the General Assembly for the Admission of a State to the United Nations: 1950 I.C.J. Rep. 4 | February 16, 1950 | March 3, 1950 | 26 days |
| Interpretation of Peace Treaties: 1950 I.C.J. Rep. 65 | Feb. 28, March 1, 2, 1950 | March 30, 1950 | 31 days |
| International Status of South-West Africa: 1950 I.C.J. Rep. 128 | May 16–23, 1950 | July 11, 1950 | 57 days |
| Interpretation of Peace Treaties (Second Phase): 1950 I.C.J. Rep. 221 | June 27, 28, 1950 | July 18, 1950 | 22 days |
| Reservations to the Convention on Genocide: 1951 I.C.J. Rep. 15 | April 10–14, 1951 | May 28, 1951 | 49 days |
| Effect of Awards of Compensation made by the United Nations Administrative Tribunal: 1954 I.C.J. Rep. 47 | June 10, 11, 12, 14, 1954 | July 13, 1954 | 34 days |
| South-West Africa—Voting Procedure: 1955 I.C.J. Rep. 67 | None. Time had been set for oral proceedings: May 10, 1955 | June 7, 1955 | 29 days** |
| Admissibility of Hearings of Petitioners by the Committee on South-West Africa: 1956 I.C.J. Rep. 23 | March 22, 1956 | June 1, 1956 | 72 days |
| Judgments of the Adminstrative Tribunal of the I.L.O. upon Complaints made against the U.N.E.S.C.O.: 1956 I.C.J. Rep. 77 | None. Time limit for written statements: July 1, 1956 | Oct. 23, 1956 | 115 days**** |

* Including day of first hearing and day of advisory opinion.
** Time elapsed has been calculated from May 10, 1955, time set for oral proceedings.
*** This total does not take into consideration possible judicial holidays.
**** Time elapsed has been calculated from July 1, 1956, time set for written statements.

| | Public Sittings | Opinion | Time Elapsed* |
|---|---|---|---|
| Constitution of the Maritime Safety Committee of the Inter-Governmental Maritime Consultative Organization: 1960 I.C.J. Rep. 150 | April 26, 27, 28, 29, May 2, 3, 4, 1960 | June 8, 1960 | 44 days |

## IV

It is not possible within the scope of a short and necessari ly summary survey of the Court to attempt an estimate of the contribution of the Court to the lessening of international tension or to the development of international law.[57] While the Court's jurisprudence has encouraged a lively and constructive controversy, there is no doubt that it has forced a greater awareness of the limits and function of law in the situations which were submitted to the Court's judgment, whether in the form of contentious or advisory proceedings. The Court's judgments and opinions have illumined the fundamental problem of order and liberty in international relations. In some instances the Court's pronouncements may have cleared the way for the codification of the law of the sea. Thus the International Law Commission based some of its draft articles on the law of the sea on the Court's judgments in the *Corfu Channel, Fisheries* and *Nottebohm* Cases,[58] which commended themselves to the subsequent Geneva Conference of 1958 in spite of the doctrinal controversy stirred up particularly by the *Fisheries* and *Nottebohm* Cases. One of the keys, if not the key, to the Court's jurisprudence is the exacting standard of customary international law which it applies. In the *Asylum* Case the Court required the complaining state, Colombia, to "prove that the rule invoked by it is in accordance with a constant and uniform usage practiced by the States in question," on the one hand, and, on the other, to "prove that this custom is established in such a manner that it has become binding on the other Party."[59] This dual standard must be combined with the holding of the Permanent Court of International Justice in the *Lotus* Case that mere abstention by states is no evidence of the rule; that, on the contrary, "only if such abstention were based on their being conscious of having a duty to abstain would it be possible to speak of an international custom."[60] This psychological element in custom which raises delicate questions of proof was applied by the present Court in the *Asylum* Case.[61] In adhering to its high standard of law and rejecting unilateral pretensions of legal rights and obligations, the Court accomplishes two objects: It manifests its conception of the judicial function as consisting in applying valid law rather than creating it, and it clears the way for appropriate law-creating activity by the states, which necessarily balances and compensates diverse interests of states.[62]

** Time elapsed has been calculated from May 10, 1955, time set for oral proceedings.

57 It may be sufficient to refer to Sir Hersch Lauterpacht, The Development of International Law by the International Court (1958); De Visscher, Théories et Réalités en Droit International Public (3rd ed., 1960); Rosenne, The International Court of Justice (1957); Schwarzenberger, International Law, Vol. 1 (3rd ed., 1957).

58 Report of the International Law Commission covering the Work of its Eighth Session, April 23–July 4, 1956. General Assembly, 11th Sess., Official Records, Supp. No. 9, pp. 13 ff., 19 f., and 24 f. (Doc. A/3159).

59 [1950] I.C.J. Rep. 276.

60 P.C.I.J., Series A, No. 10 (1927), p. 28.

61 [1950] I.C.J. Rep. 277.

62 *Cf.* De Visscher, Théories 480; Lauterpacht, *op. cit.* 197.

In the context of the *Asylum* Case the Court had the opportunity to develop the distinction between auto-interpretation and auto-decision of a state's rights and obligations under international law and treaties, a distinction which is as vital for an understanding of international law and its institutional deficiencies as it is overlooked, perhaps not altogether inadvertently, in state practice. In its first submission Colombia requested the Court to declare that it, Colombia, "as the country granting asylum, is competent to qualify the said offence for the purpose of the said asylum" on the basis of certain treaties and "of American international law in general." The Court rejected this submission "in so far as it involves a right for Colombia, as the country granting asylum, to qualify the nature of the offence by a unilateral and definitive decision, binding on Peru."[63] In its reasoning the Court sharply distinguished between the right of a state to interpret international law and treaties "for the sole purpose of determining its own conduct," which might be called auto-interpretation, and the pretended right, that is, the competence claimed by Colombia, "to qualify the nature of the offence by a unilateral and definitive decision binding on Peru."[64] It should be clear that, barring exceptional situations and special arrangements, no state has the right to lay down the law for another state. This is so because all states are equal to and independent of one another. An authoritative, that is, a binding interpretation, can only result from agreement among the states at variance or from the decision of a tribunal established by common agreement. This is one of the central features of international law today. It may not be a satisfactory one, but it is for the states to create the necessary institutional devices and to empower them to interpret their rights and obligations authoritatively and with binding effect. Such an instrument *par excellence* is the Court, and its greatest contribution has been to separate international law from pseudo-international law and to confine auto-interpretation to its necessary but limited function.

An instructive illustration of the Court's conception of its own function is afforded by the Advisory Opinion of June 27, 1950, in the case of the *Interpretation of Peace Treaties with Bulgaria, Hungary and Romania (Second Phase).* Referring to the principle of effectiveness or the maxim *ut res magis valeat quam pereat,* the Court said: "It is the duty of the Court to interpret the Treaties, not to revise them."[65]

The principle of effectiveness must be subordinated to fidelity to the text of the treaty which at once incorporates the declared intent of, and offers security to, the parties that they will not be bound to do more than they agreed to do.[66] The Court did not

[63] [1950] I.C.J. Rep. 266, at 288.

[64] *Ibid.* at 274. The distinction between auto-interpretation, which is not authoritative, and auto-decision, which is claimed to be authoritative though wholly unilateral, is indicated in the present writer's essay, "States as Organs of International Law and the Problem of Autointerpretation," in Law and Politics in the World Community 59–89 (ed. by G. A. Lipsky, 1953). See also *supra,* pp. 367–397.

[65] [1950] I.C.J. Rep. 229. See Schwarzenberger, *op. cit.* 488 ff.

[66] De Visscher, Théories 318, 475 ff., and the opinions there quoted, notably the Advisory Opinion of the Court of March 3, 1950, in the case of the Competence of the General Assembly for the Admission of a State to the United Nations, [1950] I.C.J. Rep. 4, at 8. See also Lauterpacht, *op. cit.* 290: ". . . The Advisory Opinion of the Court on the Interpreta-

hesitate to give an appropriate scope to the principle of effectiveness when it was concerned with the interpretation of an institution like the Mandates System as distinguished from interpretation of the Charter. In the Advisory Opinion on the *International Status of South-West Africa* the Court held unanimously that this territory continued to be under the Mandate assumed by the Union of South Africa on December 17, 1920, and, by twelve votes to two, that the Union "continues to have the international obligations stated in Article 22 of the Covenant" and in the Mandate, the supervisory functions to be exercised by the United Nations.[67] The Court also declared in particular that the General Assembly of the United Nations was

> legally qualified to exercise the supervisory functions previously exercised by the League of Nations with regard to the administration of the Territory, and that the Union of South Africa is under an obligation to submit to supervision and control of the General Assembly and to render annual reports to it.[68]

However, the Court did not go so far as to hold that the Union of South Africa was legally bound by Chapter XII of the Charter of the United Nations to place the territory under the Trusteeship System of the United Nations. Here the Court, faced with the text of Article 80, paragraph 2, of the Charter, adopted a strict interpretation and rejected the contention that an obligation to negotiate and conclude a trusteeship agreement was created, and said

> Had the parties to the Charter intended to create an obligation of this kind for a mandatory State, such intention would necessarily have been expressed in positive terms.[69]

In another opinion, which has been characterized as "a conspicuous example of judicial legislation,"[70] namely, that on the *Reparations for Injuries Suffered in the Service of the United Nations,* the Court was primarily concerned with the nature and character of an institution, the United Nations, and not with the interpretation of a particular treaty text. In this opinion the Court affirmed, not merely that the United Nations had international personality and was even possessed of "objective international personality," but that it also enjoyed the right to claim compensation for injuries which it, as well as the agent or those entitled to claim through him, suffered. The basis for the Court's findings may be seen in the following:

> Under international law, the Organization must be deemed to have those powers which,

tion of the Peace Treaties (Second Phase) affords an instructive example of a much needed warning of the limitations of the principle of effectiveness." But see also p. 290, note 13.

67 [1950] I.C.J. Rep. 128, at 143.

68 *Ibid.* 137.

69 *Ibid.* at 140 and 144. See also Lauterpacht, *op. cit.* 280.

70 Lauterpacht, *op. cit.* 179. See also De Visscher (Théories 478), who refers to this case as illustration of the Court's courage in breaking new ground when faced with a novel situation.

though not expressly provided in the Charter, are conferred upon it by necessary implication as being essential to the performance of its duties.[71]

To be sure, the Court referred in its opinion to the purposes and principles of the Charter and the functions which it confers upon the Organization, but it is difficult to accept the view that the Court's opinion "is merely a question of treaty interpretation."[72] The Charter is silent on the points involved in this case, as De Visscher points out.[73] Had this been just another case of treaty interpretation, it would have been unnecessary for the Court to say that it was "here faced with a new situation."[74] The Charter offered a convenient and even necessary frame of reference, but hardly more than that. The Court, rather than interpreting, it is submitted, interpolated or completed the Charter in a manner in which the framers of the Charter would have done it, had they anticipated situations such as had arisen in fact.[75]

The judgment of the Court in the *Nottebohm* Case aroused probably more controversy than any other.[76] In this case the question was not whether Nottebohm was a naturalized citizen of Liechtenstein but whether he was such a citizen for the purpose of diplomatic protection vis-à-vis Guatemala. The real issue, in the words of the Court, was "the admissibility of the claim of Liechtenstein in respect of Nottebohm."[77] The Court affirmed, without referring to it, the ruling of the Permanent Court in the case of the *Tunis-Morocco Nationality Decrees*[78] "that nationality is within the domestic jurisdiction of the State,"[79] and nothing was said by the Court to cast doubt on this fundamental principle. But where, as in the *Nottebohm* Case, nationality or naturalization projects itself on the international plane, other considerations are bound to enter into account. Again, as in the *Tunis-Morocco* Case, the recognition by, or "opposability" of nationality vis-à-vis, third states depends, and always depended, on international law.[80] In order "to be re-

[71] [1949] I.C.J. Rep. 182.

[72] Schwarzenberger, *op. cit.* 595.

[73] Théories 478. But he goes on to say in this case the Court applied the two principles of interpretation: the object and function of the treaty and the full effectiveness of its provisions, the convergence of which nearly always suffices to sway the interpreter.

[74] [1949] I.C.J. Rep. 182.

[75] That this is so is corroborated by the following statement in the Report of the Rapporteur of Committee IV/2 as approved by the Committee: "As regards the question of international juridical personality, the Committee has considered it superfluous to make this the subject of a text. In effect, it will be determined *implicity from the provisions of the Charter taken as a whole.*" Doc. 933, June 12, 1945; 13 U.N.C.I.O. Docs. 703, at 710 (emphasis supplied).

[76] *Cf.* Kunz, "The Nottebohm Judgment (Second Phase)," 54 A.J.I.L. 536–571 (1960), and the literature there cited.

[77] [1955] I.C.J. Rep. 4, at 16.

[78] P.C.I.J., Publications, Series 8, No. 4 (1923).

[79] [1955] I.C.J. Rep. at 20.

[80] On these points the Court said: "It is for Liechtenstein, as it is for every sovereign State, to settle by its own legislation the rules relating to the acquisition of its nationality, and to confer that nationality by naturalization granted by its own organs in accordance with that legislation. . . .

"But the issue which the Court must decide is not one which pertains to the legal system of Liechtenstein. It does not depend on the law or on the decision of Liechtenstein whether that State is entitled to exercise its protection, in the case under consideration. To exercise protection, to apply to the Court, is to place oneself on the plane of international law. It is international law which determines whether a State is entitled to exercise protection and to seise the Court.

"The naturalization of Nottebohm was an act performed by Liechtenstein in the exercise of its domestic jurisdiction. The question to be decided is whether that act has the international effect here under consideration." *Ibid.* at 20 ff.

spected by a State in the position of Guatemala,"[81] the naturalization of Nottebohm had to conform to applicable standards of international law. This it failed to do, because at the time when it was conferred on Nottebohm by Liechtenstein there was no "genuine connection" between Nottebohm and Liechtenstein. "It was granted," said the Court, "without regard to the concept of nationality adopted in international relations."[82] It may be noted that the Court used here the wider term, international relations *("rapports internationaux"),* rather than the more technical term, international law.

In this case, as in others, the Court acted as the guardian of the sovereignty of both the applicant and respondent states: the autonomy of Liechtenstein in matters of nationality and the autonomy of Guatemala in refusing to admit the right of Liechtenstein to protect Nottebohm on the basis of an "extremely tenuous" link.[83] To hold otherwise would have placed one state (Guatemala), in a matter which affects its interests protected by international law, under the sway of another state, and thus would have denied to the former the protection to which it was entitled under existing principles of international law.[84] To criticize the holding of the Court in the *Nottebohm* Case for introducing an element of uncertainty by relying on subjective criteria is to criticize international law and particularly that part of it relating to nationality, which exhibits all the elements of uncertainty corresponding to the prevailing degree of international integration.[85]

In considering and protecting the autonomy of both litigants in the *Nottebohm* Case, the Court merely applied a principle which it had used as a starting point in the *Fisheries* Case, where it said:

> The delimitation of sea areas has always an international aspect; it cannot be dependent merely upon the will of the coastal State as expressed in its municipal law. Although it is true that the act of delimitation is necessarily a unilateral act, because only the coastal State is competent to undertake it, the validity of the delimitation with regard to other States depends upon international law.[86]

The same principle applies to naturalization: it is an act which can be performed only by the state concerned, but the validity (opposability) of this naturalization with regard to other states depends upon international law. It is difficult to see how otherwise the principles of order and liberty can be harmonized on the international plane. The Court has no choice but to take international law and relations as it finds them at any given time, to show their essentially mutual aspect, to strengthen international institutions when it is

[81] *Ibid.* 26.

[82] The preceding passage is as follows: "That naturalization was not based on any real prior connection with Liechtenstein, nor did it in any way alter the way of life of the person upon whom it was conferred in exceptional circumstances of speed and accommodation. In both respects, it was lacking in the genuineness requisite to an act of such importance, if it is to be entitled to be respected by a State in the position of Guatemala." *Ibid.*, and at 23.

[83] *Ibid.* 25.

[84] Schwarzenberger, *op. cit.* 370: "The element of a genuine connection between a sovereign State and a naturalized individual is the common denominator of all those cases." See also *ibid.* 132.

[85] De Visscher, Théories 399.

[86] [1951] I.C.J. Rep. 132.

called upon to do so and, without revising them, to introduce progressive improvements here and there.

The Court was able to make a notable contribution of far-reaching significance along these lines in the *Corfu Channel* Case. On the one hand, the Court declared that Albania had failed to observe "certain general and well-recognized principles" which include "every State's obligation not to allow knowingly its territory to be used for acts contrary to the rights of other States."[87] On the other hand, the Court, upholding Albania's territorial sovereignty, rejected the defenses of intervention and self-protection or self-help on which the United Kingdom relied in justification of "Operation Retail." It may be worth while to quote in full the pronouncements of the Court in view of their relevance to contemporary international relations. Referring to intervention, the Court said:

> The Court cannot accept such a line of defence. The Court can only regard the alleged right of intervention as the manifestation of a policy of force, such as has, in the past, given rise to most serious abuses and such as cannot, whatever be the defects in international organization, find a place in international law. Intervention is perhaps still less admissible in the particular form it would take here; for, from the nature of things, it would be reserved for the most powerful States, and might easily lead to perverting the administration of justice itself.[88]

Referring to the defense of self-protection or self-help, the Court declared:

> The Court cannot accept this defence either. Between independent States, respect for territorial sovereignty is an essential foundation of international relations. The Court recognizes that the Albanian Government's complete failure to carry out its duties after the explosions, and the dilatory nature of its diplomatic notes, are extenuating circumstances for the action of the United Kingdom Government. But to ensure respect for international law, of which it is the organ, the Court must declare that the action of the British Navy constituted a violation of Albanian sovereignty.[89]

These pronouncements afford a glimpse into the sort of international relations which could be ours if only the governments would live up to their glib professions in favor of the rule of law, if only they would call upon the Court more frequently, even regularly, to adjudicate their disputes on the basis of the mutual respect for their sovereignty that they all claim and the reciprocal rights of which sovereignty is the accepted and traditional symbol.

The Court has made significant, if modest, contributions to the strengthening of international organizations and the clarification of the competence of their organs. To be sure, the opportunities offered the Court were far removed from the "defects in international organization" to which the Court referred above. The advisory opinions of the

[87] [1949] I.C.J. Rep. 4 at 22.
[88] *Ibid.* at 35.
[89] *Ibid.*

Court in the *Reparations* and *South-West African* cases have already been mentioned. In the second *Admissions* case the Court clarified authoritatively the respective rôles of the General Assembly and Security Council in the procedure of admission to the United Nations, and rejected the attempt "to deprive the Security Council of an important power which has been entrusted to it by the Charter." The Court, speaking generally, declared that "the Charter does not place the Security Council in a subordinate position," and stated as a general proposition "that nowhere has the General Assembly received the power to change, to the point of revising, the meaning of a vote of the Security Council."[90] The Court thus decisively spoke in order to preserve the autonomy of the Assembly and Council in the exercise of the powers and responsibilities conferred upon them by the Charter.

In two advisory opinions the Court had occasion to pronounce upon the status of members of the international civil service and in so doing to strengthen their independence and secure them from arbitrary dismissal. In the opinion of July 13, 1954, the Court rejected the contention that the General Assembly could not, in establishing an administrative tribunal, impose legal limitations upon powers with which it was charged by the Charter, *i.e.*, the budgetary power, a contention amounting to a claim of legal irresponsibility of the General Assembly.[91] As the Court construed the request, it was asked to say "whether the General Assembly is legally entitled to refuse to give effect to an award of compensation made by the Administrative Tribunal, properly constituted and acting within the limits of its statutory competence."[92] The Court, by nine votes to three, held

> that the General Assembly has not the right on any grounds to refuse to give effect to an award of compensation made by the Administrative Tribunal of the United Nations in favour of a staff member of the United Nations whose contract of services has been terminated without his assent.[93]

The Court thus put a stop to a determined effort on the part of some Members of the United Nations to vindicate for the United Nations a sort of illimitability of absolute monarchs, who invoked on its behalf the old and now discredited "Divine Right of Kings" idea. To do otherwise would not merely have cast doubt on the good faith which should govern the relations between the organization and its international staff. "It would," as the Court said

> hardly be consistent with the expressed aim of the Charter to promote freedom and justice for individuals and with the constant preoccupation of the United Nations Organization to

[90] Competence of the General Assembly for the Admission of a State to the United Nations, Advisory Opinion of March 3, 1950, [1950] I.C.J. Rep. 4, at 8–10.

[91] Effect of Awards of Compensation made by the United Nations Administrative Tribunal, Advisory Opinion of July 13, 1954, [1954] I.C.J. Rep. 47, at 59.

[92] *Ibid.* 51.

[93] *Ibid.* at 62.

> promote this aim that it should afford no judicial or arbitral remedy to its own staff for the settlement of any disputes which may arise between it and them.[94]

The Court showed complete understanding, in fact a much greater understanding than was manifested by certain Members of the Organization, of the prerequisite of a sound international civil service when it found that

> the power to establish a tribunal, to do justice as between the Organization and staff members, was essential to ensure the efficient working of the Secretariat, and to give effect to the paramount consideration of securing the highest standards of efficiency, competence and integrity. Capacity to do this arises by necessary intendment out of the Charter.[95]

The Court has shown here not merely its concern to ensure the welfare of the individual members of the Secretariat but also its characteristic penchant towards a broad and flexible "interpretation" of constitutional foundations on which the organization rests. The opinion of the Court exercised a salutary impact on the subsequent decisions of the General Assembly in this matter.[96]

The Court, when called upon to interpret a specific clause in a constitutional instrument, does not deviate from the principle of fidelity to the text. This is demonstrated again in its opinion of June 8, 1960, on the *Constitution of the Maritime Safety Committee of the Inter-Governmental Maritime Consultative Organization.* The Court, after a careful examination of the preparatory work relating to Article 28(a) of the Convention establishing this organization, refuted the attempts at a broad and functional interpretation of this provision and concluded that the term "ship-owning nations" refers "solely to registered tonnage. The largest ship-owning nations are the nations having the largest registered ship tonnage."[97] The Court refused to subscribe to a subjective test when an objective test was not merely intended but also available,[98] and in so doing expressed its preference for order as against arbitrariness.

The exacting test which the Court laid down with respect to proof of customary international law led the Court to a pronouncement on reservations to multilateral treaties which, much to the surprise of a large segment of the profession, appears to espouse arbitrariness against order. In its opinion on *Reservations to the Convention on the Prevention and Punishment of the Crime of Genocide,* the Court referred to the argument

> that there exists a rule of international law subjecting the effect of a reservation to the express or tacit assent of all the contracting parties. This theory rests essentially on a contractual conception of the absolute integrity of the convention as adopted

[94] *Ibid.* at 57.
[95] *Ibid.*
[96] See Gross, "Participation of Individuals in Advisory Proceedings before the International Court of Justice: Question of Equality between the Parties," 52 A.J.I.L. 16–40, at 26 ff. (1958). See also *infra,* pp. 705–726, at 714.
[97] [1960] I.C.J. Rep. 150, at 170.
[98] *Ibid.* at 166, 171.

and, noting that this theory cannot prevail over the intent of the parties to derogate from that rule, said:

> It does not appear, moreover, that the conception of the absolute integrity of a convention has been transformed into a rule of international law.[99]

The Court then laid down the principal test:

> that a State which has made and maintained a reservation which has been objected to by one or more of the parties to the Convention but not by others, can be regarded as being a party to the Convention if the reservation is compatible with the object and purpose of the Convention; otherwise, a State cannot be regarded as being a party to the Convention.[100]

Admittedly the test of "compatibility" is a flexible one and open to divergent interpretations.[101] But the Court does not have the function of creating rules where none exist. This is a prerogative of the states.[102] The Court can do no more useful service than to point out that no rule in fact exists where one was assumed to exist, even if in the meantime a degree of uncertainty should prevail.[103] But uncertainty is a mark of international law in the present state of integration in the society of nations.

This is an admittedly and necessarily sketchy review of some of the points on which the Court is believed to have made a significant contribution to international law and relations and thereby to a better understanding of the problem of order and liberty in the relations of states. Perhaps in the future the Court may make an even greater and more constructive contribution as an instance or organ of review of the constitutionality of acts of the United Nations and its specialized agencies. Its status as the principal judicial organ of the United Nations qualifies it pre-eminently for this rôle. That this view was shared by Members of the organization can best be shown by recalling General Assembly Resolution 171 (II) A, adopted on November 14, 1947, recommending

[99] [1951] I.C.J. Rep. 15 at 24. See Lauterpacht (*op. cit.* 186), who regards this Opinion and the Judgment in the Fisheries Case as "the two principal instances of judicial legislation in face of an admitted absence of agreed law."

[100] *Ibid.* at 29. The Court also laid down several other rules.

[101] See *ibid.* at 31, the Dissenting Opinion of Judges Guerrero, Sir Arnold McNair, Read, Hsu Mo.

[102] That governments responded to this challenge can be seen from the discussion in the General Assembly's Sixth Committee on Reservations to Multilateral Conventions and India's ratification with a condition of the Convention on the Inter-Governmental Maritime Consultative Organization. General Assembly, 14th Sess., Official Records, 6th Committee, pp. 69–159. The Court's opinion had also a remarkable impact in the International Law Commission. In his Report on the Law of Treaties, the Rapporteur, Professor H. Lauterpacht, after noting that, even prior to the Court's Advisory Opinion in the matter of Reservations to the Genocide Convention, no general agreement on the so-called "unanimity view" existed, and that some governments, including the United Kingdom, "who in the past have conspicuously advocated that principle, may be ready to admit that it is too rigid," stated: "In view of the fact that the principle of unanimous consent has ceased to be regarded as supplying a satisfactory solution of the problems which have arisen and are likely to arise in this connexion, the Commission no longer feels justified in limiting itself to the formulation, by way of codification, of a legal rule on the subject based on that principle. Nor does it consider itself justified in making the principle of unanimous consent the basis of the future law on the subject." Doc. A/CN.4/63, pp. 107 ff. See also Second Report on the Law of Treaties by H. Lauterpacht, Doc. A/CN.4/87, pp. 28 ff.

[103] Among the constant preoccupations of international tribunals De Visscher notes the considerations of order and stability which determine the judge not to sanction, without compelling reasons, interpretations which would bring about confusion and uncertainty. Théories 474 and 480.

> that organs of the United Nations and the specialized agencies should, from time to time, review the difficult and important points of law within the jurisdiction of the International Court of Justice which have arisen in the course of their activities and involve questions of principle which it is desirable to have settled, including points of law relating to the interpretation of the Charter of the United Nations or the constitutions of the specialized agencies, and, if duly authorized according to Article 96, paragraph 2, of the Charter, should refer them to the International Court of Justice for an Advisory Opinion.[104]

## V

The organs of the United Nations, including the General Assembly, have paid scant attention to this call for greater use of the Court as a sort of constitutional court. Yet, with the United Nations gaining visibly in stature and becoming increasingly a focal point of worldwide international relations, can there be any doubt that the Court is fully capable of being of service to the United Nations and its Members for resolving their differences? At least one of the principal organs of the United Nations, the Secretary General, has strongly urged the Members to make greater use of the Court. In one of his statements Mr. Dag Hammarskjöld said:

> One may recognize that the reluctance of Governments to submit their controversies to judicial settlement stems in part from the fragmentary and uncertain character of much of international law as it now exists. Where wide margins of uncertainty remain in the law, the tendency to seek a political settlement even in cases where questions of law lie at the heart of the dispute is understandable. Yet in the longer view, it is surely in the interest of all Member States to restrict as much as possible the sphere where sheer strength is an argument and to extend as widely as possible the area ruled by considerations of law and justice. In an interdependent world, a greater degree of authority and effectiveness in international law will be a safeguard, not a threat, to the freedom and independence of national States.[105]

He also recognized the contribution of the Court to development of the law of the United Nations in stating:

> The beginnings of a "common law" of the United Nations, based on the Charter, are now apparent; its steady growth will contribute to stability and orderliness. Advisory opinions of the International Court of Justice have added substantially to the law of the United Nations; their more frequent use should be encouraged. In appropriate cases, arbitral proceedings may usefully be employed in connexion with controversies on legal points; the use of such proceedings would tend both to facilitate immediate solutions and to further the long-range goal of strengthening the authority of law. The systematic examination within the

[104] General Assembly, 2nd Sess., Official Records, Resolutions, Sept. 16–Nov. 29, 1947, p. 103 (Doc. A/519). The vote on this resolution was 46 in favor, 6 against, and 2 abstentions. At that time the membership of the United Nations stood at 59. It would be interesting to know what would be the vote if the resolution or a similar one were put to the vote in the present General Assembly comprising 104 Members.

[105] Annual Report of the Secretary General on the Work of the Organization July 1, 1954–June 15, 1955. General Assembly, 10th Sess., Official Records, Supp. No. 1, p. xiii (Doc. A/2911).

United Nations of the practice of States can bring to light areas of agreement and divergence in the law and stimulate efforts to seek a reconciliation of opposing views.[106]

It is not possible to deny the strength of the argument that the growth of tensions, in particular of hegemonial tensions, adversely affected the flow of business of the Permanent Court and that it inhibits the flow of business of the present Court.[107] The dominant tension plays now between East and West and this tension would have to cool down very substantially before any disputes between East and West would be submitted to the Court.[108] The future flow of cases depends, in realistic terms, upon disputes between members of the Free World being steered in the direction of the Court. The fact that not many such disputes go to the Court cannot, it is submitted, be explained by the prevailing East-West tension.

In the past it has been fashionable to emphasize the "legislative" aspects of the Court's jurisprudence. This was natural in the context of the debate on the function of adjudication as a key factor in establishing peace on a durable basis. Today more modest expectations are attributed to the judicial function: to settle disputes on the basis of law.[109] It has been shown that the diplomatic procedures for the settlement of disputes maximize power and minimize law. The procedures now available to a large number of states in and through the United Nations to a degree neutralize the power element, but they do not enhance the rôle of law. They could do that in some measure, that is, to the extent that the advisory function of the Court is drawn upon, as suggested by the General Assembly and the Secretary General. The possibilities which lie in that direction have hardly been explored, let alone exploited. As the jurisprudence of the Court has shown, the depoliticization of the dispute, whether involving states or individuals, is achieved once the dispute is submitted to it. The Court has been scrupulous in its respect for the autonomy of states in the absence of strict proof of legal obligation.

States are autonomous and sovereign only in virtue of international law. Every increment of strength of the law is bound to make more secure the independence of states. Adjudication is no longer regarded as a cure for all the ills which currently afflict international relations. Nor is adjudication of itself the sure road to peace under the rule of law in the relations between states. On the other hand, to avoid, except in the rarest of circumstances, resort to the judicial authority, to confine states almost exclusively to diplomatic and political procedures, amounts to depriving the world of a possibility or avenue for strengthening international peace. For, as the former President of the Court, Judge

[106] *Ibid.* See also the Annual Reports of the Secretary General for 1952–1953, General Assembly, 8th Sess., Official Records, Supp. No. 1, pp. xi–xii (Doc. A/2404); for 1956–1957, *ibid.*, 12th Sess., Supp. 1 A, pp. 4–5 (Doc. A/3594/Add. 1); and for 1958–1959 *ibid.*, 14th Sess., Supp. 1 A, pp. 3–4 (Doc. A/4132/Add. 1). And see Basdevant ("La Place et le Rôle de la Justice Internationale . . . ," 5 Les Affaires Etrangères 331–351 at 346 ff. (1959), who stresses the restraining influence of Advisory Opinions.

[107] De Visscher, Théories 445 ff.

[108] But see the various efforts of the United States referred to above, p. 686, to bring such disputes before the Court.

[109] In a sense the surrender of the larger, if illusory, object for a more modest, if realistic, one, makes matters more difficult rather than easier. For, as Jenks pointed out, "the movement for a larger measure of compulsory jurisdiction can no longer draw strength from the emotional and political forces which supported it when it could be presented as an alternative to war and a guarantee of peace." Preliminary Report 179.

Basdevant, suggested, the mere fact of appearing and arguing a case before the Court constitutes an important factor in the slow process of building an international community. And to the extent that governments submit or refuse to submit disputes to the Court, they fulfill or decline to fulfill the object stated in the Preamble of the Charter of the United Nations, "to establish conditions under which justice and respect for the obligations arising from treaties and other sources of international law can be maintained."[110] Granted that in the past there may have been a tendency to overestimate the rôle of the judicial function in international relations, there is no reason for allowing the pendulum to swing in the opposite direction and to underestimate the contribution which the Court is fully capable of making towards introducing a measure of stability and predictability in the relations of the largest single group of states. At the very least the boundaries between what is law and what is advanced under the guise of law will be progressively delineated.

[110] Jules Basdevant, "La Place et le Rôle de la Justice Internationale dans les Relations entre Etats et à l'égard des Organisations Internationales," 5 Les Affaires Etrangères 331–351, at 338, 351 (Presses Universitaires de France, 1959). His statement on p. 349 may bear quotation in full: "Non seulement les Etats se présentent et sont traités comme des égaux devant la justice internationale mais ceux qui comparaissent devant celle-ci pour représenter un Etat ou une organisation internationale parlent tous le même langage, le langage du droit, pour convaincre les juges dont ils savent que ceux-ci statueront selon le droit et par une décision obligatoire. C'est tout autre chose que parler dans un débat à l'Assemblée générale des Nations Unies ou au Conseil de sécurité où, bien souvent, les représentants des Etats parlent beaucoup moins pour convaincre ceux à qui ils s'adressent directement que pour satisfaire leurs mandants, leur presse, leur opinion publique, ou encore pour le retenissement qu'ils espèrent obtenir dans l'opinion publique de tel ou tel pays. A l'opposé de cela, tous ceux qui parlent devant la Cour, s'efforçant de parler le langage du droit, tout en soutenant des thèses opposées, retrouvent ou découvrent devant le juge quelque chose qui leur est commun. Ainsi le fait d'aller devant le juge international fait apparaître ou mieux sentir ce qu'il y a de commun entre les peuples. Cela contribue à créer ou à entretenir un esprit de compréhension, de mutuelle considération, de mutuel respect, esprit qui, lui-même, sera générateur de l'esprit de mutuelle concession.

"Par cela, le recours à la justice internationale, au delà et par-dessus la solution de tel différend qui lui est déféré, apporte sa contribution à la formation d'une psychologie commune susceptible de fournir le meilleur appui au maintien de la paix et de la sécurité internationales."

# PARTICIPATION OF INDIVIDUALS IN ADVISORY PROCEEDINGS BEFORE THE INTERNATIONAL COURT OF JUSTICE: QUESTION OF EQUALITY BETWEEN THE PARTIES

## I. BACKGROUND

In its Advisory Opinion of October 23, 1956, in the matter of *Judgments of the Administrative Tribunal of the International Labour Organization upon Complaints made against the United Nations Educational, Scientific and Cultural Organization,*[1] the International Court of Justice considered the question of equality between the parties, UNESCO and the officials of this specialized agency. The question is not new. It had already arisen, albeit in a somewhat different form, before the Permanent Court of International Justice. That Court had faced the question in the case of the Danzig Legislative Decrees, 1935. The Court, "preoccupied with the establishment so far as possible of equality before the Court between the Senate of the Free City on the one hand and the petitioners . . . on the other," decided that it would receive written statements from the Government of the Free City as well as from the individuals representing three minority political parties, which submitted a petition to the Council of the League of Nations concerning certain legislative decrees of the Danzig Senate. However, "with regard to oral statements, the Court, in accordance with its normal practice in advisory cases, heard a statement by the representatives of the Free City, but decided that the terms of the Statute and Rules precluded it from hearing the petitioners. In declaring the hearings closed, however, the

[1] [1956] I.C.J. Rep. 77; A.J.I.L. 410 (1957).

President reserved the Court's right not only to ask the representatives of the Free City for further information or explanations, but also to procure them by other means at its disposal.''[2] In a dissenting opinion Judge Anzilotti, alluding to the above decision of the Court, declared:

> In this way, the two Parties to the dispute, to which the question before the Court relates, were placed on a footing of manifest inequality. The majority party, of which the Senate of the Free City is composed, was enabled not only to submit to the Court a written memorial, but also to have oral statements made on its behalf by an Agent and Counsel, whereas the three minority parties were only allowed to send explanatory notes, without taking any part in the oral procedure: neither orally nor in writing were they given an opportunity of answering the contentions of their opponents, so that the case was never argued before the Court.
>
> It may perhaps be contended that the resulting inequality between the majority party and the other parties in the proceedings before the Court is of no consequence, since the conclusion arrived at by the Court is favourable to the case of the minority parties: the latter would certainly have no reason for complaint, and it is hardly likely that the Senate of the Free City would reproach the Court for having placed it in a privileged position.
>
> It would be easy to reply that the hearing of both sides and the submission of the arguments in support of the respective contentions is designed to furnish the Court with all data for its decision and is therefore provided in the essential interests of justice and consequently of the Court. As the Agent for the Free City pointed out in his statement on October 30th, 1935, in the absence of an opponent, there can be no certainty that all doubtful points will clearly be brought out at the hearing. The arguments which the minority parties would have presented would perhaps have strengthened their case, but it is also conceivable that they might have revealed weak points to the Court.
>
> That, however, is not the point with which I am concerned. The essential point to my mind is that the Court, in order to be able to give this Opinion, was obliged either to set aside its Rules and create a procedure *ad hoc,* or to deviate from a rule so fundamental as that of the equality of parties; and the reason for this was that the case concerned a question of municipal law arising in connection with a domestic political dispute.[3]

The considerations of Judge Anzilotti have been set out rather fully, as they have lost none of their cogency through the passage of time, and merit renewed attention, as will be shown presently.

The decision of the Court regarding the petitioners in the Danzig case may not have been imposed inevitably by its Statute,[4] and in connection with the 1936 revision of its Rules, Vice President Guerrero suggested that it was desirable ''to remove any inequality between the parties, whoever they might be.''[5] This suggestion was not accepted. However, the imperative need to ensure equality of parties before the Court was recognized by

[2] P.C.I.J., Ser. E, No. 14, p. 161. See also Manley O. Hudson, The Permanent Court of International Justice 1920–1942 (1943), p. 403; ''Participation of Individuals in Proceedings before the International Court of Justice'': Memorandum submitted by the Secretary-General, U.N. Doc. A/AC. 78/L. 10 (April 13, 1955). General Assembly, 10th Sess., Official Records, 1955, Annexes, Agenda Item 49, pp. 26–28, at 27.

[3] P.C.I.J., Ser A/B, No. 65, Consistency of Certain Danzig Legislative Decrees with the Constitution of the Free City. Advisory Opinion of Dec. 4, 1935, p. 65 f.

[4] In the view of Judge Hudson ''it would seem possible for the Court to have said, down to 1936 at any rate, that national organizations and even individuals might likewise appear to furnish information in advisory proceedings.'' *Op. cit.*

[5] ''Participation of Individuals . . .'' (cited note 2 above), p. 28.

the Council of the League of Nations in connection with its request for an Advisory Opinion in the case of the complaint from five former officials of the Governing Commission of the Saar Territory. Emphasizing "the gravity of the issues involved" and recognizing that the complaint of the former officials called for the application of international law,[6] the Secretary General proposed, and the Council approved, a procedure providing for the exchange of written statements between the petitioners and the Secretary General and the submission to the Court of these documents at the same time as the request for an advisory opinion. Moreover, paragraph 4 of the resolution adopted by the Council on December 14, 1939, was couched in these terms:

> The League of Nations hereby renounces the exercise of the right to present the written and oral statements provided for by Article 66 of the Statute of the Court, if the same possibility cannot be given to the petitioners, since it does not wish to have greater opportunities of furnishing information to the Court than the petitioners themselves.[7]

The Court had no occasion to take up this matter. It is always possible to waive rights, as the League did in this case. In effect, the waiver would have resulted in a truncated procedure before the Court as the Court would have been deprived of the benefit of the "contentious" procedure provided for in Article 66 of its Statute. To be sure the procedure adopted by the Council would have resulted in equality between the parties, but it would also have resulted in the paradox of there being no parties at all before the Court. This decision raises the related issue whether and how far the parties determine the procedure before the Court or whether the Court is master of its procedure and can count on the full co-operation of the parties concerned "in the essential interests of justice and consequently of the Court."

## II. THE ISSUE OF EQUALITY BEFORE THE COURT

The substance and history of the Court's Advisory Opinion in the case of the *Judgments of the Administrative Tribunal of the I.L.O.* may be left on one side, as this paper is essentially concerned with the issue of the equality of the parties and the ancillary problem of the participation of individuals in advisory proceedings.[8] The Executive Board of UNESCO which formulated the request to the Court was made aware of the issue of equality. The legal adviser of UNESCO informed the Board that Chapter IV of the

[6] The Secretary General observed on this point: "Enquiry into the validity of the present claims involves the question whether, having regard to its constitution and the principles of international law which are applicable, it is possible that the League of Nations should have incurred financial responsibility by reason of accomplishing a function of the character given it by Section IV of Part III of the Peace Treaty of Versailles." League of Nations Official Journal, November-December, 1939, p. 502.

[7] *Loc. cit.* 503.

[8] The full title of the Advisory Opinion of Oct. 23, 1956, is "Judgments of the Administrative Tribunal of the International Labor Organization upon Complaints made against the United Nations Educational, Scientific and Cultural Organization," [1956] I.C.J. Rep. 77. For a digest see 51 A.J.I.L. 410–417 (1957); and for an analysis see Manley O. Hudson, "The Thirty-Fifth Year of the World Court," *ibid.* 4–9.

Court's Statute excluded individuals but that *"des considérations d'équité militant en faveur de l'égalité des droits des parties intéressées"* required consideration of measures designed to enable the interested individuals to present their views to the Court. He also pointed out that neither Article XII of the Administrative Tribunal of the I.L.O. nor the procedure recently adopted by the United Nations concerning the review of judgments of its Administrative Tribunal has ever been applied. In the absence of an applicable precedent, he was of opinion that the Court would not reject written statements by the interested individuals if they were included in the documentation submitted to the Court by UNESCO.[9] The representative of The Netherlands regretted a procedure *"qui interdit à la cour de La Haye d'entendre des personnes,"* and hoped that the matter would be presented to the Court in as complete a manner as possible. While the Board took no decision, the President stated that the interested individuals would be enabled to present their views to the Court as indicated by the legal adviser.[10]

In the ensuing tri-cornered correspondence between the counsel for the staff members, the Registrar of the Court and the legal adviser of UNESCO the usual viewpoints were expressed. Counsel requested facilities for presenting observations and counter-observations on behalf of his clients to the Court; the Registrar informed him that the Court was not in position to grant this request; the legal adviser at first attempted to establish limitations on the observations to be submitted by counsel,[11] but faced with the objection that this would imply a control by UNESCO, reversed himself and undertook to forward to the Court the observations of the staff members "without verifying their content."[12] Finally it was understood that if the Court called for counter-memorials or replies, the staff members would be afforded the necessary facilities, that is, they would receive the written observations submitted by UNESCO as well as by governments to the Court in order to enable them to formulate their counter-observations.[13] As a matter of fact, the observations of the staff members, beneficiaries of the judgments of the I.L.O. Administrative Tribunal, were transmitted to the Court as an "Appendix" to the State-

[9] Written Statement by UNESCO, I.C.J. Pleadings, Oral Arguments, Documents, Judgments of the Administrative Tribunal of the I.L.O., p. 70.

[10] *Ibid.*

[11] Legal Adviser, Dr. Saba, to Maître Mercier, Feb. 1, 1956: "Je vous indiquais, toutefois, qu'étant donné le caractère de la procédure à suivre devant la Cour, les observations de vos clients devraient se limiter à la réfutation d'arguments de droit sans comporter de critiques concernant, soit la politique d'un Etat membre de l'Organisation, soit les agissements de celle-ci." *Ibid.* 247.

[12] *Ibid.* 248. See also pp.235–237, 245, 249, 253, 254, 264.

[13] In this context it is interesting to recall the correspondence between counsel for staff members and the Registrar of the Court with reference to the United Nations request for an Advisory Opinion on the "Effect of Awards of Compensation made by the United Nations Administrative Tribunal." After rejecting a request by counsel concerning submission of observations to the Court, the Registrar also rejected a request for permission to receive the statements submitted on this question by Member States or the Secretary General to the Court. Referring to Arts. 82 and 44 of the Court's Rules, the Registrar declared: "In the view of the President the same principles apply to the communication of the written statements in connection with advisory opinions, and it would not be proper for the Court to order that the written statements submitted to it in the present case should be made available to members of the public without consent of the body by whom the request for the advisory opinion was submitted, namely, the General Assembly." I.C.J. Pleadings, United Nations Administrative Tribunal, p. 410. See also pp. 394, 397, 409. It will be noted that the staff members, beneficiaries of judgments of the Administrative Tribunal involved in this case, were put in the category of "members of the public."

ment submitted by UNESCO.[14] Supplementary observations by the beneficiaries were also forwarded to the Court by UNESCO.[15] The Court dispensed with public hearings in this case and accordingly no question of representation of the beneficiaries in such hearings arose.

The Court, in its Opinion, considered the question of equality between UNESCO and the officials *proprio motu,* [16] and noted at the outset that the advisory proceedings in the present case "involve a certain absence of equality between UNESCO and the officials both in the origin and in the progress of those proceedings."[17] Regarding the first aspect, namely, equality in point of origin, the Court referred to "generally accepted practice" according to which "legal remedies against a judgment are equally open to either party. In this respect each possesses equal rights for the submission of its case to the tribunal called upon to examine the matter."[18] The present proceeding was instituted under Article XII of the Statute of the Administrative Tribunal of the I.L.O. which confers "an exclusive right" on the Executive Board of UNESCO to challenge the judgments of the Administrative Tribunal by appealing to the Court. Article XII of the Statute of this Tribunal reads as follows:

> 1. In any case in which the Executive Board of an international organization which has made the declaration specified in Article II, paragraph 5, of the Statute of the Tribunal challenges a decision of the Tribunal confirming its jurisdiction, or considers that a decision of the Tribunal is vitiated by a fundamental fault in the procedure followed, the question of the validity of the decision given by the Tribunal shall be submitted by the Executive Board concerned, for an advisory opinion, to the International Court of Justice.
> 2 The opinion given by the Court shall be binding.[19]

The Court considered that the inequality in law arising from Article XII

> does not in fact constitute an inequality before the Court. It is antecedent to the examination of the question by the Court. It does not affect the manner in which the Court undertakes that examination. Also, in the present case, that absence of equality between the parties to the Judgments is somewhat nominal since the officials were successful in the proceedings before the Administrative Tribunal and there was accordingly no question of any complaint on their part. This being so, it is not necessary for the Court to express an opinion upon the legal merits of Article XII of the Statute of the Administrative Tribunal. . . .[20]

[14] I.C.J. Pleadings, Judgments of the Administrative Tribunal of the I.L.O., pp. 170–183, 258.

[15] *Ibid.* 219–223, 266. It appears from these supplementary observations that the beneficiaries and their counsel had reviewed the statements submitted to the Court by UNESCO as well as a number of governments.

[16] The question was alluded to in the French and British statements but in a somewhat different context. See *ibid.* 210, 214.

[17] Judgments of the Administrative Tribunal of the I.L.O. upon Complaints made against the U.N.E.S.C.O., Advisory Opinion of Oct. 23, 1956, [1956] I.C.J. Rep. 77 at 85.

[18] *Ibid.*

[19] *Ibid.* at 78. On Jan. 10, 1956, the declaration specified in Art. 11, par. 5, was made by WHO, ITU, UNESCO, IMO, FAO and the European Organization for Atomic Research. I.C.J. Pleadings, Judgments of the Administrative Tribunal of the I.L.O., p. 239.

[20] [1956] I.C.J. Rep. 77 at 85.

It is understandable why the Court refrained from expressing an opinion on the legal merits of Article XII, although it may appear regrettable that it has not done so in this case. For the Court, on the basis of this reasoning, will never have an opportunity to express an opinion, as the Executive Board alone has the right to challenge the validity of judgments of the Administrative Tribunal. On the contrary hypothesis—a challenge of this validity on the grounds specified in Article XII by staff members *against* whom judgment was given by the Administrative Tribunal—the Court would not have an opportunity to express an opinion because the challenge would not lead to proceedings before the Court. There is no reason to assume that only judgments in favor of staff members but never judgments adverse to staff members could be affected by a question of jurisdiction or fundamental fault in procedure. Be that as it may, concluding its examination of inequality in point of origin, the Court held that "the circumstance that only the Executive Board was entitled to institute the present proceedings does not constitute a reason for not complying with the Request for an Advisory Opinion."[21]

Turning then to the question of equality in point of the procedure before the Court, the Court noted at the outset that "here the absence of equality flows not from any provision of the Statute of the Administrative Tribunal but from the provisions of the Statute of the Court," and that "the judicial character of the Court requires that both sides directly affected by these proceedings should be in a position to submit their views and their arguments to the Court."[22] UNESCO had available to it the necessary facilities, but regarding the "different" position of the officials the Court declared:

> It was with that difficulty that the Court was confronted. The difficulty was met, on the one hand, by the procedure under which the observations of the officials were made available to the Court through the intermediary of Unesco and, on the other hand, by dispensing with oral proceedings. The Court is not bound for the future by any consent which it gave or decisions which it made with regard to the procedure thus adopted. In the present case, the procedure which has been adopted has not given rise to any objection on the part of those concerned. It has been consented to by counsel for the officials in whose favour the Judgments were given. The principle of equality of the parties follows from the requirements of good administration of justice. These requirements have not been impaired in the present case by the circumstance that the written statement on behalf of the officials was submitted through Unesco. Finally, although no oral proceedings were held, the Court is satisfied that adequate information has been made available to it. In view of this there would appear to be no compelling reason why the Court should not lend its assistance in the solution of a problem confronting a specialized agency of the United Nations authorized to ask for an Advisory Opinion of the Court. Notwithstanding the permissive character of Article 65 of the Statute in the matter of advisory opinions, only compelling reasons could cause the Court to adopt in this matter a negative attitude which would imperil the working of the régime established by the Statute of the Administrative Tribunal for the judicial protection of officials. Any seeming or nominal absence of equality ought not to be allowed to obscure or to defeat that primary object.[23]

[21] *Ibid.* at 86.
[22] *Ibid.*
[23] *Ibid.*

The Court thus concluded that in point of procedure the inequality between the parties was inconsequential and not a bar to the good administration of justice. Two observations appear in order. One is that counsel for the officials accepted the procedure after the legal adviser abandoned what might well have been regarded as prior censorship with regard to the written statements on behalf of his clients but, having no official standing before the Court, how could he have made known to the Court his objection if for substantial reasons he should have found the proposed procedure unsatisfactory?[24] The other is that it is difficult to appreciate the statement of the Court that the régime in question was established "for the judicial protection of officials," if Article XII "confers an exclusive right on the Executive Board" to apply to the Court and, as the Court noted, "officials have no such remedy against the judgments of the Administrative Tribunal."[25]

The Court decided by nine votes to four "to comply with the Request for an Advisory Opinion."[26] Four judges were of opinion that the Court should refuse to do so, although three—Judges Winiarski, Klaestad and Sir Muhammad Zafrulla Khan —concurred in the operative part of the Opinion and one, Judge Córdova, would have done so had he "not been firmly convinced that the Court should have refused to comply with the Request of UNESCO because of its lack of competence to render an advisory opinion in circumstances such as those underlying the present case."[27]

Judge Winiarski pointed out that the question before the Court was not one pending between two states and that the advisory procedure was intended to serve, as stated in the Opinion of the Court, "the object of an appeal against the four judgments (of the Administrative Tribunal), seeing that the Court is expressly invited to pronounce, in its Opinion, which will be 'binding,' upon the validity of these Judgments."[28] He also pointed out that the Court, as a judicial body, cannot depart from "two fundamental principles of procedure: *audiatur et altera pars* and the equality of the parties before a Court." These principles do not appear to have been strictly observed: on the one hand, the Court did not object to a situation "in which one of the parties to the proceedings before the Administrative Tribunal can only send its observations to the Court through the intermediary of the other party," and on the other hand, "the oral proceedings, which constitute the means by which the Court usually obtains clarification of the issue before it, have been dispensed with beforehand."[29]

[24] On this point Judge Winiarski declared in his Separate Opinion: "The fact that this unusual procedure has not given rise to any objection on the part of those concerned and that it has been consented to by counsel for the officials is irrelevant. These officials had no place in the normal advisory procedure." *Ibid.* at 108. See also Judge Sir Muhammad Zafrulla Khan's Separate Opinion, *ibid.* at 114.

[25] *Ibid.* at 85.

[26] *Ibid.* at 101.

[27] *Ibid.* 155. Two Judges, Hackworth and Badawi, disagreed with the opinion on the merits and wrote dissenting opinions.

[28] *Ibid.* at 106, 84. Judge Winiarski recalled that at the San Francisco Conference Venezuela made the following proposal which was defeated: "As a Court of Appeals, the Court will have jurisdiction to take cognizance over such cases as are tried under original jurisdiction by international administrative tribunals dependent upon the United Nations when an appeal would be provided in the Statute of such tribunals." *Ibid.* at 107. See also *ibid.* at 160.

[29] *Ibid.* at 106, 107, 108. In his Separate Opinion Judge Klaestad observed that oral hearings "have hitherto been fixed in all advisory cases which have been considered by this Court, as being a normal and useful, if not an indispensable, part of its

Judge Klaestad, reasoning along similar lines, concluded that the Court should decline the request. Noting the departures from the normal procedure, he said:

> . . . Whatever may be thought of such a departure from a normal judicial procedure, the Court cannot in any case disregard or compromise with the fundamental principle of the equality of parties—equality in law as well as in fact—a principle which is expressly confirmed by Article 35, paragraph 2, of the Statute of the Court. Nor should the Court, by answering the Questions put to it, appear to acquiesce in a review procedure which fails to observe generally recognized principles by according only to one of the parties to the judgments of the Administrative Tribunal the right to challenge the judgments.[30]

Judge Sir Muhammad Zafrulla Khan, while in general agreement with the views of Judges Winiarski and Klaestad, drew attention to the situation which might have arisen had a state requested an oral hearing:

> . . . If such a request had been received, the Court would have been confronted with a dilemma. It would have found it difficult to refuse the request. To grant it would have meant that the Court would thereby have disabled itself from delivering an Opinion. The Court finds itself able to deliver an Opinion in this case because no request for an oral hearing has been received. This means that in cases like the present, a single State or international organization to whom notice is sent under paragraph 2 or Article 66 (of the Statute) can exercise a veto upon the Court's authority to deliver an Opinion. In my humble view, the Court should not comply with a request for an Advisory Opinion in a case which necessitates its having recourse to such procedures and devices.[31]

Judge Córdova, who wrote a dissenting opinion, agreed with the arguments regarding absence of equality between UNESCO and the individuals concerned, but he draws from the inequality the consequence that the Court was incompetent to give the requested opinion. The inequalities, both in point of origin and in point of procedure, flow from the Statute of the Court which denies access to individuals. Consequently, he argues:

> . . . For individuals and international organizations to be parties in a contentious procedure it would be absolutely necessary to change the Statute, the only means of securing equality for them before the Court. This fact necessarily means that the Court, according to the present terms of the Statute, cannot legally act in compliance with the equality principle, which is the same thing as to say that the Court is incompetent or has not the legal possibility in this case to discharge its functions.[32]

Basing his dissent on very broad grounds, Judge Córdova contends that both according to Article XII of the Statute of the Administrative. Tribunal of the I.L.O. and the

proceedings." *Ibid.* at 110. Judge Sir Muhammad Zafrulla Khan pointed out in his Separate Opinion that "Oral proceedings were dispensed with not because the Court considered that it could not receive any assistance through that means, but because the inequality of the parties in respect of oral hearings could not be remedied in any manner." *Ibid.* 114.

30 *Ibid* at 112.

31 *Ibid.* at 115.

32 *Ibid.* at 168.

recently adopted new text of Article 11 of the Statute of the Administrative Tribunal of the United Nations,[33] the Court was intended to become "a judicial body reviewing the decisions of the two Administrative Tribunals in certain and specified cases."[34] It is axiomatic that the Court derives jurisdiction "entirely and exclusively from its Statute" and that other international instruments cannot "either enlarge or diminish the competence of the Court."[35] It is manifest from the preparatory work as well as the wording of Articles XII and 11 that

> their authors decided, by themselves and for themselves, that, in certain instances, the International Court of Justice should act as Court of Appeal. It is hardly necessary to comment upon the capacity or the right of the International Labour Organisation—or as far as that is concerned, of the Assembly of the United Nations—to impose upon the International Court of Justice obligations and new functions which are not provided for in its Statute or in the Charter.[36]

According to the existing Statute, the Court is "incompetent, both *ratione personae* and *ratione materiae,* to play the role of a Court of Appeal with regard to cases tried in the first instance by the Administrative Tribunals."[37] The essential function of the Court is judicial and this activity deals only with contentious cases between parties. According to Articles XII and 11 the Court is, in effect, to "render—in the guise of an advisory opinion or advice—a true judgment, a real decision binding upon those parties," *e.g.* the parties before the Administrative Tribunals. In the view of Judge Córdova:

> The confusion made by Articles XII and 11 of the Statute of both Administrative Tribunals between the judicial and advisory functions of the Court in order to transform an Advisory Opinion into a Judgment is an absolute legal impossibility according to the only applicable law: the Statute.[38]

According to Article XII what is desired is not merely an Advisory Opinion but one which is binding on the parties in the first instance, that is, before the Administrative Tribunal. "This effect," said Judge Córdova,

> can never be juridically attained unless the staff member is considered a party in the second instance. Since the Statute prevents individuals and international organizations, that is to say, UNESCO and its officials, from bringing their dispute before the Court and since the present case is undoubtedly a contentious one, the inescapable legal conclusion follows that

[33] Res. 957 (X) adopted by the General Assembly on Nov. 8, 1955. General Assembly, 10th Sess., Official Records, Supp. No. 19 (A/3116), p. 30

[34] [1956] I.C.J. Rep. 77 at 156.

[35] *Ibid.*

[36] *Ibid.* 157.

[37] *Ibid.* 158.

[38] *Ibid.* at 161. Judge Córdova dealt at some length with the Venezuelan proposal at the San Francisco Conference which was defeated, *ibid.* at 160–161; see also *supra,* note 28.

> the Court has no competence *ratione personae* to entertain and give a decision in the present case.[39]

The incompetence of the Court *ratione materiae* is the logical consequence of Article 38 of the Court's Statute. Pursuant to this, it is the function of the Court "to decide in accordance with international law such disputes as are submitted to it." In order to comply with the Request of the Executive Board of UNESCO, "the Court had to apply the Statute of the Administrative Tribunal, the Staff Regulations and the contract between the parties, UNESCO and the individual officials concerned, that is to say, it had to apply 'International Administrative Law.'" This law, as well as international criminal law,

> may form part of a wider concept of the law of nations, but they certainly concern the relations between a State and individuals and therefore they have no room within the interpretation of the words "international law" as used in Article 38 of the Statute of the Court.[40]

It is reasonably clear that the incompetence of the Court *ratione materiae* is merely a consequence of its incompetence *ratione personae*. Penetrating through the cloak of the Request, Judge Córdova found that the real parties in interest were an international organization on the one side, and individuals on the other. In a contentious proceeding where the Court exercises its true judicial function both would be barred on the threshold by Article 34 of the Court's Statute: "Only States may be parties in cases before the Court." That bar could not be by-passed by using the formal approach for an advisory opinion. Taking a broad view of the substance of the request, the international organization in fact intended the Court to exercise appellate jurisdiction in a dispute to which it and certain individuals were parties. Judge Córdova's dissenting opinion declared in substance that the Court should not assume a function by indirection which it was not authorized to undertake by the Statute. The inequalities between UNESCO and the officials concerned, both in point of origin and in point of procedure, were merely the inevitable result of the Court's rendering an opinion in circumstances in which it ought to have refused to do so in the interest of a sound administration of justice. Judge Córdova's dissent is all the more significant as it embraces not merely the actual request before the Court but also possible requests to the Court under Article 11 of the Statute of the United Nations Administrative Tribunal.

## III. THE ISSUE OF EQUALITY AND ARTICLE 11 OF THE STATUTE OF THE UNITED NATIONS ADMINISTRATIVE TRIBUNAL

Summing up, it is obvious that the Opinion of the Court, the three Separate Opinions and Judge Córdova's Dissenting Opinion point to the same characteristic feature of

[39] *Ibid.* at 164.
[40] *Ibid.* at 165–166.

the case: the inequality between the parties. There are significant differences in the interpretation of the consequences of this inequality. It is common ground that inequality existed in point of origin; the right to initiate the review procedure under Article XII is conferred exclusively upon the Executive Board of UNESCO and "is denied to the weaker party."[41] The Court considered that this inequality in law did not lead in inequality in fact before the Court and was "antecedent" to the proceedings. In the view of Judges Klaestad and Córdova this inequality can be traced to the Statute of the Court, which does not enable individuals to request an Advisory Opinion and constitutes one reason militating against entertaining the request of UNESCO.

It is to be noted that in this respect Article 11 of the Statute of the United Nations Administrative Tribunal appears to be designed to provide for a measure of equality. Paragraphs 1 and 2 of Article 11 read as follows:

> 1. If a Member State, the Secretary-General or the person in respect of whom a judgment has been rendered by the Tribunal . . . objects to the judgment on the ground that the Tribunal has exceeded its jurisdiction or competence or that the Tribunal has failed to exercise jurisdiction vested in it, or has erred on a question of law relating to the provisions of the Charter of the United Nations, or has committed a fundamental error in procedure which has occasioned a failure of justice, such Member State, the Secretary-General or the person concerned may, within thirty days from the date of the judgment, make a written application to the Committee established by paragraph 4 of this article asking the Committee to request an advisory opinion of the International Court of Justice on the matter.
>
> 2. Within thirty days from the receipt of an application under paragraph 1 of this article, the Committee shall decide whether or not there is a substantial basis for the application. If the Committee decides that such a basis exists, it shall request an advisory opinion of the Court, and the Secretary-General shall arrange to transmit to the Court the views of the person referred to in paragraph 1.[42]

It is not necessary to go here into the questions which were much debated in the United Nations regarding this text, in particular whether it accurately implements the decision of the General Assembly to establish a "judicial review" of judgments of the United Nations Administrative Tribunal [43] and whether it is "juridically well founded."[44] It is sufficient to observe that Article 11 establishes the right for the Secre-

[41] Judge Klaestad, *ibid.* 111.

[42] Res. 957 (X) of Nov. 8, 1955. General Assembly, 10th Sess., Official Records, Supp. No. 19 (A/ 3116), p. 31.

[43] The General Assembly accepted "in principle" judicial review by Res. 888 (IX) B of Dec. 17, 1954. General Assembly, 9th Sess., Official Records, Supp. No. 21 (A/2890), p. 43. For a presentation of views expressed by Members on the subject of judicial review, see Report of the Special Committee on Review of Administrative Judgments, Doc. A/2090 of June 10, 1955, General Assembly, 10th Sess., Official Records, Annexes, Agenda Item 49, pp. 1-16; for the views of the Secretary General see Suggestions by the Secretary General on Judicial Review of United Nations Administrative Judgments, Doc. A/Ac.78/L.8 of April 12, 1955, *ibid.* 16–17, and Statement made by the Secretary General at the 493rd meeting of the Fifth Committee on Oct. 17, 1955, *ibid.* 37–38.

[44] The Belgian delegation submitted a draft resolution proposing to request an advisory opinion of the Court on this question. Doc. A/L.199 of Nov. 7, 1955, *ibid.* 44. This draft was put to the vote on Nov. 8, 1955, and not adopted, there being 31 votes against, 15 in favor and 13 abstentions. General Assembly, 10th Sess., Official Records, Plenary Meetings, p. 288. The draft resolution was supported by India, Syria and Yugoslavia, see *ibid.* 280, 286, and opposed by Argentina, Iraq, the United Kingdom and the United States, *ibid.* 277, 278, 283, 284. The U. S. representative argued that, if the

tary General as well as the individual staff member concerned to initiate the review procedure before the screening committee. It thus establishes a status of equality in law between the parties to a judgment of the Administrative Tribunal. Whether it also establishes equality in fact is a different question on which judgment must be deferred. This matter was the subject of debate in the General Assembly, particularly in its Fifth Committee, where the political character of the screening committee was emphasized. According to Article 11, paragraph 3:

> The Committee shall be composed of the Member States the representatives of which have served on the General Committee of the most recent regular session of the General Assembly.

It was pointed out in the debate that the composition of the Committee introduced a political element into the review procedure and consequently inequality. Thus the representative of Norway declared:

> Since its composition would correspond to that of the General Committee of the General Assembly, which was primarily determined by political considerations, the screening committee would have a political rather than a judicial character, despite the fact that its functions would be essentially judicial. While it was possible that the representatives of the countries concerned might be appointed on the basis of their personal ability and legal competence, there was no guarantee that that would be so.[45]

The fact that the Committee was to make the preliminary decision whether there was "a substantial basis for the application for review" conferred upon it a large discretionary power. Moreover, an element of inequality was seen in the procedure,

> since in practice it would be much more difficult for a staff member requesting a review to convince the committee that there was a substantial basis for his application than it would be for a Member State. The latter might even be represented on the committee, while no provision was made for the participation of staff members in its proceedings.[46]

In support of the procedure it was contended by the representative of the United States that

> the committee's task would be to screen requests for advisory opinions for the purpose of protecting the Court from frivolous applications. The only body entitled to decide on those questions of law which might affect Tribunal judgments would be a judicial organ, the International Court of Justice.
>
> The proposed procedure would entail no unfairness to staff members. . . . Before

review procedure is used at all, "the Court automatically has the opportunity of deciding whether or not there is any legal flaw in the procedure. We can be certain that the Court will not hesitate to inform us if any important element of the procedure is contrary to the provisions of the Charter or of the Statute of the Court itself, or if it does not give the necessary protection to the parties who might be affected." *Ibid.* 284, par. 67.

[45] General Assembly, 10th Sess., Official Records, Fifth Committee, 493rd meeting, Oct. 17, 1955, p. 38, par. 34.

[46] *Ibid.* pars. 35, 37.

> any inequity could result, the Secretary-General . . . would have to make an improper decision which deprived a staff member of his contractual rights; the Administrative Tribunal would have to confirm the Secretary-General's decision and, finally, a committee of Member States constituted on the pattern of the General Committee would have to act quite arbitrarily and refuse to ask the advisory opinion of the Court. That was a whole series of assumptions which nobody would be justified in making.[47]

There is considerable persuasive force in this reasoning and it would seem to be the better part of wisdom, having drawn attention to a potential source of inequality in fact in the initial stage of the review procedure of the United Nations Administrative Tribunal, to leave the matter to the future.[47a]

It is common ground that there was inequality in the procedure before the Court, both in the written and oral stage, and that both were attributable to the Court's Statute barring individuals. The former was seen in the inability of the individuals concerned to address themselves in writing directly to the Court, and the latter in the Court's decision to dispense with oral hearings altogether, thus depriving itself as well as the parties in interest from a usual and potentially vital stage in arguing the legal aspects of the questions put to the Court. There was a difference in interpretation: The majority found this inequality merely "seeming or nominal" which did not result in a real disadvantage to the staff members, whereas Judges Winiarski, Klaestad and Sir Muhammad regarded it as a defect in procedure sufficient to warrant a refusal to render the requested opinion. In their view the Court ought not to have compromised with the fundamental and time-honored principle of equality in law and in fact. Judge Sir Muhammad furthermore pointed out that a single state or an international organization, entitled to appear before the Court under Article 66, paragraph 2, of the Statute, "can exercise a veto upon the Court's authority to deliver an Opinion," by requesting an oral hearing and thus upsetting the precarious equality between the parties.

It is now appropriate to examine whether the revised Statute of the United Nations Administrative Tribunal meets these objections. In the first place, it is to be noted that Article 11, paragraph 2, makes the transmission of the views of the interested staff members mandatory: "The Secretary-General shall arrange to transmit to the Court the views of the person referred to in paragraph 1." Moreover, the Secretary General stated before the Fifth Committee that he would consider it his "responsibility to assure as far as possi-

[47] *Ibid.* 44, pars. 17, 18. The provision conferring upon Member States the right to initiate the review procedure was much debated but it prevailed, because it was deemed an essential feature of the compromise proposal embodied in the final text of Art. 11. See remarks made by the representative of the United States, *ibid.*, p. 66, par. 11. The opposition was led by India, which also proposed amendments deleting the words "a Member State." *Ibid.* 55 ff., 66, and Plenary, p. 280.

[47a] The Committee on Applications for Review of Administrative Tribunal Judgments was convened at United Nations Headquarters on October 16, 1956, to adopt rules of procedure and consider the first application requesting a review of a judgment of the United Nations Administrative Tribunal. The Committee has since considered several applications and decided in all cases "that there was not a substantial basis for the application under Article 11 of the Statute of the Administrative Tribunal and, therefore, did not consider that the International Court of Justice should be requested to give an advisory opinion." See Docs. A/AC.86/2, A/AC.86/3, A/AC.86/4, A/AC.86 /5. For the revised Provisional Rules of Procedure of the Committee see Doc.A/AC.86/2/Rev.1.

ble an equality of rights for the staff member concerned."[48] To this end he proposed to follow the procedure adopted by the League of Nations in connection with the case of former officials of the Saar Commission.[49] It would thus appear that the United Nations endeavored to approach equality to a greater extent than is the case under Article XII of the Statute of the Administrative Tribunal of the I.L.O. On the other hand, the procedure laid down in Article 11 still falls short of the standard of equality in law and fact which was deemed to be required by Judges Winiarski, Klaestad, Sir Muhammad and Córdova. For the written statements of the staff member would reach the Court through the Secretary General, who may well be the opposing interested party. In any event, Member States, including the Member exercising the right to initiate the review procedure, would have the undoubted right to submit written observations directly to the Court. Thus the element of inequality, resulting from the Statute of the Court, is bound to be preserved in the written stage of the procedure before the Court.

Regarding the oral stage of the proceedings, the General Assembly, in paragraph 2 of the above-mentioned resolution,

> Recommends that Member States and the Secretary-General should not make oral statements before the International Court of Justice in any proceedings under the new article 11 of the Statute of the Administrative Tribunal adopted under the present resolution.

This recommendation, clearly devised to ensure a measure of equality in at least a negative sense, calls for comment. In the first place, it is not binding on the Member States and presumably not even on the Secretary General. The latter may be presumed to be inspired by a sense of fairness and desire to ensure equality, and is therefore unlikely to take any initiative in the matter.[50] The Member States are in a different position. By participating in oral hearings, if such are held by order of the Court, any one of them may create a situation in which the Court may deem it necessary to decline giving the requested opinion. In the circumstances, Judge Sir Muhammad pointed out, the Member State, any Member State, would be invested with the power of veto which, if exercised by participating in oral hearings, would have the effect of paralyzing the review procedure.

The recommendation of the Assembly is certainly not binding on the Court, which remains master of its procedure under the Statute and bears exclusive responsibility for the sound administration of justice. Equality between the parties has been admitted by the Court to be an indispensable part of it. In spite of this the Court may yet find it possible and advisable to co-operate with the United Nations and dispense with oral hearings as it did in the UNESCO case. Its opinion in the latter case is not necessarily a precedent, as the Court was careful in scrupulously limiting its reasoning to the request before it.

[48] General Assembly, 10th Sess., Official Records, Annexes, Agenda Item 49, p. 38, par. 8.

[49] See *supra*, pp. 706–707.

[50] In this connection it is relevant to recall the following statement made by the Secretary General before the Fifth Committee: "It would likewise be my intention to waive any right which the Secretary General has to further participation in the proceedings before the Court from which the staff member was excluded except, of course, as the Court might specifically require further information." *Loc. cit.*, Annexes, Agenda Item 49, p. 38, par. 10.

Should the Court, however, dispense with hearings in cases coming up for review from Administrative Tribunals of the I.L.O. or the United Nations, it might come very close to erecting into a principle what cannot but appear to be a truncated procedure. There are, as will presently be shown, important reasons why the Court may find it necessary to hold oral hearings in order to obtain the fullest possible argument from the interested parties. These might well be cases involving not merely questions of competence or jurisdiction or fundamental errors in procedure but above all cases alleging an error on a question of law relating to provisions of the Charter of the United Nations. To hold oral hearings in such cases and not to admit staff members to participate in them, might conceivably present the Court with the dilemma of refusing to give the requested opinion or impinging upon the principle of equality of the parties which it has explicitly recognized as valid. On the other hand, the present Statute leaves the Court only one alternative.

A final point remains for consideration. The Court recognized that the advisory proceeding brought into being by UNESCO appeared "as serving, in a way, the object of an appeal against the four Judgments, seeing that the Court is expressly invited to pronounce, in its Opinion, which will be 'binding,' upon the validity of these Judgments."[51] Judges Winiarski and Córdova agreed with this view of the Court's intended function, but argued that, inasmuch as the Court was not authorized by its Statute to act in this capacity, it should not allow the advisory proceeding to be used for this purpose. The binding character of the Opinion, said Judge Winiarski, "does not in itself affect the competence of the Court but constitutes further proof that what is involved is an appeal in the form of a Request for an Advisory Opinion."[52] Judge Córdova, it will be recalled, argued in even stronger terms against the competence of the Court because the appeal involved in reality a contentious case to which an international organization and certain individuals were parties, and both were excluded by the Statute; and moreover the Court was not authorized to apply international administrative law, as this was not part of international law in accordance with which the Court is to decide disputes submitted to it. "The extraordinary practical and juridical consequences of the confusion between the judicial and advisory activities," said Judge Córdova, have been the adoption of a very unusual procedure, and

> the Court, the highest judicial organ of the United Nations, was not in a position to administer justice, in cases like the present one, on the basis of strict equality between the parties.[53]

Regarding the character of the review proceedings before the Court, it is important to draw attention to a difference between Article XII and Article 11. Under the former, the Opinion of the Court is made binding, and it was this specific provision which led to the criticism that the Court was acting in the UNESCO case as an appellate organ. Arti-

[51] [1956] I.C.J. Rep. 77 at 84.
[52] *Ibid.* at 107.
[53] *Ibid.* at 166.

cle 11 is couched in terms which may well deprive this criticism of its foundation. According to Article 11, paragraph 3,

> In any case in which a request has been made for an advisory opinion, the Secretary-General shall either give effect to the opinion of the Court, or request the Tribunal to convene specially in order that it shall confirm its original judgment, or give a new judgment, in conformity with the opinion of the Court.

This text, by offering several alternatives, avoids the automaticism of Article XII, at least in a formal sense. This point deserves consideration, even if one does not share the view that the Court should decline rendering an Advisory Opinion which is to be binding upon the parties. This view would moreover have the undesirable consequence of depriving of their effectiveness the jurisdictional clauses in some important international instruments.[54]

The argument that the Court in the UNESCO case has acted, and that in cases under Article 11 it will be expected to function, as an appellate organ warrants closer analysis. The starting point should be the distinction between a case involving a challenge to the jurisdiction of an Administrative Tribunal and a case involving a challenge against the substance of the judgment of an Administrative Tribunal. The requirement of equality between the parties appears in a different light, depending upon whether a case involves one or the other kind of challenge.

The legislative history of Article XII proves conclusively that it was designed as a means of resolving a conflict of competence between two organs of an international organization, that is, as a means for determining objectively and judicially whether one organ, *i.e.*, the Administrative Tribunal, has acted *ultra vires* or in excess of the powers conferred upon it by the parent organ.[55] This point was made in the most explicit manner by the French Government in its written Statement to the Court. The French Government argued that Article XII incorporates and is based upon the "theory of the excess of power of the international judge":

> The text of Article XII envisages an examination whether the decision suffers from a "fault," whether its "validity" can be challenged; these expressions do not refer to a revision of the decision by an appeal in the ordinary sense of the term but rather to a "nullity" as in the theory of the excess of power of the international judge. It would be easy to demonstrate that among the vitiating circumstances characteristic of an excess of power one commonly finds absence of "competence" and "fundamental fault in the procedure."[56]

[54] For a list of instruments stipulating the binding force of Advisory Opinions, see I.C.J. Yearbook 1956–1957, p. 41.

[55] For the legislative history of Art. XII, which goes back to a conflict between the League of Nations and its Administrative Tribunal in 1946, see Memorandum by the International Labor Office, I.C.J. Pleadings, United Nations Administrative Tribunal, pp. 46–90, particularly pp. 71–73. The decisive statement of the Sub-Committee of the League Assembly's Second (Finance) Committee is as follows: "Although there is no ordinary appeal from the Tribunal's decision, we think it is within the power of the Assembly, which can best interpret its own decisions, by a legislative resolution, to declare that the awards made by the Tribunal are invalid and are of no effect both because they sought to set aside the Assembly's legislative act and because of their mistaken conclusion as to the intention of that act." *Ibid.* at 67.

[56] Translated by the author from the French text: "Les formules employées par l'article XII sont bien, d'autre part, celles de la théorie de l'excès de pouvoir de l'arbitre international; il s'agit dans le texte de l'article XII de rechercher si la décision est entachée d'un 'vice', si la 'validité' peut être mise en cause; ces expressions se réfèrent non pas à une

The French Government was of the opinion that the Court is not concerned with an ordinary appeal, that is, with the protection of the individual interests involved in the judgments of the Administrative Tribunal. As was recently done in connection with another Administrative Tribunal,[57] one could have provided for a genuinely judicial review of its judgments, but this was not the case here. The French Government therefore concluded:

> However deserving of respect may be the interests of the international officials, however worthy may be the efforts envisaged in order to enable them to make known to the Court their point of view, Article XII raises a question which is altogether different from that of "correctly or incorrectly adjudicated"; the definition of the "excess of power" of the international judge entails a question which above all relates to the harmonious functioning of international institutions and the future of the Organization. Whether one likes it or not, the Court, in interpreting a text, namely Article XII of the Statute of the Administrative Tribunal, is bound to give precision to concepts which are vastly more fundamental than the text itself; the theory of the excess of power of the international judge will be influenced in an important manner by the Court.[58]

The distinction between an appeal having for its sole object the determination of the competence of a tribunal and an appeal having for its object the determination whether a tribunal has correctly applied the law to the merits of a dispute, is, it is submitted, eminently sound. It also points to a solution of the problem of equality of parties. In the former case, the only issue at stake is the validity of a judgment of an Administrative Tribunal in terms of its having acted within the scope of the competence conferred upon it. The Court in the UNESCO case saw the problem put before it strictly in that light when it refused to answer Question II put to it, saying:

> Question I of the present Request for an Opinion is concerned only with a challenge of the decision confirming jurisdiction. . . . The Statute of the Administrative Tribunal could have provided for other reasons for challenging the decision of the Tribunal than those referred to in Article XII. It has not done so. In view of this, the Court cannot answer Question II within the framework of Article XII of the Statute of the Tribunal—the only Article by reference to which the opinion of the Court is involved.
>
> . . . In the Request for an Advisory Opinion, Question II has been placed within the orbit of Article XII. Actually it is outside that Article. Accordingly, it cannot be considered by the Court for the purpose of acting upon the request made to it.[59]

réformation de la décision par une voie de recours au sens habituel du terme, mais bien à une 'nullité' comme dans la théorie de l'excès de pouvoir de l'arbitre. Il serait de même facile de montrer que parmi les vices qui constituent l'excès de pouvoir de l'arbitre on rencontre le plus communément l'absence de 'compétence' et la 'faute essentielle dans la procédure.'" *Ibid.* at 210.

[57] Here the French Government had reference, albeit indirectly, to the new Art. 11 of the United Nations Administrative Tribunal.

[58] Translated by the author from the French text: "Si respectables que soient les intérets des fonctionnaires internationaux, si estimables que soient les efforts envisagés pour leur permettre de faire connaître leur point de vue à la Cour, la procédure de l'article XII pose une toute autre question que celle du 'bien ou du mal jugé'; la définition de 'l'excès de pouvoir' d'un juge est au premier chef une question qui touche au fonctionnement harmonieux des institutions internationales et à l'avenir de l'Organisation. Qu'on le veuille ou non, en interprétant un texte, l'article XII du Statut du Tribunal administratif, la Cour va préciser des notions dont la portée dépasse singulièrement ce texte; la théorie de l'excès de pouvoir de l'arbitre international sera directement influencée par l'avis de la Cour." *Ibid.*

[59] [1956] I.C.J. Rep. 77 at 99. Question II was as follows: "In the case of an affirmative answer to question I: (a) Was the Administrative Tribunal competent to determine whether the power of the Director-General not to renew fixed-term

This being so, one wonders whether it was indispensable for the Court to examine the question of the equality of the parties, that is, of UNESCO and the staff members concerned. No doubt the Court's concern with this aspect of the case is indicative of its desire to consider all aspects of the case and to maintain the administration of international justice on the highest level. The opinions of Judges Winiarski, Klaestad, Sir Muhammad and Córdova testify to the same desire. However, as the French Government argued, the case involved what might for want of a better term be called an intra-organizational dispute; one organ of UNESCO was at variance with the Administrative Tribunal of the I.L.O. as to the question of competence. The fact that the interests of certain staff members were affected was neither a reason for refusing to render the requested opinion nor a reason, strictly speaking, for making them party to the proceedings before the Court.[60]

The new Article 11 of the United Nations Administrative Tribunal raises the issue of the equality in a very cogent manner. This article, like Article XII, has its origins in a dispute over competence.[61] Like Article XII, it provides for a challenge of the judgments of the Administrative Tribunal in case it has exceeded its jurisdiction or competence or has committed a fundamental error in procedure which has occasioned a failure of justice. It goes further by including among the grounds for a challenge the failure of the Tribunal to exercise jurisdiction vested in it. All these grounds relate to the theory of excess of power in a sense which is fundamentally common to Article XII. In the event of a request to the Court for an Advisory Opinion on any of these grounds, there is no reason to suppose that the Court would change its view regarding the equality of parties. Article 11, however, deviates from Article XII in one important point: it provides that a Member State or the Secretary General or the staff member concerned may object to the judgment of the Administrative Tribunal on the ground that it "has erred on a question of law relating to the provisions of the Charter of the United Nations." An objection on this ground relates not to the validity of the judgment but to the merits of the judgment. The Court, when seized of a case of this kind, is not called upon to express an opinion on the question whether the Administrative Tribunal has stayed within the bounds of its competence, but whether it has correctly applied the law which it is competent to administer. The Court then would not pronounce upon an intra-organizational dispute, but exercise judicial review, a true appellate jurisdiction. This would be so in spite of the absence in Article 11 of the provision in Article XII that the Advisory Opinion of the Court

appointments has been exercised for the good of the service and in the interest of the Organization? (b) Was the Administrative Tribunal competent to pronounce on the attitude which the Director-General, under the terms of the Constitution of the United Nations Educational, Scientific and Cultural Organization, ought to maintain in his relations with a Member State, particularly as regards the execution of the policy of the Government authorities of that Member State?" *Ibid.* at 79.

[60] On the first point see the Written Statement of the United Kingdom, I.C.J. Pleadings, Judgments of the Administrative Tribunal of the I.L.O., p. 214.

[61] See Effect of Awards of Compensation made by the United Nations Administrative Tribunal, Advisory Opinion of July 13, 1954, [1954] I.C.J. Rep. 47; 48 A.J.I.L. 655 (1954); and Judicial Review of United Nations Administrative Tribunal Judgments, Working Paper submitted by the Secretary General, Doc. A/AC.78/L.1 and Corr. 1 (March 22, 1955), General Assembly, 10th Sess., Official Records, Annexes, Agenda Item 49, pp. 17–25. This paper reviews the history of the question as well as the issues involved.

"shall be binding." The absence of this provision in Article 11, far from weakening the appellate character of the function of the Court, on the contrary strengthens it. For Article 11, paragraph 3, true to the concept of a judicial appeal, provides that the Secretary General shall request the Tribunal to convene specially in order "that it shall confirm its original judgment, or *give a new judgment, in conformity with the opinion of the Court.*" The opinion of the Court is thus to be given a reformatory character.

The inclusion of the review of substantive legal issues by the Court in the text of the new Article 11 of the Statute of the United Nations Administrative Tribunal was the subject of much debate in the organs of the United Nations. It was considered an essential feature of the compromise among the different proponents of the review procedure. The Government of the United States understood the new text to include

> such a question as whether the Secretary-General's judgment should be upheld in regard to the conduct of a staff member under United Nations standards of efficiency, competence, and integrity as prescribed in accordance with Article 101 of the Charter; or a question whether the Secretary-General, acting as Chief Administrative Officer of the Organization under Article 97 of the Charter, should be sustained in giving directions to a staff member or taking disciplinary action against him; or a question involving the staff member's duty to refrain from any action which might reflect on his position as an international official responsible only to the Organization under Article 100, paragraph 1.[62]

Thus cases relating directly to the application of the Charter or the consistency of the application of the Staff Regulations with the Charter are to be understood as being included in the review procedure under Article 11.

Given the broad nature of the scope of the review procedure and the distinctly appellate character of the function to be exercised by the Court, the question of the equality between the parties appears in a changed context. Leaving aside the controversial and probably rather anomalous right of a Member State to initiate the review procedure, and the provision for testing merely the validity of judgments of the Administrative Tribunal, what remains in Article 11 is the new possibility of appealing to the Court against the judgment on the merits of the Administrative Tribunal. The Tribunal is to reform its judgment, which is binding upon the parties, in accordance with the opinion of the Court. In order to enable the Court to render an opinion a contentious procedure appears indispensable, giving equal opportunity of argument to the parties, *i.e.*, the Secretary General and the individual staff members. As the delegate of Sweden pointed out with reference to the broad scope given to the words "question of law relating to the provisions of the Charter":

> If the stipulation were interpreted in such a way, it would cover the whole field of a Secretariat member's activity, notwithstanding the fact that the new article 11 proposed

[62] Report of the Special Committee on Review of Administrative Tribunal Judgments, Doc. A/2909, *loc. cit.*, Annexes, Agenda Item 49, p. 11, par. 82. See also Report of the Fifth Committee, A/3016, *ibid.* 38 ff.

> by the Special Committee and the Fifth Committee does not give the Secretariat member an opportunity to defend himself orally before the reviewing body.
>
> When a person's entire conduct may be at stake, I think it is necessary that that person should have an opportunity to make an oral presentation before the reviewing body that is to judge him.[63]

The Fifth Committee, aware of the need to ensure full equality for the staff member, was content to observe that

> the Court itself would be a guardian of due process and would not give an opinion if it considered that one of the parties was at a disadvantage. The Court could itself require the evidence necessary for its opinion.[64]

It is one thing to face up to the problem and another to face up to the need of providing a solution. Here the problem is how to ensure that full equality for the international civil servant which everyone agrees is required in the interest of a sound administration of justice. It is no solution, it is submitted, to say that the Court shall find one; the Court's refusal to give an opinion on the ground of inequality is no solution either. It will be merely a finding that Article 11 or, at any rate, what was considered a vital part of it, is unworkable. It is difficult enough to call upon the Court to exercise jurisdiction on appeal from a clearly contentious case in the transparent disguise of a request for an Advisory Opinion. No matter how transparent it may be, there is probably no harm in it, for as long as the obstacle of Article 34, paragraph 1, cannot be or has not been removed, it will be by-passed. However, even this expedient still does not allow of full equality, for the advisory proceeding (unlike Article 34, paragraph 1) enables the Secretary General to participate in oral hearings, but remains closed to the individual staff member. Unless the Court decides to dispense with oral hearings altogether, which presupposes the willing co-operation of Member States, it will have to decline rendering an opinion in all cases involving review of the merits, that is, a question of law, of the judgments of the United Nations Administrative Tribunal. If that should come about, the proponents of the new Article 11 will have scored a pyrrhic victory indeed.

## IV. CONCLUSIONS

The General Assembly might have pursued an alternative course in conjunction with the new Article 11. It might have decided that, in order to ensure the judicial review of judgments of the Administrative Tribunal, a special appeal court be established.[65] Such

[63] General Assembly, 10th Sess., Official Records, Plenary Meetings, 541st meeting, Nov. 8, 1955, p. 287, pars. 107, 108. See also Report of the Fifth Committee, *loc. cit.*, Annexes, Agenda Item 49, p. 41, par. 27.

[64] *Ibid.* 40, par. 19.

[65] See the Indian proposal summarized in the Report of the Fifth Committee, *loc. cit.* 41, par. 32; the suggestions submitted by the Secretary General, *ibid.* 24, and the views of the United Nations Staff Council, *ibid.* 37, par. 16.

a solution would have avoided all the difficulties of, and objections raised against, the resolution adopted. In particular, it would have ensured complete equality, which was generally considered an essential feature of due process of law. The Assembly might also have given some thought to the possibility of amending the Statute of the Court in order to ensure due process of law in the proceedings before the Court under Article 11. Instead, the Assembly rejected the Belgian proposal to ask the Court for an opinion on the constitutionality of the proposed text, but left it to the Court to pass on this issue when seized of a particular request to exercise the review function conferred upon it by Article 11. It was the will of the Assembly that the Court should have the final word on the subject.

The Court may well decide to wait until the Assembly submits a request to it relating to a concrete issue. The Court itself might conceivably, it is submitted, take the initiative in proposing an amendment to its Statute to enable it to discharge properly and with due regard to the principle of equality the novel review function which the General Assembly has thrust upon it. It has the power to do so under Article 70 of its Statute:

> The Court shall have power to propose such amendments to the present Statute as it may deem necessary, through written communications to the Secretary-General, for consideration in conformity with the provisions of Article 69.

Such a step would place the responsibility where it belongs, namely, upon the General Assembly, and assist it in facing up to the issue of principle: the participation of individuals before the Court in proceedings initiated pursuant to Article 11. It is not necessary to review here the changing pattern of the position of individuals in international law, for here there is no intention to make a plea for throwing the Court open to individuals generally. The suggestion is strictly limited to what is believed to be the unavoidable consequence of a step already taken by the General Assembly, that is, to provide a place, undisguised and complete, for staff members of the United Nations. The international civil servant is already a subject of international law and an essential cog in the machinery of international organizations. He already has access to international tribunals, namely, the Administrative Tribunals. The Court itself "does not deny that the Administrative Tribunal is an international tribunal."[66] The present suggestion has therefore for its object to open access for the members of the Secretariat, which is a principal organ of the United Nations, to the Court, which is the principal judicial organ of the United Nations. The Court thus stands in an intimate and direct relation to the Secretariat, which is merely another way of referring to the individuals who have the honor and responsibility to be its members.

It may be useful to recall here some suggestions for amending the Statute of the Court made in connection with a study undertaken by the Institute of International Law. Professors Henri Rolin and H. Lauterpacht proposed that Article 34 of the Statute be

[66] [1956] I.C.J. Rep. 77 at 97. See also Effect of Awards of Compensation made by the United Nations Administrative Tribunal, Advisory Opinion of July 13, 1954, [1954] I.C. J. Rep. 52–53.

amended in order to make international organizations qualified to appear before the Court in contentious cases.[67] Professor Lauterpacht considered such a reform "overdue," and, going further, submitted that

> . . . in connection with Article 34 of the Statute consideration may be given to the question whether that Article ought to be maintained in its present rigid form, namely, whether individuals and private corporations ought to be excluded from being parties to disputes before the Court. I am not suggesting that the Court should entertain disputes between individuals even if such disputes raise questions of international law. Neither is it here suggested that individuals should be in a position to bring states before the Court as defendants against their will. But is there a good reason, other than the persistence of certain traditional modes of thinking, why the Court should not be able to adjudicate upon a dispute which involves a question of international law and in which one party to the dispute is a state—provided that that state agrees in the specific case to the exercise of jurisdiction by the Court?[68]

The suggestion submitted here is obviously much more modest. The subject of Charter review is still on the agenda of the General Assembly. While the force of tradition need not be minimized, a great deal of traditional thinking was jettisoned by the General Assembly when it adopted the novel review procedure directly involving staff members. Probably no one will shed any tears if a little more of the same stuff goes overboard when an even greater traditional principle is at stake. It would be presumptuous to make concrete proposals as to how the Statute should be amended. It is ventured to suggest, however, that the desired objective might better be sought through an additional chapter rather than by adding to or changing Article 34 or 66. It may be found desirable to remove the ambiguity inherent in employing the device of advisory proceedings for the purpose of judicial review of judgments of an Administrative Tribunal. Also the strictly limited and specific character of the review function might best be brought into relief by adding a chapter laying down the rules which the Court deems desirable for fulfilling the review function pursuant to Article 11 of the United Nations and Article XII of the I.L.O. Administrative Tribunals. In this order of ideas it might be possible to combine certain features of the contentious with the advisory procedure and perhaps establish a lower quorum or perhaps a special chamber of five judges for handling such cases. In any event, in the interest of justice to the staff members concerned, it would be eminently desirable to provide for the speediest possible disposition of the appeals.

[67] 45 Annuaire de L'Institut de Droit International (I) 535, 545, 553 (1954).

[68] *Ibid.* 535. For comments by the *Rapporteur,* Judge Max Huber, *cf.* p. 431. See also observations by Professor A. de La Pradelle, p. 472.

# BULGARIA INVOKES THE CONNALLY AMENDMENT

## I

One of the most persuasive arguments advanced by the advocates of the repeal of the Connally Amendment has been its "boomerang effect." While it was intended to protect the vital interests of the United States as a respondent, it also protected, on the basis of reciprocity and perhaps less intentionally, the respondent state in a case instituted before the International Court of Justice by the United States as the applicant.[1] Judge Lauterpacht called it the sanction involved in giving effect to the condition on which a state accepted the obligatory jurisdiction of the Court pursuant to Article 36, paragraph 2, of its Statute:

> . . . The United States cannot avail itself of its—legally ineffective—Declaration of Acceptance in order to bring an action before the Court against another State; but for the very reason that the Declaration is legally ineffective no State can invoke it against the United States. Such indirect sanction as there is—and it is one with which the Court cannot be concerned—is of a different nature. While it unfailingly protects the declarant Gov-

[1] See Preuss, "The International Court of Justice, the Senate, and Matters of Domestic Jurisdiction," 40 A.J.I.L. 720–736, at 733 (1946). Preuss noted that, in the Senate debate on the Connally Amendment, "Perhaps this legal situation was insufficiently comprehended for none of the proponents of the Amendment appeared to envisage the possibility that the United States would ever appear before the Court as a 'plaintiff' seeking judicial recognition of its legal claims." In his defense of the Amendment, Francis O. Wilcox was not unaware of this possibility as well as of the reciprocity impact, but concluded optimistically that "it should not be forgotten that the United States can now sue any other declaring state. Since we have always been an important claimant state this should prove a very real advantage." See "The United States Accepts Compulsory Jurisdiction," *ibid.* 699–719, at 712 and 718 f. For a discussion of the arguments for and against repeal, see Arthur Larson, When Nations Disagree 119 ff. and 136 ff. (1961).

ernment from the jurisdiction of the Court, it deprives it, with equal certainty, of the benefits of that jurisdiction in cases in which the declarant Government is the plaintiff.[2]

Since accepting the jurisdiction of the Court as compulsory on August 14, 1946,[3] the United States has been cited as respondent in two cases, and has instituted or attempted to institute action in seven cases. In one of the former cases, the *Interhandel* Case, it invoked the protection of the Connally Amendment.[4] The cases in which the United States appeared as applicant arose out of aerial incidents and were directed against the Soviet Union, Hungary, and Czechoslovakia, none of which has accepted the compulsory jurisdiction of the Court. In all these cases the offer made by the United States to adjudicate was rejected. In one case, the *Aerial Incident of 27 July 1955,* the United States on October 28, 1957, instituted action against Bulgaria on the basis of Bulgaria's declaration of acceptance of the Optional Clause of the Permanent Court of International Justice, dated July 29, 1921. And it was in this case that the sanction was invoked against the United States, as it was invoked and applied in the *Norwegian Loans* Case against France. Bulgaria, the respondent, invoked the Connally Amendment reservation as a shield against the applicant United States, while also contesting the jurisdiction of the Court on other grounds. One of them, the invalidity of the Bulgarian declaration, had already been tested and firmly established by the Court in its judgment of May 26, 1959, in the parent case arising out of the same incident between Israel and Bulgaria.[5] Following this, the United Kingdom withdrew its application against Bulgaria in a parallel action arising out of the same incident.[6] The United States, however, continued the proceedings, and the Agents of the parties were informed on March 18, 1960, that the Court had decided to open oral hearings on June 1, 1960.[7] However, a few days prior to the date fixed for oral hearings, in a communication addressed to the Registrar of the Court on May 13, 1960, the United States requested the discontinuance of the proceedings and the removal of the case from the Court's list. The Court granted the request by order of May 30, 1960.[8] As will be shown presently, the ground for this latter action was the acceptance by the United States of the Bulgarian preliminary objection based on the Connally Amendment. This case appears unique in that here, for the first time, the applicant government accepted as justified the respondent's preliminary objection to the jurisdiction of the Court.[9]

[2] Interhandel Case, Judgment of March 23, 1959, [1959] I.C.J. Rep. 6, at 119 (dissenting opinion of Sir Hersch Lauterpacht).

[3] 1959–1960 I.C.J. Yearbook 256.

[4] For a discussion of the relevant issues, see Briggs, "Reservations to the Acceptance of the Compulsory Jurisdiction of the International Court of Justice," 93 Hague Academy Recueil des Cours 223–367, at 344 ff. (1958, I). The other case in which the United States was the respondent is the Case Concerning Rights of Nationals of the United States of America in Morocco (France *v.* U.S.A.), [1952] I.C.J. Rep. 22, 176.

[5] [1959] I.C.J. Rep. 127.

[6] 1959–1960 I.C.J. Yearbook 77; [1959] I.C.J. Rep. 264. The order of the Court removing the case from the General List issued on Aug. 3, 1959.

[7] [1969] I.C.J. Rep. 146, 147.

[8] *Ibid.* 146.

[9] Rosenne, "La Cour Internationale de Justice en 1960," 65 Revue Gén. de Droit Int. Public 1–54, at 3 (1961).

## II

In order the better to appreciate the position taken from time to time by the United States with respect to the legal scope and effect of the Connally Amendment, it may be appropriate to set out some relevant data:

1. The Court gave judgment in the *Norwegian Loans Case* on July 6, 1957. It held that it lacked jurisdiction to adjudicate upon the dispute brought before it by France on the ground:

> that the Norwegian Government is entitled, by virtue of the condition of reciprocity, to invoke the reservation contained in the French Declaration of March 1st, 1949; that this reservation excludes from the jurisdiction of the Court the dispute which has been referred to it by the Application of the French Government; that consequently the Court is without jurisdiction to entertain the Application.[10]

It will be recalled that the French reservation in question followed substantially the Connally Amendment and that Judge Lauterpacht, in an individual opinion in that case, delivered a trenchant critique of the "automatic" French reservation and, by implication, of the American reservation, which culminated in the proposition that the entire French declaration was legally invalid.[11]

2. On October 11, 1957, the United States filed preliminary objections to the Swiss request, dated October 3, 1957, for the indication by the Court of interim measures of protection in the *Interhandel* Case. Specifically, Switzerland asked the Court to request the United States "not to sell the shares of the General Aniline and Film Corporation claimed by the Swiss Federal Government as the property of its nationals." Referring to this part of the Swiss request, the United States, invoking the Connally Amendment, declared that it

> has determined that such sale or disposition of the shares in the American corporation . . . is a matter essentially within its domestic jurisdiction. Accordingly, pursuant to paragraph (b) of the conditions attached to this country's acceptance of the Court's compulsory jurisdiction, dated August 14, 1946, this country respectfully declines . . . to submit the matter of the sale or disposition of such shares to the jurisdiction of the Court.[12]

In his oral argument, the Agent for the United States, Mr. Loftus Becker, elaborated the legal effects of the above objection. He stated first, relying on the judgment in the *Norwegian Loans* Case:

[10] [1957] I.C.J. Rep. 9, at 27.
[11] *Ibid.* 61. For an analysis of the case and the views of other members of the Court, see Briggs, *loc. cit.* 336–344.
[12] I.C.J. Pleadings, Interhandel Case 72, 76, 77.

> . . . This determination by the United States of America is not subject to review or approval by any tribunal. It operates to remove definitively from the jurisdiction of the Court the matter which it determines. After the United States of America has made such a determination . . . the subject-matter of the determination is not justiciable.

He stated secondly, relying on the Court's judgment in the *Anglo-Iranian Oil Company* Case, that, in order to be able to indicate provisional measures, the Court must be satisfied that the claim does not fall completely outside the scope of international jurisdiction or, in other words, that *prima facie* the Court had jurisdiction. And he concluded by saying that:

> by virtue of the Preliminary Objection filed by the United States of America, the matter of the sale or disposition of the shares . . . falls completely outside the scope of international jurisdiction, including the jurisdiction of the Court.

In fact, he argued, that determination destroys the *prima facie* jurisdiction and, therefore, the legal basis for indicating provisional measures.[13]

The Court, without considering the legal effect of the Connally Amendment reservation, declined to accede to the Swiss request on the basis of the finding "that there is no need to indicate interim measures of protection."[14] In its reasoning the Court referred to the challenge to the American objection by the Co-Agent of the Swiss Government, Professor Paul Guggenheim, and to his statement:

> il paraît difficile d'imaginer que sur une question aussi complexe et délicate que la validité de la réserve américaine, la Cour veuille se prononcer, même d'une manière sommaire, dans le cadre de la procédure en vue de l'indication de mesures conservatoires.[15]

3. On October 28, 1957, the United States filed with the Registry of the Court an application dated October 24, 1957, instituting proceedings against Bulgaria in the matter of the *Aerial Incident of July 27, 1955.*

4. In a speech delivered on April 26, 1958, before the American Society of International Law, the then Legal Adviser of the Department of State, Mr. Loftus Becker, explained and defended the United States Government's reliance on the Connally Amendment in the interlocutory proceedings in connection with the Swiss request of October 3, 1957, for an Indication of Interim Measures of Protection in the *Interhandel* Case.[16]

5. In the written preliminary objections in the *Interhandel* Case (Preliminary Objec-

[13] Public Hearing of Oct. 12, 1957, *ibid.* 452 f., and Public Hearing of Oct. 14, 1957, *ibid.* 466. See Briggs, *loc. cit.* 347 f.

[14] Interhandel Case (Interim Measures of Protection), Order of Oct. 24, 1957, [1957] I.C.J. Rep. 105, at 112. The Court took note of the statement by the United States that it "is not taking action at the present time to fix a time schedule for the sale of such shares." *Ibid.*

[15] "It seems difficult to imagine that the Court should wish to express an opinion, even in summary fashion, upon so complex and delicate a question as the validity of the American reservation in the context of the procedure for the indication of interim measures of protection." (Author's translation.) Pleadings 462 f., Oral Hearing of Oct. 14, 1957. The Court quoted part of this statement in its Order, [1957] I.C.J. Rep. at 111.

[16] 1958 Proceedings, American Society of International Law 267–269.

tions), dated simply "June 1958," and in the oral hearings before the Court held in November, 1958, the United States maintained its view regarding the legal effect of the Connally Amendment.[17]

6. The Court gave judgment in the *Interhandel* Case (Preliminary Objections) on March 21, 1959, declaring the Swiss application inadmissible on the ground of non-exhaustion of local remedies.[18] The Court also held that the preliminary objection based on the Connally Amendment, having been declared, during the oral argument of the American Agent, as "somewhat moot," "is without object at the present stage of the proceedings."[19] In a dissenting opinion, Judge Lauterpacht maintained the views he had expressed earlier in the *Norwegian Loans* Case and argued strongly the invalidity, from a legal point of view, of the Connally Amendment.[20]

7. The Bulgarian Government on September 3, 1959, filed four preliminary objections to the jurisdiction of the Court, in the second of which it availed itself of the "made in America" reservation. The United States submitted written observations, dated simply "February 1960," in which it contended, among other things, that Bulgaria was not entitled to determine that the dispute was a matter essentially within the domestic jurisdiction of Bulgaria. This position was reversed by the United States in a communication of May 13, 1960, referred to above, and discontinuance of the proceedings was requested.

## III

In its application of October 24, 1957, instituting proceedings against Bulgaria on account of certain acts committed on July 27, 1955, by the Bulgarian Air Force in the Bulgarian airspace against American nationals on board an "El Al Israel Airlines Ltd." civil airplane, the United States placed the dispute as falling within the categories of legal disputes enumerated in subparagraphs (a) to (d) of Article 36 (2) of the Statute. The dispute involved

> among other questions of international law, the scope and application of international obligations relating to the overflight of international civil aircraft; particularly, the duties of the government, and military defense authorities of the government, in whose territory the intrusion is alleged to have taken place, with respect to interception, identification signals between intercepting and intruding civil aircraft and the use of force as against passengers of intruding civil aircraft; together with issues of fact which, if resolved in favor of the United States Government, would prove breaches of international obligation by the Bulgarian Government; and the nature and extent of the reparations to be made by the Bulgarian Government to the United States Government for all these breaches.[21]

[17] Public Hearing of Nov. 6, 1958, Pleadings 320, 507; Public Hearing of Nov. 14, 1958, *ibid.* 610.

[18] [1959] I.C.J. Rep. 6, at 30.

[19] *Ibid.* at 26. For a discussion of this aspect of the Interhandel Case, see Briggs, *loc. cit.* 359 ff., and in 53 A.J.I.L. 547 at 557 ff. (1959).

[20] [1959] I.C.J. Rep. at 118.

[21] I.C.J. Pleadings, Aerial Incident of July 27, 1955 (Israel *v.* Bulgaria; United States of America *v.* Bulgaria; United Kingdom *v.* Bulgaria), p. 22 f. This volume will be cited hereinafter as "I.C.J. Pleadings, Aerial Incident."

It was further stated that the El Al Israel airplane was driven off its course by strong local winds, that the weather was poor, that the aircraft, while flying innocently over Bulgarian territory and trying to return to its course, was fired upon by Bulgarian military fighter aircraft, that all passengers, including six American nationals, were killed and their property on board the aircraft was destroyed. The United States, for these breaches of international law, demanded monetary reparation in the amount of $257,875 with interest, and such other reparations as the Court might deem to be fit and proper.[22]

The legal basis for instituting proceedings by means of a unilateral application was described in these terms:

> The United States Government, in filing this application with the Court, submits to the Court's jurisdiction for the purposes of this case. The Bulgarian Government accepted the compulsory jurisdiction of this Court by virtue of the signature of its representative to the Protocol of Signature of the Statute of the Permanent Court of International Justice, and his acceptance was completely unconditional; acceptance became effective as to the jurisdiction of the International Court of Justice by virtue of Article 36 (5) of the Statute of the Court upon the date of admission of Bulgaria into the United Nations.[23]

It will be noted that the United States refrained from specifying the basis of the Court's jurisdiction insofar as it was concerned and, while stressing the unconditional acceptance of the jurisdiction of the Permanent Court by Bulgaria of July 29, 1921, it omitted reference to the conditions which it attached to its own declaration of acceptance of 1946, including the Connally Amendment reservation.

The application was followed in due course by a memorial, filed on December 2, 1958, the contents of which are here immaterial, as are all issues of fact and law except those relating to jurisdiction. However, it is difficult to suppress a feeling of regret that all those beautiful issues relating to the rights and duties of states in the event of aerial intrusion and involuntary overflight could not have been adjudicated. Be that as it may, the proceedings on the merits were suspended when Bulgaria filed preliminary objections, dated September 3, 1959, to the jurisdiction of the Court.

Bulgaria presented four objections and a protest, which, out of deference to the Court, it did not formally designate as such:

> contre les expressions outrageuses dont l'agent du Gouvernement des Etats-Unis a cru pouvoir se servir dans sa requête, laissant aux Membres de la Cour l'appréciation de cette conduite sans précédent dans la pratique judiciaire internationale.[24]

[22] *Ibid.* at 24.

[23] *Ibid.* at 23.

[24] "against the outrageous terms which the agent of the United States Government has seen fit to use in his application, leaving to the Members of the Court the evaluation of such unprecedented conduct in international judicial practice." (Translation.) Exceptions Préliminaires du Gouvernement de la République Populaire de Bulgarie (Déclinatoire de Compétence). *Ibid* at 278 f.

## A. First Bulgarian Preliminary Objection

Bulgaria contested, first of all, the American proposition that the Bulgarian declaration of July 29, 1921, had, by virtue of Article 36, paragraph 5, of the Statute, been transferred to the present Court on December 14, 1955, when Bulgaria was admitted to membership of the United Nations. The line of argument on this point is identical with that developed by Bulgaria in the parent case (*Israel* v. *Bulgaria*), and Bulgaria relied on the judgment of the Court in that case, which upheld its contention.[25] The United States observations took issue with this argument for several reasons. In the first place, the United States correctly considered that the Court was not bound by its ruling in the case of *Israel* v. *Bulgaria,* and appealed to the Court for a re-examination of this point.[26] The question must remain moot whether the arguments submitted by the United States were of such strength and novelty as to induce the Court to change its decision. The Court was divided, twelve to four, in the *Israel* v. *Bulgaria* Case, and the dissenting opinions were of great cogency. A different holding in *United States* v. *Bulgaria* could not have been excluded *a priori,* although the chances of a reversal must have appeared nil to the British Government when it requested discontinuance of its case against Bulgaria.

It is not necessary to discuss all the reasons for the validity of the Bulgarian declaration, on which the United States elaborated in its observations. One point, however, deserves mention. In considering other states to which the transitional clause in Article 36, paragraph 5, might have applied, the United States appeared to single out Thailand for special consideration:

> Although Thailand had not become a United Nations Member and party to the Statute of the Court until a number of months after April 18, 1946,[27] Thailand considered that its declaration accepting the jurisdiction of the Permanent Court was carried over to the new Court upon Thailand's becoming a party to the present Statute.[28]

This support of the United States thesis was knocked down by the Court in its judgment of May 26, 1961, in the Case concerning the *Temple of Preah Vihear (Cambodia* v. *Thailand*). In her preliminary objections, Thailand claimed that her declaration of acceptance of May 26, had been rendered meaningless and without effect by the Court's judgment of May 26, 1959, in the Case of *Israel* v. *Bulgaria,* on the ground that all declarations, which on April 19, 1946, had not already been "transformed" by the operation of Article 36, paragraph 5, into acceptances of the compulsory jurisdiction of the present Court, had lapsed and ceased to be in force. The Court conceded that Thailand's old declaration of 1940 lapsed in any event on May 6, 1950, by its own terms, but held that

[25] See note 5 above.
[26] Observations and Submissions of the Government of the United States on the Preliminary Objections of the Government of the People's Republic of Bulgaria, I.C.J. Pleadings, Aerial Incident at 310.
[27] The date of the liquidation of the Permanent Court of International Justice.
[28] I.C.J. Pleadings, Aerial Incident at 320; see also pp. 307, 315, 316.

Thailand's declaration of May 20, 1950, constituted a new and independent instrument whereby Thailand fully intended to submit herself to the compulsory jurisdiction of the Court.[29]

### B. Fourth Bulgarian Preliminary Objection

The fourth Bulgarian objection related to local remedies. It was contended that the United States application was inadmissible because the American nationals on whose behalf the United States filed the complaint had failed to exhaust the local remedies available to them under Bulgarian law.[30] This point need not be considered here.

### C. Third Bulgarian Preliminary Objection

The third Bulgarian objection is of substantial interest from the procedural point of view. Did the United States application constitute a proper seising of the Court? The Bulgarian Government contended that it did not. It will be recalled that the United States refrained from referring to its own declaration of acceptance in its application instituting proceedings against Bulgaria, while invoking the 1921 Bulgarian declaration. The Bulgarian Government construed this as an attempt to seise the Court by means of a unilateral application on the basis of the obligatory jurisdiction provided for in Article 36, paragraph 2, of the Statute. In order to avail itself of this method of seising, the United States should have indicated in its application the provisions in force between the parties conferring such jurisdiction upon the Court. This, claimed the Bulgarian Government, is required by Article 32, paragraph 2, of the Rules of Court which reads:

> When a case is brought before the Court by means of an application, the application must, as laid down in Article 40, paragraph 1, of the Statute, indicate the party making it, the party against whom the claim is brought and the subject of the dispute. It must also, as far as possible, specify the provisions on which the applicant founds the jurisdiction of the Court, state the precise nature of the claim and give a succinct statement of the facts and grounds on which the claim is based . . .

This the United States had failed to do and this failure might have placed Bulgaria in an unfavorable position; for, according to Article 62, paragraph 1, of the Rules of Court,

> A preliminary objection must be filed by a party at the latest before the expiry of the time-limit fixed for the delivery of its first pleading.

The purpose of the requirement of Article 32, paragraph 2, of the Rules becomes clear in the context of the above clause: it is to inform the respondent fully of the provisions on

[29] [1961] I.C.J. Rep. 17, at 29.
[30] Exceptions Préliminaires at 276 ff.

which the compulsory jurisdiction is alleged to rest, and to enable it to avail itself of any reservations made by the applicant government. As stated by the Bulgarian Government:

> Autoriser la Partie requérante de passer d'abord sous silence, dans la requête, sa déclaration d'acceptation de la clause facultative pour pouvoir l'invoquer valablement, serait donc lui permettre d'induire sciemment en erreur, quant à ses intentions, le défendeur afin de mettre celui-ci dans l'impossibilité de tirer parti des réserves figurant dans la dite déclaration.[31]

There is no evidence, of course, that the United States had any such intentions nor is it necessary to assume that the Court would have admitted such an attempt. In any event, the Bulgarian Government concluded that there was no basis in the American application for invoking the compulsory jurisdiction of the Court.

The Bulgarian Government also argued that this jurisdiction must be based on a contractual bond previously established between the parties. In so doing it referred to Article 36, paragraph 4, of the Statute,[32] and to the judgments of the Court in the *Right of Passage* Case and the *Nottebohm* Case. In the former case the Court said:

> . . . The Court considers that, by the deposit of its Declaration of Acceptance with the Secretary-General, the accepting State becomes a Party to the system of the Optional Clause in relation to the other declarant States, with all the rights and obligations deriving from Article 36. *The contractual relation* between the Parties and the compulsory jurisdiction of the Court resulting therefrom are established, "*ipso facto* and without special agreement", by the fact of the making of the Declaration . . . it is on that very day that the *consensual bond, which is the basis* of the Optional Clause, comes into being. . . .[33]

In the latter case, the Court declared:

> . . . The characteristic of this compulsory jurisdiction is that it results from *a previous agreement* which makes it possible to seise the Court of a dispute without a Special Agreement, and that in respect of disputes subject to it, the Court may be seised by means of an Application by one of the parties. . . . The purpose of Article 36, paragraph 2, and of the Declarations relating thereto, is to regulate the seising of the Court: under the system of the Statute *the seising of the Court by means of an Application is not ipso facto open* to all States parties to the Statute, it is only open to *the extent defined in the applicable Declarations.*[34]

Having concluded that the United States application failed to conform to the requirements of seising under the Optional Clause of Article 36, paragraph 2, of the Stat-

[31] "If the applicant party were permitted in its application to pass over in silence its declaration of acceptance of the optional clause in order to invoke it validly [at a later stage of the proceedings], then this would be tantamount to allowing it deliberately to mislead the respondent as to its intentions for the purpose of rendering it impossible for the latter to take advantage of the reservations included in that declaration." (Author's translation.) I.C.J. Pleadings, Aerial Incident at 276.

[32] "Such declarations shall be deposited with the Secretary-General of the United Nations, who shall transmit copies thereof to the parties to the Statute and to the Registrar of the Court."

[33] Case concerning Right of Passage over Indian Territory (Preliminary Objections), Judgment of Nov. 26, 1957, [1957] I.C.J. Rep. 125, at 146. Italics in the original of the Bulgarian Exceptions Préliminaires at 274.

[34] Nottebohm Case (Preliminary Objection), Judgment of Nov. 18, 1953, [1953] I.C.J. Rep. 111, at 122. Italics in the original Bulgarian Exceptions Préliminaires at 274.

ute, the Bulgarian Government finally construed the statement quoted above[35] as an acceptance of the jurisdiction of the Court *ad hoc,* that is, solely for the purpose of this dispute. Viewed from this angle, it constituted at best an offer to conclude a special agreement and this offer the Bulgarian Government declined on the ground that the dispute related to matters essentially within the domestic jurisdiction of Bulgaria.

The United States accepted the validity of this preliminary objection, stating:

> The United States Government agrees that apart from the United States Declaration of August 26, 1946, there is not a basis for compulsory jurisdiction,

and stating further with reference to the above-quoted passage in its application:

> The United States does not contend that this statement constituted a declaration under Article 36, paragraph 2 of the Statute, providing a basis for compulsory jurisdiction. For this reason it is not necessary to consider further the third Bulgarian preliminary objection.[36]

The motive that prompted the United States to formulate its application in a manner which gave the Bulgarian Government an opening for a strong and well-reasoned objection is immaterial. It may well be that the United States, considering the preceding diplomatic negotiations and the avowed willingness of Bulgaria to make reparation to the American victims of the incident,[37] deliberately chose the method of an offer of *forum prorogatum.* It was, of course, open to the Bulgarian Government to decline this offer, but it certainly was not improper for the United States to extend it. Article 32, paragraph 2, of the Rules of Court, referred to by the Bulgarian Government, clearly and deliberately distinguishes between the mandatory and the optional contents of an application, and this distinction is intended to preserve the institution of the *forum prorogatum.*[38] The mandatory requirement is set out in Article 40 of the Statute, and the United States application complied with it. Had the United States selected this method of establishing jurisdiction, through the institution of *forum prorogatum,* it would have been not only proper but indeed necessary to refrain from invoking the Bulgarian declaration of acceptance. The United States must have been aware that it was not dealing with a friendly government with which procedural shortcomings could be ironed out.[39]

### D. Second Bulgarian Preliminary Objection

The second Bulgarian preliminary objection was based on two assumptions: one, that the American application was based on the declaration of acceptance of August 26, 1946, and, secondly, that the United States might at a later stage of the proceedings modi-

[35] See p. 732 above.
[36] Written Observations, I.C.J. Pleadings, Aerial Incident at 306 and 322.
[37] *Ibid.* at 303.
[38] Rosenne, The International Court of Justice 289–291, 368 (1957).
[39] *Ibid.* 371 f.

fy this declaration, and thus attempt to deprive the Bulgarian Government of the possibility of invoking the Connally Amendment reservation. In the first hypothesis the Bulgarian Government invoked the reservation. This was formally justified on the ground of reciprocity and the essential consensual basis of the jurisdiction of the Court. With reference to the substance of the dispute, the Bulgarian Government claimed that the defense of its territory, the security in the airspace above the Southwestern frontier region, and the disposition of its anti-aircraft defense, fall under its domestic jurisdiction, which is not limited by any conventional arrangement with the United States.[40] With respect to the second hypothesis, the Bulgarian Government argued that any unilateral modification of the declaration of 1946 would deprive Bulgaria of its rights under Article 36 of the Statute. Moreover, the Bulgarian Government insisted that the United States must not be allowed to escape the "sanction," that is, the consequences of its own declaration, and declared:

> Toute renonciation éventuelle de la part des Etats-Unis, pour une affaire concrète et à l'égard d'un Etat donné, aux éléments restrictifs de leur déclaration de 1946, est contraire au Statut et ne pourrait avoir aucune influence sur l'instance en cours. *Par une pareille renonciation* ad hoc, *motivée uniquement par des considérations d'opportunité pratique le Gouvernement des Etats-Unis entendrait garder pour l'avenir et dans tous les cas où il serait défendeur, le bénéfice des avantages que lui procureraient ses propres réserves sans avoir à en subir les inconvénients dans les cas où il serait demandeur.*[41]

Finally, the Bulgarian Government declared that it

> ne saurait admettre que soient examinées devant la Cour, de façon directe ou indirecte, des questions qu'il qualifie en bon droit comme relevant essentiellement de la compétence nationale de l'Etat bulgare. Il demande, en conséquence, à la Cour de se déclarer incompétente pour examiner la requête du Gouvernement des Etats-Unis.[42]

The United States reacted to this second preliminary objection in two stages: first, in its written observations, and second, in its communication of May 13, 1960, to the Registrar of the Court. In the first stage, the argument of the United States that Bulgaria was not entitled to determine the dispute as falling essentially within its domestic jurisdiction was summarized as follows:

[40] Exceptions Préliminaires, I.C.J. Pleadings, Aerial Incident at 271 f.

[41] "A subsequent renunciation by the United States of the restrictive clauses of its Declaration of 1946, in any concrete case and with respect to a particular State, is contrary to the Statute and could have no influence in the pending proceedings. For by dint of such an *ad hoc* renunciation, motivated solely by opportunistic considerations, the Government of the United States would aim to preserve for the future and in all cases in which it would be the respondent the benefit of its own reservation without being exposed to its drawbacks in cases in which it was the plaintiff." (Author's translation.) *Ibid.* at 273. Italics in the original.

[42] "[The Bulgarian Government] cannot admit that matters which it rightfully determines as being essentially within its domestic jurisdiction should be considered, directly or indirectly, before the Court. It requests, accordingly, that the Court declare itself without competence to adjudicate upon the application of the Government of the United States." (Author's translation.) *Ibid.* at 272.

> 1. While Bulgaria is entitled to invoke, reciprocally, any of the reservations contained in the United States declaration of 1946, Bulgaria cannot exceed their proper scope in making its defense. Bulgaria cannot determine that the United States claim based on the incident of 1955 is essentially within Bulgaria's domestic jurisdiction, since any such determination would fly in the face of actuality and would ignore the international character accorded the claim by the parties in their previous negotiations. United States reservation (b) [43] does not permit the United States or any other State to make an arbitrary determination, in bad faith.
>
> 2. In the view of the United States, Bulgaria has failed to make a showing of any valid considerations of security which would form the basis for a conclusion that the present claim lies "essentially within the domestic jurisdiction of the People's Republic of Bulgaria." The United States is prepared to show, by evidence and argument on the merits, that the facts of the incident belie any threat to Bulgarian national security.[44]

It would appear from this that, as construed by the United States, the Connally Amendment is neither automatic nor peremptory nor self-judging, but subject to the judgment of the Court. More specifically, the United States, in support of its contention that the dispute was impregnated with "international character," referred to the facts of the aerial incident, the alleged liability of Bulgaria for the acts of its Air Force, the diplomatic correspondence relating to the incident, and concluded:

> After taking these steps and entering into the international engagements referred to above, the Government of Bulgaria is not entitled now to determine that these matters are "essentially within the domestic jurisdiction of the People's Republic of Bulgaria."[45]

Whether the international character of the subject matter of the dispute is "perfectly clear" as contended by the United States is immaterial; but if Bulgaria is denied the unilateral right to hold otherwise, is it for the United States to make such a determination unilaterally and with binding effect on Bulgaria? Such a position would be contrary to common sense and basic principles of international law, including that of the sovereign equality of states. [46] Is it not then an inevitable consequence of the United States contention that this question can only be decided by the Court, and by the Court alone, in spite of the Connally Amendment?

The United States also rejected the Bulgarian assertion that the subject matter was essentially within its domestic jurisdiction because its security was involved. Here again the United States submitted

> that, in all the circumstances of the 1955 incident, the present claim based upon it could not properly be characterized as lying essentially within Bulgaria's domestic jurisdiction.[47]

[43] The Connally Amendment reservation.

[44] Written Observations at 308.

[45] *Ibid.* at 324 f.

[46] In this connection *cf.* the Judgment of the Court of Nov. 20, 1950, in the Asylum Case (Colombia/Peru), [1950] I.C.J. Rep. 266 at 275 f.

[47] Written Observations at 325.

It may well be correct, as argued by the United States, that, even if it were established that Bulgarian security was involved, "it does not automatically follow" that the dispute would enter the reserved domain and that the question of which matters fall into this domain is a "relative question."[48] But who can settle these questions? Certainly not the United States; and if they cannot be settled by Bulgaria with binding effect upon the United States, then they must be settled by the Court, and this in spite of Bulgaria's invoking the Connally Amendment reservation. That this was the burden of the United States argument appears clearly from the offer "to make an extended presentation in connection with hearing of the case on the merits."[49] Thus the Connally Amendment was not construed by the United States as an absolute bar to the jurisdiction of the Court.

In arguing against the Bulgarian plea of domestic jurisdiction on the basis of the Connally reservation, the United States relied chiefly upon its intimate knowledge of the reservation in its capacity as "the author of the reservation." As presented by the United States it was a question of the scope of the reservation. On this point the United States made two important statements. First:

> The United States does not consider that reservation (*b*)[50] authorizes or empowers this Government, or any other government on a basis of reciprocity, to make an arbitrary determination that a particular matter is domestic, when it is evidently one of international concern and has been so treated by the parties.[51]

In support of this proposition the United States quoted from a speech by Senator Connally, the author of the reservation, on the floor of the Senate in August, 1946.[52] Senator Connally's remarks fitted perfectly the position of the United States taken so far. For if the Senator meant what he said, the reservation would not be used as a bar against jurisdiction but as a ground, to be used sparingly, for non-execution of a judgment of the Court, if that judgment involved a matter of domestic law rather than of international law. The system of compulsory jurisdiction to which the United States subscribed relates solely to legal disputes on questions of international law. As stated in Article 38, paragraph 1, of the Statute, it is the function of the Court "to decide in accordance with international law such disputes as are submitted to it."

In the second statement the United States referred to the *Interhandel* Case as evidence of "a practical construction to reservation (*b*)." In that case the United States invoked the

[48] At this point the United States referred to the Case of the Tunis-Morocco Nationality Decrees, P.C.I.J. Pub., Ser. B, No. 4 (1923), but without a citation.

[49] Written Observations at 325.

[50] The Connally Amendment reservation.

[51] Written Observations at 323.

[52] The passage as quoted from 92 Cong. Rec. 10,695 (1946) is as follows:

"Several Senators have argued that by this amendment the United States would put itself in the position of corruptly and improperly claiming that a question is domestic in nature when it is not, thereby taking advantage of an international dispute and saying that since the question is domestic, we will not abide by the decision of the Court. Mr. President, I have more faith in my Government than that. I do not believe the United States would adopt a subterfuge, a pretext, or a pretense in order to block the judgment of the Court on any such grounds."

Connally reservation with respect to some issues, while agreeing that other issues were not essentially a matter of domestic jurisdiction, and concluded:

> The United States considers that the practice followed by a State with respect to its own reservation is entitled to great weight in the construction of that reservation when it is invoked by another State.[53]

In this connection it appears that the Court alone has the authority to determine what weight should be given to a state's subsequent conduct in construing an instrument to which it is a party. The United States cannot by itself legally impose its construction upon Bulgaria any more than Bulgaria can impose its interpretation upon the United States.

The last stand taken by the United States calls for a brief comment. In the *Interhandel* Case on October 12, 1957, the United States took the position that its determination was "not subject to review or approval by any tribunal," and that "the subject matter of the determination is not justiciable."[54] This attitude seems to be in complete contradiction with the position taken some two years later vis-à-vis Bulgaria, which, far from contradicting, precisely followed the construction adopted by the United States in a case in which it was, like Bulgaria, the defendant party. Furthermore, even in the *Interhandel* Case, the Swiss Co-Agent, Professor Guggenheim, questioned the propriety of invoking the automatic reservation with respect only to some aspects of the dispute, and he contested the position that such aspects were properly within the reserved domain.[55] The United States, in the second statement referred to above, after quoting Senator Connally, claimed that in fact it "has given a practical construction to reservation (*b*) which is altogether consistent with the statement just quoted."[56] It may be possible to read Senator Connally's statement with different results. If it is understood as reserving the right of the United States to decline to execute a judgment which involves its reserved domain, then clearly the "practical construction" is not altogether in Senator Connally's speech, because in the *Interhandel* Case, like Bulgaria in the *Aerial Incident* Case, the United States invoked the reservation as a plea to the jurisdiction of the Court. How a government reads Senator Connally's speech and how it interprets the reservation which bears his name may well depend upon whether it argues as applicant or respondent government in a case.

The contradiction apparent between the United States position in the *Interhandel* Case and its later position in the *Aerial Incident* Case was eliminated by the letter, dated May 13, 1960, of the Legal Adviser of the Department of State to the Registrar of the Court. The relevant part of this letter, which confirms the construction placed here on the United States position in the written observations, reads as follows:

[53] Written Observations at 323.
[54] Pleadings, Interhandel Case 452–453.
[55] Pleadings 410 ff., 580. See also the oral argument of the Swiss Agent, Professor Sauser-Hall, *ibid.* 582 ff., 597 f.
[56] Written Observations, I.C.J. Pleadings, Aerial Incident at 323.

In that part of the Written Observations which relates to the second preliminary objection of Bulgaria, a contention was advanced on behalf of the United States with respect to reservation (*b*) attached to the acceptance by the United States of the jurisdiction of the Court. That contention was to the effect that reservation (*b*) did not authorize or empower Bulgaria to make an arbitrary determination that a particular matter was essentially within its domestic jurisdiction. The necessary premise of the argument was that the Court must have jurisdiction for the limited purpose of deciding whether a determination under reservation (*b*) is arbitrary and without foundation. On the basis of further study and consideration of the history and background of reservation (*b*) and the position heretofore taken by the United States with respect to reservation (*b*) in litigation before the Court, it has been concluded that the premise of the argument is not valid and that the argument must therefore be withdrawn. As it was declared by the United States to this Court in the Interhandel Case (Switzerland *v.* United States), when the United States has made a determination under reservation (*b*) that a particular matter is essentially within its domestic jurisdiction, that determination is not subject to review or approval by any tribunal, and it operates to remove definitively from the jurisdiction of the Court the matter which it determines. A determination under reservation (*b*) that a matter is essentially domestic constitutes an absolute bar to jurisdiction irrespective of the propriety or arbitrariness of the determination. Although the United States has adhered to the policy of not making any arbitrary determination under reservation (*b*), the pursuit of that policy does not affect the legal scope of the reservation. Under the rule of reciprocity applied by the Court in the case concerning Certain Norwegian Loans (France *v.* Norway), Bulgaria is accorded the same rights and powers with respect to reservation (*b*) as the United States. Accordingly, the Government of the United States withdraws that part of its Written Observations and Submissions which relates to the second preliminary objection of Bulgaria.[57]

The United States consequently requested the discontinuation of the proceedings, which was granted by order of the Court of May 30, 1960.[58]

In thus reversing itself completely, the United States has reverted to the construction of the Connally Amendment which it deemed proper in the *Interhandel* Case, but which has not yet been the subject of a determination by the Court. This reversal is remarkable. It is based on a "further study and consideration of the history and background of reservation (*b*)" and of the United States position in the *Interhandel* Case. It is always possible, of course, to rake over the identical debate in the Senate and come up with different results, although one would have assumed that both the history of the Connally Amendment and the position of the United States in the *Interhandel* Case were well known to all concerned in the Department of State. In his address, already referred to, Mr. Loftus Becker, the Legal Adviser of the Department, said, on the one hand, that the Connally Amendment

is clearly more restrictive than a reservation of the right not to submit matters essentially within the domestic jurisdiction of the United States, *as determined by the principles of international law,*

[57] This letter, as well as the written observations, was signed by Mr. Eric H. Hager, Agent of the U.S.A. I.C.J. Pleadings, Aerial Incident at 677.

[58] [1960] I.C.J. Rep. 146.

and, on the other, he admitted of a

> serious question whether "as determined by the United States of America," if fairly applied, would mean any more in the way of excluding the International Court from passing upon truly domestic issues than the words "as determined by the principles of international law."[59]

This appears, indeed, to be the nub of the problem, and it is most regrettable that the United States not merely reversed its position, but also denied the Court and itself the benefit of a judicial determination of the scope and character of the Connally Amendment.

## IV

In the *Aerial Incident* Case between the United States and Bulgaria the issue was squarely joined. Bulgaria clearly invoked the benefit of the Connally Amendment reservation, and the United States in its submissions requested the Court to adjudge and declare:

> 1. That the Court has jurisdiction in the present case concerning the Aerial Incident of July 27, 1955;
> 2. That the first, second and fourth preliminary objections of the Government of the People's Republic of Bulgaria are overruled, and that the third preliminary objection, stated as an alternative to the second preliminary objection, need not be considered; or
> 3. That, as an alternative to the foregoing, the consideration of such preliminary objections as are not now disposed of be joined to the hearing of the present case upon the merits, in case the Court considers there are issues with respect to jurisdiction which require trial and hearing.[60]

Such was not the situation in earlier cases in which a Connally-type reservation was involved. The *Norwegian Loans* Case is not necessarily an indication of what the Court might have held in the *Aerial Incident* Case. The former case is sometimes cited as authority for the proposition that when a party to a dispute invokes the Connally-type reservation, the Court can do nothing but register this fact and declare itself incompetent. It is true that in that case the Court found that it was without jurisdiction to entertain the French application because Norway was entitled, by virtue of reciprocity, to invoke the Connally-type reservation contained in the French declaration of acceptance of March 1, 1949, and this reservation excluded from the jurisdiction of the Court the dispute referred to it by France. However, the Court also considered that it did not have to examine whether the French reservation was consistent with the undertaking of a legal obligation

[59] *Loc. cit.* at 267. Italics in the original.
[60] Written Observations, I.C.J. Pleadings, Aerial Incident at 330.

and was compatible with paragraph 6 of Article 36 of the Statute.[61] This attitude of the Court is probably best explained in the Court's own words:

> . . . The validity of the reservation has not been questioned by the Parties. It is clear that France fully maintains its Declaration, including the reservation, and that Norway relies upon the reservation.
>
> In consequence the Court has before it a provision which both Parties to the dispute regard as constituting an expression of their common will relating to the competence of the Court. The Court does not therefore consider that it is called upon to enter into an examination of the reservation in the light of considerations which are not presented by the issues in the proceedings. The Court, without prejudging the question, gives effect to the reservation as it stands and as the Parties recognize it.[62]

These findings of the Court are, it is submitted, highly significant. First of all, it will be noted that the Court fully reserved the right to reconsider its position with respect to the Connally-type reservation by saying that it was giving effect to it "without prejudging the question." Secondly, decisive weight will probably have to be given to the finding that the validity of the reservation was not questioned by either party; that, in particular, France fully maintained her reservation; and that, finally, the reservation was considered by both parties "as constituting an expression of their common will." In all these respects the *Aerial Incident* Case differed from the *Norwegian Loans* Case. To be sure, Bulgaria invoked the United States reservation and endeavored to guard itself against a possible change of the American position with reference to this reservation.[63] Considering the significance attributed by the Court to the fact that France fully maintained her declaration, including the reservation, Bulgaria had every reason to be concerned about a possible change. Moreover, in the *Norwegian Loans* Case, both parties paid what must be regarded as remarkably perfunctory attention to the reservation. The Court was able to summarize in a couple of pages their positions in both oral and written pleadings.[64] In the *Aerial Incident* Case the United States reservation was invoked by one party and effectively contested by the other, and no doubt further arguments would have been presented in oral hearings, had not the United States abandoned the case. This is not to suggest that the Court would not have sustained the Bulgarian reliance on the Connally Amendment reservation. It is suggested, however, that the Court had reserved the right to hold otherwise, and it might have held otherwise precisely in view of the construction placed on the amendment by the United States, and of the intrinsic importance of the substantive issues presented to it for adjudication. In this case it could not have been said that the amend-

[61] "In the event of a dispute as to whether the Court has jurisdiction, the matter shall be settled by the decision of the Court."

[62] [1957] I.C.J. Rep. 9, at 27.

[63] This, it is suggested, may have been the meaning of the Bulgarian contention that the United States, having failed to indicate unequivocally the basis of referring the dispute to the Court, was precluded from invoking the reservation contained in its declaration of acceptance at a later stage of the proceedings. Page 734 f. above. The Bulgarian Government might have been more concerned with the possibility that the United States might place upon the reservation an interpretation disadvantageous to Bulgaria, as it actually did, and thereby place Bulgaria in an unfavorable situation.

[64] *Ibid.* 25–26.

ment constituted as between Bulgaria and the United States "an expression of their common will relating to the competence of the Court."

The position taken by the United States in the *Interhandel* Case, abandoned or substantially modified as it was in its written observations in the *Aerial Incident* Case, was certainly not a serious obstacle. The Court had no occasion to rule on the validity or scope or rôle of the Connally Amendment either in the phase of the *Interhandel* Case relating to interim measures or in that relating to preliminary objections. In connection with the Swiss request for interim measures, the United States invoked the Connally Amendment in its preliminary objection, and maintained it in the course of the proceedings, but the Court based its negative decision on other grounds, namely, that, following information submitted by the United States and accepted by Switzerland, there was "no need to indicate interim measures of protection."[65] It will be recalled that, although Switzerland challenged the reservation on a number of grounds, its Co-Agent, for all practical purposes, invited the Court to disregard this challenge, saying that, in connection with a relatively minor matter, *i.e.,* the request for interim measures, the Court would not wish to adjudicate "upon so complex and delicate a question as the validity of the American reservation."[66]

In the phase of the *Interhandel* Case relating to preliminary objections, the United States, while maintaining the reservation in part (a) of the fourth preliminary objection, qualified it through its Agent, as "somewhat academic" and "somewhat moot." The Court took official notice of this qualification, which was in the nature of a reservation to the reservation, and having found the Swiss claim inadmissible on other grounds, namely, non-exhaustion of local remedies, declared that "part (*a*) of the Fourth Preliminary Objection is without object at the present stage of the proceedings."[67] Thus, the United States succeeded in avoiding an adjudication by the Court of the validity or invalidity, in whole or in part, of its declaration of acceptance of 1946.

In the *Aerial Incident* Case the Court would most likely have sustained the first Bulgarian preliminary objection and declared itself incompetent. There was, therefore, no reason for the United States to fear that its arguments in the *Interhandel* Case would necessarily or decisively influence the Court's construction of the Connally Amendment reservation. Nor was there any reason to assume that the Court would consider the opposite construction of the Connally Amendment presented by the United States in the *Aerial Incident* Case. However, by maintaining this construction and the request to give judgment in accordance with its submissions, the United States might have been precluded from changing its position again in possible future proceedings in the *Interhandel* Case. Bearing in mind the great significance of the issues in the *Aerial Incident* Case, whose essentially international character is scarcely open to doubt, it may appear that the United States, by submitting that the Connally Amendment reservation can be used and abused

[65] [1957] I.C.J. Rep. 105, at 112.
[66] *Ibid.* at 111.
[67] [1959] I.C.J. Rep. 6, at 26 and 29.

with equal ease, paid too high a price in order to achieve a problematical and contingent gain in the future.

Insofar as the Court is concerned, the question of the validity or the invalidity, in whole or in part, of the Connally Amendment and other reservations for which it furnished the model, is still open.[68] Judge Lauterpacht's stand, formulated most elaborately in two opinions, represents the most intransigent alternative: the complete invalidity of the United States declaration of 1946. Guggenheim is probably quite right in suggesting that the Court is unlikely to accept it.[69] It must be noted that the Court could not adopt it without reversing itself. For in the *Norwegian Loans* Case the Court very clearly assumed the validity of the French declaration, including the so-called automatic reservation.[70] The Norwegian Government could not very well have availed itself of an invalid reservation embedded in an invalid declaration. By holding that Norway was entitled to invoke the reservation in the French declaration and that, consequently, the Court was without jurisdiction to adjudicate upon the dispute brought before it in virtue of that declaration, the Court implied necessarily the validity of the French declaration.

Guggenheim is probably also quite sound in suggesting that the Court is not likely to rally to Judge Guerrero's view that such reservations "must be regarded as devoid of all legal validity" because they conflict with paragraphs 2 and 6 of the Statute.[71] The Court has not shown any penchant for radical and sweeping propositions. To be sure, Judge Guerrero's view is less uncompromising than Judge Lauterpacht's, but still the Court could not adopt it without reversing itself or, at the very least, casting a shadow on its judgment in the *Norwegian Loans* Case for the reason stated above. It must be admitted, though, that the Court's judgment in that case was sufficiently circumscribed, so much so that it might be distinguished from a future case in which the issue of the validity of the reservation was fully joined. In such a case the Court might find it difficult to hold, as it did in the *Norwegian Loans* Case, that it did not have to examine whether the reservation "is consistent with the undertaking of a legal obligation and is compatible with Article 36, paragraph 6, of the Statute."[72] The Court might, of course, find, upon such examination, that the reservation was compatible with both the undertaking of a legal obligation and paragraph 6 of Article 36. Such a holding would be diametrically opposed to the construction of both Judge Lauterpacht and Judge Guerrero and might seriously impair the system of compulsory jurisdiction of which the Court is the guardian.

There is an intermediate alternative. It was developed by Bourquin and adopted by Guggenheim, and is substantially based on the notion that a reservation of the Connally type can only be invoked in good faith and that to do otherwise would constitute an

[68] Guggenheim, "Der sogenannte automatische Vorbehalt der inneren Angelegenheiten gegenüber der Anerkennung der obligatorischen Gerichtsbarkeit des Internationalen Gerichtshofes in seiner neuesten Gerichtspraxis," in K. Zemanek (ed.), Völkerrecht und Rechtliches Weltbild 116–132, at 131 (Festschrift für Alfred Verdross, 1960).

[69] *Ibid.* at 127.

[70] [1957] I.C.J. Rep. 9, at 25 ff.

[71] *Ibid.* at 69; and Guggenheim, *loc. cit. at* 128.

[72] [1957] I.C.J. Rep. at 26.

abuse which the Court would have the power to reject. In the first preliminary objection in the *Norwegian Loans* Case the Norwegian Government contended that the dispute brought before the Court by France related to municipal and not to international law, and was therefore outside Article 36, paragraph 2, of the Statute, as well as outside the Norwegian and French declarations of acceptance. Referring in the written argument to the French reservation, Norway declared:

> . . . Il est certain que pareille réserve doit être interprétée de bonne foi et qu'un gouvernement qui se retrancherait derrière elle pour dénier compétence à la Cour dans un cas où il ne s'agirait manifestement pas d'une "affaire relevant essentiellement de la compétence nationale" commettrait un abus de droit, devant laquelle la Cour ne dénier serait pas désarmée.
>
> Mais, dans ces limites, on sera d'accord pour reconnaître que la caractère de l'affaire litigieuse. Cette liberté d'appréciation est même d'autant plus large que la formule vise les affaires qui relèvent *essentiellement* de la compétence nationale—et non celles qui en relèvent *exclusivement* (comme le faisait l'article 15, par. 8 du Pacte de la Société des Nations).[73]

Professor Guggenheim, in his capacity of Co-Agent in the *Interhandel* Case, after an analysis of the preparatory work relating to the Connally Amendment and of the doctrine of abuse of right, referred to the above-quoted statement in the *Norwegian Loans* Case and declared in the oral hearing of November 12, 1958:

> Les limites d'une application normale de la réserve dite automatique sont certes dépassées lorsqu'un Etat l'invoque dans un domaine qui est totalement étranger au domaine réservé. En affirmant que la réserve dite automatique des Etats-Unis ne peut pas être opposée à la Suisse dans le cas d'espèce, nous restons dans le cadre d'une sage application de la doctrine qui s'oppose à un exercice arbitraire du pouvoir discrétionnaire qu'une convention internationale confè à un Etat.[74]

An approach somewhat similar to that of Bourquin and Guggenheim is developed by Briggs. An application on the basis of the United States declaration constitutes a proper seisin, which gives the Court jurisdiction to adjudicate upon a plea to its jurisdiction; and no unilateral attempt on the part of the United States can deprive the Court of such juris-

[73] ". . . It is certain that a reservation of this kind should be interpreted in good faith and that a Government would commit an abuse of right if it sought the protection of the reservation in order to deny the jurisdiction of the Court in a case which manifestly did not relate to 'matters which are essentially within its domestic jurisdiction.' The Court would know how to defend itself against such an abuse.

"It is possible, however, to agree that within these limits the declarant State, under this reservation, has the right to evaluate freely the nature of the matter at issue. This freedom of appreciation is all the more comprehensive as the formula relates to matters which are *essentially*, and not merely *solely*, within the domestic jurisdiction (as was the case in Article 15, par. 8 of the Covenant of the League of Nations)." (Author's translation.) I.C.J. Pleadings, Case of Certain Norwegian Loans (France *v.* Norway), Vol. I, p. 131.

[74] "The permissible limits of a normal application of the so-called automatic reservation are certainly transgressed if a State invokes it in a matter which is totally foreign to the reserved domain. In maintaining that the so-called automatic reservation of the United States cannot be invoked validly against Switzerland in the pending case, we remain within the four corners of a prudent application of the doctrine. The doctrine does not allow for an arbitrary exercise of the discretionary powers which an international convention confers upon a State." (Author's translation.) I.C.J. Pleadings, Interhandel Case (Switzerland *v.* U. S. A.) 579. See also Guggenheim, *loc. cit.* at 129.

diction already validly established.[75] A plea of domestic jurisdiction by the United States or by the adverse party would be subject to scrutiny and binding determination by the Court in virtue of Article 36, paragraph 6, of the Statute. In the view of Briggs,

> The net effect of such a decision would be that the good faith of the United States in accepting the Court's compulsory jurisdiction would not be questioned. Its Declaration would be regarded as valid although the Court would refuse effect to possible invalid determinations of matters of domestic jurisdiction. It would not be necessary for the Court to decide specifically whether the United States domestic jurisdiction reservation was valid with or without the words "as determined by the United States". Even in the absence of a domestic jurisdiction reservation, a State can always raise the plea of domestic jurisdiction before the Court both as a jurisdictional plea and as a defense on the merits.[76]

Briggs therefore concludes his thoughtful analysis by saying:

> To the extent that the United States peremptory type domestic jurisdiction reservation merely reserves disputes as to matters which by international law are within the domestic jurisdiction, the reservation is unnecessary. To the extent that it purports to substitute declarant State for the Court in determining aspects of the Court's jurisdiction it is ineffectual and invalid since, by its Statute, the Court has jurisdiction to decide disputes as to its jurisdiction in cases pending before it.[77]

Attractive as appears to be the moderate construction of the so-called automatic reservation, there are reasons which militate against it. The judgment of the Court in the *Norwegian Loans* Case was considered as precluding the Court, unless it chooses to reverse itself, from reviewing the propriety of invoking the reservation.[78] The United States, in its pleadings in the *Interhandel* Case and in its final communication in the *Aerial Incident* Case, expressed the same view. The fact that under the reservation the matters need to be

[75] Briggs, *loc. cit.* 362–363. Briggs relies here on the following passage in the judgment in the Nottebohm Case: "When an Application is filed at a time when the law in force between the parties entails the compulsory jurisdiction of the Court—which was the case between Guatemala and Liechtenstein on December 17th, 1951—the filing of the Application is merely the condition required to enable the clause of compulsory jurisdiction to produce its effects in respect of the claim advanced in the Application. Once this condition has been satisfied, the Court must deal with the claim; it has jurisdiction to deal with all its aspects, whether they relate to jurisdiction, to admissibility or to the merits. An extrinsic fact such as the subsequent lapse of the Declaration, by reason of the expiry of the period or by denunciation, cannot deprive the Court of the jurisdiction already established." [1953] I.C.J. Rep. 111 at 123.

The essential point in Briggs' argument, as elaborated elsewhere, is that a proper seisin empowers the Court to exercise incidental jurisdiction, and this includes the power to adjudicate upon a plea to its jurisdiction pursuant to Art. 36, par. 6, of the Statute. This is so, he maintains, because the states parties to a dispute have consented to the Statute as part of the Charter, and this consent cannot be set aside by subsequent declarations of acceptance. See his "The Incidental Jurisdiction of the International Court of Justice as Compulsory Jurisdiction," in Zemanek (ed.), Völkerrecht und Rechtliches Weltbild 87–95 (Festschrift für Alfred Verdross, 1960); for a more recent and slightly modified version, see his "La Compétence Incidente de la Cour Internationale de Justice en tant que Compétence Obligatoire," 64 Revue Gén. de Droit Int. Pub. 217–229 (1960). This line of reasoning, in a somewhat modified form, is developed below.

[76] Briggs, 93 Hague Academy Recueil des Cours at 363 (1958).

[77] *Ibid.*

[78] Thus Judge Lauterpacht in his dissenting opinion in the Interhandel Case, [1959] I.C.J. Rep. 6, at 115. But see pp. 742 ff. above.

essentially and not exclusively within the domestic jurisdiction of the invoking state makes a judicial review, as noted above, particularly difficult and delicate.[79]

The compatibility of the so-called automatic reservation with Article 36, paragraph 6, of the Statute is, of course, the crux of the matter, and the essential arguments for holding the reservation, if not the entire declaration of which it is a part, invalid, are based on whatever view one takes with respect to this conflict. There is a good deal of force in the proposition that the argument, according to which, even when a government avails itself of the reservation, it is the Court which makes the decision pursuant to Article 36, paragraph 6, is of a purely "verbal" or "dialectical character," for in substance it is the government and not the Court which makes the decision; the Court merely registers it.[80]

It is true, of course, that in the *Nottebohm* Case the Court did not allow an "extrinsic fact," such as the lapse of the declaration subsequent to a seising of the Court, to deprive it of jurisdiction. However, the so-called automatic reservation is not an "extrinsic" but rather an "intrinsic" fact, for the reservation is built into and forms an integral part of the declaration of acceptance on which the jurisdiction rests. It cannot, therefore, be dismissed *a limine.* Moreover, while emphatically affirming its power to adjudicate on its own jurisdiction both by virtue of Article 36, paragraph 6, and of a rule of customary international law which would suffice even in the absence of the specific clause in its Statute, the Court also declared in the *Nottebohm* Case:

> Paragraph 6 of Article 36 merely adopted, in respect of the Court, a rule consistently accepted by general international law in the matter of international arbitration. Since the *Alabama* case, it has been generally recognized, following the earlier precedents, that, *in the absence of any agreement to the contrary,* an international tribunal has the right to decide as to its own jurisdiction and has the power to interpret for this purpose the instruments which govern that jurisdiction. . . .
>
> This principle, which is accepted by general international law in the matter of arbitration, assumes particular force when the international tribunal is no longer an arbitral tribunal constituted by virtue of a special agreement between the parties for the purpose of adjudicating on a particular dispute, but is an institution which has been pre-established by an international instrument defining its jurisdiction and regulating its operation, and is, in the present case, the principal judicial organ of the United Nations.[81]

It is clear that the Court is a jealous guardian of its jurisdiction as established by the Statute and customary international law. However, the disturbing element is the restrictive clause: "in the absence of any agreement to the contrary," which may indicate that the power of the Court to decide on its own jurisdiction can be derogated by the will of the parties manifested, for instance, in the instruments conferring jurisdiction upon the Court. Now, the Court exercises compulsory jurisdiction in virtue of unilateral declarations made by states parties to the Statute pursuant to Article 36, paragraph 2. In any

[79] Judge Lauterpacht, *Ibid.* at 113; and see also Judge Lauterpacht's individual opinion in the Norwegian Loans Case, [1957] I.C.J. Rep. 9, at 42, 52.

[80] Judge Lauterpacht in the Norwegian Loans Case, at 47 f. But see p. 743 above.

[81] Nottebohm Case (Preliminary Objection), Judgment of Nov. 18, 1953, [1953] I.C.J. Rep. 111 at 119. Italics supplied.

given dispute referred to the Court, the unilateral declarations of the parties constitute the conventional bond, the *vinculum juris,* on the basis and within the scope of which the Court exercises its judicial function in that dispute. In the event that the declarations are not identical in terms, the conventional or consensual basis is established at the level common to both declarations. This is so, as the Court repeatedly declared, by reason of the principle of reciprocity. Insofar as the Connally type of reservation is concerned, the Court applied this principle explicitly in the *Norwegian Loans* Case.

The question then must be faced, it is submitted, whether an agreement incorporating the Connally-type reservation in the juridical bond established between the parties to the dispute and conferring, within its limits, jurisdiction upon an arbitral tribunal or upon the Court is the sort of agreement the Court contemplated when it declared that, "in the absence of any agreement to the contrary," an international tribunal had the right to decide as to its own jurisdiction. In accordance with the Court's own statement, two hypotheses must be distinguished: in one, an ordinary tribunal of arbitration would be involved, whereas in the other, the Court itself. In the former case the powers of the tribunal, including the power to adjudicate pleas to its jurisdiction, would be governed by principles of general or customary international law. As stated by the Court and developed by doctrine,[82] there is little doubt that under those principles the tribunal has that power. The parties may, however, stipulate to the contrary in the instrument establishing the tribunal, and if they did, there would be little doubt that the will of the parties would prevail over customary international law, since under that law the tribunal derives its powers from the consent of the parties. The opposite conclusion, that is, that the power of the tribunal to adjudicate its own competence must prevail over the will of the parties, could only be based on the notion of a hierarchy of norms. According to this, norms of a higher rank cannot be modified or set aside by the will of the parties. It must be conceded, however, that, attractive as it may appear, the theory of the hierarchy of norms, pursuant to which norms of a lower rank in the legal order cannot derogate from norms of a hierarchically superior rank is not, or at any rate is not yet, solidly established in state practice or accepted in doctrine. Any implicit or explicit proposition based on that theory would at this time appear to be debatable.

In the second hypothesis we confront the Court and a fundamental principle of the Statute, *i.e.,* of conventional international law rather than of customary international law. The question thus becomes one of the relationship between one conventional instrument, namely, the Charter of which the Statute is an integral part, and another but conflicting conventional instrument, namely, that resulting from unilateral declarations of acceptance of the compulsory jurisdiction of the Court. Conflicts between undertakings of a conventional character on the same plane or of the same order of rank are usually resolved by resort to generally accepted rules of construction, such as the rule of *lex specialis* or the rule of *lex posterior.* The application of either maxim would yield the result that the agree-

[82] See Georges Berlia, "Jurisprudence des Tribunaux Internationaux en ce qui concerne leur compétence," 88 Hague Academy Recueil des Cours 105–157 (1955, II).

ment resulting from the conflicting declarations of acceptance and the principle of reciprocity must prevail. At this point, however, there arises the further question, which must be considered, namely, whether the Statute is hierarchically superior to the will of the parties and therefore beyond their juridical capacity to stipulate clauses in contradiction with it, except, of course, in matters for which such faculty is explicitly provided, as in Article 36, paragraph 3. In this context Article 103 of the Charter is relevant,[83] and this provision, it is submitted, may well constitute the missing link in the juristic effort to remove the road-block posed by the Connally-type reservation. Article 92 formally declares not merely that the Court "shall function in accordance with the annexed Statute,"[84] but also that the Statute "forms an integral part of the present Charter." The international agreement resulting from unilateral declarations of acceptance, one of which includes the Connally type of reservation, creates the obligation for one party to accept as valid the exercise of the unilateral right by the other to determine the subject matter of the dispute as falling essentially within its domestic jurisdiction. Such an obligation, pursuant to Article 103, cannot prevail over the obligation of Members resulting from Article 36, paragraph 6, which is to be regarded as one of "their obligations under the present Charter." On the contrary, the obligation under the present Charter, that is, the obligation to let the Court decide upon its jurisdiction with binding effect for the parties, must be deemed superior to the conflicting obligation to accept the adverse party's determination "under any other agreement." Article 103 does not speak of the validity or invalidity of obligations in conflict with the Charter; it merely provides a practical rule of thumb for choosing the obligations which shall prevail in a given situation, those under the Charter, including the Statute of the Court, or those stipulated by the parties.

It must be admitted that the legal import and range of Article 103 of the Charter has never been judicially tested, and although it may offer a practical and convenient solution of the intractable problem posed by the Connally type of reservation, the line of reasoning developed above may not commend itself to the Court. The Court has usually shown respect for the sovereignty of states, but the Court has also considered itself as guardian of the system of compulsory jurisdiction.

Reliance on Article 103 of the Charter in order to safeguard the integrity of Article 36 would require an acknowledgment of the hierarchy of norms, at least for Members of the United Nations, and the resultant limitation upon their sovereignty. The Connally type of reservation, it is submitted, could hardly stand up to the test of Article 103. It may be neither surprising nor improper to suggest that states assumed certain limitations upon their sovereignty by joining the United Nations on condition of accepting, under Article 4, paragraph 1, "the obligations contained in the present Charter." One of these obligations, and a very elementary one at that, is to let the Court decide controversies

[83] "In the event of a conflict between the obligations of the Members of the United Nations under the present Charter and their obligations under any other international agreement, their obligations under the present Charter shall prevail."
[84] The resulting duty of the Court to apply Art. 36, par. 6, was noted by Judge Lauterpacht in the Norwegian Loans Case, *loc. cit.* at 43 f., and Judge Klaestad in the Interhandel Case, *loc. cit.* at 76 f.

relating to its jurisdiction. As indicated above, the Court would and should be spared the invidious task of having to declare the Connally type of reservation invalid. By invoking Article 103 of the Charter, the Court would need only to find that there existed a conflict and that the prior and superior principle of Article 36, paragraph 6, of the Statute shall prevail.

In conclusion one might observe that, if it was undesirable to introduce a veto into the Secretariat of the United Nations, one of its principal organs, which the Soviet Union attempted to do by means of its "troika" proposal, it would appear even more undesirable for the United States to insist upon introducing a veto into the application of the system of compulsory jurisdiction administered by the Court, which is another principal organ of the United Nations.[85]

[85] Said Judge Lauterpacht: "If thus practically every matter can be plausibly, though not necessarily accurately, described as a matter essentially within the domestic jurisdiction of the State concerned and if that State is the sole judge of the question, it is clear that, as the result, the element of legal obligation is reduced to a vanishing point." Case of Certain Norwegian Loans, Judgment of July 6, 1957, [1957] I.C.J. Rep. 9, at 52. Preuss, *loc. cit.* at 729, had already observed: "The effect of the Connally Amendment is to give the United States a veto upon the jurisdiction of the Court after a dispute has been referred to it by an applicant state."

# EXPENSES OF THE UNITED NATIONS FOR PEACE-KEEPING OPERATIONS

## THE ADVISORY OPINION OF THE INTERNATIONAL COURT OF JUSTICE

*Judges must beware of hard constructions and strained inferences; for there is no worse torture than the torture of the laws.*
Francis Bacon, Of Judicature

## I. SCOPE AND SIGNIFICANCE OF THE ADVISORY OPINION

The advisory opinion of the International Court of Justice adopted by 9 votes to 5 on July 20, 1962, affirmed that the expenditures authorized for operations in the Congo (ONUC)[1] by General Assembly resolutions from December 20, 1960, to October 30, 1961, and the expenditures authorized for the operations of the UN Emergency Force (UNEF) in the Middle East from November 26, 1956, to December 20, 1960, constitute "Expenses of the Organization" within the meaning of Article 17, paragraph 2, of the Charter of the United Nations.[2] Though the Court, for reasons discussed below, re-

[1] The abbreviation ONUC is taken from the French: *Organisation des Nations Unis Congo.*

[2] *Certain Expenses of the United Nations (Article 17, paragraph 2, of the Charter), Advisory Opinion of July 20, 1962: I.C.J. Reports 1962,* p. 151. Judge Spiropoulos voted with the majority but made a declaration, *ibid.,* p. 180; Judges Sir Percy Spender, Sir Gerald Fitzmaurice, and Morelli wrote separate opinions; the President of the Court, Winiarski, and Judges Basdevant, Moreno Quintana, Koretsky, and Bustamante y Rivero wrote dissenting opinions. The volume of *Pleadings, Oral Arguments, Documents* in this case will be cited as *Pleadings.*

frained from declaring it explicitly, the opinion had the effect of holding that Members of the UN were legally bound to pay the assessments made by the Assembly to defray the costs of the two operations. The Court arrived at this conclusion by a relatively simple process of reasoning: first, it found that the text of Article 17, paragraph 2, related to expenses incurred in carrying out the purposes of the Organization; second, it examined the expenditures referred to above, and found that they were incurred with that end in view; thirdly and finally, it examined arguments which had been advanced against its conclusion and found them without merit. Some of these arguments will be examined later.

At this writing it is uncertain whether the Court's opinion will assist the Organization in solving the very real financial problem which has been confronting it since the inception of the Congo operation. The total amount of arrears on the accounts of both operations exceeds $142 million.[3] The $200 million bond issue authorized by General Assembly Resolution 1739 (XVI) of December 20, 1961, was never considered as a final solution, and the successful end of the Congo operation is not yet in sight.

Members have been divided for years over the question of how peace-keeping operations of major scope should be financed. The decision of the Court has strengthened the position of those who claimed that these expenditures were legally authorized, and that, as expenses of the Organization, their apportionment by the Assembly according to the scale of assessments applied in the regular budget or some other scale was legally binding. Some Members have strongly held the view that the permanent members of the Security Council should assume the major share of such expenditures. The Assembly over the years has endeavored through various committees and consultations to reach a consensus. This has so far eluded it. If the Court's opinion does not spur efforts to develop a method of financing current operations generally acceptable to Members, it will become an urgent necessity to take a hard look at the whole problem of financing all activities of the Organization so as to make it somewhat less dependent on the whims of Members. Use of the sanction provision in Article 19 might give psychological satisfaction to some Members while exacerbating others. It would not be likely to create a climate favorable to working out a solution of a more lasting nature for the financial ills of the Organization.

The Court's opinion, being advisory, lacks compelling binding force although it would be improper and would greatly weaken the authority of the Court for the Assembly to take a legal view of the question submitted to the Court in contradiction of the opinion. However, the Assembly is a political body. Pursuant to the statement on interpretation of the Charter adopted on June 22, 1945, at the San Francisco Conference, each organ "will interpret such parts of the Charter as are applicable to its particular functions." But it also declared that if such an interpretation "is not generally acceptable it will be without binding force" and that "in cases where it is desired to establish an au-

[3] Report of the Committee on Contributions, General Assembly *Official Records* (17th session), Supplement No. 10, p. 4. According to the statement on the collections of contributions as of November 30, 1962, the total due was reduced to about $100 million. (Document ST/ADM/SER.B/166, p. 28.)

thoritative interpretation as a precedent for the future, it may be necessary to embody the interpretation in an amendment to the Charter."[4] The application of the sanction provision in Article 19 would indirectly impart a degree of finality to the Court's opinion which strictly speaking it may not and does not claim. On the other hand, as the amendment procedure is not a practical alternative, the opinion may well serve as a starting point for a diplomatic solution of the underlying problems.

The vote on the request for the advisory opinion indicated a profound division of opinion in the Assembly. The vote in the Fifth Committee was 31 for, 10 against, with 20 abstentions; the vote in plenary was 52 for, 11 against, with 32 abstentions. It is not unusual for the Court to receive a request from a divided Assembly. But this factor does not facilitate the task of the Court, and one may wonder what the purpose of asking the Court for an opinion may be if the Assembly is as deeply divided as it was in this case. Ideally, the Court's opinion should be sought before rather than after embarking upon a controversial course of action, or at any rate very soon after disagreements come to the surface. Otherwise the Court might possibly find itself in the position of declaring actions incompatible with the Charter years after they were initiated, or of declaring that no legal obligation existed years after Members had acted on the assumption that it did.[5] In this case the Court was put in the position of being asked for an opinion on expenditures already incurred and apportionments already made and partly met by Members as expenses of the Organization within the meaning of Article 17, paragraph 2.

The opinion of the Court is remarkable for two reasons. In the first place, the Court continued to develop a legal doctrine for strengthening the Organization by elucidating a new facet—and an extremely important one at that—of what has been called "institutional effectiveness."[6] The Court started this process in the *Reparation for Injuries* case, in which it declared that the Organization had international juridical personality and could perform certain acts which have traditionally been regarded as being within the exclusive prerogative of sovereign states. The Court had been careful to point out, however, that it was not saying that the Organization was a state or " 'a super-State' whatever that expression may mean."[7] In that case the Court was able to enhance the stature of the United Nations without decreasing the stature of the States Members of the Organization. In the present case the Court went substantially further; one may be tempted to say, as the French government feared might be the case, in the direction of a sort of world government. For the Court, without giving a precise definition of the crucial term "expenses of the Organization," declared:

> In determining whether the actual expenditures authorized constitute "expenses of the Organization within the meaning of Article 17, paragraph 2, of the Charter," the Court

[4] Report of the Rapporteur of Committee IV/2, UNCIO Document 933, IV/2/42, Vol. 13, p. 710.

[5] On this point see the declaration by Judge Spiropoulos. *I.C.J. Reports 1962*, p. 180.

[6] Dissenting opinion of Judge Bustamante, *ibid.*, p. 298.

[7] *I.C.J. Reports 1949*, p. 179. See also, Leo Gross, "Some Observations on the International Court of Justice." *American Journal of International Law*, January 1962 (Vol. 56, No. 1), p. 53. See also *supra*, p. 695.

> agrees that such expenditures must be tested by their relationship to the purposes of the United Nations in the sense that if an expenditure were made for a purpose which is not one of the purposes of the United Nations, it could not be considered an "expense of the Organization."[8]

Pursuing the path of a negative functional test with determination, and after listing the purposes set forth in Article 1, the Court declared:

> The primary place ascribed to international peace and security is natural, since the fulfillment of the other purposes will be dependent upon the attainment of that basic condition. The purposes are broad indeed, but neither they nor the powers conferred to effectuate them are unlimited. Save as they have entrusted the Organization with the attainment of these common ends, the Member States retain their freedom of action. But when the Organization takes action which warrants the assertion that it was appropriate for the fulfillment of one of the stated purposes of the United Nations, the presumption is that such action is not *ultra vires* the Organization.[9]

This is a proposition of far-reaching significance for the Organization and its Members. The adjective "primary" does not appear in the Charter, though the Court's statement accurately describes only the order in which the several purposes are set forth in Article 1, and it reflects accurately the thought of the authors of the Charter. From the point of view of relevance, one might argue that the foundations of peace must be built in depth and that accordingly the economic and social objectives, the realization of self-determination of peoples and human rights, are more basic in the long run than the immediate purpose described by the Court as "primary." But this is really immaterial, as the Court itself attaches no particular significance to this purpose but in referring to "those purposes" and "one of the stated purposes" embraces all purposes. One might in fact contend that the primary purpose of the action in the Congo is to enable its people to achieve "self-determination" without interference, direct or indirect, and that "peace" is merely a means to that end. What is material is that in the Court's view the "freedom of action" of the Members is limited not by explicit provisions of the Charter but by the comprehensive ends to the attainment of which the Organization is dedicated. The Court here seems to discard the dictum of its predecessor in the *Lotus* case that "the rules of law binding upon States . . . emanate from their own free will" and that "restrictions upon the independence of States cannot therefore be presumed."[10] To be sure, progressive international lawyers have always found this dictum irksome and perhaps even retrogressive. And in giving priority to the purposes of the Charter, the Court merely made explicit and gave its imprimatur to a tendency in the United Nations which became noticeable with the adoption in 1950 of the "Uniting for Peace" resolution if not earlier.

In so doing the Court had, of course, in mind the power of the Organization to impose financial obligations upon the Members. That was the first part of the request

[8] *I.C.J. Reports 1962,* p. 167.
[9] *Ibid.*, p. 168.
[10] Permanent Court of International Justice, Series A, No. 10, p. 18.

addressed to it. The second part, however, related to certain resolutions of the Assembly and the Security Council which themselves were not construed by the Court as imposing legally binding obligations upon the Members; although, at least insofar as the Congo was concerned, there was a tendency on the part of both the Council and the Secretary-General to construe them as binding.[11] To appreciate fully the unprecedented significance of the Court's broad dictum and its specific holding in this case, it is necessary to bear in mind that in the opinion of the Court the General Assembly's power of the purse was of a radically different nature from its other powers under the Charter and the manner in which it could promote the purposes of the Organization. It has been generally accepted, and it has also been accepted by the Court, that the Assembly is empowered to do no more than to issue political or socio-economic recommendations of a general or specific character which themselves lack obligatory character.[12] The Court's holding and dictum amounts to saying that even though such recommendations are not binding upon the Members, the General Assembly has the power to commit the Members either directly or through the medium of the Secretary-General to expenditures which it is in the discretion and power of the Assembly to apportion among the Members. Thus, the General Assembly may impose upon its Members binding financial obligations for the realization of non-obligatory recommendations. The Assembly, in the Court's view, may similarly apportion expenses and thus impose financial obligations for the purpose of implementing resolutions of the Security Council such as those relating to the Congo, which the Court construed as non-obligatory. In affirming the "institutional effectiveness" of the Organization in financial matters, the Court took a great leap forward in the direction indicated above.

Anticipating the opinion of the Court, the French government warned that it "would lead to the establishment of a world legislative power." The questions which should have been put to the Court were not put and, said the French government, "It is to be feared that there may be a temptation to deduce the existence for the General Assembly of a discretionary and unlimited budgetary power from the questions which have been put to the Court." The Court, by vesting in the General Assembly such power "which States have not given to any, even more closely integrated, organization," was imposing on Member States "the obligation to tax their citizens and induce their parliaments to vote the credits fixed by the Assembly and the taxes needed to pay for them."[13]

France, however, was in the minority, as were the judges who did not share the Court's reasoning and conclusion. And even among those who shared in the conclusion, the reasoning created some difficulty. This will be taken up later. It is interesting to note,

[11] See Security Council Resolution of August 9, 1960, Document S/4426, and E. M. Miller, "Legal Aspects of U.N. Action in the Congo," *American Journal of International Law*, January 1961 (Vol. 55, No. I), p. 4.

[12] See D. H. N. Johnson, "The Effect of Resolutions of the General Assembly of the United Nations," Royal Institute of International Affairs, *British Year Book of International Law, 1955–1956* (London: Oxford University Press, 1962), Vol. 32, pp. 97–123.

[13] *Financial Obligations of Members of the United Nations (Article 17, paragraph 2, of the Charter); Written Statements*, Distr. 62/21, p. 78. English translation provided by the Registry of the Court. *Pleadings*, p. 134.

however, that some of the governments knowing full well the position and preoccupations of France, have nonetheless come out strongly in favor of what must appear to be a virtually discretionary power of the General Assembly.[14] In oral hearings the representative of Canada stated that the Charter endowed the Organization with powers adequate to its immense responsibilities.[15] In his submission the representative of the United Kingdom declared:

> It is not the case that by means of a mere financial resolution the General Assembly can create an obligation on Member States to make contributions in respect of expenses incurred in furtherance of a manifestly invalid resolution; for instance, a resolution recommending a contravention of a prohibition of the Charter. But, insofar as a resolution is clearly designed to fulfill the paramount purposes of the Charter and in pursuance of such a resolution expenses are duly incurred, for example, by the Secretary-General under an authority conferred on him under Article 98, these expenses are, then, expenses of the Organization and when made the subject of a financial resolution of the General Assembly do create on apportionment a binding obligation on Member States to pay the assessed contribution.[16]

The representative of Norway disagreed with France's fear and denied that the General Assembly had a discretionary and unlimited budgetary power under the Charter; he did not indicate, however, where the limitations were to be found. On the other hand he declared:

> To leave the financing of the main tasks of the Organization, namely, its peace-promoting functions, to voluntary contributions would, in the submission of the Norwegian Government, be an extremely dangerous road to follow. And furthermore, it would be contrary to the clear provisions of the Charter.[17]

A distinction or a limitation seems to have eluded also the representative of Australia who argued that the term "the expenses" in Article 17, paragraph 2, should be read as "*all* expenses" and the term "the Members" as "*all* Members."[18]

Of special and possibly lasting interest is the position of the United States government, not merely on the ground that it is the largest single contributor to the expenses of the Organization, but also for the reason that its stand in this case differed so sharply from that taken in an earlier and, in money terms, insignificant occasion. And this is the other reason why this opinion of the Court has been called remarkable. In 1954 the Court gave an advisory opinion in the case of the *Effects of Awards of Compensation Made by the United Nations Administrative Tribunal.*[19] This opinion was frequently invoked in the writ-

[14] See *Written Statements* for statements by Italy, p. 70; Denmark, pp. 107–108; The Netherlands, pp. 114 and 118 ff.; the United States, pp. 140, 141, 147, 149; Canada, pp. 167–169; Japan, pp. 171–173; the United Kingdom, pp. 188–189; and Ireland, p. 196. See also *Pleadings*, pp. 126, 163–164, 170, 172, 175, 193, 194, 200, 202, 220–222, 224–226, 242–243, 249.

[15] *Pleadings*, p. 309.

[16] *Ibid.*, p. 337. See also the remarks of the United Kingdom representative on pp. 138, 340, and 349.

[17] *Ibid.*, pp. 366–367. Along similar lines, see the oral statement of the representative of Ireland, *ibid.*, p. 389.

[18] *Ibid.*, p. 385. Italics in the original.

[19] *I.C.J. Reports 1954*, p. 47.

ten and oral statements and by the Court itself. The Court was seized with the question whether the General Assembly had the right to refuse to give effect to an award of compensation made by the Administrative Tribunal in favor of a dismissed staff member of the United Nations. The Court ruled that the Assembly had no right to "refuse to give effect to the obligations arising out of an award of the Administrative Tribunal." And in this context the Court said:

> The function of approving the budget does not mean that the General Assembly has an absolute power to approve or disapprove the expenditure proposed to it; for some part of that expenditure arises out of obligations already incurred by the Organization, and to this extent the General Assembly has no alternative but to honor these engagements.[20]

It is perfectly clear that the Court's statement related to obligations arising from contracts of service of staff members. It was relied upon, however, for the altogether unrelated purpose of indicating that the budgetary power of the Assembly was not "absolute."[21] Be that as it may, the opinion of the Court created a problem for the United States, inasmuch as the award had been made in favor of citizens of the United States who took the Fifth Amendment. The Congress of the United States adopted House Concurrent Resolution 262[22] to the effect that no part of the funds heretofore and hereafter appropriated by the Congress should be used for the purpose of paying these awards amounting to $179,420. Normally they would have been included in and paid out of the regular budget of the Organization. The United States delegation, mindful of the Congressional resolution, "made particular and successful efforts to insure that the awards would be financed from sources of income other than" those mentioned in the resolution.[23] These efforts were crowned with success when the Assembly adopted a resolution providing in effect for the payment of the awards from the staff assessment fund.[24] No doubt, most Members would be quite satisfied if the operations in the Middle East and the Congo could be financed in the same manner.

In the present case the United States was the strongest advocate of virtually unlimited budgetary powers for the Assembly. In his oral statement, the United States representative declared not merely his dissent from the French argument but contended that "the United Nations can pay for what it is empowered to do" and "what the United Nations can do, it can finance under the provisions of Article 17." In other words,

[20] *I.C.J. Reports 1954*, p. 59.

[21] See, for instance, the statement of the Norwegian representative. *Pleadings*, pp. 367–368.

[22] This resolution was approved by the House of Representatives on August 10, 1954, and by the Senate on August 20, 1954. *Congressional Record*, Vol. 100, Part II, p. 13949, and Part 11, p. 15486.

[23] *U.S. Participation in the UN*, Report by the President to the Congress for the year 1954. Department of State Publication 5769, p. 202.

In a speech in the Fifth Committee, Senator Fulbright declared that "if the Fifth Committee and the General Assembly refused to grant any relief with regard to awards of the Administrative Tribunal, his Government would be confronted with serious questions, for such a decision would undoubtedly arouse greater opposition to the United Nations in the United States than now exists," General Assembly *Official Records . . . Fifth Committee* (9th session), p. 302.

[24] Report of the Fifth Committee and General Assembly Resolution 888C (IX) of December 17, 1954. *Ibid.*, Annexes, p. 12.

though the Member States are not legally bound to carry out recommendations that the organs of the United Nations may adopt for the achievement of its purposes, including peace-keeping but not excluding others, they are legally bound to contribute financially to their achievement if the Assembly, in its discretion, chooses to regard the expenditures involved as expenses of the Organization within the meaning of Article 17, paragraph 2. The safeguards are to be found in the political realm and not in the provisions of the Charter. This statement, because of its far-reaching implications, warrants quotation in full:

> Member States do not find their protection against such action[25]—if protection is needed—in legal strictures of the Charter, but in the political requirement of a two-thirds majority in the General Assembly both to initiate the action and to make the necessary financial arrangements. If these majorities can be mustered; if the activities engaged in are immediately related to the express purposes of the United Nations; if they are approved in due course according to the regular procedures of one of its organs having competence over the subject matter; if they do not contravene any prohibition of the Charter nor invade the sovereign powers of individual States—if conditions such as these are satisfied, I can perceive no reason why the United Nations should be prohibited from levying assessments to pay for goods and services needed for those activities. The goods and services may be furnished by States Members. Often they will be furnished by private agencies or individuals. In neither case could the United Nations *require* that they be made available. But I do not see why, in either case, this should militate against the Organization's power to raise money by assessment to pay for them.[26]

Apart from formal requirements for the validity of acts of United Nations organs, which were not an issue in this case, the only protection offered was that such acts could not invade the sovereignty of Member States. This was an issue here, in fact the crucial one, but the representative of the United States attempted to dispose of that issue by arguing, first, that the Organization could do what it was not prohibited from doing; and secondly, that though the Organization could not require Members to furnish "goods and services," whatever they might be, it could require them to pay for these if some Member or the Secretary-General was willing to provide them. As regards the first proposition, all that needs to be said is that it inverts the basic principle of international organization: under international law an organization has no plenitude of powers like sovereign states; on the contrary, being an "artificial person" it has only such powers and competences as are conferred upon it by its constitution, which is a multilateral treaty. What is not so conferred is retained by the Member States, and this would be so even if Article 2, paragraph 1, of the Charter did not explicitly recognize it. It was a substantial relaxation of this fundamental principle when the Court, accepting a fairly narrow con-

[25] In the preceding paragraph the United States representative argued that the United Nations could appeal to Members for contingents of military forces or it could try, with the consent of the states concerned, to raise a force by direct recruitment, but, he said, "if those consents were obtained, it is hard to see what would prohibit the Organization from raising such a force and, if it did so, from paying for it by assessment."

[26] *Pleadings,* pp. 424 f. Italics in the original. See also p. 777, footnote 78, below.

cept of implied powers, said in a different case: "Under international law, the Organization must be deemed to have those powers which, though not expressly provided in the Charter, are conferred upon it by necessary implication as being essential to the performance of its duties."[27]

The advisory opinion on *Certain Expenses of the United Nations* will assuredly become a landmark in the jurisprudence of the Court and the evolution of the United Nations. Apart from its signal contribution to the "institutional effectiveness" of the United Nations, it is bound to arouse a good deal of theoretical interest. In essence it raises in an acute form a basic question of treaty interpretation. The Charter is a multilateral treaty and it is, accordingly, a matter of construction to determine exactly the competences and powers conferred upon the Organization, and the competences and powers retained by Member States. The often quoted San Francisco statement on interpretation[28] is not very helpful. It is a truism to say, as it does, that the several organs of the United Nations will have to interpret the Charter in the course of day-to-day work. At the same time, the statement deprives such interpretation of binding and authoritative character, unless it is generally acceptable or embodied in an amendment. In the absence of effective procedure for authoritative interpretation, differences are bound to arise and remain unresolved unless a general consensus emerges as it did, for instance, in connection with the abstention of permanent members of the Security Council contrary to the letter of Article 27, paragraph 2. The difficulty cannot be resolved by an advisory opinion of the Court unless it is generally accepted.[29] It cannot be resolved by practice, on which the Court relied to a considerable extent in the instant case, unless this practice is evidence of a general consensus. In the words of Judge Sir Percy Spender:

> Apart from a practice which is of a peaceful, uniform and undisputed character accepted in fact by all current Members, a consideration of which is not germane to the present examination, I accordingly entertain considerable doubt whether practice of an organ of the United Nations has any probative value either as providing evidence of the intentions of the original Member States or otherwise a criterion of interpretation. As presently advised I think it has none.[30]

Under international law, sovereign states have the right of auto-interpretation, that is, of interpreting their rights and obligations resulting from treaties or other sources of law. The situation is bad enough, as states are not generally obligated to refer disputes to

[27] *Reparation for Injuries Suffered in the Service of the United Nations, Advisory Opinion of April 11, 1949: I.C.J. Reports 1949,* p. 182.

[28] See p. 755 above.

[29] This was so, for with respect to the *Second Admissions Case,* the *Interpretation of Peace Treaties (2nd Phase) Case,* the *Reparation for Injuries Case,* and the advisory opinion granted at the request of the Intergovernmental Maritime Consultative Organization in connection with the constitutionality of the Maritime Safety Committee.

[30] *I.C.J. Reports 1962,* p. 195. But see his statement (p. 196) relating to Article 17, paragraph 2, which is not free from ambiguity. Sir Percy's view is identical with that of the French government, which, in its written statement, declared: "From the beginning of the operation of the United Nations, customary rules or practices contrary to the Charter can have become established only if such customary rules or practices have been uniform and not given rise to controversy." English translation supplied by the Registry. *Pleadings,* p. 133.

the Court or a tribunal of arbitration for authoritative resolution of their respective claims. However, without being obligated to do so, they are always free to do so, and the Court is always open and accessible to them. In the case of international organizations, the problem of interpretation is raised to a higher and even more intractable plane. The organizations, as well as member states, have the right of interpreting their respective powers and competences. In a conflict between an organization and its member states, however, there does not yet exist the possibility of referring the dispute to the Court. The United Nations and other international organizations are denied access to the Court in contentious proceedings and a provision for arbitration has been included only in some specific agreements, such as the Headquarters Agreement between the United Nations and the United States. The advisory opinion in the present case illustrates the impasse which inevitably results from conflicting interpretations of the Charter. It points up an urgent need for a generally acceptable method of construing the Charter authoritatively and thus eliminating auto-interpretation by the Member States, as well as by the Organization.[31]

## II. THE QUESTION

As formulated by the General Assembly in Resolution 1731 (XVI) of December 20, 1961, the question was: "Do the expenditures authorized" in a number of General Assembly resolutions relating to United Nations operations in the Congo (ONUC) undertaken pursuant to certain Security Council and Assembly resolutions, and "the expenditures authorized" in a number of Assembly resolutions relating to operations of the United Nations Emergency Force (UNEF) undertaken pursuant to certain Assembly resolutions "constitute expenses of the Organization within the meaning of Article 17, paragraph 2, of the Charter of the United Nations?" The purpose in requesting the Court to give an advisory opinion on this question was stated in the preamble to the request to be the need of the Assembly "for authoritative legal guidance as to the obligations of Member States under the Charter of the United Nations in the matter of financing the United Nations operations in the Congo and in the Middle East."

The formulation of the question presented some difficulties to the Court. As interpreted by the Court, the question was whether the specified "expenditures" were "expenses" of the Organization without going into the question of what are the financial obligation of the Members. This is indicated in the change of title of the case from *Financial Obligations of Members of the United Nations,* which appeared on all documents pertaining to the case, to *Certain Expenses of the United Nations (Article 17, paragraph 2, of the Charter)* which appeared on the Advisory Opinion. As Judge Sir Gerald Fitzmaurice said in his separate opinion, this change was deliberate.[32] From the Court's point of view an

[31] On this problem see Leo Gross, "States as Organs of International Law and the Problem of Auto-interpretation," in *Law and Politics in the World Community,* edited by George A. Lipsky (Berkeley: University of California Press, 1953), pp. 59 ff. See also *supra,* pp. 367–397.

[32] *I.C.J. Reports 1962,* p. 198.

opinion on "expenses" would afford the Assembly sufficient guidance. Once it was determined that certain expenditures were expenses of the Organization within the meaning of the clause, the rest, namely apportionment and obligation to pay, would necessarily follow. Or, in the concrete case, if the Court determined that the specified expenditures were expenses of the Organization, it would follow that Members would be bound to pay the assessed contributions. This view was not generally shared, as will be shown later; not even by judges who concurred in the operative part of the opinion.

Another difficulty arose from a proposed amendment to the draft resolution requesting an advisory opinion. The French delegation wished to substitute the words "were the expenditures . . . " for "do the expenditures" at the beginning of the request and to insert the words "decided on in conformity with the provisions of the Charter and, if so, do they" before the word "constitute."[33] The proposed amendment was rejected. However, it hovered over the written and oral stage of the proceedings, and the Court itself declared that if this question was found to be relevant, the Court would examine it. In fact, the Court did so to a degree. Members of the Court and representatives of governments in their written and oral statements took positions ranging from those claiming that it would be improper for the Court to deal with the question implicit in the French amendment to those who argued quite fully the question of the formal and substantive validity of the relevant financial as well as basic resolutions down to and including the way the latter were implemented by the Secretary-General, particularly in the Congo.

Some members of the Court, regarding the question itself as unduly restrictive and retrospective in spite of the need for authoritative legal guidance referred to in the preamble of the request, expressed the view that the Court should decline to give an opinion. This was urged upon the Court by Judge Basdevant, who developed his position in an ably argued dissenting opinion.[34] This aspect of the opinion will be left out of consideration here.

## III. THE BUDGET

Article 17, paragraph 1, provides that the General Assembly shall consider and approve the budget of the Organization. According to Article 18, paragraph 2, a two-thirds majority of the Members present and voting is required for budgetary questions. The arguments submitted by governments addressed themselves in substance to two points: whether Article 17, paragraph 1, is concerned with the regular budget only, and whether

[33] UN Document A/L.378. The French amendment would have had the effect of changing the request to read: "Were the expenditures authorized" in a number of General Assembly resolutions relating to ONUC . . . and UNEF "decided on in conformity with the provisions of the Charter and, if so, do they constitute 'expenses of the Organization' within the meaning of Article 17, paragraph 2, of the Charter of the United Nations?"

[34] Said Judge Basdevant: "Where it would have been possible to obtain from an opinion requested of the Court collaboration in the present work of the United Nations, it has been sought to obtain from the Court only a retrospective evaluation of what has been done up to the end of 1961." (*I.C.J. Reports 1962*, p. 237.)

the budgetary power of the Assembly is exclusive. With regard to the first question, viewed in its generality rather than in detail, in the opinion of the Court no limitation such as "regular" or "administrative" is to be found in the text of the article or elsewhere in the Charter. The Court pointed out that the drafters of the Charter were familiar with the distinction between "administrative" and "operational" budgets which appears in paragraph 3 of Article 17 with respect to specialized agencies, and had they intended to limit the term "budget" in the first paragraph they would have done so. Furthermore, the Court found that, in the practice of the United Nations, items were included in the regular budget which could not be qualified as administrative, and finally, that "it is a consistent practice of the General Assembly to include in the annual budget resolutions, provision for expenses relating to the maintenance of international peace and security."[35]

The plain meaning of the text, however, is entirely compatible with an interpretation opposite to the Court's. The drafters of the Charter, following in the footsteps of the League of Nations and familiar with the establishment of specialized agencies, intended to say "regular" or "administrative" budget. They were familiar with the distinction and did not provide for an operational budget. There were two natural reasons for it: in the first place operational functions were entrusted by governments to the specialized agencies rather than to the United Nations; and in the second place, the vital operational function of the Organization, that is enforcement of action, was especially provided for in Article 43 of the Charter.

Even the concept of a "regular" budget was not static but dynamic, and the Members were free to agree that items which might seem to be operational had become so routine or so essential to the United Nations that they should be included in the regular budget. This no doubt had happened, as the Court pointed out with respect to some activities which broadly could be classified as "peace-keeping," being related to the maintenance of international peace and security. Thus, the Working Committee of Fifteen, set up to seek a reconciliation of the diverse views with respect to financing peace-keeping operations, adopted with wide support and without a dissent the following point: "Investigations and observation operations undertaken by the Organization to prevent possible aggression should be financed as part of the regular budget of the United Nations.[36] That was the limit of the consensus.

The Court relied here as elsewhere on the "practice" of the United Nations. Two of the judges who were with the majority cautioned against reliance, or too much reliance, on practice or the "principle of subsequent practice."[37] Practice was essentially a useful tool if it supported a contention that the Members agreed or acquiesced in a certain interpretation of the Charter. However, the fact that Members voted for a certain resolu-

[35] *I.C.J. Reports* 1962, p. 160.

[36] *Ibid.*, p. 161. See also pp. 772–773 below.

[37] *I.C.J. Reports 1962,* pp. 187 ff. (Sir Percy Spender's separate opinion) and pp. 201 f. (Sir Gerald Fitzmaurice's separate opinion).

tion could not by itself be conclusive evidence that they regarded it legally as being in conformity with the Charter, or that the view of the majority was binding on the minority. In connection with financial resolutions, Sir Gerald Fitzmaurice pointed out that "it is hardly possible to infer from the mere fact that Member States *pay,* that they necessarily admit in all cases a positive legal obligation to do so."[38] It could then be argued that the financial resolutions in question, though they were adopted with the requisite majority despite impressive numbers of negative votes and abstentions, was not sufficient evidence that the expenses were deemed to fall into the "regular budget." Moreover, it could not be overlooked that a substantial number of Members did not pay their assessments and that a careful scrutiny of the relevant statistics might turn up a number of Members who voted for the resolution and yet did not pay.[39] Finally, the fact that these resolutions were adopted could not preclude the Court from examining whether they were legally binding. To argue otherwise would deprive the request addressed to the Court of all meaning.

In the written and oral statements the practice of the United Nations was carefully examined and opposite conclusions were drawn from the evidence presented. It would not be profitable to review these here. Suffice it to say that peace-keeping functions other than those mentioned above, that is observation and investigation, and with respect to which a wide consensus existed, were not, until UNEF was established, apportioned among the Members as "expenses of the Organization" and as part of the regular budget.[40] Certainly the "peace-keeping" action in Korea, probably the only applicable precedent for actual use of forces, was not financed in this manner. Since the establishment of UNEF, the Members have been divided as to the proper manner of financing it; no general consensus has resulted from the numerous debates and consultations on it; and it is not known how many Members that pay do so out of a sense of obligation or legal duty and how many Members that voted for the financial resolutions have paid their contribution. A small point, but a point which was made in argument, was that none of the resolutions relating to UNEF referred explicitly to Article 17, paragraph 2. The language

[38] *Ibid.,* p. 201.

[39] The discrepancy must have been quite substantial, as might be inferred from the following figures: as of December 31, 1961, 30 out of 81 Members, and five out of eighteen newly admitted Members, had paid in full their assessments for UNEF; seventeen out of 81 Members, and two out of eighteen newly admitted Members, had paid in full their assessments for ONUC. (*Financial Reports and Accounts for the Year ending 31 December 1961,* General Assembly *Official Records* [17th Session], Supplement No. 6, pp. 89 f. and 98 f.) The tables for the amounts for this operation would have to be examined more carefully in order to determine accurately the amounts actually contributed by Members. It has been the practice of the United Nations to reduce the assessments for a substantial number of Members by 50 to 80 percent and to apply voluntary contributions to offset deficits remaining after these reductions. See, for example, General Assembly Resolutions 1732 (XVI) and 1733 (XVI) of December 20, 1961. Judge Koretsky considered this practice as a device to influence Members in voting on the financial resolutions relating to UNEF and ONUC. (*I.C.J. Reports 1962,* pp. 266 and 267.)

[40] The Norwegian representative enumerated the various peace-keeping actions (*Pleadings,* pp. 363 f.). None of them was a clear precedent for either UNEF or ONUC, although he found a striking similarity between UNEF and the United Nations Observation Group in Lebanon (UNOGIL), the expenses of which were carried on the regular budget. There are two important points of difference, however: first, as the Secretary-General defined its mission, UNEF "would be more than an observers' corps, but in no way a military force" (Second Report of Secretary-General of November 6, 1956, approved by the General Assembly Resolution 1000 [ES-I], November 5, 1956). Secondly, the consensus among the Members included investigation and observation operations but not other peace-keeping activities. Therefore, UNOGIL was within the ambit of this consensus, and UNEF was not.

of the resolutions was quite similar; the article was invoked in the debates, but it never found its way into the final text. In connection with the Congo, a reference to Article 17, paragraph 2, appeared in General Assembly Resolution 1583 (XV) of December 20, 1960, the first resolution on the subject, but it disappeared from the following resolutions. Much was made of this in argument before the Court. The Court emphasized the language of the resolution which included the words "as expenses of the Organization," and no doubt they were apportioned; but the Court's conclusion that they were "apportioned in accordance with the power granted to the General Assembly by Article 17, paragraph 2"[41] rested on inference.

Opponents of an affirmative answer also relied on the language of the resolutions relating to the Congo and UNEF. In connection with the latter, the Secretary-General in his final report of November 6, 1956, declared that the subject of financing required further study and that certain costs would be borne by nations providing contingents, "while all other costs should be financed *outside the normal budget* of the United Nations." Later, on November 26, 1956, he expressed the opinion that the operation must "be construed as coming within the meaning of Article 17, paragraph 2."[42] The resolutions adopted by the Assembly throughout the period under consideration reflected, as the Court pointed out, continuing differences of opinion as to the manner in which UNEF should be financed on the one hand, and on the other, the conviction that the expenses should be assessed against the Members. The Court concluded that "from year to year, the expenses of UNEF have been treated by the General Assembly as expenses of the Organization within the meaning of Article 17, paragraph 2, of the Charter."[43]

The representative of the Soviet Union, which for the first time took part in oral hearings before the Court, drew the opposite conclusion. He attached decisive significance to the fact that none of the resolutions was adopted unanimously, that in spite of repeated efforts no consensus emerged, that none of the proposals to include a reference to Article 17, paragraph 2, was adopted, and that "in actual fact more than 50% of the Members of the United Nations do not take part in financing the Emergency Force."[44]

The first financial resolution relating to the Congo, General Assembly Resolution 1583 (XV), of December 20, 1960, included, as noted above, a reference to Article 17, paragraph 2. The Soviet representative attached decisive significance to the fact that this reference was superseded in subsequent resolutions by a preambular paragraph emphasizing that "the extraordinary expenses for the United Nations Operations in the Congo are essentially different in nature from the expenses of the Organization under the regular budget." In addition he quoted a statement by the Mexican delegation, one of the authors of Resolution 1732 (XVI) of December 20, 1961, which was not listed in the request for an advisory opinion, who stressed the "axiomatic" premise that the character

[41] *I.C.J. Reports 1962,* p. 178.
[42] *Ibid.,* p. 173. Italics supplied.
[43] *Ibid.,* p. 175.
[44] *Pleadings,* p. 408.

of these expenses "is fundamentally different from that of the other expenses of the Organization included in the regular budget. In other words, my delegation believes that these expenses cannot be considered as 'expenses of the Organization' within the meaning of Article 17, paragraph 2, of the Charter." While admitting that the practice of the UN with respect to the Congo was inconsistent, the Soviet representative contended that practice did not support the position taken by the proponents of an affirmative answer.[45] The Court concluded that, although the expenses were regarded as "extraordinary" and "essentially different," they were nonetheless "expenses of the Organization" and that the second part of this preambular paragraph merely "contemplated another *scale* of assessment and not some method other than assessment. 'Apportionment' and 'assessment' are terms which relate solely to the General Assembly's authority under Article 17."[46]

If the brilliant reasoning of the Court does not convince one fully, this may be explained by the fact that in order to find an answer to the Assembly's question, the Court relied heavily on the words used by the Assembly in the resolutions which were put in question by the request for the advisory opinion. The impression seems inescapable that the Court's reasoning was addressed not primarily to the question put to it but to another question which, to make the point clear, might be formulated as follows: Do the expenses authorized in a number of General Assembly resolutions relating to UN operations in the Congo . . . and . . . to operations of the UN Emergency Force . . . *constitute in the view of the General Assembly* expenses of the Organization? This question, however, was not before the Court; yet a great deal of the Court's reasoning and of the argument by governments appears to have been addressed to it. To be sure, the Assembly came very close to suggesting this question by saying "authorized," but this could be taken as no more than a statement of fact amounting to saying that the expenditures were included in the several resolutions. It could not be regarded as a statement of law. Had it been so regarded there would have been no question before the Court,[47] because undoubtedly the expenditures were "authorized," some money was collected, and even more was spent.

Granting the imperfections in the formulation of the request, the problem posed by it might have been better approached from a legal point of view if the resolutions themselves had been disregarded. In other words, if the question which indeed arose in 1956, and again in 1960, had been submitted, as ideally it should have been, to the Court for an opinion *before* the first financial resolutions on UNEF and ONUC were adopted or immediately after they were adopted, or as soon as it was established that Members were in arrears, there would not have been an impressive series of resolutions before the Court, but one or none. The question then would clearly have been whether the expenses which it was proposed to incur, or which in fact had been incurred on a provisional basis, could be regarded legally as coming within the budgetary powers of the Assembly under paragraphs 1 or 2, or both, of Article 17. The Court then would not have been able to rely on

[45] *Ibid.*, p. 123.
[46] *I.C.J. Reports 1962*, p. 179.
[47] See Judge Basdevant's dissenting opinion, *ibid.*, pp. 235 ff.

a string of resolutions and to attach probative value to them, but would have been bound to search for a criterion of "expenses of the Organization" in the Charter independent of the *ipse dixit* of the General Assembly repeated over a period of time amidst persistent controversy. This the Court did to some extent, and this part of its reasoning will be discussed in the following section.

It was indicated earlier that the question of the applicability of Article 43 was also argued in connection with the concepts of "budget" and "expenses of the Organization." Not much needs to be said on this point. No doubt the Security Council in negotiating special agreements might have tackled the issue of financing peace-keeping operations. There is nothing in Article 43 to suggest that the armed forces could be used for enforcement action only. Insofar as this clause is concerned, they could have been used for purposes of a more general peace-keeping type, such as were involved in both UNEF and ONUC. In the absence of the agreements provided for in Article 43, the transitional procedure laid down in Article 106 should have been used but, of course, it was not. The Soviet representative argued before the Court that, while UNEF was set up illegally because under Article 11 the General Assembly is barred from taking action, ONUC was illegal because it was the Secretary-General and not the Security Council who selected the states furnishing armed forces, and because he and not the Council directed the operations in the Congo.[48] At the other extreme was the contention by the Canadian representative that the Congo action at any rate could be justified in terms of Chapter VI of the Charter.[49] The Australian government and its representative devoted a *great* deal of their argument to invalidating any inference from Article 43 that would limit the budgetary power of the Assembly. They appear to have been particularly bothered by the statement in the commentary on the Charter by Goodrich and Hambro that "expenses referred to in this paragraph [i.e., Article 17, paragraph 2] do not include the cost of enforcement action."[50]

The Court dismissed Article 43 on the ground that neither UNEF nor ONUC were enforcement action within the compass of Chapter VII of the Charter. The Court relied chiefly on the consensual basis of the operations. Apart from this the Court felt that the Security Council might have agreed in one or another agreement negotiated pursuant to Article 43 that part of the financial burden should be borne by the Organization. In such a case the "expense would form part of the expenses of the Organization and would fall to be apportioned by the General Assembly under Article 17."[51]

It does not seem profitable to pursue this point further. Though Article 43 and its possible or predictable consequences were canvassed pretty thoroughly, one piece of documentation escaped attention. It is the two reports of the Collective Measures Committee

[48] *Oral Statements*, pp. 400 f. The Soviet representative relied not merely on Article 43, but on Article 48, paragraph 1, as well. See also the dissenting opinion of Judge Koretsky, *I.C.J. Reports 1962*, pp. 274 ff.

[49] *Pleadings*, p. 305.

[50] Leland M. Goodrich and Edvard Hambro, *Charter of the United Nations* (second edition revised; Boston: World Peace Foundation, 1949), p. 184, footnote 90. *Pleadings*, pp. 232, 382.

[51] *I.C.J. Reports 1962*, p. 166.

established pursuant to the "Uniting for Peace" resolution. Both are relevant in the context of this case. In its first report of 1951, the committee, referring to Articles 49 and 50 of the Charter, stressed the need for equitable sharing of the burdens resulting from United Nations action.[52] This principle was elaborated in the second report of 1952 and applied to military measures as well; and the committee, which was boycotted by the Soviet Union, made the following recommendation:

> In the Committee's view, one method which should be considered by the Security Council or the General Assembly to accomplish this objective would be the establishment of an *ad hoc* negotiating committee to *deal directly with States in respect to their contributions.* Such a committee would be analogous to the Committee established by the General Assembly to obtain contributions for the relief operations undertaken in Korea and Palestine and for the Expanded Programme of Technical Assistance . . . and now operating as the Negotiating Committee for Extra-Budgetary Funds, established under resolution 571B (VI).
>
> The basic purpose of the *ad hoc* committee would be to obtain for the United Nations the forces, manpower, assistance, facilities, services and *funds* required for the effective conduct of the military operations. . . .[53]

It is clear from this that when the question of financing peace-keeping operations under the "Uniting for Peace" resolution or otherwise was discussed dispassionately and not under the pressure of a mounting deficit, it was believed that the funds necessary to support such operations would be raised in the same way as for the voluntary programs of the United Nations. Inasmuch as the Court and most of the governments in their statements recognized that the operations in the Middle East and Congo were *not* binding enforcement action but voluntary actions, the view of the Collective Measures Committee is entitled to some weight.

## IV. EXPENSES OF THE ORGANIZATION

In its search for an independent criterion of the term "expenses of the Organization" in Article 17, paragraph 2, the Court relies in the first place on the text itself and what may be called the plain meaning of the term. The Court starts out with the proposition that it "means all the expenses and not just certain types of expenses which might be referred to as 'regular expenses.' "[54] Expenses of the Organization might and have in the past been incurred pursuant to Chapters IX and X and Article 98 of the Charter, and

> the Court does not perceive any basis for challenging the legality of the settled practice of including such expenses as these in the budgetary amounts which the General Assembly apportions among the Members in accordance with the authority which is given to it by Article 17, paragraph 2.[55]

[52] General Assembly *Official Records* (6th Session), Supplement No. 13, p. 21, paragraphs 164–165.
[53] General Assembly *Official Records* (7th Session), Supplement No. 17, p. 11, paragraphs 82 and 83. Italics supplied.
[54] *I.C.J. Reports 1962,* p. 165.
[55] *Ibid.*, p. 162.

The Court then passes to the examination of other articles of the Charter which were alleged to imply a limitation of the plain meaning of Article 17, paragraph 2. In the opinion of the Court, Article 24, which confers "primary" but not exclusive authority on the Security Council for the maintenance of international peace and security, does not preclude the Assembly from recommending measures or action. The Council has exclusive power to obligate Members to take action but the Assembly has power to recommend action without binding force. Along similar lines, Article 14 authorizes the Assembly to recommend "measures," and in the Court's opinion this clause may be regarded as the basis for UNEF.[56] Reviewing Article 11, paragraph 2, which required the Assembly to refer questions "on which action is necessary" to the Security Council, the Court finds that "the word 'action' must mean such action as is solely within the province of the Security Council."[57] Such action is only coercive or enforcement action. The Court looks to "the practice of the Organization throughout its history" for evidence that, short of coercive action, the General Assembly, whether under Article 11 or Article 14, engaged in activities in connection with the maintenance of international peace and security. The Court accordingly rejects as unfounded the argument derived from Article 11, paragraph 2, to limit the budgetary authority of the Assembly.[58] The interpretation given by the Court to Article 43 of the Charter has already been discussed. Thus having established the intrinsic meaning of the term "expenses of the Organization" and having further established that no limitation can be derived from Article 11, paragraph 2, and Articles 14, 24, and 43, the Court does "not find it necessary to go further in giving a more detailed definition of such expenses." It finally is of the opinion that the test to be applied in order to determine whether "actual expenditures" constitute "expenses of the Organization" must be their relationship to the purposes of the United Nations "in the sense that if an expenditure were made for a purpose which is not one of the purposes of the United Nations, it could not be considered an 'expense of the Organization.' "[59]

It would not be profitable to go into a detailed analysis of this part of the Court's reasoning, so much of which is reminiscent of the discussion preceding the adoption of the "Uniting for Peace" resolution in 1950. Obviously, the first step in the reasoning—equating "the expenses" with "all the expenses"—determines the subsequent steps. Since the Members did not intend to transfer unlimited financial powers to the Assembly, it would have been more in keeping with precedent to interpret "the expenses" as the "normal" or "usual" expenses and then look into the Charter for possible extensions of this concept rather than for limitations. The qualifying word "primary" in Article 24 has been the object of much heated discussion. The Court did not look into the other four equally authentic languages for a confirmation of the meaning which it chose as the cor-

[56] *Ibid.*, pp. 163 and 172.
[57] *Ibid.*, p. 165.
[58] *Ibid.*
[59] *Ibid.*, p. 167, and see pp. 755–756 above.

rect one. It may be conceded that the drafting of the Charter was largely done in English and that the other texts are essentially translations. However, they are at least contemporaneous translations and as such entitled to consideration, quite apart from the formal provision in Article III. Be that as it may, since the United States government turned to the other languages including Chinese for confirmation of the mandatory English text of Article 17, paragraph 2, it may be proper to point out that Judge Koretsky turned to the other languages except Chinese to find confirmation for his proposition that the term "primary" "is not used in Article 24 in the sense of an ordinal number (i.e., first, second, etc.) but, one may say, in the hierarchical sense."[60]

It will be recalled that the Court seemed in final analysis to prefer Article 14 to the controversial Article 11, paragraph 2, for the basis of UNEF. A good deal of the argument and reasoning reflected preoccupation with the nature of the action in the Middle East and the Congo. With respect to UNEF, the Court relied chiefly on the Secretary-General's definition of its role as being "more than an observers' corps, but in no way a military force." It was, in consequence, not to be regarded as enforcement action which would come within the jurisdiction of the Council.[61] Therefore the expenses incurred by the Secretary-General for UNEF had to be considered as "expenses of the Organization."[62] The basic resolutions of the Security Council relating to the Congo did not aim at enforcement action, though the Court declined to express an opinion on which article of the Charter they were based. "The Charter" said the Court, "does not forbid the Security Council to act through instruments of its own choice." It may establish subsidiary organs or it may, under Article 98, entrust certain functions to the Secretary-General. Furthermore, "the operations of ONUC did not include a use of armed force against a State." From these two premises the Court concluded:

> Financial obligations which, in accordance with the clear and reiterated authority of both the Security Council and the General Assembly, the Secretary-General incurred on behalf of the United Nations, constitute obligations of the Organization for which the General Assembly was entitled to make provision under the authority of Article 17.[63]

As to the function conferred upon the Secretary-General, France stressed the point that "the legal power to make recommendations to Member States does not include permission to create, by the circuitous method of a decision addressed to the Secretary-General . . . any obligations for States."[64] It is difficult to escape the logic of this position. While there is nothing in the Charter prohibiting, there is also nothing in the Charter authorizing the Security Council to delegate financial powers to the Secretary-General and thus to invade what the Court considered to be the exclusive budgetary power of the

60 *I.C.J. Reports 1962,* p. 274; *Pleadings,* p. 194.
61 *I.C.J. Reports 1962,* p. 171.
62 *Ibid.,* p. 172.
63 *Ibid.,* p. 177.
64 *Pleadings,* p. 131. English translation provided by the Registry of the Court.

Assembly. As to the position of the Court that force was not used "against a State," there is nothing in Article 39 to require that the measures to maintain international peace and security be directed against a state.[65] In fact, force was used in the Congo, and even if use of force was not implicit in the first Security Council resolution, it was made explicit in the resolution of February 21, 1961. It is characteristic of the budgetary practice of the United Nations that though ONUC was authorized by the Security Council as early as July 14, July 22, and August 9, 1960, the General Assembly did not get around to voting the first financial resolution until December 20, 1960.

The reasoning of the Court on the purview of the expression "expenses of the Organization," as on the nature of the budget, draws a good deal on the practice of the United Nations which is itself the subject of the request. As Judge Sir Gerald Fitzmaurice, who concurred in the opinion given by the Court, points out, the Court did not deal with the crucial question whether the Assembly may make *final* rulings regarding the conformity of its own resolutions with the Charter. As was indicated above, some governments argued that the Assembly had this power, and it is difficult to escape the impression that the Court made this view its own although Sir Gerald did "not read the Opinion of the Court as going so far."[66] Furthermore, in his view the Court did not deal with the crucial question whether, if certain expenditures are regarded as expenses of the Organization, there is also an obligation for Members to contribute to them as apportioned by the Assembly. In the present submission the Court assumed without argument that any expenditure which is incurred pursuant to valid General Assembly or Security Council resolutions and which is geared to one of the purposes of the United Nations becomes *ipso facto* an "expense of the Organization within the meaning of Article 17, paragraph 2." Validity of expenditure implies obligation for Members to contribute if and as apportioned by the Assembly. The non-obligatory character of valid resolutions created no problem for the Court.

And yet Sir Gerald points out,

> The core of the difficulty is how to reconcile the obligatory character of the liability to meet the expenses of the Organization with the non-obligatory character of many, indeed most, of the resolutions under which these expenses are incurred. To me, it has not seemed self-evident that Article 17, paragraph 2, on its actual wording, necessarily or automatically disposes of this difficulty; and unless it can be disposed of satisfactorily, the affirmative reply given to the question addressed to the Court must be less convincing than it ought to be.[67]

This takes us back to the basic problem: if the *ipse dixit* of the General Assembly is not sufficient to convert an expenditure into an expense, when is an expenditure an expense? With expenses included in the regular budget there is no problem. With expenses for

[65] This point is elaborated in Judge Koretsky's dissenting opinion, *I.C.J. Reports 1962*, p. 274.
[66] *Ibid.*, p. 203.
[67] *Ibid.*, p. 210.

certain peace-keeping operations such as observation and investigation there is no problem, for the Member States have acquiesced in seeing them included in the regular budget.[68] With expenses arising from binding decisions of the Security Council, there is no problem in virtue of Article 25 of the Charter. How about other expenses? The Court considers all of them obligatory. As far as essential activities are concerned, Sir Gerald arrives at the same conclusion, relying as the Court did on Article 17, paragraph 2, namely, that although the resolutions relating to such expenses are non-obligatory, "the special obligation to contribute to the expenses incurred in carrying them out prevails, and applies even to Member States voting against."[69]

Resolutions, the sole purpose of which is the making of a payment or contribution, are considered by Sir Gerald as non-obligatory. He finds support if not inspiration for this in the UN practice of relying on voluntary contributions for activities such as the UN Special Fund and the UN Children's Fund.[70] Generalizing, he distinguishes two types of functions: those which the Organization has a *duty* to carry out, such as peace-keeping and political activities generally, and those "*permissive* in character," such as social and economic activities. Expenditures incurred in connection with the former are "true expenses," and the Member States are bound to contribute. Expenditures incurred in connection with permissive activities present a problem which cannot be solved by Article 17, paragraph 2, alone. Sir Gerald appears to distinguish between Members that vote for or against or abstain on such resolutions relating to such activities. He inclines to the view that at least "the dissenting voter" could not be considered to fall under Article 17, paragraph 2. To attribute to such resolutions, as the Court in the present submission apparently did, obligatory financial effect if Article 17, paragraph 2, were applied "would be reading a lot into such a provision as Article 17, paragraph 2." Moreover, if Article 17, paragraph 2, were applied to such activities, "then it would follow that, in theory at least, the Assembly could vote enormous expenditures, and thereby place a heavy financial burden even on dissenting States, and as a matter of obligation even in the case of non-essential activities."[71] The Assembly, and here again practice comes to the rescue, has relied on voluntary contributions to finance such activities. But, of course, it may cease to do so following the opinion of the Court.

Does this approach offer from the legal point of view a satisfactory solution of the problems posed by the Court's opinion? It is submitted that it does not and this for two reasons. First, as Sir Gerald is well aware, the distinction between essential and non-essential, between obligatory and permissive, between necessary and optional activities is not easy to draw, and some of the economic and social activities may well be regarded as

[68] It should be noted though that, while in the Working Group of Fifteen eleven Members including the Soviet Union and the United States supported this statement, and none were opposed, three (Brazil, China and India) reserved their position and one (France) abstained. (UN Document A/4971, p. 7, paragraph 22.)

[69] *I.C.J. Reports 1962,* p. 212.

[70] *Ibid.,* p. 213.

[71] *Ibid.,* p. 214.

preconditions for the success of the essential political activities.[72] This being so, who would decide which activity falls into one or the other category? Clearly, the General Assembly and its ruling not only in the Court's view but also in Sir Gerald's would be binding. The only caveat entered by the Court is relationship to the purposes listed in the Charter. Sir Gerald, though more cautious, would in the final analysis let the Assembly have the final word on the matter until some other procedure is devised.[73]

The second objection against Sir Gerald's approach is that the distinction, even if it were feasible, does not reflect accurately the Charter. Article 1, the basic provision regarding purposes, does not make any distinction between political and economic or social objectives, and it does not indicate which are mandatory and which are permissive. Furthermore, the articles dealing with the political functions of the General Assembly, that is, Articles 10, 11, and 14 are couched in permissive terms: "The General Assembly may. . . ." Only Article 11, paragraph 2, Article 12, paragraph 2, and Article 13 are worded in a mandatory manner, but the first two provisions are inhibitions against certain political activities. Chapter VI does not confer any specific political functions on the Assembly. Insofar as the Security Council is concerned, some clauses are mandatory as are Articles 33, paragraph 2, and 37, paragraph 2, or hortatory as are Article 36, paragraphs 2 and 3, or permissive as are Articles 34 and 36, paragraph 1. In Chapter VII relating exclusively to the Security Council, Articles 39, 44, 45, and 46 are mandatory, but Articles 40, 41, and 42, which constitute the essence of political activities within the framework of the Organization, are permissive in language. By contrast the basic provisions relating to economic and social functions, Articles 55 and 58, are mandatory and not permissive. Thus the Charter either does not make the distinction indicated by Sir Gerald at all, or it makes it in the opposite sense; that is, it makes social and economic cooperation mandatory and political activities where the General Assembly is concerned almost wholly permissive, the exception being Article 13 which has not figured prominently in the work of the Organization. The Security Council is given some mandatory directives, but in matters of enforcement action it is given discretion. If Sir Gerald's distinction were to be relied upon as a yardstick for determining which expenses are mandatory and which are not, it would seem to follow that expenses necessary for the performance of economic and social functions of the Organization are not merely essential but mandatory, the practice of the General Assembly, so far at any rate, to the contrary notwithstanding.

It may be recalled that costs of regular technical assistance programs, as distinguished from the Expanded Program of Technical Assistance (EPTA) have been included in the regular budget. Henceforth, the legal barriers having been removed, if a two-thirds majority so wills, there is no reason against EPTA and other programs being considered

[72] *Ibid.*, p. 215.

[73] In his view there is a presumption in favor of the validity of expenditures if they are incurred "in the apparent furtherance of the purposes of the Organization. . . . Only if the invalidity of the expenditure was apparent on the face of the matter, or too manifest to be open to reasonable doubt, would such a *prima facie* presumption not arise." *Ibid.*, p. 204.

as expenses of the Organization within the meaning of Article 17, paragraph 2, and apportioned accordingly.

## V. CONCLUSIONS

The Court expressed in a firm voice its opinion on several constitutional issues of first-rate significance. It affirmed at least indirectly the validity of the "Uniting for Peace" resolution, although it found in Article 14 an alternative and perhaps more congenial and less controversial legal basis for the peace-keeping activities of the General Assembly. It affirmed the "third force" role assumed by the Secretary-General of the United Nations acting pursuant to broad directives issued by the General Assembly or the Security Council in the field of peace-keeping operations, with far-ranging financial implications for the Organization and its Member States. Article 98 was thus construed in the most comprehensive and inclusive sense. The Court in fact reversed the stand, taken by the Permanent Court of International Justice in the *Lotus* case, with its implication that what is not explicitly surrendered by states is retained, that limitations upon the sovereignty of states cannot be presumed. In substance it took the opposite position, and although it continued to regard the Charter as a multilateral treaty, it construed it in the instant case on the basis of the principle that what the Organization is not prohibited from doing, it may do. It enhanced the "institutional effectiveness" of the United Nations immeasurably by attributing to it a virtually unlimited budgetary power. It affirmed specifically that the General Assembly could and did validly and with legally binding force authorize expenditures for the purpose of effectuating legally non-obligatory resolutions of either the General Assembly or the Security Council. It affirmed that financial resolutions were presumptively not *ultra vires* the Organization if they were geared to one of the purposes stated in the Charter.

Although it is probably still true, as the United States representative declared, that a resolution which invaded the sovereign powers of Member States may be regarded as invalid, the Court gave an affirmative answer in inclusive terms to the specific question put to it and thus, it is felt, invaded the sovereign powers of Member States. To construe the advisory opinion otherwise would be tantamount to either depriving it of its meaning or rendering the concept of sovereignty meaningless. It is probably also true as the United States representative declared that a resolution which contravened any prohibition of the Charter may be regarded as invalid by Member States. The Court in construing the categoric prohibition in Article 11, paragraph 2, rendered it nugatory for all practical purposes. The prohibition of Article 2, paragraph 7, has long since been eroded by the General Assembly, and from the financial point of view it has not been and is not likely to be relevant.

It may not be inaccurate to suggest that the advisory opinion may well amount to a revision of the Charter, although as the Court itself pointed out on a different occasion "it is the duty of the Court to interpret treaties, not to revise them."[74] It will certainly be a step in this direction if it is adopted and acted upon by the General Assembly.[75]

The Court did not close any doors to political or diplomatic compromise. It would be premature to say that it opened the floodgates for the Special UN Fund for Economic Development (SUNFED) and similar programs long under consideration and clearly related to the mandatory functions of the United Nations in the sense of Judge Sir Gerald Fitzmaurice. As France pointed out, the sort of power which the General Assembly may

[74] *Interpretation of Peace Treaties with Bulgaria, Hungary, and Romania (Second Phase), Advisory Opinion of July 18, 1950: I.C.J. Reports 1950,* p. 229.

[75] The General Assembly at its 1199th meeting on December 19, 1962, by a vote of 76 to 17, with 8 abstentions, adopted Resolution 1854 A (XVII) by which it "accepts the opinion of the Court." At the same time the Assembly by a vote of 78 to 14, with 4 abstentions, adopted Resolution 1854 B (XVII) the text of which is as follows:

> *The General Assembly,*
>
> *Recognizing* that peace-keeping operations of the United Nations, such as those in the Congo and in the Middle East, impose a heavy financial burden upon Member States, and in particular on those having a limited capacity to contribute financially,
>
> *Recognizing* that in order to meet the expenditures caused by such operations a procedure is required different from that applied to the regular budget of the United Nations,
>
> *Taking into account* the advisory opinion of the International Court of Justice of 20 July 1962 in answer to the question contained in resolution 1731 (XIV),
>
> *Convinced* of the necessity to establish at the earliest possible opportunity financing methods different from the regular budget to cover in the future peace-keeping operations of the United Nations involving heavy expenditures, such as those for the Congo and the Middle East,
>
> 1. *Decides* to re-establish the Working Group of Fifteen with the same membership as that established in resolution 1620 (XV) and to increase its membership to twenty-one by the addition of six Member States to be appointed by the President of the General Assembly with due regard to geographical distribution as provided for in resolution 1620 (XV), to study, in consultation as appropriate with the Advisory Committee on Administrative and Budgetary Questions and the Committee on Contributions, special methods for financing peace-keeping operations of the United Nations involving heavy expenditures such as those for the Congo and the Middle East, including a possible special scale of assessments;
>
> 2. *Requests* the Working Group of Twenty-One to take into account in its study the criteria for the sharing of the costs of peace-keeping operations mentioned in past resolutions of the General Assembly, giving particular attention to the following:
>
> (a) The references to a special financial responsibility of members of the Security Council as mentioned in resolutions 1619 (XV) and 1732 (XVI);
>
> (b) Such special factors relating to a particular peace-keeping operation as might be relevant to a variation in the sharing of the costs of the operation;
>
> (c) The degree of economic development of each Member State and whether or not a developing State is in receipt of technical assistance from the United Nations;
>
> (d) The collective financial responsibility of the Members of the United Nations;
>
> 3. *Requests further* the Working Group of Twenty-One to take into account any criteria proposed by Member States at the seventeenth session of the General Assembly or submitted by them directly to the Working Group;
>
> 4. *Requests* the Working Group of Twenty-One to study also the situation arising from the arrears of some Member States in their payment of contributions for financing peace-keeping operations and to recommend, within the letter and the spirit of the Charter, arrangements designed to bring up to date such payments, having in mind the relative economic positions of such Member States;
>
> 5. *Requests* the Working Group of Twenty-One to meet as soon as possible in 1963 and to submit its report with the least possible delay and in any case not later than 31 March 1963;
>
> 6. *Requests* the Secretary-General to distribute the report of the Working Group of Twenty-One to Member States as soon as possible with a view to its consideration when appropriate by the General Assembly.

It will be noted that in spite of the words "taking into account the advisory opinion" in its Preamble, the resolution largely signifies a return to the *status quo* which prevailed prior to the request addressed to the Court. Whatever the retrospective effect of the advisory opinion may be, insofar as offering "authoritative legal guidance" for the future, the opinion may yet turn out to have been a Pyrrhic victory. This would be so if the Working Group felt it advisable to fall back on the recommendations of the Collective Measures Committee referred to above. In any event, the Working Group has a virtually free hand in its search for an acceptable solution.

now claim under the Court's opinion, has not been given even to more closely integrated organizations. It is stressing the obvious to say that the Organization of the United Nations has not yet excelled in integrating its Member States into a cohesive community. Whether the advisory opinion will promote greater integration will depend wholly on the statesmanship of its Member States. That it contains elements which could prove to be disruptive in fact should be obvious. The United Nations has sometimes been likened to "parliamentary diplomacy." Following this advisory opinion, it could more properly be called a species of parliamentary government, for now the General Assembly has control of the "power of the purse" in a very real sense; it may, to vary the statement made by France, control the purse of its Member States.

There were alternatives open to the Court, several of which were, as is apparent from the separate and dissenting opinions, discussed *in camera.* One was to decline to give an opinion. The Court in its capacity as one of the principal organs has always been ready to collaborate with the political organs of the United Nations. But the Court is more than that; it is the one and only truly international and permanent judicial institution open to states whether Members of the United Nations or not. If the Court could not, and in the view of one of the majority judges, it did not, dispose satisfactorily of all the difficulties encountered in giving an affirmative opinion to the request addressed to it, it might have been part of judicial caution to decline to give an opinion rather than to give an opinion which "must be less convincing than it ought to be."[76]

Another alternative would have been to declare that the expenditures incurred were expenses of the Organization without going as far as saying that they were expenses of the Organization within the meaning of Article 17, paragraph 2. In connection with some previous requests, the Court found it necessary and opportune to rephrase somewhat, by interpreting it, the question addressed to it by the Assembly. It does not seem that this possibility was urged upon the Court. Still, when seized of a request for an advisory opinion, the Court may be deemed to have greater latitude in reaching out for an appropriate answer and the legal reasons for it than it generally has in contentious cases. The starting point for this line of reasoning would have been Article 17, paragraph 1. If the term "budget" were taken to mean "regular" budget and the term "expenses" in paragraph 2 of Article 17 were construed as related to that, then it might have been possible to consider the expenditures in question as expenses of the Organization without tying them in with that clause. It may be observed in passing that the exclusive power of the General Assembly in budgetary matters was generally not disputed.[77]

An alternative urged upon the Court by governments which were concerned about possible implications of what the Soviet representative called "a supra-national financial authority"[78] would have required selecting, as a starting point, the distribution of pow-

[76] See the separate opinion of Judge Sir Gerald Fitzmaurice, *I.C.J. Reports 1962,* p. 210; quoted on p. 772 above.

[77] See the dissenting opinion of President Winiarski, *I.C.J. Reports 1962,* p. 228.

[78] *Pleadings,* p. 403. That this implication was known to and considered by governments favoring an affirmative reply has already been shown. It may, however, be useful to include here the following observation by the United States representative. Arguing against the French thesis which was shared to some extent by the Soviet government, he declared:

ers laid down in the Charter between the General Assembly and the Security Council on the one hand and that between the Organization and the Members on the other. The crux of the matter in the latter context is whether non-obligatory recommendations, the staple product of the United Nations, can be used as a legal basis for binding financial resolutions. The point was argued with admirable skill and from a variety of angles. However, the proponents of the affirmative answer ultimately rested their case on Article 17 and to a lesser or greater extent on UN practice. One could have wished for a more persuasive argument to render inoperative what had hitherto been regarded as a fundamental principle of contemporary international as distinguished from supranational organization. For the practice was inconclusive, and Article 17 itself was the heart of the controversy. Reliance on Article 17 to invalidate or severely curtail a fundamental though unwritten principle is—this scarcely needs to be pointed out—rather in the nature of a circular argument. When the Collective Measures Committee had this matter under advisement, it came to a conclusion diametrically opposite to that reached by the Court.

Turning to the distribution of powers between the General Assembly and the Security Council, it will be observed that the question put to the Court was a double-barrelled one: it contained in fact two questions, one relating to ONUC and the other to UNEF. The Court emphasized the similarity between the two actions: it reduced them to a common denominator, namely "peace-keeping" operations; it considered that neither was enforcement action, that neither was obligatory since both actions depended on the consent of the affected governments, Egypt and the Congo respectively, that therefore both were within the recommendatory powers of the General Assembly and the Security Council respectively, and therefore in conformity with the Charter.

However, it might have been possible to distinguish between the two cases on the basis of the Charter, and minimize or leave out of account altogether the practice of the United Nations. As Judge Sir Percy Spender put it in his separate opinion,

> In the present case, it is sufficient to say that I am unable to regard any usage or practice followed by any organ of the United Nations which has been determined by a majority therein against the will of the minority as having any legal relevance or probative value.[79]

> It may have a certain plausibility to say that, if the Organization cannot compel a State to contribute forces, it cannot compel it to pay for forces contributed by others. But it would be equally plausible and equally erroneous to say that, since a national government cannot compel one of its citizens to work on a dam, it cannot tax him to pay for the work of others. (*Pleadings*, p. 425).

Thus, by attempting to rebut the French fears, he furnished strong support for them by using the analogy between the power to tax of a national government, which is an attribute of sovereignty, and the budgetary power of the United Nations, which is of a different nature. Sir Gerald, referring to this, or possibly another quite similar statement—he did not identify the representative he had in mind—said with approval: "This position was aptly compared. . . . " (*I.C.J. Reports 1962,* p. 212.)

[79] *I.C.J. Reports 1962,* p. 197. Although he arrived at a different conclusion on the principal issue, he concurred with the French government in saying that once a question is put to the Court, it passes "on to the legal plane and takes on a new character, in the determination of which legal considerations and legal considerations only, may be invoked." *(Ibid.)* The statement of the French government was as follows:

According to the Charter, responsibility for the maintenance of international peace and security is conferred by the Members on the Security Council. Articles 24 and 25 are explicit and so is—leaving practice out of account for the reason indicated by Sir Percy—Article 11, paragraph 2. Strictly speaking and accepting as sound doctrine Sir Percy's proposition that "only legal considerations may be invoked and *de facto* extension of the Charter must be disregarded,"[80] it would seem to follow that UNEF must be distinguished from ONUC. The former was authorized by the General Assembly and the latter by the Security Council, and unless one accepts the view that the General Assembly may recommend action short of enforcement action, then UNEF was *ultra vires* the power of the General Assembly. Without going into the question of the legal consequences of acts *ultra vires* or the applicability of this doctrine to international law or the law of the Charter—the Court merely touched upon this problem—it would not seem to follow necessarily that the expenditures incurred for UNEF were not or have not become expenses of the Organization which it is bound to honor.[81] The good faith of third parties, the participating Members, must be protected. The expenditures may be regarded, as the Court said, as expenses of the Organization in the present submission, but it does not inevitably follow that they are expenses within the meaning of Article 17, paragraph 2, or subject to the sanction of Article 19.

The action in the Congo was undertaken pursuant to Security Council resolutions; they emanated from the competent organ of the United Nations. There have been conflicting views regarding the binding force of these resolutions.[82] The Court construed them as non-obligatory in the same manner and for the same reason as the resolutions of the General Assembly relating to UNEF. However, without venturing an opinion on the subject, it may be sufficient to suggest that the opposite construction would not be quite hopeless. Certain parts of the resolution may have binding force; others may not. The Security Council no more than the General Assembly is known for scrupulous adherence to the letter and spirit of the Charter. Suffice it to let Judge Koretsky speak on the matter: "The references made to Articles 25 and 49 of the Charter [in the Security Council resolution of August 9, 1960, Document S/4426] reaffirmed that the Council's appeals were nothing else but decisions binding on all Members of the United Nations."[83] In this context it is of special interest to note his *cris de coeur:* "Moreover, the Security Council

> The Government of the French Republic would first of all point out that too great importance should not be attached to statements *[déclarations]* voted on a political plane and during a lengthy examination of a difficult question. Just as, in negotiations between States, the Court has decided that the successive proposals of one of the States cannot be relied upon against it after the end of the negotiations and when the case passes on to the legal plane, in the same way the Government of the French Republic recognizes that a case brought before the Court as the result of a request for an advisory opinion takes on a new character, and that only legal considerations should and can henceforth be invoked. (*Pleadings*, p. 132. English translation provided by the Registry.)

[80] *I.C.J. Reports 1962,* p. 197. The whole sentence is as follows: "When, however, the Court is called upon to pronounce upon a question whether certain authority exercised by an organ of the Organization is within the power of that organ, only legal considerations may be invoked and *de facto* extension of the Charter must be disregarded."

[81] This is said without accepting fully the Court's very brief statement of the consequences of acts *ultra vires* the Organization or Judge Morelli's more elaborate analysis. (*Ibid.,* pp. 168 and 220 ff.)

[82] See p. 757 above, footnote 11.

[83] *I.C.J. Reports 1962,* p. 270.

should, from the very beginning, have acted in compliance with Article 39 of the Charter."[84]

Whether the Security Council failed to act under Chapter VII, or whether for "pragmatic reasons," that is, the usual need to collect the necessary votes, it merely refrained from crossing the t's and dotting the i's, the Council did authorize the use of force, and force has been used in fact in order to maintain peace and security. The peace-keeping operation in the Congo, in spite of constitutional blemishes, fits better into the framework of Chapter VII than any other part of the Charter. The Court might accordingly have found sufficient support in the Charter, particularly in Article 24 and Article 2, paragraph 6, in addition to Articles 25 and 49 invoked by the Security Council itself, for construing if not a cast-iron then at least a tenable basis for attributing binding force in whole or in part to the resolutions which govern ONUC.

Taking this as the point of departure the Court might then have concluded that the expenditures incurred in the larger of the two peace-keeping operations were expenses of the Organization and left it at that. This would have been the minimal solution. Or the Court might have found sufficient justification for the maximal solution and declared, as it did, the expenditures to be expenses of the Organization within the meaning of Article 17, paragraph 2. The difference between the approach outlined here and that adopted by the Court, and its advantage, lies in the link between the expenditures authorized and the Security Council's powers under Articles 24 and 25. This link would have put a limitation on the Court's holding and precluded the inference that any expenditure authorized for the attainment of any of the stated purposes of the United Nations can properly be made an expense of the Organization within the meaning of Article 17, paragraph 2, by a two-thirds majority of the General Assembly.[85] There would, in fact, have been no room for any implication of supranational financial power except in the context of the Security Council's primary responsibility under Article 24 and within the specific ambit of Chapter VII of the Charter. A reasoning along these lines, it is felt, would have been based strictly on the distribution of powers between the organs of the United Nations on the one hand, and between the United Nations and the Member States on the other. They would, as a result, have been held only to what they consented to when they joined the Organization.

It may be useful to refer to one or two points which appear relevant. In order to determine the binding effect of the resolutions of the Security Council, is it necessary or permissible, and if so to what extent, to take into account the diplomatic circumstances in which they were adopted? The point made by the French government that too much legal weight should not be attached to statements voted on a political plane or to votes cast for political reasons in search of a "pragmatic solution"[86] is sound as far as it goes but it

[84] *Ibid.*, p. 175.

[85] On this point see the observations of Judge Sir Gerald Fitzmaurice in his separate opinion. (*I.C.J. Reports 1962*, p. 203.) Sir Gerald's attempt to find a limitation in the distinction between mandatory and permissive purposes of the Organization has already been discussed (see pp. 772–774 above). In the present submission, the attempt has not been successful.

[86] See p. 778, footnote 79, above and the following statement made in the Working Group of Fifteen:

does not go very far. It is difficult to see how the Court could examine the conscience of the Members when participating in a vote in the Security Council. The habit of offering "explanations of the vote," before or after casting it, should have no bearing on the responsibility which must be borne by the Members when they cast votes which engage the corporate personality of the Organization.[87]

Similarly, the reasons advanced by Judge Koretsky for denying full force to the Security Council resolutions, namely, that it was the Secretary-General who was entrusted with the organization, direction, and financing of the Congo force, are not persuasive. Perhaps the Council should not have conferred such comprehensive authority on the Secretary-General and should have kept the reins in its hands. Presumably there were compelling considerations for selecting this course rather than another. In any event, the Council acted in this manner, and if the Soviet member really objected strongly to the delegation of authority, he would have cast a negative vote. To look beyond the vote to the explanation of the vote, as Judge Koretsky did,[88] is scarcely a sound way to invalidate a vote or to exonerate the Members from their responsibility. Members cannot have it both ways. Be that as it may, it cannot be the function of the Court to look beyond the votes and to weigh them according to pre- or post-voting explanations and to relieve members wholly or partially from their responsibility which flows for all Members from the vote. On the contrary, by holding Members to the full measure of their responsibilities, the Court may exercise a salutary effect on them; both the Members and organs may develop in the future a stronger sense for the law of the Charter than they have shown in the past. Any restraint on the widespread politicization of the United Nations will be welcome. There is room for both law and politics in the United Nations, but the Court has been well advised not to overstep the thin line which separates these interdependent but separate realms.

Judicial control of acts of international organs has been and remains an objective in the interest of the rule of law in international relations.[89] The Court exercised such control in the case involving the *Constitution of the Maritime Safety Committee of the Inter-Governmental Maritime Consultative Organization.*[90] In the present case no constitutional

As it is planned to ask the International Court of Justice for an advisory opinion on the General Assembly's financial competence outside the operational budget of the Organization itself, the French delegation feels bound to reserve its position on the substance of the legal question. For that reason it wishes to state that neither the comments it made during the discussions in the Working Group of Fifteen, nor the votes it cast, must be taken to express legal principles; they represent only the co-operation of the French representives in seeking pragmatic solutions. The positions it then adopted do not, therefore, prejudge in any way the statement of principle which the French delegation reserves the right to make on the problem if the opinion of the International Court of Justice is sought. (Report of the Working Group of Fifteen. UN Document A/4971, annex II, p. 6).

[87] For this reason the attempt to distinguish the consequences of a valid resolution for Members that vote for or against or abstain on a given resolution, as Judge Sir Gerald Fitzmaurice seems to suggest, appears unresponsive to the corporate character of the actions of the Organization. (*I.C.J. Reports 1962,* pp. 210 ff. and p. 773 above.) The General Assembly and the Security Council are more than the traditional diplomatic conferences in which, it is believed, the distinction has its origin.

[88] He said: "But at the same time the representative of the USSR made an objection against entrusting the Secretary-General with the implementation of the suggested measures." (*Ibid.,* p. 278.)

[89] See Resolutions adopted by the Institute of International Law at its session in Amsterdam, September 18–27, 1957. *American Journal of International Law,* January 1958 (Vol. 52, No. 1), pp. 103–107.

[90] *Advisory Opinion of June 8, 1960: I.C.J. Reports 1960,* p. 150. See also S. Rosenne, "La Cour Internationale de Justice en 1960," *Révue Générale de Droit Internationale Public,* 1961 (No. 3), p. 44 (of reprint).

question properly so-called was put to the Court. The Court was merely requested to give its opinion on whether or not certain financial resolutions fall under Article 17, paragraph 2. This required no more than an interpretation of that proviso. The Court of its own choice examined a constitutional question, namely, whether certain resolutions of the General Assembly and Security Council relating to UNEF and ONUC were or were not in conformity with the Charter. In a narrow sense, the Court's conclusions on this subject are *dicta.* Coming from the Court, they are entitled to the highest respect. So is, of course, the operative part of the opinion. The Court chose a starting point which led it to the adoption of a maximalist solution: an affirmative answer to both parts of the question submitted to it. Alternative approaches, which were roughly sketched above, would have led to less radical solutions. Whether the maximalist view in point of fact, and given the political realities in the United Nations, will be more helpful to the Assembly than either of the alternatives in curing the financial plight of the Organization remains to be seen. On the one hand, the good faith, credit, and future of the United Nations is at stake; interests of third parties must be protected, and essential peace-keeping operations must be continued. On the other hand, insistence on the advisory opinion and the application of Article 17, paragraph 2, and, as a consequence, of Article 19, may not fetch the money needed to cover the deficit and ensure the financing of the $200 million bond issue. The crisis can be solved if it can be solved at all—and let it be said that in the present view it ought to be solved—by the tried and tested method of diplomatic negotiations rather than by voting. The United Nations needs not to be reminded that its Members are sovereign states which will not be commanded if they cannot be persuaded.

# THE JURISPRUDENCE OF THE WORLD COURT: THIRTY-EIGHTH YEAR (1959)

## INTRODUCTION

In the first study devoted to the World Court, Manley Hudson was largely concerned with the formal steps leading to its establishment and its organization. He placed the Court in historical perspective by linking it with the fruitless efforts at the 1907 Hague Peace Conference to set up a Permanent Court of Arbitral Justice. He was not overly optimistic as to the future of the new Court, saying that "of course, the real test of the reception of the Court by the peoples of the world will come in the action of their governments as disputes arise."[1] He was concerned about the co-existence of two courts: the new Court and the Permanent Court of Arbitration, which has its roots in the 1899 Hague Peace Conference. Will the new Court "be generally utilized, in preference to arbitration before tribunals of the Permanent Court of Arbitration and tribunals independently set up by special agreement"?[2]

Hudson noted with satisfaction that the reception of the new Court among lawyers, including those in the United States, was good and he quoted with approval the words of Sir Ernest Pollock: "May we not as lawyers regard the establishment of an International Court of Justice as an advance in the science which we pursue"?[3] Writing a year later, Hudson could afford to be more affirmative and sanguine about the Court:

[1] "The First Year of the Permanent Court of International Justice," 17 A.J.I.L. 15–28, at 26 (1923).
[2] *Ibid.*
[3] *Ibid.* at 27.

> . . . such has been its progress in two years that the court now appears to be one of the established institutions in our international life. The Foreign Offices have begun to regard it as a sort of international fixture. It is fast accumulating a record of achievement indispensable to the international law of the future, and the court now bids fair to be permanent in influence as in name.[4]

He went on to point out that if the docket of the Court was not crowded, one could take comfort from the history of the Supreme Court of the United States which did not have a contested case until its sixth term.

Returning to the problem of the co-existence of the two courts, he found satisfaction in the fact "that since the court was created, no question has been referred to a tribunal of the Permanent Court of Arbitration, though various special arbitrations have been arranged."[5]

With his usual acumen Hudson discerned the significance of the Court's advisory function. Far from joining the ranks of its detractors, he demonstrated, first, that giving advisory opinions was no novelty in the Anglo-American legal system and, next, that "the court is performing a judicial function when it gives advisory opinions to the Council of a League of fifty-four nations."[6]

The Court, at its inception, was off to a promising start. Hudson noted that the nine opinions handed down in the first two years had met with "general satisfaction" and that they dealt with "vexed questions of international law." The states concerned accepted the opinions of the Court. He was quite hopeful:

> The influence of the court has been steadily growing. With forty-seven signatories to the protocol under which it exists, with lawyers everywhere viewing its record with satisfaction and hope, the court promises a fulfilment of the world's long-cherished desire.[7]

Hudson never lost faith in the Court and its vital, if modest, rôle in international relations. The Court has indeed become a fixture of our life; its jurisprudence, though sparse, has continued to grow in significance and deserves more than ever the close attention of international lawyers.

Manley Hudson continued the annual survey of the Court even after his election to the bench on October 8, 1936, until 1959, when the last of his contributions appeared. This is not the occasion to evaluate his work as a faithful chronicler of the Court over nearly four decades. Suffice it to recall Philip C. Jessup's words:

> His annual articles in the AMERICAN JOURNAL OF INTERNATIONAL LAW on the work of the Court are the studies of a jurist who was a master of the Court's law and procedure and who rendered a great service by following every development with the utmost care and with ready criticism when criticism was due.[8]

[4] "The Second Year of the Permanent Court of International Justice," 18 A.J.I.L. 1–37, at 1 (1924).
[5] *Ibid.*
[6] *Ibid.* at 25, 29.
[7] *Ibid.* at 37.
[8] "Manley Hudson, 1886–1960," 54 A.J.I.L. 603–604, at 604 (1960).

The invitation of the Board of Editors to resume and continue Manley Hudson's annual review of the Court's work is a great honor to one of his former students, and a great responsibility. It will be no easy task to come up to his exacting standards of scholarship, precision of language, and fair critical evaluation. The task is made more difficult as a hiatus of several years has occurred. Every effort will be made to catch up with the Court's jurisprudence. Some variations in organization, method and analysis will be inevitable. No two jurists view the Court in an identical manner. It remains for the writer to bespeak the indulgence of the reader and to express the hope that his surveys will be found serviceable.

During the year under review, the Court gave three judgments, two on preliminary objections and one on merits. Of the former, one, the *Interhandel* case, was the subject of extensive comment and analysis both in this JOURNAL as well as elsewhere.[9] It was therefore deemed reasonable to omit it from this survey.

## CASE CONCERNING THE AERIAL INCIDENT OF JULY 27, 1955

This case was before the Court in three phases: the principal phase was concerned with the claim of Israel, application of October 9, 1957, against Bulgaria; the second, with the claim of the United Kingdom against Bulgaria, and the third, with the United States claim against Bulgaria. As will be shown, the second and third claims were withdrawn after the Court declared itself without competence in the first phase. Although the United States claim was withdrawn in 1960, it will be discussed here briefly, as it arose out of the same facts.

### 1. Israel v. Bulgaria

The facts of the case were not in controversy. An Israeli civil aircraft, 4X-AKC, on a flight from Vienna (Austria) to Lydda (Israel), strayed from its course, penetrated Bulgarian territory on July 27, 1955, and was shot down by aircraft of the Bulgarian antiaircraft defense forces. The plane crashed and the 7-man crew and the 51 passengers of various nationalities were killed. Israel claimed compensation in the amount of $2,559,688.65 for the loss "incurred by the persons whose cause is being adopted." With respect to the submission that Bulgaria violated international law in destroying the Israeli aircraft, the Israeli Government stated "that a declaration by the Court regarding

[9] Interhandel Case (Switzerland *v.* U. S.), [1959] I.C.J. Rep. 6. A digest of the opinion appeared in A.J.I.L., Vol. 53, pp. 671–687 (1959). For an analysis of the Court's opinion see Briggs, "Interhandel: The Court's Judgment of March 21, 1959, on the Preliminary Objections of the United States," *ibid.* 547–564. For other comments on the case and its earlier phase see: Hudson, "The Thirty-Sixth Year of the World Court," 52 *ibid.* at 4 f. (1958); Briggs, "Towards the Rule of Law?" 51 *ibid.* at 519 (1957); Jacoby, "Towards the Rule of Law?" 52 *ibid.* 10 ff. (1958); Briggs, "The United States and the International Court of Justice," 53 *ibid.* 307 ff. (1959); Simmonds, "The Interhandel Case," 10 Int. and Comp. Law Q. 495–547 (1961); Charles De Visscher, "L'Affaire de l'Interhandel devant la Cour Internationale de Justice," 63 Rev. Gén. de Droit Int. Public 413–433 (1959); Jillson, note, 58 Mich. Law Rev. 467 (1960); note, Duke Law J. 73.

the international responsibility of Bulgaria . . . would be sufficient satisfaction and that it was waiving any further claim to reparation."[10]

It is interesting to note that the Israeli Government had expressed its regrets for the violation of Bulgarian sovereignty committed involuntarily and accidentally by its aircraft and that "in the interests of a speedy settlement the Government of Israel was prepared to waive its claim for damages directly suffered by the Israel Government."[11] In its application the Israeli Government reinstated its claim for "moral and material reparation,"[12] only to waive it to the extent observed above, in its memorial.[13] It would seem that the international delict which Israel alleged was committed by Bulgaria consisted, not in Bulgaria's action to enforce its sovereignty, but rather in the manner in which that sovereignty was enforced. Although this aspect of the case was not material to the proceedings, which were confined to only one of several Bulgarian preliminary objections, it may be of general interest, in view of aerial incidents, to quote the following passage from the Israel memorial:

> In this petition the Government of Israel is asking the Court to hold that in the circumstances the opening of fire on 4X-AKC on 27 July 1955 by units of the Bulgarian armed forces, resulting in the complete destruction of 4X-AKC, constitutes a violation of international law. The degree of violence used was quite out of proportion to any possible threat to Bulgaria which 4X-AKC may have presented . . . An excess of force is reprehensible in itself and would be so even without the admission by the Bulgarian Government that in so acting its armed forces manifested haste . . . and had not taken all measures necessary to constrain the aircraft to land. . . . That being so, the opening of fire on 4X-AKC was in breach of international law, and Bulgaria is accordingly obliged to make reparation therefor.
>
> The basis of this contention is the rule that when measures of force are employed to protect territorial sovereignty, whether on land, on sea or in the air, their employment is subject to the duty to take into consideration the elementary obligations of humanity, and not to use a degree of force in excess of what is commensurate with the reality and the gravity of the threat (if any). In all systems of law, including international law, this is the test for measuring the degree of violence which may justifiably be used to protect rights recognized by the law, and particularly the degree of violence used when performing acts by their very nature dangerous.[14]

[10] Case concerning the Aerial Incident of July 27, 1955, (Israel *v.* Bulgaria), Preliminary Objections, Judgment of May 26, 1959, [1959] I.C.J. Rep. 127 at 130; digest in 53 A.J.I.L. 923–937 (1959). See also, on this case, Caflisch, "Recent Judgment of the International Court of Justice in the Case concerning the Aerial Incident of July 27, 1955, and the Interpretation of Article 36(5) of the Statute of the Court," 54 A.J.I.L. 855 (1960); note, 1960 Duke Law J. 240; Conac, "L'Affaire relative à l'Incident Aérien du 27 juillet 1955 entre Israël et la Bulgarie devant la Cour Internationale de Justice," 64 Rev. Gén. de Droit Int. Public 711 (1960).

[11] Note Verbale of Feb. 14, 1956, from the Israel Legation in Sofia to the Bulgarian Ministry for Foreign Affairs. I.C.J. Pleadings, Aerial Incident of 27 July 1955 (Israel *v.* Bulgaria; United States of America *v.* Bulgaria; United Kingdom *v.* Bulgaria), p. 17 (cited hereinafter as Pleadings). The damages were described as arising from the Bulgarian action against the aircraft and the expenses incurred as a result of this action.

[12] Pleadings at 6. The extent of the government's claim is detailed *ibid.* at 112.

[13] *Ibid.* at 116.

[14] Pleadings at 84. The admissions referred to by the Israeli Government resulted from a Bulgarian commission of inquiry and were adopted in the Note Verbale of Aug. 4, 1955, from the Bulgarian Ministry for Foreign Affairs to the Israeli Legation in Sofia, *Ibid.* at 13. The Israeli Government construed these admissions as "binding and conclusive in themselves." *Ibid.* at 100. See also memorial of the United Kingdom, *ibid.* at 358 f., and generally, Lissitzyn, "The Treatment of Aerial Intruders in Recent Practice and International Law," 47 A.J.I.L. 559–589 (1953).

It is also interesting, though equally not germane, that Bulgaria countered Israel's claim for compensation by submitting that, even if the persons concerned may have been Israeli nationals, "the damage in respect of which it seeks reparation was for the most part suffered by non-Israel companies."[15] The Government of Israel briefly opposed several objections to this contention, arguing *inter alia* that, "as between States parties to the present dispute such (insurance) contracts and arrangements are *res inter alios acta,*" and did not affect Israel's claim for reparation for the destruction of the aircraft "at the hands of the Bulgarian armed forces acting *jure imperii.*"[16]

Israel, in its application, invoked the compulsory jurisdiction of the Court under Article 36 of the Statute on the basis of its own Declaration of October 3, 1956, replacing the previous Declaration of September 4, 1950, on the one hand, and the Bulgarian Declaration of July 29, 1921, on the other. Bulgaria having filed preliminary objections to the jurisdiction of the Court, the Court by order of December 17, 1958, suspended the proceedings on the merits. Both parties elected, in accordance with Article 31, paragraph 3, to appoint judges *ad hoc.* Israel chose Mr. Justice Gotein of its Supreme Court, and Bulgaria chose Mr. Jaroslav Zourek (Czechoslavakia), a member of the United Nations International Law Commission.

Of the five Bulgarian Preliminary Objections only the first was the subject of the Court's Judgment of May 26, 1959. As amended, it requested the Court to declare itself without jurisdiction to adjudicate upon the Israel application relating to the aerial incident of July 27, 1955, in the following terms:

> The Declaration of August 12th, 1921, by which the Kingdom of Bulgaria had accepted the compulsory jurisdiction of the Permanent Court of International Justice . . . ceased to be in force on the dissolution of the Permanent Court, pronounced by the Assembly of the League of Nations on April 18th, 1946; . . . that Declaration was therefore no longer in force on the date on which the People's Republic of Bulgaria became a party to the Statute of the International Court of Justice; and
>
> . . . it cannot accordingly be regarded as constituting an acceptance of the compulsory jurisdiction of the International Court of Justice, by virtue of Article 36, paragraph 5, of the Statute of that Court. . . .[17]

With respect to the Bulgarian First Preliminary Objection, Israel asked for its dismissal on the following grounds:

> (a) The jurisdiction of the Court in this case is dominated by Article 36, paragraph 5, of the Statute and by the declarations of both Parties accepting the compulsory jurisdiction;
>
> (b) Article 36, paragraph 5, of the Statute of the Court is clear and there is no difficulty in giving effect to it;
>
> (c) Article 36, paragraph 5, lays down the rule that all declarations made under Arti-

[15] [1959] I.C.J. Rep. at 131 f. and 133. *Cf.* also Pleadings at 132. For the oral statement by Professor Cot, *cf. ibid.* at 438 ff.

[16] Pleadings at 159. See also *ibid.* at 520, 524, 532–535.

[17] [1959] I.C.J. Rep. at 132. In its original form this objection was as follows: "Article 36, paragraph 5, of the Statute of the International Court of Justice is inapplicable in regard to the People's Republic of Bulgaria." *Ibid.* at 131.

cle 36 of the Statute of the Permanent Court of International Justice and which were still in force on 24 October 1945, the date of entry into force of the Charter, shall be deemed as between the parties to the present Statute to be acceptances of the compulsory jurisdiction of this Court for the period which they still had to run on 24 October 1945 and in accordance with their own terms;

(d) Article 36, paragraph 5, applies to all States parties to the present Statute whenever they become parties to it;

(e) As is recognized in the Bulgarian Preliminary Objection, the Bulgarian Declaration of 1921 was in force on 24 October 1945; it has since neither expired in accordance with its own terms, nor has it been withdrawn and, therefore, as between Israel and Bulgaria, both parties to the present Statute, it is still in force as acceptance of the compulsory jurisdiction of this Court;

(f) The operation of Article 36, paragraph 5, is quite independent of extrinsic actions and events, and in particular is not affected by the dissolution of the Permanent Court of International Justice, an event which in fact was contemplated when the present Statute was drawn up and Article 36, paragraph 5, inserted into it;

(g) Accordingly, this Objection is unfounded.[18]

The Court upheld by twelve votes to four the First Bulgarian Preliminary Objection and declared itself without jurisdiction to adjudicate upon the dispute.[19]

Vice President Zafrullah Khan wrote a brief declaration, Judges Badawi and Armand-Ugon wrote separate opinions, Judges Sir Hersch Lauterpacht, Wellington Koo and Sir Percy Spender appended a joint dissenting opinion, and Judge *ad hoc* Goitein also submitted a dissenting opinion.

The Court appears to have adopted from the outset a purpose or object-oriented approach and was, like Bulgaria, less concerned with the text of the clause on which Israel as well as the dissenting judges relied. For the sake of convenience the reasoning of the Court may be divided into two parts: in the first will be considered the question to which states paragraph 5 was intended to apply, that is, the range of this clause *ratione personae,* and in the second, the question to which declarations was paragraph 5 intended to apply, that is, the range of this clause *ratione materiae.*[20]

### a. *Range of Article 36, Paragraph 5, Ratione Personae*

The first question to which the Court addressed itself was whether Article 36, paragraph 5, of the Statute was applicable to Bulgaria and to its Declaration of 1921. The Declaration was as follows:

On behalf of the Government of the Kingdom of Bulgaria, I recognize, in relation to any other Member or State which accepts the same obligation, the jurisdiction of the Court as compulsory, *ipso facto* and without any special convention, unconditionally.[21]

[18] Oral Argument by Mr. Rosenne (Israel), Pleadings at 535 f.
[19] [1959] I.C.J. Rep. at 146.
[20] The distinction was made by the Bulgarian Advocate, Professor Cot, in oral argument. Pleadings at 392.
[21] [1959] I.C.J. Rep. 127

The fifth paragraph of Article 36 of the Statute is in the following terms:

> Declarations made under Article 36 of the Statute of the Permanent Court of International Justice and which are still in force shall be deemed, as between the parties to the present Statute, to be acceptances of the compulsory jurisdiction of the International Court of Justice for the period which they still have to run and in accordance with their terms.[22]

The Court started from the proposition that there was a basic difference between states represented at the San Francisco Conference, which drew up the Charter with the Statute, and states which were not so represented but which might be admitted subsequently. Looking at the purpose of paragraph 5, the Court found that it was adopted in anticipation of the dissolution of the old and the creation of the new Court, and was intended to perform a dual operation: first, to preserve old declarations "with immediate effect as from the entry into force of the Statute," and, secondly, to transfer them to the new Court.[23] Non-signatory states could not be affected by this accord between signatories, their declarations without their consent could not be prevented from lapsing on the dissolution of the old Court, and accordingly they could not be transferred to the new Court. The authors of the Charter could have made an offer to non-signatory states, but no such offer was made. The Court said:

> Thus to restrict the application of Article 36, paragraph 5, to States signatories of the Statute is to take into account the purpose for which this provision was adopted.[24]

If nothing had been done, the old declarations would have lapsed upon the dissolution of the Permanent Court and a retrogressive step would have been taken in the development of compulsory adjudication, unless new declarations were made forthwith upon the establishment of the new Court, an event which apparently was not anticipated at San Francisco. Instead,

> it was sought to provide for this transitory situation by a transitional provision and that is the purpose of Article 36, paragraph 5. By its nature and by its purpose, that transitional provision is applicable only to the transitory situation it was intended to deal with, which involved the institution of a new Court just when the old Court was being dissolved. The situation is entirely different when, the old Court and the acceptance of its compulsory jurisdiction having long since disappeared, a State becomes a party to the Statute of the new Court: there is then no transitory situation to be dealt with by Article 36, paragraph 5.[25]

[22] The French text, which played a significant rôle in argument, is as follows: "5. Les déclarations faites en application de l'article 36 du Statut de la Cour permanente de Justice internationale pour une durée qui n'est pas encore expirée seront considérées, dans les rapports entre parties au présent Statut, comme comportant acceptation de la juridiction obligatoire de la Cour internationale de Justice pour la durée restant à courir d'aprè ces déclarations et conformément à leurs termes."

[23] [1959] I.C.J. Rep. 127 at 137.

[24] *Ibid.* at 139.

[25] *Ibid.*

The Court found some confirmation for its view that paragraph 5 was only concerned with signatory states in the preparatory work of the San Francisco Conference.[26] It seems reasonably clear, however, that what the Court was essentially concerned about was to preserve the consensual character of its jurisdiction in general and of its compulsory jurisdiction in particular. The Court sought and found this consent in the signature and ratification of the Charter by those states which were affected by Article 36, paragraph 5:

> But when, as in the present case, a State has for many years remained a stranger to the Statute, to hold that that State has consented to the transfer, by the fact of its admission to the United Nations, would be to regard its request for admission as equivalent to an express declaration by that State as provided for by Article 36, paragraph 2, of the Statute. It would be to disregard both that latter provision and the principle according to which the jurisdiction of the Court is conditional upon the consent of the respondent, and to regard as sufficient a consent which is merely presumed.[27]

### b. *Range of Article 36, Paragraph 5, Ratione Materiae*

In the second part of its reasoning the Court addressed itself to the Israeli construction according to which, as stated by the Court, Article 36, paragraph 5, covers "a declaration made by a State, which had not participated in the San Francisco Conference, which is not a signatory of the Statute and only became a party thereto much later." However, this part of the Court's reasoning is introduced with the following statement:

> Even if it should be assumed that Article 36, paragraph 5, is not limited to the declarations of signatory States, the terms of that provision make it impossible to apply it to the Bulgarian Declaration of 1921.[28]

Having thus formulated the conclusion which would follow from its examination of the Israeli contentions even before entering upon this examination, the Court proceeded to consider whether the conditions laid down in paragraph 5 of Article 36 for the transfer of declarations made with respect to the Permanent Court to the new Court were satisfied, and whether accordingly the Bulgarian Declaration must "be deemed . . . to be an acceptance of the compulsory jurisdiction of the International Court of Justice." Insofar as the states which participated in the Conference are concerned, the Court saw no difficulty in giving effect to the provision, for: "This constituted a new obligation which was, doubtless, no more onerous than the obligation which was to disappear but it was nevertheless a new obligation."[29] Turning to the time factor, the Court found that no date was determined for the transfer, that is, for the birth of this new obligation: it could be the date of signature or the date of entry into force of the Charter. Neither date could

[26] *Ibid.* at 140–141.
[27] *Ibid.* at 142.
[28] *Ibid.*
[29] *Ibid.* at 143.

apply to a state stranger to the Charter, such as Bulgaria was until her admission on December 14, 1955. By that time the Statute of the Permanent Court had disappeared along with that Court, the legal basis for Bulgaria's Declaration had ceased to exist, and "thus, the Bulgarian Declaration had lapsed and was no longer in force."[30]

The words in Article 36, paragraph 5, "which are still in force" *("pour une durée qui n'est pas encore expirée")*, do not specify a date precisely. Bulgaria "was not privy" to either the signature or the entry into force of the Charter. The Court said on this crucial point:

> . . . it would be permissible to have reference to those dates in respect of the application of Article 36, paragraph 5, only if that provision had referred thereto expressly or by necessary implication; nothing of the kind is stated or implied in the text.[31]

It is submitted that the reason for this statement is again, as throughout the Court's Judgment, the absence of Bulgaria from the San Francisco Conference, for obviously, in spite of the lack of a precise date in Article 36, paragraph 5, it could and did apply to states which, having participated in the Conference, signed and ratified the Charter. It follows also from the Court's reasoning up to this point that it could have applied to any state which, although it did not participate in the Conference, was admitted while its declaration was still in force, that is, before it lapsed in consequence of the dissolution of the Permanent Court. What is not clear is whether Article 36, paragraph 5, would have covered the declaration of a state which participated in the Conference and signed the Charter but ratified it only after the dissolution of the Court. From the following reasoning it would seem that this would be so, although Article 36, paragraph 5, is silent on this point in the sense of not limiting its scope specifically or by necessary implication to participants in the Conference and signatories of the Charter.[32]

The Court states that Article 36, paragraph 5, expresses no intent to preserve the declarations which were "in existence" at the time of signature or entry into force of the Charter, "regardless of the moment when a State having made a declaration became a party to the Statute." The nub of the Court's reasoning appears in the following:

> Such a course would have involved the suspending of a legal obligation, to be revived subsequently: it is scarcely conceivable in respect of a State which was a stranger to the drafting of Article 36, paragraph 5. There is nothing in this provision to show any intention of adopting such an exceptional procedure. If there had been such an intention, it should have been expressed by a direct clause providing for the preservation of the declaration, followed by a provision for its subsequent re-entry into force as from the moment of admission to the United Nations: nothing of the kind is expressed in the Statute.[33]

[30] *Ibid.*
[31] *Ibid.* at 144.
[32] In a *reductio ad absurdum* of the Bulgarian contention, the joint dissenting opinion points out that Art. 36, par. 5, might have been completely frustrated if the Permanent Court had been dissolved prior to entry into force of the Charter, with the effect of invalidating all declarations which were in force at the time of the drafting of the Charter. [1959] I.C.J. Rep. at 167. The Court did not consider this fatal flaw inherent in the Bulgarian contention, nor does it seem to have been noticed by Israel.
[33] *Ibid.* at 144.

The interpretation which the Court rejects as far as a state "stranger to the drafting of Article 36, paragraph 5" is concerned, appears impliedly as tenable as regards a state which was "privy" to the drafting. However, although the requirement of consent at the time of drafting seems very much in evidence in the Court's reasoning, in final analysis it is the time element which is established as decisive. For the Court, Article 36, paragraph 5 , contains two conditions: (1) that the state having made the declaration should be a party to the Statute; and (2) that the declaration should still be in force. But

> Since the Bulgarian Declaration had lapsed before Bulgaria was admitted to the United Nations, it cannot be said that, at that time, the declaration was still in force. The second condition stated in Article 36, paragraph 5, is therefore not satisfied in the present case.[34]

The Court thus adopted the Bulgarian position in its essential aspects. This position, in all its variations, consisted of two arguments: one, that the Bulgarian Declaration was attached to the Statute of the Permanent Court like "a branch is to the tree" and therefore, when the tree was cut down on April 18, 1946, the branch fell with the tree.[35] The words in paragraph 5 of Article 36, "which are still in force," were interpreted accordingly as referring to the validity of the Bulgarian Declaration as dependent upon the existence of the Permanent Court and its Statute. The Declaration, having lost its validity with the demise of the old Court, could not have been revived by or in consequence of Bulgaria's entry into the United Nations in 1955. To argue otherwise is tantamount to saying that in joining the United Nations Bulgaria accepted the compulsory jurisdiction of the Court by reviving its old Declaration and modifying it in the sense that henceforth it would apply to the International Court of Justice rather than to the old Court, which no longer existed. That Bulgaria's entry into the United Nations would have this consequence required an express stipulation, for it limited its sovereignty, and limitations upon sovereignty cannot be presumed.[36]

The second argument, a variation of the consensual point, related to the powers of the San Francisco Conference: the Conference could and did impose obligations on the participating states; it could not impose any obligation on a state which, to use the Court's language "was not privy" to it. More particularly it could not, without the consent of such a state, preserve or modify a Declaration which is "contractual and consensual" in nature.[37]

The Israeli position, as indicated above, was based entirely on a strict interpretation of Article 36, paragraph 5, emphasizing more strongly its French rather than its English version, whereas Bulgaria preferred the English to the French version. In the French ver-

[34] *Ibid.*
[35] Pleadings at 383, 388, 393.
[36] *Ibid.* at 413.
[37] *Ibid.* at 549.

sion the words "which are still in force" appear as *"pour une durée qui n'est pas encore expirée."* As construed by Israel, Article 36, paragraph 5, encompassed all declarations and was intended to encompass all declarations the validity of which had not yet expired at the critical date. This date was October 24, 1945, when the Charter entered into force. It was common ground that the Bulgarian Declaration was still in force on that day, and therefore automatically and objectively the competence of the old Court devolved on the new Court.[38] Neither the phrase quoted nor the concluding words of Article 36, paragraph 5 ("for the period which they still have to run and in accordance with their terms"), refer to, or permit the introduction of, an extrinsic factor such as the anticipated dissolution of the Permanent Court. Accordingly, if a declaration was in force on October 24, 1945, and had, in accordance with its terms, not expired pursuant to Article 36, paragraph 5, it became operative "as between the parties to the present Statute" on the date when Bulgaria became a party to the present Statute, that is, on the day of its admission to the United Nations, December 14, 1955.

In the submission of Israel, Article 36, paragraph 5, established a legal fiction: declarations made with respect to the old Court and which are still in force "shall be deemed" to be acceptances of the compulsory jurisdiction of the new Court. This was one of the ways, perhaps the principal one, in which Israel, without resorting to notions such as preserving, reviving, or modifying the terms of old declarations, construed their binding force. Israel recognized that the binding force of such declarations must be based on the consent of the states concerned. This consent was given by some states at the time of signature and ratification of the Charter and by others at the time of their admission to the United Nations. In applying for admission to the United Nations, Bulgaria, pursuant to Article 4, paragraph 1, agreed to accept "the obligations contained in the present Charter," including those provided for in the Statute of the Court which is an integral part of the Charter. The obligation expressed in paragraph 5 of Article 36 is one of these obligations.[39]

Inasmuch as the Bulgarian Declaration of 1921 was not limited in point of time and therefore had not expired at the time of Bulgaria's admission to the United Nations, it was to be deemed an acceptance of the compulsory jurisdiction of the International Court of Justice. Israel argued, *inter alia,* that it was open to Bulgaria to withdraw her Declaration at any time and that, failing to do so, the Declaration fell under the sway of Article 36, paragraph 5.[40] Bulgaria, apart from contending that the Declaration, having lapsed, could not be withdrawn, countered with the argument that it could not have been withdrawn, on the ground that this right was not reserved in the Declaration.[41] Israel admit-

[38] *Ibid.* at 142, 475. The notion of devolution was borrowed from Kaeckenbeeck, 70 Hague Academy Recueil des Cours 212 (1947).

[39] Pleadings at 462, 469, 578. For the Bulgarian rebuttal, see *ibid.* at 542–545.

[40] *Ibid.* at 144. It may be noted in passing that Bulgaria, in support of the contention that its 1921 Declaration had lapsed, referred to the fact that the Yearbook of the I.C.J. did not include Bulgaria in the list of states still bound by old declarations. *Ibid.* at 129. Israel rejected this argument, saying that the Yearbook prepared by the Registry "is not evidence for the validity or even the existence of instruments conferring or purporting to confer jurisdiction on the Court." *Ibid.* at 149.

[41] *Ibid.* at 400, 414, 415.

ted the existence of doctrinal controversy on this matter but persisted that Bulgaria had not even attempted to withdraw its Declaration.[42] This point was not considered by the Court[43] and it is not clear what its relevance was. Prior to its admission to the United Nations or after its admission, a communication purporting to withdraw its 1921 Declaration could presumably have been addressed to the Secretary General of the United Nations, but there is no basis for doubting the good faith of Bulgaria in considering its Declaration to have lapsed. Apart from this, it is doubtful whether a withdrawal would not have been open to challenge. The fiction, to use Israel's construction, established in Article 36, paragraph 5, provides that old acceptances shall be deemed to be acceptances of the new Court "for the period for which they still have to run and in accordance with their terms." As the right to terminate or withdraw the Declaration was not reserved, it is at least doubtful whether such termination or withdrawal would have been compatible with the "terms" of the Bulgarian Declaration.[44]

The joint dissenting opinion of Judges Lauterpacht, Wellington Koo and Spender, which is substantially longer and more elaborate than the Judgment itself, deals with three points: first, the Bulgarian contention that the words "which are still in force" refer to the existence of the Permanent Court, and therefore that declarations lapsed with the dissolution of the Permanent Court; secondly, the assumption of the Court that Article 36, paragraph 5, applied only to original Members of the United Nations; and thirdly, the question of whether its own interpretation and, by the same token, that of Israel, were reasonable. Regarding the first point, the joint dissenting opinion holds that the Bulgarian contention is incompatible with both the ordinary meaning of the words "still in force," as well as with the object of paragraph 5 of Article 36. It leans, as did Israel, more heavily on the French text, but finds that both phrases refer, in their ordinary connotation, to the element of the expiration of time—not to termination as the result of an extraneous event such as the dissolution of the Permanent Court.[45] Further support for this interpretation is found in the uncontested meaning given to similar terms in Article 36, paragraph 1 ("treaties or conventions in force"), and Article 37 ("treaty or convention in force").[46] It has never been claimed that the dissolution of the Permanent Court

[42] *Ibid.* at 484, 497. For further Bulgarian and Israeli statements on this, see *ibid.* at 553 f., 581, 584. The point was also made by the United States in its observations, *ibid.* at 313, 320.

[43] It is, however, mentioned without elaboration in the joint dissenting opinion and in the dissenting opinion of Judge *ad hoc* Goitein. [1959] I.C.J. Rep. at 189–190, 202, 204.

[44] In a somewhat different context the joint dissenting opinion declares: "Admittedly, an international obligation may cease to exist for reasons other than lapse of time; it may, for instance, terminate because of the fulfilment of its object, denunciation in a manner provided in the instrument, or its dissolution by mutual agreement." [1959] I.C.J. Rep. at 162. This observation may well have a bearing on the point, that is, on the question whether legally Bulgaria could have unilaterally withdrawn her Declaration. See also Anand, Compulsory Jurisdiction of the International Court of Justice 176 ff.

It may be noted that Judges Badawi and Armand-Ugon considered that Bulgaria's Declaration was not covered by Art. 36, par. 5, precisely because it was made for an indefinite duration. As construed by them, the concluding words of that paragraph presupposed only declarations made for a definite period of time. [1959] I.C.J. Rep. at 150 and 154. For a decisive rebuttal of this view, see joint dissenting opinion, *ibid.* at 192–194.

[45] [1959] I.C.J. Rep. at 163. For the evaluation of the five languages of the Charter see *ibid.* 161–162.

[46] *Ibid.* at 163.

had any impact on those two clauses, and there was no reason to assume that the draftsmen of the Charter used the same language in a different sense in Article 36, paragraph 5.[47] The joint dissenting opinion did not consider, as was urged by Israel, that October 24, 1945, was the critical date. The words "still in force" could equally well be attached to the date on which the particular declarant state became a Member of the United Nations, that is, in the case of Bulgaria, on December 14, 1955.[48]

Considering the object of the clause, the joint dissenting opinion, agreeing with Israel, concludes that the draftsmen of the Charter wanted to preserve to the greatest possible extent the progress achieved in establishing compulsory jurisdiction. They were concerned in finding a suitable formula precisely because the dissolution of the Permanent Court was anticipated, and they were determined to prevent the termination of existing declarations as a consequence of the dissolution of the Court.[49] The three judges had no difficulty in agreeing partly with Bulgaria that: "Undoubtedly, they [*i.e.,* the declarations] lapsed so far as the Permanent Court was concerned; they did not lapse so far as the present Court is concerned." In their view

> The governing principle underlying paragraph 5 is that of automatic succession of the International Court of Justice in respect of the engagements undertaken by reference to the Statute of the Permanent Court, the dissolution of which was clearly envisaged and anticipated.[50]

Adverting to the Bulgarian contention that a dead declaration could not be revived, the joint dissenting opinion stated that

> there are obvious limits to the analogy between the death of a person and the cessation of the operation of a legal provision. Nothing can revive the dead; a short paragraph in a treaty can instill new and vigorous life into a treaty or provision of it whose operation is suspended or which had ceased to exist. . . . Legal intercourse between States—as between individuals—abounds in examples of a contractual provision being dormant, and its operation suspended, pending the accomplishment of an event by an act of a party or some extraneous occurrence.[51]

Bulgaria brought to life its 1921 Declaration by freely accepting in its application for admission to membership the Statute of the Court, including Article 36, paragraph 5. She thus "supplied the consensual basis of a declaration of acceptance of the compulsory jurisdiction of the new Court."[52]

With reference to the second point, that is, that part of the Court's Judgment ac-

[47] *Ibid.* at 164, 171, 180, 181.
[48] *Ibid.* at 164.
[49] "The intention of paragraph 5 which used the words 'shall be deemed . . . to be acceptances' is to cut clear through any cobweb of legal complications and problems which might arise in this connection." *Ibid.* at 168.
[50] *Ibid.* See also p. 173 for a statement of the importance attached to the subject of succession in international organizations.
[51] *Ibid.* at 169. The concrete example given is that of the impact of war on some treaties.
[52] *Ibid.* at 170.

cording to which the operation of Article 36, paragraph 5, is limited to original Members of the United Nations, the joint dissenting opinion could find no basis for it either in the Charter, in general principles of international law, in the legislative history of that clause or in the literature.[53] The Court, it will be recalled, was concerned with the consensual requirement for the operation of Article 36, paragraph 5. It had no difficulty, of course, in this connection with the states which signed and ratified the Charter. The joint dissenting opinion, aware of the Court's preoccupation with this requirement, is permeated with affirmations that, in adhering to the Charter on the basis of an application in which it formally accepted all the obligations of the Charter as required by Article 4, paragraph 1, of the Charter, Bulgaria had given "her consent to the jurisdiction of the Court as confirmed and continued by that provision," namely, Article 35, paragraph 5.[54] Of more general and enduring character, because it relates to the general law of international organization, is the following weighty statement which for this reason deserves to be quoted in full:

> In our opinion there is no legal basis for the assertion that, while the original Members of the United Nations could bind themselves in the matter of the transfer of the declarations under paragraph 5 of Article 36 of the Statute, they could not bind other States subsequently adhering to the Charter. It is of the very essence of the Charter that its provisions—all its provisions—bind States which adhere to the Charter subsequent to its coming into force. If Article 36 had provided unconditionally for the obligatory jurisdiction of the Court—and not merely for the maintenance of existing declarations in accordance with their terms—it would be binding not only upon original Members but also upon all States subsequently adhering. It would not be *res inter alios acta* in relation to those States. That proposition is too fundamental to require elaboration. We consider it imperative that in deciding any particular controversy, which may be of a passing character, no countenance should be given to general propositions such as that there is a difference, with regard to any obligations of the Charter, between original Members and others; or that any provision of the Charter can be *res inter alios acta* in relation to States subsequently adhering; or that the obligations of a judicial settlement must be interpreted by reference to standards more exacting than the interpretation of other obligations of the Charter.[55]

Turning now to the final point, the question whether its interpretation of Article 36, paragraph 5, meets the requirement of reasonableness,[56] the joint dissenting opinion starts with the proposition that "the test of reasonableness must itself be applied in a reasonable way."[57] The test itself "follows from the ever present duty of States to act in good faith," and therefore applies both ways, that is, against the state making a claim and

[53] *Ibid.* at 175 ff. The literature in question consisted of Judge Manley O. Hudson's article, "The Twenty-Fifth Year of the World Court," 41 A.J.I.L. 1–19, at 10 (1947). This article figured prominently in the argument of both Israel and Bulgaria. It may be noted that, as stated in the joint dissenting opinion, the limitation of Art. 36, par. 5, to original Members was not invoked by Bulgaria and not argued by the parties, although it is the alternative basis for the judgment of the Court. *Cf. ibid.* at 170, 175, 186.

[54] *Ibid.* at 186; but see also 177, 182, 187.

[55] *Ibid.* at 176. See also particularly, with reference to the last point, the forceful statement at 187.

[56] The joint dissenting opinion found it necessary to discuss this requirement because "of some considerations underlying the Judgment of the Court." *Ibid.* at 188.

[57] *Ibid.* at 189.

the state resisting a claim. So far as Bulgaria, the state resisting the claim, is concerned, the three dissenting judges declared:

> There is nothing manifestly unreasonable in itself in invoking in 1956 the Bulgarian Declaration of 1921—a declaration which in 1945 was given a new potential lease of life in the Statute of the Court and which was confirmed by the entry of Bulgaria into the United Nations in 1955 and, in the preceding years, by her repeated affirmation of the intention to be bound by the resulting obligations.[58]

The Bulgarian Declaration of 1921 was the last of the declarations to which the transitional clause could apply, and therefore it was contended that, having substantially though not fully achieved its objective, it would be unreasonable to subject Bulgaria to it. On this the three dissenting judges made two comments. In the first place,

> It matters little to that State—in the present case the applicant State—that most or all other parties have already benefited from it and acted upon it. Unless the interested State has been guilty of negligence or bad faith in pursuing its legal rights, it is entitled to expect that the treaty will be given effect.[59]

Israel's application did not fall under any of these qualifications.

The second comment, also relating to Israel's application, was based on the nature of the right to which the test of reasonableness is to be applied. On the one hand, there are substantive claims the invocation of which "causes unfair hardship or which, through an abusive reliance upon a legal right, puts in jeopardy important interests of the defendant State." On the other hand, there are claims, such as Israel's, which call for adjudication upon a controversy in accordance with international law. With reference to this the joint dissenting opinion significantly observed:

> A State ought not to be deemed to be acting improperly if in reliance—even if it be rigid reliance—upon a valid instrument it asks the Court to declare its competence to administer international law. It is only in most exceptional circumstances that a demand, based on a valid treaty, for the exercise of the primary function of the Court to administer justice based on law can be held to be unreasonable. These exceptional circumstances may include the operation of the rule of extinctive prescription after a prolonged period of inaction on the part of the applicant State. No such ground has been invoked here.[60]

Whatever one may think of the relative persuasiveness of the Bulgarian and Israeli arguments, or of the Court's reasoning in upholding Bulgaria's Preliminary Objection and the reasoning of the joint dissenting opinion in rejecting it, one can hardly be of two minds as to which (the Court's or the joint dissenting opinion) is the more elaborate in its

[58] *Ibid.* at 190.
[59] *Ibid.* at 191.
[60] *Ibid.* at 191–192. Several instances are cited in support of the argument that in the past the Court has applied the test of reasonableness "as a motive not for defeating but for upholding its jurisdiction."

depth and more instructive in its comprehensiveness and thoroughness with which the arguments *pro* and *con* were presented, related to their sources and incisively analyzed.

2. United Kingdom v. Bulgaria

The United Kingdom Government instituted proceedings against Bulgaria by an application dated November 19, 1957, on behalf of five victims, four of whom were British subjects and one, a Swedish citizen, the wife of a British subject.[61] The jurisdiction of the Court was derived from the United Kingdom Declaration of April 18, 1957, and the Bulgarian Declaration of 1921 accepting the compulsory jurisdiction of the Permanent Court, which

> became effective as to the jurisdiction of the International Court of Justice, by virtue of Article 93(1) of the Charter of the United Nations and Article 36(5) of the Statute of the Court, on the date of Bulgaria's admission to membership of the United Nations.[62]

Thus the United Kingdom, so far as the Bulgarian Declaration is concerned, adopted the same construction as that advanced by Israel. However, in addition and alternatively,

> the United Kingdom Government hereby submits specifically and unconditionally to the jurisdiction of the Court for all the purposes of the present dispute, and invokes Bulgaria's unconditional acceptance of the Court's compulsory jurisdiction, effective in the manner described in the preceding paragraph.[63]

The first part of this statement could be construed as an offer of *forum prorogatum* which, of course, was open to the British Government, and which it would have been open to Bulgaria to accept or reject. The latter part in which an attempt is made to hold Bulgaria to its unconditional Declaration of 1921 is more difficult to understand. It is hardly compatible with the concept of *forum prorogatum,* the essence of which is voluntary consent on the part of both states.[64] The clue to this attempted alternative basis of compulsory jurisdiction, which is unconditional, may be precisely the conditional character of the April 18, 1957, United Kingdom Declaration. According to this, the United Kingdom reserved disputes

> relating to any question which, in the opinion of the Government of the United Kingdom, affects the national security of the United Kingdom or any of its dependent territories. . . .[65]

This is as self-judging and automatic a reservation as the United States' Connally Amendment. And the reason for the alternative basis of jurisdiction may well have been the de-

[61] Pleadings at 35, 332.
[62] *Ibid.* at 36.
[63] *Ibid.* and 331.
[64] Rosenne, The International Court of Justice 284 (1957).
[65] [1957–1958] I.C.J. Yearbook 211.

sire to head off the "boomerang" effect which such reservations are bound to provoke when the declarant state is the plaintiff. There is no doubt that the Bulgarian Government, aware of the difference between the Israeli and United Kingdom Declarations,[66] would have availed itself of the British reservation as in fact it availed itself of the American reservation. However, before the Bulgarian Government submitted any objections to the jurisdiction of the Court, the United Kingdom on July 8, 1959, requested that proceedings be discontinued. This decision was reached in view of the Court's Judgment of May 26, 1959, in the parent case of *Israel* v. *Bulgaria,* that it had no jurisdiction.[67] The Judgment certainly justified the discontinuation insofar as the British Government relied on the Bulgarian Declaration of 1921 as the basis of jurisdiction. It does not explain the abandonment of the alternative basis insofar as it related to the *forum prorogatum* doctrine. By order of August 3, 1959, the President of the Court decided that the case be removed from the Court's list.[68]

The British alternative for founding the jurisdiction of the Court might possibly be construed in another way, namely, as the unconditional acceptance of the offer contained in the Bulgarian Declaration of 1921. Under this construction, Bulgaria would appear as making the offer and Britain as accepting it. Whether the Court, had it been free to do so, would have declared itself competent on the basis of this construction is doubtful, for the Bulgarian Declaration, although it accepted the jurisdiction of the Court "unconditionally," presumably still required the condition of reciprocity in the words: "in relation to any other Member or State which accepts the same obligation."

### 3. United States v. Bulgaria

United States proceedings against Bulgaria were initiated by an application dated October 24, 1957, in which damages were claimed for stated "breaches of international obligation." The jurisdiction of the Court was founded in the following manner:

> The United States Government, in filing this application with the Court, submits to the Court's jurisdiction for the purposes of this case. The Bulgarian Government accepted the compulsory jurisdiction of the Court by virtue of the signature of its representative to the Protocol of Signature of the Statute of the Permanent Court of International Justice, and his acceptance was completely unconditional; acceptance became effective as to the jurisdiction of the International Court of Justice by virtue of Article 36(5) of the Statute of the Court upon the date of admission of Bulgaria into the United Nations.[69]

Thus the United States, like the United Kingdom, adopted the same construction as that formulated by Israel with regard to Article 36, paragraph 5, of the Statute and its effec-

[66] Communication from the Bulgarian Government to the President of the Court of May 14, 1959. Pleadings at 695.

[67] Pleadings at 698.

[68] Case concerning the Aerial Incident of 27 July 1955 (United Kingdom *v.* Bulgaria), Order of Aug. 3, 1959, [1959] I.C.J. Rep. 264.

[69] Pleadings at 23. For a more detailed analysis of this case, see Gross, "Bulgaria Invokes the Connally Amendment," 56 A.J.I.L. 357-382 (1962). See also *supra*, pp. 727-751.

tiveness, brought about by the admission of Bulgaria to the United Nations. Unlike the United Kingdom, the United States maintained this construction even after it was rejected by the Court in *Israel* v. *Bulgaria* on the strength of Article 59 of the Court's Statute, and further on the ground that

> Particularly where the interpretation of a constitutional text (Article 36, paragraph 5) is in question, no doctrine of *stare decisis* precludes reexamination of the holding in a previous case in this court.[70]

It is generally accepted that, from a formal point of view, the doctrine of *stare decisis* does not apply in the jurisprudence of the Court, although in practice the Court has shown a strong tendency to adhere to previous holdings. It is not clear what additional support for Article 59 the United States sought to derive from singling out constitutional texts. The Court has consistently taken the position that the Charter of the United Nations is a multilateral treaty and has construed it accordingly. No authority in international law to underpin the distinction implied above was cited, although some American and Canadian cases were cited.[71]

The United States Government followed up its application with a memorial,[72] and the Bulgarian Government on September 3, 1959, submitted Preliminary Objections to the jurisdiction of the Court.[73] It will be recalled that in its application the United States did not refer to its own Declaration of August 26, 1946, accepting the compulsory jurisdiction of the Court pursuant to Article 36, paragraph 2, of its Statute. The Bulgarian Government objected to this manner of proceeding on several grounds. It did not conform to Article 32, paragraph 2, of the Rules of the Court,[74] and this defect made it impossible for Bulgaria to comply with Article 62, paragraph 1, of the Rules[75] and to formulate its preliminary objections *in limine litis*. Secondly, in order to seize the Court by means of a unilateral application, that is, by invoking the compulsory jurisdiction of the Court, it is necessary to do so on the basis of a prior acceptance of this jurisdiction. According to the constant jurisprudence of the Court, the seizing of the Court depends on and is possible only within the limits of applicable declarations. The acceptance of the ju-

[70] Observations and Submission of the Government of the United States of America on the Preliminary Objections of the Government of the People's Republic of Bulgaria, February, 1960. Pleadings at 307. See *ibid.* at 311–322, for construction of Art. 36, par. 5.

[71] *Ibid.* at 310–311.

[72] *Ibid.* at 167 ff.

[73] *Ibid.* at 265 ff.

[74] The application "must also, as far as possible, specify the provision on which the applicant founds the jurisdiction of the Court . . ."

[75] Art. 62, par. 1: "A preliminary objection must be filed by a party at the latest before the expiry of the time-limit fixed for the delivery of its first pleading." Relevant also is par. 2 of Art. 62: "The preliminary objection shall set out the facts and the law on which the objection is based, the submissions and a list of the documents in support . . ." Bulgaria was quick to seize upon the obvious insufficiency of the American application. However, it failed to conform to the requirements of Art. 62 of the Rules in submitting preliminary objections against the Israeli application. See Observations of Israel, Pleadings at 135–136.

risdiction of the Court in the United States application does not have the character of a declaration within the meaning of Article 36, paragraph 2, and was, moreover, not deposited with the Secretary General of the United Nations as required by paragraph 4 of Article 36.

Thirdly and finally, Bulgaria contended that the statement could be construed as "an offer to enter into a special agreement." This Bulgaria declined to accept on the ground that the dispute related to matters essentially within its national jurisdiction.[76] The United States admitted that the Bulgarian exceptions were well founded and "that apart from the United States declaration of August 26, 1946, there is not a basis for compulsory jurisdiction."[77] It is not often that one sees a government attempting to found the compulsory jurisdiction of the Court on a basis which could be knocked out so easily. The United States might have done better had it admitted that the statement in its application indeed constituted an offer to accept voluntarily the jurisdiction of the Court under the doctrine of *forum prorogatum,* and that this offer was rejected, thus placing the blame squarely on Bulgaria.

To the United States reliance on the Bulgarian Declaration of 1921, in substance the same line of reasoning was opposed as was developed in the case of *Israel* v. *Bulgaria.* The Judgment of May 26, 1959, in that case was invoked as confirming the thesis that the Declaration had lost its force. It is unnecessary to go further into this phase of the pleadings. The United States' view that the Court was not barred from taking a fresh look at the matter by its Judgment in the *Israel* v. *Bulgaria* case has already been mentioned.[78]

The main thrust of the Bulgarian preliminary objections was directed against the United States Declaration of August 26, 1946, as an implied basis of jurisdiction. This Declaration contains the Connally Amendment, a reservation *ratione materiae* so far as it excepts "disputes with regard to matters which are essentially within the domestic jurisdiction" of the United States, and a reservation of a self-judging and preemptory character so far as it provides that the nature of the dispute in question shall be "determined by the United States of America." Bulgaria, availing itself of the principle recognized by the Court, namely, that all jurisdictional rights which a state may invoke for itself may be invoked against it by other states, invoked the Connally Amendment. Bulgaria

> could not admit that any matters which it rightly [*"en bon droit"*] qualifies as falling essentially within its domestic jurisdiction, should be examined, directly or indirectly, before the Court. It requests, accordingly, that the Court declare itself incompetent to entertain the Application of the United States.[79]

Out of an abundance of caution and in view of the alleged unconditional acceptance of the jurisdiction of the Court in the United States application, Bulgaria submitted three sub-

[76] Pleadings at 273–276.
[77] United States Observations, *ibid.* at 306.
[78] *Cf.* p. 800 above, note 70.
[79] Pleadings at 272 (author's translation).

sidiary arguments derived from the principle of reciprocity and the norms governing the compulsory jurisdiction of the Court. First, by accepting unconditionally the jurisdiction of the Court, the United States attempted to change unilaterally the prior consensual bond created by the declarations. Such a unilateral modification of the 1946 Declaration, which is studded with several reservations, is inadmissible. Secondly, such a unilateral modification would frustrate the rights which Bulgaria is entitled to derive from Article 36 of the Court's Statute. And, thirdly, such a modification made after the event being contrary to the Statute, could have no bearing on the case at bar.[80]

The United States, in its observations on the Bulgarian Preliminary Objection, admitted the principle of reciprocity[81] but denied that the Connally Amendment could properly be invoked, on two grounds: first, the determination of the 1955 incident as falling within Bulgaria's domestic jurisdiction "would fly in the face of actuality."[82] Secondly, having taken certain steps and having entered "into the international engagements" recited by the United States, "the Government of Bulgaria is not entitled now to determine that these matters are 'essentially within the domestic jurisdiction of the People's Republic of Bulgaria' ".[83] In the second argument the United States seems to use as a counter-defense the doctrine of estoppel or preclusion. However, the United States in its observations appears to have given greater prominence to its own construction of its own Declaration on the ground that, as author of the Connally Amendment, it knew better than did Bulgaria how it was intended to be construed and under what circumstances it could properly be applied. In substance the United States in a variety of formulations argued, without using the words, that its reservation should be used sparingly and reasonably, saying it does not consider that it

> authorizes or empowers this Government, or any other government on a basis of reciprocity, to make an arbitrary determination that a particular matter is domestic, when it is evidently one of international concern and has been so treated by the parties.[84]

Opponents of the Connally Amendment would have had every reason to applaud this construction which in effect would have nullified it. By necessary implication as well as explicitly,[85] the United States must have been prepared to let the Court determine whether in the premises the reservation of domestic jurisdiction applied, thus restoring to the Court the power, under Article 36, paragraph 6, of the Statute, to determine whether it had jurisdiction, a competence which, it was believed, the Connally Amendment was intended to nullify. The approving reference to the relativity test of domestic jurisdiction

[80] *Ibid.* at 271–273. Bulgaria also said that "by dint of such an *ad hoc* renunciation motivated solely by opportunistic considerations, the Government of the United States would aim to preserve for the future and in all cases in which it would be the respondent the benefit of its own reservations without being exposed to their drawbacks in cases in which it was the plaintiff." (Author's translation.) *Ibid.*

[81] *Ibid.* at 308, 323.

[82] *Ibid.* at 308.

[83] *Ibid.* at 324 f.

[84] *Ibid.* at 323.

[85] See the United States submissions, *ibid.* at 330, where the Court is requested to overrule the Bulgarian objections.

established by the Permanent Court in the case of the *Tunis-Morocco Nationality Decrees*[86] strengthens this reading of the American observations. The jubilation would have been short-lived, for on May 13, 1960, having been informed on March 18, 1960, that oral proceedings would begin on June 1, 1960, the United States requested the Court to discontinue the proceedings against Bulgaria,[87] which request was granted by order of the Court on May 30, 1960.[88]

As stated in the request, the United States, after further study, concluded that the premise of its argument against Bulgaria was not valid, and that the position taken in the *Interhandel* case was correct. As construed now by the United States, the Connally Amendment excludes any review by the Court of the propriety or arbitrariness of the determination by Bulgaria that the dispute fell within its domestic jurisdiction. The United States accordingly withdrew its observations with respect to Bulgaria's invocation of the Connally Amendment.[89] It remains to be noted that the United States obviously desired to set the record straight with respect to its own understanding of the legal scope of the Connally Amendment as "an absolute bar to jurisdiction," irrespective of its policy not to invoke it arbitrarily or unreasonably. It could have requested discontinuation of the proceedings on the same ground as the United Kingdom had done, had discontinuation been its sole or primary objective.

## CASE CONCERNING SOVEREIGNTY OVER CERTAIN FRONTIER LAND (BELGIUM/NETHERLANDS)

Belgium and The Netherlands signed on March 7, 1957, a special agreement which entered into force on November 19, 1957, requesting the Court to determine

> whether sovereignty over the plots shown in the survey and known from 1836 to 1843 as Nos. 91 and 92, Section A, Zondereygen, belongs to the Kingdom of Belgium or the Kingdom of the Netherlands.[90]

The Court gave judgment on June 20, 1959, by a vote of 10 to 4 in favor of Belgium. Judges Sir Hersch Lauterpacht, Armand-Ugon and Moreno Quintana dissented; the first submitted a brief declaration, and the latter two wrote dissenting opinions. Judge Spiropoulos, in a declaration, stated that the case involved choosing between two hypotheses, and that in his view the Netherlands hypothesis was less speculative and

[86] *Ibid.* at 325.

[87] *Ibid.* at 676.

[88] Case concerning the Aerial Incident of 27 July 1955 (United States *v.* Bulgaria), Order of May 30, 1960, [1960] I.C.J. Rep. 146.

[89] For a fuller presentation and analysis, see Gross, *loc. cit.* at 370 ff. *Supra,* at 740.

[90] Case concerning Sovereignty over Certain Frontier Land, Judgment of June 20, 1959, [1959] I.C.J. Rep. 209, at 211; I.C.J. Pleadings, under the same title, at 8. Digest in 53 A.J.I.L. 937–943 (1959). For a succinct analysis of the case, *cf.* Verzijl, "The I.C.J. in 1959," 7 Netherlands Int. Law Rev. 1-16, at 10-15 (1960). See also note, 1960 Duke Law J. 252; and note, 13 Revista Española de Derecho Internacional 519 (1960).

should be preferred. "For this reason," he concluded, he "hesitated to concur in the Judgment of the Court."[91] This is probably an accurate description of his state of mind but not an unequivocal indication of how he voted. It must be noted that neither Belgium nor The Netherlands availed itself of the provision in Article 31, paragraph 3, of the Court's Statute to appoint a judge *ad hoc.*

The case involved two plots of land of about fourteen hectares, of ancient history,[92] which were in dispute between the Belgian Commune of Baerle-Duc and the Netherlands Commune of Baarle-Nassau, and constituted enclaves in Netherlands territory and Baarle-Nassau. The controversy between the parties did not concern a substantial material or political interest, although it affected the territorial aspect of their sovereignty. As pointed out by the Belgian Agent at the beginning of the oral hearings, the dispute was highly interesting from the viewpoints of jurisprudence and doctrine with respect to the application in international law of the concept of error in connection with the conclusion of treaties.[93]

The error in question—and both parties were in agreement on this point—arose, if it did arise, in connection with the Boundary Convention between the two countries of August 8, 1843, which resulted from the labors of a Mixed Boundary Commission set up pursuant to the Treaty of London of April 19, 1839, sanctioning the separation of Belgium from The Netherlands. The directive addressed to this Commission is contained in Article 14 of the Treaty of November 5, 1842, between The Netherlands and Belgium for the Execution of the Treaty of London of April 19, 1839. Article 14 reads:

> The *status quo* shall be maintained both with regard to the villages of Baarle-Nassau (Netherlands) and Baerle-Duc (Belgium) and with regard to the ways crossing them.[94]

Article 70 provided further that the Mixed Boundary Commission should draft the convention "in accordance with the foregoing provisions," that is, in accordance with the *status quo* prevailing between the two Baarles. The Boundary Convention consists of a text and descriptive minutes, and survey maps prepared and signed by the Commissioners, which "shall remain annexed to the present Convention and shall have the same force and effect as though they were inserted in their entirety."[95] With respect to the boundary between the two Baarles, the Convention, in paragraph 5 of Article 14, states that it was impossible to draw a continuous line between these communes because the Commission had been directed by Article 14 of the Boundary Treaty to maintain the *status quo.* For the division between these communes reference is made to Article 90 of the "Descriptive Minute" annexed to the Convention. This is the seat of the opposing con-

[91] [1959] I.C.J. Rep. at 232.
[92] For an historical sketch, *cf.* Netherlands Counter-Memorial, Pleadings at 37 ff.
[93] Pleadings at 463.
[94] Pleadings at 439, and [1959] I.C.J. Rep. at 214. The Court refers to the 1842 treaty as the "Boundary Treaty" as distinguished from the "Boundary Convention" of 1843.
[95] Art. 3 [1959] I.C.J. Rep. at 215, and Pleadings at 442.

tentions. The "Descriptive Minute" declares that, having regard to Article 14 of the Boundary Treaty requiring the maintenance of the *status quo* and the resulting impossibility of drawing a regular delimitation, the Commissioners consider

> that it may be useful to note what was established with the agreement of both sides, by the Minute of 29 November 1836, agreed to and signed on March 22, 1841 by the local authorities of the two communes.

The Commissioners' decision follows:

> a. The above-mentioned Minute, noting the plots composing the communes of Baerle-Duc and Baarle-Nassau, is transcribed word for word in the present Article.
> b. A special map . . . showing the whole detailed survey plot by plot of the two communes . . . has been made. . . .[96]

In the transcription of the Minute of 1836 and 1841, called by the Court the "Communal Minute," there appears the following listing for Zondereygen:

> Plots numbers 78 to 90 inclusive belong to the commune of Baarle-Nassau.
> Plots numbers 91 and 92 belong to Baerle-Duc
> Plots numbers 93 to 111 inclusive belong to Baarle-Nassau.[97]

However, the copy of the "Communal Minute" on which The Netherlands relied and which it submitted to the Court provides:

> Plots numbers 78 to 111 inclusive belong to the commune of Baarle-Nassau.[98]

Considering that the "Descriptive Minute" directed the transcription "word for word" of the "Communal Minute" of 1836/41 and that the transcribed text did not conform to the copy of the "Communal Minute" produced in Court, The Netherlands claimed that the "flagrant contradiction" between the two texts was due to an error, which The Netherlands explained at great length.[99]

The Netherlands, in law, derived several conclusions from the above instruments. It contended, first, that Article 90 of the "Descriptive Minute" could not create a valid title to sovereignty. The title was to be found in Article 14 of the 1842 Boundary Treaty and Article 14, paragraph 5, of the 1843 Boundary Convention, which require the maintenance of the *status quo.* This could not be changed by the "Descriptive Minute" drawn up by the Boundary Commission.[100] Secondly, even if the error which found its way into the "Descriptive Minute" was not noted at the time the Minute was drafted, insofar as it

[96] [1959] I.C.J. Rep. at 216, and Pleadings at 450.
[97] [1959] I.C.J. Rep. 216, and Pleadings at 452.
[98] [1959] I.C.J. Rep. 216.
[99] Pleadings, Netherlands Counter-Memorial at 36, 44 ff.
[100] *Ibid.* at 85 f.

related to the contested plots it was null and void *ab initio,* in spite of its being signed by the High Contracting Parties:

> C'est en effêt un principe reconnu en droit international, aussi bien que par le droit des nations civilisées, que l'erreur constitue un vice du consentement et lui enlève sa force obligatoire, tout comme le dol ou la contrainte. L'application de ce principe s'impose. L'erreur porte sur la substance même de l'engagement en ce qui concerne les parcelles litigieuses.[101]

The Netherlands requested, alternatively, that the Court nullify the clause in the "Descriptive Minute."

Thirdly, The Netherlands relied on the events which followed the 1843 Boundary Convention: it continued to collect from the owners the land tax on the contested plots, and transfers of land were registered in the Netherlands registers of land transfer deeds. From this The Netherlands argued:

> An undisputed, stable and permanent situation is capable of creating law. In particular, an exclusive and valid title of sovereignty may be the result if typical acts of sovereignty were performed without opposition and over a period of time on a certain territory. In international relations the State which provides an effective government for a territory should be preferred to a State whose jurisdiction rests on legal titles which it does not assert.[102]

On these grounds The Netherlands claimed that its sovereignty should be recognized even if the "Descriptive Minute" should be accepted as giving a title of sovereignty to Belgium.

The Court rejected all Netherlands contentions. As to the work of the Mixed Boundary Commission, the Court was satisfied that unquestionably, under both the 1839 and the 1842 treaties, the Commission had authority to delineate the boundary, and that it

> did not confine itself to a mere reference to Article 14 of the Treaty of 5 November 1842 and to the *status quo* whatever it was. From the record of its proceedings as disclosed in the minutes, it appears that the Commission went much further and proceeded to delimit the boundaries between the two States in respect of the two Baarles in the only way which was open to it.[103]

The Commission reversed an earlier minute which attributed the plots to The Netherlands, and adopted the text which attributed the plots to Belgium. Furthermore, the Commission ordered detailed survey maps; these maps show the disputed plots as belonging to Belgium, they became part of the Boundary Convention and have in virtue of

[101] *Ibid.* at 88. "It is indeed accepted as a principle of international law as well as of the law of civilized nations, that an error vitiates the consent, and, just like fraud or duress, deprives it of binding force. The error affects the very essence of the obligation so far as it relates to the contested plots." (Translation of author.)

[102] *Ibid.* at 89.

[103] [1959] I.C.J. Rep. at 220.

Article 3 the same legal force as the Convention itself.[104] The Convention represents the final and common intention of the two states.

Having concluded that the 1843 Boundary Convention made a definite allocation of the disputed plots, the Court then examined the Netherlands thesis that the Convention was vitiated by error. The Court was not satisfied with the hypothesis offered by The Netherlands with respect to the origin of the error in transcription, which it found was neither plausible nor substantiated by proof.[105] Regarding the Netherlands contention that, regardless of its origin, the mistake was apparent between the copy of the "Communal Minute" produced by it and the text appearing in the "Descriptive Minute," the Court said:

> The matter is not, however, capable of being disposed of on this narrow ground. The Court must ascertain the intention of the Parties from the provisions of a treaty in the light of all the circumstances.[106]

The Court was satisfied that no error or mistake had occurred in the process of the transcription. But what was transcribed was not the copy of the "Communal Minute" produced by The Netherlands before the Court; rather it was the copy "then in the possession of the Netherlands Commission." It was this copy which, in the view of the Boundary Commission, represented the *status quo* in relation to the disputed plots; it attributed sovereignty over them to Belgium, and was incorporated in the Boundary Convention.[107] The Court, reviewing the protracted labors of the Boundary Commission, noted the notoriety of its decisions on both the communal and state level, the signature, ratification and publication of the Boundary Convention, and concluded:

> . . . For almost a century the Netherlands made no challenge to the attribution of the disputed plots to Belgium.
>
> The Court is satisfied that no case of mistake has been made out and that the validity and binding force of the provisions of the Convention of 1843 in respect of the disputed plots are not affected on that account.[108]

Turning to the Netherlands claim to sovereignty "in derogation of the title established by treaty," the Court examined first whether Belgium ever relinquished its sovereignty. The Court found no such evidence. On the contrary, when it was discovered by a Belgian inspector of survey, who visited Baarle-Nassau some time after 1906, that the disputed plots were entered in the Netherlands survey, official inquiries were made which, after an interruption through World War I, led the Belgian Ministry of Foreign Affairs in 1921 to draw the attention of the Netherlands Government to the inclusion of the

[104] *Ibid.*
[105] *Ibid.* at 224 and 226.
[106] *Ibid.* at 225.
[107] *Ibid.* at 226.
[108] *Ibid.* at 227.

plots in the Netherlands survey. It was in reply to this that The Netherlands for the first time, on October 6, 1922, claimed that the "Communal Minute" had been inaccurately transcribed. That exchange marked the origin of the dispute.[109] Reviewing the various acts cited in support of its claim to sovereignty by The Netherlands, the Court observed:

> The weight to be attached to the acts relied upon by the Netherlands must be determined against the background of the complex system of intermingled enclaves which existed. The difficulties confronting Belgium in detecting encroachments upon, and in exercising, its sovereignty over these two plots, surrounded as they were by Netherlands territory, are manifest. The acts relied upon are largely of a routine and administrative character performed by local officials and a consequence of the inclusion by the Netherlands of the disputed plots in its Survey, contrary to the Boundary Convention. They are insufficient to displace Belgian sovereignty established by that Convention.[110]

The Court also considered the 1889–1892 negotiations between the two countries to achieve a regular boundary, which culminated in a convention signed in 1892 but not ratified. According to this convention, Belgium was to cede the disputed plots to The Netherlands. Without attaching any legal significance to the unratified convention, the Court noted that "The Netherlands did not in 1892, or at any time thereafter until the dispute arose between the two States in 1922, repudiate the Belgian assertion of sovereignty." Taking all these factors into account, the Court concluded "that Belgian sovereignty established in 1843 over the disputed plots has not been extinguished."[111]

In substance the Court's Judgment will not affect the situation which, as Professor Verzijl points out, forced "a married couple to continue to share their conjugal couch, traversed by an international frontier,"[112] a fact which, it is to be hoped, will interfere with the population growth of the Baarles no more in the future than it did in the past. From the juridical point of view, it is submitted, the Judgment illuminates the question of the impact of error or mistake on the validity of a treaty and even more decisively the controversial question of adverse prescription or, to use the words of the Court, of the acquisition of sovereignty "in derogation of title established by treaty." The Court, though not the dissenting judges, was reluctant to accept anything short of conclusive proof of error. Such proof was lacking, and the Court would not upset a treaty on the basis of an hypothesis. If the negotiators at both the local and state level, who were so close to the problems with which they had to wrestle for several years, had not found fault with the instruments recording their work, it was not for the Court to do so a hundred years later on the basis of a reconstruction which, no matter how ingenious, was not fully conclusive.[113] Nothing less would or should be allowed to interfere with the validity of a treaty duly signed, approved by parliaments, ratified, and published and applied

[109] *Ibid.* at 228.
[110] *Ibid.* at 229.
[111] *Ibid.* at 230.
[112] *Loc. cit.* at 11.
[113] It may be relevant to recall that, according to the Judgment, the error, if there was one, occurred not on the part of the Commission but on the part of the Netherlands Commissioner. [1959] I.C.J. Rep. at 225 and 226.

over a long period of years. For a similar reason the Court declined to upset the Boundary Convention on the ground that the Commission had exceeded its powers, as, according to Judge Lauterpacht, it should have done.[114] The Court laid greater stress on the broad powers conferred upon the Commission than on the specific directive to maintain the *status quo,* a seemingly precise term to describe a very imprecise situation. Again, to upset a treaty, more conclusive proof of excess of power would be required.

For the dissenting judges the "Communal Minute" was, if not conclusive, then sufficient proof of the *status quo.* The authenticity of the copy produced by The Netherlands before the Court was undisputed and this, coupled with the failure of Belgium to produce its copy, a fact to which Judge Armand-Ugon attached great significance,[115] might have been sufficient in an ordinary court of law in a litigation between private parties to tip the scale in favor of the party producing the document. But the Court is not bound by ordinary rules of evidence and has the widest authority and discretion in admitting and considering evidence in a litigation between sovereign states. What the Court appears to have accepted as proven—its own reconstruction makes this clear—is the fact that the two copies, the Netherlands and the Belgian copies, were available to the Commission when it formulated its decision laid down in the Descriptive Minute and accepted by The Netherlands and Belgium in the Boundary Convention.[116]

In considering the Netherlands claim to sovereignty over the disputed plots, it is noteworthy that the Court made it clear at the outset that it would weigh the acts of sovereignty performed by The Netherlands against the Belgian title established by treaty. This was the decisive point. The dissent of Judge Lauterpacht makes this plain, for in his opinion, "there is no room here for applying the exacting rules of prescription in relation to a title acquired by a clear and unequivocal treaty; there is no such treaty."[117] But the Court assumed that there was such a treaty and it did apply exacting rules. This it did by qualifying the Netherlands acts as "of a routine and administrative character," by stressing the difficulties confronting Belgium in detecting such acts, and making the most of the unratified treaty of 1892 and the failure of The Netherlands to repudiate the Belgian assertion of sovereignty. The Court did not deviate from the rule established in the *Eastern Greenland* case that, in evaluating the character and quantum of acts of sovereignty, the nature of the territory is to be taken into account. What characterized the nature of the territory in this case was that it was intermingled with undisputably Netherlands territory. It was this character also which explains why the Court did not attach significance

[114] [1959] I.C.J. Rep. at 231.

[115] "The non-possession of this document," he stated, "invoked by the Belgian Government, cannot create for that Government a more favourable situation. It has neither explained nor proved when and how this disappearance occurred; neither accident nor *force majeure* has been put forward by way of explanation. It is a mere assertion on its part, made in 1955." *Ibid.* at 235.

[116] Said the Court: "The Commission was not a mere copyist. Its duty was to ascertain what the *status quo* was. It had authority to fix the limits between the two States, which duty it discharged . . . it was aware of the discrepancy between the two copies of the Communal Minute . . . the Commission, by enquiries on the spot and by recourse to records and surveys of both communes, must have reached its own conclusion and determined, as was its duty, what the *status quo* was in relation to the disputed plots." *Ibid.* at 226.

[117] *Ibid.* at 231.

to the absence of protest on the part of Belgium against the acts performed by The Netherlands.[118]

Judge Armand-Ugon expressed the view that "sovereignty over the Minquiers and Ecrehos was decided by this Court exclusively on the basis of facts similar to those relied upon by the Netherlands Government in the present case."[119] This statement, it is respectfully submitted, overlooks an essential difference. In the cited case the Court was weighing acts of sovereignty performed by the United Kingdom against acts of a similar kind performed by France. Here it was weighing the acts performed by The Netherlands against a title established by treaty. Herein lies the essential difference between the two cases. This was perceived by Judge Lauterpacht who, as noted above, urged upon the Court the view that there was no occasion to apply exacting standards "in the absence of clear provisions of a treaty."[120] The Court was of the contrary opinion and, moreover, it could find no evidence that "Belgium ever relinquished its sovereignty over the disputed plots." [121] It is significant that, before even looking at the Netherlands claim, the Court desired to assure itself that there was no abandonment of sovereignty on the part of Belgium. Had the Court found evidence of it, it would have applied different standards to the acts of The Netherlands, for then it would have been considering a different situation.

To be sure, the Judgment of the Court perpetuates "a geographic anomaly,"[122] but in so doing, the Court felt bound to give effect to the common intention of the parties as expressed in the Boundary Convention. It is not for the Court to revise treaties, even though there may be appealing reasons of a practical character to do so. Having set at rest authoritatively the legal controversy, the Court cleared the path for the governments to revise the treaty.

## COMPULSORY JURISDICTION OF THE COURT

The development of the compulsory jurisdiction of the Court pursuant to Article 36, paragraph 2, of its Statute continues in the doldrums. Between 1955, when the "package deal" opened the door to many states, and 1959, the year here under review, twenty-three states were admitted to membership of the United Nations, namely: Albania, Austria, Bulgaria, Cambodia, Ceylon, Federation of Malaya, Finland, Ghana, Guinea, Hungary, Ireland, Italy, Japan, Jordan, Laos, Libya, Morocco, Nepal, Portugal, Rumania, Spain, The Sudan, and Tunisia. Of these, only five have accepted the compulsory jurisdiction of the Court, namely: Cambodia, Finland, Japan, Portugal, and The Sudan.

During the year under review no state accepted the compulsory jurisdiction of the Court. Two states, France and India submitted new Declarations dated, respectively, July

[118] Judge Armand-Ugon in his dissenting opinion would have attached weight to this fact. *Ibid.* at 250.
[119] *Ibid.* He referred to [1953] I.C.J. Rep. 67–70.
[120] *Ibid.* at 232.
[121] *Ibid.* at 227.
[122] Judge Lauterpacht, *ibid.* at 232.

10, 1959, and September 14, 1959, replacing their old Declarations. A welcome feature of the new Declarations is the elimination of the Connally Amendment type of reservation. Both states reverted to the classic type of reservation of domestic jurisdiction, with this difference: whereas France, following the League of Nations Covenant formula, exempts "disputes relating to questions which by international law fall exclusively within the domestic jurisdiction," India adopted the United Nations Charter formula in exempting "disputes in regard to matters which are essentially within the jurisdiction of the Republic of India."[123] The text of these two Declarations is as follows:

France:[124] 10 VII 59[125]

On behalf of the Government of the French Republic, I accept as compulsory *ipso facto* and without special agreement, in relation to other Members of the United Nations which accept the same obligation, that is to say, on condition of reciprocity, the jurisdiction of the Court, in conformity with Article 36, paragraph 2, of the Statute, for a period of three years and thereafter until such time as notice may be given of the termination of this acceptance, in all disputes which may arise in respect of facts or situations subsequent to this declaration, with the exception of:

(1) disputes with regard to which the Parties may have agreed or may agree to have recourse to another method of peaceful settlement;

(2) disputes relating to questions which by international law fall exclusively within the domestic jurisdiction;

(3) disputes arising out of any war or international hostilities and disputes arising out of a crisis affecting the national security or out of any measure or action relating thereto;

(4) disputes with any State which, at the date of occurrence of the facts or situations giving rise to the dispute, has not accepted the compulsory jurisdiction of the International Court of Justice for a period at least equal to that specified in this declaration.

Paris, 10 July 1959.

India:[126] 14 IX 59.[127]

I have the honour, by direction of the President of India, to declare on behalf of the Government of the Republic of India that they accept, in conformity with paragraph 2 of Article 36 of the Statute of the Court, until such time as notice may be given to terminate such acceptance, as compulsory *ipso facto* and without special agreement, and on the basis and condition of reciprocity, the jurisdiction of the International Court of Justice over all

[123] [1959–1960] I.C.J. Yearbook 240, 242.

[124] *Ibid.* at 240. This declaration replaced that dated Feb. 18, 1947, notice of the termination of which was received by the Secretary General of the United Nations on July 10, 1959. For the text of the earlier declaration, see [1957–1958] Yearbook 199.

[125] This is the date of the deposit of the declaration.

[126] *Ibid.* at 241–242. For the text of an earlier declaration by India, terminated by a notice of Feb. 8, 1957, see [1955–1956] Yearbook 186.

[127] This is the date of the deposit of the declaration.

disputes arising after 26 January 1950 with regard to situations or facts subsequent to that date, other than:

(1) Disputes, in regard to which the Parties to the dispute have agreed or shall agree to have recourse to some other method or methods of settlement.

(2) Disputes with the Government of any State which, on the date of this Declaration, is a Member of the Commonwealth of Nations.

(3) Disputes in regard to matters which are essentially within the jurisdiction of the Republic of India.

(4) Disputes concerning any question relating to or arising out of belligerent or military occupation or the discharge of any functions pursuant to any recommendation or decision of an organ of the United Nations, in accordance with which the Government of India have accepted obligations.

(5) Disputes in respect of which any other party to a dispute has accepted the compulsory jurisdiction of the International Court of Justice exclusively for or in relation to the purposes of such dispute; or where the acceptance of the Court's compulsory jurisdiction on behalf of a party to the dispute was deposited or ratified less than twelve months prior to the filing of the application bringing the dispute before the Court.

(6) Disputes with the Government of any State with which, on the date of an application to bring a dispute before the Court, the Government of India has no diplomatic relations.

New York, 14 September 1959.

# LIMITATIONS UPON THE JUDICIAL FUNCTION

## I. INTRODUCTION

The case of the *Cameroons* v. *The United Kingdom* concerning the Northern Cameroons, described, in a typical understatement, as "almost unique in the annals of international litigation,"[1] has been terminated by a judgment of the International Court of Justice which appears as well to be "almost unique." In fact, neither the Court nor any of the separate opinions referred to any precedent.

What makes the case unusual is that the Cameroons' application of May 30, 1961, requested the Court to adjudicate upon certain violations alleged to have been committed by the United Kingdom as Administering Authority for the Cameroons under a Trusteeship Agreement which expired on June 1, 1961, but failed to formulate any specific claim for reparation. What makes the judgment unusual is that the Court declined to adjudicate upon the merits and, additionally, that it did so at that stage of the proceedings devoted to preliminary objections raised by the United Kingdom, without finding it necessary "to pass expressly upon the several submissions of the Respondent, in the form in which they have been cast."[2] This statement is itself rather unusual, since the Court considered two of these submissions and found them to be without substance; moreover, in the operative clause of the judgment the Court almost textually incorporated another of these submissions.

[1] Case concerning the Northern Cameroons (Cameroon *v.* United Kingdom Preliminary Objections. Judgment of Dec. 2, 1963, [1963] I.C.J. Rep. 15. Separate opinion of Judge Sir Gerald Fitzmaurice at 98. For a digest of the judgment see 58 A.J.I.L. 488 (1964).

[2] *Ibid.* at 38.

## II. THE JUDGMENT

The history of the complaint submitted by the Republic of Cameroon is without relevance here. Suffice it to underscore the fact that, following a plebiscite held on February 11 and 12, 1961, in the Northern Cameroons at that time administered by the United Kingdom as part of the Northern Region of Nigeria, the General Assembly of the United Nations, by Resolution 1608(XV) adopted on April 21, 1961, endorsed its results and decided that the United Kingdom Administration should be terminated on June 1, 1961, upon the joining of the Federation of Nigeria as a separate province. This fact was admitted by both parties.[3] After Cameroon attained independence on January 11, 1960, and was admitted to membership of the United Nations on September 20, 1960, it objected to certain features of the United Kingdom administration both in notes addressed to the United Kingdom and in the forums of the United Nations. It may be assumed that Cameroon was of the opinion that, had the Trust Territory been administered differently and had the United Kingdom heeded General Assembly Resolution 1473 (XIV) adopted on December 12, 1959, recommending the separation of the administration of the Northern Cameroons from that of Nigeria, the result of the plebiscite might or would have been different, that is, it would have been in favor of joining the Cameroon.

An attempt by Cameroon to bring its complaints before the Court by means of a special agreement failed, as the United Kingdom felt itself unable to accede to Cameroon's request. Thereupon Cameroon brought proceedings before the Court by application dated May 30, 1961, basing itself on Article 19 of the then still valid Trusteeship Agreement.[4] The United Kingdom raised preliminary objections on August 14, 1962, and under Article 62 of the Rules of Procedure, the Court suspended proceedings upon the merits by order of September 3, 1962. As finally formulated at the hearing on October 1, 1963, the United Kingdom objections were as follows:

> 1. That there has not at any time been a dispute as alleged in the Application in this case;
> 2. That there has not been or was not on May 30, 1961, as alleged in the Application, a dispute falling within Article 19 of the Trusteeship Agreement for the Territory of the Cameroons under United Kingdom Administration;
> 3. That, in any event, there is no dispute before the Court upon which the Court is entitled to adjudicate.[5]

In addition, the preliminary objections included the point that the application was inadmissible because it did not conform to Article 40, paragraph 1, of the Statute and Article 32, paragraph 2, of the Rules of the Court. This position was not pressed during the oral hearings[6] and was not included in the final submissions of the United Kingdom.

[3] *Ibid.* at 24.

[4] The text of Art. 19 is as follows: "If any dispute whatever should arise between the Administering Authority and another Member of the United Nations relating to the interpretation or application of the provisions of this Agreement, such dispute, if it cannot be settled by negotiation or other means, shall be submitted to the International Court of Justice, provided for in Chapter XIV of the United Nations Charter."

[5] [1963] I.C.J. Rep. at 20.

[6] Dissenting opinion of Judge Bustamante, *ibid.* at 173, and separate opinion of Judge Wellington Koo, *ibid.* at 42–43.

Nevertheless, the Court, acting presumably *proprio motu*,[7] took up the point and said that in its view:

> the Applicant has sufficiently complied with the provisions of Article 32(2) of the Rules and the preliminary objection based upon noncompliance therewith is accordingly without substance.[8]

The Court found it convenient to take up only the first of the United Kingdom final objections. In one short paragraph it determined that the facts of the case and the opposing views of the parties as to the interpretation and application of the Trusteeship Agreement, expressed both in the forums of the United Nations and in direct communications between the two governments,

> reveal the existence of a dispute in the sense recognized by the jurisprudence of the Court and of its predecessor, between the Republic of Cameroon and the United Kingdom at the date of the Application.[9]

A reference to the jurisprudence of the Court and its predecessor would have been useful. The Court quite recently dealt with a similar point in the *South West Africa* cases.[10]

Normally, after the disposing of the preliminary objections to its jurisdiction found relevant by the Court, the interlocutory phase of the proceedings would have come to an end. This, however, is an unusual case and, without disposing explicitly of all the objections, the Court proceeded to discuss the propriety of exercising any jurisdiction at all. By way of introducing this part of its reasoning, the Court found that it had been properly seised of the Cameroon application but that, even though it may in consequence have jurisdiction, it was not bound to exercise it, for

> There are inherent limitations on the exercise of the judicial function which the Court, as a court of justice, can never ignore. There may thus be an incompatibility between the desires of an applicant, or, indeed, of both parties to a case, on the one hand, and on the other hand, the duty of the Court to maintain its judicial character. The Court itself, and not the parties, must be the guardian of the Court's judicial integrity.[11]

It may be noted in passing that the adjective "inherent" harks back to an earlier phase in the development of international law and tends to foreclose rather than open up the path to a fruitful analysis of the limitations upon the judicial function. Whatever one may think of the use of this term in the Charter of the United Nations, Article 38 of the

[7] With reference to the examination of jurisdictional questions *proprio motu*, see Lauterpacht, The Development of International Law by the International Court 347 (1958), and Rosenne, The International Court of Justice 359 (1957).

[8] [1953] I.C.J. Rep. at 28.

[9] *Ibid.* at 27.

[10] Judgment of Dec. 21, 1962, [1962] I.C.J. Rep. 319, at 342–344; digested in 57 A.J.I.L. 640 (1963).

[11] [1963] I.C.J. Rep. at 29.

Court's Statute is explicit that this function is to be exercised in accordance with international law.

After referring to some considerations which would lead it to decline to give judgment, and noting that in previous cases such matters had been raised *proprio motu,*[12] the Court proceeded to examine what Cameroon asked it to do and at some length what Cameroon had not asked the Court to do. Cameroon had requested the Court on the merits to

> adjudge and declare that the United Kingdom has, in the interpretation and application of the Trusteeship Agreement for the Territory of the Cameroons under British Administration, failed to respect certain obligations directly or indirectly flowing from the said Agreement, and in particular from Articles 3, 5, 6 and 7 thereof.[13]

The matters with respect to which Cameroon desired no adjudication are many: it did not ask the Court "to redress the alleged injustice"; it did not ask "to restore to the Republic of Cameroon peoples or territories claimed to have been lost"; it did not ask for an award of "reparation of any kind"; it did not ask the Court, with respect to General Assembly Resolution 1608(XV) "to revise or to reverse those conclusions of the General Assembly or those decisions as such";[14] it did not ask the Court "to criticize the United Nations" or to declare that it "was wrong in terminating the Trusteeship" or "to pronounce the annulment of resolution 1608"; it did not ask the Court "to find any casual connection between the alleged maladministration and the result of the vote favouring union with the Federation of Nigeria." "As a result" of all the things Cameroon did not ask for, said the Court, "the Court is relegated to an issue remote from reality."[15] Consequently, a judgment in favor of Cameroon would not revive the Trusteeship Agreement; it would not invalidate the union with the Northern Region of Nigeria; it would not cause the former Northern Cameroons to be joined to Cameroon; the United Kingdom would have no authority to give satisfaction to "the underlying desires of the Republic of Cameroon"; and it would not be binding on either the United Nations or Nigeria. The Court concluded this listing of negatives, stating:

> The function of the Court is to state the law, but it may pronounce judgment only in connection with concrete cases where there exists *at the time of the adjudication* an actual controversy involving a conflict of legal interests between the parties. The Court's judgment must have some practical consequence in the sense that it can affect existing legal rights or obligations of the parties, thus removing uncertainty from their legal relations. No judgment on the merits in this case could satisfy these essentials of the judicial function.[16]

[12] *Ibid.* at 29–30. On this matter see also Hudson, The Permanent Court of International Justice 1920–42, p. 588, and Rosenne, *op. cit.* 360.

[13] [1963] I.C.J. Rep. at 20 and 26.

[14] *Ibid.* at 32.

[15] *Ibid.* at 33.

[16] *Ibid.* at 33–34. Italics supplied.

This is on its face an important statement on the Court's judicial function and its limitations, but in substance it concerns the type or nature of disputes on which the Court may adjudicate. Seen in this perspective it is a significant factor in the understanding of Article 36(1) of the Statute and inevitably also of the jurisdictional clause in the Trusteeship Agreement. However, it will be recalled that, insofar as the latter is concerned, the Court had already dealt with this point in connection with the first United Kingdom preliminary objection. In that context it considered the dispute well within its jurisdiction by virtue of that clause as well as presumably of Article 36(1), to which jurisdictional clauses must be deemed to be subordinated. The Court perhaps had this relationship in mind when, after referring to the arguments of both parties relating to the Court's judgment in the *South West Africa* cases and the applicability *vel non* of its conclusions with respect to Article 7 of the Mandate for South West Africa to the interpretation of Article 19 of the Trusteeship Agreement for the Cameroons, it declined to pronounce an opinion on the ground that such an opinion

> can have only an academic interest since that Trusteeship is no longer in existence, and no determination reached by the Court could be given effect by the former Administering Authority.[17]

Apart from the fact that Cameroon did not ask and did not expect the Court to hand down a judgment which could be given effect by the United Kingdom in the defunct Trust Territory, it is clear that, by a subtle application of the *rebus sic stantibus* doctrine, the Court substituted in the two statements just quoted one critical date for another: whereas, earlier in its reasoning in dealing with the first United Kingdom preliminary objection, it considered the dispute to be within the range of its adjudicative function, the critical date being the date of the application, it now considered as the critical date the date of its judgment. The Court made this quite clear, speaking as follows:

> The Court must discharge the duty to which it has already called attention—the duty to safeguard the judicial function. Whether or not at the moment the Application was filed there was jurisdiction in the Court to adjudicate upon the dispute submitted to it, circumstances that have since arisen render any adjudication devoid of purpose. Under these conditions, for the Court to proceed any further in the case would not, in its opinion, be a proper discharge of its duties.
>
> The answer to the question whether the judicial function is engaged may, in certain cases where the issue is raised, need to wait upon an examination of the merits. In the present case, however, it is already evident that it cannot be engaged. No purpose accordingly would be served by undertaking an examination of the merits of the case for the purpose of reaching a decision which, in the light of the circumstances to which the Court has already called attention, ineluctably must be made.[18]

[17] *Ibid.* at 35.
[18] *Ibid.* at 38.

The Court accordingly, after stressing once more that any judgment which it might pronounce "would be without object," by ten votes to five "finds that it cannot adjudicate upon the merits of the claim of the Federal Republic of Cameroon."[19]

## III. ON DECLARATORY JUDGMENTS

In the course of its reasoning the Court made some significant observations on the nature and object of declaratory judgments which, though they also illustrate the Court's conception of propriety and limitation of the judicial function, may more conveniently be treated separately. The Court devoted an unusual degree of attention to the things Cameroon did not seek, before it finally came to state that all Cameroon ever wanted was a declaratory judgment with respect to the claim formulated in its application while the Trusteeship was still alive.

There is no doubt that the Court may make declaratory judgments.[20] The only question was whether in the circumstances of the instant case the Court would regard it as proper to do so. The Court decided that it would be inconsistent with its judicial function, on the ground that

> if in a declaratory judgment it expounds a rule of customary international law or interprets a treaty which remains in force, its judgment has a continuing applicability. But in this case there is a dispute about the interpretation and application of a treaty—the Trusteeship Agreement—which has now been terminated, is no longer in force, and there can be no opportunity for a future act of interpretation or application of that treaty in accordance with any judgment the Court might render.[21]

The Court, rebutting arguments advanced by counsel, said that he "seeks to minimize the forward reach of a judgment of the Court." The Court also rejected the plea that, following its judgment in the *Haya de la Torre* case,[22] it should not concern itself "with the aftermath of its judgment," saying:

> But there is a difference between the Court's considering the manner of compliance with its judgment, or the likelihood of compliance, and, on the other hand, considering whether the judgment, if rendered, would be susceptible of any compliance or execution whatever, at any time in the future.[23]

[19] *Ibid.* The dissenting judges were: Spiropoulos, Koretsky, Badawi, Bustamante y Rivero, and Beb a Don *(ad hoc).*

[20] *Ibid.* at 37. See also Hudson, *op. cit.* at 588; Rosenne, *op. cit.* at 82–83; De Visscher, Théories et Réalités en Droit International Public 361 (1960); 1 Schwarzenberger, International Law 654 (3d ed., 1957); Witenberg, L'Organisation Judiciaire, la Procédure et la Sentence Internationales 321–322 (1937); 2 Guggenheim, Traité de Droit Internationale Public 103 (1954).

[21] [1963] I.C.J. Rep. 37. The Court quoted at this point the following statement from Judgment No. 11 (Interpretation of Judgments Nos. 7 and 8, The Chorzów Factory) given by the Permanent Court of International Justice on Dec. 10, 1927, which is the *sedes materiae* for declaratory judgments: "The Court's Judgment No. 7 is in the nature of a declaratory judgment, the intention of which is to ensure recognition of a situation at law, once and for all and with binding force as between the Parties; so that the legal position thus established cannot again be called in question insofar as the legal effects ensuing therefrom are concerned." P.C.I.J., Series A, No. 13, p. 20.

[22] [1951] I.C.J. Rep. 78–79, quoted in this judgment at p. 30.

[23] [1963] I.C.J. Rep. 37.

Agreeing with the applicant's contention that "the use which the successful party makes of the judgment is a matter which lies on the political and not on the judicial plane," the Court nevertheless declared, here again elucidating another aspect of the judicial function and its limitation:

> But it is not the function of a court merely to provide a basis for political action if no question of actual legal rights is involved. Whenever the Court adjudicates on the merits of a dispute, one or the other party, or both parties, as a factual matter, are in a position to take some retroactive[24] or prospective action or avoidance of action, which would constitute a compliance with the Court's judgment or a defiance thereof. That is not the situation here.[25]

There is no doubt that a distinction between declaratory and executory judgments exists, although this distinction is not consistently maintained by the Court when it speaks of "likelihood of compliance," "any compliance," and "execution" in the future. The effect of a declaratory judgment may well be to provide the basis for political action, that is, the termination or a revision of the treaty in question or the negotiation of some settlement acceptable to the parties. It may be that, having clarified the legal situation, no action is called for by either party. That would have been so in the instant case as it was in other cases decided by this Court, if, for instance, the judgment had rejected the claim of the applicant state.

In the individual opinions, the concept and application of declaratory judgments both in domestic and international forums was discussed at some length and the views expressed therein deserve close study.[26] No attempt will be made here to analyze these opinions. One instance of a declaratory judgment, mentioned more often than others, on which the applicant placed much reliance, may be briefly referred to here. This is that part of the *Corfu Channel* case which related to the "Operation Retail." The question put to the Court was as follows:

> Has the United Kingdom under international law violated the sovereignty of the Albanian People's Republic by reason of the acts of the Royal Navy in Albanian waters on the 22nd October and on the 12th and 13th November 1946 and is there any duty to give satisfaction?

The Court held with reference to the acts performed on November 12 and 13, 1946, that

> the United Kingdom violated the sovereignty of the People's Republic of Albania, and that this declaration by the Court constitutes in itself appropriate satisfaction.[27]

[24] The French translation, "mesures visant le passé," is perhaps a clearer expression of the Court's meaning.

[25] *Ibid.* at 37–38.

[26] See separate opinion of Judge Wellington Koo, *ibid.* at 61–64; separate opinion of Judge Morelli, *ibid.* at 132, 140–141; dissenting opinion of Judge Badawi, *ibid.* at 150–153; dissenting opinion of Judge Bustamante, *ibid.* at 170–172, 182–183; and dissenting opinion of Judge *ad hoc* Beb a Don, at 193–196.

[27] [1949] I.C.J. Rep. 4 at 26, 36.

The full significance of this holding and its bearing upon the instant case become clear when it is read in the context of the Court's reasoning:

> This declaration is in accordance with the request made by Albania through her Counsel, and is in itself appropriate satisfaction.[28]

Did Counsel for Cameroon ask for more?

This judgment, which has been considered as "an example of a purely declaratory judgment, not executory,"[29] has, in the opinion of Judge *ad hoc* Beb a Don, all the characteristics of a declaratory judgment:

> the Court confined itself to stating legal truth, to finding a breach of the law; there was no claim for material reparation; there was no practical application.[30]

In the opinions of several dissenting judges, the *Corfu Channel* case was a case in point and should have been followed in the instant case.[31] Judge Morelli in his separate opinion agreed in substance with their view and hypothesized as follows:

> . . . the question arises as to what would have happened if Albania had from the beginning adopted in the matter of reparation an attitude corresponding to that which was subsequently to be taken by the Court, and had refrained from asking for any satisfaction other than that constituted by the declaration of the violation itself. It would seem difficult to suppose that in such a case the Court would have declined to do what it did do, namely declare the violation, on the grounds that in the absence of any claim for reparation there was no dispute to settle.[32]

The Court itself did not find it necessary to deal with the *Corfu Channel* case, but it may not be far-fetched to suggest that the Court had it in mind when, in the passage quoted above, it referred to a declaratory judgment in which "it expounds a rule of customary international law or interprets a treaty which remains in force" and which for that reason "has a continuing applicability."[33] In the instant case the Court was asked to interpret a treaty. To be sure, insofar as that particular treaty is concerned, the judgment would not have had "continuing applicability." However, it may be observed that treaties of a similar kind are still in force, and it cannot be excluded that what the Court might have said about that particular Trusteeship Agreement might have had relevance for other Trusteeship Agreements which are still in force. In that sense, like a judgment on a rule of customary international law, the Court's judgment might have had "continuing applicability." Secondly, even the interpretation of a treaty might well have led the

[28] *Ibid.* at 35.
[29] Rosenne, *op. cit.* at 83, note 3.
[30] [1963] I.C.J. Rep. at 195.
[31] See dissenting opinions of Judges Badawi, *ibid.* at 150–151, Bustamante, *ibid.* at 170 and 180, and Judge *ad hoc* Beb a Don, *ibid.* at 196.
[32] *Ibid.* at 141.
[33] See above, at p. 819.

Court into the realm of customary international law, since every treaty is embedded in that law.[34] And thirdly, in view of the arguments advanced by both parties, the Court might have been led to elucidate the relationship of the judicial function to the political or other function of the General Assembly.[35] If the Court had done so over and beyond its observations on this point in the present judgment, it would no doubt have given a judgment of "continuing applicability."

These considerations are speculative, of course, but so are the Court's. There is also a degree of speculation in Judge Fitzmaurice's distinction between the *Corfu Channel* case and the case at bar. The declaration in the former case,

> though it related to a past and irreversible *event,* was also relevant to *a still continuing situation* in which a repetition of the violation of sovereignty could occur, and it had operative legal effect as a prohibition or interdiction on any such repetition. This was quite a different case from the present one.[36]

It is suggested that a judgment regarding violation of a treaty has as much relevance as a judgment regarding a violation of territorial sovereignty. In both situations the Court would be dealing with fundamental principles of the international legal order: in one case with the principle of territorial integrity and in the other with the principle of *pacta sunt servanda.* In the circumstances of the *Corfu Channel* case, there was little chance of the judgment of the Court having the effect of "interdiction on any such repetition" between the same parties, though undoubtedly it might be wholly relevant in other circumstances involving other states. It is difficult to see why such an effect should *a priori* be denied to a judgment dealing with the interpretation of a treaty, even though the treaty was of a special kind, namely, a Trusteeship Agreement.

It is, according to Professor Guggenheim, a characteristic feature of a declaratory judgment that "it only authorizes the parties to draw themselves the legal consequences flowing from the judgment, unless the injured party succeeds in obtaining another judgment involving performance."[37] This is precisely one of the advantages of declaratory judgments[38] and this is what Cameroon seems to have argued, at least alternatively. At any rate, it is the impression one derives from the Court's judgment,[39] the pleadings being unavailable at this writing. To be sure, this might not have been easy for Cameroon, and further proceedings before this Court or another tribunal would have required, as Judge Fitzmaurice pointed out, the consent of the United Kingdom.[40] How-

[34] Lauterpacht, *op. cit.* at 27: "In fact, it would be a mistake to assume that the function of interpretation of treaties, consisting as it does in ascertaining what was the intention of the parties, is a process divorced from the application and development of customary international law."

[35] See, on this subject, the interesting observations of Judge Bustamante, [1963] I.C.J. Rep. at 176–182.

[36] *Ibid.* at 98, note 2. Italics in the original.

[37] *Op. cit.* at 163. The French text is as follows: "La décision autorise seulement les parties à tirer elles-mêmes les conséquences juridiques découlant du jugement, à moins que la partie lésée n'obtienne un autre jugement comportant cette fois une obligation de prestation."

[38] Guggenheim, *ibid.* at 164.

[39] And from the separate opinion of Judge Fitzmaurice, [1963] I.C.J. Rep. at 107.

[40] *Ibid.*

ever, one wonders how far the Court should or whether it should not concern itself with such matters. Predictions about contingencies are hazardous in the extreme in a state of rapidly changing diplomatic and political relations. Should the Court have refrained in the *Corfu Channel* from awarding monetary damages to the United Kingdom on the ground that, given the attitude of the respondent and the veto power of the Soviet Union in the Security Council, the likelihood of the judgment being productive was extremely marginal?

## IV. LIMITATIONS UPON THE JUDICIAL FUNCTION

As to the judgment itself, one or two preliminary remarks may be in order. First, the operative part of the judgment declining to adjudicate upon Cameroon's claim, cannot be regarded as being in the nature of a *non liquet;* it is a *non possumus* rather than a *non liquet.* [41] The Court declined to give judgment, not on the ground of a gap in or an insufficiency of the law, which is the classic view of *non liquet,* [42] but on other grounds. Secondly, the Court did not invoke "inherent" limitations upon its judicial function on the ground that Cameroon had merely used the form of a contentious procedure in order to obtain in fact only an advisory opinion. This intention seems indeed to have been attributed by the respondent to the applicant.[43] Had the Court been persuaded that such was the case, it would have been justified in declining to adjudicate.[44] Thirdly, this case cannot be subsumed under any of the earlier precedents in which the Court declined to adjudicate on the ground that it would not be drawn into making recommendations, as in the *Free Zones* case, or making choices between alternative courses of action, as in the *Haya de la Torre* case.[45] Fourthly, it does not seem to be a case—but this proposition is advanced with all necessary reservation, as the pleadings are unavailable at this writing—where the parties have made it impossible for the Court to settle the matter. The attitude of the parties and defects in the pleadings may make it impossible for the Court to settle all aspects of a dispute brought before it,[46] but this does not appear to have been so in the instant case. The Court did not decline to adjudicate on this or that aspect of the Cameroon claim; it declined to adjudicate on any of its aspects. And fifthly, the Court did not encounter the situation which it faced in the *Monetary Gold* case, when a state directly involved, *i.e.,* Albania, neither participated in the proceedings nor consented to them. In the case at bar, Nigeria did not participate in the proceedings, but the Court did not decline to adjudicate on that ground. It may well be, as has been suggested, that absence of a

[41] See Schwarzenberger, *op. cit.* at 270.

[42] For recent restatements of the doctrine, see Lauterpacht, "Some Observations on the Problem of 'Non-Liquet' and the Completeness of International Law," in Symbolae Verzijl 196–222 (1958); and Stone, "Non Liquet and the Function of Law in the International Community," 35 British Year Book of International Law 124–161 (1959).

[43] See dissenting opinion of Judge Bustamante, [1963] I.C.J. Rep. at 170.

[44] Lauterpacht, The Development of International Law by the International Court 146 (1958). But see Rosenne, *op. cit.* at 82.

[45] De Visscher, Théories et Réalités en Droit International Public (1960); Rosenne, *op. cit.* at 269-271.

[46] See Rosenne, *op. cit.* at 63–64.

state directly involved raises a question of propriety,[47] but in the *Monetary Gold* case the Court dealt with the absence of Albania as a question of jurisdiction and not as a question of propriety.[48]

From the procedural point of view it must be observed that when a question of propriety arises, involving the function of the Court as a court of law, this question has priority over all preliminary objections to the jurisdiction or to the admissibility of the claim. Questions of propriety "are of a wholly antecedent or, as it were, 'pre-preliminary' character."[49] They are independent of objections to jurisdiction submitted by the respondent, they can and have been raised *proprio motu,* and even if the Court were competent to go into the merits of the case, the Court will not do so if it considers that it ought not to do so. As Judge Fitzmaurice interpreted the judgment of the Court,

> The Court has not, I think, pronounced the claim to be formally inadmissible, but it has in effect (to make use of the French term *recevabilité*) treated it as non-receivable or unexaminable because of the consequences (i.e. strictly the lack of any) which would ensue if it was acceded to.[50]

The Court indeed did not find it necessary to go into the question of admissibility,[51] and stated that, for the reasons developed in the judgment, it has "not felt called upon to pass expressly upon the several submissions of the Respondent in the form in which they have been cast."[52] It found, nevertheless,

> that the proper limits of its judicial function do not permit it to entertain the claims submitted to it in the Application of which it has been seised, with a view to a decision having the authority of *res judicata* between the Republic of Cameroon and the United Kingdom. Any judgment which the Court might pronounce would be without object.[53]

The basis of the Court's judgment was not an affirmation of jurisdiction which would have required an express ruling by the Court, although the Court did express an opinion on two of the respondent's objections. It was an exercise of incidental jurisdiction.

It is well established that it is the duty and function of the Court, as Articles 36, paragraph 1, and 38, paragraph 1, provide, to decide in accordance with international law such disputes as are submitted to it, whereas in the matter of advisory opinions the Court, by virtue of Article 65, has the discretion whether or not to give an opinion on

[47] See Rosenne, *op. cit.* at 65.
[48] See Lauterpacht, The Development of International Law by the International Court at 342 (1958). But see separate opinion of Judge Fitzmaurice, [1963] I.C.J. Rep. at 102, note 4.
[49] Separate opinion of Judge Fitzmaurice, *ibid.* at 103.
[50] *Ibid.* at 101.
[51] *Ibid.* at 28.
[52] Judge Koretsky dissented precisely on this ground. In his opinion, the Court should have dealt with the preliminary objections before going into the merits. *Ibid.* at 39–40.
[53] *Ibid.* at 38.

legal questions. It is also well established that, in giving an opinion or in deciding contested cases, the Court is exercising a judicial function. But, as the Court put it,

> That function is circumscribed by inherent limitations which are none the less imperative because they may be difficult to catalogue, and may not frequently present themselves as a conclusive bar to adjudication in a concrete case.[54]

In the instant case the Court took a most significant step toward the delimitation of that function. Before examining it, it may be useful to recall some cases in which members of the Court or its predecessor urged it to decline adjudication. Thus, in his dissenting opinion in the *Memel* case (Preliminary Objection), Judge Rolin-Jaequemyns felt it useful

> to point out that the action of the four Governments is calculated to lead the Court to intervene in a mere divergence of views, without any *legal dispute,* in the proper sense of the term, having as yet arisen therefrom, which would justify the Court in giving a decision in conformity with Articles 13 and 14 of the Covenant of the League of Nations, in accordance with Article 17 of the Convention of 1924 and in accordance with that which is expressly laid down in Article 36 of the Court's Statute.[55]

This caution does not apply to the present case because here the Court was satisfied that a dispute existed. In the phase of the *Memel* case dealing with the merits, Judge Anzilotti dissented from the judgment of the Court, and considered the application inadmissible because

> this application does not embody the essential features of a claim for legal redress and tends to force the Court to deviate from the fundamental rules governing the activities of a judicial body.

It was his view that

> In its judicial capacity, the Court cannot answer questions; it must pass upon claims. . . . The Court could not answer the questions put to it in the application, because by so doing, it would be giving an advisory opinion for which the applicant Powers were not entitled to ask and which the Court was not entitled to give.[56]

Judge Anzilotti's concept of the judicial function was not shared by the majority of the Court. However, the point he made, namely, that the Court should confine itself to deciding claims for legal redress, is one which was made in the *Cameroon* case several times. It may be noted that in replying to the questions put to it in the *Memel* case, the Court showed no concern with the use, if any, to which its replies would be put. In other

[54] *Ibid.* at 30.

[55] Judgment (Preliminary Objection) of June 24, 1932. P.C.I.J., Series A/B, No. 47, pp. 243–258, at 258. Italics in the original.

[56] Judgment (Merits) of Aug. 11, 1932. P.C.I.J. , Series A/B, No. 49, pp. 294–360, at 349, 350.

words, it did not involve itself in considerations or speculations about the aftermath of its judgment. Its effectiveness or lack of it is a matter of history. The two dissenting opinions of Judges Rolin-Jaequemyns and Anzilotti have this in common: that the Court should confine itself to the adjudication of legal disputes rather than giving opinions on divergencies of views, and that a claim for legal redress is an essential feature of a legal dispute. If the case brought before it does not exhibit these characteristics, there is no occasion for the Court to act. The limitation of the judicial function is determined indirectly, that is, by specifying the characteristics of a legal dispute.

In a quite recent case, the *South West Africa* cases (Preliminary Objection), Judges Spender and Fitzmaurice, in their joint dissenting opinions, appear to have taken a similar stand. In their view, the Court was asked " to discharge a task which, in the final analysis, hardly appears to be a judicial one." Although the Court was considering objections to its jurisdiction, it was their view that:

> It is nevertheless legitimate for a Court, in considering the jurisdictional aspects of any case, to take into account a factor which is fundamental to the jurisdiction of any tribunal, namely whether the issues arising on the merits are such as to be capable of objective legal determination.

After looking at those issues and noting the absence of objective criteria, they concluded that the issues

> involve questions of appreciation rather than of objective determination. As at present advised we have serious misgivings as to the legal basis on which necessary objective criteria can be founded.[57]

The majority of the Court, however, thought otherwise, dismissed the objections to its jurisdiction and thus cleared the path for adjudication on the merits. Whatever one may think of the considerations expressed by Judges Spender and Fitzmaurice,[58] it must be noted that the reasons for suggesting that the Court should decline to adjudicate in the *South West Africa* cases related to the basis, or rather the absence of the legal basis, on which a judgment could be founded. Therefore, as in the *Memel* cases, the Court was seen as faced with a case which lacked an essential characteristic of a legal dispute, namely, the capability of being decided on the basis of law, and therefore was not in the nature of a legal or justiciable dispute. Judges Spender and Fitzmaurice were concerned with the possibility for the Court of giving a judgment at all and not with the aftermath of the judgment.

The limits of its judicial function as variously formulated by the Court in the *Northern Cameroons* case all seem to converge on one point: the judgment or any judgment

[57] South West Africa Cases (Ethiopia *v*. South Africa; Liberia *v*. South Africa) Preliminary Objections, Judgment of Dec. 21, 1962. [1962] I.C.J. Rep. 319, at 466–467.

[58] See the separate opinion of Judge Jessup, *ibid.* at 428.

would have been devoid of purpose; it would have been without object. Any such view is necessarily based on an anticipation of the future conduct of the parties, that is, it is speculative in character, and one may wonder how far a court of law can engage in such a line of thought and still remain within the limits of the judicial function. In the *Right of Passage* case, the situation prevailing in the Portuguese enclaves of Dadra and Nagar-Aveli was not a matter for speculation but of record: the Portuguese authority had been effectively displaced in July, 1954, and there could have been no doubt about the attitude of the Indian Government with respect to continued exercise of Portuguese sovereignty over the enclaves. The door to the exercise of any sovereignty, whether civilian or military, was shut for all practical purposes. The Court nonetheless gave judgment on the legal issues presented to it, although it could harbor no illusions as to its effect or object or purpose. One might even go further and suggest that, by splitting Portugal's right of passage into civilian and military components, by further affirming that the former was subject to Indian control, whereas the latter did not even exist, and by holding that India's conduct effectively barring Portugal from re-establishing its sovereignty in the enclaves was not contrary to its obligations vis-à-vis Portugal, the Court has locked and bolted the door.[59] The Court expressly declared that "it was no part of the judicial function of the Court to declare in the operative part of its judgment" that certain arguments are or are not well founded, but in so doing the Court did not include in the operative judgment any statement looking to the restoration of *status juris*. It thus left Portugal without a legal remedy; there was nothing executory about this judgment; it was declaratory on the points with which it dealt. Insofar as some parts of the declaration confirmed Portugal's rights as they existed in July/August, 1954, but which had *de facto* ceased to exist at the time of the judgment, this was all the satisfaction Portugal received. The Court was not concerned whether or not its judgment might have some continuing applicability. Having regard to the factual situation, India's attitude, and the absence of any ruling with respect to a course of action, the judgment was without object.[60]

One might well ask whether the Court was right in abandoning the *Right of Passage* case as a possible precedent and in concerning itself with the factual situation as it existed in the *Northern Cameroons* case at the time of the judgment rather than at the time of the application. Put in another way, one might ask whether it was compatible with the Court's function to give a judgment in a situation where possibility of compliance was remote. There is, however, a difference between these two cases. Portugal's object was certainly to obtain a legal remedy which would be a step in restoring its control over the enclaves in question, even though her submissions may not have been crystal clear or not properly formulated. In other words, Portugal desired an executory judgment and received a declaratory judgment with respect to rights which had been rendered obsolete by the course of events. Cameroon, however, wanted no more than a declaratory judgment,

[59] Case concerning the Right of Passage over Indian Territory (Merits), Judgment of April 12, 1960. [1960] I.C.J. Rep. 6, at 45–46.

[60] For a trenchant critique of this judgment, see Verzijl, in 7 Netherlands International Law Review 211–242 (1960).

which calls for no compliance, with respect to a situation which she knew could not be undone. The Court did not deem it a proper exercise of its judicial function to give her this satisfaction. To give satisfaction is, it is submitted, a proper exercise of the judicial function. [61] It lends strength to what Judge Jessup has called the legal interest of states "in the general observance of the rules of international law."[62] It is surely not far-fetched to suggest that states have also a legal interest in the observance of treaties.

Judge Badawi in his dissenting opinion adverted to the legal interest which the applicant has "to clear itself of any charge of defamation which might properly be directed against it," and he also pointed out that the establishment of the truth with regard to the alleged irregularities "could not fail to be of great legal interest both for the applicant and for the General Assembly."[63] In a similar line of thought Judge Bustamante stated:

> In declaratory suits, the pure and simple definition of the law, in favour of one or other of the parties, constitutes in itself a *judgment* which goes beyond the purely speculative or academic field and gives the successful party a truly objective element, namely the adjudication of a right with which what I call his "legal assets" are enriched, that is to say, the whole sum of rights which that party possesses in its capacity as a legal person. . . . If it is the respondent who appears in the judgment as the successful party, his legal position is consolidated and all the matters of complaint in the application become without foundation, the effect of the judgment being a public rehabilitation . . . . All these effects of a declaratory judgment become evident to the outside world in a concrete and perceptible fashion and take their place within the field of social or international life beyond any purely moral or individual confines.[64]

Thus there were strong reasons for adjudicating the issues. Had the Court done so without concerning itself with the motives for appealing to the Court or with the uses which the parties would have made of its judgment,[65] the Court as well as its judgment might have been criticized. The Court must exercise prudence in assuming jurisdiction and in limiting itself strictly to administering the law.[66] But this it must do. It will be criticized, whatever it does, but in refusing to adjudicate altogether it may have set an undesirable precedent and selected the least desirable way of escaping the dilemma. It would seem that the real dilemma here was how to draw the fine line between safeguarding and abdicating the judicial function.[67]

Clearly the Court was faced with a policy issue of first magnitude. Had the Court rejected the United Kingdom's preliminary objections as unfounded—and in view of its

[61] De Visscher, *op. cit.* at 360; Witenberg, *op. cit.* at 323.

[62] South West Africa cases, [1962] I.C.J. Rep. at 425.

[63] [1963] I.C.J. Rep. at 153.

[64] *Ibid.* at 172. Italics in the original. In this context note the observation of *ad hoc* Judge Chagla that the judgment of the Court in the Right of Passage case "in the main *vindicates* the attitude taken up by India in the controversy between herself and Portugal over the question of the right of passage." [1960] I.C.J. Rep. 6, at 118. Italics added.

[65] See De Visscher, *op. cit.* at 462.

[66] See *ibid.* at 451, 458–459.

[67] "In one famous case, the judge sought to escape the dilemma by washing his hands, but neither the precedent nor the judge has been deemed worthy of imitation." Jessup, "The Customs Union Advisory Opinion," 26 A.J.I.L. 105–110 at 105 (1932).

own finding that a dispute existed at the time of Cameroon's application and its broad interpretation of the adjudication clause in the *South West Africa* cases as comprising disputes relating to the general administration of the Mandate, there may have been no convincing or convenient way to do so—the Court might well have opened the sluice gates to a flood of litigation. If policy considerations, including the requirements of sound administration of justice, made it desirable to discourage cases such as this from being steered in the direction of the Court, some other and more restricted ground might have been found. *Quieta non movere* is an old maxim of law and probably has a place in international law. Judge Wellington Koo suggested a decision along this line when he declared that "respect is due from the Court to the situation which now obtains in regard to the former Trusteeship of the Cameroons."[68]

Another way of reaching the same result was developed by the Court itself in the judgment, but merely as an hypothesis. The Court, hypothetically speaking, declared that the decision of the General Assembly to terminate the Trusteeship Agreement [69] with the consent of the United Kingdom as the Administering Authority had the legal effect of putting an end to any procedural or substantive rights which Members of the United Nations possessed during the lifetime of the Trusteeship. The application of the Cameroon, even though filed with the Court two days prior to the expiration of the Trusteeship, could not, solely for this reason, survive the comprehensive extinction of the Trusteeship. This would be all the more so as Cameroon's application was exclusively concerned with provisions relating to the general application of the Trusteeship Agreement and not with any specific interest or right acquired under it.

To sum up, in this writer's submission, if the issue of the limitation upon the judicial function had to be faced in this case, it would have been preferable, in conformity with the jurisprudence of the Court, to resolve it by reference to the nature of the dispute rather than to the putative effect of the judgment, that is, by holding that the dispute was moot and not that the judgment would be moot. The submissions of the United Kingdom, particularly the third preliminary objection, pointed in this direction. It has already been suggested[70] that the Court virtually adopted that objection, namely, that "there is no dispute before the Court upon which the Court is entitled to adjudicate." However, instead of holding that it could not adjudicate the dispute because it was moot and therefore it was not a legal dispute within the meaning of the Statute, the Court held "that it cannot adjudicate upon the merits of the claim of the Federal Republic of Cameroon" because "any judgment which the Court might pronounce would be without object." In upholding the third United Kingdom preliminary objection, which the Court would have been able to do without affecting its judgment in the *South West Africa* cases, the

[68] [1963] I.C.J. Rep. at 64.

[69] It is suggested that the Court may have erred when it said that the General Assembly "decided on the termination of the Trust," for nothing in the Charter or the Trusteeship Agreement confers such a unilateral power on the General Assembly. The termination could only result from the joint action of the General Assembly and the Administering Authority. See *ibid* at 32, 33, 34 and 36.

[70] See p. 813 above.

Court would have rested on a reasonable objective conception of "legal disputes," whereas its actual holding rests upon rather subjective and conjectural assumptions about the effect of its judgments or the lack of it. Thus, rather than saying that the dispute was moot and therefore not suitable for the exercise of its judicial function, the Court preferred to say that its judgment would be moot and that for this reason it would be outside its judicial functions. Surely the Court ought not to adjudicate upon disputes that are moot and, as understood by this writer, the dispute between Cameroon and the United Kingdom was moot from its inception, as the application was filed after the General Assembly adopted Resolution 1608 (XV) on April 21, 1961, which provided, in agreement with the United Kingdom as the Administering Authority, for the termination of the Trusteeship on a definite date, namely, June 1, 1961. The fact that the Trusteeship Agreement was still in force when the Court was seised of the dispute could not change or alter the character of the dispute. Alternatively, it might have been possible to construe the joint decision of the General Assembly and the United Kingdom of April 21, 1961, to terminate the Trusteeship Agreement as an authentic interpretation of all outstanding issues, binding certainly upon the Members of the United Nations and thus, as of that date, putting an end to any outstanding claims with respect to the administration of the Trust Territory. The Court is not endowed with any sort of appellate jurisdiction from such decisions and would rule accordingly. Reasoning along some such line would have enabled the Court to determine the limits of its judicial function by reference to legal criteria—the Statute, the Charter, the Trusteeship Agreement or general international law—rather than by resorting to meta-juridical sources such as "inherent" limitations. In addition, it would have become unnecessary for the Court to shift the critical date from the time of the Cameroon application, to the unpredictable period of oral argument or the even more unpredictable time of the handing down of the judgment, elements over which the parties have no control and to the hazards of which their legal rights should not, without compelling reasons, be exposed.

# THE TIME ELEMENT IN THE CONTENTIOUS PROCEEDINGS IN THE INTERNATIONAL COURT OF JUSTICE

It is common knowledge that the initial time periods for the submission of written pleadings—memorial, counter-memorial, reply and rejoinder—are determined by the Court after consultation with the parties. Similarly, extensions of time limits are granted by the Court at the request of one party and after consultation with the other party or parties. The Court in both respects has been absolutely at the mercy of the parties, the formal orders made by the Court signifying its compliance with their wishes.

It is, therefore, interesting to note that in its Order of May 24, 1968, in the *Case concerning the Barcelona Traction, Light and Power Company, Ltd.* (New Application: 1962), the Court for the first time, it is believed, indicated clearly that the initiative and responsibility for further delays fell on one of the parties. The time limit fixed for the submission of the Spanish Rejoinder was May 31, 1968. The Spanish Government on May 10, 1968, requested an extension of one month. In granting this request and in fixing July 1, 1968, as the new date, the Court said:

> Although *noting with regret* that the time-limits originally fixed by the Court for the filing of the pleadings have not been observed, whereby the written proceedings have been considerably prolonged,
>
> The Court
>
> *Nevertheless* extends to 1 July 1968 the time-limit for the filing of the Rejoinder of the Government of Spain.[1]

[1] [1968] I.C.J. Rep. 13, at 14 (italics supplied).

This order illustrates the well-known fact that contentious proceedings before the Court are time-consuming, but it is moot whether they are unnecessarily so. The following table provides exact data on the time passed between the filing of a unilateral application or of a special agreement and the judgment of the Court either on preliminary objections or on the merits or on both. It also indicates the deferments requested by one party or the other.

It will be noted that in 57%—that is, in seventeen cases or phases of cases out of a total of thirty, not counting the pending phase of the *Barcelona Traction Company* case—the time limits were extended. In 37%, that is, in eleven cases, the delay due to extensions was 10% or higher; in 23% of the cases (7), delays exceeded 20%. In percentage terms, the delay due to extensions requested by one party or both parties varied from one per centum in the *Rights of Nationals of the U.S.A. in Morocco* case to seventy-one in the *Northern Cameroons* case. This case has also the distinction of holding the record for net extensions—380 days. Without any extension some of the cases required a substantial, but no more than a reasonable, period of time. Thus the *Corfu Channel (Merits)* case took 513 days, and the *Sovereignty over Certain Frontier Land* took 570 days. The disposition of preliminary objections can be as time-consuming as proceedings on the merits. This was so in the *Nottebohm* (525 days), *Aerial Incident* (587 days), *South West Africa* (615 days) and *Barcelona Traction Company* (631 days) cases. These figures clearly indicate that governments attach great significance to the exposition of their legal arguments. It is not possible to claim, however, that, in view of the complexity of the matters referred to the Court and the legal as well as political significance which governments quite naturally attach to the proceedings and even more to their outcome, the proceedings have been excessively slow. The over-all impression is bound to be on the other side: in view of all these factors the proceedings have been reasonably expeditious.

In any event, the table, it is hoped, will dispose once and for all of the criticism that proceedings before the Court are so slow as to discourage governments from submitting cases to it. They are as slow or as expeditious as the parties choose to make them. The Court, there can be no doubt about it, would like them to be expeditious and it has indicated this strongly, though with the usual restraint, in the Order deferred to above.

It would be quite pointless, I believe, to attempt a comparison between proceedings before domestic tribunals and those before the Court. The situations are not at all comparable. However, it is possible and, to a point, instructive to compare the work of the Court with that of *ad hoc* arbitral tribunals.

DURATION OF CONTENTIOUS PROCEEDINGS BEFORE THE INTERNATIONAL COURT OF JUSTICE

| | *Duration** | *Net Extensions*** | *Delay in Proceedings**** |
|---|---|---|---|
| Corfu Channel (United Kingdom *v.* Albania) (Preliminary Objection): 1947–1948 I.C.J. Rep. 15 | 176 days | None | None |
| Corfu Channel (United Kingdom *v.* Albania) (Merits): 1949 I.C.J. Rep. 4 | 513 days | None | None |
| Corfu Channel (United Kingdom *v.* Albania) (Assessment of the Amount of Compensation): 1949 I.C.J. Rep. 244 | 250 days | 6 days | 2% |
| Asylum Case (Colombia *v.* Peru): 1950 I.C.J. Rep. 266 | 402 days | 16 days | 4% |
| Request for Interpretation of the Judgment of Nov. 20, 1950, in the Asylum Case (Colombia *v.* Peru): 1950 I.C.J. Rep. 395 | 7 days | None | None |
| Haya de la Torre Case (Colombia *v.* Peru): 1951 I.C.J. Rep. 71 | 183 days | None | None |
| Fisheries (United Kingdom *v.* Norway): 1951 I.C.J. Rep. 116 | 816 days | 181 days | 29% |
| Ambatielos (Greece *v.* United Kingdom) (Preliminary Objection): 1952 I.C.J. Rep. 28 | 142 days | None | None |
| Anglo-Iranian Oil Co. (United Kingdom *v.* Iran) (Preliminary Objection): 1952 I.C.J. Rep. 93 | 423 days | 69 days | 19% |
| Rights of Nationals of the U.S.A. in Morocco (France *v.* United States): 1952 I.C.J. Rep. 176 | 670 days | 7 days | 1% |
| Ambatielos (Greece *v.* United Kingdom) (Merits: Obligation to Arbitrate): 1953 I.C.J. Rep. 10 | 629 days | 123 days | 24% |

| | *Duration** | *Net Extensions*** | *Delay in Proceedings**** |
|---|---|---|---|
| Minquiers and Ecrehos *(France v.* United Kingdom): 1953 I.C.J. Rep. 47 | *712 days* | *53 days* | *8%* |
| *Nottebohm (Liechtenstein v.* Guatemala) (Preliminary Objection): 1953 I.C.J. Rep. 111 | *525 days* | *None* | *None* |
| *Monetary Gold Removed from Rome in 1943 (Italy v.* France, United Kingdom and U.S.A.) (Preliminary Question): 1954 I.C.J. Rep. 19 | *392 days* | *45 days* | *13%* |
| *Nottebohm (Liechtenstein v.* Guatemala) (Second Phase): 1955 I.C.J. Rep. 4 | *681 days* | *268 days* | *65%* |
| *Certain Norwegian Loans (France v.* Norway): 1957 I.C.J. Rep. 9 | *732 days* | *88 days* | *14%* |
| *Interhandel (Switzerland v.* United States of America), Request for the Indication of Interim Measures of Protection: 1957 I.C.J. Rep. 105 | *24 days* | *None* | *None* |
| *Right of Passage over Indian Territory (Portugal v.* India) (Preliminary Objections): 1957 I.C.J. Rep. 125 | *529 days* | *182 days* | *52%* |
| *Application of the Convention of 1902 governing the Guardianship of Infants (Netherlands v.* Sweden): 1958 I.C.J. Rep. 55 | *506 days* | *None* | *None* |
| *Interhandel (Switzerland v.* U.S.A.) (Preliminary Objection): 1959 I.C.J. Rep. 6 | *513 days* | *104 days* | *25%* |
| *Aerial Incident of July 27, 1955 (Israel v.* Bulgaria (Preliminary Objection): 1959 I.C.J. Rep. 127 | *587 days* | *None* | *None* |
| *Sovereignty over Certain Frontier Land (Belgium v.* Netherlands): 1959 I.C.J. Rep. 209 | *570 days* | *32 days* | *6%* |
| *Right of Passage over Indian Territory (Portugal v.* India) (Merits): 1960 I.C.J. Rep. 6 | *1042 days* | *192 days* | *23%* |
| *Arbitral Award made by the King of Spain on 23 December 1906 (Honduras v.* Nicaragua): 1960 I.C.J. Rep. 192 | *872 days* | *62 days* | *8%* |

| | *Duration** | *Net Extensions*** | *Delay in Proceedings**** |
|---|---|---|---|
| *Temple of Preah Vihear (Cambodia v.* Thailand) (Preliminary Objections): 1961 I.C.J. Rep. 17 | *492 days* | *None* | *None* |
| *Temple of Preah Vihear (Merits) (Cambodia v.* Thailand): 1962 I.C.J. Rep. 6 | *491 days* | *None* | *None* |
| *South West Africa (Ethiopia v.* South Africa; Liberia *v.* South Africa) (Preliminary Objections): 1962 I.C.J. Rep. 319 | *615 days* | *None* | *None* |
| *Northern Cameroons (Cameroon v. United Kingdom) (Preliminary Objection): 1963 I.C.J. Rep. 15* | *916 days* | *380 days* | *71%* |
| *Barcelona Traction, Light and Power Company, Limited, Case (Belgium v.* Spain) (Preliminary Objections): 1964 I.C.J. Rep. 6 | *631 days* | *None* | *None* |
| *South West Africa (Ethiopia v.* South Africa; Liberia *v.* South Africa (Second Phase): 1966 I.C.J. Rep. 6 | *1468 days* | *135 days* | *10%* |
| *Sum of All Cases* | *16509 days* | *1943 days* | *13%* |

*Including the day of registration of the application and the day on which judgment was given. The cases are cited in accordance with the standardized form of citation adopted by the Court, I.C.J. Yearbook 1966–1967, pp. 89, 94–132. The data are based on that Yearbook and the I.C.J. Reports.

**Adjusted to eliminate double-counting (when an extension requested by one party is necessitated by an extension previously granted to the other party) and catch-ups (when one party stays on schedule despite an extension granted to the other party). Double-counting causes overestimation of the delay in proceedings attributable to extensions. Catch-ups also cause overestimation.

***Let Duration be T; let Net Extensions be $T_0$. Then, percent delay in proceedings due to net extensions is $\frac{(100)\,To}{T - To}$.

Since no two cases are comparable in terms of their legal complexity or political implications, it may be objected that a comparison of the time periods required for the decision by *ad hoc* arbitral tribunals and the Court is not very illuminating. However, it may be helpful to set out in a rough manner the time periods consumed in some of the well-known arbitrations selected at random:

| *Title* | *Special Agreement* | *Award* | *Duration* |
|---|---|---|---|
| Norwegian Ship Owner's Claim (U.S.A., Norway) | June 30, 1921 | Oct. 13, 1922[2] | 470 days |
| Landreau Claim (U.S.A., Peru) | May 21, 1921 | Oct. 26, 1922[3] | 524 days |
| Tinoco Case (United Kingdom, Costa Rica) | Jan. 12, 1922 | Oct. 18, 1923[4] | 644 days |
| Island of Palmas Case (U.S.A., Netherlands) | Jan. 23, 1925 | April 4, 1928[5] | 1167 days |
| Tacna-Arica Question (Chile, Peru) | July 20, 1922 | March 4, 1925[6] | 958 days |
| Salem Claim (U.S.A., Egypt) | Jan. 20, 1931 | June 8, 1932[7] | 505 days |
| Honduras Borders (Guatemala, Honduras) | July 16, 1930 | Jan. 23, 1933[8] | 922 days |
| I'm Alone Case (Canada, U.S.A.) | Jan. 28, 1932 | Jan. 9, 1935[9] | 1077 days |
| Trail Smelter Case (U.S.A., Canada) | April 15, 1935 | March 11, 1941[10] | 2157 days |
| North Atlantic Coast Fisheries Case (U.S.A., United Kingdom) | Jan. 27, 1909 | Sept. 7, 1910[11] | 588 days |
| Case of Lac Lanoux (France, Spain) | Nov. 19, 1956 | Nov. 17, 1957[12] | 363 days |

[2] 1 Int. Arb. Awards 307.
[3] *Ibid.* 347.
[4] *Ibid.* 369.
[5] *Loc. cit.,* Vol. II, p. 829.
[6] *Ibid.* 921.
[7] *Ibid.* 1161.
[8] *Ibid.* 1308.
[9] *Loc. cit.,* Vol. III, p. 1609. Jan. 28, 1932, is the date on which the procedure started, *ibid.* 1613. A joint Interim Report of the Commissioners was submitted on June 30, 1933; the Joint Final Report was submitted on Jan. 9, 1935.
[10] *Ibid.* 1905. The Tribunal met on June 21, 1937, for organization and hearing of preliminary statements, *ibid.* 1912. A partial award was given on April 16, 1938. March 11, 1941, is the date of the final award.
[11] *Loc. cit.,* Vol. XI, p. 167.
[12] *Loc. cit.,* Vol. XII, p. 281.

| *Title* | *Special Agreement* | *Award* | *Duration* |
|---|---|---|---|
| *Argentina-Chile Frontier Case (Argentina, Chile)* | *April 1, 1965* | *Dec. 9, 1966*[13] | *617 days* |
| *Rann of Kutch (India, Pakistan)* | *June 30, 1965* | *Feb. 19, 1968*[14] | *964 days* |

The periods of time elapsed between the signing of the special agreement which is the formal start of the proceedings or between the actual start of the proceedings, as in the *Trail Smelter Case,* and the delivery of awards varies then from somewhat less than a year in the case of *Lac Lanoux* to about 3 years and 9 months in the *Trail Smelter Case.* By comparison the Court gave judgments in less than one year in 4 cases: *Corfu Channel (Preliminary Objections), Corfu Channel (Assessment), Haya de la Torre, Ambatielos (Preliminary Objections).* However, the *South West Africa Cases (Second Phase)* consumed 4 years and eight days, including extensions amounting to about four and one-half months.

Without any attempt at pressing the comparison, it may be observed that many of the arbitral proceedings such as in the *Tinoco, Island of Palmas* and *Tacna-Arica* cases were before a single arbitrator. This may well be a factor in expediting proceedings. Another factor may be the composition of the tribunal. If the tribunal is composed wholly of members of the same nationality, as was the case in the Award of the Queen of England, this may also be a factor in expediting proceedings. Moreover it will be noted that in some cases the agreement to arbitrate lays down the time limits for the several stages of the procedure. Thus in the *Lac Lanoux Case* the agreement provided that memorials were to be filed within three months from the constitution of the tribunal, counter-memorials were to be filed within two months, and hearings were to commence one month later, although they could be deferred by one month but no more. In this tight schedule there were some, though very minor, delays.[15]

In the *Rann of Kutch Arbitration,* the tribunal met on February 15, 1966, and fixed the time limits for the filing of written pleadings—June 1, 1966, for memorials, August 1, 1966, for counter-memorials, September 1, 1966, for final memorials—and stipulated that "no extension of these time-limits will be granted."[16]

A source of major delays in the proceedings before the International Court of Justice is, of course, the highly sophisticated use of objections to the receivability or admissibility of unilateral applications and to the jurisdiction of the Court. All such matters of an ante-

[13] Foreign Office, Award of H.M. Queen Elizabeth II for the Arbitration of a Controversy between the Argentine Republic and the Republic of Chile concerning certain parts of the Boundary between their Territories (London, H. M. Stationery Office, 1966). The first date is that on which the British Secretary for Foreign Affairs signed the Agreement of Arbitration, *ibid.* 12. This arbitration involved an aerial survey of the area and a reconnaissance on the ground, *ibid.* 17.

[14] 7 Int. Legal Materials 633–705 (May, 1968). The first meeting of the Tribunal was held on Feb. 15, 1966.

[15] The President of the Tribunal, Judge Sture Petrén, was appointed by the King of Sweden on Jan. 25, 1957; time limits began to run from this date; the opening of oral hearings was deferred by the parties until Oct. 17, 1957; they were terminated on Oct. 23, 1957; and the award rendered about three weeks later.

[16] 7 Int. Legal Materials 640 (1968).

cedent character, that is, all pleas preceding the merits are wholly in the hands of the parties. The Court may contribute to delays growing out of such challenges by joining some preliminary objections to the merits with the result that after a considerable delay the case is disposed of without a judgment on the merits. Thus in the *Nottebohm Case* 525 days were consumed by the proceedings on preliminary objections and 681 days by the second phase, which ended in a finding that Liechtenstein's claim was inadmissible, a total of somewhat more than three years and seven months. The *South West Africa Cases* hold the record of altogether five years and eight and one-half months.

The *Barcelona Traction Company Case* required 631 days for the preliminary phase, and four years have passed since the judgment of the Court on the preliminary objections rendered on July 24, 1964. The Spanish Government submitted its counter-memorial 17 months and 7 days later, the Belgian Government filed its Reply after 16 months and 14 days. With the latest extension granted to the Spanish Government, the Rejoinder will be filed after 13 months and 14 days. In this case five requests for extensions of time limits have been made and granted, accounting for a delay of twenty months or, to be exact, 611 days.[17] As the Court has joined some preliminary objections to the merits,[18] there is the possibility that the case will be disposed of without a judgment on the merits.

Assuming that the Special Rejoinder will be filed with the Court on July 1, 1968, and on the probably unrealistic assumption that oral hearings will be held and judgment given within six months, that is, by December 31, 1968, this case will have had a duration of 1760 days with a net extension of 611 days representing a 53% delay in the proceedings.

The *North Sea Continental Shelf Cases* (Denmark/Federal Republic of Germany, Federal Republic of Germany/Netherlands) seem to be moving along agreed lines. The Special Agreements laid down that memorials by Germany shall be filed within six months and counter-memorials by Denmark and The Netherlands respectively within twelve months from February 20, 1967. These pleadings were duly filed. The German Reply was to be filed on May 31, 1968, and a single common Rejoinder by Denmark and The Netherlands on August 31, 1968.[19]

It may be noted that, as the following table indicates, the Court handled requests for advisory opinions with utmost dispatch. It will also be observed that, particularly during the first four years, the Court was able to dispose of five contentious cases (*Corfu Channel, Fisheries, Asylum, Haya de la Torre, Rights of Nationals*) and six requests for advisory opinions, a commendable performance by any standard.

[17] I.C.J. Communiqué No. 68/5, June 5, 1968.

[18] [1964] I.C.J. Rep. 6.

[19] I.C.J. Communiqué No. 68/4 (unofficial). In its Order of April 26, 1968, the Court found that Denmark and The Netherlands were parties in the same interest, joined the proceedings in the two cases and required, accordingly, a single Rejoinder by these two states. Oral hearings in this case started on Oct. 23, 1968. I.C.J. Communiqué 68/7.

*Duration of Advisory Proceedings*

| | *Adoption of Request* | *Receipt of Request* | *Advisory Opinion* | *Duration* |
|---|---|---|---|---|
| *Conditions of Admission of a State to Membership in the U.N. (Article 4 of the Charter)* | *17 Nov. 1947* | *12 Dec. 1947* | *28 May 1948* | *168 days* |
| *Reparation for Injuries Suffered in the Service of the U.N.* | *3 Dec. 1948* | *7 Dec. 1948* | *11 April 1949* | *125 Days* |
| *Interpretation of Peace Treaties with Bulgaria, Hungary and Romania, First Phase* | *22 Oct. 1949* | *3 Nov. 1949* | *30 March 1950* | *147 days* |
| *Second Phase* | | | *18 July 1950* | |
| *Competence of General Assembly for the Admission of a State to the U.N.* | *22 Nov. 1949* | *28 Nov. 1949* | *3 March 1950* | *95 days* |
| *International Status of South West Africa* | *6 Dec. 1949* | *27 Dec. 1949* | *11 July 1950* | *196 days* |
| *Reservations to the Convention on the Prevention of the Crime of Genocide* | *16 Nov. 1950* | *20 Nov. 1950* | *25 May 1951* | *186 days* |
| *Effect of Awards of Compensation made by the U.N. Administrative Tribunal* | *9 Dec. 1953* | *21 Dec. 1953* | *13 July 1954* | *204 days* |
| *Voting Procedure on Questions relating to Reports and Petitions concerning the Territory of South West Africa* | *23 Nov. 1954* | *6 Dec. 1954* | *7 June 1955* | *183 days* |

| | *Adoption of Request* | *Receipt of Request* | *Advisory Opinion* | *Duration* |
|---|---|---|---|---|
| *Judgments of the Administrative Tribunal of the I.L.O. upon Complaints made against UNESCO* | *23 Nov. 1955* | *2 Dec. 1955* | *23 Oct. 1956* | *326 days* |
| *Admissibility of Hearings of Petitioners by the Committee on South West Africa* | *3 Dec. 1955* | *22 Dec. 1955* | *1 June 1956* | *162 days* |
| *Constitution of the Maritime Safety Committee of IMCO* | *19 Jan. 1959* | *25 March 1959* | *8 June 1960* | *441 days* |
| *Certain Expenses of the U.N. (Article 17, par. 2, of the Charter)* | *20 Dec. 1961* | *27 Dec. 1961* | *20 July 1962* | *205 days* |

The proceedings in advisory cases were invariably completed in less than one year and in time for the advisory opinion to be considered by the requesting body at its session following that in the course of which the request was made. In no case was the time elapsed between the vote on the request and the delivery of opinion more than eleven months (*Judgments of the Administrative Tribunal of the I.L.O.*) and in one case (*Competence of the General Assembly*) it was less than three and a half months, the normal duration being between four and seven months. It will be noted that in some cases there was a considerable delay—as much as two months in the case of the *Constitution of the Maritime Safety Committee of IMCO*—in filing the request with the Registry of the Court. If the duration of advisory proceedings were counted from the date of the receipt of the request, the temporal record of the Court would be even better.

A similar adjustment could, of course, be performed in connection with contentious cases if, instead of the dates taken in the present table, that is, the date of the special agreement or of the filing of the unilateral application, the date of the filing of the memorial or memorials were taken as the starting point of the proceedings. True, a government becomes directly immersed in the judicial settlement from the moment it seises the Court in either of these two ways. The Court, however, does not really get involved until the first written pleadings are filed. The time between the seising of the Court and the filing of the memorial may be substantial and, if taken into account, would reduce the total period of the judicial proceedings quite substantially. The periods of time run from a minimum of two months (*Haya de la Torre Case*) to seven and a half months (*Aerial Incident Case*). In some cases there has been a considerable delay in filing the special agreement with the Court. Thus in the *Minquiers and Ecrehos Case* the Special Agreement was signed on December 29, 1950, and filed with the Court only on December 6, 1951; in the case of *Sovereignty over Certain Frontier Land* the Special Agreement was signed on March 7, 1957, and filed on November 27, 1957. However, the normal period of time between the seising of the Court and the submission of the memorial runs between four and four and one-half months to five and one-half or six months.

A final table will illustrate graphically the average duration of the three types of proceedings discussed above:

*Average Duration*

| | | |
|---|---|---|
| Arbitral awards | (13 cases) | 843 days |
| I.C.J. contentious cases | (30 cases) | 550 days |
| I.C.J. advisory opinions | (12 cases) | 203 days |

It will be noted that the average duration of proceedings in contentious cases is 171% longer than the average duration of advisory proceedings, and that the average duration of contentious proceedings in cases in which no extension has been requested would drop from 550 days to 486 days.[20]

In evaluating the efficiency of the Court's performance there is an extraneous factor which needs to be taken into consideration. The Court, since its inception, has been

[20] The time periods between the opening of oral hearings and judgments in contentious cases and advisory opinions in advisory proceedings will be found in Leo Gross's "Some Observations on the International Court of Justice," 56 A.J.I.L. 33–62, at 47–50 (1962). See also *supra.* The following table provides supplementary data for judgments and opinions rendered since 1961:

*Judgments*

| | *Public Sittings* | *Opinion* | *Time Elapsed* |
|---|---|---|---|
| South West Africa (Ethiopia *v.* South Africa; Liberia *v.* South Africa) | | | |
| Preliminary objections | Oct. 2–22, 1962 | Dec. 21, 1962 | 81 days |
| Second Phase | March 15–July 14, Sept. 20–Nov. 29, 1965 | July 18, 1966 | 504 days |
| North Cameroons (Cameroon *v.* United Kingdom) | | | |
| Preliminary objections | Sept. 19–Oct. 3, 1963 | Dec. 2, 1963 | 88 days |
| Barcelona Traction, Light and Power Company | | | |
| Preliminary objections | March 11–May, 19, 1964 | July 24, 1964 | 156 days |
| | *Advisory Opinion* | | |
| Certain Expenses of the United Nations | May 14–21, 1962 | July 20, 1962 | 68 days |

(I.C.J. Yearbook 1966–1967, pp. 127–131.)

housed in the Peace Palace in The Hague. During his recent visit to the Court, the Secretary General of the United Nations, U Thant, "visited the locations in the Peace Palace which the International Court of Justice is entitled to use."[21] The space for offices of the judges has become very confining and there may be reason to hope that as a result and a follow-up of the Secretary General's visit, serious consideration will be given to the need of providing adequate facilities for the Court.[22]

Two other points which were discussed by the Secretary General with the members of the Court deserve to be mentioned. One is the old and somewhat delicate matter of "the full recognition" of the status of the Court in The Hague, on which the Court suggested "certain possibilities" to the Secretary General. It has been common knowledge that the status of the Court in the diplomatic hierarchy at The Hague was not what the Court has thought it ought to be.[23]

Finally, there is the acute problem of the use of the Court as an organ of international law and as the principal judicial organ of the United Nations. This matter was discussed by the Court with the Secretary General.[24] As reported, the Court "suggested to the Secretary-General certain possibilities for enhancing its usefulness," and the Secretary General "assured the Court that he would always be mindful of the need which the United Nations has for this impartial tribunal which can contribute more than any other organ to the eventual triumph of law and justice for the solution of international differences." He also "made it clear that he wished to do all in his power to assist the Court in making its maximum contribution to the maintenance of peace which is the purpose of the United Nations and of all its organs."[25]

It would be most interesting to know what were the "possibilities for enhancing its usefulness" suggested to the Secretary General by the Court, and what steps the Secretary General had in mind that he could take to assist the Court "in making its maximum contribution" to peace through the development of international law. The Court has received no request for an advisory opinion since 1961 from the nineteen organs and agencies at present authorized to make such requests.[26] Since 1962 only one new conten-

[21] I.C.J. Communiqué No. 68/3, April 9, 1968.

[22] On the physical facilities of the Court, which seem to have always been inadequate see Hudson, The Permanent Court of International Justice 1920–1942 (1943), pp. 323–324.

[23] On the thorny question of protocol see Hudson, *op. cit.* 321–331. The diplomatic corps takes precedence at official ceremonies to which it and the Court are invited. According to the exchange of letters between the President of the Court and the Minister of Foreign Affairs of The Netherlands of June 26, 1946, "the question of precedence . . . remains outside the present agreement." 2 Rosenne, The Law and Practice of the International Court 875–877 (1965). In Hudson's view, the "Court has not been sufficiently exigent in this matter. The judges as a body ought not to be assimilated to a diplomatic corps, and a proper respect for the Court as an institution may be thought to require that its members be given precedence over the representatives of any single State." *Op. cit.* 331.

[24] In 1968, perhaps in order to emphasize its rôle as a principal organ of the Organization, the Court for the first time, in conformity with the long-standing practice of the other principal organs, submitted to the U. N. General Assembly a report on its activities. Report of the International Court of Justice, 1 August 1967–31 July 1968, General Assembly, 23rd Sess., Official Records, Supp. No. 17 (A/7217) and Corrigendum.

[25] Communiqué No. 68/3, April 9, 1968.

[26] These organs and agencies are: General Assembly of the United Nations, Security Council of the United Nations, Economic and Social Council of the U.N., Trusteeship Council of the U.N., Interim Committee of the General Assembly, Committee on Application for Review of Administrative Tribunal Judgments, International Labor

tious case, the *North Sea Continental Shelf Cases,* has been submitted to it. These are unusually long delays in using the Court as the principal judicial organ of the United Nations for advisory opinions and as an organ of international law for the settlement of interstate disputes. It is to be hoped that in considering using the Court in either of its two capacities the myth of long delays in the proceedings before the Court will henceforth play no rôle whatever. The Court has been extremely prompt in responding to requests for advisory opinions and as efficient in adjudicating disputes as the parties permitted it.

Organization, Food and Agriculture Organization of the U.N., United Nations Educational, Scientific and Cultural Organization, International Civil Aviation Organization, International Bank for Reconstruction and Development, International Finance Corporation, International Development Association, International Monetary Fund, World Health Organization, International Telecommunication Union, World Meteorological Organization, Inter-Governmental Maritime Consultative Organization, International Atomic Energy Agency. 1966–1967 I.C.J. Yearbook 36–37.

I wish to thank Mr. Martin S. Wishnatsky, Teaching Fellow in Government, Harvard University, for his assistance in the compilation of the tables.

# THE INTERNATIONAL COURT OF JUSTICE AND THE UNITED NATIONS

## INTRODUCTION

At the end of the second decade of its activity the International Court of Justice finds itself in a serious crisis. The Judgment of the Court in the *South West Africa* cases (18 July 1966), and the reaction thereto on the part of the international community, are not the only causes of this predicament, although it would be idle to pretend that they have not powerfully contributed to it. Even before 1966 statesmen and scholars were concerned about stagnation in the development of international adjudication of which the Court was to be the principal instrument. Lack of confidence in the composition of the Court and the law which it applied was commonly identified as a proximate cause of this situation. However, these factors were but outward manifestations of yet deeper doubts—doubts regarding the role which international adjudication could and should play in the pattern of the international relations which has evolved since the end of World War II, and particularly following the rapid achievements of decolonization, and the consequent doubling of the membership of the United Nations. The attitudes of States were seen to be determined by the prevailing international tensions, by the emergent system of international politics characterized as bipolar, the technological developments which led to reappraisal of the requirements of national security, and the disparity between developed and developing nations; these are some of the more remote factors which left their imprint on the behaviour of States.

It is not my purpose to analyze these and other factors which may and in some fashion have shaped attitudes and influenced the behaviour of States and perhaps even the

Court. I shall concern myself with the behaviour of the Court, the perceptions of its role in international relations and the expectations of the Members of the United Nations with respect to the role which the Court should play in the system, that is, the political system of the United Nations, chiefly in connection with the transformation of purposes and objectives of the Charter into juridical and political reality.

The concept which the Court has formed of its own role in the United Nations system and the attitudes of the Members concerning the role of the Court have a common basis in the Charter and the links it establishes between the Court and the Organization, and between the Court's Statute and the Organization's Charter. Of course, these links were subject to evolution, and attention will be directed to discovering whether such an evolution, has indeed taken place. This inquiry will take as its starting points the Charter, including as it does the Statute, the Advisory Opinions given by the Court in response to United Nations requests, some contentious cases which may be relevant and other materials capable of shedding light on the perceptions, attitudes and expectations above mentioned.

The central issue, it is suggested, relates to the dual function which the Court has been called upon to discharge under the relevant instruments. The Court was created to function both as an organ of the United Nations and as an organ of international law, to render advisory opinions in the former capacity and judgments in the latter. This may be the cause of a certain ambiguity relating to its role and the expectations with respect thereto. To be sure, it was assumed that there would be no tension between these two functions since there had been none, or at least none of any significance, during the life of its predecessor, the Permanent Court of International Justice. That Court had also discharged a dual role: it rendered advisory opinions at the behest of the League of Nations and judgments in contentious cases between States. At first sight the ambiguity in respect to the present Court arises from two factors: first, the links between the Court and the United Nations are much closer—some writers call them "organic"—than were those between the old Court and the League. Secondly, the separation between the advisory, or what might be called the United Nations function of the Court, and its contentious or adjudicative or international law function, has not and perhaps could not be maintained, as illustrated in the *South West Africa* cases.

Three possible outcomes may be envisioned: first, a continuation of the present ambivalence; secondly, a clearer separation between the two functions; and thirdly, an overcoming of the ambivalence as a result of the Court's becoming increasingly a United Nations Court. Which of these outcomes is more likely to emerge will depend: first, to a substantial extent on the United Nations' becoming a truly universal international organization; secondly, on the evolution of the present Organization from one of co-ordination to one of integration; and thirdly, as a consequence of the former, the degree to which international law adjusts to and absorbs United Nations law or vice versa. The latter alternative is essentially a matter of emphasis and direction of the process.

Thus, to illustrate, the different positions assumed by the majority and minority of judges in the 1962 and, particularly, in the 1966 Judgment in the *South West Africa* cases, can be presented in terms of two schools of interpretation: one favouring a flexible, extensive interpretation and the other adhering to a strict and restrictive interpretation. This antimony might be translated into terms of judicial conservatism and abstention on the one hand, and judicial liberalism and involvement on the other. But the difference can also be seen as representing two schools of legal thought, the one inclined to move in the direction of applying, in contentious cases, United Nations law or standards and objectives to what appeared to be in substance if not in form a United Nations case, and the other adhering to the traditional view that what appeared in form as a dispute between two statal parties should be decided according to international law without regard to nascent United Nations law.

Had the former school prevailed the Court would have moved closer to fulfilling the role assigned to it in the Charter, namely that of an organ of the United Nations, a United Nations Court; the latter school preferred the role assigned to the Court by the Statute in contentious cases, namely that of an organ of international law.

It may also be suggested that what divided the Court in 1966 into two equal groups may have been a difference in the basic conception of international law: one school adhering to the consensual theory whereas the other group may be seen as moving toward a consensus theory of international law. The former may be deemed to maintain substantially the principles for which the *Lotus* and *Eastern Carelia* cases stand as symbol—a part of the inheritance from the old Court, which has always been challenged by the "progressive" international lawyers. The latter appears as espousing a more elastic approach which would adapt rules of international law to the needs of international life, particularly as expressed in the General Assembly of the United Nations. Advisory Opinions, such as those in the *South West Africa,* the *Peace Treaties,* the *Reparation* and *Expenses* cases are suggested as evidence of this latter trend along with the Judgment in the *South West Africa* (Preliminary Objections) cases. The Advisory Opinion in the *Peace Treaties* (Second Phase) and that part of the *South West Africa* (Status) Opinion which denied that South Africa was under an obligation to conclude or to enter into negotiations for the conclusion of a trusteeship agreement, and the Judgment in the *South West Africa* (Second Phase) cases are indications of the former trend.

However, it may be noted that it does not seem possible to classify the members of the Court into schools. There is no alignment of judges between conservatives and liberals comparable to that which is frequently found in the Supreme Court of the United States. Thus, Judges Spender, Fitzmaurice and Morelli who were with the "conservative" majority in the 1966 *South West Africa* Judgment were also with the "progressive" majority in the *Expenses* case, while one of the judges, Koretsky, who was with the "conservative" minority in the *Expenses* case, was also with the "progressive" minority in the 1966 Judgment. Judge Winiarski was consistently with the "conservative" group in both cases. The frequent changes in the composition of the Court have so far prevented the crystallization of a predictable alignment. Several factors, then, may account singly or in combination for the varying alignments in the Court: adherence to principle, the specific characteristics of the issues which fell to be decided in the different cases, different perceptions of the role of the Court with respect to the issues and the law to be applied, and the relation of the issues to the United Nations.

I wish to thank my colleague, Professor John H. Spencer, for many helpful suggestions, and Mr. Michael H. P. Belknap, A.B. '63, LL.B. '67 (Harvard University), for his cheerful co-operation.

# CHAPTER I

## Institutional Integration

The Charter and the Statute contain a number of interlocking devices to ensure the integration between the Organization of the United Nations and the Court. The integration is virtually complete but for the postal services: the United Nations postal service does not extend to the Court.[1] The Statute is an "integral part" of the "present Charter"—(Article 92)—but it is not made explicit whether the Charter is part of the Statute.[2] The Members of the United Nations are *ipso facto* parties to the Statute and constitute the "judicial community" in the narrow sense.[3] The Court is constituted by Article 7 of the Charter as a "principal organ" of the United Nations and as "the principal judicial organ of the United Nations", by Article 92. The Court's status as an organ of the United Nations and the "judicial community" in the narrow sense are the principal innovations compared with the relations between the League of Nations and the Permanent Court of International Justice. At first sight they seem merely formal in character as does the further innovation which makes the Statute an integral part of the Charter. Whether they were destined to be the starting points for a new functional relationship would depend upon the behaviour of the Organization and of the Court, and will be explored subsequently.

The provision concerning enforcement of the Court's judgments in Article 94, paragraph 2, is different from that in Article 13, paragraph 4, of the Covenant. So far there has been no case which would have put the Charter provision to a test. Commentators seem agreed that it offers the Security Council a substantial amount of discretion. There is no consensus with respect to the question whether Article 94, paragraph 2, provides a new basis for enforcement measures or whether such measures can be taken by the Council only if nonexecution of a judgment is also qualified as a threat to the peace pursuant to Chapter VII of the Charter.[4] The Statute provides in Article 69 for its amendment thus removing the "unfortunate *lacuna*"[5] in the Statute of the Permanent Court. Article 70 of

[1] S. Rosenne, *The Law and Practice of the International Court* (1965), p. 263 (hereinafter cited as Rosenne).

[2] Article 1 of the Statute declares that the Court "shall be constituted and function in accordance with the provisions of the present Statute". This corresponds to the provision in Article 92 of the Charter: "It (the Court) shall function in accordance with the annexed Statute . . ." Rosenne's statement (p. 68) that they are to be read as one instrument does not quite meet this point.

[3] Hans Kelsen, *The Law of the United Nations* (1951), pp. 79 ff. The "judicial community" in the wider sense comprises States parties to the Statute but not members of the United Nations, like Switzerland, Liechtenstein and San Marino. *I.C.J. Yearbook 1965–1966*, p. 29.

[4] On the problem of execution see generally Kelsen, *op. cit.*, pp. 539–544; Rosenne, p. 74 and pp. 150–153; Leo Gross, "Problems of International Adjudication and Compliance with International Law," 59 *American Journal of International Law*, pp. 48–59 (1965); see also *supra*, pp. 399–410; Oscar Schachter, "The Enforcement of International Judicial and Arbitral Decisions," 54 *AJIL*, 1–24 (1960); E. K. Nantwi, *The Enforcement of International Judicial Decisions and Arbitral Awards in Public International Law* (1966).

[5] Manley O. Hudson, *The Permanent Court of International Justice*, 1920–1942 (1943), at 130.

the Statute confers upon the Court the potentially beneficial power "to propose such amendments to the present Statute as it may deem necessary".

The Charter and the Statute do not break new ground in connection with the elections of the Members of the Court[6] and its budget; the Charter does not provide for any kind of supervision by the political organs of the Organization of the activity of the Court as a judicial organ. In practice, however, the power of the purse is significant, and a debate on the budget can involve one on the jurisprudence of the Court. In point is the discussion in the Fifth Committee of the Assembly in connection with the proposal for an increase of $72,500 in the supplementary estimates for the Court for the financial year 1966. The representative of Guinea declared that for reasons "that were well known" the African group would vote against the increase. The Soviet delegate declared that he would vote against it on the ground that "in obedience to its Statute, the Court (in the *South West Africa* cases) should have rendered a decision consistent with General Assembly resolution 1514 (XV), condemning racism and colonialism". The delegate of Iran pointed out that "while it would be dangerous to refuse funds on a subjective basis . . . the issue in the present case was that legislation enacted by the United Nations had not been put into effect". The delegate of Cameroon, denying that the attitude of the African States "might set a dangerous precedent" stated: "The budget was the translation into financial terms of a certain political trend; it was permissible to condemn a trend which departed from earlier decisions. Under its Statute, the International Court was supposed to base its judgments on certain norms. The norms had not been respected. The Fifth Committee was entitled to say that the sums disbursed by the Court had not been spent as had been intended".[7]

The Committee rejected the supplementary appropriation by 40 votes to 27, with 13 abstentions.[8] It is difficult not to share the opinion of the delegate from Norway that: "It was . . . neither necessary nor proper for it (the Committee) to discuss the decisions of the International Court. It would indeed be a dangerous precedent to deny an organ funds because of disagreement with a particular decision".[9] A dangerous precedent has, indeed, been set. Those who voted against the appropriation wanted it although they knew that the sum required would have to be found in the totality of appropriations voted by the General Assembly for 1966.[10]

However, the 1966 Judgment in the *South West Africa* cases stimulated efforts to change the composition and structure of the Court with the avowed purpose of making it more responsive to the trends prevailing in the political organs and in this connection give consideration to factors which may be extraneous to the standards laid down in Article 2

[6] But note Article 13 of the Statute which introduced the system of triennial partial elections, an innovation of doubtful value. See Rosenne, pp. 184–190.

[7] *GAOR:* 21st Session, Fifth Committee, 1124th meeting, 10 October 1966, pp. 23–25.

[8] *Ibid.*, p. 25.

[9] *Ibid.*, p. 24.

[10] *Ibid.*, statement by the representative of the Secretariat.

of the Statute. Thus the representative of Pakistan expressed the view shared in one way or another by many Members:

> "The insensitivity of these judges to current international standards or legal norms, their disregard of the mode of generation of customary international law, their refusal to apply, in performance of their functions in accordance with Article 38 of the Statute, directives manifested in the resolutions of the General Assembly, are things which are bound to perturb enlightened public opinion throughout the world".[11]

Many delegations accordingly advocated a change in the composition of the Court. To cite only one statement,—the representative of Upper Volta said:

> "Created at a time when the world was altogether different from that of today, the International Court of Justice is not attuned, in its present composition, to today's realities. A change in its composition would be to the advantage of this Organization".[12]

The triennial elections held in 1966 may be deemed to reflect in some measure old preoccupations intensified by the Court's judgment.

It may be only fair to point out that judicial institutions generally, both national and international, pass through periods when they seem to lag behind social developments. Judge Alvarez, from the beginning, in his opinions urged upon the Court a new outlook of international law, the law of social interdependence. Both legal doctrine on the sources of international law and on the United Nations developed during the past 20 years in a manner which could not have been entirely anticipated in 1945 when Article 38 of the Statute was under consideration.

This Article, incidentally, was amended at the San Francisco Conference. In the old text of Article 38 the enumeration of the "sources" of international law was preceded by the words: "The Court shall apply", a language which was broad enough to encompass advisory opinions along with judgments. In 1945 the text was changed to: "The Court, whose function is to decide in accordance with international law such disputes as are submitted to it, shall apply." This was intended to emphasize the Permanent Court's own perception of its role as an "organ of international law",[13] but in the process the

[11] Doc. A/PV. 1414, p. 37.

[12] Doc. A/PV. 1425, p. 27. See also the statement of representatives of Czechoslovakia, *ibid.*, pp. 43–45 ("It is imperative to change its membership so that it reflects the legal and political realities of the present-day world."); Ireland, A/PV. 1427, p. 17 ("I feel sure that all who supported the election of those judges who voted for the decision as men who would give wise, equitable and speedy decisions, must bitterly regret that their confidence was misplaced."); Iran, *ibid.*, pp. 53–55; Ivory Coast, A/PV. 1429, p. 74; Tunisia, A/PV. 1431, p. 12; Jamaica, *ibid.*, p. 23; Syria, *ibid.*, p. 52; Indonesia, A/PV. 1449, p. 53; Guinea, A/PV. 1456, p. 21. ("Immediately after the scandalous finding of the International Court of Justice, the Africans and their friends decided to make efforts to ensure that the Court would be a reflection of international realities as they exist today.") These views are generally reflected in Ernest B. Gross, "The South West Africa Case: What Happened?" 45 *Foreign Affairs*, pp. 36–48 (1966), at 48.

[13] Manley O. Hudson, "The Twenty-fourth Year of the World Court," 40 *American Journal of International Law*, pp. 1-53 (1946), at 35.

That this was the intention of the San Francisco Conference appears from the following statement in the report of the Rapporteur of Committee IV/1/74 (1), p. 12: "The First Committee has adopted an addition to be inserted in the introductory phrase of this article referring to the function of the Court to decide disputes submitted to it in accordance with text was narrowed down to "disputes," that is, contentious cases. What "sources" of law was the Court expected to apply in advisory proceedings? In this respect the integration of the Court is somewhat less than satisfactory.

The description of the Court as the "principal judicial organ" confers upon it no pre-eminent position, neither in the area of dispute-settlement (Article 95 of the Charter) nor in that of Charter interpretation. Proposals to this effect were made but not adopted, and the well-known statement on "Interpretation of the Charter" places the Court on a footing of equality with other principal *organs and even an* ad hoc *committee* of jurists. Either the Court or such a committee could be asked for an opinion concerning the meaning of a provision of the Charter. And, "if an interpretation" says the statement, "made by any organ of the Organization or by a committee of jurists is not generally acceptable, it will be without binding force".[14] In one respect the statement makes explicit, codifies in a way, the practice of the League, which, depending on the occasion, the urgency and nature of the matter under consideration, referred questions to the Court or to a committee of jurists. But the Permanent Court was not an integral part of the League, and it does seem somewhat objectionable to suggest that committees and the Court can be used interchangeably with equal effect. What is worse, however, is that the statement endorsed the proposition that each organ may interpret the Charter in their "day-to-day" operations. Thus, the interpretation by a political organ was given as much cogency as that by the principal judicial organ, which in this context appears to be no more than another principal organ, and that, accordingly, there was no compelling reason to refer questions to the Court for an opinion. This is exactly the kind of reasoning one finds in the debates in the General Assembly in connection with proposals for requests to the Court. Finally, the statement had in mind the experience of the League, its *modus operandi* and its high respect for international law, in short, its "legalistic" character. It could not anticipate the effect it would have on what turned out to be an organization wholly different in its outlook and *modus operandi,* its very nearly "anti-legalistic" if not "anti-legal" character. But it is into such an institution that the Court has been integrated.

A matter which may be said to have been overlooked in the process of effectuating the integration of the Court into the Organization is the question of the relations between it and the other principal organs. Article 12 of the Charter contains a provision regulating the handling of disputes or situations which are simultaneously pending before the Security Council and the General Assembly. While the Assembly may discuss, it shall not make a recommendation with regard to such disputes or situations. No comparable provision has been inserted with respect to matters pending before the political organs and the judicial organ. Again, it may have been the experience of the League which suggested that this matter can be left to the good sense, restraint and tact of the political

international law. The lacuna in the old Statute with reference to this point did not prevent the Permanent Court of International Justice from regarding itself as an organ of international law; but the addition will accentuate that character of the new Court." UNCIO *Documents,* Vol. 13, p. 381, at 392.

[14] UNCIO *Documents,* Vol. XIII, p. 710: Report of the Rapporteur of Committee, IV/2, Doc. 933, IV/2/42 (2).

organs. As the handling of the *South West Africa* cases indicates this trust was misplaced. One could have expected that at the very least Article 12 would be followed, and that at worst the political organs may continue to discuss a dispute or situation which was pending before the Court for an advisory opinion or a judgment but that they would refrain from making recommendations. The principle of *sub judice* was invoked by South Africa as soon as the Court was seised of the dispute by the applications of Liberia and Ethiopia, but it was rejected by large majorities in the committee and the plenary session of the General Assembly.[15]

The General Assembly went on adopting resolutions with respect to South Africa and even approved a resolution which had, and probably was intended to have, a most direct bearing on one of the points essential to the case of the Applicants. According to Article 7, paragraph 2, of the Mandate for South West Africa, the Court had jurisdiction in any dispute arising between the Mandatory and another Member of the League relating to the interpretation or application of the Mandate "if it cannot be settled by negotiation". On 18 December 1960, after rejecting South Africa's *sub judice* plea, the Assembly adopted resolution 1560 (XV) in which it concluded "that the dispute which has arisen between Ethiopia, Liberia and other Member States on the one hand, and the Union of South Africa on the other, relating to the interpretation and application of the Mandate has not been and cannot be settled by negotiation".[16] The Applicants referred to the first part of this conclusion in support of their propositions that a "dispute" existed and that it "cannot be settled by negotiation". In fact, it constitutes the whole of their argument on this vital condition of the jurisdiction of the Court.[17]

It is not necessary here to discuss the question whether there is a rule or principle of

[15] *GAOR*: 15th Session, Fourth Committee, 14 Nov. 1960, pp. 296–299; the vote to reject was 67 to 1 (South Africa), with 11 abstentions. See, *ibid.*, p. 299, the very thoughtful speech by the representative of the United Kingdom, who said the General Assembly "could, by expressing an opinion, bring the greatest pressure to bear upon the Court, if it so wished". In his view it was the "clear duty of the General Assembly and its Committees to exercise restraint similar to the discipline which the House of Commons and similar chambers imposed upon themselves with regard to matters which were before the International Court of Justice". For discussion and vote in the 954th plenary meeting, 18 Dec. 1960, see *ibid.*, Plenary Meetings, pp. 1385–1387. The vote to reject was 82 to 1 (South Africa) with 9 abstentions. The United States favoured rejection in both votes.

The question of prejudging an opinion of the Court was not new. It arose in 1949, first in connection with the decision of the Fourth Committee to grant an oral hearing to Reverend Michael Scott, Doc. A/1180, 2 Dec. 1949. Report of the Fourth Committee, para. 23. *GAOR*, Plenary Meetings, Annex, Agenda Item 34, p. 105. Objections on the ground of prejudging were raised by several delegations. See *GAOR*, Fourth Committee, Summary Records, 132nd meeting, para. 28 (South Africa), paras. 38, 45–49 (Belgium), paras. 63–65 (Israel), para. 72 (Canada), 133rd meeting, paras. 9–11 (France), para. 29 (Thailand), para. 33 (United Kingdom), and 134th meeting, para. 37 (Australia). It arose again in connection with the Indian draft resolutions reiterating previous resolutions and inviting South Africa to resume submission of reports on its administration of South West Africa which became resolution 337 (IV) adopted on 6 Dec. 1949 by a vote of 33 in favour, 9 against, and 10 abstentions. *GAOR*, Plenary, p. 269. Objections on the ground of prejudging an advisory opinion of the Court requested at the same time were raised by several delegations in the Fourth Committee and in the Plenary. See *GAOR*, Fourth Committee, Summary Records, 135th meeting, para. 58 (United Kingdom), 136th meeting, para. 23 (Canada), 139th meeting, paras. 7, 17 (United States), and Plenary, 269th meeting, para. 37 (South Africa), para. 63 (Greece), paras. 92–95 (Belgium), paras. 104, 108–109 (United States). See Rosenne II, 751–753, regarding action of the General Assembly in connection with the two subsequent requests for advisory opinion in connection with South West Africa.

[16] *GAOR*: 15th Session, Supp. No. 16 (A/4684), p. 32.

[17] Memorial submitted by Ethiopia, International Court of Justice *Pleadings*, South West Africa, Vol. I, pp. 89 and 93.

international law corresponding to the domestic principles of *litispendence* or *sub judice* which must, in any event, be regarded as refinements appropriate for mature political-legal systems. It should be noted, however, that in this case the situation was not that the continued discussion in the forum of the Assembly was on one plane and the consideration in the judicial forum on another. Rather it was the case of one forum reaching out of its domain into that of the other.[18] Again it may be recalled that the founders of the United Nations used the League as a model, and there was not enough in its experience to suggest a need for an explicit regulation of what, heeding Professor de Visscher's warning, might be called, "quasilitispendence". They could not foresee how profoundly politicized the Organization would become almost from its inception.

One gap, however, might have been filled. During the lifetime of the League the question had never been resolved what vote was required in the Council for the adoption of a request for an opinion.[19] While it is widely believed that in practice unanimity prevailed and that this circumstance accounts for the effectiveness of advisory opinion, it is by no means certain whether the unanimity was to be understood in the sense of Article 5, paragraph 1, of the Covenant, namely the agreement of the Members represented at the meeting, or in the sense of Article 15, paragraph 6, which in calculating unanimity, did not require the agreement of one or more parties to the dispute. The latter rule prevailed in connection with requests regarding the *Acquisition of Polish Nationality* (1923) and the *Mosul* question (1925) cases.[20] The same uncertainty prevails in the United Nations although both organs operate on the basis of majority votes. However, since the founders assigned to the General Assembly and the Security Council two majority votes each, it would have been useful to state in the Charter which of the two majority votes should prevail in the Assembly and Council respectively. In the Security Council, does the mandatory abstention in Article 27, paragraph 3, apply to requests for advisory opinions?

In concluding this brief and necessarily incomplete survey of the "organic" link between the United Nations and the Court, several observations may be made. The Court has been integrated into an Organization which in its day-to-day political activities ac-

[18] In the *South West Africa* (Preliminary Objection) cases, the Court considered that although the conflicts before the United Nations and the Court "may be regarded as two different disputes, the legal questions at issue are identical". *I.C.J. Reports 1962,* pp. 319 and 345. This suggests the "two planes" theory. In the joint dissenting opinion of Judges Spender and Fitzmaurice, after referring to General Assembly resolutions 1361 (XIV) of November 1959 and 1565 (XV) of December 1960, it is said: "It is not for us to comment on this process, except in so far as we have to consider what the legal consequences are". *Ibid.,* at 548. On the question of *litispendence,* see Rosenne, pp. 83–87; 513–516; Paul Reuter, Principes de droit international public, Hague *Recueil* 1961: II, p. 649, who notes "que l'Assemblée n'a pas toujours fait preuve de discretion à l'égard des compétences de la Cour". Charles de Visscher warns against the use of the term to describe a situation such as that which developed in the *South West Africa* cases. *Aspects récents de droit procédural de la Cour International de Justice* (1966), p. 176 (hereinafter cited "Aspects récents").

[19] See Otto Göppert, *Der Völkerbund* (1938), pp. 188–191.

[20] Göppert, *loc. cit.,* Poland participated in the proceedings in the former case (Hudson, World Court *Reports,* Vol. I (1934), p. 237) but Turkey did not in the latter case. Concerning the *Mosul* case see below, p. 876). See also Hudson, *The Permanent Court of International Justice,* 1920–1942, pp. 488–494; League of Nations Assembly, Ninth Plenary Session, *Official Journal,* Supp. No. 64, pp. 38, 64, and League of Nations *Official Journal,* October 1925, pp. 1377, 1382, and *ibid.,* February 1928, p. 128.

cords only a marginal place to law, whereas the Permanent Court was loosely linked to the League which showed a keen and fairly consistent commitment to law and the procedures of law. Allowing for the fact that the founders of the United Nations could not anticipate the political climate in which the Organization would function and the pervasive East-West, North-South and decolonization tensions, it is still true, it is submitted, that while the integration between the Permanent Court and the League might have been useful but was in fact not necessary, the integration of the International Court into the United Nations was neither necessary nor useful. It was not necessary because the success of the Permanent Court showed that the Court, even though only administratively connected with the League,[21] could function effectively, as indicated by the volume of contentious cases and particularly the number of advisory opinions which it handled. The experience of the Permanent Court proved conclusively that an organic connection with the parent organization was not necessary. Has institutional integration been beneficial to the International Court?

Disregarding the "spill-over" of the political arena into the judicial arena, which points to a certain proprietary conception of the former with respect to the latter, the following points may be noted. Article 36, paragraph 3, of the Charter, a potentially significant feature of the integration, was used only once in 1947 in connection with the *Corfu Channel* case, and has remained a dead letter ever since. The organic connection between the judicial community of the United Nations has failed to produce an easy, sustained co-operation.[22] It has failed to generate a substantial acceptance of the compulsory jurisdiction of the Court.[23] Finally and most importantly, it has failed to stimulate a significant flow of cases to the Court. As of 31 July 1966, the General List of the Court contained 50 cases as having been referred to the International Court. Since then two new cases have been submitted,[24] which raises the total to 52. Of these, 12 were requests for advisory opinions (counting the two phases in the *Peace Treaties* case as one request) and 40 were contentious cases. Dividing the latter group, three are pending, eight were removed (non-acceptance of juris-

[21] This did not prevent President Loder, at the inaugural meeting of the Court, to refer to it as "one of the principal organs of the League". Quoted in Hudson, *The Permanent Court of International Justice*, 1920–1942, p. 113. Hudson also quotes, *ibid.*, p. 111, from the letter of the Council to the Committee of Jurists that the Court was "one of the principal organs of the League". Hudson himself shared these views and called the Court "the judicial organ of the League" *(ibid.)*. A. P. Fachiri looked upon the Court as "an institution distinct from the League". *The Permanent Court of International Justice*, 2nd ed. (1932), p. 330.

[22] It may be noted, however, that it provided the pretext in six cases for the United States and in two cases for the United Kingdom to seise the Court by unilateral arraignment. *I.C.J. Yearbook 1965–1966*, Folio Nos. 22, 23, 25, 26, 27, 28, 40, and 44, pp. 116, 118, 119, 128, 130. The American cases related to aerial incidents in Hungary, Czechoslovakia and the Soviet Union, and all of them fell into the cold war category. See Rosenne, p. 356, and Leo Gross, "Some Observations on the International Court of Justice," 56 *AJIL* (1962), at p. 43. See also *supra*, pp. 677–704. "It is possible", said Lauterpacht, "that applications of this nature may be mere political devices to embarrass the State which it is being sought to make defendant". *The Development of International Law by the International Court*, p. 104.

[23] As of 31 July 1967, 42 out of 125 States forming the judicial community in the wider sense, were bound by Declarations under Art. 36 (2) of the Statute. *I.C.J. Yearbook 1966–1967*, pp. 8–32; 44–72.

[24] *North Sea Continental Shelf (Denmark/Germany)* and *North Sea Continental Shelf (Germany/Netherlands)*. For text of the Special Agreements for the submission of these cases, see I.C.J. Communiqué No. 6711 of 21 Feb. 1967, and *I.C.J. Yearbook 1966–1967*, p. 131.

diction), six were discontinued (of these one was settled), 12 were decided by a judgment on the merits,[25] and in two cases judgments were designated "Second Phase" (*Nottebohm* and *South West Africa*). Finally, the Court upheld preliminary objections in six cases and gave one interpretative judgment *(Asylum)*.[26]

In contrast, the Permanent Court gave 27 advisory opinions (two-and-one-half times as many as the International Court) and 32 judgments in contentious cases. The latter involved nine disputes in which preliminary objections were ruled upon,[27] 20 decisions on the merits,[28] two interpretative judgments,[29] and one judgment granting the right to intervene.[30]

While there is a marked disparity in the number of contentious cases handled by the two courts during a comparable period of time, the *quality and significance* of the disputes decided by the International Court go some way toward mitigating it. However, the disparity in the number of requests for advisory opinions is all the more remarkable considering the fact that whereas only two organs of the League were empowered to request such opinions, currently the advisory jurisdiction of the Court is open to six organs or subsidiary bodies of the United Nations, 12 Specialized Agencies and their affiliates, and the International Atomic Energy Agency.[31] Reasons for the reluctance of these organs and particularly of the United Nations have been explored in some detail.[32] The point is, however, that the organic connection between the Court and the Organization has been

[25] *Corfu Channel, Fisheries, Asylum, Rights of Nationals in Morocco, Haya de la Torre, Ambatielos, Minquiers and Ecrehos, Right of Passage, Guardianship, Certain Frontier Land, Arbitral Award (King of Spain)* and *Temple* cases.

[26] *Anglo-Iranian, Monetary Gold, Norwegian Loans, Interhandel, Aerial Incident (Israel* v. *Bulgaria)* and *Northern Cameroons* cases. In the last case the Court declined to give a judgment on grounds of judicial propriety. See Leo Gross, "Limitations upon the Judicial Function", 58 *AJIL*, pp. 415–431 (1965). See also *supra*, pp. 813–829. The General List has two numbers each for the *Corfu Channel* and *South West Africa* cases.

[27] *Mavrommatis Palestine Concession, Certain German Interests in Polish Upper Silesia, Chorzów Factory, Mavrommatis Jerusalem Concession, Memel Statute, Borchgrave, Phosphates in Morocco, Panevezys-Saldutiskis Railway* and *Electricity Company of Sofia* cases.

[28] *Wimbledon, Treaty of Neuilly, Mavrommatis Palestine, Certain German Interests in Polish Upper Silesia, Lotus, Rights of Minorities, Chorzów Factory, Serbian Loans, Brazilian Loans, River Oder, Free Zones, Memel Statute, Eastern Greenland, Hungaro-Czechoslovak Mixed Arbitral Tribunal, Lighthouses (France/Greece), Lighthouses in Crete and Samos, Société Commerciale de Belgique* cases.

[29] Interpretation of Judgment # 3 (Treaty of Neuilly) and Interpretation of Judgments # 7 and # 8 (Germany/Poland) cases.

[30] Intervention of Poland in the *Wimbledon* case.

[31] See *I.C.J. Yearbook 1966–1967*, pp. 36–37.

[32] See Alexy, "Die Inanspruchnahme des Internationalen Gerichtshofs durch die Organe der Vereinten Nationen", 21 *Zeitschrift für Ausländisches Öffentliches Recht und Völkerrecht*, pp. 473–510 (1961); Rosenne, "On the Non-use of the Advisory Competence of the International Court of Justice", *British Year Book of International Law*, pp. 1–53 (1963); H. C. L. Merillat, *Legal Advisers and International Organization* (1966). It is interesting to note some of the objections felt among legal advisers of the Special Agencies to the greater use of the advisory opinions. Some pointed to the risk "of referring to the Court questions the resolution of which depends on compromise among the parties"; others considered reference of inappropriate questions which might debase the authority of the Court; the delay involved was also an inhibiting factor. In some organizations "one reason for reluctance to use them (the advisory opinion procedures) has been a concern that the Court, being outside the mainstream of the organizations' activity, might come to decisions not fully sensitive to the internal requirements for effective operation. In other words, the detached objective legal view may not contribute to the actual effectiveness of the organization. Added to this is the reluctance of all parties, even those in a minority position, to force an 'authoritative', definite, and presumably enduring interpretation when compromise and flexibility may be more useful. ('It does not help that the application of the legal rule is legally impeccable if it is politically impossible'!) This is reflected in the practice of adopting informal legal decisions in those organizations that have the power of 'authoritative' interpretation". *Ibid.*, pp. 10–11. Some of these considerations also carry weight with Members of the United Nations.

of no relevance to the attitude of Members when addressing themselves to the question of requesting the Court's Opinion.

The striking fact is not the large array of reasons for making as little use as possible of the "principal judicial organ", but that after 20 years no clear conception has emerged in what situations the Court could and should be consulted with any degree of predictability. It also is a striking fact that the Court was able to function in its inherited capacity of "organ of international law," that is, in contentious cases, more often and more effectively than in its new role as a principal organ and as the principal judicial organ of the Organization, that is, in advisory proceedings. The decline in the latter may not necessarily be a cause of regret and would not have been had the Court not been linked organically to the Organization.[33] However, it is quite conceivable that the organic connection "may create psychological obstacles to recourse to the Court as an organ of the United Nations even when judicial settlement is desired" and that States "may find unsatisfactory factors in the political composition of the Court which lead them to prefer to set up an *ad hoc* tribunal of their own".[34] The Court has no dependable clientele, and as its composition comes to reflect increasingly the composition of another principal organ, the Security Council (apparently the goal of some Members of the United Nations), it may become decreasingly attractive for States which seek a depoliticized procedure leading to a judgment based essentially on existing law.[35]

To sum up: the founders of the United Nations integrated the Court into the Organization and thus formalized and made explicit the relations between the Permanent Court and the League. Hopefully, by providing for *ipso facto* membership of Members of the Organization in the judicial community of the Court they expected to speed up the closing of the gap left by the rejection of compulsory jurisdiction. Indeed, the Conference accepted a recommendation to the Members of the Organization that they declare as soon as possible their acceptance of the obligatory jurisdiction of the Court.[36] This has so far remained a pious hope. On the other hand, the founders could not foresee the nature of post-World War II politics and the eminently contentious climate which has settled on the political organs of the United Nations and which has not been hospitable to the stabilizing function of the Court. Given the right opportunity, the Court could play, and has to some extent played, a legitimizing function, but the Members have preferred their own legitimizing processes to the risk entailed in having the Court express a negative opinion on their claims to legitimacy and legality. The risk was quite substantial as

[33] de Visscher thinks that the Court should congratulate itself that it has not been involved more often in the politics of the Organization and exposed to requests which are but a dangerous echo of the "political and passionate debates in New York". *Aspects récents*, p. 198.

[34] Rosenne, I, p. 10.

[35] There may, of course, be other reasons as well for preferring arbitration. Even during the inter-war period more disputes were settled through genuine arbitration, that is, not counting the tribunals set up by or in connection with the Peace Settlement of 1919, than through the Permanent Court. See Laurent Tully (J. F. Lalive), "Arbitration and Judicial Settlement: Recent Trends", 48 *AJIL*, pp. 380–407 (1954) at 381, who states that no less than 60 arbitral awards *strictu sensu* were given during the period 1920 to 1940.

[36] UNCIO *Documents*, Vol. 1, p. 612, at 627. Verbatim Minutes of the Ninth Plenary Session, 25 June, Doc. 1210, p. 16.

shown by the final outcome of the Court's handling of the *South West Africa* cases, dating from 1950 when hopes were raised to 1966 when hopes were dashed. For some Members the Court may have only a nominal existence in spite of its organic connection with the United Nations,[37] but for others the Court's usefulness may depend on the prior successful completion of a restatement and progressive development of international law.[38]

Having surveyed the institutional integration of the Court into the United Nations and its general consequences, it remains to consider whether and to what extent this integration exercised an influence on the Court's perception of its role and its jurisprudence.

[37] . . . "Indeed, there is evidence, in the records of the various organs of the United Nations, that the Court is regarded as something apart from normal United Nations organs, and its procedures something independent from customary United Nations procedures. In other words, for an important section of the Members of the United Nations, the existence of the Court, and even its status within the Organization, are nominal". Rosenne, p. 111. For a staunch advocate of the organic status of the Court in the Organization, this is a significant admission.

[38] A. E. Gotlieb, "The International Law Commission", 4 *Canadian Yearbook of International Law*, pp. 64–80 (1966) at 65: "If one were to summarize the basic legal trends of our time, it would . . . be fair to conclude that the international community has, when taken as a whole, shown less enthusiasm for the judicial settlement of disputes than for the restatement and development of the general rules of international law". Compared with United Nations successes in this area of its activities, the League was remarkably unsuccessful.

# CHAPTER II

# FUNCTIONAL INTEGRATION

## 1. Preliminary Observations

This section will examine the ways in which the Court's institutional connection with the United Nations influenced its behaviour, activities and jurisprudence. As the Statute is an integral part of the Charter and the Court a principal organ of the Organization, provisions of the Charter which apply to organs generally, such as the domestic jurisdiction clause in Article 2 (7), apply also to the Court; provisions of a more general character such as those in the Preamble, and in Articles 1 and 2, may be used by the Court as guides in its interpretative task in advisory and contentious procedures, particularly in cases relating to the United Nations, such as the *South West Africa* cases.

Although the Statute has been incorporated by reference into the Charter, it belongs to a different age than the Charter. It has its roots in the Hague Peace Conferences and was drafted almost immediately after World War I. It does not reflect trends which have developed in the doctrine in the last 40 years. Hence a degree of friction in the application of the Statute particularly with respect to the sources of law and decision, had to be expected.

As not all aspects of the possible impact of the institutional link on the behaviour of the Court can be considered, it is necessary to be selective. Among the principles which guided the Permanent Court in its jurisprudence and which have passed on to the present Court, are three which can be used as focal points of analysis: first, consent in its several applications (consent to advisory or contentious jurisdiction, to the adoption of the request for an opinion, to the applicable law); second, *audiatur et altera pars;* and third, equality of parties. The latter principle was a matter of concern only in one case, the *I.L.O. Administrative Tribunal* case, and without arousing any prolonged controversy, it was applied negatively: neither side to the proceeding participated in the oral hearings; in fact, none was held.[1]

The second principle was material in the same case and in the *Peace Treaties* case. As it appears as a specific application or derivative of the first, it will be considered in that context.

The selection of the principle of consent as an organizing principle for analysis, commends itself for two reasons, one being of a more theoretical and the other of a more practical character. First, the consensual theory of international law and the jurisdiction of the

[1] Leo Gross, "Participation of Individuals in Advisory Proceedings before the International Court of Justice: Question of Equality between the Parties", 52 *AJIL*, pp. 16–40 (1958), particularly pp. 26 ff. regarding the revised Statute of the United Nations Administrative Tribunal; see also *supra*, pp. 706–725; and Rosenne, II, p. 738, concerning the conservative attitude of the Court with respect to individuals.

Court, of which the *Lotus* and *Eastern Carelia* cases respectively are the symbols, have been and continue to be the *bêtes noires* of progressive international lawyers, and it seems therefore relevant to inquire whether and to what extent the Court, in spite of its Statute, adapted itself to current doctrinal views urged upon it for about 40 years, with respect to title of jurisdiction (in both advisory and contentious procedures) and the sources of law or decision. Secondly, as will be seen, the expectations of Members and the perception of the Court regarding its role in the United Nations can be related to both the consensual basis of jurisdiction and the more contemporary ideas concerning sources of law or of decision such as the application of General Assembly resolutions in appropriate cases, or what might be called United Nations cases.

A sample of such expectations will be presented. It is well to remind oneself that the Court is integrated into the United Nations system which operates, as pointed out, on a majoritarian principle, and that according to Article 96 of the Charter, the General Assembly and the Security Council may ask, and that according to Article 65 (1) of the Statute the Court may give, an advisory opinion on "any legal question".

## 2. Expectations and Perceptions

The Court had occasion in several pronouncements to indicate its perception of its role or roles in relation to the dual function conferred upon it: the advisory function exercised at the behest of United Nations organs—what might be called its United Nations function—and its contentious function at the behest of States and States only (Article 34, Para. 1, Statute), what might be called its international judicial community function. The Court had also occasion to define—in general terms—the limits which its judicial character, its Statute and international law impose upon it when acting in either capacity.

The Court referred to itself as an "organ of the United Nations,"[2] as the "principal judicial organ,"[3] as an organ of international law[4] and as a "Court of law".[5] The first two descriptions can be related to the Court's advisory and the latter two descriptions to the contentious function.

In the *Peace Treaties* (First Phase) case the Court gave an indication of its conception of its role as an organ of the United Nations. In that case the view was urged upon the Court that its position was different from that of its predecessor which was only loosely connected with the League of Nations.[6] The Court made five statements: first, it declared that "the reply of the Court, itself an 'organ of the United Nations' represents its participation in the activities of the Organization"; secondly, that the reply "in principle, shall

[2] *Peace Treaties* (First Phase), *I.C.J. Reports 1950,* p. 71.

[3] *Admissions, I.C.J. Reports 1948,* p. 61; *Peace Treaties* (First Phase), *I.C.J. Reports 1950,* p. 71; *Nottebohm* (Jurisdiction), *I.C.J. Reports 1953,* p. 119; and *Expenses* cases, *I.C.J. Reports 1952,* p. 156.

[4] *Corfu Channel* case, *I.C.J. Reports 1949,* p. 35.

[5] *South West Africa* (Second Phase), *I.C.J. Reports 1966,* pp. 34, 36. In the *Cameroons* case the Court saw itself as a "Court of justice". *I.C.J. Reports 1963,* p. 15, at 29.

[6] See G. G. Fitzmaurice, "The Law and Procedure of the International Court of Justice", 29 *BYIL,* pp. 1–63 (1952) at 45–46.

not be refused''; thirdly, that the reply ''is only of an advisory character: as such it has no binding force''; fourthly, ''it follows'' said the Court, ''that the State, whether a Member or not, cannot prevent the giving of an Advisory Opinion which the United Nations considers to be desirable in order to obtain enlightenment as to the course of action which it should take''; and fifthly, that while ''the consent of States, parties to a dispute, is the basis of the Court's jurisdiction in contentious cases'' the situation ''is different in regard to advisory proceedings even where the request for an opinion relates to a legal question actually pending between States''.[7] In addition, the Court, in the *Membership* case declared that it could ''not'' attribute a political character to a request which, framed in abstract terms, invites it to undertake an essentially judicial task, ''the interpretation of a treaty provision'' and that it was ''not concerned with the motives which may have inspired this request''.[8]

These are propositions of judicial policy which have far-reaching significance, and they are all traceable to the institutional connection between the Court and the Organization. The Court, a principal and a judicial organ, participates in the activities of the United Nations, that is, in its political and highly politicized activities. Thus its opinions serve as a stage in the action to be taken by the United Nations. For this reason no consent of the State or States concerned in the dispute or in the subject-matter of the request is necessary. In addition, the opinion has no binding, and in this context it may be ventured to suggest, no legal force, nor in principle should a request for an opinion be refused. The Court had occasion to reiterate the last proposition several times,[9] but it should be noted that it underscores the positive aspect of the discretion vested in the Court by Article 65 (1) of the Statute, which merely says that the Court ''may'' give an advisory opinion. Furthermore, it will be noted that as a consequence of the elimination of consent of the State or States concerned, such States may or may not—in the *Peace Treaties* case some of them did not—participate in the proceedings. The Court does not seem to consider in such cases the principle *audiatur et altera pars* essential.

Without going into detail it may be observed that in almost every respect the perception of the Court differs from that of its predecessor. In the *Eastern Carelia* case, the Permanent Court, although it was also called upon to discharge two functions, conceived its role in unitary terms: ''The Court, being a Court of Justice, cannot, even in giving advisory opinions, depart from the essential rules guiding their (sic!) activity as a Court.''[10] This unitary approach was reflected in the assimilation of the procedure between the two functions which were inherited by the present Court (Articles 82 to 85 of the Rules of the Court) and in the assimilation of the legal effect of opinions and judg-

[7] *I.C.J. Reports 1950,* p. 65.

[8] *I.C.J. Reports 1948.*

[9] See *Reservations, I.C.J. Reports 1951,* p. 19; *I.L.O. Administrative Tribunal Reports 1956,* p. 86; and *Expenses, I.C.J. Reports 1962,* p. 155, cases.

[10] *Eastern Carelia* case, *P.C.I.J., Series B, No. 5* p. 29, quoted by the present Court in the *Expenses* case, *I.C.J. Reports 1962,* p. 155.

ments. In the words of the Permanent Court: "Answering the question would be substantially equivalent to deciding the dispute between the parties."[11]

The Court has indicated that there are some limits imposed upon its co-operation with the United Nations. They flow from its role as "principal judicial organ". Thus the Court may refuse to give an opinion if the question is not a legal one and even refuse to give an opinion if the question is a legal one if "the circumstances of the case are of such a character as should lead it to decline to answer the Request".[12] On the other hand, the Court also declared, presumably having in mind its dual role as a principal organ and as a judicial organ, that only "compelling reasons" should lead it to refuse complying with a request.[13] The Court, as indicated above, is bound by its Statute and international law as well as considerations of judicial propriety. However, it is interesting to note that the Court has not yet been faced with a request with which for "compelling reasons" it would have had to refuse to comply, but that in one contentious case, the *Cameroons* case, it decided to decline to render a judgment on grounds of judicial propriety.[14]

Individual Members of the Court also stressed the new role of the Court and its limitations. To give one or two examples: Judge Azevedo considered that the Court "has been *raised* to the status of a principal organ and thus more clearly geared to the mechanism of the United Nations Organization" and that it "must do its utmost to co-operate with the other organs with a view to attaining the aims and principles that have been set forth". On the other hand he emphasized that there are "certain limits which a judicial court may not overstep, even in the exercise of an advisory function assigned to it as a *subsidiary* activity". He regarded absence of consent as one of those limits.[15]

Judge Winiarski was of the opinion that while the Court "has no doubt the duty to give the opinions which are requested of it, for this is one of the two purposes for which it has been constituted . . . there may be important legal grounds for not giving an opinion . . ."[16] In his view "the Court has its own responsibility which cannot disappear behind that of the Assembly".[17]

In an opinion which has found little if any attention, Judge *ad hoc* Dr. Ecer in the *Corfu Channel* case contended that the task of the Court "as the judicial instrument of the United Nations" was—

[11] *Ibid.* See also separate opinion of Judge Azevedo, and the dissenting opinions of Judges Winiarski, Zorocic and Krylov in the *Peace Treaties* (First Phase) case, *I.C.J. Reports 1950*, pp. 80 ff., 89 ff., 101, 111.

[12] *Expenses* case, *I.C.J. Reports 1962*, p. 155, and *Peace Treaties* (First Phase), *ibid., 1950*, p. 72.

[13] *I.L.O. Administrative Tribunal, I.C.J. Reports 1956*, p. 86, and *Expenses* case, *ibid., 1962*, p. 155.

[14] *I.C.J. Reports 1963*, p. 15, at 29. The Court said: "There are inherent limitations on the exercise of the judicial function which the Court, as a Court of Justice, can never ignore . . . The Court itself, and not the parties, must be the guardian of the Court's judicial integrity". See Leo Gross, "Limitations upon the Judicial Function", 58 *AJIL*, pp. 415–431 (1964); see also *supra*, pp. 813–829; and Charles de Visscher, *Aspects récents*, pp. 35 f.

[15] Separate opinion, *Peace Treaties* (First Phase), *I.C.J. Reports 1950*, p. 82. Italics supplied. Judge Azevedo would not go further than to "acknowledge the duty of reasonable co-operation with the other organs of the United Nations". *Ibid.*, at 88.

[16] Dissenting opinion, *ibid.*, at 92.

[17] *Ibid.*, at 97. Judge Krylov in his dissenting opinion also took exception to the view that the Court, in its new capacity of principal judicial organ "had a lesser degree of autonomy than the Permanent Court". *Ibid.*, p. 109.

> "to help to strengthen the cohesion of the international community. The instrument of cohesion of the international community is the United Nations Charter. It is true international law, with its source in the new requirements of international life and the juridical conscience of its peoples. The authority of the Judgment and that of the Court as judicial organ of the United Nations would be strengthened by a reference to the provisions of the Charter".[18]

The expectations and perceptions of the Members of the role of the Court can only be very briefly touched upon. There are several indices available. One is the number of declarations accepting the compulsory jurisdiction of the Court which indicate at best only a moderate interest. Another index is the number of ratifications of the Optional Protocols relating to the conventions elaborated by the United Nations.[19] The frequency and importance of cases referred to the Court in advisory or contentious procedure have already been discussed. The prevailing estimate is that the Court has not been used very much. The attitude of Members to the draft on arbitral procedure prepared by the International Law Commission is well known. It was, at worst, one of hostility or, at best, one of calculated reserve.[20]

At two sessions of the United Nations Special Committee on Principles of International Law concerning Friendly Relations and Co-operation among States, the role of the Court was discussed along with various non-judicial procedures for the peaceful settlement of disputes. There is no room here to review the arguments in favour of or opposed to integrating the role of the Court in the formulation of the principle relating to peaceful settlement.[21] The opponents pointed out, *inter alia,* that the willingness of States to submit legal disputes to the Court depended upon geographical areas and the degree of integration achieved by States in some areas; the greater the degree of integration, the greater the willingness and vice versa. It was observed in this context that the Charter of the Organization of African Unity had omitted mentioning judicial procedures as one of the means of peaceful settlement.[22] The atmosphere of the debate on the advantages of direct diplomatic negotiations as the fundamental—and one is tempted to say, exclusive—means of resolving disputes,[23] is revealed by an argument made by the anti-judicial settlement

[18] *I.C.J. Reports 1949,* p. 4, at 130.

[19] As of July/November 1967 the following figures may be given: 63 States are parties to the 1961 Vienna Convention on Diplomatic Relations, and 29 are parties to its Optional Protocol: 25 States are parties to the 1963 Vienna Convention on Consular Relations and 11 States are parties to its Optional Protocol. According to Article V of the 1958 Optional Protocol relating to the Geneva Conventions on the Law of the Sea only States who are parties to any of the four Conventions may become parties to the Optional Protocol. Only 20 States are both parties to one of these Conventions as well as the Optional Protocol. States bound by the Conventions are as follows: 33 by the Convention on the Territorial Sea, 40 by the Convention on the High Seas, 25 by the Convention on Fishing and 37 by the Convention on the Continental Shelf. I am obliged to UNITAR and the General Legal Division, Office of Legal Affairs, United Nations for the above information. See also Doc. UNITAR/EX/8, 1 Aug. 1967.

[20] See Leo Gross, "The United Nations and the Role of Law", 19 *International Organization,* pp. 537–561 (1965), at 545. See also *supra.*

[21] For a resumé of the different stands pro and con at the Mexico City Conference in 1964, see Report of the Special Committee, Doc. A/5746, 16 Nov. 1964, paras. 166–178, and 183, and paras. 191–194 (Composition of the Court). For a resumé of the discussion in the Sixth Committee by the General Assembly, see Doc. A/6165, paras. 32–37.

[22] *Ibid.,* para. 176.

[23] *Ibid.,* paras. 155–164.

group: to give a place of priority to the Court "would be to adopt a doctrinaire position contrary to the principle of sovereign equality and independence of States".[24] In the present submission, it would be difficult to find a procedure better calculated to ensure the equality of parties than the judicial procedure.[25] Be that as it may, the Committee at its first session failed to reach a consensus on the subject of peaceful settlement of disputes.

The second session of the Special Committee fared somewhat better. A consensus text was adopted but it contains no reference to the Court. A proposal by five Members which provided that "as a general rule" legal disputes should be referred by the parties to the Court and that States "should endeavour" to accept the compulsory jurisdiction of the Court reached no consensus.[26] The gist of the argument against a specific reference to the Court bears quoting:

> "(1) recent international practice did not justify attempts to extend the compulsory jurisdiction of the Court; (2) the need to take into account the freedom of the parties to settle each specific dispute by the means which they considered most appropriate; (3) the need for more equitable representation in the membership of the Court; (4) the still vague and fragmentary state of international law".[27]

There was no consensus concerning two proposals that States should include dispute clauses or compromissory clauses in bilateral or multilateral treaties.[28] The question of the advisory function of the Court was barely touched upon.[29]

In connection with the *Peace Treaties* case reference has already been made to the arguments advanced by governments in that case. The representative of the United States, Mr. Benjamin V. Cohen, in oral hearings, argued that the Charter, considering Article 96 (1) of the Charter, and Articles 36 (1) and 65 (1) of the Statute, "as such was an independent source of jurisdiction", that it was "the constitution of the international community". Furthermore, "the Charter of the United Nations, of which this Court is the principal judicial organ, confers jurisdiction upon this Court to give an advisory opinion on any legal question at the request of the General Assembly. That jurisdiction", he continued, "is not conditioned upon the consent of States specially concerned, be they members or non-members of the United Nations".[30] Mr. Cohen also distinguished the effect

[24] *Ibid.*, para. 174. In this connection reference may be made to the French amendment which was calculated to meet the sovereignty argument. The French proposed to add to the United Kingdom proposal which gave a prominent place to the Court, the following paragraph: "Recourse to any one of the means of peaceful settlement of disputes, in conformity with an undertaking freely entered into, shall (not) be regarded as derogating from the sovereignty of the States". *Ibid.*, para. 132. The word "not" is not in the text but this is probably due to a clerical error. See Report of the 1966 Special Committee Doc. A/6230, 27 June 1966, para. 248, where "not" appears in paragraph 5 of the agreed Text.

[25] Leo Gross, "Some Observations on the International Court of Justice", 56 *AJIL*, pp. 33–62 (2962), at 40–42. See also *supra*, pp. 677–704.

[26] Report of the 1966 Special Committee, Doc. A/6230, 27 June 1966, paras. 248 I and II B, para. 272. The five States were: Dahomey, Italy, Japan, Madagascar and the Netherlands. The consensus text contains in paragraph 5 the French proposal of 1964.

[27] *Ibid.*, para. 216. Generally for arguments pro and con, see paras. 210–220, and in connection with "explanations of vote" paras. 256–271.

[28] For text of these proposals see *ibid.*, paras. 159–161. The former included a specific reference in para. 2 *(b)* to the Court. For discussion see paras. 240–245.

[29] *Ibid.*, para. 220.

[30] *Peace Treaties, Pleadings*, p. 276. See also *ibid.*, p. 272.

of judgment from that of an advisory opinion essentially in the manner endorsed by the Court in its Opinion. In view of the mutation which the effect of advisory opinions seem to undergo in the practice of the United Nations, it may be useful to quote the following passage from Mr. Cohen's speech:

> "An advisory opinion does not have the binding force of a judgment . . . An advisory opinion is what it purports to be, advice and guidance which the Court is authorized to give under the Charter and the Statute. Even the parties to a dispute concerning which the Court gives an advisory opinion are not bound by the opinion given and there is no inherent reason in principle why their consent to the giving of the opinion should be required . . .
>
> In this instance the Advisory Opinion is sought to assist the Assembly in the performance of its Charter functions. Of course the Opinion may, and we hope it will be of use and value to the States specially concerned as well as to the Assembly but it can only persuade and cannot coerce their judgment".[31]

The representative of the United Kingdom, Mr. (as he then was) Fitzmaurice, took the position that "even if the Permanent Court was right" in declining to give an opinion in the *Eastern Carelia* case, there was a question "whether the present Court is in the same position *constitutionally* and *organically* as the Permanent Court. In other words, there is involved here not only the question of applicability of the *Eastern Carelia* principle in the circumstances of the present case, but also the question of the constitution and status of the present Court as compared with the former Permanent Court".[32] The Permanent Court was not an organ of the League, whereas the present Court is "the principal judicial organ of the United Nations" and in order to be able to deal with disputes "in conformity with the principles of justice and international law" (Article 1 (1) of the Charter), "the United Nations and its various organs must be able to turn to the Court for advisory opinions. Subject, therefore, to the inherent right of the Court as a court . . ." Mr. Fitzmaurice submitted, "the Court has unquestionably a right, and (within the same limits) an obligation, to give an opinion if it possibly can".[33] Like Mr. Cohen, Mr. Fitzmaurice distinguished judgments from advisory opinions in a language which was virtually incorporated by the Court in its Opinion.[34] There can be no doubt that these two Governments have decisively illuminated some of the implications of the organic status of the Court in its advisory, that is, its United Nations function.

During the general discussion at the twenty-first session of the General Assembly in

[31] *Ibid.*, at 272.

[32] *Ibid.*, at 305. Italics in the original.

[33] *Peace Treaties, Pleadings*, at 305–306. Cf. also p. 312.

[34] "The opinion", he said, "however great its persuasive authority, does not *formally* settle the dispute at all. It is an opinion, not a decision; it is given not to the States concerned, but to the international Organization requesting it." *Ibid.*, at 304. Italics in the original.

Later in his speech he advanced "a somewhat extreme view" that when the Assembly exercises its right to ask the Court on any legal question "the whole issue is simply a matter between the Assembly and the Court, and not one in which any individual State has, strictly speaking, any right to intervene, or to suggest that the Assembly is not competent to request an opinion or the Court not competent to give it". *Ibid.*, at 313. On the last issue see Judge Winiarski's dissenting opinion, *I.C.J. Reports 1950*, at 96–97.

connection with South West Africa, the delegations of many Members expressed their views concerning the role of the Court particularly with respect to the law and standards to be applied by it without distinguishing its advisory and judicial functions. Thus the delegate of Pakistan referring to the 1966 judgment of the Court drew attention to "the insensitivity of these judges to current international standards or legal norms, their disregard of the mode of generation of customary international law, their refusal to apply, in the performance of their function in accordance with Article 38 of the Statute, directives manifested in the resolutions of the General Assembly".[35] Some speakers felt that the Court should have considered General Assembly resolution 1514 (XV) of 1960 containing the Declaration on the Granting of Independence to Colonial Peoples, the 73 resolutions relating to South West Africa,[36] "the decisions of the United Nations",[37] "the spirit of the times",[38] "political and humanitarian considerations",[39] and the principle *ut res magis valeat quam pereat.*[40] One speaker described the Court as "one of the Organization's principal subsidiary organs" and the General Assembly, when legal remedies failed, as "the Court of last resort".[41] Another delegate described the Court's verdict as "recommendatory, not binding".[42] The delegate of Israel, Dr. Rosenne, stated that the Court has been unable "to play what it has more than once stated to be its own role as one of the principal organs of the United Nations, that is, to participate in the activities of the Organization and co-operate with the other organs in the pursuit of the aims of the United Nations" and "that insufficient attention may have been given to the circumstances which prompted the initiative of Ethiopia and Liberia and to the mutual relationships of the two principal organs of the organization concerned, the Court and this General Assembly".[43] He may have had in mind, the "grand strategy, political and legal", agreed upon at the Second Conference of African States, held in Addis Ababa in June 1960, when it was recognized that "our recourse to legal action in respect of South West Africa was to be complementary to all political efforts in the United Nations".[44]

[35] Doc. A/PV. 1414, p. 37.

[36] Ukrainian S.S.R., A/PV. 1431, p. 41, Hungary, *ibid.*, 1429, p. 48, Algeria, *ibid.*, pp. 56 f. ("The Court . . . has remained wedded to a static approach to the law . . . The Court is no longer in a position to respond to present requirements in international relations.")

[37] Byelorussian S.S.R., A/PV. 1449, pp. 63–65.

[38] Mongolia, *ibid.*, p. 26.

[39] Venezuela, A/PV. 1431, p. 61.

[40] Poland, A/PV. 1427, pp. 48–50.

[41] Ghana, A/PV. 1419, pp. 53–55, 58–60.

[42] Saudi Arabia, A/PV. 1431, p. 72.

[43] A/PV. 1439, pp. 42–47.

[44] Ethiopia, A/PV. 1414, pp. 8–10, 11. The delegate of Algeria also referred to that Conference and said that "those two countries (Ethiopia and Algeria) have instituted action on behalf of all Africa because that mission was entrusted to them by the independent African States in 1960". A/PV. 1429, p. 56.

As to the "grand strategy" it was expected that the judgment of the Court "would open the way to effective United Nations action with regard to this question". It also seemed to the Secretary-General of the United Nations "that the permanent members of the Security Council and the main trading partners of South Africa have a special responsibility as well as the means to persuade the South African Government to abandon its present course and seek a solution consistent with the Charter of the United Nations and the resolutions of the Security Council and the General Assembly". *Introduction* to the Annual Report of the Secretary-General on the work of the Organization, 1965–1966. *GAOR*, 21st Sess., No. 1 A (A/6301/Add. 1), p. 11. See also Ernest A. Gross, "The South West Africa Case: What Happened?" 45 *Foreign*

It would appear from this sample of opinions that the Court was expected to treat resolutions, decisions, declarations along with political and humanitarian considerations as part of the law to be applied by the Court in contentious cases. This matter will be considered later. However, to make sure that this would be so, Article 38 of the Statute should be amended to include General Assembly resolutions and declarations.[45] Otherwise, given the sparsity of cases the process of adjustment is bound to be slow unless the composition of the Court is changed radically. It may be recalled that the rule which the Permanent Court applied in the *Lotus* case was not formally changed until the 1958 Geneva Conference on the Law of the Sea.[46]

The various expectations voiced in the General Assembly after the 1966 Judgment had been succinctly presented to the Court by the Agent of Applicants, Mr. Ernest A. Gross, in the *South West Africa* cases in the following manner:

> "Such an approval (to regard the international consensus[47] as a general principle of law recognized by civilized nations everywhere in the world) would view the interpretation of the subdivisions of Article 38 in light of the needs of the developing international legal order, giving to Article 38 a dynamic content, and thereby giving full scope to the fact that the Statute of the Court is an integral part of the Charter . . . and is itself capable of, and entitled to, the same flexible principles of interpretation as have been applied to the remaining provisions of the Charter itself. This of course applies with even greater force to the Mandate instrument and international régime. The Statute of the Court, as an integral portion of the Charter underscores the point that this Court itself is formally constituted as an international component of the organized community thereby making it highly appropriate to give effect to the law-creating processes active in other segments of this same international community, of which the Court is the high judicial tribunal".[48]

The doctrine tends to agree with the perception of the role of the Court as developed in the *Peace Treaties* case and to stress on the one hand its duty to take part in the political activities of the political organs of the United Nations, and on the other, as the Court has done, to emphasize that this duty is not unlimited and that the Court must preserve its

*Affairs*, 36–48 (1966), p. 42, in whose opinion "it was the hope and expectation of the Applicant States . . . that a judgment would impel the United Nations—in particular, South Africa's principal trading partners—to take effective action in support of the rule of law, embodied and reflected in the judicial process".

[45] Thus the delegate of France declared: "The international community which we comprise imposes on the Court the obligation to settle, in accordance with international law, the disputes submitted to it. It has the obligation to formulate legal opinions and, so to speak, to remain indifferent to political concerns, to which, on the other hand, the Assembly cannot fail to give the greatest consideration. That serves as a guarantee for each of the States represented here . . . If this distinction, which seeks to separate clearly law from politics, were to be challenged, my delegation feels that the result of this would be a very serious modification of the balance between the respective powers of the various organs of the United Nations. Should it appear that the pertinent rules of law whose sources are enumerated in Article 38 of the Statute of the Court are no longer in keeping with the circumstances, it is for the States, and not for the Court to modify them". A/PV. 1439, p. 77. One of the innovations introduced into the Statute in 1945 is Article 70 which confers upon the Court the "power to propose such amendments to the present Statute as it may deem necessary". It is to be hoped that this clause will not remain a dead letter.

[46] The Brussels Convention of 10 May 1952 relating to Penal Jurisdiction in Matters of Collisions and Other Accidents of Navigation was signed by a handful of States. L. Oppenheim, *International Law*, Vol. I (8th ed. by H. Lauterpacht, 1954), pp. 334, 603, note 5.

[47] He was referring to the evidence presented in the Reply at pp. 274–291.

[48] Oral Hearings, *South West Africa* cases, Verbatim Records, C.R. 65/35, p. 28.

character as a court. Lauterpacht expressed the view that "the tendency to caution in matters of jurisdiction is—and ought to be—mitigated in the case of advisory opinions by the specific character of that function of the Court, namely that it is essentially advisory in nature. In addition, in relation to the International Court of Justice—as distinguished from the Permanent Court of International Justice—there is the further consideration that the Court is expressly described as the judicial organ of the United Nations and that its resulting obligations and powers must . . . be deemed to modify to some extent the previous position on the subject".[49] De Visscher is of the opinion that while the Court as the principal judicial organ should in principle reply to every request for an opinion, it should decline to do so if it were in the guise of an opinion to decide the merits of a dispute without the consent of the States concerned.[50] In Hudson's view the Court being "a part of the General Assembly . . . would seem to be bound to pay attention to the course of the United Nations".[51] Professor Green raises the rhetorical question "whether, in view of the fact that the Court is the principal judicial organ of the United Nations, it is not incumbent upon the judges to seek to give effect to the purposes of the United Nations".[52] In strongest language Rosenne expressed the view that "in its capacity of a principal organ of the United Nations . . . subject to overriding considerations of law (including judicial propriety), the Court must co-operate in the attainment of the aims of the Organization and to strive to give effect to the decisions of the principal organs, and not to achieve results which would render them nugatory".[53] Adverting to the sources of decision which the Court should apply, Rosenne on the one hand contends that the Court must not reach its decisions "on opportunistic grounds or those of expediency" but on the other hand, this does not mean that "the members of the International Court, as the judges of any domestic court, are expected to remain indifferent to prevailing trends and requirements of the society which has charged them with judicial functions". Nevertheless, "the principal objective of the political function of adjudication, and hence of the Court as an institution for that purpose, is to meet the desire for completely non-political treatment of a matter, and its solution on the basis of law".[54]

One cannot but agree with these propositions but it would be self-deceiving to believe that they solve the problem. They merely indicate the perimeters within which all judicial activity takes place. As such they necessarily lack precision and even as mere

[49] *The Development of International Law by the International Court* (1958), p. 109. But see p. 250 for a statement of the limits having a legal character.

[50] *Aspects récents,* p. 41.

[51] "The Thirty-Fourth Year of the World Court." 50 *AJIL,* pp. 1–17 (1956) at 9. The words "General Assembly" and "United Nations" evidently should be transposed.

[52] L. C. Green, "South West Africa and the World Court," 22 *International Journal* (Canadian Institute of International Affairs), pp. 39–67 (1966–1967), at 58. When two interpretations are possible the judges are exhorted to "support the operative interpretation".

[53] *The Law and Practice of the International Court* (1965), Vol. I, p. 70. It will be noted that Rosenne as diplomat (Cf. *supra,* at 866) is consistent with Rosenne as scholar.

[54] *Ibid.,* at 90–91. Elsewhere he suggests that the Court is primarily concerned, equally, in advisory and contentious procedure, with the application of international law to disputes and not "with the formulation of legal policy". *Ibid.,* at 77.

guidelines they are afflicted with ambiguity. One thing seems certain: in one way or another, the present Court, due to its organic connection with the United Nations, is expected to perform its judicial activity, both in advisory and contentious proceedings, in a manner different from that of the Permanent Court.

### 3. A New Title of Jurisdiction

The first case to come before the Court offers an instructive example of the impact of the institutional connection on its behaviour. In its composition the Court was essentially a new Court; only two members who had served on the Permanent Court were elected to the bench of the International Court, Judges Guerrero and de Visscher. The facts of the case are well known and need not be recounted. It was first brought to the Security Council by the United Kingdom. The Council on 9 April 1947 adopted a resolution in which it recalled the incident on 22 October 1946 in the Strait of Corfu in which two British war vessels were damaged by mines and recommended that the two Governments concerned—the United Kingdom and Albania—"should immediately refer the dispute to the International Court of Justice in accordance with the provisions of the Statute of the Court".[55]

The British Government brought the case before the Court by means of a unilateral application in which the jurisdiction of the Court was claimed to be founded on four grounds: (1) that under Article 36 (1) of its Statute the Court's jurisdiction comprised "all matters specially provided for in the Charter of the United Nations"; (2) the aforementioned resolution of the Council; (3) the acceptance by Albania of the Council's invitation to participate in the discussion, subject to the condition that it accept all the obligations of a Member of the United Nations; and (4) that under Article 25 of the Charter Members agree to carry out the decisions of the Security Council in accordance with the present Charter.[55]

Albania in a note of 2 July 1947 to the Court declared that it "fully accepts the recommendation of the Security Council", that Article 25 related solely to decisions of the Council taken under Chapter VII of the Charter, but that "it is prepared, notwithstanding this irregularity in the action taken by the Government of the United Kingdom, to appear before the Court".[56] The alleged irregularity consisted in the failure of the United Kingdom to proceed "in accordance with the provisions of the Statute", that is, by seeking the agreement of Albania for the conclusion of a special agreement. All these arguments were elaborated in the Preliminary Objections filed by Albania with the Court on 9 December 1947. In particular it was insisted that "a recommendation certainly cannot *ipso facto* constitute a matter specially provided for in the Charter of the United Nations to which the Court's jurisdiction extends".[57]

[55] The *Corfu Channel* case (Preliminary Objections), Judgment 25 March 1948, *I.C.J. Reports 1948*, p. 14, at 17.
[56] *Ibid.*, at 19.
[57] *I.C.J. Reports 1948*, at 22.

The Court rejected Albania's preliminary objections and affirmed jurisdiction on the basis of the 2 July note in which that Government declared that it was "prepared . . . to appear before the Court" without expressing any view on the novel ground for compulsory jurisdiction invoked by the United Kingdom.[58] However, in a separate opinion seven Judges (Basdevant, Alvarez, Winiarski, Zorocic, de Visscher, Badawi, Krylov) deemed the United Kingdom's claim of "a new case of compulsory jurisdiction" sufficiently important to receive an explicit rebuttal. They based the rejection on three grounds: first, the normal meaning of recommendation; secondly, "the general structure of the Charter and of the Statute which founds the jurisdiction of the Court on the consent of States"; and thirdly, the text of Article 36 (3) of the Charter which is merely a reminder addressed to the Security Council. For all these reasons, harking back to the outlook of the old Court, it appeared impossible to these judges "to accept an interpretation according to which this article, without explicitly saying so, has introduced more-or-less surreptitiously, a new case of compulsory jurisdiction".[59]

This is, of course, the "immutable" rule of the *Eastern Carelia* case,[60] and this group of Judges lost no time in recognizing it as such in so far as the new Court was concerned, and to reinstate the authoritative warning against any attempt to regard the advisory procedure as a means of introducing into the Charter and Statute "by a circuitous route", the idea of compulsory jurisdiction which had been deliberately excluded from it.[61] However, it is submitted that in the *Corfu Channel* case the caution may have been misplaced and that a different interpretation was possible based on consent and not solely on the new institutional status of the Court.

First of all, Article 25 of the Charter is not limited to Chapter VII although it is limited to "decisions" of the Security Council.[62] In this case the Council used the verb "recommend"; it could have used some other verb, but it is doubted that this alone would have been sufficient to create a new case of compulsory jurisdiction.[63] But certainly the new words in Article 36 (1) of the Statute relating to "all matters specially provided for in the Charter" should have received closer attention than they did and could certainly not be totally discounted as if they were due to an "error in drafting".[64] However, the missing element which was needed to enable the Court to give effect to the new text in Articles 36 (3) of the Charter and 36 (1) of the Statute was the consent of the parties. The Court may have found it more convenient to base jurisdiction in the case on a form of *forum prorogatum* but it could also have based it on the resolution of the Security

[58] *Ibid.*, at 26.

[59] *Ibid.*, at 32.

[60] Cf. Judge Azevedo's separate opinion in the *Peace Treaties* case, *I.C.J. Reports 1950*, p. 82.

[61] This warning related to the Covenant and was uttered by Å. Hammarskjöld whose authority was great. *Juridiction Internationale* (Leyden: Sijthoff, 1938) p. 284. It was quoted by Judge Azevedo, *loc. cit.*, p. 80. See also Charles de Visscher, *Theory and Reality in Public International Law*, p. 331, and note 4 on p. 331.

[62] On the meaning of "decision" see Fitzmaurice, "The Law and Procedure of the International Court of Justice", 29 *BYIL*, pp. 1-63 (1952), at 31-32.

[63] As is suggested by Rosenne, at 344.

[64] Rosenne, at 342.

Council. The United Kingdom by its application certainly gave its consent to the Council's recommendation. And Albania in its note of 2 July, declared that it "fully accepts the recommendation of the Security Council". It is suggested that the consent of the parties, United Kingdom and Albania, together with the new wording in Article 36 (1) of the Statute constitute the necessary and sufficient basis for a new title or case of compulsory jurisdiction. This new title is not introduced "by a circuitous route" or "surreptitiously" but quite openly and directly by the Charter and Statute to which all Members have consented as did Albania for that particular case, subject, of course, to their right to accept or reject the Council's recommendation. In the *Corfu Channel* case both parties explicitly accepted it and thus supplied the requisite link.

The Court, it is submitted, missed an opportunity both as an organ of international law and as principal judicial organ of the United Nations to accept a new title of compulsory jurisdiction which might have infused some vitality into Article 36 (3) of the Charter and into the whole system of peaceful settlement established in the Charter.

Changing from judicial caution to judicial boldness with respect to the recommendation of the Security Council in connection with the assessment of the amount of compensation, the Court based its judgment, given by default due to the non-participation of Albania, at least in part on that recommendation. When notified of the Special Agreement between the parties immediately after the delivery of its judgment on the Preliminary Objections, the Court made an Order on 26 March 1948 in which it placed on record that this Agreement "now forms the basis of further proceedings before the Court in this case".[65] According to the Agreement the Court was asked, *inter alia,* to decide the question "is there any duty to pay compensation" for the damage and loss of life which resulted from the explosion in Albanian waters. On its face this Agreement limited the Court to establishing the duty of Albania to pay which was indeed the position taken by Albania. The Court, however, moved by the principle of effectiveness in construing jurisdictional clauses,[66] was of the opinion that "if the Court limited itself to saying that compensation was due without fixing the amount, the dispute would not be completely settled". In support of this reasoning the Court fell back on the Security Council resolution whereby, as understood by the Court, the Council had "doubtless intended that the dispute should be resolved by the Court".[67] Unfortunately the Council had failed to express any such intent. It did not even refer to settlement; it merely recommended that the parties refer the dispute to the Court. Moreover, the Court would seem to have precluded itself from drawing any aid from the Council recommendation when it decided that "now" the further proceedings would be based on the Special Agreement. The Agreement is eloquently silent on the point of fixing the quantum of compensation. To establish the duty to pay compensation is one thing and this function was entrusted to the

[65] *I.C.J. Reports 1948,* p. 53 at 55; restated in the judgment on the merits, *ibid., 1949,* p. 4 at 6–7.

[66] See Lauterpacht, *The Development of International Law,* pp. 243–250, and de Visscher, *Aspects récents,* pp. 54–61, and the same *Theory and Reality,* pp. 345–346.

[67] *I.C.J. Reports 1949,* pp. 246–248.

Court; but to establish how much shall be paid is another and this function was not conferred upon the Court, neither explicitly nor by necessary implication.

In this case the Court made history for two reasons: first, by granting the first and only judgment by default, one which Albania has so far refused to honour; and secondly, by applying the principle of effectiveness at the wrong place. The proper place, in the present submission, would have been in connection with a new case of compulsory jurisdiction.

The Court may also have made history for two additional reasons: first, by censuring in no uncertain terms the use of force by the United Kingdom in connection with "Operation Retail" and by refusing the pleas based on "the alleged right of intervention", self-help and self-protection: "But to ensure respect for international law, of which it is the organ, the Court must declare that the action of the British Navy constituted a violation of Albanian sovereignty".[68] Secondly, by failing to refer in this context to the law of the Charter. As Judge *ad hoc* Dr Ečer, said in his dissenting opinion: "The authority of the Judgment, and that of the Court as judicial organ of the United Nations would be strengthened by a reference to the provisions of the Charter".[69]

## 4. Scope of and Consent to Request

The general impact of the institutional connection with the United Nations upon the behaviour of the Court in advisory proceedings has already been discussed. It remains to add some detailed comments. The Court remains master of its procedure. While it recognized in the *Peace Treaties* case its duty—as an organ—to participate in the political activities of the United Nations, this is subject to certain limits as the Court considers itself to be "essentially" the "principal judicial organ" of the Organization.[70] As a consequence, the Court's power to give an advisory opinion is open to certain challenges by the interested States and the Court itself may consider *ex officio* objections to its power or competence to give an opinion. As the Court put it in the *Cameroons* case, it has "the duty to safeguard the judicial function",[71] and this fundamental principle applies to both its advisory and contentious functions. As a consequence, before considering the substantive issues addressed to it in a Request, the Court will take under advisement these preliminary questions in order to determine "whether the circumstances of the case are of such a character as should lead it to decline to answer the Request".[72] Unlike the conten-

[68] *I.C.J. Reports 1949,* at 35.

[69] He had in mind Articles 2 (4) and 42. *Ibid.,* at 130–131. Judge Alvarez reminded the Court in his individual opinion that it had "a new mission which was not conferred—at least not expressly—on the Court which preceded it", namely pursuant to General Assembly resolution 171 (III) of 14 November 1947, to develop international law. *Ibid.,* at 40.

[70] *I.C.J. Reports 1950,* at 71.

[71] *Reports 1963,* at 38 and see *supra.*

[72] *Peace Treaties* case, *I.C.J. Reports 1950,* at 72; restated in *Expenses* case, *ibid., 1962,* at 155. Å. Hammarskjöld considered that the judicial character of advisory opinions had two corollaries: first, the right and the duty to determine its jurisdiction, and secondly, the absence of an unconditional duty to reply to every request even if the request is formally correct. *Loc. cit.,* at 285.

tious procedure the Court's handling of the preliminary questions in advisory cases is informal as no separate votes are apparently taken in order to dispose of them.

This informality can be embarrassing for the judges. In the *Peace Treaties* case Judge Azevedo would have preferred that the Court should abstain from giving an opinion. However, notions of a different character "have been decided by one and the same vote, namely the preliminary point regarding the Court's capacity to comply with the Request for an Opinion and the answer which the Court should give to the questions put to it".[73] As a consequence, the vote on the answer is not an accurate reflection of the division of the Court on the preliminary points. However, in the case of *I.L.O. Administrative Tribunal* the operative part of the opinion includes the decision of the Court by 9 votes to 4 to comply with the Request for an Advisory Opinion.[74]

It is well established that the Court will entertain only a request relating to a legal question. Recalling the holding in the *Eastern Carelia* case,[75] the Court in the *Expenses* case declared that in accordance with Article 65 of the Statute it can give an opinion only on a legal question and that "if a question is not a legal one, the Court has no discretion in the matter; it must decline to give the opinion".[76] The Court has never defined the meaning of the term but has provided some guidelines. First, the Court is not bound by the apparent designation of the question as a legal one by the requesting organ;[77] it is not concerned with the motives prompting the organ to make the request or the Members who vote in favour of it;[78] it is not concerned with the object of the request although it may take note of it;[79] nor can it be, in the nature of things, concerned with the use which the requesting organ or another organ of the Organization concerned, will make of the answer.

The Court will give an "opinion on any legal question, abstract or otherwise"[80] or, positively, upon "a concrete legal question".[81] In particular the Court will reply to a question involving the interpretation of the Charter,[82] or of any bilateral or multilateral treaty.[83] An objection to competence based on the principle of domestic jurisdiction in Article 2 (7) of the Charter has been overruled on the ground "that the interpretation of the terms of a treaty . . . could not be considered as a question essentially within the do-

[73] *I.C.J. Reports 1950,* at 79.

[74] *I.C.J. Reports 1956,* at 101.

[75] "The Court, being a Court of Justice, cannot, even in giving advisory opinions, depart from the essential rules guiding their (Fr. *son*) activity as a Court". *P.C.I.J. Series B, No. 5,* p. 29 (23 July 1923).

[76] *I.C.J. Reports 1962,* at 155.

[77] Rosenne, II, p. 703.

[78] The Court "is not concerned with the motives which may have inspired this request, nor with the considerations which, in the concrete cases submitted for examination to the Security Council, formed the subject of the exchange of views which took place in that body". *Admissions* case, 1948, at 61.

[79] "In the present case the Court is dealing with a Request for an Opinion, the sole object of which is to enlighten the General Assembly". *Peace Treaties* case, *I.C.J. Reports 1950,* at 72.

[80] *Membership* case, *I.C.J. Reports 1948,* at 61.

[81] *Expenses* case, *I.C.J. Reports 1962,* at 156.

[82] "Nowhere is any provision to be found forbidding the Court, 'the principal judicial organ of the United Nations', to exercise in regard to Article 4 of the Charter, a multilateral treaty, an interpretative function which falls within the normal exercise of its judicial powers". *Membership* case, *I.C.J. Reports 1948,* at 61; restated in the *Expenses* case 1962, p. 156.

[83] As it did in the *Peace Treaties* case. This can be based on Article 36 (*2a*) of the Statute of the Court.

mestic jurisdiction of a State. It is a question of international law which, by its very nature, lies within the competence of the Court''.[84]

Objections directed against the competence of the organ to make the request could also arise. For instance, it could be objected that a request from an organ of the United Nations other than the Assembly and the Council,[85] or from a specialized agency,[86] for an advisory opinion related to a legal question which had not arisen ''within the scope of their activity'' (Article 96, para. 2, of the Charter), or that the request was *ultra vires* on the ground, for instance, that it was contrary to Article 2 (7).[87] The Court had an opportunity to consider objections based on the principle *audiatur et altera pars.* This objection could arise when the interested party cannot appear and, secondly, when the interested party can, but does not appear.[88] The former situation arose in the *I.L.O. Administrative Tribunal* case, in which the Court declared: ''The judicial character of the Court requires that both sides directly affected by these proceedings should be in a position to submit their views and arguments to the Court''. The Court found that this principle can be satisfied by making available to the Court the observations of the officials concerned.[89] The latter situation arose in the *Peace Treaties* case. The principle requires, said the Court, that the parties or ''sides'' directly affected ''should be in a position'' to be heard; therefore, the voluntary non-participation of Hungary, Rumania and Bulgaria in the *Peace Treaties* case was not a bar to the proceedings.[90]

Another objection derived from the *audiatur* principle relates to the equality of the parties which ''follows from the requirements of good administration of justice''. This objection arose in the *I.L.O. Administrative Tribunal* case and was met by dispensing with oral hearings.[91] In the same case the Court considered and rejected the objection arising from Article XII of the Statute of the I.L.O. Administrative Tribunal which provided that the opinion of the Court shall be ''binding''. The Court acknowledged that ''such

[84] *Peace Treaties* case, *I.C.J. Reports 1950* at 70. In using the adverb ''essentially'' the Court indicated that it was considering the objection from the point of view of Article 2 (7) but the Court declined to pronounce on the question whether as an organ of the United Nations it was bound by that clause saying: ''These considerations also suffice to dispose of the objection based on the principle of domestic jurisdiction and directed specifically against the competence of the Court, namely that the Court, as an organ of the United Nations, is bound to observe the provisions of the Charter, including Article 2, par. 7''. *Ibid.,* at 72.

[85] All principal organs except the Secretariat have been authorized to request opinions.

[86] And the International Atomic Energy Agency.

[87] In the *Peace Treaties* case the Court considered such an objection and rejected it asserting that the Assembly justified the adoption of the resolution containing the request by reference to Article 55 of the Charter. *I.C.J. Reports 1950,* at 70.

[88] Hammarskjöld's view was that advisory opinions should not become mere consultations furnished by the Court to the political organs of the League without the guarantees of public and adversary proceedings; the practice of the Permanent Court satisfied these requirements. *Loc. cit.,* at 284.

[89] *I.C.J. Reports 1956,* p. 77 at 86.

[90] Nor was the non-participation of South Africa in the *South West Africa* (Voting) and *South West Africa* (Petition) cases an impediment. Rosenne, II, pp. 699, 706.

[91] *I.C.J. Reports 1956,* at 86. The Court relied also on the principle of effectiveness saying: ''Notwithstanding the permissive character of Article 65 of the Statute . . ., only compelling reasons could cause the Court to adopt in this matter a negative attitude which would imperil the working of the regime established by the Statute of the Administrative Tribunal for the judicial protection of officials. Any seeming or nominal absence of equality ought not to be allowed to obscure or to defeat that primary object.'' *Ibid.* In this case as in the *Reparation* and *United Nations Tribunal* cases the Court went out of its way to make a contribution to the independence and security of international officials.

effect of the Opinion goes beyond the scope attributed by the Charter and by the Statute of the Court to an Advisory Opinion'', but this ''in no wise affects the way in which the Court functions . . . nor does it affect the reasoning by which the Court forms its Opinion or the context of the Opinion itself''.[92]

Of all the objections to the admissibility of a request for an advisory opinion, absence of consent on the part of interested States has been considered by the Permanent Court to be fundamental if the request, in the words of Article 82 of the Rules of the Court, ''relates to a legal question actually pending between two or more states''[92a]. Pursuant to Article 68 of the Statute, the Court is directed to ''be guided by the provisions of the present Statute which apply in contentious cases to the extent to which it recognizes them to be applicable''. The standpoint of the present Court in respect of the requirement of consent has already been discussed.[93] It remains to fill in a few details. The *Eastern Carelia* case is the accepted starting point, and the Court as well as writers have concentrated on the issue whether the opinion in the *Peace Treaties* case constitutes a departure from the opinion of the Permanent Court. An ancillary question is whether the partial or complete abandonment of the *Eastern Carelia* ruling is due to the new institutional status of the Court.

The Permanent Court started from the positivist premise that the principle of the independence of States ''is a fundamental principle of international law'' and that ''it is well established in international law that no State can, without its consent, be compelled to submit its disputes with other States either to mediation or to arbitration, or to any other kind of pacific settlement''. The Court found that Russia had not given her consent and consequently that it was ''impossible to give its opinion on a dispute of this kind''. That was the primary reason. The second reason which ''renders it very inexpedient'' for the Court to deal with the matter, was that ''the question whether Finland and Russia contracted on the terms of the Declaration as to the nature of the autonomy of *Eastern Carelia* is really one of fact''. In the absence of Russia and its refusal to participate in the inquiry, it was doubtful whether the Court could ''arrive at any judicial conclusion upon the question of fact: What did the parties agree to?''[94] The third reason was that although the Court had been asked to give an advisory opinion and not to decide the dis-

[92] *I.C.J. Reports 1956,* at 84. On this and other issues in this case see Leo Gross, ''Participation of Individuals in Advisory Proceedings before the International Court of Justice: Question of Equality between the Parties'', 52 *AJIL,* pp. 16–40 (1958). See also *supra,* pp. 705–726.

[92a] It may be noted that in such a case Rule 82 of the Rules of Court is also relevant which provides that Article 31 of the Statute shall apply. This clause regulates the appointment of judges *ad hoc.*

[93] See *supra,* p. 860.

[94] The Court ''does not say that there is an absolute rule that the request for an advisory opinion may not involve some inquiry as to facts, but, under ordinary circumstances, it is certainly expedient that the facts upon which the opinion of the Court is desired should not be in controversy, and it should not be left to the Court itself to ascertain what they are''. *Status of Eastern Carelia,* Advisory Opinion, 23 July 1923, *P.C.I.J. Series B, No. 5,* pp. 7–29, at 28. It will be noted that the ''fact'' with which the Court was concerned did not relate to a factual situation in the ordinary sense but to the existence of a legal obligation. Rosenne, II, p. 700, seems to read this case and the *Peace Treaties* case as relating to the facts in the former sense.

pute, the question concerned the main point of the controversy between Finland and Russia, and

> "Answering the question would be substantially equivalent to deciding the dispute between the parties. (Fr. répondre à la question équivaudrait en substance à trancher un différend entre les parties.) The Court, being a Court of Justice, cannot, even in giving advisory opinions, depart from the essential rules guiding their (sic!) activity as a Court".[95]

Another litigation which is frequently linked with the *Eastern Carelia* case in connection with the *Peace Treaties,* is the *Mosul* case.[96] In that case the Court had been asked to give an opinion as to the nature of the decision to be taken by the Council (was it an arbitral award, a recommendation or a simple resolution), as to the nature of the vote (unanimous or majority), and as to whether the interested parties might participate in the vote. It responded to the request by declaring its intention "to confine itself strictly to consideration of these questions, without in any way prejudging the merits of the problem before the Council".[97]

In rendering its Opinion, the Court did not find it necessary to distinguish the *Eastern Carelia* case. However, it did consider the matter during the proceedings and "took the view that though the question under consideration offered some analogy with that of *Eastern Carelia* (Advisory Opinion No. 5), in that one of the interested parties held aloof from the proceedings, the circumstances in the present case were distinctly different, since the question before the Court referred not to the merits of the affair but to the competence of the Council, which had been duly seised of the affair and could undoubtedly ask for the Court's opinion on points of law. It was further observed that the Turkish Government had officially submitted certain "documents and information".[98] The latter statement was denied by Turkey.[99]

In the *Peace Treaties* case, its power to comply with the Request of the Assembly having been challenged, the Court distinguished the case from the *Eastern Carelia* case and found "in the opposition to it (the Request) made by Bulgaria, Hungary and Rumania no reason why it should abstain from replying to the Request".[100]

It will be recalled that the Court conceived its role in that case to be not merely that of an organ of the United Nations, but essentially that of the "principal judicial organ". It follows then that if the distinction could not be made, the Court, as a judicial organ,

[95] *Ibid.,* at 27–29.

[96] *Interpretation of Article 3, para. 2, of the Treaty of Lausanne* (Frontier between Iraq and Turkey), Advisory Opinion No. 12, 21 Nov. 1925, *P.C.I.J., Series B, No. 12,* pp. 6–35.

[97] *Ibid.,* at 18.

[98] *P.C.I.J., Series E, No. 2,* p. 164.

[99] League of Nations *Official Journal,* Feb. 1926, pp. 121, 128. Turkey also declared that it had voted against the request for an opinion. *Ibid.,* at 122. The *Official Journal,* October 1925 at 1382 merely states: "The Council adopted the conclusions of the Committee" which included the proposal for the request. It would thus appear that the vote of the parties was not counted in such decisions. See observations of Mr. Unden (Sweden) and Mr. Motta (Switzerland), League of Nations *Official Journal, Special Supp.* No. 64, pp. 38 and 64 respectively.

[100] *I.C.J. Reports 1950,* p. 72.

could not have given an opinion, although—and here appears to lie a contradiction—the Court, irrespective of the *Eastern Carelia* case, had already declared that no State could prevent it from giving the opinion requested by the Assembly which it considered necessary "in order to obtain enlightenment as to the course of action it should take".[101]

The distinction, as developed by the Court, is based on the following points: first, the request is "solely concerned with the applicability to certain disputes of the procedure for settlement instituted by the Peace Treaties"; secondly, "it is justifiable to conclude that it in no way touches the merits of those disputes"; thirdly, "the settlement of these disputes is entrusted solely to the Commission provided for by the Peace Treaties"; fourthly, "it is for these Commissions to decide upon any objections which may be raised to their jurisdiction in respect of any of these disputes"; and fifthly, "the present Opinion in no way prejudges the decisions that may be taken on those objections".[102]

The first question put before the Court was whether certain diplomatic exchanges between the States signatories to the Treaties of Peace disclose disputes within the meaning of certain articles of the Peace Treaties. The Court affirmed the existence of disputes as certain charges having been made regarding violation of articles dealing with human rights and these charges having in turn been denied, "there has thus arisen a situation in which the two sides hold clearly opposite views concerning the question of the performance or non-performance of certain treaty obligations".[103] The disputes refer, accordingly, to "the interpretation or execution of the Peace Treaties".

It is respectfully submitted that in pronouncing upon the first question, the Court decided in part upon a matter of substance in the dispute brought before the General Assembly.[104] Moreover, since the contest over the existence of a dispute within the meaning of a treaty, in this case of the Peace Treaties, usually forms the subject of preliminary objection to the jurisdiction of a tribunal in contentious cases, it is difficult to accept the reasoning of the Court that the Opinion in no way prejudges the decision of the Commission. To be sure the Court could not bind the Commission, but this is not the same thing as not prejuding its decision, unless the Court put its authority so low that the Commission would be justified in disregarding completely the pronouncement of the Court. The pronouncement does not bear directly on the question of the violation of the Peace Treaties, but it does directly involve an aspect of the dispute, namely whether the charges brought against Bulgaria, Rumania and Hungary were really concerned with human rights violations or were merely politically inspired. There is a difference between the assertion that a dispute exists within the meaning of a treaty and the existence of a dispute. It is a matter of proof.[105] It is difficult to see how the Court could pronounce on

[101] *I.C.J. Reports 1950*, p. 71; *supra*, p. 860.
[102] *I.C.J. Reports 1950*, p. 72.
[103] *Ibid.*, at 74.
[104] For a different view see de Visscher, *Aspects récents*, at 40, 42 f.
[105] *South West Africa* (Preliminary Objection) cases, *I.C.J. Reports 1962*, at 328; de Visscher, *loc. cit.*, p. 37.

so important an issue without the consent and assistance of the States concerned.[106]

Having determined the existence of a dispute, the answer to the second question followed logically. The question as formulated by the Court was whether in view of the disputes which had arisen and had not been settled, the Governments were "obligated" to comply with the disputes clauses in the Peace Treaties. The Court, guided by a purpose-oriented approach, had no hesitation in asserting that the three Governments are "obligated to carry out the provisions of those articles . . . which relate to the settlement of disputes, including the provisions for the appointment of their representatives to the Treaty Commissions".[107]

The question of the existence of the obligation to implement the disputes clauses was, like the existence of a genuine dispute, part and parcel of the situation which was under consideration by the General Assembly and on which the parties held different, opposing views. As was pointed out, "it is a question of substance; not in respect of human rights, but of the arbitration clauses".[108] The pronouncement on the existence of a dispute and of the obligation to execute the disputes clauses of the Peace Treaties was based on diplomatic notes submitted to the Court by one of the opposing parties. They have "solely the value of information", but "what the parties said or have to say must be said before the Court in proceedings which, though not contentious, do, nevertheless, call for the presentation from both sides of argument, declarations, proof and submissions".[109] Surely it is fair to suggest that the principles of equality and *audiatur et altera pars*—"the fundamental principles of law and justice"—were not observed in this case,[109] and a form of "advisory arbitration" or compulsory jurisdiction through the "indirect channel of advisory opinions" was introduced.[110]

It may be useful, in order to clarify further the points under consideration, to digress for a moment. A dispute may involve the judicial determination of several obligations each of which may constitute the subject of separate judicial proceedings and therefore the merits of such proceedings. In the *Peace Treaties* case as in the *Ambatielos* case the disputes were divided into three stages: first, was there a dispute between the parties within the meaning of the relevant instruments; secondly, was there an obligation for the parties to submit the dispute to the procedure for settlement established by these instruments; and finally, was there a substantive violation of the relevant instruments or—in the *Ambatielos* case—a dispute within the meaning of the Treaty of 1886. In the *Ambatielos* case the Court was asked to decide whether the United Kingdom was under an obligation arising from the relevant instruments to submit the dispute to arbitration.

[106] See separate opinion of Judge Azevedo: "To affirm the existence of a dispute in the present case is to begin to adjudicate upon it, and therefore to recognize the competence of the Court". *I.C.J. Reports 1950*, at 87; see also dissenting opinion of Judge Winiarski, at 92 f.

[107] *Ibid.*, at 77. The following illustrates the purpose-orientation of the opinion: "In view of the fact that the Treaties provide that any dispute shall be referred to a Commission 'at the request of either party', it follows that either party is obligated, at the request of the other party, to co-operate in constituting the Commission, in particular by appointing its representatives. Otherwise, the method of settlement by Commissions provided for in the Treaties would completely fail in its purpose". *Ibid.*

[108] Dissenting opinion of Judge Winiarski, *I.C.J. Reports 1950*, at 93.

[109] *Ibid.*, at 95.

[110] *Ibid.*, pp. 86 (Judge Azevedo), and 89, 90 (Judge Winiarski).

That was the "merits" phase of the controversy submitted to the Court for adjudication, and this phase had in turn a preliminary phase inasmuch as the United Kingdom objected to the jurisdiction of the Court to adjudicate upon the "merits". The Court held on the basis of the relevant instruments, that it was without jurisdiction "to decide on the merits of the Ambatielos claim" but that it had "jurisdiction to decide whether the United Kingdom is under an obligation to submit to arbitration, in accordance with the Declaration of 1926, the difference as to the validity of the Ambatielos claim, in so far as this claim is based on the Treaty of 1886".[111] It is no matter of concern here whether the Court was right in judging it as it did; the important point is that the Court based its jurisdiction upon the consent of the parties given in the Declaration of 1926.[112]

Thus, in the *Ambatielos* case, as Professor Verzijl pointed out, "there are two kinds of merits involved . . . which is very confusing", and he proposed "to distinguish them by writing 'merits' where Great Britain's obligation to arbitrate is at stake and merits when allusion is made to the validity of the claim of Mr. Ambatielos".[113]

In the *Ambatielos* case the Court having rejected the respondent's preliminary objections and decided that it had jurisdiction on the "merits" of the claim, adjudged accordingly that "the United Kingdom is under an obligation to submit to arbitration, in accordance with the Declaration of 1926, the difference as to the validity, under the Treaty of 1886, of the Ambatielos claim".[114] Whether in so doing the Court has departed from the attitude it had adopted in the *Peace Treaties* case and has compromised the position of the parties before the tribunal of arbitration or prejudged the jurisdiction thereof is here immaterial.[115] It is relevant to observe that in deciding a procedural issue the Court passed upon the "merits" of the controversy and that the term "merits" is used in the title of the case, in several of the separate opinions,[116] and in the joint dissenting opinion.[117]

In the *Peace Treaties* case there were also two kinds of merits: the first related to the "merits" of the two questions put to the Court in the first phase of the proceedings,[118] and the second related to the merits of the dispute, that is, the alleged violation of the human rights provisions of the *Peace Treaties* of 1947. In complying with the Assembly's

[111] *I.C.J. Reports 1952,* p. 28, at 46.

[112] In the subsequent judgment in this case the Court expressly affirmed the consensual basis of its jurisdiction as follows: "The Court is not departing from the principle, which is well established in international law and accepted by its own jurisprudence as well as that of the Permanent Court of International Justice, to the effect that a State may not be compelled to submit its disputes to arbitration without its consent". *I.C.J. Reports 1953,* p. 10, at 19. The joint dissenting opinion by Sir Arnold McNair, President, and Judges Basdevant, Klaestad and Read, expressly referred to the *Eastern Carelia* Opinion and its application on various occasions including the *Peace Treaties* case. *Ibid.*, at 28.

[113] J. H. W. Verzijl, *The Jurisprudence of the World Court,* Vol. II, *The International Court of Justice* 1947–1965 (Leyden: Sijthoff, 1966) at 151, n. 3.

[114] *Ambatielos* case (Merits: obligation to arbitrate), *I.C.J. Reports 1953,* p. 10, at 23.

[115] This aspect of the case is discussed by Fitzmaurice, "The Law and Practice of the International Court of Justice, 1951–1954. Questions of Jurisdiction, Competence and Procedure," 34 *British Year Book of International Law,* pp. 1–161 (1958) at 41 ff.

[116] *I.C.J. Reports 1952,* at 52 (Judge Levi Carneiro) and 56 (Judge Spiropoulos).

[117] *I.C.J. Reports 1953,* at 25 where it is stated: "The Court, having found that it has jurisdiction for this purpose, is called upon to adjudicate upon the merits of the difference between the Parties as to the existence or non-existence of this obligation".

[118] Professor Verzijl used the term merits in quotation marks in his analysis of the case.

request the Court pronounced upon the "merits" of the controversy between the parties without the consent of all the parties. It affirmed the existence of a dispute within the meaning of the relevant clauses as well as the obligation of Bulgaria, Hungary and Rumania to implement the settlement provisions of the Peace Treaties. In the second phase these Governments having failed to appoint their representatives within the period of 30 days prescribed by the General Assembly, the Court went still further in saying:

> "As the Court has declared in its Opinion of 30 March 1950, the Governments of Bulgaria, Hungary and Rumania are under an obligation to appoint their representatives to the Treaty Commissions, and it is clear that refusal to fulfill a treaty obligation involves international responsibility".[119]

It is not pertinent to enquire into the juridical basis of this pronouncement although it is somewhat surprising seeing that the Court has held—in the first phase—that its advisory opinion had "no binding force", and that it "is given not to the States, but to the organ which is entitled to request it", that is, to the United Nations for its "enlightenment as to the course it should take" but not as to the course the States concerned should take.[120] The essential point is that the Court has done in the *Peace Treaties* case what the Permanent Court has declined to do in the *Eastern Carelia* case, that is, to answer the question: "What did the parties agree to?" without the consent of the parties concerned.

The *Mosul* Case, it is submitted, offers no support for the Court's departure from the *Eastern Carelia* ruling.[121] In the latter case the Permanent Court was solely concerned with the voting procedure of the Council of the League, which in any event was laid down in the Covenant and according to which in calculating unanimity (Article 15, para. 6) or majority (Article 15, para. 7) the votes of the parties were excluded.

The purpose of this somewhat detailed discussion of the *Peace Treaties* case has been to consider three questions: first, the question whether the Court successfully and convincingly distinguished the *Eastern Carelia* case; secondly, whether its behaviour was influenced by its new institutional status; and thirdly, whether the Court simply set lower limits on the requirements of consent.

As regards the answer to the third question in the *Peace Treaties* case there seems to be little room for doubt that it can be subsumed under the *Mosul* case: the Court was concerned with the question of competence, not of the requesting organ, but at any rate, of another principal organ of the United Nations; it was a question of competence not under the Charter but under a treaty. These differences are of minor character.

To sum up: in answering the first two questions in the *Peace Treaties* case, the Court appears to have substantially departed from the *Eastern Carelia.* That case made no distinction between questions of procedure and substance. Nor, in the *Mosul* case, was the Permanent Court concerned with a question of procedure relating to the obligations or rights of Turkey

[119] Interpretation of the *Peace Treaties* (second phase), Advisory Opinion: *I.C.J. Reports 1950,* p. 221, at 228.
[120] *I.C.J. Reports 1950,* p. 65, at 71 and *supra,* at p. 860.
[121] *I.C.J. Reports 1952,* p. 28, at 46.

and Iraq under the instruments in question. It was solely concerned with interpreting them in so far as the Council's role was involved. The first two questions in the *Peace Treaties* case did not relate to any competence of the General Assembly or of the Secretary-General. They related directly to the rights and obligations of the States concerned under the Peace Treaties, even though they did not involve the human rights provisions. They did not concern a point of procedure in the General Assembly, but the procedural law of the parties.

Much has been made of the passage in the Opinion in the *Eastern Carelia* case to the effect that the question put to the Permanent Court "concerns directly the main point" of the controversy and that "answering the question would be substantially equivalent to deciding the dispute between the parties".[122] The International Court did declare that "the circumstances of the present case are profoundly different from those which were before the Permanent Court . . . in the *Eastern Carelia* case" and referred to the statement quoted above. However, it is submitted first that the first two questions addressed to the Court related directly to a main point of the controversy between the parties even before it was placed before the General Assembly, and secondly that the words "substantially equivalent", while not free from ambiguity, do not refer to the substance or merits, as the International Court apparently construes them, and thus distinguishes them from procedure. The Permanent Court did not say in that passage that it is not proper for it, as a Court of Justice, to handle merits without the consent of Russia. The passage in question may well relate rather to the effect of the Advisory Opinion: the Court was saying that the effect of an Opinion was "substantially equivalent" of that of a Judgment,[123] and therefore it had to decline to give an opinion in the absence of the consent of Russia. It is submitted that in the light of the preceding considerations, in which the Permanent Court made no distinction whatever between merits and procedure, and in which it was exclusively concerned with consent and participation of Russia, the Court intended to say that since the effect of an Opinion was substantially equivalent to a Judgment, it could not, as a Court of Justice, even in connection with requests for advisory opinions, depart from the fundamental rule of international law requiring consent.

However, the International Court was not bound to follow the Permanent Court in this matter. Doctrine and the practice of international organizations have changed: unanimity of consent is no longer required in any organ of the United Nations. The time may well have come to end the immutability of the *Eastern Carelia* ruling and depart, as the Court in fact did, from the requirement of consent in advisory proceedings even when there are "contending parties", and the request "relates to a legal question actually pending between States". The most important reason for change is, of course, the mutation in the prevailing estimate of the legal effect of Advisory Opinions: if they have none for the parties, if they have no longer the effect which doctrine and practice attributed to them in

[122] See *supra*, p. 875.

[123] In 1927, three of the judges who were sitting in the *Eastern Carelia* case, Loder, Moore and Anzilotti, reached the conclusion: "In reality, where there are in fact contending parties, the difference between contentious and advisory cases is only nominal . . . So that the view that advisory opinions are not binding is more theoretical than real". *P.C.I.J. Series E, No. 4, 1927*, p. 76; quoted by Judge Azevedo in the *Peace Treaties* case, *I.C.J. Reports 1950*, p. 80.

the League of Nations, then indeed there is no reason to adhere to the old rule. *Cessante ratione, lex ipsa cessat.* The argument that Members of the United Nations have *qua* Members given their consent that the Assembly and the Council may request an opinion on "any legal question"[124] is correct and should carry weight provided its limitation is also understood: in the matter of peaceful settlement of disputes, no organ of the United Nations may give a decision binding upon a Member without its consent. What the departure from unanimity has accomplished is that the United Nations now has at its disposal an effective procedure for requesting advisory opinions but not a procedure for effective advisory opinions.[125]

Paradoxically, both those who contend that the authority of the *Eastern Carelia* ruling remains unimpaired,[126] as well as those who contend that the *Peace Treaties* case stands for a relaxation or partial abandonment of the *Eastern Carelia* ruling,[127] are right: the latter because in the present submission, the Court not merely departed from the orthodoxy of an earlier era but abandoned it, and the former because answering the question is no longer substantially equivalent to deciding the dispute between parties.

## 5. Consent and Applicable Law

In the application of international law the Court's behaviour shows a duality of approach which roughly corresponds to what has been called the duality of the function: the advisory or United Nations function corresponding to its role of a principal organ, and the contentious function corresponding to its role of organ of international law. In the latter capacity the Court seems to have accepted and even fortified the consensual nature of customary international law and, following the positivist theory, applied international law as it found it. In the former capacity the Court, particularly when applying and interpreting the Charter or instruments closely related to the United Nations such as the Mandate for South West Africa, the Court appears to have adopted a dynamic or progressive, if not a frankly teleological, approach. At least it seemed to be so until the two functions crossed and fused into one as in the litigation relating to the Mandate. A detailed examination of the Court's jurisprudence in contentious and advisory proceedings is neither possible nor necessary in this context. It must be sufficient to characterize it in general terms.

It is trite to say that as an organ of international law the Court's task is to apply the

[124] Lauterpacht, *The Development*, at 357–358.

[125] Therefore Lauterpacht's affirmation: "The presumption is in favour of the effectiveness of this aspect of the jurisdiction of the Court" (*The Development*, at 249), must be taken *cum grano salis*.

[126] de Visscher, *Aspects récents*, at 200.

[127] Lauterpacht, *loc. cit.*, at 354 f. See also Rosenne, II, at 709, who accepts the proposition that there is a "general principle of international law concerning the consensual basis of the Court's jurisdiction in contentious judicial proceedings and . . . that the advisory procedure constitutes such a judicial proceeding" and that "this view rests firmly upon the reply of the Permanent Court in the *Eastern Carelia* case". However, in the present submission, it no longer rests, as far as the advisory procedure is concerned, firmly on the *Peace Treaties* case. That this can be so can be gathered from Rosenne's guarded observation that "the views of the present Court, as expounded in the *Peace Treaties* case, are of considerable importance to the future development of international judicial institutions". *Ibid.*

law, but what is the law? In facing this issue the Court generally applied a strict test. In what is probably the leading case, the *Asylum* case, the Court held: "The Party which relies on a custom of this kind must prove that this custom is established in such a manner that it has become binding on the other Party".[128] The Court did not, and did not have to, refer to the *Lotus* case. The continuity in the consensual approach is obvious. It became and has been recognized as the *leitmotif* in the contentious jurisprudence of the Court. As further instances of "the extreme positivist position" assumed by the Court in the *Asylum* case, the following have been cited in addition to the oft-lamented *Lotus* case: the *Fisheries, U.S. Nationals in Morocco,* and *Right of Passage* cases, and only one Advisory Opinion, the *Reservations* case.[129] It has been said that the Court's position in these cases "involves a frontal challenge to any possibility of the development of international law by means of international adjudication" and that "if this is indeed the logic of these decisions of the International Court we are confronted with the most tragic paradox in the development of international law and international institutions".[130]

Indeed, there is perhaps a paradox, and it may even be a tragic one in the jurisprudence of the Court and its approach to the law, but it lies elsewhere. The Court has been more successful in its contentious than in its advisory jurisdiction. All judgments based on positive international law have been respected and accepted with the exception of the judgment in the *Corfu Channel* case relating to the assessment of compensation. It is at least moot whether the Court adhered to the positivist method in that phase of the case when it allowed the United Nations through the Security Council to intrude into the interpretation of the Special Agreement.[131] Paradoxically, in its advisory jurisdiction, where the Court has displayed judicial boldness amounting to judicial legislation, it has been remarkably less successful. The argument that in the five contentious cases and one advisory opinion listed above, the Court has debarred "itself from playing a constructive part in the progressive crystallization of custom into law"[132] is not, it is submitted, wholly correct. The task of law-making still belongs essentially to the States and not to the Court. The Court can render a very useful service by saying what the law is and then leaving it to the States to change it. Thus the rule upheld in the *Lotus* case was changed in Article 11 of the 1958 Convention on the High Seas. The pronouncements of the Court

[128] *Asylum* case, *I.C.J. Reports 1950*, p. 266. The Court went on to say: "The Colombian Government must prove that the rule invoked by it is in accordance with a constant and uniform usage practised by the States in question, and that this usage is the expression of a right appertaining to the State granting asylum and a duty incumbent on the territorial State".

[129] Jenks, *Prospects*, pp. 225 ff.

[130] Jenks, *loc. cit.*, p. 237.

[131] The Court may be deemed to have learned a lesson from this in resisting attempts to apply the principle of effectiveness in interpreting the Iranian Declaration accepting the compulsory jurisdiction. *Anglo-Iranian Oil Co.* case, *I.C.J. Reports 1952*, p. 93, at 105 ff. In addition to giving a strict interpretation to the Declaration the Court rejected the British contention that the concession agreement was anything more than that (p. 112) and that it should accept jurisdiction on the basis of the principle of *forum prorogatum*. It could not find in the conduct of Iran "an element of consent regarding the jurisdiction of the Court" (p.114).

[132] Jenks, *loc. cit.*, at 237–238.

in the *Corfu Channel* and the *Fisheries* cases were largely incorporated into the 1958 Convention on the Territorial Sea. The gist of the advisory opinion in the *Reservations* case was adopted by the International Law Commission in Article 17 of the 1966 Draft Articles on the Law of Treaties.[133] The rule underlying the *Asylum* case that the State granting diplomatic asylum does not have the right to determine the degree of urgency with binding effect for the territorial States was changed by Article VII of the 1954 Caracas Convention on Diplomatic Asylum.[134]

It would seem then that the Court, as an organ applying positive international law, played a constructive role in the evolution of international law in the listed cases as well as in other judgments in which it was able to clarify and give greater precision to some aspects of customary international law.

As the principal judicial organ of the United Nations, the Court has displayed caution in relating the Charter to its judgments. It had occasion to do so in the *Corfu Channel* case but refrained from availing itself of the opportunity.[135]

In the *Right of Passage* case, both parties argued extensively the question of the applicability of Articles 1, 55, 56 and 62 of the Charter in connection with the refusal of the Indian Government to allow Portugal the authorization for the passage of reinforcements to the enclaves of Dadra and Nagar-Aveli. Professor Waldock claimed for India the right to draw "the attention of the principal judicial organ of the United Nations to . . . the relevant provisions of the Charter" and to say that "at least a Member of the United Nations is, under a separate obligation to abstain from action which is diametrically opposed to the whole purpose and spirit of the human rights provisions", particularly Articles 55 and 56 relating to self-determination.[136] For his opponent, Professor Bourquin, these provisions appeared "too embryonic to be applicable by the Court in any legal connection whatever",[137] and he required proof that the rules invoked by India have modified or abrogated the traditional principles of customary international law.[137] Referring to the Indian Counter-Memorial he said: *"N'est-ce pas reconnaître que nous sommes encore dans la brume?"*[138] Although the arguments derived from the Charter were included in the final submissions of the parties[139] and the Court referred to them,[140] it held: "It is no part of the judicial function of the Court to declare in the operative part of its Judgment that any of these arguments is or is not well-founded".[141] The arguments relating to the Charter

[133] In the *Reservations* case the Court applied the strict test which it was to apply in the *Fisheries* case, when it held that "it does not appear . . . that the conception of the absolute integrity of a convention has been transformed into a rule of international law". *I.C.J. Reports 1951*, p. 15, at 24.

[134] Tenth Inter-American Conference, 1–28 March 1954, Department of State Publication 5692, p. 180. See also C. Neale Ronning, *Diplomatic Asylum* (1965), p. 156. As only 11 States ratified the Convention there does not seem to be any enthusiasm for the new rule nor any widespread dissatisfaction with the Court's pronouncement in the *Asylum* case.

[135] See *supra*. p. 872.

[136] I.C.J. *Pleadings*, case concerning Right of Passage, Vol. IV, pp. 858–859 (Oral Hearings, 21 Oct. 1959).

[137] *Ibid.*, at 584.

[138] *Ibid.*, p. 585.

[139] *I.C.J. Reports 1960*, p. 6, at 16 (Portugal) and at 25 (India).

[140] *Ibid.*, at 31.

[141] *Ibid.*, at 32.

were accordingly not included in the three questions retained for consideration on the merits.[142] For this reason, the Court did not base its decision on the ground advanced by India, namely its alleged duty to refrain from interfering with the right of self-determination of the peoples in the enclaves. Yet this would have been plausible in the light of the developments in and out of the United Nations in this matter.[143] The Court, however, chose a positivist and a more congenial solution by dividing the right of passage into passage for civilians and passage for official and military personnel by subjecting the latter to Indian authorization which could be and has been lawfully denied.[144] The Court thus reached the desired result without involving itself in the problem of decolonization and the binding character of the Charter provisions relating to self-determination and human rights.

Doctrine and practice on the legal force of the human rights provisions in the Charter have remained divided. So have doctrine and practice in respect of the legal force of resolutions generally and those which are called "declarations", purporting to set forth rules or principles of conduct for Members and/or non-member States. For a number of years the Court had within its own ranks a persistent advocate of an innovative jurisprudence, Judge Alvarez. In his view the institutional connection with the United Nations conferred upon the Court a new mission which was made explicit by General Assembly resolution 171 (II) A of 14 November 1947.[145] Also in his view the evolution of the General Assembly is characterized by factors which "transform the Assembly into an all-powerful legislative organ".[146]

It is not possible to discuss here in any detail the legal force of resolutions of the General Assembly. There is widespread consensus that certain resolutions, namely those relating to the internal economy of the Organization such as resolutions admitting States to membership, promulgating rules of procedure, establishing subsidiary bodies and others are legally binding for all Members.[147] Beyond this, there is no agreement.[148]

[142] *Ibid.*, at 36.

[143] This approach with respect to the question of Portuguese sovereignty has been urged in the name of the Charter of the United Nations by Judge Moreno Quintana, in his dissenting opinion: "To support the Portuguese claim in this case, which implies survival of the colonial system, without categorical and conclusive proof is to fly in the face of the United Nations Charter. As judge of its own law—the United Nations Charter—and judge of its own age—the age of national independence—the International Court of Justice cannot turn its back upon the world as it is. 'International law must adapt itself to political necessities', said the Permanent Court of Arbitration in its award on indemnities to Russian individuals (11 XI 1912). That is the reason why the Charter made legal provision to cover the independence of non-self-governing territories". *I.C.J. Reports 1960*, at 95.

[144] *I.C.J. Reports 1960*, p. 6 at 45–46.

[145] This resolution somewhat inconsistently considered that the interpretation of the Charter "be based on recognized principles of international law" and the Court "should be utilized to the greatest practicable extent in the progressive development of international law, both in regard to legal issues between States and in regard to constitutional interpretation". Doc. A/519, p. 103. See separate opinion of Judge Alvarez in *Corfu Channel* (Merits) case, *I.C.J. Reports 1949*, p. 4, at 40, and his dissenting opinion in the *Reparations* case, *ibid.*, p. 174. According to Rosenne (p. 48), "it is difficult to see if this type of resolution is competent to endow the Court with functions not given to it expressly or by necessary implication by the Charter or Statute. The most it can do is to encourage nascent tendencies".

[146] *United Nations Administrative Tribunal* case, *I.C.J. Reports 1954*, p. 47, at 71.

[147] See, for instance, Waldock, *loc. cit.*, at 26; A. I. R. Tammes, "Decisions of International Organs as a Source of Law", 94 Hague *Recueil* 265 (1958), at 316; D. H. N. Johnson "The Effect of Resolutions of the General Assembly of the United Nations", 32 *BYIL* 97 (1955–56), at 121–122; Fitzmaurice, "The Law and Procedure of the International Court

Thus the Universal Declaration of Human Rights may be regarded by some but not by others as "an authoritative expression of customary international law . . . or, at least, the customary law of the United Nations on that subject" but could not be treated as "a legal instrument directly binding upon Member States".[149] In regard to some resolutions Members may record their view that they recognize the principles contained in them as constituting or reflecting international law.[150] In such a case the binding force of principles may be based on explicit acceptance of the same by such Members rather than on the binding force of the resolutions as such. Some resolutions like General Assembly resolution 1514 (XV) may be stepping stones towards a principle of international law, but it will be recalled that many Members criticized the Court's Judgment in the *South West Africa* (Second Phase) case for failing to accept it and apply it as law.[151]

It may be useful to refer to the opinion of the Office of Legal Affairs of the United Nations, on the meaning of the term "Declaration". Apart from being a more formal and solemn instrument than a recommendation, there is probably

> "no difference . . . as far as strict legal principle is concerned. A 'declaration' or a 'recommendation' is adopted by resolution of a United Nations organ. As such it cannot be made binding upon Member States, in the sense that a treaty or convention is binding upon the parties to it, purely by the device of terming it a 'declaration' rather than a 'recommendation'. However, in view of the greater solemnity and significance of a 'declaration', it may be considered to impart, on behalf of the organ adopting it, a strong expectation that Members of the international community will abide by it. Consequently, in so far as the expectation is gradually justified by State practice, a declaration may by custom become recognized as laying down rules binding upon States".[152]

In this view then, the binding character of the contents of a declaration will depend upon the development of practice accepted as law, in short, upon the growth of customary law in accordance with the consensual nature of international law. It is not self-evident that proof of custom would be substantially affected if, instead of applying the guide-lines established by the Court in the *Asylum, Fisheries* and *Reservation* cases, one were to accept the proposition that all uniform conduct of governments or abstention therefrom should be considered as evidence of custom unless it were shown that *opinio necessitatis juris* was

of Justice, 1951–1954", 4 *BYIL* 1–161 (1958), at 3–6; W. Friedmann, *Changing Structure of International Law* (1964), at 139.

[148] Leo Gross, "The United Nations and the Role of Law", 19 *International Organization,* pp. 537–561 (1965), at 555 f. See also *supra.*

[149] Waldock, *loc. cit.,* at 32. Waldock also affirms that "the resolutions of the Assembly do not have legislation force outside the Organization". *Ibid.,* at 35. It may be a matter of some difficulty to reconcile these propositions.

[150] This was done by the representative of the United States with respect to the Declaration on Principles governing the Use of Outer Space, G.A. resolution 1962 (XVIII) of 13 December 1963, 49 Department of State *Bulletin* 1005, 1007 (1963), and by the representative of Canada, 3 *Canadian Yearbook of International Law* 342 (1965).

[151] de Visscher does not see how the Court could attribute definite legal authority to that particular resolution which in many ways goes beyond the Charter. *Aspects récents,* at 207, n. 1. See also Michel Virally, "Droit International et Décolonisation Devant les Nations Unies", 9 *Annuaire Français de Droit International,* pp. 508–541 (1963), at 541.

[152] Doc. E/CN.4/L.610, 2 April 1962, entitled "Use of the Terms 'Declaration' and "Recommendation', Memorandum by the Office of Legal Affairs". In conclusion, reads the Memorandum, "it may be said that in United Nations practice, a 'declaration' is a solemn instrument resorted to only in very rare cases relating to matters of major and lasting importance when maximum compliance is expected".

absent.[153] A resolution or declaration of the General Assembly, putting it at the highest, could be regarded as *opinio juris,* but as indicated in the Memorandum quoted above, unless it results in uniform conduct could not be regarded as a rule of law. It would make little difference if a declaration were to be regarded as custom from which any Member could opt out by pursuing a contrary conduct.[154]

In the contentious *South West Africa* cases, the Court came face to face with the problem of the effect to be given to General Assembly resolutions on human rights and particularly racial discrimination. The Court had already rendered three advisory opinions on the Mandate. The first opinion found that the administrative supervision of the Mandate had passed from the League of Nations Council to the United Nations General Assembly. With respect to this finding, Judge Sir Arnold McNair (as he then was) declared that it constituted "pure inference" and that he—

> "cannot find any legal ground on which the Court would be justified in replacing the Council of the League by the United Nations for the purposes of exercising the administrative supervision of the Mandate and the receipt and examination of reports. It would amount to imposing a new obligation upon the Union Government and would be a piece of judicial legislation".[155]

With respect to the last judicial phase in these cases, the Judgment of 18 July 1966, Judge Jessup felt bound to state that he considered it "completely unfounded in law".[156] And in regard to the judgment on Preliminary Objection of 21 December 1962, Judges Sir Percy Spender and Sir Gerald Fitzmaurice expressed the opinion that in order to assume jurisdiction the Court has adopted "premises which . . . largely assume beforehand the correctness of the conclusions arrived at".[157] They also felt it necessary to state:

> "We are not unmindful of, nor are we insensible to, the various considerations of a non-juridical character, social, humanitarian and other, which underlie this case; but these are matters for the political rather than for the legal arena. They cannot be allowed to deflect us from our duty of reaching a conclusion strictly on the basis of what we believe to be the correct legal view".[158]

The case, in its two contentious phases involved "a fundamental question of judicial approach".[159] Was the Court to act in its capacity of "principal organ" and "principal

[153] Lauterpacht, *The Development,* at 380. The "mystery of custom oscillating inconclusively between being a law-creating source of legal rules and mere evidence of pre-existing law" would still, it is submitted, baffle the jurist. *Ibid.,* at 379. See Josef L. Kunz, "The Meaning and Range of the Norm *Pacta Sunt Servanda,*" 39 *AJIL,* pp. 180–198 (1945).

[154] Gross, "The United Nations and the Role of Law," *loc. cit.,* at 557. See also *supra.*

[155] *South West Africa* (Status) case, *I.C.J. Reports 1950,* p. 128 at 159, 161–162. Judge Read put it this way, stressing the consensual nature of international law: "Such a succession could not be implied, either in fact or in law, in the absence of consent, expressed or implied by the League, the United Nations and the Mandatory Power. There was no such consent". *Ibid.,* at 172.

[156] *I.C.J. Reports 1966,* p. 6, at 325.

[157] *I.C.J. Reports 1962,* p. 319, at 465.

[158] *Ibid.,* at 466. Judge Basdevant in his dissenting opinion noted at the outset that the Court's function was "to decide in accordance with international law such disputes as are submitted to it". *Ibid.,* at 459.

[159] Joint dissenting opinion of Spender and Fitzmaurice, *ibid.,* at 465. See also Richard A. Falk, "The South West African Cases: An Appraisal", 21 *International Organization,* pp. 1–24 (1967) at 7.

judicial organ" of the United Nations or as an "organ of international law"? Was the Court to handle this case as a United Nations case in conformity with the preceding advisory opinions or was it to approach it from a strictly legal point of view and disregard the preceding advisory opinion given to the General Assembly "for its further consideration of the question"?[160] The Court in the 1962 Judgment found "no valid ground for departing from the conclusion reached in the Advisory Opinion of 1950 to the effect that the dissolution of the League of Nations has not rendered inoperable Article 7 of the Mandate"[160a] whereas the joint dissenting opinion declared that "that Opinion was wrong in one or two important respects, but by no means in all".[161] Judge McNair, it will be recalled, regarded it as "pure inference" in its vital aspect.

The Court in 1962 pursued what may be called a dynamic or teleological or constitutionalist approach, which it had previously used only in advisory proceedings, but which the Court has not used in contentious cases. One or two findings in the Court's judgment will illustrate the point. On the crucial issue of the scope of Article 7 of the Mandate, the words "any dispute whatever" are linked with the words "relating to the interpretation or the application of the provisions of the Mandate" but *not* to the words "if it cannot be settled by negotiation". The Court, having thus isolated the words from their context declared in an often quoted passage: "The language used is broad, clear and precise: it gives rise to no ambiguity and it permits of no exception".[162] However, when considering the words "another Member of the League of Nations" for which the Respondent claimed "the natural and ordinary meaning" the Court said: "When such a method of interpretation results in a meaning which is incompatible with the spirit, purpose and context of the clause or instrument in which the words are contained, no reliance can be validly placed on it".[163] But from the following reasoning it appears that the Court did not interpret those words in "the spirit, purpose and context of the clause" but in the spirit, purpose and context of the "sacred trust" in Article 22 of the League Covenant and the circumstances, resolutions and declarations related to the dissolution of the League.[164]

[160] Preamble of resolution 338 (IV) of 6 December 1949, containing the request for an advisory opinion. *I.C.J. Reports 1950*, p. 128, at 129. It may be noted that the Assembly made it doubly clear to the Court where it stood on the matter first by recalling in that resolution all its previous resolutions and by adopting on the same day resolution 337 (IV) in which it reiterated "in their entirety" all its previous resolutions on South West Africa and invited the Union Government "to comply with the decisions of the General Assembly contained in" those resolutions.

[160a] *I.C.J. Reports 1962*, at 338.

[161] *Ibid.*, at 471. Spender and Fitzmaurice considered the 1950 Opinion as inapplicable because "quite different issues" were before the Court in 1962. *Ibid.*, at 473. They found it necessary to state their views on the 1950 Opinion because the judgment of the Court was "partly founded" on that Opinion and because the Applicants maintained and the Respondent denied that the Opinion "was correct in all respects and that (though not on the basis of *res judicata*) it completely and automatically governed the issues in the present proceedings". *Ibid.*, at 471.

[162] *I.C.J. Reports 1962*, at 343. But see Judge Jessup's strictures against the "clear meaning" rule in his dissenting opinion in the Second Phase, *I.C.J. Reports 1966*, at 355.

[163] *I.C.J. Reports 1962*, at 336.

[164] *Ibid.*, at 336–341. In the view of Jenks the judgment and the concurring opinions "rest essentially upon far-reaching considerations of international public policy". In regard to the scope of Article 7, Jenks finds the joint dissenting opinion

The Court comes closest to playing its role as a principal organ of the United Nations and to participating in the activities of the Organization when it applied the notion of "parliamentary diplomacy" to the requirement of prior negotiations in Article 7 of the Mandate. In answer to the Respondent's contention that direct negotiations between it and the Applicants had never taken place, the Court stated first that "it is not so much the form of negotiations that matters as the attitude and views of the Parties on the substantive issues of the question involved" and that "moreover, diplomacy by conference or parliamentary diplomacy has come to be recognized in the past four or five decades as one of the established modes of international negotiation".[165] This is of course so. One could even trace it back to the nineteenth-century European Concert.[166] But Article 7 does not provide for "international" or "collective" negotiations although for larger reasons of policy one of these adjectives used by the Court could be interpolated. However, for other reasons of policy, namely the interest in preserving the integrity of adjudication clauses, such an interpolation may be regarded as undesirable.[167] In so far as the present case is concerned one may regard the resolution of the General Assembly on the subject of negotiations as indicative of the United Nations political policy.[168] The Court's pronouncements indicate the harmony between these two principal organs of the United Nations in the First Phase of the *South West Africa* cases.

The harmony was broken in the Second Phase. For reasons which need not be gone into, the Court's composition has undergone some changes, and the defenders of the "organ of international law" role had a technical majority. In several passages the Court underscored this role and drew a sharp distinction between positive law and non-legal considerations. Some examples will be helpful:

> "Throughout this case is has been suggested, directly or indirectly, that humanitarian considerations are sufficient in themselves to generate legal rights and obligations, and that the Court can and should proceed accordingly. The Court does not think so. It is a Court of law, and can take account of moral principles only in so far as these are given a sufficient expression in legal form".[169]

not convincing. *Prospects,* at 482, 494. Could not that opinion also be regarded as based on considerations of international public policy?

165 *Ibid.,* at 346. See also Judge Jessup, separate opinion, *ibid.,* at 433–436; the joint dissenting opinion, *ibid.,* 560–563; and de Visscher, *Aspects Récents,* at 23–28, who finds the Court's Judgment on this point unacceptable for larger reasons of judicial policy. Jenks finds the views of Spender and Fitzmaurice "eminently reasonable" but agrees with the Court. *Loc. cit.,* at 494.

166 As did Judge Jessup in his separate opinion, *I.C.J. Reports 1962,* at 434.

167 These policy considerations were set out as follows in the joint dissenting opinion: "We shall conclude by pointing out that the requirements about 'disputes' and 'negotiations' are not mere technicalities. They appear in one form or another in virtually every adjudication clause that has ever been drafted, and for good reason. They are inserted purposely to protect the parties, so far as possible, from international litigation that is unnecessary, premature, inadequately motivated, or merely specious. Without this measure of protection, countries would not sign clauses providing for compulsory adjudication. This is an aspect of the matter to which we feel insufficient attention has been given". *Ibid.,* at 563.

168 See *supra,* p. 853.

169 *South West Africa* (Second Phase) cases, *I.C.J. Reports 1966,* p. 6, at 34.

The condition "sufficient expression" could conceivably relate to the array of relevant General Assembly resolutions and declarations, and if it does, one could infer that the Court does not consider them to have been cast "in legal form".[170] In another passage the Court said:

> "If, on a correct legal reading of a given situation, certain legal rights are found to be non-existent, the consequences of this must be accepted. The Court cannot properly postulate the existence of such rights in order to avert those consequences. This would be to engage in an essentially legislative task, in the service of political ends the promotion of which, however desirable in itself, lies outside the function of a court-of-law".[171]

In regard to the claim that the Court should allow a sort of *"actio popularis"* to vindicate a public interest in the proper performance of the Mandate, the Court declared that this action "is not known to international law as it stands at present", nor could the Court regard it as part of the "general principles of law" in Article 38 [1 *(c)*] of its Statute.[172]

Finally, referring to the "necessity" argument that some remedial action must be afforded to enforce the proper application of the Mandate, the Court held that now to read a remedial action into the mandates system "would be engaging in *ex post facto* process, exceeding its functions as a court of law. As is implied by the opening phrase of Article 38, paragraph 1, of its Statute, the Court is not a legislative body. Its duty is to apply the law as it finds it, not to make it".[173]

It may be observed in passing that in spite of all these considerations the Court may well have intended to preserve, in their entirety, all the earlier pronouncements on the subject of South West Africa even though it disagreed with some of them. Thus, it deliberately chose the narrowest possible ground, a matter of an "antecedent" character, in order to reject, as it felt that it must as a court-of-law, the claims of the Applicants.[174] This is not to suggest that the Court would necessarily have departed from its role as organ of international law had it adjudicated on the merits and not raised an antecedent issue. But the duty to participate in the activities of the Organization, that is, to participate actively in the achievement of its objectives, its purposes and principles, has so far

[170] With regard to the "sacred trust" concept of the Covenant which has played a prominent role in Assembly debates, in the 1950 Opinion, and in the judgment of 1962, the Court said: "To sum up, the principle of the sacred trust has no residual juridical content which could, as far as any particular mandate is concerned, operate *per se* to give rise to legal rights and obligations outside the system as a whole; and within the system equally, such rights and obligations exist only in so far as there is actual provision for them". *Ibid.,* at 35.

[171] *Ibid.,* at 36. The Court is here rejecting the argument that it would be unacceptable to conclude that there is no entity entitled to claim the performance of the Mandate inasmuch as the United Nations has no access to the contentious jurisdiction of the Court.

[172] *Ibid.,* at 47. Judge Jessup referred to some analogies in the law of the United States, which, however, are quite controversial, but agreed with the Court that "there is no generally established *actio popularis* in international law. But international law has accepted and established situations in which states are given the right of action without any showing of individual prejudice or individual substantive interest as distinguished from the general interest". *Ibid.,* at 388. The Court accepted this proposition with respect to the *Minorities Treaties* but found it inapplicable with respect to Mandates. *Ibid.,* at 32, 40, 47. See also, de Visscher, *loc. cit.,* at 21, 70 ff.

[173] *Ibid.,* at 47–48. The Court quoted here with approval the passage from the *Peace Treaties* (Second Phase), *I.C.J. Reports 1950,* p. 229.

[174] Judge Jessup's view that "the Court now in effect sweeps away this record of 16 years" contrasts with his more realistic construction of the precise legal scope of the Court's verdict elsewhere in his dissenting opinion, *ibid.* at 328, 330–331.

been recognized by the Court only in connection with its advisory, its United Nations function. In the contentious phase of the South West Africa problem, the Court may well have faced the dilemma whether and to what extent it should continue the co-operation which it had begun in 1950 and on which the General Assembly had based its policy in the matter for more than a decade.[175] Except for the fortuitous change in the relative strength of the sharply divergent schools, there is no doubt that the Court would have continued to function along the lines laid out in the 1950 Opinion and the 1962 Judgment. The Court was urged repeatedly to do so by Counsel for the Applicants.

With respect to the main issue, the practice of apartheid, the Applicants developed a somewhat ambiguous "norm and/or standard" theory. According to one of the two major branches of this case, the standard of interpretation, as finally and comprehensively restated runs:

> "This involves the standard of interpretation . . . in relation to the supervisory organ responsible for the supervision of the Mandate (i.e., the General Assembly), and also involves the *relationship between that administrative agency and the Court.* This branch of the case, therefore, involves the mandate jurisprudence, which involves the clear and virtually unanimous pronouncements and judgments of the competent international organ which the Applicants submit, for reasons which have been set out in detail, should be accepted by the Court as authoritative interpretations of the Mandate".

The second branch of the argument was restated as follows:

> "And secondly . . . with respect to the norm, the role of international law for which the Applicants contend in terms of Article 38 of the Statute—that . . . has been presented to the Court as an alternative and a cumulative, or supplemental, argument on the basis that the practice of States and the views of the competent international organs are so clear, so explicit, and so unanimous in respect of the policies against discrimination, that such standards have achieved the *status of an international rule of law,* as a legal conclusion based upon the application of Article 38".[176]

The case of the Applicants rested in part on the relationship between the Court and the "administrative agency" or "competent international organ" that is, the General Assembly or perhaps, more correctly, on the capacity of the Court as a principal organ of the United Nations.[177] As an organ of the United Nations the Court was urged to accept the

[175] Judge Jessup defended its authority: "If it be thought that in advisory proceedings the Court does not receive as full a statement or argument as it presented in contentious proceedings, it may be noted that in 1950 the Volume of *Pleadings* . . . on the question of the *International Status of South West Africa* contains 350 pages. In the course of the presentation, Dr. Steyn, representative of the Union of South Africa, spoke at four separate sessions of the Court". In another place he said: "It is apparent that there is nothing in the argument about any 'new facts' to induce the Court to alter *decisions* about the *International Status of South West Africa* which it had reached after full argument and full deliberation". *Ibid.,* at 350–351. Italics supplied. However, de Visscher, who as judge participated in the 1950 proceedings, observed recently: "Il est possible que les avis consultatifs antérieurement émis par la Cour relativement aux affaires concernant l'Union sud-africaine aient quelque peu contribueé à obscurcir la distinction entre la perspective politique et la perspective judiciaire. Que l'on en soit arrivé là n'en est pas moins regrettable". *Aspects récents,* at 27.

[176] Quoted in Judge Jessup: dissenting opinion, *ibid.,* at 431. Italics supplied.

[177] See statement quoted *supra,* pp. 867–868.

various pronouncements of the Assembly—which it did make—and "judgments"—which it could not make—as a standard of interpretation, and alternatively or cumulatively to accept these standards as a customary rule of international law. As was pointed out by Judge Jessup, the Court could not have accepted the latter proposition since the various international bodies—the Assembly, the International Labor Organisation and others—"lack a true legislative character, their resolutions alone do not create law".[178] This, it is respectfully suggested, does not quite meet the point, namely whether the practice of the Assembly and other organs has given birth to a customary rule of international law. And the answer to that question does not depend upon whether or not the General Assembly has legislative power. When faced with the alleged existence of custom, the Court would have to apply its usual standards of proof, as indicated earlier[179] and determine whether it is "opposable" with respect to South Africa. Secondly, the Court would have to determine whether its institutional connection with the United Nations constitutes a necessary and sufficient reason for departing from its usual practice in contentious cases,[180] having regard to the special circumstances of the case.

It must remain a matter for speculation what the Court would have done if the judges had not been equally divided. However, there is little doubt that had the majority of 1962 written the judgment in 1966 it would have accepted the argument of the Applicants relating to the standard of interpretation. As Judge Jessup put it:

> ". . . my conclusion does not rest upon the thesis that resolutions of the General Assembly have a general legislative character and by themselves create new rules. But the accumulation of expressions of condemnation of apartheid . . . especially as recorded in the resolutions of the General Assembly of the United Nations, are proof of the pertinent contemporary international community standard. . . . It is equally true that obtaining the disagreement, the condemnation of the United Nations, is of decisive practical—and juridical—value in determining the applicable standard. The Court is bound to take account of such a consensus as providing the standard to be used in the interpretation of Article 2 of the Mandate. Today's judgment does not ignore humanitarian considerations, or the 'moral ideal' of the sacred trust, but seeks to find where and how they have been given juridical expression and 'clothed in legal form'. With due respect, I explore these same areas, but find the 'juridical expression' and 'legal form' lead to legal conclusions different from those recorded by the Court".[181]

[178] *Ibid.*, at 432. Judge Jessup also suggests a second reason for rejecting the "norm" argument, namely that the dispute would then become one about a violation of a general rule of international law whereas the Court's jurisdiction was based on Article 7 (2) of the Mandate and limited to disputes about the interpretation of the Mandate. The finding of a norm would also have involved the practice of apartheid in South Africa.

[179] *Supra*, p. 883.

[180] See Judge Jessup's remarks *ibid.*, at 441. Judge Tanaka has addressed himself to the point raised and concluded that "the accumulation of authoritative pronouncements such as resolutions, declarations, decisions, etc., concerning the interpretation of the Charter by the competent organs of the international community can be characterized as evidence of the international custom referred to in Article 38, paragraph 1 *(b)*". *Ibid.*, at 292. This norm is binding on the Mandatory as a member of the United Nations. *Ibid.*, at 293. Judge Tanaka construes the principle of equality as having a "natural-law character" and this justified its inclusion in the Mandate. *Ibid.*, at 301.

[181] *Ibid.*, at 441. See also dissenting opinion of Judge Padilla Nervo, *ibid.*, at 468 and 470.

It is perhaps a minor flaw in this reasoning that it attributes to the Members of the United Nations in their collective capacity the power to fix the standard for the resolution of a dispute between the Members in their individual capacities.[182] It is reasonably clear, however, that had Judge Jessup and his dissenting colleagues been in the majority in the Second Phase, the Court would have accepted the resolutions of the General Assembly at least as a standard of interpretation. This would have left open the question whether they would have done so, as urged by the Applicant, because of the institutional relation between the Court and the United Nations or because of the close link between the controversy and the United Nations. However, to attribute to the General Assembly the capacity and the power to develop binding standards through non-binding resolutions would constitute a substantial development in international law even if limited, at first, to what might be called United Nations contentious cases.

In its advisory capacity the Court almost from the beginning adopted a dynamic and progressive attitude based largely on the principle of effectiveness without, however, discarding altogether the positivist approach. At the risk of oversimplification the main reasons that can be derived from the practice of the Court and that may account, it is suggested, for its behaviour appear to be the following: (1) the new institutional status of the Court as a principal organ of the United Nations; (2) the consciousness of a duty to co-operate in the political activities of the Organization; (3) the asserted power to give opinions on any legal question, whether substantive or procedural, whether abstract or concrete; (4) the emancipation from the requirement of consent, *audiatur et altera pars* and equality of parties in connection with requests relating to a pending dispute; (5) the lack of binding force of the opinion for the requesting organ and the States concerned; (6) the view that the opinion is given to the requesting organ and not to the interested States; and finally (7) that only compelling reasons dictated by its judicial character could preclude the Court from complying with the request.[183]

Instances in which adherence to the positivist emphasis on consent and judicial caution were prominent are the *Peace Treaties* (Second Phase) and the 1950 *South West Africa*

[182] In the 1962 Judgment the Court distinguished two different disputes: one before the Court and the other before the United Nations, the former between the Applicants and the Respondent, and the latter between the Respondent (more correctly, South Africa), and other Members of the United Nations. By a curious line of reasoning the Court considered the "collective negotiations" relating to the controversy in the United Nations as satisfying the requirement of prior, that is bilateral, "negotiation" in the dispute between the Applicants and Respondent. The deadlock reached in the collective negotiations in the United Nations and the fact that the continual existence of the deadlock was disclosed in the "present" pleadings "conveyed the conclusion that no reasonable probability exists that further negotiations would lead to a settlement". *Ibid.*, at 345. But as the Court correctly pointed out, "the alleged impossibility of settling the dispute obviously could only refer to the time when the Applications were filed". *Ibid.*, at 344. Obviously, if no negotiations had taken place prior to that critical time, then the deadlock disclosed in subsequent written pleadings and continued in the oral presentation seems irrelevant as proof that negotiation had disclosed a deadlock prior to the filing of the Application. *Ibid.*, at 345–346.

[183] See Lauterpacht, *The Development*, pp. 109, 249, 354–356. In view of the admittedly non-binding character of advisory opinions, Lauterpacht, perhaps somewhat inconsistently maintains that "at least in relation to the Members of the United Nations, the Charter has created a species of quasi-compulsory jurisdiction of the Court by way of Advisory Opinions the request for which may be made, by a requisite majority, in disregard of the adverse vote of the State or States affected". *Ibid.*, at 357.

(Status) cases. The former has already been discussed.[184] The observation may be added that the Court could well have affirmed the power of the Secretary-General to appoint a commissioner without exceeding the bounds of positivism and that the distinction between interpreting and revising treaties may be clear in theory but difficult in practice.[185] In the *South West Africa* (Status) case the Court held that Chapter XII of the Charter imposed no legal obligation upon South Africa to place the territory under the trusteeship system.[186] Judge de Visscher dissented from this part of the Opinion on the ground that the rules of effectiveness and context were "particularly applicable to the interpretation of a text of a treaty of a constitutional character like the United Nations Charter, above all when, as in this case, its provisions create a well-defined international régime, and for that reason may be considered as complementary to one another".[187] Having regard to the basic objectives of the trusteeship system in Article 76 and the purposes of the Charter he accordingly concluded that the provisions of Chapter XII impose upon South Africa "an obligation to take part in negotiations with a view to concluding an agreement".[188]

It has been said that in view of the Court's affirmation of continuing supervision by the United Nations, "the problem of the formal conclusion of trusteeship agreements acquired a symbolic rather than a practical significance".[189] This is true but in the opposite sense. Seeing that the Opinion lacked binding force, the conclusion of a trusteeship agreement would have, indeed, acquired a symbolic importance; it would have been symbolic of the recognition by South Africa of legal obligations for itself with respect to the mandated territory and of legal rights of supervision for the General Assembly. In short, it would have transformed the non-binding Opinion into a legally binding instrument. Without this the Opinion remained what it was and the attitude of South Africa remained what it was.

The 1950 Advisory Opinion, in its crucial aspect, namely the obligation of South Africa to submit to supervision, was based on "doctrine and logical arguments", and the "importation, on the part of the Court, of the rules of succession in relation to international organization" may have been "no more than an example of the legitimate application of the principles of effectiveness to basic international instruments".[190] But this importation was in the view of Judge McNair "pure inference" and "a piece of legislation" that amounted "to imposing a new obligation upon the Union Government (of South Africa)".[191]

[184] *Supra*, pp. 876 ff.

[185] Lauterpacht, *The Development*, p. 287 and note 10. See also dissenting opinion of Judge Read, *I.C.J. Reports 1950*, at 238–246.

[186] *I.C.J. Reports 1950*, at 140.

[187] *Ibid.*, at 187. Italics supplied. Elsewhere in this opinion he said: "In this connection one must bear in mind that in the interpretation of a great international constitutional instrument, like the United Nations Charter, the individualistic concepts which are generally adequate in the interpretation of ordinary treaties, do not suffice". *Ibid.*, at 189. One will note a certain affinity with the line of thought pursued by Judge Alvarez. de Visscher elaborated his ideas in *Problèmes d' interprétation judiciaire en droit international public* (1963), pp. 140 ff.

[188] *Ibid.*, at 186, 189–190.

[189] Lauterpacht, *The Development*, at 281.

[190] *Ibid.*, pp. 124, 280.

[191] *I.C.J. Reports 1950*, at 161–162; see also Judge Read, dissenting opinion, *ibid.*, at 172. "Such a succession could not be implied, either in fact or in law, in the absence of consent, expressed or implied by the League, the United Nations and the Mandatory Power". Cf. also *ibid.*, at 173.

Moved by a desire to find ways and means for the protection of the territory by providing for an adequate degree and method of supervision, the Court drew heavily on declarations by South Africa, the recognition of its own obligation by its subsequent conduct, the circumstances incidental to the dissolution of the League of Nations, the similarity between the functions of the League and the United Nations in the matter of mandates and trust territories, but there was conspicuously absent any unequivocal evidence of consent by South Africa to accept both accountability to and supervision by the General Assembly.[192] The authority of the Opinion could not be stronger than the materials from which it was built.[193]

However, the Court showed a degree of positivist influence in the *caveat* that

> "The degree of supervision to be exercised by the General Assembly should not therefore exceed that which applied under the Mandates System, and should conform as far as possible to the procedure followed in this respect by the Council of the League of Nations".[194]

This *caveat*, correct in itself in the context of the Opinion, could hardly have been expected to be effective. It was addressed to a body which since 1946 has demonstrated that it took a view of its supervisory authority and function in respect to trust territories and particularly the non-self-governing territories which was vastly different in degree and spirit from that of the League Council. For the Court to subject South Africa to this type and degree of supervision in the climate of opinion prevailing in the United Nations may well have amounted to subjecting it to a new sort of obligation.

The *caveat* has an interesting after-history. In arguing the necessity for judicial supervision of the general conduct as well as special interest clauses in the Mandate, the Court was faced in 1962 with the objection that the trusteeship agreements for three of the former "C" Mandates did not provide for judicial supervision. The Court met this argument which "apparently overlooks one important difference in the structure and working of the two systems" by pointing out that, under Article 18 of the Charter, the General Assembly could make "decisions" by a two-thirds majority vote whereas the unanimity rule prevailed in the Council and Assembly of the League. "Thus", concluded the Court,

> "legally valid decisions can be taken by the General Assembly of the United Nations and the Trusteeship Council under Chapter XIII of the Charter without the concurrence of

[192] *I.C.J. Reports 1950,* at 132–137. The Court, it is suggested, relied on what may be called "similarity of functions theory", somewhat comparable to "the similar clauses theory" rejected in the *Ambatielos* case. *I.C.J. Reports 1952,* p. 28, at 40.

[193] To illustrate: in a much quoted passage which deserves to rank as a classic *non-sequitur,* the Court said: "The authority which the Union Government exercises over the Territory is based on the Mandate. If the Mandate lapsed, as the Union Government contends, the latter's authority would equally have lapsed". *Ibid.,* at 133. To be sure, the Government's authority derived from the Mandate would have expired with the lapse of the Mandate, but does it follow that the Government would have no title at all to the territory? See Judge Jessup's dissenting opinion in the 1966 Judgment, *I.C.J. Reports 1966,* at 418 and 421–423 where he demonstrates the absence of reversionary rights of the Principal Allied and Associated Powers.

[194] *I.C.J. Reports 1966,* at 138.

> the trustee State, and the necessity for invoking the Permanent Court for judicial protection which prevailed under the Mandates system is dispensed with under the Charter".[195]

If it was the intent of the Court to contend that "legally *valid* decisions" were identic with "legally *binding* decisions", it must be pointed out respectfully that there is no legal basis for such an identification—for two reasons: first, the text of Article 18; and secondly, the Court's earlier Advisory Opinion of 1955 in the *South West Africa* (Voting) case.

Article 18, paragraph 2, begins with the word "decisions", and as pointed out earlier [196] the Assembly may adopt resolutions containing a decision, but the following sentence qualified "decisions" by providing "these questions shall include: recommendations with respect to . . . questions relating to the operation of the trusteeship system". Unless there is a provision elsewhere in the Charter which endows such recommendations with binding force, they have none, always excepting those relating to the internal economy of the Organization.[197]

Secondly, in its Opinion of 1955 the Court found no incompatibility between its *caveat* of 1950 and Rule F adopted by the General Assembly according to which "decisions" of the Assembly relating to reports and petitions concerning the Territory of South West Africa shall be governed by Article 18 of the Charter.[198] It has already been pointed out that these "decisions" are generally in the nature of non-binding recommendations. Additional support for this view can be derived from the separate opinion of Judge Lauterpacht who discusses the matter in full detail. Having considered virtually all the variations of the effect of Assembly resolutions, and having rejected some and adopted others ranging from full legal effect to some moral effect, he concluded, in agreement with the Court, that Rule F was in accordance with the correct interpretation of the 1950 Opinion:

> "This is so for the reason that the decisions of the General Assembly in the meaning of Rule F do not possess a degree of legal authority equal to that of the decisions of the Council of the League of Nations. In view of this, although adopted through a less stringent voting procedure, they cannot be held to involve a degree of supervision exceeding that which obtained under the Mandates System".[199]

[195] *I.C.J. Reports 1962,* at 342.
[196] *Supra,* pp. 885 f.
[197] See joint dissenting opinion, *I.C.J. Reports 1962,* at 523–524.
[198] *I.C.J. Reports 1955,* p. 67, at 77.
[199] *Ibid.,* at 123. One characteristic statement is the following: "To suggest that any such particular recommendation is binding in the sense that there is a legal obligation to put it into effect is to run counter not only to the paramount rule that the General Assembly has no legal power to legislate or bind its Members by way of recommendations, but, for reasons stated, also to cogent considerations of good government and administration". *Ibid.,* at 116. One such consideration is that "the Administering Authority, not the General Assembly bears the direct responsibility for the welfare of the population of the Trust Territory". *Ibid.* On the other hand the discretion vested in the Authority must be "exercised in good faith", and an Administering State which consistently disregards the "repeatedly expressed judgment of the Organization . . . may find that it has overstepped the imperceptible line between impropriety and illegality, between discretion and arbitrariness, between the exercise of the legal right to disregard the recommendation and the abuse of that right, and that it has

If this is so, and it is suggested that it is, then the need for judicial protection would appear even greater in the United Nations system than it was in the League System. The fact that it was jettisoned in the General Assembly without even a discussion[200] throws a curious light on the cogency of the argument quoted above from the 1962 Judgment.

The next question is the importance, if any, of the Court's institutional connection with the United Nations when requested for an advisory opinion concerning the interpretation of the Charter of United Nations. Five cases call for consideration: the *Membership, Competence of General Assembly, Reparation, United Nations Administrative Tribunal* and *Expenses* cases. The opinions rendered by the Court in the *South West Africa* cases have already been discussed. The *IMCO* case related to the constitution of the Intergovernmental Consultative Organization and the *I.L.O. Administrative Tribunal* case, concerned to some extent with the constitution of a Specialized Agency which has already been mentioned.

The *IMCO* case has some interest in the present context. The Court preferred the test of registered tonnage and rejected that of beneficial ownership favoured by some influential members of the Organization though not by the United States which is the chief beneficiary of the "flag of convenience". In adopting the registered tonnage test as "practical, certain and capable of easy application" and one might add, automatic application, the Court emphasized the consultative character of the Organization. It pointed out that recommendations for maritime regulation[201] could be made to the members only "through the Council and the Assembly". The Court may well have intended to make clear that the nature of the Organization was in any case only consultative, and that no binding regulations could ensue from the work of the Committee, the composition of which was determined by the transparent test of registered tonnage.

In regard to the other cases the Court insisted from the outset that it had the power to interpret provisions of the Charter, or to put it negatively, as the Court has done: "Nowhere is any provision to be found forbidding the Court 'the principal judicial organ of the United Nations', to exercise in regard to the Charter, a multilateral treaty, an interpretative function which falls within the normal exercise of its judicial function".[202] In the *Expenses* case the Court referred to this part of the statement in which the Charter is described as a "multilateral treaty" but added:

> "On the previous occasions when the Court has had to interpret the Charter of the United Nations, it has followed the principles and rules applicable in general to the interpretation of treaties, since it has recognized that the Charter is a multilateral treaty, albeit a treaty having certain special characteristics. In interpreting Article 4 of the Charter, the Court

exposed itself to consequences legitimately following as a legal sanction". *Ibid.*, at 120. The sanction could be legal if imposed by the Security Council but in the case of the Assembly it would be political.

200 *I.C.J. Reports 1962*, at 523.

201 *I.C.J. Reports 1960*, p. 150, at 169, 170. The Court, having reached its conclusion, rejected as "irrelevant" the "genuine link" notion as incorporated in the then unratified 1958 Geneva Law of the Sea Convention (Article 5). *Ibid.*, at 171.

202 *Membership* case, *I.C.J. Reports 1948*, p. 57, at 61. The substance of this was recalled in *Competence of the General Assembly* case, *I.C.J. Reports 1950*, p. 4, at 6.

> was led to consider, 'the structure of the Charter' and the 'relations established by it between the General Assembly and the Security Council'; a comparable problem confronts the Court in the instant matter. The Court sustained its interpretation of Article 4 by considering the manner in which the organs concerned 'have consistently interpreted the text' in their practice''.[203]

Given the Court's extensive use of the practice of organs in the *Expenses* case it is worth noting its approach in the *Membership* case. In that case, the Court found that the five conditions listed in Article 4 (1) were the necessary as well as the sufficient requirements for deciding admission to membership. In addition, it considered the text to be ''sufficiently clear'' without elaboration. But the Court went on to refer to Rule 60 of the Provisional Rules of Procedure of the Security Council and observed that the Rule ''is based on this interpretation of Article 4 (1)''.[204] Similarly in the passage quoted above, the Court did not refer to the practice of the organs but to their Rules of Procedure in support of its interpretation that a favourable recommendation of the Security Council ''is the condition precedent to the decision of the Assembly by which the admission is effected''.[205] Inasmuch as the power to adopt rules of procedure is expressly conferred by the Charter on the Assembly (Article 21) and the Council (Article 30), these rules are in the nature of legislation and binding both upon the Members and these organs. Practice as evidenced by such rules is not on the same legal plane as the practice of organs to which the Court had occasion to refer in the *Expenses* case.[206]

In the *Reparation* case which is ''regarded as marking the break between the 'traditionalist' and the 'constitutionalist' systems of interpretation of the constituent instrument of an international organization'',[207] the Court appears indeed to break new ground. In the *Membership* case, to be sure, the Court relied on the necessary implication of Article 4 of the Charter,[208] but in the *Reparation* case the doctrine of implied powers plays a key role. While this may be true, it would also seem that the doctrine was applied in the service of the principle of effectiveness which with some of the exceptions already noted in one form or another runs through the jurisprudence of the Court. In the *Reparation* case the Court participated directly in achieving the objective set forth by the Assembly in the resolution containing the request, which was that of ''ensuring to its agents the

[203] *Expenses* case, *I.C.J. Reports 1962*, p. 151 at 157. The quoted passages are from the *Competence of the General Assembly* case, *I.C.J. Reports 1950*, at 8–9.

[204] *Membership* case, *I.C.J. Reports 1948*, p. 63.

[205] *Competence of the General Assembly* case, *I.C.J. Reports 1950*, at 8. The Court noted that as provided in the Rules, applications have been sent back by the Assembly to the Council, and that an unfavourable recommendation has never been made in practice. *Ibid.*, at 9.

[206] See Rosenne, ''Is the Constitution . . .,'' *loc. cit.*, p. 76, note 136: ''There is, of course, considerable difference between a dispositive text such as the Rules of Procedure, made by virtue of power expressly conferred by the Charter, and a Resolution which represents the formulation of the action of an organ in concrete circumstances''. Cf. also Judge Azevedo's dissenting opinion, *I.C.J. Reports 1950*, at 24, and Fitzmaurice, ''Law and Procedure'', 28 *British Year Book of International Law* at 24 (1951).

[207] Rosenne, *loc. cit.*, at 75.

[208] ''The provisions of Article 4 necessarily imply that every application for admission should be examined and voted on separately and on its own merits''. *I.C.J. Reports 1948*, at 65. On the consequences of this finding and of the Opinion as a whole for the admissions problem see Leo Gross, ''Progress toward Universality of Membership in the United Nations'', 50 *AJIL*, pp. 791–827 (1956). See also *supra*, pp. 607–641.

fullest measure of protection in the future''.[209] The Court referred to the resolution in its Opinion and underscored the fact that ''the need of protection of the agents of the Organization, as a condition of the performance of its functions, has already been realized'' and that ''this was the unanimous view of the General Assembly''.[210] The theory of the functional protection of agents is a necessary means to that end but juridically it was derived from the ''necessary intendment'' of the Charter.[211] The finding of the Court that the United Nations possesses ''international personality'' and that ''it is a subject of international law'' were merely necessary stepping stones, as was the frequently cited statement that ''the rights and duties of an entity such as the Organization must depend upon its purposes and functions as specified or implied in its constituent documents and developed in practice''.[212] When dealing with the question whether the Organization has capacity to claim damages for injuries to the victim or for persons entitled through them to recover, the Court reformulated its position, declaring: ''Under international law, the Organization must be deemed to have those powers which, though not expressly provided in the Charter, are conferred upon it by necessary implication as being essential to the performance of its duties''.[213] The Court sustained this conclusion asserting: ''This principle of law was applied by the Permanent Court of International Justice to the International Labour Organisation in its Advisory Opinion No. 13 of July 3rd, 1926 (*Series B, No. 13,* p. 18), and must be applied to the United Nations''.[214]

As important as that Advisory Opinion of the Permanent Court may have been for the future development of the Labour Organisation,[215] it has no bearing on the doctrine of implied powers and offers no support for the conclusion reached by the International Court in the *Reparation* case. The Permanent Court drew certain inferences from the ''terms of the Treaty'' of Versailles (Chapter XIII) with respect to the competence of the Labour Organisation to formulate proposals and to investigate and discuss labour problems. At the same time it pointed out that the ''competence (of the Labour Organisation) is also wholly confined to that auxiliary form of activity'', that it had no legislative power, and that ''each member is free to adopt or to reject any proposal of the Organiza-

[209] *Reparation* case, *I.C.J. Reports 1949,* at 175.
[210] *Ibid.,* at 183.
[211] *Ibid.,* at 184.
[212] *Ibid.,* at 180. In the pleadings relating to this case, Mr. Feller, Counsel for the Secretary-General, drew the attention of the Court to the report of Committee IV/2 of the San Francisco Conference according to which a specific provision regarding the international personality in the Charter was unnecessary because this was ''to be determined implicitly from the provisions of the Charter as a whole''. *Pleadings,* at p. 70. The Court, however, did not refer to this in its reasoning.
[213] *Ibid.,* at 182. In connection with this line of reasoning, it is interesting to observe that Mr. Feller, without resorting to implied power, argued that the United Nations ''possesses those substantive rights of general international law which are necessary and proper for the exercise of its functions''. *Ibid.,* at 76. He, thus, seems to have anticipated Finn Seyersted's theory of ''inherent'' powers. See his article ''International Personality of International Organizations'', 4 *Indian Journal of International Law* 589 (1949); for a discussion on Seyersted's views see *Legal Advisers and International Organizations* edited by H. C. L. Merillat (1966), pp. 13-17.
[214] *I.C.J. Reports 1949,* at 182-183.
[215] See Jenks, *Prospects,* at 479, who stresses the ''long-range considerations of international public policy'' on which it was based and its similarity to the constitutional cases ''involving questions of economic and social policy before the Supreme Court of the United States''.

tion either for a national law or for an international convention''.[216] The Permanent Court thus gave only a limited endorsement in that case to the principle of effectiveness, while giving a wide interpretation to the terms of the constituent instrument with regard to its purposes.

The Court, in the *Reparation* case, could not draw upon the text of the Charter and relied on the implications of the duties and functions of the Organization and of international law. However, although on the strength of the ''objective international personality'' of the United Nations, the Court affirmed the capacity of the Organization to claim reparation from a State which is not a member, it stopped short of finding explicitly any obligation on the part of Members or non-member States to satisfy such claims. Referring to question I *(b)*—whether the Organization has the capacity to bring claims in respect of the damage caused to the victim or to persons entitled through him—the Court observed:

> ''The question lies within the limits already established; that is to say it presupposes that the injury for which reparation is demanded arises from a breach of an obligation designed to help an agent of the Organization in the performance of his duties''.[217]

It would seem then that without relying on any implied powers, the United Nations may bring a claim whenever there is a breach of an international obligation in respect of its agent or itself. The assumption that there *can be* and in specific cases that there *is* an international obligation, implies the responsibility of the State concerned under international law to pay reparation. This is in essence a circular or tautological answer to a circular or tautological question: if there is obligation, there is responsibility for violating it; and if there is responsibility, there must have been breach of an obligation. In affirming that the United Nations has international personality and is a subject of international law, the Court made explicit the implication bequeathed by the San Francisco Conference as well as the implications put by the General Assembly into its request.[218] All the same, the Court made a most useful contribution to the law of the United Nations in elucidating the theory of functional protection.

The Court had occasion to make further contribution to this theory in the *United Nations Administrative Tribunal* case and to manifest again its abiding concern for the secu-

[216] *P.C.I.J., Series B, No. 13,* p. 17. See also de Visscher, *Problèmes,* at 142, 144, note 1.

[217] *I.C.J. Reports 1949,* at 182. Similarly with respect to question I *(a)*—reparation for damage caused to the United Nations—the Court said: ''It cannot be doubted that the Organization has the capacity to bring an international claim against one of its Members which has caused injury to it by *a breach of its international obligations* towards it''. *Ibid.,* at 180. Italics supplied. Finally, when dealing with non-member States, the Court said: ''Here again the Court is authorized to *assume* that the damage suffered involves the responsibility of a State, and it is not called upon to express an opinion upon the various ways in which that responsibility might be engaged''. *Ibid.,* at 185. Italics supplied.

[218] It may be well to recall the introductory words: ''In the event of an agent of the United Nations in the performance of his duties suffering injury in circumstances *involving the responsibility* of a State . . .'' The General Assembly did not ask: in what circumstances does an injury to an agent involve the responsibility of a State. Some such circumstances were brought to the attention of the Court by Mr. Feller in his oral statement. *Pleadings,* at 79. That part of the request which related to the reconciliation of the claim by the United Nations and ''such rights as may be possessed by the State of which the victim is a national'' presented no difficulty and the Court did not think there was a ''risk of competition between the Organization and the national State'' because ''the bases of the two claims are different''. *I.C.J. Reports 1949,* at 186. It is indeed difficult to see how the national State could make a claim for an injury suffered by an agent of the United Nations in the performance of his duties. On the other hand the Organization would necessarily be confined to such a claim.

rity and independence of international officials, particularly in crisis situations. Here, as in the *Reparation* and *Competence of the General Assembly* cases, the Court considered the whole Charter and what it now called—for the first time, it is believed—"the organized legal system of the United Nations".[219] In order to answer the question put to it, the Court reformulated it as follows: "The legal power of the General Assembly to establish a tribunal competent to render judgments binding on the United Nations has been challenged. Accordingly, it is necessary to consider whether the General Assembly has been given this power by the Charter".[219] In the absence of a positive or negative provision of the Charter, the Court recalled the "necessary implication" principle laid down in the *Reparation* case, and took into account the principles and objectives of Chapter XV of the Charter, as well as "the expressed aim of the Charter to promote freedom and justice for individuals" thereby devolving a judicial remedy for the staff of the Organization in disputes between the Organization and its own staff. It concluded by stating:

> "In these circumstances, the Court finds that the power to establish a tribunal, to do justice as between the Organization and the staff members, was essential to ensure the efficient working of the Secretariat, and to give effect to the paramount considerations of securing the highest standards of efficiency, competence and integrity. Capacity to do this arises by necessary intendment out of the Charter".[220]

Conceding the implied power to establish an administrative tribunal, the Court held that "an implied power to impose legal limitations upon the General Assembly's express Charter powers is not legally admissible". While admitting that the Assembly could have created a different tribunal and a different statute to govern it, the Court proceeded to give full effect to the Statute that had been actually adopted by the Assembly. Having adopted at the outset its own version of implied powers, the Court categorically rejected contentions derived from "inherent" limitations upon those powers.[221] With respect to the budgetary power of the Assembly the Court observed that this "does not mean that the General Assembly has an absolute power to approve or disapprove the expenditure proposed for it", and that it is bound to honour obligations already incurred by the Organization as result of a final award rendered by its Administrative Tribunal.[222] No obligations were assumed by the Members of the Organization to which their consent had not already been given when the Assembly established the Tribunal to settle conclusively disputes between the Organization and its staff members.

The *Expenses* case sums up the several approaches developed by the Court in its pre-

[219] *I.C.J. Reports 1954*, p. 47, at 56.

[220] *I.C.J. Reports 1954*, at 56–57.

[221] "But the contention that the General Assembly is inherently incapable of creating a tribunal competent to make decisions binding on itself cannot be accepted". *Ibid.*, at 61. It is interesting to note that Judge Alvarez, the persistent advocate of a progressive approach to international law based on "international social justice" was led in this case to a position which must appear as reactionary. He invoked the transformation of the Assembly "into an all-powerful legislative organ", and its "omnipotence". *Ibid.*, 71. He failed to share the liberal-democratic starting point of the Court, namely the conception of the United Nations as an "organized legal system", that is, a system in which power is subjected to law.

[222] *Ibid.*, at 59.

vious opinions. They are all confirmed by the Court including the role of the Court as a participant in the activities of the Organization, the consideration of the request in the context of the "Charter as a whole", and "the structure of the Charter".[223] The new element is the heavy reliance of the Court on the practice of organs. Recognizing "its need for authoritative legal guidance as to the obligations of Members . . . in the matter of financing the United Nations operations in the Congo and in the Middle East" the Assembly requested of the Court an opinion on the question whether "the expenditures authorized" in enumerated Assembly resolutions in pursuance of enumerated Security Council and Assembly resolutions relating to the Congo and "the expenditures authorized" with respect to UNEF in enumerated Assembly resolutions in pursuance of enumerated Assembly resolutions "constitute 'expenses' of the Organization within the meaning of Article 17, paragraph 2, of the Charter". The question related to past and not to future authorizations, and it remains unclear what guidance the Assembly could derive from an opinion based on such past authorizations. The Court also found it necessary to address itself to the "obligations" of Members in respect to past or future authorizations.[224] The Court gave no definition of the term "the expenses" in Article 17 (2) although it offered a negative test: in order to determine whether authorized expenditures constitute "expenses" they "must be tested by their relationship to the purposes of the United Nations in the sense that if an expenditure were made for a purpose which is not one of the purposes of the United Nations, it could not be considered an 'expense of the Organization' ".[225] As the expenditures enumerated in the request were related to specified resolutions, the Court declared that "when the Organization takes action which warrants the assertion that is was appropriate for the fulfillment of one of the stated purposes of the United Nations, the presumption is that such action is not *ultra vires* the Organization". And, stated the Court, "if the action was taken by the wrong organ, it was irregular as a matter of that internal structure, but this would not necessarily mean that the expense incurred was not an expense of the Organization".[226]

The Court was satisfied that the action had been taken by the proper organ, that it was appropriate for achieving the stated purposes—international peace and security—and that the expenditures were therefore expenses of the Organization within the meaning of Article 17 (2).[227] The practice on which this conclusion depends with respect to "action" is not directly relevant here.[228] However, the practice on which the Court drew to sustain its principal conclusion was not practice in the sense in which it was used in the *Membership* and *Competence of the General Assembly* cases,[229] but practice in the sense that the enumerated authorized expenditures have indeed been authorized and declared to be,

[223] *I.C.J. Reports 1962*, p. 151 at 155–157.
[224] See separate opinion of Judge Fitzmaurice, at 198. This accounts for the change of title of the case which up to the Advisory Opinion was: "Financial Obligations of Members of the United Nations".
[225] *Ibid.*, at 167.
[226] *I.C.J. Reports 1962*, at 168.
[227] *Ibid.*, at 179.
[228] *Ibid.*, at 165–172.
[229] *Supra*, pp. 898 f. See also on this point Judge Spender's observations, *ibid.*, at 194–195.

by the General Assembly, expenses of the Organization within the relevant clause.[230] The Assembly hardly required any "authoritative legal guidance" on that matter. It was the constitutionality of these authorizations and practices which was in issue here[231] and if the Court could or would not see its way clear to address itself to that real question, it might have been better for it to decline to give an opinion. There is neither space nor need to examine the question discussed at some length by Judges Spender and Fitzmaurice as to whether practice pursued by an organ is in any way equivalent to so-called subsequent conduct of parties to a treaty and has or should have the same or a comparable place in ascertaining the proper interpretation of a constituent instrument like the Charter.[232]

The crucial point appears to be that as a result of the Court's finding those Members of the United Nations which had consistently opposed the contested resolutions and others which, while paying their assessments, admitted no legal obligation to do so, found themselves in the position of seeing legal financial obligations imposed upon them without their consent.[233] Furthermore, if they failed to pay, they faced the application of the sanction provided for in Article 19 of the Charter.

Article 17 furnishes no basis for a concept of either "the budget of the Organization" or "the expenses of the Organization". These concepts have a certain historical connotation derived from the experience of the League of Nations, the International Labour Organisation and a host of other inter-governmental institutions. In relying on the "practice" of the Assembly the Court assumed that both budget and expenses can be defined generally or *ad hoc* by a two-thirds majority of the Assembly with binding effect for all Members. The Assembly could thus require all Members to pay for the execution of resolutions which, as was recognized by the Court, were themselves lacking binding force, subject of course to the test set up by the Court. But that test, it will be readily conceded, is so flexible as to be of no value at all. In this Opinion the Court may have intended to legitimize the action already taken by the Assembly and thus contribute to its "institutional effectiveness".[234] Whether the Court actually made this contribution will be examined presently.

Apart from their historical connotation the concepts "budget" and "expenses" have no fixed, inherent meaning. There is no meaning inherent in those words though they have a dictionary definition. As the Court rightly pointed out,[235] there was no

[230] Thus with respect to the resolutions authorizing expenditures for UNEF (*ibid.*, at 172–175) the Court concluded "that, from year to year, the expenses of UNEF have been treated by the General Assembly as expenses of the Organization within the meaning of Article 17, paragraph 2, of the Charter". *Ibid.*, at 175. Similarly with respect to the resolutions authorizing expenditures for ONUC (*ibid.*, at 175–178) the Court concluded "that the General Assembly has twice decided that even though certain expenses are 'extraordinary' and 'essentially different' from those under the 'regular budget', they are none the less 'expenses of the Organization' to be apportioned in accordance with the power granted to the General Assembly by Article 17, paragraph 2". *Ibid.*, at 178.

[231] Thus Judge Fitzmaurice, *ibid.*, at 201.

[232] See Judge Spender, *ibid.*, at 192–197 and Judge Fitzmaurice, *ibid.*, at 201–205. See also Rosenne, "Is the Constitution . . .", *loc. cit.*, at 36.

[233] For an analysis of the Opinion from this standpoint see Leo Gross, "Expenses of the United Nations for Peace-Keeping Operations", 17 *International Organization*, pp. 1–35 (1963). See also *supra*, pp. 753–782.

[234] The words are Judge Bustamante's, *I.C.J. Reports 1962*, at 238.

[235] *Ibid.*, at 159.

compelling reason to identify the term "budget" with "administrative" or "ordinary" budgets although this would have been persuasive in view of their historical connotation. The Court was, of course, also right in drawing attention to the fact that the budget of the United Nations, as a matter of "consistent practice" included items for the "maintenance of peace and security".[236] It validly invoked the statement adopted without opposition in the Working Group of Fifteen that

> "Investigations and observation operations undertaken by the Organization to prevent possible aggression should be financed as part of the regular budget of the United Nations".[237]

The Court, it is respectfully submitted, should have given more weight to this statement than it did. For it discloses the method by which the concepts of budget and expenses are filled with substantive operational content. It is the consensus of the membership which determines what is the budget and what are the expenses of a particular organization at any given time, and not the majority vote of a representative body. In so far as the United Nations is concerned the consensus ended at financing investigation, observation, the maintenance of the United Nations cemetery in Korea, etc.[238] The consensus of the membership while not necessarily static, has not gone beyond those limits, despite the Opinion of the Court, and it is unlikely to change so long as deep-seated differences relating to the operations of the United Nations do not yield to a new consensus at a higher level. The Members of the United Nations which have withheld the payment of their assessments in respect to UNEF or ONUC or both may be presumed to have done so not because the Court has abandoned the traditionalist method of interpretation in favour of the constitutionalist approach or the frankly teleological or "emergent purpose" approach.[239] They would have done so even if the Court had based its conclusion on the traditionalist methods: the natural and ordinary meaning of Article 17 of the Charter or the clear meaning rule. They have opposed the politics which led to the request and they continue to oppose the Opinion of the Court which, to them, appeared to endorse and put the stamp of judicial legitimacy on those politics. The 9 to 5 vote in the Court was a more-than-adequate reflection of the division in the membership on the matter.

The assertions of the Court that "the Charter was a multilateral treaty" has been accepted at face value even if it were correct to say that the language were nothing but a

[236] *I.C.J. Reports 1962,* at 160.

[237] *Ibid.*, at 161.

[238] Leo Gross, *loc. cit.*, at 15, 20–26 and *supra*.

[239] Rosenne, *loc. cit.*, 77–78; Fitzmaurice, "The Law and Procedure of the International Court of Justice", 33 *British Year Book of International Law,* 203–293 (1957) at 225. The legitimate place for the doctrine of "emergent purpose", according to Fitzmaurice, is not in the theory of interpretation but in the law of treaties or, put in other words, it is not a method for interpreting treaties but for revising them "provided always that the application of the doctrine is limited to its proper scope, namely the case where the 'purpose' clearly emerges as a matter of evidence, on the basis of the acts, practices, and conduct of the parties, and is not supplied or superimposed by the tribunal". If the doctrine is understood in that sense then, of course, the Court did not apply it, for it considered the practice of organs and not of States.

convenient phraseology on which to base the Court's jurisdiction to interpret it.[240] The matter becomes of concern, however, in connection with the methods of interpretation which are claimed to attach to constitutions or constituent instruments. Most, if not all, constituent instruments contain provisions which may be called constitutional—the structure of the organization, the attribution and distribution of competence to and between its organs, the principles and purposes and similar matters—as well as provisions which may be called conventional—rights and duties of States, reserved domain, etc. Thus, it becomes a matter of some difficulty to determine which method of interpretation should apply to the constitutional and the conventional provisions. de Visscher called attention in his dissenting opinion in the *South West Africa* (Status) case to the constitutional character of the Charter and claimed that the concepts generally applied to the interpretation of ordinary treaties did not suffice.[241] Judge Jessup recalled this observation as well as the "famous apothegm of Chief Justice Marshall in *McCulloch* v. *Maryland* (4 Wheat. 407): 'We must never forget that it is a constitution we are expounding' ".[242] Reference to *McCulloch* v. *Maryland,* a landmark in the development of the United States Constitution, comes easily enough to those familiar with its history. Over 40 years ago that case was, probably for the first time, invoked in connection with the Covenant of the League of Nations, as a precedent for "bold and constructive interpretations".[243] The representative of the United States recalled the case in his oral statement in the *Expenses* case. He described it as a "general principle of law recognized by civilized nations" to which the Court has given expression in the doctrine of implied powers in the *Reparation* case.[244]

In a more recent American precedent, *Missouri* v. *Holland,* which Mr. Justice Holmes wrote the Opinion, is the famous dictum that "when we are dealing with words that also are a constituent act, like the Constitution of the United States, we must realize that they have called into life a being the development of which could not have been foreseen completely by the most gifted of its begetters".[245] In this view it has been said that "the living growth approach to the constitutional problems of international organi-

[240] As is claimed by Rosenne, *loc. cit.,* at 35. Rosenne contends "the question whether the constitution of an international organization is itself an international treaty does not permit of an unqualified answer. The reply will depend on the circumstances in which the question is raised".

[241] *I.C.J. Reports 1950,* at 189. See also his *Theory and Reality in Public International Law,* at 229–254, and his more recent work *Problèmes d' interprétation,* at 140–153. See also, F. A. Vallat who considers the "organic interpretation" of the Charter as a Constitution rather than as a treaty to be suitable for the General Assembly. "The competence of the United Nations General Assembly", 97 *Hague Recueil,* 203–291 (1959) at 269.

[242] *I.C.J. Reports 1966,* p. 353, note i. See also his references to judgments of the Supreme Court of the United States in *I.C.J. Reports 1962,* at 428–429.

[243] "The usefulness and success of our own constitution, in near a century and half of trial has largely depended upon the bold and constructive interpretation established under the lead of Chief Justice Marshall, who always found, within the four corners of that august instrument, whatever was necessary for the welfare of the federal government. Probably the Covenant of the League requires for its survival as bold and broad interpretation". Charles N. Gregory, "The Neutralization of the Aaland Islands", 17 *AJIL,* 63–76 (1923), at 75.

[244] *Pleadings,* at 426. He also referred to *Missouri* v. *Holland* but omitted the sentence following the semicolon. See below note 245 in the quotation. *Ibid.,* at 425.

[245] 252 U.S. 416 (1920). Justice Holmes continued as follows: "It was enough for them to realize or to hope that they had created an organism; it has taken a century and has cost their successors much sweat and blood to prove that they created a nation".

zations has been characteristic of the jurisprudence of the International Court from its earliest days'' and that ''it is a legitimate ambition to seek to make the jurisprudence of the International Court of Justice fulfill the great ends which the United Nations was established to accomplish''.[246]

Alas, the Charter of the United Nations is not a constitution in the sense of the American Constitution: the analogy begins with the first two words ''We the'' in the preambles of both instruments but ends with the following third word which is ''people'' in the American and ''peoples'' in the United Nations constitution. Therein lies a difference. The United Nations is not like the United States even in its infancy. The possibility, of course, cannot be excluded that after a century, and as Mr. Justice Holmes said, much sweat and blood—not to mention Sir Winston Churchill's tears—the United Nations will acquire the degree of integration which will make the comparison with the federalism of the United States more tenable. However, to return from vision to more mundane matters, since *McCulloch* v. *Maryland* has been invoked as a model for the Court to emulate, it may be useful to recall the following passage from Chief Justice Marshall's Opinion:

> ''Let the end be legitimate, let it be within the scope of the constitution, and all means which are appropriate, which are plainly adapted to that end, which are not prohibited, but *consist with the letter and spirit* of the constitution, are constitutional''.[247]

The Constitution of the United States is very flexible but even its ends must be achieved in conformity with its letter and spirit.[248] It cannot be otherwise with the interpretation of the Charter of the United Nations, as the Court itself has recognized, for example, in that part of its Opinion in the *South West Africa* (Status) case which concerned Article 80 of the Charter. Great and dynamic as the principle of effectiveness may be as a method of interpretation, effectiveness, as its chief protagonist has put it, is in general ''a principle of good faith, is a matter of circumstances and degree''.[249] As such it has its place in the interpretation of treaties in general as well as in the interpretation of constituent instruments of international organizations.[250] The Court's jurisprudence leaves no doubt

[246] Jenks, *Prospects*, at 461. Mr. Jenks refers to the Advisory Opinions of the Permanent Court in the *International Labour Organisation*, the *Tunis-Morocco Nationality Decrees* and the *Interpretation of the Treaty of Lausanne* cases, to the Opinion of the International Court in the *Reparation, United Nations Administrative Tribunal, Expenses,* and the three Opinions as well as the Judgment on Preliminary Objections in the *South West Africa* cases.

[247] Wheat. 316 at 421. Italics supplied.

[248] See Mr. Justice Black's Opinion in *Reid* v. *Covert*, 354 U.S. 1 (1957). Mr. Justice Black held that the power of the Congress to legislate in order to carry out United States obligations under international agreements was not free from the restraints of the Constitution—thus, distinguishing the present case from *Missouri* v. *Holland*—and that military trial of civilians was inconsistent with both the ''letter and the spirit of the Constitution''. He also considered that ''nothing said here contravenes the rule laid down in *McCulloch* v. *Maryland*''. See also the International Court's Advisory Opinion in the *Peace Treaties* (Second Phase), for limits of the principle of effectiveness. *I.C.J. Reports 1950,* at 229.

[249] Lauterpacht, *The Development*, at 292.

[250] It may be noted that the International Law Commission has seen no need to include the principle of ''effective interpretation'' in its General Rules of Interpretation but considered as sufficient interpretation in ''good faith in accordance with the ordinary meaning to be given to the terms of the treaty in their context and in the light of its object and Purpose''. Article 27, paragraph 1, of Draft Articles on the Law of Treaties. Report of the International Law Commission,

that as an organ of the United Nations and as an interpreter of its Charter it will carry forward the purposes and principles of the Organization. But there are limits to what a Court can expect to, and what can legitimately be expected that it should, accomplish and these are set by its role as a Court and the environment in which it, as well as the United Nations, functions.

Methods of interpretation, by whatever designation they go, are but tools in the hand of the interpreter. The Court has used a variety of methods and techniques[251] depending upon circumstances and on the procedure, the contentious or advisory, in which the case came before it. Rules of interpretation are not so much "roads to right legal solutions" as "footholds for struggling for these solutions".[252] The choice of "starting-points for argument",[253] which are themselves of a metajuridical character, will be indicated to the Court by its dual function: as an organ of the United Nations or as an organ of international law.

*GAOR*, 21st Sess., Supp. No. 9 (A/6309/Rev. i), p. 49. Cf. Article 4 which subordinates the articles to "any relevant rules" of international organizations.

[251] For an excellent survey see Edward Gordon, "The World Court and the Interpretation of Constitutive Treaties", 59 *AJIL*, 794–833 (1965).

[252] Ilmar Tammelo, "The Law of Nations and Rhetorical Tradition of Legal Reasoning", 13 *Indian Year Book of International Affairs*, 227–258 (1964) at 250.

[253] Julius Stone, *Legal System and Lawyers' Reasoning* (1964), pp. 325 ff., and *Rutgers Law Review*, 757–781 (1964) at 768 ff.

## CHAPTER III

## EFFECTIVENESS OF ADVISORY OPINIONS

Great as is the quantitative difference in the number of requests for advisory opinions addressed to the International Court as compared with those directed to the Permanent Court, the qualitative difference is no less significant. Although the Opinions of the Permanent Court preserved their "advisory" character despite the reception accorded to them, they "greatly facilitated the work of the Council of the League of Nations", they "facilitated the efficient functioning of international institutions other than the Council" and they "also proved useful to States in disputes".[1] In fact their practical effectiveness and usefulness were so impressive that they were regarded by some as "equivalent in the eyes of the Council, of public opinion and of the interested parties to a judgment".[2] The policy of assimilating the advisory to the contentious procedure was considered sound but Hudson warned against carrying this process too far, lest the advisory opinions come to be regarded as a "species of judgment", and the "advisory jurisdiction . . . be regarded as an alternative to obligatory jurisdiction, and this might result in diminishing the frequency of requests for advisory opinions".[3] He accordingly went out of his way to underscore that the opinions were not binding on the requesting body, or on the Court or on the States concerned. He even minimized the importance of a Committee of the Permanent Court composed of its President Loder, and Judges Moore and Anzilotti which in 1927 declared that "the view that advisory opinions are not binding is more theoretical than real", by placing it in the context of the problem before the Committee.[4] But that view can also be understood as a restatement of the 1923 pronouncement of the Permanent Court in the *Eastern Carelia* case that to answer the question—in the circumstances of the controversy—"would be substantially equivalent to deciding the dispute between the parties".[5] And this the Court declined to do without the consent and participation of Russia.

Turning to the effectiveness of the advisory opinions rendered by the International Court, a different picture emerges. All of the United Nations requests have come from the General Assembly and none from the Security Council. In all but one case the Assembly formally accepted or noted them.[6] The exception is the Advisory Opinion in the *Competence of the General Assembly* case, but for all practical purposes the Opinion was effective; it settled the issue of the role of the two principal organs in the admissions pro-

[1] Hudson, *The Permanent Court of International Justice 1920–1942* (1943), at 523.

[2] *Ibid.*, at 513.

[3] *Ibid.*, at 509.

[4] *Ibid.*, at 512, and note 80. See *supra*, p. 881.

[5] *P.C.I.J. Series 3, No. 5* pp. 7–29, at 29. See *supra*, p. 876.

[6] For details see Rosenne, II, 748–754.

cess. In fact, Argentina, the chief protagonist of the so-called "Argentine thesis", failed to argue its thesis before the Court.

The Advisory Opinion in the *Admissions* case was ineffective. Its impact was severely undercut by several factors: first, its authority was severely shaken by the cogently written joint dissenting opinion of five judges; secondly, the separate opinions of two judges raised a question about the internal working process of the Court in chambers: they voted for the Opinion but their individual opinions were more in accord with the dissenters than with the reasoning of the Court; thirdly, the Court, within the compass of the request, could not possibly provide an objective, functional test for evaluating a Member's vote and could not suggest who would be competent to evaluate it; and fourthly, the Court did not, and, within the four corners of the question put to it, perhaps could not distinguish conditions of admissibility or eligibility for membership in Article 4 (1) from conditions of admission in Article 4 (2).[7]

The Opinion in the *Reparation* case was effective. The Assembly authorized the Secretary-General to bring in international claims for reparation against States "alleged to be responsible".[8] The Secretary-General initiated the necessary proceedings, after communicating with the Governments of which the victims were nationals and receiving their assurance that they would not present separate claims. This procedure has been followed in eight cases, of which five related to the war in Palestine in 1948, and three concerned events in 1956 and 1958 in the Middle East. He was successful in four cases and one case is still pending. He obtained satisfaction in two cases from Israel,[9] and in one case each from Jordan[10] and the United Arab Republic.[11] The pending case relates to Lt. Col. G. A. Flint, an observer with UNTSO who was killed in 1958 in the demilitarized zone of Mt. Scopus in Jerusalem by a bullet projected from Jordanian-held territory. In three cases the Secretary-General has not been successful.[12] The claims for damage suffered by

[7] See Leo Gross, "Election of States to United Nations Membership", American Society of International Law, *Proceedings*, 37–59 (1954), at 44. In connection with the "package" admission in 1955 it needs to be pointed out that the injunction of the Court that the applications should be examined and voted on separately (*I.C.J. Reports 1948*, at 65) was followed in both the Assembly and the Council. See Leo Gross, "Progress Toward Universality of Membership in the United Nations," 50 *AJIL*, 791–827 (1956), at 822. See also *supra*, 585–606 and 607–641.

[8] General Assembly resolution 365 (V) of 1 December 1949, A/1251 at 64.

[9] Relating to the death in 1948 of Count Bernadotte and Colonel Serot; Israel paid $54,628 in satisfaction of the former and $25,233 of the latter claim; for damages suffered by the United Nations in the case of Colonel Serot an additional payment of $575 was paid in satisfaction of a separate claim filed by his father who was 89 years old.

[10] This claim concerned Lt. Col. Erik H. Thalin, Swedish Military Observer with UNTSO who suffered injuries resulting in total disability after being fired upon by members of the Jordanian National Guard. The amount of $25,518.26 covered the monetary damage borne by the United Nations, including a lump sum paid to the victim and payments of his medical expenses.

[11] This claim concerning Trooper R. A. Allen of the Canadian contingent of UNEF was settled by payment directly to the Government of Canada of a sum of $21,433 fixed by Canada. Trooper Allen was killed by gunfire in U.A.R. territory. In this case the United Nations served as intermediary. It may be doubtful whether this claim can be used in support of effectiveness.

[12] They concern Lt. Col. Joseph Queru and Capt. Pierre Jeannel, United Nations Military Observers from France who were killed on 28 August 1948 at the Gaza Airport by Saudi Arabian troops under Egyptian command, and Mr. Ole H. Bakke, a United Nations staff member of Norwegian nationality who was killed on 13 July 1948 in Jordanian-held territory while on duty with the United Nations.

the United Nations generally included expenses of the Organization such as pensions or compensations to the victim or his widow, medical and funeral expenses, etc.[13]

In the *Peace Treaties* the three *South West Africa* and the *Expenses* cases the Advisory Opinions were not effective. However, in the *Peace Treaties* case the Assembly relied on the finding as a matter of substance, although the Court had considered it to be a matter of procedure and condemned "the wilful refusal of Bulgaria, Hungary and Romania to fulfill their obligation under the provisions of the Treaties of Peace to appoint representatives to the Treaty Commissions, which obligation has been confirmed by the International Court of Justice".[14]

The *South West Africa* cases, although based on the principle of interpretation called "useful effect", produced no such effect. The Government of South Africa has continued to stand by its version of the obligations incumbent upon it as Mandatory for the territory. The attempt to convert the non-binding opinions into a binding judgment succeeded in the first and failed in the second phase. The Court failed to provide the legal basis for Security Council action pursuant to Article 94 (2). Whether the hope that the Council would be able to generate the unanimity of the Permanent Members required for any action was well-founded or misplaced must remain a matter for conjecture. The General Assembly, stung into action by the Court's judgment, adopted on 27 October 1966 resolution 2145 (XXI), by a vote of 114 in favour, 2 against with 3 abstentions. In this, it reaffirmed that resolution 1514 (XV) was fully applicable to the people of the territory and that the territory has an international status. It declared that South Africa has failed to fulfill its obligations under the Mandate and "has, in fact, disavowed the Mandate". Finally, it decided that the Mandate "is therefore terminated" and that "henceforth South West Africa comes under the direct responsibility of the United Nations".[15] The resolution clearly expresses the political will of the Assembly. The matter has once again been treated as a political and not a legal problem. The Assembly moved from the legal to the political plane and it is on that plane that the ways and means will have to be found to execute the resolution which, legally, has no binding force.

The Advisory Opinion in the *Expenses* case remains ineffective, though this is not to say that it was without effect. A flurry of intense activity concerned with the application of Article 19 of the Charter to the Soviet Union and to other Members which were significantly lagging in their payments,[16] led to the crisis in 1964 at the Nineteenth Session, the "non-session" of the General Assembly, and later to the abandonment of American efforts to enforce the Opinion of the Court. The Committees of the Assembly, established

[13] See Annual Report of the Secretary-General, *GAOR*: 4th to 10th Sessions, Supp. No. 1, Docs. A/930, p. 131; A/1287, p. 124; A/1844, p. 188; A/2141, p. 160; A/2404, p. 144; A/2663, p. 101; A/2911, p. 109; S/7867, S/7873, S/7882, and S/7886.

[14] General Assembly resolution 385 (V) of 3 November 1950, *GAOR*: 5th Sess. Supp. No. 20 (A/1775).

[15] *GAOR*: 21st Sess. Supp. No. 16 (A/6316), at 2.

[16] For the position of the United States, which played a leading role in this matter, see Memorandum of Law prepared by Office of Legal Adviser, Department of State, February 1964, see 58 *AJIL*, 753–778 (1964), and 59 *AJIL*, 622–632 (1965).

to seek and find common ground on the underlying financial and constitutional problems of peace-keeping operations, have failed.[17]

It must be a matter of profound regret that, in the aftermath of the Advisory Opinion, the United States Government felt compelled to declare on 16 August 1965, without prejudice to its position that Article 19 was applicable, that the "consensus of the membership is that the Assembly should proceed normally". Ambassador Goldberg continued:

> "At the same time, we must make it crystal clear that if any member can insist on making an exception to the principle of collective financial responsibility with respect to certain activities of the Organization, the United States reserves the same option to make exceptions if, in our view, strong and compelling reasons exist for doing so. There can be no double standard among the members of the Organization".[18]

There would have been no double standard if the United States had limited itself to the financing of UNEF and ONUC or possibly peace-keeping operations generally. The reservation introduced by the United States, which is reminiscent of the Connally Reservation in its Declaration of 1946 accepting the compulsory jurisdiction of the Court, is as sweeping as is the reasoning of the Court with respect to expenditures that may be classified as expenses within the meaning of Article 17 (2) of the Charter. It is precisely through this statement that the United States introduced a double standard. No other Member, either before or after, has claimed the right to make an exception to the principle of collective financial responsibility if, in its judgment, "strong and compelling reasons exist for doing so". This reservation is not automatic but it appears to be just as self-judging as is the Connally Reservation.

The Advisory Opinions, in the *Reservations* and *United Nations Administrative Tribunal* cases were effective. The General Assembly gave instructions to the Secretary-General "to conform his practice to the advisory opinion of the Court" in relation to reservations to the Genocide Convention and to follow substantially the Opinion with respect to future conventions concluded under the auspices of the United Nations.[19] The "most serious challenge to the authority of an advisory opinion"[20] came from the International Law Commission which regarded "the criterion of the compatibility of a reservation with the object and purpose of a multilateral convention, applied by the International Court of Justice to the Convention on Genocide, as not suitable for application to multi-

[17] See General Assembly resolution 2220 (XXI) of 19 December 1966 which continued the Special Political Committee's work of the comprehensive review of the whole question of peace-keeping operations in all their aspects. *GAOR*: 21st Sess. Supp. No. 16 (A/6316), at 21. Referring to the latest report submitted by the Committee (Doc. A/6603), the Secretary-General expressed his regrets that it "is so negative. It not only shows the continuing failure to agree on basic principles, but it also reflects a reluctance to come to grips with the problem". Introduction to the Annual Reports of the Secretary-General on the Work of the Organization, 16 June 1965–15 June 1966. *GAOR*: 21st Sess. Supp. 1A (A/6301/Add. 1), at 2.

[18] 53 Department of State *Bulletin* 454, at 456; United Nations Committee on Peacekeeping Operations, A/AC.121/Sr.15, at 6.

[19] General Assembly resolution 598 (VI) of 12 January 1949, *GAOR*: 6th Sess. Supp. No. 20 (A/2119), at 84.

[20] Rosenne, II, at 752, note 3.

lateral conventions in general''.[21] However, the Commission in elaborating the clauses on reservations in its Draft Articles on the Law of Treaties finally reversed itself and rallied to the Opinion of the Court.[22]

Following the receipt of the Court's Opinion in the *United Nations Administrative Tribunal* case, the General Assembly made arrangements for the payment of the awards and revised the Statute of the Tribunal.[23]

The Advisory Opinions given in response to requests from the International Labour Organisation and IMCO were promptly implemented. In the former case the awards were paid and in the latter case the Maritime Safety Committee was reconstituted in conformity with the Court's Opinion.

Of the total of 12 Advisory Opinions given by the Court, six proved effective in practice; of the ten opinions requested by the General Assembly only four were effective. All four related to matters which might be considered as falling within the internal economy of the Organization. Only a resolution of the General Assembly was necessary to ensure effectiveness.

It would be tempting to relate the effectiveness of the Opinions or its absence to the size of the majority by which the request was adopted. However, such an effort would be fruitless. In all cases there was more than a two-thirds majority in favour of the request; the votes ranged from 25 in favour to 11 opposed with 21 abstentions in the case of *South West Africa* (Voting) case, to 52 in favour to 11 opposed with 32 abstentions in the case of the *Expenses,* and there was unanimity in the *Reparation* case.[24] The solid feature in the negative votes has been the Soviet bloc. The resolutions leading to ineffective Opinions were backed by substantial majorities, the votes being: 40 : 8 : 2 (*Admissions* case); 47 : 5 : 7 (*Peace Treaties* case); 40 : 7 : 4 (*South West Africa* (Status) case); 25 : 11 : 21 (*South West Africa* (Voting) case); 32 : 5 : 19 (*South West Africa* (Petitions) case); and 52 : 11 : 32 (*Expenses* case). On the political level it is clear that where effectiveness depended upon the Soviet bloc, its political opposition to the request was a sure indication that it would refuse to co-operate in the execution of the Opinion or, put in another way, that it would continue its political opposition against any attempt by the Assembly to implement the Advisory Opinion on the political plane.

What has just been said suggests a correlation. Several of the requests arose from or were related to two of the profound controversies which have been carried on in the forum of the United Nations: the Cold War and Colonialism. The *Membership, Peace Treaties* and *Expenses* cases fall into the Cold War category,[25] whereas the three *South*

[21] Report of the International Law Commission covering the work of its third session 16 May–27 July 1951, *GAOR*: 6th Sess. Supp. No. 9 (A/1858), at 5.

[22] See Articles 26 *(c)* and 17 and Commentary thereon in Report of the International Law Commission on the second part of its eighteenth session, 4 May–19 July 1966, *GAOR*: 21st Sess. Supp. No. 9 (A/6309/Rev. i), at 35–40.

[23] See Leo Gross, "Participation of Individuals in Advisory Proceedings before the I.C.J.: Question of Equality between the Parties", 52 *AJIL* (1958). See *supra,* 705–726.

[24] See Rosenne, II, at 664 for the votes.

[25] But in connection with the Cuban proposal to refer certain questions relating to its "expulsion" from the Organization of American States to the Court for an Advisory Opinion, the representative of the United States on 19 March 1962

*West Africa* cases fall into the colonialism category. These issues reflect fundamental divisions in the Organization. And utilization of the Court's advisory function and the Court's willingness to contribute a judicial element to the political battles have been, predictably, without avail. Resort to the Court presupposes a disposition to depoliticize the issues; when this precondition is not attained on both sides of the fence, the Court's Advisory Opinions are bound to be ineffective.[26] The Opinions will become part and parcel of the political contest and share in its outcome.

Two issues on which requests were made were marginally related to a domestic situation which for some years had deeply preoccupied the United States: the loyalty issue of alleged Communists or sympathizers among the American citizens in the staff of international institutions. The *United Nations Administrative Tribunal* and the *I.L.O. Administrative Tribunal* cases had their origin in this situation. However, in these matters the Advisory Opinions proved helpful in burying it. In these cases and in the *Reparation* case the Court manifested its concern for the integrity and independence of international secretariats and developed the theory of functional protection.

It is obvious that in cases which related to disputes either between States or between States and the Organization, the Court's Advisory Opinions, given without the consent of the State or States concerned, could and would not be effective. This category includes all the Cold War and Colonialism Opinions. A departure from the *Eastern Carelia* case may have appeared necessary and in the light of the Court's institutional status in the Organization, inevitable, but it did not secure the effectiveness of the Advisory Opinions.

Within this context one is tempted to look for a correlation between the method of approach used by the Court in interpreting the legal issues presented to it and the effectiveness of the Opinions. In five cases the Court may be deemed to have made use of the principle of effectiveness as a principle of interpretation in varying degrees. Doctrine has tried to designate various degrees of application of this principle by terms such as "useful purpose", "organic", "emergent purpose", "logical integration", "teleological", "constitutionalist", "international public policy", and others. The Court itself has drawn a firm line between revising and interpreting treaties. But where this line is to be drawn is a matter of judgment, just as is the case with the line between judicial boldness and judicial caution.

It has already been suggested that when the Court adhered to the positivist approach, as generally in its judgments and in the *Reservations* case, it was invariably successful in settling the issues. In its advisory jurisdiction in which there seemed more room for

pointed out that "although his Government had always favoured increased recourse to the International Court, it did not favour the use of the Court for cold-war political purposes foreign to the Charter and the Statute of the Court". Annual Report of the Secretary-General, 1961–1962, *GAOR*: 17th Sess. Supp. No. 1 (A/5201) at 84.

[26] Rosenne, II, at 697, put it this way in generalizing the factors which should be decisive in considering requests: "The first is whether, in the view of the requesting organ, judicial determination of the issues presented in the request is likely to further the development of United Nations policy in the matter. The second is whether there exists sufficient general agreement that the legal problem which the Court is being asked to resolve is sufficiently ripe for judicial treatment and for the crystallization which inevitably follows the judicial pronouncement". These propositions are sound enough as guides for the future but they do not, in the present submission, reflect the actual practice of the Assembly in all cases.

boldness and a degree of experimentation, the Court's opinions showed a marked tendency to be ineffective in the political forum. The *Membership* case is rather uncharacteristic. It was not the application of the method of effectiveness which denied efficacy to the Opinion but the fact that it missed the actual issue which confronted the Assembly and the Council. In the *Reparation* case the Court developed the doctrine of implied powers which in the context appears as a form of the principle of effectiveness. The Opinion could have done without it, but as it involved no new burdens for the States it has been eminently acceptable. In the *Peace Treaties* (First Phase) the role of the principle of effective interpretation was limited to the question of jurisdiction and the distinction between procedure and merits. Though modest and highly acceptable to the doctrine, it offered no assistance to the General Assembly in its further treatment of the controversy. In the *South West Africa* (Status) case the Court employed the method of "logical integration" and gave a great deal of scope to the preservation of the international status of the territory with all the safeguards which it enjoyed under the League of Nations. However right the Court may have been in implementing certain values, the juridical basis on which the Court proceeded was open to question. There were gaps in the transition from the League to the United Nations, and those gaps were filled by the Court's making the most out of the legal materials available to it. Among these materials, however, the consent of South Africa was conspicuous by its absence. The principles of purpose and effectiveness were the guides in weaving these elements into a coherent pattern for the future conduct of both the United Nations and the Government of South Africa. The two later Advisory Opinions relating to the territory clarified some points in the 1950 Opinions. All three Opinions were ineffective in practice.

In the *Expenses* case the Court found in the practice of organs a new way to preserve and even enhance the institutional effectiveness of the Organization. More than in other cases relating to the Charter, the Court took into account the fact that it was a constituent instrument rather than an ordinary treaty and that methods of interpretation suitable for the latter were not entirely suitable for the former. The method adopted in this case could best be described as teleological. One could also perhaps suggest that the method of the Court was as teleological as was that of the General Assembly in adopting the various substantive and financial resolutions. The Advisory Opinion faced in the General Assembly the same determined opposition which the Assembly itself faced in adopting the resolutions. The absence of negative votes to which the Court seemed to attach some significance is no sure guide to determining the actual political approval to the course of action pursued in the Assembly and the Security Council. There may be compelling reasons of political opportunism for abstaining in both organs. In any case, the Assembly and the Council operate on the political plane and the votes do not necessarily reflect legal convictions.[27]

In the *Expenses* case the dynamic interpretation of the Charter by the judicial organ

[27] Leo Gross, "Expenses of the United Nations", *loc. cit.*, at 30, note 79. See also *supra*, 753–782.

of the Organization in accordance with judicial technique led to the same result as the dynamic interpretation of the Charter by the political organ in accordance with the political means available to it, and it met the same political resistance.

It is axiomatic, it is submitted, that the effectiveness of an Advisory Opinion can be no greater than the power of the requesting organ to implement it. The General Assembly, on the political plane, has only the power of recommendation and its resolutions have accordingly no binding force. In the present state-system and the current stage of integration in the international society, this is the price which had to be paid for introducing majority voting. At most the Assembly can incorporate the opinion of the Court into a resolution and this generally lacks binding force.[27a]

It might be different if the Security Council made an advisory opinion a part of a political decision. In such a contingency the opinion as such would still lack binding force, but if the decision came within the scope of Article 25 of the Charter, it would be binding on the Members. Article 25 attaches binding force to certain decisions of the Security Council but not to advisory opinions. So far that contingency has never arisen. The Security Council has turned down all proposals for requesting an opinion and so far has never seen fit to base its political action on an opinion given to the General Assembly. Under the Charter and international law the Council would certainly be competent to do so provided it could marshal the necessary political support.

On the whole experience with the effectiveness of the Advisory Opinions in the United Nations does not compare favourably with that of the League of Nations. As has been shown this is due in part to the political and intractable divisions in the United Nations and partly to the enlistment of the Court's assistance and participation in the political strategies pursued in the political contests in the United Nations. The attitude of the Court may be regarded as a contributory factor. Seeing itself, as the Court stated categorically in the *Peace Treaties* case, in the role of organ of the United Nations, albeit a judicial organ, the Court was in principle willing to participate in the activities of the Organization. It was the Court which made the categorical statement that its Opinions had no binding force, that they were not given to the State but to the requesting organ, and that no State could prevent the giving of an Advisory Opinion which, not the Court, but the United Nations "considers to be desirable in order to obtain enlightenment as to the course of action it should take". The Court maintained that the case before it, the *Peace Treaties* case, was "profoundly different" from the *Eastern Carelia* case.[28] It is suggested that it was rather the perception of its role which was "profoundly different" from that of the Permanent Court.

In the League the Advisory Opinions were formally not binding but substantially equivalent to a judgment. The statements which on the one hand minimized the difference between the contentious and advisory procedures and the warnings against introduc-

[27a] An obvious exception is the resolution implementing the opinion in the *U.N. Administrative Tribunal* case. See *supra*, at p. 913.

[28] *I.C.J. Reports 1950*, at 71–72, and *supra*, pp. 876 f.

ing into the Covenant "by a circuitous route" the idea of compulsory jurisdiction on the other must be seen and appreciated in that context. They are all reflected in the separate and dissenting opinions in the *Peace Treaties* case. The views from the past are recalled and others are added: Advisory Opinions had "certain compelling force"; the view that they are not binding "is more theoretical than real"; they were in the nature of "advisory arbitration"; they possessed "an enforceability *sui generis*";[29] "if the opinions are treated as mere utterances and freely discarded, they will inevitably bring the Court into disrepute";[30] the Permanent Court "did not intend to be merely the adviser, *ad nutum advocabilis,* of the Council or the Assembly";[31] the Advisory Opinion, in practice, "is nothing else than an unenforceable judgment". Finally Judge Zorocic stated that—

> "the Court's advisory opinions enjoy the same authority as its judgments, and are cited by jurists who attributed the same importance to them as to judgments. The Court itself refers to its previous opinions in the same way as to its judgments".[32]

To be sure the judges who wrote these opinions were concerned primarily with the case before them which related to a pending dispute between States and therefore required the parties' consent. But they were also concerned with basic issues: the role of the Court and of its advisory jurisdiction. So was, of course, the Court. The Court wrote a prologue for the future, the minority wrote an epilogue for the past.

If this be so, and it is believed that it is so, then the efforts to retrieve for the advisory opinion the authority it enjoyed in the era of the League seem unjustified. Judge Jessup recalled some of the statements quoted by Judges Azevedo and Winiarski (reproduced above) as if they still possessed some validity.[33] But it was this Court which cut the umbilical cord which tied the opinions to the States when it declared that its opinions are given to the requesting organ and not to the States. The doctrinal statements which Judge Jessup quoted can hardly be regarded as reflecting the current practice.[34] Another statement which he quoted makes it clear that "on the plane of their doctrinal authority there is hardly a distinction between judgments and opinions".[35] This may be so on the plane of doctrine but certainly not on the plane of the practice in the United Nations. Again, for purposes of Article 38 (1) *(d)* there may be no distinction between the

[29] Cf. Judge Azevedo's separate opinion, *ibid.,* 79–88. Summing up Judge Azevedo wrote: "We must build a wall between the contentious and the advisory functions".

[30] The words are Judge John B. Moore's and they were recalled by Judge Winiarski, *ibid.,* at 89.

[31] Judge Winiarski, *ibid.*

[32] *Ibid.,* at 101.

[33] *I.C.J. Reports 1966,* at 338.

[34] He quoted Rosenne, II, at 747: "It may be stated that the practical difference between the binding force of a judgment, which derives from specific provisions of the Charter and Statute apart from the *auctoritas* of the Court, and the authoritative nature of an advisory opinion possessed of that same *auctoritas,* are not significant". But when Judge Winiarski referred to the authority of the Court and its advisory opinions he was speaking of the Permanent Court. *I.C.J. Reports 1950,* at 91–92. Kelsen denies that the Court's interpretations of the Charter are authoritative. *Law of the United Nations,* at 547.

[35] de Visscher, *Aspects Récents du Droit Procédural de la Cour International de Justice* (1966), at 195.

two kinds of judicial pronouncements[36] but this proposition merely describes the use which the Court and doctrine have made of advisory opinions and not their practical effect.[36a]

As already noted elsewhere[37] Judge Lauterpacht was deeply concerned with the legal effect of advisory opinions. In his separate opinion in the *South West Africa* (Petitions) case he discussed it at some length. One passage may be quoted here:

> "No countenance can be given to the suggestion that, as the result of the attitude adopted by South Africa, the régime as established by that Opinion (1950) . . . is liable to changes—except in pursuance of the principle that that régime as a whole must be and remain effective. The Opinion of 11 July 1950 has been accepted and approved by the General Assembly. Whatever may be its binding force as part of international law—a question upon which the Court need not express a view—it is the law recognized by the United Nations. It continues to be so although the Government . . . has declined to accept it as binding upon it and although it has acted in disregard of the international obligations as declared . . . in that Opinion".[38]

In another passage the learned judge stated:

> "Finally, I do not attach any decisive importance to the possible submission that this is an instance of a Government claiming the benefit of its own wrong by declining to supply and transmit information which, according to the Opinion of 11 July 1950, it is legally bound to supply and transmit and at the same time resisting the contemplated effort to obtain alternative information. For it may not be easy to characterize precisely in legal terms a situation in which South Africa declines to act on an Advisory Opinion *which it was not legally bound to accept* but which gave expression to the legal position as ascertained by the Court and as accepted by the General Assembly".[39]

This 1950 Advisory Opinion, which followed the Court's Opinion in the *Peace Treaties* case, "established" the regime, as Judge Lauterpacht correctly describes the action of the Court, and this regime South Africa was not bound legally to accept. The regime has not been effective, and it is difficult to understand why Judge Lauterpacht stated that it "must be and remain effective". The Advisory Opinion was given to the requesting organ and not to South Africa. How is one then to understand that by a sort of mutation the Opinion has become "the law recognized by the United Nations?" Does the Assembly under the Charter or international law have the legislative power to transform the regime "established" by the Court in an Advisory Opinion which admittedly is not le-

[36] Rosenne, II, 745, note 1. Elsewhere Rosenne stated: "As a statement of what the law is, there is no difference between an advisory opinion and a judgment". "Is the Constitution", *loc. cit.*, at 69, note 123.

[36a] This seems to be Judge Jessup's point. For he admits that "an Advisory Opinion or a series of such opinions, is not or are not legally binding on a State Member of the United Nations, whether or not the opinion is accepted or endorsed by the General Assembly". On the other hand, he expressed the concern that the Court "would have been brought 'into disrepute' if it should now have attributed no weight to those prior views", formulated in the 1950 Advisory Opinion and reaffirmed in the 1962 Judgment concerning the survival of the Mandate. *I.C.J. Reports 1966*, at 338.

[37] *Supra*, pp. 868, 882.

[38] *I.C.J. Reports 1956*, at 46–47.

[39] *Ibid.*, at 47. Italics supplied.

gally binding—neither on the Assembly nor on the State concerned—into "the law recognized by the United Nations"?

It would seem as if the non-existing legislative authority of the General Assembly were enlisted in order to endow Advisory Opinions with a legal force which the Court said emphatically they do not possess. The reconciliation, it has been said, of the advisory function with the essentially judicial character of the Court poses an "eternal problem".[40] As far as the International Court itself is concerned, this problem can be resolved only on the basis of its own perception of its role and place in the United Nations: as an adviser to the political organs. It is their responsibility to endow the legal opinions which they request of and receive from the Court with the necessary force. Whether to give an opinion is a matter which, as the Court declared, it and it alone must decide. Whether and in what manner it should be used and enforced by the political organs in their further consideration of the controversy, is a matter which they and they alone must decide. The acceptance or refusal of the Opinion on the part of the State or States concerned may well prevail in that political process and cause the Opinion to be ineffective in fact. But this post-advisory phase should be of no more concern to the Court than is and has been the post-adjudicative phase of its judgments.

To sum up: there has been so far at any rate a question of the effectiveness of Advisory Opinions but no problem of their legal effect. They are certainly not *res judicata* for the Court, the requesting organ, or the State or States concerned. They undoubtedly have a place in the jurisprudence of the Court and they are received and expounded in doctrine. In so far as the United Nations is concerned neither the Charter nor general international law attaches any legal effect to the Advisory Opinions and the Court has repeatedly emphasized that they are legally not binding.

It is misleading, in this submission, to contend that a State has disregarded or failed to comply with an Advisory Opinion: that State received no Advisory Opinion; it did not request it; it was not a party before the Court; at the most, it may have acted as an informer. In reality the State or States concerned has or have disregarded or failed to comply with a resolution of the General Assembly. Members are legally entitled to decline compliance with General Assembly resolutions even if they are based on or incorporate an Advisory Opinion.

The Court has never found it necessary to apply Articles 82 and 83 of the Rules of Court relating to requests upon legal questions actually pending between two or more States. It is moot whether the Court should have applied them. It is arguable that in some cases such as *Membership, South West Africa, Peace Treaties,* and *Expenses,* the legal question put to the Court related to legal questions actually pending between States, either about the proper meaning of certain provisions of the Charter, or of the Mandate or of the Peace Treaties. But the Court has declined to look into the political motivation of the requesting organ or the political background of the request. If the Court had followed the

[40] de Visscher, *Aspects récent,* at 198.

*Eastern Carelia* precedent, the consent of the State or States to the request would have been required as well as their participation in the proceedings in accordance with Articles 82 and 83 of the Rules of Court. In such an eventuality the problem of the binding effect of the Advisory Opinion for the consenting and participating State or States might have arisen.

An Advisory Opinion may have binding effect if either the States concerned have agreed beforehand to accept it as binding or because an appropriate instrument so provides, as is the case with the Statutes of the Administrative Tribunals of the International Labour Organisation and the United Nations, or as is the case with the Headquarters Agreement between the United Nations and the United States of America of 1947. In such cases it is possible to speak of "compulsive" Advisory Opinions.[41]

In other cases effectiveness will, as it has in the past, depend upon the persuasion or, to put it frankly, pressure which the requesting organ chooses to bring to bear on the State or States concerned. But this is a matter of politics and not of law.[42] So far, at any rate, the political organs have not seen fit to take appropriate action which—on the political plane—might have brought about compliance. In the *South West Africa* cases it was hoped that by transforming the Advisory Opinions into judgments this inertia would be overcome. That hope might have turned out to be vain. In the *Expenses* case the diplomatic and political efforts to apply the sanction of Article 19 were abandoned for lack of consensus. In the *Peace Treaties* case the General Assembly recognized the limits of possible political action by burying the issue through a non-binding though condemnatory resolution.

However, whichever view one takes of their impact on the behaviour of the States, it must be acknowledged that the opinions of the Court have made a substantial contribution to the development and clarification of relevant international law.

[41] See Rosenne, II, 682–690.

[42] As the Court put it: "The persuasive force of Assembly resolutions can indeed be very considerable—but this is a different thing. It operates on the political and not the legal level; it does not make these resolutions binding in law". *I.C.J. Reports 1966*, at 50–51. See also Leo Gross, "Domestic Jurisdiction, Enforcement Measures and the Congo", 1 *Australian Year Book of International Law*, 137–158 (1966), at 144. See also *infra*, 1173–1191.

# CHAPTER IV

## CONCLUSIONS

The expectations of Members with respect to the Court as an organ of the United Nations and perhaps, beyond that, simply as a Court, clearly point in one direction: the Court should contribute to the realization of the objectives of the Organization, as laid down in the Charter and as, dynamically, interpreted and expounded in resolutions and declarations of the political organs. Some Members envisaged the possibility of amending Article 38 of the Statute of the Court and in the process of clarifying the standing of United Nations resolutions and declarations as sources of law or as subsidiary means for the determination of rules of law. This could be done generally or with some emphasis on the advisory function of the Court.

The attitude of Members toward the Court has been ultra-conservative. They manifest a great and persistent restraint in accepting the compulsory jurisdiction of the Court, in formulating requests for advisory opinions, and in incorporating disputes clauses in multilateral conventions. When such clauses are included in optional protocols, there is again restraint in accepting them as binding.

There may be a cause and effect relationship between expectations and attitudes; the attitudes may change as the expectations are fulfilled. This must remain for the time being a matter of conjecture. Perhaps the Court will, without any formal change in its Statute, make a step or two towards meeting the expectations in appropriate cases. It has been noted that in some of its Advisory Opinions the Court, on the judicial level, gave expression to the "living law" approach which the General Assembly has manifested on the political level. In some cases, the Opinions, as noted above, were effective, in others they were not. The Members that opposed the dynamic, purpose-oriented "living law" approach on political grounds continued to do it, and on the same grounds, when confronted with the Advisory Opinions of the Court.

However, in order to realize their expectations Members put emphasis, as a first step, on changing the composition of the Court and speeding up the work of the International Law Commission for the codification and progressive development of the law. The General Assembly, with the latter objective in mind, set up the Special Committee. It remains to be seen what the effect of the first step taken in the Twenty-first General Assembly Session in the triannual election of the members of the Court will be. One could contemplate an expansion of the Court from 15 to 18 members to make it possible for the changed membership of the United Nations to be reflected on the Court. As noted earlier a change in the composition or size of the Court could discourage some States from submitting their disputes to the Court without necessarily overcoming the reluctance of the qualified organs of the United Nations and authorized agencies to make a greater use of the Court in its capacity as principal judicial organ of the United Nations.

The Court, which, in the present submission, has substantially lived up to the expectations of the Members in its advisory procedure, has failed to do it in the contentious procedure in the Second Phase of the *South West Africa* cases. However, it is doubtful whether the political organs of the United Nations would have found the will, as well as the ways and means, to enforce a judgment which would have substantially upheld the submissions of the Applicants. As it happened, the Court offered itself and was seized upon by the Members, as a convenient scapegoat. The progress in implementing the resolution of the General Assembly divesting South Africa, and providing for the taking over by the United Nations, of the responsibility for administration of South West Africa illuminates once again the chasm between the political objectives of the Assembly and the means available for their achievement. An overwhelming majority in the United Nations General Assembly may be very impressive, but it is not necessarily a reliable indicator of the will of the essential Members to place the interest of the United Nations over and above their national interests. The experience with Rhodesia is relevant in this context.

The *malaise* which has existed for some time with respect to the Court and the function of adjudication has been accentuated, and the challenge "to fit the Court for the tasks which it is called upon to perform in the vastly changed international society"[1] has lost none of its urgency. However, in establishing the institutional connections between the Court and the Organization, the founders of the United Nations did hardly anything more than to give, in constitutional terms, expression to the relations which have existed in fact between the Permanent Court and the League of Nations. Had the 1919 Peace Conference found the time to draft the Covenant as well as the Statute of the Court, there can be little doubt that the Court would, legally speaking have been as much part of the League as the present Court is part of the United Nations. However, what the San Francisco Conference could have done is to define more precisely and imaginatively the tasks which the new Court should perform as a principal organ of the United Nations. Having failed in this creative enterprise, it remains for the United Nations to undertake it.

So far in the Special Committee, at its Mexico City and New York City meetings, the attitude of the Members has been largely negative.[2] This negative attitude persisted in connection with the Draft Covenant on Civil and Political Rights. According to Article 44 the Human Rights Committee was to have the right to recommend to the Economic and Social Council that it ask the Court for an advisory opinion on a legal question connected with a matter of which the Committee is seized. This clause was opposed on the ground that it would introduce into the Covenant of Human Rights, a "strong element of compulsion" and that if an article were also adopted on the individual right of petition, the Court would be given "a right to adjudicate on a complaint by an individual against his State of Nationality, which would be an unprecedented departure from the accepted rules of international law". Article 44 was accordingly deleted in the Third Committee of the Assembly by a vote of 51 to 32 with 7 abstentions.[3]

[1] Rosenne, I, 113–114.
[2] See *supra*, pp. 863 F.
[3] Doc. A/6546, pp. 131–133. The quotation is from para. 520 on p. 132.

One might have thought that it was the adoption of the Covenant that constituted an unprecedented departure on a world-wide scale and that the provision for adjudication was merely consequential. To provide rights without remedies is of course convenient, but it perpetuates an old system, one against which so much has been spoken at that same session of the General Assembly.[4] On the other hand, the International Convention on the Elimination of All Forms of Racial Discrimination adopted by General Assembly resolution 2106 (XX) of 21 December 1965, provides in Article 22 that disputes over the interpretation or application of the Convention shall, at the request of any of the parties to the dispute, be referred to the Court, if it is not settled by negotiation and if no other mode of settlement is accepted by the parties.[5]

Members of the United Nations might be interested in examining whether the Court, as its principal judicial organ, could not be given some of the tasks discharged so successfully by the Court of Justice of the European Communities. To be sure, the latter represents a higher type of organization and integration than the United Nations but this need not be an absolute reason for refusing to learn from its experience.[6] Even in an organization of co-ordination, but aspiring toward the rule of law, certain things may be possible.[7]

It might be possible and desirable to grant access to the Court to staff members of the United Nations and specialized agencies. As a first step in this direction one could envisage granting individual staff members access in advisory proceedings on a footing of equality with the Organization. Such a change would satisfy two principles of sound administration of justice: equality of "parties" and *audiatur et altera pars.* As a second step one could think of allowing the individual staff members to bring before the Court a question arising from the award of an Administrative Tribunal. So far this access is open only to the Organization and only indirectly, through a screening committee, to the staff members. This screening process may not really be necessary. The Court could establish a Chamber to hear and adjudicate staff member controversies.[8]

A proposal which has frequently been made and which was aired by some delegates at the 1966 session of the General Assembly would involve an amendment of Article 34 of the Statute in order to permit the United Nations and possibly the specialized agencies and other intergovernmental organizations to institute proceedings in contentious cases against States or other international organizations. It would be a major problem to define

[4] Adverting to the argument of the Applicants that judicial supervision was essential to provide securities against abuse, the Court said: "In the international field, the existence of obligations that cannot in the last resort be enforced by any legal process, has always been the rule rather than the exception,—and this was even more the case in 1920 than today". *I.C.J. Reports 1966,* at 46. The Assembly, by its action, confirmed brilliantly the view of the Court that things have not changed.

[5] *GAOR*: 20th Sess., Supp. No. 14 (A/6014), at 51.

[6] See de Visscher, *Problèmes d'interprétation judiciaire en droit international public* (1963), at 153–158; and generally Gerhard Bebr, *Judicial Control of the European Communities* (1962), and Stuart A. Scheingold, *The Rule of Law in European Integration* (1965).

[7] See Jenks, *The Propects of International Adjudication* (1964), pp. 119–185 for some proposals for a wider range of procedures and remedies.

[8] See Leo Gross, "Participation of Individuals . . .", *loc. cit.,* at 38–40, and *supra.*

precisely the categories of controversies in respect of which such a right has become necessary, or, looking to the future, such a right would be desirable. Agreements to which the United Nations may become, is a party or is considered to be a party, such as the Trusteeship Agreements, may be a convenient starting point for the study of this problem. A related problem is of course the reciprocal right of the State, or other organizations, parties to such agreements to institute contentious proceedings against the United Nations.

In connection with requests for advisory opinions it would seem to be desirable that questions which are considered material by a minority of Members—as in the *Expenses* case—should be included in the request along with the questions proposed by the majority of Members. A more equitable approach in this matter might create a better climate for the reception of the opinion. In this connection it may be noted that in most instances only a very small number of Members has participated in the advisory proceedings. Participation has ranged from one Member in written and oral proceedings to a high of 23 in the written and 9 in the oral hearings in the *Expenses* case.[9] The Applicants in the *South West Africa* cases participated in none of the three advisory proceedings in that case.

In connection with the effect of advisory opinions relating to the interpretation and application of the Charter, it is perhaps useful to recall the San Francisco statement on interpretation of the Charter. According to that statement if an interpretation "is not generally acceptable it will be without binding force". In such circumstances, declared the statement, "or in cases where it is desired to establish an authoritative interpretation as a precedent for the future, it may be necessary to embody the interpretation in an amendment to the Charter".[10] Short of a formal amendment one could envisage a procedure whereby the advisory opinion or its operative part would be accepted as authoritative for the future by a vote which corresponds to the requirement in Article 108 for the ratification of amendments, namely a vote of two-thirds of the Members of the United Nations including all the permanent members in the Security Council.

It will be objected that that would give the permanent members a veto. This is correct but the permanent members have in any event a political veto as the experience with advisory opinions has shown conclusively. That political veto is exercised by Great Powers whenever they decline to conform in their behaviour to resolutions adopted by overwhelming majorities even if they incorporate the opinions of the Court. Such a procedure would offer safeguards to all permanent members as well as to those that were in a minority in the vote on the request. A vote on a request is taken in conformity with Article 18 (2), that is, a two-thirds majority of the members present and voting. This proce-

[9] Rosenne, II, 742. Rosenne's statement that "participation by States in the advisory proceedings has been wide" (*ibid.*, at 741) is open to question as the participation of some Members has been nominal. Thus in the *Expenses* case the Governments of Upper Volta, Japan, Portugal, Spain, the Byelorussian S.S.R., Bulgaria, the Ukrainian S.S.R., and Luxembourg limited themselves to simple letters and some other governments transmitted an exposé comprising a couple of pages. See the Chart for details regarding participation in written and oral proceedings in connection with advisory opinions.

[10] Doc. 933, 12 June 1945, in UNCIO Documents, Vol. 13, p. 709. See also Judge Spender's separate opinion and Judge Winiarski's dissenting opinion in the *Expenses* case, *I.C.J. Reports 1962,* at 196 and 229.

## INTERNATIONAL COURT OF JUSTICE: ADVISORY OPINIONS
## STATEMENTS TO THE COURT[1]

| | Membership (1948) | Reparation (1949) | Peace Treaties (1950) Phase 1 | Peace Treaties (1950) Phase 2 | Competence of the General Assembly (1950) | South West Africa (Status) (1950) | Reservations (1951) | U.N. Administrative Tribunal (1954) | South West Africa (Voting Procedure) (1955) | ILO Administrative Tribunal (1956) | South West Africa (Petitioners) (1956) | IMCO (1960) | Expenses (1962) |
|---|---|---|---|---|---|---|---|---|---|---|---|---|---|
| WRITTEN: | | | | | | | | | | | | | |
| Number of *States* submitting written Statements | 15 | 5 | 10 | 1 | 8 | 5 | 13 | 18 | 6 | 4 | 3 | 13 | 20 |
| *Secretariat of the U.N.* | No | No | No | No | S | No | S | S | D | No | D | No | D |
| Other Internat. Organizations? | No | No | No | No | No | No | S | S | No | DS | NO | D | No |
| Number of Briefs | 15 | 5 | 10 | 1 | 8 | 5 | 13 | 18 | 3 | 6 | 2 | 11 | 18 |
| Number of Statements referring to previous Statement in U.N. | 6 | 0 | 8 | 0 | 8 | 4 | 7 | 12 | 2 | 0 | 1 | 0 | 7 |
| Number of Pages: | | | | | | | | | | | | | |
| *States* | 19 | 31 | 82 | 27 | 54 | 88 | 93 | 148 | 24 | 33 | 13 | 237 | 158 |
| *Secretariat* | 0 | 0 | 0 | 0 | 67 | 0 | 118 | 61 | 0 | 0 | 0 | 0 | 0 |
| *Others* | 0 | 0 | 0 | 0 | 0 | 0 | 73 | 45 | 0 | 161 | 0 | 0 | 0 |
| *Total* | 19 | 31 | 82 | 27 | 121 | 88 | 284 | 254 | 24 | 194 | 13 | 237 | 158 |
| ORAL: | | | | | | | | | | | | | |
| Oral Hearings | Yes | Yes | Yes | Yes | Yes | Yes | Yes | Yes | No | No | Yes | Yes | Yes |
| Number of States Participating | 5 | 3 | 2 | 2 | 1 | 2 | 3 | 5 | — | — | 1 | 7 | 9 |
| *Secretariat* | Yes | Yes | Yes | Yes | No | Yes | Yes | Yes | — | — | No | No | No |
| Other Internat. Organizations? | No | No | No | No | No | No | No | No | — | — | No | No | No |
| Number of public hearings in case | 3 | 3 | 3 | 2 | 1 | 6 | 5 | 4 | — | — | 1 | 7 | 7 |
| Number of Pages | | | | | | | | | | | | | |
| *States* | 60 | 37 | 74 | 42 | 12 | 79 | 106 | 77 | — | — | 12 | 172 | 139 |
| *Secretariat* | 17 | 44 | 11 | 3 | 0 | 79 | 22 | 21 | — | — | 0 | 0 | 0 |
| *Others* | 0 | 0 | 0 | 0 | 0 | 0 | 0 | 0 | — | — | 0 | 0 | 0 |
| *Total* | 77 | 81 | 85 | 45 | 12 | 158 | 128 | 98 | — | — | 12 | 172 | 139 |
| *Combined Total of written + oral argument* | 96 | 112 | 167 | 72 | 133 | 246 | 412 | 352 | 24 | 194 | 25 | 409 | 297 |

1. D = Dossier; S = Statement.

dure may result in a vote which is quite unrepresentative of the membership. For instance the vote on the request in the *Expenses* case was 52 : 11 with 32 abstentions; it precipitated a very serious constitutional crisis. The new procedure would provide a corrective by introducing a vote on accepting the advisory opinion by a qualified two-thirds majority vote. If it is adopted by such a vote, the advisory opinion would become part of the law of the United Nations; in case of failure it would be laid aside and possibly grave crises avoided. This again reflects only political realities and the *Expenses* opinion is a case in point.

It has often been observed, sometimes with regret, that the Charter has not provided for judicial control or review of the constitutionality of acts of the political organs of the United Nations. There was no need for it when the Organization was set up. This is a matter which has assumed major significance with the rapid development of the United Nations and the increasingly dynamic conception of its role. The United Nations desires to promote the rule of law in the life of nations. It is perhaps not too soon to start thinking whether and in what form and in what circumstances such a control or review could be established. When the General Assembly requested advisory opinions in the *United Nations Administrative Tribunal* and in the *Expenses* cases, it did, in fact, invite the Court to pass upon the constitutionality of past or future acts. These are precedents of great significance. However, constitutional review is also, if not primarily, a protection of the minority against the majority. It would be in harmony with the expressed aim of the Members to promote the rule of law and the objective of the Charter "to establish conditions under which justice and respect for the obligations arising from treaties and other sources of international law can be maintained" to give consideration to this problem. A review procedure along the lines indicated here in barest outline would not, of course, interfere with the Security Council's responsibilities for taking action under Chapter VII of the Charter.[10a]

What effect, if any, would changes in the role of the Court as a United Nations organ have upon the Court's other role as an organ of international law in disputes outside the framework of the United Nations? So far—with the possible exceptions of the *South West Africa* cases—the Court has had no problem in discharging its two roles, following generally the line of positive international law in one capacity and another more dynamic and flexible in the other.

There have been many disputes in the last two decades which the States concerned submitted to arbitration instead of to the Court. Many disputes are settled by procedures

[10a] It may be recalled that according to Article 96 (2) of the Havana Charter for an International Trade Organization of 24 March 1948, "any decision of the Conference under this Charter shall, at the instance of any Member whose interests are prejudiced by the decision, be subject to review by the International Court of Justice by means of a request, in an appropriate form, for an advisory opinion pursuant to the Statute of the Court". Pursuant to para. 5 of Article 96 the Organization "shall consider itself bound by the opinion of the Court on any question referred by it to the Court. In so far as it does not accord with the opinion of the Court, the decision in question shall be modified". Department of State *Publication* 3117, p. 50. As a corollary to this one could provide that if a Member does not request that a decision of an organ be reviewed by the Court, that Member shall be bound by the decision. The Havana Charter failed to enter into force. On the subject of judicial review of acts of international organs including the IMCO case see E. Lauterpacht, "The Legal Effect of Illegal Acts of International Organizations", in *Cambridge Essays on International Law* (Oceana, 1965), pp. 88–122.

which are internal to specialized agencies. The World Bank has recently established a Centre for the Settlement of Investment Disputes between private investors and States.[11] This is another instance where orthodoxy in the matter of standing of individuals in international procedures has been abandoned. The Court is not without rivals and the drift towards arbitration may continue or even gain momentum. It may well become more pronounced if the Court were to apply in contentious cases—outside the United Nations framework—methods of interpretation or concepts of law which are appropriate in its capacity as an organ of the United Nations. The Court in the *South West Africa* (Second Phase) Judgment appeared equally divided in this matter.

However, the Court would preserve the confidence it has earned from the States if, in its capacity of organ-of-international law, it continued to adhere to generally accepted methods of interpretation, if it would interpret treaties and not revise them, in short if it continued to function on the basis of consent both to jurisdiction and applicable law. For as one of the keenest students and judges of the Court, having noted the voluntary nature of the jurisdiction of international tribunals, observed:

> "An international court which yields conspicuously to the urge to modify the existing law—even if such action can be brought within the four corners of a major legal principle—may bring about a drastic curtailment of its activity".[12]

Similar warnings have been expressed by other learned writers.[13] It is true that "the judicial process has stood still",[14] compared with the developments of the political institutions. But this is largely due to circumstances beyond the control of any single institution, be it political or judicial. The Court's tasks as an organ-of-international-law cannot be other than to give judgments on the basis of law and in a manner which will be acceptable as expositions of international law as it stands. The Court is hardly in the position, through judicial legislation, to compete with the States in creating new rules or principles of international law. The responsibility and authority for law-making, for international legislation, belong to the States and to the United Nations and other international organizations. Being essentially a political function it is through political, and not the judicial institutions, that it must be tackled. The United States Supreme Court is not yet a model for the International Court. Both of them have to function in the society, and in the constitutional-political systems to which they are institutionally connected. But there is no reason why the International Court should not play a greatly more active and significant role in the society of which it is the judicial organ.

The adjudication process in the *South West Africa* cases has revealed some weak-

[11] See Nigel S. Rodley, "Some Aspects of the World Bank Convention on the Settlement of Investment Disputes", 4 *Canadian Year Book of International Law*, pp. 43 f. (1966).

[12] Lauterpacht, *The Development of International Law by the International Court* (1958), at 76.

[13] J. H. W. Verzijl, *The Jurisprudence of the World Court*, Vol. I (1965), at 504, 509–510, 512; C. Wilfred Jenks, *Prospects*, at 458; G. Schwarzenberger, *International Law*, Vol. I (3rd ed. 1957), at 66.

[14] Sir Humphrey Waldock, General Course on Public International Law, Hague *Recueil* II (1962), p. 120. This is the theme developed fully by Jenks in his book *Prospects*, p. xii of the Introduction.

nesses in the Court's procedure in contentious cases. Some complaints have been voiced in respect of the time involved in reaching the final disposition. Such complaints should be addressed to the parties and not to the Court. The Court will not, and probably should not, impose rigid time-limits for the filing of written pleadings by the litigants. The Court could exercise a more effective control over the conduct of oral hearings and the presentation of experts and witnesses without interfering with the right of the parties to make as full a statement of their case as they deem necessary. But the Court could ask the parties to elucidate the points which in the Court's views need clarification. The time lapse between the closing of the hearings on 29 November 1965 and the reading of the judgment in the *South West Africa* case on 19 July 1966, a total of 230 days,[15] is not unreasonable in view of the voluminous documentation, pleadings, oral testimony and statements, and 446 pages of separate and dissenting opinions. There is a good deal of duplication and repetition in the pleadings both written and oral but again this is a matter which escapes the effective control by the Court whose clients are sovereign States.

The Court has the power pursuant to Article 70 of its Statute to propose amendments to the Statute and it is master of the Rules of Court. As noted earlier, the Statute was elaborated some 40 years ago, and has remained substantially unchanged. It may be eminently desirable for the Court itself to subject it and the Rules of Court to a close review. One matter which occupied the attention of the Permanent Court concerns the treatment of preliminary objections to jurisdiction and their separation from the merits. It has been regarded as axiomatic that a party which contests the jurisdiction of the Court should not have to plead to the merits.[16] However, it has also been taken for granted that as much of the merits must be pleaded as may be necessary for the Court to rule on the preliminary objections. In some cases this minimum has been insufficient and some or all preliminary objections were joined to the merits.

One of the interesting experiences of the Court has been the degree of sophistication developed by States in this matter. There may be objections to jurisdiction, admissibility or receivability, and there may be pre-preliminary as well as preliminary objections.[17] It is little wonder that the Members of the United Nations were perplexed and upset when, instead of a judgment on the merits in the Second Phase of the *South West Africa* cases, the Court handed down a judgment on a "matter that appertained to the merits of the case but which had an antecedent character, namely the question of the Applicants' standing in the present phase of the proceedings".[18] The Court in its 1962 Judgment (Preliminary Objections) held "that it has jurisdiction to adjudicate upon the merits of the dispute".[19] This created the legitimate expectation that all preliminary objections, that is, all ques-

[15] For periods of time in other cases see Leo Gross, "Some Observations on the International Court of Justice", 56 *AJIL*, 33–62 (1962) at 47–50, and *supra*. The previous longest period was 205 days in the *Right of Passage* case.

[16] Therefore, Article 62 (2) of the Rules of Court provides that upon the filing of a preliminary objection, proceedings on the merits shall be suspended.

[17] See Judge Fitzmaurice's separate opinion in the *Cameroons* case, *I.C.J. Reports 1963*, p. 15, at 103 ff.

[18] *I.C.J. Reports 1966*, at 18.

[19] *Ibid., 1962*, at 347.

tions of an antecedent character, having been rejected, the Court would give judgments on the merits. Instead, the Court carrying the sophistication a step further, discovered that there was still a matter of an antecedent character but this one pertained to the merits and not to jurisdiction.

It would seem desirable, if it were possible, for the sake of sound administration of justice, to avoid complexities which delight jurists but baffle governments, and to devise a procedure which would be not only fair but also generally intelligible particularly to governments, the actual and potential clients of the Court.[20] In such a procedure all manner of objections (to jurisdiction, admissibility, receivability and their subdivisions), whether raised by the parties or *ex officio* by the Court, as well as all matters of an antecedent character such as standing and judicial propriety, would form part of one phase of the proceedings so that no objections of any kind would be admitted in the second phase that should be confined to the merits.[21] This proposal does not intend to prevent the Court from joining certain matters of an antecedent character—to use the most comprehensive description—to the merits. But no new matter would be permitted to be raised by the parties or by the Court in the second phase if indeed there is a second phase. The Court, in its own interest both as an organ of the United Nations and as an organ of international law, would do well to avoid "a procedure of utter futility"[22] as well as rendering judgments "on grounds of high technicality and abstraction".[23] Nothing could be more fatal to the Court than a reputation of excessive formalism.

The Court has not been used by governments as much as it might and should have been used. It is well to remind ourselves that it requires a political decision to submit a dispute to the Court, but it also requires a political decision *not* to submit a controversy to the Court. Much has been written on the reasons for the latter, the negative decision. It has been pointed out that a decision to go to the Court involves a risk. Undoubtedly this is so. But it is equally true that a negative decision also entails a risk.

The point has been made that governments prefer the political processes of the United Nations to the juridical process of the Court. This is also true but it would require some research in order to determine whether the controversies channelled to the United Nations could equally well have been channelled to the Court. In any event, without run-

[20] Judge Jessup may have had this in mind when he asked: "Why should the Court tolerate a situation in which the parties would be put to great trouble and expense to explore all the details of the merits, and only thereafter be told that the Court would pay no heed to all their arguments and evidence because the case was dismissed on a preliminary ground which precluded any investigation of the merits?" *I.C.J. Reports 1966,* at 382. Of course, this possibility is inherent in the Court's procedure. It can and does arise when preliminary objections are joined to the merits, as was done in the *Barcelona Traction Company* case. Judge Jessup concurred in that Judgment. *I.C.J. Reports 1964,* p. 6, at 49 f. No doubt that Judgment put the parties "to great trouble and expense" without any predictable certainty that the Court will not uphold one or both of the preliminary objections joined to the merits and consequently decline to rule on the merits.

[21] A somewhat analogous proposal was made by Judge Loder in connection with the proposed revision of the Rules of the Permanent Court and rejected by seven votes to four. Publications of the P.C.I.J., *Series D, Add. to No. 2, Revision of the Rules of Court* (1926), pp. 81, 92.

[22] The words are Judge Jessup's in his dissenting opinion in the *South West Africa* (Second Phase) cases, *I.C.J. Reports 1966,* at 382.

[23] The representative of Israel (Mr. Rosenne) in Doc. A/PV. 1439, at 47.

ning much risk, one can suggest that, as a forum for the settlement of disputes, the United Nations has been singularly unsuccessful.

Another reason which has been advanced in rationalizing the attitude of the governments toward the Court is that the law is very uncertain and therefore the judgment unpredictable. This too contains an element of truth. However, there is a vicious circle here: the smaller the number of cases submitted to the Court and the narrower the range of legal problems on which the Court is asked to give a ruling, the less opportunity is afforded to the Court to clarify the law. If it is true, at least to a degree, that the judgments of the Court are unpredictable, they have been in practice effective; on the other hand, it is quite predictable that the resolutions adopted by the political organs of the United Nations in connection with the settlement of disputes, will be ineffective.

It is, of course, for the governments to make the choice between the procedures available to them. However, I wonder whether governments really make a rational choice, whether the arguments for and against a recourse to the Court are as fully considered as they ought to be. I suspect that there has developed a certain inertia in this respect. And I wonder whether governments receive the sort of advice which will enable them—on the political level—to make a rational decision. It requires a very thorough knowledge, not merely of international law, but also of the jurisprudence of the Court, its Statute and the Rules of Court, to come to an enlightened conclusion on the potential which adjudication offers in connection with a pending dispute. It may, for instance, make a very great difference whether a government appears before the Court as applicant or as respondent.

If a controversy can be settled by diplomatic negotiations, of course, that procedure should be adopted. However, it should be borne in mind that that method offers special attraction to Great Powers. They have the power, the resources, the staff, the expertise, the time, which are necessary for successful negotiations. States which are not equally well endowed may find that they will come out at the short end of diplomatic negotiations unless they can take advantage of the antagonism between the Great Powers or some other contingency. But apart from special situations, it would seem that the judicial procedure has advantages which diplomatic negotiations do not offer. Adjudication is the only procedure in which the power of the litigants is minimized and legal considerations including principles of equity are maximized.[24] The Court has also shown that it is aware of social and economic factors and that it will take them into consideration in appropriate situations.

I am not arguing that recourse to the Court is always and invariably preferable to other alternatives. What I am suggesting is much more modest. I am suggesting that

[24] This point was stressed by proponents of judicial settlement in the Special Committee on Principles of International Law concerning Friendly Relations and Co-operation among States: "It was clear that resort to the Court offered considerable advantage and greater guarantees than other means of settlement. For one thing, in the light of the objectivity and impartiality of the Court, the real inequality in the strength of States would not affect the outcome as in the case of other means of settlement and final settlement, being based on law, could be accepted by unsuccessful parties without feeling that they had lost prestige". Doc. A/5746, 16 November 1964, p. 93, para. 172.

governments should consider recourse to judicial procedure, advisory or contentious, as one of the alternatives and that in *making their choice* they should take into account *their long range interest* in promoting the development of a society in which law will increasingly come to controlling and civilizing the exercise of power. In this development the function of the Court is inevitable, both as an organ of the United Nations and an organ of international law.

# THE INTERNATIONAL COURT OF JUSTICE: CONSIDERATION OF REQUIREMENTS FOR ENHANCING ITS RÔLE IN THE INTERNATIONAL LEGAL ORDER

## I. ARBITRATION AND ADJUDICATION AS A SUBSTITUTE FOR WAR

It is commonplace to say that the Court has not lived up to the expectations expressed at its creation, although it could also be said that the governments in and out of the United Nations have not lived up to those expectations. In presenting the Statute of the Court to the Fourth Commission at the United Nations Conference on International Organization, the Rapporteur of its First Committee said that the Committee "ventures to foresee a significant role for the new Court in the international relations of the future." He went on to say: "The judicial process will have a central place in the plans of the United Nations for the settlement of international disputes by peaceful means."[1]

I wish to thank the American Society of International Law for inviting me to undertake, in my capacity as rapporteur of the Society's Panel on the Future of the International Court of Justice, a study on the Court from the point of view of requirements for enhancing its rôle in the international legal order. Also, my thanks to Dietrich E. Franke (LL.M. Harvard '70), Richard E. Bissell (B.A. Stanford '68, M.A. Fletcher '69) and Michael Doyle (B.A. Harvard '70) for their research assistance.

I wish to thank Professor Norman J. Padelford of M.I.T. for permission to use his tables on the composition of the Court and the qualifications of the judges. The tables were brought up to date by Harold Payson, III (B.A. Harvard '61, M.A. Fletcher '68, M.A.L.D. Fletcher '69).

I am particularly indebted to Judge Philip C. Jessup, who was good enough to read the entire manuscript. His numerous comments were most helpful in revising the manuscript.

[1] Doc. 913, 13 U.N.C.I.O. Doc. 381, at 393.

This prediction has not become true: "Since the Second World War, remarkable advances have been made in virtually every sector of international organization except the judicial sector."[2] This lack of progress is commonly ascribed to a lack of confidence in the Court, its composition, and the law which it applies. The problem of compulsory jurisdiction "is political and psychological," and

> The essence of the question is confidence; confidence in the stability and adequacy of the law, and confidence in the integrity and predictability of the courts and tribunals administering the law.[3]

The question is:

> How can we contribute to creating in a world of cataclysmic change and acute mutual distrust, the wider and fuller confidence necessary to the further progress of international adjudication? Only by so doing can we enable international adjudication to play a more effective part in promoting and securing the rule of law.[4]

On the level of predictability we face, we are told, a dilemma, which is as old as adjudication but which has assumed baffling proportions in the present international order, that includes so many new states which share a certain distrust of customary international law. A tribunal which boldly strikes out in new directions will be accused of lack of predictability, but a tribunal which applies the law as it finds it, and fosters "stability of law and predictability of outcome" of international litigation may "fall soon into disuse and sterility."[5]

Lack of confidence is not merely a matter of scholarly appreciation and analysis. On the level of practical statesmanship the discussion relating to the Court in the Special Committee on Friendly Relations is revealing. The main arguments explaining the reluctance of states to accept compulsory jurisdiction were the following: (a) recent international practice did not justify attempts to extend the compulsory jurisdiction of the Court; (b) the need to take into account the freedom of the parties to settle each specific dispute by the means which they consider most appropriate; (c) the need for more equitable representation in the membership of the Court; (d) the still vague and fragmentary state of international law.[6]

The Special Committee pointed out with respect to (a) that compulsory jurisdiction was rejected at the San Francisco Conference and by the 1958, 1961 and 1963 Conferences on the Law of the Sea, on Diplomatic Relations and on Consular Relations, respectively; that the compulsory jurisdiction of the Convention on Consent to Marriage, Minimum

[2] C. Wilfred Jenks, The Prospects of International Adjudication 1 (1964).
[3] *Ibid.* at 101.
[4] *Ibid.* at 3.
[5] *Ibid.* at 107.
[6] Report of the 1966 Special Committee . . . Doc. A/6230. P. 102, par. 217.

Age for Marriage and Registration of Marriages of 1962 depended on the consent of all the parties to the disputes; that most states adopted a negative attitude towards the Draft Articles on Arbitral Procedure; and, finally, that many states attached reservations to their acceptances of compulsory jurisdiction which deprived them "of any real value."[7]

A "more equitable representation" was understood to mean "a more equitable representation of the main forms of civilization and of the principal legal and social systems of the present-day world."[8] The question of the composition of the Court will be discussed later, but it may be useful to state that Article 9 of the Court's Statute does not refer to representation of "social" systems.

With respect to point (d), several views were expressed: the need for accelerating the progressive development of international law and its codification; the fear of states "that they would be subject to customary international law which they did not recognize and which they had played no part in forming;" and the expectation "that codification and progressive development of international law would facilitate the elimination of outdated and unjust treaties by which the colonial Powers were guaranteed advantageous positions and economic, political and military privileges and would thus strengthen the confidence of the new States in international law and in the legal settlement of disputes."[9]

There is no elaboration of point (b) in the Report, but freedom of choice is the idea which permeates the consensus text which was adopted by the Committee[10] and which will be referred to later.

The views expressed in the Special Committee are presented here not because they are necessarily right but because it is important to consider views which are believed to be right by a substantial number of Members of the United Nations. They address themselves to the question of confidence in the Court, its composition and the law which it applies.

There is, finally, another way of looking at the problem which has been commonplace for a long time, and that is that the Court has a rôle to play in the preservation of peace. This thought was expressed at the San Francisco Conference by the Rapporteur of the First Committee of Commission IV as follows:

> In establishing the International Court of Justice, the United Nations hold before the war-stricken world the beacons of Justice and Law and offer the possibility of substituting orderly judicial process for the vicissitudes of war and the reign of brutal force.[11]

[7] *Ibid.* 103, par. 218.
[8] *Ibid.*, par. 219.
[9] *Ibid.*, par. 219.
[10] *Ibid.* 113, par. 248. The text adopted in 1966 was incorporated into the "Declaration on Principles of International Law concerning Friendly Relations and Cooperation among States in accordance with the Charter of the United Nations" and adopted by the General Assembly on Oct. 24, 1970. Doc. A/Res/2625 (XXV); reprinted in 65 A.J.I.L. 243 (1971).
[11] See note 1 above.

The notion that arbitration or adjudication is or may be a substitute for war as dispute-settling procedure was developed by the 19th-century peace movement. It received a sort of official *imprimatur* in the 1899 Hague Convention for the Pacific Settlement of Disputes,[12] in the Covenant of the League of Nations,[13] and in the Geneva Protocol for the Pacific Settlement of International Disputes of 1924.[14] Much of the League efforts to consolidate peace was summed up in the formula: arbitration, security and disarmament. Outside the League the Kellogg-Briand Pact of 1928 expressed the same idea when it condemned "recourse to war for the solution of international controversies" and posited the principle that the solution of such controversies "shall never be sought except by pacific means."

Writing on the contribution of the League Court, the Permanent Court of International Justice, Judge Hudson, while recognizing that it was conceived "as a great bulwark of peace, and popular support was enlisted for it on that basis," concluded with the understatement that "On the record of its eighteen years of useful service, however, some doubt may be entertained with reference to the Court's fulfillment of such a rôle."[15] It is interesting to note that so shrewd a student of international affairs as William E. Rappard could write on the eve of World War II of the same Court that its "constitution and actual working . . . are a very significant triumph of supernationalism over nationalism."[16]

The essence of the provisions of the Kellogg-Briand Pact reappears in paragraphs 3 and 4 of Article 2 of the U.N. Charter. The Court was presented at the San Francisco Conference as a substitute "for the vicissitudes of war and the reign of brutal force," and it was predicted that "the judicial process will have a central place in the plans of the United Nations for the settlement of international disputes by peaceful means."[17] The experience of the past 25 years is otherwise. The Court did not become a substitute for the reign of brutal force, although the Court was enabled to adjudicate some tension-laden disputes, and it has not occupied a "central" place in the procedures for the settlement of disputes. To be sure, the Security Council is to take into consideration, when making recommendations with respect to high-tension disputes,[18] "that legal disputes

[12] Art. 1: "With a view to obviating, as far as possible, recourse to force in the relations between States, the Signatory Powers agree to use their best efforts to insure the pacific settlement of international differences." And Article 27, par. 1: "The Signatory Powers consider it their duty, if a serious dispute threatens to break out between two or more of them to remind these latter that the Permanent Court is open to them." Scott, The Hague Conventions and Declarations of 1899 and 1907, at 42 and 61 (1915).

[13] Art. 12, par. 1: "The Members of the League agree that, if there should arise between them any dispute likely to lead to a rupture, they will submit the matter either to arbitration or judicial settlement or to inquiry by the Council, and they agree in no case to resort to war until three months after the award by the arbitrators or the judicial decision, or the report by the Council."

[14] Art. 2: "The signatory States agree in no case to resort to war either with one another or against a State which, if the occasion arises, accepts all the obligations hereinafter set out. . . ."

[15] International Tribunals at 238 (1944).

[16] "What is the League of Nations," in: The World Crisis at 44 (1938).

[17] See note 1 above.

[18] This follows from the reference to Art. 33 in Art. 36 (1) which deals with "any dispute, the continuance of which is likely to endanger the maintenance of international peace and security. . . ." The disputes thus covered are essentially identical with those described in Art. 12 of the Covenant as "likely to lead to a rupture."

should as a general rule be referred by the parties to the International Court of Justice in accordance with the provisions of the Statute of the Court." This clause calls for comment: First, the Security Council has used this authority only in one case, which is a far cry from the "central" place the Court was to occupy; secondly, in that case the *Corfu Channel* case, the Court based its jurisdiction first on the *forum prorogatum* doctrine and then on to the special agreement between the United Kingdom and Albania, and not on the Security Council resolution,[19] and, thirdly, Article 36 (2) of the Statute of the Court was amended in San Francisco to read "in all legal disputes" in lieu of "in all or any of the classes of legal disputes," which may restrict the range of disputes in which the Court could exercise compulsory jurisdiction: high-tension disputes, some assert, are not legal but political disputes, even though they relate to questions of international law.[20]

The relation between paragraphs 3 (settlement of disputes) and 4 (nonresort to force or threat of force) of Article 2 of the Charter has been interpreted in two ways: On the one hand, it has been argued that the principle in paragraph 4 "has had an adverse effect on the willingness of States to submit to adjudication or arbitration" in the sense that "In many cases the alternative is no longer arbitration on the one hand or war or other forcible measures of redress on the other, but adjudication or arbitration on the one hand or stalemate on the other,"[21] The other interpretation was adopted by the Institute of International Law on September 11, 1959, at its Neuchâtel session. According to this, the renunciation of the use of force or threat of force should have as its corollary recourse to arbitration or to adjudication by the Court.[22]

It is not surprising that there is no contradiction between these two interpretations: the former describes the practical effect of paragraph 4 on paragraph 3, whereas the latter describes the ideal effect which paragraph 4 should have on paragraph 3. Both views reflect the traditional link between arbitration and adjudication on the one hand and recourse to force or threat on the other. There is a suggestion here, to go no higher than that, that states should either agree to have recourse to arbitration or adjudication or else face coercion as a means of obtaining a settlement of the dispute.[23]

The prevailing trend in international lawmaking is, however, in the opposite direction. Three illustrations may be given. First, there is Article 52 of the 1969 Vienna Convention on the Law of Treaties which declares:

[19] Leo Gross, "The International Court of Justice and the United Nations," 121 Hague Academy, Recueil des Cours 351–355 (II, 1967). See also *supra*.

[20] Leo Gross, "Some Observations on the International Court of Justice," 56 A.J.I.L. 33-62 at 39 (1962). See also *supra*, pp. 677–704.

[21] Jenks, *op. cit.* at 104.

[22] The relevant paragraph reads as follows: "In an international community the members of which have renounced recourse to force and undertaken by the Charter of the United Nations to settle their international disputes by peaceful means in such a manner that international peace and security, and justice, are not endangered, recourse to the International Court of Justice or another international court or arbitral tribunal constitutes a normal method of settlement of legal disputes as defined in Article 36, paragraph 2, of the Statute of the International Court of Justice." 48 Institute of International Law, Annuaire at 381 (II, 1959).

[23] That was in fact the essence of the 1907 Hague Convention respecting the Limitation of the Employment of Force for the Recovery of Contract Debts. See Scott, note 12 above, at 89.

> A treaty is void if its conclusion has been procured by the threat or use of force in violation of the principles of international law embodied in the Charter of the United Nations.[24]

Secondly, there is the Declaration on the Prohibition of Military, Political or Economic Coercion in the Conclusion of Treaties adopted by the United Nations Conference on the Law of Treaties, which

> Solemnly condemns the threat or use of pressure in any form, whether military, political, or economic, by any State in order to coerce another State to perform any act relating to the conclusion of a treaty in violation of the principles of the sovereign equality of States and freedom of consent.[25]

And, thirdly, there is the Declaration on Principles of International Law concerning Friendly Relations and Co-operation among States which, with reference to paragraph 4 of Article 2 of the Charter, declares:

> Such a threat or use of force constitutes a violation of international law and the Charter of the United Nations and shall never be employed as a means of settling international issues,[26]

Considering that the term "treaty" as used in the Vienna Convention embraces every kind of written international agreement between states, including exchanges of notes, and considering the specific clause relating to the settlement of disputes, the conclusion seems inescapable that the prevailing trend is to eliminate coercive methods as an acceptable alternative to peaceful methods for the settlement of international disputes. The wisdom of this and its practicability in the contemporary international system may be open to doubt. The viability of such an approach may be questioned in view of its total one-sidedness, leaving wide open the alternative, peaceful method of settlement.

To be sure there have been many resorts to force since 1945. The reasons vary from simple to complex, but one may wonder in which cases resort to force was an alternative to settlement by arbitration or adjudication. Put in another way, in how many of them did there exist a dispute taken in its simplest meaning as a conflict between states as to their respective rights? No doubt, in many cases issues of this nature were involved, but they were not the issues which provoked or led to the use of force. It seems no longer even to be relevant whether the use of force was legal under international law. For in declaring that "States have a duty to refrain from acts of reprisal involving the use of force," the 1970 Declaration proscribes the use of force as a reaction against a prior illegal use of force or some other violation of international law.[27] This goes very far indeed in view of the absence of a working system for peaceful settlement of such violations of in-

[24] Doc. A/CONF. 39/27 (May 23, 1969), at 25; 63 A.J.I.L. 891 (1969).
[25] Doc. A/CONF. 39/26 (May 23, 1969), at 7.
[26] *Loc. cit.* note 10 above.
[27] *Ibid.*

ternational law, but one is forced to concede that the Declaration expressed what is a widely shared attitude in the United Nations.

This being so, it would seem unprofitable to relate the need for or desirability of a greater and regular use of arbitration or adjudication to the renunciation of force or threats of force as was done by the Institute of International Law. Though framed in the most innocuous terms, such a link must be seen as unacceptable to a large number of states, old and new, and harks back to the policies of colonialism and imperialism. If states are to be induced to make a greater use of the Court, other ways and means must be sought. In any event it would seem that the commonplace assumption of arbitration and adjudication as a substitute for war or other methods of coercion should be abandoned. The proper rôle for the Court lies in promoting unification in the interpretation and application of international law, both customary and conventional and contributing thereby to the rule of law and greater integration of the international society.

If the Court will contribute to the achievement of these objectives it will make a contribution to peace; it will not be, except perhaps in rare cases, a direct contribution to peacemaking but an indirect one by strengthening the underpinnings of law on which a secure peace can eventually be based.

## II. PROGRESS OR RETROGRESSION

It may be useful to clear away another misconception. As indicated earlier, it is believed that there have been "remarkable advances . . . in virtually every sector of international organization except the judicial sector."[28]

As the general field of international organization is outside the scope of this paper, it is only necessary to see to what extent the proposition is correct with respect to the judicial sector. It will be argued that, following a period of progress in the development of peaceful methods for the settlement of disputes, a retrogressive trend has set in, and that the retrogression concerns not merely the judicial sector but is discernible in the whole area of peacemaking. As the Legal Counsel of the United Nations pointed out:

> . . . As regards the pacific settlement of disputes, it must be said that experience over the past 25 years has been generally very discouraging. This is not for want of machinery within the Charter itself. Besides the Security Council and the General Assembly, which offer a forum for political settlement, the International Court of Justice, established as one of the principal organs of the United Nations, provides a means of judicial settlement. States have not, however, shown in the great majority of cases the will to avail themselves of these means for a genuine resolution of their international disputes. . . . At the present the International Court of Justice does not have a single case before it, although this is not, as we all know, for lack of disputes. Nor can it be said that this reluctance has been accompanied by a compensating growth in recourse to the alternative means of settlement listed in Article 33 of the Charter, ranging from negotiation and arbitration to resort to regional agencies or peaceful means of the parties' own choosing. In this sphere, if no other, the past

[28] See Jenks, note 2 above.

> 25 years have witnessed a disappointing lack of progress and it is difficult to envisage any sudden change in the preference of States for keeping a dispute alive, rather than entrusting it to some form of third party settlement which might not come out wholly in their favor.[29]

The standstill amounting to retrogression covers the whole range of procedures for the settlement of disputes and goes back to the founding of the United Nations. Some aspects of this situation will be indicated briefly after a sketch of the era of progress.

The century opened hopefully with the 1899 Hague Convention for the Pacific Settlement of International Disputes setting forth procedures for good offices, mediation, and commissions of inquiry, and establishing the Permanent Court of Arbitration. The Second Hague Peace Conference adopted the Draft Convention relative to the Creation of a Judicial Arbitration Court and the Convention relative to the Creation of an International Prize Court neither of which materialized.[30] In spite of its obvious shortcomings, 17 disputes were brought before tribunals of the Permanent Court between 1902 and 1914. Sixteen states were involved in voluntary arbitrations before panels composed of jurists of recognized competence: Renault (France) was involved in seven cases, de Savonnin Lohman (The Netherlands), Hammarskjöld (Sweden), and Fusinato (Italy) in five cases each, Lammasch (Austria), Kriege (Germany), and Taube (Russia) in four cases each.[31]

The Central American Court was established in 1907 and functioned until 1917, and many bilateral treaties of arbitration were concluded during the same period. Following World War I there was a great activity in the area of dispute settlement: thousands of cases were adjudicated by Mixed Arbitral Tribunals set up in connection with the Peace Treaties of 1919, by the Tribunal in Upper Silesia and by numerous claims commissions. The League of Nations Covenant provided a measure of compulsory settlement of disputes by arbitration, adjudication or inquiry by the Council, and established the Permanent Court of International Justice as a separate institution. The Optional Clause providing for the compulsory jurisdiction was a breakthrough in the development of international adjudication and as of December 31, 1938, out of 54 Members of the League, 38 were bound by the Optional Clause. In Judge Hudson's opinion "the willingness of so many States to confer compulsory jurisdiction on the Court . . . marks a substantial advance in the history of the law of pacific settlement of disputes."[32] The Court was fairly active: it received 27 requests for advisory opinions, it was seized in 65 contentious cases, it gave 20 judgments on merits, 2 judgments interpreting an earlier

[29] Constantin A. Stavropoulos, "The United Nations and the Development of International Law 1945–1970," in 7 U. N. Monthly Chronicle 78–84 (June, 1970) at 80–81. On July 29, 1970, the Security Council for the first time requested of the Court an advisory opinion on a question relating to Namibia. Res. 284 (1970), 1969–1970 I. C. J. Yearbook at 112.

[30] Scott, note 12 above, at 31, 41 and 188.

[31] W. J. M. van Eysinga, "Evolution Rétrograde," Varia juris gentium, Liber Amicorum J. P. A. Francois, 6 Netherlands International Law Review (Special Issue) 100–102 at 100–101 (1959). Five additional disputes were settled between 1920 and 1932. A. M. Stuyt, Survey of International Arbitrations, 1794–1938, at 325, 330, 388, 415, 418 (1939). One dispute was settled in 1956, XII Reports of International Arbitral Awards 155 (U.N. Pub. Sales No. 63, V. 3).

[32] The Permanent Court of International Justice 1920–1942, at 482.

judgment, and 9 on preliminary objections, including one declaring the application inadmissible. The League handled over 40 political questions involving conflicts or complaints with varying degrees of success.

The League tried to improve procedures for the peaceful settlement of disputes, and its greatest achievement in this field was the General Act for the Pacific Settlement of International Disputes adopted by the Assembly on September 26, 1928. The Act entered into force on August 16, 1929, and was accepted by 23 states, including France, the United Kingdom and Italy. Of these, 21 states acceded to the Act as a whole; The Netherlands and Sweden acceded to parts of the Act. The Act provides in Chapter I a procedure of conciliation for all disputes; in Chapter II, a procedure of judicial settlement or arbitration for legal disputes; and in Chapter III, a procedure of arbitration for other disputes. The League manifested great respect for legal issues involved in disputes of a mixed, political-legal character. One indication of this concern is the fact that all but five, it would seem, of the requests for advisory opinions related to disputes pending before the Council.

The Kellogg-Briand Pact of 1928 was hailed as a milestone in the progress of peace. A great number of treaties—about 300—providing for the peaceful settlement of disputes were concluded during the period of the League.[33]

The common feature of the endeavors of the League and of states during the interwar period was the introduction of an element of compulsion in the processes for dispute settlement, and it is this that distinguished them from the voluntarism which was characteristic of the Hague system. The substitution of firm commitments for agreements to agree, and the reliance on arbitration and adjudication as against the diplomatic procedures of negotiations, good offices and mediation, were the elements of progress. The substitution clearly involved a willingness to depoliticize the conflicts between states, adjudication by the Court being regarded as the highest possible and desirable degree of depoliticization.

A reversal of both these tendencies, amounting to retrogression, marks the current period of the United Nations. This became evident as early as the Dumbarton Oaks Proposals. With reference to settlement of disputes, "[t]he Security Council should be empowered at any stage of a dispute of the nature referred to in paragraph 3 above [disputes the continuance of which is likely to endanger the maintenance of international peace and security], to recommend appropriate procedures or methods of adjustment."[34] The degree of retrogression can be measured by comparison with the Covenant of the League. Unlike the Council of the League, the Security Council was not empowered to recommend terms of settlement. The omission was made good to some extent at the San Francisco Conference, and the Charter provides in Article 37 that, if the parties fail to settle the dispute voluntarily or by arbitration or judicial means, "they" shall refer it to the

[33] Habicht, Post-War Treaties for the Pacific Settlement of International Disputes, at xix (1931); Systematic Survey of Treaties for the Pacific Settlement of International Disputes, 1929–1948, at 1180 (U.N. Pub. Sales No. 1949. V. 3).

[34] Chap. VIII, Sec. A, par. 5. Department of State Pub. 2257, Conf. Ser. 60, at 12; 39 A.J.I.L. Supp. 51 (1945).

Council, which may then decide whether to recommend procedures or "to recommend such terms of settlement as it may consider appropriate." Here again there is a degree of retrogression: The Covenant made it clear that "any party to the dispute" is authorized to submit the dispute to the Council. The Charter is ambiguous and unnecessarily so. Strictly speaking "they" means all the parties to the dispute. Article 35(1) provides that "Any Member of the United Nations may bring any dispute, or situation of the nature referred to in Article 34, to the attention of the Security Council or of the General Assembly;" but it is doubtful whether the Council, in such a case, can do more than apply Article 36 and "recommend appropriate procedures or methods of adjustment" only or whether it may recommend terms of settlement as well.[35]

The Court was made one of the principal organs of the United Nations and its "principal judicial organ," and all Members of the United Nations are "*ipso facto* parties to the Statute" of the Court. The organic link between the Court and the United Nations and the enlargement of the judicial community appear progressive steps but only on the surface. It has yet to be demonstrated that the Court benefited from this link and from the wider judicial community.[36] The jurisdiction of the Court remained optional. Out of the 130 parties to the Statute—Liechtenstein, San Marino and Switzerland in addition to 127 Members of the United Nations—not more than 46 have accepted the jurisdiction of the Court as compulsory. This compares very unfavorably with the 1938 ratio of 54 to 38 in the League. Moreover, 25 other states which were bound by the jurisdiction of the present Court or of its predecessor "have withdrawn their acceptance or have not renewed it."[37] The Court has delivered 13 advisory opinions and one request is pending.[38] The Court, during the period 1946–1970, was seized in 39 contentious cases and gave 31 judgments,[39] of which 14 were on merits, two were judgments designated "Second Phase" (*Nottebohm* and *South West Africa*), and one was an interpretative judgment. The others were concerned with preliminary objections, of which 6 were upheld.

The declarations by which states accepted the jurisdiction of the Court as compulsory are studded with reservations, the most damaging of which is probably still the so-called self-judging and automatic Connally Amendment to the United States Declaration of 1946. The extent of harm done to the legal framework constituted by such reservation will be appreciated if it is borne in mind that most reservations are available on the basis of reciprocity to states which have not made them. Thus the United States reservation can

[35] Hans Kelsen, The Law of the United Nations at 415–416 (1950).

[36] See Gross, note 19 above, at 323–336, and *supra*.

[37] Report of the I.C.J., Aug. 1, 1968–July 31, 1969. GAOR, 24th Sess., Supp. No. 5 (A/7605), at 1.

[38] See note 29 above. The total number of requests was in fact only 12 but in the Peace Treaties case the Court gave 2 opinions.

[39] The judgments in the Continental Shelf cases and South West Africa (Second Phase) cases are each counted as one. Eight cases were simply removed because there was no acceptance of the jurisdiction on the part of the impleaded states. By the Court's own count, the number of cases "with which the Court has had to deal can really be reckoned as 24; since in eight of the cases shown on its list the applicant State itself recognized in its Application that the other side had not recognized the Court's jurisdiction, and the cases which have a common origin but which have separate entries on the list can be counted as a single case." Report of the International Court of Justice, August 1, 1969–July 31, 1970. GAOR, 25th Sess., Supp. No. 5 (A/8005), at 2. The number of states involved was 33. *Ibid.*

be invoked, and has been invoked in one case,[40] by any other state against which the United States has instituted or will in the future start proceedings before the Court. While there were reservations to the instruments relating to the Optional Clause, those included in the post-1945 era are particularly rampant and retrogressive, for they constitute so many attempts to re-introduce voluntarism through the back door of reservations to the declarations, which, it was hoped, would establish firm commitments.

The application of the Charter procedures for peaceful settlement has been generally disappointing. It would be an exaggeration, perhaps, to say that the United Nations has failed to settle any disputes by its political organs.[41] A recent study examined 55 "disputes" referred to the United Nations during the 20-year period and concluded that 18 were settled by the United Nations or with its assistance.[42] How one evaluates success or failure in settling a dispute or adjusting a situation is to a large extent a matter of judgment. In what sense could the United Nations be credited with the settlement or aid to settlement of such matters as Korea, Suez or the India-Pakistan war which are listed in that study in the "success" column? In my view the performance of the United Nations in dispute settlement as distinguished from stopping hostilities is very unsatisfactory. It would require a very detailed study and agreement on relevant criteria in order to determine whether there has been progress or retrogression compared with the League.[43]

The late Secretary General of the United Nations, Dag Hammarskjöld, in several of his *Annual Reports on the Work of the Organization,* called attention to the unsatisfactory state of affairs relating to the Court, and the paucity of declarations accepting its jurisdiction and the far-reaching reservations attached to some of them. He regretted in particular the reluctance of states to separate the legal from the political aspects of a dispute and to submit the former to the Court. In 1957 he wrote: "Even in the present state of international society there are many disputes which would be closer to settlement if the legal issues involved had been the subject of judicial settlement."[44] In 1959 he was even more explicit. Referring to his concern about the Court, he observed that "the development and acceptance of international law impartially administered by judicial tribunals is essential to progress toward a more just and peaceful international order," and he stressed the possible separability of legal and political aspects of disputes as follows:

> It should also be recognized that there are many international disputes which involve legal questions along with the political elements and the submission of such questions to the Court for judicial determination would clear the ground for processes of peaceful negotiations in the political organs of the United Nations. Neglect of the legal elements in interna-

[40] See Leo Gross, "Bulgaria Invokes the Connally Amendment," 56 A.J.I.L. 357–382 (1962). See also *supra.*

[41] Synopses of United Nations Cases in the Field of Peace and Security 1946–1967, compiled by C. G. Teng, published by the Carnegie Endowment for International Peace (rev. ed., 1969) lists 71 cases, some of which may be disputes and others situations.

[42] E. B. Haas, Collective Security and the Future International System. University of Denver: The Social Science Foundation and Graduate School of International Studies, Monograph Series in World Affairs, Vol. 5, No. 1 (1967–1968), at 46.

[43] *Cf.* note 29 above, for the view of the U.N. Legal Counsel.

[44] GAOR, 12th Sess., Supp. No. 1A (A/3594) Add. 1, at 4–5.

> tional conflicts, and of the means by which they may be clarified, thus stands in the way of progress in the political field and, in the long run, may tend to weaken the weight of law in international affairs.[45]

A reversal of progressive tendencies can also be seen in other aspects of dispute settlement. The General Act of 1928, the high-water mark of League efforts in this field, was restored with some amendments to adapt it to the United Nations organs by Resolution 268 A (III) of April 28, 1949, and remained virtually a dead letter. The Scelle Draft on Arbitral Procedure of 1953 was totally emasculated and every element of compulsion was expurgated from it. The negative attitude of Member Governments and their preference for liberty of action was expressed by Professor Scelle as follows:

> . . . as the number of States Members of the United Nations increases, so the majority hostile to the Commission's draft seems bound to increase, for the more recently the new Members required [*sic*] their sovereignty the greater will be their desire to maintain it whole and entire.[46]

The accuracy of this appraisal could be questioned only on the ground that the attitude of new states is shared in large measure by old states.

The Optional Protocols to the Geneva and Vienna Conventions have been ratified by a small number of states. This lack of enthusiasm, shared by the United States, is all the more significant as the obligation to adjudicate is limited to the disputes relating to the interpretation or application of conventions in the drafting of which the new states participated on a footing of equality with the old states.[47]

Most illuminating of the retreat from the adjudicative process altogether is the 1970 Declaration of Principles of International Law concerning Friendly Relations and Co-operation among States with respect to the settlement of disputes. It reads as follows:

> 1. Every State shall settle its international disputes with other States by peaceful means, in such a manner that international peace and security and justice are not endangered.
>
> 2. States shall accordingly seek early and just settlement of their international disputes by negotiation, inquiry, mediation, conciliation, arbitration, judicial settlement, resort to regional agencies or arrangements, or other peaceful means of their choice. In seeking such a settlement the parties shall agree upon such peaceful means as may be appropriate to the circumstances and nature of the dispute.
>
> 3. The parties to a dispute have the duty, in the event of failure to reach a solution by any one of the above peaceful means, to continue to seek a settlement of the dispute by other peaceful means agreed upon by them.
>
> 4. States parties to an international dispute, as well as other States, shall refrain from any action which may aggravate the situation so as to endanger the maintenance of interna-

[45] *Ibid.*, 14th Sess., Supp. No. 1A (A/4132) Add. 1, at 3–4. See also the Annual Reports of 1953 and 1955, *ibid.*, 8th Sess., Supp. No. 1 (A/2404) at xi–xii, and *ibid.*, 10th Sess., Supp. No. 1 (A/2911) at xiii.

[46] (1958) I.L.C. Yearbook (II) at 2; see also pp. 3, 80, and G. A. Res. 1262 (XIII), No. 14, 1958.

[47] For an illuminating discussion of the arguments for and against the Optional Protocols and disputes clauses, see H. W. Briggs, "Reflections on the Codification of International Law by the International Law Commission and by Other Agencies," 126 Hague Academy, Receuil des Cours 244–256, 267–283 (I, 1969).

> tional peace and security, and shall act in accordance with the purposes and principles of the United Nations.
>
> 5. International disputes shall be settled on the basis of the sovereign equality of States and in accordance with the principle of free choice of means. Recourse to, or acceptance of, a settlement procedure freely agreed to by States with regard to existing or future disputes to which they are parties shall not be regarded as incompatible with sovereign equality.
>
> 6. Nothing in the foregoing paragraphs prejudices or derogates from the applicable provisions of the Charter, in particular those relating to the pacific settlement of international disputes.[48]

Attempts to include a reference to the Court or the desirability of including jurisdictional clauses in treaties were rebuffed and dropped for the sake of reaching a consensus. The result is a paean to the liberty of states in which Vattel would have rejoiced.

A total emasculation of jurisdictional clauses may be seen in Article 8 of the Convention on Consent to Marriage, Minimum Age for Marriage and Registration of Marriages, which provides that any dispute relating to its interpretation or application, shall, "at the request of *all* the parties to the dispute," be referred to the Court.[49] The model for this clause was obviously Article 1 (1) of the convention, which provides that "no marriage shall be legally entered into without the full and free consent of *both* parties . . .," and not the model clause for conferring compulsory jurisdiction upon the Court for inclusion in conventions, adopted by the Institute of International Law in 1956 and reaffirmed in 1959.[50] The essence of such jurisdictional clauses is that disputes can be submitted to the Court by unilateral application.

In this context it may be noted that the dispute clause in the recent Convention on the Law of Treaties relating to the application or interpretation of the *jus cogens* (Articles 53 and 63) is not free from ambiguity. Article 66 provides for two procedures: in paragraph (a) for arbitration or adjudication, and in paragraph (b) for conciliation. It is not clear which procedure has priority over the other and which procedure shall be applied in case one party follows paragraph (a) and the other, paragraph (b). Furthermore, paragraph (a) merely provides that any one of the parties to a dispute may "by a written application submit it to the International Court of Justice for a decision."[51] This is a far cry from conferring upon the Court compulsory jurisdiction.[52] For obviously any party is free to submit a dispute to the Court by a written application, and the Court will remove it if the other party fails to consent to jurisdiction. This has happened in eight unrelated cases.

Outside the United Nations, the trend seems to be also in favor of the liberty of states. The Charter of the Organization of African Unity fails to provide for judicial set-

[48] *Loc. cit.* note 10 above, at 5–6; 65 A.J.I.L. 247 (1971). For comment, see Briggs, note 47 above, at 284–301.

[49] Annex to General Assembly Res. 1763 (XVII) of Nov. 7, 1962. GAOR, 17th Sess., Supp. No. 17 (A/5217) at 29. Italics supplied.

[50] 48 Annuaire, note 22 above, at 382.

[51] Doc. A/CONF. 39/27 (May 23, 1969), at 33.

[52] But see Briggs, note 47 above, at 308, who concludes that Art. 66(a) "provides for the compulsory adjudication of *jus cogens* issues." In view of its history (*ibid.* at 302–309), it may be doubtful whether it is indeed so or whether Art. 66(a) is merely a face-saving formula.

tlement of disputes. The Charter of the Organization of American States (O.A.S.) was recently revised and the discussions relating to dispute-settlement indicated a marked tendency toward voluntarism and against obligation. Articles 23–26 and Articles 84–90 on peaceful settlement of disputes are very general in character and do not seem to go beyond fact-finding and good offices. The application of the latter depends normally upon acceptance by both parties to the dispute.[53] The failure to achieve anything of significance evoked this eloquent comment from the United States Delegation:

> While the United States would have preferred that the amendments had given broader powers to the pertinent O.A.S. organs with respect to the peaceful settlement of disputes . . . it is recognized that these points were too controversial for incorporation into a treaty which all of the Member States would be expected to ratify.[54]

The lowest common denominator was very low indeed.

The fact has often been commented upon that the most remarkable retrogression, compared with the Permanent Court, has been in the advisory jurisdiction of the present Court. The Permanent Court received 27 requests between 1922 and 1942, or between 1922 and 1935, the last year in which a request was made. Only two organs of the League were empowered to make requests, the Assembly and the Council. In fact, all requests were made by the Council, five of them on behalf of the International Labor Organization. In the United Nations, on the other hand, four principal organs, two subsidiary organs of the General Assembly, 12 specialized agencies, and the International Atomic Energy Agency—altogether 19 organs—are authorized to request advisory opinions. So far the General Assembly has requested 11 advisory opinions, the Security Council one, and of the 12 specialized agencies only two (UNESCO and IMCO) have requested opinions.

This remarkable reluctance of specialized agencies was a topic of discussion at an informal conference of legal advisers sponsored by the American Society of International Law. It was pointed out that

> one reason for reluctance to use them (the advisory opinion procedures) has been a concern that the Court, being outside the mainstream of the organization's activity, might come to decisions not fully sensitive to the internal requirements for effective operation. In other words, the detached objective legal view may not contribute to the actual effectiveness of the organization. Added to this is the reluctance of all parties, even those in a minority position, to force an "authoritative," definite, and presumably enduring interpretation when compromise and flexibility may be more useful. ("It does not help that the application of a legal rule is legally impeccable if it is politically impossible.") This is reflected in the practice of adopting informal legal decisions in those organizations that have a power of "authoritative" interpretation.[55]

[53] Protocol of Amendment to the Charter of the OAS. Pan American Union, Treaty Series, No. 1-B, OAS Official Records, OEA/Ser. A/2, Add. 2,1967; 64 A.J.I.L. 996 (1970).

[54] Report of the U. S. Delegation to the Third Special Inter-American Conference, Feb. 15–27, 1967, Dept. of State ARA/IPA, at 38.

[55] H. C. L. Merillat (ed.), Legal Advisers and International Organizations at 10 (1966). The words between parentheses are attributed by the editor to Edvard Hambro, *ibid.* at 8.

In view of this somewhat parochial attitude of legal advisers, it would be unrealistic to expect that specialized agencies will make a better use of the Court's advisory function in the foreseeable future. It may be noted that the International Bank for Reconstruction and Development has recently (1965) established an "International Centre for Settlement of Investment Disputes," but no requests for settling any dispute have been submitted so far.[56] The possibility cannot be excluded that some cases which otherwise might have found their way to the Court will go to the Center.

Finally, the effect of the Court's judgment in the *South West Africa* case (Second Phase) on the Members of the United Nations should be mentioned. The dissatisfaction was profound and widespread. It was expressed in criticism of the composition of the Court and its insensitivity to anti-colonial and anti-apartheid sentiments as formulated in resolutions and declarations of the General Assembly.[57] As was to be expected, this criticism is also reflected in learned articles. Thus in one of them it was said, with respect to the hopeful view that "in five or six years' time, it will be realized that this (judgment) was a great turning point because (the Court) did not give way to political pressure," that:

> If this Judgment proves to be a "turning point," this will be, it is submitted, because the Judges now being elected, and likely to be in the future, come from a generation of legal scholars which recognizes the significance of functional and sociological approaches, and as such are determined to bring the Court and the law they are called upon to apply up-to-date and suitable for the mid-century world. If they do not, then there is the danger that the Court and the world will split into two different schools of international law to the disadvantage of both and the further collapse of the rule of law.[58]

It is too early to say what the reaction will be to the Court's most recent judgment in the case of the *Barcelona Traction Company.*[59] The judgment in the *North Sea Continental Shelf* case[60] has not provoked violent criticism on one side or excessive praise on the other. In any event, it has helped the parties to come to an amicable resolution of their respective claims. On the Danish side it was said that

> In the present Judgment, the Court has proved extremely restrictive in its attitude towards the progressive development of international law. Viewed abstractly as a theoretical proposition, the restrictive concept of international law appears highly justified. It is not to be expected that States will esteem a court which by its judgments imposes obligations which the States have not expressly or tacitly accepted as legally binding.[61]

[56] ICSID Press Release, Sept. 29, 1969. The Convention for the creation of the Center has been ratified by 52 states.

[57] For a sample of the views of Members, see Gross, note 19 above, at 346–349. See also *supra.*

[58] L. C. Green, "The United Nations, South West Africa and the World Court," 7 Indian J. of Int. Law 491–525 at 522 (1967). The words in the text to which Prof. Green addressed himself are Sir F. Vallat's.

[59] [1970] I.C.J. Rep. 3; 64 A.J.I.L. 653 (1970).

[60] [1969] I.C.J. Rep. 3; 63 A.J.I.L. 591 (1969).

[61] Isi Foighel, "The North Sea Continental Shelf Case," 39 Nordisk Tidsskrift for International Ret 109–127 at 125 (1969). For an analysis of the contribution of this judgment to the theory of sources of international law, see Krystyan Marek, "Le Problème des Sources du Droit International dans l'Arrêt sur le Plateau Continental de la Mer du Nord," 6 Revue Belge du Droit International 44–78 (1970).

On the German side it was emphasized that the Court has avoided rigidity and tried to find a just and equitable solution. "In this sense," it is said, "the judgment represents one of the highest achievements of international jurisprudence and will significantly enhance confidence in the potential of international dispute settlement.[62]

It may be fitting to close the presentation of regressive tendencies in international peacemaking on this optimistic note. It may be noted in passing that the Court has achieved its best results when it applied the law and did not engage in judicial lawmaking in a pronounced manner.[63] While the judicial function made no spectacular advances in the last 25 years and the optimistic forecasts of the great rôle it was to play in maintaining peace were not fulfilled, it held its ground and fared better than the political procedures of the United Nations for the settlement of disputes. The question is whether the absence of contentious cases on its docket is a sign that the stagnation and regressive trend have now extended to the Court or whether it is merely a fortuitous lull without portents for its future.

It may be noted in this context that, whereas the number of arbitral decisions since 1945 was not spectacular, it was not insignificant, although it is probably true that, as the Secretary General of the United Nations pointed out, "most of them concerned minor questions, many of them of a commercial nature, which were not in the least likely to disturb peace and security."[64] The total figure is 22, including the *Gut Dam* claim, which was before a United States-Canada Tribunal but was settled by negotiations.[65] In addition, there were three Postal Arbitrations, and many cases were settled by various Conciliation Commissions or Property Commissions established pursuant to peace treaties terminating the second World War.[66]

## III. THE COURT AT A CROSSROADS

The choice is thus presented: Should one opt for remedial action in improving procedures and opening ways of access to the Court or should one opt for what may appear to be structural changes? In substance, one has to make up one's mind whether the Court can make a greater contribution to the clarification, and thereby to the development of international law, by relying on states as its clientèle in contentious cases, and international organizations in advisory proceedings, or whether a new and additional function should be conferred upon the Court. Those who argue in favor of the first alternative remain in the

[62] E. Menzel, "Der Festlandsockel der Bundesrepublik Deutschland und das Urteil des Internationalen Gerichtshofs vom 20. Februar 1969," 14 Jahrbuch für Internationales Recht 13–121 at 96 (1969).

[63] Gross, note 19 above, at 370 ff.

[64] Introduction to the Annual Report of the Secretary General on the Work of the Organization, June 16, 1969–June 15, 1970 (A/8001/Add. 1), at 38.

[65] U. N. Reports of International Arbitral Awards, Vols. 12–16. The figure of 22 includes the Ottoman case which was settled in 1956 by a tribunal of the Permanent Court of Arbitration. The figure given by the Secretary General is 14. *Ibid.*

[66] The Commissions and number of cases decided are as follows: France-Italy: 284; Italy-U.S.A.: 235; Italy-Netherlands:1; United Kingdom-Italy: 190; U.S.A.-Japan: 8; Netherlands-Japan: 2; United Kingdom-Japan: 7; Arbitral Commission on Property, Rights, and Interests in Germany: 52; Arbitral Tribunal for the Agreement on German External Debts, Italy-Switzerland: 1. This material is as of 1962 and culled from the source cited in note 65 above.

tradition of the Hague system. Those who prefer the latter would appear as advocating a progressive step, the first since 1899, if one leaves out of account the permanency of the Court along with optional, compulsory and advisory jurisdiction introduced by the League about 50 years ago. Important as these innovations were and continue to be, they were in line with the thinking of 1899 that arbitration and adjudication were civilized substitutes for war or the solution of conflicts between states. More imaginative innovations may be needed to take into account the unprecedented interdependence of states in their international relations, due above all to the phenomenal growth of transnational activities of individuals and corporations. Here is a resource of the first magnitude which has never been tapped for international judicial business. In order to tap this natural resource, it seems necessary to establish a link between the traditional forum of litigation, national tribunals, and the international forum, the World Court, in cases of international law, conventional and customary. Such a link has been established in the European Communities between the Court of Justice and the domestic tribunals of the six member states. Reviewing that Court and the Court of Human Rights, Jenks suggested that "the jurisdiction and procedures of the European tribunals and those of the International Court represent different epochs in the development of international adjudication."[67]

This is indeed so, inasmuch as the International Court is the outgrowth of the Hague system and its concern is with inter-state relations governed by law. The concern of the new European Court, however, is not limited to inter-state relations and inter-state conflicts, but extends to interpersonal (natural and juristic) relations and relations between individuals, the states and international organizations governed by law. The function of the European Court is to ensure that the law be applied uniformly throughout the European Community. The new function for the World Court, it is suggested, should be that of an authoritative interpreter of that part of international law, largely conventional, which governs business transactions and the relations between individuals, both natural and corporate, *inter se,* and between them on the one hand and states on the other. Relations between individuals who are international civil servants and international organizations are already to some extent within the purview of the Court, but there is room for improvement even here.

It is not suggested that, as one epoch succeeds another, the traditional function of the Court should be replaced by the new function. What is suggested is that, first of all, the idea should be explored whether, to what extent, and in what ways the new function could be grafted on the old one. There is no reason to assume, in the present submission, that the two functions are incompatible. The International Court, subject to a slight amendment in its Statute, could discharge both functions and thus establish a central position in the vastly expanded and still expanding area of transnational activities. There is no need for a multiplicity of tribunals whose jurisprudence, far from bringing uniformity

[67] Jenks, note 2 above, at 148. See p. 987 below.

and predictability in the interpretation of the law, might merely contribute to its fragmentation.

An extension of the Court's jurisdiction along the lines tentatively indicated above should be considered on its merits in spite of the retrogressive tendencies in the General Assembly of the United Nations manifested in connection with the supervision of the application of the International Covenant on Civil and Political Rights. As adopted this Covenant gives states parties the option under Article 41 to allow the Human Rights Committee to receive claims of one state party against another state party that the latter is not fulfilling its obligations under the Covenant, provided both parties have accepted the Committee's competence to consider such claims. The Committee may offer its good offices to the parties, make a report, or, under Article 42, refer the claim with the consent of both parties to a Conciliation Commission. The Commission may in turn try to bring about an "amicable solution" and failing this, submit a report embodying its views on the possibilities of an amicable solution.[68] An Optional Protocol opens the possibility for individual claims against a state party which is also a party to the Protocol.[69] More far-reaching proposals to provide for a reference of legal questions raised in claims by states against states, or individuals against states, to the Court by means of a request for an advisory opinion were rejected.[70] This is a far cry from the optional provisions which make possible recourse to the European Court of Human Rights in order to obtain a judgment and not merely an advisory opinion.[71] However, failure in one area does not necessarily preclude success in another. Progress does not thrive on defeatism.

In accordance with these considerations it is proposed to explore some of the ways and means for enhancing the Court's traditional, Hague system, function[72] and of grafting a new function on the old one.[73]

## IV. BUILDING CONFIDENCE IN THE COURT

Leadership is required for any improvement in the existing situation. It may be possible to make some headway by means of a General Assembly resolution, or, what will be more difficult, by means of an amendment to the Statute of the Court, or by filling the present vacuum by submitting some contentious cases to the Court. In any event, no progress is likely to materialize unless one of the leading Powers or a group of Powers takes the necessary initiative. In view of its adamant stand vis-à-vis the Court and the judicial function in general, the Soviet Union and its bloc must be ruled out, although its acquies-

[68] General Assembly Res. 2200 (XXI) of Dec. 16, 1966. GAOR, 21st Sess., Supp. No. 16 (A/6316), at 57; 61 A.J.I.L. at 882 (1967).

[69] GAOR, 21st Sess., Supp. No. 16 (A/6316), at 59; 61 A.J.I.L. 887 (1967).

[70] Gross, note 19 above, at 424.

[71] The text of the relevant provisions is reproduced in Brownlie, Basic Documents in International Law at 194–219. The American Convention on Human Rights, "Pact of San José, Costa Rica" signed Nov. 22, 1969, follows the European model. O.A.S. Official Records, OEA/SER. A/16, Articles 33–73.

[72] See below, p. 981 ff.

[73] See below, p. 987 ff.

cence in some changes of the Statute may become necessary. This leaves the United States and the group of liberal, democratic nations with a tradition of arbitration and adjudication, as well as those new nations which through their acceptance of the compulsory jurisdiction have manifested their sense of appreciation of the judicial function.

The United States, however, has precluded itself from playing an active rôle in the promotion of judicial settlement through the Court. The United States Declaration of August 14, 1946, struck a most damaging blow at the Court. It expresses a virtually total lack of confidence in the Court. To be sure, other states hedged with reservations their acceptances of the Court's compulsory jurisdiction, but they had enough confidence in the objectivity and impartiality of the Court to let it decide whether these reservations were applicable in a given case. The United States expressed its total lack of confidence in the Court by claiming for itself the right to determine whether its reservations applied in a given case. The United States may or may not have foreseen—as one of its imitators, France, has certainly not—that what it claimed for itself it was bound to concede to its adversary. This is not relevant here. Nor is it relevant whether, as Judge Lauterpacht argued in the *Interhandel* case,[74] the whole Declaration was invalid because it was incompatible with the principle of customary international law, of which Article 36(6) of the Statute is the expression, namely, that in case of a challenge to its jurisdiction, "the matter shall be settled by the decision of the Court;" or whether as I have argued, only the self-judging clause in the Declaration is invalid.[75] What does matter is that any United States representative who raised the issue of the present stalemate in the contentious jurisdiction of the Court would decidedly lack credibility in the General Assembly or in any other forum. A state which would encourage other states to show confidence in the Court must itself show confidence. And this no United States representative can do as long as the present reservations stand.[76] Therefore, if there is any validity in the considerations set out above, these reservations must be removed. They are unnecessary; they offer no protection to the United States; and they show lack of confidence in the Court. Moreover, the self-judging reservation is violative of a cardinal principle of the international judicial process, so essential and so widely accepted that it could rank as a peremptory norm of international law, and the reservation on multilateral treaties shows merely lack of knowledge of the Statute of the Court and particularly Article 63.

It has been said that, as the reservations originated in the Senate of the United States, the initiative for their repeal must come from the same body. It is not necessary to

[74] [1959] I.C.J. Rep. 6 at 101.

[75] Gross, note 40 above, at 375 ff. See also *supra*.

[76] The Declaration provides:

". . . that this declaration shall not apply to

(a)disputes the solution of which the parties shall entrust to other tribunals by virtue of agreements already in existence or which may be concluded in the future; or

(b) disputes with regard to matters which are essentially within the domestic jurisdiction of the United States of America as determined by the United States of America; or

(c) disputes arising under a multilateral treaty, unless (1) all parties to the treaty affected by the decision are also parties to the case before the Court, or (2) the United States of America specially agrees to jurisdiction." 1969–1970 I.C.J. Yearbook at 80.

express an opinion on the merits of this argument: It may be valid as far as it goes or it may be merely a pretext for tolerating an unworthy situation, or it may have elements of both. However, it is certainly within the authority of the Executive Branch of the Government to give notice to terminate the Declaration of August 14, 1946, and to submit a new Declaration to the Senate for its advice and consent. First steps must come first, and surely the claim of the United States to be the champion of the free world and a staunch advocate of the rule of law in international relations will have a hollow ring unless and until the United States removes those crippling reservations. Other governments have done so, but what other governments have done is no substitute for the initiative which the United States should take for its own sake and in order to break the present deadlock.[77]

Before closing this section it is important to note some encouraging indications of renewed interest in the Court. The Secretary of State of the United States, Mr. William Rogers, has called for greater use of the Court's advisory and contentious jurisdiction and has made some constructive proposals, most of which will be found elsewhere in this essay.[78] The Secretary General of the United Nations, U Thant, regretting the infrequent use of the Court, appealed "to the Members to give serious consideration to the advantages of a final settlement by an impartial tribunal on the basis of the law binding on both sides" and encouraged Members to accept the compulsory jurisdiction of the Court "with as few reservations and limitations as possible."[79] Finally, mention should be made of the initiative of several delegations to the 25th Anniversary Session of the General Assembly proposing the establishment of an *Ad Hoc* Committee to undertake "an appropriate study with a view to enhancing the effectiveness of the Court" which would complement the study of the Rules of Court on which the Court has been engaged for several years.[80] The Assembly decided by a resolution adopted unanimously on December 15, 1970, to defer the proposal until the next session; but it authorized the Secretary General to request the Members to submit their views and suggestions concerning the rôle of the Court; it invited the Court, should it so desire, to state its views; and it requested a comprehensive review by the Secretary General.[81]

[77] It may be recalled that in 1959 the Institute of International Law called for the withdrawal of self-judging reservations and called attention to the judgments given and the opinions expressed in the Norwegian Loans and Interhandel cases. 48 Institute of International Law, Annuaire, 381 (1950, II); reproduced in 54 A.J.I.L. 136 (1960).

[78] In particular he proposed consideration to be given to additional intergovernmental and particularly regional organizations as well as states access to the advisory jurisdiction. He also suggested greater use of chambers and summary proceedings. In his view chambers could meet outside The Hague and chambers could be established for handling disputes arising within the Latin American, Asian and African regions. "The Rule of Law and the Settlement of International Disputes," 62 Dept. of State Bulletin 623 f. (1970); printed in 64 A.J.I.L 285 f. (September, 1970).

[79] Introduction to Annual Report of the Secretary General on the Work of the Organization, June 16, 1969–June 15, 1970, GAOR, 25th Sess. Supp. No. 1(A/8001/Add. 1), at 38.

[80] See Doc. A/8042 of Aug. 14, 1970, and the same, Add. 1 and 2.

[81] Res. 2723 (XXV), U.N. Press Release GA/4355 (Dec. 17, 1970), Pt. VIII, p. 32.

## V. DEPOLITICIZING THE RECOURSE TO THE COURT

It is generally agreed that adjudication by the Court ensures the greatest degree of objective and impartial consideration of an international dispute on the basis of the law.[82] Political factors are involved, however, in the election of judges, possibly in the framing of a *compromis,* but above all in the desicion whether or not to choose the judicial method or another method which may be available. It has been said that one of the factors which impedes recourse to the Court, particularly by unilateral application in reliance upon compulsory jurisdiction, is the consideration that such action may be regarded as an unfriendly act by the respondent government. This is not an idle exaggeration of the sensitivity of states. At the inauguration of the Hague system it was found necessary to stipulate that the offer of good offices and mediation and the advice offered to conflicting parties "to have recourse to the Permanent Court, can only be regarded as friendly actions."[83]

It would be extremely difficult to provide factual proof that governments have refrained from having recourse to the Court for fear of offending the susceptibilities of their adversaries. However, the Institute of International Law, which includes members of the legal and political elite, found it desirable and perhaps even necessary to declare in 1959 that recourse to the Court constitutes "a normal method of settlement of legal disputes" as a consequence of paragraphs 3 and 4 of Article 2 of the Charter, and that

> Consequently, recourse to the International Court of Justice or to another international court or arbitral tribunal can never be regarded as an unfriendly act towards the respondent State.[84]

Inasmuch as the Court is a descendant of the Hague system, it makes sense to go back to it in order to advance beyond it. An appeal along the lines of the Institute's resolution may therefore be the logical first step in order to get the Court off dead center.[85] The appeal should come from the General Assembly and be addressed to all states. It should contain two simple propositions: first, that the Court is open to all states members of the international judicial community, and, second, that recourse to the Court shall never be regarded as an unfriendly act when other procedures for resolving legal disputes have failed.

There are two additional reasons for a resolution of this kind. First, the General Assembly has not expressed itself on the Court since its Resolution 171(II) of November 14, 1947, which called upon the Members and organs of the United Nations and specialized

[82] Gross, note 20 above, at 39–42.

[83] Arts. 3 and 27 of the Convention for the Pacific Settlement of International Disputes, Scott, note 12 above, at 43, 61. See also Philip C. Jessup, "International Litigation as a Friendly Act," 60 Columbia Law Rev. 24–34 (1960).

[84] 48 Institute of International Law, Annuaire 381 (1959, II). Reproduced in 54 A.J.I.L. 136 (1960).

[85] Jenks, note 2 above, at 108.

agencies to make greater use of the Court's contentious and advisory jurisdictions. This resolution had no apparent impact upon the Members and organs. The proposed resolution, like that of 1947, would state a general principle. The second reason is that the Declaration on Friendly Relations is silent on the Court, although it is eloquent on the liberty and sovereignty of states. It might be well to remind the members of the international legal community that resort to the Court, whether by means of a special agreement or a unilateral application, is not a surrender but an exercise of sovereignty. The proposed resolution would remind the members that judicial settlement is one of the options and that use of this option can never be regarded as an unfriendly act. This is implicit in Article 33, which is restated in the Declaration on Friendly Relations. The time has come to make it explicit. It is also implicit in Article 92(1) whereby the Court is instituted as "the principal judicial organ of the United Nations," that is, of the Members of the United Nations.

Finally, it may be worth while to ponder the question of whether the proposed resolution or another resolution should remind the Security Council of Article 36(3). The fact that this clause was used only once (*Corfu Channel* case) in nearly twenty-five years is eloquent testimony to the high degree of the politicization of the handling of international disputes by the United Nations. More frequent use of this option available to the Security Council would be an essential first step in its depoliticization.

The appeal outlined above may appear as weak compared with an appeal for general ratification of the Optional Clause, with no conditions except reciprocity and the exclusion of disputes arising out of the past and belonging thereto."[86] However, in this writer's view such an appeal would be premature and likely to fall on deaf ears, as did the 1947 resolution of the General Assembly. Such an appeal might well be considered at a later stage, when the present situation is unfrozen and some momentum gained in recourse to the Court.

## VI. POSSIBLE APPROACHES AND SOME PROPOSALS

Proposals for facilitating and encouraging recourse to the Court in contentious and advisory proceedings fall into two categories: those which involve a change in the Statute and those which do not. Changes in the Statute are equivalent to amendments of the Charter (Article 69 of the Statute) and require "a vote of two thirds of the members of the General Assembly" and ratification by two thirds of the Members, including all the permanent members of the Security Council (Article 108 of the Charter). The initiative may come from Members or from the Court (Article 70 of the Statute). The Court has already taken such an initiative for amending Articles 22(1), 23(2) and 28 of its Statute, which provide that the seat of the Court shall be at The Hague.[87]

It may be possible to devise some changes with respect to access to the Court or

[86] Jenks, note 2 above, at 109 and 124–125.

[87] Report of the International Court of Justice, August 1, 1968–July 31, 1969, GAOR, 24th Sess., Supp. No. 5 (A/7605) at 3, 5.

procedural matters which do not necessarily involve formal amendments. There is some flexibility in this matter under Article 36(1) of the Court's Statute:

> The jurisdiction of the Court comprises all cases which the parties refer to it and all matters specially provided for in the Charter of the United Nations or in treaties and conventions in force.

It has been pointed out that the Permanent Court for fourteen years, from 1922 to 1936, delivered advisory opinions at the request of the Council of the League, in spite of the fact that the Statute which was in force during the period was silent on the subject of advisory proceedings.[88] The 1922 Rules of the Court contained provisions for advisory proceedings, and these were included in the Revised Statute of 1936.[89] The Statute of the Permanent Court did not include in its Article 36 a specific reference to the Covenant; the Covenant, being Part I of the Treaty of Versailles, was covered by the words "treaties and conventions in force," and Article 14 of the Covenant dealt with advisory opinions. Relying on this precedent and on the broad scope of Article 36, paragraph 1, it has been asked whether some innovations in procedures and remedies might be brought about "by means of an instrument or instruments supplementary to the Statute giving jurisdiction in respect of matters provided for in treaties and conventions in force within the meaning of Article 36."[90]

A simple and well-known example is the provision in some agreements between states, such as the General Convention on the Privileges and Immunities of the United Nations, and in agreements between states and international organizations, such as the Headquarters Agreement between the United States and the United Nations, which attach binding force to the advisory opinions of the Court. In the UNESCO case the Court stated that "the fact that the Opinion of the Court is accepted as binding provides no reason why the Request for an Opinion should not be complied with."[91] This case is also authority for the proposition that the requested opinion may in fact relate to a dispute between individuals and international organizations.[92]

The Committee on Applications for Review of Administrative Tribunal Judgments, established by General Assembly Resolution 957(X) of November 8, 1955, which was authorized to request advisory opinions in certain defined circumstances and with defined consequences, is a useful precedent. It has been suggested that, drawing upon this, the General Assembly might "create an organ of the United Nations specially for the purpose of requesting advisory opinions in defined circumstances, instruct such an organ to request an opinion whenever satisfied that certain conditions exist and make such an opinion binding on the parties substantively interested in the matter."[93] Such a method of

[88] Hudson, note 32 above, at 210–213; Jenks, note 2 above, at 127.
[89] Hudson, note 32 above, at 680–681, 730–732.
[90] Jenks, note 2 above, at 124.
[91] [1956] I.C.J. Rep. 77 at 84.
[92] Leo Gross, "Participation of Individuals in Advisory Proceedings before the International Court of Justice: Question of Equality between the Parties," 52 A.J.I.L. 16-40 (1958). See also *supra*, pp. 705–726.
[93] Jenks, note 2 above, at 160–161.

"outflanking" Article 34 of the Statute of the Court, which provides that "only States may be parties in cases before the Court," could be used in disputes between individuals and organizations, and between states and organizations or individuals.[94]

Such an organ might also be used in order to obtain, on the basis of an appropriate instrument, an interpretation of the instrument in a case arising before a domestic tribunal of a party. It could be provided in the instrument that the advisory opinion would have the effect of a declaratory judgment[95] or simply that it would be binding upon the domestic court.

It has been suggested that international organizations other than specialized agencies might be authorized to request advisory opinions of the Court. It may be noted that Article 96(2) of the Charter provides that organs of the United Nations other than the General Assembly or the Security Council and organs of specialized agencies may be authorized to request advisory opinions. In fact the International Atomic Energy Agency, which is not a specialized agency of the United Nations, has received this authorization. This may not appear to be strictly in accordance with Article 96(2). However, Article 65(1) of the Statute is broader than Article 96(2) of the Charter and it could be argued that the Court would be guided by its Statute rather than by the Charter. Article 65(1) provides that:

> The Court may give an advisory opinion on any legal question at the request of whatever body may be authorized by or in accordance with the Charter of the United Nations to make such a request.

It all depends on how strictly the Court would construe the words "in accordance with the Charter." This is obviously a doubtful point. However, since the General Assembly saw fit to authorize IAEA to request advisory opinions, there is no reason why the Assembly could not, if requested, authorize regional or functional organizations to request advisory opinions of the Court upon any legal question.[96]

Finally the suggestion has been made that the Court could handle requests for advisory opinions before chambers, already constituted or to be constituted *ad hoc* (Article 26(2) of the Statute), or by summary procedure (Article 29 of the Statute).[97] Usually the Court has been able to render an opinion within a year of the request, and it may not be easy to accelerate the advisory proceedings very much. Furthermore, some stretching may be required to apply the procedure before chambers or the summary procedure to advisory proceedings. However, the Court would seem to have authority under Article 68 of the Statute to apply provisions governing contentious cases in its advisory function.

In this connection attention may be drawn to a provision in the Statute which has

[94] *Ibid.* at 161.
[95] *Ibid.*
[96] Jenks, note 2 above, at 160; and Rogers, note 78 above.
[97] *Ibid.*

never been used in contentious cases but which may assume importance in connection with a wider use of the advisory function by regional organizations and specialized agencies. Article 30(2) of the Statute reads: "The Rules of the Court may provide for assessors to sit with the Court or with any chambers, without the right to vote." According to Article 7(1) of the Rules of the Court,

> The Court may, either upon its own initiative or upon the request of a party made not later than the end of the written proceedings, decide, for the purpose of a particular case, to appoint assessors to sit with it but without the power to vote.

The remaining paragraphs of Article 7 deal with the selection and appointment of assessors by secret ballot. The same procedure applies to the appointment and selection of assessors by chambers. According to Article 8 of the Rules the assessors shall make a declaration which is substantially identical with that required of members of the Court by Article 20 of the Statute and Article 5 of the Rules. It is well to recall that the Court has also the power to carry out an inquiry or call for an expert opinion (Article 51 of the Statute and Articles 54 and 57 of the Rules). Unlike such experts, the assessor may participate in the private deliberations of the Court and in this fashion, presumably, in the drafting of the judgment.

The legal advisers of specialized agencies have appeared reluctant to use the advisory function of the Court on the ground that the Court, "being outside the mainstream of the organization's activity, might come to decisions not fully sensitive to the internal requirements for effective operation."[98] This is certainly a legitimate concern. It is believed that the use of assessors and possibly also of experts should go a long way toward providing the Court or one of its chambers with the sort of expertise which would enable the Court to appreciate the particular sensitivities of any functional agency. In truth, there may be some advantage in seeking the legal opinion of a relatively detached but knowledgable tribunal. In any event the point here is that, pursuant to Article 68 of the Statute and the corresponding Article 82 of the Rules, the Court would seem to have authority to use assessors and experts in advisory proceedings.[99]

There are also possibilities for developing recourse to the contentious jurisdiction of the Court which do not require explicit changes of the Statute. One improvement is seen in accelerating the process of litigation. The Court is sensitive to the issue.[100] *Barcelona Traction* is the landmark case and provoked some comment from the Court in its judgment.[101] Such inordinate delays which increase the cost of litigation are due to the parties in the first place, but there may be opportunities for the Court in co-operation with the parties to expedite the written and often repetitous oral phase of the proceedings. The

[98] Merillat, note 55 above, at 10–11.

[99] On the status of international organizations in relation to the Court see Jenks, note 2 above, at 185–208.

[100] Leo Gross, "The Time Element in the Contentious Proceedings in the International Court of Justice," 63 A.J.I.L. 74-86 (1969). See also *supra*, pp. 831–843.

[101] [1970] I.C.J. Rep. 3 at 6. See also Separate Opinions of Judges Fitzmaurice, at 113, and Jessup, at 221.

Statute provides that "the hearings shall be under the control of the President" (Article 45), but it is well known that this control has been nominal in most cases.

Article 29 requires the Court to set up chambers for summary procedure. It has been proposed that summary proceedings could be held before the full Court at the request of the parties or if provided for in instruments.[102] This is neither specially provided for nor excluded by the Statute. However, Article 82(2) of the Rules provides that "If the Court is of the opinion that a request for an advisory opinion necessitates an early answer, it shall take the necessary steps to accelerate the procedure." What is possible for advisory proceedings without a special clause in the Statute should be possible in contentious cases with the consent *ad hoc* of the parties or in the applicable jurisdictional clause. The Court has resources, hitherto largely untapped, for speedier conduct of its business in Article 49 of the Statute: "The Court may, even before the hearing begins, call upon the agents to produce any document or to supply any explanations. Formal note shall be taken of any refusal." In using the possibilities opened up by this clause the Court would be in a position to develop contacts with the parties which might expedite the proceedings without depriving them of their "day in court," as it were.

Other proposals on access to the Court would take the "adversary" out of contentious proceedings. A jurisdictional clause could be inserted in a treaty providing that proceedings instituted thereunder by one party would be regarded "as proceedings instituted jointly for the determination of a question rather than as proceedings instituted by an applicant against a respondent." The question could be defined, if necessary, "under the control of the Court by an officer acting on behalf."[103] This approach is hardly distinguishable from proceedings instituted pursuant to a special agreement. In such proceedings there are no adversaries in the sense of applicant and respondent, and the procedure has the added advantage that the agreement defines the question on which the Court is requested to rule and, conceivably, the law to be applied.[104] Usually the subject matter of a special agreement is a concrete dispute, in the sense of a difference between the parties as to their respective rights. However, there is no reason why the special agreement should not invite the Court to define the legal principles on the basis of which the parties shall seek a settlement rather than provide the solution itself.

An example of this sort of approach is the recent *North Sea Continental Shelf* case. This case came before the Court by means of Special Agreements concluded February 2, 1967, between Denmark and the Federal Republic of Germany and between the Federal Republic and The Netherlands. Differences having arisen between the parties concerning the delimitation of their shares in the continental shelf in the North Sea, the parties requested the Court "to decide the following question: What principles and rules of inter-

[102] Jenks, note 2 above, at 132.

[103] Jenks, note 2 above, at 155. The model for this is the Master of the Supreme Court of England and the *juge d'instruction* in France.

[104] The parties could certainly agree that the Court apply provisions of a treaty even though the treaty has not been ratified by them or, if ratified, has not yet entered into force. This would seem compatible with the language of Art. 38, par. 1 a, of the Court's Statute.

national law are applicable to the determination as between the Parties of the area of the continental shelf in the North Sea which appertains to each of them. . . ."

In the Special Agreements the parties also agreed that they "shall delimit the continental shelf in the North Sea as between their countries by agreement in pursuance of the decision requested from the International Court of Justice."[105] The Court was not asked to resolve the dispute—that is, it was not asked to delineate the boundaries, this task being reserved to the parties. The Court in its judgment of February 20, 1969, laid down applicable principles and rules of international law and also "the factors to be taken into account in the course of negotiations."[106] The dispute was eventually settled by negotiations between the parties. The method adopted by the parties in this case is a useful precedent for the future.

Another procedure would also require the prior consent of the states to an instrument providing "for the citation of nominal respondents." Thus an agreement might authorize any party to bring before the Court questions relating to the interpretation or application of the agreement, naming "automatically . . . as repondent all the other parties to the instrument." The respondents having thus been named, all or some could appear before the Court; and if none appeared, judgment would be given by default.[107]

A similar approach (advance consent in a treaty) could be used for obtaining judgments relating to the interpretation of constituent instruments of international organizations, through *ex parte* proceedings. This method avoids naming any other party to the treaty as respondent, but in accordance with Article 34(3) of the Statute the organization concerned would be notified, and in virtue of Article 63 of the Statute, any interested state could apply to the Court for permission to intervene.[108] The interests of the organization and of states concerned could be fully safeguarded in this manner.

The feature common to these proposals is that they depend upon consent. In that respect they are analogous to proceedings based upon special agreements, in which there are no adversaries in the sense of proceedings instituted by unilateral application. But they depend upon prior consent, given in advance of a dispute or question, as do proceedings instituted by unilateral application. They require, in short, a jurisdictional clause of a special kind, the distinctive virtue of which is that they permit institution of contentious proceedings by unilateral application not directed against any particular state. Through this device it is hoped to overcome the hesitation of a state to call another state before the Court and thus appear as committing an unfriendly act toward it. Such procedures may well be criteria of a mature system of law, even though they start from the premise of the immaturity of the states or, at the lowest, of their extreme sensitivity.

In the same manner, that is, through a separate instrument or clauses in conventions, states could agree to accept as binding provisional measures indicated by the Court

[105] [1969] I.C.J. Rep. 3, at 6.
[106] *Ibid.* at 53; reprinted in 63 A.J.I.L. 591 (1969).
[107] Jenks, note 2 above, at 157 f.
[108] *Ibid.* at 156–157.

pursuant to Article 41(1) of the Statute.[109] It will be recalled that in the *Anglo-Iranian Company* case the question of the legal effect of such measures was controversial, and the matter has not yet been clarified. Short of amending the statute, states would generally in a treaty, or perhaps even in special agreements, agree to accept provisional measures as binding. In view of the frequently protracted nature of litigation, an agreement of that sort would make sense and might encourage states to have recourse to the Court, knowing that their interests would be protected pending the final disposition of the case.

It remains to note that most of these proposals were discussed by an informal study group on the International Court of Justice. The group was unable to consider all of them in detail but there was support particularly for an extension and wider use of advisory proceedings. The study group was convinced, as was the Institute of International Law, that one way of promoting progress was through the dissemination of a "wider and more thorough knowledge of the working and decisions of the International Court of Justice and other international courts and tribunals" and that public and private national and international bodies can play an important rôle in this task.[110]

## VII. COMPOSITION OF THE COURT

Confidence in the Court, its impartiality and objectivity has been widely identified as a crucial factor in the rôle which it might play in the changing pattern of international relations. In this context the composition of the Court is of central significance. The principles and procedures governing the composition of the Court are contained in Chapter I (Articles 2–33) of the Statute. There has been on the whole satisfaction with the composition of the Court through the application of these principles and procedures, but there has also been consideration of proposals designed to ensure the independence of the Court from political and other influences.[111] Some of the desired objectives might be attained by means of General Assembly resolutions, which Members would be free to accept as binding and act accordingly. Others might require an amendment of the Statute. Judge Huber suggested that the former method would be acceptable in matters which by the statute are left to the discretion of the Members such as the functioning of the national groups for the nomination of candidates for the Court. Some of the more significant considerations will be discussed below.

[109] *Ibid.* at 157–158.
[110] 48 Annuaire at 380–386 (1959).
[111] M. Huber, 45 Institute of International Law, Session of Aix-en-Provence, Annuaire at 407 (I, 1954).

## 1. Qualification of Judges

### (Articles 2 and 9 of the Statute)

The basic principle is in Article 2, which states the personal and professional requirements; high moral character, eligibility to highest judicial office, recognized competence in international law.[112] Such persons should be elected "regardless of their nationality." Article 9, however, reminds the electors that "in the body as a whole the representation of the main forms of civilization and of the principal legal systems of the world should be assured." In a perfect world such a combination of factors would present no insuperable problem. In the actual world of the United Nations nationality has always been a factor—nationals of the Four Big Powers were elected—a fact which provoked no criticism, as nationality seemed to go hand in hand with the other requirements. However, generally speaking, the feeling arose that the "forms and systems" requirement seemed of greater concern to the electors than the personal and professional requirements. In the climate of the United Nations all requirements tended to be submerged in the considerations which generally govern elections, namely, the preference for representation of voting blocs, regional and/or social, economic and political "affinity" groups. As the balloting is secret, it would be impossible for an outsider to test the validity of this feeling. However, an outspoken demand exists for a more equitable representation in the Court of various political and social systems,[113] which are not mentioned anywhere in the Statute.

Indeed from Table 1 a shift in the geographical origins or affiliations of judges can be detected.[114] The most striking expression of this can be seen in the election of one judge from Africa in each of the last three triennial elections. By comparison there are two judges from Latin America and two from Western Europe (apart from judges from the United Kingdom, the U.S.A. and France). No judge from a non-Member State has ever been elected, although candidates of outstanding ability and competence have been nominated.

The Secretary General of the United Nations, U Thant, stated that the present composition of the Court satisfies not merely the requirements of representation of the main forms of civilization and the principal legal systems, "but, even from the geographic standpoint, it may be noted that the composition of the Court is *exactly* the same as that agreed on in 1963 for the Security Council. Since the composition of the Council is generally considered balanced, there appears little justification for objecting to that of the Court."[115]

[112] For qualifications of judges see Table in Annex 2, p. 1004.
[113] Report of the Special Committee on Principles . . . (A/6230), June 27, 1966 at 103, par. 219. See note 6 above.
[114] See Table, Annex 1, p. 1003.
[115] Introduction to the Annual Report, note 79 above, at 38, par. 147. Italics supplied. The Secretary General presumably referred to General Assembly Resolution 1991 A (XVIII) of Dec. 17, 1963, pursuant to which the ten non-permanent

The question, then, has arisen whether somehow the political climate pervading the United Nations can be eliminated and the pre-eminence of the "character" and "competence" requirement can be established over the "forms and systems" requirement. With this end in view the Institute of International Law made two suggestions, one relating to the election process itself and the other concerning the relation between Articles 2 and 9. After rejecting radical proposals (such as that Article 9 be altogether eliminated or at least that the words "principal legal systems," which had come to be regarded as synonym a for geographical areas, be deleted) the Institute adopted in 1954 the following resolution:

> Without prejudice to the need for maintaining a certain geographical representation within the International Court of Justice, as provided for in Article 9 of the Statute, judges of the Court should be elected primarily on the basis of their personal qualifications in accordance with Article 2.
>
> In the event of the Statute being revised, a clarification covering this point could usefully be added to Article 9.[116]

The sense of this resolution might well be expressed, short of a formal amendment, in a resolution of the General Assembly. It is open to question, however, whether deeply ingrained habits could be changed by a resolution, if it were to be adopted (which is doubtful), or even by an amendment of Article 9. As Judge Spiropoulos observed, it would be "chimerical to believe that one could eliminate the political combinations in connection with the election of judges by a simple revision of the text of Articles 2 and 9, for the Assembly and the Council are political bodies in which political considerations prevail."[117]

Other proposals tending to influence the election of judges in accordance with the "character and competence" criteria will be discussed in their context. However, one proposal may be mentioned here. In the wideranging discussion of the Principles of Friendly Relations in the Sixth Committee of the General Assembly, the representative of Japan, Mr. Hattori, outlined several steps that would strengthen the rule of law and the rôle of the Court. He covered some well-known ground but also included the following: "to examine the possibility of making acceptance of the Court's compulsory jurisdiction a factor in deciding its composition, albeit with the utmost care to avoid any damage to its prestige."[118]

members shall be elected according to the following geographical pattern: (a) five from African and Asian states, (b) one from Eastern European states, (c) two from Latin American states, and (d) two from Western European and other states. GAOR, 18th Sess., Supp. No. 15 (A/5515) at 21–22.

[116] 45 Annuaire at 296, and at 412, 414, 509, 523, 542 (II, 1954); 49 A.J.I.L. 14 (1955).

[117] J. Spiropoulos, "Les Resolutions de l'Institut de Droit International sur les Amendements à Apporter au Statut de la Cour International de Justice," in W. Schätzel and H. J. Schlochauer (eds.), Rechtsfragen der Internationalen Organisation, Festschrift für Hans Wehberg 374–384, at 376 (1956).

[118] GAOR, 18th Sess., Sixth Committee, 821st Meeting, Nov. 27, 1963, at 226.

This stipulation could, if found acceptable, be included in a revised Article 9 or in a General Assembly resolution. This would add another factor to the "character and competence" and "forms and systems" factors. It would not be wholly without precedent. Article 23 (1) of the Charter lays down the factors to be taken into account in the election of nonpermanent members of the Security Council: "in the first instance . . . the contribution of Members of the United Nations to the maintenance of international peace and security and to the other purposes of the Organization and also to equitable geographical distribution." Both factors were relevant in the formative stage of the United Nations; then the second seemed to take precedence over the first, and currently the elections are governed by the resolution of the General Assembly of 1963 allocating places among geographic regions. Still, within geographic areas, political, social and economic affinities seem to play an important rôle.

It may well be that the consideration advanced by Japan would, like other criteria, come to be dominated by the factor of affinity, whether it were incorporated in a revised Article 9 or in a resolution of the General Assembly. Its merit would be to remind the electors of the distinction between the nominal international judicial community and the effective one, the latter being comprised of those states which have manifested a disposition to settle their disputes by adjudication by accepting the compulsory jurisdiction of the Court.

It is impossible to determine objectively whether the electors have had the compulsory-jurisdiction factor in mind when casting their secret ballot. It can be objectively determined whether the elected members of the Court are nationals of states which have or have not accepted the compulsory jurisdiction of the Court. In the triennial election the ratio of states that had accepted its compulsory jurisdiction to those that had not was 4:1 (Senegal) in 1963, 3:2 (Lebanon, Poland) in 1966; and 2:3 (Dahomey, U.S.S.R., Spain) in 1969. By going back to 1946 one might be able to determine whether the last 3 triennial elections indicate a trend.

Article 7 of the Statute directs the Secretary General to prepare a list in alphabetical order of all persons nominated in accordance with Article 5. It also states that, with the exception of Article 12 (2), "these shall be the only persons eligible." However, while this is so, it does not follow that all of them are equally eligible. It might be worth considering the desirability of requesting the Secretary General, through a resolution of the General Assembly, to prepare a second list for the guidance of the electors which would separate the persons nominated from countries which have accepted the compulsory jurisdiction from those which have not. Article 98 of the Charter would be ample authority for such a resolution. There is, after all, a difference between the 46 countries which accept the judicial process and those which do not. The former have a greater stake in the composition of the Court than the latter. The non-election of a candidate from China indicates that permanent members of the Security Council have no vested right in being "represented" on the Court. The veto-free vote in the Security Council is further evidence that it was not the intention of the founding fathers of the United Nations to provide for such "representation."

What impact a Court constituted along the lines indicated above would have on the advisory function is problematical. It could hardly lead to a less frequent recourse to it than during the last 10 years or so. It might have an encouraging effect on some of the specialized agencies. Conceivably, it might spur some states to accept the compulsory jurisdiction of the Court. To be sure, the possibility cannot be excluded that some of these acceptances may be accompanied by reservations of a far-reaching character. However, as noted in a different context, there may still remain a residuum of usable compulsory jurisdiction.[119]

### 2. Number of Members of the Court

### (Article 3 of the Statute)

The Statute provides that the Court shall consist of 15 members. The Permanent Court consisted of the same number of judges. Since 1945, when the present Statute was drafted, the number of Members of the United Nations has risen from 51 to 127. The question then is whether the increase in the nominal membership of the international judicial community, which stands at 130, should be reflected in an increase in the number of members of the Court. The question was discussed in the Institute of International Law in 1954 and the informal study group on the Court in 1963. The result was a resolution which reads:

> It is desirable to avoid an increase of the number of judges, which would be calculated to make the deliberations of the International Court of Justice more difficult.
>
> Should new circumstances make some increase necessary, the number of judges should not exceed eighteen.[120]

As to the method for achieving this increase, there were two views in the Institute. According to one, the increase should be accomplished through a revision of the Statute fixing the number at 18; and according to the other, supported by Judge Huber, the Statute should be amended by a change in Article 3, declaring that the Assembly and Council may, in agreement, raise the number to 18. The former view prevailed. It is obvious that a larger number than 15 might threaten the cohesion and efficiency of the Court.[121] This danger could be mitigated. One proposal was to split the Court into two "cham-

[119] See p. 993 below.

[120] 45 Annuaire at 297 (1954); 49 A.J.I.L. 14 (1955).

[121] See 45 Annuaire at 504, 525, 532 and 529, for the views respectively of Castberg, Kaeckenbeeck, Lauterpacht and Olivan. See also Spiropoulos, note 117 above, at 377.

bers'' of nine judges each.[122] Obviously the term ''chambers'' is not used in the sense of Article 26 of the Statute. Rather it is used in the sense of sections, and the Statute makes no provision for them. Article 25 says that ''the full Court shall sit except when it is expressly provided otherwise in the present Statute.'' If the Court were to be split into sections, a revision of this clause would be necessary.

A more practical proposal would rely on keeping the operational membership at no more than 15 judges by use of Article 23 (2) which states: ''Members of the Court are entitled to periodic leave, the dates and duration of which shall be fixed by the Court. . . .''[123] This seems certainly feasible as long as ''the number of judges available to constitute the Court is not . . . reduced below eleven''(Article 25 (2)), and a quorum of nine judges is assured (Article 25 (3)). Another method is indicated in Article 25 (2), namely, that ''the Rules of the Court may provide for allowing one or more judges, according to circumstances and in rotation, to be dispensed from sitting,'' provided that the number of available judges is not thereby reduced below eleven.

It is clear, then, that an enlargement of the membership of the Court need not necessarily produce an unwieldy tribunal. However, there is still a possibility that the cohesion and efficiency of the Court might suffer. The manipulation of leaves of absence and dispensations from sitting might result in a tribunal the composition of which might be quite unpredictable. As will be argued below, the introduction of triennial elections has already introduced a degree of uncertainty and unpredictability. This would be increased by leaves and dispensations from sitting. States would like to have their disputes settled by the same Court. As litigation becomes protracted by reason of preliminary objections and delays in the written stage of the proceedings, the likelihood decreases of having the same judges at the start and at the finish.

The need for continuity is recognized in Article 13 (3), dealing with triennial elections: ''The members of the Court shall continue to discharge their duties until their places have been filled. Though replaced, they shall finish any cases which they may have begun.'' This clause has not prevented a different bench from indicating provisional measures and hearing objections to jurisdiction, or from ruling on preliminary objections and rendering judgments on merits.[124] It would seem that the term ''case'' does not mean the whole litigation but certainly includes hearings in a case and the rendering of the judgment. Since the composition of the bench is without doubt one of the factors taken into account by the party or parties instituting proceedings, the various schemes propounded for mitigating the adverse effects of an enlarged Court might fall short of their objective; they might even become counter-productive.

[122] E. Hambro, ''Should the Membership of the International Court of Justice be Enlarged?'' in Festgabe für A. N. Makarov, 19 Zeitschrift für Ausländisches Öffentliches Recht and Völkerrecht 141–152 at 149 (1958).

[123] Hambro, *loc. cit.* at 148.

[124] For examples, see 1 Rosenne, The Law and Practice of the International Court 199–200 (1965). To the examples there listed should be added the Barcelona Traction Company and the South West Africa cases, where judgments on preliminary objections were rendered in 1963 and 1962 and final pronouncements in 1970 and 1966, respectively.

An enlargement of the Court was primarily considered as a response to demands of the new states for "more equitable representation." In the last three triennial elections for the first time—if one does not consider India and Pakistan as "new" states—three judges from Africa, and one each from the Philippines and Lebanon were elected. To be sure, this has been possible at the expense of Western European and other states. Surely the three elections gave "equitable representation" to new states. They now have one-third of the seats on the bench. The situation raises the question whether other areas and systems of law and politically related groups of states can be said to have "equitable representation" on the Court. One test for determining the effect of the change in the composition of the Court will be whether contentious cases are submitted to the Court from the ranks of the new states as well as from the traditional clients of the Court in the West. If there are no cases from new states, then the lack of "equitable representation" was not the cause for their reticence, although it may have become a cause for the reticence of the West. If that turns out to be the case, then an enlargement of the Court's membership may have to be carried out in order to restore a more "equitable representation" to the traditional clients of the Court.

### 3. Nomination of Candidates

### (Articles 4, 5 and 6 of the Statute)

The process of nominating qualified persons for election to the Court was not changed when the Statute was drafted in 1945. An alternative method was proposed, namely, nomination directly by governments; but the preference was for the old method of indirect nomination, and the question was decided accordingly at the San Francisco Conference.[125] It was felt that the old method had worked well. Whether the same method has worked well in the United Nations seems less clear. Everything in the United Nations tends to be politicized in the sense that everything, including elections to the Court, becomes stakes in the never-ending process of bargaining for whatever is on the market. The process of nomination, it is felt, has also been infected, and the national groups and their equivalents (Article 4(2)) are not as autonomous in their selections as they were reputed to have been in the League of Nations period. It may not be much of an exaggeration to suggest that the difference between the direct and indirect nominations is the difference between direct and indirect political influences. It seems more important to governments that the Court should reflect accurately the strength of the several "affinity" groups in the United Nations than that it should be an effective organ of the United Nations.

[125] N. J. Padelford, "The Composition of the International Court of Justice: Background and Practice," in K. W. Deutsch and S. Hoffmann, the Relevance of International Law 219–250, at 224–227 (1968).

In the Institute of International Law several ideas to improve the nomination process were discussed. Little support was given to La Pradelle's proposal that the Court itself should draw up a list of candidates.[126] Gidel's proposal that Article 5 be revised to provide that members of the national groups and their equivalents shall be considered *ipso facto* as eligible[127] did not fare better. Lauterpacht suggested that the national groups should be encouraged to set up a committee of five persons to assist them in making the nominations. The Committee should include two judges, one practicing lawyer and two teachers of international law. Such a committee "would offer some guarantees of independence and expert knowledge."[128] This proposal was not adopted. Obviously it has some merit. Under Article 6, the national groups have leeway to establish such committees. They could be encouraged to do so by means of a resolution of the General Assembly. They could also be encouraged to publish the consultations undertaken pursuant to Article 6 and the responses they received, without necessarily mentioning names.[129]

None of these proposals was accepted by the Institute. It has been claimed that only those nominees are likely to be elected who are supported by their governments. "Moreover the collaboration between the national groups of the Permanent Court of Arbitration and the governments is extremely close, and as a consequence the decision concerning persons to be nominated cannot be insulated from political influences."[130] Still, an appeal to the national groups to discharge their task independently and responsibly might serve a useful purpose.

One more point may be made in connection with the nominating process. The Statute sets an upper limit on the number of persons to be nominated in each of the two categories—no more than two co-nationals and no more than four altogether (Article 5(2)). Some national groups nominate only one co-national which lends some credence to the suspicion that political influence is at work. It would decidedly be an improvement if the national groups would regularly nominate two of their co-nationals.[131] This would give the electors a better choice. A resolution of the General Assembly might well make an appeal along these lines to the national groups, and the Secretary General of the United Nations could be instructed to remind the national groups of such a resolution when inviting them, pursuant to Article 5(1) of the Statute, to make the nominations. The national groups and their equivalents could also be reminded that in fulfilling this task they are acting as international organs and not as organs of the state which appointed them. In free and democratic societies such an appeal should not fall on deaf ears.

The Secretary General, under Article 7, is to "prepare a list in alphabetical order of all the persons thus nominated." It has already been suggested that he could be instructed

[126] 45 Annuaire 407–554 at 491 (II, 1954).

[127] *Ibid.* at 450–451. See also 44 Annuaire at 64 (II, 1952).

[128] 45 Annuaire at 476 (II, 1954).

[129] In this context *cf.* R. R. Baxter, "The Procedures Employed in Connection with the United States Nominations for the International Court in 1960," 55 A.J.I.L. 445–446 (1961). This is the only such account of which the writer is aware.

[130] Spiropoulos, note 117, above, at 378.

[131] This was proposed by the Institute of International Law in 1952, 44 Annuaire at 64 (II, 1952), but not adopted at its 1954 session.

by the Assembly to prepare another list which would indicate which persons are nationals of countries which have accepted the compulsory jurisdiction of the Court. The Secretary General could also be instructed to include in the list short biographies of the nominated persons. Lauterpacht contended that the greatest flaw in the present procedure is that the elections are "not preceded by any organized collective examination of the merits of the individual candidates" nor "by any fully responsible and orderly attempt to balance the claims of representation as conceived under Article 9 and the personal requirements as laid down in Article 2." He suggested that a "preparatory and explanatory body" be established to carry out the scrutiny and report to the General Assembly and Security Council. The report would not be binding. The committee could be composed of eleven members—three members each from the Assembly and the Council, three members of the Court, the Secretary General of the United Nations, and one international lawyer of acknowledged authority who could be nominated by the Bureau of the Institute of International Law.[132]

No doubt such procedure would provide some guidance for the electors in choosing the judges from the raw list prepared by the Secretary General. From the purely constitutional point of view, it seems unobjectionable.[133] A committee could be set up by the General Assembly or by the Assembly upon a recommendation of the Security Council. The question is whether it is feasible from the political point of view. What Lauterpacht and others were concerned about is to take politics and politicking out of the election process. Other proposals yet to be discussed all tend in the same direction. Some may deny that there has been politicking; others may admit it and argue that it is inevitable. A tribunal which satisfies the political instincts and reflects the political deals of the members, but is not the kind of court to which they would entrust the settlement of their disputes, is obviously of no use to anybody. Political affinity groups may score victories, but they may turn out to be Pyrrhic victories. The crisis of confidence in the Court may indeed be the result of the extent to which the process of politicizing the elections has gone. The electors know it and they have no confidence in what they have created.

### 4. The Timing of Elections

### (Article 8 of the Statute)

Article 8 merely provides that the Assembly and the Council "shall proceed independently of one another to elect the members of the Court." Proposals to let the Assembly alone elect the judges were considered at various times but found no acceptance.[134]

[132] 45 Annuaire at 481 (II, 1954). Fitzmaurice supported this proposal. *Ibid.* at 511.

[133] In this context it may be recalled that Art. 6 of the I.L.C. Statute provides: "The Secretary General shall as soon as possible communicate to the Governments of States Members the names submitted, as well as any statements of qualifications of candidates that may have been submitted by the nominating Governments." The Work of the I.L.C. (U.N. Pub. 67.V.40), at 56.

[134] 45 Annuaire at 420, 544 (II, 1954). Rolin, Kaeckenbeeck and Olivan supported the proposal.

Article 8 is silent on the question of timing. The practice has been to include elections of judges on the agenda of the regular sessions of the Assembly along with the election of the members of a miscellaneous array of other organs. It is in this practice that political bargaining on the composition of the Court had its origin. Election of a candidate to the Court is traded off for support of another candidate to another body. And the Court became just one more body. To counter this practice, proposals have been made to separate the election of members of the Court from other elections. Elections to the Court should be held within eight days of the opening of the Assembly session.[135] With the same objective in mind the Institute at its Siena Session in 1952 adopted a resolution stating that

> . . . in order to comply with the letter and spirit of Article 2 and 8 of the Statute, the following administrative measures should be taken at once:
>
> 1. By reason of its non-political character, the election of the Members of the Court, being concerned with persons, not with States, should be kept altogether apart from the elections relating to other organs of the United Nations, and should take place at the nearest possible date to the opening of the Session of the Assembly and immediately after the closure of the general opening debate.
>
> 2. In order to ensure independence for the voting in the two organs which have to carry out the elections of the judges simultaneously, steps should be taken to prevent any communications passing between them, save only the official announcements made by each body to the other, of the results of their respective electoral meetings.[136]

It should be noted that this proposal was made in 1952, when the membership of the United Nations stood at sixty. It proceeds from the assumption that the elections are "concerned with persons, not with States." If that had been correct in 1952, there would have been no need for the resolution. Currently it is probably closer to the true situation to say that the elections are concerned with states and with political affinity groups rather than with persons. The groups bargain about which will get what, and it is not an exaggeration to say that the effective nominations are made by the groups. The notion of the Institute that there should be no communication between the two electoral organs loses much of its meaning in view of the current practice. It simply does not make much sense to say that the 127 Members of the United Nations and the three non-Members, on the one side, and the fifteen members of the Council will be guided by an "invisible hand." Some preparation and consultation are inevitable and unavoidable, particularly as long as the present bicameral system of elections is maintained. Lauterpacht's suggestion, discussed in the preceding section, assumed correctly that some screening and guidance are necessary. If this is not done by an independent body with the best interest of the Court in mind, it will be and has been done instead on the basis of the perceived best interests of the affinity groups.

The suggestion to separate the judicial from other elections by scheduling them early in the session may have been useful in 1952 when the bargaining process for elective

[135] See Judge Guerrero's proposal, *ibid.* at 544.

[136] 44 Annuaire at 474 (II, 1952); 47 A.J.I.L. 463 (1953).

posts was less intense. Currently it would make no difference when the elections for the Court are held because the bargaining process has become a year-round business. Also the general debate has expanded and covers four to six weeks, during which lobbying between and within groups takes place.

However, it would at least be an acknowledgement of the special position of the Court as the principal judicial organ, not of the United Nations alone but indeed of the world, if the election of its members were held at a special session of the Assembly and the Council. The members of the Court should ideally be elected at a meeting of the international judicial community and without the Security Council. Assuming that a unicameral system of elections is not practical at this juncture, the least that could be done is to convene the parties to the Statute every three years for the purpose of electing members of the Court and of dealing with other matters relating to the Court, such as possible revisions of the Statute or the consideration of resolutions relating to the Court. This could certainly be done without any revision of Article 8. Preferably the Assembly and the Council would agree by resolutions to hold special sessions in the spring of the year in which triennial elections are to be held. If that were too expensive or inconvenient, the special session could be held a week before the opening of the regular session of the Assembly. This is suggested without any fond expectation that the electors would then be guided solely by the spirit of Articles 2 and 8. But at least they would be reminded of their solemn obligation as members of the international judicial community to elect a bench which would command the confidence of the international community and to which as a consequence, they would be willing to submit their disputes.

### 5. Voting in Elections of Members of the Court

### (Articles 10 to 12 of the Statute)

The rules laid down in these articles, although of some complexity, do not eliminate all difficulties. In triennial elections, when five judges are to be elected, it is possible for more than five persons to receive the requisite majorities—an absolute majority of votes—in both the Assembly and the Security Council. The case of the election of Judge Ammoun is well known.[137] The Statute provides in Article 10(2) that a vote in the Security Council "shall be taken without any distinction between permanent and non-permenant members of the Security Council." The Statute provides for the eventuality that one or more seats remain to be filled after a third meeting (Article 12), but does not deal with the situations which have actually arisen.

The Institute of International Law considered a proposal to abolish Articles 11 and

[137] W. N. Hogan, "The Ammoun Case and the Election of Judges to the International Court of Justice," 59 A.J.I.L. 908–912 (1965).

12 in favor of co-optation of the judges by the Court itself from among those candidates who received a certain minimum of votes.[138] It proposed in 1954 the following rule:

> When several seats are to be filled, successive votes for each seat seem more likely to prevent unexpected results. This method is not incompatible with the present Statute.[139]

The second sentence is correct, although clearly Article 10 and following are so drafted as to convey the impression that several candidates are voted upon simultaneously. This has been the understanding which has prevailed in the practice of both the League and the United Nations. However, a different interpretation is not excluded. In supporting the election of "one man at a time" Judge Huber recalled the example of the Swiss Federal Council, which for a hundred years has been elected in this manner.[140] If this method took more time, the results of the elections would be "more mature and more just."[141] In this as in all its other proposals the Institute was guided by the concern of reducing the political element in the elections. Doubt was expressed whether the new scheme would indeed be successful in this regard.[142] On the other hand, Professor Rudzinski, who has the advantage of an insider's experience, suggested that:

> . . . A sequence of five separate one-man elections instead of one five-man election would strain substantially the trust needed for election deals. . . . Anyhow, splitting of multiple ballots may be the least objectionable basic remedy and is worth considering.[143]

Inasmuch as no formal revision of the Statute is involved but only a change in the practice, a change for the better might be accomplished through appropriate amendments in the Rules of Procedure of the Assembly and the insertion of an appropriate rule in the Provisional Rules of Procedure of the Council. Rule 40 of the latter simply refers to the Statute, and Rule 152 of the former blatantly underscores the defects of the present system by stipulating that any meeting of the Assembly "shall continue until as many candidates as are required for all the seats to be filled have obtained *in one or more ballots* an absolute majority of votes."[144] At the very least the "one man at a time" scheme would do away with this objectionable feature, and it may well tend to reduce the politicking of the various affinity groups.

[138] 45 Annuaire at 422 (II, 1954). Rolin suggested two fifths of the vote. *Ibid.* at 544.

[139] *Ibid.* at 297.

[140] 45 Annuaire at 421–422 (II, 1954).

[141] *Ibid.* at 422.

[142] Spiropoulos, note 117 above, at 379.

[143] A. W. Rudzinski, "Election Procedure in the United Nations," 53 A.J.I.L. 81–111 at 84 (1959).

[144] Doc. A/520/Rev. 4. Italics supplied. Rule 152 defeats the purpose and raison d'être of Art. 12 of the Statute and its constitutionality is, therefore, open to question.

## 6. Term of Office

### (Articles 13 and 15 of the Statute)

The present Statute provides for a term of nine years, one third of the judges to be elected every three years after an initial transitional period, which has expired. The nine-year term is the same as that of the judges of the Permanent Court. The triennial election is an innovation designed to secure continuity. The Statute has been criticized on both counts. The triennial elections introduced an element of uncertainty in the composition of the Court which is apt to discourage states from submitting cases to the Court. A further adverse effect of this innovation has been that preliminary objections may be decided upon by one bench and the merits by another.[145] Forty-seven judges have served on the Court between 1946 and 1970, including judges elected to fill unexpired terms caused by death. During the roughly comparable period of 1922–1942, thirty-two judges served on the Permanent Court. There has been a significantly larger turnover on the bench of the Court than on that of its predecessor. Since triennial elections multiply the opportunities for political bargains, they are also objectionable on that score.

Various proposals were canvassed by the Institute of International Law, which in 1954 adopted the following resolution:

> With a view to reinforcing the independence of the judges, it is suggested that members of the Court should be elected for fifteen years and should not be re-eligible. In this event, an age-limit should be laid down; it might be fixed at seventy-five years.
>
> Provisions should also be made whereby, contrary to the present text of the Statute, new members of the Court would be elected for terms of fifteen years, subject to the age-limit, irrespective of the terms for which their predecessors held office.
>
> It is not intended to suggest that these new provisions should apply to judges now in office, except in cases of re-election for a new term of office.[146]

The first and obvious consequence implied in this text is the elimination of Article 15 of the Statute, according to which a replacement for a member whose term of office has not expired "shall hold office for the remainder of his predecessor's term." This particular provision has been criticized on the ground "that the relatively short term of office inevitably offered to members elected to fill occasional vacancies may deter qualified persons from agreeing to be candidates."[147] This is certainly a consideration. However, whether qualified persons have indeed been deterred would require an analysis of the facts, all of which may not be in the public domain. The suggested remedy, namely, that members elected at occasional elections should serve a full term of nine years,[148] is not feasible as long as the system of triennial elections remains in force.

[145] See above, at p. 965.
[146] 45 Annuaire at 297 (II, 1954); 49 A.J.I.L. 14 (1955).
[147] I Rosenne, The Law and Practice of the International Court at 191 (1965).
[148] *Ibid.*

It is not clear from the Institute's resolution whether it implies the abolition of the present system of triennial elections or whether it presupposes a return—perhaps after a transitional period—to the old system of electing all 15 members every fifteen years. In any event, the application of the age limit would require occasional elections to replace retiring members either for the balance of their unexpired term or for a full term of fifteen years.

As to the proposal to extend the term of judges to 15 years, abolish re-election and fix an age limit, it was inspired, as were all the proposals of the Institute, by the desire to reduce the political hazards of frequent elections and to ensure the independence of the judges. The first question which comes to mind, is, of course, whether the present system of a nine-year term, re-eligibility and no age limit has, in fact, affected the independence of the judges. Absent any reliable data, any attempt to give an answer would be highly speculative and conceivably harmful to the prestige of the Court. One must confine himself to the general proposition that judges elected for life, as are for instance, the members of the Supreme Court of the United States and of high magistratures in other countries, are generally regarded as more independent than judges for whom considerations of re-election might be a factor.

The Institute may also have been impressed with the thought that the proposed reform could conveniently lead to a system of individual elections.[149] Obviously, such a system would tend to reduce the influence of the manipulations of affinity groups and perhaps focus on the qualifications of the single member to be elected. The reform proposed by the Institute might lead to greater stability in the composition of the Court, and this in turn might promote a greater understanding and spirit of co-operation among the Members. The jurisprudence of the Court might, as a consequence, become more predictable, a factor which, as has already been pointed out, is ever present in the calculations of governments whether to submit a dispute to the Court.[150] For all these reasons the general idea of the proposed reform, if not its exact formulation, deserves close scrutiny. There is no point, obviously, for governments to go on electing a Court to which they are not prepared to submit their disputes.

## 7. Incompatibility of Functions and Disqualification of Members

## (Articles 16, 17, and 24 of the Statute)

The provisions contained in these three articles appear to have worked well in practice. Those in Article 16 regarding incompatibility of current activities or previous functions are self-evident, although there may be room for some doubt whether they have been applied by the Court with precision. In the opinion of Rosenne, Article 17 "may also require a judge to divest himself of financial and other material holdings which could

[149] 45 Annuaire at 424 (II, 1954).
[150] Rosenne, note 147 above, at 189 and 199, note 2.

lead to a conflict of interests."[151] In view of the significance which this matter assumed in the United States recently, there may be some advantage in stating explicitly a principle which can be read into Article 17 only with some difficulty.

The operation of Article 24 and Article 17 (2) "is an internal matter for the Court."[152] On the whole, they have worked smoothly. However, in view of the controversy surrounding the stepping down of Judge Sir Zafrulla Khan in the Second Phase of the *South West Africa* cases, it may be useful to take a fresh look at the subject. In that case, it is widely assumed, his absence proved fatal to the applicant governments.

As it is, it may be argued, Article 24 (2) places a very great burden on the President of the Court in providing that: "If the President considers that for some special reason one of the members of the Court should not sit in a particular case, he shall give him notice accordingly." It is only in case of disagreement between the President and the member that, according to paragraph 3 of Article 24, "the matter shall be settled by the decision of the Court." The procedure envisaged in paragraph 2 is surely more delicate, but that of paragraph 3 is more judicious. One may wonder whether it would not be preferable to sacrifice the delicacy and thus relieve the President of what must be an unwelcome burden and to provide simply that in such matters the Court shall have the power of decision. This could be accomplished by dropping paragraph 2 and by a slight re-wording of paragraph 3. As there is no particular reason why the President alone should have the right to raise the matter, it could also be provided that any member of the Court could initiate the appropriate proceedings.

The Court appointed on May 10, 1967, a committee of three members to study the question of functions which are incompatible with the office of a judge and the "circumstances in which a Member of the Court should refrain from participating in a case." The three members (Sir Gerald Fitzmaurice, M. Gros and Mr. Ammoun) submitted a report, which was adopted on July 3, 1968. "The recommendations approved by the Court relate to the following matters: other forms of peaceful settlement of disputes, scientific activities; public function and occupation of a professional nature; private activities."[153]

It is merely a speculation to suggest that this re-examination of the practice of the Court was brought about in part by the incident which arose in connection with the *South West Africa* cases (Second Phase). Since details of the report are not available, it is impossible to say whether the new rules are designed to prevent future such incidents.

[151] See note 147 above, at 196 and *ibid.*, note 2.

[152] Rosenne, *ibid.*

[153] Report of the I.C.J., Aug. 1, 1967–July 31, 1968, GAOR, 23rd Sess., Supp. No. 17 (A/7217), at 4, and 1967–1968 I.C.J. Yearbook at 91.

## 8. Judges *ad hoc*

## (Article 31 of the Statute)

The institution of judges *ac hoc* in contentious cases and in advisory proceedings under Articles 68 of the Statute and 83 of the Rules of Court has been a matter of controversy between those who would suppress it for the sake of enhancing the impartiality of the Court[154] and those who, for a variety of reasons, would maintain it.[155] There are also those who, occupying a middle ground, assert that the abolition of judges *ad hoc* should be combined with the exclusion of "national" judges from the bench, that is, judges who are nationals of one or both parties before the Court.[156] In this view, the essential objective is equality between the parties; this can be achieved either by adding to the bench a judge *ad hoc* or by excluding the "national" judge. The right of a party to appoint a judge *ad hoc* has also been urged on the ground that it gives practical expression to the maxim *audiatur et altera pars.* This, it has been claimed, has become a general principle of law within the meaning of Article 38, paragraph 1(c) of the Statute, and necessarily entails "the right of a party to be represented in the composition of the Court."[157] On the other hand, the Indian judge *ad hoc* in the *Right of Passage* case expressed himself against this institution.[158]

The Institute of International Law discussed the matter at its sessions in 1952 and 1954. Judge Huber regarded the system of *ad hoc* judges as being "undoubtedly . . . contrary to the conception of a magistrature" and as reflecting the notion of arbitration.[159] Those who seemed resigned to the system, like Castberg, stressed the obvious politico-psychological reasons,[160] or emphasized, like De La Pradelle, that its retention would facilitate recourse to the Court.[161] On the opposing side, Lauterpacht argues that:

> there can be no question, within the Court, of any representation of particular interests. The judges present only the impersonal interest of justice. This means that the question of the nationality of the judges adjudicating any given case must be ignored.[162]

[154] For a recent view see F. L. Grieves, Supranationalism and International Adjudication at 180 (1969).

[155] See Rosenne, note 147 above, at 202–205.

[156] Erik Castrén, "Revision de la Charte des Nations Unies," 7 Revue Hellénique de Droit International 20–34 at 32 (1954).

[157] V. S. Mani, "Audi Alteram Partem: Journey of a Principle from the Realms of Private Procedural Law to the Realms of International Procedural Law," 9 Indian Journal of International Law 381–412 at 400 (1967).

[158] M. A. C. Chagla, "Rule of Law and the International Court of Justice," 1960 Proceedings, Am. Soc. Int. Law 237–242 at 242 (1960): "I think the system of *ad hoc* judges is bad."

[159] 45 Annuaire at 428 f. (I, 1954). This was the view of the Committee of Jurists which drafted the P.C.I.J. Statute. The following passage in Hudson, note 32 above, at 354–355, traces the origin of the institution of judges *ad hoc* to the Hague Peace Conference of 1907, where "the well-known rule that 'no one can be judge in his own suit' has been advanced as a reason for excluding all participation by national judges. This view was strongly urged at the Hague Peace Conference of 1907, but it was not adopted in The Hague *projet* of 1907. It was included, however, in Article 27 of the draft proposed by the Five-Power Conference which met at The Hague in February 1920. The 1920 Committee of Jurists put its decision to permit participation by judges of the nationality of the parties on the ground that this would protect the character of the Court as a World Court, and would avoid 'ruffling national susceptibilities'; it then proceeded to defend the admission of judges *ad hoc* on the ground that this was necessary to 're-establish equality.' The Committee emphasized that 'States attach much importance to having one of their subjects on the bench when they appear at the Court of Justice,' though it admitted the results to be that the Court envisaged 'more nearly resembles a court of arbitration than a national court of justice.' "

[160] 45 Annuaire at 506 (I, 1954).

[161] *Ibid.* at 528.

Fitzmaurice attacked the system on similar grounds, arguing in particular two points: First, those who advocate its retention on the ground that it increases confidence in the Court argue from an impermissible premise that judges, particularly *ad hoc* judges, will necessarily espouse the view of their government. Secondly, once a case is terminated, a judge *ad hoc* may feel himself free of every obligation of confidence and may reveal to his government what had been said in the deliberations of the Court. This could have harmful consequences for the independence of judges, particularly if such relevations occurred shortly before elections to the Court.[163]

The upshot of this review of the reasons for and against the system of *ad hoc* judges was that the Institute confined itself to methods designed to ensure a better selection of such judges. A proposal made in 1952 to allow the Court itself, by analogy to Article 12(3) of the Statute, to select the judge *ad hoc* from the national groups which make the nominations[164] was not adopted. Instead, the following resolution was adopted in 1954:

> If the system of *ad hoc* judges cannot be abandoned, it is as a minimum highly desirable that the appointment of such judges should be subject to guarantees as nearly as possible equivalent to those governing the election of titular judges. The appointment of such judges might, for instance, be entrusted to the national group of the Permanent Court of Arbitration of the State concerned, or to the national group appointed by the Government in pursuance of Article 4, paragraph 2, of the Statute.[165]

This proposal found some favor,[166] but doubt was expressed whether it would have any effect in terms of the independence of the judges *ad hoc.*[167]

The fact of the matter is that in every case where the majority of the Court gave a favorable judgment for the appointing state, the judge *ad hoc* concurred, and he dissented in nearly every case where the judgment went against it. Such voting alignments, even if the *ad hoc* judge is the only dissenting judge, as was the case in the recent *Barcelona Traction* judgment, do not necessarily reflect on the independence of the judge concerned. Even the majority of 14 in that case could be wrong, and, despite concurrence in the result, there was wide disparity in the actual reasoning of the various judges. In the matter of advisory proceedings, there is no experience to be drawn upon so far as the present Court is concerned.[168] This is not surprising, since the Court so thoroughly devalued the rôle and effect of advisory opinions in the *Peace Treaties* case. Since advisory opinions are strictly advisory, are given to the requesting body and not to the states at variance, and

[162] *Ibid.* at 528.

[163] *Ibid.* at 444 f.

[164] 44 Annuaire at 65 (II, 1952).

[165] 45 *ibid* at 298 (II, 1954).

[166] H. J. Schlochauer, "Bemerkungen zur Revision der Charter of the United Nations," 19 Zeitschrift für Ausländisches Öffentliches Recht and Völkerrecht (Festgabe für A. N. Makarov) 416–448 at 446 (1958).

[167] Spiropoulos, note 117 above, at 383.

[168] In the Jurisdiction of Danzig Courts, both *ad hoc* judges appointed by Poland and Danzig joined in the unanimous opinion of the Court. Hudson, note 32 above, at 356.

represent the participation of the Court (itself an "organ" of the United Nations) in the activities of the organization, there is no need for states to appoint judges *ad hoc.*[169]

It has often been observed that where two parties appoint judges *ad hoc,* their votes cancel each other out.[170] In litigation where only one party appoints a judge *ad hoc,* the other party having a national as a titular judge, his vote could make a difference in marginal cases, but there have been no such cases.

The most constructive view on the rôle of judges *ad hoc* has been expressed in two forms. According to one, such judges, while not representing their own countries, "fulfill a useful function in supplying local knowledge and a national point of view."[171] The other sees the task of an *ad hoc* judge not so much in his influence upon the judgment as upon its formulation. It rests with such judges "to represent their countries' interests in the whole process through which the decision is produced and the reasons formulated. If the role of the judges *ad hoc* could be more accurately designated as that of assessors, the grant to them of the status of judge (with the right to vote) represents a concession to diplomatic susceptibilities."[172]

It is recognized on all sides that diplomatic susceptibilities and politico-psychological considerations are involved, and if one takes them seriously, then the system of judges *ad hoc* should be left alone. To the purist it will remain objectionable as a survival of the basic idea of arbitration in the system of international adjudication. It is open to question, however, whether the rest of the argument is still convincing in view of the fact that the practice in the matter of appointing and selecting judges *ad hoc* seems to have undergone a change, a change which might be interpreted as indicating that the states themselves did not or do not attach the significance attributed to the system. In the first place, in three cases no *ad hoc* judges were appointed: *Nottebohm* (Preliminary Objections), *Frontier Land,* and *Temple of Preah Vihear.* In at least the latter two cases there would have been room for "local knowledge and a national point of view." In the second place, in six cases the judges *ad hoc* were not of the nationality of the appointing party, namely: *Corfu Channel, Nottebohm* (Merits), *Aerial Incident, King of Spain, South West Africa,* and *Barcelona Traction.* In these cases the judges *ad hoc* neither supplied "local knowledge and a national point of view" nor represented their "countries' interests" in the process of decision-making. To be sure, in some of these cases the judge *ad hoc* belonged to the affinity group of the appointing state: a Czech judge in the *Corfu* and *Aerial Incident* cases was appointed by Albania and Bulgaria respectively; a Swiss was appointed by Liechtenstein; and first a Pakistani and then a Nigerian were chosen by Ethiopia and

[169] Gross, note 19 above, at 339. The appointment of judges *ad hoc* in advisory proceedings is based on a combination of Art. 83 of the Rules of the Court and Art. 68 of the Statute. By an order of Jan. 29, 1971, the Court, by 10 votes to 5 (Fitzmaurice, Gros, Petrén, Onyeama, Dillard), rejected the application of South Africa for leave to choose a judge *ad hoc* to sit in the proceedings concerning the pending request for an Advisory Opinion in the matter of Namibia (South West Africa). [1971] I.C.J. Rep. 12.

[170] Rosenne, note 147 above, at 203.

[171] Informal Inter-Allied Committee, Report, par. 39; 39 A.J.I.L. Supp 1 at 11 (1945); quoted in Rosenne, cited above, at 203.

[172] *Ibid.* at 204.

Liberia. It would be more difficult to explain on affinity grounds the selection of an Italian by Honduras, a Columbian by Nicaragua (*King of Spain*), or of a Uruguayan by Spain (*Barcelona Traction*).

At best, one can see the judge *ad hoc* acting, as suggested by Rosenne, as a sort of an assessor. In that case there would seem to be no reason why he could not be chosen by the Court. Provision for assessors is made in Article 30(2) of the Statute, although, according to it, they have no right to vote. If diplomatic susceptibilities are involved, assessors chosen by the Court to function as judges *ad hoc* could be given the right to vote. It would be even simpler to propose that judges *ad hoc* be selected by the Court from members of the national nominating group or from persons nominated but not elected, or from a slate of two or three persons submitted by the government concerned. A proposal to abolish the system altogether might be inopportune at a time when the fortunes of the Court are at a low ebb. So too would be the proposal to abolish the system and, at the same time, to drop the "national" judge from the bench. To be sure, if the number of judges were raised to 18, then the argument against such reform—namely, that dropping the "national" judge might make it difficult for the Court to have a quorum—would lose much of its force. But the reform would be a radical one and inopportune at this time.

Perhaps the system of judges *ad hoc* is dying a quiet death anyhow. And if states continue to select qualified persons who are not their nationals as judges *ad hoc* then the main argument against the system, that in some fashion such judges represent "their" governments on the Court, would lose much of its persuasiveness. This would be so even if, as might well be the case, the government has beforehand ascertained the views of the prospective judge *ad hoc*. For all one knows, the national, titular judge of the other party may also entertain a friendly disposition towards his country's case. For these reasons it would be appropriate to note the changes which have already taken place in the form of non-appointment of judges *ad hoc* and the appointment of non-nationals and to encourage states to continue this enlightened practice. A resolution by the General Assembly is suggested as the appropriate method.

## VIII. THE SEAT OF THE COURT
(Article 22 of the Statute)

In 1969 the Court took the initiative under Article 70 of its Statute to propose an amendment to Article 22 which designates The Hague as the seat of the Court. The Court proposed adding to Article 22, paragraph 1, the words "or at such other place as shall at any time be approved by the General Assembly on the recommendation of the Court," and making consequential changes in Article 23(2) and 28. Article 22 was originally by the Committee of Jurists which drafted the Statute of the Permanent Court of International Justice in 1920. It undoubtedly reflects the spirit of the Hague system of 1899 and 1907.

The Court in an explanatory memorandum gave several reasons for its proposal. First, it considered the provision discriminatory inasmuch as "no other principle organ of the United Nations and none of the specialized agencies has its seat specifically designated in its constitutional instrument."[173] Secondly, "the special qualities attached to The Hague in 1922 are less distinctive now, and the importance of other places as legal centres has been enhanced"; and thirdly, "it is an uncontroverted fact that the Peace Palace, while a noble national monument with an historic past, is totally unsuited to the needs of the International Court of Justice."[174] The Court did not advert the delicate question of precedence at ceremonial receptions to which the Court and the diplomatic corps are invited.[175]

There are two aspects to the problem: one, of symbolic significance, is the removal of a provision which the Court considers "invidious," and the other, of practical significance, is to move the Court to another "legal center." With respect to the latter, the Court made it clear that it "is not now recommending that its seat should be established elsewhere than at The Hague," but the Court clearly had this possibility in mind when it said that it should be made possible for the Court "to be established at whatever place, in the course of the years, it may be considered that it could function most harmoniously and effectively."[176] Thus it seems that the symbolic aspect merges with the practical. For obviously, if the Court cannot "function most harmoniously and effectively" at The Hague, it should be moved to the place where it can.

On the other hand, the Netherlands Government has made proposals since 1966 for a new building for the Court. If it were possible to negotiate an agreement with The Netherlands for the erection of a new building at or near The Hague and if the question of precedence could be solved in favor of the Court, there would be no objection to a revision of Article 22(1) of the Statute. Otherwise the clause should be revised, even if there is objection in some quarters. The Court is entitled to a location where it can "function most harmoniously and effectively."

The second sentence in Article 22(1) of the Statute provides that the establishment of the Court at The Hague "shall not prevent the Court from sitting and exercising its function elsewhere whenever the Court considers it desirable." Article 28 contains an analogous provision regarding chambers. The Court did undertake an inspection *in loco* in the *Meuse* case and refused an invitation from South Africa to visit South West Africa, but neither it nor any of its chambers has sat elsewhere than at The Hague. On this matter the Court expressed the view that

[173] Report of the I.C.J. August 1, 1968–July 31, 1969, GAOR, 24th Sess., Supp. No. 5 (A/7605), at 3 and 5. Following the letter from the Minister of Foreign Affairs of The Netherlands of Sept. 15, 1969, the Court accepted the correction that by their constituent instruments of 1952 and 1947 respectively, the Universal Postal Union has its seat fixed at Berne and the International Telecommunications Union at Geneva. The Minister also pointed out that the headquarters of the International Bank for Reconstruction and Development and the International Monetary Fund are to have their seat in the country maintaining the largest financial contribution. GAOR, 24th Sess., Agenda item 93, pp. 3 and 4.

[174] Report, *ibid.*, at 5.

[175] See Leo Gross, "The Time Element in the Contentious Proceedings in the International Court of Justice," 63 A.J.I.L. 74–85 at 84 (1969). See also *supra*, pp. 831–843.

[176] *Ibid.*

> the Court would naturally exercise this option for a particular case when consideration of the convenience of the Parties and of the effective administration of its judicial functions made such a departure from its headquarters desirable.[177]

It would seem that in no case have the parties taken the initiative to propose that the Court sit elsewhere and the Court has seen no advantage, such as hearing of witnesses, for a more effective administration of justice in sitting outside The Hague. What remains then is the "demonstration effect" of the Court sitting in different localities to publicize, as it were, its existence and availability. For this reason, indeed, it has been thought that the Court should seize a suitable occasion and show itself to different segments of the world. Whether the Court could afford to do it within its stringent budget is a different matter. Conceivably the country which invited the Court would be prepared to share in the expenses. Were the Court to function temporarily in New York City or Geneva, it could use the facilities of the United Nations. There is a precedent for cost-sharing in connection with diplomatic conferences convened outside the American or European headquarters of the United Nations.

## IX. INTERNAL JUDICIAL PRACTICE OF THE COURT (Article 30 of the Statute)

The Court has applied since 1946 the amended resolution of 1936 of its predecessor concerning the internal judicial practice of the Court. The resolution is drawn up pursuant to Article 30(1) of the Statute and "it is intended for the use of the Court alone and is concerned with the method by which the Court proceeds in each case to hold its deliberations in private and to prepare its decision."[178] The Court initiated in 1964 a review of the 1936 resolution and on July 5, 1968, approved the text of a new resolution which "is designed to render its deliberations more efficient and more rapid."[179]

The length of the proceedings has been a matter of concern to the Court, governments, and the profession.[180] Some of the delays are substantially due to the parties. The Court is responsible for the time it takes for its private deliberations and the drafting of the judgment. No doubt the work of the Court has been complicated by the large number and remarkable length of separate and dissenting opinions.

The Court closed the oral hearings in the *South West Africa* cases (Second Phase) on November 29, 1965, and delivered judgment on July 18, 1966, some six months and a half later. The Court moved more promptly in the *North Sea Continental Shelf* cases, in which hearings were closed on November 11, 1968, and judgment was delivered on February 20, 1969, some three months later. In the *Barcelona Traction* case (Second Phase),

[177] *Ibid.*

[178] Report of the ICJ., August 1, 1967–July 31, 1968, GAOR, 23rd Sess., Supp. No. 17 (A/7217) at 4.

[179] *Ibid.* The text of the resolution will be found in 1967–1968 I.C.J. Yearbook at 87–91; also in 63 A.J.I.L. 407 (1969).

[180] Leo Gross, note 175 above. See also the observations of the Court in the Barcelona Traction case (Second Phase), [1970] I.C.J. Rep. 30, par. 27, Judge Jessup, P. 221 (Note), and Judge Fitzmaurice, p. 113 (Postscriptum).

hearings were terminated on July 22, 1969, and the judgment delivered on February 5, 1970, about six months later. In this case the Court had no other demands upon its time. The amount of papers submitted to the Court is extremely large, perhaps excessive. In *Barcelona Traction,* the written documents ran to 18–19,000 pages; about 4,000 pages of "new" documents were introduced by the two parties during the oral proceedings.[181] Such mountains of written material and lack of law clerks, research assistants, and even individual typist-secretaries make it very difficult for the Court to work more efficiently and rapidly. And that is about as far as an outsider's opinion can go. However, it may be worth while to note here that some dissatisfaction has been observable at the length and frequency of separate and dissenting opinions and at the difficulty of determining what the majority of votes was on some segments of the operative part of the judgment. These matters are governed by Articles 55, 56 and 57 of the Statute. Whether there is room, as some believe, for remedial action here is a matter of opinion.[182] It is also a matter of opinion whether such action, if it is deemed advisable in the interest of a sound administration of justice, can be or should be taken through revision of the Court's rules for its internal judicial practice or by formal amendment of Articles 55, 56 and 57.

## X. ACCESS TO THE COURT—PART 1
### (Article 34 of the Statute)

The most significant feature in the Statute reflecting the enduring hold of the Hague system over the minds of its draftsmen is probably to be found in paragraph 1 of Article 34: "Only States may be parties in cases before the court." It ignores the change which has occurred with respect to the subjects of international law, notably the recognition of the United Nations and other public inter-governmental organizations and conceivably of individuals as subjects of international law. It reflects the doctrine which was dominant in the 19th century that states and states only were subjects of international law. This doctrine was vigorously attacked in the inter-war period, but the San Francisco Conference ignored both doctrine and practice in maintaining the old text of Article 34(1), although the International Labor Office in 1944 suggested that the jurisdiction of the Court be extended to disputes between two or more public international organizations.[183] In view of the large and growing rôle which such organizations have come to play in international relations, it is time to consider a revision of Article 34(1) and thus free the Statute from the vestiges of the Hague system.

The Institute of International Law in 1954 and the International Law Association in 1956 adopted resolutions to this effect. The Institute resolved that:

[181] *Ibid.* 215, par. 97 of Judge Jessup's opinion.

[182] See President Sir Percy Spender's declaration in the South West Africa cases, [1966] I.C.J. Rep. 6 at 51-57; but *cf.* Jessup, *ibid.* 323–324.

[183] Jenks, note 2 above, at 208 and 217–218.

> It is a matter of urgency to widen the terms of Article 34 of the Statute so as to grant access to the Court to international organizations of States of which at least a majority are Members of the United Nations or Parties to the Statute of the Court.[184]

The Association proposed that Article 34 of the Statute of the international Court of Justice should be amended to give the United Nations and its specialized agencies direct access to the Court in contentious cases.[185]

The qualification in the Institute's resolution seems unnecessary, and in any event there are few international organizations the majority of whose members are not also Members of the United Nations. The Institute's resolution is ambiguous, however, in that it does not clearly refer to the contentious procedure, as the Association's does, and does not mention the United Nations. However, the reference to Article 34 would seem to be sufficient to eliminate the first ambiguity. As to the second, it stands to reason that if international organizations are to have access to the Court, the United Nations, which, as the Court said in the *Reparation* case, "is at present the supreme type of international organization,"[186] should be granted access along with other organizations. Jenks has proposed a simple amendment to Article 34(1) to make it read: "Only States or public international organizations may be parties in cases before the Court."[187]

Even this text could be still further simplified and possibly improved by omitting "only" and substituting "and" for "or" so that it would read: "States and public international organizations may be parties in cases before the Court." A text along these lines would accommodate those who wish international organizations to have access to the Court, but it would not satisfy those who advocate access to the Court to certain individuals such as international civil servants, or those who would like to see the Court able to give authoritative interpretations of international law questions arising before domestic tribunals, by analogy to the "evocation" procedure in the European Court of Justice or the Arbitral Tribunal of Upper Silesia of 1922.[188] In order to provide for a progressive evolution along such contemporary lines, it would be necessary to find a more flexible formulation for Article 34, one which would make "the parties to the original proceedings eligible parties to the proceedings before the Court,"[189] it being understood that the original proceedings were proceedings before domestic courts. Such proceedings may involve states, individuals,[190] or corporations. In order to include cases brought before the Court by reference from a domestic tribunal the text of Article 34(1) would run somewhat along these lines:

[184] 45 Annuaire at 298 (II, 1954); 49 A.J.I.L. 15 (1955).

[185] I.L.A., 47th Report, at viii (1956). This resolution was based on a background memorandum provided by a committee of the American Branch. Proceedings of the American Branch of the I.L.A., 1955–1956, at 70–75.

[186] [1949] I.C.J. Rep. 174, at 179.

[187] Jenks, note 2 above, at 209.

[188] See Jenks, note 2 above, at 165–166. The "evocation" terminology is that of Jenks.

[189] *Ibid.* at 166.

[190] For a strong plea in favor of opening up access to the Court for individuals, see T. Franck, The Structure of Impartiality 220 ff. (1968).

> The Court shall exercise its judicial function with respect to disputes between States, between States and international organizations, and between international organizations *inter se;* the Court shall also be competent to exercise its judicial function with respect to any question of international law brought before it by means of evocation.

It may well be, however, that the evocation procedure could be better accommodated in another article of the Statute, a matter which will be discussed in the following section.[191]

Disputes involving international organizations could come before the Court by means of a special agreement between the organizations concerned or between an organization and a state. There is some support for a consequential amendment in Article 36 of the Court's Statute to enable international organizations to accept the compulsory jurisdiction of the Court. Thus the International Law Association in its resolution of 1954 proposed that

> Article 36 of the Statute should be amended to empower the General Assembly to establish the conditions under which the United Nations, its specialised agencies and other public international organisations might make declarations accepting the jurisdiction of the Court under paragraph 2 of that Article.[192]

This amendment may be further revised to say that, by analogy to Article 93(2) of the Charter and Article 35(2) of the Statute, the General Assembly shall establish the conditions upon a recommendation of the Security Council.[193] However, there may be doubt as to the timeliness of this proposal. It may be argued that if international organizations are to be accepted as full-fledged subjects of the law, they should have also the power to make declarations pursuant to Article 36(2). On the other hand, it may be urged that some caution is needed and that most of the objectives of the proposed reform would be achieved if the organizations had access to the Court on the basis of special agreements or of jurisdictional clauses.

One of the chief reasons for giving organizations access to the Court is to terminate the widespread practice of restricting them to access to the Court through the device of the advisory proceedings. Beginning with the Headquarters Agreement between the United States and the United Nations, a number of agreements came to "embody rather artificial arrangements for giving such proceedings the form of a request for an advisory opinion in order to overcome the difficulty that the United Nations and specialized agencies have no *locus standi in judicio* before the Court."[194] It is these artificialities—proceedings advisory in form but binding in substance—which are to be eliminated by amending Article 34(1) and a subversion of the Court's advisory jurisdiction terminated.

[191] See below, p. 987.
[192] I.L.A., note 185 above, at viii.
[193] Seidl-Hohenveldern, "Der Zugang Internationaler Organisationen zum Internationalen Gerichtshof," 54 Die Friedenswarte 16–28 at 26 (1957/1958).
[194] Jenks, note 2 above, at 212.

Existing instruments providing for such indirect access to the Court could be revised as soon as Article 34(1) is amended. Whether further steps, as proposed by the International Law Association, are needed and desirable may be a matter for later consideration after some experience has been gained in litigations involving states and international organizations.

Another consequential amendment relates to Article 38 of the Statute. Under paragraph 1(a), the Court shall apply conventions "establishing rules expressly recognized by the contesting states." This clause could be amended to read "the contesting parties," but in the opinion of Jenks "such an amendment would not appear to be indispensable."[195] Clearly it is undesirable to take a dogmatic stand on the subject, and perhaps the matter would be better handled in connection with possible changes in Article 38. However, the amendment would have a solid foundation in the fact that states and international organizations are parties to many international instruments and, if appropriate, such instruments should be considered by the Court. On the other hand, one can also argue that the Court could do so in any event, as the disputes likely to arise and to come before the Court would relate to the application or interpretation of specific instruments.

The study group on the International Court of Justice supported the opening of access to the Court to international organizations, but doubts arose as to how such recourse to the Court could be practically handled. Two objections or questions were raised, one relating to the type of cases which could be litigated and the other to the conduct of the litigation. As to the first, it was pointed out that the proposed amendment to Article 34 is concerned merely with removing a procedural barrier against organizations' appearing as parties in contentious proceedings before the Court. The type of cases or the specific case which would be submitted to the Court would depend upon the sort of jurisdictional clause which would be inserted in an agreement between states and international organizations or between international organizations *inter se*,[196] or upon the special agreement between such parties. In case of a consequential revision in Article 36 of the Statute which would make it possible for international organizations to accept the compulsory jurisdiction of the Court, the required declaration would be carefully considered by the competent bodies on which the Member States would be represented. It is most unlikely that such declarations would be made or that they would be made without compelling reasons and careful deliberation.

The second objection is equally irrelevant at this stage, which is concerned with the removal of procedural barriers. It would be for each organization to determine, in accordance with its constitutional instrument and practice, which organ would be competent to initiate litigation or represent the agency in contentious proceedings brought against it before the Court. It could be the chief executive organ of the agency alone or that organ assisted by another organ or by an *ad hoc* organ. There is probably some, but no fundamental difference in this respect between making a request for an advisory opinion and

[195] *Ibid.* at 209, note 68.
[196] Jenks, *ibid.* at 220.

initiating contentious proceedings. The advisory procedure is an established feature of many agreements to which international organizations are parties. Under the relevant clauses only the organization can make a request for an advisory opinion. In the case of the United Nations, such a request would probably be made by the Security Council or the General Assembly. The initiation of contentious proceedings could be regulated in a similar manner. No request for an advisory opinion has even been made under any of the instruments in force, and therefore there is no practice as to who would represent the United Nations in such advisory proceedings. Presumably it would be the chief executive, the Secretary General of the United Nations or the Director General of the specialized agency. It has been pointed out that "there is nothing novel in the executive head of an international organization having to act in this manner; he is in a similar position . . . when instituting or defending legal proceedings (the other party to which may be a public authority of a member) in a municipal Court."[197] He is acting in a similar manner when settling claims against the organization arising, for instance, out of peacekeeping operations, or initiating or defending proceedings before a tribunal of arbitration or defending proceedings before the Administrative Tribunal of the United Nations or similar tribunals of other agencies. It may be readily conceded that problems will arise, but there is no reason to assume that they will be insoluble. According to Jenks:

> Progress in the matter must be made empirically but can be made only when the procedural incapacity of international organizations has been eliminated. Any developments which occur must occur by a process of natural growth, but there can be no such growth while Article 34, paragraph 1 of the Statute remains unchanged.[198]

To revise Article 34(1) and to give to international organizations access to the contentious jurisdiction of the Court is merely to make good a long overdue omission, for as international legal persons they have a right to defend themselves in the judicial forum of the world.

## XI. ACCESS TO THE COURT—PART 2
## (Articles 34(1), 35(1 and 2) and 36(1) of the Statute)

It may be proper to raise the question whether it would be advisable in the process of revising the Statute ro review the clauses which, under the heading "Competence of the Court," deal with access to the Court and its jurisdiction. Perhaps a more rational arrangement and greater clarity could be achieved. There is no room here for a detailed analysis of these several provisions,[199] but some tentative ideas may be offered for consideration.

Thus far, Article 34(1) has been regarded merely from the point of view of the desir-

[197] Jenks, *ibid.* at 221.
[198] *Ibid.*
[199] For this see Rosenne, note 147 above, Chaps. VIII–X.

ability of opening access to international organizations and, possibly, individuals. But the more basic question is whether greater rationality and economy could be achieved by cutting out this remnant of the Hague system altogether. There may be a question about the remaining paragraphs 2 and 3; but if they are deemed worth preserving, even though they have never been applied,[200] a place for them could doubtless be found elsewhere in the Statute. Article 34(1) serves no useful purpose; the Court need not be surrounded by a fence.

The Statute, in a section entitled "Competence of the Court," should affirmatively and simply declare the extent or scope of the Court's competence *ratione personae, materiae,* and *temporis.*

Article 35(1) is concerned with competence *ratione personae:* "The Court shall be open to States parties to the present Statute." This is clear enough, but it does not say which states are parties. This is stated in Article 93 of the Charter. According to paragraph 1 of that article, the parties are all Members of the United Nations; and, according to paragraph 2, states which are not Members may under certain conditions become parties. The Court is, however, also open to states which are neither Members of the United Nations nor parties to the Statute under Article 93(2) of the Charter. This is stated in Article 35(2) of the Statute. One may question the propriety of including the third paragraph of Article 35 in the Statute. It deals with "housekeeping," and its substance could more rationally be included in the conditions laid down by the Security Council pursuant to paragraph 2 of Article 35 or elsewhere in the Statute.

If the proposal is accepted to grant access to international organizations, a clause to this effect should be included in a revised Article 35, as discussed above. It may also be desirable to provide access to individuals and corporations in cases which would come before the Court by evocation or, by analogy to Article 177 of the E.E.C. Treaty, by case-stated procedure. Alternatively, a clause should be included stating that the Court is open to entities or persons other than states on conditions laid down by the General Assembly upon recommendation of the Security Council.

The competence of the Court *ratione materiae* is defined in two separate articles instead of being dealt with comprehensively in one provision. Article 36(1) provides:

> The jurisdiction of the Court comprises all cases which the parties refer to it and all matters specially provided for in the Charter of the United Nations or in treaties and conventions in force.

The competence of the Court *ratione materiae* is also alluded to in Article 38(1):"The Court, whose function is to decide in accordance with international law such disputes as are submitted to it, shall apply. . . ."

The conservatory or transitional provision of Article 37 is also relevant, as it explains the last words of Article 36(1), "treaties and conventions in force." Finally, one

[200] Rosenne, *ibid.* at 287.

may question whether the description of disputes contained in paragraph 2 of Article 36 is only relevant in connection with compulsory jurisdiction or with competence *ratione materiae* in general. The structure and content of this article appear more concerned with the perennial problem of voluntary as against compulsory jurisdiction than with the competence of the Court *ratione materiae.* It is, of course, obvious that if such disputes as are generically listed in Article 36(2) are fit for the compulsory jurisdiction of the Court, they are also fit for its voluntary jurisdiction. It would make for a more economical and rational arrangement if the question of consent to jurisdiction were kept distinct from the matter of material jurisdiction in contentious cases. It would be sufficient to state that, as Article 38(1) says, the competence of the Court comprises disputes submitted to it by the parties or that it comprises disputes concerning any question of international law, as stated in Article 36, paragraph 2 b. The latter formula would seem preferable, as it concerns itself with the subject matter and leaves the question of parties open for whatever changes are acceptable to the international community. Questions of consent could, if necessary, be treated in a separate clause.

The Statute provides no limitation of the competence of the Court *ratione temporis.* Exclusion of disputes *ratione temporis* is a frequent feature of declarations made by states pursuant to Article 36(2) of the Statute, and there is a rich jurisprudence on the subject. However, it would be unwise to introduce any rule into the statute that would prevent the Court from adjudicating a dispute between states, which they would otherwise be willing to submit to the Court, on the ground that it arose before, or related to facts which arose prior to, some arbitrary date. As regards such disputes there is no statute of limitations. The question whether a rule should be written into the Statute limiting the discretion of states in including or excluding disputes *ratione temporis* (Article 36(3)) is a different matter altogether.[201]

## XII. ACCESS TO THE COURT—PART 3
## (Preliminary Decision Procedure)

The discussion of the composition of the Court was based on the assumption that, if the judges were elected in a somewhat different manner, by which high qualifications and independence were ensured, governments would feel more confidence in the Court, refer cases to it more frequently, and thus enable the Court to play a more active rôle in the development of law, in the promotion of stability, and ultimately in the maintenance of peace. It is clearly impossible to predict the outcome of reforms. But one may have some doubt whether such reforms are likely to have great impact on the attitude of states toward the Court.

Similarly, granting to international organizations access to the Court, while long overdue, may not result in a substantial increase in the flow of cases. The attitude of legal

[201] See below, at pp. 993 ff.

advisers, discussed earlier,[202] is not promising, and there is, indeed, no compelling reason why organizations with their own procedures for the settlement of disputes should address themselves to the Court.

It remains to consider a novel approach which, in a manner of speaking, would abandon the pattern of the Hague system and base itself on the pattern of the European Court of Justice.[203] It may be useful to recall the acute observation of Jenks, quoted earlier, that "the jurisdiction and procedures of the European tribunals and those of the International Court represent different epochs in the development of international adjudication."[204] It is no part of the proposal to be submitted that the epoch of the Hague system should be abandoned. Rather, the Court should be adapted to a new age, characterized by an unparalleled increase in transnational relations and in international agreements. What is really needed is an organ which can ensure the authoritative and uniform interpretation of conventions in the domestic forum. Indeed the Court could and should play this rôle, and beyond interpreting conventions in a uniform manner, the Court could also be empowered to give authoritative interpretations on questions of customary international law involved in disputes before domestic tribunals.[205] It should be emphasized that these are two different steps which could be taken, the first being more modest than the second. Whether one step is taken or both, the important objective is to integrate the Court with the mainstream of judicial settlement of international legal problems.

It is perfectly in tune with the spirit of the Hague system to regard the Court as "part of the institutional structure which modern diplomacy may—indeed should—take into account as one of the means to its end. . . ."[206] As such, the decline in the business of the Court would indicate that modern diplomacy prefers other means of achieving its ends. It is suggested that the Court could also play a more vital rôle as part of the judicial machinery available to litigants on the more humble level of municipal tribunals. As long as diplomacy makes no greater demands upon it, there is no reason why the Court should not perform this additional rôle.

Article 177 of the Rome Treaty of March 25, 1957, establishing the European Economic Community, and Article 150 of the Treaty of the same date establishing the European Atomic Energy Community, read as follows:

> The Court of Justice shall be competent to make a preliminary decision concerning:
> (a) the interpretation of this Treaty;
> (b) the validity and interpretation of acts of the institutions of the Community; and

[202] Above, p. 946.

[203] Judge Jessup has drawn attention to a similar proposal advanced by Lauterpacht as early as 1929. Philip C. Jessup, "The International Judicial Process," 52 Judicature 140–145, at 142 (1968).

[204] Note 2 above, at 148.

[205] Reference of questions of customary international law, such as issues of sovereign immunity, is suggested by Jessup, note 203 above, at 145.

[206] Rosenne, note 147 above, at 6. Part One of Rosenne's book is entitled "The Court as Part of the Machinery of Diplomacy."

(c) the interpretation of the statutes of any bodies set up by an act of the Council, where such statutes so provide.

Where any such question is raised before a court or tribunal of one of the Member States, such court or tribunal may, if it considers that its judgment depends on a preliminary decision on this question, request the Court of Justice to give a ruling thereon.

Where any such question is raised in a case pending before a domestic court or tribunal from whose decisions no appeal lies under municipal law, such court or tribunal shall refer the matter to the Court of Justice.[207]

This novel procedure has attracted a great deal of attention among jurists in the European Community and elsewhere. It has some affinity with, or precedent in the English "procedure by case stated" and possibly in the American *certiorari* procedure. However, the distinction between these procedures is more significant than any similarity. Both the case stated and *certiorari* are concerned with moving a question of law from a lower to a higher domestic tribunal. This is not at all the case with the preliminary decision procedure. The question of interpretation is not sent by a lower court to a higher court, for the European Court of Justice is in no sense a court which, in the hierarchy of tribunals, is superior to the domestic courts of the members of the European Community. It is altogether a different court, an international court of the Community whose function it is, as stated in Article 164 of the E.E.C. Treaty and Article 136 of the Euratom Treaty, to "ensure observance of law and justice in the interpretation and application of this Treaty."[208] Uniformity in the interpretation of the treaty is the principal objective of the preliminary decision procedure under Article 177. The application of the treaty, as interpreted by the Court of Justice, is left to the domestic tribunals.

It is therefore extremely important to insist that building this procedure into the Statute of the Court would not in any sense make the International Court superior to the domestic tribunals of the states. It is not at all part of the preliminary decision procedure that the Court would or should become a court of appeal from judgments of domestic tribunals, a feature of the stillborn International Prize Court of 1907. What would be achieved would be the appropriate observance of law in the decision of international issues by domestic tribunals.

There is a good deal of case law on the subject.[209] There are unresolved controversies about the exact application of Article 177, the relevance of the theory of the *"acte claire,"* the scope of inquiry into the facts of the case by the Court of Justice, and related matters. But in the cases in which it has been applied, the procedure has worked well and has contributed to the acceptance of the integrity of the Community law. The Court of

[207] 298 U.N.T.S. 11, 76 (1958); *ibid.* at 167, 215. Art. 177 may well have served as a model for Art. 56 of the U. S. Draft of United Nations Convention on International Seabed Area (Aug. 3, 1970), which reads as follows: "When a case pending before a court or tribunal of one of the Contracting Parties raises a question of the interpretation of this convention or of the validity or interpretation of measures taken by an organ of the Authority, the court or tribunal concerned may request the Tribunal to give its advice thereon." 9 Int. Legal Materials 1046, at 1062 (1970).

[208] 298 U.N.T.S. 11, 73 (1958); *ibid.* at 167, 212. Art. 31 of the earlier European Coal and Steel Community Treaty provides: "The function of the Court is to ensure the rule of law in the interpretation and application of the present Treaty and of its implementing regulations." 261 U.N.T.S. 140, 165 (1957).

[209] Eric Stein and Peter Hay, Law and Institutions in the Atlantic Area 180 (1967).

Justice interprets the abstract question of law submitted to it by the domestic tribunal and the domestic tribunal applies the interpretation to the case before it.

According to Article 20 of the Protocol on the Statute of the Court of Justice of the Community:

> In cases provided for under Article 177 of this Treaty, the decision of the domestic court or tribunal which suspends its proceedings and makes a reference to the Court shall be notified to the Court by the domestic court or tribunal concerned. Such decision shall then be notified by the registrar to the parties in the case, to the Member States and to the Commission, and also to the Council if the act whose validity or interpretation is in dispute originates from the Council.
>
> The parties, the Member States, the Commission and, where appropriate, the Council are entitled to submit to the Court, within a period of two months after the latter notification, memoranda or written comments.[210]

By means of this provision the original parties as well as the interested governments may and, indeed, have participated in the proceedings before the European Court. It is to be emphasized that under Articles 169 and 170 of the E.E.C. Treaty, the Commission and the Member States, respectively, have the right to refer to the European Court Cases alleging violations of a Member's obligations under the treaty. As the European Court declared in the *van Gend en Loos* case:

> The fact that the Treaty, in the aforementioned Articles [169 and 170], allows the Commission and the member-States to bring before the Court a State which has not carried out its obligations, does not imply that individuals may not invoke these obligations, in appropriate cases, before a national court; and likewise, the fact that the Treaty puts at the disposal of the Commission means to ensure respect for the duties imposed on those subject to it does not exclude the possibility of invoking violation of these obligations in litigation between individuals before national courts. . . . Reliance on these Articles would risk being ineffective if it had to be exercised after the enforcement of a national decision which misrepresented the requirements of the Treaty. The vigilance of individuals interested in protecting their rights creates an effective control additional to that entrusted by Articles 169 and 170 to the diligence of the Commission and the member-States.[211]

One of the chief virtues of the preliminary decision procedure is that it is prophylactic in effect; it is designed to prevent a decision by national tribunals which could be regarded as violative of a treaty. The procedure also involves the real persons in interest, the individuals or corporations who are at variance as to their respective rights under a convention. While it does not preclude state-against-state litigation, it normally takes the "adversary" out of adversary proceedings, for no state is required to decide whether or not to cite another state before the bar of international justice. The preliminary decision procedure completely depoliticizes the appeal to the Court. No state appears before the

[210] 298 U.N.T.S. 147, 152 (1958).

[211] N. V. Algemene Transporten Expeditie Onderneming van Gend en Loos *v.* Nederlandse Tariefcommissie, 2 Common Market Law Reports 105, 130 (1963).

Court as applicant or respondent. No state need appear in the procedure at all unless it desires to submit written comments. The preliminary decision procedure has some features of advisory proceedings—such as the absence of parties—and an important feature of the contentious procedure—a binding decision on the proper interpretation of a treaty.

The difficulty national tribunals may face when called upon to interpret a treaty or a principle of international law is that, being national institutions, their impartiality may not be above suspicion. The point need not be labored. Suffice it to recall the divergent judgments of the courts in Aden, Rome and Tokyo in the wake of the purported nationalization of the Anglo-Iranian Oil Company, or the divergent judgments of the courts in Hamburg and Rotterdam on the Indonesian nationalization of Dutch tobacco plantations. The point was put with complete clarity by the Supreme Court of the United States in the *Sabbatino* case. Referring to the respondent's contention "that United States courts could make a significant contribution to the growth of international law, a contribution whose importance, it is said, would be magnified by the relative paucity of decisional law by international bodies," Mr. Justice Harlan declared:

> But given the fluidity of present world conditions, the effectiveness of such a patchwork approach toward the formulation of an acceptable body of law concerning state responsibility for expropriations is, to say the least, highly conjectural. Moreover, it rests upon the sanguine presupposition that the decisions of the courts of the world's major capital exporting country and principal exponent of the free enterprise system would be accepted as disinterested expressions of sound legal principle by those adhering to widely different ideologies.[212]

One may wonder whether the Supreme Court of other tribunals faced with similar problems would not have been glad to refer the question to the International Court of Justice for a preliminary decision. Moreover, the judgment of national tribunals on controversial aspects of international law must not only be impartial but they must also appear to be impartial.

The preliminary decision procedure of Article 177 applies in three situations, of which the first two appear relevant in the present context—the interpretation of treaties and the validity and interpretation of acts of organs of the United Nations or other international institutions. A third category would embrace the interpretation of principles of customary international law. The introduction of the preliminary decision procedure into the Statute of the International Court would probably be least resisted with respect to treaties, whether bilateral or multilateral. Once the Statute is revised so as to admit this procedure, it would be up to states to take advantage of it and include a suitably drafted jurisdictional clause. The question of the validity and interpretation of acts of international organizations might present greater difficulty. One can easily imagine a case before a domestic tribunal involving an embargo upon trade with a given state imposed, say, by the Security Council or the General Assembly. To confer upon the Court competence to

[212] Banco Nacional de Cuba *v.* Sabbatino, 376 U.S. 398, 434–435 (1964); 58 A.J.I.L. 795 (1964).

give a preliminary decision on the validity of such a resolution would be equivalent to instituting a system of judicial review of the constitutionality of acts of organs of the United Nations.[213] Proposals to this effect have been considered but have not garnered much support.

The third category, questions of customary international law, may appear as involving too radical an innovation.[214] On the other hand, it would be the easiest to implement. For once the Court is made competent to give preliminary but binding interpretations on such questions, it could be left to the discretion of each state whether, through national legislation, it desired to empower its tribunals to refer such questions to the Court.[215] States which have shown a predisposition for the development of the rule of law might be among the first to take the necessary initiative. As in connection with giving access to the Court to international organizations, the important first step appears to be to make the necessary changes in the Statute of the Court. Other matters may be worked out as need and experience indicate. Surely a revision along these lines would be most likely to increase the volume of business before the Court. It need hardly be emphasized that it would be strictly legal business and completely in line with the function of the Court as the principal judicial organ of the international community. The Court could establish chambers, if it saw fit, to handle such cases and, if necessary, such chambers could meet at the seat of the national tribunal which referred the question to the International Court. The Statute already provides in Article 26 for the establishment of chambers for dealing with particular categories of cases, for example, labor cases and cases relating to transit and communications. A chamber for dealing with disputes relating to bilateral or multilateral trade agreements might be useful. Questions of the validity or interpretation of acts of international organs and of general international law might be left to the full Court.

A reform along these lines would not involve any curtailment of national sovereignty. Consent of the state or states concerned would be required in any event, and the application of the law would remain in the hands of national tribunals. It is well to remember that the judgment of a national tribunal on a question of international law is not conclusive on other states and may, indeed, be the first step in a diplomatic controversy which may ultimately be submitted to an international tribunal for a decision. The preliminary decision procedure has the virtue of preventing such controversies and of removing from busy foreign offices an often unwelcome burden. In any event, no better guarantee could be offered to litigants before national tribunals that justice will be done in accordance with the highest available standards.

[213] See E. Lauterpacht, "The Legal Effect of Illegal Acts of International Organizations," in Cambridge Essays in International Law; Essays in Honour of Lord McNair 88–102 (1965).

[214] Jenks, note 2 above, at 167.

[215] It may be noted that, if states were authorized to request advisory opinions (see p. 1000 below), this procedure could be used to obtain authoritative interpretations of international law pending before a national tribunal.

## XIII. COMPULSORY JURISDICTION
## (Article 36 (2) of the Statute)

The question of compulsory jurisdiction has already been discussed earlier in this paper. It remains to point out possible ways of strengthening it.

In 1954 Lauterpacht expressed a widely held view that the absence of compulsory jurisdiction "signifies a fundamental defect in the organization of international society" which "should be subject to repeated examination." He proposed, as a first step, to elevate "the compulsory jurisdiction of the Court to the position of a governing principle" and to give " individual states the right to contract out from that principle by a special declaration."[216] That proposal was before the San Francisco Conference, which did not adopt it and gave preference to the old system of contracting-in.[217] If it is true that the chief importance of the system of compulsory jurisdiction is psychological,"[218] then it might be worth while to consider the possibility of introducing the contracting-out principle in place of the contracting-in principle which has now been in force for close to 50 years. The change may not increase decisively the effectiveness of the system of compulsory jurisdiction but its psychological value may be quite substantial. It would also have the beneficial effect of showing to the world at large that the Members of the United Nations attach great significance to the settlement of disputes by the judicial technique. States which, for a variety of reasons, may have hesitated to contract in might be glad to have the decision made for them, and they may be under no pressure to contract out. But even if they did, they would not be likely to contract out completely. It is more likely that the contracting-out would take the form of formulating reservations which, even at their worst, might still leave a residuum of usable compulsory jurisdiction.

The frequent use of reservations of increasingly arbitrary character in declarations accepting the compulsory jurisdiction of the Court has been a matter of serious concern to publicists and governments.[219] The self-judging reservation of domestic jurisdiction has already been discussed, along with the 1959 Resolution of the Institute of International Law.[220] The Institute, besides calling for the withdrawal of this type of reservation, also declared:

> In order to maintain the effectiveness of the engagements undertaken, it is highly desirable that declarations accepting the jurisdiction of the International Court of Justice in virtue of Article 36, paragraph 2, of the Statue of the Court should be valid for a period which, in principle, should not be less than five years. Such declarations should also provide that on

[216] 45 Annuaire 536–537 (II, 1954). In this sense also Schlochauer, note 166 above, at 447.

[217] Rosenne, note 147 above, at 365 f.

[218] Rosenne, *ibid.* at 419. Rosenne goes on to say: "It is an instrument for disseminating among the public and among professional diplomats, the idea that judicial settlement of international disputes is both possible and desirable. It enhances the general prestige and standing of the Court."

[219] Waldock, "The Decline of the Optional Clause," 32 British Year Book of International Law 244–287 (1955–1956).

[220] Above, pp. 949, 950.

> the expiration of each such period they will, unless notice of denunciation is given not less than twelve months before the expiration of the current period, be tacitly renewed for a new period of not less than five years.[221]

It would seem highly desirable if the General Assembly could be induced to consider and eventually adopt a resolution on the subject of reservations *ratione temporis.* Particularly objectionable are reservations which provide that the declaration can be terminated or amended *ratione materiae* by notice to the Secretary General of the United Nations and that such notice should have immediate effect. It is well established that states may make such reservations, but they nonetheless "appear to be inconsistent with the effectiveness of the (Optional) Clause."[222] The Assembly could propose a model clause to states or amend the Statue by including such a model clause in the Statute itself.[223]

Until and unless the inventiveness of states in hedging their declarations is curbed, other states can take, and have taken, defensive measures. Thus the Government of Portugal, almost immediately upon being admitted to membership of the United Nations, deposited on December 19, 1955, a Declaration of the same date, in which it stated: "The present declaration enters into force at the moment it is deposited with the Secretary-General of the United Nations."[224] Portugal promptly instituted proceedings against India in what has come to be known as the *Right of Passage* case, and the Court upheld the validity of the Declaration.[225] The Court did this while admitting

> that during the interval between the date of a notification to the Secretary-General and its receipt by the Parties to the Statute, there may exist some element of uncertainty. However, such uncertainty is inherent in the operation of the system of the Optional Clause . . .[226]

There is no need to be fatalistic about annoying uncertanties. All that is needed is a slight change in Article 36 (4) to provide that declarations shall be deposited with the Registrar of the Court and that in any event they shall not enter into force until a month or so after their deposit.

The defense of the United Kingdom against this form of reservation *ratione temporis* appears in paragraph (iii) of its Declaration of January 1, 1969, whereby disputes are excluded

> where the acceptance of the Court's compulsory jurisdiction on behalf of any other Party was deposited or ratified less than twelve months prior to the filing of the application bringing the dispute before the Court.[227]

[221] 48 Annuaire 382 (II, 1959); 54 A.J.I.L. 135 at 136–137 (1960).

[222] Jenks, note 2 above, at 108. While the term "Optional Clause" is still widely used, it is inappropriate in connection with the present Court and its Statute. Rosenne, note 147 above, at 365, note 6.

[223] C. Derbasch, "La Compétence Ratione Temporis de la Cour Internationale de Justice dans le Système de la Clause Facultative de Juridiction Obligatoire," 64 Revue Générale de Droit International Public 230–259, at 234 (1960).

[224] 1968–1969 I.C.J. Yearbook 66.

[225] Right of Passage case [Preliminary Objections], (1957) I.C.J. Rep. 125, at 141.

[226] *Ibid.* at 143.

[227] 1968–1969 I.C.J. Yearbook at 71.

The point hardly needs to be labored that a uniform regulation of the temporal elements of declarations would be superior to individual solutions.

As regards exclusions *ratione materiae* or *personae*[228] there have been no complaints, although the former have frequently led to arguments before the Court and to preliminary objections to jurisdiction. It is moot whether it is still necessary to exclude disputes relating to matters which are claimed to fall within the domestic jurisdiction of the applicant or respondent states.[229]

The validity of reservations may be challenged by states which have accepted the compulsory jurisdiction of the Court, as was done by Sweden with respect to the afore-cited Declaration of 1955 made by Portugal. It has been said that "theoretically, in the event of a difference arising, the Secretary-General or the State concerned could bring it before the General Assembly."[230] This is certainly possible, but it is open to question whether a political body should be seized of a delicate and essentially legal matter. It may be desirable to consider, in connection with a revision of the Statute, whether the Court itself should not be enabled to rule on the conformity of declarations with its own system of compulsory jurisdiction. The Court could be empowered to do so *ex officio* or at the request of any state which is a party to the system of compulsory jurisdiction.

Article 36 (2) lists four classes of disputes with respect to which compulsory jurisdiction may be accepted. It has been proposed to enlarge the listing to 30 specific subjects with respect to which states would have the option to accept compulsory jurisdiction.[231] This proposal merits consideration, particularly if it is deemed that a particularization of the present list would stimulate a wider acceptance of compulsory jurisdiction. To include a long list in the text of the Statute may not be the best way to accomplish the proposed objective. It may be possible, however, to draw the attention of states to the proposed list. To reconcile this with the present Article 36 (2), it may be necessary to change its wording in such a manner that parties to the Statute would have the option of accepting the compulsory jurisdiction of the Court with respect to "all legal disputes concerning any question of international law." As it is, sub-paragraphs a, c, and d of Article 36 (2)

[228] An example of the latter exclusion is the Declaration of Israel which does not apply to "any dispute between the State of Israel and any other State . . . which does not recognize Israel or which refuses to establish or to maintain normal diplomatic relations with Israel . . ." *Ibid.* at 53. Frequent also are exclusions of disputes between members of the Commonwealth. See Declarations of India, *ibid.* at 52, and the United Kingdom, *ibid.* at 71. For an example of the former exclusion *cf.* the Canadian Declaration of April 7, 1970, par. 2(d), 1969–1970 I.C.J. Yearbook at 55: "disputes arising out of or concerning jurisdiction or rights claimed or exercised by Canada in respect of the conservation, management or exploitation of the living resources of the sea, or in respect of the prevention or control of pollution or contamination of the marine environment in marine area adjacent to the coast of Canada."

[229] Rosenne, note 147 above, at 393–395.

[230] *Ibid.* at 391–392.

[231] L. B. Sohn, "Step-by-Step Acceptance of the Jurisdiction of the I.C.J.," 1964 Proceedings, Am. Soc. Int. Law at 131. For a detailed elaboration of several alternatives along similar lines, see International Law Association, Report of the Fifty-first Conference, Tokyo, pp. 65–96, 79–117, and xiii–xiv, which is the text of the unanimously adopted resolution on this subject.

are in a sense redundant, for they are mere particularizations of sub-paragraph b, which would be preserved in the proposed formulation.

As an alternative to the above proposal or in addition to it, declarations could accept the jurisdiction of the Court with respect to disputes relating to the interpretation and application of specific treaties. States could include such a list in the declaration or in an annex thereto.

## XIV. SOURCES OF LAW
## (Article 38 of the Statute)

The criticism of the Court's conception and application of law relates to its jurisprudence and not to Article 38. To be sure, there are suggestions for re-wording sub-paragraph b of paragraph 1 of Article 38 relating to customary international law, and to include judicial decisions or, at any rate, decisions of international tribunals among the formal sources of law. Insofar as the complaint is concerned with the lack of confidence in the law which the Court has applied, three areas may be distinguished: first, the application of customary international law, second, codifiction of this law, and third, the Court's attitude toward United Nations law.

Taking the second point, codification, first, it has been said that states would have greater confidence in the law which the Court applies if the law were brought up to date and reflected the interest not merely of the states which were dominant in the era of colonialism and imperialism but of the new states as well.[232] No doubt the certainty of the law and its predictability would be enhanced if it were codified and progressively developed to a greater extent than is the case at present. The International Law Commission has achieved remarkable results, but they seem to fall short of the expectation of new states. If any measures can usefully be taken to accelerate progress in this work, they should receive the most serious consideration from the General Assembly and the Commission. However, as long as the Commission is organized as it is and holds only one session annually, it is unreasonable to expect more rapid progress.

Turning to the first point, the concept and application of customary international law, it is well to recall that, when the Permanent Court of International Justice was established, it was expected that it would not merely clear up dubious points but also, in the absence of an international legislature, contribute to the development of the law. It is generally agreed that in some of its judgments—for instance, the *Corfu Channel* and the *Fisheries* cases—the International Court has made significant contributions to the development of the law. The same may be said of some of its advisory opinions, such as those in the *Reparation* and *Reservations* cases. However, there is still a sense of disappointment with the performance of the Court over the years. Nowhere has this been expressed more cogently than in the words of Jenks:

[232] See p. 934 above.

> Taken together these nineteen propositions may appear to verge upon the extreme positivist position that no State is bound by custom in the absence of proof of its own recognition of the alleged custom in deference to an *opinio juris sive necessitatis.* This position involves a frontal challenge to any possibility of the development of international law by means of international adjudication. If this is indeed the logic of these decisions of the International Court we are confronted with the most tragic paradox in the development of international law and international institutions. A court which holds that international law permits whatever it does not specifically prohibit, which will not presume that consent to a rule in the absence of proof of a sense of legal obligation, which accepts dissent from or repudiation of a custom as proof that it is inapplicable, which regards a divergence of views in a political assembly as evidence that there is no generally accepted rule of law, and which views with reserve as constituent elements of custom treaty obligations, the practice of international organisations, municipal judicial decisions and the views of publicists, thereby debars itself from playing a constructive part in the progressive crystallisation of custom into law. . . .[233]

It must not be overlooked, however, that consent to the law is still a crucial requirement, and while it may appeal to a progressive audience to urge the Court to abandon the "sovereign state" oriented approach in favor of a "community" oriented approach, the time has not yet come for so radical a reorientation. There is a real dilemma here: If the Court should indulge in judicial lawmaking and should make light of the consent of states to the law, it might abruptly find itself in the position of a leader without a following.[234] In a typical situation, one state before the Court may seek security through existing law while its opponent may seek satisfaction through a change in the law. It is not easy for the Court to find a solution which will seem solidly based in existing law and yet be innovative at the same time. We are here, to some extent, in an area of subjectivities.

In any event, a change for the better is not likely to come from a revision of Article 38 of the Statute. If a better mix of law and international public policy is desired than is found in the jurisprudence of the Court, such a change can come only from the Court. And this brings us back to the question which has already been aired at length, namely, the question of the composition of the Court.

The attitude of the Court to United Nations law brings us back to what has already been said about codification, progressive development, and customary international law. Typically, changes in the law are the result of treaties, but such changes, barring exceptions, are slow. Therefore, the possibility of achieving progressive development of the law through resolutions and declarations of the United Nations seems enormously attractive to states and academic circles. It is unnecessary to review here the arguments *pro* and *con* on the attribution of legislative competence to the General Assembly or the Security Council and the legal force of their resolutions.[235] The question was extensively analyzed

[233] Jenks, note 2 above, at 237 f.

[234] Gross, "The International Court of Justice and the United Nationa," note 19 above, at 370 and 430. See also p. 946 above.

[235] Gross, *ibid.* at 374 ff., and see Rosalyn Higgins, "The United Nations and Lawmaking: The Political Organs," 64 A.J.I.L. (Proceedings, Am. Soc. Int. Law) at 37–48 (1970).

in the Dissenting Opinions of Judge Jessup and Judge Tanaka in the *South West Africa* cases (Second Phase).[236] It is a pity that the Court did not give an authoritative pronouncement on the subject. The Court, in a different composition, may see fit, and indeed may have to come to grips with the question in connection with the pending request of the Security Council for an advisory opinion on the question: "What are the legal consequences for States of the continued presence of South Africa in Namibia (South West Africa), notwithstanding Security Council resolution 276 (1970)?"[237]

In view of this it may seem advisable to postpone consideration of the matter. On the other hand, one could consider possible ways in which Article 38 could be amended so as to include "United Nations Law." Two possibilities seem to be open: One would be to include it among the formal sources of law: the other would be to include a reference to United Nations law in sub-paragraph d of paragraph 1 of Article 38. In the latter case, the Court would be called upon to consider resolutions and declarations of the General Assembly and Security Council (and conceivably equivalent acts of specialized agencies, regional organizations, etc.) "as subsidiary means for the determination of rules of law."[238] It would be well to place these words ahead of judicial decisions and publicists. A revision along these lines would express the conviction, which may well be universal, that resolutions and declarations of the Assembly and Council play a significant rôle in the development of the law.

The first alternative would require a paragraph directing the Court to apply "lawmaking resolutions and declarations of the General Assembly and the Security Council" and equivalent acts of other international agencies. Whether a particular resolution or declaration is indeed "lawmaking" would be decided as are all questions of law and fact, by the Court on the basis of the written and oral pleadings of the parties to a dispute. Obviously not all resolutions and declarations are lawmaking in intent or character. Nothing might be lost if the qualification "lawmaking" were omitted from the proposed text, at least so long as the opening paragraph in Article 38(1) provides that the Court's function is "to decide in accordance with international law such disputes as are submitted to it." It may be argued that this is inherent in the Court's adjudicative function.

Finally, reference may be made to the view that the distinction in Article 38(1) between binding and non-binding sources of law "was becoming increasingly irrelevant and unrealistic."[239] This may be so, and in any event the distinction, if it has been made, may be not so much irrelevant as incorrect. A more tenable distinction may be made between sources of law and evidence of law, and between sources of law and sources of obligation. It would be beyond the scope of this paper to examine the latter distinction. As to

[236] For Judge Tanaka's view *cf.* [1966] I.C.J. Rep. 6, at 291–294; and Judge Jessup's views, *ibid.* at 432–433, 441. See also Gross, *loc. cit.* above, at 380 ff. See also *supra.*

[237] 1969–1970 I.C.J. Yearbook at 5.

[238] This has been proposed by the writer in "The United Nations and the Role of Law," 19 International Organization 537–561, at 557 (1965). See also *supra.*

[239] Oliver J. Lissitzyn, in R. N. Swift (ed.), Annual Review of United Nations Affairs, 1963–1964, at 127 (1965).

the former, it would appear that it is the distinction which is actually made in Article 38(1), sub-paragraphs a (treaties), b (customary international law) and c (general principles of law) being statements of the sources of law, and sub-paragraph d being a statement of the evidence of the law.

A discussion of the general principles of law in the jurisprudence of the Court must be omitted for lack of space.[240] If the Court is to be called upon to make more frequent use of general principles, the judges can accomplish this on their own, and no statement in Article 38 is needed. The composition of the Court and the kind of cases which the Court may have occasion to adjudicate in the future will be the determinants.

## XV. ADVISORY PROCEEDINGS

### (Article 96 of the Charter and Articles 65–68 of the Statute)

The Charter confers authority upon the General Assembly and the Security Council to request advisory opinions on any legal question (Article 96 (1)). Furthermore, the Charter empowers the Assembly to confer authority upon other organs of the United Nations and specialized agencies to request opinions "on legal questions arising within the scope of their activities" (Article 96 (2)). Six organs of the United Nations (including the Assembly and Council) and 13 agencies (including the International Atomic Energy Agency)—a total of 19 organs and agencies—are at present authorized to request opinions. However, only twelve requests have been made and one, the first to be made by the Security Council, is pending. It is not necessary to review once again the reasons for this conspicuous non-use of the advisory function of the Court.[241]

One proposal for widening access to the advisory jurisdiction of the Court, made by the International Law Association in 1956, would amend Article 96 of the Charter in order "to empower the General Assembly to authorize public international organizations, whether general or regional, to request advisory opinions of the Court."[242] It has also been proposed to extend this faculty to organizations and organs which are not wholly composed of states or representatives of states.[243] Both proposals would require only an amendment of Article 96 (2) of the Charter, as Article 65 of the Statute is broad enough to enable the Court to receive requests "of whatever body may be authorized . . . in accordance with the Charter of the United Nations to make such a request." The informal study group on the International Court of Justice expressed itself in 1963 as being in favor of conferring the necessary authority on public international organizations, including regional organizations.

The International Law Association in 1956 also proposed that

[240] See p. 997 above.

[241] See Alexy, "Die Inanspruchnahme des IGH durch die Organe der Vereinten Nationen," 21 Zeitschrift für Ausländisches Öffentliches Recht und Völkerrecht 473–510 (1961); Pierre L. Zollikofer, Les Relations Prévues entre les Institutions Spécialisées des Nations Unies et la Cour Internationale de Justice at 72–75 (1955).

[242] Report, at viii (1956). See also p. 955 above.

[243] K. Herndle in 3 Strupp-Schlochauer, Wörterbuch des Völkerrechts at 34 (1962).

> Article 96 of the Charter should be amended so as to impose upon the organs of the United Nations the obligation to request from the International Court of Justice and [*sic!*] advisory opinion concerning any situation in which the claim is made by a member that the organ had exceeded its jurisdiction under the Charter.[244]

This attempt to make a Member "put up or shut up" is not likely to achieve its object, even if the Charter were amended. No request could be made without the necessary majority, and there is no way to compel the majority of Members to vote in favor of a request.

The informal study group on the Court considered the possibility of making the advisory procedure available to states.[245] There would be some advantage in this innovation, which would require amendments of both the Charter and the Statute. As long as states consider being brought before the Court as an unfriendly act, a request for an advisory opinion made jointly or even unilaterally under a sort of compulsory advisory jurisdictional clause in a treaty might seem a more acceptable way of settling a dispute than the adversary procedure in a contentious case. It could be left open to states, and indeed states could be urged to agree to consider the opinion given by the Court as binding. Such an agreement "to abide by the result of advisory proceedings is valid."[246] Consequential changes will have to be made in the Statute. It would be a matter for further reflection whether advisory opinions accepted in advance as binding by the states concerned should be placed under the authority of the Security Council pursuant to Article 94 (2) of the Charter. The obvious argument against this notion is that it would deprive the suggested innovation of its flexibility and reintroduce the element of coercion inherent in contentious proceedings and in the ensuing judgment, which many states regard as unacceptable. On the other hand, the dignity and authority of the Court must be safeguarded; and unless this is done, the Court may decline, on the ground of judicial propriety, to give the requested opinion.

The desired objective could be achieved in a more informal way, and without any amendment of either Charter or Statute, if the General Assembly could be persuaded to act as a channel for states which desire the assistance of the Court. In the dispute between the United Kingdom and France over the latter's nationality decrees in Tunisia and Morocco, the League of Nations in substance channeled the dispute to the Court in the form of a request for an advisory opinion, and the opinion given by the Court enabled the two

[244] Note 242 above.

[245] In this connection attention may be drawn to Art. 64 of the American Convention on Human Rights which reads as follows:

"1. The Member States of the Organization may consult the [Inter-American] Court [of Human Rights] regarding the interpretation of this Convention or of other treaties concerning the protection of human rights in the American states. Within their spheres of competence, the organs listed in Chapter X of the Charter of the Organization of American States, as amended by the Protocol of Buenos Aires, may in like manner consult the Court.

"2. The Court, at the request of a member State of the Organization, may provide that state with opinions regarding the compatibility of any of its domestic laws with the aforesaid international instruments." See note 78 above, p. 952.

[246] Jenks, note 2 above, at 141.

governments to reach an agreement. There is no reason why the General Assembly should not be willing to assist states at variance in a similar fashion. It may be desirable for the Assembly to delegate this task to a subsidiary organ by analogy to the existing Committee on Applications for Review of Administrative Tribunal Judgments, and to confer upon such a subsidiary body the authority to request an advisory opinion. In fact, though not in form, this body would act on behalf of the states at variance.[247]

A further step along these lines might involve an amendment of Article 36 (3) of the Charter. This clause has been used only once, in the *Corfu Channel* case. The political organs of the United Nations might be enabled to recommend to the parties to refer the dispute to the Court for an advisory opinion through the channel outlined above. It is conceivable that the political organs might feel more at ease in recommending such a procedure and consequently make more frequent use of it than they have of the existing Article 36 (3). It may be better attuned to the sensitivities of states, both old and new.

Finally, for the sake of assuring equality of the "parties" and a sound administration of justice, it seems desirable to open access to the Court to individuals whose interests are involved in a request for an advisory opinion. The starting point for this is the *Complaints against UNESCO* case. It will be recalled that the officials concerned could not address written statements directly to the Court, and the Court dispensed with oral hearings because it could not permit the officials or their counsel to participate in them. The Court, in that case, was satisfied that the principle of equality of the parties which follows from the requirements of good administration of justice "has not been impaired."[248] This is so, but all the same the procedure was a truncated one. It has been suggested that it may be "feasible to hear both sides as witnesses only," or the Court may hear, on the basis of Article 66 (2) of its Statute, the Federation of International Civil Servants' Associations.[249] These are palliatives at best. Moreover, the first alternative may be resented by the international organization on the ground that it is reduced to the status of a witness, and the latter might be unacceptable to the Court on the ground that the "international organization" referred to in Article 66 (2) clearly means the sort of international organization which normally appears in advisory proceedings.

If this is so, the Statute should be amended to enable the organization and its officials to participate in both the written and oral phases of the advisory procedure on a footing of complete equality. They enjoy equality before the Administrative Tribunal, and they should continue to do so before the Court, when it acts, in substance though not in form, as a court of appeal from the Administrative Tribunal. Officials still remain at a disadvantage because only the organization or, in the case of the United Nations, only the Committee on Applications for Review of Administrative Tribunal Judgments is competent to make the request to the Court for an advisory opinion.

Finally, the question may be raised whether arbitral tribunals or permanent interna-

[247] See p. 955 above.
[248] [1956] I.C.J. Rep. at 86.
[249] Jenks, note 2 above, at 144.

tional tribunals established pursuant to treaties should have access to the Court in advisory proceedings. In this connection Article 46 of the "United States Draft of United Nations Convention on the International Seabed Area" of August 3, 1970, is pertinent. Paragraph 1 of Article 46 defines the jurisdiction of the tribunal to be established pursuant to this Draft and declares that "in its decisions and advisory opinions the Tribunal shall also apply relevant principles of international law." Paragraph 2 of Article 46 reads as follows:

> Subject to an authorization under Article 96 of the Charter of the United Nations, the Tribunal may request the International Court of Justice to give an advisory opinion on any question of international law.[250]

Presumably this proposal assumes that the General Assembly will be inclined to interpret broadly its power under Article 96 (2), as it has done in authorizing the International Atomic Energy Agency to request advisory opinions of the Court. As there is room for doubt as to the propriety of such an interpretation,[251] it may be preferable to consider an amendment to Article 96 (2) of the Charter so as to enable the Assembly to authorize intergovernmental organizations, international public corporations, states, international officials, and international tribunals to request advisory opinions.

In the case of a tribunal of arbitration, it is obvious that the states concerned would have to include in the special agreement the authorization for the tribunal to request an advisory opinion of the Court. In this case, as well as in the case of a permanent tribunal as envisioned in the Draft Seabed Convention, the autonomy of the States would be fully safeguarded. What needs to be done is to open the advisory jurisdiction of the Court to judicial organs, be they permanent or *ad hoc,* truly international or regional.

[250] 9 Int. Legal Materials 1046, at 1060 (1970).
[251] See pp. 955–956, 1001 above.

## ANNEX 1
Judges Elected to the International Court of Justice

| Year | G.A. Session | Afro-Asian | Commonwealth | Latin American | Eastern European | Western European | Others |
|---|---|---|---|---|---|---|---|
| 1946 | I | Abdul Hamid Badawi* (Egypt) | Arnold McNair (U.K.)<br>John Read (Canada) | Jose G. Guerrero (El Salvador)<br>J. P. de Barros Azevedo (Brazil)<br>Alejandro Alvarez (Chile)<br>Fabela Alfaro** (Mexico) | Sergei Krylov** (USSR)<br>Bohdan Winiarski* (Poland)<br>Milovan Zoricic* (Yugoslavia) | Jules Basdevant (France)<br>Charles de Visscher** (Belgium)<br>Helge Klaestad** (Norway) | Green H. Hackworth** (U.S.)<br>Hsu Mo* (China) |
| 1948 | III | Abdul Hamid Badawi (Egypt) | John Read (Canada) | | Bohdan Winiarski (Poland)<br>Milovan Zoricic (Yugoslavia) | | Hsu Mo (China) |
| 1951 | VI | Benegal R. Rau (India) [C] | | Levi F. Carneiro*** (Brazil)<br>E. C. Armond-Ugon (Uruguay) | Sergei A. Golunsky (USSR) | Helge Klaestad (Norway) | Green H. Hackworth (U.S.) |
| 1953 | VIII | | | | Feodor I. Kojevnikov*** (USSR) | | |
| 1954 | IX | M. Zafrulla Khan*** [C] (Pakistan) | Hersch Lauterpacht (U.K.) | Jose G. Guerrero (El Salvador)<br>Roberto Cordova (Mexico)<br>Lucio M. M. Quintana (Argentina) | | Jules Basdevant (France) | |
| 1956 | XI | | | | | | V. K. Wellington Koo*** (China) |
| 1957 | XII | Abdel Hamid Badawi (Egypt) | Percy Spender (Australia) | | Bohdan Winiarski (Poland) | Jean Spiropoulos (Greece) | V. K. Wellington Koo (China) |
| 1959 | XIV | | | Ricardo J. Alfaro*** (Panama) | | | |
| 1960 | XV | Kotaro Tanaka (Japan) | Sir Gerald Fitzmaurice (U.K.)*** | Jose Luis Bustamente y Rivero (Peru) | Vladimir M. Koretsky (USSR) | Gaetano Morelli (Italy) | Philip C. Jessup (U.S.) |
| 1963 | XVIII | Muhammed Zafrullah Khan (Pakistan)<br>Isaac Forster (Senegal) | Sir Gerald Fitzmaurice (U.K.) | Luis Padilla Nervo (Mexico) | | André Gros (France) | |
| 1965 | XX | Fouad Ammoun*** (Lebanon) | | | | | |
| 1966 | XXI | Fouad Ammoun (Lebanon)<br>Cesar Benqzon (Philippines)<br>Charles I. Onyeama (Nigeria) | | | Manfred Lachs (Poland) | Sture Petrén (Sweden) | |
| 1969 | XXIV | Louis Ignacio-Pinto (Dahomey) | | Eduardo Jiménez de Aréchaga (Uruguay) | Platon D. Morozov (USSR) | Federico de Castro (Spain) | Hardy C. Dillard (U.S.) |

* Elected for 3-year term;
** Elected for 6-year term;
*** Elected to fill an unexpired term.
[C] Also Commonwealth country.

ANNEX 2
Qualifications of Judges

| | President, Prime Min., Sec. of Foreign Aff., or Cabinet Member in own Country | Solicitor, Legal Advisor, or Ambassador | Judge in High Court in own Country | United Nations Delegation | President of General Assembly | Attended UNCIO (San Francisco) 1945 | Washington Conference of Jurists 1945 | Member, Permanent Court of Arbitration | Judge of Permanent Ct. of International Justice | Member, International Law Commission | Professor of International Law in own Country |
|---|---|---|---|---|---|---|---|---|---|---|---|
| *Judge* | *1* | *2* | *3* | *4* | *5* | *6* | *7* | *8* | *9* | *10* | *11* |
| Guerrero (El Sal.) | X | | | | | | | X | X | | |
| Basdevant (France) | | X | | | | X | X | X | X | | X |
| Alvarez (Chile) | | | | | | | | X | | | X |
| McNair (U.K.) | | X | | | | | | X | | | X |
| Hackworth (U.S.) | | X | | | | X | X | X | | | |
| Winiarski (Poland) | | X | | | | | | | | | X |
| Zoricic (Yugo.) | | X | X | X | | | | X | | | |
| Klaestad (Norway) | | X | ·X | | | | | X | | | |
| Badawi (Egypt) | X | X | | X | | X | | | | | X |
| Read (Canada) | | X | | X | | | X | | | | X |
| Hsu Mo (China) | | X | X | X | | X | X | | | | X |
| de Visscher (Belgium) | | X | | | | X | X | X | X | | X |
| Krylov (U.S.S.R.) | | X | | X | | X | X | | | X | X |
| Azevedo (Brazil) | | X | X | | | | | | | | X |
| Fabela (Mexico) | X | X | | | | | | X | | | X |
| Carneiro (Brazil) | | X | | | | | | X | | | X |
| Armond-Ugon (Uruguay) | | | X | X | | | | | | | X |
| Rau (India) | | X | X | X | | | | | | X | |
| Golunsky (U.S.S.R.) | | X | | | | X | X | | | | X |
| Kojevnikov (U.S.S.R.) | | X | | | | | | | | X | X |
| Khan (Pakistan) | X | X | | X | X | | | | | | |
| Koo (China) | X | X | | X | | X | X | X | | | |
| Lauterpacht (U.K.) | | X | | | | | | X | | X | X |
| Quintana (Argentina) | | X | X | X | | | | X | | | X |
| Cordova (Mexico) | | X | | X | | X | X | | | X | |
| Spender (Australia) | X | X | | X | | | | | | | |
| Spiropoulos (Greece) | | X | | X | | X | X | X | | X | X |
| Alfaro (Panama) | X | X | | X | | X | | | | X | X |
| Fitzmaurice (U.K.) | | X | | X | | X | X | | | X | |
| Koretsky (U.S.S.R.) | | X | | X | | | | | | X | X |
| Tanaka (Japan) | | X | X | | | | | | | | X |
| Bustamante y Rivero (Peru) | X | | | | | | | | | | X |
| Jessup (U.S.) | | X | | X | | X | X | | | | X |
| Morelli (Italy) | | X | | | | | | X | | | X |
| Forster (Senegal) | | X | X | | | | | | | | |
| Nervo (Mexico) | X | | | X | X | X | | | | X | |
| Gros (France) | | X | | X | | | | X | | X | X |
| Ammoun (Lebanon) | X | X | X | X | | | | | | | |
| Benqzon (Philippines) | | | X | | | | | | | | X |

ANNEX 2—*(Continued)*

| | President, Prime Min., Sec. of Foreign Aff., or Cabinet Member in own Country | Solicitor, Legal Advisor, or Ambassador | Judge in High Court in own Country | United Nations Delegation | President of General Assembly | Attended UNCIO (San Francisco) 1945 | Washington Conference of Jurists 1945 | Member, Permanent Court of Arbitration | Judge of Permanent Ct. of International Justice | Member, International Law Commission | Professor of International Law in own Country |
|---|---|---|---|---|---|---|---|---|---|---|---|
| *Judge* | *1* | *2* | *3* | *4* | *5* | *6* | *7* | *8* | *9* | *10* | *11* |
| Oneyeama (Nigeria) | | | X | | | | | | | | |
| Lachs (Poland) | | X | | X | | | | X | | X | X |
| Petrén (Sweden) | | X | X | X | | | | X | | | X |
| Ignacio-Pinto (Dahomey) | X | X | X | X | | | | | | X | |
| Jimenez de Arechaga (Uruguay) | X | | | X | | | | | | X | X |
| Morozov (U.S.S.R) | | X | | X | | | | | | | |
| de Castro (Spain) | | X | | X | | | | X | | | X |
| Dillard (U.S.) | | | | | | | | | | | X |

The foregoing charts are reproduced, with permission, from Norman J. Padelford, "The Composition of the International Court of Justice," in Karl W. Deutsch and Stanley Hoffmann (eds.), The Relevance of International Law 232–234 (1968). They have been brought up to date by Harold Payson III of The Fletcher School of Law and Diplomacy.

# WHAT FUTURE FOR THE INTERNATIONAL COURT OF JUSTICE

## A COMMENT

I would like to remind you all of one fact which relates to the present composition of the International Court of Justice. The present composition of the Court, geographically speaking, is exactly the same as that of the Security Council of the United Nations. Whether that should be a factor which would encourage states to have confidence in the Court, or whether it would work in the opposite direction we shall find out in the next few years.

Our main speaker, Judge Jessup, and the commentators were right in stressing the flexibilities which are built into the Statute and which have not been sufficiently explored: the chambers, assessors, experts, commissions of inquiry and so on. They have all been there for fifty years and they have not been used or not been used very frequently. Therefore, I find that the Statute does need revision. I would like to suggest how it may be changed. We have to think in terms of removing some of the rigidities which are inherent in the present Statue. Unless we begin to think in terms of some rather drastic reform, the outlook for the Court is very dim.

I would like to make three suggestions. One relates to the advisory jurisdiction of the Court. In reference to the advisory jurisdiction I would suggest the possibility of amending the relevant articles of the Charter and the Statute to make it possible for states to include in a treaty a new form of jurisdictional clause whereby the states would agree that any one of the contracting parties could ask the Court for an advisory opinion on any question relating to the application or interpretation of that treaty. It might also be useful to consider the possibility of including in such a jurisdictional clause a provision which would make it possible for the states to agree in advance to accept the advisory opinion of the Court as binding.

My second proposal is for another type of jurisdictional clause which might be included in treaties or conventions which provide for a procedure of conciliation as the Vienna Convention on the Law of Treaties does. The new feature for such a commission would be to include a clause whereby the contracting states could agree that the conciliation commission may ask the International Court of Justice for an advisory opinion on the legal aspects of the issues pending before the commission. As you know, conciliation commissions are not necessarily bound to base their proposals on the applicable law. It might be helpful for some states to have the possibility to use the essential function of the commission and yet to make sure that law will get due attention. It seems that a useful way to achieve this would be to enable such commissions at the request of one party or both parties to ask the International Court of Justice for an advisory opinion on such related or underlying legal issues.

The third suggestion which I would like to put before you relates to a jurisdictional clause that states may include a treaty whereby they would agree to allow their domestic tribunals to refer questions of international law to the International Court of Justice for preliminary binding decisions on the interpretation of the law. It is not a question of delegating any jurisdiction to the International Court as to the application of the law. My suggestion merely follows in the footsteps of Article 177 of the Rome Treaty which established the European Economic Community and which provides for this type of procedure.

Governments should have a choice between the traditional jurisdictional clause whereby they agree to confer compulsory jurisdiction on the International Court. In addition to such a traditional clause they might include one or two or all three of the new clauses which I have suggested to you. I am very much impressed with the sentiment which has been expressed in the United Nations time and time again, and that is that governments are very much attached to the idea of freedom of choice. My proposals are based exactly on this notion of freedom of choice. Those states which want to include such jurisdictional clauses should have the facility to do so. No one would be bound to accept such clauses. No one is bound to accept the traditional clause. What I am proposing is merely to broaden the choice of procedures that could be used by governments which are so disposed. In order for states to have this greater freedom of choice it would be necessary to change one or two clauses in the Charter and Statute. This is not a superhuman task. It does not require states to do anything more than to open the way to the Court to those states which are willing to go to the Court.

# REVIEW OF THE RÔLE OF THE INTERNATIONAL COURT OF JUSTICE

The stagnation in the functioning of the International Court of Justice[1] is only one of several indicators of the neglect by Members of the United Nations of the development and modernization of adjective law. There has been gratifying progress in the codification and progressive development of substantive law through the International Law Commission and other bodies, but substantive law without an adequate adjective law is bound to lack in effectiveness and uniform and predictable application.

With a view to promoting a more balanced evolution of those interdependent branches of the law, the United States and eleven other Members[2] took the important initiative of requesting the inclusion in the agenda of the Twenty-Fifth Session of the General Assembly of an item entitled: "Review of the Rôle of the International Court of Justice." In an explanatory Memorandum they stated:

> A review of the role of the International Court of Justice, the principal judicial organ of the United Nations is urgently needed. The lack of business currently before the Court is evidence of this fact. This situation is not commensurate with either the distinction of the judges or the needs of the international community. A study should be undertaken, therefore, of the obstacles to the satisfactory functioning of the International Court of Justice, and ways and means of removing them. Such a study should also include an exploration

[1] There are two cases pending before the Court, namely: Appeal Relating to the Jurisdiction of the ICAO Council (India *v.* Pakistan), see I.C.J. Communiqué No. 71/12, Sept. 16, 1971. For background of the case instituted by India on Aug. 30, 1971, see *ibid.*, No. 71/11, Sept. 1, 1971. On April 14, 1972, the United Kingdom instituted proceedings against Iceland relating to the latter's decision to extend as of September, 1972, the exclusive fishing limits to a distance of fifty miles. I.C.J. Communiqué No. 72/2, April 14, 1972.

[2] To wit: Argentina, Canada, Finland, Italy, Japan, Liberia, Mexico, Uruguay, Australia, Ivory Coast, the United Kingdom. Doc. A/8042, Aug. 14, 1970, and Add. 1 and 2.

of additional possibilities for the use of the Court that have not yet been adequately explored.[3]

Anticipating a point that has been made quite frequently in the ensuing debates, namely, that the Court has been engaged since 1967 in the revision of its Rules, and that, consequently, it would be inappropriate for the Members or the Assembly to encroach upon the prerogative of the Court, the sponsoring Members declared that "an appropriate study with a veiw to enhancing the effectiveness of the Court would complement the revision that the judges are undertaking of its rules." And they proposed the establishment of an *ad hoc* committee to undertake the study.[4]

The item was duly placed on the Agenda of the Assembly and debated in the Sixth Committee at its 1210th to 1218th and 1224th to 1230th meetings, held from October 29 to November 5, and from November 12 to November 18, 1970. An analytical survey of the different points of view will be found in the Report of the Sixth Committee on the item by its Rapporteur, Hisashi Owanda (Japan).[5] The Committee, after informal consultation, reached the consensus agreement to recommend to the Assembly the adoption of a draft resolution submitted by a group of Members of which the original twelve formed the nucleus. The recommendation was adopted "by acclamation" and the Committee decided to include in its Report to the Assembly the statement:

It has been possible for the Sixth Committee to adopt a consensus draft resolution on the International Court of Justice on the understanding that this draft resolution is without prejudice to whatever action may be taken in 1971.[6]

The Assembly took note of the Committee's statement and unanimously adopted on December 15, 1970, Resolution 2723(XXV), incorporating the committee's recommendation. The Assembly, "considering the desirability of finding ways and means of enhancing the effectiveness of the Court," proposed several steps "bearing in mind that a study of the Court will in no way impair its authority, but should seek to facilitate the greatest possible contribution by the Court to the advancement of the rule of law and the promotion of justice among nations." The concrete steps included an invitation to Member States and States parties to the Court's Statute to submit to the Secretary General "views and suggestions concerning the role of the Court on the basis of the questionnaire to be prepared by the Secretary-General," an invitation to the Court "to state its views, should it so desire," a request to the Secretary General to prepare a comprehensive report

[3] *Ibid.*, p. 3, par. 1.

[4] *Ibid.*, par. 2. The initiative of the twelve Members was followed by the decision of the American Society of International Law to establish a Panel on the Future of the International Court of Justice. Judge Philip C. Jessup was Chairman of the Panel until the autumn of 1971. He was succeeded by Ambassador Edvard Hambro. The present writer serves as Rapporteur of the Panel.

[5] Doc. A/8238, Dec. 11, 1970.

[6] *Ibid.*, p. 27, pars. 69–71.

of the opinions expressed by states and the Court, and a decision to place the items on the provisional agenda of its Twenty-Sixth Session.[7]

It will be noted that the Sixth Committee and the Assembly had so far appeared to support the initiative and substantive program of the twelve Members. No guidelines for the opinions of Members were formulated, no limitations proposed or imposed, no distinction was drawn between proposals for a revision of the Statute and the Rules of Court or merely for their re-interpretation. On the procedural side, however, the enlarged group of twelve suffered a setback. The draft resolution submitted by it in the Sixth Committee would have had the Assembly establish an *ad hoc* committee, but this provision was deleted.[8] What was more important, however, was the outspoken and insistently hostile tone of the arguments of a group of states around the Soviet Union. It opposed *a limine* any attempt or consideration of proposals aiming at a revision of the Statute which is an integral part of the Charter. As summarized by the Rapporteur, in the view of these delegations,

> Any attempt to change the role of the Court, and consequently to amend the Charter, would be an attempt to change the delicate balance in powers of the principal organs of the United Nations, and such an endeavour might jeopardize international peace and security and undermine the entire United Nations system and did not seem calculated to serve the interests of the international community.[9]

This group of delegations also opposed any consideration of changes in the Court's procedure since any changes in the Rules of Court were within the competence of the Court. I do not see any merit in either argument.

As stated at the outset, there was no doubt that only the Court may change its Rules. But a discussion of possible improvements in the *ad hoc* committee and eventually in the Assembly might well have assisted the Court in its own work. In the process of such a consideration it might be found useful to place some rules of procedure in the Statute. And a revision of the Statute is without doubt within the competence of the Assembly. As to the first argument, the *ad hoc* committee was intended to have general terms of reference but no one doubted that it could amend neither the Statute nor the Charter. All it could do was to make a report, possibly including recommendations for amendments, but obviously such recommendations would have to go through the procedure for amending the Charter provided for in Article 108.[10]

The second phase in the Review of the Court was initiated by the Secretary General, who by a circular letter dated March 5, 1971, transmitted a questionnaire to the states

[7] GAOR, 25th Sess., Supp. No. 28(A/8028), p. 128.

[8] See Docs. A/C.6/L.800/Rev. 1 and A/C.6/L.808/Rev. 2, in Report of the Sixth Committee, Doc. A/8238, pp. 5, 9.

[9] Doc. A/8238, p. 24, par. 63.

[10] The conditions for coming into force of amendments to the Statute of the Court are laid down in General Assembly Res. 2520(XXIV) of Dec. 4, 1969. GAOR, 24th Sess., Supp. No. 30 (A/7630), p. 4.

mentioned in Assembly Resolution 2723(XXV).[11] The questionnaire was intended to elicit the states' views on four substantive points[12] and one of procedure: future action on the item by the General Assembly. In view of the sharp division on this point in the Sixth Committee, this procedural angle seemed more important than the substantive.[13] For obvious reasons, the comments which governments might make on the basis of the questionnaire would not differ substantially from comments already made in the 1970 Sixth Committee or which they would make in the 1971 session of the Sixth Committee. What was needed was a forum for a sustained study of all the ramifications of the problem raised by the twelve Members, and for the eventual formulation of proposals.

Thirty-one states—thirty Member States and one non-Member party to the Statute, Switzerland—responded to the questionnaire. The analytical report was prepared by the Secretary General on the basis of twenty-six responses which had reached him in time,[14] and it served as a basis for the discussion of the item at the 1277th to 1284th and 1293rd and 1296th meetings of the Sixth Committee held from November 9 to 17, and from November 29 to December 1, 1971.

A little procedural skirmish relating to the question of the right of Switzerland to participate in the work of the Sixth Committee is worth mentioning. The issue was raised by Switzerland in its reply to the Secretary General's questionnaire. While not questioning the procedure followed in 1970 when non-Members of the United Nations parties to the Court's Statute were not invited, and while conceding that, according to the letter of Article 69 of the Statute and General Assembly Resolution 2520(XXIV),[15] such states may participate only in the adoption of amendments to the Statute, Switzerland considered that the spirit of the Statute suggested a more liberal interpretation. Moreover, the circulation of the questionnaire and the authorizing Resolution 2723(XXV) "changed the situation for the future." In the Swiss view there would be

> no justification for allowing States which are Parties to the Statute but are not Members of the United Nations to participate only in the discussion and voting on amendments to the Statute and not permitting them to take part in the debate on the other aspects of the proposed reform. In both cases, the international community concerned is the group of Parties

[11] See Review of the Role of the International Court of Justice, Report of the Secretary General, Doc. A/8382, Sept. 15, 1971, p. 4. Although a copy of the questionnaire was transmitted to the Registrar of the Court by the Legal Counsel of the United Nations, the Court, under par. 3 of the Resolution, was invited "to state its views, should it so desire," irrespective of the questionnaire. The letter from the President of the Court to the Secretary General, dated June 18, 1971, is printed in 1970–1971, I.C.J. Yearbook, 116, and Doc. A/8382, p. 130.

[12] Namely: I. The role of the International Court of Justice within the framework of the United Nations; II. Organization of the Court; III. Jurisdiction of the Court; and IV. Procedures and methods of work of the Court. Doc. A/8382, cited note 11 above, p. 6.

[13] This, at any rate, was the conviction of the Society's Panel on the Future of the Court. After due deliberation, the Chairman of the Panel, acting on its behalf, in the summer of 1971 addressed a communication to the legal officers of the states which received the questionnaire, as well as to the President of the Court. Accompanying it was a reasoned Memorandum on "The Future of the International Court of Justice" and a "Summary of Points." In the Panel's view the establishment of an *ad hoc* committee to advance the study of the Court was "profoundly desirable."

[14] The Report of the Secretary General, Doc. A/8382, is cited, note 11 above. The responses received from the United Kingdom and Senegal are reproduced in Doc. A/8382/Add. 1, the responses from Ivory Coast, Turkey and New Zealand are *ibid.*, Add. 2–4, respectively.

[15] For citation see note 10 above.

to the Statute of the Court and each State in this group has an equal right to participate in the discussion of all problems concerning the community.[16]

The Swiss request was reiterated in a note verbale to the Secretary General, who on October 6, 1971, transmitted it to the Chairman of the Sixth Committee.[17] The Committee, presumably after some informal discussions, at its 1279th meeting, on November 16, decided to invite the Swiss Delegation "to present its views and suggestions on the item." Thereupon the Soviet delegate pointed out that his delegation "as a matter of courtesy . . . was prepared to agree that Switzerland be allowed to take part in the work of the Sixth Committee on the question, provided of course that it did not have the right to vote or to submit formal proposals."[18] While grateful to the Soviet Union for its courtesy, the Swiss delegate maintained the position of his government "that it had a right to be associated to the same extent as the other Parties to the Statute in any future work on the role of the Court."[19] Without going into the merits of the issue, one may welcome the decision of the Committee, for it made it possible for the Swiss Delegation to enrich the discussion with some thoughtful comments.

The proponents of an *ad hoc* committee to study in depth the question of the rôle of the Court suffered a further setback at the 1971 session of the General Assembly. The choice before the Sixth Committee was among a draft resolution supported by the United States, among others, which would have had the Assembly set up an *ad hoc* committee to study the rôle of the Court, a resolution by eight "Socialist" Members, including the Soviet Union, which would have postponed further consideration of the question until the Court completes the revision of its rules, and one sponsored by nine Members, including France, which simply would have postponed consideration of the question until the Twenty-Seventh Session of the Assembly.[20] The Committee adopted by a vote of 57 to 40, with 12 abstentions, the French-sponsored draft resolution.[21] The General Assembly adopted the resolution, numbered 2819(XXVI) on December 15, 1971, without objection. Before this decision was taken, the representative of the United States said that his "delegation will . . . be pleased to vote for the draft resolution proposed by the Sixth Committee in order to establish the unanimous nature of the Assembly's desire to have the item discussed next year. We look forward to useful and productive debate on this vital item next year."[22] Those Member States which had not responded to the Secretary

[16] Doc. A/8382, note 11 above, p. 124, par. 375.

[17] Doc. A/C.6/407, Oct. 11, 1971.

[18] "He hopes," he said, "that in the same spirit of courtesy other States which had been the victims of discrimination would be allowed to participate in the activities of the United Nations." Doc. A/C.6/SR.1279, Nov. 16, 1971, p. 2. One wonders whether the Soviet delegate had in mind states parties to the Statute of the Court which are not Members of the United Nations or only certain non-member states.

[19] Doc. A/C.6/SR.1283, Nov. 19, 1971, p. 8.

[20] Review of the Role of the International Court of Justice. Report of the Sixth Committee. Doc. A/8568, Dec. 10, 1971, pp. 4–8.

[21] *Ibid.*, p. 28.

[22] A/PV.2019, Dec. 15, 1971, pp. 3–5.

General's questionnaire in 1971 will have until July 1, 1972, to transmit to him their comments.

It is not the purpose of this paper to analyze the reasons for the temporizing action of the Sixth Committee. Certainly the fact that not more than 31 states replied to the questionnaire was repeated over and over again. Although it is true that more than 50 delegations participated in the debate, not all of them spoke in favor of the *ad hoc* committee. The danger remains, as the Belgian delegate pointed out, that the Committee would become "trapped in a vicious circle in which each year the same arguments were presented from all sides."[23] No doubt many delegations were reluctant to support the establishment of the *ad hoc* committee on the ground that the whole effort might be useless, "since two permanent members of the Security Council had expressed their unalterable opposition to any such project," which might involve a revision of the Statute and therefore of the Charter.[24] No doubt the more privately than publicly announced intention to "veto" any amendments to the Statute and Charter cast a pall over the discussion of this item from the outset. There is no doubt also that the argument made, among others, by the President of the Court that the use of the Court depended upon the willingness of the states, and that there was no compelling reason to assume that changes in procedure and related matters would produce a dramatic shift in the subjective attitude of the states, found much support.

Be that as it may, two points can be confidently affirmed: On the one hand, it would be difficult to maintain that a reform of the Court is the most urgent business before the United Nations or that it would contribute significantly or even marginally to international peace and security, economic and political development, and similar matters which rank high on the priority list of many if not most Members of the Organization. On the other hand there is profound truth in the observation of Mr. Ritter, the Observer for Switzerland, that the purpose of the review of the rôle of the Court

> was not merely to enhance the authority and prestige of the Court but rather *to make the Court better able to respond to the actual needs of those whe were prepared to have recourse to it*. . . . Since there was nothing in the work under way which should raise any difficulties for those States which were reluctant to have recourse to the Court, his Government hoped that those *States for which international jurisdiction played a fundamental role would be allowed to continue unhindered their efforts to perfect the instrument which was to them of primary importance.*[25]

This, in a nutshell, is the heart of the matter. But the question remains whether Members who have so far opposed or not sufficiently supported the study will rise above their negativistic attitude and take a more far-sighted view of the problem. Since recourse to the

[23] Doc. A/C.6/SR.1294, Dec. 3, 1971, p. 6.

[24] Report, Doc. A/8568, cited note 20 above, p. 27, par. 67. The "unalterable opposition" to any revision of the Charter should, of course, be taken with some grains of salt. For at the same Twenty-Sixth Session the General Assembly adopted on Dec. 20, 1971, an amendment to the Charter which would increase the membership of the Economic and Social Council from 27 to 54 (Res. 2847(XXVI)). U.N. Press Release GA/4548, Dec. 28, 1971, Part IV, p. 63.

[25] Doc. A/C.6/SR.1283, pp. 8–9. Italics supplied.

Court will remain voluntary, it is merely a matter of making the Court more accessible and more attractive for those who want to use it in their own best interest and to foster an ever-spreading area for the rule of law.

It is not the purpose of this paper to analyze systematically the great variety of useful and thoughtful comments made by Members in their replies to the Secretary General's questionnaire and in the debates in the Sixth Committee in 1970 and in 1971. They cover pretty well the spectrum of ideas and suggestions to be found in the literature[26] and ably put together in the reports covering the 1970 and 1971 meetings of the Committee.[27] Some points may be mentioned at random. With respect to the composition of the Court some Members emphasized the need for depoliticizing the election process,[28] while other considered that Members of the Court should be elected to ensure the representation of "various legal cultures" rather than "principal legal systems" as provided in Article 9 of the Statute of the Court.[29] One Member suggested that the number of judges from Black Africa—currently three—was inadequate and "should be raised to five, even if that were to entail an increase in the number of members of the Court."[30] In connection with the suggestion for granting preferential treatment in the election of judges to states that have accepted the compulsory jurisdiction of the Court,[31] the opposing comments of Switzerland should be noted.[32] In connection with various proposals concerning the terms of office of judges, their re-eligibility, mandatory retirement age, and similar matters, several Members stressed the need to ensure continuity in the composition of the Court when adjudicating on successive phases—such as preliminary objections and merits—of the same case.[33] Such identity of composition could be ensured without any amendment of Article 13(3) of the Statute.

In connection with the procedures and methods of work of the Court a large array of critical and constructive comments were made. Among those who addressed these matters there was a desire for greater use of summary proceedings of *ad hoc* chambers of regional chambers, in order to expedite the handling of cases and reduce costs. Those who

[26] See Leo Gross, "The International Court of Justice: Consideration of Requirements for Enhancing Its Rôle in the International Legal Order," 65 A.J.I.L. 253, *passim* (1971) and *supra* at 933–1005. See also "What Future for the International Court of Justice?" Proceedings, American Society of International Law, 65, A.J.I.L. 261–285 (Sept., 1971) and *supra* at 1007.

[27] Docs. A/8238, note 5 above, and A/8568, note 20 above.

[28] *E.g.*, Cyprus, the United States, Switzerland, Sweden, Doc. A/8382, pars. 113, 116, 120–123.

[29] Report, Doc. A/8568, note 20 above, p. 15, par. 30. The significance of the proposal emerges with greater clarity from the following passage: "The Court's composition should therefore be enlarged or modified so that it would reflect the structure of the international community. In that respect, the view was expressed that the criterion of geographical distribution was difficult to define; rather than referring to the principal legal systems of the world, it would have been preferable to speak of legal cultures, since the old dichotomy of the Anglo-Saxon and Roman systems had been superceded in part of the western hemisphere with the emergence of an independent Latin American legal culture which had made far-reaching contributions to international law. Similarly, the young countries of Africa were forging their own legal culture. In considering the share which should fall to any legal culture in the composition of the Court, it was suggested that the guiding consideration should be a judicious balance between them all, and not the number of States which subscribed to any one." Report, note 5 above, par. 37. See also note 11 above, par. 112 (Yugoslavia).

[30] Senegal, Doc. A/8382/Add.1, p. 11, par. 4.

[31] Cyprus, Doc. A/8382, p. 58, par. 160.

[32] *Ibid.*, pp. 58–60, pars. 161–166.

[33] Switzerland and Sweden in Doc. A/8382, pp. 60–62, pars. 167–172, and Israel in Doc. A/C.6/SR.1278/Corr. 1, p. 3.

favored regional chambers were concerned with the danger of fragmentation of the law and proposed that an appeal to the full Court be provided for. In connection with the high cost of litigation, several Members pointed out that the cost of going to the Court was less than submitting the case to a tribunal of arbitration,[34] whereas other suggested some form of United Nations assistance.[35]

In connection with possible ways of rationalizing the procedure, thoughtful comments were made with respect to the handling of preliminary objections to jurisdictions, objections to receivability and their joinder to the merits.[36] With respect to the rendering of judgments some delegations were of the opinion "that the decisions reached by the casting vote of the President were unsatisfactory and that States would have greater confidence in the Court if its judgments were based on the unanimous opinion of the judges, referred to in Article 57 of the Statute."[37] Two related comments may be mentioned in this context. One relates to separate and dissenting opinions and the other to the vote on the judgment. With respect to the former, the statement of the President of the Court in the *South West Africa* cases (Second Phase)[38] was recalled and it was suggested that individual opinions, whether concurring or dissenting, "must bear on the issue on which the Court has passed judgment."[39] With respect to the latter, the United States stated that "the Court might decide cases by a two-thirds rather than a simple majority, thereby ensuring the views of all legal systems be fully taken into account in the Court's deliberation."[40] Commenting on Articles 25 and 55 of the Statute, the delegate of Israel suggested that "consideration should be given to raising the quorum (of nine judges) slightly and abandoning the somewhat brutal and arbitrary system whereby the President had a casting vote when the Court was equally divided." In the event of an equally divided Court, "in a contentious matter the Court might declare the case lost or, in an advisory matter, state that the Court was unable to give an adequate reply." In any event, "no decisions by the Court should be possible without the concurrence of at least half its members."[41]

[34] Mexico and Switzerland in Doc. A/8382, p. 116, pars. 348–349, New Zealand, *ibid.*, Add. 4, p. 4.

[35] United States in Doc. A/8382, p. 115, par. 346, Sweden, *ibid.*, p. 116, par. 350, Canada, *ibid.*, p. 126, par. 380, Turkey, *ibid.*, Add. 3, p. 5, par. 18, and New Zealand, *ibid.*, Add. 4, p. 4; Japan in Doc. A/C.6/SR.1280, p. 9, and Turkey, *ibid.*, SR1283, p. 21.

[36] United States in Doc. A/8382, p. 105, par. 322, Switzerland, *ibid.*, pp. 106–110, pars. 323–332, Sweden, *ibid.*, p. 111, par. 333, Canada, *ibid.*, par. 334, Austria, *ibid.*, par. 335, United Kingdom, *ibid.*, Add. 1, pp. 8–9, pars. 22–23. The Swiss Government suggested that "in the absence of any imperative reason to the contrary, an objection relating to the existence of compulsory jurisdiction should be ruled upon as a preliminary matter, whereas an objection regarding the extent of a compulsory jurisdiction that has already been established can more conveniently be joined to the merits of the case. The adoption of such a rule would not necessarily require an amendment to the Statute, but could take the form of a recommendation in a resolution." *Ibid.*, p. 110, par. 332.

[37] Report, Doc. A/8283, cited note 5 above, p. 14, par. 32.

[38] [1966] I.C.J. Rep. 6, at 51–57.

[39] Switzerland in Doc. A/8382, p. 118, par. 353.

[40] Doc. A/8382, p. 37, par. 100. The United States went on to state: "A judgment based on less than a two-thirds majority might be delivered in a declaratory form, on the basis of which the parties would negotiate a settlement. This alternative might be studied further." Indeed, further study of this surprising suggestion would seem eminently desirable. For a reasoned statement in favor of declaratory judgments see Switzerland, *ibid.*, pp. 81–85, par. 238–247.

[41] Doc. A/C.6/SR.1278/Corr. 1, pp. 3–4.

The questions of the compulsory jurisdiction of the Court and of broadening access to the advisory and contentious jurisdiction received a good deal of attention. One government proposed that the jurisdiction of the Court be made compulsory,[42] but generally there seems to have been a realization that such a sweeping proposal had little chance of being seriously considered. In a more modest but interesting vein the Canadian Government offered the possibility for "groups of like-minded states to consult among themselves in a effort to reach agreement on co-ordinated declarations wherein they would list those instances in which they could accept the jurisdiction of the Court to adjudicate on problems arising from their mutual interrelations."[43] Other governments favored fewer reservations and clarification of existing ones. It was also suggested—by Canada—that the General Assembly declare "unequivocally that recourse to the jurisdiction of the Court was not *per se* an unfriendly act but was prompted by the desire to advance the rule of law."[44]

In the view of many governments access to the contentious jurisdiction of the Court should be open to international organizations,[45] generally or in specific instances. The United Kingdom invited consideration "to the possibility of enabling private individuals and corporations to be parties before the Court or to intervene in certain cases and on certain conditions." It also suggested "conferring on the International Court an appellate jurisdiction from the decisions of other international tribunals."[46] Governments which, on principle, opposed amendments to the Statute, were also opposed to this group of proposals.[47]

There was also widespread support for granting access to the advisory jurisdiction of the Court to international organizations but somewhat more reserved support for access being granted to regional organizations, states, and even individuals.[48] Pending or in the absence of an amendment, it was suggested that international organizations could obtain access to the Court through the instrumentality of a committee of the General Assembly.[49] The Swedish Government deemed it worthwhile

> to examine the question whether the Court should be authorized to give an advisory opinion at the request of the supreme national court of a State party to the Statute before its

[42] Laos, in Doc. A/8382, p. 66, par. 184. But see the comment of the same government, *ibid.*, p. 120, par. 359, which indicates that there may be a misunderstanding in the use of the term "compulsory."

[43] Doc. A/8382, p. 68, par. 191; see also Ambassador Hambro (Norway), in Doc. A/C.6/SR.1279, p. 8.

[44] Doc. A/C.6/SR.1279, pp. 11–12; see also Finland, *ibid.*, SR.1277, p. 6.

[45] *E.g.*, Cyprus, Denmark, Guatemala, the United States, Switzerland, Sweden, Austria, Argentina, Finland, Mexico, the United Kingdom, in Doc. A/8382, pp. 70–77, and *ibid.*, Add. 1, p. 6. See also Greece, Norway and Turkey in Doc. A/8382, pp. 70–77, and *ibid.*, Add. 1, p. 6. See also Greece, Norway and Turkey in doc. A/C.6/SR.1279, pp. 6, 7 and *ibid.*, SR.1283, p. 20.

[46] Doc. A/8382/Add. 1, p. 7, pars. 14–15.

[47] *E.g.*, France, Doc. A/8382, pp. 76–77, pars. 220–222.

[48] *E.g.*, Cyprus, Laos, Denmark, Guatemala, United States, Argentina, Italy, Finland, Switzerland, Netherlands, Sweden, Canada, Madagascar, Iraq, Austria, Yugoslavia, Belgium, in Doc. A/8382, pp. 90–101.

[49] The United Kingdom in this context, recalled that the Committee on Applications for the Review of Administrative Tribunal Judgments established by General Assembly Resolution 957(X), provides a precedent. Doc. A/8382/Add. 1, p. 7, par. 16. See also Canada, Doc. A/8382, p. 98, par. 292.

giving judgment on a question of international law, provided, of course, that the national court accepts in advance the ruling of the International Court of Justice as binding.[50]

In any debate on the rôle of the Court, whether past or future, there are bound to be voices expressing dissatisfaction with the jurisprudence of the Court and the law which it applies. The *bête noire* is, of course the 1966 Judgment of the Court in the *South West Africa* cases although some delegations were prepared to regard it as an isolated incident of unresponsiveness to the climate in the United Nations and the needs of the international community. In the eyes of many delegations the Court "redeemed" itself through its advisory opinion in the *Namibia* case.[51] However, there is no use in closing one's eyes to the fact that the issue of the law is likely to be both important and controversial in an *ad hoc* committee which, hopefully, will be established at the 1972 session of the General Assembly. It is not merely the attitude of many new states that international law is essentially Western in its orientation and was developed without their participation and regard for their interests, although this argument is going to be pressed for all it is worth. The discussion may well turn on the weight to be given to declarations and resolutions of United Nations organs and probably of other international organizations as well. To select, at random, one or two observations. The delegate of Cyprus stated that, "in addition to the sources cited in Article 38 of the Statute, the Court should give due weight to the law-making resolutions and declarations of the General Assembly and the Security Council."[52] In a more cautious vein, Ambassador Hambro (Norway) stated:

> As to the sources of law enumerated in Article 38 of the Statute, while it was clear that the General Assembly had not been given legislative authority, it was equally clear that no country, *having voted in favour of a declaration,* could ignore it or act inconsistently with it on the basis that General Assembly resolutions were mere recommendations. The solemn declarations could not and should not be considered as having no validity.[53]

Addressing the same issue, Mr. Rosenne (Israel) stated that the declarations and resolution would

> acquire a status which did not flow from either the provisions of the Charter or the rules of international law concerning the creation of the legal norms applied in international relations. Such a change would not be effectuated through the re-interpretation of existing provisions but being a fundamental amendment of the Charter would have to be achieved in accordance with the procedure laid down in Article 108.[54]

[50] Doc. A/8382, p. 98, par. 291. This idea merited consideration in the opinion of the Austrian Delegation, see Doc. A/C.6/SR.1278, p. 12.

[51] [1971]I.C.J. Rep. 16.

[52] Doc. A/C.6/SR.1283, p. 18. See also statements by Iran, *ibid.*, p. 10, Afghanistan, *ibid.*, p. 16, Sudan, *ibid.*, p. 6.

[53] Doc. A/C.6/SR.1279, p. 7. Italics supplied.

[54] Doc. A/C.6/SR.1278/Corr. 1, p. 2. For a summary of views on the state of international law, see also Report A/8238, cited note 5 above, pp. 14–15; Report A/8568, cited note 20 above, pp. 13–15; and Report A/8382, and Report A/8382, cited note 11 above, pp. 22–27.

It is obvious that this may well become as contentious an issue on the governmental level as it has already become on the doctrinal one.

It has been pointed out that some of the proposals made in the course of the written and oral debates in the last two years may require an amendment to the Statute and of the Charter. Others may require an agreed re-interpretation of these instruments or of the Rules of Court or of its judicial practice. The Court is master of its Rules and practice, and conceivably the Court may find some of the comments sufficiently persuasive to include them in a suitable form in the current revision of its Rules. Changes or adjustments in its judicial practice may be made gradually and over time and without any formality. The Court is fully aware of the opinion of governments, but the governments have no knowledge of the Court's work on the revision of its Rules.[55] The Court has not seen fit to respond to the invitation of the Assembly to state its views on the pending review of its rôle. The President of the Court indicated, however, that "if the General Assembly were to consider that the Court could usefully be asked for particular observations on legal questions, the Court would be prepared to meet such requests."[56]

The Court has lately embarked on a variety of activities designed to establish more sustained contacts with the United Nations and its larger constituency. For some of these it has been roundly criticized.[57] The practice, initiated in 1968, to submit reports covering its activities to the United Nations, has been the subject of searching and critical evaluation.[58] Also the Court in 1967 established a "Committee on Relations," composed of Judges Lachs, Onyeama and Dillard, which "is responsible for preparing plans and programmes with a view to the wider dissemination of information on the work of the Court and the development of its relations with other United Nations organs and other international organizations and bodies."[59]

The United Kingdom called attention to one aspect of the Court's relations with its professional constituency, namely its publications. Although written and oral pleadings in one of the two official languages (French and English) are unofficially translated by the Registry of the Court into the other for the use of the judges and parties, they are published only in their original language. "This means," observed the United Kingdom, "that scholars and practitioners who find it easier to work in one language rather than the other are deprived of the opportunity of making use of the translations which have been made."[60] Since the publications of the Court are governed by the Rules of Court

[55] See remarks by the representative of Israel, Doc. A/C.6/SR.1278/Corr. 1, p. 3.

[56] Doc. A/8382, p. 130, and 1970–1971, I.C.J. Yearbook 116. In this connection it may not be amiss to quote the comment by Iraq on the question of the future action of the General Assembly: "Under the Charter, the General Assembly could request the International Court of Justice to give an advisory opinion on legal questions. Surely, the Statute of the International Court of Justice is pre-eminently such a question. Consequently, the General Assembly could, if it so decides, request an advisory opinion from the Court on the question of the latter's Statute and Rules." Doc. A/8382, p. 129, par. 389. With respect, what is the question?

[57] See the remarks of the delegate of Israel, Doc. A/C.6/SR.1278, Corr. 1, p. 3.

[58] Salo Engel, "Annual Reports of the International Court of Justice to the General Assembly?" 44 Brit. Yr. Bk. Int. Law 193–201 (1970).

[59] 1970–1971 I.C.J. Yearbook 87.

[60] Doc. 8382/Add. 1, cited note 11 above, p. 9, par. 24.

(Articles 22 and 59(2)), this reform could easily be introduced by the Court itself. There is no doubt that it would be greeted with enthusiasm by those practitioners and scholars who, as the United Kingdom puts it so delicately and gracefully , "find it easier to work in one language rather than the other." However, the pleadings in some cases are enormously and, as some governments pointed out, unnecessarily bulky and there is no blinking the fact that the additional cost of introducing even this modest reform may run into trouble in the Fifth Committee of the General Assembly,[61] which determines the budget of the Court—the principal judicial organ of the United Nations and the only judicial organ of the wider international community.

[61] As it did on a previous occasion in the wake of the Court's judgment in the South West Africa cases. See Leo Gross, "The International Court of Justice and the United Nations," 120 Hague Academy of International Law, Recueil des Cours 324 f. (I, 1967). *Supra*, pp. 845–931.

# THE DISPUTE BETWEEN GREECE AND TURKEY CONCERNING THE CONTINENTAL SHELF IN THE AEGEAN

## I. INTRODUCTION

On August 10, 1976, Greece addressed a communication to the President of the Security Council requesting an urgent meeting of the Council on the ground that "following recent repeated flagrant violations by Turkey of the sovereign rights of Greece in the continental shelf in the Aegean, a dangerous situation has been created threatening international peace and security."[1] On the same day, by unilateral application, Greece instituted proceedings in the International Court of Justice against Turkey in "a dispute concerning the delimitation of the continental shelf appertaining to Greece and Turkey in the Aegean Sea, and concerning the respective legal rights of those states to explore and exploit the continental shelf of the Aegean."[2] Also on the same day Greece filed a request for interim measures of protection asking the Court to direct that both Greece and Turkey

> (1) unless with consent of each other and pending the final judgment of the Court in this case, refrain from all exploration activity or any scientific research with respect to the continental shelf areas within which Turkey has granted such licenses or permits or adjacent to the Islands, or otherwise in dispute in the present case,[3]

[1] UN Doc. S/12167

[2] Aegean Sea Continental Shelf, Interim Protection Order of 11 Sept. 1976. [1976] ICJ Rep. 3 (hereinafter cited as [1976] Rep.), 15 ILM 985 (1976).

[3] In the French version the passage is clearer: ". . . la Turquie a accordé des concessions ou des permis, ou qui sont adjacentes aux iles, ou qui se trovent à d'autres égards en litige dans la présente espèce."

> (2) refrain from taking further military measures or actions which may endanger their peaceful relations.[4]

While this procedure—a simultaneous appeal to the most political of the political organs of the United Nations, the Security Council, and its principal judicial organ, the Court—may strike one as a bit unusual, it may have been useful, as the outcome shows, to seek, as Judges Lachs and Elias put it, "both legal and political relief."[5] Greece was successful in obtaining some relief from the Security Council in paragraphs 1 and 2 of Resolution 395(1976) although it failed to receive from the Court satisfaction for its request for interim measures. Turkey was successful before the Court in so far as the denial of the Greek request was concerned though it failed to persuade the Court that the Greek Application was "premature," that the Court lacked jurisdiction, and that, for this reason, the case should be removed from the Court's list.[6] Turkey was also partly successful in the Council inasmuch as paragraph 3 of Resolution 395(1976) called for resumption of direct negotiations and paragraph 4 invited both governments "to take into account the contribution that appropriate judicial means, in particular the International Court of Justice, are qualified to make the settlement of any remaining legal differences which they may identify in connection with their present dispute." This could be interpreted as an indication that the Council considered, as did Turkey, that the Greek Application was premature and that in any event the Court should be seised, as contended by Turkey in the Council as well as in the preceding diplomatic exchanges with Greece, by means of a special agreement rather than, as it was, by unilateral application.[7]

[4] [1976] REP at 4–5.
[5] *Id.* at 19 and 27. Judge Elias thought this case was "probably unique" from this angle. *Id.*
[6] *Id.* at 5, paras. 8 and 13, paras. 45 and 46.
[7] In the Council the Turkish representative, referring to this, said:

> The position of the Turkish Government on this matter has always been clear and consistent. If it becomes necessary, Turkey does not exclude recourse to the International Court of Justice to settle certain relevant aspects of the problem, but maintains that the dispute should first be negotiated between the two countries. Those aspects of the problem that cannot be resolved through negotiations conducted meaningfully and in good faith could then and only then be referred to the International Court of Justice or to any other legal or judicial instance. It is obvious that such a referral can only be made jointly.

U.N. Doc. S/PV.1950, Aug. 13, 1976, at 12. The representative quoted the following passage from the *Continental Shelf* case on the meaning of "meaningful" negotiations:

> The parties are under an obligation to enter into negotiations with a view to arriving at an agreement, and not merely to go through a formal process of negotiations as a sort of prior condition for the automatic application of a certain method of delimitation in the absence of agreement, they are under an obligation so to conduct themselves that the negotiations are meaningful, which will not be the case when either of them insist upon its own position without contemplating any modification of it.

[1969] ICJ REP. 3, at 47, para. 85(a). The text in UN Doc. S/PV.1950 is not quite accurate. For earlier evidence of Turkey's position, see Notes Verbales from the Turkish Ministry of Foreign Affairs to the Greek Embassy in Ankara of Feb. 6, 1975, Sept. 30, 1975, and Nov. 18, 1975 in UN Doc. S/12173, Aug. 12, 1976, Annexes II and III.

Paragraphs 3 and 4 of Resolution 395(1976) raise an issue of principle, namely that of the relations between the Security Council and the Court which will be discussed below. But it may be useful first to survey briefly some substantive aspects of the Greco-Turkish dispute.

It appears from documents submitted to the Council and the Court that the dispute relates to the shelf of the two countries and more particularly, as stated in the Greek submission to the Court, to the shelf appertaining to Greek islands in the Aegean.[8] In its first submission to the Court, Greece claims "that these islands . . . as part of the territory of Greece, are entitled to the portion of the continental shelf which appertains to them according to the applicable principles and rules of international law."[9] It is in the shelf area of these islands, though outside their territorial waters, that since November 1, 1973, Turkey has granted to the Turkish State Petroleum Company (TPAO) exploration permits which Greece claimed "encroached upon the continental shelf" of the islands.[10] In the Turkish view, "at the present time Greece possesses no delimited sovereign rights in the Aegean beyond its own territorial waters."[11] Turkey also contended that whereas since the 1960's Greece has granted numerous exploration licenses and drilled for oil in the Aegean "outside Greek territorial waters," Turkey had "started its research activities on the natural prolongation of Anatolian peninsula in 1974, 11 years later than Greece."[12]

Although in its second submission Greece asked the Court to declare "what is the course of the boundary (or boundaries) between the portions of the continental shelf appertaining to Greece and Turkey in the Aegean Sea in accordance with the principles and rules of international law which the Court shall determine to be applicable,"[13] it also affirmed: "The dispute is confined to the continental shelf adjacent to the said Islands and does not concern any other part of the Aegean Sea or seabed thereof."[14] While both Governments based their views on international law,[15] the Turkish Government, as under-

[8] The Islands are listed in the Greek Application at 4, 5, and 10 and in [1976] Rep. 6, para. 15(i).

[9] *Id.* 4, para. 1(i).

[10] *Id.* 7, para. 16, and Greek Application at 4.

[11] The Turkish representative in the Security Council, UN Doc. S/PV.1950, Aug. 13, 1976, at 7–10.

[12] Letter from the permanent representative of Turkey to the Secretary-General of the UN of Aug. 18, 1976, UN Doc. S/12182.

[13] [1976] Rep. at 4, para. 1(ii). Submissions (iii) to (vi) are consequential: the Court is asked to adjudge that Greece has exclusive rights in the shelf, that Turkey is not entitled to undertake any activities without the consent of Greece, that Turkish activities constitute infringements of Greek sovereign rights, and finally that Turkey shall not continue its activities.

[14] Greek Application, 18, para. 31. Islands are listed in para. 29. It may be that the position of Greece was motivated by its reservation to the accession of the General Act for the Pacific Settlement of International Disputes of September 28, 1928. This excluded certain disputes "in particular disputes relating to its rights of sovereignty over its ports and lines of communications." [1976] Rep. 8, para. 19. Turkey's position was that the General Act was "no longer a treaty in force between Greece and Turkey" and alternatively that the dispute fell within the terms of the reservation. *Ibid.* This point is elaborated in the Observations of the Government of Turkey on the Request by the Government of Greece for Provisional Measures of Protection, transmitted to the Court on August 25, 1976, at 8 and 10 ff. The Court found that "it is not necessary for the Court to reach a final conclusion at this stage of the proceedings on the questions thus raised concerning the application of the 1928 Act as between Greece and Turkey . . ." . [1976] Rep. 8, para. 21

[15] Greece could invoke Article 1 of the 1968 Geneva Convention on the Continental Shelf which defines in Article 1(b) the term "continental shelf" as referring "to the seabed and subsoil of similar submarine areas adjacent to the coasts of

stood by Greece, maintained that some of the islands "could not have a continental shelf, the reason being either that those islands constituted mere elevations (protuberances) on what Turkey considered to be its own continental shelf, or that a long time ago they belonged geologically to the continent of Asia."[16] This, in rough outline, is the substance of the dispute which provides the background for the tension that came before the Security Council.

## II. THE APPEAL OF GREECE TO THE SECURITY COUNCIL

As indicated earlier[17] the Greek appeal to the Security Council was based on the dangerous situation created by the "seismological explorations" conducted since August 6, 1976 by Turkey "with the vessel *Sismik-I* on the Aegean continental shelf, which Greece considers her own."[18] Greece, invoking Article 35 of the Charter, appealed to the Council "in order to avert the danger of disturbing the peace, which is being seriously threatened."[19] In an Explanatory Memorandum Greece referred to "the already very serious Greco-Turkish dispute, the Turkish naval and air manoeuvres preceding or accompanying the movements of the vessel *Sismik-I,* the presence and concentration of Turkish naval and air units 'covering' the activities of that vessel, the precautions inevitably taken by the Greek Government, and Turkey's insistence on continuing the tests" as elements "creating a situation of confrontation the prolongation of which is likely to endanger the maintenance of international peace and security."[20] In the Council, Greece maintained its stand and asked the Council to let Turkey know "that it must suspend its provocative acts. The United Nations was not in time to stop the tragedy of Cyprus. It can now prevent a new tragedy in the Aegean."[21]

Turkey responded by restating its position with respect to the substantive dispute, namely that in the absence of an agreed delimitation of the continental shelf "the Greek claim of violation of the Greek sovereign rights is completely unfounded" and "that

islands." 15 UST 471; TIAS No. 5578; 499 UNTS 311, 52 AJIL 858 (1958).

Turkey, although not a party to the Convention, could rely on Article 6, as interpreted by the Court in the *Continental Shelf* case, which, in cases of both coasts which are opposite each other and coasts adjacent to the territories of two adjacent states, stressed the principle that delimitation shall be determined by agreement and that "special circumstances" may require consideration. *See* Turkish Note Verbale, Feb. 27, 1974, in Greek Application, at 37–39, referring to [1969] REP. 31, paras. 43 and 44 and 47, para. 85.

16 Greek Note Verbale, March 22, 1976, in Greek Application, at 81. As understood by Greece, Turkey denied the applicability of the median line to the delimitation of the shelf in the Aegean between opposite states, also on the ground that there was "a discontinuity in the seabed." Statement by the Greek Delegation at the Meeting of Experts of the Governments of Greece and Turkey in Berne on June 19 and 20, 1976, in Greek Application, at 84–86.

17 *Supra,* p. 1021.

18 UN Doc. S/12168, Aug. 10, 1976, at 1.

19 *Id.* at 3, and UN Doc. S/PV.1949, Aug. 12, 1976, at 6.

20 UN Doc. S/12173, Aug. 12, 1976, at 5. The movements of *Sismik-I* are detailed in this document at 2 as well as in its Annex I, at 2–3.

21 UN Doc. S/PV.1949, Aug. 12, 1976, at 16. The Greek representative summarized the substantive dispute at 6–15.

*MTA Sismik-I* is carrying out its researches outside the territorial waters in the Aegean where the Continental Shelf is yet to be delimited."[22] Turkey also claimed "that since August 6, 1976, the vessel was under the harassment of vessels and aircraft belonging to the Greek Navy and Air Force."[23] In addition, Turkey complained that Greece, in violation of the Treaty of Lausanne of July 24, 1923, and the Treaty of Peace with Italy of February 10, 1947, had militarized the islands which pursuant to these treaties were to be demilitarized.[24] In the Council Turkey maintained its position and also recalled that "a Greek vessel named *Nautilus* is at this very moment conducting very similar activities in a neighboring region" and "that at the present time Greece possesses no delimited soveign rights in the Aegean beyond its own territorial waters."[25] Turkey hoped that the Council would invite Greece to enter into "meaningful negotiations" and "that the Council will examine Greece's flagrant violations of its international obligations under the treaty regarding the demilitarization of the islands in the eastern Aegean and will take the steps required to put an end to a threat to peace and security in that region."[26]

The Security Council did not attempt to assess blame on one side or the other for the situation in the Aegean nor did it attempt to deal directly with the substance of the dispute,[27] although it made a recommendation with respect to the procedure which it considered appropriate. After consultations outside the Council, France, Italy, the United Kingdom and the United States, submitted on August 24, 1976 a draft resolution (UN Doc. S/12187) which would, if adopted, "provide a framework in which the dispute between Greece and Turkey can be resolved."[28] As there was no unanimity in its favor, on the one hand, and no objection on the other, the President declared the draft resolution adopted by consensus.[29]

Resolution 395(1976), as is so often the case with Security Council resolutions, does not indicate on which article of the Charter it is based. Members of the Council expressed different views. France, one of the sponsors, referring to paragraph 4 of the resolution,

22 UN Doc. S/12172, Aug. 11, 1976, Annex I and Annex II, at 1.

23 *Id.* Annex II, at 2. Turkey submitted "a list of illustrative nature of the harassment and intimidation actions" by Greece. UN Doc. S/12175, Aug. 13, 1976.

24 UN Doc. S/12176, Aug. 13, 1976. Turkish charges of Greek explorations in the Aegean "outside the territorial waters" of the specified islands are detailed in UN Doc. S/12182, Aug. 20, 1976.

25 UN Doc. S/PV.1950, at 6, 7–10. The representative of Turkey also alluded to "illegal acts" of Greece "aimed at transforming the international air space of the Aegean into national Greek air space, thus depriving Turkey and other countries of their inherent and traditionally established rights to use the international air space over the Aegean." *Id.* at 17.

26 *Id.* at 21. Some details on the violations of the treaties of 1923 and 1947 will be found *id.* at 16. Concerning "meaningful negotiations," see *supra* note 7.

27 The statement by the representative of the United Kingdom, UN Doc. S/PV.1953, Aug. 25, 1976, at 8. The representative of the United States did not believe that the Council was the place "to analyze such complex issues of international law" as those relating to the continental shelf which "are among the most sensitive in the entire field of international law."*Id.* at 14–15.

28 UN Doc. S/PV.1953, Aug. 25, 1976, at 8.

29 *Id.* 47. Pakistan objected to paragraph 4 of the draft resolution and to the unilateral application of Greece to the Court and hoped that Greece "will now find it possible to reconsider." *Id.* 43. Libya indicated that if a vote were taken, it would abstain. *Id.* 47. As adopted, the resolution was numbered 395(1976).

mentioned specifically Article 36(3).[30] Panama referred to Article 33(1) and (2), Tanzania and Japan referred to Article 33 of the Charter.[31]

Clearly, as indicated earlier, Resolution 395(1976) has two parts: In the first part, paragraphs 1 and 2, the Council calls, as the United Kingdom representative put it, "for restraint on both sides and must then go on to urge them to do everything in their power to reduce the present tensions."[32] Turkey, which had considered the Greek appeal to the Council "completely pointless," put an interpretation on this part that was most favorable to itself, saying that the Council "did not accept the contention that the Turkish research vessel 'Sismik-I', in its activities, had infringed on the sovereign rights of any country."[33] In the style which usually prevails in such matters in the United Nations, one could add that the Council had not rejected the Greek contention. In any event, Greece appeared satisfied,[34] and, as far as one knows, the tension was defused. As the French representative put it: "Since fever does not make for a clear head, it must first be reduced."[35]

In paragraphs 3 and 4, Resolution 395(1976) addresses itself to the legal aspects of the dispute. As indicated earlier, this part of the resolution appears to support partly the Turkish stand, although it was also acceptable to Greece.[36] Turkey objected to paragraph 4 saying that "the core of the resolution can be found in operative paragraph 3. While we

[30] The French representative stated that the authors of paragraph 4 "had a great deal of trouble with the two parties regarding it" and went on to say:

> The Charter in Chapter VI, lists the various peaceful ways of settling disputes. Article 36(3) specifically singles out the specific role to be played by the International Court of Justice in dealing with legal disputes, which is clearly what the limitation of the continental shelf is. What we have tried to recall in the last operative paragraph of our draft, which is the logical outcome of the preceding paragraph, is that when the parties, in their negotiations, encounter problems which they are unable to resolve, they have available to them the judicial channels laid down in the Charter—and, in the case of the International Court of Justice at The Hague—those enunciated in the Court's Statute. This reminder seems reasonable to us and in accordance with the position previously taken by both Greece and Turkey.

UN Doc. S/PV.1953 at 21.

[31] *Id.* 24–25, 26, 51, and 52.

[32] *Id.* 7. The last preambular and the first two operative paragraphs read as follows:

*Conscious* of the need for the parties both to respect each other's international rights and obligations and to avoid any incident which might lead to the aggravation of the situation and which, consequently, might compromise their efforts towards a peaceful solution,

1. *Appeals* to the Governments of Greece and Turkey to exercise the utmost restraint in the present situation;
2. *Urges* the Governments of Greece and Turkey to do everything in their power to reduce the present tensions in the area so that the negotiating process may be facilitated;

[33] *Id.* 53–55.

[34] *Id.* 57.

[35] *Id.* 18.

[36] *See supra*, p. 1022, at note 7. For the Greek statement, see UN Doc. S/PV.1953, at 57. The text of paras. 3 and 4 is as follows:

> 3. *Calls on* the Governments of Greece and Turkey to resume direct negotiations over their differences and appeals to them to do everything within their power to ensure that these result in mutually acceptable solutions;
> 4. *Invites* the Governments of Greece and Turkey in this respect to continue to take into account the contribution that appropriate judicial means, in particular the International Court of Justice, are qualified to make to the settlement of any remaining legal differences which they may identify in connexion with their present dispute.

feel that this paragraph is in accord with our policy, we do not consider that we are bound by any other provision that could be construed as constituting any precondition or constraint, nor could we accept any provision that would be likely to prejudge the process of negotiation or its outcome or that might involve any unilateral recourse to a judicial body."[37]

It has been suggested that paragraphs 3 and 4 raise a question of principle, namely the propriety, to put it no higher, of the Council making a recommendation with regard to the method of settling a dispute when the same dispute was subjudice in the International Court of Justice. It may be doubtful whether this was a situation which comes under the technical rubric of *lis pendens.*[38] In any event, although the parties as well as the members of the Council were aware that the legal aspects of the dispute had been brought before the Court by the application of Greece, no objection was raised in the Council against paragraph 3 and more particularly, against paragraph 4 of Resolution 395(1976). On an earlier occasion, in 1960 in connection with the *South West Africa* cases, South Africa raised the issue of sub judice in the General Assembly without avail. In the view of some commentators, neither the principle of *lis pendens* nor the cognate sub judice have become general principles of law or part of the law of the United Nations.[39] Indeed it has been said that "while there is sufficient experience in the United Nations to indicate that *litispendence may* constitute a temporary obstacle to effective political treatment, it is now clear that the fact that a dispute is simultaneously being dealt with by the General Assembly and by the Court is not in itself regarded in either organ as a bar to its further action."[40]

Yet it does not seem wholly satisfactory to let the latter rest there. Article 36 (2) refers to methods for the settlement of disputes and the Council "should take into consideration any procedures for the settlement of the dispute which have already been adopted by the parties." In this case the parties have been engaged in negotiations for a substantial

[37] UN Doc. S/PV.1953, at 56. The Turkish representative went on to say:

> It should also be borne in mind that Turkey has not recognized the jurisdiction of the International Court of Justice as binding. Furthermore, it is undeniable that the resumption of negotiations implies that no unilateral action should be undertaken that would be in flagrant contradiction with the concept of negotiations as I have just defined it.

*Id.* 57.

[38] Concerning this, see Ciobanu, *Litispendens between the International Court of Justice and the Political Organs of the United Nations*, in L. Gross (ed), 1. THE FUTURE OF THE INTERNATIONAL COURT OF JUSTICE 209–75, esp. 219–26 (1976) (hereinafter cited as GROSS). *See also* S. ROSENNE, THE LAW AND PRACTICE OF THE INTERNATIONAL COURT 83–87, 516, 752, n.2 (1965).

[39] ROSENNE, *supra* note 38, at 752, 851; Ciobanu, *supra* note 38, at 225–26. Gross 120 REC.DES COURS 313–439, at 329 (I, 1967).

[40] ROSENNE, *supra* note 38, at 87. Rosenne continues as follows:

> This is illustrative of the extent of the integration with the Organization and its work of the Court as a principal organ and the principal judicial organ of the United Nations. It well illustrates the functional parallelism of two principal organs of the United Nations, each of which has competence, under the combined Charter and Statute, to deal with the same "dispute".

period of time, and no matter what the preferred meaning of this clause may be[41] the appeal in paragraph 3 of Resolution 395(1976) does not appear to be helpful in the absence of any guidance concerning the applicable principles of international law. To be sure, Greece did not seek such guidance from the Council but from the Court. There is no doubt that it was quite proper for the Council to deal with the tension which had arisen in the Aegean but it is another thing altogether for the Council to make a recommendation which, if it has any meaning at all, invites certainly Greece and to an extent Turkey, to withdraw the case from the Court.[42]

If doubt is possible about the real intent of the Council in connection with paragraph 3, no doubt seems possible with respect to paragraph 4. It may be recalled that France in this context referred specifically to Article 36(3) of the Charter.[43] As is well known, the Council has only once, in the *Corfu Channel* case, adopted a resolution under Article 36(3).[44] Though practice is therefore extremely scarce, there can be no doubt about the intent and purpose of this clause: the Council should, as a general rule, encourage the parties to take legal disputes to the Court and not to discourage them from so doing. But "discourage" is precisely, in the specific circumstances of the Greco-Turkish dispute, what the Council appears to have done. As the dispute was pending before the Court and, as it included "remaining legal differences" which the parties have been unable to resolve in bilateral negotiations, what could possibly be the intent of the Council unless it was to invite the parties to go back to square one and/or invite Greece to withdraw its application so that negotiations could start *ab novo* without the sword of Damocles—the Court—hanging over their heads? In casting the Court in this role, the Council has not contributed to the enhancement of the stature of the Court or the strengthening of its precarious position. Even if from the constitutional point of view, the Council acted within its rights, a matter on which there is, in the present submission, room for doubt, the Council showed a remarkable lack of respect and sense of propriety for the Court in the advice which it offered to the parties. It is odd, indeed, for the Security Council to criticize a state, even though by indirection,[45] for resorting to the Court

[41] Thus, Ciobanu concluded that

> the *travaux préparatoires* of the San Francisco Conference seem to indicate that it was not the intent of the conferees to restrict the jurisdiction of the Security Council to deal with any dispute falling under its jurisdiction for the sole reason that other means and procedures for its peaceful settlement (among them the judicial settlement by the International Court of Justice) have been adopted by the parties.

*Supra* note 38, at 222.

[42] The inclusion of Turkey is made with some diffidence but it may be justified by the fact that on August 25, 1976, the day on which Resolution 395 (1976) was adopted in the Council, Turkey transmitted to the Registrar of the Court its Observations on the Request of Greece for Provisional Measures of Protection. The Observations are dated August 10, 1976.

[43] *Supra,* p. 1024, at note 30.

[44] Resolution 19(1947), Feb. 27, 1947, 2 SCOR, RES. DEC. 3 (1947).

[45] It is impossible not to see a veiled criticism of Greece in the remarks of the United States representative:

> I believe it is also clear that both parties recognize the potentially valuable role of the International Court of Justice to consider matters which remain unresolved after negotiations. The important thing is that the parties find a basis

on what it believed to be sufficient legal grounds and after extensive diplomatic efforts have proved fruitless in the search for the solution of legal problems of vital interest to it as well as to the other side. Greece, in appealing to the Court, has taken a step in the direction of depoliticizing the dispute; the Security Council has taken a step in repoliticizing it, the effect of which remains to be seen.[46]

## III. THE APPEAL OF GREECE TO THE INTERNATIONAL COURT OF JUSTICE

As stated earlier, Greece submitted an Application to the Court on August 10, 1976 in the dispute with Turkey concerning the continental shelf in the Aegean. At the same time Greece requested interim measures of protection pending judgment on the merits. Only this request will be considered here and it seems convenient to separate the action of the Court with respect to this request from the question of jurisdiction.

### A. Request for Interim Measure of Protection

The Greek request had two objectives: to enjoin both Greece and Turkey (a) from conducting further exploration or research in the contested areas and (b) from taking measures likely to endanger their peaceful relations.[47] The request was based on Article 33 of the General Act of 1928 for the Pacific Settlement of International Disputes, on Article 41 of the Statute of the Court, and Article 66 of the Court's Rules of Procedure.[48] Although the applicability of the General Act was contested by Turkey because it was no longer in force and if it was, the dispute was excluded by the Greek reservation,[49] the Court found it unnecessary "to reach a final conclusion at this stage of the proceedings"

> through direct contacts between them for whatever combination of direct talks and supporting adjudication may be necessary to achieve the peaceful settlement that my Government is confident both Governments seek.

UN Doc. S/PV.1953, at 17.

[46] It may be pertinent to draw attention to G.A. Resolution 3232(XXIX) of November 12, 1974 entitled "Review of the role of the International Court of Justice" which in a general way was designed to encourage states and UN organs to make greater use of the Court. 29 GAOR, Supp. (No. 31) 141, UN Doc. A/9631 (1974). In paragraph 6 the Assembly "reaffirms that recourse to judicial settlement of legal disputes, particularly referral to the International Court of Justice, should not be regarded as an unfriendly act." "Referral" in this context cannot mean anything but seising the Court by means of a unilateral application. It is difficult to escape the impression that both Turkey and the Security Council tended to regard the Greek Application as an unfriendly act which they should not have done had they heeded the Assembly resolution. For a recommendation of diplomatic and judicial procedures, see G.A. Res. 1497(XV), October 31, 1960, "The status of the German-speaking element in the Province of Bolzano (Bozen); implementation of the Paris agreement of 5 September 1946." 15 GAOR, Supp. (No. 16) 5, UN Doc. A/4684 (1960). In that case, however, no judicial proceedings were pending before the Court. In the Special Political Committee reference was made to Article 36(3) of the Charter by the representatives of Paraguay, Liberia and Ireland. 15 GAOR, Spec. Pol. C. at 19, 26, and 47 (1960).

[47] *See supra*, p. 31, at notes 3 and 4 for text of the Greek request.

[48] [1976]REP. 4, para. 2. It is not clear whether provisional measures indicated by the Court under Article 41 of the Statute are binding. *See Conclusions* in GROSS, *supra* note 38, at 739, and H. LAUTERPACHT, THE DEVELOPMENT OF INTERNATIONAL LAW BY THE INTERNATIONAL COURT 110–13, 253–54 (1958). Therefore, the invocation of Article 33(1) of the General Act had the object of eliminating any doubt on this score for it provides: "The parties to the dispute shall be bound to accept such measures."

[49] [1976]REP. 8, para. 19. *See supra* note 14.

on the question and decided to examine the Greek request "only in the context of Article 41 of the Statute."[50]

The Court then defined its powers under Article 41:

> Whereas the power of the Court to indicate interim preasures under Article 41 of the Statute presupposes that irreparable prejudice should not be caused to rights which are the subject of dispute in judicial proceedings and that the Court's judgment should not be anticipated by reason of any initiative regarding the matters in issue before the Court.[51]

The Court has used similar language on other occasions[52] and while the principles set out in the abstract may be clear enough, there may be problems when they are applied to particular situations. In the present case the Court examined in particular whether the concessions granted and the seismic explorations undertaken by Turkey were in the nature of causing or threatening an irreparable prejudice to the rights claimed by Greece as its own. The Court found that these activities cannot "be creative of new rights or deprive the other State of any rights to which in law it may be entitled."[53] Turning to the seismic explorations conducted by Turkey, the Court was of the opinion that their illegality depended upon a prior finding that they were conducted in an area which the Court, in proceedings on the merits, may find to appertain to Greece.[54] The Court appears to have broken new ground, however, when it applied the test of "irreparable prejudice" as a condition for the application of Article 41. The Court stated that a prejudice is not irreparable if it is "capable of reparation by appropriate means,"[55] that in the present case there was no threat of irreparable injury, and therefore no need or justification for applying Article 41.

The Court seems to have taken the cue offered it by Turkey which, in its Observations, argued that interim measures may be indicated when one of these two situations arises:

> either the damage that is caused to one party is irreparable in the sense that it cannot in the future be remedied by the payment of a sum of money; or the execution of the eventual judgment of the Court will be made impossible by the actions undertaken by the State against which the interim measures are requested. It is evident that neither of these two situations is present in this case. Even if one were to admit that the explorations conducted by Turkey did cause any harm to the rights of Greece, there would be no reason why such prejudice could not be compensated and one fails to see how it could possibly affect the execution of any judgment that the Court might give in the present case.[56]

[50] *Id.* 8, para. 21.

[51] *Id.* 9, para. 25.

[52] Fisheries Jurisdiction case (United Kingdom v. Iceland) Interim Protection, Order of Aug. 17, 1972, [1972] ICJ Rep. 12, at 16, para. 21, and Nuclear Tests case (Australia v. France), Interim Protection, Order of June 22, 1973, [1973] Rep. 99, at 103, para. 20.

[53] [1976] Rep. 10, para. 29.

[54] *Id.* 10–11, para. 31.

[55] *Id.* 11, para. 33.

[56] Turkish Observations, 14–15, para. 20. The quoted passage is summarized by the Court in [1976] Rep. 8, para. 18.

Applying this test to the case in hand, the Court declared that "the alleged breach by Turkey of the exclusivity of the right claimed by Greece to acquire information concerning the natural resources of areas of continental shelf, if it were established, is one that might be capable of reparation by appropriate means," that "it follows that the Court is unable to find in that alleged breach of Greece's rights such a risk of irreparable prejudice to the rights in issue before the Court as might require the exercise of its power under Article 41 of the Statute to indicate interim measures for their preservation,"[57] and on these grounds the Court declined to indicate such measures.

It is open to question whether the Court, in saying what it did, opened the proverbial Pandora's box or opened the way to a rational application of the test of "irreparable prejudice." One wonders, in this specific case, how the Court could have arrived at the conclusion that the prejudice, if one was found to have been created by Turkey, was "capable of reparation by appropriate means" without some inquiry and expert opinions,[58] and how Greece could be compensated for the "information" acquired by Turkey?[59] "Information" acquired by Turkey could affect negotiations on delimitation even if it were disclosed to Greece. Be that as it may, it is sufficient to point out that the test of compensation or reparations has not been applied by the Court in cases in which it did indicate provisional measures. There is at least no evidence of any reasoning along some such lines in the *Anglo-Iranian Oil Company,*[60] the *Fisheries Jurisdiction,* [61] or the *Nuclear Tests* cases.[62] There was a strong probability, to put it no higher, that the prejudice which may have been caused to the United Kingdom in the first two cases could have been "remedied by the payment of a sum of money." And even in the last case reparation could not be excluded if Australia were able to prove specific damage.[63] However, as Judge Elias pointed out in a trenchant criticism of the Court, the possibility of compensation depends upon a state's capacity to pay and this additional test would require the Court to make possibly invidious distinctions between states as to their capacity to pay compensation. Judge Elias said:

> Finally, the apparent acceptance by the majority of the Court that once any damage resulting from the exploration and/or exploitation by Turkey is capable of being compensated for in cash or kind, Greece cannot be said to have suffered irreparable damage does not seem to me to be a valid one. It means that the State which has the ability to pay can under

[57] *Id.* 11, para. 33.

[58] The Court does go into the question of nature and physical effect of seismic exploration "according to the information before the Court." *Id.* 10, para. 30.

[59] In his Dissenting Opinion, Judge *ad hoc* Stassinopoulos considered "equally irreparable the prejudice caused by the gathering of information on the resources of the Greek shelf and the possibility of disclosing them [*sc.* information; in French original: "des renseignements"], which would raise an insurmountable obstacle to their exploitation by Greece." *Id.* 37.

[60] Order of July 5, 1951. [1951] ICJ Rep. 89. On the question of compensation, see Lauterpacht, *supra* note 48 at 252.

[61] Order of Aug. 17, 1972. [1972] ICJ Rep. 12.

[62] Order of June 22, 1973. [1973] ICJ Rep. 99.

[63] The United States paid *ex gratia* compensations in the 1954 incident of the Japanese fishing boat *Diago Fukurya Maru,* the crew of which suffered injuries from radiation fallout. For details, see 4 Whiteman, Digest of International Law 565 ff. (1965). In the *Nuclear Tests* case, the Court noted that no claim of damages was raised by Australia. [1974] ICJ Rep. 270, para. 53.

> this principle commit wrongs against another State with impunity, since it discounts the fact that the injury by itself might be sufficient to cause irreparable harm to the national susceptibilities of the offended State. The rightness or wrongness of the action itself does not seem to matter. This is a principle upon which contemporary international law should frown: might should no longer be right in today's inter-State relations.[64]

The President of the Court, Judge Jiménez de Aréchaga, construed the words "if it considers that circumstances so require" in Article 41 of the Statute as meaning that before the interim measures can be granted "all relevant circumstances must be present—including the possibility of jurisdiction over the merits. However, to refuse interim measures it suffices for only one of the relevant circumstances to be absent." In the present case, one of the "absent" circumstances was apparently the circumstance of "irreparable injury," for, in his view, the Court's finding that interim measures were not required was based on "the existence of appropriate means of reparation or satisfaction."[65] That is, on the presence of a circumstance which, so far at any rate, has not been considered as included in Article 41. The question of jurisdiction will be taken up presently but, in view of the foregoing, one may agree with Judge Elias that "there are substantive as well as procedural questions raised in the consideration of the application of Article 41 of the Statute of the Court which require urgent and serious re-thinking by the Court."[66]

There remains for consideration the second part of the Greek request for provisional measures, namely "the right of Greece to the performance by Turkey of its undertaking contained in Article 2, paragraph 4, and Article 33 of the Charter of the United Nations and Article 33 of the General Act[67] . . . to abstain from all measures likely to react prejudicially upon the execution of any judicial decision given in these proceedings and to abstain from any sort of action which may aggravate or extend the present dispute between Greece and Turkey."[68] The Court declared that whereas this right "is not the subject of any of the several claims submitted to the Court by Greece in its Application; whereas it follows that this request does not fall within the provisions of Article 41 of the Statute."[69] The Court is no doubt on solid ground in saying that this right is not specifically included in the submissions formulated by Greece in its Application relating to the dispute. But this does not conclude the matter, for in another case, the *Anglo-Iranian Oil Company*, the Court did include among the provisional measures "which will apply on the basis of reciprocal observance:

> . . .
>
> 2. That the Iranian Government and the United Kingdom Government should each

[64] [1976] Rep. 30.
[65] *Id.* 16.
[66] *Id.* 29.
[67] It will be recalled that the Court had decided to confine its examination of the request to Article 41. *Id.* 8, para. 21 and *supra*, p. 1030.
[68] [1976] Rep. 6, para. 15(ii).
[69] *Id.* 11, para. 34.

> ensure that no action of any kind is taken which might aggravate or extend the dispute submitted to the Court.[70]

In its reasoning, the Court pointed out that as the object of Article 41 "is to preserve the respective rights of the Parties pending the decision of the Court," it follows "that the Court must be concerned to preserve by such measures the rights which may be subsequently adjudged by the Court to belong either to the Applicant or to the Respondent."[71] The decisive link seems to be between the measure and the *petita* and not between the measure and the ground on which the party, rightly or wrongly, bases its request for interim measures.

The reason for the statement that "the Court does not find it necessary to examine" the question whether it has "an independent power" to indicate measures "in order to prevent the aggravation or extension of the dispute" is the adoption by the Security Council of Resolution 395(1976) on August 25, 1976, the day when the Court began public hearings.[72] The Court was, of course, fully aware of the proceedings in the Council; it referred to the fourth and sixth preambular paragraphs and to operative paragraphs 2 and 3, as well as to the statements by Turkey and Greece made after the adoption of the resolution.[73] The Court then went on to say:

> 41. Whereas both Greece and Turkey, as Members of the United Nations, have expressly recognized the responsibility of the Security Council for the maintenance of international peace and security; whereas, in the above-mentioned resolution, the Security Council has recalled to them their obligations under the United Nations Charter with respect to the peaceful settlement of disputes, in the terms set out in paragraph 39 above; whereas, furthermore, as the Court has already stated, these obligations are clearly imperative in regard to their present dispute concerning the continental shelf in the Aegean; and whereas it is not to be presumed that either State will fail to heed its obligations under the Charter of the United Nations or fail to heed the recommendations of the Security Council addressed to them with respect to their present dispute;
>
> 42. Whereas, accordingly, it is not necessary for the Court to decide the question whether Article 41 of the Statute confers upon it the power to indicate interim measures of protection for the sole purpose of preventing the aggravation or extension of a dispute; . . .[74]

[70] [1951] ICJ REP. 89, at 93. *See also* Fisheries Jurisdiction case, [1972] ICJ REP. 17, para 1(a) of operative clause. For earlier cases, see LAUTERPACHT, *supra* note 48, at 282–83.

[71] [1951] ICJ REP. 89, at 93. The Court invoked Article 61(6) of its old Rules of Procedure, now Article 66(6), which authorizes the Court to indicate interim measures *proprio motu* as additional basis for its indication.

[72] [1976] REP. 5, paras. 6 and 9. The hearings were continued on August 26 and 27.

[73] *Id.* 12–13, paras. 37–40. The text of the preambular paragraphs referred to in paragraph 39 of the Order is as follows:

> *Bearing in mind* the principles of the Charter of the United Nations concerning the peaceful settlement of disputes, as well as the various provisions of Chapter VI of the Charter concerning procedures and methods for the peaceful settlement of disputes, . . .
>
> *Conscious* of the need for the parties both to respect each other's international rights and obligations and to avoid any incident which might lead to the aggravation of the situation and which, consequently, might compromise their efforts towards a peaceful solution, . . .

[74] *Id.* 13. In paragraph 43, the Court recalled Article 66(5) of its Rules of Procedure according to which a party may make a fresh request for interim measures "based on new facts."

It is clear that the Court left open the question of whether its power under Article 41 extends to the indication of measures "for the sole purpose of preventing the aggravation . . . of a dispute."[75] In the present case the Court did not feel compelled to take a stand because of the prompt or relatively prompt action by the Council. The Court found nothing in Article 41 or elsewhere in its Statute against the incorporation by reference, in its Order, of the relevant parts of Resolution 395.[76] On the other hand, the Court chose to ignore operative paragraph 4 of the resolution which includes a questionable reference to the potential role of the Court in the settlement of the dispute pending before it.[77]

Although the action of the Court with respect to the Council resolution was supported by all of the 12 sitting judges—the Order was adopted by 12 votes to 1 (the Greek judge *ad hoc*)—Judge Mosler had some reservations about it.[78] Judge Lachs would have wished the Court to have made "a positive contribution to the solution of the dispute." There is nothing in the Statute to preclude the Court from assisting states in the peaceful settlement of a dispute otherwise than by adjudication; in view of the intimate connection of the Court with the United Nations, the Court, he said, "should the more readily seize the opportunity of reminding the member States concerned in a dispute referred to it of certain obligations deriving from general international law or flowing from the Charter"; and while the Court "has given due prominence to this resolution" of August 25, 1976 in its reasoning,[79] there was, in his view, "no statutory bar to its spelling out the

[75] Rosenne seems to think that the Court has the power but should not exercise it in view of the availability of the political organs of the United Nations: "Nor, normally, ought this jurisdiction to be invoked to prevent 'incidents'. That was the rationale of the decision of the Permanent Court in the *South-Eastern Greenland* case, It applies with greater force when the Court is a principal organ of the United Nations, which has other organs—the Security Council and the General Assembly—equipped, to varying degrees, with competence to prevent 'incidents'." *Supra*, note 38, at 426. This is persuasive as far as it goes but if an applicant state in a Contentious proceedings also requests interim measures to prevent an aggravation of the dispute, it may well be part of the Court's judicial function to indicate such measures and not expect the applicant to appeal to the General Assembly, which may not be in session, or to the Security Council which may be prevented from taking useful action by a veto of one of its permanent members which may be in a patron-client relation to the respondent state. It seems pointless to procrastinate proceedings by referring the requesting party to Article 66(5) of the Court's Rules of Procedure.

[76] Thus Judge Elias, after referring to paragraph 41 of the Order—cited *supra*, note 74—said: "Since this must be the main object of the Greek Government's request and since the substance of the Security Council resolution which has thus been incorporated had been accepted as such by the Applicant, the Order has gone far towards achieving the desired result." [1976] REP. 30.

[77] It will be recalled that the Court denied the Turkish request to remove the case from its list. *Supra*, p. 1022. The Court in the operative part of its Order reserved "the fixing of time-limits for the said written proceedings [addressed to the jurisdiction of the Court], and the subsequent procedure, for further decisions." [1976] REP. 14. The time-limits were fixed by an Order of October 14, 1976, the Court fixed April 18, 1977 and October 24, 1977 for the delivery of the Greek Memorial and the Turkish Memorial respectively. ICJ Communiqué No. 77/10, Oct. 14, 1976.

[78] While agreeing with the Court that the seismic exploration of the shelf "does not cause, of itself and in isolation, irreparable damage" justifying the application of Article 41, he said:

> But I must express doubts regarding the Court's separation of the infringement of alleged Greek rights to exploration from the military measures, taken by both sides for purposes of the protection or supervision of the vessel, which involve a risk of armed conflict. I consider the military aspect not as a distinct element but simply as an aggravating circumstance additional to the basic element of continued exploration. In my view the Court should have considered that it was part of its overall responsibility to consider the situation as a whole, quite apart from its assessment of the Security Council's resolution and the reactions thereto of Greece and Turkey.
> [1976] REP. 26.

[79] Judge Tarazi also stressed that the Court being "an integral part of the United Nations," ought "if the circumstances so require . . . collaborate in the accomplishment of this fundamental mission," namely the responsibility of the

legal consequences of the Security Council's resolution and the official statements of the representatives of the two States. The pronouncements of the Council did not dispense the Court, an independent judicial organ, from expressing its own view on the serious situation in the disputed area.''[80] Judge Lachs concluded his view of the proper role of the Court as a judicial organ in the following words:

> While it would not be proper specifically to advise Greece and Turkey ''as to the various courses'' they should follow (*I.C.J. Reports 1951,* p. 83), the Court, acting *proprio motu,* should even while not indicating interim measures have laid greater stress on, in particular, the need for restraint on the part of both States and the possible consequences of any deterioration or extension of the conflict. In going further than it has, the Court, with all the weight of its judicial office, could have made its own constructive, albeit indirect, contribution, helping to pave the way to the friendly resolution of a dangerous dispute. This would have been consonant with a basic role of the Court within the international community.[81]

This is not the first time that the Court or its individual members have given voice to what might be called a dynamic conception of the role of the Court as a judicial organ. The emphasis on the connection between this Court and the United Nations was first made by the Court in connection with its advisory function.[82] There may be room for some flexibility in interpreting the words in Article 38(1) of the Statute: ''The Court, whose function is to decide in accordance with international law such disputes as are submitted to it'' in accordance with, broadly speaking, the international law in force. Conceivably some jurists might be moved to decline to serve on a tribunal with so narrowly defined a mission. But if that is not the mission of this Court, then what is it? To offer advice to the parties which come before it seeking a judgment?

It is not easy to discern in Judge Lachs' cryptic observations what additional advice he wanted the Court to offer to the parties. In the present submission, the Court's weighty observations on the obligations flowing from Articles 2(4) and 33 of the Charter could have been completed only by adding the Court's ''weight of its judicial office'' to paragraph 4 of Resolution 395(1976) and advise the parties, or rather Greece, to withdraw its application and put an end to the judicial proceedings, if not *ad calendas graecas*

Security Council for the maintenance of peace and security, and concluded that he ''would have thought it necessary to mention this resolution in the operative part.'' *Id.* 33–34. There are apparently no limits to the consequences to be derived from the integration of the Court in the United Nations.

[80] *Id.* 20. One cannot fail to be reminded of the legal consequences which the Court spelled out in the *Nuclear Tests* case with respect to the statements made by several French officials. [1974] ICJ Rep. 253, at 267, paras. 43 and 269, paras. 50–52. With regard to this case, *see* A. Rubin, *The International Legal Effects of Unilateral Declarations,* 71 AJIL (1977), pp. 1–30.

[81] *Id.* 20. The reference in the quotation is to the *Haya de la Torre* case in which the Court was asked to declare how its judgment in the *Asylum* case of November 20, 1950, should be executed.

[82] In *Peace Treaties* case, the Court declared:

> The Court's Opinion is given not to States, but to the organ which is entitled to request it; the reply of the Court, itself an ''organ of the United Nations'', represents its participation in the activities of the Organization, and, in principle, should not be refused.

[1950] ICJ Rep. 65, at 71.

then at least until the end of the current Third Law of the Sea Conference. Judge Tarazi may have expressed this intent quite clearly when he suggested that the Court should have mentioned "this resolution," the whole resolution, including its deleterious paragraph 4, in the operative part of its Order.

The desire of the Court to integrate itself ever more closely in the political activities of the United Nations may well be due, to some extent at any rate, to the growing number of *onusiens* elected to membership of the Court,[83] the greater emphasis on this principle of balanced or equitable geographical representation which has become pervasive in the United Nations, and the diminished concern with the personal qualification of the judges who should be, as Article 2 of the Statute provides, "jurisconsults of recognized competence in international law."[84] The integration process may well transform the Court into just another unit of the United Nations far removed from the center of its activities but the Court might as well pay heed to the import of this trend on its judicial business and the trend for states to submit disputes to arbitral tribunals rather than to the Court.[85]

## B. Jurisdiction of the Court

The impressive degree of cohesion exhibited by the judges in the 12 to 1 vote on the indication or, rather, nonindication of interim measures of protection stands in sharp contrast to the disarray with respect to the question of jurisdiction. Of the twelve judges who constituted the majority, eight wrote separate opinions of which three seem to support and five to oppose the decision of the Court on this question. The Greek *ad hoc* judge also dissented. The Court deals with this important matter in a single sentence which is as follows:

[83] Rosenne, *The Composition of the Court* in GROSS, *supra* note 38, at 428. The term refers to members of the Court "with a long history of personal involvement in United Nations affairs" and, "who by way of experience and intellectual inclination possess an intangible psychological relationship with the United Nations." *Id.* 388.

[84] Sir Gerald Fitzmaurice in *Enlargement of the Contentious Jurisdiction of the Court* (in GROSS, *supra,* note 38, at 469) stresses the need to elect jurists with expertise in public international law. Experience in international affairs and other branches of law does "not furnish an adequate substitute. It cannot be a good thing for the Court that members of it have to start learning—or re-learning—their public international law after they come to it." For comments on the suggestion of Fitzmaurice, see INSTITUT DE DROIT INTERNATIONAL LIVRE DU CENTENNAIRE 1893–1973, at 277, 391 (Bindschedler), 391–95 (Petrén), 395–96 (Reuter), 397 (Ruegger), and 400 (Rosenne) (1973).

Having been a member of the Court from 1960 to 1973, Fitzmaurice speaks from experience. Rosenne maintains that the qualifications of the candidates and "the records of the judges as are apparent from their separate and dissenting opinions (the only proper source of information on this subject) will show that the exacting standards of professional qualification and competence imposed by the Statute (Article 2) are generally reached." On the other hand, he notes that in trying to strike the balance between personal criteria and the demands of balanced geographical representation "not surprisingly perhaps, the two electoral colleges, being political organs, have come down heavily in favor of the politically directed criteria . . .". GROSS, *supra* 382. Membership in the International Law Commission, which Rosenne lists as a factor (*id.* 381), is not necessarily a criterion of professional competence as the elections to this organ have also come to be dominated by political criteria and considerations of balanced geographical representation. On the subject of the composition of the Court, see also GROSS, *supra,* 729–30.

[85] The revised Rules of Court have in fact acknowledged this trend but tried to capture it by opening up an opportunity for arbitral tribunals functioning within the framework of the Court. *See* E. Hambro, *Will the Revised Rules of Court Lead to Greater Willingness on the Part of Prospective Clients?* in GROSS, *supra,* note 38, at 365–76. It is not suggested that the trend noted in the text is the only or a primary reason why states eschew recourse to the Court. On this subject, as well as possible remedies, see GROSS, *supra, passim.*

Whereas, in order to pronounce on the present request for interim measures of protection, the Court is not called upon to decide any question of its jurisdiction to entertain the merits of the case; . . .[86]

In recent cases the Court specifically addressed the question of jurisdiction in connection with requests for indication of provisional measures. Thus in the *Fisheries Jurisdiction* case the Court said while it "need not, before indicating them, *finally* satisfy itself that it has jurisdiction on the merits of the case, yet it ought not to act under Article 41 of the Statute if the absence of jurisdiction on the merits is *manifest.*"[87] Having considered the basis of jurisdiction invoked by the United Kingdom, the Court said that this provision "in an instrument emanating from both Parties to the dispute appears, prima facie, to afford a *possible* basis on which the jurisdiction of the Court might be founded."[88] Similarly, in the *Nuclear Tests* cases, the Court held "that the provisions invoked by the Applicant appear, prima facie, to afford a basis on which the jurisdiction of the Court might be founded."[89].

In an earlier case, the *Anglo-Iranian Oil Company,* the Court granted the British request for interim measures, although its jurisdiction was contested by Iran, after having satisfied itself that "it cannot be accepted *a priori* that a claim based on such a complaint falls completely outside the scope of international jurisdiction."[90] Judges Winiarski and Badawi Pasha in their Dissenting Opinion objected to the decision of the Court saying: "The question of interim measures of protection is linked, for the Court, with the question of jurisdiction; the Court has power to indicate such measures only if it holds, should it be only provisionally, that it is competent to hear the case on its merits."[91]

[86] [1976] REP. 13, para. 44. The rest of the sentence is unobjectionable and reads as follows: "—and whereas the decision given in these proceedings in no way prejudges any such question, or any question relating to the merits, and leaves unaffected the rights of the Greek and Turkish Governments to submit arguments in respect to any of these questions."

[87] [1972] ICJ REP. 12, at 15, para. 15 (emphasis supplied).

[88] *Id.* 16, para. 17 (emphasis supplied).

[89] [1973] ICJ REP. 99, at 102, para. 17. In the *Trial of Pakistani Prisoners of War* case, the Court did not refer to the basis of jurisdiction invoked by Pakistan, if there was one, and found it unnecessary to deal with the Pakistani request for provisional measures on the ground that Pakistan requested postponement of its request. *Id.* 328, at 330, para. 14. Nevertheless, Judge Petrén, in his Dissenting Opinion, expressed the view that "the first question to which the Court should have attended was that of its own jurisdiction on the merits of the case." *Id.* 334.

[90] [1951] ICJ REP. 89, at 93. The Court continued that "the considerations stated in the preceding paragraph suffice to empower the Court to entertain the Request for interim measures of protection." This case is unusual because the President of the Court addressed a telegram to the Prime Minister of Iran on June 23, 1951, the day after receiving the British request, suggesting that no measures be taken which might impede the execution and eventual judgment or aggravate the dispute. The hearing in this case was held on June 30. *Id.* 91 and 92.

[91] *Id.* 96. These two judges, elaborating the cited statement, pointed out that the text of Article 41 presupposes the competence of the Court, inasmuch as there must be "proceedings" and "parties" within the meaning of the Statute. The Court need not pronounce "finally" on its jurisdiction "but the Court must consider its competence reasonably probable," and "its opinion on this point should be reached after a summary consideration." *Id.* 96 and 97. The judges rejected any presumption in favor of the Court's power by pointing out that under Article 41 the power of the Court is not unconditional and that generally speaking

We find it difficult to accept the view that if *prima facie* the total lack of jurisdiction of the Court is not patent, that is, if there is a possibility, however remote, that the Court may be competent, then it may indicate interim measures of protection. This approach, which also involves an element of judgment and which does not reserve to any greater extent the right of the Court to give a final decision as to its jurisdiction, appears however to be based

In *Interhandel,* the only case in which this Court found "that there is no need to indicate interim measures of protection," the Court, at the outset of its consideration of the Swiss request, declared that both Switzerland and the United States "have, by Declarations made on their behalf, accepted the compulsory jurisdiction of the Court on the basis of Article 36, paragraph 2, of the Statute."[92] The United States invoked its self-judging reservation, known as the Connally reservation, even against the indication of provisional measures, but the Court felt relieved of the need to examine its validity by the Swiss Co-Agent. He challenged the reservation on several grounds but also stated at the hearing, "that, in its examination of a request for the indication of interim measures of protection, the Court would not wish to adjudicate 'upon so complex and delicate a question as the validity of the American reservation'."[93] Judge Lauterpacht, in his Separate Opinion, agreed with the U.S. contention that the objection "removed the basis for any assumption of a *prima facie* jurisdiction of the Court on the merits of the dispute and that the Court therefore lacked the power to exercise jurisdiction under Article 41 of the Statute." In his view, governments "have the right to expect that the Court will not act under Article 41 in cases in which absence of jurisdiction on the merits is manifest." He stated that

> The correct principle . . . which has been uniformly adopted in international arbitral and judicial practice is as follows: The Court may properly act under the terms of Article 41 provided that there is in existence an instrument such as a Declaration of Acceptance of the Optional Clause, emanating from the Parties to the dispute, which *prima facie* confers jurisdiction upon the Court and which incorporates no reservations obviously excluding its jurisdiction. These conditions do not exist in the case now before the Court.[94]

In the opinion of Judge Lauterpacht this principle applies whether the Court exercises jurisdiction "by granting the request for an indication of interim measures or by declining it."[95] He argued that the Court had assumed jurisdiction with regard to the Swiss request and although "it has declined to grant it," the Order is "contrary to a conclusive condition under which the jurisdiction of the Court has been accepted."[96]

> on a presumption in favour of the competence of the Court which is not in consonance with the principles of international law. In order to accord with these principles, the position should be reversed: if there exists weighty arguments in favour of the challenged jurisdiction, the Court may indicate interim measures of protection; if there exists serious doubts or weighty arguments against this jurisdiction such measures cannot be indicated.

*Id.* 97. For argument against the probability test, see LAUTERPACHT, *supra* note 48, at 255, particularly nn. 41 and 42.

[92] [1957] ICJ REP. 105, at 110.

[93] *Id.* 111. The Court also said that the decision given under Article 61 of Rules of Court—Article 66 of the revised Rules—does not prejudge the question of jurisdiction on the merits.

[94] *Id.* 118–19 (emphasis in the original). *See also* LAUTERPACHT,*supra* note 48, at 111–12 for an identical statement, and also *id.* at 255.

[95] [1957] ICJ REP. 119 and also at 120.

[96] *Id.* 120. Some of the material presented here is contained in the Turkish Observations at 5–8. Turkey argued that the Court lacked prima facie jurisdiction because the General Act was no longer in force and the Brussels Agreement did not constitute a commitment to submit the dispute to the Court without a special agreement. *Id.* 8–9.

It appears from this survey that although opinions differ about the proper construction of instruments conferring jurisdiction upon it, the Court itself considered that no matter how tenuous—as in the *Anglo-Iranian Oil Company* case, where it is most tenuous—there must be a link between jurisdiction on the merits and the power to indicate provisional measures or to deny them. The present case departs from what may be regarded as the constant jurisprudence of the Court. The President, Judge Aréchaga, in explaining this departure in his Separate Opinion, argued that "Article 41 is an autonomous grant of jurisdiction to the Court, independent from its jurisdiction over the merits of the dispute," that the possibility of jurisdiction is only one of the relevant circumstances, and that it would make no sense to indicate measures unless there was "reasonable possibility, prima facia ascertained by the Court, of jurisdiction on the merits." In this case interim measures were not required because there was no danger of irreparable injury in view of the existence of appropriate means of satisfaction, and "having reached this conclusion it was not necessary for the Court to make any determination as to the prospect of its jurisdiction with regard to the merits, even on a prima facie basis."[97] In a nutshell, if the Court rejects a request for provisional measures, it need not concern itself with the question of jurisdiction.

It is not necessary to examine the proposition that under Article 41 the Court enjoys power independent from jurisdiction on the merits. Judge Mosler correctly pointed out, it is believed, that the power under Article 41 is not "an independent source of jurisdiction on the same footing and of the same legal quality as Article 36." In his view, it is "an autonomous grant of jurisdiction" only to the extent "that it permits that the grounds conferring jurisdiction in conformity with the basic Article [Art. 36 of the Statute] are to be examined only to the extent that this can be done without endangering the urgency with which a request for interim measures must be considered."[98]

[97] [1976] REP. 15–16. As a further reason for declining the request the Court relied on the action taken by the Security Council.

[98] *Id.* 24. The link between jurisdiction on merits and provisional measures was developed persuasively by Judges Winiarski and Badawi Pasha in their Dissenting Opinion in the *Anglo-Iranian Oil Company* case where the link was stretched by the Court to the breaking point. In view of the confusion reflected in the present case, it seems worthwhile to quote their statement:

> In international law it is the consent of the parties which confers jurisdiction on the Court; the Court has jurisdiction only in so far as that jurisdiction has been accepted by the parties. The power given to the Court by Article 41 is not unconditional; it is given for the purposes of the proceedings and is limited to those proceedings. If there is no jurisdiction as to the merits, there can be no jurisdiction to indicate interim measures of protection. Measures of this kind in international law are exceptional in character to an even greater extent than they are in municipal law; they may easily be considered a scarcely tolerable interference in the affairs of a sovereign State. For this reason, too, the Court ought not to indicate interim measures of protection unless its competence, in the event of this being challenged, appears to the Court to be nevertheless reasonably probably. Its opinion on this point should be reached after a summary consideration; it can only be provisional and cannot prejudge its final decision, after the detailed consideration to which the Court will proceed in the course of adjudicating on the question in conformity with all the Rules laid down for its procedure.

[1951] ICJ REP. 97. Rosenne affirmed "that there is no essential interconnexion" between the jurisdiction of the Court under Article 41 and its jurisdiction on the merits, but concludes as follows: "Having regard to the exceptional power which this jurisdiction [under Art. 41] involves, it may be arguable that it ought to be more closely integrated with the principal jurisdiction to deal with the case on the merits then it now is." *Supra,* note 38, at 428. *See also* Briggs, *The Inciden-*

Judge Nagendra Singh agreed with the President's view that the question of competence does not arise if the Court finds that no circumstances exist which would justify exercise of its powers under Article 41.[99] Judge Elias, without referring to the distinction between a positive or a negative decision on a request, agrees with the majority view that "it is not necessary to decide the question [of jurisdiction to entertain the Greek request for interim measures] for the purpose of indicating provisional measures of protection under Article 41 of the Statute of the Court."[100]

Judge Lachs, disagreeing with the Court, stated that the Court was "under an obligation to consider the issue [of jurisdiction] *proprio motu* and make clear its provisional view thereon, notwithstanding the negative answer it felt bound to give the request for interim measures."[101] Judge Ruda, in a remarkably short Separate Opinion, expressed his agreement with Lauterpacht's view in the *Interhandel* case[102] and, disagreeing with the Court, stated that "the Court cannot decide on a request for interim measures of protection, without having considered, at least prima facie, the basic question of its own jurisdiction to entertain the merits of the dispute."[103] Judge Mosler, whose views on the question of principle have already been presented, appears to disagree with the President's view that the question of jurisdiction is a circumstance within the meaning of Article 41. In his opinion it is "a preconditon of the examination whether such circumstances exist." He also rightly, it is submitted, declared:

> If the Court however, as in the present Order, rejects the request because the circumstances are not considered to require interim measures, it examines the legal situation existing between the parties to the dispute and thus, to that extent, also assumes jurisdiction. But in this hypothesis the Court has only to satisfy itself that it does not manifestly lack jurisdiction, since the Order does nothing to interfere with the rights of the respondent party.[104]

Judge Tarazi dissented from the view that under Article 41 "the Court possesses a special competence which is in some way different from its basic, specific jurisdiction as

*tal Jurisdiction of the International Court of Justice as Compulsory Jurisdiction,* in K. ZEMANEK (ed.), VÖLKERBRECHT UND RECHTLICHES WELTBILD. FESTSCHRIFT FÜR ALFRED VERDROSS 87, at 92 ff. (1960). In his view, states by becoming parties to the Statute have consented to the incidental jurisdiction of the Court of which Article 41 is a part. *Id.* 93 f.

[99] [1976] REP. 17. Judge Nagendra Singh would require a more exacting degree of jurisdiction for the indication of measures than "prima facie" jurisdiction or "no manifest lack" of it. "The acid test," in his view, "of the Court's competence . . . is that the judgment be within clear prospect."

[100] *Id.* 27.

[101] *Id.* 19.

[102] *See supra,* p. 1038, at note 94.

[103] [1976] REP. 23.

[104] *Id.* 25. In order fully to understand Judge Mosler's point, it may be useful to quote his "attempted definition of the criteria of a positive prima facie test" which is as follows:

> In view of the provisional character of the requested Order and bearing in mind that it in no way prejudges the decisions to be taken in the forthcoming proceedings, it is in my view sufficient that the Court, when it actually indicates interim measures, should have reached the provisional conviction, based on a summary examination of the material before it (including written observations of a party not represented) and subject to any objections which may be raised in subsequent proceedings, that it has jurisdiction on the merits of the case.

*Id.* 24. *See also* Judge Lauterpacht's view, *supra,* at note 95.

conferred by Article 36'' of the Statute. In his view ''the power conferred upon it by Article 41 to indicate interim measures when appropriate is merely a corollary of its jurisdiction under Article 36''; only ''a more thoroughgoing examination'' of the relevant instruments, would enable the Court to pronounce upon the issue of jurisdiction. Existing ambiguities could be resolved only ''after written and oral proceedings had taken place in the normal way.''[105]

Taken literally, Judge Tarazi would break with the jurisprudence of the Court which has been content with some preliminary tests such as prima facie. There is no doubt whatever that this is the position of Judge Morozov, who, without writing a separate or dissenting opinion, participated in the three recent cases in which the Court applied a provisional or summary test to the question of jurisdiction in connection with the application Article 41 measures.[106] Briefly, Judge Morozov's argument was that the provisions in Chapter III of the Statute entitled ''Procedure'' have no independent significance from Chapter II entitled ''Competence of the Court,'' that as the Turkish Government had suggested lack of jurisdiction, ''it was the primary duty of the Court to consider the question of its jurisdiction'' and he stressed ''that the Court has no right to consider either the question of appointment of a judge *ad hoc* under Article 31, paragraph 3, of the Statute, or the question of interim measures of protection, before it has satisfied itself that it has jurisdiction in accordance with Articles 36 and 37 of the Statute.''[107] He also objected to the statement of the Court[108] that the absence of Turkey from the hearings ''cannot by itself constitute an obstacle to the indication of interim measures of protection'' on the ground that pursuant to Article 52(2) of the Statute, the Court, in such a case, ''must satisfy itself that it has jurisdiction.''[109]

The judge *ad hoc* in this case joined the group of judges who urged the necessity of finding some basis of jurisdiction. As Judge Stassinopoulos put it:

> the Court must satisfy itself, by an extremely summary examination, that it has prima facie jurisdiction to deal with the merits of the case. Not only does that rule emerge from the Court's jurisprudence, but it also constitutes a general principle governing all analogous institutions.[110]

[105] *Id.* 32.

[106] These cases are summarized, *supra*, p. 1031. Referring to this practice in which he participated, Judge Marozov pointed out that neither the Statute nor the Rules of Court ''contain any provisions which provide that the request for interim measures of protection has any priority over the question of jurisdiction. The precedents afforded by cases in which the Court has sometimes made Orders on the question of interim measures of protection contrary to its Statute and Rules cannot be regarded as having any value in the argument.'' [1976] Rep. 22.

[107] *Id.* 21.

[108] *Id.* 6, para. 13.

[109] *Id.* 22. It may be of interest to note that Judge Gros participated in the Order in the present case although in his Dissenting Opinion in the *Nuclear Tests* case he argued strongly that it was not ''in accordance with the rules of procedure to suspend the application of Article 53 provisionally in the present case on the ground that this is an interim measure phase.'' [1973] ICJ Rep. 99, at 117. It may be that Article 53 could be suspended if the Court declined to indicate the requested measures and to that extent his earlier emphatically expressed view may appear to be modified.

[110] [1976] Rep. 39.

It is obvious that some middle ground will have to be found between a more or less mechanical and superficial test of jurisdiction prior to the indication of provisional measures or the rejection of a request for it and the desire of Judges Tarazi and Morozov for a test which would amount to a full airing of the question of jurisdiction on merits in extended written and oral pleadings. Judge Elias was certainly right, seeing the disarray of opinions on this matter, in suggesting that it requires "urgent and serious re-thinking by the Court."[111] As there is no other case pending before the Court and this case is not likely to come up for a hearing on the question of jurisdiction before the end of 1977,[112] the Court has ample time, if it so desires, to examine the question with the thoroughness that it deserves. The prestige of and the confidence in the Court suffer if the judges are as divided as they were in this case on a relatively simple, but from the point of view of the state interests involved, fundamental issue. However, considering the fluctuations in the composition of the Court due to the triennial system of elections, it would be desirable, if the Court finds a formula for the future, to include it in the Rules of Court. Then governments would be on notice with respect to the test of jurisdiction which the Court requires for entertaining a request for interim measures and be prepared to furnish the Court with the necessary written and oral arguments.

## IV. CONCLUDING OBSERVATIONS

A further point may deserve consideration in this context. Pursuant to Article 35(2) of the Rules of Court (Art. 32(2) of the 1964 Rules), in case of unilateral arraignment, the application "must also, as far as possible, specify the provision on which the applicant founds the jurisdiction of the Court." The flexibility built into this rule—"must . . . as far as possible"—opens the way to the assumption of jurisdiction on the basis of *forum prorogatum*. It is not necessary to examine this doctrine here in all its ramifications[113] but one aspect of it may help explain the reason why with some regularity, one might be tempted to say with alarming regularity, states abstain from participating in the proceedings before the Court initiated by a unilateral application. In the present Court, the *forum prorogatum* doctrine was first applied in the *Corfu Channel* case. Proceedings in this case were instituted by a unilateral application transmitted to the Court on May 22, 1947, in which the United Kingdom founded the jurisdiction on the combined effect of four factors: Article 36(1) of the Statute, the resolution of the Security Council of April 9, 1947, the participation of Albania in the Council proceedings under Article 32 of the Charter, and, finally, Article 25 of the Charter.[114]

The Albanian Government, in a letter of July 23, 1947, rejected the British argument and contended that the case could be brought before the Court only by special

[111] *Id.* 29. *See supra*, p. 1031.
[112] *See supra*, note 77 for the time-limits fixed for the filing of written pleadings.
[113] The doctrine is discussed by ROSENNE, *supra*, note 38, at 344–63.
[114] [1947–48] ICJ REP. 17 and 1 Corfu Channel Case, ICJ Pleadings 8 (1947).

agreement. However, it also stated that, inspired by certain lofty principles, "it is prepared, notwithstanding this irregularity in the action taken by the Government of the United Kingdom, to appear before the Court" and "that its acceptance of the Court's jurisdiction for this case cannot constitute a precedent for the future."[115] The first reaction to this letter was an Order made by the President of the Court on July 31, 1947, which stated:

> Whereas having regard to the Resolution of the Security Council of April 9th, 1947, the said note of the Albanian Government may be regarded as constituting the document mentioned in Article 36 of the Rules of Court.[116]

Thus Albania, probably unwittingly, supplied the missing link which established it as the respondent in the proceedings. This is apparent from the Memorial of the United Kingdom in which it interpreted the Albanian letter as accepting "the jurisdiction of the Court in the present dispute" and for this reason "the difference of opinion as to the effect of Article 25 of the Charter is of no practical importance for the purposes of the present case."[117] Albania endeavored to retrieve its slip, if that is what it was, in its Preliminary Objections[118] and in the oral hearings, which was of no avail.[119] In its statement on the Preliminary Objection, the United Kingdom held Albania to the letter[120] and declared: "Having once consented to the jurisdiction, the Albanian Government cannot afterwards withdraw its consent."[121]

The Court rejected the Albanian charge that the proceedings were irregularly instituted[122] and declared:

> In submitting the case by means of an Application, the Government of the United Kingdom gave the Albanian Government the opportunity of accepting the jurisdic-

[115] [1947–48] ICJ Rep. 19 and 46. Albania reiterated its reservations but also appointed its Agent. *Ibid.* The full text of Albania's letter is in 2 Pleadings 25 (1947).

[116] [1947–1948] ICJ Rep. 20. For the full text of the Order, see *id.*4.

[117] 1 Pleadings 20 (1947).

[118] [1947–48] ICJ Rep. 20–23.

[119] *See* the statement by the representative of Albania, Vochoč, in 3 Pleadings 48 (1947).

[120] "Even if (which is not admitted) there was any formal irregularity in the mode of commencement of the present proceedings, this irregularity has been *cured* because the Albanian Government by its letter of 2nd July, 1947, has *waived* any possible objection and has consented to the jurisdiction of the Court. An irregularity in the manner in which a case is introduced may be cured by subsequent events . . ." [1947–48] ICJ Rep. 24 (emphasis supplied).

[121] *Id.* This theme, that Albania was trying to go back on its acceptance, was elaborated by Sir Hartley Shawcross in the hearings. *See* 3 Pleadings 56, 76, 154 (1947).

[122] Rejecting the Albanian assumption that "the institution of proceedings by application is only possible where compulsory jurisdiction exists and that, where it does not, proceedings can only be instituted by special agreement," the Court declared:

> This is a mere assertion which is not justified by either of the texts cited. Article 32, paragraph 2, of the Rules does not require the Applicant, as an absolute necessity, but only "as far as possible," to specify in the application the provision on which he founds the jurisdiction of the Court. It clearly implies, both by its actual terms and by the reasons underlying it, that the institution of proceedings by application is not exclusively reserved for the domain of compulsory jurisdiction.

[1947–48] ICJ Rep. 27.

> tion of the Court. This acceptance was given in the Albanian Government's letter of July 2nd, 1947 . . .
>
> Furthermore, there is nothing to prevent the acceptance of jurisdiction, as in the present case, from being effected by two separate and successive acts, instead of jointly and beforehand by a special agreement.[123]

It may be idle to speculate, thirty years later, whether the Court was inspired by the maxim *boni judicis est ampliare jurisdictionem* or whether it was unduly harsh on Albania. In any event the outcome in the *Corfu Channel* case[124] left traces which can be seen in a later case, the *Anglo-Iranian Oil Company* case. In the application of May 26, 1951, instituting proceedings against Iran, the United Kingdom invoked the declaration of September 19, 1932 whereby the Government of Persia had accepted the jurisdiction of the Permanent Court of International Justice as compulsory under Article 36(2) of its Statute. Referring to the *Corfu Channel* case, it also submitted:

> Alternatively, whether or not the Court has the right to exercise jurisdiction in this case by virtue of the terms of the aforementioned declaration . . . the Government of the United Kingdom expects that Iran as a Member of the United Nations[125] . . . will appear before the Court voluntarily in order to hear and answer on their merits the arguments of the Government of the United Kingdom.[126]

The Iranian Government, which seems to have been better served by expert advice than had been the Albanian Government, declined the profferred bait and in carefully conceived language, submitted observations dated February 4, 1952, the sole purpose of which was to demonstrate the lack of competence of the Court and reject its jurisdiction. It went on to say:

> Il ne s'agit donc pas ici d'un contremémoire dont on pourrait induire qu'il lie la procédure devant la Cour, mais seulement de refuter le mémoire du Gouvernement anglais en date du 10 octobre 1951 et uniquement sur les points qui ont trait à la compétence de la Cour.[127]

[123] *Id.* 27–28. The Court went on to quote from Judgment No. 12, of April 26, 1928 in the *Minority Schools in Upper Silesia* case of the PCIJ:

> The acceptance by a State of the Court's jurisdiction in a particular case is not, under the Statute, subordinated to the observance of certain forms, such as, for instance, the previous conclusion of a special agreement.

*See* 2 Hudson, World Court Reports 284 (1935).

[124] It may be recalled that the outcome must have appeared sufficiently doubtful to both parties because they did conclude a special agreement in which Albania was able to include a complaint against the United Kingdom relating to the "Operation Retail" on which the Court gave judgment in favor of Albania. [1949] ICJ Rep. 4 at 36.

[125] There follow citations to Articles 1(1) and 36(3) of the Charter.

[126] Anglo-Iranian Oil Company case, Pleadings 8, at 17–18 (1951).

[127] *Id.* 281. In the author's translation:

> There can be no question here of a counter-memorial which could be construed as completing the procedure before the Court, rather it is intended for the sole purpose of rejecting the Memorial of the British Government dated October 10, 1951, and is limited exclusively to the jurisdiction of the Court.

It is interesting to note that Iran characterized the nationalization of the Company as "an act of national liberation." *Id.* 306.

In order to make doubly sure that the doctrine of *forum prorogatum* would be excluded by any act which could be construed as tacit or implied consent to jurisdiction, the Iranian Government chose to be absent from the proceedings.[128] The Court indicated interim measures of protection which, as is well known, were ignored. At a later stage the Court found, as was predicted by Judges Winiarski and Badawi Pasha, that it had no jurisdiction on the merits.[129]

In the instant case, the *Aegean* dispute, the Turkish Government took its precautions against any possible application of the *forum prorogatum.* It was absent from the hearing but this may well be explained, as indeed it was, by the short notice given by the Court.[130] In its letter of transmittal, dated August 25, 1976, it is stated:

> On the assurance which was given by the President of the International Court of Justice to the Turkish Ambassador at The Hague during their informal conversation on 18 August 1976, it is understood that the presentation of the attached observations to the International Court of Justice shall not imply any commitment as to the jurisdiction of the Court.

This express reservation was restated in the Observations.[131] The unsettling effect of the *forum prorogatum* doctrine may also be gauged from the fact that in acknowledging the receipt of the Greek Application and Request for interim measures, Turkey felt bound to declare, through its Ambassador, that it did so "with the understanding that this would commit neither himself nor his Government."[132] It may well be correct that, according to a general principle of international law applicable also in international litigation, and therefore in proceedings before the Court, "a party is not permitted to benefit from its

[128] It is pertinent to cite in this context the following statement from the Dissenting Opinion of Judges Winiarski and Badawi Pasha:

> There are certainly cases in which the objection to the jurisdiction is regarded as a mere ground of defence, and in which the party overruled in its objection continues to take part in the proceedings. But in this case the facts are quite different. Iran affirms that it has not accepted the jurisdiction of the Court in the present matter and that it is in no way bound in law; it has refused to appear before the Court and has put forward reasons for its attitude. The Court ought therefore to decide, in a summary way and provisionally, for the purpose of arriving at the decision which it must take on the question of interim measures of protection, which is the more probable of the two conclusions which it may finally come to on the question of its jurisdiction.

[1951] ICJ Rep. 98.

[129] [1952] Rep. 93, at 111. For the prediction, see [1951] ICJ Rep. 98. An attempt by the United Kingdom to apply the doctrine of *forum prorogatum* to certain submissions by Iran was firmly rejected by the Court in holding:

> The principle of *forum prorogatum,* if it could be applied to the present case, would have to be based on some conduct or statement of the Government of Iran which involved an element of consent regarding the jurisdiction of the Court. . . . It is true that it has submitted other Objections which have no direct bearing on the question of jurisdiction. But they are clearly designed as measures of defence which it would be necessary to examine only if Iran's Objection to the jurisdiction were rejected.

[1952] ICJ Rep. 101, at 113–14. *See* Rosenne, *supra* note 38, at 360–61.

[130] Turkish Observations, 2, para. 5.

[131] "Nevertheless, so that the Court may be informed that, in the view of the Turkish Government, the Greek request is without merit, Turkey is submitting the present observations without commitments." *Ibid.*

[132] *Id.* 1, para. 2.

own inconsistencies."[133] However, no inconsistency is involved when a state declares it has not agreed to jurisdiction and it is undesirable to attempt to erode the principle of consent by indirection as long as it is resistant to a frontal attack.[134]

The question then is whether any lesson can be learned from past experience. It is suggested that a lesson can be learned by an analogy from domestic judicial practice. It is well established in Anglo-American jurisprudence that a foreign sovereign cannot be impleaded in the courts of another country without its consent. There are various ways for asserting this sovereign immunity from suit. One of these is for the foreign sovereign to appear in court "specially," that is for the sole purpose of asserting its immunity. An appearance so made precludes any imputation of submission, tacitly or by implication, to the jurisdiction of the court on the merits. It would seem that a procedure along these lines might go a long way towards restoring confidence in the fairness of the International Court's procedure on jurisdiction, particularly, but not necessarily exclusively, in connection with requests for interim measures of protection.[135] By appearing voluntarily to contest a claimed title to jurisdiction, the state should not be held to have consented, by *this appearance alone,* to the jurisdiction of the Court to indicate measures of protection or to jurisdiction on the merits.

It is submitted that in the *Corfu Channel* case the Albanian letter of July 2, 1947, could easily have been interpreted in the sense of willingness "to appear before the Court," as it explicitly stated, for the sole purpose of contesting the title of jurisdiction invoked by the United Kingdom in its application. The Iranian Government in its observations expressed itself with greater prudence but did not appear in Court. The Turkish Government in the *Aegean* dispute might conceivably have appeared in Court in spite of the extremely tight time-limit, if that could have been done without any risk that its appearance could or would be construed as admission of jurisdiction. The issue may not be as clear cut in the other case. The suggestion here made would probably be less helpful in cases like the *Fisheries Jurisdiction* case. It might have had some relevance in the *Nuclear Tests* case. In that case Australia invoked two bases of jurisdiction. One was the French Declaration of May 20, 1966 made pursuant to Article 36(2) of the Statute. This excluded explicitly "disputes concerning activities connected with national defence." This clause would fall into the category suggested by Lauterpacht, namely that the prima facie as-

[133] ROSENNE, *supra,* note 38, at 348.

[134] After reviewing the relevant cases and their aftermath, Rosenne concludes: "No doubt the connexion between these instances of the failure of the judicial process and the doctrine of *forum prorogatum* is purely fortuitous. Nevertheless, hesitation over the practical wisdom of the Court's attitude is necessarily strong and, so far, unresolved." *Id.* 363. It may be added that this hesitation has been reinforced by the Court's jurisprudence in more recent years.

[135] This point was made by Sir Hartley Shawcross, who reviewing the alternatives open to Albania, stated:

> The second course was that the Government of Albania might have appeared and objected to the jurisdiction—appearing only in order to argue its objection on the grounds of competence; not submitting itself to the jurisdiction of the Court at all, but appearing before the Court in order to argue that the Court was not competent. Clearly that course was open to the Government of Albania if it chose to take it.

3 Corfu Channel case, ICJ Pleadings 56 (1947).

sumption of jurisdiction is permissible if the Declaration "incorporates no reservations obviously excluding jurisdiction."[136] The other title of jurisdiction invoked by Australia in the *Nuclear Tests* case, as it was in the present case by Greece, is the General Act of 1928. Its continued validity is certainly not clear nor is its invalidity "obviously" clear, as was claimed by France in the former[137] and suggested by Turkey in the latter case.[138] The matter was further complicated by the Turkish claim that the French reservation to its acceptance of the General Act clearly excluded the jurisdiction of the Court[139] and by the French claim that its later reservation in the 1966 Declaration should be applied to its earlier acceptance of the General Act.[140] Perhaps the interests of a sound administration of justice in disputes between sovereign states would have been served better if both France and Turkey could have had the possibility open to them to appear specially before the Court for the sole purpose of arguing the validity of the General Act, leaving open the way for arguments on the applicability of the reservation to the jurisdiction of the Court founded on the General Act. This Act may well have ceased to be a usable basis of jurisdiction of this Court but it cannot be excluded that states may find in their archives jurisdictional clauses which they may consider of some validity in instituting proceedings before the Court. The procedural remedy here suggested might well be useful to dispose of such clauses without risk to the respondent party.

If the Court takes the question of the relationship between jurisdiction and Article 41 measures under consideration, it might also consider providing in its Rules for the possibility of "respondent" states appearing specially, in conformity with the principle that no state may be impleaded without its consent.

[136] *Supra*, p. 1038, at note 94.
[137] [1973] ICJ REP. 102 para. 15.
[138] Turkish Observations 10, para. 16.
[139] *Id.* 10–12, and *supra*, note 14.
[140] [1973] ICJ REP. 102, para. 15.

# ON THE JUSTICIABILITY OF INTERNATIONAL DISPUTES

Hans Morgenthau recently affirmed his belief "in the eternal truth of Hobbes' insight into the nature of society and of the relation between law and politics to the effect that there can be no legal order, that there can be no peace within society, without the existence of a government which can give the law, formulate the law, apply, and enforce it." Applying this insight to international relations, he contended: "There can be no stable political order, there can be no permanent peace, there can be no viable legal order without a government. As long as nations deal with each other and more particularly oppose each other on the basis of equality without having a sovereign superior to them which can give, apply, and enforce the law, the international order, international peace, and international law are bound to be in a precarious state."[1]

This is not exactly and probably was not intended to be a novel proposition. For centuries, certainly since Dante's *De Monarchia* (1312–1313), plans have been formulated for a world government or federation that, to use the words of the 1928 Kellogg-Briand Pact, would do away with war as an instrument of national policy. At the two Hague Peace Conferences of 1899 and 1907, the nineteenth-century peace movement and governments themselves fostered the idea of arbitration as a substitute for, or alternative to, war as a means of settling disputes. At the same time governments tried to limit arbitration to the solution of those conflicts that have come to be known as legal disputes and that usually did not cause wars, and to exempt from commitments to arbitrate those con-

* "I wish to thank my Research Assistant, Farrokah Jhabvala, B.S., B.E. (Bombay), M.A. (Delhi), A.M., M.A.L.D. (Tufts-Fletcher) for his help in preparing this paper.

[1] "International Law and International Politics: An Uneasy Partnership." Address by Hans J. Morgenthau, American Society of International Law, *Proceedings*, 68th Annual Meeting, pp. 331–333 (1974) p. 333

flicts that have come to be known as political disputes, such as those affecting vital interests or honor, which may lead to war. This dual approach to the problem of war avoidance was reflected in the Covenant of the League of Nations and in a rich literature devoted to the classification of disputes into two groups, those that were suitable for arbitration or adjudication—the latter became possible with the establishment by the League of the Permanent Court of International Justice—and those that were not. It is to this problem of classification between legal and political or, to use the terminology that came into vogue in the interwar period, between justiciable and nonjusticiable disputes, that Morgenthau devoted himself nearly 50 years ago in his book on the judicial function in international law.[2] He refined his views a few years later and elaborated the concept of the "political." His hope was to formulate the basis for determining the limits of international dispute settlement by providing, in a theoretical manner, "a scientifically unassailable classification of international disputes."[3] The principal results of these erudite monographs were later incorporated in his magnum opus, *Politics Among Nations.*

One of the first, propositions is that the capacity of the international judge to decide disputes is unlimited. This Morgenthau calls justiciability in the objective sense and this is strictly limited to the capacity to decide disputes.[4] Legal disputes are then defined as differences in which the parties are at variance about matters that are susceptible of decision on the basis of legal norms unless the grounds disclose a legal norm the existence of which cannot be substantiated with legal arguments.[5] Obviously, in the latter case, there would be no dispute or no dispute in the legal sense. Another category of disputes is defined as "tensions." These are conflicts between states with respect to an alleged discrepancy, in the relations of one state with another, between the concrete ratio of power and the prevailing legal situation.[6] Such conflicts are often imprecise in their contours, rationally ill-defined, and not amenable to peaceful settlement procedures. Tensions, as de Visscher paraphrasing Morgenthau put it, "defy rational expression, they assume a passionate quality that makes them refractory to pacific settlement."[7]

It is this "passionate quality" and not something inherent in the subject matter[8] that characterizes political disputes. Typically they arise between a state pursuing a policy of increasing its power and a state bent on preserving its power, that is, between an imperialist and a *status quo* state.[9]

Having thus defined his concept of the political in opposition to the prevailing doctrine that sought in the nature of the subject matter the criterion that distinguished legal

[2] Die internationale Rechtspflege, ihr Wesen und ihre Grenzen. In: Frankfurter Abhandlungen zum Kriegsverhütungsrecht (Leipzig: Robert Noske, 1929). The English translation was offered by Morgenthau, *supra,* n. 1, p. 332.

[3] La Notion du "Politique" et la Theorie des Differends Internationaux (Paris: Recueil Sirey, 1933), p. 89. Morgenthau's name is consistently, from the title page on, misprinted as "Morgenthan."

[4] *Supra,* note 2, at p. 42; *Supra,* n. 3, at p. 86f.

[5] *Supra,* n. 2, p. 53.

[6] *Supra,* n. 2, p. 78, *supra* n. 3, p. 78.

[7] Charles de Visscher, *Theory and Reality in Public International Law* (Princeton: Princeton University Press; 1968, revised ed.) p. 79.

[8] *Supra,* 3, pp. 36–37.

[9] *Ibid.,* pp. 42, 61.

from political disputes, Morgenthau proceeds to formulate his three-part classification of disputes in terms of their relationship to tensions. In the first group are "pure disputes," comprising disputes between states that have no tension or where the tension has been separated from or absorbed in the dispute that can be rationally formulated and thus become susceptible of a judicial decision on the basis of generally applicable norms.[10,11]

The second group comprises "disputes with the substance of a tension" and is defined as follows: "The subject matter of the dispute may be identical with a certain segment of the subject matter of the tension. The tension may be compared to an iceberg, the main part of which is submerged while the top stands out about the surface of the ocean."[12] The third group, called "disputes representing a tension," resembles, on the surface, pure disputes: "As a matter of fact, pure disputes often transform themselves into disputes representing a tension, and vice versa. The subject matter of such a dispute has no relation at all to the subject matter of the tension. It is in the representative and symbolic function alone that the relation between tension and dispute consists."[13]

The second and third class of disputes are political disputes "in which, therefore, the overall distribution of power between two nations is at stake" and such disputes, related as they are, by definition, to a tension, "cannot be settled by judicial methods."[14] They are, in the usual terminology, nonjusticiable. However, they are not nonjusticiable in any absolute or final sense. They are nonjusticiable only as long as one or both states at variance remain locked in a tension. This is what Morgenthau calls justiciability in the subjective sense. Whereas, objectively speaking, all disputes are justiciable, political disputes, defined as disputes in relation to a tension, are nonjusticiable in the subjective sense.[15]

It would be tempting to examine this classification of disputes and determine whether it is theoretically unassailable; but this, as will be shown presently, is unnecessary. It may be worth pointing out, however, that Lauterpacht, who, after Morgenthau, subjected the various attempts regarding the classification of disputes by their justiciability to a most thorough examination, arrived at substantially the same conclusion as did Morgenthau. He rejected all such attempts as untenable and concluded that "it is the refusal of the State to submit the dispute to judicial settlement, and not the intrinsic nature of the controversy, which makes it political" and "that the only decisive test of the justiciability of the dispute is the willingness of the disputants to submit the conflict to the arbitrament of law."[16]

Be that as it may, the concept of tension in the context of peaceful settlement of disputes has come to be widely accepted. Another concept that Morgenthau contributed

[10] *Supra*, n. 2, p. 80; *Supra*, n. 3, pp. 79–80.
[11] *Politics Among Nations* (New York: Knopf, 5th ed., 1973) p. 422.
[12] *Politics, supra*, n. 11, p. 422.
[13] *Politics, supra*, n. 11, p. 423.
[14] *Politics, supra*, n. 11, p. 425.
[15] *Supra*, n. 2, p. 90.
[16] H. Lauterpacht, *The Function of Law in the International Community* (Oxford:Clarendon Press, 1933) p. 164.

to the discussion is that of depoliticization. Speaking of political disputes, he concedes that in certain cases such disputes, by the very fact of being submitted to an organ of peaceful settlement, may be deprived of their political character; in particular, disputes of the third category—disputes representing a tension—may thus be "depoliticized," that is, deprived of their link with a tension.[17] He accordingly amends his proposition that all political disputes are nonjusticiable. He suggests that the concept of political disputes be limited to a group that cannot be further defined and, in the case of the others, that states are psychologically reluctant to submit political disputes to international adjudication or arbitration.[18] In *Politics Among Nations* there is no elaboration of the eminently useful concept of depoliticization, and statesmen are explicitly exempted from responsibility "for the failure of most nations, particularly the great powers, to accept the compulsory jurisdiction of international courts. It is not the stupidity or wickedness of statesmen or nations that must be held responsible for this failure, but the nature of international politics and of the society within which it operates."[19]

This exculpation may not be wholly warranted and, depending on one's viewpoint, history, particularly modern history, is not lacking in instances of wickedness and shortsightedness, if not downright stupidity. Morgenthau supplies an impressive list of vices of the new diplomacy.[20] However, the vice of neglecting the judicial process as a possible means of settling disputes is conspicuous by its absence. There are not many who would argue that international tribunals can control the struggle for power or resolve disputes in which it is not the existing law that divides the states but deeply felt positions about what the law ought to be. Those who hold or held such views misconceived the nature of adjudication in the international field. As Kunz observed, in order to preserve peace the acceptance of compulsory adjudication "would constitute the greatest, deepest advance. But it alone cannot eliminate war; it can decide, but not settle, all conflicts. It is an illusion to believe that it ever will be possible to transform world history into nothing but a court procedure."[21]

While it is true that adjudication has not become an alternative to war, it is also true that both the Permanent Court of International Justice and the International Court of Justice have handled many disputes of substantial political significance or, to use Morgenthau's terminology, disputes in relation to a tension.[22] It is nevertheless also true that "so long as the individualistic distribution of power among sovereign States endures, peace will serve justice better than justice will serve peace."[23] Everything depends on the will of the states at variance to depoliticize a dispute, to separate a dispute from a tension,

[17] *Supra,* n. 3, p. 87.
[18] *Ibid.,* p. 88.
[19] *Supra,* n. 11, p. 419.
[20] *Ibid.,* pp. 532–540.
[21] Joseph L. Kunz "Compulsory International Adjudication and Maintenance of Peace" 38 *American Journal of International Law,* 673–678 (1944) p. 678.
[22] See Shabtai Rosenne, *The Law and Practice of the International Court* (Leyden: Sijthoff, 1965), pp. 1, 11, 12–13, 15–16, 18.
[23] de Visscher, *supra,* n. 7, p. 367.

and to submit it to third-party settlement. In this sense, it is as Politis pointed out, the agreement to arbitrate or to adjudicate, the *compromis,* as it is called, that is more important than the award or the judgment.[24] On the other hand, the International Court of Justice, through its permanence, represents not only, as Morgenthau says, the most important step "toward the centralization of functions in the field of international law"[25] but it is also "the most refined instrument at present existing for the depoliticization of the process of pacific settlement and its implementation through the application of legal techniques. . . ."[26]

It is certainly accurate to describe the International Court of Justice as part "of the institutional structure which modern diplomacy may—indeed should—take into account as one of the means to its end,"[27] that is, the peaceful settlement of disputes. Another part of the contemporary institutional structure, however, consists of the political organs of the United Nations. They have turned out to be more attractive to modern diplomacy than the depoliticized judicial process. Despite the lack of success in achieving a settlement of disputes through "parliamentary diplomacy,"[28] governments persist in their negative attitude towards judicial settlement.

This negative attitude can easily be illustrated. Of the 147 state members of the international judicial community—the 144 members of the United Nations plus Switzerland, Liechtenstein, and San Marino—only 45 have accepted the jurisdiction of the International Court of Justice.[29] Many states have done so with reservations and the United States pioneered the widely and rightly deplored self-judging type of reservation in its Declaration of 1946 whereby it accepted the jurisdiction of the Court as compulsory. Only two of the five permanent members of the Security Council—the United States and the United Kingdom—have accepted compulsory jurisdiction.[30] Lest it be thought that reservations are a practice confined to great powers that may be involved in international tensions, the case of El Salvador may be recalled which, speedily followed by India, submitted an unusually comprehensive list of reservations.[31]

Judicial statistics offer an equally dismal picture. In the course of 30 years only 15 requests for advisory opinions have been addressed to the Court by five of the 19 international organs authorized by the Charter—the General Assembly and the Security Council—or by the General Assembly under Article 96(2) of the Charter.[32] The Court was seised in 60 contentious cases (1947–1973), of which only 16 have been terminated by judgments on the merits.[33] In two cases—the *South West Africa* and the *Barcelona Traction*

[24] *Ibid.*, at 369. De Visscher quoted N. Politis, *La justice internationale* (Paris: Hachette, 1924) p. 49.
[25] *Politics, supra,* n. 11, p. 285.
[26] Rosenne, *supra,* n. 22, p. 9.
[27] Rosenne, *ibid.*, p. 6.
[28] *Politics, supra,* n. 11, p. 532.
[29] I.C.J. Yearbook 1974–1975, p. 49.
[30] France terminated her acceptance on January 2, 1974. I.C.J. Yearbook 1973–1974, p. 49.
[31] I.C.J. Yearbook, 1974–1975, p. 55. For the text of the Indian declaration of September 15, 1974, see *ibid.*, p. 59.
[32] They are listed in I.C.J. Yearbook 1974–1975, p. 41.
[33] Among the 60 cases there were 8 that disclosed no title of jurisdiction; 8 were withdrawn. In the remaining judgments the Court gave one on interpretation, upheld objections to jurisdiction, or declared the application inadmissible.

cases—after prolonged litigation the applicants were denied *jus standi;* in one case—*Cameroons*—the Court declined to give judgment on the ground of judicial propriety; and in the last contentious cases—the *Nuclear Test* cases—the Court found that the applications of Australia and New Zealand against France had become without object.[34] These statistics illustrate not merely the utmost reluctance of international organizations and of governments to invoke the jurisdiction of the Court, but also the utmost caution with which the Court exercised its jurisdiction. At present the Court's docket is bare.

The hand-offs attitude of members of the United Nations towards the Court which, according to Article 92 of the Charter, "shall be the principal judicial organ of the United Nations," has been demonstrated on two recent occasions. In a resolution entitled "Declaration on Principles of International Law concerning Friendly Relations and Cooperation among States in accordance with the Charter of the United Nations," adopted by the Assembly at its twenty-fifth anniversary session, the principle is that "international disputes shall be settled on the basis of the sovereign equality of States and in accordance with the principle of free choice of means."[35]

The second occasion on which the members of the United Nations expressed their attitude on the judicial function presented itself in connection with the proposal of the United States made at the same session of the Assembly to set up an *ad hoc* committee to study "the obstacles to the satisfactory functioning of the International Court of Justice, and ways and means of removing them."[36] After several postponements, the Assembly, on November 12, 1974, adopted by consensus Resolution 3232 (XXIX) in which it reaffirmed "that recourse to judicial settlement of legal disputes, particularly referral to the International Court of Justice, should not be considered as an unfriendly act between States."[37] Considering that the Court has been functioning for over fifty years, this is not exactly a ringing endorsement of judicial settlement. In an era of rampant nationalism perhaps no more could be expected.

The obvious and persistent reluctance of states to have recourse to judicial settlement of their disputes has been subjected to careful analysis. Cultural attitudes towards law and courts no doubt play an important part, as do the lack of confidence in the impartiality of the Court and, especially among many of the new states, in the adequacy of international law. Since judges of the Court are elected by the General Assembly and the Security Council, it is the responsibility of the members to elect judges in whom they can have confidence. As to the state of the law, it no doubt remains underdeveloped, but notable advances have been made in both the codification and progressive development of important segments of international law, and much law has been created by international

[34] I.C.J. *Reports* 1974, (*Australia* v. *France*) p. 253 at 272, (*New Zealand* v. *France* ) p. 457 at 478. In this paper all further reference to the *Nuclear Test* case is to that between Australia and France.

[35] General Assembly Resolution 2625(XXV) of October 24, 1970. General Assembly Official Records: 25th Session, Supplement no. 28 (A/8028), pp. 121, 123.

[36] U.N. Document A8042, August 14, 1970. The proposal and the comments of governments are briefly discussed in Leo Gross, "Review of the Role of the International Court of Justice," 66 *American Journal of International Law* 479–490 (1972). See also *supra* at 1009–1019.

[37] General Assembly Official Records: 29th Session Supplement No. 31 (A/9631) p. 142.

conventions in new areas of international concern such as human rights. To a substantial extent new states have participated in the shaping of such conventions. However, the provisions for the settlement of disputes relating to interpretation and application are either ineffective or are not readily acceptable. Thus, in order not to jeopardize the ratification of some conventions, the provisions for compulsory dispute settlement have been put into so-called Optional Protocols that require separate ratification. However, the Optional Protocols to such bread-and-butter conventions as the 1961 and 1963 Vienna Conventions on Diplomatic and Consular Relations have only met with limited appeal.[38] The most notable achievement of the law-making efforts of the United Nations, the 1969 Vienna Convention on the Law of Treaties, contains, as an integral part, provisions for a conciliation procedure for the settlement of some, and provisions for the compulsory judicial settlement of other, disputes arising from its interpretation or applications. This convention, dealing with a vital aspect of international relations, has been ratified or accepted by only 24 states, far below the minimum of 35 required for its entry into force.

In addition to the reasons for the marginal function of judicial settlement in contemporary international relations already discussed, there are some that are less theoretical and more practical in character. One is obviously the fear of losing a case. This is a risk that not every government feels strong enough, domestically or internationally, to take. Then there is the lawyer's preference for settling disputes out of court rather than facing the rigors of adversary proceedings before a judicial organ, so that they will advise a client government accordingly. Fitzmaurice provides still another explanation that seems very persuasive. Drawing upon his experience as legal adviser, he concludes that "apart from the natural reluctance to litigate felt by almost everyone, governments prefer to deal with disputes by political means rather than by submission to adjudication, and fight shy of the *commitment* involved by going to law: they dislike the loss of control that is entailed over the future of the case, the outcome of which they can no longer influence politically once it is before a court of law, since this will depend upon legal considerations with which they do not find themselves at home."[39] It may well be that this fear of losing control is the most important psychological factor in determining the justiciability of disputes in the *subjective* sense.

This factor, fear of loss of control, needs to be elucidated. First of all in compromissory clauses in treaties or conventions, governments usually include a provision making recourse to compulsory jurisdiction of the Court dependent upon prior diplomatic negotiations. At this stage governments are in full control and may refine the issue that divides them and through negotiations explore appropriate solutions. Diplomats have a full opportunity to try their skills in achieving a solution through means con-

[38] The Convention on Diplomatic Relations was ratified by 115 States; the Optional Protocol on Compulsory Settlement of Disputes was ratified by 45 States; the figures for the Consular Relations Convention are 76 and 29 respectively.

[39] "The Future of Public International Law and of the International Legal System in the Circumstances of Today," Special Report by Sir Gerald Fitzmaurice, *Livre du Centenaire 1873–1973*. Institut de Doit International, p. 279. Italics in the original.

genial to them and with which they are supposedly quite familiar. The Court, when seised of the dispute, will determine whether or not the requirement of prior diplomatic negotiations has been satisfied. There is no absolute test, for as the Permanent Court of International Justice stated, "the question of the importance and chances of success of diplomatic negotiations is essentially a relative one."[40] It may be useful to recall that recourse to the compulsory jurisdiction of the Court need not be and usually is not the first but the last step in the search for a solution. Governments, in accepting the jurisdiction of the Court as compulsory under Article 36(2) of its Statute, may and do make the reservation that their acceptance excludes disputes with respect to which the governments at variance have agreed to some other method of peaceful settlement. At this state of the process, that is, prior to the seising of the Courts, what the governments and diplomats may fear is not loss of control but, at most, loss of face.

Furthermore, states litigating before the Court retain a measure of control over the proceedings. Under conditions laid down in the Rules of Court, Articles 73–74, the applicant alone or with the consent of the respondent may ask for a discontinuance of the proceedings. "Discontinuances," says Fitzmaurice, "usually occur because the case is settled after proceedings have been commenced, or in order to enable further negotiations to take place, free from the 'shadow of proceedings'."[41] It is also understood that even during the proceedings the parties are free to continue the search for a solution of the dispute through the diplomatic process. If a mutual agreement is reached by the parties at any time before the judgment has been delivered, they will inform the Court that they are not going on with the proceedings. In accordance with Article 73 of the Rules of Court, the Court shall make an order officially recording the conclusion of the settlement and this brings the proceedings to an end.

Moreover, the parties are also free to negotiate an agreement that is not a final settlement of the dispute without interrupting or concluding the proceedings before the Court. Thus, the United Kingdom and Iceland concluded on November 13, 1973, an "Interim Agreement in the Fisheries Dispute" while the dispute was actually pending before the Court. Under its terms, the Agreement was worked out "pending a settlement of the substantive dispute and without prejudice to the legal position or rights of either Government in relation to it."[42] The question arose as to whether the Agreement rendered the case before the Court moot and whether the Court should refrain from pronouncing judgment in the case. The Court declined to do so on the grounds that "the inevitable result would be to discourage the making of interim agreements in future disputes with the object of reducing friction and avoiding risk to peace and security. This would run counter to the purposes enshrined in the provisions of the United Nations Charter relating to the pacific settlement of disputes."[43]

[40] The *Mavrommatis Palestine Concession* (Jurisdiction) case, Judgment of August 30, 1924. Publications of the PCIJ, Series A, No. 2, p. 13.

[41] *Supra,* n. 39, p. 281.

[42] *Fisheries Jurisdiction* case, Judgment of July 24, 1974, I.C.J. *Reports* 1974, p. 3, at 17, paragraphs 35–36.

[43] *Ibid.,* p. 20, paragraph 41.

Another aspect of the matter is illustrated by the *Continental Shelf* case in which the parties, the Federal Republic of Germany on one side and the Netherlands and Denmark on the other, requested the Court to define the principles and rules of international law applicable to the delimitation of certain contested areas of the continental shelf in the North Sea.[44] The Court was asked to assist the parties in clarifying the applicable rules of law about which the parties held different views and thus assist them in finding a mutually acceptable solution to the dispute. The Court responded to the request and a settlement was achieved by two treaties signed on January 28, 1971.[45] This is an innovative and potentially useful example of the use of the Court as part of the institutional tools available to modern diplomacy.

In the usual cases, the governments exercise a measure of control over the judicial proceedings, typically by raising objections to the jurisdiction of the Court or the admissibility of the application. All objections are, in virtue of Article 36(6) of the Statute of Court, decided by the Court: This clause invests the Court, as the saying goes, with *la compétence de la compétence.* Since the Court is also the guardian of its judicial character, objections may be raised by the Court itself and, as indicated earlier, the Court may decline to adjudicate on the grounds of judicial propriety.[46] The Court must also be satisfied that the application, in case of a unilateral citation on the basis of a specific clause or a declaration under Article 36(2) of its Statute conferring compulsory jurisdiction on the Court, discloses the existence of a genuine dispute. The mere fact that a state filed an application and thus alleged the existence of a dispute is not conclusive. In the *Mavrommatis* case, the Court gave the following definition: "A dispute is a disagreement on a point of law or fact, a conflict of legal views or interests between two persons."[47] Although subject to refinements in subsequent judgments, the question "whether a dispute exists or not is a matter of fact for objective determination by the Court itself, being dependent neither upon the subjective assertion by one party that a dispute exists nor upon an equally subjective denial by a party that a dispute exists."[48] The dispute must be of a legal character. This follows not merely from Article 36(2), which provides for compulsory jurisdiction "in all legal disputes" falling into one or several classes of disputes, but also from Article 38 of the Statute: "The Court, whose function is to decide in accordance with international law such disputes as are submitted to it . . ." Clearly only disputes as defined by the Court or what Morgenthau calls "pure disputes" are susceptible of a decision on the basis of legal criteria established by treaty or customary law or derived from general principles of law. The parties, however, have also the option of agreeing that the Court shall decide a case *ex aequo et bono* as provided for in paragraph 2 of Article 38 of the Statute. There has never been a case before the Court in which both parties have agreed to such a

[44] Judgment of February 20, 1969. I.C.J. *Reports* 1969, p. 3, at 6.
[45] I.C.J. *Yearbook* 1970–1971, pp. 117–126.
[46] See *supra*, p. 1053.
[47] See *supra*, n. 40, p. 11.
[48] Rosenne, *supra*, n. 22, p. 292. See also *Nuclear Test* case (*Australia* v. *France*) Judgment of December 20, 1974, I.C.J. *Reports* 1974, p. 253, at 270, paragraph 55 and 271, paragraph 57.

decision. It would be particularly suitable in disputes in which the parties desire the Court to base its judgment on broader criteria that, although presumably derived from existing law, would indicate a progressive development of the law. In this sense the Court could be used as an organ of peaceful change provided the demand for change is mutual and of modest scope. It may be worth noting that the General Assembly in the resolution 3232 (XXIX), referred to earlier, recalled "opportunities afforded by the power of the International Court of Justice, under Article 38, paragraph 2, of its Statute, to decide a case *ex aequo et bono* if the parties agree thereto." It would be the task of the parties to argue responsibly the inadequacy of existing law with respect to the conflict and indicate the direction in which the law should be developed in order to meet the needs of a changing international society.

In determining the character of a dispute as legal or political the Court will, of course, disregard the motivation of the party or parties, which is invariably political. This is not always a simple matter and judges may and do differ in their appreciation, in a given dispute, of the extent to which, if at all, it is based on a principle or rule of international law. This occurred in the *Nuclear Test* cases. The applicants were Australia and New Zealand, respectively, against France. They asked the Court to adjudge that "the carrying out of further atmospheric nuclear weapon tests in the South Pacific Ocean is not consistent with applicable rules of international law."[49] The Court declared in its judgment that the Australian claim "no longer has any object" in view of certain statements by ministers of the French Government and the President of the French Republic that the current round would be the last of the atmospheric tests.[50]

Among the judges were several who voted in favor of ending the case on the ground, as Judge Gros put it, "of the nonexistence, from the outset of the case submitted to the Court, of any justiciable dispute."[51] The French Government, which did not participate in the proceedings at all, claimed that the dispute concerned a political and military problem and not a legal one,[52] nor did Australia claim any injury.[53] As Judge Petren pointed out in his separate opinion, "one of the first prerequisites" for a valid seising of the Court "is that the dispute should concern a matter governed by international law. If this were not the case, the dispute would have no object falling within the domain of the Court's jurisdiction, inasmuch as the Court is only competent to deal with disputes in international law."[54] He also argued that, although disputes concerning the interpretation and application of international law "may possess great political importance without thereby losing their inherent character of being legal disputes," it was "nonetheless necessary to distinguish disputes revolving on norms of international law and tensions between States caused by measures taken in a domain not yet governed by international

[49] See *supra*, n. 48, p. 256, paragraph 11.
[50] The statements are cited in the Judgment, pp. 265–266.
[51] *Ibid.*, p. 276.
[52] *Ibid.*, Joint Dissenting Opinion, p. 360.
[53] *Ibid.*, Separate Opinion of Judge Gros, p. 279.
[54] *Ibid.*, p. 302.

law."[55] This, it is submitted, is a most useful distinction between disputes and tensions. Thus the question of the justiciability *vel non* of the dispute hinged on the existence of a rule of conventional or customary international law opposable to France; that is, a rule which could be relied on against France. As France had not become a party to the Test Ban Treaty of August 5, 1963, and since there was no evidence of a rule of customary international law having evolved since then and in opposition to the stand of France and other states, the dispute was nonjusticiable and should have been declared inadmissible on that ground.[56]

To return to the question of control, it needs to be borne in mind that the parties exercise a measure of control over the proceedings by formulating the submissions on which the Court is asked to adjudicate. Submissions may be formulated and amended in the course of written and oral pleadings and some may be withdrawn in the course of oral hearings.[57]

Once proceedings come to an end, whether on jurisdiction, admissibility, or receivability, the parties are faced with a judgment that, under Article 60 of the Court's Statute, "is final and without appeal." Pursuant to customary international law and Article 94(1) of the Charter of the United Nations, the parties are bound to comply with decisions of the Court. However, while the judgment is irrevocable[58] and the loss of political control seems complete, the parties find themselves, in the postadjudicative phase of the dispute, again on the diplomatic plane.[59] To comply or not to comply is a political question. The record of international arbitration and adjudication clearly shows that even in the absence of an executive organ capable of enforcing compliance, states have generally carried out awards and judgments. In case of noncompliance, the other party may appeal to the Security Council of the United Nations under Article 94(2) of the Charter, and the Council "may, if it deems it necessary, make recommendations or decide upon measures to be taken to give effect to the judgment." This clause has never been tested. It is therefore moot whether the Council is empowered to make recommendations relating to the substance of the dispute. Obviously the Council cannot change the judgment or overrule the Court, but the Council may, taking the whole situation into account—including the judgment and the interests of the international community—recommend how the dispute should be settled. There is force in the argument of Fitzmaurice that "in the absence of any true international legislature, it is not infrequently only by breaking the law that the law can be changed, or rather that those processes can be set in motion which will ultimately lead to the emergence of a new and more generallly acceptable rule."[60] The Council, under appropriate conditions, could play a useful role in that process.[61] In any

[55] *Ibid.*, p. 303.
[56] See Judge Gros, *ibid.*, pp. 288 and 304, and Judge Petren, p. 305.
[57] See *Barcelona Traction* (Preliminary Objections), I.C.J. *Reports* 1964, p. 25, and Fitzmaurice, *supra*, n. 39, p. 281.
[58] See Fitzmaurice, *supra*, n. 39, p. 281.
[59] See Leo Gross, "Problems of International Adjudication and Compliance with International Law: Some Simple Solutions," 59 *American Journal of International Law* 48–59 (1965). See also *supra*, pp. 399–410.
[60] See *supra*, n. 39, p. 229.
[61] See Lauterpacht, *supra*, n. 16, pp. 337–338.

event, if both parties share the desire to achieve a settlement of the dispute, they could take the judgment as the starting point for a new round of negotiations. Having depoliticized the dispute by submitting it to the Court, it would seem unreasonable for *diplomats* to repoliticize it by raising the stakes.

At this point it is pertinent to recall the observation of Fitzmaurice that governments "do not find themselves at home" with legal considerations. This observation is somewhat surprising as a reason for not going to law. Surely there has been no period in the history of international relations when statesmen were more deeply involved in the making and application of international law than the decades since the Hague Peace Conferences or the century and a half since the Congress of Vienna. The growth of interdependence of states has produced an unprecedented mass and, for jurists, a maze of treaties, conventions, exchanges of notes, and other instruments freely negotiated by diplomats and accepted by states.

The language of modern diplomacy is replete with legal arguments and allusions. To suggest that governments are not at home with legal considerations may indicate a severe case of amnesia or, more likely, that governments, while freely dispensing their views on the legal obligations of other states, are unwilling to submit their own claims to the impartial scrutiny of an international judicial body. For as Lauterpacht pointed out: "International tribunals do not impose new obligations. They ascertain existing law. They give effect and expression to the will of the State by ascertaining what legal obligations it has undertaken by way of express or tacit consent."[62]

If states then are unwilling to submit their subjective legal views, their autointerpretation of legal rights and obligations, to objective third-party judgment, this can only indicate that states, in spite of their professions to the contrary, are still unwilling to accept international law as the standard by which their conduct is to be measured. Statesmen do not seem to have grasped the basic characteristic of international law and relations, namely that the sovereignty or independence of states has "nothing to do with a State's subordination to international law. . . ."[63] The decentralized character of international law is not the cause of the weakness of the judicial function but a reflection of the desire of States to view international law as a body of rules limiting the independence and sovereignty of other states but not their own. It is the opposition to international law itself that accounts, in the present submission, for the unwillingness of most states to submit to judicial proceedings not merely high-or-low-tension disputes but even disputes of a routine or minor character arising from the interpretation and application of freely negotiated and freely accepted treaties. This, and not any theory, is the heart of the problem of the justiciability of international disputes. The principle "of free choice of means," affirmed by the General Assembly in 1970,[64] for the peaceful settlement of international

[62] See *supra,* n. 16 at 420, and Charles de Visscher, Aspects recents du droit procedural de la Cour internationale de Justice. (Paris: Pedone, 1966) p. 54.

[63] Judge Anzilotti in his Separate Opinion in the *Customs Regime between Austria and Germany* case, Permanent Court of International Justice, Advisory Opinion, September 5, 1931. *Publications* of the P.C.I.J. Series A/B No. 41, 37–103, p. 58.

[64] See *supra,* p. 1054.

disputes appears to be understood by some states as free choice in the fulfillment of their international legal obligations as they see them and not as they might be interpreted by an impartial judicial tribunal. As long as states persist in this attitude, whether out of fear, or ignorance about international adjudication, or stupidity or wickedness, the international legal order and even peace will be more precarious than they need be even in the existing international system. World government might cure the disease and kill the patient.

# THE CASE CONCERNING UNITED STATES DIPLOMATIC AND CONSULAR STAFF IN TEHRAN: PHASE OF PROVISIONAL MEASURES

## I. INTRODUCTION

This case, instituted by the United States on November 29, 1979, by means of a unilateral Application under Article 40 of the Statute of the Court and Article 38 of the Rules of Court, relates to the takeover of the American Embassy in Tehran and the American Consulates in Tabriz and Shiraz and the detention as hostages of some 50 Americans by so-called militants. According to one doctrine of the justiciability of disputes, it would be difficult to imagine a more tension-laden and therefore non-justiciable dispute, considering that, as contended by the United States both in the Application and the Request of November 29, 1979, for the indication of provisional measures under Article 41 of the Court's Statute and Articles 73 and 74 of the Rules of Court, the Iranian Government was involved in the takeover and continues to be involved in the detention of the hostages. The circumstances, which in the view of the United States required the indication of provisional measures, were summarized by the Court in paragraph 34 of its Order of December 15, 1979,[1] as follows:

> (i) On 4 November 1979, in the course of a demonstration outside the United States Embassy compound in Tehran, demonstrators attacked the Embassy premises; no Iranian security forces intervened or were sent to relieve the situation, despite repeated calls for help

[1] The Order of the Court, December 15, 1979, [1979] ICJ REP. 7, *reprinted in* 74 AJIL 266 (1980) [it will be cited hereinafter as Order]. The U.S. Application and Request for Interim Measures are *reprinted in id.* at pp. 258 and 264, respectively.

from the Embassy to the Iranian authorities. Ultimately the whole of the Embassy premises was invaded. The Embassy personnel, including consular and non-American staff, and visitors who were present in the Embassy at the time were seized. Shortly afterwards, according to the United States Government, its consulates in Tabriz and Shiraz, which had been attacked earlier in 1979, were also seized, without any action being taken to prevent it;

(ii) Since that time, the premises of the United States Embassy in Tehran, and of the consulates in Tabriz and Shiraz, have remained in the hands of the persons who seized them. These persons have ransacked the archives and documents both of the diplomatic mission and of its consular section. The Embassy personnel and other persons seized at the time of the attack have been held hostage with the exception of 13 persons released on 18 and 20 November 1979. Those holding the hostages have refused to release them, save on condition of the fulfilment by the United States of various demands regarded by it as unacceptable. The hostages are stated to have frequently been bound, blindfolded, and subjected to severe discomfort, complete isolation and threats that they would be put on trial or even put to death. The United States Government affirms that it has reason to believe that some of them may have been transferred to other places of confinement;

(iii) The Government of the United States considers that not merely has the Iranian Government failed to prevent the events described above, but also that there is clear evidence of its complicity in, and approval of, those events;

(iv) The persons held hostage in the premises of the United States Embassy in Tehran include, according to the information furnished to the Court by the Agent of the United States, at least 28 persons having the status, duly recognized by the Government of Iran, of "member of the diplomatic staff" within the meaning of the Vienna Convention on Diplomatic Relations of 1961; at least 20 persons having the status, similarly recognized, of "members of the administrative and technical staff" within the meaning of that Convention; and two other persons of United States nationality not possessing either diplomatic or consular status. Of the persons with the status of member of the diplomatic staff, four are members of the Consular Section of the Embassy;

(v) In addition to the persons held hostage in the premises of the Tehran Embassy, the United States Chargé d'Affaires in Iran and two other United States diplomatic agents are detained in the premises of the Iranian Ministry for Foreign Affairs, in circumstances which the Government of the United States has not been able to make entirely clear, but which apparently involve restriction of their freedom of movement, and a threat to their inviolability as diplomats.

The alleged nonjusticiable character of the dispute was underscored by Iran in its letter of December 9, 1979, to the Court. Iran urged the Court "not [to] take cognizance of the case," which "only represents a marginal and secondary aspect of an overall problem." Iran argued that the problem is "not one of the interpretation and application of the treaties upon which the American Application is based," and that any examination of the numerous repercussions of the Islamic revolution is "a matter essentially and directly within the national sovereignty of Iran."[2] How the Court dealt with these arguments

[2] The text of the letter is in paragraph 8 of the Order; the passages quoted are in paragraphs 1, 2, and 3, and the concluding paragraph of the letter.

will be discussed later; they are presented here to indicate Iran's view of the nonjusticiability of the dispute.

However, as the Iranian Government itself at least partially admitted in the above letter, the dispute can also be regarded as a classic example of a justiciable dispute involving the application and interpretation of articles of conventions in force between the parties, the violation of which is claimed by the United States in its Application.[3] Moreover, as the Court pointed out in its Order, the rights for which the United States requested protection relate to fundamental principles and institutions of positive international law. The Court formulated them as follows in paragraphs 38 to 40 of its Order:

> 38. Whereas there is no more fundamental prerequisite for the conduct of relations between States than the inviolability of diplomatic envoys and embassies, so that throughout history nations of all creeds and cultures have observed reciprocal obligations for that purpose; and whereas the obligations thus assumed, notably those for assuring the personal safety of diplomats and their freedom from prosecution, are essential, unqualified, and inherent in their representative character and their diplomatic function;
>
> 39. Whereas the institution of diplomacy, with its concomitant privileges and immunities, has withstood the test of centuries and proved to be an instrument essential for effective co-operation in the international community, and for enabling States, irrespective of their differing constitutional and social systems, to achieve mutual understanding and to resolve their differences by peaceful means;
>
> 40. Whereas the unimpeded conduct of consular relations, which have also been established between peoples since ancient times, is no less important in the context of present-day international law, in promoting the development of friendly relations among nations, and ensuring protection and assistance for aliens resident in the territories of other States; and whereas therefore the privileges and immunities of consular officers and consular employees, and the inviolability of consular premises and archives, are similarly principles deep-rooted in international law.

In the view of the United States, the case was eminently justiciable. "We believe," said U.S. Agent Roberts B. Owen in closing his oral presentation on December 10, 1979,

> that this case presents the Court with the most dramatic opportunity it has ever had to affirm the rule of law among nations and thus fulfill the world community's expectation that the Court will act vigorously in the interest of international law and international peace. The current situation in Tehran demands an immediate, forceful, and explicit declaration by the Court, calling upon Iran to conform to the basic rules of international intercourse and human rights. Only in that manner, I respectfully suggest, can the Court discharge its high responsibilities under the Charter of the United Nations.[4]

[3] *See* paragraph 1(a) of the Order. The treaties are: the 1961 Vienna Convention on Diplomatic Relations, the 1963 Vienna Convention on Consular Relations, the 1973 Convention on the Prevention and Punishment of Crimes against Internationally Protected Persons, including Diplomatic Agents, and the 1955 Treaty of Amity, Economic Relations, and Consular Rights between the United States and Iran. The Application also refers to Articles 2(3), 2(4), and 33 of the Charter.

[4] ICJ Public Sitting, December 10, 1979, Verbatim Record (uncorrected) 44 (Doc. CR79/1, 1979) [hereinafter cited as Verbatim Record].

It would seem that the Court lived up to these expectations. It delivered the unanimous Order indicating provisional measures on December 15, 16 days after the filing of the Request on November 29. To be sure, as Mr. Owen recalled, the Court has acted with even greater dispatch in other cases.[5] However, in this case, both the U.S. team and the Court had to make a substantial effort to glean the relevant facts. Thus, the Court became a more active participant in these proceedings than in others. As early as December 4, the President of the Court addressed several questions to the Agent of the United States.[6] On that day he asked for information about the then pending discussion in the Security Council which resulted in the adoption of Resolution 457 (1979),[7] and at the opening of the public sitting, he asked Mr. Owen to comment on the significance that should be attached by the Court, "for the purpose of the present proceedings, to resolution 457 adopted by the Security Council on 4 December 1979."[8] At the conclusion of the public sitting, further and searching questions were formulated by Judge Mosler and the President.[9]

While Mr. Owen, as Agent, represented the United States, the factual information was supplied by David D. Newsom, Under-Secretary for Political Affairs in the Department of State. This appears from the certificate transmitted to the Court by Secretary of State Cyrus Vance on November 29, 1979, along with the application. It reads as follows:

> I, David D. Newsom, certify and declare the following:
>
> 1. I am Under-Secretary for Political Affairs in the United States Department of State. I have been vested by the Secretary of State with overall responsibility within the Department for matters relating to the crisis in Iran.
>
> 2. In this capacity, I have closely monitored events since the attack on the United States Embassy in Tehran began. The facts stated in the Application of the United States to the Court are, to the best of my knowledge, true.[10]

The Request for Interim Measures of Protection of November 29, 1979, contains in paragraph 2 the statement: "The facts set forth therein have been verified in the appended statement of David D. Newsom. . . ." The existence of what appears to be a somewhat unusual division of labor, if not of responsibility, did not escape the attention of the President of the Court.[11]

[5] Without identifying the cases, Mr. Owen said that in one case the period between the filing of the request and the indication of the measures was 13 days, in another, 9, and in a third, 6. *Id.* at 43.

[6] *Id.* at 8–9.

[7] *Id.* at 9.

[8] *Ibid.*

[9] *Id.* at 45–46.

[10] This certificate is reproduced in U.S. DEP'T OF STATE, PUB. NO. 9001, SELECTED DOCUMENTS NO. 14, at 5 (Near East & South Asian Series 92, 1979).

[11] In the telegram addressed to the Agent, Mr. Owen, on December 4, 1979, there are these words in paragraph 2: "The President, while noting the certificate of Mr. David D. Newsom appended to the United States Application, asks the Agent of the United States. . . ." Verbatim Record, *supra* note 4, at 8.

Whatever the reasons may be, it appears from the Order of the Court that certain important facts, such as the diplomatic or consular status of the hostages—see paragraph 34 of the Order quoted above—became clear to all concerned only in the course of the proceedings.[12]

To sum up: the strongest evidence of the justiciability of the dispute may be seen in the fact that the Order was adopted unanimously and without any individual opinion.[13]

## II. CONDITIONS FOR THE INDICATION OF INTERIM MEASURES OF PROTECTION

These conditions are laid down in Article 41 of the Statute and Articles 73 through 78 of the Rules of Court. The Court has had occasion to express its views on this subject in several recent cases,[14] and it has been considered in several learned analyses of the jurisprudence of the Court.[15] However, it is not the purpose of this paper to contribute to this discussion but rather to present the issues in this most unusual case[16] and the manner in which they were handled by the Court.

Before taking up some of the issues connected with Article 41, it may be well to note that the Court made the usual pronouncement about the absence of Iran from the hearing: "the non-appearance of one of the States concerned cannot by itself constitute an obstacle to the indication of provisional measures" (Order, para. 13). The Court cited no precedent, but the respondent was absent in all the recent cases mentioned above (in note 14). The Court also restated the prima facie test, saying: "Whereas on the request for provisional measures in the present case the Court ought to indicate such measures only if the provisions invoked by the Applicant appear, *prima facie,* to afford a basis on which the jurisdiction of the Court might be founded."(Order, para. 15).

The Court did not advert to the view expounded in connection with some of the earlier cases that in the absence of the Respondent, Article 53 of the Statute comes into

[12] Thus, paragraph 2 of the Request for Interim Measures contains this general statement: "At least fifty United States citizens, virtually all of whom are diplomatic agents or administrative and technical staff of the Embassy, are being held hostages."

[13] In the *Aegean Sea Continental Shelf* case (Greece v. Turkey), the Court denied the Greek request for the indication of interim measures of protection by a vote of 12 to 1 (the judge *ad hoc* appointed by Greece), but there were 8 separate opinions. [1976] ICJ REP. 3, 14. *See* Gross, *The Dispute Between Greece and Turkey Concerning the Continental Shelf in the Aegean,* 71 AJIL 31 (1977). See also *supra,* pp. 1021.

[14] The most recent case is mentioned in the preceding note. The present Court was faced first with the issue in the *Anglo-Iranian Oil Co.* case (United Kingdom v. Iran), and more recently in the *Fisheries Jurisdiction* cases (United Kingdom v. Iceland, and German Federal Republic v. Iceland) and the *Nuclear Tests* cases (Australia v. France, and New Zealand v. France).

[15] Reference may be made to the following: Elkind, *French Nuclear Testing and Article 41—Another Blow to the Authority of the Court?,* 8 VAND. J. TRANSNAT'L L. 39 (1974); Merrilis, *Interim Measures of Protection and the Substantive Jurisdiction of the International Court,* 36 CAMB. L.J. 86 (1977); Mendelson, *Interim Measures of Protection in cases of Contested Jurisdiction, 46* BRIT. Y.B. INT'L L. 259 (1972–73); Lellouche, *The Nuclear Tests Cases, 16* HARV. J. INT'L L. 614 (1975); Obol, Note in 18 *id.,* at 649 (1977); Adede, *The Rule on Interlocutory Injunctions Under Domestic Law and the Interim Measures of Protection Under International Law: Some Critical Differences,* 4 SYRACUSE J. INT'L L. COM. 277 (1977).

[16] There may be a parallel of sorts in the *Pakistani Prisoners of War* case which, however, was withdrawn before it came for adjudication.

play and therefore more than a prima facie test should be applied.[17] As will be shown presently, the Court was satisfied that the clauses invoked by the Applicant furnished the necessary basis for jurisdiction (Order, paras. 17 and 18).

## Jurisdiction

The first condition for applying Article 41 is that the Court must satisfy itself that the *Application* discloses a basis for assuming jurisdiction on the merits. In this case the United States invoked the four conventions mentioned above, but primarily it relied on the identical Article I of the Optional Protocols on the Compulsory Settlement of Disputes attached to the Vienna Conventions on Diplomatic and Consular Relations, respectively. Article I of the protocols provides: "Disputes arising out of the interpretation or application of the Convention shall lie within the compulsory jurisdiction of the International Court of Justice and may accordingly be brought before the Court by an application made by any Party to the dispute being a Party to the present Protocol."

Articles II and III provide alternative methods for settlement—arbitration or conciliation—but the right of unilateral arraignment in Article I is in no way modified by Articles II and III. The Court accordingly concluded that Article I provides "in the clearest manner for the compulsory jurisdiction" of the Court (Order, para. 17) and that, as stated in paragraph 18 of the Order,

> it is manifest from the information before the Court[18] and from the terms of Article I of each of the two Protocols that the provisions of these Articles furnish a basis on which the jurisdiction of the Court might be founded with regard to the claims of the United States under the Vienna Conventions of 1961 and 1963.

Having thus established one leg of jurisdiction, it remained to show that the persons concerned, by their status, were covered by the two conventions. As has been seen from paragraph 34(iv) of the Order quoted above, the Court was satisfied that 28 of the hostages had the status, recognized by the Government of Iran, of "member of the diplomatic staff" and 20 persons, similarly recognized, of "members of the administrative and technical staff." Thus, 48 hostages were covered by the two conventions. There still remained the question of two private U.S. nationals. Could the United States make claims on their behalf under the Vienna Conventions or under the bilateral Treaty of Amity, Economic Relations, and Consular Rights? The dispute clause in that treaty, Article XXI(2), required attempts at adjustment by diplomacy prior to an appeal to the International Court of Justice. The Agent of the United States argued, however, that because Iran had rejected "the repeated efforts of the United States to deal with the dispute by

[17] In case of a default judgment the Court, pursuant to Article 53 (2), must "satisfy itself, not only that it has jurisdiction in accordance with Articles 36 and 37, but also that the claim is well founded in fact and law."

[18] The Court may have referred here to paragraph 16 of the Order in which it found that Iran and the United States are parties to the two conventions and to their protocols without any reservation.

diplomacy . . . it seems indisputable that under the Treaty of Amity, this case is properly before the Court."[19]

The Court did not pursue this line of reasoning. In fact, it found a more elegant solution. In analyzing the case of these private individuals, the Court held that their seizure and detention also fell within the scope of the applicable Vienna Conventions relating to the inviolability of the premises of embassies and consulates, and more specifically within the scope of Article 5 of the Vienna Convention on Consular Relations, which provides for consuls to assist nationals of the sending state, and to protect and safeguard their interests. The Court accordingly concluded that Article I of the protocols "furnishes a basis on which the jurisdiction of the Court might be founded with regard to the claims of the United States in respect of the two private individuals in question" (Order, paras. 19 and 20).

The jurisdiction of the Court under Article I of the protocols to the two Vienna Conventions relates to disputes arising under the substantive provisions of the conventions themselves. The Application of the United States contains a list of articles alleged to have been infringed, but has it been established that there arose a dispute over which the Court could exercise jurisdiction? The best known definition of a dispute was given by the Permanent Court of International Justice in the *Mavrommatis* case: "A dispute is a disagreement on a point of law or fact, a conflict of legal views or of interests between two persons."[20] It is, as Rosenne pointed out,

> inherent in the conception of "dispute" . . . that some diplomatic negotiations had preceded the institution of the proceedings, in the course of which the points of fact or of law on which the parties were in disagreement had become identified. Indeed, without some diplomatic negotiations, there will frequently be difficulty in establishing the existence of the dispute.[21]

One may surmise from the questions addressed to the Agent of the United States on December 4,[22] and the request made on the same day for "copies of any official statements of the President of the United States, the Secretary of State or any of the other United States authorities relating to the matters alleged in the United States Application of November 29, 1979; and any statements by Iranian authorities evidencing those mat-

[19] *See* Verbatim Record, *supra* note 4, at 28.
[20] The Mavrommatis Palestine Concessions, [1924] PCIJ, ser. A, No. 2, at 11.
[21] S. Rosenne, 2 The Law and Practice of the International Court 513 *ff.* (1965).
[22] They were:

> (a)What, if any, exchanges have taken place between the Governments of the United States and Iran regarding recourse to arbitration, conciliation or any other pacific means for the settlement of their present differences; and to furnish the Court with copies of any documents relating thereto;
>
> (b) whether the government of either the United States or Iran has formally broken off diplomatic relations between the two governments since the matters which are the subject of their present differences arose; and, if so, to furnish the Court with copies of any documents thereto.

Verbatim Record, *supra* note 4, at 8.

ters,"[23] that the Court was anxious to be enlightened on the existence and scope of the dispute. The information received from Mr. Newsom on December 9 was not wholly satisfactory, for at the end of the public sitting the Court asked for further information.[24] It seems fairly obvious that the Court was interested in getting the sort of factual information on which a finding that a dispute exists can be made. However, it would seem that taking a realistic rather than a formalistic view of the matter, the Court must have satisfied itself about the existence of a dispute. This leaves open the question as to the critical date when the dispute arose. Perhaps the letter from the Iranian Government to the Court of December 9, 1979, may be regarded as the formal acknowledgment of the existence of the dispute. In this letter Iran asked the Court not to take cognizance of the case submitted by the United States on two grounds.[25]

As mentioned earlier in connection with the question of the justiciability of the dispute,[26] Iran drew the attention of the Court "to the deep-rootedness and the essential character of the Islamic revolution of Iran" and contended that "any examination of the numerous repercussions thereof is a matter essentially and directly within the national sovereignty of Iran." Whether this argument should have been regarded as being in the nature of a plea to the jurisdiction of the Court on the merits, and considered in that context, need not be examined here. The Court rejected it in no uncertain terms, saying (in paragraph 25 of the Order):

> Whereas it is no doubt true that the Islamic revolution of Iran is a matter "essentially and directly within the national sovereignty of Iran"; whereas however a dispute which concerns diplomatic and consular premises and the detention of internationally protected persons, and involves the interpretation or application of multilateral conventions codifying the international law governing diplomatic and consular relations, is one which by its very nature falls within international jurisdiction.

The Court also considered another Iranian objection, which will be discussed below in connection with Security Council Resolution 457 (1979), and, having found it without merit, concluded that neither objection could "be accepted as constituting any obstacle to the Court's taking cognizance of the case brought before it by the United States Application of 29 November 1979" (Order, para. 26). Stated in positive terms: the Court was satisfied that it had prima facie jurisdiction on the merits of the case.

[23] *Id.* at 9.

[24] *Id.* at 45. The Court asked for a copy of the message intended to be delivered by Ramsey Clark and of any documents or questions which Mr. Newsom stated had been communicated to the Iranian Chargé d'Affaires. In his oral statement Mr. Owen referred to the Ramsey Clark mission. *Id.* at 26.

[25] The letter will be found in paragraph 8 of the Order.

[26] Text at note 2 *supra*.

## Some Other Aspects of Procedure for the Indication of Interim Measures

The United States was aware that its Request for Interim Measures might run into two seemingly substantial difficulties. One of these related to the possible impact of Security Council Resolution 457, adopted unanimously on December 4, 1979,[27] and the other to the fact that in both its Application and its Request the United States asked for the release of the hostages, which seemed to be contrary to the principle that a Request for Interim Measures should not anticipate the judgment on the merits.

It will be recalled that at the opening of the public sitting on December 10, the President of the Court said that he had given prior notice to the U.S. Agent of the Court's request that it be informed of his Government's view on the question: What significance should be attached by the Court, for the purpose of the present proceedings, to the Security Council resolution?[28] The question was obviously motivated by the role that a Security Council resolution had played in the *Aegean Sea Continental Shelf* dispute. In that case, apart from its request for provisional measures to ensure the preservation of its rights, Greece also had asked the Court to indicate provisional measures to prevent an aggravation of the dispute. The Court then reviewed the proceedings in the Security Council initiated by Greece on August 10, 1976, the day on which the Greek Application and Request for Interim Measures were filed in the Court, and found that in view of the adoption by the Security Council of the consensus Resolution 395 (1976) and the positive attitude of both Turkey and Greece to it, "it is not necessary for the Court to decide the question whether Article 41 of the Statute confers upon it the power to indicate interim measures of protection for the sole purpose of preventing the aggravation or extension of a dispute.[29] As the Court, for various reasons, had already determined that Article 41 of the Statute was inapplicable, the Court declined to accede to the Greek request.[30]

Resolution 457 was adopted on December 4, 1979, following an initiative by the Secretary-General under Article 99 of the Charter. After noting the "dangerous level of tension between Iran and the United States" and reaffirming the obligation "of all State Parties" to the Vienna Conventions to respect the sanctity of diplomatic personnel and premises, the Security Council in the resolution "*[u]rgently calls on* the Government of Iran to release immediately the personnel of the Embassy of the United States of America being held in Tehran, to provide them protection and to allow them to leave the country."

In view of the close relationship between this resolution and the U.S. request for the release of the hostages and the use made by the Court of the Security Council resolution in the *Aegean Continental Shelf* case, and in view of the above-mentioned request to the

[27] *Reprinted in* 18 ILM 1644 (1979).
[28] Verbatim Record, *supra* note 4, at 11.
[29] [1976] ICJ REP. 12–13. For comments on this case, see articles listed in notes 13 and 15.
[30] [1976] ICJ REP. 11 and 14, paras. 32 and 46.

Agent of the United States, one would have been justified in expecting the Court to give this matter close consideration. Nothing of the sort happened. To be sure, the Agent of the United States distinguished the *Aegean* case from the present one on several grounds and stressed the judicial function of the Court "to decide in accordance with international law such disputes as are submitted to it" (Article 38(1) of the Court's Statute).[31] However, the Order contains only one incidental reference to the Security Council resolution in the context of one of the Iranian objections to the Court's jurisdiction.

In its letter of December 9, Iran asked the Court not to take cognizance of the dispute on the ground that the hostages question formed only "a marginal and secondary aspect of an overall problem" relating to the activities of the United States over a period of 25 years. The Court stated that, "having regard to the importance of the legal principles involved," the seizure of the American Embassy and Consulates and the detention of internationally protected persons cannot be regarded as "secondary" and "marginal." The Court then went on to refer to the initiative of the Secretary-General, who had characterized the events as "a grave situation" posing "a serious threat to international peace and security"; the Court concluded "that the Security Council in resolution 457 (1979) expressed itself as deeply concerned at the dangerous level of tension between the two States, which could have grave consequences for international peace and security" (Order, para. 23). Thus disappeared what appeared to be an obstacle to the American case, serious enough to warrant the request from the President of the Court to the Agent of the United States. Whether this means that the ruling of the Court in the *Aegean Continental Shelf* case has been abandoned remains to be seen. In any event, its value as a precedent may never be the same.

The duplication of the appeal for the release of the hostages in the Application and the Request did not escape the attention of Iran. In its letter of December 9, it contended that this action by the United States implied "that the Court should have passed judgment on the actual substance of the case submitted to it, which the Court cannot do without breach of the norms governing its jurisdiction."[32] In the *Chorzów* case, the Permanent Court of International Justice held that the German request "cannot be regarded as relating to the indication of measures of interim protection, but as designed to obtain an interim judgment in favor of a part of the claim formulated in the Application."[33] The

[31] Verbatim Record, *supra* note 4, at 37–39. Mr. Owen quoted a statement by U.S. Ambassador Donald McHenry, which was discussed with all members of the Security Council. It reads as follows:

> The United States wishes to place on the record that the adoption of this resolution by the Security Council clearly is not intended to displace peaceful efforts in other organs of the United Nations. Neither the United States nor any other Member intends that the adoption of this resolution shall have any prejudicial impact whatever on the request of the United States for the indication of provisional measures of protection by the International Court of Justice.

*Id.* at 39. As the Court made no comment on the statement, it is difficult to assess the significance it may have attached to it.

[32] *See* Order, para. 8 (4).

[33] Order of November 21, 1927, [1927] PCIJ, ser. A, No. 12, 9–11, at 10. *See* in this connection the ICJ Order of June 22, 1973, in the *Nuclear Tests* cases, in which the Court called upon France to avoid nuclear tests causing the deposit of radioactive fallout on Australian territory. [1973] ICJ REP. 99, 106. And *see also* the dissenting opinions of Judges Forster

Agent of the United States in his oral argument admitted the overlap in the Application and Request in that "both pleadings ask in effect for an Order calling for an immediate release of the hostages and their safe departure from Iran." He explained that this overlap resulted "from an excess of caution on the part of the United States" and admitted that the request for the release of the hostages "should have appeared only in our pending request for an indication of provisional measures."[34]

The Court disposed of the Iranian objection in a single, short paragraph; the heart of it is in a sense of reinterpretation of the *Chorzów* dictum. The Court quoted the *Chorzów* ruling but distinguished it from the present case, saying that "the circumstances of that [*Chorzów*] case were entirely different from those of the present one, and the request there sought to obtain from the Court a *final* judgment on part of a claim for a sum of money."[35] The Court continued:

> whereas, moreover, a request for provisional measures must by its very nature relate to the substance of the case since, as Article 41 expressly states, their object is to preserve the respective rights of either party; and whereas in the present case the purpose of the United States request appears to be not to obtain a judgment, interim or final, on the merits of its claims but to preserve the substance of the rights which it claims *pendente lite.*[36]

The Court thus removed the last substantial obstacle facing the United States request and in doing so may well have made a significant contribution to a better understanding of a complex problem.

The Iranian Government in the above-cited letter also maintained that "since provisional measures are by definition intended to protect the interests of the parties, they cannot be unilateral, as they are in the request submitted by the American Government" (Order, para. 8(4)). The Court rejected this argument as Article 41 of the Statute speaks specifically of measures "which ought to be taken to preserve the respective rights of *either* party" (emphasis by Court, Order, para. 29). The Court referred to Article 73 of its Rules as recognition of the fact that "the whole concept of an indication of provisional measures . . . implies a request from one of the parties for measures to preserve its own rights against action by the other party calculated to prejudice those rights *pendente lite,*" and declared that it follows from this consideration "that a request for provisional measures is by its nature unilateral." Finally, the Court referred to Article 75 of its Rules pursuant to which the Court may indicate provisional measures *proprio motu* which ought to be taken by any or all of the parties. The fact that Iran did not appear before the Court and made no request for provisional measures "does not, and cannot, mean that the Court is precluded from entertaining a request from a party merely by reason of the fact that measures which it requests are unilateral" (Order, para. 29). In short, a party in the

and Gros, who recalled the *Chorzów* principle and based their dissent partly on that ground. *Id.* at 113 and 123, respectively.

[34] Verbatim Record, *supra* note 4, at 36.

[35] Order, para. 28 (emphasis supplied).

[36] *Ibid.*

position of Iran has no veto over the indication of provisional measures requested by the other party to the dispute.

## III. CONCLUDING OBSERVATIONS

In examining the Request for provisional measures, as formulated by the United States in its final submissions filed with the Registry on December 12, 1979, that is, after the oral hearing, the Court turned first to the "circumstances," that elusive term in Article 41(1). The Court has the power to indicate provisional measures "if it considers that circumstances so require." The Court understood the term in a factual sense and gave a summary of the circumstances, which is quoted at the beginning of this paper. It then examined another requirement of Article 41(1), namely, that the measures be designed "to preserve the respective rights of either party." This requirement caused some difficulty in the past as it may seem to refer implicitly to the *Chorzów* ruling. Were the rights to be preserved those rights that a party claimed as appertaining to it but that were the very subject of litigation? If so, would it not be a matter to be determined only in the judgment on the merits?

In this case, the United States in its Application claimed that Iran had violated numerous provisions in the conventions mentioned above, as well as obligations flowing from customary international law, and asked the Court to adjudge and declare that Iran by its action and inaction had indeed violated these legal obligations, that it should pay reparations to the United States for these violations, and that the persons who seized the premises and staff of the Embassy and Consulates should be prosecuted. It will be recalled that the United States had also, albeit unnecessarily, included in the Application a request for the release of the hostages. In its final submissions, the United States somewhat amended its earlier formulation in the Request of November 29, of the provisional measures it regarded as required to "preserve" its rights.[37] The Court did not deem it neces-

[37] In the final submissions filed with the Court on December 12, 1979, the United States asked the Court to indicate the following measures:

> "First, that the Government of Iran immediately release all hostages of United States nationality and facilitate the prompt and safe departure from Iran of these persons and all other United States officials in dignified and humane circumstances.
>
> Second, that the Government of Iran immediately clear the premises of the United States Embassy, Chancery and Consulate in Tehran of all persons whose presence is not authorized by the United States Chargé d'Affaires in Iran, and restore the premises to United States control.
>
> Third, that the Government of Iran ensure that, to the extent that the United States should choose, and Iran should agree, to the continued presence of United States diplomatic and consular personnel in Iran, all persons attached to the United States Embassy and Consulates should be accorded, and protected in, full freedom of movement, as well as the privileges and immunities to which they are entitled, necessary to carry out their diplomatic and consular functions.
>
> Fourth, that the Government of Iran not place on trial any person attached to the Embassy and Consulates of the United States and refrain from any action to implement any such trial; and that the Government of Iran not detain or permit the detention of any such person in connection with any proceedings, whether of an 'international commission' or otherwise, and that any such person not be required to participate in any such proceeding.
>
> Fifth, that the Government of Iran ensure that no action is taken which might prejudice the rights of the United States in respect of carrying out of any decision which the Court may render on the merits, and, in particular,

sary to engage in what might have become a time-consuming and possibly controversial exercise of examining in detail how or to what extent the requested measures related to rights that the United States sought to have protected. Instead, the Court did two things: first, it made the most emphatic statement possible (quoted above, page 1065) on the universal significance of the institutions and principles pertaining to the conduct of relations between states (Order, paras. 38–40). Obviously, these institutions and principles deserve protection.

In the second place, without saying so explicitly, the Court appears to have accepted the following statement submitted by the United States of the rights entitled to protection by the indication of provisional measures: "The right [of the United States] to maintain a working and effective embassy in Tehran, the right to have its diplomatic and consular personnel protected in their lives and persons from every form of interference and abuse, and the right to have its nationals protected and secure."[38]

As the Court pointed out, there is no obligation under general international law for states to maintain embassies and consulates, and both Vienna Conventions contain elaborate clauses for the termination of diplomatic and consular relations in times of peace and war (Order, para. 41). Iran, however, has not chosen to act in accordance with the law but has acted and continues to act in brutal violation of the law. The rights to which, in the Court's judgment, the United States is entitled, and which its Agent, Mr. Owen, put in a nutshell in almost moving language, are indeed rights that deserve protection in accordance with Article 41 of the Statute of the Court.

There remains one point to be considered, which figured prominently in the *Aegean Continental Shelf* case, namely, the question whether "the circumstances of the case disclose the risk of an irreparable prejudice to rights in issue in the proceedings."[39] In that case, the Court was unable to find in the alleged breach by Turkey "of Greece's rights such a risk of irreparable prejudice to rights in issue before the Court as might require the exercise of its power under Article 41 of the Statute to indicate interim measures for their preservation."[40] On the contrary, the Court was of the opinion that the breach "might be capable of reparation by appropriate means."[41]

These statements made it inevitable that the United States would stress that the rights claimed in this case were threatened with irreparable injury. With the *Aegean Continental Shelf* case perhaps in mind, Mr. Owen declared with reference to the above-mentioned rights[42] that

> with each passing hour those rights are being destroyed, and the injury, once incurred, is plainly and completely irreparable. The trauma of being held hostage day after day in condi-

neither take, nor permit, action that would threaten the lives, safety, or well-being of the hostages" [quoted by Court, Order, para. 12].

[38] This is from Mr. Owen's oral statement, Verbatim Record, *supra* note 4, at 31.
[39] [1976] ICJ REP. 11, para. 32.
[40] *Id.*, para. 33.
[41] *Ibid.*
[42] Text at note 38 *supra*.

> tions of danger cannot be erased, the weeks of interruption of diplomatic functions cannot be repaired. If the hostages are physically harmed, this Court's decision on the merits cannot possibly heal them. Given the nature of the rights involved, an ultimate award of monetary damages simply could not make good the injuries currently being sustained as this case awaits the Court's judgment.[43]

It was obviously necessary to stress in this phase of the case the irreparable character of the threatened injuries, inasmuch as the United States, in its Application, requested that the Court adjudge and declare, *inter alia,*

> [t]hat the Government of Iran shall pay to the United States, in its own right and in the exercise of its right of diplomatic protection of its nationals, reparation for the foregoing violations of Iran's international legal obligations to the United States, in a sum to be determined by the Court.

On its face, there seems to be a contradiction here, but a claim for reparation in the usual sense for a breach of an international obligation may well be distinguished from the threat of an irreparable prejudice, particularly to the detained individuals.

This, it seems to the present writer, is the approach adopted by the Court in this case. The Court accepted the view that the power to indicate provisional measures under Article 41 of the Statute "presupposes that irreparable prejudice should not be caused to rights which are the subject of dispute in judicial proceedings" (Order, para. 36). The Court then found that the "continuance of the situation the subject of the present request exposes the human beings concerned to privation, hardship, anguish and even danger to life and health and thus to a serious possibility of irreparable harm" (Order, para. 42). It is significant that the Court required "a serious possibility" and not certainty, which in many cases would raise questions of proof.

In finally deciding upon the request, the Court said that, for unstated reasons, it "cannot fail to take note of the provisions of the Convention on the Prevention and Punishment of Crimes against Internationally Protected Persons, including Diplomatic Agents, of 1973, to which both Iran and the United States are parties." This convention, it will be recalled, was included by the United States, along with the Vienna Conventions of 1961 and 1963, among the bases of jurisdiction of the Court. However, the Court found that it was not necessary to examine the question whether a basis for the exercise of its powers under Article 41 of the Statute might also be found in the above convention or in the bilateral treaty between the United States and Iran (Order, para. 21).

Having satisfied itself that "in the light of the several considerations set out above, . . . the circumstances require it to indicate provisional measures, as provided by Article

[43] Verbatim Record, *supra* note 3, at 31. In support of this position, Mr. Owen referred to the case concerning the *Denunciation of the Treaty of November 2nd, 1865, between China and Belgium* decided by the Permanent Court of International Justice. In that case, which involved protection for nationals and property, and performance of consular functions, the Court granted measures on the ground that the injury expected to occur during the pendency of the case "could not be made good by the payment of an indemnity or by compensation or restitution in some other material form." [1927] PCIJ, ser. A, No. 8, at 6.

41 of the Statute,'' and having made the usual disclaimer that ''the decision given in the present proceedings in no way prejudges the question of the jurisdiction of the Court to deal with the merits'' (Order, paras. 44 and 45), the Court unanimously indicated the following provisional measures:

> A. (i) The Government of the Islamic Republic of Iran should immediately ensure that the premises of the United States Embassy, Chancery and Consulates be restored to the possession of the United States authorities under their exclusive control, and should ensure their inviolability and effective protection as provided for by the treaties in force between the two States, and by general international law;
>
> (ii) The Government of the Islamic Republic of Iran should ensure the immediate release, without any exception, of all persons of United States nationality who are or have been held in the Embassy of the United States of America or in the Ministry of Foreign Affairs in Tehran, or have been held as hostages elsewhere, and afford full protection to all such persons, in accordance with the treaties in force between the two States, and with general international law;
>
> (iii) The Government of the Islamic Republic of Iran should, as from that moment, afford to all the diplomatic and consular personnel of the United States the protection, privileges and immunities to which they are entitled under the treaties in force between the two States, and under general international law, including immunity from any form of criminal jurisdiction and freedom and facilities to leave the territory of Iran;
>
> B. The Government of the United States of America and the Government of the Islamic Republic of Iran should not take any action and should ensure that no action is taken which may aggravate the tension between the two countries or render the existing dispute more difficult of solution.

It will be noted that these measures do not coincide entirely with the measures requested by the United States in its final submissions of December 12, 1979. The first and probably the most significant request for release of the detained personnel appears in A(ii) of the Court's Order; the second U.S. request appears in A(i), albeit in a more elaborate form; the third U.S. request may be covered in A(iii). The latter request was addressed to reports that some or all of the hostages might be subjected to trial in Iran. This possibility is not included specifically in any of the measures indicated by the Court. However, it may well come under A(iii), where the Court calls upon Iran to afford the United States personnel full protection under treaties and general international law, ''including immunity from any form of criminal jurisdiction and freedom and facilities to leave the territory of Iran.'' The fifth U.S. request may well be subsumed under paragraph B of the measures indicated by the Court.

No doubt the Order of the Court in this case, even if it is not implemented by Iran, will come to be regarded as a landmark in the jurisprudence of the Court relating to Article 41 of the Statute. The Court's Order is not argumentative. It is left to students of this subject to find the points in which the Court clarified the principles governing the indication of provisional measures. There is nothing in the Order, for instance, on whether the power to indicate such measures is an ''independent'' or ''inherent'' or ''incidental'' power. On the other hand, in the present writer's provisional opinion, there is a good deal here to clarify the relation between jurisdiction on merits and jurisdiction under Article 41, on the relation between provisional measures and judgment on merits, on the meaning of "irreparable harm," and on the relevance of Security Council action.

Be that as it may, there is no doubt that this case represents a landmark in the relations between the United States and the Court. There has never been any doubt about the interest of the United States in promoting adjudication by the court.[44] However, the actual use of the Court by the United States is another matter. Over a period of years, from 1954 to 1958, the United States brought several cases before the Court against Hungary, Czechoslovakia, and the Soviet Union arising out of aerial incidents—knowing full well that there was no basis on which the Court could assume jurisdiction. In one case, the *Aerial Incident of 27 July 1955,* the United States cited Bulgaria before the Court on the basis of a Bulgarian declaration under Article 36 of the Statute of the Permanent Court of International Justice, which the present Court, in a companion case—Israel v. Bulgaria—found to have lapsed. However, the American Application was withdrawn when Bulgaria invoked the so-called Connally Amendment against the United States.[45] This then is the first time in 35 years that the United States has turned to the Court. Is there reason to hope that the United States will henceforth demonstrate its devotion to the cause of international adjudication by deeds as well as by words? Would this be a propitious time for the United States to submit a new declaration under Article 36(2) of the Statute of the Court from which the Connally Amendment would be conspicuous by its absence?

[44] *See* recent study by the DEPARTMENT OF STATE, PUB. NO. 8940, THE SECRETARY'S REPORT TO THE PRESIDENT ON REFORM AND RESTRUCTURING OF THE U.N. SYSTEM 16 and 18 (1978).

[45] *See* Gross, *Bulgaria Invokes the Connally Amendment,* 56 AJIL 357 (1962). See also *supra*, pp. 727–751.

# VIII

# SETTLEMENT OF DISPUTES BY THE POLITICAL ORGANS OF THE UNITED NATIONS: SOME ASPECTS OF THE ARAB-ISRAEL DISPUTE

# PASSAGE THROUGH THE SUEZ CANAL OF ISRAEL-BOUND CARGO AND ISRAEL SHIPS

## I. INTRODUCTION

The purported nationalization of the Universal Company of the Suez Maritime Canal by the Egyptian Decree of July 26, 1956, refreshed the interest of the international community in the long-lingering dispute over restrictions imposed by Egypt on the passage of cargoes bound for Israeli ports and the prohibition of the passage of Israeli ships through the Suez Canal. At the 22-Power London Conference, August 16–23, 1956, representatives of several governments referred to these restrictions[1] and

> it was pointed out that Egypt is in defiance, really, of a decision by the Security Council of the United Nations, taken in 1951 . . . which was reaffirmed again . . . in 1953, that under the terms of the Treaty of 1888 the Israeli shipping was entitled to go through and that Egypt was not entitled to bar it as it was doing.[2]

It is probably not altogether speculative to assume that it was with this situation in mind that the eighteen governments participating in the London Conference included in their Statement the following principle: "Insulation of the operation of the Canal from

[1] See remarks made by the representatives of France, New Zealand, Iran, Netherlands and India. The Suez Canal Problem, July 26–September 22, 1956, pp. 91, 112, 128, 145, 164 (State Dept. Pub. 6392).

[2] Secretary of State John Foster Dulles at the news conference Aug. 28, 1956. *Ibid.* 298. The statement by Mr. Dulles, which is inaccurate in part, was in response to the following question: "Mr. Secretary, was Israel's right of passage through the Suez (Canal) in any way discussed at the London Conference?"

the influence of the politics of any nation."[3] This principle, one of the six which were to form the basis of any settlement of the Suez question, was voted upon in the Security Council on October 13, 1956, and received unanimous approval.[4]

In the recent Middle East situation, which assumed the character of an acute crisis with the military action of Israel launched on October 29, 1956, to remove the bases of the guerrilla raiders in the Gaza strip, and which was followed by the combined Anglo-French action to secure the Canal, the restrictions imposed by Egypt in the Canal also played a significant role. The first resolution adopted on November 2, 1956, by the General Assembly during its First Emergency Special Session, urged that

> upon the cease-fire being effective, steps be taken to reopen the Suez Canal and restore secure freedom of navigation.[5]

The Egyptian view that the state of war, initiated by Egypt on March 15, 1948, continued in spite of the General Armistice Agreement with Israel of February 24, 1949, and that Egypt derived from this certain rights of belligerency, namely, the right of visit, search and seizure, was an important element in the debates of the General Assembly and the negotiations leading to the withdrawal of Israeli troops from Egypt and the Gaza strip. It is unnecessary to review in detail the various relevant statements. Suffice it to recall that President Dwight D. Eisenhower in his address to the nation of February 20, 1957, recalled that "Egypt ignored the United Nations in exercising belligerent rights in relation to Israeli shipping in the Suez Canal and in the Gulf of Aqaba." After noting that Egypt, "by accepting the Six Principles adopted by the Security Council last October in relation to the Suez Canal bound itself to free and open transit through the Suez Canal without discrimination, and to the principle that the operation of the Canal should be insulated from the politics of any country," he declared:

> We should not assume that if Israel withdraws, Egypt will prevent Israeli shipping from using the Suez Canal or the Gulf of Aqaba. If, unhappily, Egypt does hereafter violate the Armistice Agreement or other international obligation, then this should be dealt with firmly by the society of nations.[5a]

When announcing in the General Assembly, on March 1, 1957, the plans of her government for withdrawal from Egypt, the representative of Israel, Mrs. Golda Meir, declared with reference to the above statement: "This declaration has weighed heavily with

[3] *Ibid.* 308.

[4] As adopted by the Security Council, principle (3) is phrased as follows: "The operation of the Canal should be insulated from the politics of any country." In this connection principle (1) is also directly relevant: "There should be free and open transit through the Canal without discrimination, overt or covert—this covers both political and technical aspects." Security Council, Official Records, 743rd Meeting, Oct. 13, 1956, p. 18, par. 105, and Doc. S 3671.

[5] Resolution 997 (ES-I). General Assembly, Official Records, First Emergency Spec. Sess., Supp. No.1, p.2 (Doc. A3354).

[5a] 36 Dept. of State Bulletin 390 (1957).

my Government in determining its action today."[6] However, neither the various resolutions adopted by the General Assembly in relation to the recent crisis nor the withdrawal of Israeli troops appear to have quieted public apprehension as to the continuation of Egypt's claim to belligerent rights. Repeated requests of the Government of Israel to secure assurances from Egypt, through the office of the Secretary General of the United Nations, "to the mutual and full abstention from belligerent acts, by land, air and sea,"[7] have been of no avail. The Secretary General reported to the General Assembly that

> the Government of Egypt reaffirms its intent to observe fully the provisions of the Armistice Agreement to which it is a party, as indicated earlier in its acceptance (A/3266) of the 2 November resolution of the General Assembly, on the assumption, of course, that observance will be reciprocal.[8]

A reaffirmation of this kind is of no practical value, since the Government of Egypt has at all times insisted that its restrictive practices and belligerent rights were compatible with the Armistice Agreement. It continued to do so even after the Security Council on September 1, 1951, called upon it to terminate such practices and declared that "neither party can reasonably assert that it is actively a belligerent or requires to exercise the right of visit, search, and seizure for any legitimate purpose of self-defence."[9] The position of the United States and other Members of the United Nations has also remained unchanged, and they continue to hold the view that Egypt, under the Armistice Agreement, does not possess belligerent rights.[10] It may be noted, however, that the Security Council resolution of September 1, 1951, does not express this simple view directly. The Council may have deemed it unnecessary to labor the obvious after having rejected explicitly every one of the specific arguments marshaled by Egypt in support of its practices. It is nonetheless remarkable that neither the Council nor the Assembly has yet seen its way to declare clearly and unequivocally that, between Members of the United Nations, a state of war, after termination of hostilities, is incompatible with the Charter. This, it is submitted, appears from the legal point of view to be the most promising point of departure for resolving the controversy over the Egyptian restrictions in the Suez Canal.[11] The controversy since 1949 has been the focus of legal argument principally between Israel and

[6] New York Times, March 2, 1957, p. 10.

[7] U.N. Doc. A3527, Annex I: Aide-mémoire dated Feb. 4, 1957, transmitted to the Secretary General by the Permanent Representative of Israel to the United Nations.

[8] U.N. Doc. A3527, Feb. 11, 1957, p. 6. Resolution 997 (ES-I), referred to above, urged "the parties to the armistice agreements promptly to withdraw all forces behind the armistice lines, to desist from raids across the armistice lines into neighbouring territory, and to observe scrupulously the provisions of the armistice agreements." Official Records, First Emergency Spec. Sess., Supp. No. 1, p. 2 (Doc. A3354).

[9] Official Records, 6th Year, 558th Meeting, Sept. 1, 1951, p. 2.

[10] See, *e.g.*, the statement by Secretary of State Dulles at his news conference March 26, 1957. 36 Dept. of State Bulletin 596 (1957).

[11] This paper is not concerned with the question of passage through the Straits of Tiran and the Gulf of Aqaba. Insofar as the restrictions practiced by Egypt in that area hinge juridically on the "state of war" doctrine, the arguments advanced with reference to the Suez Canal are equally applicable to it.

Egypt, and since 1951 between Egypt and the Security Council, as the latter has made its own the principal theses advanced by Israel. These arguments and counter-arguments will now be examined.

## II. EGYPTIAN RESTRICTIONS AND THEIR JUDICIAL JUSTIFICATION

On May 15, 1948, Egypt announced its "armed intervention in Palestine with a view to restoring law and order, and with the object of putting an end to acts of violence committed by the Zionist bands."[12] At the same time a state of siege was proclaimed, a shipping inspection service in the Ports of Alexandria, Port Said and Suez was established, and by Proclamation No. 38 of July, 1948, a Prize Court was set up. The Court was to "apply the rules of public international law, in their absence . . . it should decide in accordance with the principles of equity."[13]

Nearly one year after the conclusion of the General Armistice Agreement with Israel, these regulations were consolidated in the decree issued by King Farouk I on February 6, 1950 "on the procedure of ship and airplace searches and of seizure of contraband goods in connection with the Palestine War."[14] Article 2 provides for inspection by customs officers of the ship's manifest and cargo "so as to ensure that it contains no arms, munitions, war material or other articles considered war contraband and shipped directly to institutions or persons on Palestinian territory under Zionist control." Article 10 lists the categories of articles to be deemed war contraband, including fuel of every kind and "seized as prize." According to Article 3 of the decree,

> *force* may at all times be used against any ship attempting to avoid search, where necessary by *firing* so as to *force* it to stop and submit to search. Where the search subsequently reveals that the ship is not carrying any contraband it shall be permitted to continue its voyage.

Article 4 provides that

> if the crew of the ship resists the search by force, the ship shall be deemed to have lost its neutrality by reason of the hostile act. In that event the ship may be arrested, even if the search reveals that it was not carrying contraband and the cargo may be impounded for that reason, unless the owner proves his innocence.

[12] *The Flying Trader*, Egypt, Prize Court of Alexandria, Dec. 2, 1950, Lauterpacht (ed.), International Law Reports 1950 (hereafter cited as 1950 Int. Law Rep.), p. 444. See also cablegram from the Minister of Foreign Affairs of Egypt to the President of the Security Council dated May 15, 1948, U.N. Doc. S743; Security Council, Official Records, 3rd Year, No. 66, 292nd Meeting, May 15, 1948, p. 2.

[13] *The Fjeld*, Egypt, Prize Court of Alexandria, Nov. 4, 1950, 1950 Int. Law Rep. 345 at 346.

[14] Text published in the Journal Officiel, No. 36, April 8, 1950. The English translation was submitted to the Security Council by the representative of Israel on Feb. 15, 1954, U.N. Doc. S3179; Security Council, Official Records, 9th Year, Supp. Jan.–March, 1954, p. 6. The representative of Egypt referred to this decree as dated Feb. 9, 1950, Security Council, Official Records, 549th Meeting, July 26, 1951, p. 18, par. 69. He also listed there the regulations promulgated earlier by Military Proclamations No. 5 of May 15, 1948, No. 13 of June 6, 1948, No. 38 of July 8, 1948, and one of Nov. 4, 1949.

The decree contains other rules customarily found in prize regulations, which are of no direct interest for the dispute. It is important, however, to stress the two facts: One is that the search is to be carried out by customs officials, and the other that force may be used, including firing, in order to force the ship to submit to search.

The representative of Israel also communicated to the Security Council an amendment to this decree, promulgated by the Council of Ministers on November 28, 1953, that is, more than four and one-half years after the conclusion of the Armistice Agreement. This amendment added to the list of contraband "foodstuffs and all other commodities which are likely to strengthen the war potential of the Zionists in Palestine in any way whatever." It also appeared to broaden the territorial applicability of the amended decree by providing as follows:

> All the commodities heretofore enumerated shall be regarded as war contraband even when passing Egypt's territory or territorial waters in transit.[15]

These aggravations, in scope and geographical extent, of the restrictive measures were commented upon by the members of the Security Council and the Government of Israel, and they were not denied by the Government of Egypt.[16]

The legal basis of the Egyptian restrictions was discussed "from a purely academic point of view" by the Prize Court of Alexandria in the case of *The Fjeld*. Claimant argued that the seizure was null and void, as the procedure for inspection was carried out "at a time when no state of war existed"; that prior to May 15, 1948, no state of war could have existed between "the Zionist armed bands and the Arabs" and none could exist after that debate because Egypt had not recognized the "Zionist State."[17] The Prize Court held that "the Palestinian conflict had begun some time before 15 May 1948 and that the Palestinian Arabs and States of the Arab League actively participated therein," and that "Egypt, in her capacity of member of the Arab League and ally of members of the League, found herself in a state of war with the Zionists, before 15 May 1948."[18] Regarding the claimant's second argument the Prize Court held that it was contradicted by the facts:

> Not only has the State of Israel been admitted to the United Nations but also on 15 May, the United States of America and Russia recognized the new State. Such recognition was unqualified and conferred upon Israel the capacity to proceed according to the laws of war, to seizures and to taking in prize so far as her enemies were concerned. The exercise of such rights by Israel against Egypt and the group of Arab States gives, no doubt, a corresponding right to Egypt to exercise the same rights against Israel. The non-recognition by Egypt of Israel as a State cannot prevent Israel from being regarded as a belligerent. Nothing in international law requires that the status of belligerency should be expressly pro-

[15] Security Council, Official Records, 9th Year, Supp. Jan.-March, 1954, p. 9.

[16] See remarks by the representatives of New Zealand, Official Records, 662nd Meeting, March 23, 1954, p. 3, par. 10; Brazil, *ibid.*, 664th Meeting, March 29, 1954, p. 5, par. 17; Israel, *ibid.*, 659th Meeting, Feb. 15, 1954, p. 17, par. 94; and Egypt, *ibid.*, 661st Meeting, March 12, 1954, p. 6, par. 28.

[17] 1950 Int. Law Rep. 345 at 347.

[18] *Ibid.* 348.

> claimed; such a status can result from circumstances. The Egyptian government, by creating a Prize Court governed by the principles of international law, and by applying the rules of war in so far as concerns the treatment of prisoners and wounded and so far as concerns the conduct of hostilities, has clearly shown its desire to follow the rules laid down by international law in the Palestinian conflict.
>
> It now remains to decide the consequences of the conflict in so far as neutrals are concerned. It is established that the Palestinian conflict constitutes, from the legal point of view, a true war with international aspects. This imposes upon neutrals the duties resulting from neutrality and requires them to submit to the rights of the belligerents, whether or not such neutrals have officially proclaimed their neutrality, for neutrality is only one of the consequences of a state of war, and subjects neutrals, by reason only of their knowledge of such a state, to the action of the belligerents.[19]

It is important to note that the Prize Court took no notice of the General Armistice Agreement between Egypt and Israel. The Court presumably assumed, as the Egyptian Government did, that the Armistice had no effect on continued validity of the legislation concerning visit, search and seizure. If the Prize Court had taken the opposite view, that the conclusion of the Armistice Agreement put an end to the legislation of 1948, the re-enactment of virtually the identical measures by the Decree of February 6, 1950, after the conclusion of the Armistice Agreement, left the Court no choice. On this point the Court held:

> The existence of a state of war or of neutrality in so far as non-belligerents are concerned cannot be discussed by the Prize Court, for it is the duty of the Court to apply the law without examining its legality.[20]

It may well be that the Court, under the Egyptian system of law, was precluded from discussing the "existence of a state of war," both before and after the Armistice Agreement entered into force. The existence or non-existence of a state of war after the entry into force of the Agreement has been and continues to be the first point in the debates before the international forum.

It will be noted that the Egyptian decrees referred to do not deal especially with "enemy" ships. This is perhaps unnecessary as customary international law and the applicable Hague Conventions provide the necessary legal basis in time of war. The question whether and to what extent the Constantinople Convention of October 29, 1888, respecting the Free Navigation of the Suez Maritime Canal derogates from the usual rules regarding visit, search and seizure, has been considered by the Prize Court of Alexandria and debated even more extensively before the U. N. Security Council. The views expressed in the latter forum will be discussed below. In *The Flying Trader,* the Prize Court of Alexandria, after reviewing Articles 1, 4, 5, 7, 8, 9, 10, and 11 of the Convention, concluded:

[19] *The Fjeld,* Prize Court of Alexandria, Nov. 4, 1950. *Ibid.* 345 at 348 *ff.*
[20] *The Fjeld, loc. cit.* 347.

It falls to this Court to interpret the expression "the defence of Egypt and the maintenance of public order,"[21] a situation which involves the non-application of Article 4 of the Convention.

The Court has already ruled that Egypt was truly a belligerent State possessing the right of capture *jure belli.* It follows that Egypt has in this connexion the right to take any measures necessary for its defence. The exercise of this right in no way runs counter to the provisions of Articles 4, 5, and 7, for the prohibitions contained in those articles cannot interfere with the natural right of a State to preserve its own existence, a right which cannot be the subject even of express renunciation. Egypt is the sole judge of the existence of a state of danger menacing her existence and rendering necessary certain acts referred to in Article 4.[22] All that the Convention requires, in the event of the carrying out of particular measures, is notification to the Powers signatory to the Declaration of London of 17 March 1885. Every armed conflict to which Egypt is a party, and especially a conflict with its neighbors, raises inevitably the question of the defence of its own territory, whatever the origin of the hostilities may be. The entire territory, land or sea, becomes, in the eyes of international law, a theatre of war authorizing the enemy to commit such acts of war therein as it may judge expedient.[23] There flows from this the necessity of repelling aggression, whether by repulsing enemy attacks, or in preventing such attacks from taking place, which includes interrupting the means of reinforcing such attacks.

The provisions of Article 11 of the Convention, which states that measures taken by Egypt and Turkey in the exceptional cases contemplated by Articles 9 and 10 must not interfere with the free use of the Canal, cannot be construed as a restriction upon the rights of Egypt. The signatories of the Convention intended by this Article to confirm what is said in Article 1[24] about free passage through the Canal in time of war and peace; but reasonable and necessary measures taken by Egypt do not interfere with such passage.[25]

Here again is a failure to take into account the existence of a complete armistice between Egypt and Israel, by land, sea and air.[26] Whatever may have been the rights of the parties during the stage of active hostilities, the commission of hostile or warlike acts has been rendered illegal by the Armistice.[27] If the commission of such acts is prohibited as between the parties to the Armistice, it follows *a fortiori* that they are prohibited also in relation to third states, strangers to the conflict. The legality of Egypt's restrictions

[21] In Art. 10 of the Convention.

[22] In order to avoid a possible misunderstanding of the Court's argument, reference must be had to Art. 4 of the Constantinople Convention: "The Maritime Canal remaining open in time of war as a free passage, even to ships of war of the belligerents, under the terms of Article I of the present Treaty, the High Contracting Parties agree that no right of war, act of hostility or act having for its purpose to interfere with the free navigation of the Canal, shall be committed in the Canal and its ports of access, or within a radius of 3 nautical miles from those ports, even though the Ottoman Empire should be one of the belligerent Powers." The Suez Canal Problem, *op. cit.* 17; 3 A.J.I.L. Supp. 124 (1909). It will be seen that contrary to a possible implication in the Court's language, Art. 4, far from authorizing Egypt to take any action in the Canal, expressly prohibits the exercise of any right of war.

[23] The Court referred here to 2 Oppenheim, International Law 187 (1944 ed.).

[24] Art. 1 of the Convention: "The Suez Maritime Canal shall always be free and open, in time of war as in time of peace, to every vessel of commerce or of war, without distinction of flag."

"The Canal shall never be subject to the exercise of the right of blockade." *Op. cit.* 17; 3 A.J.I.L. Supp. 123 (1909).

[25] 1950 Int. Law Rep. at 446 *ff.*

[26] Art. II, par. 1, of the Egyptian-Israeli General Armistice Agreement, Rhodes, Feb. 24, 1949. U.N. Doc. S/1264/Rev. 1; Security Council, Official Records, 4th Year, Spec. Supp. No. 3, p. 2.

[27] The following articles of the General Armistice Agreement are relevant in this context: Art. I, par. 2: "No aggressive action by the armed forces—land, sea, or air—of either Party shall be undertaken, planned, or threatened against the people or the armed forces of the other"; Art. II, par. 2: "No element of the land, sea or air military or para-military forces of either Party, including non-regular forces, shall commit any warlike or hostile act against the military or para-military forces of the other Party, or against civilians in territory under the control of that Party." *Ibid.*

against third states, strangers to the conflict. The legality of Egypt's restrictions against third states has been open to question even during the hostilities, as evidence by the protests addressed to Egypt.[28] They have become even more problematical after the end of hostilities.[29] On the strength of the Court's reasoning, Israel would have the legal right to commit acts of war—by land, sea and air—against Egypt as if the Armistice Agreement did not exist. If such acts are deemed prohibited—as they rightly are—to one party, by parity of reasoning they are also prohibited to the other.

The Court's contention that Egypt "is the sole judge" is untenable. Only the Convention of Constantinople could have conferred such an exclusive right (auto-decision), that is, the right to interpret the Convention with binding force for the other parties to it and the world at large. In the absence of such an exclusive competence, Egypt has merely the right of auto-interpretation.[30] That this was the intent of the authors of the Convention clearly appears from its Article 8, paragraph 1:

> The Agents in Egypt of the Signatory Powers of the present Treaty shall be charged to see that it is carried out . . . In any case, they shall meet once a year to take note of the due execution of the Treaty.

The acts of the Egyptian Government have thus been placed under the supervision of the Contracting Parties.

It follows that the exception in favor of Egypt provided in Article 10 of the Convention does not escape the general supervision by the other Contracting Powers. Moreover, as the Court recognizes, the measures which Egypt "might find it necessary to take to assure by their own force the defense of Egypt and the maintenance of public order" under Article 10 of the Convention, are restricted by the requirement of Article 11 namely, such measures "shall not interfere with the free use of the Canal." The Court's statement that "reasonable and necessary measures taken by Egypt do not interfere with such passage" is for this reason not altogether in harmony with the Convention. Whether measures taken by Egypt do or do not interfere with "the free use of the Canal" is a question of fact. Certainly Egypt is authorized to take "reasonable and necessary" measures but these measures must not interfere with the "free use" of the Canal. It cannot be assumed, as the Prize Court apparently does, that any measures which Egypt regards as "reasonable and necessary" will not interfere with "free use." They very well may so interfere and in the case under consideration they have been found to do so by a large number of states.

[28] Mr. Fawzi (Egypt) stated in the Security Council: "Most of the protests were lodged with the Egyptian Government even while the hostilities in Palestine were still taking place." Official Records, 553rd Meeting, Aug. 16, 1951, p. 24, par. 101.

[29] Referring to the Egyptian contention that a dispute existed between the protesting Powers and Egypt, Sir Gladwyn Jebb (United Kingdom) said: "If there were any dispute within the meaning of the Charter between one of the five delegations mentioned and Egypt, the Armistice Agreement and the whole question of Palestine would be quite irrelevant." Official Records, 555th Meeting, Aug. 27, 1951, p. 3, par. 10.

[30] *Cf.* Leo Gross, "States as Organs of International Law and the Problem of Auto-Interpretation," in George A. Liosky (ed.), Law and Politics in the World Community, pp. 59–89 (1953). See *supra*, pp. 367–397.

## III. EFFECTIVENESS OF EGYPT'S RESTRICTIONS AND PROTESTS AGAINST THEM

Members of the Security Council have on four different occasions discussed the Egyptian restrictions from the legal, political and practical points of view.[31] Members of the United Nations from the very beginning of the restrictions have also protested directly to the Government of Egypt against them. Speaking in the Security Council the representative of Egypt stated:

> Up to today, the Netherlands has protested to the Egyptian Government no less than three times; Turkey, at least once; the United Kingdom, at least ten times; the United States, twelve times; and France, twenty-two times. Most of the protests were lodged with the Egyptian government even while the hostilities in Palestine were still in progress.[32]

Israel's complaints, chiefly juridical in nature, obviously also stressed the adverse effect on its economy. In 1951 the representative of Israel stated that "vessels found to have called at any port in Israel are placed on a black list" and that the "threat of forcible interference acts as a deterrent to the normal trade which would otherwise have passed through the Suez Canal to or from Israel."[33] The blacklist, according to the Government of Israel, contains 104 ships of "British, United States, Swedish, Greek, Norwegian, Dutch, Danish, Panamanian, Liberian, Swiss, Costa Rican and Italian nationality."[34] The effect of blacklisting is that

> cargo carried on these ships shall "be deemed intended for the enemy" and subject to confiscation and seizure, while the ships themselves would be denied the essential facilities necessary for passage through the Suez Canal. The existence of the Blacklist is, therefore, the most stringent of the deterrents whereby Egypt has prevented trading with Israel through an international waterway.[35]

[31] The first debate took place in October–November, 1950, in connection with the Israeli complaint: "Violations by Egypt of the Egyptian-Israeli General Armistice Agreement through the maintenance for seventeen months of blockade practices inconsistent with the letter and spirit of the armistice agreement," U.N. Doc. S/1974, Sept. 16, 1950. The second debate took place at several meetings held between July 26, 1951, and Sept. 1, 1951, following the Israeli complaint: "Restrictions imposed by Egypt on the Passage of Ships through the Suez Canal," U.N. Doc. S/2241, July 11, 1951, Official Records, 6th Year, Supp. July–Sept., 1951, p. 9. The third debate occurred at several meetings between Feb. 5 and March 29, 1954, regarding the Israeli complaint: "Enforcement by Egypt of Restrictions on the Passage of Ships trading with Israel through the Suez Canal," U.N. Doc. S/3168, Jan. 28, 1954, Official Records, 9th Year, Supp. Jan.–March, 1954, p. 1. The final debate was concerned with the complaint by Israel arising from "the illegal arrest and detention of the Israel vessel, the *Bat Galim*, on 28 September 1954" and was spread over meetings held Nov. 3, 1954–Jan. 13, 1955, U.N. Doc. S/3300, Official Records, 9th Year, Supp. Oct.–Dec., 1954, pp. 1 *ff.*

[32] Official Records, 553rd Meeting, Aug. 16, 1951, p. 23, par. 98. Similarly, the representative of the United Kingdom said: "During the past two years a number of maritime countries have made almost continuous representations to the Eqyptian Government through the diplomatic channels, but all these have been of no avail." Official Records, 552nd Meeting, Aug. 16, 1951, p. 4, par. 12.

[33] Official Records, 549th Meeting, July 26, 1951, p. 3.

[34] Letter dated Oct. 13, 1956, from the representative of Israel to the President of the Security Council, U.N. Doc. S3673, p.6.

[35] *Ibid.* The blacklist includes 75 tankers. *Ibid.* Blacklisting of ships is provided for in Art. 11 of the Royal Decree of 1950: Cargo shall be "deemed intended for the enemy whenever . . . (2) It is being shipped indirectly to such persons or

In the view of Israel, "some 90 per cent of the trade which would have normally flowed through the Canal to and from Israel in the past eight years has been effectively obstructed."[36] Several ships were visited and searched, and "Egypt has confiscated and held goods of the value of $5,600,000 seized from ships exercising innocent passage in the Suez Canal."[37]

The representative of Egypt, while admitting that "some maritime Powers are, to our regret affected, although slightly, by the exercise by Egypt of its right of visit and inspection," and that "it is natural for them to want to complain," argued that "it is natural for us to want to survive."[38] Generally, the position taken by Egypt was to stress the small number of ships affected, the lenient manner in which she exercised what she claimed as her rights, and to hold out the prospect of relaxation of the measures in force. Thus the representative of Egypt spoke of "the relatively microscopic action of Egypt,"[39] and offered to show that "Egypt does little more than delay only a few ships for only a few minutes."[40] During the period

> 15 May 1948 to 24 February 1949, out of 8,009 merchantmen which arrived at Port Said, 548 ships were visited and only 71 ships were unloaded of contraband of war. During the same period, 282 ships reached Suez, and only two ships were visited and none was even partly unloaded. In the following three months, 2,139 ships arrived at Port Said, 195 of them were visited and only 25 were partly unloaded. During the same period 1043 ships reached Suez, nine of them were visited and none at all unloaded.[41]

In the course of the 1954 debate, the representative of Egypt declared that "since the Security Council adopted its resolution of 1 September 1951, no ship or cargo has been confiscated by Egypt" and that since then "only 55 suspected ships have been subjected to the inspection procedure out of 32,047 ships passing through the Suez Canal."[42] After quoting figures showing an increase in the tonnage of goods passing through the Canal he said: "It is clear, therefore, that the measures of visit and search taken by Egypt have not in the least restricted the free use of the Canal."[43]

Relaxation of the restrictions was referred to several times by the representative of Egypt.[44] After the Security Council failed to adopt the New Zealand draft resolution ow-

institutions (on Palestinian territory occupied by the enemy). This shall be presumed in any of the following circumstances: . . . (g) If the consignor or consignee is listed on the *black list* kept for that purpose as a carrier of contraband for the Zionists."

[36] *Ibid.* 7.

[37] *Ibid.* 9. For a list of some of these ships, *cf. ibid.* 7–9. The representative of Israel said in the Security Council that "about 95 per cent of Israel's normal trade in products other than oil has been throttled through these restrictions, and, in the case of oil, 100 per cent of that aspect of Israel's import trade has been completely set at naught." Official Records, 661st Meeting, March 12, 1954, p. 31, par. 152.

[38] Official Records, 549th Meeting, July 26, 1951, p. 21, par. 79.

[39] *Ibid.*, 553rd Meeting, Aug. 16, 1951, p. 15, par. 62.

[40] *Ibid.*, 550th Meeting, Aug. 1, 1951, p. 3, par. 11.

[41] *Ibid.*, 549th Meeting, July 26, 1951, p. 20, par. 75.

[42] Official Records, 661st Meeting, March 12, 1954, p. 17, pars. 88–89.

[43] *Ibid.*, p. 18, par. 91.

[44] *Ibid.*, 659th Meeting, Feb. 15, 1954, p. 24, par. 130; 661st Meeting, March 12, 1954, p. 20, par. 105; 662nd Meeting, March 23, 1954, p. 12, par. 43.

ing to the Soviet Union's negative vote, he declared that "now Egypt . . . will of its own free will move towards tolerance."[45] The representative of Lebanon stressed that "this positive note which the representative of Egypt has afforded us . . . is something which we can all welcome and stress and end upon as a happy note."[46] As the seizure of the Israeli ship *Bat Galim* by Egypt on September 28, 1954, was to show, Egypt's spontaneous offer of "tolerance" was either shortlived or fell far short of the Security council resolution of September 1, 1951.

The statistics adduced by Egypt, far from proving the absence of any serious interference with non-Israeli shipping through the Suez Canal, were regarded by the representative of Israel and eight members of the Security Council as proof of the opposite, namely, the substantial effectiveness of the restrictions in deterring trade with Israel.

## IV. NATURE OF THE RESTRICTIONS

The legal nature of the Egyptian restrictions was discussed in several instances in the Security Council. Israel characterized these measures as blockade or "blockade practices" on several occasions.[47] This point is of some relevance in view of Article 1, paragraph 2, of the Constantinople Convention of 1888 which provides categorically: "The Canal shall never be subject to the exercise of the right of blockade." The Egyptian Government was accordingly at pains to show that the practices in question were technically and juridically not a blockade. Thus its representative declared in the Security Council:

> Egypt has never decreed or applied a blockade of the Suez Canal. Its action is confined to the boarding and inspection by customs employees of a very small number of suspected merchant vessels.[48]

This statement fails to mention the right of seizure or confiscation, which is also claimed by Egypt as a consequence of belligerency, and that the action of customs officers may be supported by force.[49]

It can readily be conceded that the right of visit, search and seizure which Egypt

[45] *Ibid.*, 664th Meeting, March 29, 1954, p. 23, par. 157.

[46] *Ibid.*, p. 24, par. 164.

[47] The Israeli complaint of Sept. 16, 1950 (U. N. Doc. S/1794), referred to "blockade practices." See also statements by the representative of Israel at 433rd Meeting, Aug. 4, 1949, p. 16; 517th Meeting, Oct. 30. 1950, p. 10 f.; 522nd Meeting, Nov. 13, 1950, p. 23; 549th Meeting, July 26, 1951, p. 13; 658th Meeting, Feb. 5, 1954, p. 12, par. 49; 659th Meeting, Feb. 15, 1954, p. 14, pars. 80, 88, 89. See also statement by the representative of the United Kingdom in which he referred to the "blockade practices in the Suez Canal," *ibid.*, 522nd Meeting, Nov. 13, 1950, p. 17.

[48] *Ibid.*, 658th Meeting, Feb. 5, 1954, p. 31, par. 163. See also 659th Meeting, Feb. 15, 1954, p. 24, pars. 127, 128; 661st Meeting, March 12, 1954, p. 6, par. 27 f., p. 15, par. 77.

[49] Arts. 1 and 3 of the Royal Decree of Feb. 6, 1950, see *supra*, p. 1084. Another representative of Egypt stressed strongly the right of confiscation, saying: "To judge whether Egypt is entitled to practise the right of visit, search and confiscation of war contraband, reference must be made to the rules of international law. A state of war gives the belligerents certain rights. Foremost amongst these is the incontestable right of visit and search of ships in territorial waters, in ports, in mid-ocean, and in enemy waters, with a view to the confiscation of what is legally considered war contraband." Official Records, 659th Meeting, Feb. 15, 1954, p. 3, par. 9.

admittedly enforces in the Suez Canal is not identical with the right of blockade as the term is normally understood in the law of naval war. However, this is true only insofar as ships of nations other than Israel are concerned; for Israeli ships have been barred absolutely from even entering the Canal, and to that extent and in that sense it is not improper to say that Egypt has subjected the Canal to a blockade against Israeli ships within the meaning of the second paragraph of Article 1 of the Constantinople Convention. The normal meaning of blockade would, in any event, not make much sense in connection with that clause.[50]

Israel attempted only once to send a merchant vessel, the *Bat Galim*, flying her flag, through the Canal. The ship, described by the Egyptian Government as an "armed Israel vessel," during the night of September 27/28, 1954, "entered the Gulf of Suez through Egyptian territorial waters and advanced through the Gulf on its way to Suez."[51] It was further alleged that "the crew attacked two Egyptian fishing boats by automatic fire . . . sinking one of them, thus causing the death of two Egyptian fishermen," and that "this hostile act committed by armed Israelis inside Egyptian territorial waters constitutes a flagrant violation of the General Armistice Agreement.[52] The Commission investigated the allegations and by a majority vote—the Israeli delegate and the Chairman voting in favor—adopted the Israeli draft resolution and found "the Egyptian complaint regarding the *Bat Galim* case to be unfounded and that no provision of the General Armistice Agreement has been violated by Israel."[53] After the vote the Chairman stated:

> I have voted for the Israel draft resolution because conclusive evidence has not been produced that the *Bat Galim* attacked the Egyptian fishermen in the Gulf of Suez. I shall call on both parties to come quickly to an agreement for the release of the *Bat Galim* and its crew.[54]

After its judicial authorities "set aside, owing to insufficient evidence," the various charges against the crew of murder and unlawful carrying of weapons, the Egyptian Government declared on December 4, 1954, that it was prepared to release crew and cargo,

[50] The Egyptian representative quoted C. John Colombos, The International Law of the Sea, p. 539: "Blockade is the interception by sea of the approaches to the coasts or ports of an enemy with the purpose of cutting off all his overseas communications. Its object is not only to stop the importation of supplies but to prevent export as well." Official Records, 661st Meeting, March 12, 1954, p. 6, par. 29.

[51] Report dated Nov. 25, 1954, by the Chief of Staff of the United Nations Truce Supervision Organization in Palestine to the Secretary General concerning the *Bat Galim* incident, U. N. Doc. S/3323; Official Records, 9th Year, Supp. Oct.–Dec., 1954, p. 30 at p. 32, par. 8.

[52] *Ibid.* at 30, par 2.

[53] *Ibid.* at 40, 41, pars. 34, 40. The Egyptian delegate appealed against this decision to the Special Committee provided for in the Armistice Agreement. This committee decided on Nov. 25, 1954, as follows: "The Special Committee finds that the words in the resolution, 'the Egyptian complaint regarding the *Bat Galim* case to be unfounded and' should be omitted, for the following reasons: The Mixed Armistice Commission should not adopt resolutions defining a complaint as 'unfounded,' as this may appear as restricting the right of either side to submit any complaint it may deem necessary; furthermore, it is unnecessary to describe a complaint in such terms after the non-adoption of the complaining party's resolution. This decision is not intended as a judgment on the facts of this particular case, as to which the Special Committee has no competence, nor is it intended as a reversal of the findings of the Mixed Armistice Commission in the resolutions as to the facts." *Ibid.* at 42 f., par. 48.

[54] *Ibid.* at 41, par. 41.

and on December 23, 1954, it also declared that it was prepared to release the ship.[55] It appears that the crew was released but, according to the Israeli Governent, Egypt violated her undertakings regarding the cargo and the ship.[56]

This incident appears to show that the Egyptian Government's practices regarding Israeli ships are more akin to the concept and purpose—interception of enemy ships—of a blockade than to visit and search and seizure of war contraband. If Egypt were concerned merely with visit and search, there was no reason for not allowing the *Bat Galim* to proceed on its voyage through the Canal after Egypt had satisfied itself that the ship was unarmed and that its cargo was not subject to seizure.[57] In view of these facts, admitted by Egypt, there remains the Israeli flag as the sole reason for not permitting the ship to proceed through the Canal. This has indeed been freely conceded by Egypt and defended in terms of the state of war or belligerency which she claims to exist.[58] In addition to the state of war as a ground for barring and intercepting Israeli ships, Egypt also claimed that the security of the Canal required the exclusion of such ships, as they might commit acts of sabotage within the approaches *to* the Canal or *within* the Canal itself.[59] It follows then that as long as Egypt maintains the state of war with Israel, rights of belligerency are claimed which are in the range of economic warfare. As far as the ships of what Egypt calls "neutral" states are concerned, they are subjected to visit, search and seizure, whereas the ships of Israel are subjected to complete exclusion and interception in fact. Therefore, as far as Israeli ships are concerned, the effect of these measures appears indistinguishable from that of a blockade prohibited generally by the Constantinople Convention. The fundamental thesis of Egypt is the continuation of the state of war and exercise of belligerent rights in the Suez Canal as incidental to the former. It is therefore necessary to examine the validity of this thesis.

[55] See U.N. Docs. S/3326 and S/3335, *ibid.* at 44, 45.

[56] See U.N. Doc. S/3673, p. 8: "The Egyptian Government appropriated the cargo to itself, and has now commissioned the confiscated ship to the Egyptian Navy."

[57] Statement by Egyptian representative at 686th Meeting, Dec. 7, 1954, p. 16, par. 79.

[58] Said the representative of Egypt: ". . . in the state of belligerency which in our opinion still exists between Egypt and Israel, how can we allow Israel vessels to pass through the Suez Canal without interference, as the Israel representative demands." *Ibid.* 24, par. 132.

[59] Said the representative of Egypt: "What guarantee have we that an Israel merchant vessel passing through the Canal will not be tempted to scuttle itself and thus obstruct the Canal for a considerable period, causing material losses and gravely damaging the interests of maritime Powers in general! Who can say that Israel vessels passing through the Canal will not be tempted even to lay mines in Egyptian territorial waters, either before reaching the Suez Canal or in the Canal itself? Lastly, who can say that Israel nationals on such a vessel will not try to find a way of landing in Egypt in order to damage the Canal or commit acts of sabotagė in Egyptian territory?" *Ibid.*, par. 133.

## V. CONTINUATION OF STATE OF WAR BETWEEN EGYPT AND ISRAEL AS LEGAL JUSTIFICATION FOR RESTRICTIVE PRACTICES

There has never been a deviation from the Egyptian thesis that a state of war continues to prevail between Egypt and Israel, and this thesis has been the chief target of the Government of Israel and of the Security Council, particularly in its resolution of September 1, 1951.

The General Armistice Agreement of February 24, 1949, with Israel "which put an end to hostilities and which was accepted as an indispensable step towards the liquidation of the armed conflict," in the opinion of the Egyptian Government, "did not put an end to the conflict and contains no provision concerning the right of visit and inspection.[60] Moreover, "the principles of international law uphold this view,"[61] and the practice, "which is designed to ensure the defence of Egypt and the maintenance of public order there, cannot be construed as an infringement of the provisions of the Convention signed in 1888 concerning the Suez Canal."[62]

As regards Israeli ships in particular, Egypt contended that the Security Council resolution of September 1, 1951, which in any event it did not carry out, was inapplicable, as it was concerned with "the passage of neutral merchant vessels through the Canal for the purpose of trading with Israel, and not the passage of Israel vessels."[63]

### 1. Compatibility of the Restrictive Practices with General International Law

It may be conceded that according to general international law an armistice does not put an end to a state of war. It may also be conceded, although this was contested by Israel,[64] that the *de facto* hostilities which developed as a result of the military intervention of Egypt and other Arab States[65] resulted in a *de facto* state of war. However, what may be the effect of the Charter on the traditional doctrine of war and belligerent rights, particularly when some or all of the belligerents are Members of the United Nations, is a moot question. State practice has not always been uniform, and in some cases the cessation of hostilities has ended the state of war itself.[66] The general armistice is

[60] *Ibid.* 20, par. 100, and 21, par. 113.
[61] *Ibid.*,pars. 101, 103, 113.
[62] *Ibid.* 20, par. 104, and 21, pars. 105–111.
[63] *Ibid.* 23, par. 123. See also pars. 124–131.
[64] Security Council, Official Records, 549th Meeting, July 26, 1951, p. 10, pars. 10–36.
[65] This intervention has been regarded as aggression. Said the representative of the United States in the Security Council: "Probably the most important and best evidence we have on that subject is contained in the admissions of the countries whose five armies have invaded Palestine that they are carrying on a war. Their statements are the best evidence we have of the international character of this aggression; it is a word which is not included in the text but which has been mentioned in the statements of these aggressors." Official Records, 3rd Year, No. 72, p. 41. The former Secretary General of the United Nations said: "The invasion of Palestine by the Arab States was the first armed aggression which the world had seen since the end of the war." Trygve Lie, In the Cause of Peace 174 (1954); *cf.* also 178 *ff.*
[66] Julius Stone, Legal Controls of International Conflict 639 (1954).

> a living, dynamic war convention . . . . The elaborate armistice agreements of recent years have, in effect, rendered the preliminaries of peace obsolete. It is not inconceivable that the formal treaty of peace will suffer the same fate and that wars will one day end at the armistice table.[67]

It is, therefore, far more important to concern ourselves with the intended effect and scope of particular armistice agreements ending particular hostilties, than with the general question of the effect of an armistice on the existence of a state of war. It has been suggested that the question whether a particular armistice agreement has the effect of terminating the war is one of "construction of the particular armistice agreement concerned."[68] It may well be that an armistice agreement, even without terminating the state of war in the legal sense, puts an end to certain hostile acts such as blockade or visit, search and seizure.

### 2. Compatibility of the Restrictive Practices with the General Armistice Agreement between Egypt and Israel.

The Egyptian-Israeli General Armistice Agreement was signed at Rhodes on February 24, 1949, and entered into force on that date.[69] The Agreement was concluded pursuant to the Security Council resolution of November 16, 1948, calling upon the parties "as a further provisional measure under Article 40 of the Charter of the United Nations, and in order to facilitate the transition from the present truce to permanent peace in Palestine, to negotiate an Armistice."[70] The Agreement, pertinent provisions of which have already been quoted,[71] recognizes "the right of each party to its security and freedom from fear of attack by the armed forces of the other."[72] The Agreement prohibits all "warlike or hostile" acts against military, para-military forces and civilians, but does not specifically refer to blockades, or visit, search and seizure of vessels. Whether in the absence of a specific prohibition such acts are permitted, as Egypt argues, or are to be deemed prohibited by inclusion in the acts specifically banned, will be discussed presently. It is useful to recall, however, that the Armistice with Germany of November 11, 1918, specifically continued "the existing blockade conditions."[73] The Armistice Agreement in Korea of July 27, 1953, concluded "with the objective of establishing an armistice which will insure a complete cessation of hostilities and of all acts of armed force in Korea," provides in Article 2 A, paragraph 15, that the naval forces of the opposing parties "shall not engage in blockade of any kind of Korea."[74] The United Nations Command accordingly

[67] Colonel Howard S. Levie, "The Nature and Scope of the Armistice Agreement," 50 A.J.I.L. 880–906 at 906(1956). This day, however, in the view of the author, has not yet come. *Ibid.* 884.

[68] Stone, *op. cit.* 641.

[69] Art. 12, par. 1, U.N. Doc. S/1264/Rev. 1; Official Records, 4th Year, Spec. Supp. No. 3, p. 8.

[70] Preamble, *ibid.*, p. 1.

[71] See *supra*, p. 1087.

[72] Art. 1, par. 3.

[73] Sir Frederick Maurice, The Armistices of 1918, p. 98 (1943).

[74] U.N. Doc. S/3079, Aug. 7, 1953; reprinted in 47 A.J.I.L. Supp. 186 (1953). It has been said that this "is probably one of the most complete naval provisions ever included in an armistice agreement." Levie, *loc. cit.* 906.

gave orders to its naval forces "to cease hostilities and blockade operations."[75] As the Egyptian-Israeli Agreement was concluded under orders from the Security Council, some light might be shed on its intended meaning by referring to the Council's debates and resolutions.

### (a) The Armistice Agreement before the Security Council: Interpretation and Construction

The United Nations Acting Mediator on Palestine, Dr. Ralph J. Bunche, who actively participated in the armistice negotiations, stated in the Security Council on August 4, 1949:

> The Armistice Agreements are not the final peace settlement, but the only possible interpretation of their very specific provisions is that they signal the end of the military phase of the Palestine situation . . . . The entire heritage of restrictions which developed out of the undeclared war should be done away with. There should be normal access . . . there should be free movement for legitimate shipping, and no vestiges of the wartime blockade should be allowed to remain as they are inconsistent with both the letter and the spirit of the Armistice Agreements.[76]

The representatives of Israel, the United Kingdom and the United States concurred in this interpretation. The latter also stated that "the Armistice Agreements contain provisions which make them in fact non-aggression pacts." And the representative of China said: "We rejoice in the restoration of normal relations" between the parties to the Agreements.[77] It may be added here that in the course of the recent crisis in the Middle East, the Secretary General of the United Nations expressed the view, echoing the above statement by the United States representative, that Article 1 "assimilates the Armistice Agreement to a non-aggression pact, providing for mutual and full abstention from belligerent acts."[78]

The Security Council, by nine votes in favor, with two abstentions (Ukrainian S.S.R., U.S.S.R.), adopted a resolution on August 11, 1949, in which, making its own the interpretation submitted by the Acting Mediator, it

> Reaffirms, pending the final peace settlement, the order contained in its resolution of 15 July 1948 to the Government and authorities concerned, pursuant to Article 40 of the Charter of the United Nations, to observe an unconditional cease-fire and, bearing in mind that the several armistice agreements include firm pledges against any further acts of hostility between the parties and also provide for their supervision by the parties themselves, relies upon the parties to ensure the continued application and observance of these agreements.[79]

[75] U.N. Doc. S/3185; Official Records, 9th Year, Supp. Jan.–March, 1954, p. 40 at 42.

[76] Official Records, 4th Year, No. 36, p. 6. See also Shabtai Rosenne, Israel's Armistice Agreement with the Arab States 45 (1951).

[77] Official Records, 4th Year, No. 36, pp. 16, 19, 25, 27, 33.

[78] U.N. Doc. A/3512, Jan. 24, 1957, p. 5, par. 15.

[79] U.N. Doc. S/1367; Official Records, 4th Year, No. 37, p. 2 f., No. 38, p. 13.

It follows then that, although the Agreement itself is silent on the point, it has been interpreted authoritatively as prohibiting belligerent acts of visit, search and seizure. This construction is all the more indicated as the statement by the Acting Mediator was made and the resolution of the Security Council was adopted after the matter of restriction had first been raised by Israel before the Mixed Armistice Commission. No dissent was voiced from this interpretation in the Security Council. No claim was made regarding the existence or continued existence of a state of war.

### (b)The Armistice Agreement before the Mixed Armistice Commission

The question of the compatibility of the Egyptian restrictive practices with the General Armistice Agreement was first considered by the Mixed Armistice Commission in June, 1949, at the request of Israel in connection with a particular incident. At that time the Commission decided that "the blockade of the Suez Canal was not a subject that could be discussed in the Mixed Armistice Commission."[80] In August, 1949, Israel submitted a second complaint of a specific character and the Commission decided:

> The Mixed Armistice Commission did have the right to demand that the Egyptian Government should not interfere with the passage of goods to Israel through the Suez Canal.[81]

Egypt appealed to the Special Committee. The Security Council, in consequence of the Israeli complaint before it, on November 17, 1950, adopted a resolution reiterating the substance of its resolution of August 11, 1949, and, "bearing in mind that the several armistice agreements include firm pledges against any further act of hostility between the parties," reminded Egypt and Israel of their obligations under the Charter and requested the Chief of Staff to report "on the compliance given to this resolution" and decisions of the Special Committee.[82]

The Chief of Staff, General Riley, reported to the Security Council on June 12, 1951, the decision of the Special Committee "on the question as to whether or not the Mixed Armistice Commission has the right to demand from the Egyptian Government not to interfere with the passing of goods to Israel through the Suez Canal." In view of the significance of this Report on the compatibility of Egyptian restrictions with the Armistice Agreement and the conflicting interpretations placed upon it by the Security Council, Egypt and Israel, its operative part is reproduced *in extenso:*

> In explanation of his vote, which was contrary to the stand taken by Israel, the Chief of Staff made the following statement:
>
> It is quite clear to me that action taken by Egyptian authorities in interfering with passage of goods destined for Israel through the Suez Canal must be considered an aggres-

[80] General W. E. Riley, Chief of Staff, Truce Supervision Organization, in Security Council, Official Records, 516th Meeting, Oct. 30, 1950, p. 22.

[81] *Ibid.*, and Official Records, 518th Meeting, Nov. 6, 1950, p. 20.

[82] U.N. Doc. S/1907; Official Records, 524th Meeting, Nov. 17, 1950, p. 15.

sive action. However, due to the limitation imposed by the text itself on the words "aggressive action," this action is not necessarily against article 1, paragraph 2 of the General Armistice Agreement which states in part "No aggressive action by armed forces—land, sea, or air—of either party shall be undertaken, planned, or threatened against the people or the armed forces of the other."

Similarly, I must of necessity consider that interference with the passage of goods destined for Israel through the Suez Canal is a hostile act, but not necessarily against the General Armistice Agreement, because of the limitations imposed on the term "hostile act" in the text of article 2, paragraph 2 of the General Armistice Agreement, which says "No element of the land, sea or air military or para-military forces of either party including non-regular forces, shall commit any warlike or hostile act against the military or para-military forces of the other party . . ."

It follows, therefore, that I have no other choice but to cast my vote with Egypt that the Mixed Armistice Commission does not have the right to demand from the Egyptian Government that it should not interfere with the passage of goods to Israel through the Suez Canal.

. . . . .

As Chief of Staff of the United Nations Truce Supervision Organization, I am forced to base my position in this matter on the specific provisions of the General Armistice Agreement signed by Egypt and Israel. I deliberately avoid, therefore, any consideration of the status of the Suez Canal or the rights of any party with regard to it.

While I feel bound to take this technical position on the basis of the relevant provisions of the General Armistice Agreement I must also say that the action of the Egyptian authorities in this instance, is, in my view, entirely contrary to the spirit of the General Armistice Agreement and does, in fact, jeopardize its effective functioning. It was certainly never contemplated at Rhodes that what is, in effect, an act of blockade or at least an act undertaken in the spirit of a blockade and having the partial effect of one, would be continued by one of the parties to the General Armistice Agreement more than two years after it had been signed.

Although, in my view, there is no adequate basis for agreeing that the Mixed Armistice Commission has competence to deal with the question, it must be clear, and it certainly is to me, that the question cannot rest here. Either the Egyptian Government must, in the spirit of the General Armistice Agreement, relax the practice of interference with the passage of goods destined for Israel through the Suez Canal, or the question must be referred to some higher competent authority such as the Security Council or the International Court of Justice.

. . . . .

Because of the effect which such continued action will have on the implementation of the Armistice Agreement and the future operations of the Mixed Armistice Commission, I am compelled to direct a strong request to the Egyptian delegate to intercede with his Government to desist from the present practice of interfering with goods destined for Israel through the Suez Canal, since such acts can only be construed as inconsistent with the spirit of the Armistice Agreement.[83]

[83] U.N. Doc. S/2194: Cablegram dated June 12, 1951, to the Secretary General from the Chief of Staff of the Truce Supervision Organization, transmitting a report to the Security Council; Official Records, 6th Year, Supp. April–June, 1951, pp. 162–164.

The representatives of Egypt, while belittling the significance of the Chief of Staff's finding that the interference is "an aggressive and hostile act" and "contrary to the spirit of that (General Armistice) Agreement,"[84] argued that the Report constituted a vindication of the Egyptian contention that the restrictive practices were not contrary to the Armistice Agreement.[85] Contrary to the views of Israel and other members, who argued that the Armistice Agreement was *sui generis,* the Egyptian representative claimed:

> The fact that the Armistice Agreement is silent on this point. (i.e. the right of visit and search), although it is fairly common practice to include a provision on this subject in armistice agreements, shows, as indeed the Mixed Armistice Commission has confirmed, that the armistice agreement of classical type concluded between Egypt and Israel expressed the joint will of the signatories and left them free to exercise their legitimate right of visit and search.[86]

Although this view was explicitly rejected by Israel (a fact which makes the assertion of the joint "will" rather problematical)[87] and also by the Security Council in its resolution of September 1, 1951,[88] Egypt persisted in invoking the Report in justification of its restrictive practices. It may therefore be useful to examine the Report in some detail.

The Report clearly does not state that the Egyptian practices, which are called "an act of blockade . . ." are consistent with the Armistice Agreement as claimed by Egypt. It explicitly states that they are "contrary to" and "inconsistent with" the spirit of the Agreement. The Report does state, however, after what must have been careful consideration,[89] that "there is no adequate basis for agreeing that the Mixed Armistice Commission has competence to deal with the question." Members of the Security Council generally construed the Report in this sense, although some expressed a reservation on this point.[90]

The decisive consideration in determining the compatibility of the Egyptian actions with the Armistice Agreement should be, it is submitted, their aggressive and hostile

[84] The representative of Egypt claimed that these findings relate "exclusively to his activities as a self-appointed jurist and as a gentleman-at-large." Official Records, 549th Meeting, July 26, 1951, p. 17. The United Kingdom representative, on the contrary, believed that "any opinion which he expresses should command great respect in this Council." *Ibid.,* 550th Meeting, Aug. 1, 1951, p. 20 f, par. 95 f.

[85] *Ibid.,* 553rd Meeting, Aug. 16, 1951, p. 13, par. 52, and p. 25, par. 108.

[86] *Ibid.,* 661st Meeting, March 12, 1954, p. 9, par. 43 f. and p. 13, par. 64.

[87] *Ibid.,* 549th Meeting, July 26, 1951, pp. 9–11, and 661st Meeting, March 12, 1954, p. 29, par. 144. Israel's representative, after referring to Dr. Bunche's view, quoted *supra,* p. 545, and the Report of the Chief of Staff, declared: ". . . all these are unanimous in asserting that whatever may be the character of other armistice agreements, this Armistice Agreement is not compatible with active belligerency or with the exercise by either party of visit, search or seizure." See also statement by Peruvian delegate, Official Records, 688th Meeting, Jan. 13, 1955, p. 7, par. 27.

[88] As well as by a majority of members of the Security Council in voting in 1954 for the reaffirmation of the 1951 resolution.

[89] The Egyptian representative stated in the Security Council that "This decision of 12 June 1951 was taken after consultation with the United Nations Secretariat, particularly with the Legal Department." Official Records, 662nd Meeting, March 23, 1954, p. 9, par. 34. This consultation does not appear in public documents of the United Nations.

[90] See, *e.g.,* the remarks by the American representative: "My Government believes that this may be technically correct, but it is difficult to consider the Egyptian actions as thereby justified merely because the officials who enforce the restrictions cannot be classified as military or para-military forces of Egypt." Official Records, 552nd Meeting, Aug. 16, 1951, p. 10, par. 45. See also remarks by the New Zealand delegate, *ibid.,* 662nd Meeting, March 23, 1954, p. 5, par. 19.

character, as well as the fact that, being performed by the official forces of Egypt, they are attributable to the Government of Egypt. On the basis of these two tests and in view of the circumstance that the Government of Egypt openly insists on performing the belligerent right of visit, search and seizure, there should be no difficulty in concluding that Egyptian restrictive practices are incompatible with the Armistice Agreement.

### 3. Compatibility of the Restrictive Practices with the Convention of Constantinople of 1888

During the debates in the Security Council the question was frequently raised whether the Egyptian restrictions were compatible with the provisions of the Constantinople Convention. The resolution of September 1, 1951, itself makes no explicit reference to this Convention.

One of the outstanding characteristics of the Convention is the "neutralization" of the Canal, that is, the establishment in Article 1 of the principle of freedom of navigation in both peace and war for ships of all nations. Thus, even assuming the correctness of the Egyptian contention, namely, that a state of war continues to exist, Israeli ships have a right of passage through the Canal. Articles 9 and 10 authorize the Egyptian Government, as an exception to Articles 4, 5, 6, 7, and 8, to take "the necessary measures for enforcing the execution of the said Treaty" and to take such measures which it might find necessary to assure by its own forces the defense of Egypt and the maintenance of public order." It will be noticed that the exceptions listed in Articles 9 and 10 do not include Article 1, which is therefore one which Egypt is bound to respect in all circumstances. This would be so even without the specific statement in Article 11:

> The measures taken in the cases provided for by Articles 9 and 10 of the present Treaty shall not interfere with the free use of the Canal.

It follows then, as the Prize Court of Alexandria held, that Egypt may exceptionally take "reasonable and necessary measures,"[91] but such measures must "not interfere with the free use of the Canal." The Convention thus lays down the limit beyond which Egypt is not authorized to go. Egypt argued, of course, that visit and search, as well as seizure, "cannot be regarded as prejudicing free passage through the Canal, and therefore as contrary to the Convention of Constantinople of 1888."[92] As pointed out already, Egypt is not the final arbiter in determining whether these measures conform to the requirements of the Convention.[93] Members of the Security Council did contend that they are "undoubtedly incompatible" with the Convention.[94]

The restrictive practices of Egypt having been considered at variance with the

[91] *Cf. supra*, pp. 1086–1087.
[92] Official Records, 661st Meeting, March 12, 1954, p. 15, par. 74, and p. 17, par. 87.
[93] See *supra*, p. 1088.
[94] *Cf., e.g.*, the remarks of the Netherlands representative, Official Records, 553rd Meeting, Aug. 16, 1951, p. 5, pars. 16–17; of the representative of Ecuador, *ibid.*, p. 27, par. 123.

Constantinople Convention, an even stronger case can be made against the complete prohibition of passage of Israeli ships through the Canal. The power to take reasonable and necessary measures is power to regulate, not to prohibit, passage through the Canal. In this context reference may be made to the judgment of the International Court of Justice in the *Corfu Channel* case which clearly established this essential distinction. After holding that the North Corfu Channel "should be considered as belonging to the class of international highways through which passage cannot be prohibited by a coastal State in time of peace," the Court went on to declare as follows:

> On the other hand, it is a fact that the two coastal States did not maintain normal relations, that Greece had made territorial claims precisely with regard to a part of Albanian territory bordering on the Channel, that Greece had declared that she considered herself technically in a state of war with Albania, and that Albania, invoking the danger of Greek incursions, had considered it necessary to take certain measures of vigilance in this region. The Court is of opinion that Albania, in view of these exceptional circumstances, would have been justified in issuing regulations in respect of the passage of warships through the Straits, but not in prohibiting such passage or in subjecting it to the requirement of special authorization.[95]

As the parallelism between this case and the Suez Canal situation, grounded on the pretended existence of a technical state of war, is obvious, several conclusions suggest themselves: First, if the principle laid down by customary international law and applied by the Court governs passage through the Corfu Straits, it follows *a fortiori* that it governs passage through the Suez Canal. In the latter case the principle of customary international law is reinforced by the conventional principle of Article 1 of the Constantinople Convention. Secondly, if the principle governs the passage of warships, it follows *a fortiori* that is must govern the lesser case, namely, the passage of merchantmen. Thirdly, if in consequence of the existence of a technical state of war Albania was justified in regulating the passage of warships but not in prohibiting or subjecting it to the requirement of special authorization, the authorization granted to Egypt by the Constantinople Convention appears to be similarly limited. If Egypt claims to be entitled to impose stricter regulations, the burden of proof rests on the claimant state. Fourthly, if the measures indicated by the Court are excluded even in the case of warships, it follows *a fortiori* that they are excluded in the case of merchant vessels.

Since the view of many members of the Security Council was based on a reasoning along the lines suggested above, it may arouse some astonishment that the resolution of September 1, 1951, does not explicitly pronounce on the question of compatibility of the Egyptian practices with the Constantinople Convention. The reason may well be that the members were unsure whether the Council had competence to make such a direct pronouncement. Article 8 of the Convention provides:

[95] [1949] I.C.J. Rep. 4 at 29; 43 A.J.I.L. 558 at 577 (1949).

> The Agents in Egypt of the Signatory Powers of the present Treaty shall be charged to see that it is carried out. In any circumstance threatening the security and free passage of the Canal, they shall meet at the summons of three of them and under the presidency of their Doyen, to make the necessary verifications. They shall inform the Khedivial Government of the danger perceived, in order that it may take proper steps to assure the protection and the free use of the Canal.

It would require going beyond the compass of this paper to examine the applicability of this procedure to the problem posed by the Egyptian restrictions.[96]

Suffice it to point out that Egypt, strongly supported by the Soviet Union, challenged the competence of the Security Council to deal with Israel's complaints on the ground that they related to the Constantinople Convention and that the procedure provided for in the Convention should be utilized.[97] Israel, the complaining state, is not a party to the Convention and could therefore not invoke the procedure of the Convention.[98] The Security Council did not, however, accept the Egyptian viewpoint regarding its competence in the matter. As was pointed out by several members, the Council is competent to deal with threats to the peace, including threats arising out of the non-observance of the Constantinople Convention. As the French representative stated:

> The Council is not competent to impose observance of the Constantinople Convention as such. It is, primarily and solely, the organ mainly responsible for the maintenance of international peace and security. More particularly, the Council has the paramount right of supervising the execution of the armistice agreements negotiated under its auspices between Israel and the neighboring Arab States.
>
> . . . . .
>
> . . . *The Council is competent to supervise its application in this case* in view of the special situation created between Egypt and Israel under the General Armistice Agreement of 1949.[99]

In view of this strong statement, which was shared by other members of the Council both as to the competence of the Security Council and the incompatibility of Egypt's pre-

[96] Also, and for the same reason, an analysis is omitted of the regime established for the Canal by the United Kingdom in two World Wars, a matter which was raised at some length, though inconclusively, by the representatives of Egypt. See Official Records, 555th Meeting, Aug. 27, 1951, p. 8 f. On this aspect see R. R. Baxter, "Passage of Ships through International Waterways in Time of War," 31 Brit. Yr. Bk. of Int. Law 187–216 at 196, 206–208 (1954).

[97] The representative of Egypt said: "It is Article 8 which you should bring into operation, not the Security Council. Apply to the signatories' representatives in Cairo. You are perfectly entitled to complain of obstacles to the free passage of shipping through the Canal. I believe you know that the signatories are France, Germany, Austria-Hungary, Spain, Great Britain, Italy, the Netherlands, Russia and the Ottoman Empire. These countries exist. They even have successors . . . You can find three to call together the signatories' representatives in Cairo. Take your complaint to them. But to raise the question of free passage through the Suez Canal in the Security Council is wrong. It is completely at variance with Article 24 of the United Nations Charter." Official Records, 662nd Meeting, March 23, 1954, p. 14, par. 47. For the remarks of the Soviet representative see *ibid.*, 664th Meeting, March 29, 1954, p. 10, pars. 52–56.

[98] The Egyptian representative said: "For so far as the Egyptian Government is concerned, the State of Israel has nothing to do with the 1888 Convention. It was not a signatory to the Convention; at the time the Convention was signed it was not yet in existence." *Ibid.*, 659th Meeting, Feb. 15, 1954, p. 23, par. 123.

[99] Official Records, 687th Meeting, Jan. 4, 1955, p. 10, pars. 56–57. See also the French statement *ibid.*, 663rd Meeting, March 25, 1954, p. 8, pars. 34–35. Italics supplied.

tended rights with its obligations under the Constantinople Convention,[100] it is probably regrettable that the Council chose not to include an explicit finding to this effect in its resolution of September 1, 1951, or in the draft resolution of 1954, and, in connection with the *Bat Galim* incident, deemed it inexpedient to declare so unequivocally.[101] Nevertheless, in the public mind the impression persists that the Security Council based its action against Egypt squarely on that ground.

### 4. Egypt's Right of Self-Defense or Self-Preservation as Basis for Restrictive Practices

In the course of the several debates centered on Israel's complaints, it became standard practice for Egyptian representatives to invoke the right of self-preservation or self-defense as a juridical justification for Egypt's restrictive practices. This right, said the representative of Egypt, "is universally recognized and known to transcend all other rights";[102] it is

> at the root of all existence, of all survival, individual or national . . . it is part and parcel of the Charter and the very concept of the United Nations, and . . . it is the main patrimony and the highest privilege of every individual, every community, every nation and every group of nations, except the damned and the fools.[103]

Members of the Security Council generally rejected this claim on the ground that no actual hostilities were in progress.[104] the representative of The Netherlands stated that two years after signing the Armistice Agreement Egypt

> does not require to exercise the belligerent right of visit, search and seizure for any legitimate purpose of self-defence. Besides, as far as self-defence is concerned, something has changed in our world since the closing years of the nineteenth century. Today we, the Members of the United Nations, live—or at least should live—by the Charter of our Organization.[105]

The position of the Council found expression in the resolution of September 1, 1951. It has, moreover, been restated recently by the Secretary General of the United Nations. Interpreting the assurances given him by Israel and Egypt to respect unconditon-

[100] On the first point, the representative of Belgium stated: "As has been pointed out, the Security Council is clearly not competent to enforce the observance of the Constantinople Convention as such. It does, however, possess such competence through the Charter, insofar as it has to carry out the provisions of the Charter in order to ensure the maintenance of peace and international security. The 1951 resolution was therefore the outcome of a proper use of the Council's powers, and was not *ultra vires*." *Ibid.*, 688th Meeting, Jan. 13, 1955, p. 3, par. 9.

[101] This may well have been due to the belief that a resolution would be opposed by the Soviet Union.

[102] Official Records, 549th Meeting, July 26, 1951, p. 21, par. 78.

[103] *Ibid.*, 550th Meeting, Aug. 1, 1951, p. 8, par. 42. See pp. 6–8 for authority cited by the representatives. See also the representative's observation *ibid.*, 661st Meeting, March 12, 1954, p. 14, pars. 67–73; 659th Meeting, Feb. 15, 1954, p. 9, par. 50.

[104] See remarks by the British representative *ibid.*, 550th Meeting, Aug. 1, 1951, p. 20, par. 93.

[105] *Ibid.*, 553rd Meeting, Aug. 16, 1951, p. 4, par. 15.

ally the cease-fire injunction, subject to the right of self-defense under Article 51, the Secretary General declared that this reserve applies

> in cases of non-compliance by the other party with its obligations under the Charter, or under the Armistice Agreement, only if and when such non-compliance is found to be a reason for the exertion *[Sic!] of the right of self-defence as recognized in Article 51 of the Charter. The Security Council alone can decide whether this is the case or not. The reserve for self-defence in the several cease-fire assurances and the significance it may give to compliance with the Charter, other clauses in the Armistice Agreement or relevant Security Council decisions, is thus under the sole jurisdiction of the Security Council, in accordance with the rules established.*

In particular, the reservation of self-defense "could not derogate from the obligations assumed under Article 2, paragraph 2, of the Armistice Agreement between Egypt and Israel." Neither, according to his interpretation, said the Secretary General, does it "permit acts of retaliation, which repeatedly have been condemned by the Security Council."[106]

The Secretary General's interpretation is particularly illuminating and to the point as Egypt appeared to justify its practices of restriction and interception by invoking the right of self-defense or self-preservation with respect to alleged infringements of various clauses of the Armistice Agreement by Israel.[107] These acts then assume the character of retaliation, which, in the case of Israel, have been condemned by the Security Council. By parity of reasoning, such retaliatory actions by Egypt, whether or not based on or derived from the right of self-defense, are equally inadmissible.[108]

## VI. SECURITY COUNCIL ACTION WITH RESPECT TO EGYPT'S RESTRICTIVE PRACTICES

### 1. Resolution of September 1, 1951

When Israel lodged its first complaint with the Security Council, a resolution was adopted on November 17, 1950, reminding the parties of their pledges of "no hostilities" and postponing further consideration until the submission of a report by the Mixed Armistice Commission.[109] In July, 1951, the Council began the consideration of the second Israeli complaint in the light of the Report of the Special Committee of June 12, 1951,[110] the relevance of which has already been discussed.[111] The Council debated the

[106] U. N. Doc. S/3596, May 9, 1956: Report of the Secretary General to the Security Council pursuant to the Council's resolution of April 4, 1956, on the Palestine Question, pp. 13, 14.

[107] See remarks by the Egyptian delegate in Official Records, 686th Meeting, Dec. 7, 1954, p. 25, par. 136 *et seq.*

[108] Said the Brazilian representative: "Should we accept the Egyptian thesis, we would be bound to recognize any measures of reprisal adopted by the Israel Government." Official Records, 552nd Meeting, Aug. 16, 1951, p. 12, par. 56.

[109] U. N. Doc. S/1899; Official Records, 522nd Meeting, Nov. 13, 1950, p. 15, and 524th Meeting, Nov. 17, 1950, p. 15.

[110] U.N. Doc. S/2194; Official Records, 6th Year, Supp. April–June, 1951, pp. 162–164.

[111] *Cf. supra*, pp. 1097 *ff.*

issues from political as well as juridical points of view. The majority of the members of the Security Council firmly rejected every one of the Egyptian contentions as unfounded.

The Council voted on the tripartite draft resolution, as amended,[112] on September 1, 1951. The vote was eight in favor (Brazil, Ecuador, France, Netherlands, Turkey, United Kingdom, United States of America, Yugoslavia), none against, and three abstentions (China, India, U.S.S.R.). China and India abstained because on the one hand they did not feel that the legal issues had been adequately dealt with, and on the other hand they were not convinced in view of the opposition of Egypt that the resolution would contribute towards peace and stability in the area. Soviet Russia never participated in the discussion.[113]

The resolution as adopted[114] reads as follows:

> The Security Council,
>
> 1. Recalling that in its resolution of 11 August 1949 (S/1376) relating to the conclusion of Armistice Agreements between Israel and the neighboring Arab States it drew attention to the pledges in these Agreements "against any further acts of hostility" between the Parties,
>
> 2. Recalling further that in its resolution of 17 November 1950 (S/1907and Corr. 1), it reminded the States concerned that the Armistice Agreements to which they are parties contemplate "the return of permanent peace in Palestine," and therefore urged them and other States in the area to take all such steps as will lead to the settlement of the issues between them,
>
> 3. Noting the report of the Chief of Staff of the Truce Supervision Organization to the Security Council of 12 June 1951 (S/2194),
>
> 4. Further noting that the Chief of Staff of the Truce Supervision Organization recalled the statement of the senior Egyptian delegate in Rhodes on 13 January 1949, to the effect that his delegation was "inspired with every spirit of co-operation, conciliation and a sincere desire to restore peace in Palestine," and that the Egyptian Government has not complied with the earnest plea of the Chief of Staff made to the Eqyptian delegate on 12 June 1951, that it desist from the present practice of interfering with the passage through the Suez Canal of goods destined for Israel,
>
> 5. Considering that since the armistice regime, which has been in existence for nearly two and a half years, is of a permanent character, neither party can reasonably assert that it is actively a belligerent or requires to exercise the right of visit, search, and seizure for any legitimate purpose of self-defence,

[112] The amendment, which was adopted, related to par. 3 of the draft resolution, the original text of which was: Noting that the Chief of Staff of the Truce Supervision Organization in his report to the Security Council of 12 June 1951 considered interference with the passage through the Suez Canal of goods destined for Israel to be a hostile and aggressive act, and contrary to the spirit of the Armistice Agreement, the effective functioning of which is thereby jeopardized." The Yugoslav delegate found this passage to be of exceptional gravity, and the American representative introduced the revision which was adopted. Official Records, 553rd Meeting, Aug. 16, 1951, p. 30, par. 142; p. 31, par. 145, and note 3.

[113] On one occasion, for unexplained reasons, the Soviet Union insisted on a postponement of the debate for 48 hours. Official Records, 556th Meeting, Aug. 29, 1951, p. 6.

[114] U.N. Doc. S/2298/Rev. 1; Official Records, 558th Meeting, Sept. 1, 1951, p. 2. The resolution was subsequently issued as a separate document under the symbol S/2322.

6. Finds that the maintenance of the practice mentioned in paragraph 4 above is inconsistent with the objectives of a peaceful settlement between the parties and the establishment of a permanent peace in Palestine set forth in the Armistice Agreement;

7. Finds further that such practice is an abuse of the exercise of the right of visit, search and seizure;

8. Further finds that that practice cannot in the prevailing circumstances be justified on the ground that it is necessary for self-defence;

9. And further noting that the restrictions on the passage of goods through the Suez Canal to Israel ports are denying to nations at no time connected with the conflict in Palestine valuable supplies required for their economic reconstruction, and that these restrictions together with the sanctions applied by Egypt to certain ships which have visited Israel ports represent unjustified interference with the rights of nations to navigate the seas and to trade freely with one another, including the Arab States and Israel,

10. Calls upon Egypt to terminate the restrictions on the passage of international commercial shipping and goods through the Suez Canal wherever bound and to cease all interference with such shipping beyond that essential to the safety of shipping in the Canal itself and to the observance of the international conventions in force.

The resolution notes the Report of the Chief of Staff which declared the exercise of restrictions by Egypt to be "in effect, an act of blockade," a "hostile and aggressive action" contrary to the spirit of the General Armistice Agreement.[115] It also noted the appeal addressed by the Chief of Staff to the Egyptian delegate to desist from the "present practice." The resolution rejects the Egyptian claim that it or Israel is still "actively a belligerent," and that "the exercise of the right of visit, search and seizure" is required "for any legitimate purpose of self-defense." But it will be noted that the resolution does not directly repudiate the Egyptian contention that, in spite of the Armistice, a "state of war" continues to exist, although it rejects all the consequential rights which Egypt claimed as flowing from it.[116] It must, of course, be conceded that the Security Council is free to choose the juridical or political ground on which it desires to take a stand on an

[115] See *supra*, p. 1098. Commenting on this on behalf of the three sponsoring Powers, the British delegate said: "The Armistice Agreement was meant to terminate all hostile acts, and it was so understood both by the parties and by the Security Council itself. . . . The restrictions which applied to Egypt were terminated by the Security Council resolution (S/1376) of August 1949, and there can be no justification for the attempt by Egypt to maintain against Israel restrictions similar to those from which Egypt itself was released two years ago." Official Records, 552nd Meeting, Aug. 16, 1951, p. 4, par. 12.

[116] In commenting upon it the British delegate expressed himself as follows: "Egypt claims that there is a state of war and that it is therefore entitled to exercise belligerent rights. It is not necessary, in our view, for the Council to pronounce on this. Even if it were self-evident that a state of war existed—which is by no means the case, of course—this would in itself afford no justification for the maintenance of the restrictions at the present time and in the light of the present situation. What matters is not whether there is some technical basis for the restrictions, but whether it is reasonable, just and equitable that they should be maintained. This is the principle on which the draft resolution before the Council has been formulated, and it is on this issue that we consider the Council should pronounce." *Ibid.*, p. 3, par. 7. Adverting to the same theme later in his speech, he said: "For the reasons which I have already stated, the draft resolution does not attempt to say whether or not Egypt can technically claim to be entitled to belligerent rights. What the draft resolution does say is that, in the light of the Armistice Agreement and of what has taken place since it was signed, the maintenance of the present restrictions is unjustified and unreasonable and must be held to constitute an abuse of any rights which Egypt may claim to possess." *Ibid.*, par. 10.

issue of which it is seized. In this case the Council chose not to pronounce on what it considered a technical and probably secondary aspect of the issue, although it was pressed earnestly by Israel. It believed itself to be—and no doubt it is—legally on solid ground when it ruled in paragraphs 5, 6, 7 and 8 that the belligerent rights of visit, search, and seizure claimed by Egypt were inconsistent with the armistice regime and could not be justified on grounds of self-defense. It thus construed the Armistice Agreement as one *sui generis* and in so doing rejected the Egyptian contention that it was of the classical variety and that, since it did not expressly prohibit the right of visit, search and seizure, the exercise of this right was permissible. Having done so, one may wonder why the Council found it necessary to characterize the exercise of this right of visit, search and seizure as an "abuse." While the doctrine of abuse of right is gaining ground in international law, its rôle in the system of the resolution is not clear. If the right in question is declared to be inconsistent with the armistice regime and cannot be justified as legal, was it necessary to affirm that it constituted an abuse of right?

The meaning of this affirmation becomes clear when related to the final paragraph of the resolution and to the debate in the Council regarding the compatibility of Egyptian restrictions with its obligations and rights under the Constantinople Convention of 1888. In this debate it was conceded that Egypt has certain rights under the Convention, but it was argued that these rights are limited by Article 11, which reserves the right of "free use." Both Egypt's rights and obligations are reaffirmed in paragraph 10 of the resolution, which calls on Egypt to terminate all interference with shipping through the Suez Canal "beyond that essential to the safety of shipping in the Canal itself and to the observance of international conventions in force." One of the "conventions in forcc" is, of course, the Constantinople Convention. It is precisely because Egypt's interference exceeded the measures permissible under the Constantinople Convention that the Council qualified the interference as "abuse of the exercise of the right of visit, search and seizure." It is for the same reason that the United Kingdom representative declared, on behalf of the three sponsoring governments, that, in calling upon Egypt to terminate the restrictions in the Suez Canal,

> we are not asking the Egyptian Government to give up any of the rights which it can legitimately claim to exercise in regard to the passage of ships through the Canal. The normal administration of the Canal must obviously continue, and the proper precautions must be taken to safeguard the Canal itself and the ships which pass through it. All this is specifically provided for in the draft resolution. The relevant international conventions must also be observed, including the Suez Canal Convention itself and any others, such as sanitary conventions, which may apply. What we want to see is the restoration of normal peacetime conditions in the Canal, providing for the unhindered passage of the ships of all nations.[117]

[117] *Ibid.*,p. 3, par. 11.

The Security Council thus drew a line between "reasonable and necessary" measures for safeguarding freedom of passage for ships of all nations, including Israel, and the imposition of measures of visit, search and seizure, and qualified the latter as an "abuse of right." Thus eleven months after Israel first appealed to the Security Council against Egypt's restrictions, the Council finally found the complaint well founded. There can be no doubt that the Council proceeded slowly but it also moved deliberately.[118] Egypt's reaction consisted in restating its position that "the assumptions on which the claim of Israel was based—or on which it tried to base itself—have yet to be proved," and in fully reserving "its rights in connexion with the present debate."[119] More specifically, the Egyptian representative argued that the resolution "is in flagrant violation of the purposes of the United Nations, as formulated in Article 1 of the Charter, which govern the functions and powers of the Security Council"; that these powers and functions mentioned in Article 24, paragraph 2, "are limited and should be strictly regulated and governed by the fundamental principles and purposes laid down in" Article 1, paragraph 1; and that the resolution "in fact proposes that the Council violate the principles and practices of international law and the stipulations of Articles 1 and 24 of the Charter of the United Nations."[120]

That the Security Council has, as the United Kingdom representative maintained, the "paramount right of supervising the execution of the Armistice Agreement"[121] cannot and has not been doubted. In adopting the resolution the Council exercised this right. And the obligatory character of the findings laid down by the Council stems from the binding character of the Armistice Agreement and the Suez Canal Convention as well as from the fact that the former was concluded by Egypt and Israel pursuant to a resolution adopted by the Council under Chapter 7 of the Charter.[122]

[118] After the adoption of the resolution, the French representative recalled that several postponements were granted "to give the Egyptian Government time to find a way of adapting its behavior to the obligations incumbent upon it, on the one hand under the Armistice Agreement which it had concluded with Israel, and on the other hand under the international statute of the Suez Canal," and expressed disappointment that Egypt had failed to do so. *Ibid.*, 558th Meeting, Sept. 1, 1951, p. 5, pars 18–19.

[119] *Ibid.*, p. 7, pars. 28–29.

[120] *Ibid.*, 553rd Meeting, Aug. 16, 1951, p. 22, pars. 94–95. The Egyptian representative referred to Art. 1, par. 1, which states as one of the purposes "to bring about by peaceful means, and in conformity with the principles of justice and international law, adjustment or settlement of international disputes or situations which might lead to a breach of the peace." The sentence referred to in par. 2 of Art. 24 reads: "In discharging these duties the Security Council shall act in accordance with the purposes and principles of the United Nations."

[121] Official Records, 687th Meeting, Jan. 4, 1955, p. 10, par. 56. The French representative referred to the Council as the "guardian" of the Armistice Agreement. *Ibid.*, 663rd Meeting, March 25, 1954, p. 8, par. 35.

[122] With respect to the Constantinople Convention, it is relevant to recall the following statement by the Belgian delegate: "The 1951 resolution was therefore the outcome of a proper use of the Council's powers, and was not *ultra vires*. It could not, indeed, be represented in that light, since it contained nothing new and merely restated the provisions of the Convention of 1888. Actually, it restated them only in part, for it referred only to commercial shipping, whereas the Convention was also applicable to warships. Even if the resolution itself were not binding, its provisions would be, since they correspond to provisions which have been binding since 1888." *Ibid.*, 688th Meeting, Jan. 13, 1955, p. 3, par. 9.

## 2. Egypt's Failure to Carry out the Security Council Resolution of September 1, 1951

On January 28, 1954, Israel again complained to the Security Council that, in violation of the resolution of September 1, 1951, Egypt "has persisted in its illegitimate interference with shipping passing through the Suez Canal and has since extended the blockade to shipping passing to and from the Israeli port of Eilat on the Gulf of Aqaba"; and that moreover, these "illegal practices have been . . . recently aggravated."[123] Egypt freely admitted that it continued to act in defiance of the Security Council resolution of September 1, 1951, and its representative, in an effort to clear up the "misunderstanding" that the Egyptian measures are "entirely contrary" to the Security Council's decision of 1 September 1951," declared:

> Egypt is taking action which is perhaps not in conformity with the Security Council's decision of 1 September 1951; I am prepared to recognize that. But at the same time, I would like to point out—and this is the misunderstanding I want to clear up—that when the Security Council's decision was taken, Egypt received it in a certain spirit. That spirit is illustrated in the statement made by the Egyptian representative who attended the meeting of the Security Council of 1 September 1951, at which this decision was taken.[124]

What the Egyptian representative said, in substance, was that Egypt never intended to carry out the decision of the Security Council of September 1, 1951, that it had so declared immediately after that decision was adopted, and that it would continue to do so. In a debate which was remarkable for the absence of any "tenable reason" for Egypt's refusal to comply with that resolution and equally for the absence of any "new legal argument,"[125] members rejected the Egyptian "reservations" and indeed repudiated its right to make any such "reservations." Thus the New Zealand representative declared:

[123] U.N. Docs. S/3168 and S/3168/Add. 1; Official Records, 9th Year, Supp. Jan.-March, 1954, p. 2, par. 2 and p. 3, par. 4. The aggravation, that is, the extension of confiscatory measures to the Gulf of Aqaba and the inclusion of food among the items to be regarded as "war contraband" was instituted, said the Israeli representative, on Jan. 25, 1954. *Ibid.*, p. 3, par. 3. The decision referred to declares that "Egypt has to take sterner measures to attain the desired end" (*ibid.*, pp. 4, 5), and contrasts sharply with the alleged voluntary relaxation of the restrictive measures by Egypt. See also statement by Israel's representative, Official Records, 658th Meeting, Feb. 5, 1954, pp. 1 ff.

[124] He went on to say: "Thus Egypt accepted the Security Council's decision of 1 September 1951, within the limits of that statement, which made it clear that Egypt was not convinced that the discussion was ended, that in its view the question was not closed and that the decision did not rest on fixed and final foundations. That was our conviction in September 1951. That is still our conviction and we accordingly maintain the same viewpoint and the same position. It is therefore beside the point to state now that Egypt is acting in a manner incompatible with the decision taken by the Security Council on 1 September 1951. Egypt will continue to maintain the same position because it is convinced, as its representative said at the very moment the decision was taken, that the decision was not based on exhaustive studies or on clear opinions." Official Records, 659th Meeting, Feb. 15, 1954, p. 25, Par. 135, and p. 26, par. 136. For the Egyptian representative's statement at the Sept. 1, 1951, meeting see *supra*, p. 1108.

[125] See remarks by British and French representatives, Official Records, 663rd Meeting, March 25, 1954, p. 5, par. 23, and p. 7, par. 31. For Egyptian restatements see *ibid.*, 658th Meeting, Feb. 5, 1954, p. 26; 659th Meeting, Feb. 15, 1954, pp. 1 ff., 23 ff.; 661st Meeting, March 12, 1954, pp. 2 ff.

> We cannot accept the argument that Egypt is entitled to disregard the terms of the resolution of September 1951 by reason of a reservation entered at the time of its adoption.[126]

The Danish representative referred to Article 25 of the Charter and pointed out:

> There is no reservation to this. The obligation to accept and carry out is not limited to such decisions as you agree with and consider legal.[127]

The New Zealand representative accordingly introduced a draft resolution on March 23, 1954, which addressed itself primarily to the "incontestable and indeed uncontested fact that the clear and precise provisions of the 1951 resolution have not been complied with."[128] The draft resolution, after recalling the whole of the resolution of September 1, 1951,[129] "notes with grave concern that Egypt has not complied with that resolution," and "calls upon Egypt in accordance with its obligations under the Charter to comply therewith."[130] This paragraph, noted the French representative, "is manifestly based on Article 25 of the Charter."[131]

The United Kingdom representative, while refraining from submitting a formal amendment to the New Zealand draft resolution, put on record his government's view "that if, as I sincerely hope will not be the case, Egypt has not within ninety days complied with the resolution, the Council should stand ready to take the matter up again."[132]

The Egyptian representative declared the adamant opposition of his government, saying: "This draft resolution is not accepted by Egypt. Egypt rejects it with utmost vigour, just as it rejected the 1951 resolution,"[133] The Soviet representative, intervening for the first time in the substantive discussion of the issue, challenged the jurisdiction of the

[126] *Ibid.*, 662nd Meeting, March 23, 1954, p. 4, par. 17.

[127] *Ibid.*, 663rd Meeting, March 25, 1954, p. 3, par. 12. He continued as follows: "All Member States in ratifying the Charter agreed to a limitation of their sovereignty. If the Council accepted that a Member State that disagreed with one of its decisions, by calling such decisions illegal was not bound by the decision, the work of the Council would become chaotic. For any State ready to shoulder the responsibility for aggression surely would be only too willing to accuse the Council of acting illegally. We might then foresee an entire technique of evasion develop. The smaller nations cannot possibly want such developments to take place."(p. 4, par. 13.)

[128] *Ibid.*, 662nd Meeting, March 23, 1954, p. 3, par. 9. See also remarks by the U. S. representative, *ibid.*, 663rd Meeting, March 25, 1954, p. 1, par. 1, p. 2, par. 5; the French representative, *ibid.*, p. 7, par. 31, p. 9, par. 41; the Brazilian delegate, *ibid.*, 664th Meeting, March 29, 1954, p. 5, par. 16; and the Colombian delegate, *ibid.*, p. 5, par. 22.

[129] Statement by the New Zealand representative, *ibid.*, 662nd Meeting, March 23, 1954, p. 5, par. 21.

[130] U.N. Doc. S/3188 and Corr. 1; Official Records, 9th Year, Supp. Jan.-March, 1954, p. 44. The final paragraph of the draft resolution refers, "without prejudice to the provisions of the resolution of 1 September 1951," Israel's complaint regarding passage through the Gulf of Aqaba to the Mixed Armistice Commission. According to statements by the American, French, and British representatives, the passage of ships through the Gulf was covered by the same principles already enunciated with respect to the Suez Canal. As the question had not yet been considered by the Commission and in order to maintain the normal procedure, it was proposed to refer the question first of all to the Commission. Official Records, 663rd Meeting, March 23, 1954, p. 2, par.6; p. 6, pars. 27, 28; p. 9, pars. 38, 39.

[131] *Ibid.*, p. 9, par. 41.

[132] *Ibid.*, 664th Meeting, March 29, 1954, p. 11, par. 61; see also 663rd Meeting, March 25, 1954, p. 6, par. 26, for a similar statement.

[133] And for the same reason: "It is convinced that the two texts do not deal with the question as it should be dealt with. The legal element, which is fundamental to this dispute, is completely ignored in both." *Ibid.*, 662nd Meeting, March 23, 1954, p. 15, par. 49.

Council,[134] and proposed that instead of attempting to impose a decision upon one of the parties which "has been stated by that party to be absolutely unacceptable from the outset," the Council should "appeal to both parties to take steps to settle their difference on this question by means of direct negotiations."[135]

The draft resolution was put to the vote on March 29, 1954, and not adopted, the vote being eight in favor (Brazil, Colombia, Denmark, France, New Zealand, Turkey, United Kingdom, United States), two against (Lebanon, U.S.S.R.), and one abstention (China).[136] This was the second time that the Soviet Union interposed its veto in a vote on a question relating to Palestine.[137] It marked the change from the position of abstention which the Soviet Union had followed since 1948 to one of active support of the Arab States against Israel. It must be admitted, however, that the Soviet proposal to call for direct negotiations between Israel and Egypt had some merit, particularly if these negotiations were to be conducted on the basis of the resolution of September 1, 1951. In view of the persistent refusal of the Arab States to enter into such direct negotiations with Israel, it may be doubtful that a call from the Council would have been heeded by Egypt.

It remains to note that after the vote the French representative observed that the Soviet veto "could not have caused repeal of a legally adopted resolution."[138] The representative of Israel similarly expressed his government's understanding that

> the law of the United Nations in the Suez Canal and in the Gulf of Aqaba is . . . the valid and unrepealed resolution of the Security Council adopted on 1 September 1951.[139]

### 3. The Security Council and the Interception of the Israeli Ship, *Bat Galim,* by Egypt

At the end of the Security Council debate on March 29, 1954, the representative of Egypt declared that, freed from the pressure of the New Zealand draft resolution, Egypt "will of its own free will move towards tolerance." As a token of this spontaneous tolerance Egypt, six months later, on September 28, 1954, intercepted the first Israeli ship, the *Bat Galim,* which, on the strength of the September 1, 1951, Security Council resolution, attempted to pass through the Suez Canal with a cargo of meat.[140] The Egyptian charges against the *Bat Galim,* namely, that its crew attacked two fishing boats with automatic fire and killed two fishermen, are immaterial, as they were dismissed by the Mixed Armistice Commission as "unfounded."[141] The incident was discussed at several meetings

[134] This challenge, based on Art. 8 of the Constantinople Convention, has already been dealt with. See *supra,* p. 1102.

[135] Official Records, 664th Meeting, March 29, 1954, p. 9, pars. 45–50; p. 10, pars. 52–56.

[136] *Ibid.,* p. 12, par. 69.

[137] The first Soviet veto occurred in connection with the question of water from the River Jordan, at the 656th Meeting, Jan. 22, 1954, p. 27, par. 135.

[138] *Ibid.,* 664th Meeting, March 29, 1954, p. 18, par. 113.

[139] *Ibid.,* par. 141.

[140] The facts of this incident are discussed above, pp. 1092 ff.

[141] U.N. Doc. S/3323; Official Records, 9th Year, Supp. Oct.–Dec. 1954, p. 30 at 41.

of the Security Council. The discussion revealed a good deal of satisfaction at the high standard of Egyptian administration of justice in dismissing the charges against the Israeli seamen and their release, as well as at the unfulfilled promise to release the cargo and the ship. There was remarkably little disposition to examine the heart of the matter, to wit, that, contrary to the resolution of September 1, 1951, the Armistice Agreement as construed by the Mixed Armistice Commission and the Security Council, and the Constantinople Convention, Egypt had intercepted an Israeli merchantman and by separating the crew from the ship had prevented its passage through the Suez Canal. The representative of the United Kingdom, to be sure, did express his hope that the grave charges against the crew having been "withdrawn when they could not be substantiated . . . the Egyptian Government could thereafter have seen its way to letting the ship proceed on its course through the Canal, under such security restrictions as seemed appropriate in the circumstances."[142] The French delegate correctly interpreted the Egyptian statements regarding the release of the cargo and the ship "to mean that the Egyptian Government maintains its claim that it is entitled to forbid passage through the Suez Canal to any vessel flying the Israel flag and manned by an Israel crew," and asked "that Egypt should abide by the Council's decision" of September 1, 1951, to terminate the restrictions on the passage of "international commercial shipping."[143] The United States representative declared:

> Further action to give full effect to the decision of 1 September 1951, to allow the passage of the *Bat Galim*, an Israel ship, to Israel and to cease interference with Israel shipping as well as with neutral shipping carrying goods to and from Israel, will confirm our respect for Egypt as the legitimate custodian of the Suez Canal, only recently reasserted by Egypt's historic agreement with the United Kingdom. Anything less than this will not be consistent with the spirit and intent of the resolution of 1 September 1951, nor, in our opinion, with its express terms.
>
> . . .Israel has shown forbearance and restraint in the conduct of its case here. Israel might well have shown impatience and resentment that it was not granted immediate satisfaction in such a case as this, where the majority of the members of the Council have shown that they believe the right to be on Israel's side.[144]

Similar views were voiced by the representatives of Belgium,[145] New Zealand,[146] and Brazil.[147] The Egyptian contention that the 1951 resolution did not apply to Israeli

[142] Official Records, 687th Meeting, Jan. 4, 1955, p. 8, par. 46. He went on to say: "Though it would, of course, have left all the questions of principle untouched, this would at least have settled the adventures of this particular ship in a more or less satisfactory manner."

[143] *Ibid.*, p. 9, par. 52, and p. 10, pars. 58–59. The Egyptian statement will be found *ibid.*, pp. 5 ff., pars. 33–34.

[144] *Ibid.*, p. 12, pars. 69–70.

[145] "The Belgian delegation cannot but assume that this suggestion is inspired by a desire to bring about a settlement in conformity with the Constantinople Convention." *Ibid.*, 688th Meeting, Jan. 13, 1955, p. 4, par. 11.

[146] "May I say, quite frankly, that for Israel to set out deliberately to damage the Canal would be an act so patently against its own interests as to put the possibility beyond serious consideration . . . . There is no justification, therefore, for an Egyptian policy of exclusion against Israel ships desiring to pass through the Canal—a policy which we regard as entirely inconsistent with the intent of the 1951 resolution." *Ibid.*, p. 10, par. 46. For statements made by Peru, which endorsed the 1951 resolution, and Iran, which avoided the issue, see *ibid.*, p. 7, par. 27, and p. 8, pars. 35–7.

[147] The Brazilian delegate said: "In any case we cannot accept a breach of the Constantinople Convention, any more than we can pass over in silence the fact that a Security Council resolution is being ignored." *Ibid.*, 687th Meeting, Jan. 4, 1955, p. 14, pars. 99–100.

ships[148] was explicitly or implicitly rejected by the representatives of all these governments. The representative of Israel expressed the hope

> that the Security Council will decide to reaffirm its 1951 resolution and will continue to oppose any interference with or discrimination against the ships or cargoes of any nation or flag, including Israel.[149]

This the Council failed to do. In spite of all the brave words, no member of the Council introduced an appropriate draft resolution expressing the views of the majority and none was therefore voted upon. Instead the President of the Council summed up the sense of the discussion: On the one hand, "it is evident that most representatives here regard the resolution of 1 September 1951 as having continuing validity and effect, and it is in this context and that of the Constantinople Convention that they have considered the *Bat Galim* case"; on the other hand, "hope has been expressed that a continued attitude of conciliation on both sides will speedily bring about an agreement on the arrangements for the release of the ship and the cargo."[150]

Thus, when faced with a clear test of its authority, the Security Council bowed to the *fait accompli* completely and without any reservation. It may well be that this was done in the certain knowledge of an impending Soviet veto. But this had never in the past nor has it ever in the succeeding years discouraged the Council from letting the Soviet Union shoulder the responsibility before the bar of public opinion, even when lesser issues were involved. Here there was open defiance of treaties and of a standing policy and decision of the Council formulated as early as August, 1949, when it placed the seal of its approval and construction upon the Egyptian-Israeli General Armistice Agreement. Here there was an issue which has been a primary cause of the chronic and endemic tension in the Middle East, and, as subsequent events were to show, a grave threat to international peace and security. Why, then, this unmitigated fiasco, why this shirking of the Council's "primary responsibility for the maintenance of international peace and security" and the taking of "prompt and effective action by the United Nations"? A possible explanation, it is ventured to suggest, may be found in the competitive wooing of the Arab States which set in with the first and second veto cast by the Soviet Union in order to shield its prospective clients in the Middle East. An exploration of the validity of this hypothesis lies, however, outside the compass of this paper.

[148] *Ibid.*, 686th Meeting, Dec. 7, 1954, pp. 22 ff., pars. 120–133.
[149] Official Records, 688th Meeting, Jan. 13, 1955, p. 16, par. 77.
[150] *Ibid.*, p. 20, pars. 99–100.

## VII. CONCLUSIONS

Several conclusions emerge from the preceding analysis. The Security Council is undoubtedly competent to deal with the issues arising from the Egyptian restrictions. Egypt has seen fit to challenge such competence when its point of view appeared certain not to be sustained by the Council. However, at the first stage of the dispute, Egypt freely admitted that

> the General Armistice Agreement between Egypt and Israel took place under the auspices of the Security Council. The Council is therefore obviously the umpire in all matters relating to the armistice agreement. It is indeed obviously competent to deal with all matters relating to world peace and security.[151]

It is even arguable that the General Assembly would have competence under the Uniting for Peace Resolution of November 3, 1950,[152] if the Council failed to exercise its primary responsibility for the maintenance of international peace and security, owing to lack of unanimity of the permanent members. The dangers to Middle East peace were often emphasized in the Council in connection with Egypt's restrictions.[153] Indeed, the General Assembly might well be better qualified to pronounce upon the larger issue arising from the continuation of Egypt's hostile and aggressive action.

Before taking up this larger aspect of the matter, it may be well to point out that it might be profitable for the Mixed Armistice Commission to take a fresh look at the Israeli complaints and to adjust its decidedly myopic construction of June 12, 1951, of the Armistice Agreement in the light of the specific findings and general tenor of the Security Council resolution of September 1, 1951. Several members made this point specifically with reference to the Gulf of Aqaba, but there is no reason why this should not be done also in relation to the Suez Canal. Thus the United States representative said:

> We believe that the Mixed Armistice Commission, in considering the specific complaint with respect to actions in the Gulf of Aqaba, must be bound not only by the provisions of the General Armistice Agreement but should act also in the light of paragraph 5 of the resolution of 1 September 1951.[154]

If the Commission has to consider the Israeli complaint regarding the Gulf of Aqaba in the light of the Security Council resolution, there is every reason for it to reconsider its earlier position regarding the Suez Canal in the same light. In so doing it might conceivably remove what has turned out to be a cause of persistent, albeit fruitless, misunder-

[151] Official Records, 514th Meeting, Oct. 20, 1950, p. 17.

[152] General Assembly Resolution 377 A (V), Official Records, 5th Year, Supp. 20, pp. 10–12 (Doc. A/1775).

[153] See Official Records, 552nd Meeting, Aug. 16, 1951, p. 12, par. 56 (Brazil); *ibid.*, p. 10, par. 45 (U.S.A.); 553rd Meeting, Aug. 16, 1951, p. 3, par. 9 (Netherlands); 663rd Meeting, March 25, 1954, p. 8, par. 34 (France).

[154] *Ibid.*, 663rd Meeting, March 25, 1954, p. 2, par. 6. See also the British statement, *ibid.*, p. 6, par. 27, and the French statement, *ibid.*, p. 9, par. 39.

standings on the part of Egypt and also lift the cloak which it unwittingly put on the true nature of Egyptian actions.

The Security Council, in considering the legal aspects of the Egyptian restrictions in general and of the seizure of the *Bat Galim* in particular, has chosen to rest its reasoning and conclusions on its own resolutions concerning the truce in Palestine and the subsequent Armistice Agreement on the Armistice Agreement itself and other "international conventions in force," including the Convention of Constantinople of 1888. It thus placed itself on solid ground. Even statements made more recently in connection with the Middle East crisis, in which the Israeli complaint against Egyptian restrictions and exclusions in the Suez Canal played an important part, proceeded from the same ground. Thus, in the view of the Secretary General of the United Nations:

> It follows from the finding of the Security Council in 1951 that under such circumstances the parties to the Armistice Agreement may be considered as not entitled to claim any belligerent rights. Were the substantive clauses of the Armistice Agreement, especially articles VII and VIII, again to be implemented, the case against all acts of belligerency, which is based on the existence of the Armistice régime, would gain full cogency. With such a broader implementation of the Armistice Agreement, the parties should be asked to give assurances that, on the basis established, they will not assert any belligerent rights (including, of course, such rights in the Gulf of Aqaba and the Straits of Tiran).
>
> As a conclusion from paragraphs 24–27, it may be held that, in a situation where the Armistice régime is partly operative by observance of the provisions of the Armistice Agreement concerning the armistice lines, possible claims to rights of belligerency would be at least so much in doubt that, having regard for the general international interest at stake, no such claim should be exercised in the Gulf of Aqaba and the Straits of Tiran . . .[155]

The solution of the apparent conflict between two principal organs of the United Nations, to wit, the Secretary General's view that the prohibition of belligerent rights is not unconditional and that in some way "the parties" may assert such rights,[156] and the view of the Security Council that Egypt is unconditionally prohibited from exercising belligerent rights by the Armistice Agreement as construed by the Acting Mediator, the Security Council itself, and the Mixed Armistice Commission, is of no immediate concern here. What is of direct interest is that this conflict indicates the insufficiency of the ground on which the issue of belligerency has so far been debated and on which the Security Council based its resolution of 1951.

Between Members of the United Nations, the first standard for determining the propriety of their conduct is not an armistice agreement, not even a peace treaty, but the

[155] Report by the Secretary General in pursuance of the resolution of the General Assembly of Jan. 15, 1957. U.N. Doc. A/3512, Jan. 24, 1957, p. 9, pars. 27–28; 36 Dept. of State Bulletin 278 (1957).

[156] See *e.g.* his statement: "Under these circumstances, it is indicated that whatever rights there may be in relation to the Gulf and Straits, such rights be exercised with restraint on all sides. Any possible claims of belligerent rights should take into account the international interests involved and, therefore, if asserted, should be limited to clearly non-controversial situations." *Ibid.*, p. 8, par. 25. Under the Armistice Agreement, what would be "clearly non-controversial situations" in which belligerent rights could be asserted?

Charter of the United Nations. In the conflict in Palestine, the hostilities, to be sure, were brought to a close by the truce ordered by the Council and by the Armistice Agreements concluded pursuant to a Council resolution. The decisive factor, however, was the admission of Israel to membership of the United Nations on May 11, 1949.[157] Without wishing to belittle the political and legal significance of the Armistice Agreements, particularly the Egyptian-Israeli Agreement of February 24, 1949, it is submitted that the admission of Israel to membership is of decisive significance for determining the issue of belligerent rights, whether in the Suez Canal, the Gulf of Aqaba or anywhere else in the air, on sea or land. Egypt asserts categorically: "A state of belligerence exists between Egypt and Israel."[158] It asserts equally that this state of belligerency has not been terminated by the Armistice Agreement, and consequently it is authorized to exercise the belligerent right of visit, search and seizure, although Israel is not authorized to exercise belligerent rights on land or in the air. The Security Council completely and in every respect rejected these pretensions, but it did so on the basis of the Armistic Agreement. The untenable character of the Egyptian assertion of a state of belligerency becomes even more obvious if it is examined in the light of the law of the Charter which is equally binding upon Egypt and Israel as Members of the Organization governed by that law. The question then can properly be formulated as follows: In the absence of authorization by the Security Council, are a state of belligerency between Members claimed unilaterally by one of them and the exercise of belligerent rights by one Member against another, compatible with the law of the Charter?[159a]

If the first submission is accepted, namely, that the relations between Egypt and Israel are governed by the law of the Charter,[159] then the conclusion seems inescapable that no rights can be asserted under an agreement which is in conflict with the law of the Charter. Article 103 of the Charter clearly establishes the supremacy of the law of the Charter over obligations under any other agreement.[160] It follows *a fortiori* that in case of a conflict between an asserted right under an agreement and obligations under the Charter, the latter must prevail. A treaty or agreement inconsistent with the Charter is null and void,

> for such a treaty is an attempt to amend or abolish the Charter or parts of it in the relations of the Members, parties to this treaty. Such an effect, however, can be reached only by an amendment to the Charter the procedure of which is determined in Articles 108 and 109.

[157] General Assembly Resolution 273 (III), Official Records, 3rd Sess., Pt. II, p. 18 (Doc. A/900).

[158] Official Records, 686th Meeting, Dec. 7, 1954, p. 21, par. 113.

[159a] "The primary issue is not what rights Egypt could exercise as a belligerent under international law, but whether it could assume the status of a belligerent at all without thereby violating fundamental obligations of the United Nations Charter." Lawyers' Committee on Blockades: The United Nations and the Egyptian Blockade of the Suez Canal, p. 18 (New York, 1953). See also Rosenne, *op. cit.* 82 ff.

[159] The question of recognition of Israel by Egypt and the other Arab States is irrelevant with regard to rights and duties of membership. By Egypt's own admission, legal relations—namely a state of war—exist between Egypt and Israel which are governed by international law.

[160] Art. 103: "In the event of a conflict between the obligations of the Members of the United Nations under the present Charter and their obligations under any other international agreement, their obligations under the present Charter shall prevail."

In no other way can the obligations and rights of the Members stipulated by the Charter be changed or abolished.[161]

It follows, then, that rights and obligations claimed under the Armistice Agreement between Israel and Egypt which are in conflict with the Charter have been abrogated by it.[162]

It hardly needs any argument to point out the incompatibility of the Egyptian claim to a unilateral state of belligerency with the purposes and principles of the Charter. In particular, it requires no prolonged discussion to find the execution by Egypt of belligerent rights, such as visit, search and seizure, and of acts such as interception of merchantmen, incompatible with Article 2, paragraph 4, of the Charter. The acts themselves have already been authoritatively determined as aggressive and hostile acts. Moreover, Article 2, paragraph 2, applies, for the Armistice Agreement concluded pursuant to a Security Council resolution constitutes obligations assumed by Egypt and Israel "in accordance with the present Charter," which must be fulfilled in good faith. Failure to do so constitutes not merely a violation of the Agreement but of a basic principle of the Charter and of international law. Under general international law repeated and serious breaches of an armistice agreement give the injured party the right of reopening hostilities.[163] If the Armistice Agreement of 1949 is of the "classic" type, as Egypt argued so persistently, and if general international law, but not the Charter, governs the relations between Egypt and Israel, then the Israel intervention of October, 1956, could be regarded as a lawful exercise of rights derived from the state of belligerency, which Egypt never fails to invoke in support of its restrictions. But that has not been the position either of Egypt or of the United Nations in the face of the Israeli intervention.[164]

In conclusion it is submitted that the time has come for the United Nations to face squarely the Egyptian claim that a state of belligerency exists with a fellow Member, and that in consequence it is entitled to exercise the belligerent right of visit, search and seizure of ships of fellow Members, and of intercepting ships of Israel, a fellow Member. In determining this basic claim, it is suggested, recourse should be had to the Charter of the United Nations rather than to the Armistice Agreement or to general international law. For what is illegal under the Charter cannot be made legal by the Armistice Agreement or general international law. In case of conflict, the higher law of the Charter must prevail juridically and consequently must be made to prevail politically and effectively. The organs of the United Nations, primarily the Security Council and the General Assembly, have an ample reservoir of power in the Charter for remedial action to remove a standing challenge to law and order, peace and justice in the Middle East.

[161] Hans Kelsen, The Law of the United Nations 113 (1951).

[162] See also statements by the Israeli representative, Official Records, 516th Meeting, Oct. 30, 1950, p. 11, and 549th Meeting, July 26, 1951, p. 11; and statement by Peruvian delegate, 688th Meeting, Jan. 13, 1955, p. 7, par. 27.

[163] Stone, Legal Controls of International Conflict 644 (1954): "Certain rules seem to be established with regard to violations of armistice agreements. First, a serious breach, engaging the responsibility of the State which has committed it, gives the other belligerent state a right of withdrawal, if it so elects, and in urgent cases a right of re-opening hostilities."

[164] See Quincy Wright, "Intervention, 1956," 51 A.J.I.L. 257–277 (1957).

# THE GENEVA CONFERENCE ON THE LAW OF THE SEA AND THE RIGHT OF INNOCENT PASSAGE THROUGH THE GULF OF AQABA

Since the United Nations Emergency Force moved in and occupied the heights overlooking the Straits of Tiran, the Gulf of Aqaba has been quiet. Ships, including Israel flag ships, move freely in and out. The right of passage claimed by Israel and other states was discussed in the Security Council in 1954, in the International Law Commission in 1956, in the General Assembly in 1956–57, and again at the Geneva Conference on the Law of the Sea February 24–April 27, 1958, and will be analyzed here. It should be stated at the outset that Israel's boundaries, including the strip at the northern end of the Gulf of Aqaba, are not an issue here. Nor is the Arab claim that a state of war continues to exist pertinent in determining the legal status of the Gulf and the Straits, although it obviously has some bearing on the availability to Israel of the right of "innocent" passage.

## 1. THE GULF OF AQABA BEFORE THE SECURITY COUNCIL, 1954

On January 28, 1954, Israel submitted to the Security Council two complaints: one referred to the continued interference by Egypt with ships trading with Israel while passing through the Suez Canal, in contravention of the Security Council resolution of September 1, 1951;[1] and the other concerned interference by Egypt with shipping proceeding to the Israel port of Elath on the Gulf of Aqaba.[2] A draft resolution submitted by New Zealand proposed that "without prejudice to the provisions of the resolution of

[1] See Gross, "Passage through the Suez Canal of Israel-Bound Cargo and Israel Ships," 51 A.J.I.L. 530–568, particularly 564–568 (1957). See also *supra*, pp. 1081–1117, particularly 1114–1117.
[2] U.N. Doc. S/3168. Security Council, 9th Year, Official Records, Supp., January–March, 1954, p. 1.

1 September 1951, the complaint . . . should in the first instance be dealt with by the Armistice Commission established under the General Armistice Agreement between Egypt and Israel.[3] In the vote on March 29, 1954, this draft resolution was not adopted there being eight votes in favor (Brazil, Colombia, Denmark, France, New Zealand, Turkey, United Kingdom, United States), two against (Lebanon, U.S.S.R.), and one abstention (China).[4] The debate was largely concerned with the question whether the 1951 resolution applied to Egyptian interference in the Suez Canal only or was of a general character. Typical of the view held by members of the Council which supported the New Zealand proposal was the observation of the representative of the United States. He quoted paragraph 5 of the 1951 resolution:

> Considering that since the armistice regime, which has been in existence for nearly two and half years, is of a permanent character, neither party can reasonably assert that it is actively a belligerent or requires to exercise the right of visit, search, and seizure for any legitimate purpose of self-defense . . .[5]

and said:

> In our opinion, this principle is equally applicable to the Suez Canal and to any waters outside the Canal . . . . We believe that the Mixed Armistice Commission, in considering this specific complaint with respect to actions in the Gulf of Aqaba, must be bound not only by the provisions of the General Armistice Agreement but should also act in the light of paragraph 5 of the resolution of 1 September 1951.[6]

Egypt, in the same order of ideas, based its objections to the draft resolution, not on the legal status of the waters involved, but on the alleged rights of belligerency. While admitting the right of innocent passage through territorial waters, the representative of Egypt said:

> The passage of contraband of war through the national and territorial waters of Egypt to Israel is certainly not a case of innocent passage. It violates the most explicit provisions of Egyptian law and strengthens Israel's war effort.[7]

It is suggested that no other legal basis was open to the Egyptian representative, as, in reply to an inquiry by the United States Government, he stated that his government

[3] U.N. Docs. S/3188 and Corr. 1, March 19, 1954. *Loc. cit.*, p. 44.

[4] Official Journal, 664th Meeting, March 29, 1954, p. 12. This was the second Soviet veto in the Palestinian question; the first was cast on Jan. 22, 1954, and indicated a shift in the position of the Soviet Union from abstention to active support of the Arab states against Israel.

[5] U.N. Doc. S/2298/Rev. 1. Official Records, 558th Meeting, Sept. 1, 1951, p. 2.

[6] Official Records, 663rd Meeting, March 25, 1954, p.2. For statements to the same effect by representatives of Great Britain and France, see *ibid.*, pp. 6, 9.

[7] *Ibid.*, 661st Meeting, March 12, 1954, p. 19. The law referred to is presumably the decision of the Egyptian Council of Ministers of Nov. 28, 1953, enlarging the list of contraband goods to include food. *Cf.* U.N. Doc. S/3168, note 2 above, at p. 2.

had explicitly and formally recognized the right of innocent passage through the Straits of Tiran in the following statement of January 28, 1950:

> This occupation (of the Islands of Tiran and Sanafir) being in no sense intended to interfere in any way whatever with innocent traffic through the stretch of sea separating these two islands from the Sinai Coast of Egypt, it goes without saying that this passage, the only practicable one, will remain free, as in the past; which is in conformity with international practice and with recognized principles of international law.[8]

There is no reference here to "national" waters. The above-quoted statement was explicitly included in the United States Memorandum to Israel of February 11, 1957,[9] which forms an integral part of the official exchanges between the two governments on the basis of which Israel finally agreed to withdraw from Sharm el Sheikh. The representative of Israel argued in the Security Council on February 15, 1954, with reference to the Strait of Tiran, that

> Where a narrow waterway is the only junction between two parts of the high seas, or the only outlet to a part of the high seas, then its international character has to be preserved, and no sovereign rights based upon the doctrine of territorial waters is inherent in any country from the viewpoint of holding up free maritime traffic.[10]

Referring to the Gulf of Aqaba, Israel's position was stated to be as follows:

> Any claim by Egypt that in the Gulf of Elath (Aqaba) it is merely exercising the rights of sovereignty in territorial waters would of course be totally frivolous since it is a physical geographical fact that there is no way for a ship to approach any place on the northern shore of that narrow gulf without passing through the territorial waters of any or all of four countries—Egypt, Israel, Jordan and Saudi Arabia.
>
> We should thus arrive at the absurdity that any of those four countries could at any time use its armed force in the straits of Aqaba to prevent a ship from reaching any other of the three littoral States. It is not difficult to conceive what a maritime jungle would be created by such a ludicrous theory. International law and practice on such questions is quite clear and explicit.[11]

Israel's position appeared to rest on the view that the Straits of Tiran constitute an international waterway which is open to navigation in spite of the fact that it passes through the territorial sea of Egypt; and that freedom of navigation through the Gulf is based on the theory of access to the port or ports of the coastal states. The position of the Arab states denying freedom of navigation seemed to have been based either on the existence of a state of war and consequential belligerent rights or on the "national" character of the water involved, without specifying sharply whether this character was attributed

[8] Quoted by the Israel representative in the Security Council, Official Records, 659th Meeting, Feb. 15, 1954, p. 19.

[9] "Aide-Memoire Handed to Israeli Ambassador Eban by Secretary of State Dulles, February 11, 1957," U.S. Policy in the Middle East September 1956–June 1957, Documents, p. 290 (Dept. of State Pub. 6505).

[10] Offical Records, 659th Meeting, Feb. 15, 1954, p. 18.

[11] Official Records, 658th Meeting, Feb. 5, 1954, p. 16, and *ibid.*, 659th Meeting, Feb. 15, 1954, p. 18

to the Straits or the Gulf. Juridically the latter position does not seem very persuasive, particularly in view of the Egyptian assurances of 1950 to the United States. It was, however, developed more concretely by Saudi Arabia which claimed the Gulf as a "closed sea."

## 2. THE GULF OF AQABA AS *MARE CLAUSUM*

In a "Memorandum registering the Saudi Arabian Government's legal and historical rights in the Straits of Tiran and the Gulf of Aqaba,"[12] it was claimed that both the Straits and the Gulf constitute an Arab *mare clausum,* and not an international waterway. This is based in the first place on the configuration of the area: The Gulf is 100 miles long with widths varying between 7 and 14 miles; the entrance does not exceed 9 miles and is "intercepted by the two Islands of Tiran and Sanafir" under Saudi Arabian sovereignty; the only navigable channel lies between the Island of Tiran and the Egyptian shore and does not exceed half a mile or 500 meters.[13] In the second place, Saudi Arabia claimed that the Gulf "is of the category of historical Gulfs that fall outside the sphere of international law." The basis for this is seen in the character of the Gulf as

> the historical route to the holy places in Mecca. Pilgrims from different Muslim countries have been streaming through the Gulf, year after year, for fourteen centuries. Ever since, the Gulf has been an exclusively Arab route under Arab sovereignty. It is due to this undisputed fact that not a single international authority makes any mention whatsoever of the Gulf as an international waterway open for international navigation.[14]

The Saudi Arabian Government might have added, for completeness' sake, which "international authority makes any mention whatsoever" of the Gulf as a historic gulf or bay.[15]

Juridically as well as historically this statement is of dubious value, as it would be difficult to reconcile the sovereignty of the Ottoman Empire over the whole area with "Arab sovereignty" during fourteen centuries. However, it is unnecessary to evaluate its significance, as juridically Saudi Arabia appears to derive the historical character of the Gulf from the Suez Canal Convention of 1888:

> . . . The territorial character of the Gulf, its waters, entrance and straits, was affirmed by the Treaty of Constantinople of 1888 concerning the Suez Canal. Article 10 (par.3) of the said Treaty specified that the stipulations contained in that Treaty do not apply to the

[12] U.N. Doc. A/3575, April 15, 1957.

[13] *Ibid.,* pp. 3–4; see also statement by the representative of Saudi Arabia in General Assembly, 12th Sess., Official Records, 697th Plenary Meeting, Oct. 2, 1957, p. 233, par. 92; and at Geneva Conference on the Law of the Sea, Official Records, Vol. III, First Committee, 3rd Meeting, March 3, 1959, p. 3, par. 30: "The Gulf of Aqaba came under exclusive Arab jurisdiction."

[14] Statement in the General Assembly; *cf.* note 13 above, p. 233, par. 93.

[15] The "Memorandum concerning Historic Bays," prepared by the U.N. Secretariat for the Geneva Conference on the Law of Sea, does not mention the Gulf of Aqaba among the bays regarded as historic bays or claimed as such by the state concerned. U.N. Doc. A/Conf. 13/1 (Sept. 20, 1957), pp. 9–28.

> Arabic States lying on the Red Sea and the Gulf of Aqaba. The records of the negotiations leading to the said Treaty clearly reveal that the Gulf of Aqaba and its straits were intended to be excluded from the proposed freedom of international navigation in the Suez Canal, thus acknowledging that the waters of the Gulf, its entrance and straits, are territorial and implying no freedom of international navigation through them.[16]

Finally, the possession of a strip of the Gulf by Israel is "nothing but a military control without sovereignty whatsoever. Israel has no sovereign status in the Gulf of Aqaba."[17]

The first and last arguments are interdependent and will be discussed presently. The Suez Canal Convention provides no juridical basis for the asserted "territorial" character of the Gulf. Article 10, paragraph 3, does not have the significance attributed to it by Saudi Arabia. It declares:

> It is also understood that the provisions of the four Articles in question [4, 5, 7 and 8] shall in no case stand in the way of measures which the Imperial Ottoman Government considers it necessary to take to assure by its own forces the defense of its other possessions situated on the eastern coast of the Red Sea.[18]

The articles in question—4, 5, 7 and 8—are concerned with the rights and duties of belligerents in the Suez Canal and its approaches and measures of supervision. They are not concerned with freedom of navigation. Assuming, as the Saudi Arabian Government does, that the Convention relates to the Gulf, then the opposite conclusion from that drawn by Saudi Arabia appears more plausible. The principle of freedom of navigation in time of war and peace is established by Article 1 of the Convention. As this article is not excluded by Article 10, paragraph 3, it would follow, on the basis of the Saudi Arabian assumption, that it applies equally in the Suez Canal and the Gulf of Aqaba. Thus, far from supporting the claim to the "territorial character" of the Gulf, the Convention, if it applies at all, would negate it and substantiate the Israel claim to freedom of navigation, which is asserted by the United States and other maritime Powers as well.

Turning now to the first and last Saudi Arabian arguments, it can be admitted that historical titles are not unknown in international law. The International Court of Justice, in the Anglo-Norwegian Fisheries dispute, held:

> By "historic waters" are usually meant waters which are treated as internal waters but which would not have that character were it not for the existence of an historic title. The United Kingdom Government refers to the notion of historic titles both in respect of territorial waters and internal waters, considering such titles, in both cases, as derogations from general international law. In its opinion Norway can justify the claim that these waters are territorial or internal on the ground that she has exercised the necessary jurisdiction over them for a long period without opposition from other States, a kind of *possessio longi temporis,* with the result that her jurisdiction over these waters must now be recognized

[16] Memorandum, note 12 above, p. 4.
[17] Statement in the General Assembly; *cf.* note 13 above, p. 233, par. 96.
[18] The Suez Canal Problem July 26–September 22, 1956, p. 19 (Dept. of State Pub. 6392).

> although it constitutes a derogation from the rules in force. Norwegian sovereignty over these waters would constitute an exception, historic titles justifying situations which would otherwise be in conflict with international law.[19]

The historic title to a gulf or bay was affirmed by the Central American Court of Justice in its Judgment of March 9, 1917.[20] The Court held;

> The legal status of the Gulf of Fonseca having been recognized by this Court to be that of a historic bay possessed of the characteristics of a closed sea, the three riparian States of El Salvador, Honduras and Nicaragua are, therefore, recognized as coöwners of its waters, except as to the littoral marine league which is the exclusive property of each . . .[21]

The Court arrived at the conclusion that the Gulf of Fonseca "belongs to the special category of historic bays and is the exclusive property of El Salvador, Honduras and Nicaragua" on the theory

> that it combines all the characteristics or conditions that the text writers on international law, the international law institutes and the precedents have prescribed as essential to territorial waters, to wit, secular or immemorial possession accompanied by *animo domini* both peaceful and continuous and by acquiescence on the part of other nations, the special geographical configuration that safeguards so many interests of vital importance to the economic, commercial, agricultural and industrial life of the riparian States and the absolute, indispensable necessity that those States should possess the Gulf as fully as required by those primordial interests and the interest of national defense.[22]

Three pillars, then, support the historic character of the Gulf of Fonseca: first, immemorial possession established by the Spanish Crown in 1522 and continued by the three successor states;[23] secondly, the *animus domini* "both peaceful and continuous"; and, finally, acquiescence by other nations. It will be noted, however, that the Court did not attribute to the waters in the Gulf the character of internal waters and therefore did not exclude the right of innocent passage. The doctrine, even in the case of historic bays the coasts of which belong to a single state, does not seem to be unanimous whether the waters are to be regarded as "internal waters," thus excluding the right of innocent passage, or partly

[19] Fisheries Case (United Kingdom *v.* Norway), Judgment of Dec. 18, 1951. [1951] I.C.J. Rep. 116, at 130. See also 46 A.J.I.L. 348, at 358, 366, 369 (1952).

[20] The Republic of El Salvador *v.* The Republic of Nicaragua, 11 A.J.I.L. 674–730 (1917).

[21] *Ibid.,* at 716; see also 707.

[22] *Ibid.,* at 705.

[23] On this point the Court said: "The historic origin of the right of exclusive ownership that has been exercised over the waters of the Gulf during the course of nearly four hundred years is incontrovertible, first, under the Spanish dominion—from 1522, when it was discovered and incorporated into the royal patrimony of the Crown of Castile, down to the year 1821—then under the Federal Republic of the Center of America, which in that year attained its independence and sovereignty down to 1839; and, subsequently, on the dissolution of the Federation in that year, the States of El Salvador, Honduras and Nicaragua, in their character of autonomous nations and legitimate successors of Spain, incorporated into their respective territories, as a necessary dependency thereof for geographical reasons and purposes of common defense, both the Gulf and its archipelago, which nature had indented in that important part of the continent, in the form of a gullet." *Ibid.* at 700.

as "internal waters" and partly as territorial sea.[24] In the latter case there would presumably be a right of innocent passage in the territorial sea.[25]

It is doubtful whether the claim to the Gulf of Aqaba as a closed sea meets these three facts. Immemorial possession could not easily be established, although, in a sense, all the four states abutting on the Gulf may be considered as successors to the Ottoman Empire. Did the Ottoman Empire, however, manifest *"aminus domini"* and was the claim to regard the Gulf as Turkish acquiesced in by other nations? Unless the advocates of the Gulf as a closed sea prove both *animus* and recognition at the time the area was under Ottoman sovereignty, the states which emerged from the progressive dismemberment of the Ottoman Empire did not succeed to a historical title to the gulf or bay. In this respect the Gulf of Aqaba situation presents no analogy at all to the Gulf of Fonseca. Failing this, it would be necessary to show that a "historic" claim arose and was recognized some time after the emergence of Egypt and Saudi Arabia as independent states and the creation of the British Mandate in Palestine out of which developed both Jordan and Israel. This would be a hopeless task and in fact has not been attempted. Egypt's official declaration of 1950 stands in the way of any such attempt. Certainly since the establishment of Israel in 1948 there has been neither a "peaceful and continuous" *animus* nor acquiescence by other nations. Unlike in the case of the Gulf of Fonseca, where all littoral states assert a historic title against outsiders, in the Gulf of Aqaba Saudi Arabia is asserting a claim against one of the littoral states, with general support from Jordan, and Egypt being precluded from supporting it.[26] In this respect, too, there is no analogy whatsoever between the juridical situation of the Gulf of Fonseca and the Gulf of Aqaba.

Certainly, the Gulf of Aqaba could be transformed into a closed sea by agreement among all the littoral states and recognition by other nations. As the then Secretary of State, Mr. John Foster Dulles, said: "If the four littoral States which have boundaries upon the Gulf should all agree that it should be closed, then it could be closed."[27] Whether in such a case the littoral states would also agree to consider the entire body of water in the Gulf or only that part outside their respective territorial seas as included in co-ownership is probably not decisive. In the case of the Gulf of Fonseca the Court assumed that Nicaragua and El Salvador exercised sovereignty individually in the maritime belts.[28] In principle, it would appear that the existence of belts of territorial seas, insofar as the littoral states in their relations *inter se* are concerned, is not incompatible with the

[24] Memorandum concerning Historic Bays, note 15 above, at 63–79.

[25] See 3 Gidel, Le Droit International Public de la Mer 606 (1934). Gidel interprets the Judgment of the Central American Court in the Fonseca case in this sense.

[26] At the Geneva Conference on the Law of the Sea, the representative of Jordan expressed "his complete agreement with the observations made by the representative of Saudi Arabia" and his hope that Israel's possession of a share of the coast "would prove transient." Official Records, Vol. III, First Committee, 8th Meeting, March 7, 1958, p. 18, pars. 6 and 7. The representative of Egypt stated that, contrary to the assertion of the representative of Israel, "no single aspect of the Palestine question had yet been the object of any settlement whatever."*Ibid.*, p. 67, par. 9.

[27] News Conference Statements by Secretary of State Dulles, Feb. 19, 1957. United States Policy in the Middle East September 1956–June 1957, p. 299 (Dept. of State Pub. 6505). But see 3 Gidel, Le Droit International Public de la mer 604, where the author considers acquiescence by other states as essential even in such a case.

[28] See note 20 above, at 711, and also the fifteenth question and the answer, at 694.

character of a gulf or bay as a closed sea *erga omnes.*[29] The enactment of regulations concerning the extent of the territorial sea does not necessarily militate against a historic claim to the Gulf of Aqaba, as all states but Jordan have a coast outside the Gulf. However, the Fisheries Act No. 25 of December 2, 1943, which in Article 2 defines the territory of "Transjordan" as including that part of the sea lying within three miles from the low-water line and is maintained in force by Jordan, which has no other coastline,[30] would be a strong indication that, in the juridical view of Jordan or of the British Mandatory Administration at any rate, the historic character of the Gulf was an afterthought.

Recognition or acquiescence by third states was considered as an element in the historic title to the Gulf of Fonseca in addition to *animus* and "immemorial possession." Recognition or acquiescence or absence of protest appears to be a necessary ingredient, since a claim to a historic sea or bay appears as an encroachment upon the principle of the freedom of the high seas, or, as the International Court of Justice put it in the above-quoted passage, as "a derogation from the rules in force." Certainly the burden of proof with respect to all the elements of a historic title rests with the government or governments which claim it.[31] Certainly in the case of the Gulf of Aqaba this proof would be difficult to furnish in view of the successive changes in the number of the coastal states.[31a] The discussion at the Eleventh Session of the General Assembly on the Gulf of Aqaba failed to disclose any evidence of recognition. In any event the weight of such evidence, if it could be adduced, would have to be measured against the opposite view of Israel, which has emerged as one of the coastal states.

The Central American Court of Justice based its finding, among other factors, on the "many interests of vital importance" of the Gulf of Fonseca to the coastal states. The concept of "vital bays," that is of bays which are claimed as national or internal waters on the ground of the vital interests of the coastal state or states, does not seem to have any basis in the practice of states or in the doctrine.[32] Even if the concept were acceptable, it would be extremely difficult, in practice, to establish as national or internal the waters of a "vital bay" in the absence of agreement among the coastal states. There is obviously no such agreement with respect to the Gulf of Aqaba, although this gulf may well be vital to all or some of the coastal states. However, the interest which is considered as "vital" by them is not identic.

[29] For the opposite view see Charles B. Selak, Jr., "A Consideration of the Legal Status of the Gulf of Aqaba," 52 A.J.I.L. 660–698, at 693 (1958).

[30] U.N. Legislative Series, Laws and Regulations on the Regime of the Territorial Sea, p. 522 (Sales No.: 1957.V.2).

[31] Memorandum concerning Historic Bays, note 15 above, at 91. See also *ibid.* 83–85, for doctrinal views regarding the requirement of recognition or acquiescence, and 98–102 for an analysis of the judgment of the International Court of Justice with respect to this requirement. See also the Japanese proposal of April 1, 1958, relating to Art. 7, par. 4, which, in defining historic bays, combines the elements of usage and recognition: "The term 'historic bays' means those bays over which coastal State or States have effectively exercised sovereign rights continuously for a period of long standing, with explicit or implicit recognition of such practice by foreign States." U.N. Doc. A/Conf. 13/C.1/L. 104, Conference on the Law of the Sea, Official Records, Vol. III, First Committee, p. 241.

[31a] According to Alexander Melamid, "Legal Status of the Gulf of Aqaba," 53 A.J.I.L. 412–413 (1959), there would seem to be no basis whatever for any historic or exclusive title to the Gulf in any of the riparian states.

[32] Memorandum concerning Historic Bays, note 15 above, at 85–88.

In conlusion, it is one thing to claim a bay as historic but another to establish a valid claim. The International Law Commission, in view of the inherent difficulties, did not attempt to include a definition of historic bays in its draft.[33] The Geneva Conference itself did not fill the gap. Instead it adopted a resolution recognizing the juridical importance of historic waters, including historic bays, and requested the General Assembly of the United Nations "to arrange for the study of the juridical régime of historic waters, including historic bays, and for the communication of the result of such study to all States Members of the United Nations."[34] However, the Conference may be deemed to have implicitly rejected the claim to the Gulf of Aqaba as a historic gulf or bay when it adopted paragraph 4 of Article 16 of the Convention on the Territorial Sea, which has been generally regarded as fitting that particular gulf.[35]

## 3. THE JURIDICAL STATUS OF THE GULF OF AQABA BEFORE THE INTERNATIONAL LAW COMMISSION

The question was raised by the Government of Israel in connection with the provisional articles concerning the regime of the territorial sea adopted by the International Law Commission at its Seventh Session in 1955. Article 18 provided that the coastal state may take measures in the territorial sea "to protect itself against any act prejudicial to its security" and for the same reason may even "suspend temporarily and in definite areas of its territorial sea the exercise of the right of passage if it should deem such suspension essential." Article 18, paragraph 4, on the other hand, read:

> There must be no suspension of the innocent passage of foreign vessels through straits normally used for international navigation between two parts of the high seas.[36]

The Government of Israel, in commenting on this, pointed out that, while agreeing with the substance, it objected to the arrangement which made it appear as if the freedom of navigation through straits were a derogation from the sovereignty of the littoral state or states, whereas it considered the latter subordinate to the former. Accordingly,

> What this means is that where access to a given port—whether an existing one or one which at some future date a State may wish to establish—is only possible by traversing a strait (in the geographical sense), then it is quite immaterial whether that strait is or is not within the waters classed as territorial sea of one or more of the littoral States, or what is the legal nature (gulf, bay, high seas) of the waters on which the harbour is situated. In such circumstances the right of passage for the ships of all nations, and quite regardless of their cargo, is and must remain absolutely unqualified, and the littoral State or States have no right whatsoever, so long as the matter is not regulated by Convention, to hinder, ham-

[33] See Statement by Professor François, Expert to the Secretariat of the Conference, U.N. Doc. A/Conf. 13/C.1/L.10 U.N. Conference on the Law of the Sea, Official Records, Vol. III, First Committee, p. 69, pars. 13, 14.

[34] U.N. Doc. A/Conf. 13/L.56, p. 8 (April 30, 1958). *Loc. cit.*, Vol. II, Plenary Meetings, p. 145.

[35] *Cf.* pp. 1140–1142 below.

[36] General Assembly, 10th Sess., Official Records, Supp. No. 9 (A/2934); and 50 A.J.I.L. 232 (1956).

> per, impede or suspend the free passage of those ships. The same rule is also true as regards warships.[37]

It is reasonably clear that the Government of Israel commented not so much on the legal status of straits in general and passage through them from one part of the high sea to another as on the legal status of a specific kind of strait, namely, that which affords the only navigable access to a port in a gulf or bay. In short, it set forth its view concerning the Straits of Tiran and the Gulf of Aqaba with emphasis on the right of access.

The International Law Commission weighted the provisions in Article 18 heavily, probably too exclusively in favor of the littoral state's right of protecting its security.[38] This imbalance was corrected to some extent at the Geneva Conference. In the Commission the comments submitted by Israel were recognized as referring to the Gulf of Aqaba, the position of which, in the view of the *Rapporteur,* Professor François, was "exceptional—possibly unique."[39] He also pointed out that

> paragraph 4 of Article 18 related to straits between two parts of the high seas, and so did not apply to the Gulf of Aqaba which, though open to the high seas at one end, merely gave access to a port at the other.[40]

Faris Bey el-Khouri agreed that the case was "exceptional" but, disagreeing with Israel, said:

> A port was not a natural feature existing from time immemorial, and if a State saw fit to establish a port at a point to which the only access was through the territorial waters of other States, it must accept the consequences. It was always open to the State in question to establish a port elsewhere or to conclude agreements with the other coastal States on the question of access to the port.[41]

Sir Gerald Fitzmaurice disagreed. In his view

> vessels would in any case enjoy the right of innocent passage through a gulf consisting entirely of the territorial waters of coastal States to a port belonging to a third State. He wondered whether the situation envisaged by the Israel Government was not already covered by article 18.[42]

[37] U.N. Doc. A/CN.4/99/Add.1; 2 I.L.C. Yearbook 1956, pp. 52, 56; 50 A.J.I.L. 998 at 1005 (1956). The comment concluded as follows: "The interests of the international community must here have absolute predominance over those of the littoral States whose territorial waters have to be traversed in making for a given harbour. In this respect the passage through straits of this character is assimilated to the high seas themselves."

[38] See Myres S. McDougal, "The Crisis of the Law of the Sea," 67 Yale Law Journal 546 (1958), on the conflict between "internationalist" and "provincial" myopia.

[39] 336th Meeting, June 13, 1956, 1 I.L.C. Yearbook 1956, Summary Records of its 8th Sess., April 23-July 4, 1956, p. 202, par. 89.

[40] *Ibid.,* par. 96.

[41] *Ibid.,* par. 93.

[42] *Ibid.,* par. 94.

After a brief and desultory discussion the Commission decided that "the question raised by the Israel Government related to an exceptional case which did not lend itself to the formulation of a general rule."[43] However, in its Report on the Eighth Session the Commission included the following comment to Article 17 (formerly Article 18):

> The question was asked what would be the legal position of straits forming part of the territorial sea of one or more States and constituting the sole means of access to a port of another State. The Commission considers that this case could be assimilated to that of a bay whose inner part and entrance from the high seas belong to different States. As the Commission felt bound to confine itself to proposing rules applicable to bays, wholly belonging to a single coastal State, it also reserved consideration of the above-mentioned case.[44]

This comment, along with the Commission's draft of Article 17, was before the Geneva Conference, which did not adopt it. It was also, prior to the Conference, available to the Members of the United Nations during the Eleventh Session in 1956–1957, of the General Assembly, when Israel's demand for free and unimpeded passage through the Straits of Tiran and the Gulf of Aqaba was discussed in connection with its withdrawal from the Sinai Peninsula.

What the Commission appeared to be saying can be summarized under five heads:

> 1. The Straits of Tiran were not straits within the meaning of Article 17, paragraph 4, because they did not connect two parts of the high seas but a part of the high sea with a gulf or bay; therefore Article 17, paragraph 4, prohibiting the suspension of innocent passage did not apply.
> 2. The Straits of Tiran could be assimilated to a bay bordered by several states; therefore Article 17, paragraph 4, did not apply.
> 3. States had a right of innocent passage through the territorial seas of other states under Article 16, but a coastal state was authorized by the Commission to suspend temporarily such passage "in definite areas of its territorial sea" under Article 17, paragraph 3.
> 4. Inasmuch as the only navigable channel in the Straits of Tiran and the Gulf of Aqaba to the Israel port of Elath passed through territorial seas, therefore access to that port could be suspended by the coastal states concerned under Article 17, paragraph 3.
> 5. Be that as it may, it was not the task of the Commission to lay down rules for particular or even unique cases.

## 4. THE JURIDICAL STATUS OF THE GULF OF AQABA BEFORE THE ELEVENTH SESSION OF THE GENERAL ASSEMBLY 1956–1957

Attempts to clarify the juridical status of the Straits of Tiran and the Gulf of Aqaba were made by Israel and a number of other Members in connection with the withdrawal of Israel from the Sharm el Sheikh area. It is not necessary to trace the deliberations of the General Assembly through its various phases, though it may be useful to indicate the principal juridical arguments for and against the right of free and unimpeded passage claimed by Israel.

[43] *Ibid.*, par. 102.
[44] General Assembly, 11th Sess., Official Records, Supp. No. 9 (A/3159), p. 20.

A key to the understanding of the debates appears to be the views expressed by the Secretary General. In a note dated January 15, 1957, he stated:

> The international significance of the Gulf of Aqaba may be considered to justify the right of innocent passage through the Straits of Tiran and the Gulf in accordance with recognized rules of international law.[45]

This statement, which appeared fully to endorse the position of Israel, was somewhat modified in the Secretary General's Report dated January 24, 1957, in which, after repeating it, the following was added:

> However, in its Commentary to Article 17 of the articles of the law of the sea (A/3159, p. 20), the International Law Commission reserved consideration of the question "what would be the legal position of straits forming part of the Territorial sea of one or more States and constituting the sole means of access to the port of another State." This description applies to the Gulf of Aqaba and the Straits of Tiran. A legal controversy exists as to the extent of the right of innocent passage through these waters.[46]

On the other hand, after reviewing the Security Council resolution of September 1, 1951, in which the Council called upon Egypt to terminate the restictions which it imposed on shipping through the Suez Canal destined for Israel,[47] the Secretary General declared that

> . . . it may be held that, in a situation where the armistice régime is partly operative by observance of the provisions of the Armistice Agreement concerning the armistice lines, possible claims to rights of belligerency would be at least so much in doubt that, having regard for the general international interest at stake, no such claim should be exercised in the Gulf of Aqaba and the Straits of Tiran.[48]

The Secretary General thus formulated three propositions: First, there was a right of innocent passage through the Straits and the Gulf; secondly, there was a controversy as to the extent of this right; and thirdly, no belligerent rights should be exercised in the Gulf and the Straits. These views were to weigh heavily in the subsequent debate, although different delegations attached different weight to each of them. The second proposition, a palpable truism, was invested with an importance which appears to be quite out of proportion to its real significance. For "legal controversy" exists not merely regarding the right of innocent passage but also regarding a good deal of the law of the sea and international law in general. It is also remarkable that the positive statement made by the Commission, to wit, that "this case could be assimilated to that of a bay whose inner port and

[45] U.N. Doc. A/3500, p. 5, par. 14. General Assembly, 11th Sess., Official Records, Annexes, Agenda Item 66, p. 44. The Secretary General added that he "has not considered that a discussion of the various aspects of this matter, and its possible relation to the action requested in the General Assembly resolutions on the Middle East crisis, falls within the mandate established for him in the resolution of 4 November (1956)."

[46] U.N. Doc. A/3512, p.8, par. 24. Annexes, Agenda Item 66, p. 49.

[47] On this subject see Leo Gross, "Passage through the Suez Canal of Israel-Bound Cargo and Israel Ships," 51 A.J.I.L. 530–568 (1951). *Supra*, pp. 1081–1117.

[48] U.N. Doc. A/3512, p. 9, par. 28. Annexes, Agenda Item 66, p. 50.

entrance from the high seas belong to different states," was virtually passed over with silence. Had this statement been given its due weight, the Members might have found it easier to disentangle the situation, for if there is a rule of international law regarding which there is practically no controversy, it is the rule that bays and gulfs with several littoral states, "however narrow their entrance may be, are non-territorial. They are parts of the open sea, the marginal belt inside the gulfs and bays excepted." Such gulfs and bays "are in time of peace and war open to vessels of all nations, including men-of-war."[49] Had this principle been taken as the starting point, the issues which remained for consideration would have been confined to the question of innocent passage and possibly the question of belligerent rights in a state of armistice.

Regarding freedom of passage, in and out of the Assembly debates, two schools of thought emerged. One, led by the United States, supported the Israeli position of freedom of passage, and the other, led by India, opposed it. The United States Government in an *Aide-Mémoire* handed to Israeli Ambassador Eban by Secretary of State Dulles on February 11, 1957, stated:

> With respect to the Gulf of Aqaba and access thereto—the United States believes that the Gulf comprehends international waters and that no nation has the right to prevent free and innocent passage in the Gulf and through the Straits giving access thereto.

After recalling the Egyptian declaration of January 28, 1950, with respect to freedom of passage through the Straits,[50] the *Aide-Mémoire* continued:

> In the absence of some overriding decision to the contrary, as by the International Court of Justice, the United States, on behalf of vessels of United States registry, is prepared to exercise the right of free and innocent passage and to join with others to secure general recognition of this right.[51]

This declaration, which President Eisenhower stated "related to our intentions, both as a Member of the United Nations and as a maritime power having rights of our own,"[52] was decisive. The first part of it was repeated textually by the Foreign Minister

[49] 1 Oppenheim, International Law 508 (8th ed., H. Lauterpacht, 1955). See also Gidel, *op. cit.* 593–608.

[50] See p. 1120 above.

[51] United States Policy in the Middle East Sept. 1956–June 1957, Documents, p. 290 (Dept. of State Pub. 6505).

[52] White House News Statement issued at Thomasville, Georgia, Feb. 17, 1957. *Ibid.*, p. 293. The position of the U. S. Government was restated in the Statement by the Department of State of June 27, 1957, which was delivered to the Washington missions of the eleven Arab nations in reply to their collective démarche submitted to the Secretary of State on May 24, 1957, on the problems of Algeria, Palestine, the Gulf of Aqaba and the Suez Canal. The writer is indebted for copies of these statements to the Chief, Historical Division, Department of State, and the Arab States Delegations Office, respectively. Parts of the American statement were printed in the New York Times, June 29, 1957. With respect to the U.S. position concerning the Gulf of Aqaba, see also the Circular sent by the Department of State on June 5, 1957, to Clarence G. Morse, Maritime Administrator, Department of Commerce, and Ralph E. Casey, American Merchant Marine Institute, New York, N. Y., in which the Department declared: "A denial of free and innocent passage through those waters [*i.e.*, the Straits of Tiran and the Gulf of Aqaba] to vessels of United States registry should be reported to the nearest available United States diplomatic or consular officer." 37 Dept. of State Bulletin 112 (1957). This Circular referred to the Notice to Mariners No. 44 of Oct. 29, 1955, by the U. S. Hydrographic Office, which repeats the substance of the "Ports and Lighthouses Administration Circular to Shipping No. 4 of 1955," issued by the Director General, Rear Admiral

of Israel in announcing on March 1, 1957, Israel's plans for full withdrawal from the Sharm el Sheikh area,[53] and the representative of the United States repeated textually all relevant parts of the statement at the same meeting of the Assembly, with this addtion:

> These views are to be understood in the sense of the relevant portions on the law of the sea of the report of the International Law Commission covering the work of its eighth session from 23 April to 4 July 1956 (A/3159).[54]

The American view was endorsed in substance though in varying formulas by the representatives of France,[55] Costa Rica, [56] the United Kingdom,[57] Italy,[58] The Netherlands,[59] New Zealand,[60] Australia,[61] Belgium,[62] Canada,[63] Norway,[64] Sweden, [65] Denmark,[66] and Iceland.[67] An opposite view was taken by several Members, though for reasons which are far from clear. The representative of the Soviet Union spoke of "a gross violation of the indisputable rights of Egypt and other Arab States in relation to the territorial waters of the Gulf of Aqaba and the Straits of Tiran."[68] In the opinion of the delegate of Iraq "we cannot consider passage through the Gulf as different from the passage of the refugees to their own homes."[69] The representative of Colombia, in a rea-

Youssef Hammad. According to this Egyptian Circular, by "Orders dated 7th of July 1955, issued by the Minister of War and the Commander-in-Chief of the Armed Forces, the Regional Boycotting Office for Israel is appointed to be the sole authority for issuing permission to vessels to pass through the Egyptian Territorial Waters in the Gulf of Aqaba." The Circular requires notification of at least 72 hours prior to the entry of the vessel into the Gulf of Aqaba. *Ibid.* The State Department's Circular would seem to indicate that U. S. vessels need not comply with the Egyptian requirement.

[53] 666th Plenary Meeting. General Assembly, 11th Sess., Official Records, p. 1276, par. 11. The Minister added the words: ". . .in accordance with the generally accepted definition of those terms in the law of the sea." See also the statement by the Israeli representative at the 668th Meeting, March 8, 1957. *Ibid.*, p. 1325, par. 252.

[54] *Ibid.*, p. 1277, par. 33.

[55] *Ibid.*, p. 1280, pars. 58, 59.

[56] *Ibid.*, p. 1281, par. 72.

[57] *Ibid.*, 667th Meeting, p. 1284, par. 13.

[58] *Ibid.*, p. 1287, par. 51.

[59] *Ibid.*, p. 1288, pars. 56–61. The detailed reasoned statement by the representative of The Netherlands bears quoting in full: "First, inasmuch as the Gulf of Aqaba is bordered by four different States and has a width in excess of the three miles of territorial waters of the four littoral States on either side, it is, under the rules of international law, to be regarded as part of the open sea. Secondly, the Straits of Tiran consequently are, in the legal sense, straits connecting two open seas, normally used for international navigation. Thirdly, in regard to such straits, there is a right of free passage even if the straits are so narrow that they fall entirely within the territorial waters of one or more States. This rule was acknowledged by the International Court of Justice in the case of the Corfu Channel (Judgment of December 15, 1949; I.C.J. Reports 1949, p. 244) and also by the International Law Commission in its report for 1956 (A/3159). Fourthly, if a strait falls entirely within the territorial waters of one or more of the littoral States, there is still a right of innocent passage, but then the littoral States have the right, if necessary, to verify the innocent character of the passage. Fifthly, this right of verification, however, does not exist in those cases where the strait connects two parts of the open sea. It must, therefore, be concluded that all States have the right of free and unhampered passage for their vessels through the Straits of Tiran."

[60] *Ibid.*, p. 1292, par. 103.

[61] *Ibid.*, p. 1594, par. 124.

[62] *Ibid.*, p. 1296, par. 139.

[63] *Ibid.*, p. 1296, par. 148. It should be noted, however, that Canada's position was based on political rather than legal considerations, as in its view the Assembly should not attempt to determine legal rights in the Gulf and the Straits.

[64] *Ibid.*, p. 1300, par. 196. Norway's position was somewhat akin to that of Canada's in holding that the legal status of these waters "should be dealt with only by a legal body."

[65] *Ibid.*, p. 1303, par. 224.

[66] *Ibid.*, par. 234.

[67] *Ibid.*, 668th Meeting, p. 1319, par. 187.

[68] *Ibid.*, 667th Meeting, p. 1297, par. 159.

[69] *Ibid.*, p. 1294, par. 116.

soned statement weighing the "commercial right" of passage against "the right of security," argued that the latter, "that is to say, the State's right to control navigation in its territorial waters must prevail."[70] On the other hand, he also argued "that no country has the right to prevent passage if it is innocent. A country may control it, regulate it, in order to ensure that the passage is innocent; but if it is established that the passage is innocent we would consider it an abuse of right to prevent passage."[71] This raises the issue of what constitutes innocent passage, to which the representative of India devoted some remarks. He contended, first, that the Gulf of Aqaba was an "inland sea";[72] secondly, that it would "be possible for Egypt, in agreement with Saudi Arabia, to fill up the Gulf of Aqaba";[73] and thirdly, that Article 17, paragraph 4, of the International Law Commission's draft articles concerning the law of the sea, did not apply to the Gulf because it does not connect two high seas;[74] and, finally, without disputing the right of innocent passage, that

> this right of innocent passage, so-called, actually means that, first of all, one must prove innocence. Innocence depends upon the character of the party claiming the passage; it depends upon the purpose of the passage, and also upon the freight that is carried.[75]

The opinions put forward by India's representatives were not unchallenged. The United Kingdom representative pointed out that the Straits of Tiran were bordered by two countries—Egypt and Saudi Arabia—and not by Egypt alone and that the Gulf of Aqaba was surrounded by four littoral states.[76] The delegate of Italy challenged India's opinion concerning innocent passage and stated correctly, it is believed, that

> This interpretation would nullify the rule of innocent passage, since it is obvious that, if it were valid, the littoral States would no longer have the duty of justifying their refusal of passage to a vessel on specific occasions and for specific reasons; rather, it would rest with the vessel to prove that its passage was innocent.[77]

The question of what constitutes innocent passage was debated at some length at the Geneva Conference on the Law of the Sea and clarified along the lines indicated by the delegate of Italy.

[70] *Ibid.*,p. 1290, par. 78.
[71] *Ibid.*,p. 1291, par. 88. It may be noted here that the representative of Iraq fully subscribed to the statements made by the representatives of Colombia and India. *Ibid.*, p. 1293, par. 116.
[72] *Ibid.*, 665th Meeting, p. 1269, par. 49.
[73] *Ibid.*, p. 1270, par. 56. In his enthusiasm, the delegate of India overlooked the remaining littoral states, Jordan and Israel.
[74] *Ibid.*, p. 1271, par. 62.
[75] *Ibid.*, At the 667th Meeting the representative of India specifically declared that access to the Gulf through the Straits of Tiran "cannot be arranged except with Egypt's consent," inasmuch as the waters in the Straits are Egypt's territorial waters. *Ibid.*,p. 1301, par. 210. In his view, it was not within the province of the General Assembly to decide legal controversies. *Ibid.*, p. 1269, par. 48, and p. 1301, par. 209.
[76] *Ibid.*, p. 1284, par. 12.
[77] *Ibid.*, p. 1287, par. 51.

With regard to the question of belligerent rights in a state of armistice, there also emerged two positions, although the affirmative view was not pressed for obvious reasons. Though this particular issue is not directly relevant to the question of the legal status of the Gulf and the Straits, it may be useful to refer to it briefly. As on the issue of the right of passage, the United States position on belligerency was accepted by a substantial number of Members.

The position of the United States was made clear in the *Aide-Mémoire* of February 11, 1957, in which it declared that, after Israel's withdrawal, the United States "has no reason to assume that any littoral State would under these circumstances obstruct the right of free and innocent passage."[78] In stronger terms President Eisenhower stated on February 20, 1957, as follows:

> We should not assume that if Israel withdraws, Egypt will prevent Israeli shipping from using the Suez Canal or the Gulf of Aqaba. If unhappily, Egypt does hereafter violate the Armistice Agreement or other international agreements, then this should be dealt with firmly by the society of nations.[79]

The representative of the United States declared in the General Assembly:

> Once Israel has completed its withdrawal in accordance with the resolutions of the General Assembly, and in view of the measures taken by the United Nations to deal with the situation, there is no basis for either party to the Armistice Agreement to assert or exercise any belligerent rights.[80]

Several Members, including France,[81] the United Kingdom,[82] Italy,[83] New Zealand,[84] Belgium,[85] Canada,[86] and Sweden,[87] spoke in the same vein. In this context reference should be made also to the statement by the Secretary General in his Report of January 24, 1957,[88] and the resolution of the Security Council of September 1, 1951, which includes the following:

> Considering that since the armistice regime, which has been in existence for nearly two and a half years, is of a permanent character, neither party can reasonably assert that it is actively

[78] United States Policy in the Middle East Sept. 1956–June 1957, Documents, p. 291 (Dept. of State Pub. 6505).

[79] Radio and television address by President Eisenhower, Feb. 20, 1957, *Loc. cit.*, p. 307.

[80] 666th Meeting, March 1, 1957. General Assembly, 11th Sess., Official Records, Plenary, p. 1278, par. 36. *cf.* also p. 1277, par. 32.

[81] *Ibid.*, par. 60.

[82] *Ibid.*, 667th Meeting, p. 1284, par. 14.

[83] *Ibid.*, p. 1287, par. 50.

[84] *Ibid.*, p. 1292, pars. 99–101.

[85] *Ibid.*, p. 1296, par. 140. The Belgian representative based his view also on the Charter itself: "I pointed out on 1 February that each party to the Armistice Agreement must, in accordance with one of its fundamental provisions, refrain completely from any aggressive action against the people or the armed forces of the other. This is, moreover, an overriding principle of the Charter, except, of course, in the case of self-defence against armed aggression."

[86] 660th Meeting, Feb. 26, 1957. *Ibid.*, p. 1203, par. 48.

[87] 667th Meeting, March 4, 1957. *Ibid.*, p. 1303, par. 225.

[88] *Cf.* p. 1130 above.

> a belligerent or requires to exercise the right of visit, search and seizure for any legitimate purpose of self-defence.[89]

The contrary view was expounded by India. Its representative contended that the Armistice Agreement between Egypt and Israel of 1949 did not exclude belligerent or hostile action, and that the Secretary General's statement referred to above

> is based on the false conception that the exercise of sovereign rights in a sovereign territory, in territorial waters, is an act of belligerency. Such an exercise of sovereign rights would be no more an act of belligerency than if it were an act on the highways of Cairo. It would be an act of belligerency if it were committed anywhere else. Therefore, in the submission of my Government, the statement is based on that false conception.[90]

With respect to India's Government, it may be said that rarely has a new state committed itself to so ancient a view of sovereignty. An act of belligerency may be committed on the "highways of Cairo" as well as on the highways leading through the territorial waters of a strait. If it is a belligerent act, it does not lose this character by reason of the place where it is committed.

The views expressed by Members on the international character of the waters in the Gulf, the right of innocent passage through the Straits of Tiran unimpeded by any claim to exercise belligerent rights, were not embodied in a draft resolution. [91] They remained, therefore, the view of these Members and did not become the position of the United Nations. They are nonetheless significant. The failure of the General Assembly to take a position on this vital aspect of the Middle East crisis is all the more remarkable if one considers that one of the purposes of the United Nations is "to bring about by peaceful means, and in conformity with the principles of justice and international law, adjustment or settlement of international disputes or situations which might lead to a breach of the peace."[92]

## 5. THE JURIDICAL STATUS OF THE GULF OF AQABA AND THE STRAITS OF TIRAN BEFORE THE UNITED NATIONS CONFERENCE ON THE LAW OF THE SEA

The Geneva Conference succeeded in unraveling the tangled question of innocent passage through waters corresponding closely to the Straits of Tiran and the Gulf of Aqaba. In addition, it made more precise the meaning of innocent passage, of the duties and rights of the coastal state or states and the duties of foreign ships during their inno-

[89] U.N. Doc. S/2298/Rev. 1, Official Records, 558th Meeting, Sept. 1, 1951, p. 2.

[90] 665th Meeting, March 1, 1957. General Assembly, 11th Sess., Official Records, Plenary, p. 1270, par. 55. See also p. 1269, pars. 46, 47.

[91] The representative of Canada appeared to advocate the opposite course at the 660th Meeting on Feb. 26, 1957. *Ibid.*, p. 1203, pars. 41 *ff.*

[92] Art. 1, par. 1, of the Charter.

cent passage. As all these rules bear upon the particular case here under consideration, they will be briefly considered.

## a. Innocent Passage

Article 15, paragraph 3, of the International Law Commision's draft related the innocence of the passage to conduct of the ship.[93] Several amendments were proposed to clarify its meaning. A United States proposal[94] aimed at indicating "that the sole test of the innocence of a passage was whether or not it was prejudicial to the security of the coastal State."[95] It was recognized in the debate that a close link existed between the definition of innocent passage, the rights of the coastal state, and the duties of the foreign ship regulated in Articles 17 and 18 of the Commission's draft. The American proposal was opposed as "inconsistent with existing international law" on the ground it "would enable a State to claim that the actual passage of a ship was prejudicial to its security," whereas the real test of innocence was "the manner in which passage was carried out."[96] The First Committee appeared to be anxious to eliminate as far as possible any subjective tests which might restrict the traditional scope of innocent passage. It was probably for this reason that an eight-Power amendment submitted by Mexico to insert the words "or the interests" after the word "security" in the American proposal was defeated.[97] On the other hand, amendments submitted by India[98] and Turkey[99] were adopted. The American proposal as amended by India and Turkey became Article 14, paragraph 4, of the Convention on the Territorial Sea after adoption at the Twentieth Plenary Meeting,[100] and reads as follows:

> Passage is innocent so long as it is not prejudicial to the peace, good order or security of the coastal State. Such passage shall take place in conformity with these articles and with other rules of international law.[101]

[93] "Passage is innocent so long as a ship does not use the territorial sea for committing any acts prejudicial to the security of the coastal State or contrary to the present rules, or to other rules of international law." Report of the International Law Commission Covering the Work of Its Eighth Session, April 23–July 4, 1956. General Assembly, 11th Sess., Official Records, Supp. No. 9 (A/3159), p. 19 (hereinafter referred to as I.L.C. Report 1956).

[94] "Passage is innocent so long as it is not prejudicial to the security of the coastal State. Such passage shall take place in conformity with the present rules." Doc. A/Conf.13/C.1/L.28/Rev.1. U.N. Conference on the Law of the Sea, Official Records, Vol. III, First committee, p. 216.

[95] *Op. cit.*, p. 82, par. 22.

[96] Representative of Denmark, *ibid.*, p. 83, par. 27.

[97] Text of the eight-Power proposal in U.N. Conf., Official Records, Vol. III, p. 85, par. 4. For result of the vote see *ibid.*, p. 98, par. 37. The co-sponsors were: Chile, Ecuador, Haiti, Panama, Peru, Uruguay, Venezuela and Mexico. Speaking on this point, the representative of the United Kingdom "considered that any reference to the interests of the coastal State was also unacceptable, since it widened the whole concept to a degree which would make a farce of the right of innocent passage." *Ibid.*, p. 85, par. 7.

[98] The Indian representative proposed to insert after the word "prejudicial to" the words "the peace, good order or." *Ibid.*, p. 85, par. 3. For result of the vote see *ibid.*, p. 98, par. 39.

[99] The Turkish amendment proposed to add in the second sentence of the American proposal the words "and to the other rules of international law." *Ibid.*, p. 98, par. 40.

[100] *Ibid.*, par. 41, and Official Records, Vol. II, Plenary Meetings, p. 65, par. 3.

[101] U.N. Doc. A/Conf. 13/L.52, p. 6 (April 28, 1958). Official Records, Vol. II, Plenary Meetings, p. 133; also 52 A.J.I.L. 837 (1958).

After the vote in committee the representative of Israel formulated a reservation on the definition of innocent passage.[102] A drafting change, proposed originally by Burma and later supported by Saudi Arabia, was accepted in the First Committee by the representative of the United States but does not appear in the final text. Burma proposed "a positive fact" for the "negative proof" called for by the American text by substituting the words "passage is innocent unless it is prejudicial . . ." for the words "passage is innocent so long as it is not prejudicial . . ."[103] This wording would have given somewhat more emphasis to the original intent to make the passage itself rather than the ship the test of innocence. However, even without it, the text as adopted clearly puts the burden on the coastal state to show that the passage itself rather than the passage of a particular ship, its purpose or cargo, was prejudicial to the stated values of the coastal state. Thus the text rules out the concept of innocent passage propounded by India in connection with the question of passage through the Straits of Tiran and the Gulf of Aqaba.[104] It represents a stage in the struggle for a greater measure of objectivity and a corresponding reduction in the degree of subjectivity which generally characterizes the rules regarding innocent passage formulated by the International Law Commission.[105]

### b. Duties of Coastal State

Draft Article 16, paragraph 1, of the International Law Commission included a negative and a positive duty.[106] The United States proposed to strike out the latter, stated in the second sentence, on the grounds that it went beyond existing principles of international law, that it might be construed as constituting absolute liability on the part of the coastal state, and that, contrary to the view of the Commission,[107] it was not supported

[102] Official Records, Vol. III, p. 99, par. 43. He considered that in spite of certain improvements introduced by the American amendment, the text of the Commission's draft was more precise than the first sentence of the American amendment. The reservation was not repeated in the Plenary Meeting when the final text of Art. 14 was adopted. The final articles of the Convention do not provide for reservations.

[103] *Ibid.*, p. 83, par. 32, p. 85, par. 15; and Doc. A/Conf. 13/C.1/L.75, *ibid.*,p. 231. The acceptance of the Burmese drafting change by the representative of the United States is contained *ibid.*, p. 84, par. 46. There was no formal vote on the proposal.

[104] *Cf.* p. 1133 above. But see Max Sørensen, "Law of the Sea," International Conciliation, No. 520, p. 234 (Nov. 1958). *Cf.* note 179, p. 1147, below.

[105] That the Committee was concerned with this problem and was anxious to eliminate subjective judgment, although it was divided on the text best calculated to realize this objective, can be seen from the observation of the representative of the Soviet Union, who "shared the misgivings expressed by several representatives regarding the revised United States proposal, which, by referring to the passage itself as not being prejudicial to the security of the coastal State, makes a subjective interpretation of the rule possible. The text drafted by the International Law Commission was much more objective because it referred to a ship using the territorial sea for committing acts prejudicial to the security of the coastal State." Official Records, Vol. III, p. 84, par. 38. He finally voted in favor of the revised American proposal. *Ibid.*, p. 99, par. 42, In this context reference should also be made to the French amendment which introduced the concept of intent. Doc. A/Conf. 13/C.1/L.6, *ibid.*, p. 212. It was not voted upon. For observation on it by the Danish representative see *ibid.*, p. 86, par. 24; see also 3 Gidel, Le Droit International Public de la Mer 206 f.

[106] "The coastal State must not hamper innocent passage through the territorial sea. It is required to use the means at its disposal to ensure respect for innocent passage through the territorial sea, and must not allow the said sea to be used for acts contrary to the rights of other States." 1956 I.L.C. Report 19.

[107] Expressed in its commentary to Art. 16, par. 1. *Ibid.*

by the Judgment of the International Court of Justice in the *Corfu Channel* Case.[108] This proposal was adopted in Committee I,[109] and also by the Conference.[110] The first sentence of Article 16, paragraph 1, in the Commission's draft became Article 15, paragraph 1, in the Convention on the Territorial Sea.

For the purpose of this paper it is unnecessary to determine whether the adoption of the United States amendment adds to or detracts from the traditional principles. Paragraph 1 of Article 15 categorically imposes upon the coastal state the duty not to hamper innocent passage as defined in Article 14, paragraph 4. Beyond this duty the First Committee did not desire to go.[111]

### c. Rights of Protection of the Coastal State

Article 17, particularly its paragraph 1, 3 and 4 in the Commission's draft, was of greatest significance for the principle of innocent passage in general and the rights claimed by Israel in the Straits of Tiran and the Gulf of Aqaba in particular. Here, as in connection with the definition of innocent passage, several representatives were concerned to establish an objective standard and to eliminate subjective criteria as far as this is possible in a juridical text and in the present stage of the organization of the society of nations. As far as the first paragraph of Article 17 was concerned, the Committee's task was seen as establishing harmony and consistency with Article 14, paragraph 4, defining innocent passage. To this end the six-Power proposal to Article 17, paragraph 1,[112] was submitted, reading as follows:

> The coastal State may take the necessary steps in its territorial sea to prevent passage which is not innocent.[113]

This text met with some opposition[114] but was adopted in committee,[115] and in the Plenary Meeting,[116] and incorporated in Article 16, paragraph 1, of the Convention.

[108] U.N. Doc. A/Conf. 13/C.1/L.38, Official Records, Vol. III, p. 220. The United States referred particularly to the Court's *dicta* on p. 22 of the Judgment, [1949] I.C.J. Rep. 4.

[109] Official Records, Vol. III, p. 115, par. 10. The First Committee did not adopt the joint proposal of Bulgaria and the U.S.S.R., which elaborated the second sentence and excluded warships from its scope. Doc. A/Conf. 13/C.1/L.46, *ibid.*, p. 223, and p. 115, par. 9. The United Kingdom proposed to delete the second part of the second sentence beginning with "and." Doc. A/Conf. 13/C.1/L.37, *ibid.*, p. 218. In view of the adoption of the U. S. proposal, the British proposal was not put to the vote. *Ibid.*, p. 115, par. 11.

[110] Official Records, Vol. II, Plenary Meetings, p. 65, par. 3.

[111] And consequently it rejected the Yugoslav proposal, which required the coastal state "to take the steps which are necessary for the safety of navigation." U.N. Doc. A/Conf.13/C.1/L.16, *ibid.*, p. 213, p. 114, par. 7, and p. 115, par. 12.

[112] "The coastal State may take the necessary steps in its territorial sea to protect itself against any act prejudicial to its security or to such other of its interests as it is authorized to protect under the present rules and other rules of international law." 1956 I.L.C. Report 19.

[113] U.N. Doc. A/Conf. 13/C.1/L.72; Official Records, Vol. III, p. 231. The sponsors were: Greece, Netherlands, Portugal, United Kingdom, United States, and Yugoslavia.

[114] Thus the Soviet and Mexican representatives favored the text formulated by the Commission. Official Records, Vol. III, p. 96, par. 8, and p. 99, pars. 6–9.

[115] *Ibid.*, p. 100, par. 16.

[116] *Ibid.*, Vol. II, Plenary Meetings, p. 65, par. 7.

Article 17, paragraph 2, of the Commission's Draft presented no difficulty and, as adopted, became Article 16, paragraph 2, of the Convention.[117]

Paragraph 3 of Article 17 as submitted by the Commission[118] met with substantial criticism. Here clearly the Commission proposed a subjective test, namely, the untrammeled opinion of the coastal state as sole condition for suspending the right of innocent passage. Amendments were introduced by several delegations "to make the condition in the first sentence more objective"[119] and to foreclose discrimination between different flags.[120] The Netherlands delegate, in introducing the four-Power amendment to Article 17, paragraph 3, emphasized also that the proposed text was intended to incorporate the tenor of the Commission's commentary to that paragraph[121]and thus to render it more objective.[122] In the opposing view, the Commission's text merely indicated who was to take the decision, and that

> Given the absence of an independent organ which could arbitrate in the matter of the application of an objective rule, the only practical possibility was to maintain a subjective criterion as contained in the International Law Commission's draft. The coastal State should certainly substantiate any action it might take, but it undoubtedly had the right to initiate action at its own discretion.[123]

This view was shared by the delegates of the Soviet Union[124] and India. The latter delegate, arguing the unavoidability of subjective discretion, stated:

> That did not, however, mean that the coastal State could act with impunity, for suspension of the right of passage would be *bona fide* only if ordered for the reasons given in paragraph 3, and the burden of proof would rest on the State alleging that such action was not *bona fide*.[125]

[117] The text of Art. 16, par. 2, is as follows: "In the case of ships proceeding to internal waters, the coastal State shall also have the right to take the necessary steps to prevent any breach of the conditions to which the admission of those ships to those waters is subject." For the votes see Official Records, Vol. III, p. 100, par. 17, and *ibid.*, Plenary Meetings, p. 65, par. 7.

[118] "The coastal State may suspend temporarily in definite areas of its territorial sea the exercise of the right of passage if it should deem such suspension essential for the protection of the rights referred to in paragraph 1. Should it take such action, it is bound to give due publicity to the suspension."

[119] Official Records, Vol. III, p. 79, par. 7, observations by the British delegate.

[120] *Ibid.*, par. 6, observation by the Greek delegate.

[121] The delegate probably had this comment in mind: "In exceptional cases a temporary suspension of the right of passage is permissible if compelling reasons connected with general security require it." I.L.C. Report, 1956, p. 20. The words "if compelling reasons . . . require it," imply a measure of accountability which is totally absent in the Commission's draft. See also the Netherlands delegate's observations in Official Records, Vol. III, p. 94, par. 17.

[122] *Ibid.*, p. 88, par. 15. The text of the proposal sponsored by the four Powers (Netherlands, Portugal, U.K., U.S.A.) is as follows: "Subject to the provisions of paragraph 4, the coastal State may suspend temporarily in specified areas of its territorial sea the innocent passage of foreign ships if such suspension is essential for the protection of its security. Such suspension shall take effect only after having been duly published." U.N. Doc. A/Conf. 13/C.1/L.70; Official Records, Vol. III, p. 230.

[123] Observation by the Indonesian delegate, *ibid.*, p. 94, pars. 18 and 19.

[124] *Ibid.*, p. 94, par. 29.

[125] *Ibid.*, p. 96, par. 3.

The Indian delegate clearly indicated the strength of the coastal state and the weakness of the state claiming innocent passage which was implied in the Commission's draft. The four-Power proposal was intended to restore a balance between the two interests involved. As the delegate of the United States pointed out, this proposal had been made "to ensure that a coastal State had the right to enforce its own regulations, but the doctrine of innocent passage must never be allowed to depend on the caprice of such a State."[126] The delegate of the United Kingdom "considered that it would be wrong to leave a coastal State to judge when and in what circumstances it should deem the suspension of innocent passage essential."[127] The four-Power proposal, as amended by Greece,[128] was adopted in the First Committee by a narrow margin,[129] and in the Plenary Meeting the whole Article 17 was adopted by a very large majority,[130] and became paragraph 3 of Article 16 of the Convention.

Paragraph 4 of the Commission's Article 17 was subjected to careful scrutiny and substantial changes.[131] It will be recalled that this provision was the subject of some debate in the Commission in connection with Israel's comment thereon and in the General Assembly in connection with Israel's claim that the passage through the Straits of Tiran and the Gulf of Aqaba was not subject to suspension by the coastal state or states concerned.[132] The decision of the Conference to adopt the four-Power amendment to paragraph 3 beginning with the words "subject to the provision of paragraph 4 . . ." had already settled a point, namely, that the right of suspension was further limited by the rule to be laid down in paragraph 4. This would have been so in any event, but the inclusion of these words made the point even clearer. With reference to paragraph 4 the debate centered on two main aspects of the Commission's draft: its inclusion of the word "normally" and its omission of a rule governing access to a port through straits forming part of the territorial sea of one or more states.

The United States proposed to eliminate the word "normally" on the ground that the Judgment of the International Court of Justice in the *Corfu Channel* Case, the acknowledged basis of paragraph 4 of Article 17, did not use this qualifying term.[133] The retention of "normally" was urged by the delegate of Saudi Arabia on the ground that "the right of innocent passage could be exercised only in recognized international seaways."[134] The delegate of Portugal, while supporting its omission, would bow to the

[126] *Ibid.*, p. 95, par. 33.

[127] *Ibid.*, p. 95, par. 38.

[128] The Greek proposal was to insert after the word "may" and before the word "suspend" the words "without discrimination among foreign ships." U.N. Doc. A/Conf. 13/C.1/L.31; Official Records, Vol. III, p. 93, par. 4, and p. 100, par. 18.

[129] The vote was 31 for, 27 against, with 5 abstentions. *Ibid.*, p. 100, par. 20.

[130] *Ibid.*, Vol. II, Plenary Meetings, p. 65, par. 7. The vote was 62 for, 1 against, with 9 abstentions.

[131] Its text is as follows: "There must be no suspension of the innocent passage of foreign ships through straits normally used for international navigation between two parts of the high seas."

[132] See p. 1127 above.

[133] U.N. Doc. A/Conf. 13/C.1/L.39; Official Records, Vol. III, p. 220. It was also dropped in the Netherlands proposal, Doc. A/Conf. 13/C.1/L.51, *ibid.*,p. 224. See comment by the Netherlands representative, *ibid.*, p. 79, par. 15, and the three-Power (Netherlands, Portugal, United Kingdom) proposal, Doc. A/Conf. 13/C.1/L.71, *ibid.*, p. 231.

[134] *Ibid.*, p. 94, par. 23; see also his remarks, p. 93, par. 9.

majority.[135] The delegate of the Soviet Union deemed the word "very important" and favored its retention.[136] Defending the American proposal, Mr. Dean recalled that "the Commission had not taken a vote on the insertion of the word 'normally,' which had been proposed by the USSR member at the Commission's seventh session and accepted without discussion. He therefore considered that the Committee was free to delete or retain the word in question."[137] The British delegate, supporting the deletion, pointed out that "it was vague, and might well become a future source of argument, friction and dispute between nations as to what was or was not the 'normal' use of a particular strait."[138] The decision of the Committee and the Conference was to drop the qualifying word "normally," as it was omitted from the three-Power proposal to paragraph 4 which was adopted by the Committee and the Conference. The suppression of "normally" was certainly justified in terms of the *Corfu Channel* Judgment. Whether it is likely to make much difference in practice only the future will show. For it can be contended with a degree of persuasiveness that some such qualifying concept is inherent in the phrase used by the Court, the Commission and the Conference: "straits which are *used* for international navigation . . ." In other words, the prohibition of suspension applies only to straits which are "used . . ." When or which straits are used? Does the answer depend upon the density of the traffic,[139] the habitual choice of a strait by a particular flag, the location of a recognized route or some such criterion or a combination of several criteria? It may also be noted that the word "international" qualifies navigation and is itself not free of ambiguity.[140]

The question of securing access to a port appears to have been raised first by the Netherlands delegate saying:

> His delegation was convinced that the only just solution of the regime of gulfs, bays and estuaries bordered by two or more States was to proclaim the principle of the free access of foreign ships to every port situated on their coasts, whether the water area in question included a central part which must be regarded as the high seas, or as being placed under the undivided co-sovereignty of the coastal States, or whether it was divided up into distinct territorial maritime zones.[141]

[135] *Ibid.*, p. 94, par. 27.
[136] *Ibid.*, p. 94, par. 30.
[137] *Ibid.*, p. 95, par. 31.
[138] *Ibid.*, p. 95, par. 36. This argument was rejected by the delegate of Saudi Arabia, who recalled that the term "normally" had been used in several international instruments, and had been specifically included in the Convention and Statute on the International Régime of Maritime Ports, adopted at Geneva in 1923, to remove any doubts and ambiguity. *Ibid.*, p. 96, par. 5.
[139] See Arthur H. Dean, "The Geneva Conference on the Law of the Sea: What Was Accomplished," 52 A.J.I.L. 607–629, at 623 (1958).
[140] The Saudi Arabian delegate's point is borne out by the fact that the Geneva Convention used the word "normally" in spite of its vagueness. Thus in the Convention on the Territorial Sea, Art. 3 speaks of "normal" baselines and Art. 9 of roadsteads which are "normally" used. The Convention on the Continental Shelf states in Art. 5, par. 8, that the coastal state shall not "normally" withhold its consent.
[141] 6th Meeting, March 6, 1958, Official Records, Vol. III, p. 11, par. 13. At the preceding meeting, March 5, 1958, the British delegate observed in connection with the right of innocent passage through international straits: "In his delegation's view, no established and customary right of passage or access could be done away with by the unilateral action of any of the neighboring coastal States." *Ibid.*, p. 9, par. 33.

Amendments introduced by the British and Netherlands delegations to Article 17, paragraph 4, were intended to make this objective clear.[142] The British delegate, commenting upon the amendments, declared:

> Their object was to ensure that passage was not impeded in waters which were essential to maritime communications. The main purpose of any maritime voyage was, after all, to arrive at the port of destination.[143]

The Netherlands amendment had a similar purpose, namely,

> to stress that ships should always be authorized to traverse the territorial sea for the purpose of entering a port.[144]

At the suggestion of the Chairman of the First Committee, proposals by different delegations relating to "the same questions of principle"[145] were consolidated into a single text. The resulting three-Power proposal included the words "straits or other sealanes" from the Portuguese, and the words "or the territorial waters of a foreign State" from the Netherlands, amendments.[146] The United States decided to support this text.[147] In presenting it to the Committee the Netherlands delegate declared that

> it was insufficient to declare the high seas open to traffic without also guaranteeing the right of entry into seaports. If the right of access to ports was to be assured to landlocked States, *a fortiori,* should it be guaranteed to the maritime countries.[148]

The use of the term "sealanes" was supported by some delegations[149] and opposed by others.[150] Its use was defended by the Netherlands delegate on the ground that, although it had no special juridical significance,

[142] The British proposed to add the words "or waters constituting the sole means of access to a port." U.N. Doc. A/Conf. 13/C.1/L.37, March 25, 1958; Official Records, Vol. III, p. 218. The Netherlands proposed a new text for Art. 17, par. 3 of which read: "There shall be no suspension of the innocent passage of foreign ships through sealanes which are used for international navigation between a part of the high seas and another part of the high seas or the territorial waters of a foreign State." U.N. Doc. A/Conf. 13/C.1/L.51, March 25, 1958; Official Records, Vol. III, p. 224. It may be noted that Portugal suggested that Art. 17, par. 4, be modified to read: "through straits and sea lanes . . ." U.N. Doc. A/Conf. 13/C.1/L.47, March 25, 1958; Official Records, Vol. III, p. 223.

[143] Official Records, Vol. III, p. 79, par. 12.

[144] *Ibid.,* p. 79, par. 15.

[145] *Ibid.,* p. 80, par. 21.

[146] U.N. Doc. A/Conf. 13/C.1/L.71, March 28, 1958; Official Records, Vol. III, p. 231. This text was sponsored by The Netherlands, the United Kingdom and Portugal. The words in the British proposal were dropped. *Ibid.,* p. 93, par. 11.

[147] *Ibid.,* par. 5.

[148] *Ibid.,* p. 88, par. 16.

[149] See the Danish delegate's observation that he would support the text "on the understanding that it referred to straits only in so far as they constituted sealanes." *Ibid.,* p. 93, par. 7.

[150] Thus the delegate of Saudi Arabia declared that "so far as he knew, the word did not constitute a legal term, and was not defined by any writer on international law." *Ibid.,* p. 93, par. 9, and p. 94, par. 22. See also the remark by the Soviet delegate, *ibid.,* p. 94, par. 30.

> it was a term that would be easily understood by all concerned with international navigation. The term "straits" was much too narrow, because there were sea-lanes used for international navigation elsewhere than in straits.[151]

However, the reference to sea lanes was deleted and, following a proposal by the Indonesian delegate, the words "territorial waters" were replaced by "territorial sea."[152]

The fundamental part of the three-Power proposal, with which the United States had associated itself, was strongly criticized by the delegate of Saudi Arabia. He opposed it on two grounds: first, on the ground that whereas international law provided for the right of innocent passage through straits linking two parts of the high seas, "it did not provide for such a right in the case of straits linking the open sea with an internal sea or with the territorial sea of a particular State."[153] He appeared to base this position on the Judgment of the International Court of Justice in the *Corfu Channel* Case,[154] which he accepted. According to that decision he urged

> the right of innocent passage could be exercised in straits linking two areas of the high seas, but not in those linking a part of the high seas with the territorial waters of a State.[155]

It may be noted that this represents an attempt to use a judgment of the Court as authority for both what it decides, which is the usual case, and for what it does not decide, which is a most unusual case. Clearly the Court, in the Corfu Channel dispute, was not concerned with the situation envisioned in the three-Power proposal.

The second ground for the Saudi Arabian objection was that

> in his opinion the amended text no longer dealt with general principles of international law, but had been carefully tailored to promote the claims of one State. His delegation would be unable to support a text that covered only one specific case.[156]

This contention does not appear to be borne out by the published record of the discussion in the Committee. On the contrary, in the view of the three Powers proposing the amendment, as stated by the Netherlands representative,

> the addition of the words "or the territorial waters of a foreign State" reflected existing usage safeguarding the right to use straits linking the high seas with the territorial sea of a State.[157]

[151] *Ibid.*, p. 94, par. 16.

[152] *Ibid.*, p. 93, par. 14, and p. 96, par. 7. It may be noted that the term "sea lanes" appears in Art. 5, par. 6, of the Convention on the Continental Shelf adopted by the Conference. U.N. Doc. A/Conf. 13/L.55.

[153] *Ibid.*, p. 93, par. 9.

[154] [1949] I.C.J. Rep. 4.

[155] Official Records, Vol. III, p. 96, par. 4.

[156] *Ibid.*, p. 96, par. 6. He also declared that "his government's participation in the final act of the Conference would be conditional, among other things, on the rejection of the amendments to Article 17 at present before the Committee." *Ibid.*, p. 94, p. 25.

[157] *Ibid.*, p. 94, par. 16.

On the other hand, clearly the affirmation of this principle by the Conference gave strong support to one particular controversial case, namely, the right of passage through the Straits of Tiran and the Gulf of Aqaba to the Israeli port of Elath. The committee adopted the three-Power proposal, with the amendments already indicated, by a roll-call vote of 31 votes to 30, with 10 abstentions.[158] In the Plenary Meeting, the delegate of the United Arab Republic asked for a separate vote on paragraph 4 of Article 17. This was opposed by the delegate of Denmark on the ground that

> the principle of freedom of navigation was indivisible, and when vessels crossed a portion of the high seas on their way to a port, it was irrelevant whether or not they had to pass through the territorial sea of another State. The effect of a separate vote would be to discriminate between ships passing through the territorial sea of a State other than their flag State on their way from one part of the high seas to another, and ships passing through the same territorial seas on their way from a portion of the high seas to the territorial sea of a third State. The coastal State would be under an equal obligation to respect the right of innocent passage in both cases.[159]

The motion for a separate vote on the paragraph was defeated by 34 votes to 32, with 6 abstentions, and the whole Article 17 was then adopted by 62 votes to 1, with 9 abstentions.[160]

As adopted by the Conference, Article 17, paragraph 4, became Article 16, paragraph 4, and reads:

> There shall be no suspension of the innocent passage of foreign ships through straits which are used for international navigation between one part of the high seas and another part of the high seas or the territorial sea of a foreign State.[161]

Whatever may have been the motives which prompted the three-Power proposal,[162] it is clear that, rather than deal with the broad problem of bays or gulfs the coasts of which were under the sovereignty of several states, the Conference concentrated on the specific problem of the nature and extent of the right of innocent passage. In doing so it filled a gap left by the International Law Commission, and the solution which it adopted did not follow the direction indicated by the commission in its comment to Article 17, paragraph 4, relating to the particular question raised by Israel. The Conference showed

[158] *Ibid.*, p. 100, par. 21.

[159] Official Records, Vol. II, Plenary Meetings, p. 65, par. 5. He went on to justify this position by reference to Denmark's practice: "Part of the Danish coast bordered an international strait joining two parts of the high seas, and for more than one hundred years his country had maintained freedom of navigation through that strait in the interest of international trade. Such an obligation as that which his country had assumed should be counterbalanced by corresponding rights in other parts of the world, and Denmark accordingly expected that there would be free passage for its ships through straits in the territorial seas of other States." *Ibid.*, par. 6.

[160] *Ibid.*, p. 65, par. 7. In explaining his abstention, the delegate of Saudi Arabia reiterated his argument that par. 4 "had been drafted with one particular case in view," and concluded: "Saudi Arabia would take the necessary steps to protect its national interests against the interpretation and application of paragraph 4." *Ibid.*, par. 8.

[161] U.N. Doc. A/Conf. 13/L.52; Official Records, Vol. II, Plenary Meetings, p. 134.

[162] It may be noted that the question of the Gulf of Aqaba was injected into the deliberation of the First committee at their very outset by the delegate of Saudi Arabia, who claimed that this gulf "came under exclusive Arab jurisdiction." *Ibid.*, Vol. III, 3rd Meeting, March 4, 1958, p. 3, par. 30.

concern for ensuring the right of innocent passage in all conceivable situations and, while mindful of the interest of the coastal states, for protecting its character as an independent right not subordinate to any claim of sovereignty on the part of coastal states.[163] In proceeding along this line and also in insisting on objective criteria for both the right of innocent passage and the right of protection of the coastal states, the Conference corrected in some measure the overly exclusive concern of the Commission with the latter.

### d. Duties of Ships during Innocent Passage

Article 18, the last clause in the International Law Commission's draft devoted to an aspect of innocent passage, reads as follows:

> Foreign ships exercising the right of passage shall comply with the laws and regulations enacted by the coastal State in conformity with the present rules and other rules of international law and, in particular, with the laws and regulations relating to transport and navigation.[164]

Here, as in the case of other provisions bearing on the right of innocent passage, the aim was to ensure the application of objective standards. The Commission's draft contained that standard in providing, in substance, that the national laws and regulations shall be "in conformity with the present rules and other rules of international law." In the battle of amendments in the First Committee the lines were drawn between those who supported the international standard and the supporters of the national standard, that is, between those who favored the supremacy of international law and those advocating the primacy of municipal law. In short, the old contest respecting the treatment of foreigners was re-enacted with reference to innocent passage. The protagonist of national treatment was Mexico. It submitted a proposal in which the international standard was transposed from the laws enacted by the coastal state to the duty of foreign ships to observe them.[165] Explaining this proposal, the delegate of Mexico pointed out that

> there was no doubt in his delegation's view that the words "in conformity with the present rules and other rules of international law" should apply to the exercise of the right of passage by foreign ships, and not to the enactment of laws and regulations by the coastal State.[166]

He also argued that

[163] *Cf.* the observations of the delegates of The Netherlands, the United States and the United Kingdom, *ibid.*, p. 9, par. 33; p. 94, par. 15; p. 95, pars. 33 and 37.

[164] 1956 I.L.C. Report 20.

[165] The Mexican proposal for a new text of Art. 18 was worded as follows: "Foreign ships exercising the right of passage shall comply, in conformity with the present rules and other rules of international law, with the laws and regulations enacted by the coastal State, and, in particular, with those relating to transport and navigation." U. N. Doc. A/Conf. 13/C.1/L.45; Official Records, Vol. III, p. 222.

[166] *Ibid*, p. 96, par. 15.

> the obligation on coastal States to comply with rules of international law in enacting domestic laws and regulations was clearly expressed in Article 1, paragraph 2, and in Article 17, paragraph 1, of the Commission's draft.[167]

The principal argument against the Mexican proposal was the six-Power proposal, which consolidated various individual amendments and which differed only slightly from the Commission's text.[168] Commenting upon these two texts, the British delegate said that their essence

> was that foreign ships must comply with laws and regulations enacted by the coastal State, subject to the one proviso that such legislation was in conformity with the present and other rules of international law. If that proviso were omitted, there would be no limitation whatsoever on the laws which the coastal State could enact. The Mexican amendment, far from making the enactment of laws and regulations by the coastal State subject to their conformity with the rules of international law, contained a quite different proposal: that the qualification should apply exclusively to ships exercising their right of passage.[169]

In proceeding to vote on the different proposals the Committee maneuvered itself into a procedural *cul-de-sac,* the result of which was that there remained no text for Article 18 before the Committee. The Committee first adopted the Mexican amendment by 33 votes to 30, with 10 abstentions.[170] Thereupon five delegations withdrew their support from the six-Power proposal,[171] which the Chairman declared to have been rejected, in any event, as the result of the adoption of the Mexican amendment.[172] The Committee then adopted one part of a joint amendment submitted by Greece and The Netherlands and rejected another.[173] After a procedural discussion in which the incompatibility of the two adopted proposals was stressed, the Committee rejected both by 34 votes to 28, with 10 abstentions.[174] A graceful retreat by the Chairman enabled the Committee to adopt, by 59 votes to none, with 3 abstentions, the original text of the International Law Commission.[175] This text, with a consequential change ("in conformity with these articles" in place of "the present rules"''and the insertion of the word "innocent" in the phrase "right of passage" suggested by the Drafting Committee,[176] was adopted by the Confer-

[167] *Ibid.,* p. 97, par. 16.

[168] U.N. Doc. A/Conf. 13/C.1/L.72; Official Records, Vol. III, p. 231. It ran as follows: "1. Foreign ships exercising the right of passage shall comply with the laws and regulations made and published by the coastal State in conformity with the present rules and other rules of international law. 2. The Coastal State has the right to take in its territorial sea the necessary steps in order to prevent infringements of the laws and regulations mentioned in paragraph 1, and to ensure the enforcement of such laws and regulations." See also *ibid.,* p. 96, par. 13. The sponsoring Powers were: Greece, Netherlands, Portugal, United Kingdom, United States, and Yugoslavia.

[169] *Ibid.,* p. 97, par. 18.

[170] *Ibid.,* p. 101, par. 27.

[171] *Ibid.,* p. 101, par. 28. Yugoslavia apparently remained the sole supporter.

[172] *Ibid.,* p. 101, par. 31.

[173] U.N. Doc. A/Conf. 13/C.1/L.32; Official Records, Vol. III, p. 217. The Committee adopted the words: "The coastal State may not, however, apply these rules or regulations in such a manner as to discriminate between foreign vessels of different nationalities," and rejected the words "nor, save in matters relating to fishing and shooting, between national vessels and foreign vessels." *Ibid.,* p. 101, pars. 34, 35.

[174] *Ibid.,* p. 102, par. 16.

[175] *Ibid.,* p. 109, par. 57.

[176] *Ibid.,* p. 256.

ence by 72 votes to none, with 2 abstentions, and became Article 17 of the Convention.[177] This completed the Conference's work on innocent passage. There can be little doubt that, in preferring the Commission's text rather than the Mexican proposal, the Conference scored a point in favor of the international standard as against the national-treatment principle. Whether the text of Article 17 will obviate disputes relating to the applicable national enactments and their conformity with the Convention and customary international law remains to be seen. In particular it remains to be seen whether the right to enforce these enactments, implicitly recognized in Article 17, includes the right to prevent a ship from passing through the territorial Sea.[178] It would seem that the Conference's solution leaves room for supplementary regulation by bilateral or multilateral instruments.

## 6. CONCLUSIONS

There is obviously room for differing evaluations of the work of the Conference discussed above and in particular of its contribution to the solution of the question of passage through the Straits of Tiran and the Gulf of Aqaba. The intent of the Conference to reduce the element of subjectivism and to provide a better balance between the interests involved—security on the one side and freedom of navigation on the other—will probably meet with general approval. The large majorities in favor of the several articles are indicative of it. Whether the Conference actually succeeded in translating this intent into the articles dealing with vital aspects of innocent passage is debatable.[179]

Concerning the specific problem of passage through the Straits of Tiran and the Gulf of Aqaba, the contribution of the Conference is significant. The Conference, in Article 16, paragraph 4, decidedly gave its support to the point of view of all those governments which have taken their stand on the right of transit through the Straits and the Gulf. The reproach of the Arab states that the Conference was concerned with this specific problem, though approaching it through a general formula, seems to be well founded.[180] However, it is still a question whether the Conference adopted a rule the validity of which depends upon ratification of the Convention, or whether it merely confirmed an existing principle the validity of which is independent of acceptance of the Convention. The Conference received from the United Nations General Assembly the broad mandate to examine the law of the sea, "taking account not only of the legal, but

[177] Official Records, Vol. II, Plenary Meetings. pp. 65 and 134.

[178] *Cf.* Max Sorensen, "Law of the Sea," International Conciliation, No. 520, p. 234 (Nov. 1958). He apparently assumes that "the coastal State is authorized to *enforce* its laws and regulations on foreign ships passing through its territorial sea, but is not allowed to prevent a ship from passing through merely on the ground of a violation of such laws or regulations."

[179] Thus Sørensen argues that Art. 14, par. 4, far from restricting, "now extends the rights of the coastal State and allows it to interfere with passage on such grounds as the nature of the cargo and its ultimate destination—provided, of course, that such factors are genuinely of a character to prejudice the security of the coastal State in the specific case." *Ibid.* This view, if correct, would go a long way towards nullifying the right of innocent passage.

[180] See Sorensen, *loc. cit.*, p. 236.

also of the technical, biological, economic and political aspects of the problem."[181] The Conference does not seem to have come to any conclusion as to whether its work was primarily codificatory or in the nature of progressive development, although it debated this matter in connection with the number of ratifications to govern the entry into force of the conventions, and the inclusion of denunciatory clauses or reservations.[182] The Convention on the Territorial Sea does not state, as does the Convention on the High Seas, that it codifies the pertinent rules of international law and that its provisions are "generally declaratory of established principles of international law."[183] On the other hand, it contains no provision regarding reservations, as do the Conventions on Fishing and the Continental Shelf.[184]

With respect to the last part of Article 16, paragraph 4, however, it has been said that the Conference "adopted a new rule which clearly applied to the Israeli-Arab controversy," and that "the result reached was in accord with the general position of the United States" as laid down in the *Aide-Mémoire* of February 11, 1957.[185] This might be taken to mean that, unless ratified, that rule would not be binding, On the other hand, the debates at the Conference would seem to give substance to the view that the rule was part of international law. This evidentiary value is significant.[186] The latter view would certainly correspond quite closely to the position taken by the Members of the United Nations in the General Assembly in favor of the right of passage through the Straits and the Gulf as a right based upon existing international law.

There is a difference between their position, however, and the rule of Article 16, paragraph 4. Whereas the Members urged freedom of passage on the basis that the Gulf "comprehends international waters and that no nation has the right to prevent free and innocent passage in the Gulf and through the Straits giving access thereto,"[187] thus resting their claim essentially on the *Corfu Channel* Judgment, the Geneva Conference, while retaining this, added the further principle that there shall be "no suspension of the innocent passage of foreign ships through straits which are used for international navigation between one part of the high seas and . . . the territorial sea of a foreign State." This is a simpler way to the same port. It has the advantage which, particularly in the case of the Gulf of Aqaba, should not be overlooked, of rendering unnecessary proof of the affirmation or fact that the Gulf "comprehends international waters," about which there was some uncertainly in the International Law Commission.[188]

Should exception be taken to the validity of the principle formulated by the Geneva

[181] Res. 1105 (XI), Feb. 21, 1957; Official Records, Vol. II, Plenary Meetings, p. xi.

[182] *Ibid,* Plenary Meetings, pp. 26, 27, 52, 56, 57, 58, 59, 60.

[183] *Ibid.*, p. 135.

[184] *Cf.* Art. 19 of the former and Art. 12 of the latter. *Ibid.*, pp. 141, 143.

[185] Arthur H. Dean, "The Geneva Conference on the Law of the Sea: What Was Accomplished," 52 A.J.I.L. 607–629, at 623 (1958). For the Aide-Mémoire, see p. 1131 above.

[186] Philip C. Jessup, "The Geneva Conference on the Law of the Sea: A Study in International Law-Making," 52 A.J.I.L. 730–733, at 732 (1958): "The debates in the Conference would naturally contribute further evidence of what states consider to be 'a general practice accepted as law'."

[187] *Cf.* U.S. Aide-Mémoire, p. 1131 above.

[188] *Cf.* p. 1127 above.

Conference, then the right of passage would rest, as it did before, solidly on the fact that the Straits of Tiran connect with a gulf or bay the coasts of which are under the sovereignty of several states. Such gulfs or bays have traditionally had the character of open seas, and under international law, if not under the holding in the *Corfu Channel* Case, there is a right of innocent passage through such straits to such bays or gulfs.[189]

[189] Gidel, note 49 above, at p. 601, affirms the right of innocent passage to the different littoral states situated on a bay. Concerning passage through straits connecting with such a bay, he says: "À partir du moment où plusieurs riverains se partagent les côtes de cette mer, celui qui détient l'entrée a, en vertu du droit international, et à moins de limitation de régimes conventionnels spéciaux, l'obligation de laisser les Etats tiers passer par cette entrée. Il parait devoir en être de même dans le cas d'une baie . . . On ne doit pas facilement présumer pour des espaces maritimes la condition d'eaux 'intérieures,' puisque le passage inoffensif peut n'y être pas accordé par l'Etat riverain." *Ibid.* at 603. See also the statement by the delegate of The Netherlands, p. 1141 above.

# PASSAGE THROUGH THE STRAIT OF TIRAN AND IN THE GULF OF AQABA

## INTRODUCTION

The crisis in the Middle East which opened on May 18, 1967, with the request from the Government of the United Arab Republic to the Secretary-General of the United Nations to withdraw the United Nations Emergency Force (UNEF) "from the territory of the United Arab Republic and Gaza Strip,"[1] and which was decisively aggravated by the announcement of the President of the Republic on May 22, 1967 that "the United Arab Republic had decided to prevent Israeli ships and other ships carrying strategic cargoes to Israel, from passing through the mouth of the Gulf of Aqaba"[2] was brought under control by the unanimous adoption on November 22, 1967 in the Security Council of Resolution 242.[3] This resolution contains at least two principles which are directly relevant to the question here under consideration. According to the first, the Council affirmed that the establishment of a just and lasting peace in the Middle East requires the application of the principle:

> Termination of all claims or states of belligerency and respect for and acknowledgment of the sovereignty, territorial integrity and political independence of every State in the area and their right to live in peace within secure and recognized boundaries free from threats of act of force.

[1] Special Report of the Secretary-General, U.N. Doc. A/6669, at 1 (1967).
[2] N.Y. Times, May 23, 1967, at 1, col. 8.
[3] S.C. Res. 242 (1967). *See* full text in Rosenne. The Middle East Crisis: Test of International Law. In *Law & Contemporary Problems.* School of Law. Duke University, Vol. XXXIII, 1968, pp. 44–68, at 56.

In the second principle the Council affirmed the necessity "[f]or guaranteeing freedom of navigation through international waterways in the area."

A settlement implementing these two principles will have to include the controversies which were aired once again in the Security Council prior to the outbreak of hostilities on June 5, 1967 and in the Fifth Emergency Special Session which followed their termination. These controversies related to the status in international law of the Gulf of Aqaba, the status of Israel as a coastal state in the Gulf, the right of innocent passage through the Strait of Tiran and, of course, the right claimed by the United Arab Republic to exercise belligerent rights in the Strait and Gulf. These problems will now be considered in that order.

## I. STATUS OF GULF OF AQABA IN INTERNATIONAL LAW

Since 1957 the Gulf has been claimed by various governments and writers as an historic gulf or bay under exclusive Arab domination, more precisely the domination of the three Arab coastal states: the United Arab Republic, Jordan and Saudi Arabia. The position was first formulated by Saudi Arabia,[4] and was restated by the representative of the United Arab Republic in the Security Council on May 29, 1967.[5] What is involved is a mixed question of fact and law. By its configuration the Gulf of Aqaba has some similarity to the Gulf of Fonseca, which is usually relied upon as an analogue and precedent. It is about 100 miles long, the width varies from seven to fifteen miles, and it is connected with the Red Sea through the narrow Straits of Tiran, about nine miles wide. In the Fonseca case the Central American Court of Justice established three criteria in support of the historic character of the Gulf: first, immemorial possession, secondly, *animus domini* and thirdly, acquiescence by other nations.[6] The Gulf of Aqaba meets none of these requirements.[7] The Gulf has been said to have been Arab in character from 700 to 1517. It was under Ottoman control from 1517 to 1918, and since then it has been bounded by two littoral states and the British Mandate of Palestine, out of which Jordan and the state of Israel arose.[8] There is no evidence of an *animus domini* on the part of the Ottoman Empire. Even if it is assumed that all four present littoral states succeeded to the Ottoman Empire, they succeeded to no verifiable claim or right.[9]

What evidence there is points in the opposite direction. Up to 1917 the Gulf of Aqaba seems to have been a backwater rather than an historic bay. Since that time British

[4] U.N. Doc. A/3575 (1957).

[5] U.N. Doc. S/PV.1343, at 31–42 (1967).

[6] Judgment of March 9, 1917, The Republic of El Salvador v. The Republic of Nicaragua, 11 AM. J. INT'L L. 674, 705 (1917).

[7] *But see* Hammad, *The Right of Passage in the Gulf of Aqaba*, 15 REVUE EGYPTIENNE DE DROIT INTERNATIONAL 118, 132 (1959), who finds that "in considering the legal status of the Gulf of Aqaba the analogy of the case of the Gulf of Fonseca is reasonable and logical." For a recent study of the subject, see H. SULTAN, LE PROBLEME DU GOLFE D'AKABA (Institut de Récherche et Études Arabologiques, Cairo, 1967).

[8] Selak, *A Consideration of the Legal Status of the Gulf of Aqaba*, 52 AM. J. INT'L L. 660, 692 (1958).

[9] Gross, *The Geneva Conference on the Law of the Sea and the Right of Innocent Passage Through the Gulf of Aqaba*, 53 AM. J. INT'L L. 564, 569 (1959). *Supra*, pp. 1119–1149, at 1119 and 1124.

ships began to sail through the Gulf, joined by Scandinavian, German and others; ships of Arab states seem to have been rare users of the Gulf.[10] In view of this, the proposition that "foreign Powers probably were not interested in navigation in the Gulf, since it apparently had no commercial importance to them"[11] seems without foundation. Whatever trade existed was "foreign, rather than local."[12] Similarly, the view that because the Gulf is used for pilgrimages to Mecca it "enjoys a specific character that justifies the claim to be regarded as historical bay"[13] is hardly persuasive. Moreover, some of the pilgrims seem to travel on non-Arab ships, and at least one of them, "the British ship *Anchun,* carrying Jordanian pilgrims from Aqaba to Jidda, was fired on by Egyptian shore batteries as a result of a misunderstanding."[14]

All these facts indicate that no juridical analogy can be drawn between the Gulf of Aqaba and the Gulf of Fonseca; there is no acceptable evidence of immemorial usage, of *animus domini* and of acquiescence. When Saudi Arabia formulated the claim to the historic character of the Gulf, the UNEF was stationed on the Strait of Tiran and Israel and other maritime nations passed freely through the Gulf.

In the debate in the General Assembly in 1957 only India seems to have taken the position that the Gulf was "an inland sea," but without any relevant supporting evidence.[15]

India also supported the claim of the United Arab Republic in 1967. It justified it on several grounds, first that the Republic "is not a party to any agreement recognizing the Gulf of Aqaba as an international waterway or guaranteeing the freedom of passage to Israeli ships."[16] This is obviously correct but the Republic is not a party to any agreement establishing the Gulf as an historic or closed bay.[17] Furthermore, in view of Israel's coastline on the Gulf no such agreement could be arrived at and relied upon vis-á-vis Israel without her consent.[18] The legal status of Israel in this context will be considered later.

The second Indian argument was that "there is no universally recognized rule of international law on freedom of navigation applicable to such bodies of water as Aqaba."[19] This is correct but irrelevant. The principle of freedom of the seas applies to all waters which qualify as high seas or parts thereof. States which desire to exclude parts of

[10] Melamid, *Legal Status of the Gulf of Aqaba*, 52 AM. J. INT'L L. 412 (1959). Melamid concludes that his research "supports the view that navigation rights have definitely been established in the Gulf of Aqaba by nations other than the Arab states. Use of the Gulf by Arab states, particularly for pilgrim travel, followed only upon the pioneering efforts of other nations." *Id.* at 413.

[11] Selak, *supra* note 8, at 692.

[12] Melamid, *supra* note 10, at 413.

[13] Hammad, *supra* note 7, at 133.

[14] Selak, *supra* note 8, at 670. Mr. Selak may have confused the facts. As stated in the House of Commons on July 6, 1955, by Mr. Nutting, Minister of State for Foreign Affairs, this ship was on the pilgrim run between Jedda and Aqaba but when fired upon and hit it was returning empty to Aqaba. 543 PARL. DEB., H.C. (5th ser.) 1134 (1955), quoted in 4 M. WHITEMAN, DIGEST OF INTERNATIONAL LAW 478 (1965).

[15] Selak, *supra* note 8, at 674, points out that all the water areas cited by the Indian delegates are "indentations in the territory of one state only."

[16] U.N. Doc. A/PV.1530, at 81 (1967).

[17] The absence of any agreement among the Arab littoral states was noted by Selak, *supra* note 8, at 692.

[18] Gross, *supra* note 9, at 570. See also *supra*, p. 1125.

[19] U.N. Doc. A/PV.1530, at 81 (1967).

the high seas from the regime of customary international law on historical or others grounds have the burden of the proof. As suggested earlier no such evidence has been made available by the governments concerned or writers who support them.[20]

Moreover, there is strong evidence that the Arab coastal states as well as Israel have considered the Gulf to be part of the high seas; all of them proclaimed belts of territorial sea in the Gulf varying from three (Jordan) to six (Saudi Arabia, Egypt and Israel) miles.[21] Claims to territorial sea imply that the Gulf is part of the high sea[22] although there are exceptions on historical grounds as in the case of the Gulf of Fonseca.[23] But no comparable exception has been established in favor of the Gulf of Aqaba before or after the establishment of the state of Israel.

In the debates in the General Assembly in February and March, 1957, a great number of Members have formally gone on record that the Gulf of Aqaba comprehends international waters and that there is a right of free and innocent passage in the Gulf.[24] Similar views were expressed at the 1967 Fifth Emergency Special Session.[25]

The third Indian argument was that the status of the Gulf of Aqaba was "still a matter of controversy," and in support of this, the Indian delegate referred to a recent publication of the State Department,

> the *Digest of International law,* released by the Department of State in April 1965 (vol. IV, p. 233) containing a letter from the Secretary of State dated 15 January 1963, to the Attorney-General setting forth the views of the Department regarding the extent of territorial waters and the closing width of bays. On Aqaba, the letter states as follows: "The Gulf of Aqaba—the exact status of this body of water is still a matter open to controversy." I am sure there are many international lawyers in this august gathering and I make them a present of this quotation from an authoritative American textbook.[26]

This present, in spite of the generosity of the giver, should be accepted, if at all, with caution. It is true that there is a letter from the Secretary of State on the subject but it ends on page 232. The passage quoted by the Indian delegate is not from this letter but from a Memorandum prepared by Frank Boas, Attorney Adviser, Office of the Legal Adviser, Department of State, dated August 1957.[27]

After the passage quoted by the Indian delegate, Mr. Boas goes on to say that the Department of State in a recent statement published in *The New York Times* on June 24, 1957, declared that:

[20] No evidence is to be found in Murti, *The Legal Status of the Gulf of Aqaba,* 7 The Indian Journal of International Law 201 (1967), who supports the Indian Government's viewpoint. Murti does not consider the arguments developed in my article cited *supra* note 9.

[21] *See* Selak, *supra* note 8, at 666 for relevant information.

[22] *Id.* at 693.

[23] Gross, *supra* note 9, at 1125.

[24] Gross, *supra* note 9, at 1131, and Selak, *supra* note 8, at 671–75.

[25] *See e.g.,* U.N. Docs. A/PV.1531, at 29–30 (1967) (Belgium); A/PV.1541, at 13–15 (1967)(Peru); A/PV.1542, at 41 (1967). (Australia); *id.* at 58–60 (Costa Rica).

[26] U.N. Doc. A/PV.1530, at 81 (1967).

[27] *See* 4 M. Whiteman, *supra* note 14, at 239.

> The United States position is that the Gulf of Aqaba comprehends international waters. That no nation has the right to prevent free and innocent passage in the Gulf and through the Straits giving access thereto. A denial of those waters to vessels of United States registry should be reported to the nearest United States diplomatic or consular offices.[28]

Still, it is true to say that a controversy exists although it is probably not sustained by any serious doubts as to the applicable law. The Arab claims, as one Egyptian writer put it, might not have arisen "except for the fact of Arab hostility toward Israel."[29]

## II. STATUS OF ISRAEL AS A COASTAL STATE IN THE GULF OF AQABA

It is part and parcel of the position of some governments and writers that Israel is not entitled to a stretch of the coast of the Gulf, that its presence there lacks legitimacy or is tainted with illegality. Thus the delegate of the United Arab Republic charged in the Security Council on May 29, 1967, that Israel's "presence lacks legitimate foundation."[30] After referring to the resolutions of the Security Council adopted on July 15, 1948 and August 19, 1948, the same delegate declared: "In view of these specific orders, Israel's possession of the coastal strip does not entitle it to any claim to sovereignty. This is in conformity with the well-established doctrine in international law that belligerent occupation cannot legally be converted into sovereignty over the occupied territory."[31]

These arguments suffer from a common but fatal defect. They confuse the deployment of military forces which may or may not be compatible with various resolutions of the Security Council or provisions in the relevant Armistice Agreements with exercise of sovereignty over territory. There may be armistice demarcation lines but there are also frontiers in the usual sense of the word, and while the territory of Israel may be determined by such lines it does not mean that the territory itself or parts of it are "armistice territories." No armistice lines were drawn along the coasts of Israel on the Mediterranean and the Gulf of Aqaba. Insofar as the coastline on the Gulf is concerned, it was provided in the 1947 Partition Plan Resolution of the General Assembly that the territory of the new state should extend to and include a stretch of coast which corresponded to the territory of the Mandate for Palestine. The Armistice Agreements with Egypt and Jordan define only the western and eastern demarcation lines or frontiers of this part of the state of Israel.

Thus the General Armistice Agreement of February 24, 1949 between Egypt and

[28] *Id.* at 233. For material on the Gulf of Aqaba and Strait of Tiran, see *id.* at 465. *See also* "The United States Reply to the Arab States Representations Concerning the Suez Canal and the Gulf of Aqaba: Statement Delivered to the Heads of Mission of the Arab States at Washington, June 27, 1957," in STAFF OF SENATE COMM. ON FOREIGN RELATIONS, 90TH CONG., 1ST SESS., A SELECT CHRONOLOGY AND BACKGROUND DOCUMENTS RELATING TO THE MIDDLE EAST 112–15 (Comm. Print 1967).

[29] Hammad, *supra* note 7, at 137.

[30] U.N. Doc. S/PV.1343, at 31 (1967).

[31] *Id.* at 33–35.

Israel provides in article II, paragraph 2: "No element of the land, sea or air military . . . forces . . . shall advance beyond or pass over for any purpose whatsoever the *Armistice Demarcation Line* set forth in Article VI of this Agreement . . . and elsewhere shall not violate the *international frontier*. . . ."[32]

Article VI, paragraph 1, of this Agreement also refers to "the Egyptian frontier" and article VIII, paragraph 2, refers three times to the Egypt-Palestine frontier. Article VII establishes in "certain sectors of the total area involved" a western and eastern front. This relates to the southern part of the territory of Israel, the western front being governed by the Armistice Agreement with Egypt whereas the eastern front comes under the regime of the Agreement with the "third party," namely, Jordan. Annex II to the Egyptian-Israel Armistice Agreement defines the demarcation between the two fronts. The eastern front is defined as "The area east of the line described in paragraph *a* above, and from point 402 down to the southernmost tip of Palestine, by a straight line marking half the distance between the Egypt-Palestine and Transjordan-Palestine frontiers."[33]

Moreover, the Armistice Agreement explicitly recognizes Israeli possession of the territory by providing in article VII, paragraph 4 as follows: "In the area of the western front under Israeli control, Israeli defensive forces only, *which shall be based on the settlement,* may be maintained. All other Israeli forces shall be withdrawn from this area. . . ."[34] Clearly, a distinction is made between deployment of forces and control. Control remains even if forces are to be withdrawn.

The Jordan-Israel Armistice Agreement of April 3, 1949 follows to some extent the earlier Agreement between Egypt and Israel. The demarcation lines are indicated on maps annexed to the Agreement and it is to be noted that there is no demarcation line along the coast on the Gulf of Aqaba. In the area concerned the lines run from north to south and not from east to west. Thus article V, paragraph 1 (d), provides: "In the sector from a point on the Dead Sea . . . to the southernmost tip of Palestine, the Armistice Demarcation Line shall be determined by existing military positions . . . and shall run from north to south as delineated on map 1 in the annex I to this Agreement."[35]

Furthermore, and quite explicitly, article VII stipulates: "The military forces of the Parties to this Agreement shall be limited to defensive forces only in the areas extending ten kilometres from each side of the Armistice Demarcation Lines, except where geographical considerations make this impractical, as at the southernmost tip of Palestine and the *coastal strip*."[36]

This coastal strip cannot be any other than that of Palestine under Israel control and part of its territory. Finally, mention may be made of Annex II which in paragraph II, section 4, defines the defensive forces in the "Sector Engeddi to Eylat" as three battalions each and various vehicles.[37]

[32] 4 U.N. SCOR, Spec. Supp. 3, at 2, U.N. Doc. S/1264/Rev. 1 (1949). (Emphasis added.)
[33] *Id.* at 11.
[34] *Id.* at 5. (Emphasis added.)
[35] 4 U.N. SCOR, Spec. Supp. 1, at 3–4, U.N. Doc. S/1302/Rev. 1 (1949).
[36] *Id.* at 5. (Emphasis added.)
[37] *Id.* at 10.

A distinction between Armistice Demarcation Lines and international frontiers was made several times by the Secretary-General of the United Nations in his Special Report of May 18, 1967. Thus, he noted, "UNEF has been deployed in Gaza and Sinai for more than ten years for the purpose of maintaining quiet along the Armistice Demarcation Line and the International Frontier," and "All UNEF Observation Posts along the Armistice Demarcation Line and International Frontier were manned as usual."[38]

The state of Israel is not and was not an "armistice state" but a state with a territory delineated partly by armistice lines and partly by international frontiers. Certainly its maritime boundaries belong to the latter category. Thus there can be no question of the legitimacy in international law of its presence and its port on the Gulf of Aqaba. It certainly is not foreign territory conquered in violation of the Briand-Kellogg Pact or other treaties to which the doctrine of non-recognition may be applicable.

More specifically the delegate of the United Arab Republic referred to Security Council Resolution 89 (1950) as proof of the "illegal occupation" of the port of Elath on the Gulf of Aqaba. In that resolution the Council took note of the declaration of the government of Israel "that Israel armed forces will evacuate Bir Qattar pursuant to the 20 March 1950 decision of the Special Committee provided for in article X, paragraph 4, of the Egyptian-Israel General Armistice Agreement. . . ."[39] The delegate went on "to clarify that the reference to Bir Qattar includes the vicinity of Om Rashrash which the Israelis called 'Elath' after their illegal occupation of the territory."[40]

Apart from the confusion between "occupation" and military deployment this clarification is somewhat misleading. The locality "Om Rashrash" on the Armistice map is on the Israeli side of the demarcation line of the Palestine-Transjordan frontier. There can be no question, therefore, of any "illegal occupation of the territory." Furthermore, the locality is in that sector of the area which has been called "eastern front" and is, therefore, within the legal scope of the Jordan-Israel Armistice Agreement. The distance between Bir Qattar and Om Rashrash may be close enough to permit the delegate to say that the former is in the vicinity of the latter, but this can be only geographic and not juridical vicinity. Inasmuch as the Security Council referred to the Egyptian-Israel General Armistice Agreement, therefore, juridically as well as geographically, Bir Qattar must be in the "western front" area. This Security Council Resolution cannot support any inference whatsoever with respect to Om Rashrash, which the Israelis called Elath.

The delegate of the United Arab Republic also charged that

> The Israeli armed forces on 10 March 1949 usurped and occupied the village of Om Rashrash, along with a stretch of about five miles overlooking the Gulf of Aqaba. . . . This illegal act was perpetrated two weeks after the signing of the Egyptian-Israeli General Armistice Agreement on 24 February 1949. This action completely and drastically violated the letter and spirit of the Agreement. . . .[41]

[38] U.N. Doc. A/6669, at 3 (1967). Further references will be found in *id.* at 7, 9.
[39] U.N. Doc. S/PV.1343, at 32 (1967).
[40] *Id.*
[41] *Id.* He referred also to paragraphs 1 and 2 of Article IV of the Agreement.

This incident is the trump card in the reasoning designed to show that legally speaking Israel's territory does not comprise the coastal strip on the Gulf.[42] It formed the subject of an investigation by the Truce Supervisory Organization and of a Report from the Acting Mediator of Palestine to the Secretary-General of the United Nations of March 22, 1949. This report deals with complaints made by Transjordan. It confirms that an Israel force reached "Umm Reshresh" and that "the eastern front, pending the conclusion of an armistice agreement with Transjordan, remains fully subject to the existing truce."[43] The Acting Mediator, referring to the Aqaba area, stated: "It is clear on the evidence available to me as a result of the investigation by United Nations observers since 7 March that Israeli forces have effectively occupied this area since that date."[44]

Referring to a couple of incidents, he reported: "I am quite convinced that, other than those at Aqaba, any positions established in this area either by Transjordan or by Israeli forces have all been established since the existing truce came into effect on 18 July 1948 . . . and have, therefore, been established contrary to the terms of that truce."[45]

However, this incident occurred prior to the signing of the Jordan-Israeli Armistice Agreement on April 3, 1949 and in an area covered by it. The charge of the delegate of the United Arab republic that the deployment of the Israeli troops in the area of Om Rashrash was contrary to the Egyptian-Israeli General Armistice Agreement is without foundation. As the Acting Mediator pointed out, "Umm Reshresh" is in the eastern front area, therefore outside that Agreement. Moreover, it will be recalled, by virtue of the Jordan-Israeli Armistice Agreement that area along with the coastal strip fell within the territory of Israel.[46] The demarcation line follows the old frontier between the Palestine Mandate and Transjordan, and ends on the shores of the Gulf. There would seem to be, therefore, juridically no reason to doubt Israel's right to this part of its territory. True enough, the Armistic Agreements did not pretend to draw political boundaries. But apart from the fact that they did not delineate all the boundaries of Israel—the coastlines being one exception[47]—and even if it is admitted that the armistice lines are normally provisional and subject to confirmation or revision in a peace settlement, Israel was admitted to the United Nations as a state with a territory. The coastline has been, with or without military deployment, part of its territory. As long as this continues to be so it will be legally one of the four riparian states on the Gulf of Aqaba and entitled to the use of its waters as well as ingress and egress through the Strait of Tiran.[48]

[42] After recounting the above incident, Hammad concludes: "In view of these prohibitions it is clear that Israel's possession of the coastal strip, gained by the employment of the military instrument, is in the nature of a military occupation only, without lawful claim to sovereignty." Hammad, *supra* note 7, at 146.

[43] 4 U.N. SCOR, Supp. March 1949, at 46–47, U.N. Doc. S/1295 & Corr. 1 (1949).

[44] *Id.* at 47.

[45] *Id.* at 47–48.

[46] According to Selak, "in terms of the Armistice Agreements, a strong argument can be made for Israel's right to possession of its coastline on the Gulf of Aqaba. Just what is the legal nature of this possession, however, is somewhat unclear." Selak, *supra* note 8, at 681.

[47] Selak thinks it unlikely that the coastline on the Gulf is of a different legal nature than the land frontier without, however, elaborating the reasons for his doubts. *Id.* at 697.

[48] A line of reasoning that has not been explored and that cannot be explored here is whether the United Arab Republic and Jordan, which on May 15, 1948, illegally prevented the execution of the Partition Plan, can derive any advantages from

## III. STATE OF WAR AND RIGHTS OF BELLIGERENCY

No passage in a textbook or treatise on international law has been more often cited in the Middle East crisis over the past few years than that in Oppenheim-Lauterpacht that an armistice does not end the juridical state of war.[49] Predictably it was quoted by the delegate of the United Arab Republic. After emphasizing the essentially military nature of the 1949 General Armistice Agreement, the continued violations thereof "which culminated in the cowardly attack on Sinai in 1956," he contended that "a state of overt war has been existing. Hence my Government has the legitimate right, in accordance with international law, to impose restrictions on navigation in the Strait of Tiran with respect to shipping to an enemy."[50]

If there was nothing more to worry about than the question whether the imposition of the blockade was or was not in accordance with Oppenheim's views on armistices, there would not be much of a problem. However, the delegate claimed that the restrictions were "in accordance with international law," which is another matter. To begin with, if one takes Oppenheim's statement as authoritative then one would be bound to accept also as authoritative his statement that according to article 40 of the Hague Regulations respecting the Laws and Customs of War on Land of 1899 and 1907:

> Any serious violation of the armistice by one of the parties gives the other party the right of denouncing it, and even, in cases of urgency, of recommencing hostilities. . . .[51]
>
> Since the terms "serious violation" and "urgency" lack precise definition, the course to be taken is in practice left to the discretion of the injured party.[52]

Consequently, the war of June 1967 would be a lawful war for the same reason as the restrictions imposed by the United Arab Republic were claimed to be lawful. However, this was not the view taken by the Republic at the time and since. In fact, it would seem that the Republic abandoned Oppenheim's international law on armistices which he formulated in the second edition published in 1912, that is, even before World War I,[53]

their own action. Under the Plan the Jewish state was to comprise territory including the strip of the coast of the Gulf of Aqaba which has been under its sovereignty since 1948.

[49] The full text is as follows: "Armistices or truces, in the wider sense of the term, are all agreements between belligerent forces for a temporary cessation of hostilities. They are in no wise to be compared with peace, and ought not to be called temporary peace, because the condition of war remains between the belligerents themselves, and between the belligerents and neutrals on all points, beyond the mere cessation of hostilities. In spite of such cessation the right of visit and search over neutral merchantmen therefore remains intact, as does likewise the right to capture neutral vessels attempting to break a blockade, and the right to seize contraband of war." 2 L. Oppenheim, International Law 546–47 (H. Lauterpacht ed. 1952).

[50] U.N. Doc. S/PV.1343, at 36–37 (1967).

[51] The Hague Convention and Declarations of 1899 and 1907, at 122 (J. Scott ed. 1915).

[52] 2 L. Oppenheim, International Law 556 (H. Lauterpacht ed. 1952).

and placed its case on the basis of the Charter of the United Nations, that is, the new international law. The armistice agreements must then be construed and applied in the framework of the Charter. This was done by the Security Council in its resolution of September 1, 1951, and its competence to interpret and apply the armistice agreements cannot be doubted.[54] This resolution declared generally that "since the armistice regime . . . is of a permanent character, neither party can reasonably assert that it is actively a belligerent or required to exercise the right of visit, search, and seizure for any legitimate purpose of self-defence. . . ."[55] The Council made some additional findings of a general character and addressing itself to the specific complaint of Israel regarding Egypt's restrictions in the Suez Canal, called upon Egypt

> to terminate the restrictions on the passage of international commercial shipping and goods through the Suez Canal wherever bound and to cease all interference with such shipping beyond that essential to the safety of shipping in the Canal itself and to the observance of the international conventions in force.[56]

Egypt's non-compliance with this resolution is a matter of record. When Israel on January 28, 1954, complained to the Security Council about illegitimate interference with shipping passing to and from Israel through the Gulf of Aqaba, it was not contested by Egypt that the 1951 resolution applied to that waterway as well.[57] Egypt on that occasion rejected again the 1951 resolution as well as the proposed resolution on the Israeli complaint, which in any event failed of adoption as a permanent member of the Council, the Soviet Union, voted against it.

On May 30, 1967, replying to the representative of the United States, who described the first above-quoted passage from the 1951 Security Council resolution[58] as a "fundamental principle,"[59] the delegate of the United Arab Republic recalled that "two highly important factors affected the resolution":

> First, four of the nine States that voted for the adoption of the resolution were parties to the dispute, and according to Article 27, paragraph 3, of the Charter, "a party to a dispute shall abstain from voting." It follows that, according to the provisions of the Charter, the resolution should not have been adopted. . . .
>
> Secondly, the resolution was based on the assumption that for two and a half years no fighting had occurred between Egypt and Israeli authorities. Again, for political aims, those members of the Council at that time flagrantly disregarded the numerous aggressive

[53] 2 L. OPPENHEIM, INTERNATIONAL LAW 290 (2d ed. 1912). Mr. Selak mistakenly attributes Oppenheim's statement on armistices to "the British jurist, Sir Hersch Lauterpacht." Selak, *supra* note 8, at 681.

[54] *See* Gross, *Passage Through the Suez Canal of Israel-bound Cargo and Israel Ships*, 51 AM. J. J. INT'L L. 530,545 (1957). *Supra*, pp. 1081, 1096. Professor R. R. Baxter is of the opinion that this resolution can be regarded "as a legislative or law-creating act, rather than a judicial or law-declaring one," but "its burden is that the Armistice has placed special obligations upon the parties." R. BAXTER, THE LAW OF INTERNATIONAL WATERWAYS 230, 235 (1964).

[55] S.C. Res. 95, para. 5.

[56] *Id.*, para. 10.

[57] Gross, *supra* note 54, at 559–61, in this text, pp. 1109–1111. R. BAXTER, *supra* note 54, at 211–12.

[58] See text accompanying note 55 *supra*.

[59] U.N. Doc. S/PV.1344, at 57 (1967).

> acts committed by the Israelis during those two and a half years, in spite of the fact that they were presented to the Council in detail by the representative of Egypt. However, even the assumption on which the resolution was based must have been completely invalidated by the treacherous Israeli attack on Sinai in 1956.[60]

The second argument is incorrect. The Council did not assume that for two and a half years no fighting had occurred, but stated merely as a factual proposition that the armistice regime "has been in existence" for that period of time, which is undeniable. As long as the armistice regime is in force, the conclusions of the Council rest on a firm juridical foundation. It would be open to the United Arab Republic to argue that the hostilities including those of 1956 had destroyed the armistice regime but this it did not do.

The first argument raises a matter of the internal procedure of the Council. In this case the objections of Egypt were heard by the members and not accepted. The Council is master of its own procedure and the September 1, 1951 resolution was declared adopted by the President. Of course, it is open to members to follow their own interpretation of the constitutional law of the United Nations but they do so at their own risk and peril. Certainly one member cannot impose its auto-interpretation on another member or on the Security Council.

The General Assembly in establishing UNEF and directing its deployment has neither explicitly rejected the Egyptian contentions regarding belligerency and incidental rights of visit, search and seizure nor has it explicitly adopted the opposite Israeli contentions. However, the stationing of UNEF along the Armistice Demarcation Line and in the Sharm El Sheikh area gave substantial satisfaction to the Israeli request that there should be no interference with innocent passage and no assertion of belligerent rights in the Strait of Tiran. The General Assembly and the Secretary-General could do no less without violating the letter and spirit of the Security Council resolution of September 1, 1951.

In this connection it is interesting to note that the withrawal of UNEF from the Strait of Tiran and the imposition of the blockade on May 22, 1967, were presented by the United Arab Republic as "a return to the conditions prevailing prior to 1956."[61] The delegate of Pakistan, speaking at the Fifth Emergency Special Session of the General Assembly on June 22, 1967, stated the point more precisely as follows:

> The action of the United Arab Republic did not create an entirely new situation; it merely restored the *status quo ante* and sought to liquidate a consequence of Israel's aggression in 1956. Israel had enjoyed no right of passage through the Strait of Tiran before 1956, and this position had not aroused opposition on the part of most maritime Powers.[62]

The representative of the United Arab Republic, speaking in the Security Council on May 29, 1967, referred to several statements made in connection with the 1957 discussion

[60] U.N. Doc. S/PV.1345, at 53–55, 56 (1967).
[61] Report by the Secretary-General, U.N. Doc. S/7906, at 3 (1967).
[62] U.N. Doc. A/PV.1531, at 47 (1967).

in the General Assembly and argued: "The 1956 aggression did not change the legal status of the Gulf of Aqaba and consequently did not affect the United Arab Republic's rights over its territorial waters."[63]

The factual situation which obtained in the Strait and the Gulf prior to the stationing of the UNEF at Sharm El Sheikh must, of course, be distinguished from the juridical situation. The latter was expressed by most of the maritime powers in 1957 and the above mentioned 1951 resolution of the Security Council. The juridical point of view was also formulated by the United States authoritatively and formally with respect to both the pre-1956 conditions and the effect of the Security Council resolution as follows:

> The attitude of the United States with respect to the right of free and innocent passage has not been altered by the events of last October and November. Those rights previously existed and are in no way based on the results of military action. It is, of course, clear that the enjoyment of rights of free and innocent passage is inconsistent with aggression. Thus, in the United States view Israel's right to free and innocent passage was dependent upon withdrawal of its forces behind the armistice lines in accordance with the United Nations resolutions. Once the situation envisaged by the General Armistice Agreements was restored, the principles of international law regarding free and innocent passage again became applicable to Israeli traffic in the Gulf of Aqaba. The Security Council resolution of September 1, 1951, set forth the principle that a party to the armistice agreements could not assert that it was actively a belligerent.[64]

The establishment in 1957 of the right of free passage through the Strait and Gulf was correctly described as follows: "The legal situation which prevailed constituted a re-establishment of the régime which was established *de jure* by the resolution of the Security Council of September 1, 1951, but not hitherto implemented."[65]

The United Arab Republic by re-imposing the closure of the Strait of Tiran and the Gulf of Aqaba, far from restoring the *status juris quo ante,* has reverted to the *status injuriae.*

The liquidation of UNEF operations and the resumption of belligerent practices by the United Arab Republic in May 1967 thus revived the old problem. The Secretary-General was obviously concerned about the revival of tensions in the area and recognized that "the situation in the Strait of Tiran represents a very serious potential threat to peace." He also urged all the parties to "forego belligerence."[66] The keynote which was echoed by several Members in the discussions in the Security Council and the Assembly was formulated by President Lyndon B. Johnson on May 23, 1967, when he declared:

> The purported closing of the Gulf of Aqaba to Israeli shipping has brought a new and very grave dimension to the crisis. The United States considers the Gulf to be an international

[63] U.N. Doc. S/PV.1343, at 37 (1967).

[64] The United States Reply to the Arab States Representations Concerning the Suez Canal and the Gulf of Aqaba: Statement Delivered to the Heads of Mission of the Arab States at Washington, June 27, 1957. STAFF OF THE SENATE COMM. ON FOREIGN RELATIONS, 90TH CONG., 1ST SESS., A SELECT CHRONOLOGY AND BACKGROUND DOCUMENTS RELATING TO THE MIDDLE EAST 113 (Comm. Print 1967).

[65] R. Baxter, *supra* note 54, at 215.

[66] Report of the Secretary-General, U.N. Doc. S/7906, at 4–5 (1967).

> waterway and feels that a blockade of Israeli shipping is illegal and potentially disastrous to the cause of peace. The right of free, innocent passage of the international waterway is a vital interest of the entire international community.[67]

The President formulated this as one of the five principles for peace on June 19, 1967: "The right of innocent maritime passage must be preserved for all nations."[68]

The representative of the United States elaborated the President's statements in the Security Council. On May 24, 1967, he stated that the "conditions in the area have taken a still more menacing turn because of a threat to customary international rights which have been exercised for many years in the Gulf of Aqaba."[69] On May 29, 1967, referring to the Secretary-General's report he said, "forgoing belligerence must mean forgoing any blockade of the Gulf of Aqaba," and "surely, stopping, searching and preventing the passage of ships through the Strait would clearly fall within the category of acts against which this [the Secretary-General's] appeal is directed."[70]

It is interesting to note that these statements do not refer to the Egyptian-Israeli General Armistice Agreement but seem to be based on broader grounds. The President simply considered the blockade "illegal," that is, presumably, contrary to international law. The representative of the United States considered "stopping, searching and preventing passage" as belligerent acts and presumably contrary to international law or the law of the Charter of the United Nations. The Security Council, in its resolution of September 1, 1951, squarely based itself on the Armistice Agreement and the Constantinople Convention but not on the law of the United Nations.[71] And yet it would have been logical and advantageous for the Security Council to adopt the latter position and to declare the Egyptian belligerent practices to be contrary not merely to the Armistice Agreement but above all contrary to the Charter of the United Nations.[72]

While Members of the United Nations do not appear to have expressed themselves on the subject of the compatibility of an active state of war, that is, of the exercise of belligerent acts, with the Charter, it is all the more remarkable that the resolution adopted by the Security Council on November 22, 1967, and referred to earlier in this paper, proceeds from the point of view of the Charter. It does so in the third preambular paragraph which reads: "Emphasizing further that all Member States in their acceptance of the *Charter* of the United Nations have undertaken a commitment to act in accordance with Article 2 of the *Charter*."[73] Article 2 of the Charter includes the twin principles of refraining from the threat of or use of force and of settling international disputes "by

[67] 56 DEP'T STATE BULL. 870–71 (1967).

[68] 57 DEP'T STATE BULL. 33 (1967).

[69] U.N. Doc. S/PV.1342, at 6 (1967).

[70] U.N. Doc. S/PV.1343, at 16, 18–20 (1967). A request for compliance with the Secretary-General's appeal was included in the United States draft resolution introduced on May 31, 1967. *See* U.N. Doc. S/PV.1345, at 22 (1967).

[71] *See* Gross, *supra* note 54, at 564–68. In text at pp. 1114–1117.

[72] *See also* N. FEINBERG, THE LEGALITY OF A "STATE OF WAR" AFTER THE CESSATION OF HOSTILITIES UNDER THE CHARTER OF THE UNITED NATIONS AND THE COVENANT OF THE LEAGUE OF NATIONS (Jerusalem, 1961).

[73] S.C. Res. 242 (1967); 4 U.N. MONTHLY CHRON. 19 (Dec. 1967). (Emphasis added).

peaceful means in such a manner that international peace and security, and justice are not endangered."

Furthermore, in operative paragraph 1, the Security Council "[a]ffirms that the fulfillment of *Charter* principles requires the establishment of a just and lasting peace in the Middle East which shall include the application of both the following principles."[74] While the first principle relates to the "withdrawal of Israeli armed forces from territories occupied in the recent conflict" without any reference to the Armistice Agreements which figured prominently in the General Assembly resolutions with respect to the 1956 Middle East conflict,[75] the second principle states: "Termination of all claims or states of belligerency . . ."[76] The law of the Charter is the law common to all parties in the conflict and it was high time for the Security Council to declare that the state of belligerency which was claimed by the United Arab Republic to exist, and against which Israel always objected, must be terminated because of incompatibility with Charter principles. Whatever may be the outcome of negotiations between the parties, this declaration in itself is a substantial gain for the United Nations.[77]

## IV. FREEDOM OF PASSAGE THROUGH THE STRAIT OF TIRAN AND IN THE GULF OF AQABA

It has been shown that the claim to exclusive control of the Gulf of Aqaba on historic or other grounds was without merit. It has also been demonstrated that the territory of Israel includes a coast on the Gulf. There remains to be considered the question of passage through the Strait and the Gulf.

One problem can be eliminated. No government has contested the proposition that the entrance to the Gulf "is situated in the joint territorial waters of Saudi Arabia and the United Arab Republic. Due to navigational hazards the only navigable route to the Gulf runs less than one mile from the Sinai Peninsula. Hence it crosses our undisputed territorial waters."[78] These are undisputed facts. As regards passage through the Strait of Tiran, it might be well to begin with the position of Egypt. On February 11, 1957, the Secretary of State of the United States handed the Israeli Ambassador an aide mémoire in which he stated: "[T]he United States believes that the Gulf comprehends international waters and that no nation has the right to prevent free and innocent passage in the Gulf and through the Straits giving access thereto."[79] He went on to say:

[74] *Id.* (Emphasis added.)

[75] Resolutions adopted by the General Assembly during its First Emergency Special Session from November 1 to 10, 1956, U.N. GAOR (Emer. Spec. Sess. 1), Supp. 1, U.N. Doc. A/3354 (1956).

[76] S.C. Res. 242, *supra* note 73.

[77] It may be noted that none of the three draft resolutions before the Security Council in November 1967 referred to the armistice agreements or armistice lines. 4 U.N. MONTHLY CHRON. 8–9 (Dec. 1967).

[78] Mr. El Kony (U.A.R.), U.N. Doc. S/PV.1343, at 31 (1967). Mr. El Kony gives the length of the Gulf as being about 96 miles and its widest breadth as less than 15 miles.

[79] 4 M. WHITEMAN, *supra* note 14, at 466.

> The United States recalls that on January 28, 1950, the Egyptian Ministry of Foreign Affairs informed the United States that the Egyptian occupation of the two islands of Tiran and Senafir at the entrance of the Gulf of Aqaba was only to protect the islands themselves against possible damage or violation and that "this occupation being in no way conceived in a spirit of obstructing in any way innocent passage through the stretch of water separating these two islands from the Egyptian coast of Sinai, it follows that this passage, the only practicable one, will remain free as in the past, in conformity with international practice and recognized principles of the law of nations."[80]

Thus by its own admission, Egypt considered the Strait of Tiran as open to passage and consequently recognized the right of passage in the Gulf. Clearly, were Egypt or now the United Arab Republic or Saudi Arabia actively involved in a war, they could deny passage to the ships of their opponent. But apart from this, there is no right to deny or obstruct passage. When the Government of Egypt in 1955 issued instructions requiring prior notice from ships, the United States Government maintained its position that "no nation has the right to prevent free and innocent passage in the Gulf and through the Straits giving access thereto."[81] The British Government in 1955 "never recognized the legality of the Egyptian blockade either of the Canal [Suez] or other waters, such as the Gulf of Aqaba, leading to Israeli ports,"[82] and made no formal agreement with Egypt "about shipping proceeding to the Gulf of Aqaba," but rather it "adopted a *de facto* arrangement" while maintaining its legal position.[83]

At that period only the alleged existence of a state of war with Israel seemed to motivate Egypt to deny passage through the Strait.

In connection with the liquidation of the Middle East crisis in 1956–57, a good deal of attention in the General Assembly was focused on Israel's grievances with respect to the passage through the Strait of Tiran and in the Gulf of Aqaba. Fourteen Members, including those with the greatest interests in maritime freedom, expressed themselves in one form or another in favor of freedom of innocent passage through the Strait and in the Gulf.[84] As indicated earlier, the deployment of UNEF in the area of the Strait was designed to and in fact did, ensure freedom of passage as long as it lasted but the General Assembly did not adopt a formal resolution on the subject.

However, shortly thereafter at the 1958 Geneva Conference on the Law of the Sea, the question was formally settled.[85] The claim to exclusive control of the Gulf of Aqaba by the three littoral Arab states which was reiterated at the Conference found no subject. On the contrary, it was generally taken for granted that there were four littoral states, including Israel. Nor was there any concern with the allegation that Israel had no legal

[80] *Id.*
[81] *Id.* at 469.
[82] 543 PARL. DEB., H.L. (5th ser.) 1135 (1955), quoted in 4 M. WHITEMAN, *supra* note 14, at 478.
[83] 546 PARL. DEB., H.C. (5th ser.) 2288 (1955), quoted in 4 M. WHITEMAN, *supra* note 14, at 480.
[84] Gross, *supra* note 9, at 576–78. *Supra* in text at pp. 1131–1133.
[85] "The seeming general consensus indicated by this debate [in the General Assembly] in favor of preserving a right of access to straits free of the arbitrary competence of the coastal state nevertheless found impressive confirmation shortly in the outcome of the 1958 Conference on the Law of the Sea." M. MCDOUGAL & W. BURKE, THE PUBLIC ORDER OF THE OCEANS 210–11 (1962).

right to its share of the coast. Whatever the status of the Gulf may have been prior to the establishment of Israel, it could not be regarded as a historic bay after establishment of the new state.[86]

The Conference boldly tackled the issues raised by the conflict between Egypt, Israel and the rest of the maritime community, which so far the International Law Commission and the General Assembly have avoided. In full awareness of these issues the Conference by a vote of 65 for, 1 against and 1 abstention,[87] adopted article 16 of the Convention on the Territorial Sea and the Contiguous Zone.[88] The first paragraph of this article accords to the coastal state the right to "take the necessary steps in its territorial sea to prevent passage which is not innocent," the second paragraph deals with control over ships proceeding to internal waters, the third paragraph permits temporary suspension of innocent passage "if such suspension is essential for the protection of its security," and finally paragraph four, which may be called the Aqaba article, reads as follows: "There shall be no suspension of the innocent passage of foreign ships through straits which are used for international navigation between one part of the high seas and another part of the high seas or the territorial sea of a foreign State."

In addition this Convention, which entered into force on September 10, 1964, and had been ratified by more than thirty states, including the United States, the United Kingdom, the Soviet Union, and France, lays down rules concerning innocent passage (articles 14 and 15) and the permissible laws and regulations applicable to foreign ships exercising the right of innocent passage. Such law and regulations must conform to the articles of the Convention and "other rules of international law" (article 17).[89]

The Conference made some changes in the relevant draft articles of the International Law Commission and "all the changes . . . were clearly in the direction of promoting more inclusive use of straits and of restricting the authority of coastal states."[90] The Conference deleted the word "normally"—the deletion was proposed by the United States—from the Commission's draft,[91] on the ground that the word was not used by the International Court of Justice in its Judgment in the *Corfu Channel* case.[92] The effect of the deletion is "to assure passage through straits which were actually used and to avoid friction over the concept of normal use."[93]

The other important change related to the Commission's words "between two

[86] "It would no doubt be argued . . . that even if the claim to historic rights were justified the emergence of a new state bordering on the gulf altered the scope of authority normally associated with historic waters." *Id.* at 444. A similar change occurred in the Black Sea when Russia established itself on its shores. *See* Selak, *supra* note 8, at 693.

[87] U.N. Conference on the Law of the Sea, Official Records, Vol. II, Plenary Meetings, at 65, para. 3 (1958).

[88] U.N. Doc. A/Conf.13/L.52 (1958).

[89] Concerning these provisions, *See* Gross, *supra* note 9, at 580–92, and *supra* in text at 1135–1147, and M. McDougal & W. Burke, *supra* note 85, at 174–304.

[90] M. McDougal W. Burke, *supra* note 85, at 211.

[91] This draft was as follows: "There must be no suspension of the innocent passage of foreign vessels through straits normally used for international navigation between two parts of the high seas." 10 U.N. GAOR, Supp. 9, at 20, U.N. Doc. A/2934 (1955).

[92] [1949] I.C.J. 4. *See also* Gross, *supra* note 9, at 586 and *supra* at 1140 in text.

[93] M. McDougal & W. Burke, *supra* note 85, at 212.

parts of the high seas'' which qualified the word ''straits.'' This was of particular importance with respect to the Gulf of Aqaba. Although in the view of some governments, notably of the United States, the Gulf was considered to comprehend international waters, this could be contested by others, and the argument became a casualty when Egypt and Saudi Arabia extended their territorial sea from six to twelve miles. The greatest width of the Gulf being between fifteen and seventeen miles, there is not room left for international waters. The point was made by several governments at the Conference that the essential aspect of the traditional principle of freedom of navigation was for ships to enter the port of destination and to have the right, for this purpose, to pass through the territorial sea.[94] This point was met by changing the words in the Commission's draft to read ''between one part of the high seas and another part of the high seas or the territorial sea of another State.'' In this manner passage in the Gulf of Aqaba was secured. The principle of freedom of navigation was spelled out and placed on a more secure basis. By prohibiting suspension of innocent passage through straits, the Conference rejected decisively the competence of the coastal state ''to control the strait as a means of projecting its influence for purpose of special national policy, not necessarily reflecting common interest.''[95]

The relevance of article 16, paragraph 4, of the 1958 Convention on the Territorial Sea for the controversy over the Strait of Tiran and the Gulf of Aqaba was contested in the Security Council and in the General Assembly in the debates in 1967.

In arguing the illegality of the blockade measures announced by the United Arab Republic, the representative of the United States referred to article 16, para. 4, of the 1958 Convention as evidence of international law. He described the *status quo* which existed from 1957 to 1967 as being ''in accordance with international law.'' ''Such law, indeed,'' he said, ''has been expressed in the 1958 Convention on the Territorial Sea and the Contiguous Zone, to which many nations are parties.''[96]

The representative of the United Arab Republic did not deny that the rule laid down in artile 16, paragraph 4, was declaratory of customary international law but contended that the Convention was inapplicable ''to our case'' because it lacked any reference ''to the consequences of armed conflict.'' He supported his view by quoting from the report of the International Law Commission the sentence: ''This draft regulates the law of the sea in time of peace only.[97]

This is, of course, correct but the relevant point is that the 1958 Conference did not adopt the Commission's proposal. Thus, quite deliberately, the Convention was intended to apply generally without reference to states of war and peace. But, as has been pointed out, the Convention, within limits, respects the security interests of the coastal states and in case of actual armed conflict the necessary consequences would have to be

[94] Gross, *supra* note 9, at 587–89 and *supra* in text at 1141–1144.

[95] M. McDougal & W. Burke, *supra* note 85, at 189. These authors also note that ''[i]t is evident that there has been a fairly strong tendency over the past century to restrict the competence of coastal states over straits.'' *Id.* at 213.

[96] U.N. Doc. S/PV.1343, at 16–17 (1967).

[97] U.N. Doc. S/PV.1344, at 47 (1967).

drawn. In this case, however, the existence of a state of war which would justify appropriate measures by the coastal state has not been recognized and its seems unnecessary to go over the same ground again.

Another argument against article 16, paragraph 4, is that it is a "new rule."[98] The source of this is an article on the 1958 Conference by Arthur H. Dean, who was head of the American delegation, in which he said with reference to this clause: "The Geneva Conference thus, in a politically charged area, achieved agreement sufficient to write a new and beneficent rule into international law."[99]

There is room for argument whether article 16, paragraph 4, creates a new rule which would be binding on the contracting states only or whether it merely specifies or particularizes a rule which is deemed implicit in customary international law, that is, the general principle of freedom of the seas and navigation. At the Conference itself there was substantial evidence that some delegates merely desired to make explicit the right of ships to sail from port to port through international waterways, this right being implicit in the general principle.[100] In this sense there is nothing new in article 16, paragraph 4.

What is undeniably true, however, is that the rule is new in the sense that it differs in important respects, as indicated earlier, from the draft submitted by the International Law Commission. This is indeed the interpretation of Mr. Dean as appears from this clarification:

> In making this statement I was thinking mainly in terms of fact that the question of innocent passage through straits between one part of the high seas and the territorial sea of a foreign state had not been covered by the decision of the International Court in the *Corfu Channel* case or in the draft articles prepared by the International Law Commission. I did not intend to pass upon the question of whether or not this rule represented a codification of customary international law.[101]

In the present submission the rule does represent a codification of customary international law although it could also be argued that it contains an element of progressive development of the law. The very substantial vote in favor of the rule at the Conference must also be considered as an expression of the Conference in favor of free and innocent passage through international waterways. That the Conference was also aware that in article 16, paragraph 4, it "adopted a rule which clearly applied to the Israeli-Arab controversy" is undeniable.[102] More than that, for in Mr. Dean's view, "it specifically *determines* the heated controversy between Israel and Arab states as to the right of Israeli shipping to pass through the Strait of Tiran to the Gulf of Aqaba."[103]

[98] *See* the speech of the representative of the Sudan, U.N. Doc. A/PV.1530, at 28 (1967); Murti, *supra* note 20, at 203. Concerning the pro-Arab position of the Indian Government, *cf.* Kozicki, *Indian Policy Toward the Middle East*, II ORBIS 786 (1967).

[99] Dean, *The Geneva Conference on the Law of the Sea: What Was Accomplished*, 52 AM. J. INT'L L. 607, 623 (1958).

[100] Gross, *supra* note 9, at 587–89, 592–94 and *supra* in text at 1141–1143, 1147–1149.

[101] Letter from Arthur H. Dean to Leo Gross, Feb. 29, 1968.

[102] Dean, *supra* note 99, at 623.

[103] *Id.* at 621. (Emphasis added.)

Obviously, the rule could not achieve this purpose if it depended upon ratification of Arab states involved in that controversy.

## V. CONCLUSIONS

There is no need to summarize the results of this analysis of the controversy over the right of free and innocent passage through the Gulf. In the present submission none of the propositions advanced by the United Arab Republic and its supporters can be accepted as juridically persuasive: neither the claim that the Gulf of Aqaba has been from time immemorial an historic gulf, a discovery which at least on the juridical plane was made only in 1957, nor the claim that Israel's territory does not comprise a stretch of the coast of the Gulf, neither the existence of belligerent rights and of a continuing state of war, nor the claim that the Strait of Tiran is not an international waterway.

Apart from the specific issues relating to the conflict, there emerged in the 1958 Geneva Conference and in the 1967 debates in the Security Council and the General Assembly a concern for ensuring free and innocent passage through international waterways for all states. For if it is admitted that a coastal state is entitled to use waterways as an instrument of national policy no state would contemplate the future with equanimity. While many delegations addressed themselves, in the 1967 debates, to the concrete issue of innocent passage through the Suez Canal and the Strait of Tiran and in the Gulf of Aqaba, the delegate of Italy formulated the problem in comprehensive terms when he said:

> There are, moreover, questions which affect the more general interests of the international community. I have in mind the problems of international waterways, the freedom of which is guaranteed by international law and is a matter of primary interest for the whole world and particularly for those countries which, like Italy, are separated from the oceans by canals and straits.[104]

The issue is of transcendent importance for the welfare of all nations, the developed and the developing ones.

At the 1958 Geneva Conference the proposal had already been made to include in article 16, paragraph 4, the words "straits or other sea-lanes," on the ground that "[t]he

[104] U.N. Doc. A/PV.1530, at 66 (1967). In this connection mention may be made of the statement of the British representative:

> "In addition, there is one most urgent and most dangerous issue of all: the question of the right of passage for shipping of all nationalities through the Strait of Tiran. The maintenance of the provisions of the Geneva Convention on the Territorial Sea dealing with international navigation between the high seas and territorial waters is of the gravest concern to my Government, as it must be to all engaged in international trade."

U.N. Doc. S/PV.1342, at 18–20 (1967). *See also* statements by the delegations indicated in U.N. Docs. A/PV.1531, 22 June 1967, at 29–30 (Belgium); A/PV.1537, 27 June 1967, at 46 (Nigeria); A/PV.1541, 29 June 1967, at 13–15 (Peru); A/PV.1542, 29 June 1967, at 41 (Australia); and *id.* at 58–60 (Costa Rica).

term 'straits' was much too narrow, because there were sea-lanes used for international navigation elsewhere than in straits."[105]

The inclusion of the word "sea-lanes" would have had the same justification as the deletion of the word "normally," that is, avoidance of technical controversies over meanings of "strait" or "canal" and concentration on the use as a highway for international navigation.

In view of this precedent and the concern for freedom of navigation on the high seas, it was probably no mere accident that the resolution of the Security Council adopted on November 22, 1967, used the comprehensive term "international waterways" when it affirmed the necessity "[f]or guaranteeing freedom of navigation through international waterways in the area."[106]

It may also have been a matter of intent rather than mere choice of words that the resolution expresses the concern of the Security Council for guaranteeing freedom of navigation through international waterways "in the area." For while the conflict between Israel and its Arab neighbors in the past has related, insofar as freedom of navigation was involved, to the Suez Canal, the Strait of Tiran, and the Gulf of Aqaba, there are "in the area" other international waterways such as the Straits of Bab El Mandeb.

These straits have a vital function in the area for they "join the high seas of the Gulf of Aden to those of the Red Sea and form part of the international route from the Mediterranean to the Far East."[107] Four states border on these Straits: Ethiopia and French Somaliland on the African side, and Yemen and the Republic of South Yemen, the former British Aden Protectorate, on the Arabian side. Perim Island itself was formerly part of the British Colony of Aden and has become part of the Republic of South Yemen.

As concerns freedom of passage through these straits, one would assume that in the contemplation of the United States they would be covered by article 16, paragraph 4, of the 1958 Convention. This would follow from the traditional policy of the United States in favor of freedom of transit through international waterways including international straits.

Insofar as the United Kingdom and the new Republic of South Yemen are concerned, the following statement by the British Foreign Secretary, Mr. George Brown, in the House of Commons on November 29, 1967 may be quoted:

> There is as yet no new Government, but the delegation from the N.L.F., in the course of discussions in Geneva, as the communiqué shows, had agreed to accept the international obligations which we have extended to Aden, and one of those is the Geneva Convention

[105] The words are those of the delegate of the Netherlands, U.N. Conf. on the Law of the Sea, Off. Rec., vol. III, 1st Comm. 94, U.N. Doc. A/Conf.13/39 (1958). *See* Gross, *supra* note 9, at 588 and *supra* at 1142 in text.

[106] S.C. Res. 242 (1967), *supra* note 73. It is worth noting that all three draft resolutions before the Council—a three-power (India, Mali, and Nigeria) draft, a United States draft and a Soviet Union draft—emphasized in one way or another freedom of navigation or innocent passage. *See* 4 U.N. MONTHLY CHRON. 9 (Dec. 1967). The resolution which was unanimously adopted issued from a United Kingdom draft. *Id.* at 15, 17.

[107] Kennedy, *A Brief Geographical and Hydrographical Study of Straits Which Constitute Routes for International Traffic*, 1 United Nations Conference on the Law of the Sea, Official Records, U.N. Doc. A/Conf.13/6, at 115 (1958). The length of the Straits is 50 miles, the Large Strait between Perim Island and the African coast is about 9¼ miles wide, and the Small Strait between Perim Island and Arabia is about 1½ miles wide. *Id.*

> which seeks to ensure free passage through international waterways. One of these is the waterway of the Straits of Perim.[108]

The situation appears then to be adequately covered by the devolution or inheritance agreement between the United Kingdom and the Republic of South Yemen, although it is not clear from the statement whether the agreement is a formal one or sufficiently formal to be registered with the United Nations.

Conflict among nations has often contributed to the strengthening and revitalization of international law and organization. One has to remind himself of the major wars in the modern era which promoted the growth of law and organization: the Napoleonic Wars contributed through the Congress of Vienna to the development of international river law and gave birth to the Concert system; the First World War gave birth to the League of Nations and the Permanent Court of International Justice; the Second World War created the United Nations; the Indus River conflict between India and Pakistan contributed powerfully to the study and development of the law of river basins. Examples could be multiplied. Problem-solving has been a constructive experience for nations. It may then be legitimate to expect that the solution of the conflict in the Middle East will hasten the establishment of the law governing international waterways on a firm foundation by the application of the principle that such waterways shall not be used as an instrument of national policy but for the benefit of all nations. In the long run an increasingly interdependent world cannot settle for less.

[108] PARL. DEB., H.C. (5th ser.) 438 (1967). Concerning the politics of the area, see Klieman, *Bab Al-Mandab: The Red Sea in Transition*, II ORBIS 758 (1967).

# IX

# DOMESTIC JURISDICTION AND PEACE-KEEPING OPERATIONS

# DOMESTIC JURISDICTION, ENFORCEMENT MEASURES AND THE CONGO

## 1. INTRODUCTION

The so-called "peace-keeping" operation of the United Nations in the Congo has from the outset provoked a lively controversy, in and out of the United Nations, over the relevance of the domestic jurisdiction reservation in article 2 (7)[1] of the Charter, especially in connexion with the problem posed by the intended secession of Katanga. In particular it was questioned whether, and to what, extent the United Nations or its Force could "intervene" in the domestic affairs of the Congo, whether the several Security Council and General Assembly resolutions conferred such authority on the Secretary-General and the Force, and more particularly whether the Force, pursuant to the several resolutions, could go beyond self-defence in its military operations. The first part of article 2 (7) has been the subject of debates in the various organs of the United Nations from the start of the Organization and has been analysed extensively in the literature. In the Congo crisis, however, it was the second part of article 2 (7), that is the exception to the reservation, which was, for the first time, it is believed, the focal point of the debates. Both parts of article 2 (7) will be discussed in this paper though what needs to be said on the first part serves merely as a background to the analysis of the second part.

[1] Article 2 (7) reads:— "7. Nothing contained in the present Charter shall authorise the United Nations to intervene in matters which are essentially within the domestic jurisdiction of any State or shall require the Members to submit such matters to settlement under the present Charter; but this principle shall not prejudice the application of enforcement measures under Chapter VII.".

## 2. DOMESTIC JURISDICTION

The analysis of the first part of Article 2 (7) can be organized under several heads: (a) meaning of intervention; (b) meaning of matters "essentially within the domestic jurisdiction"; (c) who decides whether there is intervention or whether the matter is "essentially within the domestic jurisdiction". In the course of debates in the United Nations and in learned commentaries the legislative history and the relevant preparatory documents have been raked over time and again. [2]

As to the first point the answer depends upon the position one takes on the question whether the reservation is in the nature of a limitation on the competence, or on the powers of the United Nations. Both positions have been advocated. In the first hypothesis—limitation on the competence—the United Nations in case of a dispute relating essentially to domestic matters can do nothing about it except state the fact. This was so in the League of Nations when the Council found that the plea of domestic jurisdiction pursuant to article 15 (8) was well founded.[3] The United Nations—that is, its organs—cannot discuss or consider the matter, they cannot investigate, conciliate or make recommendations; in short, they cannot use any of the powers conferred upon them by the Charter. They can of course discuss, consider and investigate in order to determine whether the objection is well founded. If they are satisfied that it is, that is the end of the matter; in the contrary case, they can proceed and use the powers conferred upon them. In the practice of the United Nations the process of determining the competence and the process of discussing a recommendation are fused into one, and the decision on the recommendation implies a decision on competence.[4] This seems an objectionable practice but one which is too well entrenched and not likely to be changed. In this writer's opinion, article 2 (7) is in the nature of a limitation on the competence, and when invoked it would be better handled separately as a preliminary question.

The second hypothesis, namely, that the reservation relates to the powers, is a prevailing one, and the discussion then turns on the meaning of intervention. Is discussion intervention?[5] Are consideration, investigation, conciliation or recommendation intervention? The trend of discussion has been decisively influenced by Lauterpacht's view

[2] For a useful survey of doctrine and practice see *Report* of the United Nations Commission on the Racial Situation in the Union of South Africa. GAOR 8th Sess., Supp. No. 16 (A/2505 and A/2505/Add. 1) pp. 16–34. (Henceforth cited as *Report.*) For a recent discussion see Rosalyn Higgins, *The Development of International Law through the Political Organs of the United Nations* (1963), pp. 58–130, and the literature there cited.

[3] Text of article 15 (8): "If the dispute between the parties is claimed by one of them, and is found by the Council to arise out of a matter which by international law is solely within the domestic jurisdiction of that party, the Council shall so report, and shall make no recommendation as to its settlement".

[4] The view has been expressed that while the inclusion of an item in the agenda did not prejudice the question of competence, "a United Nations organ should not include an item in the agenda if, at the time of the adoption of the agenda, it was clear beyond any doubt that the item fell essentially within domestic jurisdiction and, consequently, that the organ concerned was not competent to deal with it"; Repertory of Practice of United Nations Organs, Supp. No. 1 (1958) vol. 1, p. 57, par. 122. It is not clear, however, whether the decision of the General Assembly in the case of Cyprus and of the Security Council in the case of Algeria, not to include the question in the agenda was based on political or legal grounds. Ibid., p. 44, par. 68; and p. 54, par. 116.

[5] Quincy Wright, "Is Discussion Intervention?" 50 *American Journal of International Law* (1956), 102–10. See also Repertory of Practice of United Nations Organs, vol. 1 (1955), p. 131, par. 347; pp. 132–33, pars. 350–58.

that intervention is a term of art meaning "dictatorial intervention" and that consequently only dictatorial intervention is excluded.[6] Accordingly, discussion, consideration, investigation and conciliation are not intervention nor are recommendations whether general or specific because they are not legally binding and neither enforceable nor enforced. The obvious flaws in this reasoning are first that the organs of the United Nations, particularly the General Assembly, have no power of dictatorial intervention, leaving on one side the consequences which might flow from the 1950 "Uniting for Peace" Resolution, and secondly, that the power of the Security Council to take enforcement action, that is, to intervene dictatorially, is specifically provided for. These flaws have not discouraged the adherents of Lauterpacht's view. They prefer a narrow interpretation of "intervention" in order to promote the effectiveness of the United Nations even though, in the process, article 2 (7) is emasculated—which runs counter to another canon of interpretation, namely, that "an interpretation is not admissible which would make a provision meaningless, or ineffective".[7] And they are not deterred by the obvious contradiction which results from arguing on the one hand that resolutions of the General Assembly do not constitute intervention because "there is . . . no legal obligation to accept any such recommendation", and on the other hand that the General Assembly was "not precluded from 'dictatorial intervention,' since it may use measures of coercion or enforcement by way of recommendations . . . when a matter is not essentially within the domestic jurisdiction."[8] The vital point here is, of course, who determines whether a matter is essentially within the domestic jurisdiction of a State, a point which will be considered presently.

Regarding the second point—the meaning of "essentially within the domestic jurisdiction"—two views hold sway: according to one, the formula is broader than the phrase used in the Covenant;[9] according to the other, the opposite is true. The United Nations has tended to the view that matters covered by treaties or referred to in the Charter, such as human rights and self-determination, are no longer within the reserved domain. Any other view would run counter to the express purpose of promoting respect and co-operation in these areas.[10] The General Assembly can be and has been active, with a surprising degree of success, in formulating general principles, declarations, resolutions and conventions on human rights, self-determination and related matters, without interference from article 2 (7). But it must be noted that all of these were general in nature—not

[6] H. Lauterpacht, "The International Protection of Human Rights", Hague Academy of International Law, *Recueil des Cours*, vol. 1 (1947, vol. 70 of the Series), pp. 5–107, at p. 19 *et seq.*

[7] Oppenheim, *International Law*, vol. 1 (8th ed. by H. Lauterpacht, 1955), p. 955. Lauterpacht warned against considering article 2 (7) meaningless because, human rights having been included in the Charter, they could no longer be regarded as essentially domestic matters. Measures of protection and implementation recommended by the General Assembly must, he claimed, "fall short of coercive intervention". *Recueil*, p.30.

[8] *Report*, p. 17, pars. 136 and 140. The Commission cited in this context Resolution 39 (1) concerning Franco-Spain and Resolution 377 (V) "Uniting for Peace". See also ibid., p. 21, par. 162.

[9] *Report*, pp. 18, 21.

[10] Ibid.

addressed to any particular State in a particular situation—and dependent for their implementation on the voluntary co-operation of Members. However, consistent with the desire to expand the authority of the United Nations, a narrow interpretation of the clause was selected to serve a liberal interpretation of the purpose of the Charter. The means to that end was the concept of "international concern," an omnibus concept if there ever was one.[11] Any matter, regardless of its being "essentially" domestic, could at the will of the majority of the General Assembly or the Security Council be characterized, and with good reason, as being of international concern, for there are few matters which are not of this nature in the present age of transnational interdependence.

However, Lauterpacht when sitting as a judge declared that "practically every matter can be plausibly, though not necessarily accurately, described as a matter essentially within the domestic jurisdiction of the States concerned" and that it was—

> "possible for a State to maintain, without necessarily laying itself open to an irresistible charge of bad faith, that practically every dispute concerns a matter essentially within its domestic jurisdiction."[12]

This would seem to be the better view but it is not that which found favour with the United Nations, which throughout the years preferred to operate consciously or unconsciously on the basis of "international concern." As a result the area of matters covered by article 2 (7) has been reduced to the vanishing point. Reliance on the expression "international concern" is, however, misplaced. Article 2 (7) would normally be invoked in connexion with the pacific settlement of disputes pursuant to Chapter VI of the Charter. This chapter follows in principle article 15 of the Covenant of the League, limiting the jurisdiction of the United Nations to disputes or situations of a certain gravity. Where the Covenant used the words "disputes likely to lead to a rupture," the Charter speaks of disputes or situations "likely to endanger the maintenance of international peace and security" (articles 33 and 34). The only exception is in article 38, pursuant to which "any dispute" may be submitted to the Security Council "if all parties . . . so request." In the latter case there probably and reasonably would be no occasion to invoke article 2 (7). In connection with other disputes or situations article 2 (7) could be and has been invoked. As the Charter does not define the degree of gravity intended to be conveyed by the words "likely to endanger . . .", the words "international concern" could well be used as another way to describe the sort of disputes or situations over which the United Nations could legitimately claim jurisdiction, although on their face these words would seem to be more inclusive and exacting a lower degree of intensity of conflict than the words actually used in the Charter.

It would have been better from the point of view of legislative technique to abandon altogether the precedent of the League and to allow the United Nations to handle dis-

[11] *Repertory,* vol. 1, p. 142, par. 409; and Supp. vol. 1, p. 62, par. 148; *Report,* p. 22, par. 174.

[12] Separate Opinion in the *Case of Certain Norwegian Loans,* Judgment of July 6, 1957, I.C.J. Reports, 1957, p. 9 at 52.

putes regardless of their intensity. However, no matter what words are used and no matter what degree of intensity is laid down as the threshold of United Nations jurisdiction, there remains article 2 (7). If article 2 (7) can be invoked as a bar against United Nations jurisdiction in case of disputes or situations of substantial intensity as described in Chapter VI[13] then *a fortiori* it can be invoked in case of disputes or situations of lesser intensity as described by the words "international concern."[14]

Whatever the yardstick for determining which matters fall within the area of the reserved domain and between which parties, whether it was a legal or political or politico-legal test, conceived narrowly or broadly, the all important question is who applies it and with what effects. We turn now to this question.

By design rather than by oversight the San Francisco Conference decided not to follow the precedent of the League Covenant which provided that the Council or Assembly shall determine that a plea to jurisdiction is well taken.

It was assumed, and rightly so, at the Conference and ever since that each organ of the United Nations would interpret the articles of the Charter relating to its functions.[15] This is not the same as conferring upon an organ the power to make an authoritative interpretation to which the Charter or general international law attaches finality, that is, binding force.[16] In order to secure such an effect the Charter should have followed the League precedent in article 15 (8) of the Covenant or appointed another organ, perhaps the International Court of Justice, to give a binding ruling on the applicability of article 2 (7). This was not done. The omission was not due to an oversight but was deliberate [17] as indicated in the Conference's rejection of a Greek amendment to give the Court compulsory jurisdiction as to the matter. Furthermore, the same document which is usually cited in support of the proposition that each organ is entitled to interpret such clauses of the Charter as relate to its functions, also declares in a passage which for obvious reasons has been but rarely quoted that—

> "It is to be understood, of course, that if an interpretation made by any organ of the Organization or by a committee of jurists is not generally acceptable it will be without binding

[13] It may be well to recall that article 2 (7) was originally included in the Dumbarton Oaks Proposal in the section dealing with the peaceful settlement of disputes in a somewhat different wording, one which was more closely patterned on article 15 (8) of the Covenant.

[14] It is a different matter whether the Security Council may apply the provisions of Chapter VII of the Charter in a situation like Franco-Spain in 1946, which though not constituting a "threat to the peace . . . has become ostensibly one of international concern by constituting an actual or potential threat to international peace" and thereby "ceases to be a matter essentially within the domestic jurisdiction of States". Lauterpacht, *Recueil*, pp. 33–34. This relates, it is believed, to the second part of art. 2 (7) and the threshold for Security Council action laid down in art. 39.

[15] The basis for this is the well-known San Francisco statement on interpretation of the Charter; United Nations Conference on International Organization (San Francisco) Documents vol. 13, p. 709; Doc. 933, 12 June 1945, Report of the Rapporteur of Committee IV/2 to Commission IV/2, ibid., pp. 703 *et seq.*

[16] An example of the former is art. 25 of the Charter and of the latter is art. 36 (6) of the Statute of the International Court of Justice which is declaratory of the principle of general international law that decisions of the Court on its own jurisdiction are final. See Leo Gross, "Bulgaria Invokes the Connally Amendment", 56 *American Journal of International Law* (1962), 357, at p. 382. See also *supra* at pp. 727–751.

[17] See *Report*, p. 15, par. 121, for the reasons that motivated the rejection of the Greek amendment at United Nations Conference on International Organization (San Francisco) which would have conferred compulsory jurisdiction on the Court with respect to art. 2 (7).

> force. In such circumstances, or in cases where it is desired to establish an authoritative interpretation as a precedent for the future, it may be necessary to embody the interpretation in an amendment to the Charter."[18]

The contention seems therefore untenable that because the San Francisco Conference rejected the Greek amendment referred to above, it "affirmed the *absolute right* of each of the main organs to settle the point itself."[19] It may well be that the General Assembly acted as if it had the right, absolute or otherwise, to decide on the interpretation of article 2 (7) and accordingly on its own competence, but neither the Charter nor the preparatory work nor the theory of international law on which the Charter is firmly based can be regarded as a sufficient basis for the arrogation of such a competence. To argue otherwise is to confuse autointerpretation which pertains to international institutions as well as to States with autodecision which does not, unless explicitly conferred.[20]

Moreover, practice which is not generally accepted is not conclusive with respect to the proper interpretation of a multilateral treaty such as the Charter. As Judge Sir Percy Spender pointed out:—

> "it cannot be altered at the will of the majority of the Member States, no matter how often that will is expressed or asserted against a protesting minority and no matter how large the majority of the Member States which assert its will in this manner and how small the minority."[21]

Addressing himself to the specific practice of the General Assembly with respect to the reserved domain Judge Spender declared:—

> "So if the General Assembly were to intervene in matters which are essentially within the domestic jurisdiction of any State within the meaning to be given these words, that intervention would be entering a field prohibited to it under the Charter and be beyond the authority of the General Assembly. This would continue to be so, no matter how frequently and consistently the General Assembly had construed its authority to permit it to make intervention in matters essentially within the domestic jurisdiction of any State. The majority has no power to extend, alter or disregard the Charter."[22]

[18] See Document at p. 8, cited in note [15] *ante*. See also Dissenting Opinion of Judge Winiarski in the *Expenses Case*, I.C.J. Reports, 1962, p. 151, at 229.

[19] *Report*, p. 23, par. 175, and p. 16, par. 122 (emphasis added). In par. 176, p. 23, the *Report* also declares that in practice by rejecting proposals to refer questions involving art. 2 (7) to the I.C.J. for advisory opinions, the General Assembly "affirmed its sovereign power to decide the question of competence itself".

[20] Thus Rosalyn Higgins argues: " . . . there seems to be little doubt that it is for the organ concerned to decide whether the matter is or is not essentially within the domestic jurisdiction of a state"; *op. cit.*, 67. Concerning the distinction maintained in the text above, see Leo Gross "States as Organs of International Law and the Problem of Autointerpretation", in Lipsky (ed.), *Law and Politics in the World Community*, 59–89 at p. 76 (1953) and also *supra*, pp. 367–397; and Myres S. McDougal and Associates, *Studies in World Public Order* (1960), pp. 188, *et seq.*

[21] Separate Opinion in the *United Nations Expenses* Case, I.C.J. Reports, 1962, 151, at p. 196.

[22] Ibid. But see M.S. Rajan, *United Nations and Domestic Jurisdiction* (1958), pp. 466 and 512. It is interesting to recall that in supporting an amendment to the United States declaration accepting the jurisdiction of the International Court of Justice as compulsory which was not adopted, Mr. John Foster Dulles who had a good deal to do with the drafting of art. 2 (7) at the United Nations Conference on International Organization (San Francisco) stated as follows: "If condition 3 (requiring prior agreement as to what are the applicable principles of international law) is expressed in the declaration that would make it unnecessary to stipulate who decides what is domestic, for that condition would prevent encroachment on

In addtion to these general jurisprudential arguments which militate against the attribution to the organs of the United Nations of the power to interpret article 2 (7) authoritatively,[22a] there is one which derives from the text itself. According to it "nothing contained in the present Charter . . . shall require the Members to submit such matters (i.e. which are essentially within the domestic jurisdiction) to settlement under the present Charter." This part of article 2 (7), frequently and conveniently overlooked in discussions thereon, reinforces the interpretation outlined above. If the Assembly or any other organ of the United Nations had the power to interpret authoritatively the applicability of the domestic jurisdiction reservation, the release of the Member from the submission of such matters would make no sense. It does make sense if it is accepted that the United Nations has no such power. The juxtaposition of the two parts of the first sentence in article 2 (7) yields a curious but, it is submitted, correct conclusion: both the United Nations as well as the Member concerned are legally entitled to interpret the question whether the reservation applies but neither is legally empowered to decide the question with binding effect for the other. The interpretation of the United Nations organs cannot legally oust the interpretation of the Member and the Member's interpretation cannot legally oust that of the United Nations organs. This is so, it is submitted, not only because the Charter fails to attach finality or binding force to the interpretation of the United Nations but because this failure is compounded by the provision which expressly and unconditionally releases the Members from any obligation otherwise provided for in the Charter "to submit such matters to settlement under the present Charter."[23]

Thus a Member cannot "block action" by the United Nations but it may decline to comply. This is not necessarily "fatal to the effectiveness of the United Nations"[24] but if it is, this is due not to article 2(7) but to the absence of compulsory settlement of international disputes. One may reject the interpretation suggested above and for the sake of

domestic jurisdiction by an alleged unwritten growth of international law not recognized by the United States"; Memorandum of John Foster Dulles Concerning Acceptance by the United States of the Compulsory Jurisdiction of the International Court of Justice, 10 July 1946. Hearings before a Sub-committee of the Committee on Foreign Relations, 79th Cong. 2nd sess., Senate Resolution 196 (1946), p. 45.

[22a] See S. Engel, "Procedure for the *de facto* Revision of the Charter." American Society of International Law Proceedings 1965, pp. 108–116.

[23] The conclusion reached by Fincham and adopted by Rajan "that there is no warrant for the view that a member State can make a decision legally binding on other members or on the Organization as a whole, to the effect that a particular matter is one which is essentially within its domestic jurisdiction" is correct, but the contention that "such a decision must be taken by the Organ to which the dispute has been submitted, on the general principle that it is the sole judge of its own competence under the relevant provisions of the Charter" is in error. C. B. H. Finchan, *Domestic Jurisdiction* (1948) 95; and Rajan, *loc. cit.*, 117. Similarly, Kelsen's statement: "This is one of the absurd consequences of the interpretation, compatible with the wording of the Charter, that it is upon the state concerned to decide for itself whether a matter is essentially within the domestic jurisdiction" is incorrect if the word "decide" is to be taken in its technical legal sense. *The Law of the United Nations* (1950), p. 783. Lauterpacht rightly criticized Kelsen on this point on the assumption that Kelsen intended to say that "every Member of the United Nations retains the power to determine with finality whether a matter is or is not one of essentially domestic jurisdiction"; *loc. cit.*, p. 31. There is no "finality" in the legal sense of having legally binding force though there may be "finality" for the contention of both the organ and the State in the political sense.

[24] Rajan, ibid.

rescuing the "effectiveness" of the United Nations accept the current practice of the United Nations as legally correct. A standoff or non-settlement is the result in both cases. And this is so not exclusively for the reason that article 2 (7) is ambiguous at best, but because Chapter VI of the Charter fails—and again by design and not by oversight—to confer upon the General Assembly or the Security Council or on both the power to make a binding decision either on the preliminary objection—as was the case in the League—or on the merits. Whether a Member bends to the will of these organs is a matter of politics and not of law. Even if article 2 (7) did not exist, and for all practical purposes it has been treated as non-existent except in the Congo affair which will be discussed separately, the result would be substantially the same. When the United Nations or interested Members could bring to bear pressure upon a State seeking shelter behind article 2 (7) or the notoriously weak Chapter VI, the Member gave in. Where a Member or a State, like Franco-Spain, chose to resist persuasion, the result was non-compliance with the recommendation of the General Assembly or the Security Council as the case may be. One only has to look at the roster of cases in which article 2 (7) was invoked to test this hypothesis.[25]

The weakness of the Organization would seem to reflect the strength and intractability of the environment in which it was set up and has been functioning. To be sure once set up, one may safely suspect, that a sort of reciprocal interaction developed between the State system and the United Nations but during the first twenty years the United Nations has probably made no significant dent in the more sensitive areas of the system. This is no reason for not trying, though set-backs are bound to occur where the Organization tries to press beyond the available consensus and for this to be potent it must comprise the generality of Members including the essential Members.

There is one area, that of action with respect to non-self-governing territories, where the United Nations has been credited with a substantial measure of success. Whether this may have been due to a recognition by the Members of the authority of the United Nations[26] or to the policy of the Members concerned to liquidate colonial or semi-colonial holdings, inspired and urged on by a realization that the era of colonialism was over, that the "wind of change" blew irresistibly, is a matter for more detailed analysis than is possible here.[27]

[25] Repertory of Practice of U.N. Organs, vol. 1, pp. 55–7, and Supp. No. 1, pp. 25–7.

[26] Oscar Schachter, with the inestimable advantage of close and continued familiarity with its work observed that "the right of the United Nations General Assembly to determine which territories fall within the scope of Article 73 has received such continuing support that it may now be regarded as fairly well settled". "The Relation of Law, Politics and Action in the United Nations", Hague *Recueil des Cours,* vol. 2 (1963), p. 187. Whether this affirmation would meet the test of having been generally accepted, discussed above, raises a question.

[27] For a minimal assessment of the role of the United Nations, see Rupert Emerson, "Colonialism, Political Development, and the United Nations", 19 *International Organization* (1965), 484–504.

## 3. ENFORCEMENT MEASURES

The second part of the reservation of domestic jurisdiction contains an exception in favour of "enforcement measures under Chapter VII." This exception was due to an Australian amendment at the San Francisco Conference the purpose of which was to exclude even in case of a threat to or breach of the peace or an act of aggression the authority of the Security Council to make a recommendation under article 39 to the parties as to the methods or terms of settlement of the underlying dispute or situation.[28]

It was not intended, it is submitted, to restrict otherwise the authority of the Council to take whatever action—preventive or coercive—it is empowered specifically or by necessary implication to take by way of recommendation or decision under Chapter VII. The use of the words "enforcement measures" has caused in the literature and the debates in the United Nations organs some confusion as to the range of the exception. Before going further it may be useful to say a word to clarify the effect of the exception. Does it permit "intervention" in matters essentially within the domestic jurisdiction or does it lift, as it were, the situation or dispute out of the reserved domain to the plain of "international concern?" The answer may depend on the facts of a case but in principle, it is suggested, the former view seems preferable.[29] In case of a threat to peace the Security Council may take action in a matter which is claimed to be essentially within the domestic jurisdiction of the State concerned, for a threat to the peace may arise precisely within the domestic context. The fence which the first part of article 2 (7) erects around these matters is breached by the second part. This conclusion could be fortified by reference to the principle of effectiveness but the textual analysis and the preparatory work seem sufficient.

Now the words "enforcement measures", have sometimes been construed as hav-

[28] The following statement of the Canadian delegation to United Nations Conference on International Organization (San Francisco) describes the background and effect of the exception as follows: "In its original form as proposed by the Sponsoring Powers, the exception applies not merely to enforcement measures under Chapter VII, but to *any action* taken under Chapter VII. It was felt by many delegations, and particularly those of Australia and New Zealand, that this might imply the possibility of serious encroachment on the internal jurisdiction of Members . . . What concerned them was that under Chapter VII the Security Council has not only the power to impose sanctions but also the power to 'make recommendations'. Their fear was that this might empower the Security Council to interfere in the domestic affairs of a state and dictate terms to it over a dispute arising out of a matter of internal jurisdiction. They also argued that it might encourage aggressor states to use or threaten force in any dispute arising out of a matter of domestic jurisdiction in the hope of inducing the Security Council to extort concessions from the state that was threatened. Accordingly, after considerable debate, the exception to the principle of non-interference in domestic questions was *limited* to 'the application of enforcement measures under Chapter VII,' and in this form it appears in the Charter . . . The protection accorded to the domestic jurisdiction of member states is now very complete as it is clear that there can be *no interference in the domestic economy or internal legislation* of Members". Canada, Department of External Affairs, Report on the United Nations Conference on International Organization (San Francisco), Conference series, 1945, No. 2, pp. 18 *et seq.* See also, 1945 Commonwealth of Australia, United Nations Conference on International Organization, Report by the Australian Delegates (Commonwealth Government Printer, Canberra), pp. 29 and 99; and see also, Lawrence Preuss, "Article 2, par. 7 of the Charter of the United Nations and Matters of Domestic Jurisdiction", Hague *Recueil des Cours* Vol. 1 (1949), pp. 553 *et seq.*

[29] See also Kelsen, *loc. cit.*, p. 786. But in Lauterpacht's view "a matter is no longer essentially within domestic jurisdiction of a State if it has become a matter of international concern to the extent of becoming an actual or a potential danger to the peace of the world." *Loc. cit.*, pp. 26–8.

ing the technical meaning of "sanction" or of "coercive" action "against a State." No doubt the measures envisaged could in a given situation amount to "sanction" or "coercive" action but there is no more reason to give them a technical meaning than there is in connexion with "intervention."

More significantly, these words have been interpreted restrictively as referring only to such action or measures as the Council may take especially pursuant to articles 41 and 42. This interpretation was considered determinant in connexion with the so-called peace-keeping operation in the Congo. Thus in interpreting the authority conferred upon him by the Security Council, the Secretary-General, Mr. Hammarskjold said:

> "Certainly, the Council cannot be deemed to have instructed the Secretary-General, without stating so explicitly, to act beyond the scope of his own respect or contrary to the specific limitation regarding non-intervention in internal conflicts which he stated to the Council. Moreover, in the light of the domestic jurisdiction of the Charter, it must be assumed that the Council would not authorize the Secretary-General to intervene with armed troops in an internal conflict, when the Council had not specifically adopted enforcement measures under Articles 41 and 42 of Chapter VII of the Charter."[30]

Similarly, at a later stage the Secretary-General expressed the view that if the Council desired to take action "against a State" it should apply article 42 and remove the obstacle of article 2 (7) against intervention in internal conflicts.[31]

Even after the Council adopted on 21 February 1961 the resolution which provided for the use of force,[32] the Secretary-General was of the opinion that "it does not seem . . . to derogate from the position that United Nations troops should not become parties to armed conflict in the Congo."[33] Although the Court in the *United Nations Expenses Case* was not concerned with the question of article 2 (7), it shared the view that the operations did not involve action "against a State" and, therefore, presumably, were not based on article 42:

> "It is not necessary for the Court to express an opinion as to which article or articles of the Charter were the basis for the resolutions of the Security Council, but it can be said that the

[30] SCOR 887th Meeting, August 21, 1960, par. 44, pp. 9–0.

[31] Schachter, "The Relation of Law, Politics and Action in the United Nations", Hague *Recueil des Cours* (vol. 2, 1963), p. 222, and SCOR 920th Meeting, Dec. 13/14, 1960, par. 73, pp. 18–19 . . . "I have pointed out that the Council has never explicitly referred to the Charter Article on the basis of which it took action in the Congo. In particular, it is significant that the Council did not invoke Articles 41 and 42 of Chapter VII, which provide for enforcement measures and which would override the domestic jurisdiction limitation of art. 2 (7). I mention this as one of the reasons why some far-reaching interpretations of the mandate of the Force . . . are . . . difficult to understand. Those interpretations would require at least that the Security Council had clearly taken enforcement measures under Articles 41 and 42".

[32] Operative par. 1: "Urges that the United Nations take immediately all appropriate measures to prevent the occurrence of civil war in the Congo, including arrangements for cease-fires, the halting of all military operations, the prevention of clashes, and the use of force, if necessary, in the last resort". Doc. S/4741.

[33] Doc. S/4752, Annex VII, February 24, 1961. See also his remarks in the Security Council, 887th Meeting, 21 August 1960, pp. 10–12; and 913th Meeting, 7 December 1960, pp. 5–6.

operations of ONUC did not include a use of armed force against a State which the Security Council, under article 39, determined to have committed an act of aggression or to have breached the peace. The armed forces which are utilized in the Congo were not authorized to take military action against any State. The operation did not involve 'preventive or enforcement measures' against any State under Chapter VII and therefore did not constitute 'action' as that term is used in Art. II."[34]

While the main thrust of the Court's strong statement was directed against the allegations that the delegation of authority to the Secretary-General and the expenditures incurred by him were unconstitutional, it is important to note the implication that measures to qualify for "action" must be taken in case of a breach of the peace or an act of aggression, against a State and presumably after an explicit finding based on article 39. The further inference was also drawn that the Court "did not think article 42 or article 43 were applicable."[35] This inference in turn strengthens the stand that there was no dispensation from the restriction of article 2 (7).

There is some difficulty in following the reasoning of the Secretary-General and of the Court on several points.

What actually happened in the Congo is one thing and what the Secretary-General or ONUC were authorized by the Security Council to do is another. The Council in its resolution of 21 February 1961, urged in operative paragraph A.2,

"measures to be taken for the immediate withdrawal and evacuation from the Congo of all Belgian and other foreign military and paramilitary personnel and political advisers not under the United Nations command, and mercenaries."[36]

Contrary to the Secretary-General's interpretation, the Council in its resolution of 24 November 1961, interpreted this directive as follows in operative paragraph 4:

"Authorizes the Secretary-General to take vigorous action, including the use of a requisite measure of force, if necessary, for the immediate apprehension, detention pending legal action and/or deportation of all foreign military and paramilitary personnel and political advisers not under the United Nations Command, and mercenaries as laid down in Part A, operative paragraph 2 of the Security Council resolution of 21 February 1961."[37]

Thus on two occasions the Council authorized measures meaning "the requisite use of force, if necessary" against "military" personnel as distinguished from para-military personnel and mercenaries. Now military personnel is usually personnel of a State whereas para-military personnel, such as *Gendarmerie* may belong to a State, a political party or a provincial subdivision of a State. Does it not follow then that the United Na-

[34] *Certain Expenses of the United Nations* (article 17, par. 2, of the Charter). Advisory Opinion of 20 July 1962, I.C.J. Reports, 1962, p. 151, at p. 177. The Court had in mind all the resolutions including that of 24 November 1960, ibid., p. 176.

[35] Schachter, *loc. cit.*, p. 221.

[36] *Loc. cit.*

[37] Doc. S/5002.

tions Command was authorized in two relevant resolutions to take military action or enforcement measures against a State, specifically against the military personnel of Belgium? It is immaterial, it is submitted, whether this personnel vanished from the scene completely or reappeared partially in the ranks of the para-military personnel or mercenaries.[38] It is also immaterial in order to determine the nature of the action that the United Nations command could use force in self-defence. The legal nature of the measures or action cannot depend upon fortuitous circumstances which arise in day-to-day operations but upon the explicit authorization granted by the Council. In the premises the conclusion appears, to this writer at any rate, inescapable, that the Council authorized the Command to take measures or action against a State,[39] that is, against its military forces in the Congo. If it was necessary to argue that in order to come within the purview of article 42 and article 11, the Command was to take action against a State, then the measures authorized by Council by the resolution of 21 February 1961, may be regarded as action within the meaning of article 42 and article 11, to "maintain or restore international peace and security."[39a] Article 42 does not depend juridically upon article 43, that is, the existence of prior agreements concluded between the Security Council and members pursuant to this clause.[39b] The essential requirement, a purely factual one, is that there be armed forces at the disposal of the Council.

The next point is that the Court seems to imply that the measures must be taken against a State, in case of a breach of the peace or an act of aggression. This qualification is wholly imported by the Court, but is it based on the Charter?[39c] It is true that in the Congo action no finding was made under article 39 that there was a breach of the peace or an act of aggression, although the latter expression was freely used in the debates. However, the important point is that according to article 39 the Council may take action in accordance with article 41 and 42 also in case of a threat to peace, and not merely in case of a breach of the peace or an act of aggression.[40] Thus there is no legal ground arising from the Charter for limiting the competence of the Security Council to take action only in case of a breach of the peace or an act of aggression. As will be argued presently, article 2 (7) also militates against such a restrictive interpretation.

Furthermore, the Court seems to imply a further limitation in saying that the operations of ONUC did not include a use of armed force against a State which the Security Council "under article 39, determined to have committed an act of aggression or to have breached the peace." This is of course true but is the Council legally required to do so? The Court seems to imply that it is. From a strictly legal point of view it would be eminently desirable

[38] Or whether ONUC was authorized to "apprehend criminals" as Schachter suggests *loc. cit.*, p. 226.

[39] See Dissenting Opinion of Judge Koretsky in the *United Nations Expenses Case*, *loc. cit.*, p. 274.

[39a] In the same sense Finn Seyersted, "United Nations Forces. Some Legal Problems", 37 *British Year Book of International Law*, pp. 351–475 (1963), at p. 446.

[39b] Ibid., at pp. 438–9, 468.

[39c] For a negative answer see Seyersted, *op. cit.*, at p. 446, and J. W. Halderman, "Legal Basis for United Nations Armed Forces", 56 *American Journal of International Law*, pp. 971–996 (1962), at p. 982.

[40] Although, be it noted, such a restriction as to the use of armed forces is made in Part A, par. 1 of the "Uniting for Peace" Resolution of 3 November 1950. Resolution 377A(V), GAOR 5th Sess. Supp. 20 (A/1775) pp. 10–12.

for the Council as well as the Assembly to be specific in indicating on which clause in the Charter they have based the necessary authority. But it is too well known that the organs of the United Nations are allergic to such specific invocation of Charter articles. In the Congo action the first resolution of the Council of 14 July 1960 did not contain a finding that there existed a threat to the peace. This appears for the first time in the resolution of 22 July 1960. In none of these resolutions did the Council refer to article 39. Yet the Court had no difficulty at all in finding with respect to the resolution of 14 July 1960:—

> "The resolution, in the light of the appeal from the Government of the Congo, the report of the Secretary-General and the debate in the Security Council, was clearly adopted with a view to maintaining international peace and security."[41]

If a specific reference to article 39 or article 40 for that matter[42] was not necessary to clarify the basic authority of the Council to take any action at all in the Congo, why then is such specific reference necessary with respect to article 42 at subsequent stages?[43] If the Council urges and authorizes use of force, that is, of armed force against opposing military personnel may one not relate this to article 42 which deals especially with the use of force? Such attribution seems particularly justified in view of the fact that the resolution of 9 August 1960 referred to articles 25 and 49 as suggested by the Secretary-General.[44] As has been pointed out there were persuasive political reasons not to strain to the breaking point the consensus of the Council members and the inclusion of a reference to article 42 might well have been such a point.[45] A Soviet draft resolution referring to article 41 was defeated in the Council on 14 February 1961 by a vote 8 to 1 with 2 abstentions.[46] It might have been preferable then not to refer to any article as justification for an authorization to use force. But such self-restraint has no probative valuc, one way or the other, as against the actual mandates conferred explicitly on ONUC.

If the absence of a specific reference to article 42 is not determinant for the juridical

[41] *Loc. cit.*, p. 175. See also, First Report of the Secretary-General of 18 July 1960, S/4389 to the same effect. It may also be useful to recall that the Congo problem was brought before the Security Council by the Secretary-General who for the first time specifically referred to art. 99 of the Charter. Article 99 authorizes the Secretary-General to "bring to the attention of the Security Council any matter which in his opinion may threaten the maintenance of international peace and security".

[42] "My own view" said the Secretary-General, "is that the resolutions may be considered as implicitly taken under Article 40 and, in that sense, as based on an implicit finding under Article 39. But what I should like to emphasize is that neither the Council nor the Assembly has ever endorsed this interpretation, much less put such endorsement in a resolution. What is even more certain is that the Council in no way directed that we go beyond the legal basis of Article 40 and into the coercive action covered by Articles 41 and 42"; SCOR 15th Year, 820th Meeting, 13/14 December 1960, p. 19, par. 75. For a discussion of art. 40 in the context of the Congo operation see D. W. Bowett, *United Nations Forces* (1964), p. 177. Kelsen considers recourse to art. 40 as excluded by the wording of the second part of art. 2 (7). *Loc. cit.*, p. 787.

[43] But see Rosalyn Higgins, *loc. cit.*, p. 236: "It still seems very doubtful that the grave sanction of Article 42 could be brought into play so casually, and via the 'backdoor', though the less rigorous terms of Article 40 may well be invoked in this manner". It seems difficult to follow this line of reasoning considering the possibly extremely rigorous consequences which art. 40 may have for the parties.

[44] Schachter, *loc. cit.*, p. 218. The contention in the text is opposed to the position taken by the Secretary-General: "It is true that, in its resolution of 9 August (S/4426), the Council referred to Articles 25 and 49 as the basis for the legal obligation imposed on the States concerned by the Council's action, but this is certainly not the same as invoking enforcement measures"; SCOR 15th Year, 920th Meeting, 13/14 December 1960, p. 19, par. 74.

[45] Schachter, ibid., p. 223.

[46] Doc. S/4706, SCOR 16th Year, 934th Meeting, pp. 23–4.

character of the use of force, it is still less so in so far as the release from the inhibition of article 2 (7) is concerned. The Secretary-General from the first construed any mandate given to him and to ONUC as imposing non-interference in the internal conflicts of the Congo.[47] The Security Council presumably at his behest, included in the resolution of 9 August 1960 operative paragraph 4 in which it—

> "*Reaffirms* that the United Nations Force in the Congo will not be a party to or in any way intervene in or be used to influence the outcome of any internal conflict, constitutional or otherwise."[48]

This disclaimer was preceded by the declaration "that the entry of United Nations Force into the province of Katanga is necessary for the full implementation of this resolution." Although a distinction has been made between the problem posed by Katanga's secession and internal conflict other than that, a distinction which the Council was to make clear with growing vigour in subsequent resolutions, the Secretary-General invoking the precedent of Lebanon which in the present view was totally inapplicable, stated in his "unilateral declaration of interpretation" that it followed from paragraph 4 "that the United Nations Force cannot be used on behalf of the central Government to subdue or to force the provincial government to a specific line of action."[49]

It has been noted sometimes regretfully that the United Nations itself did not adhere strictly to its own and the Secretary-General's policy of non-intervention in the internal conflict of the Congo. Certainly the General Assembly Resolution 1474 (ES-IV) of 20 September 1960,[50] and all of Part B of the Security Council Resolution of 21 February 1961 constitute significant although certainly not drastic departures from this policy. This cannot be said of Security Council Resolution of 24 November 1961, the first adopted after the death of Mr. Hammarskjold, and the last adopted in the Congo affair. If there ever was intervention in the internal conflicts of a Member country this was the case here,[51] and even more in the manner in which the Resolution was interpreted and applied in practice.[52] But the question whether this constitutes an intervention in violation of article 2 (7) still awaits an answer.

[47] See SCOR 15th Year, 920th Meeting, December 13/14 1960, par. 73, p. 18–19; and Schachter, *loc. cit.*, p. 222.

[48] Doc. S/4426, SCOR, 15th Year, Supp., p. 91. See also SCOR, 15th year, 886th Meeting, August 8/9, 1960, p. 32.

[49] Memorandum of the Secretary-General of 12 August 1960, on the Implementation of the Security Council Resolution of 9 August 1960, S/4417/Add. 6, para. 8–9.

[50] GAOR 4th Emergency Special Sess., Supp. 1 (A/4510), p. 1.

[51] See p. 1188, *ante*, for a distinction between at least two sets of internal problems, those posed by dissention within the Congo Government and those posed by the attempted secession of Katanga. See also Bowett, *loc. cit.*, p. 197.

[52] It may be noted hat the 24 November 1961 resolution recalled all the previous resolutions adopted by the Council and the Assembly, reaffirmed "the policies and purposes of the United Nations with respect to the Congo", set out in these resolutions, and listed among the five policies and purposes in the first place: "To maintain the territorial integrity and the political independence of the Republic of the Congo". This may be construed as an authentic interpretation by the Council itself of its previous resolutions. It furnishes an appropriate introduction to the preambular and operative paragraphs of the resolution and adequate legal basis for ending the secession of Katanga. Doc. S/5002, 24 November 1961.

On the face of it, there is no reason to assume that the Security Council deliberately set out to act in contravention of the domestic jurisdiction limitation. It has been argued earlier that the first part of this reservation should be construed as a limitation upon the competence and not the powers of the organs of the United Nations. The limitation ceases to apply when the Council decides on "the application of enforcement measures under Chapter VII,"[53] but the limitation upon the powers continues, as pointed out earlier, with respect to a recommendation on the underlying dispute or situation. Concerning the meaning of "enforcement measures" two observations may be made. First, they can be directed against a State but, depending on the situation, they need not be directed against a State. In the Franco-Spain case, for instance, the Security Council could have taken measures against the régime, that is, measures the object of which would have been to remove Franco from power and to restore to the people the opportunity for self-determination. A precondition of such action would have been a finding that there existed a threat to peace and not merely a potential threat.[54] Similarly in the Indonesian case, the Council could have found a threat to the peace and directed measures against the Netherlands to prevent it from taking a "police action" against the Republic of Indonesia even though the latter formed an integral part of the Netherlands.[55] This would have constituted "intervention" in the material sense, and, if accompanied by a threat to use force in case of non-compliance, a "dictatorial intervention."[56] But the Council could also have found that the aspiration for self-determination of the Republic of Indonesia and not the police action undertaken by the Netherlands constituted the threat to the peace. In such a hypothesis the measures taken by the Council would not have been directed "against a State" and yet they would have been measures taken under Chapter VII as provided for in article 2 (7).

A similar situation developed in the Congo with respect to Katanga's design to secede. If there was any doubt about the fact that this secession and its prevention was the objective of the Council from the start, it was certainly dispelled by the resolution of 24 November 1961, which is almost entirely concerned with "secessionist" activities carried on in Katanga. Without mincing words the Council in paragraph 8—

> "Declares that all secessionist activities against the Republic of the Congo are contrary to the *Loi fondamentale* and Security Council decisions are specifically *demands* that such activities which are now taking place in Katanga shall cease forthwith."[57]

This certainly constitutes intervention in the material sense. To the extent that the authorization in paragraph 4[58] for "the use of requisite measures of force" embraced the use of force to give effect to the demanded cessation of secessionist activities, it was "dictato-

[53] See also Kelsen, *op. cit.*, p. 789.
[54] Repertory, vol. 1, p. 151.
[55] Ibid., vol. 1, pp. 151-2.
[56] See p. 1176, *ante*.
[57] Document S/5002.
[58] See p. 1185, *ante*.

rial intervention''; it was not directed against a State because in the preamble of this resolution the Council completely rejected the claim of Katanga that it was a ''sovereign independent nation''; and it was taken in the context of a finding of a threat to peace and therefore under Chapter VII; and it was compatible with article 2 (7).[59] The measures actually taken will be discussed presently.

Secondly, the words ''enforcement measures under Chapter VII'' do not refer to any particular article. They are, it is submitted, used in a non-technical sense, as a sort of short title for the heading of Chapter VII, ''Action with respect to threats to the peace, breaches of the peace, and acts of aggression.'' The words ''enforcement measures'' occur only in article 50[60] and in that context do not refer to any grant of authority or specific kind of measures. Otherwise the word ''measure'' occurs in article 39–41 and 49–51. The word ''action'' occurs in the title of Chapter VII, and in article 42, 45, 48 (1), 51. Unless the words in article 2 (7) are to be deprived of all meaning since they refer to nothing in particular *in* Chapter VII, they should be taken to mean to refer to *all* the measures, provisional and coercive, hortatory and decisional, which the Council is authorized to take under Chapter VII with the exception of the recommendations covered by the Australian amendment to article 2 (7).

The measures taken by the Council in the Congo case with respect to Katanga were measures taken under Chapter VII. They may not have been taken directly against a State but as pointed out above when the Security Council intervenes in the domestic domain the measures may, but need not be directed against a State. They may be intended to assist a State to quell a rebellion, insurrection, a guerilla campaign or a secessionist movement which endangers international peace.

Certainly a settlement of the Katanga problem by persuasion would have been preferable and Mr. Hammarskjold did not abandon the hope that it could be so settled. Hence his insistence as a corollary of his non-intervention doctrine but perhaps also independently of it, that the United Nations Force would use force only in self-defence and to secure freedom of movement.

## 4. END OF KATANGA SECESSION

The second period of United Nations involvement in the Congo, with U Thant as Secretary-General, may be said to begin with his consultations with the Advisory Com-

[59] Rosalyn Higgins states with reference to par. 8 quoted above: ''The United Nations has thus taken it upon itself to pass judgment on the *Loi fondémentale [sic.]* The only defence that can be raised in favour of this paragraph is that it must be read in the context, and as the rest of the resolution is full of references to the illegal action of the mercenaries in Katanga, this particular paragraph must be taken to embrace this element. One can only regret that it is necessary to raise such defensive arguments, for inevitably the paragraph gives support to those who insist that the United Nations wants to end the Katanga secession and not merely to expel the foreign elements from influence in Katanga so that the Congolese may negotiate among themselves''. *Op. cit., p. 109.* Similar regrets were also expressed by Bowett, *op. cit.*, p. 282. There would seem to be no reason for regrets and no need for defensive arguments, as there was hardly any room for doubt that the purpose of the United Nations was to end the threat of secession and not merely to provide a sort of a *cordon sanitaire* for Katanga and its claim to self-determination. The resolution may, of course, be criticized on political grounds but from a legal standpoint there is no reason for regarding it as a ''disservice'' and ''lapse.'' Rosalyn Higgins, *op. cit.*, p. 231.

[60] ''If preventive or enforcement measures against any State are taken by the Security Council . . .''.

mittee in the summer of 1962.[61] In his view while a solution of the Katanga problem had become urgent for both the United Nations and the Congo, "there was no mandate for the United Nations to take the initiative in the use of force to achieve the political objective of ending secession . . . . However, the consensus in the Advisory Committee was that the existing United Nations mandate was adequate and that there was no need for further action by the Security Council."[62] There was, it is submitted, need for a re-interpretation of the mandate.[63] In August 1962 the Secretary-General formulated the "Plan of National Reconciliation"[64] for submission on a take-it-or-leave-it basis to the Central Government of the Congo and Mr. Tshombe. The Plan covered in outline proposals for constitutional arrangements, apportionment of revenues and other matters for the peaceful integration of Katanga in the Republic of the Congo. According to point C of phase 1, the "Course of Action"outlined in the Plan, Katanga would be informed that "the United Nations resolutions give the United Nations a right to free movement of its military forces throughout the Territory of the Congo" and "that the United Nations will exercise its right to freedom of movement should a need for it arise." Pursuant to phases 2 and 3, Katanga, if the proposal were not accepted within ten days, would be subjected to increasingly coercive measures culminating in an economic blockade and suspension of communications. Finally, if these steps failed, additional measures might be taken according to phase 4.[65]

In the ensuing months there were various incidents, the United Nations on 28 December 1962 embarked on implementing the Plan and its primary objective by clearing all Katanganese roadblocks around Elisabethville and establishing effective control in an area extending about 20 miles around the city.[65a] In the Katanga area, United Nations contin-

[61] The earlier military operations in which the United Nations became involved in Katanga during Mr. Dag Hammarskjold's administration known as "Operation Rumpunch", 28 August 1961 and "Operation Morthor" (a Hindu word for "smash"), 13 September 1961, as well as the 5–18 December 1961 military action undertaken at the beginning of U Thant's administration are omitted for lack of space. "Operation Morthor" may well be justified in terms of the 21 February 1961 Security Council Resolution. On all three of these actions see Ernest W. Lefever, *Crisis in the Congo* (1965), pp. 77–99, and Catherine Hoskyns, *The Congo Since Independence* (1965), pp. 404–8; 413–28; 447–58.

[62] Annual Report of the Secretary-General on the Work of the Organization, 16 June 1962—15 June 1963, GAOR 18th Sess., Supp. No. 1 (A/5501), p. 1.

[63] It may be noted that while the Security Council Resolution of 22 July 1960, commended the Secretary-General for prompt action and the Resolution of 9 August 1960, confirmed the authority given to him, subsequent resolutions contain no such language. For background on the gradual stiffening of the attitude of the Security Council and the increasing pressure from Afro-Asian Members, see Hoskyns, *loc. cit.*, pp. 318 *et seq.*, 350 f and 440 *et seq.*

[64] Document S/5053/Add. 13, 26 November 1962, Annex I, and Report of the Secretary-General to the Security Council, 4 February 1963, Document S/5420. Bowett correctly points out, *op. cit.*, p. 229, that the Plan was never endorsed by the Security Council. He argues that therefore "there was room for doubt whether the termination of secession was, *per se*, the proper objective for the United Nations to pursue". On this point hardly any doubt seems possible if one reads the resolutions of the United Nations and not merely the interpretation placed on them by the late Secretary-General. With respect to the first observation two remarks may be made: first, it is reasonable to assume that the Plan was discussed with the Governments most directly concerned in the Congo; and secondly, in view of the widely applauded expansion of the powers of the Secretary-General by Mr. Dag Hammarskjold, it seems hardly fair to criticize his successor for taking the initiative to end the secession of Katanga even though this required a re-interpretation of the several mandates conferred upon the United Nations Command by the Security Council. In the present submission, the overhaul was long overdue and the Secretary-General acted in unison with his Advisory Committee in carrying it out.

[65] Document S/5053/Add. 13, Annex I, SCOR, 17th year, Supp. Nov.-Dec. 1962, p. 37*et seq.*

[65a] For details of the harassment of the Force see Annual Report of the Secretary-General cited in note [62] *supra*, pp. 7–8.

gents advanced "in a two-pronged attack." The further phase of the operations is best stated in the words of the official summary:

> "The first phase, which called for the removal of roadblocks, had been successfuly concluded in two days. Finding that all opposition had crumbled and disappeared, the United Nations troops started to move forward, and what was to have been essentially a probing and patrol operation merged, in unanticipated and almost unavoidable manner, into Phase II of the plan, which called for the troops to move to Jadotville and Kolwezi. It was therefore found necessary to revise the plan on the spot and to do some improvising. Indeed, the commanding officers in the field had decided, in accordance with good military practice, to exploit the situation and continue to advance . . . . From 28 December to 4 January inclusive, a total of seventy-six sorties . . . were carried out . . . . The Katanganese Air Force was virtually annihilated . . . as were all vital installations at the Kolwezi Kengere base."[66]

In short, a brilliant military operation carried out for the first time in history by a truly multinational armed force under United Nations command. In order to make it possible, not merely military but some juridical roadblocks had to be removed. After referring to the differences of interpretation among Member States and one might add the Secretary-General Mr. Hammarskjold, the official summary states as follows:

> "The Organization, for its part, had adhered closely to two fundamental principles laid down by the Council. First, it had respected the principle of non-interference in the internal political affairs of the Congo and had therefore refrained from intervening, beyond opposing secession in general, as required by the Council's resolutions. Secondly, it had also adhered to the principle of avoiding the use of force for political purposes.[67] It was true, however, that the very presence and activity of the United Nations Force in the Congo had been an important factor in giving effective weight to the United Nations opposition to secession. Not only had the United Nations never used arms at its disposal to further the political aims of any group or to interfere with the country's political processes, but force had been used only in the most limited manner, with limited objectives, and no military initiative had ever been taken except as a last resort."[68]

A remarkable metamorphosis of the principles that the Force should use arms only in self-defence,[69] should be impartial and concerned about its freedom of movement,[70] had grad-

[66] Annual Report, p. 9.

[67] Except, presumably, for opposing secession.

[68] Ibid., p. 13.

[69] Referring to an earlier use of force, Rosalyn Higgins and Bowett claim that it fell under the conditions prescribed for the exercise of an "anticipatory right of self-defence" whereas the January 1963 action "falls less readily within the scope of self-defence": Rosalyn Higgins, *op. cit.*, p. 233 f, and Bowett, *op. cit.*, p. 202. Neither proposition seems persuasive unless one clings to the view expounded by the late Secretary-General Dag Hammarskjold that self-defence was the only condition for a permissible use of force. Referring to the 21 February and 24 November 1961 Resolutions, Bowett observes: "Whilst these Resolutions clearly entitled ONUC to go beyond mere self-defence, they cannot properly be regarded as authorising 'enforcement action,' or shifting the constitutional basis of Article 42; both the Opinion of the Court and the fact that no re-negotiation with contributing States took place support this view, and, indeed, the Secretary-General throughout denied that enforcement measures under Article 42 were authorised". *Op cit.*, p. 176. As to the Opinion, the Court deliberately declined to express any view as to which articles supported the resolutions of the Security Council, and moreover, the Opinion was handed down before the re-interpretation of these resolutions and the final action had taken place. A formal re-negotiation may not have taken place, but was it necessary? One can easily surmise that the contributing Members

ually but, one might say, inexorably taken place. A casualty of the final operations was Katanga's "right of self-determination."[71] However, as to the nature of these operations there can be little doubt: they were not merely a "policing"[72] action or "peace-keeping operation." They were enforcement measures in the material sense regardless whether based on article 42 formally and expressly.

## 5. CONCLUSION

Was the achievement of the political objective of the territorial integrity and independence of the Congo contrary to article 2 (7)? As noted above, the wording of the final clause of this paragraph was intended to exclude recommendations under article 39 relating to the underlying dispute or situation. The "Plan of National Reconciliation" seems to run counter to this exclusion. However, it is submitted that there was no incompatability. The Plan did not implicate another State party to the dispute, only the Congo which accepted it on the one hand and a rebellious province on the other. Therefore the situation or dispute, although giving rise to a threat to international peace, was domestic and internal.

The popular title "peace-keeping operation" or "policing operation" frequently conferred upon the United Nations Force in the Congo has obscured legal analysis. It is hardly necessary to insist that these terms do not occur in the Charter, were not used in any of the Security Council Resolutions with respect to the Congo, have no meaning other than that given to them by whoever uses them, and, above all, they cannot provide the starting point for any deductions concerning the nature, scope, objective or limitation of the action actually authorized and undertaken. The Advisory Opinion of the Court in the *United Nations Expenses Case* should be treated with caution in construing the legal implications of the Congo action as it was handed down on 20 July 1962, that is, before the final phase of the operation which, in the present submission, illuminated decisively its legal character.

For the purpose of legal analysis it would certainly have been desirable for the Security Council to make explicit the grounds on which it operated in the Congo. It is generally appreciated that the political consensus in the Council was tenuous. Hence, more leeway was given to the two Secretaries-General who were charged with implementing

served on the Advisory Committee and were in an excellent position to make their stands known to the Secretary-General without embarking on formal re-negotiation.

[70] *Quaere,* whether there is legal justification for the final action of the United Nations Force in the "right of freedom of movement" provided for in the Agreements between the United Nations and the Congo of 29 July 1960 and 27 November 1961. Cf. Bowett, *op. cit.,* p. 203–5. See also Schachter, *loc. cit.,* pp. 227–8. This proviso was imported from the UNEF experience and was presumably concerned with port and communications facilities, in other words, with the logistical and "house-keeping" requirements of the Force. If one looks to "freedom of movement" for a legal basis for the December 1962-January 1963 phase, one must take it in the sense in which it was used in the "Plan of National Reconciliation" referred to at p. 1191, *ante.*

[71] Annual Report, p. 5. In the light of subsequent events it might be said that Mr. Tshombe lost Katanga but gained the Congo for a while at any rate.

[72] *Expenses Case, loc. cit.,* p. 167.

the several mandates given to the Force, than might have been necessary had the members of the Security Council been in the position to compromise effectively their positions.

In construing article 2 (7), the Security Council's reference to articles 25 and 49 is of no help except as an indication that the Council operated within the ambit of Chapter VII of the Charter. The Security Council referred, however, neither to article 39 nor to article 40. Yet in spite of this reticence, neither Secretary-General Dag Hammarskjold nor writers found any difficulty in locating the legal basis for the several mandates given to the United Nations Force in these articles. Reliance on article 40 seems to this writer at any rate hardly tenable, as it is primarily concerned with provisional measures to be taken by the parties involved in a situation. Be that as it may, neither article 39 nor article 40 require directly or by necessary implication the limitations as to self-defence and domestic jurisdiction under which the Force operated for a long time.

If in spite of the silence of the Security Council resolutions regarding articles 39 and 40, the operations in the Congo were construed as being based on or derived from them, there seems to be no compelling reason why a construction based on article 42 should be excluded. In any event, in so far as the second part of article 2 (7) is concerned it is not necessary to invoke article 42 specifically in order to bring the United Nations action relating to Katanga within the orbit of the second part of that clause. All that is required is that the measures authorized and taken be substantively if not formally in the nature of "enforcement measures under Chapter VII." It is submitted that they were, and accordingly, it would seem to follow that the action of the United Nations Force was legally unfettered by the domestic jurisdiction limitation contained in the first part of article 2 (7).

# INDEX

GPSR Compliance

*The European Union's (EU) General Product Safety Regulation (GPSR) is a set of rules that requires consumer products to be safe and our obligations to ensure this.*

*If you have any concerns about our products, you can contact us on ProductSafety@springernature.com*

In case Publisher is established outside the EU, the EU authorized representative is:

Springer Nature Customer Service Center GmbH
Europaplatz 3
69115 Heidelberg, Germany

**Batch number: 10824482**

Printed by Printforce, the Netherlands